Lecture Notes in Computer Science 4642

Commenced Publication in 1973
Founding and Former Series Editors:
Gerhard Goos, Juris Hartmanis, and Jan van Leeuwen

Seong-Whan Lee   Stan Z. Li (Eds.)

Advances in Biometrics

International Conference, ICB 2007
Seoul, Korea, August 27-29, 2007
Proceedings

Volume Editors

Seong-Whan Lee
Korea University, Department of Computer Science and Engineering
Anam-dong, Seongbuk-ku, Seoul 136-713, Korea
E-mail: swlee@image.korea.ac.kr

Stan Z. Li
Chinese Academy of Sciences, Institute of Automation
Center for Biometrics and Security Research
& National Laboratory of Pattern Recognition
95 Zhongguancun Donglu, Beijing 100080, China
E-mail: szli@cbsr.ia.ac.cn

Library of Congress Control Number: 2007933159

CR Subject Classification (1998): I.5, I.4, K.4.1, K.4.4, K.6.5, J.1

LNCS Sublibrary: SL 6 – Image Processing, Computer Vision, Pattern Recognition, and Graphics

ISSN 0302-9743
ISBN-10 3-540-74548-3 Springer Berlin Heidelberg New York
ISBN-13 978-3-540-74548-8 Springer Berlin Heidelberg New York

Springer is a part of Springer Science+Business Media

springer.com

Printed in Germany

Typesetting: Camera-ready by author, data conversion by Scientific Publishing Services, Chennai, India
Printed on acid-free paper SPIN: 12114641 06/3180 5 4 3 2 1 0

Preface

Many applications in government, airport, commercial, defense and law enforcement areas have a basic need for automatic authentication of humans both locally or remotely on a routine basis. The demand for automatic authentication systems using biometrics, including face, fingerprint, gait, and iris, has been increasing in many aspects of life. The purpose of the 2007 International Conference on Biometrics (ICB 2007) was to provide a platform for researchers, engineers, system architects and designers to report recent advances and exchange ideas in the area of biometrics and related technologies.

ICB 2007 received a large number of high-quality research papers. In all 303 papers were submitted from 29 countries around the world. Of these 34 papers were accepted for oral presentation and 91 papers were accepted for poster presentation. The program consisted of seven oral sessions, three poster sessions, two tutorial sessions, and four keynote speeches on various topics on biometrics.

We would like to thank all the authors who submitted their manuscripts to the conference, and all the members of the Program Committee and reviewers who spent valuable time providing comments on each paper. We would like to thank the conference administrator and secretariat for making the conference successful. We also wish to acknowledge the IEEE, IAPR, Korea Information Science Society, Korea University, Korea University BK21 Software Research Division, Korea Science and Engineering Foundation, Korea University Institute of Computer, Information and Communication, Korea Biometrics Association, Lumidigm Inc., Ministry of Information and Communication Republic of Korea, and Springer for sponsoring and supporting this conference.

August 2007

Seong-Whan Lee
Stan Z. Li

Organization

ICB 2007 was organized by Center for Artificial Vision Research, Korea University.

Executive Committee

General Chair	Seong-Whan Lee (Korea University, Korea)
General Co-chairs	Anil Jain (Michigan State University, USA)
	Tieniu Tan (Chinese Academy of Sciences, China)
Program Co-chairs	Ruud Bolle (IBM, USA)
	Josef Kittler (University of Surrey, UK)
	Stan Li (Chinese Academy of Sciences, China)
Tutorials Chair	Patrick J. Flynn (University of Notre Dame, USA)
Publications Chair	Bon-Woo Hwang (Carnegie Mellon University, USA)
Finance Chair	Hyeran Byun (Yonsei University, Korea)
Sponsorship Chair	Dongsuk Yook (Korea University, Korea)
Registration Chair	Diana Krynski (IEEE, USA)

Program Committee

Josef Bigun (Sweden)
Frederic Bimbot (France)
Mats Blomberg (Sweden)
Horst Bunke (Switzerland)
Hyeran Byun (Korea)
Rama Chellappa (USA)
Gerard Chollet (France)
Timothy Cootes (UK)
Larry Davis (USA)
Farzin Deravi (UK)
John Daugman (UK)
Xiaoqing Ding (China)
Julian Fierrez (Spain)
Sadaoki Furui (Japan)
M. Dolores Garcia-Plaza (Spain)
Dominique Genoud (Switzerland)
Shaogang Gong (UK)
Venu Govindaraju (USA)
Steve Gunn (UK)
Bernd Heisele (USA)
Kenneth Jonsson (Sweden)
Behrooz Kamgar-Parsi (USA)
Takeo Kanade (USA)
Jaihie Kim (Korea)
Naohisa Komatsu (Japan)
John Mason (UK)
Jiri Matas (Czech Republic)
Bruce Millar (Australia)
Mark Nixon (UK)
Larry O'Gorman (USA)
Sharath Pankanti (USA)
Jonathon Phillips (USA)
Matti Pietikinen (Finland)
Ioannis Pitas (Greece)
Salil Prabhakar (USA)
Ganesh N. Ramaswamy (USA)
Nalini Ratha (USA)
Marek Rejman-Greene (UK)
Gael Richard (France)
Arun Ross (USA)

Zhenan Sun (China)
Xiaoou Tang (China)
Massimo Tistarelli (Italy)
Patrick Verlinde (Belgium)
Juan Villanueva (Spain)
Yunhong Wang (China)
Harry Wechsler (USA)
Wei-Yun Yau (Singapore)
David Zhang (Hong Kong)

Organizing Committee

Yong-Wha Chung (Korea)
Hee-Jung Kang (Korea)
Jaewoo Kang (Korea)
Chang-Su Kim (Korea)
Daijin Kim (Korea)
Hakil Kim (Korea)
Hanseok Ko (Korea)
Heejo Lee (Korea)
Chang-Beom Park (Korea)
Jeong-Seon Park (Korea)
Myung-Cheol Roh (Korea)
Bong-Kee Sin (Korea)
Sungwon Sohn (Korea)
Hee-Deok Yang (Korea)

Additional Reviewers

Andrea Abate
Mohamed Abdel-Mottaleb
Aditya Abhyankar
Andy Adler
Mohiuddin Ahmad
Timo Ahonen
Haizhou Ai
Jose Alba-Castro
Fernando Alonso-Fernandez
Meng Ao
Babak Nadjar Araabi
Arathi Arakala
Banafshe Arbab-Zavar
Vutipong Areekul
Vijayakumar Bhagavatula
Manuele Bicego
Imed Bouchrika
Ahmed Bouridane
Christina Braz
Ileana Buhan
Raffaele Cappelli
Modesto Castrillón-Santana
Ee-Chien Chang
Jiansheng Chen
Weiping Chen
Jin Young Choi
Seungjin Choi
Rufeng Chu
Jonathan Connell
Tim Cootes
Sarat Dass
Reza Derakhshani
Jana Dittman
Wenbo Dong
Bernadette Dorizzi
Timothy Faltemier
Pedro Gómez-Vilda
Javier Galbally
Xiufeng Gao
Yongsheng Gao
Georgi Gluhchev
Berk Gokberk
Abdenour Hadid
Miroslav Hamouz
Asmaa El Hannani
Pieter Hartel
Jean Hennebert
Javier Hernando
Sakano Hitoshi
Heiko Hoffmann
Vincent Hsu
Jian Huang

Yonggang Huang
Yuan Huaqiang
Jens Hube
David Hurley
Yoshiaki Isobe
Jia Jia
Kui Jia
Andrew Teoh Beng Jin
Changlong Jin
Alfons Juan
Pilsung Kang
Tomi Kinnunen
Klaus Kollreider
Ajay Kumar
James T. Kwok
Andrea Lagorio
J. H. Lai
Kenneth Lam
Jeremy Lecoeur
Joon-Jae Lee
Zhen Lei
Alex Leung
Bangyu Li
Yongping Li
Zhifeng LI
Shengcai Liao
Almudena Lindoso
Chengjun Liu
James Liu
Jianyi Liu
Rong Liu
Wei Liu
Xin Liu
Zicheng Liu
Xiaoguang Lu
Sascha Müller
Bao Ma
Sotiris Malassiotis
Sébastien Marcel
Gian Luca Marcialis
Ichino Masatsugu
Peter McOwan
Kieron Messer
Krzysztof Mieloch
Sinjini Mitra
Pranab Mohanty
Don Monro
Pavel Mrazek
Daigo Muramatsu
Vittorio Murino
Isao Nakanishi
Anoop Namboodiri
Loris Nanni
Kenneth Nilsson
Lawrence O'Gorman
Tetsushi Ohki
Nick Orlans
Carlos Orrite
Gang Pan
Roberto Paredes
Kang Ryoung Park
Jason Pelecanos
John Pitrelli
Norman Poh
Xianchao Qiu
Ajita Rattani
Jose Antonio Rodriguez
Yann Rodriguez
Fabio Roli
Sujoy Roy
Mohammad Sadeghi
Albert Salah
Raul Sanchez-Reillo
Michael Schuckers
Stephanie Schuckers
Caifeng Shan
Shiguang Shan
Weiguo Sheng
Takashi Shinzaki
Terence Sim
Sridha Sridharan
Fei Su
Eric Sung
Nooritawati Md Tahir
Dacheng Tao
Daniel Thorpe
Jie Tian
Kar-Ann Toh
Sergey Tulyakov
Kaoru Uchida

Andreas Uhl
Umut Uludag
Sekar V.
Mayank Vatsa
Raymond Veldhuis
Alessandro Verri
Claus Vielhauer
Hee Lin Wang
Jian-Gang Wang
Seadrift Wang
Yiding Wang
Zhuoshi Wei
Jing Wen
Damon Woodard
Xiangqian Wu
Wenquan Xu
Yong Xu
Shuicheng Yan
Xin Yang
Dong Yi
Lijun Yin
Jane You
Xiaotong Yuan
Khalil Zebbiche
Bingjun Zhang
Changshui Zhang
Chao Zhang
Jianguo Zhang
Taiping Zhang
Yangyang Zhang
Guoying Zhao
Wei-Shi Zheng
Jie Zhou
Xiangxin Zhu
Xuan Zou

Sponsoring Institutions

IEEE Computer Society
IEEE Systems, Man and Cybernetics Society
International Association for Pattern Recognition
Korea Information Science Society
Korea Science and Engineering Foundation
Korea University
Korea University BK21 Software Research Division
Korea University Institute of Computer, Information and Communication
Korea Biometrics Association
Lumidigm Inc.
Ministry of Information and Communication Republic of Korea

Table of Contents

Face Recognition

Poster I

Gait and Signature Recognition

Systems and Applications

Poster II

Fingerprint Recognition

Iris Recognition

Pattern Analysis and Learning

Poster III

Other Modalities

Super-Resolved Faces for Improved Face Recognition from Surveillance Video

Frank Lin, Clinton Fookes, Vinod Chandran, and Sridha Sridharan

Image and Video Research Laboratory
Queensland University of Technology
GPO Box 2434 Brisbane, QLD 4001 Australia
{fc.lin,c.fookes,v.chandran,s.sridharan}@qut.edu.au

Abstract. Characteristics of surveillance video generally include low resolution and poor quality due to environmental, storage and processing limitations. It is extremely difficult for computers and human operators to identify individuals from these videos. To overcome this problem, super-resolution can be used in conjunction with an automated face recognition system to enhance the spatial resolution of video frames containing the subject and narrow down the number of manual verifications performed by the human operator by presenting a list of most likely candidates from the database. As the super-resolution reconstruction process is ill-posed, visual artifacts are often generated as a result. These artifacts can be visually distracting to humans and/or affect machine recognition algorithms. While it is intuitive that higher resolution should lead to improved recognition accuracy, the effects of super-resolution and such artifacts on face recognition performance have not been systematically studied. This paper aims to address this gap while illustrating that super-resolution allows more accurate identification of individuals from low-resolution surveillance footage. The proposed optical flow-based super-resolution method is benchmarked against Baker et al.'s *hallucination* and Schultz et al.'s super-resolution techniques on images from the Terrascope and XM2VTS databases. Ground truth and interpolated images were also tested to provide a baseline for comparison. Results show that a suitable super-resolution system can improve the discriminability of surveillance video and enhance face recognition accuracy. The experiments also show that Schultz et al.'s method fails when dealing surveillance footage due to its assumption of rigid objects in the scene. The *hallucination* and optical flow-based methods performed comparably, with the optical flow-based method producing less visually distracting artifacts that interfered with human recognition.

Keywords: super-resolution, face recognition, surveillance.

1 Introduction

Faces captured from surveillance footage are usually of poor-resolution as they typically occupy a small portion of the camera's field of view. It is extremely challenging for a computer or even a human operator to accurately identify an

S.-W. Lee and S.Z. Li (Eds.): ICB 2007, LNCS 4642, pp. 1–10, 2007.

individual from a database in such a situation. In addition, a human operator is usually responsible for monitoring footage from several cameras simultaneously, increasing the chance of human error. One solution to the problem would be to complement our natural ability to recognise faces with the computers' power to process large amounts of video data.

This paper presents an intelligent surveillance system aided by optical flow-based super-resolution and automatic face recognition. The system operates in a semi-automatic manner where it enhances the surveillance video through super-resolution and displays a list of likely candidates from a database together with the enhanced image to a human operator who then makes the final verification.

Super-resolution is aimed at recovering high frequency detail lost through aliasing in the image acquisition process. As the reconstruction process is ill-posed due to the large number of variables, visual artifacts are usually generated as a result. These artifacts can be visually distracting to humans and/or affect machine recognition algorithms. Although it has been shown that face recognition accuracy is dependent on image resolution [1, 2, 3] and it is known that super-resolution improves image fidelity, the effects of super-resolution on recognition performance has not been systematically studied. This paper aims to address this gap while illustrating that super-resolution allows more accurate identification of individuals from low-resolution surveillance footage. Experiments were conducted to compare the performance of the proposed optical flow-based super-resolution system [12] against two existing methods – a face-specific recognition-based method [10] and a reconstruction-based algorithm that supports independently moving rigid objects [14].

Images from the Terrascope surveillance database [4] were used to illustrate the reconstruction performance of the tested methods and demonstrate the importance of accurate registration in super-resolution. Face identification performance were tested on an Eigenface [5] and Elastic Bunch Graph Matching (EBGM) [6] system using images from the XM2VTS database [7]. The Eigenface method is a baseline holistic system that new methods are usually benchmarked against while EBGM a newer technique that is less sensitive to pose and lighting changes. Traditional interpolation methods were also tested for comparison.

The outline of the paper is as follows. Section 2 provides background information on super-resolution, the inherent difficulties associated with surveillance footage as well as an overview of the super-resolution algorithm tested. Experimental methodology and results are presented in Section 3 and concluding remarks are discussed in Section 4.

2 Super-Resolution

Super-resolution image reconstruction is the process of combining low-resolution (LR) images into one high-resolution image. These low-resolution images are aliased and related to each other through sub-pixel shifts; essentially representing different *snapshots* of the same scene which carry complementary information

[8]. The challenge is to find effective and computationally efficient methods of combining two or more such images.

2.1 Observation Model

The relationship between the ideal high-resolution (HR) image and the observed LR images can be described by the following observation model,

$$y_k = DB_kM_kx + n_k, \tag{1}$$

where y_k denotes the $k = 1 \ldots p$ LR images, D is a subsampling matrix, B_k is the blur matrix, M_k is the warp matrix, x is the ideal HR image of the scene which is being recovered, and n_k is the additive noise that corrupts the image. D and B_k simulate the averaging process performed by the camera's CCD sensor while M_k can be modelled by anything from a simple parametric transformation to motion flow fields. Essentially, given multiple y_k's, x can be recovered through an inversion process. The problem is usually ill-posed however, due to the large number of pixel values to be be estimated from a small number of known pixels. Generally, reconstruction of a super-resolved image is broken up into three stages – motion compensation (registration), interpolation and blur and noise removal (restoration) [8].

2.2 Approaches to Super-Resolution

Super-resolution techniques can be classed into two categories – *reconstruction-* and *recognition-based.* Most super-resolution techniques are reconstruction-based, dating back to Tsai and Huang's work in 1984 [9]. These methods operate directly with the image pixel intensities following the principles of Equation 1 and can super-resolve any image sequence provided the motion between between observations can be modelled. Their useful magnification factors are usually low however, in that the super-resolved image becomes too smooth or blurred when the scale is chosen to be more than 4 [10].

Recognition-based methods approach the problem differently by learning features of the low-resolution input images and synthesising the corresponding high-resolution output [10]. Training is performed by looking at high-resolution and downsampled versions of sample image patches. The reconstruction process involves looking at a patch of pixels in the low-resolution input and finding the closest matching low-resolution patch in the training set, then replacing that patch with the corresponding high-resolution patch. An advantage of these methods is that only input image is required. Although they output images with sharp edges, visually distracting artifacts are often produced as by-product.

2.3 The Problem with Human Faces in Surveillance Video

As super-resolution is inherently an ill-posed problem, most methods operate within a constrained environment by assuming that the objects are static and only modeling global parametric motion such as translations/rotations, affine and projective transformation between frames. While they work well with static scenes, performance degrades severely when applied to human faces in surveillance video as human faces are non-planar, non-rigid, non-lambertian, and subject to self occlusion [11]. Optical flow methods can be used to overcome the non-planarity and non-rigidity of the face by recovering a dense flow field to describe local deformations while the remaining two problems need to be addressed through robust estimation methods.

2.4 Systems Tested

Three super-resolution methods have been included in this set of experiments.

Lin et al. – The proposed system is a reconstruction-based method [12] that uses a robust optical flow method developed by Black et al. [13] to register the local motion between frames. Optical flow techniques operate on the concept of constant intensity, meaning that although the location of a point maybe change over time, it will always be observed with the same intensity. They also assume that neighbouring pixels in the image are likely to belong to the same surface, resulting in a smoothness constraint that ensures the motion of neighbouring pixels varies smoothly. Most optical flow algorithms break down when these two assumptions are not satisfied in practice. This occurs when motion boundaries, shadows and specular reflections are present. The robust optical flow method used here addresses these two constraint violations through a robust estimation framework. A graduated non-convexity algorithm is proposed to recover the optical flow and motion discontinuities.

Schultz et al. – Schultz et al.'s [14] system is a reconstruction-based system capable of handling independently moving objects. However, each object is assume to be rigid. The system is expected to perform very poorly when applied to surveillance footage where the subjects' faces not only move around freely, but also change in orientation and shape as they turn around and change facial expressions. The system was included in this set of experiments to highlight the importance of accurate image registration, and that more flexible motion models like optical flow are required to obtain good results with surveillance video.

Baker et al. – The *hallucination* algorithm developed by Baker et al. [10] is a face-specific recognition-based method. The system is trained using full frontal face images and hence the super-resolved images are generated with a face-specific prior. The super-resolved output of the system always contains an outline of a frontal face even when the input images contain none, hence the term *hallucination*. The method works well if the input image is precisely aligned as shown in [10]. However, when applied to faces that are not full frontal pose normalised, distracting visual artifacts are expected to be produced and the appearance of the face may even change completely.

3 Experimental Results

Videos from the Terrascope database were used to investigate if the super-resolution methods were applicable to surveillance footage. The database consists of videos captured by surveillance cameras placed in an office environment. Due to the database containing only twelve subjects, the speech sequences from the XM2VTS database were used for the face recognition experiments to obtain more statistically significant results. The XM2VTS database is a multi-modal (speech and video) database created to facilitate testing of multi-modal speech recognition systems. It contains 295 subjects recorded over four sessions in four months. As the speech sequences contain only frontal faces, they represent the situation where the face detector has found a frontal face suitable for recognition whilst scanning through surveillance footage. The experiments were conducted to simulate a production environment, with no manual human interventaion required.

3.1 Preparation

The Terrascope video sequences were captured in colour at 640×480 pixels (px) at 30 frames/sec. These were converted to grayscale without any downsampling before processing since they accurately reflect real-world surveillance footage. The original XM2VTS videos were captured in colour at a resolution of 720×576px with the subject sitting close to and facing the camera, resulting in very high-resolution faces. Hence these frames needed to be downsampled first to simulate surveillance conditions more closely. The images were resized and converted to grayscale as uncompressed ground-truth images at three different resolutions – 180×144px, 120×96px and 90×72px as ground-truth high-resolution images. These images were then downsampled by a factor of two through blurring and decimation to simulate the low-resolution images which were then used as the input for the super-resolution and interpolation stages.

To super-resolve using Schultz et al. and Lin et al.'s methods , the respective algorithms were applied to a moving group of five frames, with the third frame being the reference. Five frames were chosen because it was a good trade-off between reconstruction quality and computation time [14]. Baker et al.'s method was applied using a single frame – the reference frame for the other two super-resolution methods. To compare the performance of the super-resolution algorithm with interpolation methods, upsampled images were also generated for the reference frame of each 5-frame sequence using bilinear and cubic spline interpolation.

For the face recognition experiment, an object detector [15] trained using frontal faces was applied to each of the enhanced images individually. Each image was then segmented and normalised. The CSU Face Identification Evaluation system [16] was then used to evaluate recognition performance of the super-resovled, interpolated and ground-truth images. Frontal face images from the Face Recognition Grand Challenge (FRGC) [17] Fall2003 and Spring2004 datasets were used to train the facespace for the Eigenface system. A range

(10–500) of values for the Eigenvectors retained were tested. The normalised images from the XM2VTS database were then projected into the facespace and the distance to the enrolment images computed. Both Euclidean (EUC) and Mahalinobis Cosine (MCOS) distance metrics were tested. For the EBGM system, the gabor jets used to detect the facial features were trained using 70 handmarked images from the FERET database [18]. The predictive step (PS) and magnitude (MAG) distance metrics were used.

3.2 Results

Figure 1 shows selected enhanced images from the Terrascope database. As expected, all super-resolution algorithms produced sharper images than the interpolation methods. However, Schultz et al.'s method's assumption of rigid objects has resulted in a grid-like noise pattern. The hallucinated face looks reasonably sharp and clean but the subjects take on a different appearance. Lin et al.'s method shows some sharpening noise but it is most visually correct and suitable for human inspection.

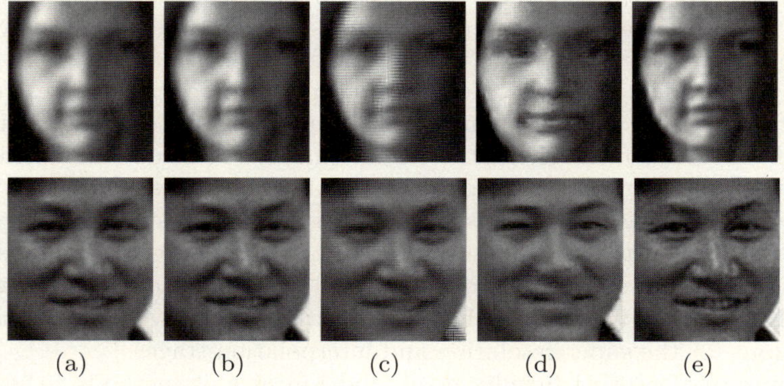

Fig. 1. Comparison between enhanced images. (a) bilinear interpolation, (b) cubic spline interpolation, (c) Schultz et al., (d) Baker et al., (e) Lin et al.

Figure 2 contains selected enhanced images from the XM2VTS database at the three resolutions. Schultz et al.'s method no longer generates the grid pattern noise due to the XM2VTS speech sequences containing only frontal faces, making the faces more or less rigid. Baker et al.'s *hallucination* algorithm didn't do so well as it is quite sensitive to misalignment of the low-resolution face. While the hallucinated faces looked sharper than those generated by other methods, the faces take on a different appearance and distracting artifacts are present upon closer inspection.

Table 1 presents the face recognition rates (ranks 1 and 10) for all combinations of face recognition algorithm, distance metric, resolution and image enhancement method. The recognition rate for a given rank N is the probability

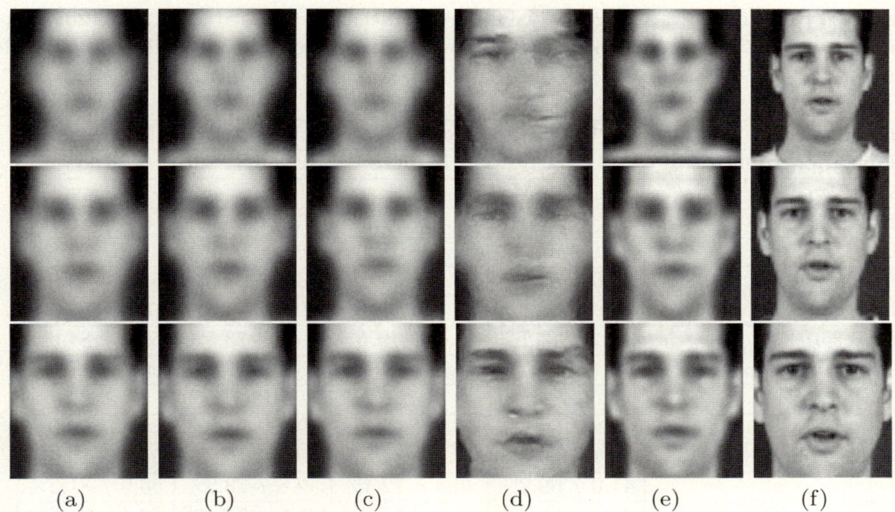

Fig. 2. Comparison between enhanced images. First row 90×72, second row 120×96, third row 180×144. (a) bilinear interpolation, (b) cubic spline interpolation, (c) Schultz et al., (d) Baker et al., (e) Lin et al., (f) ground-truth.

that the true subject is identified in the top N matches returned by the system. For example, by examining the last cell in the bottom hand corner of the table, it can be seen that when testing the ground-truth images on the EBGM method with the magnitude distance metric, the probability of returning the correct subject is 72.6%, increasing to 88.8% if the list is expanded from 1 to 10. The Eigenface system results given will be for 250 retained Eigenvectors as it gave the best overall recognition performance.

Schultz et al's method in general does not improve recognition performance over simple interpolation techniques, most likely due to its inability to handle non-rigid objects. The optical flow-based method worked very well as expected, since it accurately registers the motion between frames and produces the most visually appealing images. Once again this highlights the importance of accurate registration. The hallucinated images performed surprisingly well despite the presence of severe artifacts. This seems to suggest that the face recognition methods tested aren't sensitive to the type of visual artifacts generated by this particular algorithm. The important thing to note here is that while *hallucination* works well to improve machine recognition, the severe visual artifacts make it less desirable for the proposed application where a human operator makes the final verification.

For the two higher resolutions, the ground-truth and super-resolved images actually lose the lead to interpolated ones in some instances. This can be attributed to the Eigenface and EBGM methods being quite robust to downsampling and that the downsampling process actually smoothes out some illumination variations and noise. The authors obtained similar results, where

Table 1. Recognition rates for the two face recognition methods at 90×72px, 120×96px and 180×144px. Values in **bold** indicate best performing method (excluding ground-truth).

Recognition method	**Eigenface**		**EBGM**	
Distance metric	**EUC**	**MCOS**	**PS**	**MAG**
90×72px	Rank 1 / 10			
Bilinear	30.3 / 57.1%	34.6 / 62.2%	35.8 / 66.4%	50.2 / 78.1%
Cubic spline	30.1 / 57.3%	34.8 / 61.2%	36.3 / 66.6%	51.3 / 77.8%
Schultz et al.	31.0 / 59.2%	35.4 / 63.6%	36.4 / 67.3%	53.4 / 79.0%
Baker et al.	35.2 / **66.1%**	32.3 / 64.8%	**51.7** / **77.0%**	**61.4** / **87.3%**
Lin et al.	**37.2** / 64.6%	**41.0** / **69.5%**	45.5 / 73.5%	60.6 / 84.6%
Ground-truth	40.1 / 67.2%	43.2 / 71.4%	53.9 / 79.5%	66.3 / 87.5%
120×96px	Rank 1 / 10			
Bilinear	40.2 / 68.6%	46.5 / 72.7%	49.2 / 73.9%	56.6 / 80.9%
Cubic spline	40.7 / 69.3%	47.6 / 72.8%	49.2 / 73.8%	57.2 / 80.9%
Schultz et al.	41.0 / 69.2%	46.4 / 72.1%	49.8 / 73.3%	56.9 / 81.2%
Baker et al.	42.3 / 68.3%	50.6 / **75.2%**	**57.8** / **77.8%**	60.4 / 81.6%
Lin et al.	**47.3** / **73.3%**	**51.7** / **75.2%**	52.8 / 73.8%	**63.8** / **85.2%**
Ground-truth	49.2 / 76.5%	49.9 / 74.5%	55.2 / 74.3%	67.4 / 87.6%
180×144px	Rank 1 / 10			
Bilinear	49.1 / 73.8%	58.3 / 80.1%	57.2 / 74.9%	65.7 / 85.2%
Cubic spline	50.2 / 75.0%	59.0 / **80.4%**	57.7 / 74.3%	66.3 / 85.7%
Schultz et al.	49.9 / 75.0%	**59.5** / 79.5%	58.8 / 75.2%	67.7 / 85.7%
Baker et al.	45.6 / 72.5%	52.7 / 75.5%	**66.3** / **83.4%**	67.1 / 84.9%
Lin et al.	**53.4** / **76.9%**	**59.5** / 79.4%	60.1 / 75.9%	**70.6** / **87.6%**
Ground-truth	52.9 / 77.3%	58.0 / 77.7%	62.9 / 78.4%	72.6 / 88.8%

performance improved by smoothing the images when the resolution was sufficient [19]. This suggests that higher resolution isn't necessarily better beyond a certain limit and can actually introduce unwanted noise depending on the face recognition algorithm used.

4 Conclusion

This paper has presented a simple yet effective way to assist a human operator in identifying a subject captured on video from a database by intelligently narrowing down the list of likely candidates and enhancing the face of the subject. Visual artifacts are often generated due to the super-resolution reconstruction process being ill-posed. These artifacts can be visually distracting to humans and/or affect machine recognition algorithms. As the rank 1 recognition rates are still likely to be poor despite the improvement provided by super-resolution, a fully-automated recognition system is currently impractical. To increase accuracy to a usable level, the surveillance system will need to operate in a semi-automated manner by generating a list of top machine matches for subsequent human recognition. Therefore it is important for the enhanced images to be visually pleasing and not contain excessively distracting artifacts.

The proposed optical flow-based super-resolution method has been shown to be superior when compared against two other existing algorithms in terms of visual appearance and face recognition performance on an Eigenface and EBGM system. The system's performance was the most consistent, resulting in visually pleasing images and recognition rates comparable to the *hallucination* method. Baker et al.'s *hallucination* algorithm results in good recognition performance despite the generation of distracting artifacts due to its sensitivity to misalignment of the input images as often occurs in an automated environment. Schultz et al.'s method has been found to be unsuitable for application to surveillance footage due to its object-rigidity constraint. Its performance was no better than interpolation in many cases, highlighting the importance of accurate registration.

References

1. Gunturk, B., Batur, A., Altunbasak, Y., M III, H., Mersereau, R.: Eigenface-domain super-resolution for face recognition. IEEE Transactions on Image Processing 12(5), 597–606 (2003)
2. Lemieux, A., Parizeau, M.: Experiments on eigenfaces robustness. In: Proc. ICPR-2002, vol. 1, pp. 421–424 (August 2002)
3. Wang, X., Tang, X.: Face Hallucination and Recognition. In: Kittler, J., Nixon, M.S. (eds.) AVBPA 2003. LNCS, vol. 2688, pp. 486–494. Springer, Heidelberg (2003)
4. Jaynes, C., Kale, A., Sanders, N., Grossmann, E.: The Terrascope dataset: scripted multi-camera indoor video surveillance with ground-truth. In: Proc. Visual Surveillance and Performance Evaluation of Tracking and Surveillance, pp. 309–316 (October 2005)
5. Turk, M., Pentland, A.: Eigenfaces for recognition. Journal of Cognitive Neuroscience 3(1), 71–86 (1991)
6. Wiskott, L., Fellous, J., Krüger, N., Malsburg, C.: Face recognition by elastic bunch graph matching. In: Sommer, G., Daniilidis, K., Pauli, J. (eds.) CAIP 1997. LNCS, vol. 1296, pp. 456–463. Springer, Heidelberg (1997)
7. Messer, K., Matas, J., Kittler, J., Luettin, J., Maitre, G.: XM2VTS: The Extended M2VTS Database. In: Proc. AVBPA-1999, pp. 72–76 (1999)
8. Park, S., Park, M., Kang, M.: Super-resolution image reconstruction: a technical overview. IEEE Signal Processing Magazine 25(9), 21–36 (2003)
9. Tsai, R., Huang, T.: Multiframe image restoration and registration. Advances in Computer Vision and image Processing 1, 317–339 (1984)
10. Baker, S., Kanade, T.: Limits on Super-Resolution and How to Break Them. 24(9), 1167–1183 (2002)
11. Baker, S., Kanade, T.: Super Resolution Optical Flow. Technical Report CMU-RI-TR-99-36, The Robotics Institute, Carnegie Mellon University (October 1999)
12. Lin, F., Fookes, C., Chandran, V., Sridharan, S.: Investigation into Optical Flow Super-Resolution for Surveillance Applications. In: Proc. APRS Workshop on Digital Image Computing 2005, pp. 73–78 (February 2005)
13. Black, M., Anandan, P.: A framework for the robust estimation of optical flow. In: Proc. ICCV-1993, pp. 231–236 (May 1993)

14. Schultz, R., Stevenson, R.: Extraction of High-Resolution Frames from Video Sequences. IEEE Transactions on Image Processing 5(6), 996–1011 (June 1996)
15. Viola, P., Jones, M.: Rapid object detection using a boosted cascade of simple features. In: CVPR (2001)
16. Bolme, D., Beveridge, R., Teixeira, M., Draper, B.: The CSU Face Identification Evaluation System: Its Purpose, Features and Structure. In: Proc. International Conference on Vision Systems, pp. 304–311 (April 2003)
17. Phillips, P., Flynn, P., Scruggs, T., Bowyer, K., Chang, J., Hoffman, K., Marques, J., Min, J., Worek, W.: Overview of the face recognition grand challenge. In: Proc. CVPR '05, vol. 1, pp. 947–954 (2005)
18. Phillips, P., Moon, H., Rizvi, S., Rauss, P.: The feret evaluation methodology for face-recognition algorithms. IEEE Transactions on Pattern Analysis and Machine Intelligence 22, 1090–1104 (2000)
19. Lin, F., Cook, J., Chandran, V., Sridharan, S.: Face Recognition from Super-Resolved Images. In: Proc. ISSPA 2005, pp. 667–670 (August 2005)

Face Detection Based on Multi-Block LBP Representation

Lun Zhang, Rufeng Chu, Shiming Xiang, Shengcai Liao, and Stan Z. Li

Center for Biometrics and Security Research & National Laboratory of Pattern Recognition
Institute of Automation, Chinese Academy of Sciences
95 Zhongguancun Donglu Beijing 100080, China

Abstract. Effective and real-time face detection has been made possible by using the method of rectangle Haar-like features with AdaBoost learning since Viola and Jones' work [12]. In this paper, we present the use of a new set of distinctive rectangle features, called Multi-block Local Binary Patterns (MB-LBP), for face detection. The MB-LBP encodes rectangular regions' intensities by local binary pattern operator, and the resulting binary patterns can describe diverse local structures of images. Based on the MB-LBP features, a boosting-based learning method is developed to achieve the goal of face detection. To deal with the non-metric feature value of MB-LBP features, the boosting algorithm uses multi-branch regression tree as its weak classifiers. The experiments show the weak classifiers based on MB-LBP are more discriminative than Haar-like features and original LBP features. Given the same number of features, the proposed face detector illustrates 15% higher correct rate at a given false alarm rate of 0.001 than haar-like feature and 8% higher than original LBP feature. This indicates that MB-LBP features can capture more information about the image structure and show more distinctive performance than traditional haar-like features, which simply measure the differences between rectangles. Another advantage of MB-LBP feature is its smaller feature set, this makes much less training time.

1 Introduction

Face detection has a wide range of applications such as automatic face recognition, human-machine interaction, surveillance, etc. In recent years, there has been a substantial progress on detection schemes based on appearance of faces. These methods treat face detection as a two-class (face/non-face) classification problem. Due to the variations in facial appearance, lighting, expressions, and other factors [11], face/non-face classifiers with good performance should be very complex. The most effective method for constructing face/non-face classifiers is learning based approach. For example, neural network-based methods [10], support vector machines [9], etc.

Recently, the boosting-based detector proposed by Viola and Jones [12] is regarded as a breakthrough in face detection research. Real-time performance is achieved by learning a sequence of simple Haar-like rectangle features. The Haar-like features encode differences in average intensities between two rectangular regions, and they can be calculated rapidly through integral image [12]. The complete Haar-like feature set is large and contains a mass of redundant information. Boosting algorithm is introduced to

S.-W. Lee and S.Z. Li (Eds.): ICB 2007, LNCS 4642, pp. 11–18, 2007.

select a small number of distinctive rectangle features and construct a powerful classifier. Moreover, the use of cascade structure [12] further speeds up the computations. Li et al. extended that work to multi-view faces using an extended set of Haar features and an improved boosting algorithm [5]. However, these Haar-like rectangle features seem too simple, and the detector often contains thousands of rectangle features for considerable performance. The large number of selected features leads to high computation costs both in training and test phases. Especially, in later stages of the cascade, weak classifiers based on these features become too weak to improve the classifier's performance [7]. Many other features are also proposed to represent facial images, including rotated Haar-like features [6], census transform [3], sparse features [4], etc.

In this paper, we present a new distinctive feature, called Multi-block Local Binary Pattern (MB-LBP) feature, to represent facial image. The basic idea of MB-LBP is to encode rectangular regions by local binary pattern operator [8]. The MB-LBP features can also be calculated rapidly through integral image, while these features capture more information about the image structure than Haar-like features and show more distinctive performance. Comparing with original Local Binary Pattern calculated in a local 3×3 neighborhood between pixels, the MB-LBP features can capture large scale structure that may be the dominant features of image structures. We directly use the output of LBP operator as the feature value. But a problem is that this value is just a symbol for representing the binary string. For this non-metric feature value, multi-branch regression tree is designed as weak classifiers. We implement Gentle adaboost for feature selection and classifier construction. Then a cascade detector is built. Another advantage of MB-LBP is that the number of exhaustive set of MB-LBP features is much smaller than Haar-like features (about 1/20 of Haar-like feature for a sub-window of size 20×20). Boosting-based method use Adaboost algorithm to select a significant feature set from the large complete feature set. This process often spends much time even several weeks. The small feature set of MB-LBP can make this procedure more simple.

The rest of this paper is organized as follows. Section 2 introduces the MB-LBP features. In section 3, the AdaBoost learning for feature selection and classifier construction are proposed. The cascade detector is also described in this section. The experiment results are given in Section 4. Section 5 concludes this paper.

2 Multi-Block Local Binary Pattern Features

Traditional Haar-like rectangle feature measures the difference between the average intensities of rectangular regions (See Fig.1). For example, the value of a two-rectangle filter is the difference between the sums of the pixels within two rectangular regions. If we change the position, size, shape and arrangement of rectangular regions, the Haar-like features can capture the intensity gradient at different locations, spatial frequencies and directions. Viola an Jones [12] applied three kinds of such features for detecting frontal faces. By using the integral image, any rectangle filter types, at any scale or location, can be evaluated in constant time [12]. However, the Haar-like features seem too simple and show some limits [7].

In this paper, we propose a new distinctive rectangle features, called Multi-block Local Binary Pattern (MB-LBP) feature. The basic idea of MB-LBP is that the

Fig. 1. Traditional Haar-like features.These features measure the differences between rectangular regions' average intensities.

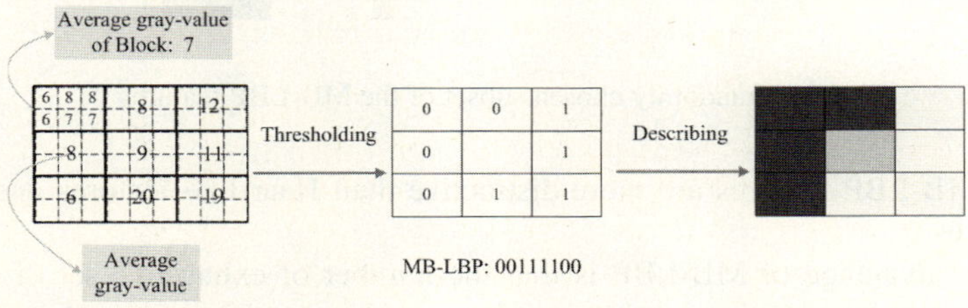

Fig. 2. Multi-block LBP feature for image representation. As shown in the figure, the MB-LBP features encode rectangular regions' intensities by local binary pattern. The resulting binary patterns can describe diverse image structures. Compared with original Local Binary Pattern calculated in a local 3×3 neighborhood between pixels, MB-LBP can capture large scale structure.

simple difference rule in Haar-like features is changed into encoding rectangular regions by local binary pattern operator. The original LBP, introduced by Ojala [8], is defined for each pixel by thresholding the 3×3 neighborhood pixel value with the center pixel value. To encode the rectangles, the MB-LBP operator is defined by comparing the central rectangle's average intensity g_c with those of its neighborhood rectangles $\{g_0, ..., g_8\}$. In this way, it can give us a binary sequence. An output value of the MB-LBP operator can be obtained as follows:

$$MB - LBP = \sum_{i=1}^{8} s(g_i - g_c)2^i \tag{1}$$

where g_c is the average intensity of the center rectangle, g_i $(i = 0, \cdots, 8)$ are those of its neighborhood rectangles,

$$s(x) = \begin{cases} 1, if\ x > 0 \\ 0, if\ x < 0 \end{cases}$$

A more detailed description of such MB-LBP operator can be found in Fig. 2. We directly use the resulting binary patterns as the feature value of MB-LBP features. Such binary patterns can detect diverse image structures such as edges, lines, spots, flat areas and corners [8], at different scale and location. Comparing with original Local Binary Pattern calculated in a local 3×3 neighborhood between pixels, MB-LBP can capture large scale structures that may be the dominant features of images. Totally, we can get 256 kinds of binary patterns, some of them can be found in Fig. 3. In section 4.1, we conduct an experiment to evaluate the MB-LBP features. The experimental results

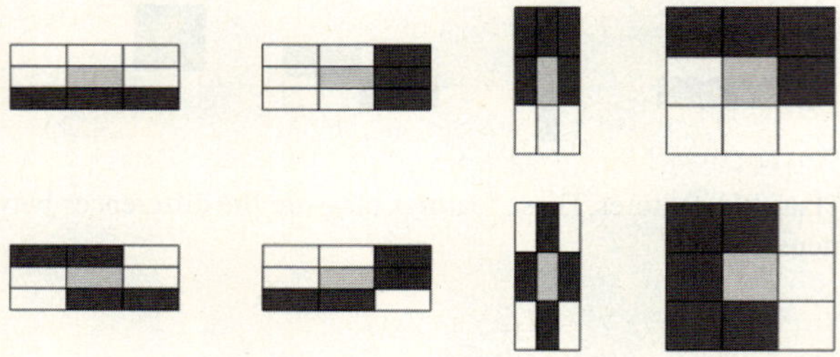

Fig. 3. A randomly chosen subset of the MB-LBP features

show the MB-LBP features are more distinctive than Haar-like features and original LBP features.

Another advantage of MB-LBP is that the number of exhaustive set of MB-LBP features (rectangles at various scales, locations and aspect ratios) is much smaller than Haar-like features. Given a sub-window size of 20×20, there are totally 2049 MB-LBP features, this amount is about 1/20 of Haar-like features (45891). People usually select significant features from the whole feature set by Adaboost algorithm, and construct a binary classifier. Owing to the large feature set of haar-like feature, the training process usually spends too much time. The fewer number of MB-LBP feature set makes the implementation of feature selection significantly easy.

It is should be emphasized that the value of MB-LBP features is non-metric. The output of LBP operator is just a symbol for representing the binary string. In the next section, we will describe how to design the weak classifiers based on MB-LBP features, and apply the Adaboost algorithm to select significant features and construct classifier.

3 Feature Selection and Classifier Construction

Although the feature set of MB-LBP feature is much smaller than Haar-like features, it also contains much redundant information. The AdaBoost algorithm is used to select significant features and construct a binary classifier. Here, AdaBoost is adopted to solve the following three fundamental problems in one boosting procedure: (1) learning effective features from the large feature set, (2) constructing weak classifiers, each of which is based on one of the selected features, (3) boosting the weak classifiers into a stronger classifier.

3.1 AdaBoost Learning

We choose to use the version of boosting called gentle adaboost [2] due to it is simple to be implemented and numerically robust. Given a set of training examples as $(x_1, y_1), ..., (x_N, y_N)$, where $y_i \in \{+1, -1\}$ is the class label of the example $x_i \in R^n$. Boosting learning provides a sequential procedure to fit additive models of the form $F(x) = \sum_{m=1}^{M} f_m(x)$. Here $f_m(x)$ are often called weak learners, and $F(x)$ is called a strong learner. Gentle adaboost uses adaptive Newton steps for minimizing the cost

Table 1. Algorithm of Gentle AdaBoost

1. Start with weight $w_i = \frac{1}{N}, i = 1, 2, ..., N, F(x) = 0$
2. Repeat for m = 1, ... ,M
(a) Fit the regression function by weighted least squares fitting of Y to X.
(b) Update $F(x) \leftarrow F(x) + f_m(x)$
(c) Update $w_i \leftarrow w_i e^{-y_i f_m(x_i)}$ and normalization
3. Output the Classifier $F(x) = sign[\sum_{m=1}^{M} f_m(x)]$

function: $J = E[e^{-yF(x)}]$, which corresponds to minimizing a weighted squared error at each step.

In each step, the weak classifier $f_m(x)$ is chosen so as to minimize the weighted squared error:

$$J_{wse} = \sum_{i=1}^{N} w_i (y_i - f_m(x_i))^2 \tag{2}$$

3.2 Weak Classifiers

It is common to define the weak learners $f_m(x)$ to be the optimal threshold classification function [12], which is often called a stump. However, it is indicated in Section 2 that the value of MB-LBP features is non-metric. Hence it is impossible to use threshold-based function as weak learner.

Here we describe how the weak classifiers are designed. For each MB-LBP feature, we adopt multi-branch tree as weak classifiers. The multi-branch tree totally has 256 branches, and each branch corresponds to a certain discrete value of MB-LBP features. The weak classifier can be defined as:

$$f_m(x) = \begin{cases} a_0, & x^k = 0 \\ & \ldots \\ a_j, & x^k = j \\ & \ldots \\ a_{255}, & x^k = 255 \end{cases} \tag{3}$$

Where x^k denotes the k-th element of the feature vector x, and a_j, $j = 0, \cdots, 255$, are regression parameters to be learned. These weak learners are often called decision or regression trees. We can find the best tree-based weak classifier (the parameter k, a_j with minimized weighted squared error as Equ.(2)) just as we would learn a node in a regression tree.The minimization of Equ.(2))gives the following parameters:

$$a_j = \frac{\sum_i w_i y_i \delta(x_i^k = j)}{\sum_i w_i \delta(x_i^k = j)} \tag{4}$$

As each weak learner depends on a single feature, one feature is selected at each step. In the test phase, given a MB-LBP feature, we can get the corresponding regression value fast by such multi-branch tree. This function is similar to the lookup table (LUT) weak classifier for Haar-like features [1], the difference is that the LUT classifier gives a partition of real-value domain.

4 Experiments

In this section, we conduct two experiments to evaluate proposed method. (1) Comparing MB-LBP features with Haar-like features and original LBP features. (2) Evaluating the proposed detector on CMU+MIT face database.

A total of 10,000 face images were collected from various sources, covering out-of-plane and in-plan rotation in the range of [$-30°$,$30°$]. For each aligned face example, four synthesized face examples were generated by following random transformation: mirroring, random shifting to +1/-1 pixel, in-plane rotation within 15 degrees and scaling within 20% variations. The face examples were then cropped and re-scaled to 20×20 pixels. Totally, we get a set of 40,000 face examples. More than 20,000 large images which do not contain faces are used for collecting non-face samples.

4.1 Feature Comparison

In this subsection, we compare the performance of MB-LBP feature with Haar-like rectangle features and conventional LBP features. In the experiments, we use 26,000 face samples and randomly divide them to two equally parts, one for training the other for testing. The non-face samples are randomly collected from large images which do not contain faces. Our training set contains 13,000 face samples and 13,000 non-face samples, and the testing set contains 13,000 face samples and 50,000 non-face samples.

Based on Adaboost learning framework, three boosting classifiers are trained. Each of them contains selected 50 Haar-like features, conventional LBP features and MB-LBP features, respectively. Then they are evaluated on the test set. Fig. 4(a) shows the curves of the error rate (average of false alarm rate and false rejection rate) as a function of the number of the selected features in the training procedure. We can see the curve

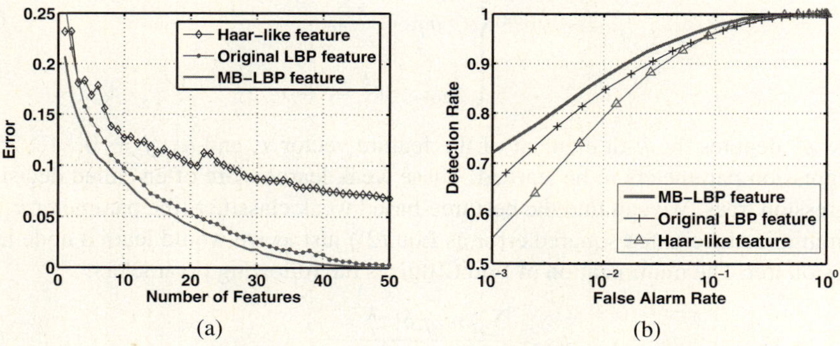

Fig. 4. Comparative results with MB-LBP features, Haar-like features and original LBP features. (a) The curves show the error rate as a function of the selected features in training process. (b) The ROC curves show the classification performance of the three classifiers on the test set.

corresponding to MB-LBP features has the lowest error rate. It indicates that the weak classifiers based on MB-LBP features are more discriminative. The ROC curves of the three classifiers on the test set can be found in Fig. 4(b). It is shown that in the given false alarm rate at 0.001, classifier based on MB-LBP features shows 15% higher correct rate than haar-like feature and 8% higher than original LBP feature. All the above shows the distinctive of MB-LBP features. It is mainly because the MB-LBP features can capture more information about the image structures.

4.2 Experimental Results on CMU+MIT Face Set

We trained a cascade face detector based on MB-LBP features and tested it on the MIT+CMU database which is widely used to evaluate the performance of face detection algorithm. This set consists of 130 images with 507 labeled frontal faces. For training the face detector, all collected 40,000 face samples are used, the bootstrap strategy is also used to re-collect non-face samples. Our trained detector has 9 layers including 470 MB-LBP features.Comparing with the Viola's cascade detector [12] which has 32 layers and 4297 features, our MB-LBP feature is much more efficient. From the results, we can see that our method get considerable performance with fewer features. The processing time of our detector for a 320x240 image is less than 0.1s on a P4 3.0GHz PC.

Table 2. Experimental results on MIT+CMU set

False Alarms	6	10	21	31	57	78	136	167	293	422
Ours	80.1%	-	85.6%	-	90.7%	-	91.9%	-	93.5%	-
Viola	-	78.3%	-	85.2%	-	90.1%	-	91.8%	-	93.7%

Fig. 5. Some detection results on MIT+CMU set

5 Conclusions

In this paper, we proposed multi-block local binary pattern(MB-LBP) features as descriptor for face detection. A boosting-based detector is implemented. Aims at the non-metric feature value of MB-LBP features, multi-branch regression tree is adopted to construct the weak classifiers. First, these features can capture more information about image structure than traditional Haar-like features and show more distinctive performance. Second, fewer feature number of the completed feature set makes the training process easier. In our experiment, it is shown that at the given false alarm rate 0.001, MB-LBP shows 15% higher correct rate than Haar-like feature and 8% higher than original LBP feature. Moreover, our face detector gets considerable performance on CMU+MIT database with fewer features.

Acknowledgements

This work was supported by the following funding resources: National Natural Science Foundation Project #60518002, National Science and Technology Supporting Platform Project #2006BAK08B06, National 863 Program Projects #2006AA01Z192 and #2006AA01Z193, Chinese Academy of Sciences 100 people project, and the AuthenMetric Collaboration Foundation.

References

1. Wu, B., Ai, H.Z., Huang, C., Lao, S.H.: Fast rotation invariant multi-view face detection based on real adaboost. In: FG (2004)
2. Friedman, J., Hastie, T., Tibshirani, R.: Additive logistic regression: A statistical view of boosting. Annals of Statistics (2000)
3. Froba, B., Ernst, A.: Face detection with the modified census transform. In: AFGR (2004)
4. Huang, C., Ai, H., Li, Y., Lao, S.: Learning sparse features in granular space for multi-view face detection. In: IEEE International conference on Automatic Face and Gesture Recognition, April 2006. IEEE Computer Society Press, Los Alamitos (2006)
5. Li, S.Z., Zhu, L., Zhang, Z.Q.: Statistical learning of multi-view face detection. In: Tistarelli, M., Bigun, J., Jain, A.K. (eds.) ECCV 2002. LNCS, vol. 2359. Springer, Heidelberg (2002)
6. Lienhart, R., Maydt, J.: An extended set of haar-like features for rapid object detection. In: ICIP (2002)
7. Mita, T., Kaneko, T., Hori, O.: Joint haar-like features for face detection. In: ICCV (2005)
8. Ojala, T., Pietikainen, M., Harwood, D.: A comparative study of texture measures with classification based on feature distributions. Pattern Recognition (January 1996)
9. Osuna, E., Freund, R., Girosi, F.: Training support vector machines: an application to face detection. In: CVPR (1997)
10. Rowley, H.A., Baluja, S., Kanade, T.: Neural network-based face detection. IEEE Transactions on Pattern Analysis and Machine Intelligence (1998)
11. Simard, P.Y., Cun, Y.A.L., Denker, J.S., Victorri, B.: Transformation invariance in pattern recognition - tangent distance and tangent propagation. Neural Networks: Tricks of the Trade (1998)
12. Viola, P., Jones, M.: Rapid object detection using a boosted cascade of simple features. In: IEEE Conference on Computer Vision and Pattern Recognition. IEEE Computer Society Press, Los Alamitos (2001)

Color Face Tensor Factorization and Slicing for Illumination-Robust Recognition

Yong-Deok Kim and Seungjin Choi

Department of Computer Science
Pohang University of Science and Technology
San 31 Hyoja-dong, Nam-gu, Pohang 790-784, Korea
{karma13,seungjin}@postech.ac.kr

Abstract. In this paper we present a face recognition method based on multiway analysis of color face images, which is robust to varying illumination conditions. Illumination changes cause large variations on color in face images. The main idea is to extract features with minimal color variations but with retaining image spatial information. We construct a tensor of color image ensemble, one of its coordinate reflects color mode, and employ the higher-order SVD (a multiway extension of SVD) of the tensor to extract such features. Numerical experiments show that our method outperforms existing subspace analysis methods including principal component analysis (PCA), generalized low rank approximation (GLRAM) and concurrent subspace analysis (CSA), in the task of face recognition under varying illumination conditions. The superiority is even more substantial in the case of small training sample size.

1 Introduction

Face recognition is a challenging pattern classification problem, which is encountered in many different areas such as biometrics, computer vision, and human computer interaction (HCI). Cruxes in practical face recognition systems result from varying illumination conditions, various facial expressions, pose variations, and so on. Of particular interest in this paper is the case of varying illumination conditions in color face image ensemble.

Various approaches and methods have been developed in face recognition. Subspace analysis is one of the most popular techniques, demonstrating its success in numerous visual recognition tasks such as face recognition, face detection and tracking. Exemplary subspace analysis methods include singular value decomposition (SVD), principal component analysis (PCA), independent component analysis (ICA), nonnegative matrix factorization (NMF), and Fisher linear discriminant analysis (LDA). All these methods seek a linear representation of face image ensemble such that basis images and encoding variables are learned, satisfying a certain fitting criterion with each face image represented by a vector.

Face images are formed by the interaction of multiple factors related to illuminations, color information, various poses, facial expressions, identities. Portion of such information are embedded in 2D spatial structure. Thus, face images,

S.-W. Lee and S.Z. Li (Eds.): ICB 2007, LNCS 4642, pp. 19–28, 2007.

intrinsically fit in multiway representation, known as *tensor*, reflecting various interactions between different modes. However, aforementioned subspace analysis methods are confined to at most 2-way representation. For example, color face images are converted to gray scale-valued vectors. This vectorization is a typical pre-processing in conventional subspace methods. It leads to high-dimensional vectors with losing some spatial structure, which results in a curse of dimensionality problem, making such methods to suffer from the small sample size problem.

Recently, there are a great deal of studies on multiway analysis in computer vision. These include 2D-PCA [1], generalized low rank approximation (GLRAM) [2], concurrent subspace analysis (CSA) [3], tensor faces [4] which employs the multilinear SVD (a.k.a HOSVD) [5,6], and multilinear ICA [7]. The basic idea of tensor analysis goes back to Tucker decomposition [8,9]. See [10] for a recent review of tensor factorization.

In the case of color face images, illumination change yields large variations on color in face images, even through they have exactly the same pose and facial expression. In this paper, we present a tensor factorization-based method for illumination-robust feature extraction in a task of color face image recognition. The method is referred to as *color face tensor factorization and slicing* (CFTFS). We form a 4-way tensor whose coordinates are associated with rows and columns of face images, color, and samples. The CFTFS employs the multilinear SVD in the 4-way tensor, simultaneously analyzing subspaces corresponding to rows, columns, and color. Then it chooses slices where the information about variations on row and column modes remain but variations on color mode are minimized. We demonstrate that CFTFS outperforms existing methods, including PCA, GLRAM, and CSA. The useful behavior of the method becomes more substantial, especially in the case of small training sample size.

The rest of this paper is organized as follows. In the next section we describe a brief overview of tensor algebra and Tucker decomposition. The proposed method, CFTFS is presented in Sec. 3. In Sec. 4, numerical experimental results are presented, showing that CFTFS is an indeed effective method for illumination-robust face recognition. Finally conclusions are drawn in Sec. 5.

2 Background: Multiway Analysis

2.1 Tensor Algebra

A tensor is a multiway array of data. For example, a vector is 1-way tensor and a matrix is 2-way tensor. The N-way tensor $\boldsymbol{\mathcal{X}} \in \mathbb{R}^{I_1 \times I_2 \times \cdots \times I_N}$ has N indices $(i_1, i_2, \ldots, i_N)$ and its elements are denoted by $x_{i_1 i_2 \ldots i_N}$ where $1 \leq i_n \leq I_n$. Mode-n vectors of an N-way tensor $\boldsymbol{\mathcal{X}}$ are I_n-dimensional vectors obtained from $\boldsymbol{\mathcal{X}}$ by varying index i_n while keeping the other indices fixed. In matrix, column vectors are referred to as mode-1 vectors and row vectors correspond to mode-2 vectors.

The mode-n vectors are column vectors of the matrix $\boldsymbol{X}_{(n)}$ which is the mode-n matricization (matrix unfolding) of the tensor $\boldsymbol{\mathcal{X}}$. The mode-n

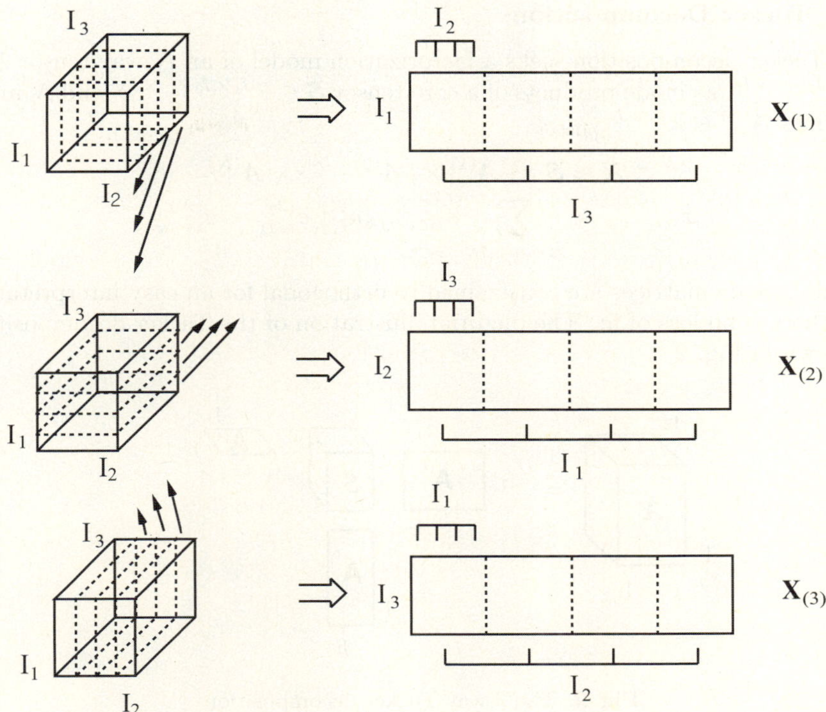

Fig. 1. Matricization of a 3-way tensor $\boldsymbol{\mathcal{X}} \in \mathbb{R}^{I_1 \times I_2 \times I_3}$ leads to $\boldsymbol{X}_{(1)} \in \mathbb{R}^{I_1 \times I_2 I_d}$, $\boldsymbol{X}_{(2)} \in \mathbb{R}^{I_2 \times I_3 I_1}$, and $\boldsymbol{X}_{(3)} \in \mathbb{R}^{I_3 \times I_1 I_2}$ which are constructed by the concatenation of frontal, horizontal, vertical slices, respectively

matricization of $\boldsymbol{\mathcal{X}} \in \mathbb{R}^{I_1 \times I_2 \times \cdots \times I_N}$ is denoted $\boldsymbol{X}_{(n)} \in \mathbb{R}^{I_n \times I_{n+1} I_{n+2} \cdots I_N I_1 I_2 \cdots I_{n-1}}$ where $I_{n+1} I_{n+2} \cdots I_N I_1 I_2 \cdots I_{n-1}$ is the cyclic order after n. The original index i_{n+1} runs fastest and i_{n-1} slowest in the columns of the matrix $\boldsymbol{X}_{(n)}$. Pictorial illustration of the mode-n matricization of a 3-way tensor is shown in Fig. 1.

The scalar product of two tensors $\boldsymbol{\mathcal{X}}, \boldsymbol{\mathcal{Y}} \in \mathbb{R}^{I_1 \times I_2 \times \cdots \times I_N}$ is defined as $\langle \boldsymbol{\mathcal{X}}, \boldsymbol{\mathcal{Y}} \rangle = \sum_{i_1, i_2, \ldots, i_N} x_{i_1 i_2 \cdots i_N} y_{i_1 i_2 \cdots i_N}$. The Frobenius norm of a tensor $\boldsymbol{\mathcal{X}}$ is given by $\|\boldsymbol{\mathcal{X}}\| = \sqrt{\langle \boldsymbol{\mathcal{X}}, \boldsymbol{\mathcal{X}} \rangle}$.

The mode-n product of a tensor $\boldsymbol{\mathcal{S}} \in \mathbb{R}^{J_1 \times J_2 \times \cdots \times J_n \times \cdots \times J_N}$ by a matrix $\boldsymbol{A}^{(n)} \in \mathbb{R}^{I_n \times J_n}$ is defined by

$$\left[\boldsymbol{\mathcal{S}} \times_n \boldsymbol{A}^{(n)} \right]_{j_1 \cdots j_{n-1} i_n j_{n+1} \cdots j_N} = \sum_{j_n=1}^{J_n} s_{j_1 \ldots j_{n-1} j_n j_{n+1} \cdots j_N} a_{i_n j_n}, \tag{1}$$

leading to a tensor $\boldsymbol{\mathcal{S}} \times_n \boldsymbol{A}^{(n)} \in \mathbb{R}^{J_1 \times J_2 \times \cdots \times I_n \times \cdots \times J_N}$. With the mode-$n$ product, a familiar matrix factorization $\boldsymbol{X} = \boldsymbol{U} \boldsymbol{S} \boldsymbol{V}^\top$ is written as $\boldsymbol{X} = \boldsymbol{S} \times_1 \boldsymbol{U} \times_2 \boldsymbol{V}$ in the tensor framework.

2.2 Tucker Decomposition

The Tucker decomposition seeks a factorization model of an N-way tensor $\boldsymbol{\mathcal{X}} \in \mathbb{R}^{I_1 \times I_2 \times \cdots \times I_N}$ as mode products of a core tensor $\boldsymbol{\mathcal{S}} \in \mathbb{R}^{J_1 \times J_2 \times \cdots \times J_N}$ and N mode matrices $\boldsymbol{A}^{(n)} \in \mathbb{R}^{I_n \times J_n}$,

$$\boldsymbol{\mathcal{X}} \approx \boldsymbol{\mathcal{S}} \times_1 \boldsymbol{A}^{(1)} \times_2 \boldsymbol{A}^{(2)} \cdots \times_N \boldsymbol{A}^{(N)} \tag{2}$$

$$x_{i_1 i_2 \cdots i_N} \approx \sum_{j_1, j_2, \ldots, j_N} s_{j_1 j_2 \cdots j_N} a^{(1)}_{i_1 j_1} a^{(2)}_{i_2 j_2} \cdots a^{(N)}_{i_N j_N}. \tag{3}$$

Usually, mode matrices are constrained to orthogonal for an easy interpretation and there is no loss of fit. The pictorial illustration of the Tucker decomposition is shown in Fig. 2.

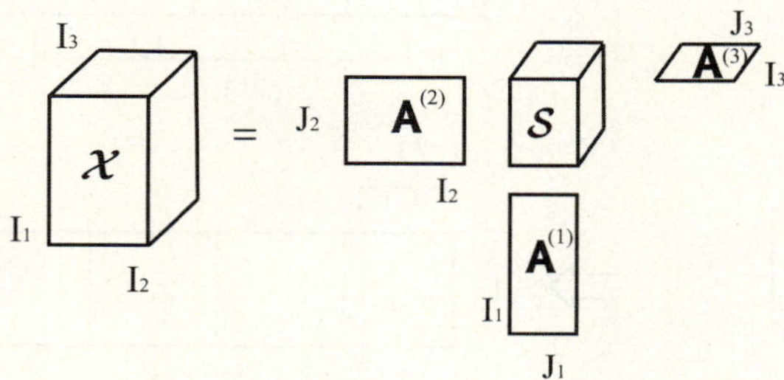

Fig. 2. The 3-way Tucker decomposition

In Tucker decomposition, all modes don't need to be analyzed. If mode-n is not analyzed, then associated component matrix $\boldsymbol{A}^{(n)}$ becomes $I_n \times I_n$ identity matrix $\boldsymbol{I}_{I_n}$. Now, we introduce new terminology 'N-way Tucker M decomposition' where *N-way* means we incorporate N-way tensor and *M* is the number of analyzed modes. This new terminology explains PCA, 2D-PCA, GLRAM, CSA, and HOSVD in general framework. Table 1 summarizes each method using this new terminology in the case of general multiway data and face image ensemble.

Suppose that $\boldsymbol{\Omega}$ is the set of analyzed modes. If all mode matrices are orthogonal, minimizing least square discrepancy between the data and model in Eq. (2) is equivalent to maximizing the function:

$$\mathcal{G}(\boldsymbol{A}^{(1)}, \boldsymbol{A}^{(2)}, \ldots, \boldsymbol{A}^{(N)}) = \|\boldsymbol{\mathcal{X}} \times_1 \boldsymbol{A}^{(1)\top} \times_2 \boldsymbol{A}^{(2)\top} \cdots \times_N \boldsymbol{A}^{(N)\top}\|^2, \tag{4}$$

over $\boldsymbol{A}^{(n)}$ for all $n \in \boldsymbol{\Omega}$. In the Tucker decomposition, Eq. (4) has no closed form solution, except for PCA, so local solution is found iteratively with Alternative Least Squares(ALS). In each step, only one of the component matrix is optimized, while keep others fixed. Suppose $n \in \boldsymbol{\Omega}$ and $\boldsymbol{A}^{(1)}, \ldots, \boldsymbol{A}^{(n-1)}, \boldsymbol{A}^{(n+1)}, \ldots, \boldsymbol{A}^{(N)}$ are fixed. Then Eq. (4) is reduced to a quadratic expression of $\boldsymbol{A}^{(n)}$, consisting of orthonormal columns. We have $\mathcal{G}(\boldsymbol{A}^{(n)}) = \|\boldsymbol{\mathcal{K}}^{(n)} \times_n \boldsymbol{A}^{(n)\top}\|^2 = \|\boldsymbol{A}^{(n)\top} \boldsymbol{K}_{(n)}\|^2$, where

$$\boldsymbol{\mathcal{K}}^{(n)} = \boldsymbol{\mathcal{X}} \times_1 \boldsymbol{A}^{(1)\top} \cdots \times_{n-1} \boldsymbol{A}^{(n-1)\top} \times_{n+1} \boldsymbol{A}^{(n+1)\top} \cdots \times_N \boldsymbol{A}^{N\top}, \tag{5}$$

Table 1. Tucker decomposition explains PCA, 2D-PCA, GLRAM, CSA, and HOSVD in general framework. Assume the last mode is associated with samples. The grayscale face image ensemble constructs the 3-way tensor(rows, columns, samples) and color face image ensemble does the 4-way tensor(rows, columns, color, samples).

Data type	Method	Tucker decomposition	Remark
N-way tensor	PCA	N-way Tucker 1	$\boldsymbol{A}^{(n)} = \boldsymbol{I}_{I_n}$ for $n \in \{1, \ldots, N-1\}$
	CSA	N-way Tucker $N-1$	$\boldsymbol{A}^{(N)} = \boldsymbol{I}_{I_N}$
	HOSVD	N-way Tucker N	$J_n \leq I_n$ for all n
Face image ensemble	PCA	3-way Tucker 1	$\boldsymbol{A}^{(1)} = \boldsymbol{I}_{I_1}, \boldsymbol{A}^{(2)} = \boldsymbol{I}_{I_2}$
	2D-PCA	3-way Tucker 1	$\boldsymbol{A}^{(1)} = \boldsymbol{I}_{I_1}, \boldsymbol{A}^{(3)} = \boldsymbol{I}_{I_3}$
	GLRAM	3-way Tucker 2	$\boldsymbol{A}^{(3)} = \boldsymbol{I}_{I_3}$
	CSA	4-way Tucker 3	$\boldsymbol{A}^{(4)} = \boldsymbol{I}_{I_4}$

Table 2. ALS algorithm for Tucker decomposition

Input: $\boldsymbol{\mathcal{X}}$, $\boldsymbol{\Omega}$, J_n for all $n \in \boldsymbol{\Omega}$.
Output: $\mathcal{S}$, $\boldsymbol{A}^{(n)}$ for all $n \in \{1, 2, \ldots, N\}$.

1. Initialize
- $\boldsymbol{A}^{(n)} \leftarrow \boldsymbol{I}_{I_n}$ for all $n \notin \boldsymbol{\Omega}$.
- $\boldsymbol{A}^{(n)} \leftarrow \mathrm{SVDS}(\boldsymbol{X}_{(n)}, J_n)$ for all $n \in \boldsymbol{\Omega}$.
- $\boldsymbol{\mathcal{S}} \leftarrow \boldsymbol{\mathcal{X}} \times_1 \boldsymbol{A}^{(1)\top} \times_2 \boldsymbol{A}^{(2)\top} \cdots \times_N \boldsymbol{A}^{(N)\top}$.

2. Repeat until converges
for all $n \in \boldsymbol{\Omega}$
- $\boldsymbol{\mathcal{K}}^{(n)} \leftarrow \boldsymbol{\mathcal{X}} \times_1 \boldsymbol{A}^{(1)\top} \cdots \times_{n-1} \boldsymbol{A}^{(n-1)\top} \times_{n+1} \boldsymbol{A}^{(n+1)\top} \cdots \times_N \boldsymbol{A}^{N\top}$.
- $\boldsymbol{K}_{(n)} \leftarrow$ mode-n matricization of $\boldsymbol{\mathcal{K}}^{(n)}$.
- $\boldsymbol{A}^{(n)} \leftarrow \mathrm{SVDS}(\boldsymbol{K}_{(n)}, J_n)$.

3. $\boldsymbol{\mathcal{S}} \leftarrow \boldsymbol{\mathcal{X}} \times_1 \boldsymbol{A}^{(1)\top} \times_2 \boldsymbol{A}^{(2)\top} \cdots \times_N \boldsymbol{A}^{(N)\top}$.

and $\boldsymbol{K}_{(n)}$ is the mode-n matricization of $\boldsymbol{\mathcal{K}}^{(n)}$. Hence the columns of $\boldsymbol{A}^{(n)}$ can be found as an orthonormal basis for the dominant subspace of the column space of $\boldsymbol{K}_{(n)}$. The resulting algorithm is presented in Table 2.

3 Color Face Tensor Factorization and Slicing

In the case of color face images, illumination change yields large variations on color in face images, even through they have exactly the same pose and facial expression. Conventional methods, such as PCA and GLRAM, convert color image into grayscale image and then reduced the dimension. As the illumination changes, the intensity value also varies extremely. However there is no way to reduce this fluctuation in garyscale image based method, since they already

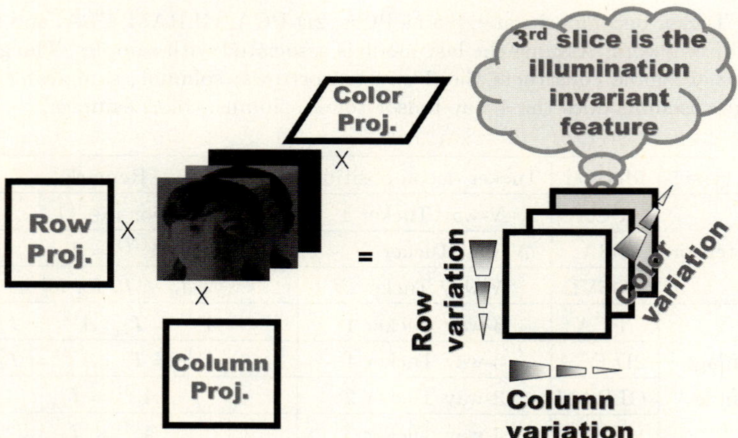

Fig. 3. CFTFS finds a transformation which reduces the size of image and minimizes the variation on color

thrown away the information on color. If there are large illumination changes but only small number of samples are available, then these methods can't prevent a sharp decline on face recognition performance. Our propose method, *color face tensor factorization and slicing* (CFTFS), solves these problem by conserving the color information and the spatial structure of original color face image ensemble.

With the help of multiway analysis, the CFTFS simultaneously analyzes the subspace of rows, columns, and color. Then CFTFS slices a feature tensor where information about variations on rows and columns modes are retained but on color mode are minimized. Basic idea of CFTFS is illustrated in Fig. 3.

CFTFS uses the 4-way tensor $\boldsymbol{\mathcal{X}}$ in which (I_1, I_2) is the size of face image, $I_3 = 3$ is the number of color coordinates(RGB), and I_4 is the number samples. The face image data is centered so that it has zero mean:

$$\boldsymbol{\mathcal{X}}_{:,:,:,i_4} \leftarrow \boldsymbol{\mathcal{X}}_{:,:,:,i_4} - \boldsymbol{\mathcal{M}} \text{ for all } 1 \leq i_4 \leq I_4, \tag{6}$$

where $\boldsymbol{\mathcal{M}} = \frac{1}{I_4} \sum_{i_4}^{I_4} \boldsymbol{\mathcal{X}}_{:,:,:,i_4}$.

As its name hinted, CFTFS consists two stage: dimension reduction and slicing. At dimension reduction stage, it play the 4-way Tucker 3 decomposition, where mode-4 is not analyzed and $J_1 < I_1$, $J_2 < I_2$, and $J_3 = I_3 = 3$. In fact, it is equivalent to CSA which minimizes

$$\sum_{i_4=1}^{I_4} \|\boldsymbol{\mathcal{X}}_{:,:,:,i_4} - \boldsymbol{\mathcal{S}}_{:,:,:,i_4} \times_1 \boldsymbol{A}^{(1)} \times_2 \boldsymbol{A}^{(2)} \times_3 \boldsymbol{A}^{(3)}\|^2 \tag{7}$$

over $\boldsymbol{A}^{(1)}, \boldsymbol{A}^{(2)}, \boldsymbol{A}^{(3)}$, and $\boldsymbol{\mathcal{S}}_{:,:,:,i_4}$ for all $1 \leq i_4 \leq I_4$. The color face tensor $\boldsymbol{\mathcal{X}}_{:,:,:,i_4}$ is projected to an intermediate feature tensor $\boldsymbol{\mathcal{S}}_{:,:,:,i_4} = \boldsymbol{\mathcal{X}}_{:,:,:,i_4} \times_1 \boldsymbol{A}^{(1)\top} \times_2 \boldsymbol{A}^{(2)\top} \times_3 \boldsymbol{A}^{(3)\top}$. Hence the dimension is reduced from $I_1 \times I_2 \times 3$ to $J_1 \times J_2 \times 3$.

Since we use SVDS in our algorithm, the first columns in mode matrices represent the most dominant subspace, the second columns do the second most subspace orthogonal to the first one, and so on. Thus the third slice $\boldsymbol{\mathcal{S}}_{:,:,3,i_4}$ of an intermediate feature tensor is a final illumination-robust feature matrix. In the final feature matrix, information of $\boldsymbol{\mathcal{X}}_{:,:,:,i_4}$ about variations on rows and columns are retained but on color are minimized.

The illumination-robust feature extraction for a test color face tensor $\boldsymbol{\mathcal{Y}} \in \mathbb{R}^{I_1 \times I_2 \times 3}$ is summarized to

$$\boldsymbol{\mathcal{T}} = (\boldsymbol{\mathcal{Y}} - \boldsymbol{\mathcal{M}}) \times_1 \boldsymbol{A}^{(1)^\top} \times_2 \boldsymbol{A}^{(1)^\top} \times_3 \boldsymbol{a}_3^{(3)\top}, \tag{8}$$

where $\boldsymbol{a}_3^{(3)}$ is the third column vector of $\boldsymbol{A}^{(3)}$.

4 Numerical Experiments

Our MATLAB implementation of the CFTFS partly uses the tensor toolbox [11]. We show the effectiveness of our proposed method for the illumination-robust face recognition, with CMU PIE face database [12], comparing it PCA,

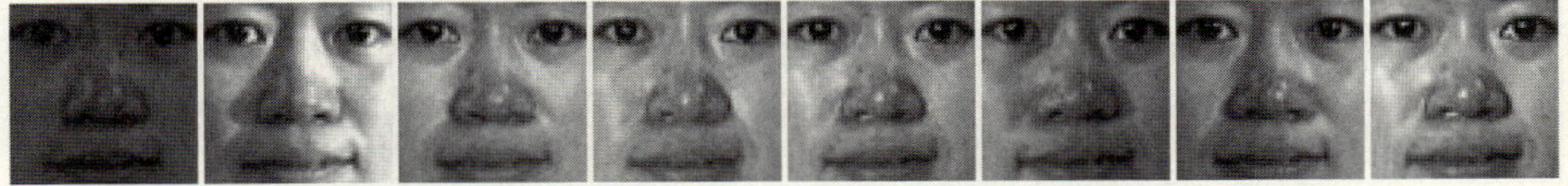

Fig. 4. Sample face images are shown. Illumination change yields large variations on color in face images, even through they have exactly the same pose and facial expression.

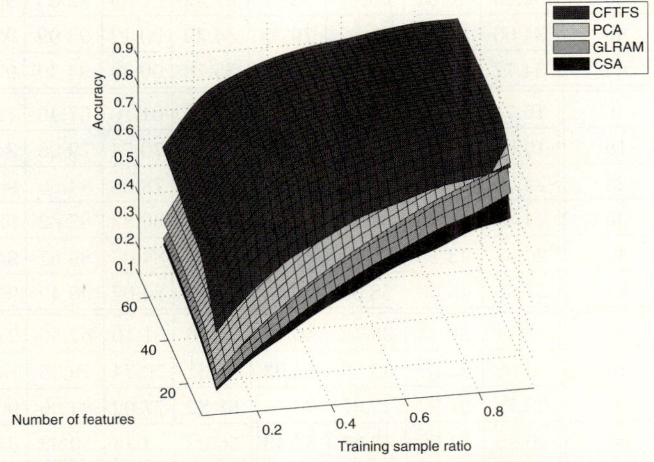

Fig. 5. From top to bottom, face recognition accuracy of CFTFS, PCA, GLRAM, and CSA. CFTFS has the highest accuracy and robust to lack of training samples.

GLRAM, and CSA. CMU PIE database contains 41,368 face images of 68 peoples. In our experiment, we use the sub-database contains 1,632 face images. It has 24 varying illumination condition with exactly same pose(C27) and facial expression(neutral) for each person. We fix the location of the two eyes, crop the face, and resize to 30×30 pixel. Sample face images are shown in Fig. 4.

Fig. 5 and Table 3 show the recognition result for 4 methods. The (x, y, z) axis represent the number of features, training sample ratio, and recognition accuracy. The number of features are $\{9, 16, 25, 36, 49, 64\}$ and training sample ratio are

Table 3. Recognition accuracy over various number of features and training sample ratio. CFTFS has the higher recognition accuracy than others in the most of the time. Moreover superiority becomes more substantial, especially in the case of small training sample size.

	# of features	training sample ratio(%)								
		10	20	30	40	50	60	70	80	90
CFTFS	9	36.67	50.85	61.27	68.04	74.75	78.74	83.06	85.32	88.19
	16	45.32	63.63	73.45	80.81	85.63	89.81	93.01	95.54	97.45
	25	52.99	70.82	80.50	86.46	90.88	94.19	96.56	98.10	99.14
	36	54.62	72.90	82.42	87.87	91.84	95.17	97.03	98.51	99.69
	49	58.45	75.62	85.07	90.20	93.67	95.97	97.43	99.13	99.63
	64	61.41	78.12	85.80	90.74	93.79	95.58	97.75	99.23	99.45
PCA	9	21.37	35.31	46.41	55.95	64.27	71.62	78.59	84.22	89.85
	16	26.44	41.71	54.17	65.26	74.04	80.54	87.89	91.89	96.93
	25	30.14	47.25	59.86	70.21	78.52	85.65	90.48	94.43	97.73
	36	32.10	50.62	63.77	73.47	81.42	87.89	92.63	96.12	98.50
	49	34.06	52.32	65.92	76.39	84.32	90.12	93.99	97.70	98.99
	64	34.72	54.47	67.35	78.28	85.28	90.38	94.49	97.58	99.60
GLRAM	9	16.74	28.44	38.18	46.97	54.76	61.10	67.46	72.42	78.90
	16	19.68	32.87	44.53	54.93	63.31	70.74	79.06	84.46	91.44
	25	22.76	37.89	50.01	60.25	69.30	78.08	84.58	90.05	95.09
	36	24.38	40.69	53.62	63.68	72.94	80.82	87.02	92.67	96.84
	49	26.65	43.19	55.74	67.46	76.53	84.03	89.67	94.54	97.30
	64	27.90	45.50	58.09	69.45	78.13	84.62	90.49	95.38	98.83
CSA	9	16.74	28.44	38.18	46.97	54.76	61.10	67.46	72.42	78.90
	16	19.68	32.87	44.53	54.93	63.31	70.74	79.06	84.46	91.44
	25	22.72	37.99	49.67	60.59	68.82	77.02	84.06	90.37	95.06
	36	20.85	34.78	46.62	57.43	66.02	73.84	80.92	87.16	92.55
	49	18.34	31.11	41.50	51.35	59.67	67.19	74.55	79.57	86.53
	64	15.59	26.33	34.61	42.67	49.14	56.00	60.76	66.53	69.63

$\{0.1, 0.2, \ldots, 0.9\}$. The experiments are carried out 20 times independently for each case and the mean accuracy are used.

It is known that GLRAM and CSA are has more image compression ability than PCA. However, our experiment results show that they are not suitable for the face recognition under varying illumination conditions. Especially, CSA shows the poorest result since it captures the feature where dominant variations on color remain. The slicing, difference between CFTFS and CSA, dramatically increases the recognition performance. As Fig. 5 and Table. 3 show, CFTFS has the higher recognition accuracy than others in the most of the time. Moreover superiority of our methods becomes more substantial, especially in the case of small training sample size.

5 Conclusions

In this paper, we have presented a method of *color face tensor factorization and slicing* which extracts an illumination-robust feature. Revisiting the Tucker decomposition, we have explained our algorithm in general framework with PCA, 2D PCA, GLRAM, CSA, and HOSVD. Using the 4-way Tucker 3 decomposition, subspaces of rows, columns, and color are simultaneously analyzed and then feature, in which information about variations on rows and columns are retained but on color are minimized, is extracted by slicing. Numerical experiments have confirmed that our method indeed effective for face recognition under a condition in which a large illumination change exists and only small number of training samples are available.

Acknowledgments. This work was supported by Korea MIC under ITRC support program supervised by the IITA (IITA-2006-C1090-0603-0045).

References

1. Yang, J., Zhang, D., Frangi, A.F., Yang, J.Y.: Two-dimensional PCA: A new approach to appearance-based face representation and recognition. IEEE Trans. Pattern Analysis and Machine Intelligence 26, 131–137 (2004)
2. Ye, J.: Generalized low rank approximations of matrices. In: Proceedings of International Conference on Machine Learning, Banff, Canada, pp. 887–894 (2004)
3. Xu, D., Yan, S., Zhang, L., Zhang, H.J., Liu, Z., Shum, H.Y.: Concurrent subspace analysis. In: Proceedings of IEEE International Conference on Computer Vision and Pattern Recognition, San Diego, CA, pp. 203–208. IEEE Computer Society Press, Los Alamitos (2005)
4. Vasilescu, M.A.O., Terzopoulos, D.: Multilinear subsapce analysis of image ensembles. In: Proceedings of IEEE International Conference on Computer Vision and Pattern Recognition, Madison, Wisconsin (2003)
5. de Lathauwer, L., de Moor, B., Vandewalle, J.: A multilinear singular value decomposition. SIAM J. Matrix Anal. Appl. 21, 1253–1278 (2000)
6. de Lathauwer, L., de Moor, B., Vandewalle, J.: One the best rank-1 and rank-$(R_1, R_2, \ldots, R_N)$ approximation of higher-order tensros. SIAM J. Matrix Anal. Appl. 21, 1324–1342 (2000)

7. Vasilescu, M.A.O., Terzopoulos, D.: Multilinear independent component analysis. In: Proceedings of IEEE International Conference on Computer Vision and Pattern Recognition, San Diego, California (2005)
8. Tucker, L.R.: Some mathematical notes on three-mode factor analysis. Psychometrika 31, 279–311 (1966)
9. Kroonenberg, P.M., de Leeuw, J.: Principal component analysis of three-mode data by means of alternating least squares algorithms. Psychometrika 45, 69–97 (1980)
10. Kolda, T.G.: Multilinear operators for higher-order decompositions. Technical Report SAND2006-2081, Sandia National Laboratories (2006)
11. Bader, B.W., Kolda, T.G.: Algorithm 862: MATLAB tensor classes for fast algorithm prototyping. ACM Trans. Mathematical Software 32, 635–653 (2006)
12. Sim, T., Baker, S., Bsat, M.: The CMU pose, illumination, and expression database. IEEE Trans. Pattern Analysis and Machine Intelligence 25, 1615–1618 (2003)

Robust Real-Time Face Detection Using Face Certainty Map

Bongjin Jun and Daijin Kim

Department of Computer Science and Engineering
Pohang University of Science and Technology,
{simple21,dkim}@postech.ac.kr

Abstract. In this paper, we present a robust real-time face detection algorithm. We improved the conventional face detection algorithms for three different steps. For preprocessing step, we revise the modified census transform to compensate the sensitivity to the change of pixel values. For face detection step, we propose difference of pyramid(DoP) images for fast face detection. Finally, for postprocessing step, we propose face certainty map(FCM) which contains facial information such as facial size, location, rotation, and confidence value to reduce FAR(False Acceptance Rate) with constant detection performance. The experimental results show that the reduction of FAR is ten times better than existing cascade adaboost detector while keeping detection rate and detection time almost the same.

1 Introduction

Face detection is an essential preprocessing step for face recognition[1], surveillance, robot vision interface, and facial expression recognition. It also has many application areas such as picture indexing, tracking, clustering and so on. However face detection has its intrinsic difficulties for the following reasons. First, face is not a rigid object, i.e. every person has different facial shape and different form/location of facial features such as eyes, nose, and mouth. Second, face of the same person looks differently as the facial expression, facial pose, and illumination condition changes. Finally, it is almost impossible to train infinite number of non-face patterns, consequently unexpected false acceptance or false rejection could be occurred.

The procedure of face detection could be divided as preprocessing step, face detection step, and postprocessing step. First, for preprocessing step, illumination compensation techniques like histogram equalization[2], normalization to zero mean and unit variance on the analysis window[3], and modified census transform[4] have been proposed. Second, for detecting faces, many classification algorithms have been proposed to classify the face and non-face patterns such as: skin color based approaches[5][6], SVM[7][8], gaussian mixture model[9], maximum likelihood[10], neural network[11] [8], and adaboost[3][4]. Finally, for postprocessing step, the algorithms usually group detected faces which is located in the similar position. Then, they select only one face from each face group and

S.-W. Lee and S.Z. Li (Eds.): ICB 2007, LNCS 4642, pp. 29–38, 2007.

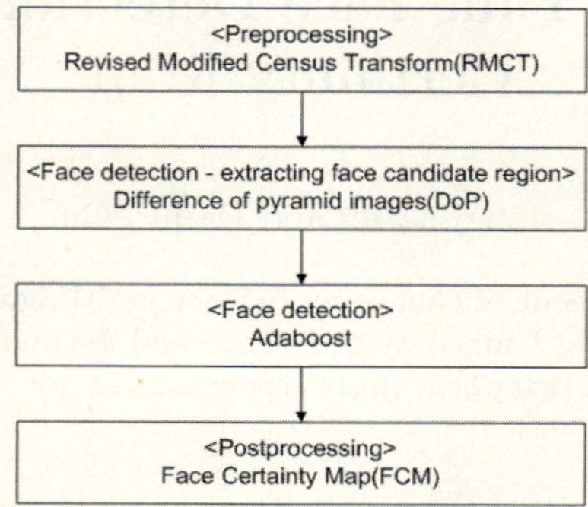

Fig. 1. The overall procedure of the proposed algorithm

determine the size, location, and rotation of the selected face. These methods usually show good performance, but have difficulties in learning every non-face patterns in natural scene. In addition, these methods are somewhat slow due to much computation steps.

In this paper, we present a novel face detection algorithm. For preprocessing step, we revise the modified census transform to compensate the sensitivity to the change of pixel values. For face detection step, we propose we propose difference of pyramid(DoP) images for fast face detection. Finally, for postprocessing step, we propose face certainty map(FCM) which contains facial information such as facial size, location, rotation, and confidence value to reduce FAR(False Acceptance Rate) with constant detection performance(Fig. 1).

The outline of this paper is as follows: in section 2, we explain modified census transform and our proposed revised modified census transform for preprocessing step. In section 3, we explain face detection using adaboost[4], our proposed face detection method, and the combined system. In section 4, we propose face certainty map for postprocessing step. In section5, we show the experimental results and analysis. Finally, some conclusions of this work are given in section 6.

2 Preprocessing Step

2.1 Revised Modified Census Transform

Zabin and Woodfill proposed an illumination insensitive local transform method called census transform(CT) which is an ordered set of comparisons of pixel intensities in a local neighborhood representing which pixels have lesser intensity than the center[12]. Let $N(x)$ define a local spatial neighborhood of the pixel at x so that $x \notin N(x)$, a comparison function $C(I(x), I(x'))$ be 1 if $I(x) < I(x')$, and $\bigotimes$ denote the concatenation operation, then the census transform at x is defined as

$$T(x) = \bigotimes_{y \in N} C(I(x), I(y)). \tag{1}$$

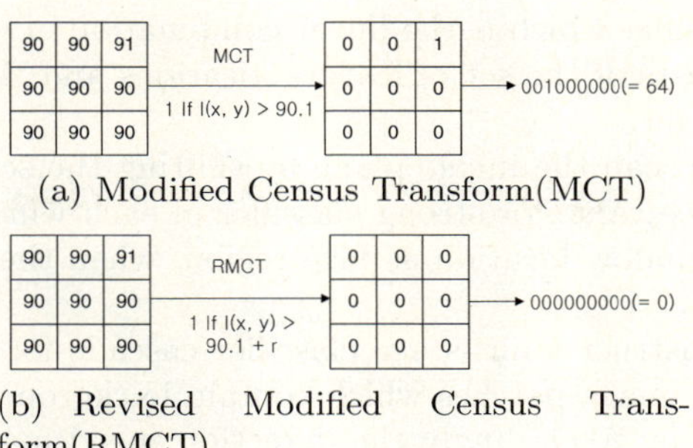

(a) Modified Census Transform(MCT)

(b) Revised Modified Census Transform(RMCT)

Fig. 2. Comparison of MCT and RMCT

Since census transform transforms pixel values by comparison with center pixel value, it can not transforms the pixel values equal to center pixel value.

Fröba and Ernst proposed modified census transform(MCT) to solve this problem[4]. Let $N'(x)$ be a local spatial neighborhood of the pixel at x so that $N'(x) = N(x) \cup x$. The intensity mean on this neighborhood is denoted by $\bar{I}(x)$. With this, they reformulate equation 1 and write the modified census transform as

$$\Gamma(x) = \bigotimes_{y \in N'} C(\bar{I}(x), I(y)). \tag{2}$$

Using equation 2, they could determine all of the 511 structure kernels defined on a 3×3 neighborhood, while CT has only 256 structure kernels. However, as you can see in Fig 2-(a), MCT is sensitive to subtle changes of pixel values in local region. To solve this problem, we revised MCT by addition of a small value r(=2 or 3) as

$$\Upsilon(x) = \bigotimes_{y \in N'} C(\bar{I}(x) + r, I(y)). \tag{3}$$

We call equation 3 as revised modified census transform(RMCT). RMCT transforms the pixel values to one of 511 patterns in 3×3 neighborhood. Since the local pixel value changes in 3×3 neighborhood is insensitive to illumination change, this transform is robust to illumination change(Fig 2-(b)). Moreover, since RMCT has regular patterns which can represent facial features, it is good to classify face and non-face patterns.

3 Face Detection Step

3.1 Face Detection Using RMCT and Adaboost

In this section, we present our proposed face detection algorithm using RMCT and adaboost. RMCT transforms the pixel values to one of 511 patterns in 3×3 neighborhood. Then, using the training images transformed by RMCT, we construct the weak classifier which classifies the face and non-face patterns and the strong classifier which is the linear combination of weak classifiers. The weak classifier consists of the set of feature locations and the confidence values for each RMCT pattern.

In test phase, we scan the image plane by shifting the scanning window and obtain the confidence value for strong classifier in each window location. Then, we determine the window location as face region, when the confidence value is above the threshold.

Moreover, we construct multi-stage classifier cascade for fast face detection. We expect that the image patches which contain background are rejected from early stage of cascade. Accordingly the detection speed may increase[3][4]. For training multi-stage classifier cascade, the non-face training images for first classifier are composed of arbitrary non-face images, while that of later classifiers are composed of the images which is falsely accepted by the former classifiers.

3.2 Speed Up the Algorithm

The face detector analyzes image patches of pre-defined size. Each window has to be classified either as a face or non-face. In order to detect faces in the input image, conventional face detection algorithms have been carried out by scanning all possible analysis windows. In addition, to find faces of various size, the image is repeatedly down-scaled with a pre-defined scaling factor. This is done until the scaled image is smaller than the sub window size. Although face detection by this full-search algorithm shows optimal performance, it is computationally expensive and slow.

To solve this problem, we propose difference of pyramid(DoP) images coupled with two-dimensional logarithmic search. First, we obtain face candidate region using DoP. Since the algorithm does not search the whole input image but the face candidate region, we expect it will reduce the computational time.

Difference of Pyramid Images. Extracting face candidate region using motion difference has been adopted for fast face detection in many previous works. However this method assumes that the location of camera is fixed and the background image is constant. Accordingly, it is difficult to adopt this method to still image or image sequence from moving camera. We propose difference of pyramid images(DoP) for compensating this problem. In order to obtain face candidate region using motion difference, at least two images are required such as background image and input image or image of previous frame and image of current frame. However, we can obtain face candidate region from single image using DoP, since it is computed not from image sequence but from single image. Thus, we are able to adopt this algorithm to still image and image sequence from moving camera as well.

Many face detection algorithms construct several numbers of down-scaled pyramid images and then scan each pyramid image using scanning window with pre-defined size. In this paper, we construct n down-scaled images which constitute an image pyramid. Then we obtain $n-1$ DoP image by subtract $i-th$ pyramid image from $(i-1)-th$ pyramid image. Since the size of $i-th$ pyramid

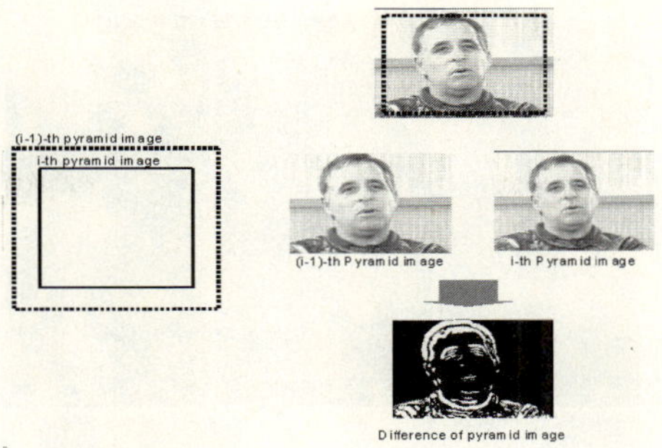

Fig. 3. Difference of Pyramid Images

image and $(i-1)-th$ pyramid image are different, we first align each image with the center point then obtain the DoP image by subtracting corresponding pixel points. Since plain background has little changes in DoP image, we can perform fast face detection. The pixel points in DoP image which have higher value than threshold are selected as face candidate region. Fig. 3 shows some example images of DoP.

4 Postprocessing Step

4.1 Face Certainty Map

For minimizing FAR(False Acceptance Rate) and FRR(False Rejection Rate), existing face detection algorithms concentrate on learning optimal model parameters and devising optimal detection algorithm. However, since the model parameters are determined by the face and non-face images in the training set, it is not guaranteed that the algorithms work well for novel images. In addition, there are infinite number of non-face patterns in real-world, accordingly it is almost impossible to train every non-face patterns in natural scene. As a result, the face detection algorithms, which showed good performance during the training phase, show high FRR and FAR in real environment.

The face detector we described in section 3.1 determines the image patch in the current scanning window as face when the confidence value is above the threshold and determines it as non-face when the confidence value is beyond the threshold. We call the scanning window of which the confidence value is above the threshold as detected face window. Fig. 4 shows some examples of the face detection algorithm proposed in section 3.1: the rectangles in each figure represent the detected face windows. We can see that while the face regions are detected perfectly, there are several falsely accepted regions(blue circle regions). In addition, when we investigate the figures precisely, there are numbers of detected face windows near real face region, while few detected face windows are near falsely accepted regions. With this observation, we propose face certainty

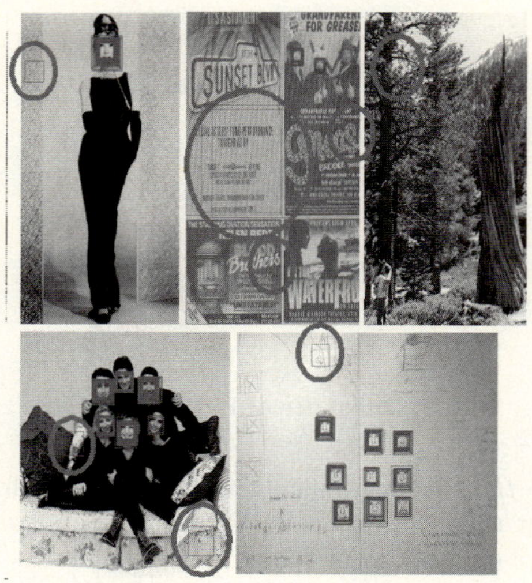

Fig. 4. Face Detection Results Without FCM

map(FCM) which can reduce FAR with constant detection performance and no additional training.

As you can see in Fig. 4, there are multiple detected face windows, even though there is only one face in the input image. For real face region, there are detected face windows with same location but different scale(Fig. 5-(a)) and detected face windows with same scale but different location(Fig. 5-(b)). However, falsely accepted regions do not show this property. Consequently, we can determine the regions where multiple detected face windows are overlapped as face region and the regions with no overlapped detected face windows as falsely accepted region. By adopting this methodology, we can reduce FAR greatly.

For now, we explain how to adopt FCM to the face detection algorithm we described in section 3.1. The detailed explanation of the procedure is given below.

1. For each scanning window centered at (x, y), we compute the confidence value.
$$H_i(\varUpsilon) = \sum_{p \in S_i} h_p(\varUpsilon(p)),$$
where i represents the $i-th$ cascade, p represents the $p-th$ feature location, and S_i is the set of feature locations, respectively.
2. The confidence value cumulated for all n cascade is like following:
$$S(x, y) = \sum_{i=1}^{n} H_i(\varUpsilon), \tag{4}$$
if $H_i(\varUpsilon)$ for all i is above threshold, otherwise 0.

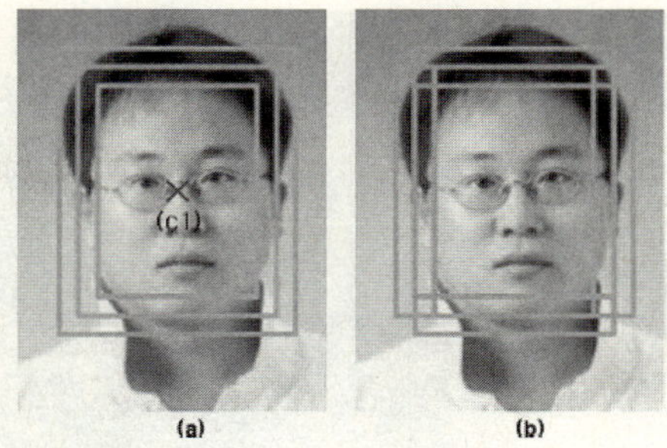

Fig. 5. Detected Face Windows;(a)Detected face windows which have the same center point(C1) but different scale (b) Detected face windows which have the same scale but different center point

We compute the cumulated confidence value for every pixel position in the image.

3. We also compute equation 4 for all pyramid images, then we have $S_p(x, y), p = 1, \ldots, m$, where m is the total number of constructed pyramid images and the pixel locations (x, y) of each down-scaled pyramid image are translated to its corresponding original image locations.
4. The FCM for location (x, y) consists of four items such as $S_{max}(x, y)$, $W_{max}(x, y)$, $H_{max}(x, y)$, and $C(x, y)$. $S_{max}(x, y)$ is the maximum confidence value among $S_p(x, y), p = 1, \ldots, m$, $W_{max}(x, y)$ and $H_{max}(x, y)$ is the width and height of the detected face window which has the maximum confidence value, and $C(x, y)$ is the confidence value cumulated for all m pyramid images $C(x, y) = \sum_{p=1}^{m} S_p(x, y)$.
5. Since we constructed FCM, we can determine the face region using it. First, we look for the values above threshold in $S_{max}(x, y)$. Then we determine the location (x, y) as the center of face when $C(x, y)$ is above threshold. The non-face region where the maximum confidence value is above threshold is not classified as a face region, since $C(x, y)$ is lower than the threshold. Consequently, we can reduce the FAR using our proposed FCM.

5 Experimental Results and Discussion

For constructing training face data, we gathered 17,000 face images from internet and Postech DB[13]. Gathered face images contain multiple human species, variety of illumination conditions, and expression variation. Each image is aligned by eye location, and we resize images to 22×22 base resolution. In addition, for the robustness to image rotation, we generated another 25,060 face images by rotating gathered face images to -3, 0, 3 degrees.

For non-face training data, we collected 5,000 images which include no face image from internet. Then, we extracted image patches from collected internet images by random size and position. After that, we generated 60,000 non-face

Fig. 6. Experimental Results

images by resizing extracted image patches to the same scale of training face images. We used these 60,000 non-face images as the training non-face data for the first stage of cascade. For the next stages of cascade, we used non-face data which are considered as face image by the previous cascade(i.e. we used false positives of previous cascade as training non-face data for training current cascade). A validation training data set is used for obtaining threshold value and stop condition of each stage of cascade. The validation set face and non-face images exclude the images used for training. We constructed validation set of 15,000 face images and 25,000 non-face images by the same way as we used for training data.

For each cascade, we preprocessed each face and non-face image using RMCT. Then we chose the feature positions for classification (S_i) and obtained classification value($H_i(\Upsilon)$) and threshold value(T_i) for each position. We constructed the face detector with 4 cascade and the maximal number of allowed position for each cascade is 40, 80, 160, and 400, respectively. In addition, the RMCT is defined 511 patterns in 3×3 neighborhood. Accordingly, we can not apply the 3×3 RMCT to the training images which have the size 22×22. Thus, we excluded the outer areas of each image and used the inner 20×20 areas of it.

We tested our algorithm on CMU+MIT frontal face test set. Fig. 6 and table 1 represents the results of face detection. When we used FCM, the reduction of FAR

Table 1. Results of Face Detection

Detector	Number of False Detection
RMCT, adaboost and FCM	3
RMCT and adaboost	93
Viola-Jones	78
Rowley-Baluja-Kanade	167
Bernhard Froba	27

is ten times better than the cascade adaboost detector with the same detection rate, while the detection time is almost the same. The cascade adaboot detector needs computations for grouping and eliminating overlapped face candidate region. In contrast, proposed detector does not need these computations but needs the computation for FCM. Operating on 320 by 240 pixel images, faces are detected at 23 frames per second on a conventional 3.2 GHz Intel Pentium IV system and 6 frames per second on OMAP5912(ARM9 system).

6 Conclusion

In this paper, we proposed a face and robust face detection algorithm using difference of pyramid(DoP) images and face certainty map(FCM). The experimental results showed that the reduction of FAR is ten times better than existing cascade adaboost detector while keeping detection rate and detection time almost the same. Existing adaboost face detection algorithms have to add more cascade stages for non-face images in order to reduce FAR. However, since it needs more weak classifier for constructing strong classifier, the processing time increases. Moreover, as the number of stages in cascade increase, FRR also increase. We were free from these drawbacks and increased detection performance by applying FCM to existing adaboost face detection algorithm. Since we can reduce FAR, the number of stages in cascade is also minimized, while preserving the same performance as existing algorithm which has more stages of cascade. Accordingly training time and processing time is faster than existing algorithm. Furthermore, FCM can be applied to any face detection algorithm beside adaboost which obtains confidence value or probability.

In this work, we applied the algorithm to only frontal faces. A future extension of this work could be pose and rotation invariant face detection algorithm

Acknowledgements

This work was partially supported by the Korea Science and Engineering Foundation (KOSEF) through the Biometrics Engineering Research Center (BERC) at Yonsei University. Also, It was financially supported by the Ministry of Education and Human Resources Development(MOE), the Ministry of Commerce, Industry and Energy(MOCIE) and the Ministry of Labor(MOLAB) through the fostering project of the Lab of Excellency.

References

1. Lee, H.-S., Kim, D.: Facial expression transformations for expression-invariant face recognition. In: Proc. of International Symposium on Visual Computing, pp. 323–333 (2006)
2. Sung, K.K.: Learning and Example Selection for Object and Pattern Recognition. PhD thesis, MIT, AI Lab, Cambridge (1996)
3. Viola, P., Jones, M.: Fast and Robust Classification using Asymmetric Adaboost and a Detector Cascade. In: Advances in Neural Information Processing System, vol. 14, MIT Press, Cambridge (2002)
4. Froba, B., Ernst, A.: Face detection with the modified census transform. In: Sixth IEEE International Conference on Automatic Face and Gesture Recognition. IEEE Computer Society Press, Los Alamitos (2004)
5. Yang, J., Waibel, A.: A real-time face tracker. In: Proc. 3rd Workshop on Appl. of Computer Vision, pp. 142–147 (1996)
6. Dai, Y., Nakano, Y.: Face texture model based on sgld and its application in face detection in a color scene. Pattern Recognition 29, 1007–1017 (1996)
7. Osuna, E.: Support Vector Machines: Training and Applications. PhD thesis, MIT, EE/CS Dept., Cambridge (1998)
8. Mohan, A., Papageorgiou, C., Poggio, T.: Examplebased object detection in images by components. IEEE Transactions on Pattern Analysis and Machine Intelligence 23, 349–361 (2001)
9. Sung, K.K., Poggio, T.: Example-based learning for view-based human face detection. IEEE Transactions on Pattern Analysis and Machine Intelligence 20, 39–51 (1998)
10. Schneiderman, H., Kanade, T.: A statistical method for 3d object detection applied to face and cars. In: Computer Vision and Pattern Recognition, pp. 746–751 (2000)
11. Rowley, H., Baluja, S., Kanade, T.: Neural network-based face detection. IEEE Transactions on Pattern Analysis and Machine Intelligence 20, 23–38 (1998)
12. Zabih, R., Woodfill, J.: A non-parametric approach to visual correspondence. IEEE Transactions on Pattern Analysis and Machine Intelligence (1996)
13. Kim, H.C., Sung, J.W., Je, H.M., Kim, S.K., Jun, B.J., Kim, D., Bang, S.Y.: Asian Face Image Database PF01. Technical Report, Intelligent Multimedia Lab, Dept. of CSE, POSTECH (2001)

Motion Compensation for Face Recognition Based on Active Differential Imaging

Xuan Zou, Josef Kittler, and Kieron Messer

Centre for Vision, Speech and Signal Processing
University of Surrey, United Kingdom
{x.zou,j.kittler,k.messer}@surrey.ac.uk

Abstract. Active differential imaging has been proved to be an effective approach to remove ambient illumination for face recognition. In this paper we address the problem caused by motion for a face recognition system based on active differential imaging. A moving face will appear at two different locations in the ambient illumination frame and combined illumination frame and as result artifacts are introduced to the difference face image. An approach based on motion compensation is proposed to deal with this problem. Experiments on moving faces demonstrate that the proposed approach leads to significant improvements in face identification and verification results.

1 Introduction

The illumination problem in face recognition, is one of those challenging problems which remain to be addressed [8]. The variation in face appearance caused by illumination change can be much larger than the variation caused by personal identity [5]. The approaches to this problem can be divided into "Passive" and "Active". In "Passive" approaches, attempts are made to process images which have already been affected by illumination variations. Such approaches are either based on illumination modelling, photometric normalisation, or the use of illumination-insensitive features. "Active" approaches usually involve additional devices (optical filters, active illumination sources or specific sensors) that actively obtain modalities of face images that are insensitive to or independent of illumination change. These modalities include face shape (depth map or surface normal) and thermal/near infrared images.

Active differential imaging is an important variant of active sensing to minimise the illumination problem. An active differential imaging system consists of an active illuminant and an imaging sensor. During the imaging process, two images are captured: the first one is taken when the active illuminant is on, the second one is taken when the illuminant is off. In the first image the scene is illuminated by the combination of both the ambient illumination and the active illumination, while in the second image the face is illuminated only by ambient illumination. Therefore the difference of these two images contains the scene viewed under active illumination only, which is completely independent of ambient illumination. Some sample images are shown in Fig. 1. Near-Infrared is often

S.-W. Lee and S.Z. Li (Eds.): ICB 2007, LNCS 4642, pp. 39–48, 2007.

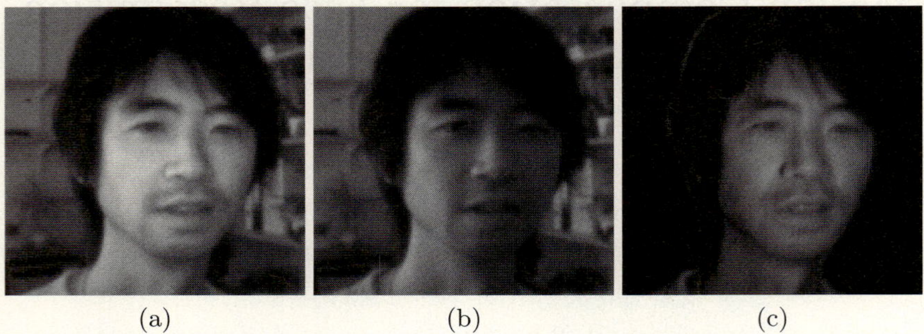

(a) (b) (c)

Fig. 1. Face images under combined illumination(a), ambient illumination(b) and their difference image(c), without any motion

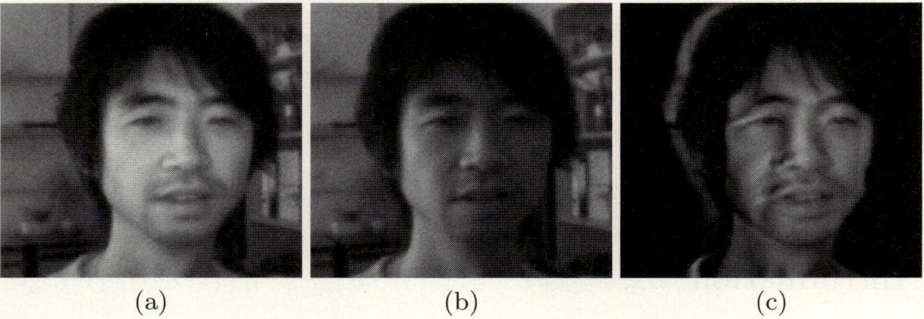

(a) (b) (c)

Fig. 2. Face images under combined illumination(a), ambient illumination(b) and their difference image(c), when the face is moving

chosen as the active illumination source for active differential imaging due to its invisibility, which makes the whole system unobtrusive.

Recently, the idea of active differential imaging has been applied to illumination invariant face recognition[9][10][1][6] and significant advantages on face recognition performance are reported for faces under varying illuminations. Specific sensors which can perform differential imaging have been proposed[3][7].

However, despite its success in removing ambient illuminations for a still scene, the active differential imaging system is detrimentally affected by any motion of the subject in the field of view. A moving subject will appear at two different locations in the combined illumination frame(C-frame) and ambient illumination frame(A-frame), respectively, which results in a difference image with "artifacts" as shown in Fig. 2.

To the best of our knowledge, this problem has not been addressed before. In this paper, we propose a motion compensation technique developed to cope with this problem. The face capture system captures a C-frame and an A-frame alternately. The motion between two C-frames is estimated, and a "virtual" C-frame is computed by performing motion interpolation. The difference image between this "virtual" C-frame, and the A-frame captured between the above two C-frames is used for recognition. The advantage of applying the proposed approach is proved by the improvement in face recognition results on a database containing moving face sequences.

The paper is organised as follows: A detailed look at the problem caused by motion is given in Section 2. Section 3 describes the proposed approach to deal with the motion problem. The information about a moving face database for our experiments is provided in Section 4. The details and results of the experiments carried out are presented in Section 5. Conclusions are drawn in Section 6.

2 Motion Problem of Active Differential Imaging

Two problems can be introduced by a motion for a capture system based on active differential imaging. The first one is motion blur for each captured image. However, this is a general problem for all imaging systems. Fortunately face recognition based on the commonly adopted subspace approaches is relatively robust to the degradation in resolution and consequently it is not seriously affected by motion blur. Therefore motion blur is not a major problem to be addressed. The second one is posed by the motion artifacts in the difference image. Since the C-frame and A-frame are captured at different times, the difference image will be quite different to what it is supposed to be due to the position change of the object. The displacement between object positions in two frames is directly related to the time interval between this two successive captures and the moving speed. As shown in Fig. 2, this problem is significant for a face capture system based on differential imaging. Artifacts are prominent especially around the edges, such as eyelids, nose and mouth. This paper focuses on the second problem.

An example is given below to show how the face similarity degrades due to displacement of the faces. A C-frame and an A-frame are taken for a still face with 60 pixels in inter-occular distance as shown in Fig. 3. We manually shifted A-frame by 1 to 10 pixels from its original position horizontally, or vertically. The faces in the resulting difference images are registered with reference to the original position in the C-frame, cropped and normalised to 55*50 patches, and histogram equalised, as shown in Fig. 4. Fig. 5 shows that the similarities between

(a) (b)

Fig. 3. Combined illumination frame (a) and ambient illumination frame (b)

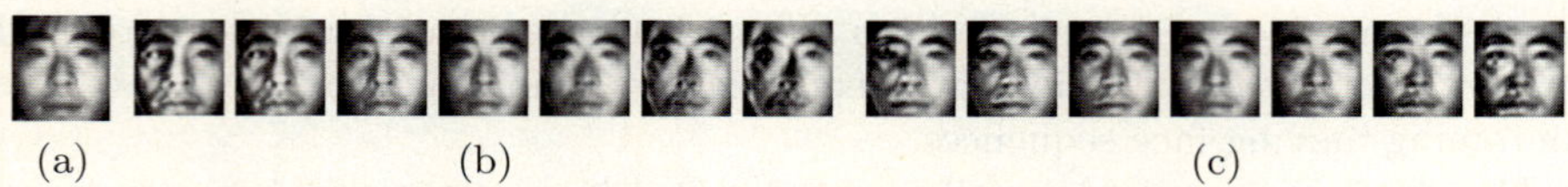
(a) (b) (c)

Fig. 4. original face template (a), and resulting difference image when A-frame shifted (-10, 7, 3, 0, 3, 7, 10) pixels horizontally (b) and vertically (c) from C-frame

the resulting difference images and the face template keep decreasing when displacement between the C-frame and A-frame in any direction (left, right, up or down) increases. The similarity is measured by the Normalised Correlation (NC) score in the original image space, Principal Component Analysis(PCA) subspace, and Linear Discriminant Analysis(LDA) subspace. PCA and LDA subspaces are built from an near-infrared face database with 2844 images of 237 people. NC in an LDA subspace usually gives much better results for face recognition than NC in the image space and PCA subspace, however, NC in the LDA subspace is much more sensitive to the displacement than in the other two spaces, according to Fig. 5.

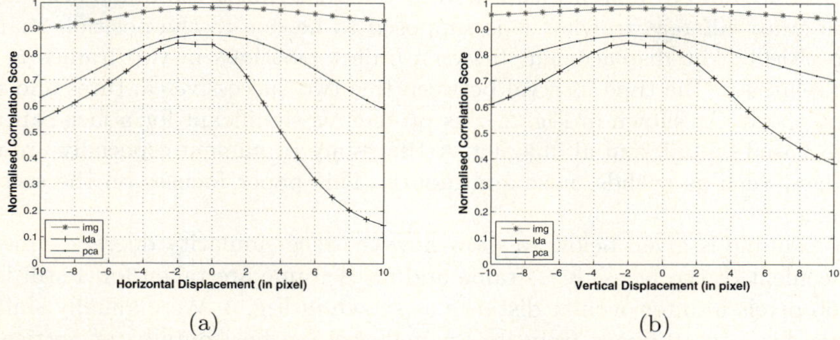

(a) (b)

Fig. 5. NC score drops when A-frame shifts from C-frame horizontally(a) and vertically(b)

Therefore, the performance of a face recognition system based on active differential imaging will degrade when faces are moving. For a general-purpose camera, the time interval between two frames is 40ms (CCIR) or 33ms (EIA), which is so long that the motion effect maybe significant. A hardware solution is specific high speed sensors, such as the sensor developed by Ni[7], which can provide a capture speed of 100 images per second. However, due to the high price of custom designed devices, a software solution is always desirable.

The problem cannot be solved using only the difference image. First, simply applying subspace approaches does not work: as discussed above, none of the commonly used face subspace representations is both insensitive to this motion effect and discriminative enough for face recognition. Second, motion information cannot be recovered from the difference image to remove the motion effect. It is also impossible to align the faces in the successive C-frame and A-frame because faces are in different illuminations in these two frames. We propose to use two nearest C-frames to obtain motion information and interpolate a virtual C-frame, the motion effect can then be removed from the difference image of the A-frame and the virtual C-frame.

3 Motion Compensation for Moving Face

Assuming the face is moving at the same speed in the same direction between t_i, the time when the first C-frame C_i is captured, and t_{i+2}, the time when the second C-frame C_{i+2} is captured. We can apply interpolation to obtain a virtual C-frame C'_{i+1} as "captured" at t_{i+1}, which is the same time when the frame A_{i+1} is captured. Therefore, the faces in the frame C'_{i+1} and frame A_{i+1} are exactly at the same location. As a result, the motion effect is removed in the difference image between the frame C'_{i+1} and frame A_{i+1}. This approach is illustrated in Fig. 6.

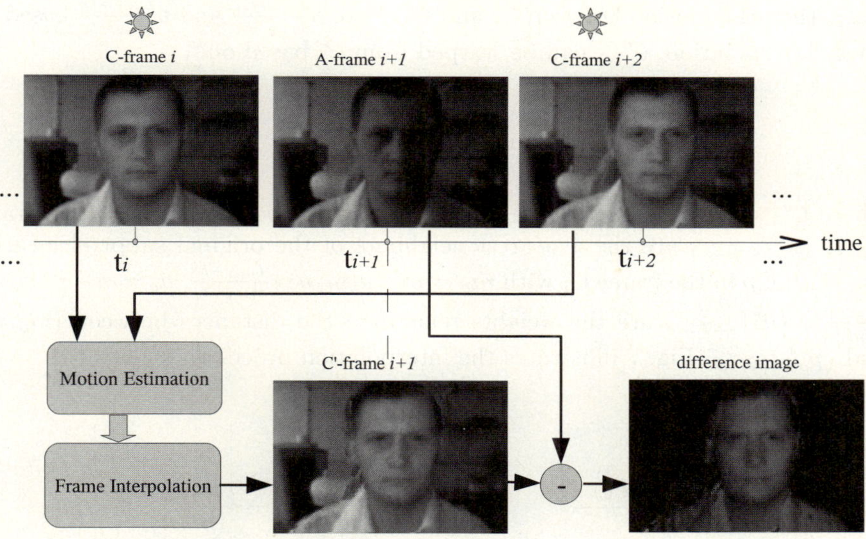

Fig. 6. Illustration of our proposed approach

The robust optical flow estimation method by Black and Anandan [4] is applied to obtain a dense motion field between two successive C-frames: C_i and C_{i+2}. For the image intensity function $I(x, y, t)$ defined on the region S, the estimation of optical flow field $U = \{(u_s, v_s) \mid s \in S\}$ can be treated as a minimization problem of a cost function $E(u, v)$ of the residual errors from the data conservation constraint and the spatial coherence constraint. The robust formulation presented in [4] is as below:

$$E(u,v)=\sum_{s\in S}\left[\lambda_{\mathrm{D}}\rho_{\mathrm{D}}(I_x u_s+I_y v_s+I_t,\sigma_{\mathrm{D}})+\lambda_{\mathrm{S}}\left(\sum_{n\in\mathcal{G}_s}\rho_{\mathrm{S}}(u_s-u_n,\sigma_{\mathrm{S}})+\sum_{n\in\mathcal{G}_s}\rho_{\mathrm{S}}(v_s-v_n,\sigma_{\mathrm{S}})\right)\right] \tag{1}$$

where I_x, I_y and I_t are the partial derivatives of $I(x,y,t)$. Both ρ_{D} and ρ_{S} are Lorentzian function:

$$\rho(x,\sigma)=\log(1+\frac{1}{2}(\frac{x}{\sigma})^2) \tag{2}$$

λ_D and λ_S are weights for the data conservation term and spatial coherence term, respectively. σ_{D} and σ_{S} are the parameters controling the shape of Lorentzian function and the threshold for outliers. Using Lorentzian function instead of the quadratic function used in Least Square Estimation, the influence of the outliers for the data conservation constraint and the spatial coherence constraint can be reduced. A coarse-to-fine strategy is employed to cope with large motions.

If u and v represent the horizontal and vertical motion between frame C_i and C_{i+2}, then the motion between C_i and C'_{i+1} are $u\frac{t_{i+1}-t_i}{t_{i+2}-t_i}$ and $v\frac{t_{i+1}-t_i}{t_{i+2}-t_i}$ based on linear interpolation. C'_{i+1} can be warped from C_i based on:

$$C'_{i+1}(p)=\sum_{s=0}^{3}d^s C_i(p_o^s) \tag{3}$$

where $C'_{i+1}(p)$ is the grey value of a pixel p with coordinates (m,n) in frame C'_{i+1}, $\{p_o^s\}_{s=0,..,3}$ are the 4 nearest neighbors of the original subpixel location (m_o,n_o) of p in the frame C_i with $m_o=m-u(m,n)*\frac{t_{i+1}-t_i}{t_{i+2}-t_i}$, $n_o=n-v(m,n)*\frac{t_{i+1}-t_i}{t_{i+2}-t_i}$. $\{d^s\}_{s=0,..,3}$ are the weights related to the distances between (m_o,n_o) and $\{p_o^s\}_{s=0,..,3}$. Fig. 7 illustrates the interpolation process.

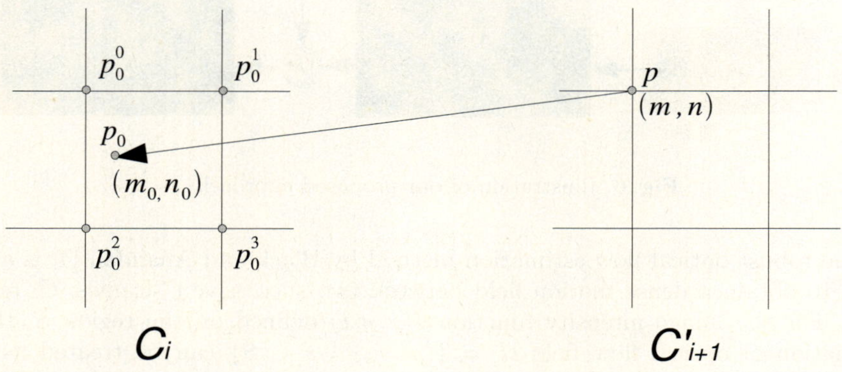

Fig. 7. Illustration of the interpolation process

4 Capture System and Database Capture

An experimental face capture system based on active differential imaging was used to capture moving face data for our experiments. The image sensor has a high resolution of 755*400 pixels. A face database of 37 subjects was captured in an indoor environment near the window with sunlight coming in. Each subject sat 1 meter away from the camera, and was asked to keep moving his/her face. Two sessions of data were recorded for each subject, with 29 C-frames and 29 A-frames captured continuously for each session. Ambient illumination was mainly from left for one session and from right for the other. Another 6 difference images for each subject were captured when the subject sat still. These images will serve as gallery images for the identification and verification experiments.

5 Experiments

To show the advantage brought by the proposed motion compensation approach, face recognition experiments are conducted on two sets of difference face images for comparison. The first set contains the original difference face images between every pair of C-frame and A-frame, without considering the motion issue. For the second set, the proposed approach is applied to obtain the difference images without motion effect. Faces in both sets are geometrically normalised based on the manually marked eye positions in the corresponding C-frame, cropped to

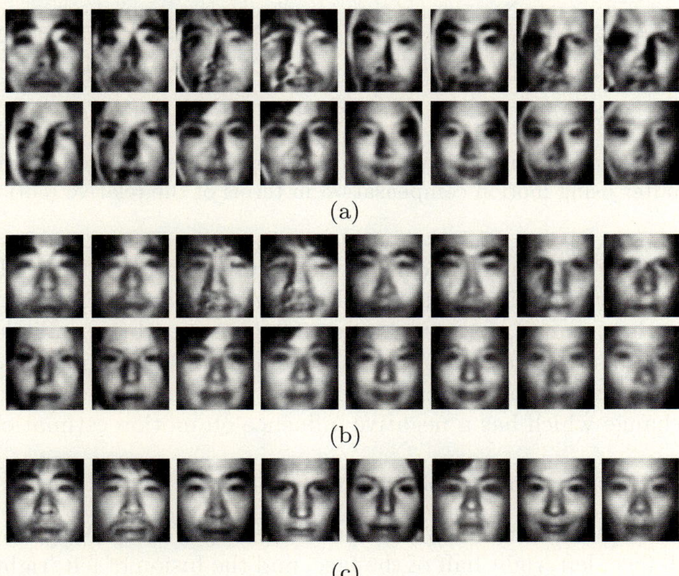

Fig. 8. Faces in difference images without motion compensation (a) and with motion compensation (b), and corresponding template images(c) for subjects in (a) and (b)

55*50 image patches, and photometrically normalised using histogram equalisation. Examples for faces in both sets are shown in Fig. 8 and it can be seen that the motion artifacts have been removed after motion compensation. Each set contains 2072 faces(37 subjects×2 sessions×28 difference images).

5.1 Improvement in Face Similarity to Template

A histogram of the motion between every two frames for the whole database is shown in Fig. 9.(a). For every pair of C-frames, the motion value recorded in the histogram is the average length of all those motion vectors of the motion foreground pixels (pixels with motion vector magnitude above a threshold 0.8). Since faces are normalised based on the eye positions for recognition, the same absolute displacement will have different influence for faces with different inter-ocular distances. Therefore relative motion, which is the motion value over the inter-ocular distance, is applied here to measure motion.

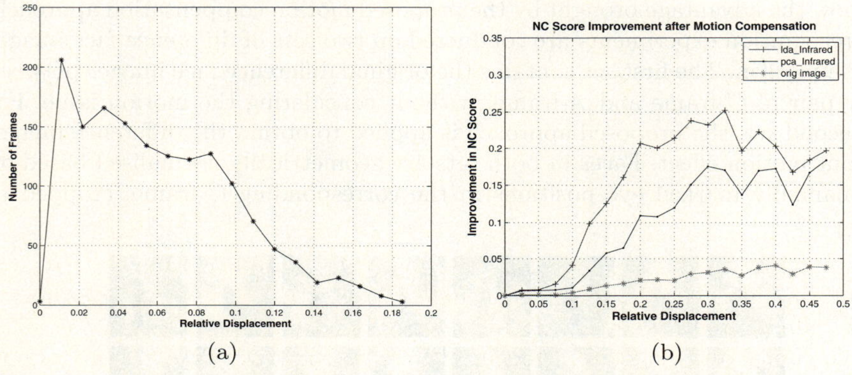

Fig. 9. (a)Histogram of the relative motion in all sequences. (b)Average improvement in NC score after using motion compensation in terms of the relative motion.

According to Fig.9.(b), NC score in LDA subspace is improved by motion compensation more significantly than in PCA subspace and original image space. When motion is too small, applying motion compensation brings a little improvement. But for moderate motion, the improvement is significant. When motion is too large the improvement decreases because large motion tends to introduce large pose change which has a negative influence on motion estimation.

5.2 Face Identification Experiments

Face identification experiments are carried out using Nearest Neighbor classifier based on full face, left/right half of the face, and the fusion of left/right halves of the face. The similarity is measured by NC score in the respective LDA subspaces for full face, left face, or right face. For the fusion case, the Sum rule[2] is applied to fuse the similarity score in the LDA subspace for left face and right face. As

Table 1. Face Identification Rank-1 Error Rates(%) on Moving Faces

	with motion compensation	without motion compensation
full face	12.07	31.71
left face	14.23	32.09
right face	10.28	26.93
fusion of left/right faces	6.13	14.96

Table 2. Verification Half Total Error Rates(%) on Moving Faces

	with motion compensation	without motion compensation
full face	7.88	14.13
left face	8.69	15.63
right face	8.72	15.33
fusion of left/right faces	6.42	10.95

shown in Table 1, after motion compensation the errors decrease to less than half of the errors achieved without performing motion compensation. Applying fusion technique gives the best identification result with an error rate 6.13%.

5.3 Face Verification Experiments

For the first round of verification experiment, the data of one session is used for evaluation, and the other session for testing. Then evaluation and testing sessions are switched for the other round of testing. Every test image is used to make claim to all 37 identities in the gallery. So in total there are 1036 instances of true claims and 1036*36 instances of false claims during evaluation and the same numbers of true claims and false claims in the testing stage. The average verification errors are reported in Table 2. Again, significant improvement is achieved by applying motion interpolation. Fusion has the best performance with the lowest error rate 6.42%.

6 Conclusion and Future Work

Motion causes problems for face recognition systems based on active differential imaging. The similarities between probe images and the template decrease due to the artefact in the captured face image caused by motion. In this paper we proposed an approach based on motion compensation to remove the motion effect in the difference face images. A significant improvement has been achieved in the results of face identification and verification experiments on moving faces. Since the motion artifact also introduces difficulties in automatic face localisation, we are now investigating the performance boost of the system in the fully automatic operation scenario.

Acknowledgement

The support from the Overseas Research Students Awards Scheme (ref. 2003040015) is gratefully acknowledged.

References

1. Hizem, W., Krichen, E., Ni, Y., Dorizzi, B., Garcia-Salicetti, S.: Specific sensors for face recognition. In: Proceedings of IAPR International Conference on Biometric (2006)
2. Kittler, J., Hatef, M., Duin, R.P.W., Matas, J.: On combining classifiers. IEEE Transactions on Pattern Analysis and Machine Intelligence 20(3), 226–239 (1998)
3. Miura, H., et al.: A 100frame/s cmos. active pixel sensor for 3d-gesture recognition system. In: Proceeding of IEEE Solid-State Circuits Conference, pp. 142–143. IEEE Computer Society Press, Los Alamitos (1999)
4. Black, M.J., Anandan, P.: The robust estimation of multiple motions: Parametric and piecewise-smooth flow fields. Computer Vision and Image Understanding 63(1), 75–104 (1996)
5. Moses, Y., Adani, Y., Ullman, S.: Face recognition: the problem of compensating for the illumination direction. In: Eklundh, J.-O. (ed.) ECCV 1994. LNCS, vol. 801. Springer, Heidelberg (1994)
6. Ni, Y., Krichen, E., Salicetti, S., Dorizzi, B.: Active differential imaging for human face recognition. IEEE Signal Processing letter 13(4), 220–223 (2006)
7. Ni, Y., Yan, X.L.: Cmos active differential imaging device with single in-pixel analog memory. In: Proc. IEEE Eur. Solid-State Circuits Conf., pp. 359–362. IEEE Computer Society Press, Los Alamitos (2002)
8. Zhao, W., Chellappa, R., Rosenfeld, A.: Face recognition: A literature survey. ACM Computing Surveys 35, 399–458 (2003)
9. Zou, X., Kittler, J., Messer, K.: Face recognition using active Near-IR illumination. In: Proceedings of British Machine Vision Conference, pp. 209–219 (2005)
10. Zou, X., Kittler, J., Messer, K.: Ambient illumination variation removal by active Near-IR imaging. In: Proceedings of IAPR International Conference on Biometric, January 2006, pp. 19–25 (2006)

Face Recognition with Local Gabor Textons

Zhen Lei, Stan Z. Li, Rufeng Chu, and Xiangxin Zhu

Center for Biometrics and Security Research & National Laboratory of Pattern Recognition,
Institute of Automation, Chinese Academy of Sciences,
95 Zhongguancun Donglu, Beijing 100080, China
{zlei,szli,rfchu,xxzhu}@nlpr.ia.ac.cn
http://www.cbsr.ia.ac.cn

Abstract. This paper proposes a novel face representation and recognition method based on local Gabor textons. Textons, defined as a vocabulary of local characteristic features, are a good description of the perceptually distinguishable micro-structures on objects. In this paper, we incorporate the advantages of Gabor feature and textons strategy together to form Gabor textons. And for the specificity of face images, we propose local Gabor textons (LGT) to portray faces more precisely and efficiently. The local Gabor textons histogram sequence is then utilized for face representation and a weighted histogram sequence matching mechanism is introduced for face recognition. Preliminary experiments on FERET database show promising results of the proposed method.

Keywords: local textons, Gabor filters, histogram sequence, face recognition.

1 Introduction

Face recognition has attracted much attention due to its potential values for applications as well as theoretical challenges. Due to the various changes by expression, illumination and pose etc, face images always change a lot on grey level. How to extract representation robust to these changes becomes an important problem.

Up to now, many representation approaches have been introduced, including Principal Component Analysis (PCA) [11], Linear Discriminant Analysis (LDA) [2], Independent Component Analysis (ICA) [3] etc. PCA provides an optimal linear transformation from the original image space to an orthogonal eigenspace with reduced dimensionality in sense of the least mean square reconstruction error. LDA seeks to find a linear transformation by maximizing the ratio of between-class variance and the within-class variance. ICA is a generalization of PCA, which is sensitive to the high-order relationships among the image pixels.

Recently, the textons based representations have achieved great success in texture analysis and recognition. The term texton was first proposed by Julesz [6] to describe the fundamental micro-structures in natural images and was considered as the atoms of pre-attentive human visual perception. However, it is a vague concept in the literature because of lacking a precise definition for grey level images. Leung and Malik [7] re-invent and operationalize the concept of textons. Textons are defined as a discrete set which is referred to as the vocabulary of local characteristic features of objects. The goal is to build the vocabulary of textons to describe the perceptually distinguishable

S.-W. Lee and S.Z. Li (Eds.): ICB 2007, LNCS 4642, pp. 49–57, 2007.

micro-structures on the surfaces of objects. Various of this concept have been applied to the problem of 3D texture recognition successfully [4,7,12].

In this work, we propose a novel local Gabor textons histogram sequence for face representation and recognition. Gabor wavelets, which capture the local structure corresponding to spatial frequency, spatial localization, and orientation selectivity, have achieved great success in face recognition [13]. Therefore, we incorporate the advantages of Gabor feature and textons strategy to form Gabor textons. Moreover, In order to depict the face images precisely and efficiently, we propose local Gabor textons (LGT) and then utilize LGT histogram sequence for face representation and recognition.

The rest of this paper is organized as follows. Section 2 details the construction of local Gabor textons. Section 3 describes LGT histogram sequence for face representation and recognition. The experimental results on FERET database are demonstrated in Section 4 and in Section 5, we conclude this paper .

2 Local Gabor Textons (LGT) Construction

Texture is often characterized by its responses to a set of orientation and spatial-frequency selective linear filters which is inspired by various evidences of similar processing in human vision system. Here, we use Gabor filters of multi-scale and multi-orientation which have been extensively and successfully used in face recognition[13,8] to encode the local structure attributes embedded in face images. The Gabor kernels are defined as follows:

$$\psi_{\mu,\nu} = \frac{k_{\mu,\nu}^2}{\sigma^2} \exp(-\frac{k_{\mu,\nu}^2 z^2}{2\sigma^2})[\exp(ik_{\mu,\nu}z) - \exp(-\frac{\sigma^2}{2})] \tag{1}$$

where μ and ν define the orientation and scale of the Gabor kernels respectively, $z = (x, y)$, and the wave vector $k_{\mu,\nu}$ is defined as follows:

$$k_{\mu,\nu} = k_\nu e^{i\phi_\mu} \tag{2}$$

where $k_\nu = k_{max}/f^\nu$, $k_{max} = \pi/2$, $f = \sqrt{2}$, $\phi_\mu = \pi\mu/8$. The Gabor kernels in (1) are all self-similar since they can be generated from one filter, the mother wavelet, by scaling and rotating via the wave vector $k_{\mu,\nu}$. Each kernel is a product of a Gaussian envelope and a complex plane wave, and can be separated into real and imaginary parts. Hence, a band of Gabor filters is generated by a set of various scales and rotations.

In this paper, we use Gabor kernels at five scales $\nu \in \{0, 1, 2, 3, 4\}$ and four orientations $\mu \in \{0, 2, 4, 6\}$ with the parameter $\sigma = 2\pi$ [8] to derive 40 Gabor filters including 20 real filters and 20 imaginary fitlers which are shown in Fig. 1. By convoluting face images with corresponding Gabor kernels, for every image pixel we have totally 40 Gabor coefficients which are successively clustered to form Gabor textons.

Textons express the micro-structures in natural images. Compared to the periodic changes of texture images, for face images, different regions of faces usually reflect different structures. For example, the eye and nose areas have distinct differences. If we cluster the textons over the whole image used in texture analysis, the size of textons vocabulary could be very large if one wants to keep describing the face precisely, which will increase the computational cost dramatically. In order to depict the face in

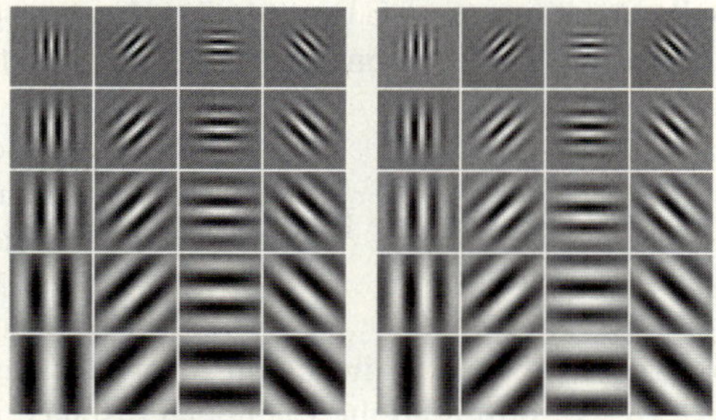

Fig. 1. Gabor filters with 5 scales and 4 orientations. Left are the real parts and right are the imaginary ones.

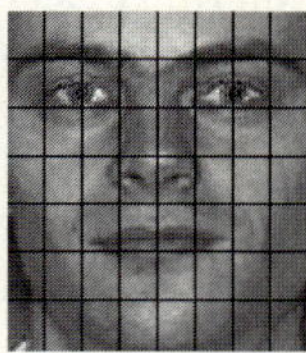

Fig. 2. An example of face image divided into 7×8 regions with size of 20×15

a more efficient way, we propose local Gabor textons to represent the face image. We first divide the face image into several regions with the size of $h \times w$ (Fig. 2), then for every region, the Gabor response vectors are clustered to form a local vocabulary of textons which are called local Gabor textons (LGT). Therefore, a series of LGT can be constructed corresponding to different regions. Specifically, we invoke K-means clustering algorithm [5] to determine the LGT among the feature vectors. K-means method is based on the first order statistics of data, and finds a predefined number of centers in the data space, while guaranteing that the sum of squared distances between the initial data points and the centers is minimized. In order to improve the efficiency of the computation, the LGT vocabulary L_i corresponding to the region R_i is computed by the following hierarchical K-mean clustering alogrithm:

1. Suppose we have 500 face images in all. These images are divided into 100 groups randomly, each of which contains 5 images. All of them are encoded by Gabor filters.
2. For each of the group, the Gabor response vectors at every pixel in region R_i with the size of $h \times w$ are concatenated to form a set of $5 \times h \times w$ feature vectors. The K-mean clustering algorithm is then applied to these feature vectors to form k' centers.
3. The centers for all the groups are merge together and the K-mean clustering algorithm is applied again to these $100 \times k'$ centers to form k centers.
4. With the initialization of the k centers derived in step 3, apply K-means clustering algorithm on all images in region R_i to achieve a local minimum.

These k centers finally constitute the LGT vocabulary L_i corresponding to region R_i and after doing these operations in all regions, the local Gabor textons vocabularies are constructed.

3 LGT Histogram Sequence for Face Representation and Recognition

With the LGT vocabularies , every pixel in region R_i of an image is mapped to the closest texton element in L_i according to the Euclidean distance in the Gabor feature space. After this operation in all regions, a texton labeled image $f_l(x, y)$ is finally formed with the values between 1 and k .

The LGT histogram, denoted by $H_i(\ell)$, is used to describe the distribution of the local structure attributes over the region R_i. A LGT histogram with the region R_i of the labeled image $f_l(x, y)$ induced by local Gabor textons can be defined as

$$H_i(\ell) = \sum_{(x,y)\in R_i} I\{f_l(x,y) = \ell\}, \ell = 0, \ldots, k-1, \tag{3}$$

in which k is the number of different labels and

$$I\{A\} = \begin{cases} 1, & \text{A is true} \\ 0, & \text{A is false} \end{cases}$$

The global description of a face image is built by concatenating the LGT histograms $\mathcal{H} = (H_1, H_2, \ldots, H_n)$ which is called local Gabor textons histogram sequence. The collection of LGT histograms is an efficient face representation which contains information about the distribution of the local structure attributes, such as edges, spots and flat areas over the whole image. Fig. 3 shows the process of face representation using LGT histogram sequence. The similarity of different LGT histogram sequences extracted from different images is computed as follows:

$$S(\mathcal{H}, \mathcal{H}') = \sum_{i=1}^{n} S_{\chi^2}(H_i, H_i') \tag{4}$$

where

$$S_{\chi^2}(H_i, H_i') = \sum_{\ell=1}^{k} \frac{(H_i(\ell) - H_i'(\ell))^2}{(H_i(\ell) + H_i'(\ell))} \tag{5}$$

is the Chi square distance commonly used to match two histograms, in which k is the number of bins for each histogram.

Pervious work has shown different regions of face make different contributions for face recognition [14,1], e.g., the areas nearby eyes are more important than others. Therefore, different weights can be set to different LGT histograms when measure the similarity of two images. Thus, (4) can be rewritten as:

$$S'(\mathcal{H}, \mathcal{H}') = \sum_{i=1}^{n} W_i S_{\chi^2}(H_i, H_i') \tag{6}$$

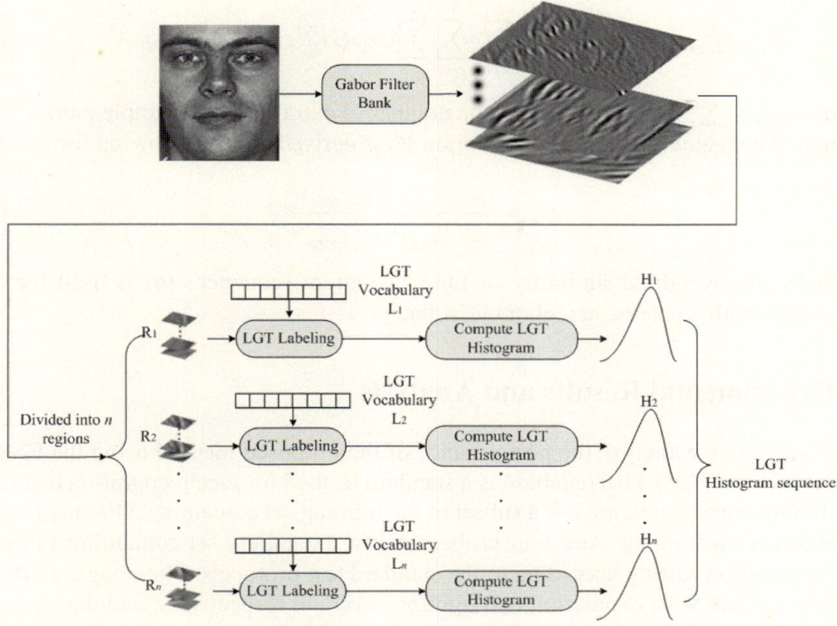

Fig. 3. Face representation using local Gabor textons histogram sequence

where W_i is the weight for i-th LGT histogram and is learned based on Fisher separation criterion [5] as follows.

For a C class problem, the similarities of different images from the same person compose the intra-personal similarity class and those of images from different persons compose the extra-personal similarity as introduced in [9].

For the i-th LGT histogram H_i, the mean and the variance of the intra-personal similarities can be computed by

$$m_{i\_intra} = \frac{1}{N_{intra}} \sum_{j=1}^{C} \sum_{p=1}^{N_j-1} \sum_{q=p+1}^{N_j} S_{\chi^2}(H_i^{p,j}, H_i^{q,j}) \tag{7}$$

$$\sigma_{i\_intra}^2 = \frac{1}{N_{intra}} \sum_{j=1}^{C} \sum_{p=1}^{N_j-1} \sum_{q=p+1}^{N_j} (S_{\chi^2}(H_i^{p,j}, H_i^{q,j}) - m_{i\_intra})^2 \tag{8}$$

where $H_i^{p,j}$ denotes the i-th LGT histogram extracted from the p-th image from the j-th class and $N_{intra} = \sum_{j=1}^{C} \frac{N_j(N_j-1)}{2}$ is the number of intra-personal sample pairs.

Similarly, the mean and the variance of the extra-personal similarities of the i-th LGT histograms can be computed by

$$m_{i\_extra} = \frac{1}{N_{extra}} \sum_{j=1}^{C-1} \sum_{s=j+1}^{C} \sum_{p=1}^{N_j} \sum_{q=1}^{N_s} S_{\chi^2}(H_i^{p,j}, H_i^{q,s}) \tag{9}$$

$$\sigma^2_{i\_extra} = \frac{1}{N_{extra}} \sum_{j=1}^{C-1} \sum_{s=j+1}^{C} \sum_{p=1}^{N_j} \sum_{q=1}^{N_s} (S_{\chi^2}(H_i^{p,j}, H_i^{q,s}) - m_{i\_extra})^2 \tag{10}$$

where $N_{extra} = \sum_{j=1}^{C-1} \sum_{s=j+1}^{C} N_j N_s$, is the number of extra-personal sample pairs.

Then, the weight for i-th LGT histogram W_i is derived by the following formulation

$$W_i = \frac{(m_{i\_intra} - m_{i\_extra})^2}{\sigma^2_{i\_intra} + \sigma^2_{i\_extra}} \tag{11}$$

Finally, the weighted similarity of LGT histogram sequences (6) is used for face recognition with a nearest neighbor classifier.

4 Experimental Results and Analysis

In this section, we analyze the performance of the proposed method using the FERET database. The FERET [10] database is a standard testbed for face recognition technologies. In our experiments, we use a subset of the training set containing 540 images from 270 subjects for training. And four probes against the gallery set containing 1196 images are used for testing according to the standard test protocols. The images in fb and fc probe sets are with expression and lighting variation respectively, and dup I, dup II probe sets include aging images. All images are rotated, scaled and cropped to 140×120 pixels according to the eye positions and then preprocessed by histogram equalization. Fig. 4 shows some examples of the cropped FERET images.

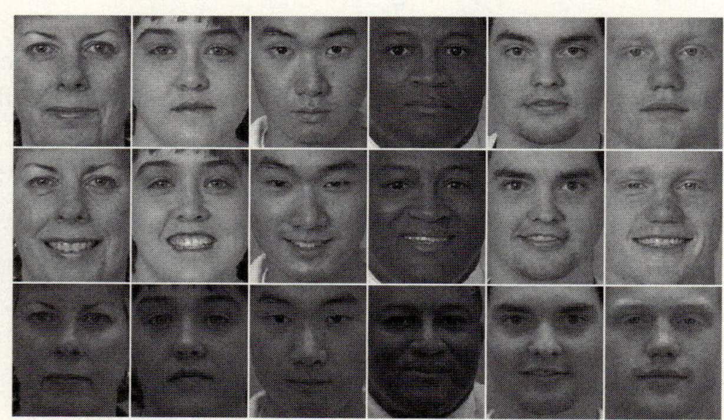

Fig. 4. Example FERET images used in our experiments

There are some parameters which influence the performance of the proposed algorithm. The first one is the size of the local region. If the size is too big (e.g. the whole image), it could lose the local spatial information and may not reveal the advantage of the local analysis. On the other hand, if the region is too small, it would be sensitive to the mis-alignment. Another parameter needed to be optimized is the size of LGT vocabulary (the number of local Gabor textons in every vocabulary). To determine the value

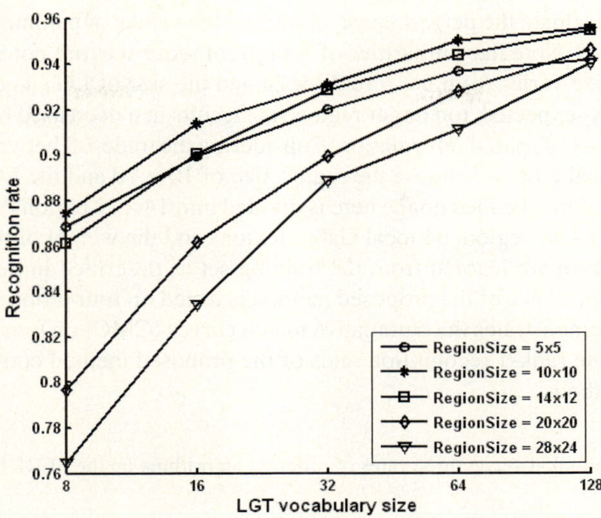

Fig. 5. The recognition rates of varying the values of parameters: the size of LGT vocabulary and the region size

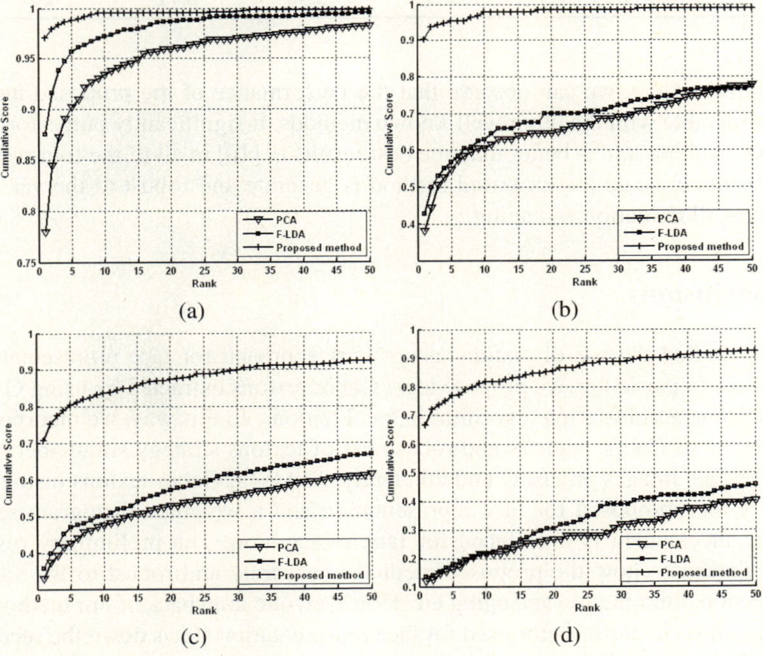

Fig. 6. Cumulative match curves on fb (a), fc (b), dup I (c) and dup II (d) probe sets

of the parameters, we use the training set to cluster the local Gabor textons and test on fb probe set to evaluate the performance of varying the values of parameters. The result is shown in Fig. 5. Note the similarities of histogram sequences are not weighted here.

The region size varies from 5×5 to 28×24 and the size of LGT vocabulary varies from 8 to 128. As expected, too larger region size results in a decreased recognition rate because of the loss of spatial information. Considering the trade-off between recognition and computational cost, we choose the region size of 10×10 and the LGT vocabulary size of 64. Therefore, the face image here is divided into 14×12 regions with the size of 10×10 and for every region, 64 local Gabor textons and the weight of the corresponding LGT histogram are learned from the training set as described in Section 2 and 3. Finally, the performance of the proposed method is tested on four probe sets against the gallery. Fig. 6 demonstrates the cumulative match curves (CMC) on four probe sets and Table 1 shows the rank-1 recognition rates of the proposed method compared to some well-known methods.

Table 1. The rank-1 recognition rates of different algorithms on the FERET probe sets

Methods	fb	fc	dup I	dup II
PCA	0.78	0.38	0.33	0.12
LDA	0.88	0.43	0.36	0.14
Best Results of [10]	0.96	0.82	0.59	0.52
The proposed method	**0.97**	**0.90**	**0.71**	**0.67**

From the results, we can observe that the performance of the proposed method is very comparable with the other well-known methods. It significantly outperforms PCA and LDA methods and is better than the best results in [10] in all of the four probe sets. These results indicate the proposed method is accurate and robust to the variation of expression, illumination and aging.

5 Conclusions

We have studied the use of textons as a robust approach for face representation and recognition. In particular, we propose local Gabor textons extracted by using Gabor filters and K-means clustering algorithm in local regions. In this way, we incorporate the effectiveness of Gabor features and robustness of textons strategy simultaneously and depict the face images precisely and efficiently. The local Gabor textons histogram sequence is then proposed for face representation and a weighted histogram sequence matching mechanism is introduced for face recognition. The preliminary results on FERET database show the proposed method is accurate and robust to the variations of expression, illumination and aging etc. However, one drawback of our method is that the length of the feature vector used for face representation slows down the recognition speed indeed. A possible choice is to apply subspace methods such as PCA, LDA etc. to reduce the dimensionality of the feature vectors which will be tested in our future work.

Acknowledgements. This work was supported by the following funding resources: National Natural Science Foundation Project #60518002, National Science and Technology Supporting Platform Project #2006BAK08B06, National 863 Program Projects #2006AA01Z192 and #2006AA01Z193, Chinese Academy of Sciences 100 people project, and the AuthenMetric Collaboration Foundation.

References

1. Ahonen, T., Hadid, A., Pietikainen, M.: Face recognition with local binary patterns. In: Proceedings of the European Conference on Computer Vision, Prague, Czech, pp. 469–481 (2004)
2. Belhumeur, P., Hespanha, J., Kriegman, D.: Eigenfaces vs. fisherfaces: recognition using class specific linear projection. IEEE Trans. PAMI 19(7), 711–720 (1997)
3. Comon, P.: Independent component analysis - a new concept? Signal Processing 36, 287–314 (1994)
4. Cula, O., Dana, K.: Compact representation of bidirectional texture functions. In: Proceedings of IEEE Computer Society Conference on Computer Vision and Pattern Recognition, pp. 1041–1047. IEEE Computer Society Press, Los Alamitos (2001)
5. Duda, R.O., Hart, P.E., Stork, D.G.: Pattern Classification, 2nd edn. Wiley, Chichester (2000)
6. Julesz, B.: Texton, the elements of texture perception, and their interactions 290(5802), 91–97 (March 1981)
7. Leung, T., Malik, J.: Representing and recognizing the visual appearance of materials using three-dimensional textons. International Journal of Computer Vision 43(1), 29–44 (2001)
8. Liu, C., Wechsler, H.: Gabor feature based classification using the enhanced fisher linear discriminant model for face recognition. IEEE Transactions on Image Processing 11(4), 467–476 (2002)
9. Moghaddam, B., Jebara, T., Pentland, A.: Bayesian face recognition. Pattern Recognition 33(11), 1771–1782 (2000)
10. Phillips, P.J., Moon, H., Rizvi, S.A., Rauss, P.J.: The FERET evaluation methodology for face-recognition algorithms. IEEE Transactions on Pattern Analysis and Machine Intelligence 22(10), 1090–1104 (2000)
11. Turk, M.A., Pentland, A.P.: Eigenfaces for recognition. Journal of Cognitive Neuroscience 3(1), 71–86 (1991)
12. Varma, M., Zisserman, A.: Classifying images of materials: achieving viewpoint and illumination independence. In: Proceedings of the European Conference on Computer Vision, pp. 255–271 (2002)
13. Wiskott, L., Fellous, J., Kruger, N., malsburg, C.V.: Face recognition by elastic bunch graph matching. IEEE Trans. PAMI 19(7), 775–779 (1997)
14. Zhang, W.C., Shan, S.G., Gao, W., Zhang, H.M.: Local gabor binary pattern histogram sequence (lgbphs): a novel non-statistical model for face representation and recognition. In: Proceedings of IEEE International Conference on Computer Vision, pp. 786–791. IEEE Computer Society Press, Los Alamitos (2005)

Speaker Verification with Adaptive Spectral Subband Centroids

Tomi Kinnunen[1], Bingjun Zhang[2], Jia Zhu[2], and Ye Wang[2]

[1] Speech and Dialogue Processing Lab
Institution for Infocomm Research (I^{2}R)
21 Heng Mui Keng Terrace, Singapore 119613
ktomi@i2r.a-star.edu.sg
[2] Department of Computer Science
School of Computing, National University of Singapore (NUS)
3 Science Drive 2, Singapore 117543
{bingjun,zhujia,wangye}@comp.nus.edu.sg

Abstract. Spectral subband centroids (SSC) have been used as an additional feature to cepstral coefficients in speech and speaker recognition. SSCs are computed as the centroid frequencies of subbands and they capture the dominant frequencies of the short-term spectrum. In the baseline SSC method, the subband filters are pre-specified. To allow better adaptation to formant movements and other dynamic phenomena, we propose to adapt the subband filter boundaries on a frame-by-frame basis using a globally optimal scalar quantization scheme. The method has only one control parameter, the number of subbands. Speaker verification results on the NIST 2001 task indicate that the selection of the parameter is not critical and that the method does not require additional feature normalization.

1 Introduction

The so-called *mel-frequency cepstral coefficients* [1] (MFCC) have proven to be efficient feature set for speaker recognition. A known problem of cepstral features, however, is noise sensitivity. For instance, convolutive noise shifts the mean value of the cepstral distribution whereas additive noise tends to modify the variances [2]. To compensate for the feature mismatch between training and verification utterances, normalizations in feature, model and score domains are commonly used [3].

Spectral subband centroids [4; 5; 6; 7] (SSC) are an alternative to cepstral coefficients. SSCs are computed as the centroid frequencies of subband spectra and they give the locations of the local maxima of the power spectrum. SSCs have been used for speech recognition [4; 5], speaker recognition [7] and audio fingerprinting [6]. Recognition accuracy of SSCs is lower in noise-free conditions compared with MFCCs. However, SSCs can outperform MFCCs in noisy conditions and they can be combined with MFCCs to provide complementary information.

S.-W. Lee and S.Z. Li (Eds.): ICB 2007, LNCS 4642, pp. 58–66, 2007.

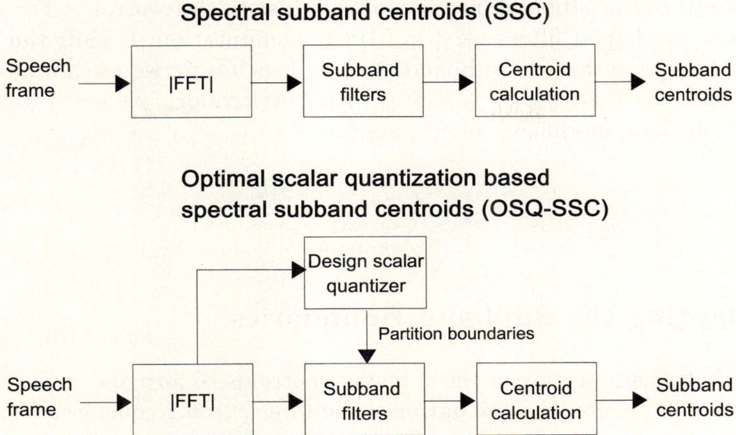

Fig. 1. Computation of the SSC and the proposed OSQ-SSC features. In SSC, the subband boundaries are fixed and in OSQ-SSC, the boundaries are re-calculated for every frame by partitioning the spectrum with optimal scalar quantization.

The key component of the SSC method is the filterbank. Design issues include the number of subbands, the cutoff frequencies of the subband filters, the shape of the subband filters, overlapping of the subband filters, compression of the spectral dynamic range and so on [5]. The parameters of the filterbank can be optimized experimentally for a given task and operating conditions.

In this study, our aim is to simplify the parameter setting of the SSC method by adding some self-adaptivity to the filterbank. In particular, we optimize the subband filter cutoff frequencies on a frame-by-frame basis to allow better adaptation to formant movements and other dynamic phenomena. We consider the subbands as *partitions* or *quantization cells* of a *scalar quantizer*. Each subband centroid is viewed as the representative value of that cell and the problem can be defined as joint optimization of the partitions and the centroids. The difference between the conventional SSC method and the proposed method is illustrated in Fig. 1.

2 Spectral Subband Centroids

In the following, we denote the FFT magnitude spectrum of a frame by $S[k]$, where $k = 1, \ldots, N$ denotes the discrete frequency index. The index $k = N$ corresponds to the half sample rate $f_s/2$. The mth subband centroid is computed as follows [5]:

$$c_m = \frac{\sum_{k=q_l(m)}^{q_h(m)} k W_m[k] S^{\gamma}[k]}{\sum_{k=q_l(m)}^{q_h(m)} W_m[k] S^{\gamma}[k]}, \tag{1}$$

where $W_m[k]$ are the mth bandpass filter coefficients, $q_l(m), q_h(m) \in [1, N]$ are its lower and higher cutoff frequencies and γ is a dynamic range parameter.

The shape of the subband filter introduces bias to the centroids. For instance, the triangular shaped filters used in MFCC computation [1] shift the centroid towards the mid part of the subband. To avoid such bias, we use a uniform filter in (1): $W_m[k] = 1$ for $q_l(m) \leq k \leq q_h(m)$. Furthermore, we set $\gamma = 1$ in this study. With these modifications, (1) simplifies to

$$c_m = \frac{\sum_{k=q_l(m)}^{q_h(m)} kS[k]}{\sum_{k=q_l(m)}^{q_h(m)} S[k]}. \tag{2}$$

3 Adapting the Subband Boundaries

To allow better adaptation of the subband centroids to formant movements and other dynamic phenomena, we optimize the filter cutoff frequencies on a frame-by-frame basis. We use scalar quantization as a tool to partition the magnitude spectrum into K non-overlapping quantization cells. The subband cutoff frequencies, therefore, are given by the partition boundaries of the scalar quantizer.

The expected value of the squared distortion for the mth cell is defined as

$$e_m^2 = \sum_{q(m-1)<k\leq q(m)} p_k(k - c_m)^2, \tag{3}$$

where $p_k = S[k]/\sum_{n=1}^{N} S[n]$ is the normalized FFT magnitude, c_m is the subband centroid as defined in (2) and $q(m-1), q(m)$ are the subband boundaries: $0 = q(0) < q(1) < q(2) < \cdots < q(K) = N$. The scalar quantizer design can then be defined as the minimization of the total error:

$$\min_{(q(0),q(1),\ldots,q(K))} \sum_{m=1}^{K} e_m^2. \tag{4}$$

The number of subbands (K) is considered as a control parameter that needs to be optimized experimentally for a given application.

We have implemented a globally optimal scalar quantizer which uses matrix searching technique to solve (4) [8]. The time complexity of the method is $O(KN)$ and our implementation runs 18 times faster than realtime on a 3 GHz Pentium processor for $(K, N) = (8, 128)$. It is interesting to note that optimal algorithms for vector quantization [9] require exponential time but globally optimal scalar quantizer can be designed in polynomial time. This theoretically interesting property, in fact, was one of our initial motivations to apply the method to feature extraction. We term the proposed method as *optimal scalar quantization based spectral subband centroids* (OSQ-SSC).

Figure 2 shows the centroids from both the SSC with mel filterbank and the OSQ-SSC method. The spectrogram is also shown as a reference. It can be seen that the OSQ-SSC features are better adapted to local dynamic changes of the spectrum compared with SSC. In particular, the centroids from OSQ-SSC tend to follow the F0 harmonics and the formant frequencies during voiced regions.

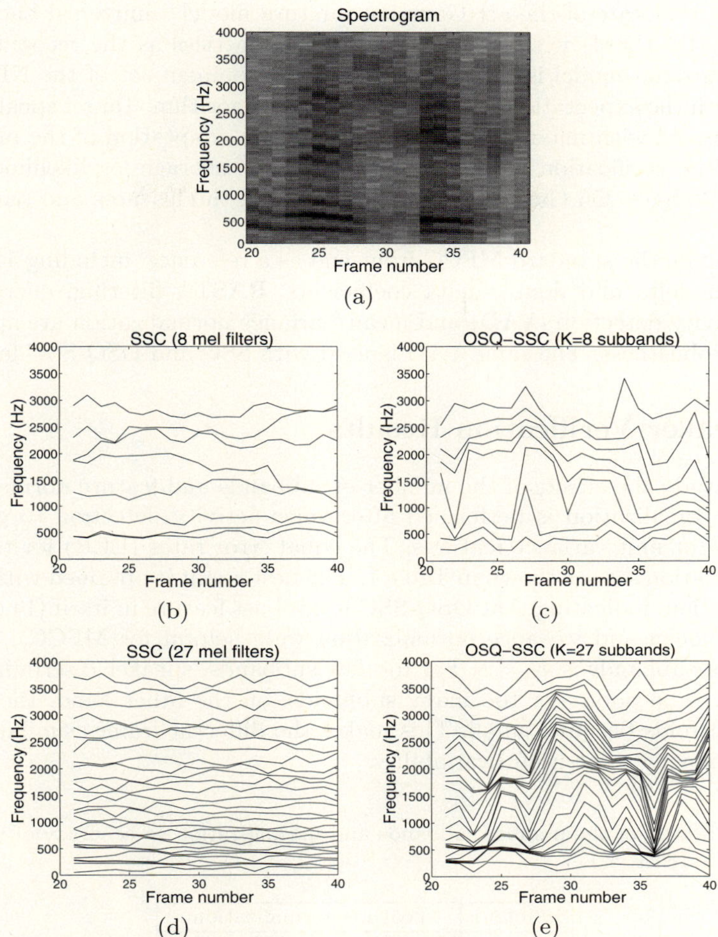

Fig. 2. Illustrations of conventional spectral subband centroids with fixed filterbank (SSC) and the proposed method with adapted subband boundaries (OSQ-SSC)

4 Speaker Verification Setup

We use the NIST 2001 speaker recognition evaluation corpus, a conversational cellular phone corpus, in our experiments[1]. The 1-speaker detection task as defined by NIST consists of 174 target speakers and 22418 verification trials with a genuine/impostor ratio of 1:10. The amount of training data per speaker is about 2 minutes and the duration of the test segments varies from a few seconds up to one minute.

[1] http://www.nist.gov/speech/tests/spk/

We use the state-of-the-art Gaussian mixture model - universal background model (GMM-UBM) with diagonal covariance matrices as the recognizer [10]. The background model is trained using the development set of the NIST 2001 corpus with the expectation-maximization (EM) algorithm. Target speaker models are derived with maximum a posteriori (MAP) adaptation of the mean vectors and the verification score is computed as the average log-likelihood ratio. The GMMs have 256 Gaussian components for all the features and parameters tested.

We include the standard MFCC front-end as a reference, including 12 MFCC with their delta and double-delta coefficients. RASTA filtering, energy-based voice activity detection (VAD) and mean/variance normalization are applied to enhance robustness. The same VAD is used with SSC and OSQ-SSC features.

5 Speaker Verification Results

We first study the effects of the number of subbands and feature normalization. Feature normalization is performed after voice activity detection to give zero mean and/or unit variance features. The equal error rates (EER) for the NIST 2001 evaluation set are shown in Table 1. The best result is obtained without any normalization, indicating that OSQ-SSC is a robust feature in itself (In contrast, both the mean and variance normalization were helpful for MFCC). Optimal number of subbands is $K = 8$. For too few subbands, speaker discrimination is expected to be poor. For too many subbands, on the other hand, the spacing of the centroids becomes small. This makes the different frames similar to each other, removing some useful variability.

Table 1. Effects of the number subbands and normalization to accuracy of the OSQ-SSC feature (EER %)

Subbands	Feature normalization			
	None	Mean	Var	Mean+Var
4	19.4	27.5	31.7	27.5
8	18.0	24.8	29.8	24.5
16	19.1	23.1	27.5	23.3
32	19.8	24.6	28.4	24.2

We next compare OSQ-SSC, their delta coefficients and the concatenation of the static and delta coefficients at the frame level. Based on Table 1, we turn off the normalizations. The results are given in Table 2. The delta coefficients yield higher error rates compared with the static coefficients which is expected. We did, however, expect some improvement when combining static and delta features which is not the case. The error rates of the delta coefficient are relatively high compared with the static coefficient which partly explains why the fusion is not successful. The simple differentiator method for computing deltas may not be robust enough and other methods like linear regression should be considered.

Table 2. Comparison of static and delta features of OSQ-SSC (EER %)

Subbands	Feature set		
	OSQ-SSC	ΔOSQ-SSC	OSQ-SSC + Δ
4	19.4	26.9	20.3
8	18.0	22.2	19.7
16	19.1	23.4	20.3
32	19.8	24.0	21.3

Table 3. Comparison of MFCC, OSQ-SSC and ΔOSQ-SSC under additive white noise condition (EER %)

Noise weight (α)	Feature set		
	MFCC	OSQ-SSC	ΔOSQ-SSC
0	8.3	18.0	22.2
0.3	15.7	19.9	26.6
0.6	18.4	22.6	29.2
0.9	25.6	28.7	47.9

We next study noise robustness of the OSQ-SSC feature. We contaminated all the training and testing files with additive white noise with three different noise levels. The noise was added with linear combination of the speech and noise as $x_{\text{noisy}}[n] = \alpha z[n] + (1 - \alpha)x_{\text{orig}}[n]$, where $x_{\text{noisy}}[n]$, $z[n]$ and $x_{\text{orig}}[n]$ denote the noisy speech, noise and the original speech signals, respectively. The results for $K = 8$ subbands and their delta coefficients are given in Table 3. The MFCC result is shown as a reference.

All the three features degrade when noise level is increased, which is expected. The MFCC feature gives the best result in all cases and ΔOSQ-SSC gives the worst result in all conditions. However, relative degradation of OSQ-SSC is much smaller compared with MFCC. For instance, the relative increase in EER from $\alpha = 0$ to $\alpha = 0.3$ is 89 % for MFCC, whereas for OSQ-SSC it is only 11 %. This is interesting since the MFCC features have 36 dimensions, including deltas and double deltas, mean and variance normalization and RASTA filtering. In turn, OSQ-SSC has only 8 dimensions and is without any normalizations. We interpret the result so that the intrinsic resistance to additive noise of OSQ-SSC is better than that of MFCC. On the other hand, speaker discrimination of MFCC is clearly higher.

Finally, we compare OSQ-SSC with SSC. We consider the following three filterbank configurations for the SSC feature:

– SSC(1) : linear frequency scale, non-overlapping rectangular filters
– SSC(2) : mel frequency scale, non-overlapping rectangular filters
– SSC(3) : mel frequency scale, overlapping triangular filters

According to [7], mean subtraction helps SSC. We confirmed this experimentally and we apply it in all the three cases. The results are shown in Table 4.

Table 4. Comparison SSC and OSQ-SSC (EER %)

Subbands	Feature set			
	OSQ-SSC	SSC(1)	SSC(2)	SSC(3)
4	19.4	24.8	23.9	24.8
8	18.0	19.7	21.9	15.4
16	19.1	21.0	25.3	17.5
32	19.8	24.2	26.3	22.5

The performance of the SSC method strongly depends on the parameter setting. The best SSC result (EER=15.4 %) is obtained by using eight overlapping filters on the mel-scale. Overall, SSC(3) gives the best result among the three filterbank configurations, followed by SSC(1) and SSC(2), respectively. Overlapping filters are useful for SSC.

Comparing OSQ-SSC with SSC, OSQ-SSC is less sensitive to parameter setup. The method has only one control parameter and the results incidate that the method is not sensitive to it. For SSC(3), the error rate varies between 15.4% - 24.8 % whereas for OSQ-SSC, the range is 18.0 % - 19.8 %. The OSQ-SSC method has a built-in "self-optimizing" property of the filterbank. The success of the SSC method, on the other hand, depends on the correct setting of the filterbank parameters.

6 Discussion

The different settings for SSC presented in Table 4 indicate that SSC gives the best results when the filterbank resembles the one used with MFCC features (mel-frequency scale with triangular overlapping filters). For OSQ-SSC, this is not the case by definition (filters are rectangular and non-overlapping).

The advantage of the OSQ-SSC feature over the baseline SSC feature, in theory, is that the subband boundaries are adapted for each frame. The partitions of the scalar quantizer, however, are themselves non-overlapping. This forces the centroid frequencies to be monotonically increasing, thereby limiting their dynamic range. The results of Table 4, on the other hand, indicate the usefulness of overlapping filters. A possible future direction would be studying optimization of the filterbank parameters using a probabilistic clustering model such as the GMM.

Does the centroid information provide complementary information that is not captured by the MFCCs? Overall, the accuracies of both the SSC- and OSQ-SSC-based recognizers are significantly lower compared with the MFCC-based features which is disappointing. We did several pairwise fusion experiments, combining both the SSC and OSQ-SSC classifier output scores with the MFCC scores by weighted sum. None of these lead to improvement even when the fusion weights were optimized on the evaluation set. This suggests that the cepstrum- and centroid-based classifiers are redundant. The centroid information seems to be already absorbed into the MFCCs.

In [7] SSCs yielded comparable results to MFCCs in noise-free condition. Moreover, SSCs outperformed MFCCs under additive noise conditions with low signal-to-noise ratios. We did not observe similar pattern; MFCCs outperformed both the SSCs and OSQ-SSCs with a wide margin in all cases. One source for this disparity may arise from implemetation differences of the feature extraction, in particular, the channel compensation methods applied. In [7], mean subtraction was used with the SSC features, but no channel compensation was mentioned in conjunction with the MFCC features. Our MFCC front-end, on the other hand, includes RASTA filtering and utterance level mean/variance normalization to increase robustness. Our MFCC front-end is comparatively more robust and the centroid information does not seem to yield additional gain in this case.

7 Conclusions and Future Work

We have studied subband centroid based features for the speaker verification task. In particular, we simplified the spectral subband centroid (SSC) method by adding self-adaptivity to the filterbank. The proposed feature (OSQ-SSC) has one control parameter and the experiments indicated that the method is not sensitive to it. It was also found that the proposed feature does not require normalization like MFCC and SSC. This is beneficial for real-time applications.

Our experiments indicate that the centroid-based features have limited use in speaker verification if a robust MFCC front-end is used. The theoretical advantage of SSCs over MFCCs would be that they have a direct physical interpretation. Therefore, SSCs and/or OSQ-SSCs might be used as alternatives to traditional LPC-based formant estimation in forensic speaker recognition [11]. Another potential application would be speech recognition. The subband centroids are related to formant frequencies, and they depend, in addition to the speaker, on the text spoken. Recently SSC-based features have shown promise as an additional feature in noisy speech recognition tasks [12; 4].

From the theoretical side, relation of the OSQ-SSC centroid frequencies to poles of the LPC model would be an interesting future direction. The cepstral coefficients derived from the LPC model [13] have been successful in speaker verification in addition to MFCCs. The centroids given by OSQ-SSC might be an alternative, numerically stable, "pole" presentation of speech signals.

References

[1] Davis, S., Mermelstein, P.: Comparison of parametric representations for monosyllabic word recognition in continuously spoken sentences. IEEE Trans. Acoustics, Speech, and Signal Processing 28(4), 357–366 (1980)

[2] Pelecanos, J., Sridharan, S.: Feature warping for robust speaker verification. In: Proc. Speaker Odyssey: the Speaker Recognition Workshop (Odyssey 2001), Crete, Greece, pp. 213–218 (2001)

[3] Bimbot, F., Bonastre, J.F., Fredouille, C., Gravier, G., Magrin-Chagnolleau, I., Meignier, S., Merlin, T., Ortega-Garcia, J., Petrovska-Delacretaz, D., Reynolds, D.: A tutorial on text-independent speaker verification. EURASIP Journal on Applied Signal Processing 2004(4), 430–451 (2004)
[4] Gajić, B., Paliwal, K.: Robust speech recognition in noisy environments based on subband spectral centroid histograms. IEEE Trans. Audio, Speech and Language Processing 14(2), 600–608 (2006)
[5] Paliwal, K.: Spectral subband centroid features for speech recognition. In: Proc. Int. Conf. on Acoustics, Speech, and Signal Processing (ICASSP 1998), Seattle, USA, vol. 2, pp. 617–620 (1998)
[6] Seo, J., Jin, M., Lee, S., Jang, D., Lee, S., Yoo, C.: Audio fingerprinting based on normalized spectral subband centroids. In: Proc. Int. Conf. on Acoustics, Speech, and Signal Processing (ICASSP 2005), vol. 3, pp. 213–216 (2005)
[7] Thian, N., Sanderson, C., Bengio, S.: Spectral subband centroids as complementary features for speaker authentication. In: Zhang, D., Jain, A.K. (eds.) ICBA 2004. LNCS, vol. 3072, pp. 631–639. Springer, Heidelberg (2004)
[8] Wu, X.: Optimal quantization by matrix searching. Journal of Algorithms 12(4), 663–673 (1991)
[9] Gersho, A., Gray, R.: Vector Quantization and Signal Compression. Kluwer Academic Publishers, Boston (1991)
[10] Reynolds, D., Quatieri, T., Dunn, R.: Speaker verification using adapted gaussian mixture models. Digital Signal Processing 10(1), 19–41 (2000)
[11] Rose, P.: Forensic Speaker Identification. Taylor & Francis, London (2002)
[12] Chen, J., Huang, Y., Li, Q., Paliwal, K.: Recognition of noisy speech using dynamic spectral subband centroids. IEEE Signal Processing Letters 11(2), 258–261 (2004)
[13] Atal, B.: Effectiveness of linear prediction characteristics of the speech wave for automatic speaker identification and verification. Journal of the Acoustic Society of America 55(6), 1304–1312 (1974)

Similarity Rank Correlation for Face Recognition Under Unenrolled Pose

Marco K. Müller, Alexander Heinrichs, Andreas H.J. Tewes, Achim Schäfer, and Rolf P. Würtz

Institut für Neuroinformatik, Ruhr-Universität, D–44780 Bochum, Germany

Abstract. Face recognition systems have to deal with the problem that not all variations of all persons can be enrolled. Rather, the variations of most persons must be modeled. Explicit modeling of different poses is awkward and time consuming. Here, we present a subsystem that builds a model of pose variation by keeping a model database of persons in both poses, additionally to the gallery of clients known in only one pose. An identification or verification decision for probe images is made on the basis of the rank order of similarities with the model database. Identification achieves up to 100% recognition rate on 300 pairs of testing images with 45 degrees pose variation within the CAS-PEAL database, the equal error rate for verification reaches 0.5%.

1 Introduction

Despite significant progress automatic face recognition still suffers from the multitude of variations a face undergoes when images are taken. This article aims at improving face recognition in the presence of head pose variation. Rather than creating a 3D model explicitly like in [1] or by introducing a manifold using many views of each subject [2,3] an approach is presented where the only preprocessing necessary is to find facial landmarks in the image followed by pose estimation. This is realised by bunch graph matching, but more sophisticated methods like EFOM matching [4,5] are available.

Contrary to approaches with explicit models for this variation, it is not necessary to collect many images showing different head poses in order to enroll a subject into the database. To generalize to different poses, images showing subjects in a variety of different head poses are additionally collected. These model images are taken offline in a preprocessing step.

As explicit modeling of pose variation is awkward and computationally expensive, a simpler approach is studied, which relies on the assumption that similar people in one pose will also be similar in another one. Then, the pose variation can be learned by a list of persons known in both poses. Recognizing a client is now achieved by comparing him with all model identities showing the same head pose, and the ranking of similarities creates a similarity function, which can be transferred to the new pose. Thus, the expensive process of enrollment for different head poses has therefore been shifted from the recognition task itself to a preprocessing step. This similarity is a special case of *rank correlation*,

S.-W. Lee and S.Z. Li (Eds.): ICB 2007, LNCS 4642, pp. 67–76, 2007.

one example being Spearman's rank order correlation coefficient [6]. This sort of statistics is used for the evaluation of biometric systems [7] and for face matching in [8]. Here, we apply it to pose generalization.

2 Method

We describe a person's identity by a list containing identity numbers from a large number of reference persons (the model database M). These lists describing a new identity are orderd according to the similarity values to our model database, they build a rank list. To model pose variation, the model database must contain one image per pose for every model identity.

Beside this model there is a gallery T_G of enrolled subjects which contains only one pose. During recognition or verification of an image of an unknown person in an unenrolled but estimated pose these ranks are calculated for the corresponding view. All these persons make up the testing probes T_P, the combination of both is the testing database T. For two poses, the model database M is structured analogous into M_G and M_P (see fig. 1). A similarity function measuring the correlation of the rank lists then measures how similar the new images of persons with different poses are.

The advantage of such a model is that no views need to be generated to deal with pose variation. New images are only compared to model images of the same kind (pose), and the between-poses comparison is done by correlation of two rank lists containing the person's identity.

2.1 Landmark Finding

The main data structure used in the algorithm is the *model graph* with nodes on facial landmarks that are labeled with Gabor jets [9]. A set of such model graphs for different faces constitutes a bunch graph [10]. The method proposed here needs galleries of known people in different poses. These galleries have been created with an automatic bunch graph generator, which works as follows.

Starting with a couple of manually labeled graphs, which are processed to a bunchgraph, the system finds the best position for the bunchgraph on the first image. If the similarity of the graph with the jets at that point crosses a threshold, matching has worked fine and the found landmarks are a potential face graph. At the beginning of the process this threshold is high, so that only a few potential graphs pass the test. To counter the problem that the similarity rises statistically with the size of the bunchgraph, another test checks the result for consistency, meaning that each node of the bunch graph should be most similar to the landmark it is placed on. Combination of these two tests leads to a stable system.

The correctly matched graph is then used to improve the bunch graph. For this purpose, a *Growing Neural Gas* (GNG) [11] is used as a clustering method.

It generates representatives of the shown data and has the very helpful property, that the optimal number of representatives need not be given by the user, but is determined according to the distribution of the data. At the beginning, a GNG is created for every node of the bunchgraph. The neurons of these GNGs are initialized on the values of the jets at the according node. The nodes of every correctly matched graph in the later process are used as input for the respective GNG. After processing of the input, the values of the neurons of the GNG are assigned to the jets of the bunchgraph.

Using the GNG delivers two main advantages compared to the simpler approach of enhancing the bunchgraph by the correctly matched graph directly. First, the bunchgraph grows more slowly and reaches a stable size once the number of representatives at each node is enough for a good representation of the data. The size of the bunchgraph determines the speed of the matching. Second, the influence of a failed matching on the bunchgraph is minimal. Since the corresponding jets are only used as an input to the GNG, the GNG will in fact move a little bit to the wrong direction, but this can be compensated fast by new and correct input.

Whenever a correctly matched graph is stored and used as input for the GNG, the corresponding image is removed from the list of images to be processed. In this way, the whole set of images is treated. After this first run, the remaining images are processed again. As the increased bunch graph covers the face space better, faces on images with incorrect matches in first run now may be matched correctly. These runs are repeated until no face is matched correctly in a whole run. Then both threshold values of the tests are lowered a little bit and the next run is started. This is repeated, until every image of the database is processed. A comparison of the position of the eye nodes of the found graphs with ground truth data showed that all faces were located with adequate accuracy. A simpler version of this is described in [12].

2.2 Rank Correlation Function

Given a testing set $T = (T_G, T_P)$ consisting of N_G gallery images $(0 \leq t_G < N_G)$ and N_P probe images$(0 \leq t_P < N_P)$. A model set $M = (M_G, M_P)$ of N_M identities is given providing both kinds of images as in gallery $(0 \leq m_G < N_M)$ and probe $(0 \leq m_P < N_M)$. From the model graphs only those N_N nodes are selected that are visible in both poses, corresponding nodes have the same node index n $(1 \leq n \leq N_N)$. For compact notation, in the following X is to be substituted by either "G" or "P". Jets are denoted by $J(\cdot,\cdot,\cdot)$ and depend on node number, identity number, and image set.

The similarities of each test image to all corresponding model images can be calculated nodewise with the jet similarity $S(J_1, J_2)$ as in [9,10]. On the resulting vectors of similarities

$$X^S(n, t_X, m_X) = S(J(n, m_X, M_X), J(n, t_X, T_X)) \tag{1}$$

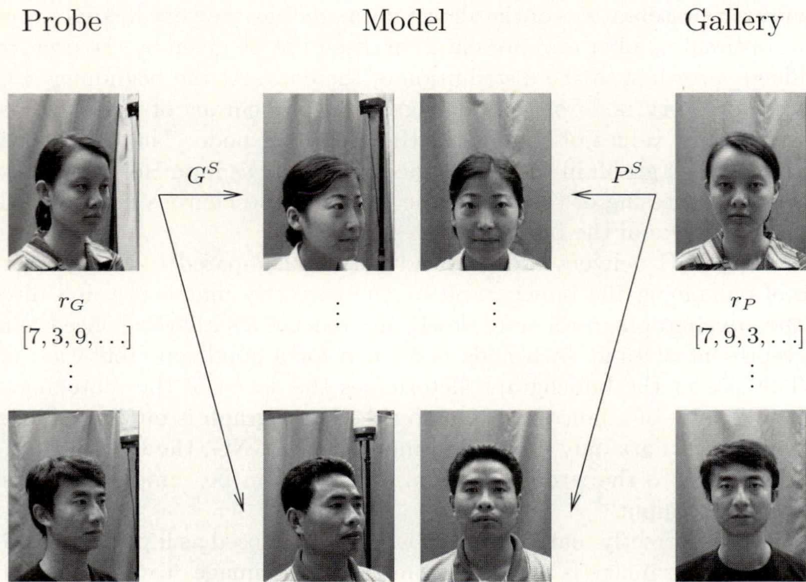

Fig. 1. For each test image the jet similarities X^S to all corresponding model jets can be calculated. Sorting the model indices according to these similarities results in a field $r_X(n, t_X)$ which contains for all test images nodewise the most similar model images. For one node these ranklist may be like the example in the figure.

the ranking $r_X(n, t_X; m_X)$ is defined by the sorting permutation such that

$$m_X > m'_X \Rightarrow X^S(n, t_X; r_X(n, t_X; m_X)) \leq X^S(n, t_X; r_X(n, t_X; m'_X)) . \quad (2)$$

Similarity between two test images is then given by:

$$S(t_G, t_P) = \frac{1}{F} \cdot \sum_{n} \sum_{m_G, m_P} \frac{\delta\big(r_G(n, t_G; m_G), r_P(n, t_P; m_P)\big)}{\sqrt{m_G + m_P + 1}} , \quad (3)$$

the normalization factor F is defined as the maximal possible similarity:

$$F = N_N \cdot \sum_{i=1}^{N_M} \frac{1}{\sqrt{2i - 1}} . \quad (4)$$

To give an example, let $r_g(n, t_G)$ be $[1, 3, 2]$. This means (for node n) the most similar model images to the test image t_G are number 1, then 3 and then 2. If r_p is $[1, 2, 3]$ the similarity for this node would be

$$S = \frac{\frac{1}{\sqrt{1}} + \frac{1}{\sqrt{4}} + \frac{1}{\sqrt{4}}}{\frac{1}{\sqrt{1}} + \frac{1}{\sqrt{3}} + \frac{1}{\sqrt{5}}} = \frac{2}{2.02} = 0.99. \quad (5)$$

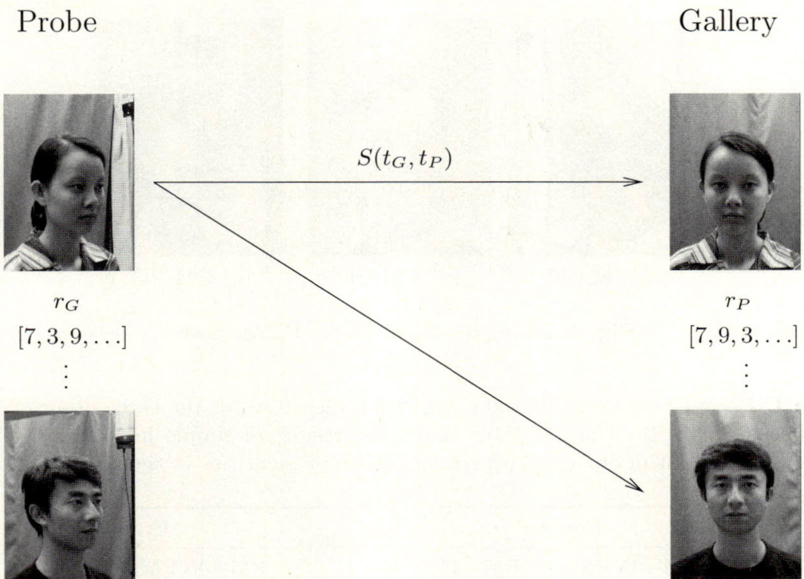

Fig. 2. Once the rank lists have been calculated, they are describing the person's identity. For each probe image showing a person in a very different pose than the image in the gallery the similarity to all gallery images can be calculated by the similarity function $S(t_G, t_P)$

3 Experiments

3.1 Data

Three poses of the CAS-PEAL face Database [13] have been used: PM+45, PM+00 and PM−45. The first N_M identities build the model database, the last N_T identities the testing database. In most experiments $N_M = N_T = 500$ has been used, variations are shown in table 2. Twelve of the remaining identities have been labeled manually to find the landmarks in the model and testing databases, as described in section 2.1.

3.2 Identification Results

Recognition rates are shown in the right half of table 1. For comparison, the results of direct jet comparison (which is not appropriate for large pose variation), are shown on the left half of that table.

Table 2 shows the recognition rates for the case album PM+00 – probe PM−45 for different numbers of identities in model and testing database. In general, recognition rates increase if the number of model identities increases or the number of testing images decreases. If the model size is equal to the test size, the results are even better with a higher number of identities, at least up to 500

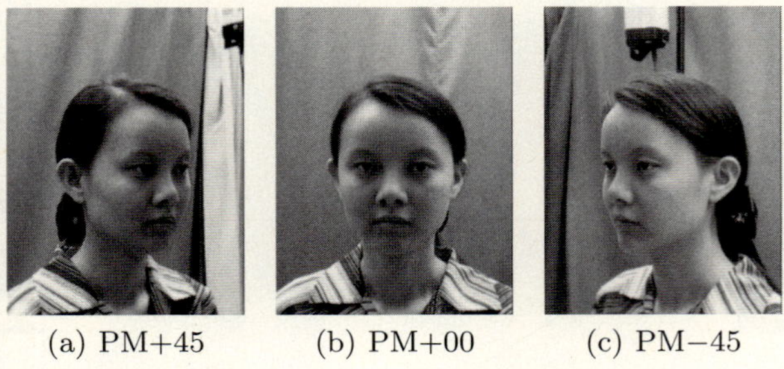

(a) PM+45 (b) PM+00 (c) PM−45

Fig. 3. Examples of used CAS-PEAL poses

Table 1. Recognition rates for 500 CAS-PEAL identities for the three poses PM+45, PM+00 and PM−45. The left table shows the results of simple jet comparison, the right one the result of our system with 500 different identities in the model database.

Gallery	Probe		
	PM+45	PM+00	PM−45
PM+45	100.0	8.0	2.6
PM+00	33.0	100.0	54.2
PM−45	3.2	24.4	100.0

Gallery	Probe		
	PM+45	PM+00	PM−45
PM+45	100.0	85.0	39.4
PM+00	98.0	100.0	99.0
PM−45	56.4	96.4	100.0

Table 2. Recognition rates for PM+00 – PM−45 for different numbers of model and test identities. The model database consists of the first N_M identities, the testing database of the N_T last ones of the 1000 used images.

Model	Test								
	100	200	300	400	500	600	700	800	900
100	96.0	95.5	89.7	88.5	83.8	81.2	79.6	78.3	75.9
200	99.0	97.5	96.7	95.3	93.4	92.0	90.4	89.6	—
300	99.0	97.5	97.3	96.8	96.8	96.5	96.1	—	—
400	100.0	98.0	100.0	98.8	98.6	98.3	—	—	—
500	99.0	98.5	99.0	99.0	99.0	—	—	—	—
600	99.0	98.0	99.7	99.5	—	—	—	—	—
700	100.0	99.0	99.3	—	—	—	—	—	—
800	100.0	99.5	—	—	—	—	—	—	—
900	98.0	—	—	—	—	—	—	—	—

identities. Figure 4 shows the cumulative match scores for the closed identification scenario we used. Our method performs quite well for pose differences of 45°, pose variations of 90° are difficult, because the number of visible landmarks in both images decreases. Experiments with node independent rank lists have been made, but combination of node dependent with node independent rank

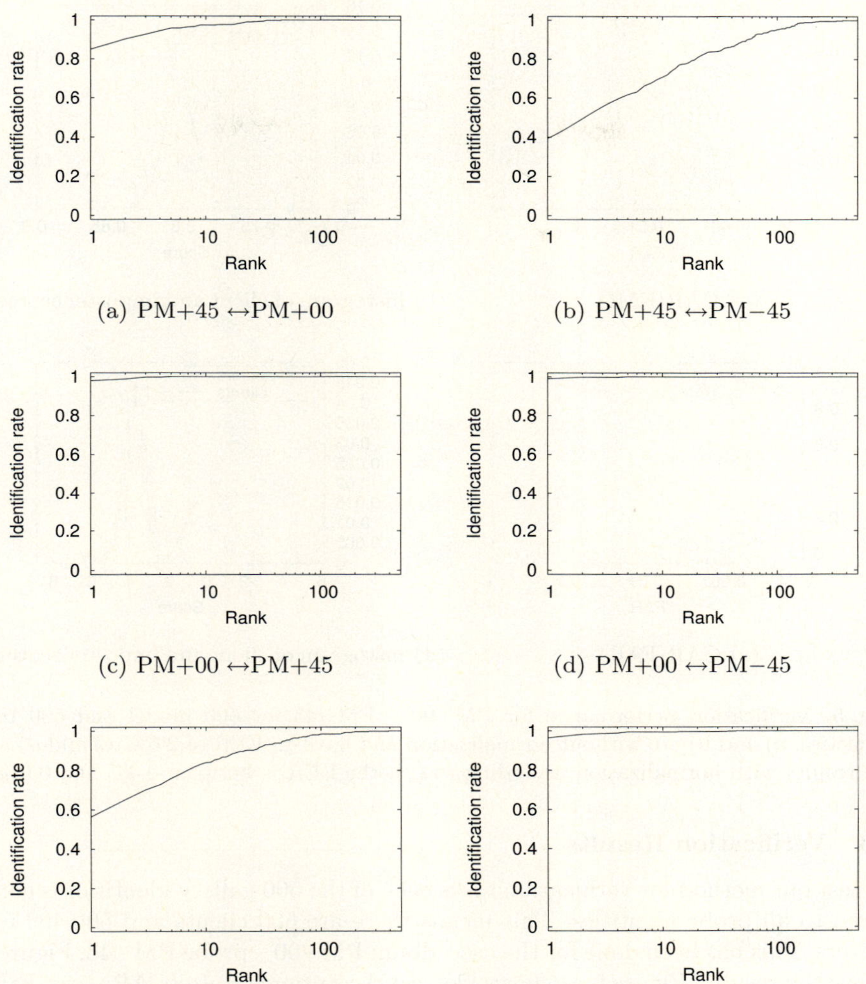

(a) PM+45 ↔PM+00

(b) PM+45 ↔PM−45

(c) PM+00 ↔PM+45

(d) PM+00 ↔PM−45

Fig. 4. Identification performance (cumulative match scores) for different poses in gallery (left of ↔) and probe (right of ↔) set. The model database consists of 500 identities, the testing database of 500 different ones.

similarities lead to better recognition rates for even bigger pose differences than 90°. What can be observed, as already in Table 1, is that recognition is generally better if the gallery consists of frontal pose. In our experiments, the rank similarity function as defined in (3) performed best. For PM+00↔PM−45 it reached 99% of recognition rate. The Spearman rank-order correlation coefficient lead to only 93.4%.

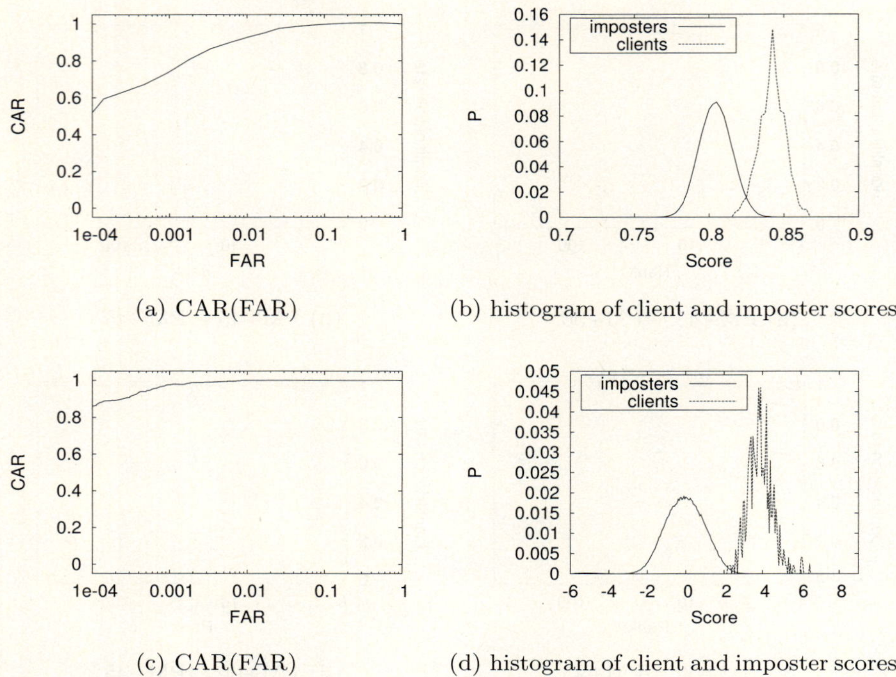

(a) CAR(FAR) (b) histogram of client and imposter scores

(c) CAR(FAR) (d) histogram of client and imposter scores

Fig. 5. Verification performance for PM+00 – PM−45 for 500 model and 500 test identities. a) and b) are without normalization and have an EER of 2.6%. c) and d) are the results with normalization according to (7); the EER is between 0.4% and 0.6%.

3.3 Verification Results

To test our method for verification tasks each of the 500 gallery identities is compared to all probe identities. This means there are 500 clients and 500·499 imposters. This has been done for the case album PM+00 – probe PM−45. Figure 5 shows the results. Figure 5 a) shows Correct Acceptance Rate (CAR) over False Acceptance Rate (FAR), Figure 5 b) the probability distributions for clients and imposters to attain a certain score. The Equal Error Rate (EER) is 2.6%.

To improve the EER in verification experiments, one can use the distribution of similarities to all gallery images to normalize the similiarity values of each probe image. For that, each probe image is tested against all gallery identities, and the resulting 500 similarities for each probe image are normalized in the following way:

$$\bar{S}(t_P) = \frac{1}{N_G} \sum_{t_G=0}^{N_G-1} S(t_G, t_P) \tag{6}$$

$$S_n(t_G, t_P) = \frac{S(t_G, t_P) - \bar{S}(t_P)}{\sqrt{\frac{1}{N_G} \cdot \sum_{t_G=0}^{N_G-1} \left(S(t_G, t_P) - \bar{S}(t_P)\right)^2}} \tag{7}$$

Fig 5 shows the resulting improvement for CAR and EER, the latter lies between 0.4 and 0.6%.

4 Discussion

We have presented a module for a face recognition system which can recognize or verify persons in a pose which is very different from the one enrolled. We have demonstrated the efficiency on 45° pose variation. An interesting side result is that the frontal pose is the best to be used as a gallery. For a complete system, the recognition step must be preceded by a rough pose estimation and look-up in the respective pose model. As the database used has considerable scatter in the actual pose angles it can be concluded that our method is robust enough to expect that the full range of poses can be covered with relatively few examples.

Acknowledgments

We gratefully acknowledge funding from Deutsche Forschungsgemeinschaft (WU 314/2-2 and MA 697/5-1), the European Union, the European Regional Development Fund, and the land of Northrhine-Westphalia in the program "Zukunftswettbewerb Ruhrgebiet" and the "Ruhrpakt". Portions of the research in this paper use the CAS-PEAL face database collected under the sponsorship of the Chinese National Hi-Tech Program and ISVISION Tech. Co. Ltd.

References

1. Blanz, V., Vetter, T.: Face recognition based on fitting a 3d morphable model. IEEE Transactions on Pattern Analysis and Machine Intelligence 25(9), 1063–1074 (2003)
2. Saul, L.K., Roweis, S.T.: Think Globally, Fit Locally: Unsupervised Learning of Low Dimensional Manifolds. Journal of Machine Learning Research 4, 119–155 (2003)
3. Okada, K., von der Malsburg, C.: Pose-invariant face recognition with parametric linear subspaces. In: Proceedings of the International Conference on Automatic Face and Gesture Recognition, Washington D.C., pp. 71–76 (2002)
4. Tewes, A.: A Flexible Object Model for Encoding and Matching Human Faces. Shaker Verlag, Ithaca, NY, USA (2006)
5. Tewes, A., Würtz, R.P., von der Malsburg, C.: A flexible object model for recognising and synthesising facial expressions. In: Kanade, T., Jain, A., Ratha, N.K. (eds.) AVBPA 2005. LNCS, vol. 3546, pp. 81–90. Springer, Heidelberg (2005)
6. Press, W., Flannery, B., Teukolsky, S., Vetterling, W.: Numerical Recipes in C — The Art of Scientific Programmming. Cambridge University Press, Cambridge (1988)
7. Andrew, L., Rukhin, A.O.: Nonparametric measures of dependence for biometric data studies. Journal of Statistical Planning and Inference 131, 1–18 (2005)
8. Ayinde, O., Yang, Y.H: Face recognition approach based on rank correlation of gabor-filtered images. Pattern Recognition 35(6), 1275–1289 (2002)

9. Lades, M., Vorbrüggen, J.C., Buhmann, J., Lange, J., von der Malsburg, C., Würtz, R.P., Konen, W.: Distortion invariant object recognition in the dynamic link architecture. IEEE Transactions on Computers 42(3), 300–311 (1993)
10. Wiskott, L., Fellous, J.M., Krüger, N., von der Malsburg, C.: Face recognition by elastic bunch graph matching. IEEE Transactions on Pattern Analysis and Machine Intelligence 19(7), 775–779 (1997)
11. Fritzke, B.: A growing neural gas network learns topologies. In: Tesauro, G., Touretzky, D.S., Leen, T.K. (eds.) Advances NIPS 7, pp. 625–632. MIT Press, Cambridge, MA (1995)
12. Heinrichs, A., Müller, M.K., Tewes, A.H., Würtz, R.P.: Graphs with principal components of Gabor wavelet features for improved face recognition. In: Cristóbal, G., Javidi, B., Vallmitjana, S. (eds.) Information Optics: 5th International Workshop on Information Optics; WIO'06, American Institute of Physics, pp. 243–252 (2006)
13. Gao, W., Cao, B., Shan, S., Zhou, D., Zhang, X., Zhao, D.: The CAS-PEAL large-scale Chinese face database and baseline evaluations. Technical Report JDL-TR-04-FR-001, Joint Research & Development Laboratory for Face Recognition, Chinese Academy of Sciences (2004)

Feature Correlation Filter for Face Recognition

Xiangxin Zhu, Shengcai Liao, Zhen Lei, Rong Liu, and Stan Z. Li

Center for Biometrics and Security Research & National Laboratory of Pattern Recognition,
Institute of Automation, Chinese Academy of Sciences,
95 Zhongguancun East Road, 100080 Beijing, China
{xxzhu,scliao,zlei,rliu,szli}@nlpr.ia.ac.cn
http://www.cbsr.ia.ac.cn

Abstract. The correlation filters for pattern recognition, have been extensively studied in the areas of automatic target recognition(ATR) and biometrics. Whereas the conventional correlation filters perform directly on image pixels, in this paper, we propose a novel method, called "feature correlation filter (FCF)", by extending the concept of correlation filter to feature spaces. The FCF preserves the benefits of conventional correlation filters, i.e., shift-invariant, occlusion-insensitive, and closed-form solution, and also inherits virtues of the feature representations. Moreover, since the size of feature is often much smaller than the size of image, the FCF method can significantly reduce the storage requirement in recognition system. The comparative results on CMU-PIE and the FRGC2.0 database show that the proposed FCFs can achieve noteworthy performance improvement compared with their conventional counterpart.

Keywords: Feature correlation filters, Correlation filters, MACE, Face recognition.

1 Introduction

Face recognition has received much attention due to its potential values for applications as well as theoretical challenges. However, despite the research advances over these years, face recognition is still a highly difficult task in practice due to the large variability of the facial images. The variations between images of a same face can generally be divided into two categories: *the appearance variations*, and *the man-made variations*. The appearance variations include facial expression, pose, aging, illumination changes, etc. And the man-made variations are mainly due to the imperfections of the capture devices and image processing technologies, e.g. the noises from the cameras and the face registration error resulting from imperfect face detections [1]. The performances of many recognition algorithms degrade significantly in these cases.

A common approach to overcome the effect of the appearance variations is to use face representations that are relatively insensitive to those variations. To deal with the man-made variations, using correlation to characterize the similarity

S.-W. Lee and S.Z. Li (Eds.): ICB 2007, LNCS 4642, pp. 77–86, 2007.

between faces is a natural choice, because of its shift-invariant property and the optimality in the presence of additive white Gaussian noise [2].

As far as correlation is mentioned, we often think of the Matched Filter (MF), which is essentially a template image designed to match with a specific pattern. The correlation peak value provides the likelihood measure, and a shift of the test image simply produces a shift of the correlation peak. However the MFs are very sensitive to even slight deformations [3]. Hence, to capture all possible image variations, a huge number of MFs are needed, which is definitely computational and storage impractical [4]. To solve these problems, more sophisticated correlation filter design techniques are proposed in various literatures [5][6][7]. The advanced correlation filters construct a single filter or template from a set of training images and can be computed analytically and effectively using frequency domain techniques. Among such advanced correlation filters, Minimum Average Correlation Energy(MACE) filter [8] is one of the most well known. Savvides *et al.* showed that the MACE is, to some extent, robust to illumination variations [4]. However, since the correlation filters (including MACE) operate directly on the raw image pixel data (sometimes with illumination normalization [9]) without feature extraction, it may not achieve stability with respect to deformations caused by expression and pose variations, thus may not gain good generalization ability. We think this might be the Achilles heel of this approach [10].

The motivation of this work is to explore potentials of MF types of matchers by combining the advantages of the correlation method and the feature representations of faces. This leads to the idea of the proposed feature correlation filter (FCF) method. To overcome the limitation of the correlation filters, we extend the concept of correlation filter to the feature space; we do the correlation using face image features rather than directly using image pixel values. "The most common motivation for using features rather than the pixels directly is that features can act to encode ad-hoc domain knowledge that is difficult to learn using a finite quantity of training data"(Viola and Jones [11]). Moreover, the FCF method could significantly reduce the size of templates stored in the system, because the size of feature is often much smaller than the size of image.

Many representation approaches have been introduced, such as Eigenface (PCA) [12], Fisherface (LDA) [3], ICA [13], Haar features [11], Gabor wavelet features [14], etc. Among these, we choose to use the PCA features and Gabor wavelet features for constructing FCFs and to demonstrate the effectiveness of the method.

By combining the advantages of the correlation filter and feature representation of faces, we expect to gain improved generalization and discriminant capability. First, we formulate the feature extraction procedure as inner products, then perform the correlation on features rather than raw image pixel values. The FCF is constructed by solving an optimization problem in frequency domain. Finally a closed-form solution is obtained.

While the focus of this work will be on the MACE filter criterion, it should be stated that all of the results presented here are equally applicable to many other kinds of the advanced correlation filters with appropriate changes to the respective optimization criteria.

The rest of this paper is organized as follows. Section 2 reviews the conventional MACE filter briefly. In Section 3, we introduce the basic concept of the FCF, and explain in detail how to construct the FCF. In Section 4, the experiments on PIE and FRGC2.0 database are presented. Finally, we conclude this paper and point out some further research in Section 5.

2 Minimum Average Correlation Energy (MACE) Filter

Notation: In this and the following section, we denote matrices by light face characters and vectors by bold characters. Uppercase symbols refer to the frequency domain terms, while lowercase symbols represent quantities in the space domain.

Suppose we have N facial images from a certain person. We consider each 2-dimensional image as a $d \times 1$ column vector $\mathbf{x}_i$ $(i = 1, 2, \ldots, N)$ by lexicographically reordering the image, where d is the number of pixels. The discrete Fourier transform (DFT) of $\mathbf{x}_i$ is denoted by $\mathbf{X}_i$, and we define the training image data matrix in frequency domain as $X = [\mathbf{X_1}\ \mathbf{X_2}\ \ldots\ \mathbf{X_N}]$. X is a $d \times N$ matrix.

Let the vector $\mathbf{h}$ be the correlation filter(correlation template) in the space domain and $\mathbf{H}$ be its Fourier transform. The correlation result of the ith image and the filter could be written as

$$\begin{aligned} c_i(m,n) &= \mathbf{h}(m,n) \circ \mathbf{x}_i(m,n) \\ &= \langle \mathbf{h}, \mathbf{x}_i^{m,n} \rangle \end{aligned} \tag{1}$$

where $\circ$ denotes *correlation*, and $\langle\ ,\ \rangle$ denotes *inner product* of two vectors. Here $\mathbf{x}_i^{m,n}$ is a vector obtained by circularly shifting the ith training image by m pixels horizontally and n pixels vertically, and reorder it to a 1-dimensional vector. Keep in mind that $\mathbf{h}$ and $\mathbf{x}_i$ are both 1-dimensional vectors obtained by reordering a 2-dimensional array. Since the correlation actually operates on a 2-dimensional plane, here we use two indices, m and n, to indicate the elements in these vectors. From Eq. (1), we can see that each value in the correlation output plane is simply a inner product of the filter and the shifted input image.

By Parseval's theorem, the correlation energy of $c_i(m,n)$ can be rewritten as follows using its frequency domain representation $C_i(u,v)$:

$$\begin{aligned} E_i &= \sum_m \sum_n |c_i(m,n)|^2 = \frac{1}{d} \sum_u \sum_v |C_i(u,v)|^2 \\ &= \frac{1}{d} \sum_u \sum_v |\mathbf{H}(u,v)|^2 |\mathbf{X}_i(u,v)|^2 \\ &= \frac{1}{d} \mathbf{h}^\dagger D_i \mathbf{h} \end{aligned} \tag{2}$$

where D_i is a $d \times d$ diagonal matrix containing the power spectrum of training image $\mathbf{X}_i$ along its diagonal. The superscripts $\dagger$ denote *conjugate transpose*.

The objective of the MACE filter is to minimize the average correlation energy over the image class while simultaneously satisfying an linear constraint that the correlation values at the origin due to training images take on pre-specified values stored in vector $\mathbf{u}$, where $\mathbf{u} = [u_1\ u_2\ \cdots\ u_N]^T$. i.e.

$$c_i(0,0) = \mathbf{X}_i{}^{\dagger}\mathbf{H} = u_i \tag{3}$$

The average correlation energy over all training images is

$$E_{avg} = \mathbf{H}^{\dagger} D \mathbf{H} \quad \text{where} \quad D = \frac{1}{N}\sum_{i=1}^{N} D_i \tag{4}$$

Minimize E_{avg} subject to the constraint, $X^{\dagger}\mathbf{H} = \mathbf{u}$. The solution can be obtained using Lagrange multipliers [8]:

$$\mathbf{H} = D^{-1}X(X^{\dagger}D^{-1}X)^{-1}\mathbf{u} \tag{5}$$

3 Feature Correlation Filter for Face Recognition

3.1 MACE in Feature Space

All the linear feature extraction method can be expressed as follows:

$$\mathbf{y}_i = v^{\dagger}\mathbf{x}_i \tag{6}$$

where $v = [\mathbf{v_1}\ \mathbf{v_2}\ \ldots\ \mathbf{v_M}]$ is a $d \times M$ feature extraction matrix. $\mathbf{y}_i \in \mathbb{R}^M$ is the feature vector of length M. M depends on what feature to use. The discrete Fourier transform (DFT) of $\mathbf{v}_j$ is denoted by $\mathbf{V}_j$, and define $V = [\mathbf{V_1}\ \mathbf{V_2}\ \ldots\ \mathbf{V_M}]$.

Note that, if we use PCA feature, the columns of v in Eq. (6) should be the eigenfaces. Extracting Gabor features could also be formulated using Eq. (6), since applying Gabor wavelet kernel to the input image is simply an inner product.

As described in Eq. (1), the correlation plane is a collection of correlation values, each one is obtained by performing an inner product of the image and the template. In our FCF method, each correlation value is obtained by performing inner product of two feature vectors. The feature correlation output of the input image $\mathbf{x}_i$ $(i = 1, 2, \ldots, N)$ and the template $\mathbf{h}$ in spatial domain can be formulated as

$$\begin{aligned} c_i(m,n) &= \langle \mathbf{y}_h, \mathbf{y}_i \rangle = \langle v^{\dagger}\mathbf{h}, v^{\dagger}\mathbf{x_i}^{m,n} \rangle \\ &= \sum_{j=1}^{M} \mathbf{v_j}^{\dagger} h \cdot \mathbf{v_j}^{\dagger} x_i^{m,n} \end{aligned} \tag{7}$$

Here $\cdot$ denotes simply *scalar product.* $\mathbf{y}_h$ is the feature vector extracted from the template $\mathbf{h}$. Comparing Eq. (7) with Eq. (1), we can see the difference in definition between our FCF method and the conventional correlation method.

The frequency representation of $c_i(m,n)$ is,

$$C_i(u,v) = \frac{1}{d}\sum_{j=1}^{M}\mathbf{V_j^{\dagger}H}\cdot\mathbf{V}_j(u,v)\cdot\mathbf{X}_i{}^*(u,v) \tag{8}$$

where the superscript $*$ denotes *complex conjugation.*

With Eq. (8), we can obtain the expression of the correlation plane energy :

$$\begin{aligned} E_i &= \frac{1}{d}\sum_u\sum_v |C_i(u,v)|^2 \\ &= \frac{1}{d^3}\mathbf{H}^{\dagger}VV^{\dagger}D_iVV^{\dagger}\mathbf{H} \end{aligned} \tag{9}$$

The average correlation plane energy is

$$E_{avg} = \mathbf{H}^{\dagger}VV^{\dagger}DVV^{\dagger}\mathbf{H} \tag{10}$$

And the constraint at the origin is

$$X^{\dagger}VV^{\dagger}\mathbf{H} = \mathbf{u} \tag{11}$$

We let $\mathbf{P} = V^{\dagger}\mathbf{H}$, the objective function and constraint function can be rewritten as

$$E_{avg} = \mathbf{P}^{\dagger}V^{\dagger}DV\mathbf{P} \tag{12}$$

subject to

$$X^{\dagger}V\mathbf{P} = \mathbf{u} \tag{13}$$

Minimize E_{avg} in Eq. (12), subject to the constraint in Eq. (13), we get the closed-form solution:

$$\mathbf{P} = (V^{\dagger}DV)^{-1}V^{\dagger}X(X^{\dagger}V(V^{\dagger}DV)^{-1}V^{\dagger}X)^{-1}\mathbf{u} \tag{14}$$

Then, we obtain the *feature correlation filter* $\mathbf{P}$, which is a $M\times 1$ complex vector. Remind that M is the number of the features used.

Let $\tilde{D} = V^{\dagger}DV$ and $\tilde{X} = V^{\dagger}X$, Eq. (14) can be rewritten as:

$$\mathbf{P} = \tilde{D}^{-1}\tilde{X}(\tilde{X}^{\dagger}\tilde{D}^{-1}\tilde{X})^{-1}\mathbf{u} \tag{15}$$

Comparing Eq. (15) with Eq. (5), we can see that the FCF and MACE share the same formulation.

Note that, for each person we only need to store $\mathbf{P}$ in the recognition system, while the conventional correlation filter based system stores a template(filter) $\mathbf{H}$. Typically the size of $\mathbf{P}$ is much smaller than the size of $\mathbf{H}$. Thus the FCF can significantly reduce the size of the templates stored in the system. However, in FCF system, the $d\times M$ matrix V is also needed to be stored for verification. So this advantage on storage may not show up until the number of people enrolled in the system grows larger than M.

3.2 Face Verification Using FCF

Given a test image $\mathbf{x}_t$, the output correlation plane can be obtained using Eq. (16),

$$\begin{aligned} c_t(m,n) &= \mathfrak{F}^{-1}(C_t(u,v)) \\ &= \mathfrak{F}^{-1}(\sum_{i=1}^{M} \mathbf{V}_i(u,v) \cdot \mathbf{P}(i) \cdot \mathbf{X}_t{}^*(u,v)) \end{aligned} \tag{16}$$

where The superscript T denotes *nonconjugate transpose* of a complex vector. $\mathfrak{F}^{-1}(\cdot)$ is *inverse Fourier transform.* $\mathbf{X}_t$ is the DFT of $\mathbf{x}_t$.

We compute the peak-to-sidelobe ratio (PSR) of $c_t(m,n)$ to measure the peak sharpness.

$$PSR = \frac{peak - mean}{\sigma} \tag{17}$$

where the peak is the largest value in the correlation output, the mean and σ are the average value and the standard deviation of all the correlation outputs, excluding a 5×5 region centered in the peak.

4 Experiments

To demonstrate the effectiveness of our proposed FCF method, several experiments are carried out on the illumination subset of the CMU-PIE database [15] and two subsets of FRGC2.0 data [16]. The experiments on the CMU-PIE is to show that the FCFs preserve the advantages of the conventional MACE, including shift-invariant and insensitive to partially occlusion. The experiments on the FRGC2.0 database, which has much larger size and is more difficult, will show the improved performance of our FCF methods. In the following experiments, the centers of the eyes of an image are manually detected firstly, then rotation and scaling transformations align the centers of the eyes to predefined locations. Finally, the face image is cropped to the size of 100×100 to extract the facial region, which is further normalized to zero mean and unit variance.

We choose the most representative holistic and local features , i.e. Eigenface(PCA) and Gabor wavelets, to construct the FCFs. For PCA, we used the eigenfaces that retain 98% of the total variation, i.e., totally 134 eigenfaces for experiments on CMU-PIE database, and 400 for experiments on FRGC2.0. The three most significant eigenfaces are discarded, since they capture the variation due to lighting [3]. The first 5 eigenfaces used for the CMU-PIE database are shown in Fig. 1. We used Gabor kernels at 5 scales and 4 orientations. In order to obtain a reasonably small-size feature vector, we extract the Gabor features at 49 predetermined positions, shown in Fig. 1. The total number of the Gabor features we used is 980.

The two kinds of FCFs are termed as PCA-FCF and Gabor-FCF, respectively.

The correlation outputs of MACE, PCA-FCF and Gabor-FCF of typical genuine and imposter images are shown in Fig. 2. The storage costs are listed in Table 1.

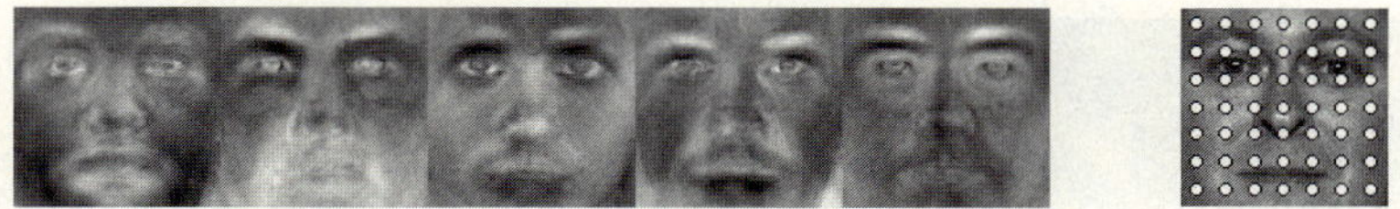

Fig. 1. Left: the first 5 Eigenfaces used for PIE database. Right: The 49 predetermined positions for Gabor feature extraction.

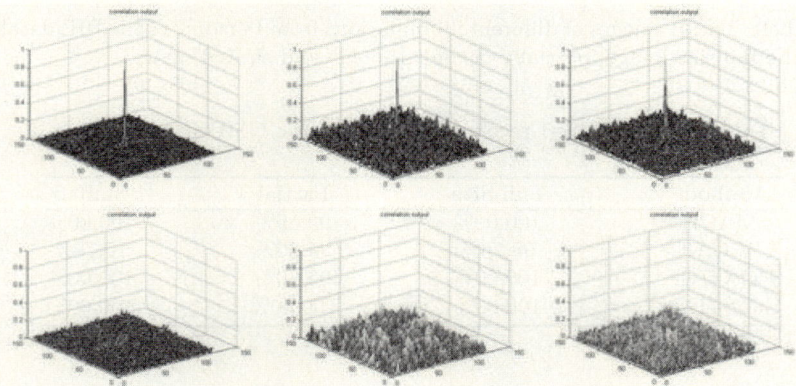

Fig. 2. The correlation output planes of MACE, PCA-FCF and Gabor-FCF, respectively(from left to right). Upper row: The correlation outputs of a typical genuine image. Lower row: The correlation outputs of a typical imposter image.

Table 1. The Storage Cost of Each Template (In KBytes)

MACE	PCA-FCF	Gabor-FCF
80.0	3.2	7.8

4.1 CMU-PIE Database

The illumination subset of the CMU-PIE database we used consists of 67 people with 21 illumination variation (shown in Fig. 3). We use 3 images per person to construct the MACE filter and the FCFs. The other 18 images are used for testing.

The test is carried out in three scenarios (shown in Fig. 3). (1) Using full size facial images for testing. (2) The testing images are partially occluded(10 pixels from top, and 15 pixels from bottom). (3) The testing images are shifted(10 pixels to the left) to simulate the situation of registration error. All these three cases are often encountered in real applications. Note that we train the MACE and the FCFs using full size images. The results are shown in Table 2.

The performance of PCA method degrades significantly in occlusion and shifting scenarios, while the MACE and the FCF methods still perform well. The

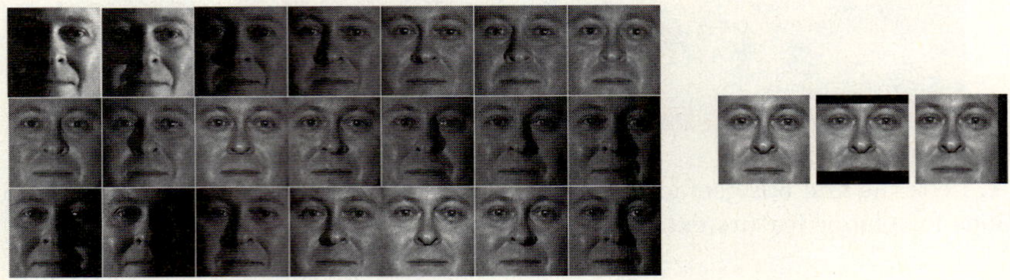

Fig. 3. Left: The 21 images of different illuminations from Person 2 of the PIE database. Right: the full size image, partially occluded image and shifted image.

Table 2. The Rank-1 recognition rates on the CMU-PIE database

Methods	Full Size	Partial	Shifted
MACE	100.00%	99.59%	100.00%
PCA	98.76%	24.30%	10.78%
PCA-FCF	100.00%	96.60%	100.00%
Gabor-FCF	100.00%	100.00%	100.00%

results demonstrate that the FCFs preserve the MACE's advantages, i.e., insensitive to occlusion and shift-invariant, which are desired in real applications.

Since there are only 67 people in the CMU-PIE database, and only illumination variation is involved(the 21 images are taken almost simultaneously, thus the expression and pose in the images are exactly the same), both MACE and FCF obtain nearly perfect recognition rates.

4.2 FRGC2.0 Database

To further evaluate the performance of the FCF-based method and show its improved recognition ability, we use the FRGC2.0 database [16], which is much larger and more difficult. Two subsets are used: the controlled subset and uncontrolled one. The controlled images were taken in a studio setting, are full frontal facial images taken under two lighting conditions and with two facial expressions. The uncontrolled images were taken in varying illumination conditions; e.g., hallways, atria, or outdoors. Each set of uncontrolled images contains two expressions. The images are taken in different semesters, and some images are blurred. Some sample images are shown in Fig. 4.

From each subset, we randomly select 222 people and 20 images per person. 5 images of each person are used for training, and the other 15 for testing. The test results are summarized in the Table 3.

The results show that the FCF methods significantly outperform the MACE. This is mainly derived from the combination of the advanced correlation filters and the feature representation.

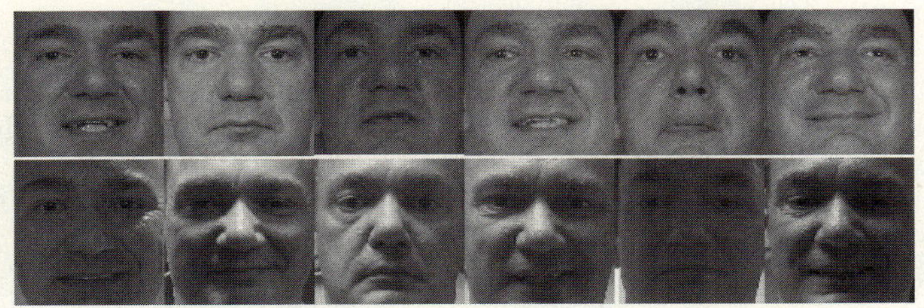

Fig. 4. Some example image for FRGC database. Top row, controlled images. Bottom row, uncontrolled images.

Table 3. The Rank-1 recognition rates on the FRGC2.0 database

Methods	Controlled	Uncontrolled
MACE	80.99%	34.29%
PCA	76.73%	51.11%
PCA-FCF	**91.92%**	**64.14%**
Gabor-FCF	**93.84%**	**67.57%**

5 Conclusions

This work aims to bring a promising perspective for using correlation filters in biometric recognition. The major contribution is the idea of incorporating the feature representations of faces into correlation filter, to take the advantages of advanced correlation filter and feature representation. We formulated the feature extraction as inner products, and obtained a closed-form solution by solving an optimization problem in frequency domain. The experimental results show that the proposed FCF methods significantly outperform their conventional counterpart. Working with fewer features, the FCF method can significantly reduce the size of the template stored in the system.

While the FCFs in this paper is in essence a linear method, in future work, we would consider the nonlinear extension. We would also consider other types of features to used, and selection of the best features and combinations of different feature types for correlation.

Acknowledgments. This work was supported by the following funding resources: National Natural Science Foundation Project #60518002, National Science and Technology Supporting Platform Project #2006BAK08B06, National 863 Program Projects #2006AA01Z192 and #2006AA01Z193, Chinese Academy of Sciences 100 people project, and the AuthenMetric Collaboration Foundation.

References

1. Rentzeperis, E., Stergiou, A., Pnevmatikakis, A., Polymenakos, L.: Impact of Face Registration Errors on Recognition, presented at Artificial Intelligence Applications and Innovations (AIAI06) (2006)
2. Vanderlugt, A.: Signal detection by complex spatial filtering. IEEE Trans. Inf. Theory 10, 139–145 (1964)
3. Belhumeur, P.N., Hespanha, J.P., Kriegman, D.J.: Eigenfaces vs. Fisherfaces: recognition using class specific linear projection. Pattern Analysis and Machine Intelligence, IEEE Transactions 19, 711–720 (1997)
4. Savvides, M., Kumar, B.V.K.V., Khosla, P.K.: Corefaces - Robust shift invariant PCA based correlation filter for illumination tolerant face recognition. IEEE Comp. Vision and Patt. Rec (CVPR) (2004)
5. Kumar, B.V.K.V., Mahalanobis, A., Juday, R.D.: Correlation Pattern Recognition. Cambridge Univ. Press, Cambridge, U.K. (2005)
6. Vijara Kumar, B.V.K.: Minimum variance synthetic discriminant functions. J. Opt. Soc. Amer. A 3, 1579C1584 (1986)
7. Mahalanobis, A., Vijaya Kumar, B.V.K., Song, S., Sims, S.R.F., Epperson, J.: Unconstrained correlation filters. Appl. Opt. 33, 3751C3759 (1994)
8. Mahalanobis, A., Kumar, B.V.K.V., Casasent, D.: Minimum average correlation energy filters. Appl. Opt. 26, 3630–3633 (1987)
9. Savvides, M., Kumar, B.V.K.V.: Illumination normalization using logarithm transforms for face authentication. In: 4th Int. Conf. AVBPA (2003)
10. Vijaya Kumar, B.V.K., Savvides, M., Xie, C.: Correlation Pattern Recognition for Face Recognition. Proceedings of the IEEE 94, 1963–1976 (2006)
11. Viola, P., Jones, M.: Rapid object detection using a boosted cascade of simple features. In: Computer Vision and Pattern Recognition (CVPR) (2001)
12. Turk, M., Pentland, A.: Eigenfaces for recognition. J. Cognitive Neuroscience 3, 72–86 (1991)
13. Bartlett, M.S., Lades, H.M., Sejnowski, T.J.: Independent component representations for face recognition. In: Proceedings of the SPIE, Conference on Human Vision and Electronic Imaging (1998)
14. Wiskott, L., Fellous, J., Kruger, N., malsburg, C.V.: Face recognition by elastic bunch graph matching. Pattern Analysis and Machine Intelligence, IEEE Transactions 19, 775–779 (1997)
15. Sim, T., Baker, S., Bsat, M.: The CMU Pose, Illumination, and Expression (PIE) Database of Human Faces, Robotics Institute, Carnegie Mellon University CMU-RI-TR-01-02 (2001)
16. Phillips, P.J., Flynn, P.J., Scruggs, T., Bowyer, K.W., Jin, C., Hoffman, K., Marques, J., Jaesik, M., Worek, W.: Overview of the face recognition grand challenge. In: Proc. IEEE Conf. Comp. Vision Pattern Rec. (CVPR) (2005)

Face Recognition by Discriminant Analysis with Gabor Tensor Representation

Zhen Lei, Rufeng Chu, Ran He, Shengcai Liao, and Stan Z. Li

Center for Biometrics and Security Research & National Laboratory of Pattern Recognition,
Institute of Automation, Chinese Academy of Sciences,
95 Zhongguancun Donglu, Beijing 100080, China
{zlei,rfchu,rhe,scliao,szli}@nlpr.ia.ac.cn
http://www.cbsr.ia.ac.cn

Abstract. This paper proposes a novel face recognition method based on discriminant analysis with Gabor tensor representation. Although the Gabor face representation has achieved great success in face recognition, its huge number of features often brings about the problem of curse of dimensionality. In this paper, we propose a 3rd-order Gabor tensor representation derived from a complete response set of Gabor filters across pixel locations and filter types. 2D discriminant analysis is then applied to unfolded tensors to extract three discriminative subspaces. The dimension reduction is done in such a way that most useful information is retained. The subspaces are finally integrated for classification. Experimental results on FERET database show promising results of the proposed method.

Keywords: discriminant analysis, Gabor tensor representation, face recognition.

1 Introduction

Face images lie in a highly nonlinear and nonconvex manifolds in the image space due to the various changes by expression, illumination and pose etc. Design a robust and accurate classifier in such a nonlinear and nonconvex distribution is difficult work. One approach to simplify the complexity is to construct a local appearance-based feature space, using appropriate image filters, so that the distributions of faces are less affected by various changes. Gabor wavelet-based features have been used for this purpose [5,14,8].

The Gabor wavelets, whose kernels are similar to the two-dimensional (2D) receptive field profiles of the mammalian cortical simple cells, exhibit desirable characteristics of spatial locality and orientation selectivity. It is robust to variations due to expression and illumination changes and is one of the most successful approaches for face recognition. However, Gabor features are usually very high-dimensional data and there are redundancies among them. It is well known that face images lie in a manifold of intrinsically low dimension; therefore, the Gabor feature representations of faces could be analyzed further to extract the underlying manifold by some statistical approach such as subspace methods.

S.-W. Lee and S.Z. Li (Eds.): ICB 2007, LNCS 4642, pp. 87–95, 2007.

Subspace methods such as PCA, LDA [1,13] have been extensively studied in face recognition research. PCA uses the Karhunen-Loeve transform to produce the most expressive subspace for face representation and recognition by minimizing the residua of the reconstruction. However, it does not utilize any class information and so it may drop some important clues for classification. LDA is then proposed and it seeks subspace of features best separating different face classes by maximizing the ratio of the between-classes scatter to the within-class scatter. It is an example of the most discriminating subspace methods.

However, because of the usually high dimensions of feature space (e.g. the total number of pixels in an image) and small sample size, the within-class scatter matrix S_w is often singular, so the optimal solution of LDA cannot be found directly. Therefore, some variants of LDA have been proposed such as PCA+LDA (Fisher-LDA), Direct LDA (D-LDA), Null space LDA (N-LDA) [1,19,2] etc. However, these LDAs all try to solve the singular problem of S_w instead of avoiding it. None of them can avoid losing some discriminative information helpful for recognition. Recently, Two-Dimensional Linear Discriminant Analysis (2D-LDA) method [18,6] has been discussed as a generalization of traditional 1D-LDA.[1] The main idea of the 2D method is to construct the scatter matrices using image matrices directly instead of vectors. As the image scatter matrices have a much smaller size, 2D-LDA significantly reduces the computational cost and avoids the singularity problem. Further generalization has also been proposed to represent each object as a general tensor of second or higher order, such as PCA and discriminant analysis with tensor representation [15,16].

Previous work usually [3,9,12] performs subspace analysis with Gabor vector representation. Because of the high-dimension of Gabor feature vectors and the scarcity of available data, it leads to the curse of dimensionality problem. Moreover, for objects such as face images, a vector representation ignores higher-order structures in the data. Yan et al. [16] proposed discriminant analysis with tensor representation. It encoded an object as a general tensor and iteratively learned multiple interrelated subspaces for obtaining a lower-dimensional space. However, the computational convergence of the method is not guaranteed and it is hard to extend it to kernel form.

In this paper, we propose a novel discriminant analysis method with Gabor tensor representation for face recognition. Compared to the method in [16], we introduce an alternative way for feature extraction on Gabor tensor in such a way that we can derive a non-iterative way for discrimination and extend it to kernel learning easily. The algorithm is divided into three steps. First, a face image is encoded by Gabor filters to form a 3rd-order tensor; Second, the 3rd-order tensor is unfolded into three 2nd-order tensors and 2D linear/kernel discriminant analysis is conducted on them respectively to derive three discriminative subspaces; and finally these subspaces are integrated and reduced further for classification with a nearest neighbor classifier.

The rest of the paper is organized as follows: Section 2 describes the Gabor tensor representation. Section 3 details the discriminant analysis method with Gabor tensor representation. The experimental results on FERET database are demonstrated in Section 4 and in Section 5, we conclude the paper.

[1] LDA based on vectors is noted as 1D-LDA.

2 Gabor Tensor Representation

The representation of faces using Gabor features has been extensively and successfully used in face recognition [14]. Gabor features exhibit desirable characteristics of spatial locality and orientation selectively and optimally localized in the space and frequency domains. The Gabor kernels are defined as follows:

$$\psi_{\mu,\nu} = \frac{k_{\mu,\nu}^2}{\sigma^2} \exp(-\frac{k_{\mu,\nu}^2 z^2}{2\sigma^2})[\exp(ik_{\mu,\nu}z) - \exp(-\frac{\sigma^2}{2})] \quad (1)$$

where μ and ν define the orientation and scale of the Gabor kernels respectively, $z = (x, y)$, and the wave vector $k_{\mu,\nu}$ is defined as follows:

$$k_{\mu,\nu} = k_\nu e^{i\phi_\mu} \quad (2)$$

where $k_\nu = k_{max}/f^\nu$, $k_{max} = \pi/2$, $f = \sqrt{2}$, $\phi_\mu = \pi\mu/8$. The Gabor kernels in (1) are all self-similar since they can be generated from one filter, the mother wavelet, by scaling and rotating via the wave vector $k_{\mu,\nu}$. Each kernel is product of a Gaussian envelope and a complex plane wave, while the first term in the square brackets in (1) determines the oscillatory part of the kernel and the second term compensates for the DC value. Hence, a band of Gabor filters is generated by a set of various scales and rotations of the kernel.

In this paper, we use Gabor kernels at five scales $\nu \in \{0, 1, 2, 3, 4\}$ and eight orientations $\mu \in \{0, 1, 2, 3, 4, 5, 6, 7\}$ with the parameter $\sigma = 2\pi$ [9] to derive the Gabor representation by convoluting face images with corresponding Gabor kernels. For every image pixel we have totally 40 Gabor magnitude coefficients which can be regarded as a Gabor feature vector of 40 dimensions. Therefore, a $h \times w$ 2D image can be encoded by 40 Gabor filters to form a $40 \times h \times w$ 3rd-order Gabor tensor. Fig. 1 shows an example of a face image with its corresponding 3rd-order Gabor tensor.

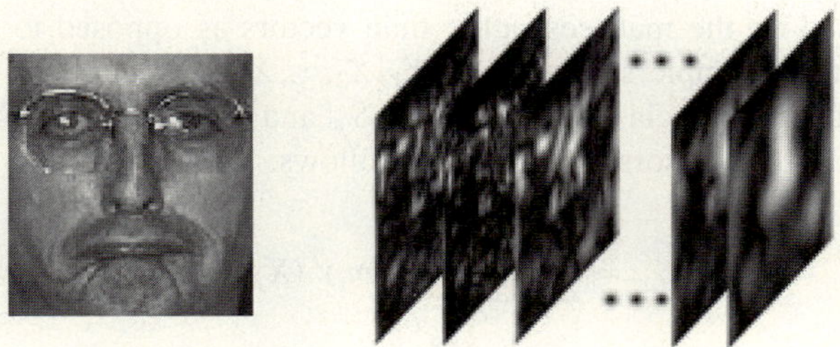

Fig. 1. A face image and its corresponding 3rd-order Gabor tensor

3 Discriminant Analysis with Gabor Tensor Representation

Since it is hard to apply discriminant analysis directly in the 3rd or higher-order tensor space, we here adopt an alternative strategy. The 3rd-order Gabor tensor is first unfolded into three 2nd-order tensors (matrices) along different axes. Fig. 2 shows the modes of the Gabor tensor unfolding. After that 2D linear/kernel discriminant analysis is conducted on these 2nd-order tensors respectively to extract effective and robust subspaces which will be combined further for classification.

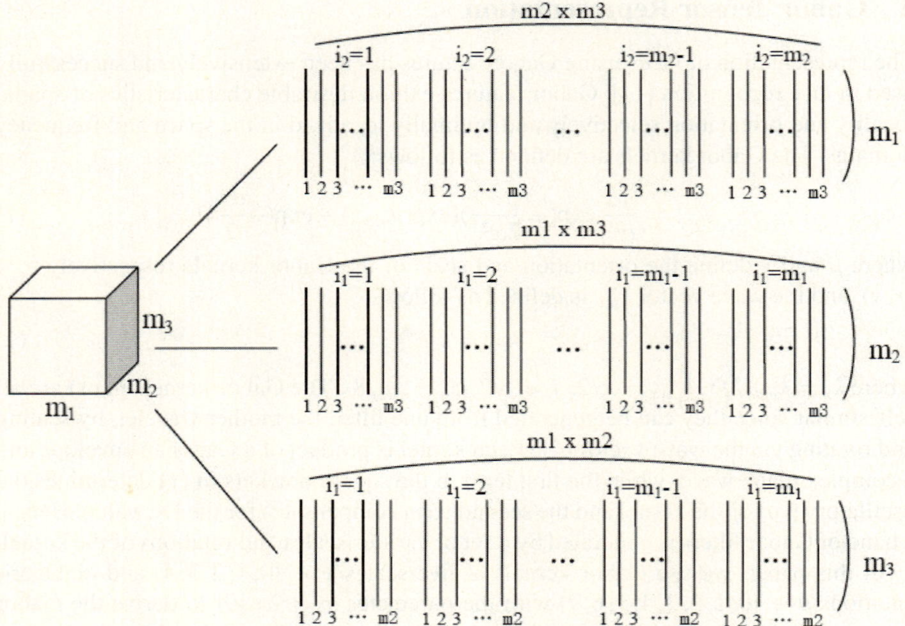

Fig. 2. Illustration of the three feature matrices unfolded from a 3rd-order tensor along different axes m1,m2,m3

3.1 2D Linear Discriminant Analysis (2D-LDA)

2D-LDA is based on the matrices rather than vectors as opposed to 1D-LDA based approaches. Let the sample set be $X = \{X_1, X_2, ..., X_n\}$, and X_i is an $r \times c$ unfolded Gabor matrix. The within-class scatter matrix S_w and the between-class scatter matrix S_b based on 2nd-order tensors are defined as follows:

$$S_w = \sum_{i=1}^{L} \sum_{X_j \in C_i} (X_j - m_i)^T (X_j - m_i) \tag{3}$$

$$S_b = \sum_{i=1}^{L} n_i (m_i - m)^T (m_i - m) \tag{4}$$

where $m_i = \frac{1}{n_i} \sum_{X_j \in C_i} X_j$ is the mean of data matrices in class C_i, and $m = \frac{1}{n} \sum_{i=1}^{L} \sum_{X_j \in C_i} X_j$ is the global mean matrix. The 2D-LDA searches such optimal projections that after projecting the original data onto these directions, the trace of the resulting between-class scatter matrix is maximized while the trace of the within-class scatter matrix is minimized. Let W denote a $c \times d$ $(d < c)$ projection matrix, and the $r \times c$ unfolded Gabor matrix X is projected onto W by the following linear transformation:

$$Y = XW \tag{5}$$

where the resulting Y is a $r \times d$ matrix smaller than X. Denote $\tilde{S}_w$, $\tilde{S}_b$ the with-class and between-class scatter matrices of the projected data Y respectively. 2D-LDA then chooses W so that the following object function is maximized:

$$J = \frac{tr(\tilde{S}_b)}{tr(\tilde{S}_w)} = \frac{tr(\sum_{i=1}^{L} n_i W^T (m_i - m)^T (m_i - m) W)}{tr(\sum_{i=1}^{L} \sum_{X_j \in C_i} W^T (X_j - m_i)^T (X_j - m_i) W)} = \frac{tr(W^T S_b W)}{tr(W^T S_w W)} \tag{6}$$

The optimal projection matrix W_{opt} can be obtained by solving the following generalized eigen-value problem

$$S_w^{-1} S_b W = W \Lambda \tag{7}$$

where Λ is the diagonal matrix whose diagonal elements are eigenvalues of $S_w^{-1} S_b$.

3.2 2D Kernel Discriminant Analysis (2D-KDA)

It is well known the face appearances may lie in a nonlinear low-dimensional manifold due to the expression and illumination variations [7]. The linear methods may not be adequate to model such a nonlinear problem. Accordingly, a 2D non-linear discriminant analysis method based on kernel trick is proposed here. Like other kernel subspace representations, such as Kernel PCA (KPCA) [11], Kernel 2DPCA [4], Kernel FDA (KFDA) [17], the key idea of 2D Kernel Discrimannt Analysis (2D-KDA) is to solve the problem of 2D-LDA in an implicit feature space F which is constructed by the kernel trick:

$$\phi : x \in R^d \rightarrow \phi(x) \in F \tag{8}$$

Given M training samples, denoted by $r \times c$ unfolded Gabor matrices A_k $(k = 1, 2, \ldots, M)$. A kernel-induced mapping function maps the data vector from the original input space to a higher or even infinite dimensional feature space. The kernel mapping on matrices is defined as:

$$\Phi(A) = [\phi(A^1)^T, \phi(A^2)^T, \ldots, \phi(A^M)^T]^T \tag{9}$$

where A^i is the i-th row vector $(1 \times c)$ of the matrix A and ϕ is kernel mapping function on vectors. Performing 2D-LDA in F means to maximize the following Fisher discriminant function:

$$J(W) = argmax \frac{tr(W^T S_b^\phi W)}{tr(W^T S_w^\phi W)} \tag{10}$$

where S_b^ϕ and S_w^ϕ represent the between-class scatter and the within-class scatter respectively in F.

$$S_b^\phi = \sum_{i=1}^{L} n_i (\Phi_i - \Phi)^T (\Phi_i - \Phi) \tag{11}$$

$$S_w^\phi = \sum_{i=1}^{L} \sum_{A_j \in C_i} (\Phi(A_j) - \Phi_j)^T (\Phi(A_j) - \Phi_j) \tag{12}$$

where, $\Phi_i = \frac{1}{n_i} \sum_{j=1}^{n_i} \Phi(A_j)$, $\Phi = \frac{1}{n} \sum_{i=1}^{L} n_i \Phi_i$.

If we follow the conventional kernel analysis as in 1D-KFDA, there exist $r \times M$ samples to span the kernel feature space $\{\phi(A_k^i)^T, i = 1, \ldots, r; k = 1, \ldots, M\}$, which will result in heavy computational cost for subsequent optimization procedure. To alleviate the computational cost, following [20], we use M samples to approximate the kernel feature space: $\Phi_f = [\phi(\overline{A}_1)^T, \ldots, \phi(\overline{A}_M)^T]^T$, here $\overline{A}_k$ is the mean of the r row vector of A_k. Thus, (10) can be rewritten as:

$$J(\alpha) = argmax \frac{tr(\alpha^T K_b \alpha)}{tr(\alpha^T K_w \alpha)} \tag{13}$$

and the problem of 2D-KDA is converted into finding the leading eigenvectors of $K_w^{-1} K_b$.

$$K_b = \sum_{i=1}^{L} n_i (z_i - z)^T (z_i - z) \tag{14}$$

$$K_w = \sum_{i=1}^{L} \sum_{\zeta_j \in C_i} (\zeta_j - z_i)^T (\zeta_j - z_i) \tag{15}$$

where $\zeta_j = [\varsigma_{1j}^T, \varsigma_{2j}^T, \ldots, \varsigma_{rj}^T]^T$, $\varsigma_{ij} = [k(\overline{A}_1, A_j^i), k(\overline{A}_2, A_j^i), \ldots, k(\overline{A}_M, A_j^i)]$, k is the kernel function to compute the inner product of two vectors in F; $z_i = \frac{1}{n_i} \sum_{\zeta_j \in C_i} \zeta_j$, and z is the mean of all ζ_j. Three classes of kernel functions are widely used, i.e. Gaussian kernels, polynomial kernels, and sigmoid kernels and here, we use Gaussian kernels in the following experiments.

3.3 Discriminant Analysis with Gabor Tensor Representation

The 2nd-order tensors, which were obtained by unfolding the 3rd-order Gabor tensor along different axes, depict faces from different aspects, so the subspaces derived from the different modes of 2nd-order tensor spaces may contain complemental information helpful for discrimination. Considering this, the subspaces are integrated and reduced further using PCA method. Suppose Y_1, Y_2, Y_3 are the three subspaces obtained for each image, they are first transformed into 1D vectors respectively, denoted as y_1, y_2, y_3, and concatenated into one 1D vector $y = [y_1^T, y_2^T, y_3^T]^T$, PCA is then performed on these combined vectors. Finally, the shorter vectors derived from PCA are used for classification with a nearest neighbor classifier.

As mentioned above, we proposed a novel linear/kernel discriminant analysis method with Gabor-tensor representation noted as GT-LDA and GT-KDA respectively. It inherits the advantages of the 2D discriminant analysis methods and therefore can effectively avoid the singularity problem. The algorithm is described with the Gabor tensor representation but not limit to it. In fact, it can be extended to arbitrary N-order tensor. Specifically, it's not hard to find that 2D-LDA and LDA are both special forms of our proposed method with $N = 2$ and $N = 1$.

4 Experimental Results and Analysis

In this section, we evaluate the performance of the proposed algorithm (GT-LDA/GT-KDA) using the FERET database [10]. The FERET database is a standard test set for

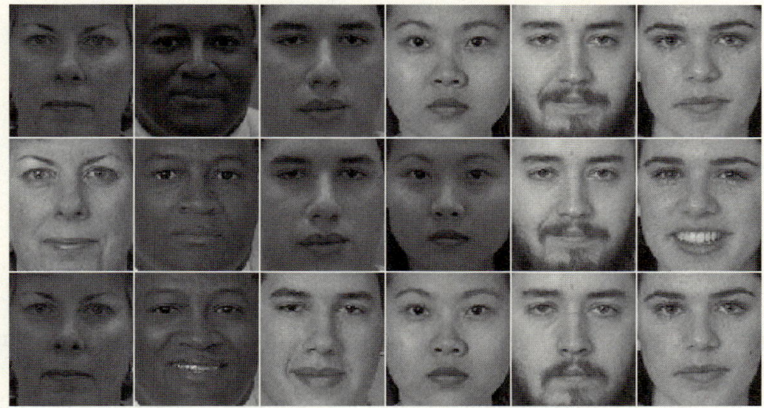

Fig. 3. Example cropped FERET images used in our experiments

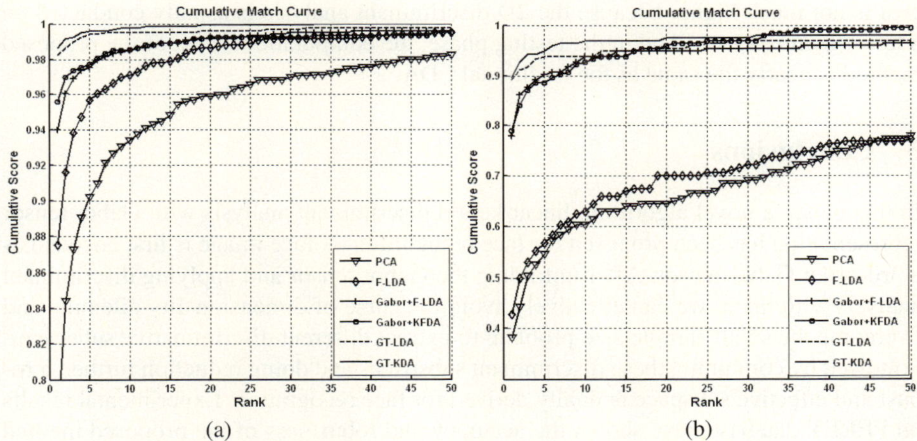

(a) (b)

Fig. 4. Cumulative match curves on fb (a) and fc (b) probe sets

face recognition technologies. In our experiments, we use a subset of the training set containing 540 images from 270 subjects for training. Two probe sets named fb (expression) and fc (lighting), which contains images with expression and lighting variation respectively, are used for testing against the gallery set containing 1196 images . All images are cropped to 88 × 80 pixels according to the eye positions. Fig. 3 shows some examples of the cropped FERET images.

To prove the advantage of the proposed method, we compare our method (GT-LDA/ GT-KDA) with some other well-known methods: PCA, LDA, Gabor+LDA and Gabor+KFDA. Fig. 4 demonstrates the cumulative match curves (CMC) of these methods on the fb and fc probe sets and the rank-1 recognition rates are shown in Table 1. From the results, we can find the proposed method, GT-LDA and GT-KDA, all outperform

Table 1. The rank-1 recognition rates on the FERET fb and fc probe sets

Methods	fb(Expression)	fc(Lighting)
PCA	77.99%	38.14%
F-LDA	87.53%	42.78%
Gabor+F-LDA	93.97%	77.84%
Gabor+KFDA	95.56%	78.87%
GT-LDA	**98.24%**	**89.18%**
GT-KDA	**98.66%**	**89.69%**

significantly to the other methods both in fb and fc probe sets and the kernel method, GT-KDA, achieves the best result: 98.66% in fb and 89.69% in fc. These results indicate the proposed method is accurate and robust to the variation of expression and illumination. Moreover, in contrast to the traditional LDA method, the computational cost of the proposed algorithm is not increased very much. In the training phase, although it needs to do three discriminant analysis rather than once in traditional LDA, the computational cost is not much higher because the 2D discriminant analysis is usually conducted on a lower feature space. And in the testing phase, the computational cost of the proposed method is nearly the same as the traditional LDA.

5 Conclusions

In this paper, a novel algorithm, linear/kenerl discriminant analysis with Gabor tensor representation has been proposed for face recognition. A face image is first encoded as a 3rd-order Gabor tensor. After unfolding the Gabor tensor and applying discriminant analysis with them, we can effectively avoid the curse of dimensionality dilemma and overcome the small sample size problem to extract different discriminative subspaces. Followed by combining these discriminant subspaces and doing reduction further, a robust and effective subspace is finally derived for face recognition. Experimental results on FERET database have shown the accuracy and robustness of the proposed method to the variation of expression and illumination.

Acknowledgements. We would like to thank Wei-shi Zheng for helpful discussion. This work was supported by the following funding resources: National Natural Science Foundation Project #60518002, National Science and Technology Supporting Platform Project #2006BAK08B06, National 863 Program Projects #2006AA01Z192 and #2006AA01Z193, Chinese Academy of Sciences 100 people project, and the AuthenMetric Collaboration Foundation.

References

1. Belhumeur, P., Hespanha, J., Kriegman, D.: Eigenfaces vs. fisherfaces: recognition using class specific linear projection. IEEE Trans. PAMI 19(7), 711–720 (1997)
2. Chen, L., Liao, H., Ko, M., Lin, J., Yu, G.: A new lda-based face recognition system which can solve the small sample size problem. Pattern Recognition (2000)

3. Ki-Chung, C., Cheol, K.S., Ryong, K.S.: Face recognition using principal component analysis of gabor filter responses. In: Proceedings of International Workshop on Recognition, Analysis, and Tracking of Faces and Gestures in Real-Time Systems, pp. 53–57 (1999)
4. Kong, H., Li, X., Wang, L., Teoh, E.K., Wang, J.G., Venkateswarlu, R.: Generalized 2d principal component analysis. In: Proc. International Joint Conference on Neural Networks (2005)
5. Lades, M., Vorbruggen, J., Buhmann, J., Lange, J., von der Malsburg, C., Wurtz, R.P., Konen, W.: Distortion invariant object recognition in the dynamic link architecture. IEEE Transactions on Computers 42, 300–311 (1993)
6. Li, M., Yuan, B.: 2d-lda: A novel statistical linear discriminant analysis for image matrix. Pattern Recognition Letters 26(5), 527–532 (2005)
7. Li, S.Z., Jain, A.K. (eds.): Handbook of Face Recognition. Springer, New York (2005)
8. Liu, C.: Gabor-based kernel PCA with fractional power polynomial models for face recognition. IEEE Transactions on Pattern Analysis and Machine Intelligence 26(5), 572–581 (2004)
9. Liu, C., Wechsler, H.: Gabor feature based classification using the enhanced fisher linear discriminant model for face recognition. IEEE Transactions on Image Processing 11(4), 467–476 (2002)
10. Phillips, P.J., Moon, H., Rizvi, S.A., Rauss, P.J.: The FERET evaluation methodology for face-recognition algorithms. IEEE Transactions on Pattern Analysis and Machine Intelligence 22(10), 1090–1104 (2000)
11. Schölkopf, B., Smola, A., Müller, K.R.: Nonlinear component analysis as a kernel eigenvalue problem. Neural Computation 10, 1299–1319 (1999)
12. Shen, L., Bai, L.: Gabor wavelets and kernel direct disciminant analysis for face recognition. In: Int'l Conf on Pattern Recognition (ICPR'04), pp. 284–287 (2004)
13. Swets, D., Weng, J.: Using discriminant eigenfeatures for image retrieval. IEEE Trans. on PAMI 16(8), 831–836 (1996)
14. Wiskott, L., Fellous, J., Kruger, N., malsburg, C.V.: Face recognition by elastic bunch graph matching. IEEE Trans. PAMI 19(7), 775–779 (1997)
15. Xu, D., Yan, S.C., Zhang, L., Zhang, H.J., Liu, Z.K., Shum, H.Y.: Concurrent subspaces analysis. In: Proceedings of IEEE Computer Society Conference on Computer Vision and Pattern Recognition, pp. 203–208. IEEE Computer Society Press, Los Alamitos (2005)
16. Yan, S.C., Xu, D., Yang, Q., Zhang, L., Zhang, H.J.: Discriminant analysis with tensor representation. In: Proceedings of IEEE Computer Society Conference on Computer Vision and Pattern Recognition, pp. 526–532. IEEE Computer Society Press, Los Alamitos (2005)
17. Yang, M.H.: Kernel eigenface vs. kernel fisherface: Face recognition using kernel methods. In: Proc. IEEE Int. Conf on Automatic Face and Gesture Recognition. IEEE Computer Society Press, Los Alamitos (2002)
18. Ye, J., Janardan, R., Li, Q.: Two-dimensional linear discriminant analysis. In: Proceedings of Neural Information Processing Systems (2004)
19. Yu, H., Yang, J.: A direct lda algorithm for high-dimensional data with application to face recognition. Pattern Recognition (2001)
20. Zhang, D., Chen, S., Zhou, Z.: Recognizing face or object from a single image: Linear vs. kernel methods on 2d patterns. In: S+SSPR06, in conjunction with ICPR06, HongKong, China (2006)

Fingerprint Enhancement Based on Discrete Cosine Transform

Suksan Jirachaweng and Vutipong Areekul

Kasetsart Signal & Image Processing Laboratory (KSIP Lab),
Department of Electrical Engineering, Kasetsart University, Bangkok, 10900, Thailand
{g4885038,fengvpa}@ku.ac.th
http://ksip.ee.ku.ac.th

Abstract. This paper proposes a novel fingerprint enhancement algorithm based on contextual filtering in DCT domain. All intrinsic fingerprint features including ridge orientation and frequency are estimated simultaneously from DCT analysis, resulting in fast and efficient implementation. In addition, the proposed approach takes advantage of frequency-domain enhancement resulting in best performance in high curvature area. Comparing with DFT domain, DCT has better signal energy compaction and perform faster transform with real coefficients. Moreover, the experimental results show that the DCT approach is out-performed the traditional Gabor filtering, including the fastest separable Gabor filter, in both quality and computational complexity.

Keywords: Fingerprint Enhancement, Discrete Cosine Transform Enhancement, Frequency-Domain Fingerprint Enhancement.

1 Introduction

Inevitably, many fingerprint identification applications are playing an important role in our everyday life from personal access control, office time attendance, to country boarder control. To pursue this goal, automatic fingerprint identification system (AFIS) must be proved to be highly reliable. Since most automatic fingerprint identification systems are based on the minutiae and ridge matching, these systems rely on good quality of input fingerprint images for minutiae and ridge extraction. Unfortunately, bad quality of fingerprint and elastic distortion are now major problems for most AFISs especially large database systems. In order to reduce the error accumulated from false accept rate and false reject rate, quality of fingerprint must be evaluated and enhanced for better recognition results.

Based on filtering domains, most fingerprint enhancement schemes can be roughly classified into two major approaches; i.e. spatial-domain and frequency-domain. Filtering in spatial-domain applies convolution directly to fingerprint image. On the other hand, filtering in frequency-domain need Fourier analysis and synthesis. Fingerprint image is transformed, then multiplied by filter coefficients, and inverse transformed Fourier coefficients back to enhanced fingerprint image. In fact if employed filters are the same, enhancement results from both domains must be exactly the same by signal processing theorem. However, for practical implementation, these

S.-W. Lee and S.Z. Li (Eds.): ICB 2007, LNCS 4642, pp. 96–105, 2007.

two approaches are different in terms of enhancement quality and computational complexity of algorithms.

Practical performing fingerprint enhancement based on each domain has different advantage and disadvantage. For example, most popular Hong's Gabor filters [1], with orientation and frequency spatially adaptable, are applied to partitioning fingerprint image. However, this Gabor filter model is based on unidirectional ridge enhancement, resulting in ridge discontinuity and blocking artifacts around highly curvature region. On the other hand, for frequency domain approaches, natural fingerprint image is localized in some frequency coefficients. Gabor filter can be easily designed to cooperate with high curvature area. For example, Kamei et al. [2] introduced fingerprint filter design based on frequency domain using discrete Fourier transform. Chikkerur et al. [3] applied short time Fourier transform and took advantage from 2-dimensional filter shaping design, adapted with highly curvature area, resulting in better enhanced results. However, comparing with spatial-domain approaches, this scheme suffers from high computational complexity in Fourier analysis and synthesis even though Fast Fourier Transform (FFT) is employed.

In order to take advantage from frequency-domain fingerprint enhancement with low computational complexity, we propose fingerprint enhancement based on Discrete Cosine Transform (DCT). The DCT is a unitary orthogonal transform with real coefficients. It is closely related to the Discrete Fourier transform (DFT) which has complex coefficients. Moreover, it has been known that DCT provides a distinct advantage over the DFT in term of energy compaction and truncation error [4]. Thus is why DCT has been widely employed in general image and video compression standards. Hence, in this paper, we investigated DCT-base fingerprint enhancement for practical implementation. We expected best enhanced quality results with low computational complexity. This paper is organized as follows. Section 2 describes several processes in order to implement enhancement filtering in DCT domain including intrinsic estimation and practical filtering. Section 3 shows experimental evaluation. Finally, section 4 concludes our works and future research.

2 Proposed Approach

The fingerprint enhancement approach consists of 4 concatenated processes; i.e. discrete cosine transform of sub-blocks of partitioning fingerprint, ridge orientation and frequency parameters estimation, filtering in DCT domain, and inverse discrete cosine transform of sub-blocks. The advantages of the proposed approach are as follows.

- Fingerprint ridges form a natural sinusoid image, which its spectrums are packed or localized in frequency domain. Hence these spectrums can be easily shaped or filtered in this domain. Moreover, filter can be specially designed in order to handle high curvature ridge area such as singular points. This is the great advantage over the spatial-domain filtering approach.
- Comparing with discrete Fourier transform, discrete cosine transform performs better in term of energy compaction. Moreover, DCT coefficients are real number comparing with complex number of DFT coefficients. Therefore, we can handle DCT coefficients easier than DFT coefficients. Besides, fast DCT

requires less computational complexity and less memory usage comparing with fast Fourier transform (FFT).

- By partitioning fingerprint into sub-blocks, the proposed approach utilizes spatially contextual information including instantaneous frequency and orientation. Intrinsic features such as ridge frequency, ridge orientation, and angular bandwidth can be simply analyzed directly from DCT coefficients.

Each process of the proposed fingerprint enhancement is explained as follows.

2.1 Overlapping DCT Decomposition and Reconstruction

Conventional fingerprint enhancement schemes, applying with non-overlapping blocks of partitioning fingerprint, often encounter with blocking artifacts such as ridge discontinuity and spurious minutiae. To preserve ridge continuity and eliminate blocking artifacts, overlapping block is applied to both DCT decomposition and reconstruction, similar to the DFT approach in [3]. However, there is no need to apply any smooth spectral window for DCT because overlapping area is large enough to prevent any blocking effects, corresponding with its energy compaction property.

2.2 Intrinsic Parameter Estimation on DCT Domain

Ridge frequency, ridge orientation, and angular bandwidth can be analyzed from DCT coefficients directly. Therefore DCT analysis yields appropriate domain to perform fingerprint enhancement and provides filtering parameters as the same time.

Ridge Frequency Estimation: The ridge frequency (ρ_0) is simply obtained by measuring a distance between the origin (0,0) and the highest DCT peak of high-frequency spectrum as following equation,

$$\rho_0 = \sqrt{u_0^2 + v_0^2} \tag{1}$$

where (u_0 ,v_0) is the coordinate of the highest peak of high-frequency spectrum.

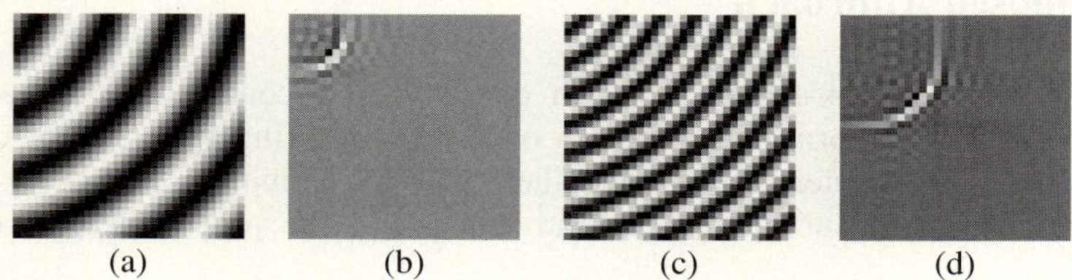

Fig. 1. Figure (a) and (c) represent blocks of a fingerprint model with different frequency. Figure (b) and (d) are DCT coefficients of figure (a) and (c), respectively. Note that DC coefficient is set to zero in order to clearly display high-frequency spectrum.

Ridge orientation estimation: The dominant orientation of parallel ridges, θ, are closely related to a peak-angle, ϕ, in DCT coefficients, where ϕ is measured counterclockwise (if $\phi > 0$) from the horizontal axis to the terminal side of the highest spectrum peak of high frequency (DC spectrum is not included). However, θ and ϕ relationship is not one-to-one mapping. The ridge orientation, which θ varies in the range of *0* to π, is projected into the peak-angle, which ϕ varies in the range of *0* to $\pi/2$. Relationship between θ_0 ridge orientation in spatial domain and ϕ_0 peak angle in frequency domain are described in equation (2) with some examples in Fig. 2.

$$\phi_0 = \tan^{-1}\left(\frac{v_0}{u_0}\right), \quad \phi_0 = \left|\frac{\pi}{2} - \theta_0\right| \text{ where } 0 \le \theta_0 \le \pi \tag{2}$$

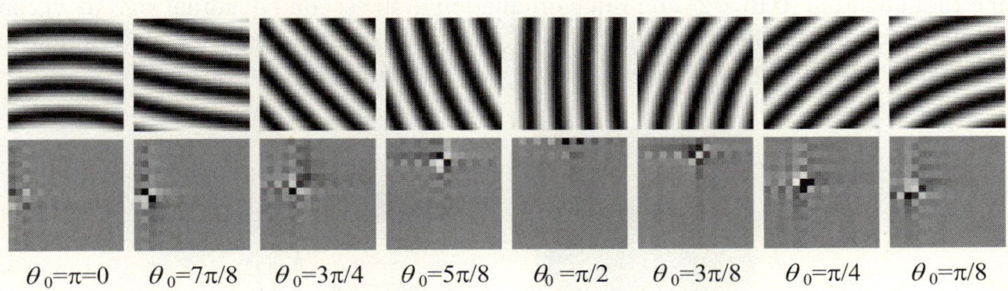

Fig. 2. Examples of relationship between ridge orientation in spatial domain and peak-angle in DCT domain, all ridge angles refer to horizontal axis and DC coefficient is set to zero in order to show high-frequency spectrum. (Note that only the top-left quarters of DC coefficients are zoomed in for clear view of high-frequency peak behavior.)

From Fig. 2, ridge orientation at π-θ has the highest spectrum peak with the same location as ridge orientation at θ. However, their phase patterns are distinguishable by observation. Therefore additional phase analysis is needed to classify the quadratics of ridge orientation in order to correctly perform fingerprint enhancement. Since Lee et al. [5] proposed edge detection algorithm based on DCT coefficients, our fingerprint enhancement modified Lee's approach by modulation theorem in order to detect quadrant of fingerprint ridge orientation.

According to Lee's technique, the orientation quadrant of a single line can be determined by the polarities of two first AC coefficients, G_{01} and G_{10}, where G_{uv} is the

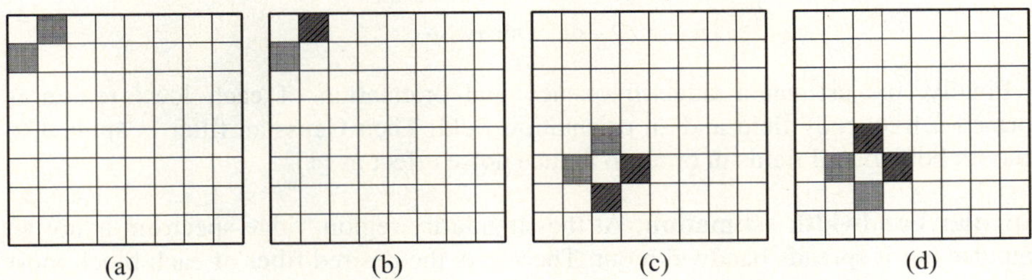

Fig. 3. Four polarity patterns indicate (a) a single line orientation ranging from 0 to $\pi/2$, (b) a single line orientation ranging from $\pi/2$ to π, (c) parallel ridge orientation ranging from 0 to $\pi/2$, and (d) parallel ridge orientation ranging from $\pi/2$ to π

DCT coefficient at coordinate (u,v), as shown in Fig. 3. In case of a single line, polarity of product of G_{01} and G_{10} coefficients indicates the line orientation. If $G_{01}\times G_{10} \geq 0$, this line orientation is in the first quadrant (0 to $\pi/2$) as shown in Fig. 3(a). On the other hand, if $G_{01}\times G_{10} < 0$, this line orientation is in the second quadrant ($\pi/2$ to π) as shown in Fig. 3(b). This technique can be applied to detect orientation of parallel lines or ridges by modulation theorem with the pattern of polarities around the high peak DCT coefficients. To be precise, ridge orientation in the first quadrant (0 to $\pi/2$) and ridge orientation in the second quadrant ($\pi/2$ to π) can be indicated by the same polarities of 45° and 135° diagonal coefficients referred to the highest absolute peak as shown in Fig. 3(c) and (d), respectively.

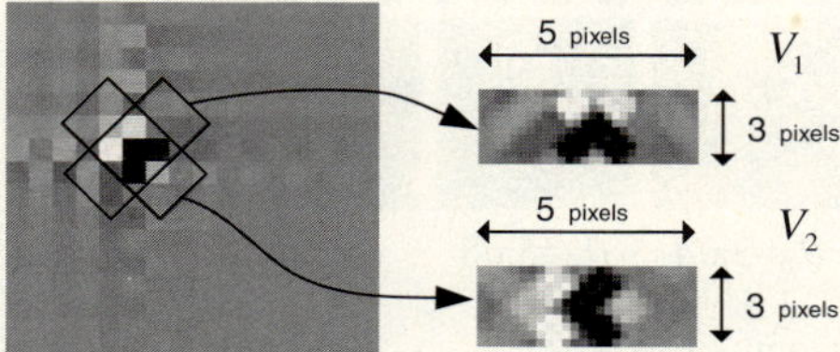

Fig. 4. Demonstrate 2-D perpendicular diagonal vectors, V_1 at 45° and V_2 at 135°, referred to the highest absolute spectrum peak (the center black pixel (negative value))

In order to identify the quadrant and avoid influence of interference, two 2-D perpendicular diagonal vectors, V_1 and V_2, are formed with size of 5×3 pixels, center at the peak position as shown in Fig. 4. The average directional strengths of each vector (S_1, S_2) are then computed by equation (3). Then the quadrant can be classified and the actual fingerprint ridge orientation can be identified as shown in equation (4).

$$S_i = \underset{n=-1,0,1}{Max} \frac{\left| \sum_{m=-2}^{2} V_i(u_0+m, v_0+n) \right|}{5} \quad \text{where} \quad i=1,2 \tag{3}$$

$$\theta = \begin{cases} \pi/2-\phi & \text{where } S_1 \geq S_2 \\ \pi-(\pi/2-\phi) & \text{Otherwise} \end{cases} \tag{4}$$

Finally, the estimated ridge frequency and orientation of each local region is formed a frequency field and an orientation field. Then Gaussian filter is applied to smooth both global fields in order to reduce noise effect as [1].

Angular bandwidth estimation: At the singularity region, ridge spectrum is not an impulse but it spreads bandwidth out. Therefore, the desired filter of each block must be adapted based on its angular bandwidth. We slightly modified the coherence parameter from Chikkerur's concept in [3], called non-coherence factor. This non-coherence factor represents how wide ridge orientation can be in the block that has more than one dominant orientation. This factor is in the range of 0 to 1, where 1 represents highly non-coherence or highly curved region and 0 represents uni-orientation region. The non-coherence factor can be given by

$$NC(u_c,v_c)=\frac{\sum_{(i,j)\in W}\left|\sin(\theta(u_c,v_c)-\theta(u_i,v_j))\right|}{W\times W} \tag{5}$$

where (u_c,v_c) is the center position of block, (u_i,v_j) is the ith and j^{th} positions of neighborhood blocks within $W\times W$, and the angular bandwidth, ϕ_{BW}, can be estimated by the equation (6) as follows,

$$\phi_{BW}(u_c,v_c)=\sin^{-1}(NC(u_c,v_c)). \tag{6}$$

2.2 Enhancement Filtering in DCT Domain

In DCT domain, filtering process is not simply as in DFT domain [2,3], which required only coefficient multiplication. The Gabor filter in [1] is modified in order to cooperate with DCT domain based on Cartesian-form representation. The enhancement filtering in DCT domain can be separated into two arithmetic manipulation; i.e. multiplication and convolution.

1) Filtering by Multiplication: The enhancement filter can be expressed in term of product of separable Gaussian functions, similar to the frequency-domain filtering technique in [2] as follows.

$$F_{fd}(\rho,\phi)=F(\rho,\phi)H_f(\rho)H_d(\phi) \tag{7}$$

where $F(\rho,\phi)$ is DCT coefficients in polar-form representation, directly related to DCT coefficients, $F(u,v)$, in rectangular-form representation. $F_{fd}(\rho,\phi)$ is DCT coefficients of the filtering output. The $H_f(\rho)$ filter, which performs the ridge frequency filtering in Gaussian shape, is given by

$$H_f(\rho|\rho_0,\sigma_\rho,Z)=\frac{1}{Z}\exp\left(-\frac{(\rho-\rho_0)^2}{2\sigma_\rho^2}\right),\ \rho_0=\sqrt{u_0^2+v_0^2};\rho_{\min}\le\rho_0\le\rho_{\max} \tag{8}$$

where ρ_0 and σ_ρ are the center of the high-peak frequency group and the filtering bandwidth parameter, respectively. The ρ_{min} and ρ_{max} parameters are minimum and maximum cut-off frequency constraints, which suppress the effects of lower and higher frequencies such as ink, sweat gland holes, and scratches in the fingerprint. The Z is a filtering normalization factor, depending on filtering energy result.

The $H_d(\phi)$ filter, which performs the ridge orientation filtering, is given by

$$H_d(\phi|\phi_0,\sigma_\phi,\phi_{BW})=\begin{cases}\exp\left(-\frac{(\phi-\phi_0)^2}{2\sigma_\phi^2}\right) & \text{where } |\phi-\phi_0|\ge\phi_{BW}\\ 1 & \text{Otherwise}\end{cases} \tag{9}$$

where the ϕ_0 is the peak orientation for bandpass filter, σ_ϕ is the directional bandwidth parameter, and ϕ_{BW}, the angular bandwidth, is given by equation (6).

2) Filtering by Convolution: Since the θ and π-θ ridge orientation coefficients are projected into the same DCT-domain region. Therefore, both directional coefficients still remain from the previous filtering. In order to truncate inappropriate directional coefficients, two diagonal Gabor filters are exploited by convolution operation. The finally enhanced DCT coefficients are given by

$$F_{Enh}(u,v) = F_{fd}(u,v) * H_q(u,v) \tag{10}$$

where $F_{Enh}(u,v)$ is enhanced DCT coefficients in rectangular-form. $F_{fd}(u,v)$ is the previous result of enhanced DCT coefficients in rectangular-form, by converted from $F_{fd}(\rho,\phi)$ in polar-form. The quadrant correction filter, $H_q(u,v)$, is given by

$$H_q(u,v) = \begin{cases} \cos\left[\dfrac{(u+v)\pi}{2}\right]\exp\left(-\dfrac{(u+v)^2}{2\sigma_q^2}\right) & \text{where } \theta \geq \pi/2 \\ \cos\left[\dfrac{(u-v)\pi}{2}\right]\exp\left(-\dfrac{(u-v)^2}{2\sigma_q^2}\right) & \text{Otherwise} \end{cases} \tag{11}$$

where σ_q is the quadratic parameter and $\cos(n\pi/2)$ only has three values -1, 0 and -1. Indeed, this convolution operation requires low computation because most of bandpass filtered coefficients are truncated to zero from the previous operation. In case of highly curved ridges, the transformed coefficients are projected into widely curved subband of DCT domain as shown in Fig. 5.

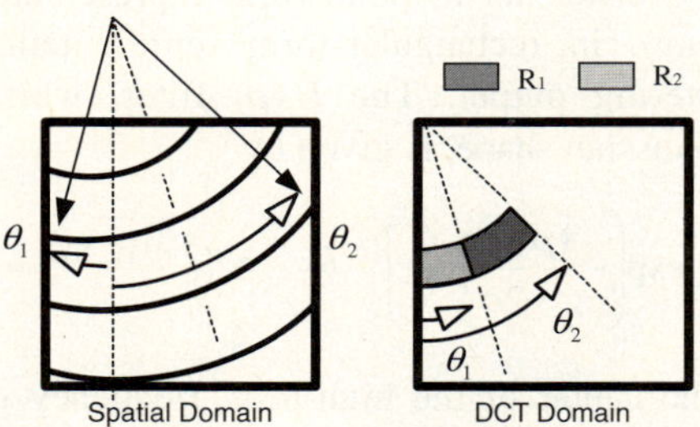

Fig. 5 Highly curved ridges in spatial and frequency (DCT) domain. Signal is localized in widely curved subband, which can be classified into the principal region (R_1) and the reflection region (R_2).

From Fig. 5, we approximate the orientation range from θ_1 to θ_2 by non-coherence factor from the equation (6). The curved subband can be classified into two regions; i.e. principal region (R_1) and reflection region (R_2). The principal region (R_1) contains only one diagonal component (45° or 135°) as mentioned before. The 45° or 135° diagonal components are the phase pattern of the oriented ridges in the range of 0° to 90° or 90° to 180°, respectively. The reflection region (R_2) composes of both of 45° and 135° diagonal components from the reflection property of DCT coefficients. Then the convolution is applied only in the principal region.

3 Experimental Evaluation

The experimental results have been evaluated on public fingerprint database FVC2002 Db3a [6] (100 users, 8 images each) in term of enhancement quality, matching performance, and computational complexity. The fingerprint image is partitioned into blocks of 16×16 pixels, and a simple segmentation scheme using mean and variance is employed. Five fingerprint enhancement filtering types are evaluated as follows; Traditional Gabor filtering with non-quantized orientation (**TG**)[1], Separable Gabor filtering with non-quantized orientation (**SG**)[7], Separable Gabor filtering with 8-quantized orientation (**SG8**)[8], Short-Time Fourier Transform approach (**STFT**)[3], and proposed approach (**DCT**). In the spatial domain approaches, the discrete Gabor filters are the same 25×25 fixed-window size. Note that the separable Gabor filter [7,8] was implemented on the fly using a set of priori created and stored filters. Moreover, symmetric of 2-D Gabor filter [1] was also exploited in this process. These filtering schemes accelerated execution speed of the traditional Gabor enhancement process as fast as possible. For the STFT [3] and the DCT approaches in frequency domain, fingerprint image is also partitioned into 16×16 blocks but each block is transformed with 32×32 overlapped window to reduce blocking artifacts. Note that the probability estimation in [3] is not included.

In order to compare the performance of various enhancement algorithms, three evaluation methodologies are used; i.e. the goodness index [1] of minutiae extraction, the matching performance, and the average execution time. First, the goodness index (*GI*) from [1] is employed to measure the extracted minutiae quantity from each fingerprint enhancement algorithm. In this case, we needed to manually mark minutiae of all fingerprints in FVC2002 Db3a. The goodness index is given by

$$GI = \frac{\sum_{i=1}^{r} q_i \left[M_i - L_i - S_i\right]}{\sum_{i=1}^{r} q_i T_i}, \tag{12}$$

where r is the number of 16×16 windows in the input fingerprint image, q_i represents the quality factor of ith window (good = 4, medium = 2, poor = 1) which estimated by partitioning and thresholding of the dryness factor (mean × variance of block) and the smudginess factor (mean / variance of block). M_i represents the number of minutiae pair, which match with human expert in a tolerance box in the ith window. L_i and S_i represent the number of lost and spurious minutiae in the ith window, respectively. T_i represents the number of minutiae extracted by experts.

Second, enhancement results are tested with our minutiae matching verification algorithm based on Jiang's concept of [9], and the equal error rate (EER) is reported. Finally, the average execution time of fingerprint enhancement process is measured for FVC2002 Db3a (image size 300×300 pixels) on Pentium M 1.5GHz with 376Mb RAM. Note that execution time includes filter parameter estimation (frequency and orientation), transform (if required), and filtering process. However, segmentation process is not included and we used the same segmentation process for all comparison schemes. The objective test results are summarized in Table 1. Contradict to our belief; overall execution time of DCT approach is faster than the separable Gabor

Table 1. Summary of the performance comparison among various fingerprint enhancement algorithms over FVC 2002 Db3a Fingerprint Database, Pentium M 1.5GHz, 376Mb RAM

Fingerprint Enhancement Algorithm	Average Goodness Index (GI) [1]	Our Matching (% EER)	Execution Time (Second)
TG [1]	0.160	9.716	0.973
SG [7]	0.167	9.326	0.278
SG8 [8]	0.181	12.196	0.160
STFT (modified from [3])	0.250	7.713	0.172
DCT (Proposed Approach)	0.336	6.846	0.151

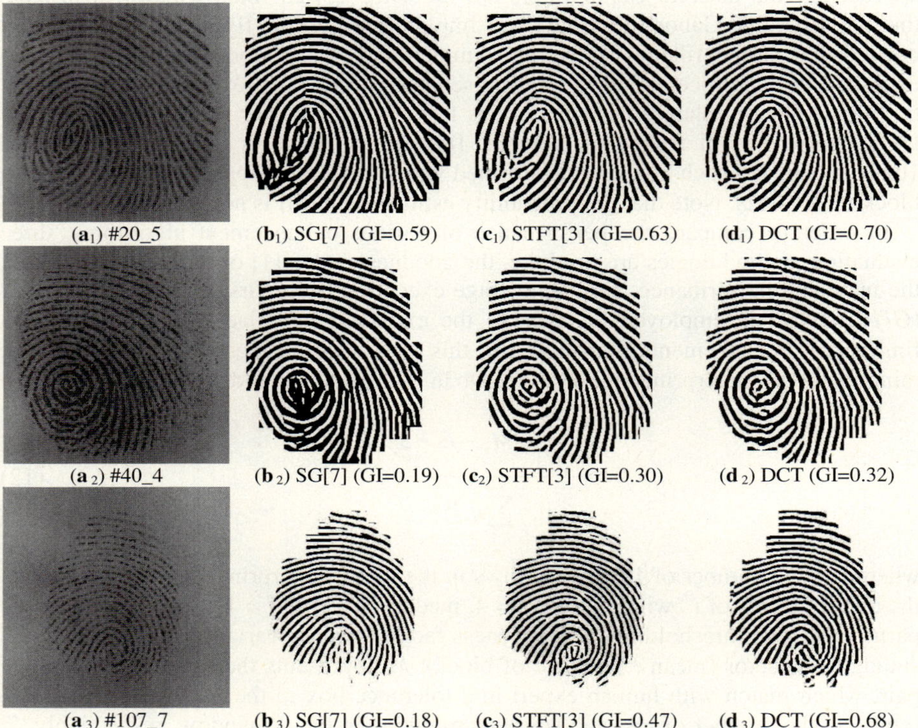

(a_1) #20_5 (b_1) SG[7] (GI=0.59) (c_1) STFT[3] (GI=0.63) (d_1) DCT (GI=0.70)

(a_2) #40_4 (b_2) SG[7] (GI=0.19) (c_2) STFT[3] (GI=0.30) (d_2) DCT (GI=0.32)

(a_3) #107_7 (b_3) SG[7] (GI=0.18) (c_3) STFT[3] (GI=0.47) (d_3) DCT (GI=0.68)

Fig. 6. (**a**) Original fingerprint #20_5, #40_4 and #107_7 from FVC2002 Db3a, (**b**) Enhanced results from SG[7], (**c**) Enhanced results from STFT modified from [3], (**d**) Enhanced results of our proposed DCT based method

filtering with 8-quantized orientation. We investigated in depth and we found that even though separable 2-D convolution alone is faster than both FFT and Fast DCT analysis and synthesis, the fingerprint intrinsic parameter estimation was slow this approach down since these parameters are evaluated in frequency domain.

Fig. 6 shows enhancement results for subjective tests with GI values for objective tests. Note that the quality of enhanced fingerprints is improved based on frequency-domain filtering, especially in highly curved ridges. Overall of FVC2002, DB3a database, both STFT and DCT based performed very well around highly curved area with slightly different results around singular point area.

4 Conclusion and Future Research

In conclusion, this paper proposes a novel fingerprint enhancement approach based on discrete cosine transform (DCT). The enhancement takes advantage of filtering real DCT coefficients with high-energy compaction in frequency-domain. Hence filtering can be specially designed to cooperate highly curvature area resulting in less discontinuity and blocking artifacts comparing with spatial-domain filtering.

For future research, we will conduct exhaustive experiments based on all FVC databases in order to prove the efficient of DCT-based fingerprint enhancement. To achieve this goal, all minutiae in all FVC databases need to be manually marked. We will also exploit orientation adaptive filter in DCT Domain in the near future.

Acknowledgments. This work was partially supported by Department of Electrical Engineering, Kasetsart University, Thailand Research Fund (TRF) through the Royal Golden Jubilee Ph.D. Program (Grant No.PHD/0017/2549), and the Commission on Higher Education through the TRF Research Scholar (Grant No. RMU4980027).

References

1. Hong, L., Wang, Y., Jain, A.K.: Fingerprint Image Enhancement: Algorithm and Performance Evaluation. IEEE Trans. on Pattern Analysis and Machine Intelligence 20(8), 777–789 (1998)
2. Kamei, T., Mizoguchi, M.: Image Filter Design for Fingerprint Enhancement. In: Proc. ISCV'95, pp. 109–114 (1995)
3. Chikkerur, S., Cartwright, A.N., Govindaraju, V.: Fingerprint Enhancement Using STFT Analysis. Pattern Recognition 40, 198–211 (2007)
4. Rao, K.R., Yip, P.: Discrete Cosine Transform: Algorithms, Advantages, Applications. Academic Press, Boston, MA (1990)
5. Lee, M., Nepal, S., Srinivasan, U.: Role of edge detection in video semantics. In: Proc. Pan-Sydney Workshop on Visual Information Processing (VIP2002). Conferences in Research and Practice in Information Technology, Australia (2003)
6. Maltoni, D., Maio, D., Jain, A.K., Prabhakar, S.: Fingerprint Verification Competition 2002. Database Available: Handbook of Fingerprint Recognition. Springer, Heidelberg (2003)
7. Areekul, V., Watchareeruetai, U., Suppasriwasuseth, K., Tantaratana, S.: Separable Gabor filter realization for fast fingerprint enhancement. In: Proc. Int. Conf. on Image Processing (ICIP 2005), Genova, Italy, pp. III-253–III-256 (2005)
8. Areekul, V., Watchareeruetai, U., Tantaratana, S.: Fast Separable Gabor Filter for Fingerprint Enhancement. In: Zhang, D., Jain, A.K. (eds.) ICBA 2004. LNCS, vol. 3072, pp. 403–409. Springer, Heidelberg (2004)
9. Jiang, X., Yau, W.Y.: Fingerprint Minutiae Matching Based on the Local and Global Structures. In: Proc. Int. Conf. on Pattern Recognition (15th), vol. 2, pp. 1042–1045 (2000)

Biometric Template Classification: A Case Study in Iris Textures

Edara Srinivasa Reddy[1], Chinnam SubbaRao[2], and Inampudi Ramesh Babu[3]

[1,2] Research Scholar
[3] Professor
Department of Computer Science, Acharya Nagarjuna Univerity,
Guntur, A.P, India
{edara_67,rinampudi}@yahoo.com

Abstract. Most of the biometric authentication systems store multiple templates per user to account for variations in biometric data. Therefore, these systems suffer from storage space and computation overheads. To overcome this problem the paper proposes techniques to automatically select prototype templates from iris textures. The paper has two phases: one is to find the feature vectors from iris textures that have less correlation and the second to calculate DU measure. Du measure is an effective measure of the similarity between two iris textures, because it takes into consideration three important perspectives: a) information, b) angle and e) energy. Also, gray level co occurrence matrix is used to find the homogeneity and correlation between the textures.

Keywords: Shaker iris, Jewel iris, Flower iris, Stream iris, gray level co-occurrence matrix, Spectral information divergence, Spectral angle mapper, DU measure.

1 Introduction

A typical iris biometric system operates in two distinct stages: the enrollment stage and the authentication stage [2]. During enrollment stage iris textures are acquired and processed to extract a feature set. The complex iris textures carry very distinctive information. The feature set includes some distinguished features like nodes and end point in the iris texture. The stored feature set, labeled with the user's identity, is referred as a template. In order to account for variations in the biometric based authentication system relies on the stability from an individual is susceptible to changes due to distance from the sensor, poor resolution of the sensor and alterations in iris texture due to cataract operations and others.

Multiple iris features pertaining to different portions of iris must be stored in data base. There is a trade off between the number of templates, and the storage and computational overheads introduced by multiple templates. An efficient system must in fact select the templates automatically.

2 Basic Types of Iris Textures

Depending on the texture of different human iris, we can group the irises into four basic groups. They are a) Stream iris, b) Jewel iris, c) Shaker iris and d) Flower iris.

S.-W. Lee and S.Z. Li (Eds.): ICB 2007, LNCS 4642, pp. 106–113, 2007.

Also, there are different combinations of there groups. As a preliminary study we have concentrated to group the given data base into the above four classes.

a) Stream Iris: It contains a uniform fiber structure with subtle variations or streaks of color as shown in fig. 1.c. The structure of the iris is determined by the arrangement of the white fibers radiating from the center of the iris (or pupil). In this image one can notice that they are uniform and reasonably direct or parallel.

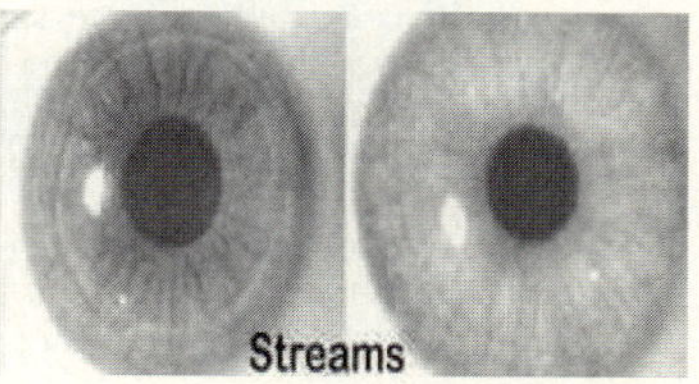

Fig. 1. a & b. Stream Iris

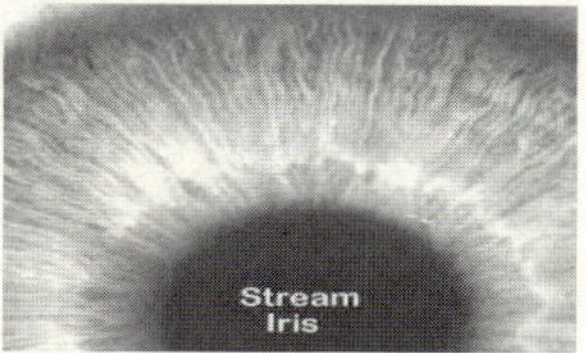

Fig. 1. c. Stream iris Texture

b) Jewel Iris: It contains dot-like pigments in the iris. The jewel iris can be recognized by the presence of pigmentation or colored dots on top of the fibers as shown in fig. 2.c. The dots (or jewels) can vary in color from light orange through black. They can also vary in size from tiny (invisible to the naked eye) to quite large.

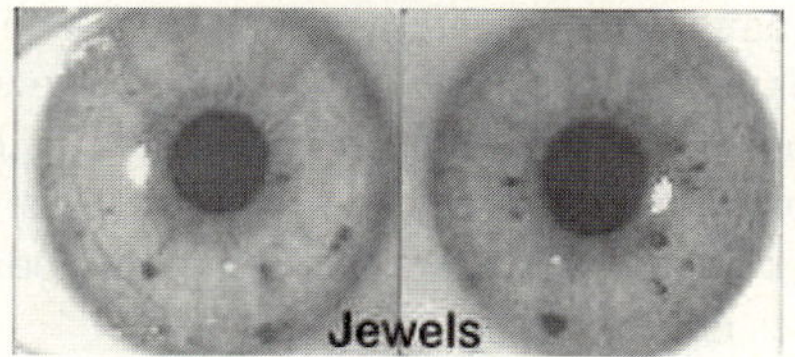

Fig. 2.a & b. Jewel iris

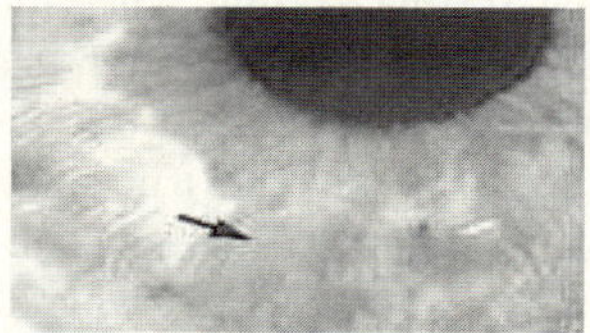

Fig. 2. c. Jewel iris Textures

c) Shaker iris: It contains dot-like pigments and rounded openings. The shaker iris is identified by the presence of both flower like petals in the fiber arrangement and pigment dots or jewels is shown in fig. 3.c. The presence of even one jewel in an otherwise Flower iris is sufficient to cause the occupant to exhibit shaker characteristics.

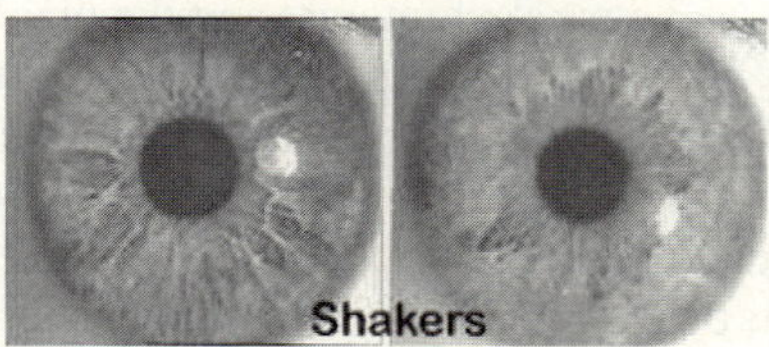

Fig. 3.a & b. Shaker iris

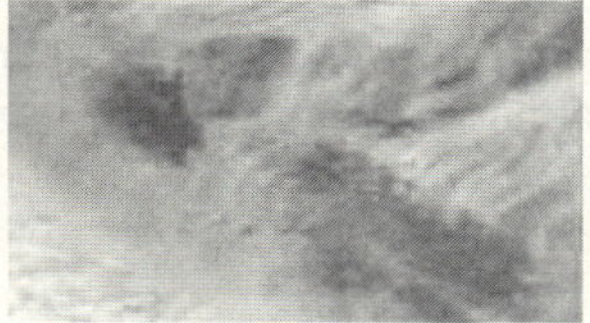

Fig. 3. c. Shaker iris textures

d) Flower iris: It contains distinctly curved or rounded openings in the iris. In a flower iris the fibers radiating from the center are distorted (in one or more places) to produce the effect of petals (hence the name flower) shown in fig. 4. In this image one can notice that they are neither regular nor uniform. A flower iris may have only one significant petal with the remainder of the iris looking like a stream

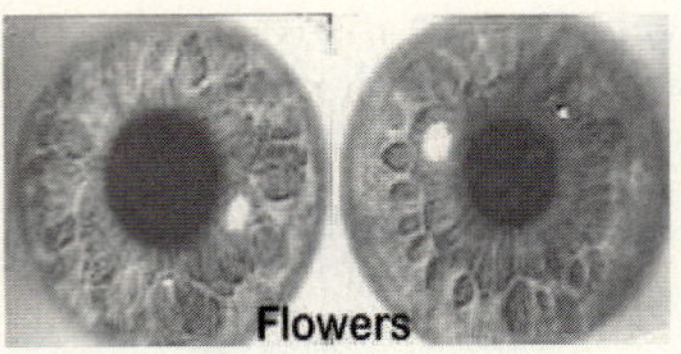

Fig. 4.a & b. Flower iris

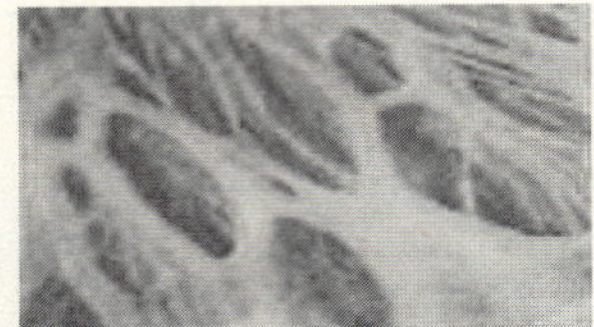

Fig. 4. c. Flower iris textures

3 Template Selections and Updating

The size of the same iris taken at different times may be different in the image as a result of changes in the camera to face distance. Due to simulation by light or for other reasons, such as hippos, natural continuous movement of the pupil, the pupil may be constricted or dilated [3]. The problem of template selection means, given a set of N iris images corresponding to a single human iris, selected k templates that best represent the similarity observed in N images. The selected templates must be updated time to time, since most of the users may under go cataract operations due to aging. To account for such changes, old templates must be replaced with newer ones. Some of the minutiae points like nodes and end points of iris textures may be added or deleted from the iris template. Thus template selection refers to the process by which iris textures are chosen from a given set of samples, where as template update refers to the process by which existing templates are replaced.

4 Selection of Feature Vectors

GLCM(gray-level co-occurrence matrix)[4], also known as the gray-level spatial dependence matrix, is a statistical measure used to characterize the texture of an image by calculating how often pairs of pixel, with specific values and in a specified spatial relationship occur in an image and then by extracting statistical measures from this matrix.

By default, the spatial relationship is defined as the pixel of interest and the pixel to its immediate right (horizontally adjacent), but one can specify other spatial relationships between the two pixels. Each element (i,j) in the resultant GLCM is simply the sum of the number of times that the pixel with value I occurred in the specified spatial relationship to a pixel with value j in the input image.

Initially, the dynamic range of the given image is scaled to reduce the number of intensity values in intensity image from 256 to 8. The number of gray-levels, determine the size of the GLCM.

The gray-level co-occurrence matrix can reveal certain properties about the spatial distribution of the gray levels in the texture image. For example, if most of the entries in the GLCM are concentrated along the diagonal, the texture is coarse with respect to the specified offset.

However, a single GLCM might not be enough to describe the textual features of the input image. For example, a single horizontal offset might not be sensitive to texture with a vertical orientation. For this reason, gray co-matrix [5] can create multiple GLCMs for a single input image. TO create multiple GLCMs, specify an array of offsets to the gray co-matrix function. These offsets define pixel relationships of varying direction and distance. For, example, one can define an array of offsets that specify four directions (horizontal, vertical and two diagonals) and four distances. In this case, the input image is represented by 16 GLCMs. The statistics are calculated from these GLCMs and then the average is taken.

Statistical description of GLCM:

The statistical parameters that can be derived for GLCM are contrast, correlation, energy and homogeneity.

a) Contrast measures the local variations in the gray-level co-occurrence matrix.
b) Correlation measures the joint probability occurrence of the specified pixel pairs.
c) Energy provides the sum of squared elements in the GLCM.

Homogeneity measures the closeness of the distribution of elements in the GLCM to the GLCM diagonal.

We have derived only correlation to identify the length of the feature vector which has unique information from iris texture. A typical iris exhibits rich texture information in the immediate vicinity of the pupil which tapers away in intensity as one move away from the pupil. Thus, the iris templates are taken by segmenting a

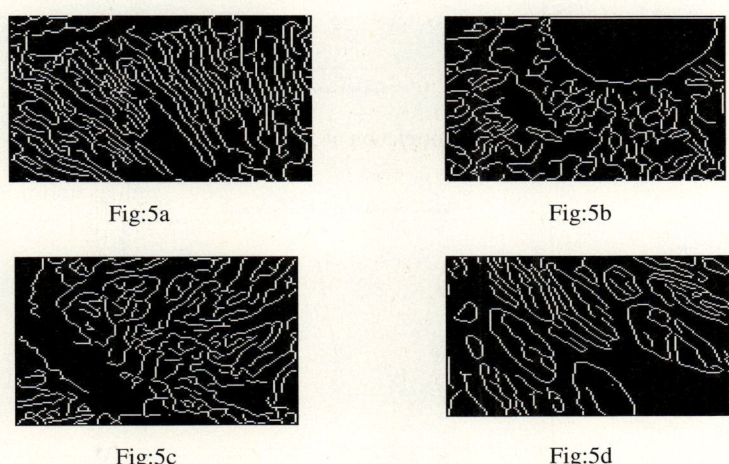

Fig. 5. Iris textures after canny edge detection a)Stream iris b)Jewel iris c)Shaker iris d)Flower iris

portion of iris texture near the pupil and from them the feature vectors are derived, by using correlation function. This is implemented by performing canny edge detection technique to produce binary image or respective iris texture and also by calculating the probability of occurrence of pixels.

The correlation Vs offset plot for different iris textures are given below.

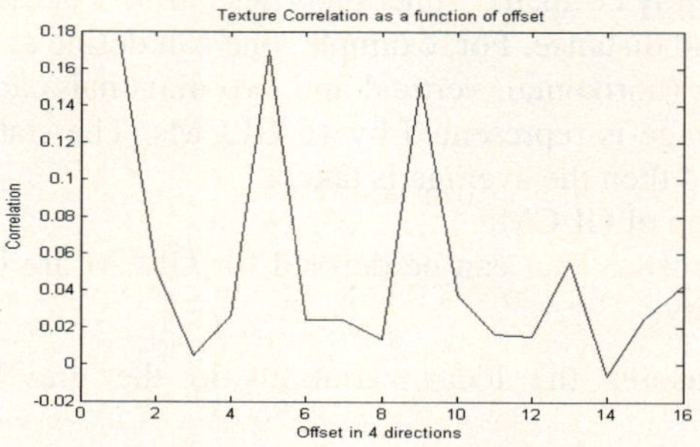

Fig. 6a. Correlation of Shaker iris texture

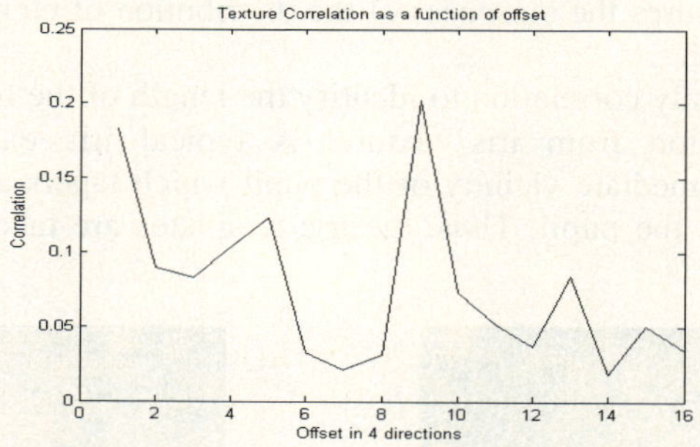

Fig. 6b. Correlation of Jewel iris texture

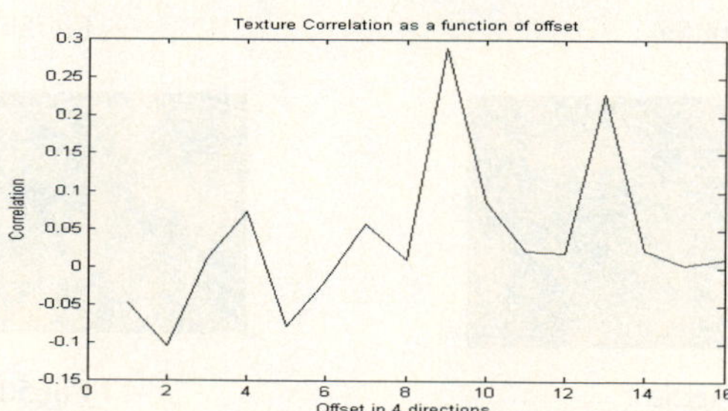

Fig. 6c. Correlation of Stream iris texture

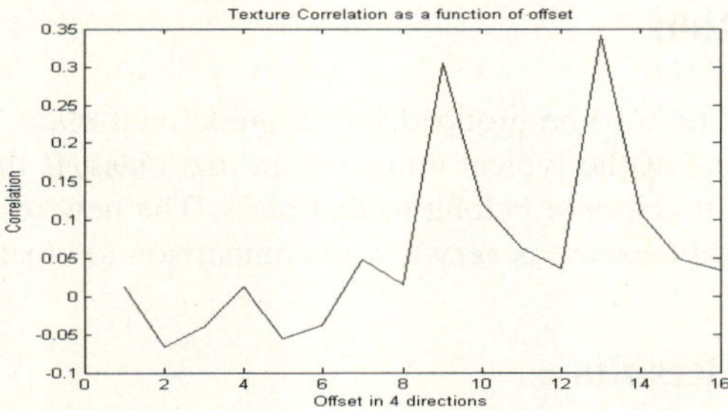

Fig. 6d. Correlation of Flower iris texture

From the above correlation plots, we can see the peak offsets which represent the periodic patterns that repeat for every set of pixels. Correlation function can be used to evaluate the coarseness. Larger texture primitives give rise to coarse texture and small primitives give fine texture. However if the primitives are periodic, then the correlation increases and decreases periodically with the distance [12]. For example, in the case of flower iris, the peak offsets are at 9 and 13 pixels. But, a common offset is observed at 9 for all textures. So, we can take a 9 pixel nearest neighbor as a feature vector to estimate DU measure in the case of iris textures.

5 Du Measure

Du measure[1] is an effective measure of the similarity between two iris textures, because it takes into consideration three important perspectives: a) information b) angle and c) energy.

a)Information: It is measured in terms of SID (spectral information divergence) between probability mass functions of the two textures f, g.

SID(f,g) = D(d||g) + D(g||f);

Here D(f||g) is the relative entropy of g with respect to f.

Where $D(f||g) = \Sigma (f * \log(f/g))$ and $D(g||f) = \Sigma (g * \log(g/f))$

b) Angle: It is measured in terms of spectral angle mapper. It measures the angle between two vectors f and g given by,

$SAM(f,g) = acos(\langle f,g\rangle/(||f||*||g||)$

Where $\langle f,g\rangle = \Sigma f_i*g_i$, and $||f||_2$ is the 2-norm of vector f, $||f||_2=\langle f,f\rangle^{1/2}$

Mixed Measure:

Du et al[26] developed SID-SAM mixed measure. It is defined by a mixed measure, M = SID(f,g) * tan(SAM(f,g)).

c) Energy: It is measured in terms of average power difference. Instead of using 2-norm, we can use 1-norm. APD (average power difference) is given by,

$APD(f,g) = ||f-g|| *1/N$, where $||x||_1=\Sigma|x|$.

Finally DU measure is given by,

Du(f,g)=APD * Mixed measure.

6 Iris Classification

When a new iris texture is to be grouped into a predefined class, the Du measure is calculated with any one of the typical templates in that class. If the Du score is very high, we can say that it does not belong to that class. The new template belongs to a class, with which its Du measure is very low in comparison to others[1].

7 Experimental Results

We have taken for our study the iris image data base from CASIA iris image Data base[CAS03a] and MMU iris data base[MMU04a]. CASIA iris image data base contributes a total number of 756 iris images which were taken in two different time frames. Each of the iris images is 8-bit gray scale with resolution 320 x 280. MMU data base contributes a total number of 450 images which were captured by LG Iris Access ® 2200.

Our studies conclude that all the iris images in the database have four different types of textures: Flower, Jewel, Stream and shaker. Thus there occur 6 different combinations for matching. Hence SID, SAM, APD values, for these 6 combinations, are given in the table.

Table 1. Du measures for different combinations of iris textures

Combination	SID	SAM	MM	APD	DU
Stream, Jewel	1.51657	0.34578	0.54618	8.3483	4.55997
Stream, Flower	1.60659	0.26289	0.43236	14.859	6.4244
Stream, Shaker	1.8626	0.29232	0.56053	4.4424	2.4901
Flower, Jewel	1.41048	0.40956	0.6123	6.491	3.9744
Flower, Shaker	2.08906	0.27165	0.58188	10.397	6.0498
Jewel, Shaker	2.14638	0.38986	0.88193	3.9059	3.447

When a new template belongs to the same class, then the SID (relative entropy) and APD (average power difference) become zero; thus Du measure automatically becomes zero or very less.

References

[1] NIST: Advanced Encryption Standard, AES (2001), http:// csrc.nist.gov/ publications/ fips/fips-197.pdf

[2] Heijmans, H.: Morphological Image Operators. AcademiPress, San Diego (1994)

[3] Juels, A., Sudan, M.: A Fuzzy Vault Scheme. In: Lapidothand, A., Teletar, E. (eds.) proc. IEEEInt'l. Symp. Inf. Theory, p. 408 (2002)

[4] Gonzalez, R.C., Woods, R.E.: Digital Image Processing, 3rd edn. Addison-Wesley, Reading (1992)

[5] De Mira Jr, J., Mayer, J.: Image Feature Extraction for application of Biometric Identification of Iris – A Morphological Approach. In: proc. IEEE. Int'l. Symp. on Computer Graphics and Image processing, SIBGRAPI'03.
[6] Uludag, U., Jain, A.K.: Fuzzy Finger Print Vault. In: Proc. Workshop: Biometrics: Challenges Arising from Theory to practice, pp. 13–16. W.H. Press, New York (2004)
[7] Teukolsky, S.A., Vetterling, W.T., Flannery, B.P.: Numerical Recipes in C, 2nd edn. Cambridge University press, Cambridge (1992)
[8] Teo, C.C., Ewe, H.T.: An efficient One Dimensional Fractal Analysis for Iris Recognition, WSCG'2005, January 31 Feb4, 2005, Plzen, Czech Republic (2005)
[9] LiMA,Tieniu: Efficient Iris Recognition by Characterizing Key Local Variations, IEEE trans., Image Processing (2004)
[10] Ives, R., Etter, D., Du, Y.: Iris Pattern Extraction using Bit Planes and Standard Deviations. In: IEEE conference on Signals, systems and computers (2004)
[11] Tian, Q.-C., Pan, Q., Cheng, Y.-M.: Fast algorithm and application of Hough Transform in iris segmentation. In: proceedings of third IEEE conference on machine learning and Cybernetics, Shangai, pp. 26–29 (2004)
[12] Sharma, M., Markou, M., Singh, S.: Evaluaion of Texture Methods For Image Analaysis, pattern recognition letters.

Protecting Biometric Templates with Image Watermarking Techniques

Nikos Komninos and Tassos Dimitriou

Athens Information Technology,
GR-19002 Peania Attiki, Greece
{nkom,tdim}@ait.edu.gr

Abstract. Biometric templates are subject to modifications for identity fraud especially when they are stored in databases. In this paper, a new approach to protecting biometric templates with image watermarking techniques is proposed. The novelty of this approach is that we have combined lattice and block-wise image watermarking techniques to maintain image quality along with cryptographic techniques to embed fingerprint templates into facial images and vice-versa. Thus, protecting them from being modified.

Keywords: Biometric templates, fingerprints, face pictures, authentication, watermarking.

1 Introduction

Visual based biometric systems use feature extraction algorithms to extract the discriminant information that is invariant to as many variations embedded in the raw data (e.g. scaling, translation, rotation) as possible. Template-based methods crop a particular subimage (the template) from the original sensory image, and extract features from the template by applying global-level processing, without a priori knowledge of the object's structural properties. Compared to geometric feature extraction algorithms, image template approaches need to locate far fewer points to obtain a correct template. For example, in the probabilistic decision-based neural network (PDBNN) face recognition system, only two points (left and right eyes) need to be located to extract a facial recognition template. An early comparison between the two types of feature extraction methods was made by Brunelli and Poggio [1]. They found the template approach to be faster and able to generate more accurate recognition results than the geometric approach.

In practice, there is not always a perfect match between templates and individuals. One speaks of a false positive if the biometric recognition system says 'yes', but the answer should be 'no'. A false negative works the other way round: the system says 'no', where it should be a 'yes'. One of the main challenges with biometric systems is to minimise the rates of both false positives and of false negatives. In theory one is inclined to keep the false positives low, but in practical situations it often works the other way round: people that operate these systems dislike false negatives, because they slow down the process and result in extra work and people complaining.

S.-W. Lee and S.Z. Li (Eds.): ICB 2007, LNCS 4642, pp. 114–123, 2007.

A potential protection approach of biometric templates is feasible with image watermarking techniques in visual-based biometric systems. Watermarking techniques attempt to protect the copyrights of any digital medium by embedding a unique pattern or message within the original information. The embedding method involves the use of a number of different authentication, encryption and hash algorithms and protocols to achieve the validity and copy protection of the particular message.

One of the most important requirements of watermarking is the perceptual transparency between the original work and the watermarked. Especially for images that objective metrics are widely used [6]. The watermark message may have a higher or lower level of perceptibility, meaning that there is a greater or lesser likelihood that a given observer will perceive the difference.

In this paper, we apply watermarking techniques to biometric templates to overcome serious cases of identity theft. In particular, we embed a person's fingerprint template into his facial image with the form of a cryptographic encoder that utilizes encryption algorithms, hash functions and digital signatures. Once the facial image has been watermarked, it can be stored in public databases without risking an identity modification or fabrication.

Following this introduction, the paper is organized as follows. Section 2 presents current work that combine watermarking and biometrics techniques. Section 3 discusses the requirements for efficient watermarking and briefly describes lattice and block-wise embedding methods and how these can be used along with cryptographic techniques to protect biometric templates. Section 4 evaluates the performance and the efficiency of the two embedding methods, through simulation tests. Section 5 concludes with remarks and comments on the open issues in watermarking and biometric templates.

2 Related Work

Current research efforts in combining watermarking techniques and visual-based biometric systems follow a hierarchical approach, with the most explored area being that of biometrics. Watermarking techniques on the other hand have been explored less in conjunction with biometrics templates. Despite the fact that several attempts of combining watermarking techniques and biometric systems have already been proposed.

In Lucilla et al. [5], a technique for the authentication of ID cardholders is presented, which combines dynamic signature verification with hologram watermarks. Two biometric features are already integral parts of ID cards for *manual* verification: the user's face and signature. This technique embeds dynamic features of the cardholder's signature into the personal data printed on the ID card, thereby facilitating automated user authentication based on the embedded information. Any modification of the image can also be detected and will further disallow the biometric verification of the forger.

Jain and Uludag [2] worked with hiding fingerprint minutiae in images. For this purpose, they considered two application scenarios: A set of fingerprint minutiae is transferred as the watermark of an arbitrary image and a face image is watermarked with fingerprint minutiae. In the first scenario, the fingerprint minutiae are transferred via a non-secure channel hidden in an arbitrary image. Before being embedded into the host image, the fingerprint minutiae are encrypted, which further increases the security of the data. The produced image is sent through the insecure communication channel. In the end, the image is received and the fingerprint minutiae are extracted, decrypted and ready for any further processing.

In the second scenario, a face scan is watermarked with fingerprint minutiae data and the result is encoded in a smart card. For the authentication of a user, the image is retrieved from the smart card, the fingerprint minutiae are extracted from it and they are compared to the minutiae obtained from the user online. The user is authenticated based on the two fingerprint minutiae data sets and the face image.

Jain et al. [3] have presented a fingerprint image watermarking method that can embed facial information into host fingerprint images. The considered application scenario in this case is as follows: The fingerprint image of a person is watermarked with face information of the same person and stored on a smart card. At an access control site, the fingerprint of the user is sensed and compared with the one stored on the smart card. After the fingerprint matching has successfully been completed, the facial information can be extracted from the fingerprint image on the smart card and can be used for further authentication purposes.

3 Combining Image Watermarking Techniques with Visual Based Biometric Systems

Visual-based biometric systems use feature extraction techniques to collect unique facial patterns and create biometric templates. However, biometric templates are subject to fraud especially in passport cloning and illegal immigration. Image watermarking techniques along with cryptographic primitives can be used to verify the authenticity of a person and also detect any modification to biometric templates when these are securely stored.

Biometric templates of a fingerprint and a face scan can be hashed and encrypted with cryptographic algorithms and then embedded into an image. For example, with the use of hash functions and encryption methods, the owner of a facial image can embed his/her template. The recipient can extract it by decrypting it and therefore can verify that the received image was the one intended by the sender. Encrypting and hashing watermarked information can guarantee the authentication of the owner and the image itself since the purpose of watermarks is two-fold: (i) they can be used to determine ownership, and (ii) they can be used to detect tampering.

There are two necessary features that all watermarks must possess [7]. First, all watermarks should be detectable. In order to determine ownership, it is imperative that one be able to recover the watermark. Second, watermarks must be robust to various types of processing of the signal (i.e. cropping, filtering, translation, compression, etc.). If the watermark is not robust, it serves little purpose, as ownership will be lost upon processing. Another important requirement for watermarks is the perceptual transparency between the original work and the watermarked; and for images objective metrics are widely used. The watermarked message may have a higher or lower level of perceptibility, meaning that there is a greater or lesser likelihood that a given observer will perceive the difference. The ideal is to be as imperceptible as possible and it is required to develop models that are used to compare two different versions of the works and evaluate any alterations. Evaluating the perceptibility of the watermarks can be done with distortion metrics.

These distortion metrics do not exploit the properties of the human visual system but they provide reliable results. Also, there is an objective criterion that relies on the sensitivity of the eye and is called *Watson* perceptual distance. It is also known as just noticeable differences and consists of a sensitivity function, two masking components based on luminance, contrast masking, and a pooling component. Table 1 gives the metrics that are used more often.

Table 1. Quality Measurements

		Mean Square Error (MSE)	$MSE = \frac{1}{MN} \sum_{m,n} \left(I_{m,n} - \tilde{I}_{m,n}\right)^2$
Signal to Noise Ratio (SNR)	$SNR = \sum_{m,n} I_{m,n}^2 / \sum_{m,n} \left(I_{m,n} - \tilde{I}_{m,n}\right)^2$	Normalized Cross Correlation (NC)	$NC = \sum_{m,n} I_{m,n}\tilde{I}_{m,n} / \sum_{m,n} I_{m,n}^2$
Peak Signal to Noise Ratio (PSNR)	$PSNR = MN \max I_{m,n}^2 / \sum_{m,n} \left(I_{m,n} - \tilde{I}_{m,n}\right)^2$	Correlation Quality (CQ)	$CQ = \sum_{m,n} I_{m,n}\tilde{I}_{m,n} / \sum_{m,n} I_{m,n}$
Image Fidelity (IF)	$IF = 1 - \sum_{m,n} \left(I_{m,n} - \tilde{I}_{m,n}\right)^2 / \sum_{m,n} I_{m,n}^2$	Watson Distance (WD)	$D_{wat}(c_0, c_w) = \left(\sum_{i,j,k} \lvert d[i,j,k] \rvert^4\right)^{1/4}$

There are plenty of image watermarking techniques available in the literature but we have combined ***lattice*** and semi-fragile, or ***block-wise***, embedding methods to take advantage of their unique features. Briefly, the lattice watermarking system embeds only one bit per 256 pixels in an image. Each bit is encoded using the trellis code and produces a sequence of four bits. The trellis coding is a convolution code and the number of states is 2^3=8 with possible outputs 2^4=16. After the encoding procedure, the bits need to be embedded in 256 pixels which means that each of the four bits is embedded in 256/4=64 pixels [6].

The *block-wise method* involves the basic properties of the JPEG compression where DCT domain takes place. Four bits are embedded in the high-frequency DCT of each 8x8 (64 pixels) block in the image and not in the low-frequency in order to avoid any visual differences that would lead to unacceptably poor fidelity. By using the block-wise method, the image can host 16 times more information than lattice. Specifically 28 coefficients are used which means that each bit is embedded in seven coefficients. The seven coefficients that host one bit are chosen randomly according to a seed number and thus, each coefficient is involved in only one bit [6].

By combing the two methods, we can exploit their advantages particularly, in circumstances where both the quality and the ability to notice the corrupted blocks is essential. In an image, the part that is likely to be illegally altered is watermarked with the block-wise method while the rest of the image is watermarked with the lattice method. In a facial image, for example, the areas of the eyes, mouth and jaw can be used to embed the fingerprint template. The round area of the face can be used to embed additional information, such as the name and/or address of the person shown in the photo with the lattice method. If an adversary changes for example the color of the eyes or some characteristics of the face (e.g. adding a moustache) the combined algorithm is able to determinate the modified pixels. This is achieved by comparing the extracted message with the original.

The combination of the two embedding methods is implemented in a *cryptographic encoder-decoder*. The authority that wishes to protect a face or fingerprint photo, extracts the biometric template(s) of that person and along with a short description and a unique feature of the image are inserted in a hash function and the result is encrypted with a 1024-bit secret key. The signature, together with the short and the extracted unique description, is embedded with the lattice method while the biometric template is embedded with the block-wise algorithm. As a unique description we have used the sum of the pixel values of the four blocks in the corners. The Secure Hash Algorithm (SHA) and the Rivest, Shamir, Aldeman (RSA) [8] have been used to hash and sign the fingerprint template, short and unique descriptions. The design of the encoder is illustrated in Fig. 1a.

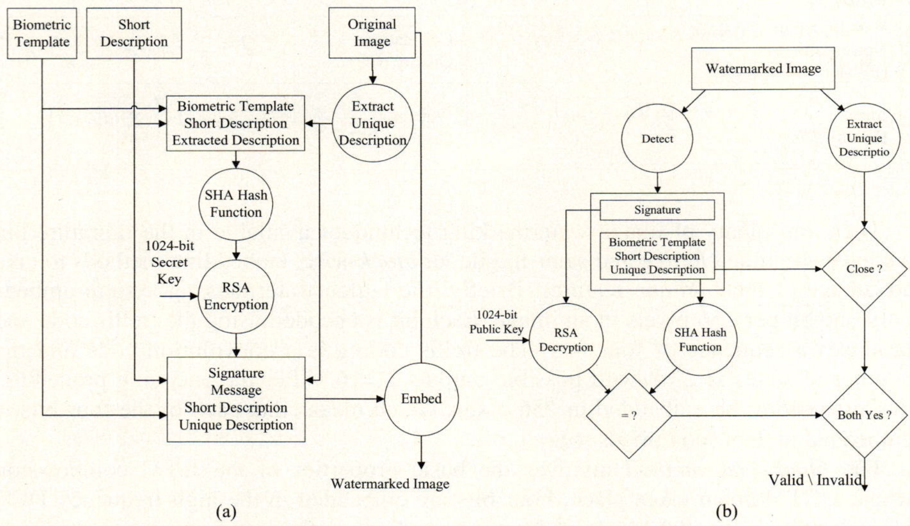

Fig. 1. Cryptographic Encoder / Decoder

From the watermarked version of the image, at the decoder's side, the signature, the short and unique descriptions are extracted with the lattice method while the biometric template is extracted with the block-wise algorithm. Then, the unique description is compared with the extracted one. Thus, the first step is to verify whether the unique descriptions match. In the case of the watermark being copied and embedded in another image, the extracted description will not be the same. This is due to the fact that the pixel values of the image have been slightly changed to host the watermark, the extracted description cannot be exactly the same, but can be very close. Therefore, some upper and lower boundaries have been determined for this step of verification.

The next step is to decrypt the signature using the 1024-bit RSA public key and retrieve the hash value. The biometric template, short and unique descriptions that have been extracted, is again the input to the hash function. The obtained hash value is then compared with the one decrypted from the signature. The third step of the decoder is to verify whether the decrypted hash value matches exactly with the one calculated by the decoder. If both hash values and unique descriptions are valid, the authentication process is successful. The whole design of the decoder is presented in Fig. 1b.

4 Experimental Results

In order to evaluate the performance and the efficiency of the embedding methods, excessive tests have taken place. A number of cases have been considered each with a different variable parameter. A grayscale bitmap image with 300x300 (Fig. 2a) resolution has been used for the experiments. The difference between the original and the watermarked image was evaluated by the ideal values of the original image that are presented in Table 2.

Table 2. Ideal Values of the test Image

Quality Measurements	Ideal Values	Quality Measurements	Ideal Values
MSE	0	NC	1
SNR (dB)	97	CQ	129.923
PSNR (dB)	104	Watson Distance	0
IF	100		

Cases have also been considered once again each with a different variable parameter, independent of lattice and block-wise methods in order to maintain image quality. When combined image watermarking is performed, a small part of the image is watermarked with the block-wise method and the rest is watermarked with the lattice method. We assume that the most vulnerable to illegal modifications, is the small part. The biometric template is embedded in the small part while the short and extracted descriptions are embedded in the large part of the image. The experimental tests of the quality measurements were performed using: only lattice; only block-wise; combined block-wise and lattice.

It was found that the lattice method achieves better results than the block-wise and expected that the produced result values of the combined case would be in between the values of those produced by the two methods. Particularly, in the case of the lattice algorithm the maximum number of the embedded bit can be 351 (one bit per 256 pixels). The formulas that are used to evaluate the differences between two images are presented in Table 1. The tests were executed using a range of values for the parameter in order to conclude what the best values are. The parameters are the embedding strength (β) and the lattice spacing (α). The range of the α value was from 0.35 to 5.33 and the range of β from 0.7 to 1.1. The incensement steps for a was 0.02 and for β 0.1.

The measurement values for the lattice method are very close to the ideal ones. More specifically, the direction towards zero is achieved using low values of α in the case of MSE. If at the same time the value of β that is used is low, the MSE is decreased even further. In the case of SNR and PSNR, the result values are higher when the parameters α and β are low. The image fidelity (IF), which is defined as a percentage of how identical the images are, the value of 100% is considered to be the optimum and as can be noticed from Table 3, the results are very close to this. Utilizing the NC and the CQ quality measurements, it is observed that their measurements are closer to the ideal ones (Table 2), as the values of α and β are decreased. The above observations are also justified from the Watson measurement which is based on luminance, contrast, and pooling masking.

Table 3. Results From Lattice, Block-Wise and Combined Embedding Methods

alpha(α)=0.93, beta(β)=1.0, alpha(a)=0.1	**Lattice alpha(α), beta(β)**	**Block-Wise alpha(a)**	**Combined alpha(α),beta(β) alpha(a)**
MSE	0.353	1.428	0.389
SNR	47.13	39.33	45.14
PSNR	53.27	45.29	52.52
IF	99.969	99.983	99.966
NC	0.99999	0.99992	0.99994
CQ	129.925	129.916	129.922
Watson-Distance	31.436	58.262	32.453

(a)

alpha(α)=1.53, beta(β)=0.8, alpha(a) =0.2	**Lattice alpha(α), beta(β)**	**Block-Wise alpha(a)**	**Combined alpha(α),beta(β), alpha(a)**
MSE	0.545	4.951	0.72
SNR	43.18	33.62	41.97
PSNR	50.77	41.18	49.55
IF	99.9952	99.9563	99.9936
NC	0.99998	0.99985	0.99998
CQ	129.921	129.903	129.921
Watson-Distance	48.901	157.506	49.136

(b)

Therefore, it could be suggested that the optimum parameter values are those that give the best results. They could even be the zero values. But at the decoder's side not all the bits are extracted correctly. Specifically when using low values of α and β, the decoder is not able to get the correct embedded bits. In conclusion it can be said that a trade-off between the quality results and the decoder's result is necessary in order to determine the optimum values. From the tests we concluded that suggested values could be $\alpha \approx 1.53$ and $\beta = 0.8$ (Table 3b).

Similarly, in the case of the block-wise method, the tests were executed for the same image in order to be comparable with those of the lattice method. One major difference is the number of bits that are embedded. Since the method embeds four bits in every 64 pixels and the image has 90000 pixels in total, the number of bits can be hosted in 5625. The size of the information that can be watermarked is significantly higher and in fact is 16 times greater than the size in the lattice method. Therefore, before even executing the test, it is expected that the results will not be as good. The information in the block-wise method is much more, which means that the alterations in the image will produce worse values in the quality measurements.

The observation of the results proves what is being stated in the beginning. The values of the quality measurements are not as good in comparison with those of the lattice method since the measurement of the MSE is higher than the ideal value, which is zero. The values of the SNR and PSNR, which are widely used, show that as the value of the parameter alpha (a) is increased, the result becomes worse. In the case of the IF, NC, and CQ, the measurements seem to be distant from the ideal values as alpha (a) takes higher values. The same conclusion can be phrased for the perceptual distance given by the Watson model, where the results are worse as the value of alpha (a) is increased.

It seems that as the value of alpha is increased, the watermarked image has poorer fidelity. So the optimum value of the parameter should perhaps possibly be a small one e.g. 0.01. However, it seems that values below 0.05 do not allow the decoder to get the right message. The chosen value of alpha depends on how sensitive the user wants the method to be in order to locate the corrupted bits and mark the corresponding blocks. Higher values increase the sensitivity but at the same time the quality of the image is reduced. So it is again necessary to make a trade-off between the results and the sensitivity. A possible suggested value could be a ≈ 0.2 (Table 3b).

Indeed the results were not as good as those of the lattice method but they were better than those of the block-wise method. In Table 3 some result values of the combination are given in order to compare them with those of the two methods when they are applied individually. Table 3 justifies that the combination produces quality measurements between the two methods. Table 4 presents the maximum number of bits that can be hosted in the image using the two embedding methods and a combination of them.

Table 4. Maximum Number of Embedded Bits

	Lattice	**Block-Wise**	**Combined**
Max Embedded Bits	351	5625	2752

The last test was to verify that in case somebody modifies the block-wise part of the image, which is the biometric template, the decoder realizes the modification, informs the authority that the authentication application failed and outputs a file with the modified blocks marked. The part that is likely to be illegally altered is the eyes or jaw and the biometric template(s) of the facial and/or fingerprint images which are embedded with the block-wise method (Fig. 2b). In the watermarked version the distance between the eyes was changed and this image was inserted in the decoder in order to verify its authenticity. The authentication process failed and a marked image was produced (Fig. 2c). By observing the last image it is clear that the decoder has successfully located the modified blocks.

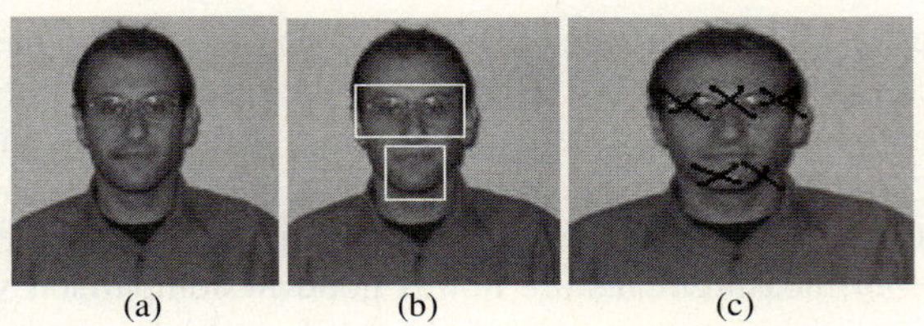

Fig. 2. Original Image (a), Watermarked Image (b), Marked Image (c)

Throughout the paper we have considered the case where a fingerprint and/or facial template is embedded into a facial image. That does not mean that a facial image cannot be embedded with our method into a fingerprint image, which is illustrated in Fig. 3. Similar to Fig. 2, Fig. 3a is the original image, Fig. 3b is the watermarked and Fig. 3c is the marked image generated by our testbed.

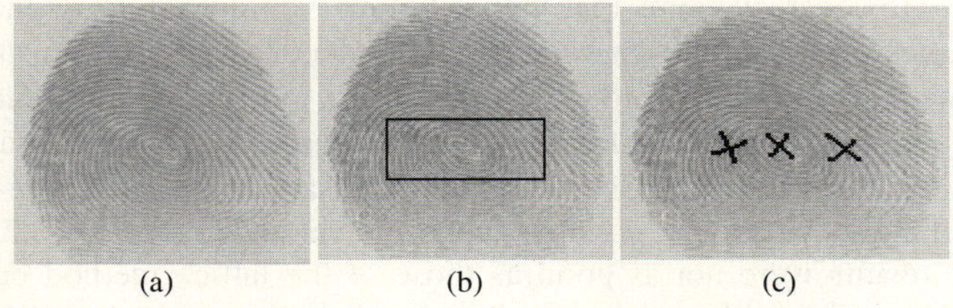

Fig. 3. Original Image (a), Watermarked Image (b), Marked Image (c)

The potential danger with sensitive databases containing biometric identifiers, such as facial, fingerprint images and templates, is that they are likely to be attacked by hackers or criminals. Watermarking the information in these databases can allow the integrity of the contents to be verified. Another danger is that this critical data can be attacked while it is being transmitted. For example, a third party could intercept this data and maliciously alter the data before re-transmitting it to its final destination. The transmission problem is even more critical in cellular and wireless channels. The channels themselves are quite noisy and can degrade the signal quality.

Additionally, data transmitted through wireless channels is far from secure as they are omni-directional, and as such can be eavesdropped with relative ease. The growth of the wireless market and e-commerce applications for PDAs requires a robust cryptographic method for data security. There are compact solid state sensors already available in the market, which can capture fingerprints or faces for the purpose of identity verification. These devices can also be easily attached to PDAs and other hand-held cellular devices for use in identification and verification.

Considering all the noise and distortion in cellular channels, our combined watermarking technique along with the cryptographic encoder/decoder will mainly work in smudging, compression and filtering. Our cryptographic encoder/decoder will only fail when noise and distortion is detected in the sensitive areas of the images that have been embedded with the block-wise algorithm. If our watermarked image is transferred in a noisy channel, then we need to reduce the amount of information inserted with the block-wise method to have a high rate of success.

5 Conclusion

Watermarking biometric data is of growing importance as more robust methods of verification and authentication are being used. Biometrics provides the necessary unique characteristics but their validity must be ensured. This can be guaranteed to an extent by watermarks. Unfortunately, they cannot provide a foolproof solution especially when the transmission of data is involved. A receiver can not always determine whether or not he has received the correct data without the sender giving access to critical information (i.e., the watermark).

In this paper we have presented a cryptographic encoder/decoder that digitally signs biometric templates, which are embedded with combined lattice and block-wise image watermarking techniques into an image. Combining image watermarking techniques with cryptographic primitives enables us to protect biometric templates that have been generated by a visual-based biometric system without any distortion of the image. Since biometric templates are essential tools for authenticating people, it is necessary to protect them for possible alterations and fabrications in conjunction with their biometric image(s) when these are stored in private/public databases.

Image watermarking techniques in conjunction with cryptographic primitives provide a powerful tool to authenticate an image, its biometric template and any additional information that is considered important according to a particular application. In the passport-based scenario, for example, the photograph and the private information (i.e. name/address) of an individual can be protected with the proposed approach. Our results showed that we can combine watermarking techniques to securely embed private information in a biometric image without fading it out.

References

1. Brunelli, R., Poggio, T.: Face recognition: features versus templates. IEEE Trans. On Pattern Analysis and Machine Intelligence 15, 1042–1052 (1993)
2. Jain, A.K., Uludag, U.: Hiding Fingerprint Minutiae in Images. In: Proc. Automatic Identification Advanced Technologies (AutoID), New York, pp. 97–102 (March 14-15, 2002)
3. Jain, A.K., Uludag, U., Hsu, R.-L.: Hiding a face in a fingerprint image. In: Proc. International Conference on Pattern Recognition (ICPR), Canada, (August 11-15, 2002)
4. Kung, S.Y., Mak, M.W., Lin, S.H.: Biometric Authentication: A Machine Learning Approach. Prentice Hall Information and System Sciences Series (2005)
5. Lucilla, C.F., Astrid, M., Markus, F., Claus, V., Ralf, S., Edward, D.J.: Biometric Authentication for ID cards with hologram watermarks. In: Proc. Security and Watermarking of Multimedia Contents SPIE'02, vol. 4675, pp. 629–640 (2002)
6. Peticolas, F., Anderson, R., Kuhn, M.: Information hiding – a survey. IEEE Proceedings 87(7), 1062–1078 (1999)
7. Wong, P.H.W., Au, O.C., Yueng, Y.M.: Novel blind watermarking technique for images. IEEE Trans. On Circuits and Systems for Video Technology 13(8), 813–830 (2003)
8. Hao, F., Anderson, R., Daugman, J.: Combining Crypto with Biometrics Effectively. IEEE Transaction on Computers 55(9), 1081–1088 (2006)

Factorial Hidden Markov Models for Gait Recognition

Changhong Chen[1], Jimin Liang[1], Haihong Hu[1], Licheng Jiao[1], and Xin Yang[2]

[1] Life Science Research Center, School of Electronic Engineering, Xidian University
Xi'an, Shaanxi 710071, China
[2] Center for Biometrics and Security Research, Key Laboratory of Complex Systems and Intelligence Science, Institute of Automation, Chinese Academy of Sciences, P.O. Box 2728, Beijing 100080, China
jimleung@mail.xidian.edu.cn

Abstract. Gait recognition is an effective approach for human identification at a distance. During the last decade, the theory of hidden Markov models (HMMs) has been used successfully in the field of gait recognition. However the potentials of some new HMM extensions still need to be exploited. In this paper, a novel alternative gait modeling approach based on Factorial Hidden Markov Models (FHMMs) is proposed. FHMMs are of a multiple layer structure and provide an interesting alternative to combining several features without the need of collapse them into a single augmented feature. We extracted irrelated features for different layers and iteratively trained its parameters through the Expectation Maximization (EM) algorithm and Viterbi algorithm. The exact Forward-Backward algorithm is used in the E-step of EM algorithm. The performances of the proposed FHMM-based gait recognition method are evaluated using the CMU MoBo database and compared with that of HMMs based methods.

Keywords: gait recognition, FHMMs, HMMs, parallel HMMs, frieze, wavelet.

1 Introduction

Hidden Markov models had been the dominant technology in speech recognition since 1980s'. HMMs provide a very useful paradigm to model the dynamics of speech signals. They provide a solid mathematical formulation for the problem of learning HMM parameters from speech observations. Furthermore, efficient and fast algorithms exist for the problem of computing the most likely model given a sequence of observations.

Gait recognition is similar with speech recognition in time-sequential space. Due to the successful application of HMMs to speech recognition, A. Kale, et al, [1, 2] introduced HMMs to gait recognition in recent years and gained inspiring performance. Some other recognition methods [3-5] based on HMMs were proposed one after the other.

There are some possible extensions to the HMMs, such as factorial HMMs (FHMMs) [6], coupled HMMs [7], and so on. FHMMs were first introduced by Ghahramani [6] and attempt to extend HMMs by allowing the modeling of several stochastic random processes loosely coupled. FHMMs are of a multiple layer structure

S.-W. Lee and S.Z. Li (Eds.): ICB 2007, LNCS 4642, pp. 124–133, 2007.

and provide an interesting alternative to combining several features without the need of collapse them into a single augmented feature. In this paper we explore the potential of FHMMs for gait modeling.

This paper is structured as follows. Section II introduces the image preprocessing and feature extraction methods. Section III describes the FHMMs in details and the realization in gait recognition. In section IV, the proposed method is evaluated using the CMU MoBo database [8], and its performances are compared with that of HMMs based methods. Section V concludes the paper.

2 Feature Extraction

2.1 Preprocessing

The preprocessing procedure is very important. The CMU MoBo database [8] offers human silhouettes segmented from the background images. However, the silhouettes are noisy and need to be smoothed.

Firstly, mathematical morphological operations are used to fill the holes and remove some noise.

Secondly, we remove some big noise blocks though filtering, which can't be eliminated by simple morphological operations.

Finally, all the silhouettes are aligned and cropped into the same size. The size can be chosen manually which varies with different databases. For CMU MoBo database, we choose 640*300, which contains most useful information and less noise for most people. An example is showed in Fig. 1.

(a)

(b)

Fig. 1. (a) is an example of the original silhouette; (b) is the processed silhouette of (a)

2.2 Feature Extraction

B. Logan [9] pointed out that "there is only an advantage in using the FHMM if the layers model processes with different dynamics; if the features are indeed highly correlated FHMMs do not seem to offer compelling advantages". The choice of features is critical to FHMMs, however, it is really a challenge to choose uncorrelated features from a sequence of gait images.

In this paper, two kinds of different feature extraction methods are employed for different layers of FHMM.

2.2.1 Frieze Feature

The first gait feature representation is a frieze pattern [10]. A two-dimensional pattern that repeats along one dimension is called a frieze pattern in the mathematics and geometry literature. Consider a sequence of binary silhouette images $b(x, y, t)$ indexed spatially by pixel location (x, y) and temporally by time t.

The first frieze pattern is calculated as $F_C(x,t) = \sum_y b(x, y, t)$, where each column (indexed by time t) is the vertical projection (column sum) of silhouette image. The second frieze pattern $F_R(x,t) = \sum_x b(x, y, t)$ can be constructed by stacking row projections. It is considered that F_R contains more information than F_c and some obvious noise can be filtered from F_R as shown in Fig.2. We choose F_R as the feature for the first FHMM layer.

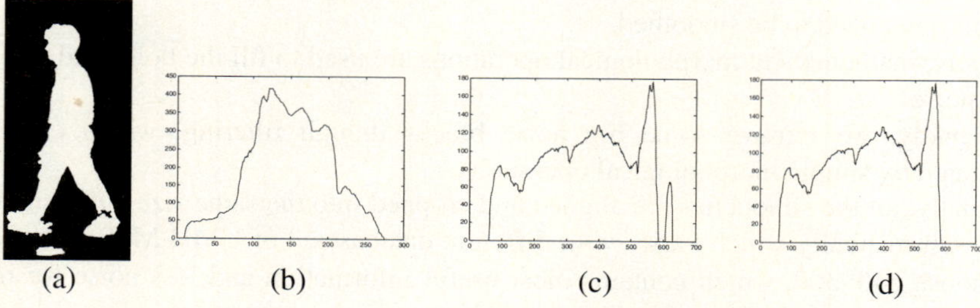

Fig. 2. (a) is a silouette image, its frieze features are F_c (b) and F_R (c). (d) is F_R after filtering noise.

2.2.2 Wavelet Feature

Wavelet transform can be regarded as a temporal-frequency localized analysis method, which has good time resolution in high frequency part and good frequency resolution in low frequency part. It has the property of holding entropy and can change the energy distribution of the image without damaging the information. Wavelet transform acts on the whole image, which can eliminate the global relativity of the image as well as separate the quantization error to the whole image avoiding artifacts.

The wavelet transform suits image processing very much, so we choose the vectors obtained from wavelet transform of the silhouette images as the feature for the second FHMM layer.

3 FHMM-Based Gait Recognition

FHMMs were first described by Ghahramani[6]. They present FHMMs and introduce several methods to efficiently learn their parameters. Our effort, however, is focused on exploiting the application of FHMMs in gait modeling.

3.1 FHMMs Description

The factorial HMM arises by forming a dynamic belief network composed of several layers. Each layer can be considered as an independent HMM. This is shown in Fig. 3. Each layer has independent dynamics but that the observation vector depends upon the current state in each of the layers. This is achieved by allowing the state variable in HMM to be composed of a collection of states. That is, we now have a "meta-state" variable which is composed of states as follows:

$$S_t = S_t^{(1)}, S_t^{(2)}, \cdots S_t^{(M)}, \tag{1}$$

where S_t is the "meta-state" at time t , $S_t^{(m)}$ is the state of the mth layer at time t and M is the number of layers.

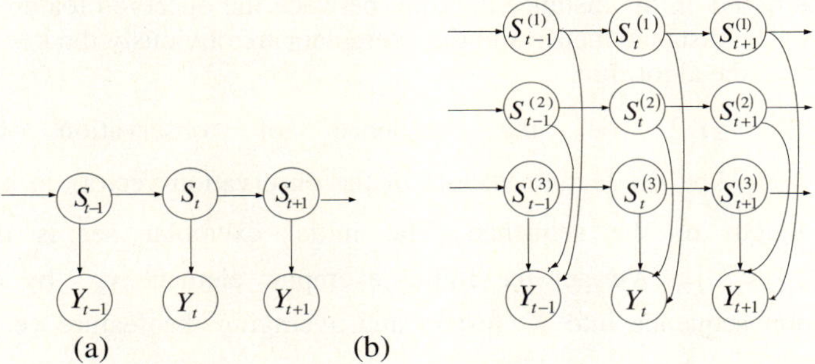

Fig. 3. (a) Dynamic Belief Network representation of a hidden markov model; (b) Dynamic Belief Network representation of a factorial HMM with M=3 underlying Markov chains

It is assumed for simplicity that the number of possible states in each layer is equal. Let K be the number of states in each layer. A system with M layers requires M $K \times K$ transition matrices with zeros representing illegal transitions. It should be noted that this system could still be represented as a regular HMM with a $K^M \times K^M$ transition matrix. It is preferable to use the M $K \times K$ transition matrices over the $K^M \times K^M$ equivalent representation for the computational simplicity.

It is also assumed that each meta-state variable is a priori uncoupled from other state variables:

$$P(S_t \mid S_{t-1}) = \prod_{m=1}^{M} P(S_t^m \mid S_{t-1}^m). \tag{2}$$

As for the probability of the observation given the meta-state, there are two different ways of combining the information from the layers. The first method assumes that the observation is distributed according to a Gaussian distribution with a common covariance and the mean being a linear combination of the state means, which is went by the name of "linear" factorial HMM. The second combination method, the "streamed" method, assumes that $P(Y_t \mid S_t)$ is the product of the distributions of each layer (Y_t is the observation at time t). More details can be found in [9].

3.2 Initialization of Parameters

(1) Number of states K and layers M : Five state numbers are chosen for CMU MOBO database. The number of layers depends on the feature vectors extracted. We extracted two kinds of feature vectors, so the number of layers is two.

(2) The transition matrices: The transition matrices are M $K \times K$ matrices. Each of the initial $K \times K$ matrices is set as a left-to-right HMM, which is only allowed transition from one state to itself and its next state.

(3) Output probability distribution: A gait sequence is always large in size. The large dimension makes it impossible to calculate a common covariance of the observation. So we employ the "streamed" method in 3.1. $P(Y_t \mid S_t)$ is calculated as the product of the distributions of each layer. The models we used are exemplar-based models [2]. The motivation behind using an exemplar based model is that the recognition can be based on the distance measure between the observed feature vector and the exemplars. The distance metric and the exemplars are obviously the key factors to the performance of the algorithm.

Let $Y = \{Y_1, Y_2, \cdots, Y_T\}$ be the sequence of observation vectors, $F^m = \{f_1^m, f_2^m, \cdots, f_T^m\}$ be the feature vectors of the observation vectors in layer m, and T be the length of the sequence. The initial exemplar set is denoted as $S^m = \{s_1{}^m, s_2{}^m, \cdots s_K{}^m\}$. We get the initial exemplar element $s_K{}^m$ by equally dividing observation sequence into K clusters and averaging the feature vectors of each cluster.

We estimate the output probability distribution by an alternative approach based on the distance between the exemplars and the image features. In this way we avoid calculating high-dimensional probability density functions. The output probability distribution of the mth layer is defined as:

$$b_n(f_t^m) = \alpha \delta_n^m e^{-\delta_n^m \times D(f_t^m, S_n^m)}, \tag{3}$$

$$\delta_n^m = \frac{N_n}{\sum_{f_t^m \in e_n^m} D(f_t^m, S_n^m)}, \tag{4}$$

where α is a constant, $D(f_t^m, S_n^m)$ is the inner product distance between the tth feature vector f_t^m and the nth state S_n^m in the mth layer. δ_n^m is defined as equation (4). N_n is the number of frames belonging to the nth cluster, which is constant to all layers. e_n^m represents the nth cluster of the mth layer.

Let β be a constant. The output probability distribution can be represented as:

$$P(Y_t \mid S_t) = \beta \prod_{m=1}^{M} b_n(f_t^m). \tag{5}$$

3.3 Estimation of Parameters

The factorial HMMs we use are exemplar-based. The model parameters are denoted as λ, which include the exemplars in each layer, the transition probabilities between states in each layer and the prior probabilities of each state. The exemplars are initialized as mentioned above and remain unchangeable when estimate other parameters. The transition probabilities and the prior probabilities can be estimated using the Expectation Maximization (EM) algorithm. The algorithm steps can be referred to [6]. The exact Forward-Backward algorithm [6] is used in the E-step. The naive exact algorithm, consisting of translating the factorial HMM into an equivalent HMM with K^m states and using the forward-backward algorithm, has the time complexity of $O(TK^{2M})$. The exact Forward-Backward algorithm has time complexity $O(TMK^{(M+1)})$ because it makes use of the independence of the underlying Markov chains to sum over M $K \times K$ transition matrices. Viterbi algorithm is used to get the most probable path and the likelihood. New exemplars can be obtained through the most probable path, also the new output probability distribution. The whole process is iterated until the likelihood converges to a small threshold.

3.4 Recognition

Firstly, the probe sequence $y = \{y(1), y(2) \cdots y(T)\}$ is preprocessed and extracted features are used as the train sequence.

Then the output probability distribution of the probe sequence can be calculated using the states of the train sequence. We can get the log likelihood P_j that the probe sequence is generated by the FHMM parameters λ_j of the jth person in the train database:

$$P_j = \log(P(y \mid \lambda_j)). \tag{6}$$

The above procedure is repeated for every person in the database. Suppose P_m is the largest one among all P_j's, then we can assign the unknown person to be person m.

A key problem during calculate the log likelihood P_j is how to get the clusters of the probe sequence given the FHMM of the train sequence. We calculate the distance between the features of probe sequence and the exemplars of a train sequence to confirm the clusters. The clusters of the same probe sequence vary with different train sequences.

4 Experiment Results

We use CMU MoBo database [8] to evaluate the proposed method. Fronto-parallel sequences are adopted and the image size is preprocessed to be 640×300. Besides the experiment on the proposed method, other three comparative experiments are conducted. When using only one of the two features, the one layer FHMMs deteriorates to standard HMMs. We give the experiment results of the two HMMs of the two features separately. As showed in Fig. 4, we also give the results of merging the results of the two HMMs. We call this system 'parallel HMM' as [11]. If the judgments of the two HMMs are same, their results will be the results of the 'parallel HMM'. Otherwise, we sum the corresponding likelihoods of the two HMMs and rearrange them to get the final results. Also, the experimental results are compared with that of [1] and [12].

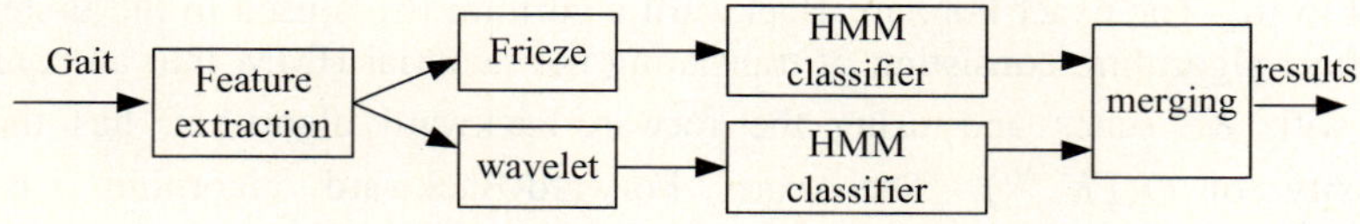

Fig. 4. Parallel HMM

4.1 Same Styles Experiments

The train and probe data sets are of the same motion style. For this type of experiments, we use two cycles to train and two cycles to test.

(a) S vs. S: Training on slow walk of some cycles and testing on slow walk of other cycles.

(b) F vs. F: Training on fast walk of some cycles and testing on fast walk of other cycles.

(c) B vs. B: Training on walk carrying a ball of some cycles and testing on walk carrying a ball of other cycles.

(d) I vs. I: Training on walk in a incline of some cycles and testing on walk in a incline of other cycles.

The results for same style experiments are shown as:

Table 1. The results for same styles experiments

P(%) at rank	HMM[12]		HMM[1]		HMMf		HMMw		pHMM		FHMM	
	1	5	1	5	1	5	1	5	1	5	1	5
S vs. S	100	100	72.0	96.0	100	100	100	100	100	100	100	100
F vs. F	96.0	100	68.0	92.0	88.0	100	100	100	96.0	100	100	100
B vs. B	100	100	91.7	100	95.8	100	100	100	100	100	100	100
I vs. I	95.8	100	---	---	92.0	100	96.0	100	96.0	100	100	100

4.2 Different Styles Experiments

The train and probe data sets are of the different motion styles. For this type of experiments, we use four cycles to train and two cycles to test. The CMC curves for the four experiments of different styles are given in Fig. 5 and the performance comparison with other methods is shown in table 2.

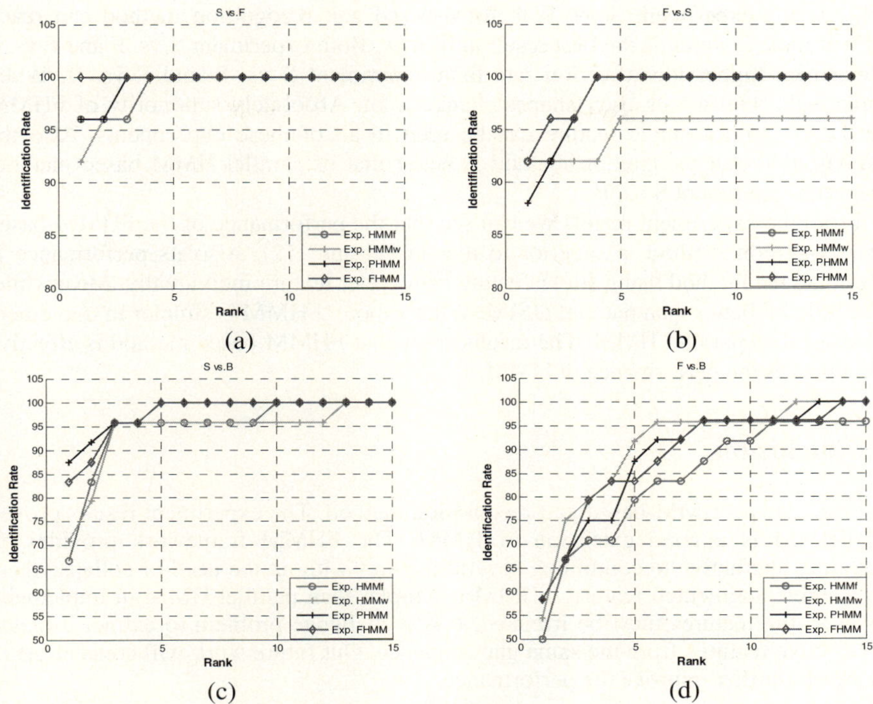

Fig. 5. The cumulative matching characteristics for different styles experiments. Exp.HMMf represents HMM with frieze vectors. Exp.HMMw represents HMM with wavelet transform vectors. Exp. PHMM represents parallel HMM. Exp. FHMM represents factorial HMM. (a) shows the results of S vs. F. (b) shows the results of F vs. S. (c) shows the results of S vs. B. (d) shows the results of F vs. B.

Table 2. The results for different styles experiments

P(%) at rank	HMM[12]		HMM[1]		HMMf		HMMw		pHMM		FHMM	
	1	5	1	5	1	5	1	5	1	5	1	5
S vs. F	---	---	32.0	72.0	96.0	100	92.0	100	96.0	100	100	100
F vs. S	---	---	56.0	80.0	92.0	100	88.0	96.0	88.0	100	92.0	100
S vs. B	52.2	60.9	---	---	66.7	95.8	70.8	95.8	87.5	100	83.3	100
F vs. B	---	---	---	---	50.0	79.2	54.2	91.7	58.3	75.0	58.3	83.3

(a) S vs. F: Training on slow walk and testing on fast walk.
(b) F vs. S: Training on fast walk and testing on slow walk.
(c) S vs. B: Training on slow walk and testing on walking with a ball.
(d) F vs. B: Training on fast walk and testing on walking with a ball.

For same styles experiments, the performance of FHMM-based gait recognition method is excellent, which can reach 100% at rank 1. For different styles experiments, more experiments are done and much better results are obtained than reference [1] and

[12]. For the experiment S vs. F, FHMM-based gait recognition method can reach 100% at rank 1, which is the best result until now. Both experiment S vs. F and F vs. S have gained higher identification rate than experiment S vs. B and F vs. B. When people walk with a ball, their shapes change a lot. Absolutely superiority of FHMM over HMM with a single feature can be seen in all of these experiments. Also the FHMM-based gait recognition method is better that of parallel HMM based method, except the experiment S vs. B.

From the experiment results we can see that the performance of the FHMM-based gait recognition method is superior to that in [1] and [12]. Also its performance is better than the method using frieze feature or wavelet feature individually. Meanwhile, it is a little bit better than parallel HMM. What's more, FHMM is simpler in implement and faster than parallel HMM. The results show that FHMM-based method is effective and improves the performance of HMM.

5 Conclusion

We presented a FHMM-based gait recognition method. The experiment results proved that FHMM is a good extension of HMM. The FHMM framework provides an interesting alternative to combining several features without the need of collapse them into a single augmented feature. FHMM is simpler than parallel HMM in implement. However, the features must be irrelated. It is a challenge problem to extract irrelated but effective features from the same gait sequence. Out future work will concentrate in this area to further improve the performance.

Acknowledgments. This work was partially supported by the Natural Science Foundation of China, Grant Nos. 60402038 and 60303022, the Chair Professors of the Cheung Kong Scholars, and the Program for Cheung Kong Scholars and Innovative Research Team in University (PCSIRT).

References

1. Kale, A., Cuntoor, N., Chellappa, R.: A framework for activity-specific human identification. In: Proc. of the Int. Conf. on Acoustics, Speech and Signal Processing (May 2002)
2. Sundaresan, A., RoyChowdhury, A., Chellappa, R.: A Hidden Markov Model Based Framework for Recognition of Humans from Gait Sequences. In: Proceedings of IEEE International Conference on Image Processing. IEEE Computer Society Press, Los Alamitos (2003)
3. Liu, Z., Malave, L., Sarkar, S.: Studies on Silhouette Quality and Gait Recognition. In: Proceedings of the 2004 IEEE Computer Society Conference on Computer Vision and Pattern Recognition (CVPR'04). IEEE Computer Society Press, Los Alamitos (2004)
4. Iwamoto, K., Sonobe, K., Komatsu, N.: A Gait Recognition Method using HMM. In: SICE Annual Conference in Fukui, Japan (2003)
5. Chen, C., Liang, J., Zhao, H., Hu, H.: Gait Recognition Using Hidden Markov Model. In: Jiao, L., Wang, L., Gao, X., Liu, J., Wu, F. (eds.) ICNC 2006. LNCS, vol. 4221, pp. 399–407. Springer, Heidelberg (2006)

6. Ghahramani, Z., Jordan, M.: Factorial Hidden Markov Models. Computational Cognitive Science Technical Report 9502 (Revised) (July 1996)
7. Brand, M.: Coupled hidden Markov models for modeling interacting processes. MIT Media Lab Perceptual Computing/Learning and Common Sense Techincal Report 405 (Revised) (June 1997)
8. Gross, R., Shi, J.: The Cmu Motion of Body (mobo) Database. Technical report, Robotics Institute (2001)
9. Logan, B., Moreno, J.: Factorial Hidden Markov Models for Speech Recognition: Preliminary Experiments. Cambrige Research Laboratory Technical Research Series (September 1997)
10. Liu, Y., Collins, T., Tsin, Y.: Gait Sequence Analysis using Frieze Patterns, CMU-RI-TR-01-38
11. Logan, B., Moreno, P.: Factorial HMMs for Acoustic Modeling, Acoustics Speech and Signal[C]. In: Proceedings of the IEEE International Conference, vol. 2 (S), pp. 813–816. IEEE Computer Society Press, Los Alamitos (1998)
12. Zhang, R., Vogler, C., Metaxas, D.: Human Gait Recognition. In: Proceedings of the IEEE Computer Society Conference on Computer Vision and Pattern Recognition Workshops. IEEE Computer Society Press, Los Alamitos (2004)

A Robust Fingerprint Matching Approach: Growing and Fusing of Local Structures

Wenquan Xu, Xiaoguang Chen, and Jufu Feng

State Key Laboratory on Machine Perception,
Center for Information Science,
School of Electronics Engineering and Computer Science,
Peking University, Beijing 100871, P.R. China
{xuwq,chenxg,fjf}@cis.pku.edu.cn

Abstract. This paper proposed a robust fingerprint matching approach based on the growing and fusing of local structures. First, we obtain candidate of minutiae triangles, the smallest local structure in our approach; and then all candidates of minutiae structures grow into larger local structures (we call *growing regions*) based on which we define the *credibility* of minutiae triangles and introduce a competition strategy; finally, *growing region*s compete and fuse into a much larger local structures (called *fusion region*). The matching score is calculated based on the evaluation of growing and fusing of local structures. Results on FVC2004 show that the proposed approach is robust to fingerprint nonlinear deformation and is efficient.

Keywords: fingerprint, nonlinear deformation, robust, local, global, grow, fuse.

1 Introduction

The nonlinear deformation of a fingerprint introduced by the elastic feature of the finger and the non-uniform pressure on the finger during the fingerprint acquisition makes finger matching algorithm less efficient and less accurate. Based on the idea that the local may be less affected by the global deformation, a lot of fingerprint matching algorithms adapt the local and global matching scheme. In this scheme we first define the local structure which is at least invariant as to affine transformation; after obtaining candidates of local structures which are possibly matched, we combine them into a global match result. The efficiency of this matching scheme depends on two critical points: first, how reliable the local structure is; second, how well the local match becomes a global match. Many works have been made on the former point. AKJ [2] use a local structure consisting of a minutiae and a list of sampling points on the same ridge of the minutiae. En Zhu[3] constructs a local structure with the orientation information near the minutiae. X. Jiang[4] suggests that the minutiae triangle local structure is less affected by the non-linear deformation. Y.He && J. Tian[5] construct a local structure with two minutiae which he assumes would be more reliable when concerning the information of ridge count. Xuefeng Liang and Tetsuo Asano [8] introduce the minutiae polygons by including more information

S.-W. Lee and S.Z. Li (Eds.): ICB 2007, LNCS 4642, pp. 134–143, 2007.

near the bifurcation minutiae. As for the latter point, there is relatively less work. AKJ [2] adapt the explicit alignment method in global matching procedure. Bazen and Gerez [6] introduce an implicit alignment using *thin plate template spline*. Both explicit and implicit alignments need reference points. Sharat Chikkerur [7] introduces a graph matching algorithm *CBFS* without alignment. Y. Feng and J. Feng [1] give a definition of local compatibility in an attempt to measure the coherence of local structure pairs and embed it in global matching process.

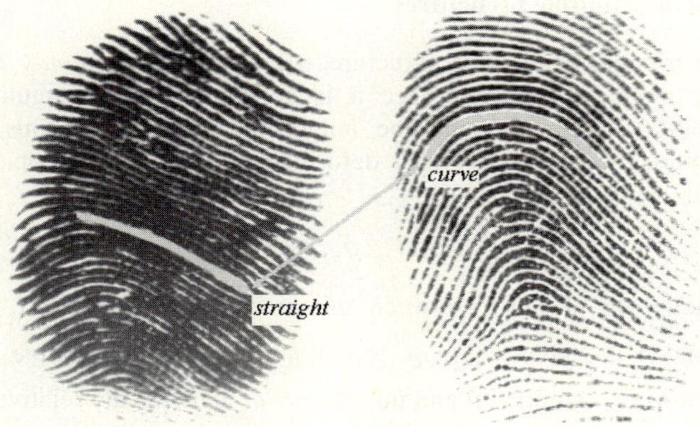

Fig. 1. Two impressions of the same fingerprint (FVC2004 DB1_A 14_3 and 14_6). Because of nonlinear deformation, the ridge in the left impression is closed to a straight line while the correspondent ridge in the right impression is a curve.

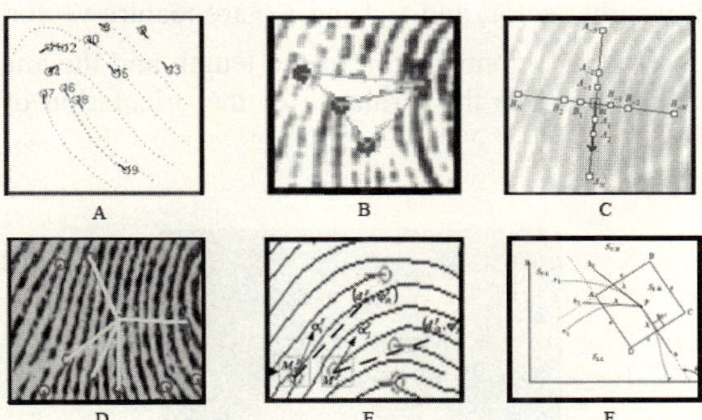

Fig. 2. Minutiae structures: A, minutiae whip; B, minutiae triangle; C, minutiae orientation cross: minutiae structure with local orientation; D, K-plet; E, minutiae stick; F, minutiae polygon.

2 Proposed Method

This paper shows the natural way in which local matches grow into global match using a competition strategy. First, candidates of minutiae triangle are obtained; and then we let candidates of minutiae structures grow into larger local structures (called *growing regions*), based on which we define the *credibility* of each minutiae triangle; finally, *growing regions* compete and fuse into a much larger local structure (called *fusion region*). The matching score is calculated based on the evaluation of both the *growing region* and the *fusion region*. In this way, we obtain the match result without alignment. The following part of this paper is arranged by the flow of the growing and fusing sequence of local, from minutiae to minutiae triangles, to *growing region*, to *fusion region*.

2.1 Matching of Minutiae Structures

With minutiae triangle being local structure, we adopt the *Delaunay Triangulation* method to get minutiae triangles since it is an equiangular triangulation method concerning both of the angle and the length of the triangle, thus making the triangulation more robust for nonlinear deformation. We define a rotation-invariant feature vector:

$$V_{tri} = (d_{pm}, d_{pn}, \rho_p, \rho_m, \theta_{pm}, \theta_{pn})$$

where d_{pi} denotes the distance between minutiae p and minutiae i, ρ_p is $\angle mpn$, ρ_m is $\angle nmp$ and ρ_n is $\angle mnp$ ($\rho_p \geq \rho_m \geq \rho_n$), θ_{pi} denotes the relative radial angle between directions of minutiae p and minutiae i, θ_{pm} denotes the relative radial angle between directions of minutiae p and minutiae m, as in Fig. 3. Now the distance of minutiae triangles can be defined by the following equation:

$$D_{tri}(V_{tri}^1, V_{tri}^2) = W_{tri}^T | V_{tri}^1 - V_{tri}^2 |,$$

where W_{tri} is a 1×6 weight vector, and V_{tri}^1 and V_{tri}^2 are feature vectors of two minutiae triangles. We can increase the contribution of the length and the angle of the triangle while at the same time decrease the influence of the orientation of the minutiae by adjusting W_{tri}.

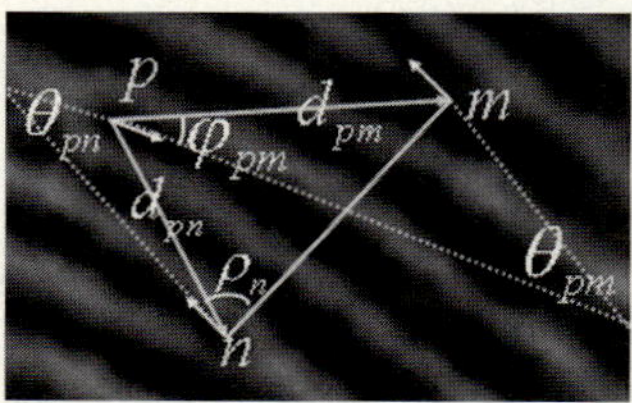

Fig. 3. Minutia triangle constructed by three minutiae *p, m* and *n*

2.2 Growing Region and Credibility of Minutiae Structures

In this stage, the minutiae triangle grows into *the growing region*, a larger matched local. In according to the similarity of *growing regions*, we define the *credibility* of the minutiae structure.

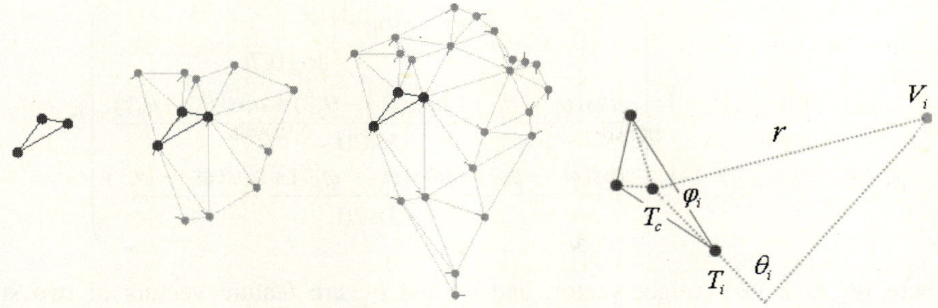

Fig. 4. Left: A *core candidate triangle* grows into a *growing region*; Right: The feature vector of a star point in the *growing region* is defined by the affine transform invariant feature vector $V_{sp} = \{\theta_1, \theta_2, \theta_3, \varphi_1, \varphi_2, \varphi_3\}$

In the work of Y.S. Feng and J.F. Feng [1], they implicitly use the neighbor minutiae triangle to define the credibility of minutiae triangle. But due to the independent construction of minutiae triangles in template fingerprint and query fingerprint, a candidate triangle can be elected only when their neighbor minutiae triangles are candidate minutiae triangles.

In this paper, we give a more reasonable definition of the *credibility* of a candidate of minutiae structure with the neighbor minutiae of the minutiae triangle. *The growing region* is developed from *a core candidate triangle* by including all the other minutiae triangles that satisfying either one of the following condition: a) the minutiae triangle has at least one common vertex with the *core candidate triangle*; b) neighboring triangles of the minutiae triangle has at least one common vertex with the *core candidate triangle* as in Fig. 4 left. For each pair of core candidate triangles, we get a pair of *growing regions* which is actually a pair of point sets. Calculating the similarity of two *growing regions* can be treated as calculating the similarity of two point sets. Since the correspondence of the three vertex of the *core candidate triangle is known*, we can further simplify it to a string matching question. For each Minutiae point (V_i, we call it star point) in the *growing regions*, it can be identified by the affine transformation invariant feature vector:

$$V_{sp} = \{r, \theta_1, \theta_2, \theta_3, \varphi_1, \varphi_2, \varphi_3\},$$

where r is the Euler distance between the star point, T_c is the center of the core candidate structure, θ_i is the angle between line T_iT_c and the minutiae direction of V_i, and φ_i is the angle between line T_iT_c and line V_iT_c as in Fig.4 right. Then we have the definition of the distance between two star points:

$$D_{sp}(V_{sp}^1, V_{sp}^2) = W_{sp1}^T f(V_{sp}^1, V_{sp}^2),$$

$$f\left(V_{sp}^{\ 1},V_{sp}^{\ 2}\right)=\begin{pmatrix} \left|\log r^1-\log r^2\right| \Big/ \left|\log 0.7\right| \\ \dfrac{abs(\theta_1^{\ 1}-\theta_1^{\ 2})+abs(\theta_2^{\ 1}-\theta_2^{\ 2})+abs(\theta_3^{\ 1}-\theta_3^{\ 2})}{3\times 30} \\ \dfrac{abs(\varphi_1^{\ 1}-\varphi_1^{\ 2})+abs(\varphi_2^{\ 1}-\varphi_2^{\ 2})+abs(\varphi_3^{\ 1}-\varphi_3^{\ 2})}{3\times 20} \end{pmatrix},$$

where W_{sp1} is a 1×3 weight vector, and $V_{sp}^{\ 1}$ and $V_{sp}^{\ 2}$ are feature vectors of two star points. We can further define the similarity of two star points as:

$$\sigma(V_{sp}^{\ 1},V_{sp}^{\ 2})=\begin{cases} 100\times\exp\left\{-W_{sp2}^{\ T}f^2(V_{sp}^{\ 1},V_{sp}^{\ 2})\right\} & if\ D_{sp}(V_{sp}^{\ 1},V_{sp}^{\ 2})<b_{sp} \\ 0 & else \end{cases}$$

In our experiment on FVC2004, $W_{sp1}=(1.2,1.2,0.8)^T$, $W_{sp2}=(0.5,0.5,0.5)^T$, and $b_{sp}=1.8$.

We convert the unordered star points of *the growing region* into an ordered sequence by arranging them in the increasing order of φ_1. And then we adopt the dynamic programming approach [6], which bases on string matching, to get matched number of star points.

The creditability of the core candidate triangle pair is determined by the similarity of *growing regions* which represent local areas. In our experiment, the creditability of the minutiae structure pair is defined as:

$$CR=n,$$

where n is the number of matched minutiae in the pair of *growing regions*. In this way, the minutiae structure pair gain more credit if it have more matched minutiae in its *growing regions*. The *growing region* has a larger area than the minutiae triangle; therefore it is more affected by the nonlinear deformation; but compare to the global region it is still less affected by the nonlinear deformation.

2.3 Fusing of Growing Regions and the Compatibility of Minutiae Structure

Human experts usually pay special attention to the interrelation of some candidate minutiae structures and double check the neighborhood of the minutiae structure. In order to imitate this human behavior, we propose a measurement for the coherence of local structure pairs, called *local structure compatibility*. In according to the compatibility of minutiae structures, all *growing regions* are fused into a *fusion region*. The fusing process is done by a majority voting among candidate local structures during which candidate local structures compete against each other.

2.3.1 The Compatibility of Minutiae Structure

Some candidates of minutiae triangle pairs we get from the local matching process may not be compatible. They are not compatible because of the relative position or relative pose or both. In order to depict this difference, we first define the feature vector of two minutiae structure as:

$$V_{mm} = \{r, \varphi_1, \varphi_2, \varphi_3, \theta_1, \theta_2, \theta_3\}$$

where r is the distance between minutiae triangles, φ_i is the angle from line $p_c m_c$ to the line $p_c p_i$, θ_i is the angle from line $p_c m_c$ to line $m_c m_i$ as in Fig. 5 left. Then we define the compatibility of minutiae triangles as:

$$CO = G\left(W \cdot \left|V_{mm}^{\ 1} - V_{mm}^{\ 2}\right|\right),$$

where $G(x)$ is monotonically decreasing function and W is a weight vector. We simply choose $G(x)$ as:

$$G(x) = \begin{cases} 1 & x < b_{co} \\ 0 & else \end{cases}.$$

where b_{co} is predefined boundary. Since V_{mm} only accounts for the Euler distance of two minutiae triangles, it can not discriminate the topological difference of two pairs of minutiae triangles. Therefore, we define three types of topological condition to check the compatibility of minutiae triangles as in Fig. 5 right: A, separate; B, share one vertex; C, share two vertices.

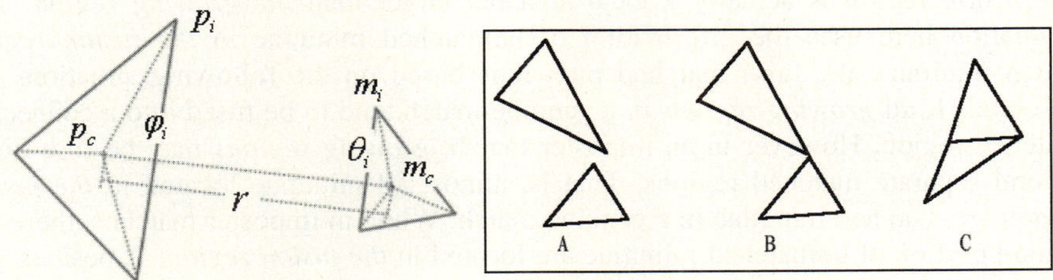

Fig. 5. Left, the feature vector of two triangle local structure can be defined by $\{r, \{\varphi_i\}, \{\theta_i\}\}$; Right, three kinds of topological conditions to check the compatibility of minutiae triangles: A, separate; B, share one vertex; C, share two vertices.

2.3.2 Majority Voting Among Minutiae Structure

In the fusing process, the possibly largest group of minutiae structures that are most compatible with each other are selected. We hold the majority voting with competition strategy, in which every pair of minutiae structures scores another one and only those candidate minutiae structure pairs that have a score larger than a certain value b_{mv} can survive and be fused into a global match region. And then all three vertices of compatible minutiae triangles together with their matched neighbor minutiae are labeled as matched minutiae. Sometimes a minutia in the template fingerprint may several possible matched minutiae in the query fingerprint obtained by different LMR. In this case, these minutiae correspondences are not reliable and are omitted.

```
Algorithm: Majority Voting among Minutiae structures
1, Let Vote[i], i=1,2,...,n represent the vote of each pair of
   minutiae structure, and let {Q_i,T_i,CR_i},i=1,2,...,n represent
   candidate minutiae structures and their credibility
2, Initialization: Vote[i]=CR_i ;
3, Scoring:
   for i = 1 to n-1
      for j = i+1 to n
            CO = the compatibility of {Q_i,T_i}and{Q_j,T_j}
            Vote [i] = Vote[i] + CR_j × CO
            Vote[j] = Vote[j] + CR_i × CO
      end
  end
```

After the fusing process, all the compatible *growing regions* are fused into a larger local (called *fusion region). The fusion region* is a circle area that can just hold all the matched minutiae inside.

2.3.3 Evaluation of the Fusion Region

The fusion region is actually a local area but larger than *the growing region*. The evaluation here uses the information of unmatched minutiae in *the fusion region* which minimize the false matched rate. It is based on the following situations we observed: 1, all *growing regions* in a genuine match tend to be fused into a connected matched region. However in an imposter match, *growing regions* may be fused into several separate matched regions. That is, almost all minutiae located in *the fusion region* are matched minutiae in a genuine match. While in imposter matches, there are a good portion of unmatched minutiae are located in *the fusion region*; 2, besides, the deformation of *the fusion region* is consistent in a genuine match, either squeezing, tensing, or rotating in the same direction. And it is not true for an imposter match.

A critical function is used to evaluate the fusing result:

$$C_{GMA} = \frac{n}{\max(n_{ft}, n_{fq})},$$

where n is the number of matched minutiae between the template fingerprint and the query fingerprint, and n_{ft} and n_{fq} are the numbers of minutiae located in *the fusion region* in the template fingerprint and query fingerprint correspondingly.

2.4 Scoring

The scoring process uses the information lying in the local as well as in the global to measure the similarity of local structures when they grow. The match score is calculated as:

$$Score = 100\frac{n^2}{n_t n_q} n_{LMR} C_{GMR} ,$$

where n_{LMA} is the number of *growing regions* and C_{GMR} is the evaluation of *the fusion region*.

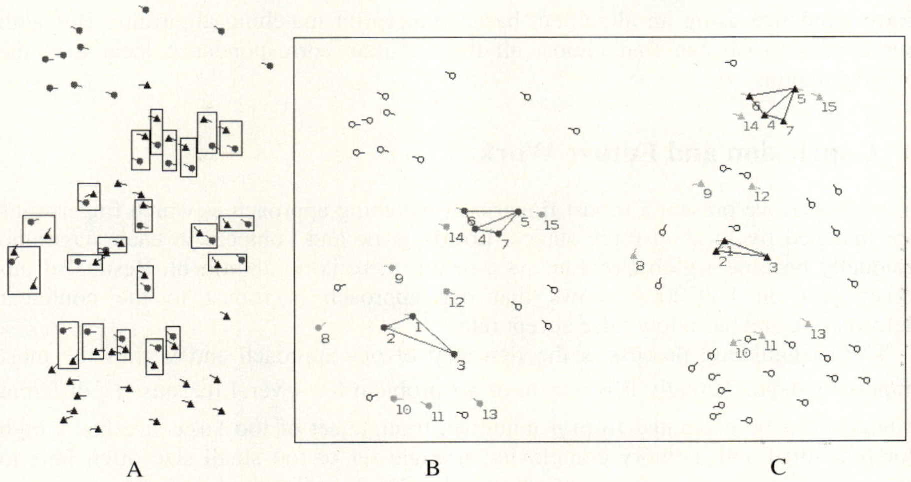

Fig. 6. Comparing the matching result of fingerprints with large nonlinear deformation between the alignment base method and our method: A, shows minutiae correspondence of two impressions of a fingerprint after alignment manually; B and C, show minutiae correspondences obtained by our approach

Table 1. Result of our method on the database of FVC2004

Database FVC2004	EER (%)	FMR100 (%)	FMR1000 (%)	ZeroFMR (%)
DB1_a	3.819	7.363	7.354	12.200
DB2_a	4.712	8.854	8.961	15.769
DB3_a	2.923	4.201	4.249	7.592

3 Experiments and Results

Our experiment is performed on fingerprint databases of FVC2004 (DB1_A, DB2_A, DB3_A). Each of the three fingerprint databases has 8 fingerprints of 100 fingers totally 800 fingerprints. This dataset is available on website of FVC 2004, and is proved to be the most difficult for most methods because no efforts were made to control image quality and the sensor platens were not systematically cleaned [9]. And we take the standard performance evaluation indicators of FVC: genuine and imposter score distribution, equal error rate (EER) and ROC [10].

With only minutiae information, our approach has EER of 3.8%, 4.7%, 2.9% on the three databases of FVC2004 (DB1_a, DB2_a, DB3_a correspondingly). The average processing time is 0.03 seconds per matching on an AMD64 3200+ 1GB PC under Windows 2003. There are two impression of a fingerprint from FVC2004 DB1_A (14_3 14_6) as in Fig.1. Because of nonlinear deformation, the ridge in the left impression is approximately a straight line while the correspondent ridge in the right impression is curve. The minutiae correspondences are pointed out manually after alignment in Fig.6 left from which we can see that it is hard to find the correspondence using an alignment based fingerprint matching algorithm. But with our approach, we can find almost all the minutiae correspondence located in the overlap region.

4 Conclusion and Future Work

In the paper, we present a robust fingerprint matching approach in which fingerprints are matched by local in three stages. Locals grow and compete in each stage and gradually become a global region. As a result, there is no alignment. Results of our experiment on FVC2004 shows that our approach is robust to the nonlinear deformation and has a low false accept rate.

The triangulation process is the first step of our approach and is thus the most important stage. Actually it is a state-of-art problem for several reasons: C_n^3 different triangles can be generated from n minutiae; triangle set of too large size has a high computational and memory complexity; triangle set of too small size often fails to have common triangles. In our experiment the Delaunay Triangulation can get a more reliable triangle set than the k-neighbor method [1][4].

The evaluation and the growing strategy applied to the matched local estimate how well locals match. So it has to account for the deformation of fingerprint which unfortunately lacks efficient description. In our method we skip this problem by stress more on the number of matched minutiae. In future work, we will understand the nonlinear deformation of fingerprint and give a more reasonable definition of the matched local.

Acknowledgments. This work was supported by NSFC(60575002、60635030) and NKBRPC (2004CB318000) and Program for New Century Excellent Talents in University. Thanks all reviewers for their useful comments.

References

1. Feng, Y., Feng, J.: A Novel Fingerprint Matching Scheme Based on Local Structure Compatibility. In: ICPR2006, vol. 4, track 4, Thu-O-II-1b (2006)
2. Jain, A., Hong, L.: On-line fingerprint verification. IEEE Trans. PAMI. 19(4), 302–314 (1997)

3. Zhu, E.: Fingerprint matching based on global alignment of multiple reference minutiae. Pattern Recognition 38, 1685–1694 (2005)
4. Jiang, X., Yau, W.-Y.: Fingerprint minutiae matching based on the local and global structures. In: ICPR2000, vol. 2, pp. 1038–1041 (2000)
5. He, Y., Tian, J.: Fingerprint Matching Based on Global Comprehensive Similarity. IEEE Trans. PAMI 28(6), 850–862 (2006)
6. Bazen, A.M., Gerez, S.H.: Fingerprint matching by thin-plate spline modeling of elastic deformations. Pattern Recognition 36, 1859–1867 (2003)
7. Chikkerur, S., Govindaraju, V., Cartwright, A.N.: K-plet and Coupled BFS: A Graph Based Fingerprint Representation and Matching Algorithm. In: ICB2006 (2006)
8. Liang, X., Asano, T.: Fingerprint Matching Using Minutia Polygons. In: ICPR2006, vol. 1, track 4, Mon-O-IV-2 (2006)
9. Fingerprint Verification Competition: (FVC2004) (2004), http://bias.csr.unibo.it/fvc2004
10. Cappelli, R., Maio, D., Maltoni, D., Wayman, J., Jain, A.K.: Performance Evaluation of Fingerprint verification systems. IEEE Trans. PAMI. 28(1), 3–18 (2006)

Automatic Facial Pose Determination of 3D Range Data for Face Model and Expression Identification

Xiaozhou Wei, Peter Longo, and Lijun Yin

Department of Computer Science,
State University of New York at Binghamton, Binghamton, NY

Abstract. Many of the contemporary 3D facial recognition and facial expression recognition algorithms depend on locating primary facial features, such as the eyes, nose, or lips. Others are dependent on determining the pose of the face. We propose a novel method for limiting the search space needed to find these "interesting features." We then show that our algorithm can be used in conjunction with surface labeling to robustly determine the pose of a face. Our approach does not require any type of training. It is pose-invariant and can be applied to both manually cropped models and raw range data, which can include the neck, ears, shoulders, and other noise. We applied the proposed algorithm to our created 3D range model database, the experiments show the promising results to classify individual faces and individual facial expressions.

Keywords: Surface Normal Difference, Facial Pose Detection; 3D range model.

1 Introduction

The facial pose estimation is a first critical step towards developing a successful system for both face recognition [21] and facial expression recognition [15]. The majority of existing systems for facial expression recognition [21, 12] and face recognition [13, 14, and 18] operate in 2D space. Unfortunately, 2D data is unsatisfactory because it is inherently unable to handle faces with large head rotation, subtle skin movement, or lighting change with varying postures. With the recent advance of 3D imaging systems [23, 11], research on face and facial expression recognition using 3D data has been intensified [8, 9, 10, 16, 19, and 22]. However, almost all existing 3D-based recognition systems are based on *static* 3D facial data. We are interested in researching the face and facial expression recognition in a *dynamic* 3D space.

One of the prerequisites of dynamic 3D facial data analysis is to design an algorithm that can robustly determine a face's pose. Previously, a number of methods have been proposed for determining the pose of a face in 2D and 3D space. Most can be broadly categorized as being either feature-based [2] or appearance-based [6]. The feature-based methods attempt to relate facial pose to the spatial arrangements of significant facial features. The appearance-based methods consider the face in its entirety [5]. Recently, approaches have been developed that combine feature-based and appearance-based techniques [8, 9], the results are very encouraging. Some

S.-W. Lee and S.Z. Li (Eds.): ICB 2007, LNCS 4642, pp. 144–153, 2007.

Support Vector Regression based approaches [3] have shown impressive results, but they require the use of a training set.

In this paper, we describe a pose and expression invariant algorithm that can robustly determine a face's pose. We have tested our algorithm on preprocessed, manually cropped 3D facial models and on unprocessed raw 3D data coming directly from our dynamic 3D imaging system.

The general framework of our approach is outlined in Figure 1. The first step is to remove the image's boundary since there is no guarantee that it is smoothly cropped. Then, we apply our novel Surface Normal Difference (SND) algorithm, which produces groups of triangles. The groups containing the fewest triangles are ignored, and the triangles in the other groups are labeled as "potentially significant." The Principal Component Analysis (PCA) algorithm is run on the vertices of the "potentially significant" triangles in order to align the model in the Z direction and determine the location of the nose tip. Finally, we label the very concave "potentially significant" triangles as "significant," and use the resulting groups, as well as the symmetry property of the face, to find the nose bridge point. At final, we evaluate the proposed algorithms through the experiments on our developed systems of dynamic 3D face recognition and dynamic 3D facial expression recognition. Each part of our framework will be elaborated on in the following sections.

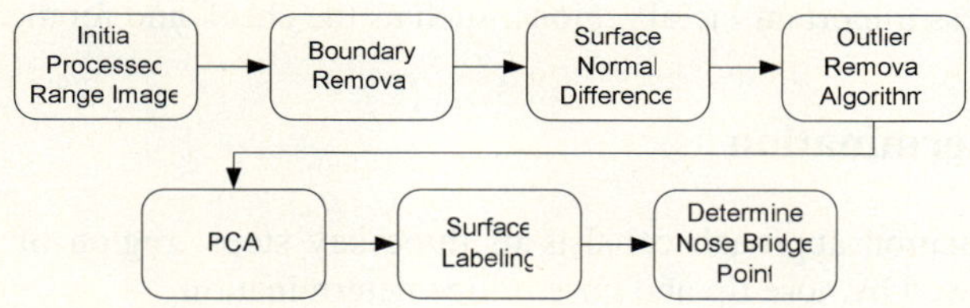

Fig. 1. Pipeline for determining the pose of a 3D facial range model

2 Surface Normal Difference (SND)

Let us define a spatial triangle as a tuple of three vertices. Assume a triangle t = (v1, v2, v3), which has a three dimensional normal vector, n_t, consisting of x, y, and z components. Assume a triangle s = (s1, s2, s3). We call s a "neighbor of" t if the sets {v1, v2, v3} and {s1, s2, s3} are not disjoint.

$$neighbor\quad (s,t) \longrightarrow \{v1, v2, v3\} \cap \{s1, s2, s3\} \neq 0$$

Assume a set of triangles, N, which contains all of t's neighboring triangles. For each triangle, u with normal n_u, in N, we determine the angle, θ_{tu}, between the normal vectors of t and u.

$$\theta_{tu} = \cos^{-1}((n_t \bullet n_u)/(|n_t| \times |n_u|))$$

We determine the maximum value of θ_{tu} and call it θ_{max}. If θ_{max} is greater than a specified angular tolerance, δ, we add t to set G. Otherwise, we add t to set L.

We repeat this procedure for all triangles in the facial mesh. Upon completion, we label the triangles in G as "potentially significant" and the triangles in L as "not significant."

Fig. 2. Neighbor normal illustration: (a) Mesh comprising part of a cheek; (b) Mesh comprising part of an eye

Figure 2a shows a mesh comprising part of a cheek and Figure 2b shows a mesh comprising part of an eye. In both figures, *t* is the blue triangle. The triangles in *N* are colored black. n_t is represented by the thick yellow line protruding from the blue triangle. n_u, for each triangle in *N*, is represented by the thick green line protruding out of each black triangle.

θ_{max} is much less in Figure 2a than in Figure 2b. This is what we expect and what our approach is based on. We have found that many of the triangles in important facial regions, including the nose, eye, and lip regions, have much larger θ_{max} values than those in less important facial regions, such as the cheek and forehead regions.

3 Pose Determination

Our pose estimation approach consists of three key steps: region of interest (ROI) detection followed by nose tip and nose bridge determination.

Figure 3 illustrates a processed range image going through our pipeline, with Figure 3a showing a processed image from our database.

3.1 Determination of Region of Interest

The first step is to remove the 3D range image's boundary triangles since the boundary may be rough, and a rough boundary would negatively affect our approach's accuracy. Figure 3b shows the result of this initial step.

Next, the Surface Normal Difference (SND) algorithm is applied. The normal of every remaining triangle in the 3D mesh is determined, and the maximum angle that each triangle's normal makes with an adjacent triangle's normal is calculated. If this maximum angle is greater than an angular tolerance, δ, both triangles whose normal vectors made the angle are marked as "potentially significant." Otherwise, the corresponding triangle is marked as "not significant." This procedure is repeated, by incrementing δ, until the number of "potentially significant" triangles is less than α. We initially set δ to 10 degrees and have empirically set α to 3000. Figure 3c shows the "potentially significant" triangles after applying the SND algorithm.

Usually, the SND algorithm will keep a number of small, connected surfaces that are not part of a significant facial region. For example, it may keep a surface corresponding to a pimple on the forehead or a cut on the cheek. Most of the time, these outlying surfaces are composed of a very small number of triangles relative to the largest remaining connected surface, which usually contains, minimally, the eye and nose regions. In order to filter out these outlying surfaces, the maximum number of triangles contained in any connected surface ρ is determined. Any surface composed of fewer than κ percent of ρ triangles is considered an outlying surface, and all of the triangles in these outlying surfaces are marked as "not significant." We have empirically set κ to 0.1.

At this point, a vertex is labeled as "significant" if it is part of a "potentially significant" triangle. All other vertices are labeled as "not significant." We call the mesh comprised of the remaining "potentially significant" triangles a Sparse Feature Mesh (SFM). The SFM is shown in Figure 3d.

3.2 Determination of Nose Tip

The PCA algorithm is run on the SFM vertices in order to align the model in the Z direction and determine the location of the nose tip (NT). Figure 3e shows the result of this step.

$$NT \in V_{sig} \mid \max(z)$$

where V_{sig} denotes the set of "significant" vertices. Note that the principal depth direction (Z) of a model can be reliably estimated with the minimum eigen-value, given the SFM vertices, even though the X and Y components may not be aligned to the correct model orientation.

The shape index [1], which is a surface primitive based on surface curvatures, is calculated at each "significant" vertex. All triangles that have at least one very concave vertex (a shape index less than -.50) are marked as "significant." All other triangles are marked as "not significant." A number of discreet groups of triangles, usually numbering around 20, remain. These groups usually include the corners of the eyes and the sides of the nose and mouth. The "significant" triangles are shown in Figure 3f.

3.3 Determination of Nose Bridge

In order to locate the nose bridge point, all pairs of groups meeting certain general geometric criteria are iterated over, and the symmetry of the shape indices of the vertices near each line connecting a pair of candidate groups (L_{CG}) and near that line translated to the nose tip (L_{NT}) is calculated. The sum of these two symmetry values is minimized and the line perpendicular to the L_{CG} that passes through the nose tip (H_{NT}) is inspected.

All the "significant" vertices within an XY distance of γ_1 from a line connecting two candidate groups are the vertices that compose a L_{CG}.

$$L_{CG}(g1, g2) = \forall (v \in V_{sig} \mid |dist_{xy}(v, \overline{g_1 g_2})| < \gamma_1)$$

where g1 and g2 are candidate groups and γ_1 is the 3D length of an arbitrary mesh triangle's side. The two points of maximum concavity on either side of the midpoint of the L_{CG}, at least a certain distance, γ_2, from the midpoint, are found, and the point between these two maximums with the greatest Z value is referred to as the PBMZ.

$$PBMZ(V) = v \in V \mid \max(z)$$

where V denotes the vertices in the region of interest. Let B be the set containing the L_{CG} vertices between these two maximums.

$$B = v \in V \mid v \geq (\max\ 1) \wedge v \leq (\max\ 2)$$

The symmetry of the shape indices of B about the PBMZ is determined by summing the mean squared differences of the shape indices of the 0.50*|B| vertices in B closest to the PBMZ. If there are not at least 0.25*|B| vertices between the PBMZ and either maximum, the L_{CG} is rejected because the nose bridge point is expected to be a point of close to maximum Z almost exactly in-between two maximum concavities (i.e. the eye corners). The L_{CG} is translated to the nose tip and the above procedure is repeated for determining the symmetry of the L_{NT}.

$$sym(B) = \sum_{i=1}^{.25*|B|} (b_{PBMZ(V)-i} - b_{PBMZ(V)+i})^2 / |B|$$

The optimal groups are found by using the symmetry minimization method, as defined below:

$$g1_{opt}, g2_{opt} \in G_{sig} \mid \min(sym(L_{CG}(g1,g2)) + sym(L_{NT}(g1,g2)))$$

If the sum is minimal, we inspect the corresponding H_{NT}, which is composed of the "significant" vertices within an XY distance of γ_1 from the line perpendicular to the L_{CG} that passes through the nose tip.

$$H_{NT}(g1,g2) = \forall (v \in V_{sig} \mid |dist_{xy}(v, \perp_{NT}(\overline{g1g2}))| < \gamma_1)$$

where $\perp_{NT}(\overline{g1g2})$ denotes the line perpendicular to $\overline{g1g2}$ that passes through the nose tip. The variances of shape indices of the 0.25*|H_{NT}| vertices closest to the nose tip on each side of the L_{NT} are calculated and compared. The side with the lesser variance is considered the nose bridge side. If either side has fewer than three vertices, the H_{NT} is rejected because the optimal H_{NT} is expected to have a large number of "significant" vertices.

NB_1 is a set containing all of the H_{NT} vertices on one side of the L_{NT} and NB_2 is a set containing all of the H_{NT} vertices on the other side of the L_{NT}. Of these two sets, the one containing the H_{NT} vertices on the nose bridge side of the L_{NT} is renamed $NB_{candidates}$ and the other is renamed $NB_{non\text{-}candidates}$.

$$NB_1 = \forall (v \in H_{NT}(g1,g2) \mid dist_{xy}(v, L_{NT}(g1,g2)) < 0)$$
$$NB_2 = \forall (v \in H_{NT}(g1,g2) \mid v \notin NB_1)$$
$$\text{var}'(V,L) = \text{var}(v \in V \mid dist_{xy}(v,L) <= dist_{xy}(middle(V),L))$$
$$NB_{candidates} = \text{var}'(NB_1, L_{NT}) <= \text{var}'(NB_2, L_{NT})\ ?\ NB_1 : NB_2$$

If a set of nose bridge candidates was found, all the vertices on the "nose bridge side" of the H_{NT} are iterated over. The point with the greatest absolute difference in maximum and minimum curvature that is not the nose tip is concluded to be the nose bridge point (NB).

$$NB \in NB_{candidates} \mid \max(|k_{\max}(NB) - k_{\min}(NB)|) \wedge NB \neq NT$$

where k_{min} is the minimum surface curvature and k_{max} is the maximum surface curvature

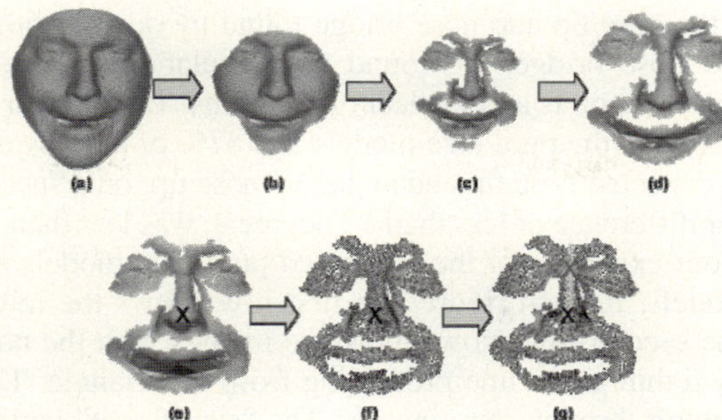

Fig. 3. Finding the pose of a 3D range image. (a) The initial range model; (b) The range model after initial boundary removal; (c) The range image after application of our SND algorithm; (d) The range image after running our outlier removal algorithm; (e) The range image after running the PCA algorithm (the nose tip is marked with a large black "X"); (f) "significant" vertices in blue and "significant" triangles in red; (g) The nose bridge is marked with a large red "X".

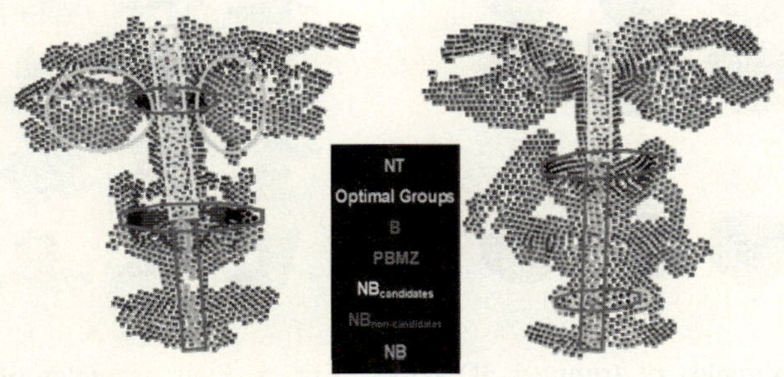

Fig. 4. Two models wit0068 the NT, Optimal Groups, B, PBMZ, $NB_{candidates}$, $NB_{non\text{-}candidates}$, and NB labeled

Figure 4 shows the key groups involved in pinpointing the nose bridge point. The result of this procedure is shown in Figure 3g, where the nose bridge point is marked with a large red "X." The optimal L_{CG} is represented by the green and pink line passing through the nose bridge and the optimal L_{NT} is represented by the black and white line passing through the nose tip. The optimal H_{NT}, on which the nose bridge point lies, is the yellow line.

As a result, the model Z direction, nose tip and nose bridge points uniquely determine the facial pose.

4 Experimental Results

We tested our approach on our created 3D facial expression database [7], which contains 2,500 models. Each model has two types of data: a face data which contains pure face region and a raw data which includes the face region and shoulder. The test subjects cover a wide variety of ethnicities and ages. The subjects expressed seven prototypic facial expressions (neutral, anger, disgust, fear, happiness, sadness, and surprise).

After comparing the nose tip and nose bridge found by our algorithm with a manually labeled nose tip and nose bridge, we found the angular difference between the lines connecting the former two points and the latter two points. The angular difference was less than 10 degrees for 98% of the pure face models and 87% of the raw data. The maximum distance between an expected nose tip and an actual nose tip, on a successful test (one that resulted in an angular difference of less than 15 degrees), was less than 7 units.

Figure 5 shows four examples of the processed pure face models and Figure 6 shows examples of raw models. In each figure, the first row shows the initial texture-mapped 3D range image. The second row shows the same images with the normal of each mesh triangle indicated by a thin green line protruding from the triangle. The third row shows the image after passing it through our pipeline. The "significant" vertices are represented by blue dots and the "significant" triangles are represented by red triangles. The nose tip is marked with a large black "X" and the nose bridge is marked with a large red "X." The fourth row shows the nose tip and the nose bridge marked on the original texture-mapped range images.

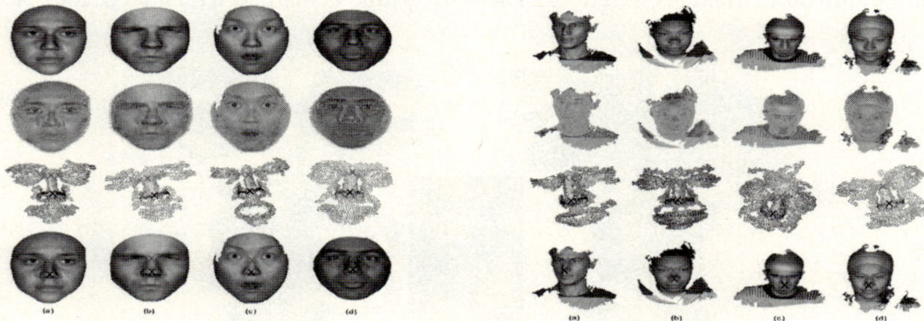

Fig. 5. Four examples of trimmed 3D range models with different expressions. The second row shows normals of the models.

Fig. 6. Four examples of raw 3D range models with different head poses

5 Applications of Pose Estimation for Identification of Range Models and Their Expressions

We applied our pose estimation algorithm to the 3D model sequences, which are created from our facial expression database [7] using our structure-lighting based capture system. There are 600 model sequences with 100 subjects. Examples are shown in Figure 7.

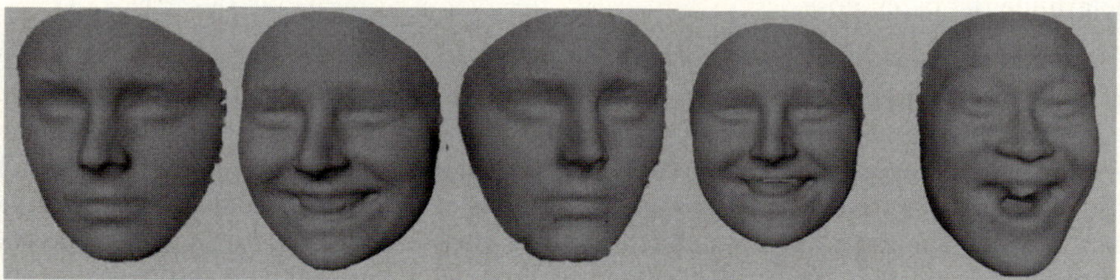

Fig. 7. Example frames of model sequences of two subjects with different poses and different expressions

5.1 Face Model Classification

We applied a generic-model based tracking approach to estimate the motion of facial surfaces. The poses of range models in each frame are estimated. Since the poses of all the frames of a model sequence are estimated, we normalize them to the front view and applied the model adaptation algorithm [20] to fit a low-resolution generic model to the high-resolution range models. The characteristics of the facial surface are captured by the adapted tracking model. Since a model sequence contains various facial expressions, we warp them to a standard shape which exhibits a neutral expression. Then, the entire warped frame models of the sequence are averaged, resulting in the individual's representative model, based on which the subsequent face recognition is carried out. We used 600 3D model sequences to test our face recognition algorithm. Based on our previous approach used in [17], we conduct the optimal feature selection, and compare the individual's representative models to the database models. The recognition is based on the feature correlation criterion. The average correct recognition rate is 90.7%. About 94 percent of facial poses of the entire database have been correctly estimated.

5.2 Face Model Expression Classification

We applied our developed approach as in [20] to analyze facial model expressions. The approach is briefly described as follows: (1) Estimate model poses in each frame; (2) Fit a tracking model to the 3D facial scan sequence; (3) Label the facial surface model using curvature information and generate a label histogram map; (4) Construct a facial expression descriptor using the tracked motion vectors and the facial surface feature label map.

Given the face scan's pose and the positions of its eyes and nose from the previous stage, we can rigidly adapt the tracking model to the face scan via the affine transformation. Then a fine adaptation procedure can be conducted in order to deform the tracking model into a non-rigid facial surface area. This procedure is realized by using the energy minimization method based on the dissimilarity (error function) between the tracking model and the face scan [20]. As a result, the 3D motion trajectories are estimated by vectors from the tracked points of the current frame to the corresponding points of the first frame with a neutral expression. Each motion trajectory is represented by a three-tuple vector v_i. Sixty-four feature points on the facial regions (e.g., eyes, nose, mouth, eyebrows, and chin) are selected to construct a facial expression motion vector $\mathbf{t} = [t_1,\ldots,t_{64}]$. It represents the *temporal* facial expression information. In addition, the *spatial* facial expression information, so called facial expression label map (FELM), is created using small scale curvature based labeling approach. The different label distributions show the different facial expression characteristics. For each expression, a FELM vector $\mathbf{s} = [s_1,\ldots,s_n]$ is generated after the model is labeled. Each element e_i of a FELM is a ratio of the number of vertices with a specific label type to the number of vertices in the whole facial region. n denotes the 12 label types (detail in [20]). Given the same facial expression from different subjects, the FELMs of expressive regions exhibit the similar characteristics of histograms.

To this end, a spatio-temporal facial expression descriptor $\mathbf{E_d}=[\mathbf{t}, \mathbf{s}]$ is constructed for each expression model. We conducted person-independent facial expression recognition experiments using our dynamic 3D facial expression database, and applied linear discriminant analysis (LDA) to classify the six prototypic facial expressions. The data from 70 subjects are used for training. The remaining 30 subjects are for test. The average correct recognition rate is 84.7%.

6 Limitations and Conclusion

Automatically locating the nose tip and the orientation of a face is crucial for face and facial expression recognition. We have developed an algorithm that decreases the search space needed to find the primary features of a face. This is the first step towards developing an automatic facial and facial expression recognition system. Our approach could be used as a preprocessing step in pose-variant systems to determine the pose of the face and make these systems pose-invariant. Note that the PCA based approach could be potentially used for the pose estimation. However, it may not achieve the satisfactory results since it requires the 'clean' data with a rigid symmetric property, which is not always the case for many of our models.

After using our SND algorithm to eliminate a large number of triangles, we use a curvature-based approach to further decrease the search space. Future improvements could be obtained by applying more accurate curvature estimation methods [4, 6].

Note that in some cases, the nose tip was incorrectly labeled. Since our algorithm is dependent on correctly locating the nose tip, it is not surprising that it found the wrong nose direction. Most of these images contained a large percentage of extraneous data, such as the shoulders and neck, which was not removed by our boundary removal algorithm. Our future work will investigate a method to have our boundary removal algorithm automatically adjust itself depending on the perceived noise of a range model using approaches based on machine learning in order to improve the robustness of the algorithm.

Acknowledgments. This material is based upon work supported by the National Science Foundation under grants IIS-0541044 and IIS 0414029, and the NYSTAR's James D. Watson Investigator Program.

References

[1] Dorai, C., Jain, A.: COSMO-A representation scheme for 3D free-form objects. IEEE Trans. on PAMI 19(10), 1115–1130 (1997)

[2] Hattori, K., Sato, Y.: Estimating pose of human face based on symmetry plane using range and intensity images. In: ICPR 1998 (1998)

[3] Rajwade, A., Levine, M.D.: Facial Pose from 3D Data. Journal of Image and Vision Computing 2007 (to appear)

[4] Razdan, A., Bae, M.: Curvature estimation scheme for triangle meshes using biquadratic Bezier patches. Computer-Aided Design 37(14) (2000)

[5] Srinivasan, S., Boyer, K.L.: Head pose estimation using view based eigenspaces. In: ICPR'02 (2002)

[6] Tanaka, H.T., Ikeda, M.: Curvature-based face surface recognition using spherical correlation-principal directions for curved object recognition. In: ICPR'96, pp. 25–29 (1996)

[7] Yin, L., Wei, X., Sun, Y., Wang, J., Rosato, M.: A 3D facial expression database for facial behavior research. In: IEEE FGR 2006, Southampton, UK, pp. 211–216. IEEE Computer Society Press, Los Alamitos (2006)

[8] Bowyer, K., Chang, K., Flynn, P.: A survey of approaches and challenges in 3D and multi-modal 3D+2D face recognition. CVIU 101(1), 1–15 (2006)

[9] Bronstein, A., Bronstein, M., Kimmel, R.: Three dimensional face recognition. IJCV 5(30) (2005)

[10] Blanz, V., Vetter, T.: Face Recognition Based on Fitting a 3D Morphable Model. IEEE Trans. on PAMI 25(9) (2003)

[11] Chang, Y., Vieira, M., Turk, M., Velho, L.: Automatic 3D facial expression analysis in videos. In: IEEE ICCV05 Workshop on Analysis and Modeling of Faces and Gestures. IEEE Computer Society Press, Los Alamitos (2005)

[12] Cohen, I., Sebe, N., Garg, A., Chen, L., Huang, T.: Facial expression recognition from video sequences: temporal and static modeling. CVIU 91(1) (2003)

[13] Gross, R., et al.: Quo vadis face recognition? In: Workshop on empirical evaluation methods in computer vision (2001)

[14] Li, S., Jain, A.: Handbook of face recognition. Springer, New York (2004)

[15] Pantic, M., et al.: Automatic analysis of facial expressions: the state of the art. IEEE Trans. PAMI 22(12) (2000)

[16] Phillips, P., Flynn, P., Scruggs, T., Bowyer, K., Chang, J., Hoffman, K., Marques, J., Min, J., Worek, W.: Overview of the face recognition grand challenge. In: IEEE CVPR. IEEE Computer Society Press, Los Alamitos (2005)

[17] Sun, Y., Yin, L.: 3d face recognition using two views face modeling and labeling. In: CVPR05 Workshop on A3DISS.

[18] Tang, X., Li, Z.: Video based face recognition using multiple classifiers. In: IEEE FGR04. IEEE Computer Society Press, Los Alamitos (2004)

[19] Lu, X., Jain, A., et al.: Matching 2.5D face scans to 3D models. IEEE Trans. PAMI 28(1), 31–43 (2006)

[20] Yin, L., Wei, X., Longo, P., Bhuvanesh, A.: Analyzing facial expressions using intensity-variant 3d data for human computer interaction. In: ICPR 2006, Hong Kong.

[21] Zhao, W., Chellappa, R., Phillips, P., Rosenfeld, A.: Face recognition: A literature survey. ACM Computing Surveys 35(4) (December 2003)

[22] Kittler, J., Hilton, A., et al.: 3D Assisted Face Recognition: A Survey of 3D Imaging, Modelling and Recognition Approaches. In: CVPR 2005 Workshops on A3DISS.

[23] Wang, Y., Samaras, D., Metaxas, D., Elgammal, A., et al.: High resolution acquisition, learning, transfer of dynamic 3D face expression. In: Eurographics (2004)

SVDD-Based Illumination Compensation for Face Recognition

Sang-Woong Lee[1] and Seong-Whan Lee[2,⋆]

[1] The Robotics Institute, Carnegie Mellon University,
5000 Forbes Ave., Pittsburgh, PA 15213, USA
rhiephil@cs.cmu.edu

[2] Center for Artificial Vision Research, Korea University,
Anam-dong, Seongbuk-ku, Seoul 136-713, Korea
swlee@image.korea.ac.kr

Abstract. Illumination change is one of most important and difficult problems which prevent from applying face recognition to real applications. For solving this, we propose a method to compensate for different illumination conditions based on SVDD(Support Vector Data Description). In the proposed method, we first consider the SVDD training for the data belonging to the facial images under various illuminations, and model the data region for each illumination as the ball resulting from the SVDD training. Next, we compensate for illumination changes using feature vector projection onto the decision boundary of the SVDD ball. Finally, we obtain the pre-image under the identical illumination with input image. By repeated for each person, we can recognize a person with facial images under same illumination. We also perform the face recognition in order to verify the efficacy of proposed method.

Keywords: Illumination compensation, face reconstruction, noise, support vector data description, face recognition.

1 Introduction

With various biometric methods such as finger print, iris, palm, gait and so forth, face recognition technologies have been one of most interesting fields up to recently. While finger print systems are generally used in our life, any face recognition system has not made an attraction to our daily life. Even though several products using face analysis for entertainments, it seems that it takes long times to use face recognition in real life.

The delay of a common product is caused by such actual problems as illumination changes, facial pose variation, facial expression changes, facial aging, different ethnic groups, etc. In the last decade, many researchers have brought up these problem and solution. Recently, Gross and Cohn surveyed the current state of the art in face recognition and made several experiments with variations of these problem and facial databases. They experimentally found that pose and illumination

⋆ Corresponding author.

S.-W. Lee and S.Z. Li (Eds.): ICB 2007, LNCS 4642, pp. 154–162, 2007.

changes are the most affective to the recognition rate [1]. Zhao et al. also identified two key problems with the illumination and pose problem in their survey paper [2]. Tan et al. mentioned the problem from a single image per person in training step and introduced holistic, local, and hybrid method for solving this problem [3]. They have paid much attention to illumination and pose changes.

We focus on solving an illumination problem based on holistic methods. In the holistic methods, while these keep all essential information of facial images, these should consider the variation of illumination using small number of training data. If trained faces have quite a different illumination with a gallery image, recognition rate decreases drastically. In earlier day, Pentland et al. proposed view-based face recognition. They prepared various training data in each change [12]. However, view-based method can not have all training data.

In order to compensating for unknown illumination changes, many approaches have tried to synthesize a new face or remove illumination effect. Gross and Brajovic proposed an image processing approach compensating illumination change. They tried to obtain facial images under consistent illumination condition based on weber's law [4]. Xudong and Lam proposed a local normalization of uneven illumination [5]. Georghiades et al. proposed illumination cone models, which can render an arbitrary illumination using several bases [6]. Zhou et al. proposed an illumination-invariant face recognition using generalized photometric stereo [7]. This also carried out the iteration steps, which takes 2-3 seconds. Song et al. also used photometric stereo method and compensated for the difference between different illumination conditions by linear combination of facial images under different lighting [8]. Both of two approaches combines linear combination of models with Lambertian reflectance and have the limit of linear analysis. Zhang and Samaras proposed harmonic image exemplars, which assume that there is no pose variation [9].

We aim to also synthesize a facial image of each trained person under the same illumination condition as one of input face. In order to accomplish this goal, we extend the concept of SVDD to illumination problem. In section 2, we address a SVDD-based training with general concepts. We explain our compensation approach using vector projection and pre-image synthesis in section 3 and make some experiments to verify our idea in section 4. Finally we make a conclusion on our intuition and experimental proof.

2 Training Diverse Illumination Condition

The SVDD method trains data belonging normal class and defines the region including these data. With trained region, it is possible to detect abnormal data and outlier. This region is called as the ball, B with the center $a \in \Re^d$ and the radius R, and the training data set D consisting of facial images, $x_i \in \Re^d$, $i = 1, \cdots, N$ under diverse illumination. SVDD method used to find a ball which can meet two constraints concurrently. The ball should be as small as possible and should contain as many training data as possible. The trained ball can includes ideally most illumination conditions of one person.

Since it is generally said that illumination change lies on the domain of non-linear problem, balls can wrap very limited class of subsets in SVDD method, which deals with linear problem. To represent more complex decision regions in $\Re^d$, one can use the so-called feature map $\phi : \Re^d \to F$ and hyper-balls, B_F with the center, a_F and the radius, R_F defined on the feature space F. We use the concepts of the slack variable ξ_i, the trade-off constant C, and kernel function K for optimal B_F which contains reasonably large portion of the (transformed) training face data set $D_F = \{\phi(x_i)|i = 1, \cdots, N\} \subset F$. Finally, we can obtain the solution by the following QP:

$$\begin{aligned} &\min_\alpha \textstyle\sum_{i=1}^N \sum_{j=1}^N \alpha_i \alpha_j K(x_i, x_j) - \sum_{i=1}^N \alpha_i K(x_i, x_i) \\ &\text{s. t.} \ \textstyle\sum_{i=1}^N \alpha_i = 1, \ \alpha_i \in [0, C], \ \forall i \end{aligned} \tag{1}$$

The criterion for the normality can be summarized as follows:

$$\begin{aligned} f_F(x) &\triangleq R_F^2 - \|\phi(x) - a_F\|^2 \\ &= R_F^2 - 1 + 2\textstyle\sum_{i=1}^N \alpha_i K(x_i, x) \\ &\quad - \textstyle\sum_{i=1}^N \sum_{j=1}^N \alpha_i \alpha_j K(x_i, x_j) \\ &\geq 0. \end{aligned} \tag{2}$$

This explanation is similarly referred from the paper of Park et al., where they use this SVDD concept for de-noising. They considered noised numeric images as abnormal data and clear numeric images as normal data, respectively in feature space. The projection of the vector of abnormal data is transformed to image space. The pre-image of projected vector results in de-noising one [10]. Lee et al. applied this knowledge to low resolution face recognition. They trained facial images of high resolution. A facial vector is moved to feature space, projected on the surface of the ball, and returned in image space [11].

3 Illumination Compensation

Briefly introducing our approaches, we train several facial images of a person in different illumination as normal class on off-line stage. In Fig. 1, training data set was composed of facial images of same person with various illuminations. As on-line stages, when a facial image is given, this is transformed in feature space and projected onto surface of trained ball, B_F. With this projected vector, we imitate illumination condition of arbitrary facial images (as abnormal) of another person.

The support is expressed by a reasonably small ball containing a reasonably large portion of face feature vectors, $\phi(x_i)$, of different illumination in a feature space. When an abnormal facial image is given as a test input, x, of different person from training class, the network resulting from the SVDD is supposed to recognize the fact that the x does not belong to the normal class; apparently all images in the ball has the same identity. If input image is used from another person under unknown illumination, it may be out of the ball because it has

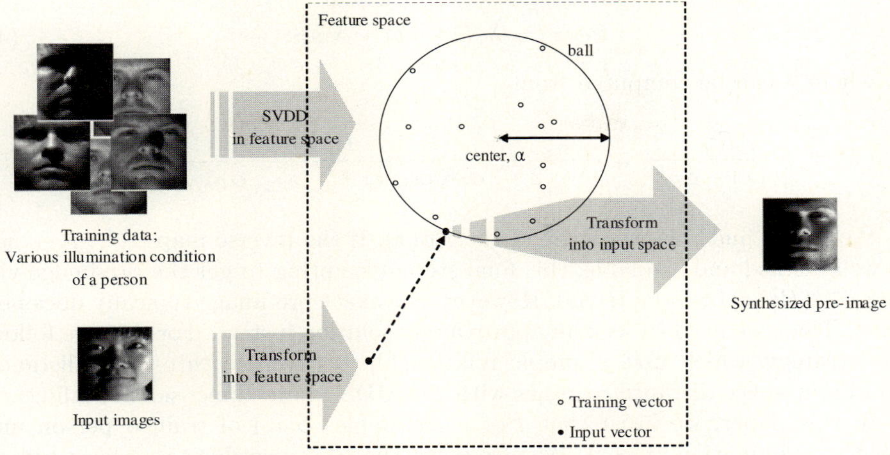

Fig. 1. Basic idea in example for illumination compensation

different shape. When input vector, x is transformed to input feature vector, $\phi(x)$, our intuition is the followings with regard to the vector projection.

- Pre-image of projected input vector, $\phi^{-1}(P\phi(x))$ resembles the facial shape of the trained person
- The illumination condition of $\phi^{-1}(P\phi(x))$ is similar with one of input images, x.

For vector projection and pre-image synthesis, we adopt Park and Kwok's method [10]. It is quite easy to let the feature vector, $\phi(x_i)$, of the abnormal image move toward the center, a_F, of the SVDD ball, B_F, until it reaches the decision boundary, so that it can be tailored enough to be considered as normal[1]. Of course, since the movement starts from the feature, $\phi(x_i)$, there are plenty of reasons to believe that the tailored feature, $P\phi(x_i)$, still contains essential information about illumination condition. In the concrete, when the decision function f_F of Eq. (2) yields a nonnegative value for x, the test input is accepted normal as it is. In the otherwise case, the test input x is considered to be abnormal. For illumination compensation, we move the feature vector $\phi(x)$ toward the center a_F up to the point where it touches the ball B_F. Thus, the outcome of this movement is the following:

$$P\phi(x) = a_F + \frac{R_F}{\|\phi(x) - a_F\|}(\phi(x) - a_F). \tag{3}$$

As a result of the projection, we have the obvious result $\|P\phi(x) - a_F\| = R_F$. Also, note that with $\lambda \triangleq R_F/\|\phi(x) - a_F\|$, the Eq. (3) can be further simplified into

[1] In this paper, we use Gaussian kernel where projected feature vector is located on the surface of the hyper-ball.

$$P\phi(x) = \lambda\phi(x) + (1 - \lambda)a_F, \tag{4}$$

where λ can be computed from

$$\lambda^2 = \frac{R_F^2}{\|\phi(x) - a_F\|^2} = \frac{R_F^2}{(1 - 2\sum_i \alpha_i K(x_i, x) + \sum_i \sum_j \alpha_i \alpha_j K(x_i, x_j))}. \tag{5}$$

We try to find the pre-image of the $P\phi(x)$. If the inverse map $\phi^{-1} : F \rightarrow \Re^d$ is well-defined and available, this final step attempting to get the pre-image via $\hat{x} = \phi^{-1}(P\phi(x))$ will be trivial. However, the exact pre-image typically does not exist. Thus, we need to seek an approximate solution instead. For this, we follow the strategy, which uses a simple relationship between feature-space distance and input-space distance together with the MDS (multi-dimensional scaling).

In this paper, we insist that $P\phi(x_i)$ resembles $\phi(x_i)$ of trained person under the illumination of $\phi(x)$. We also insist that it is possible to perform better recognition with $P\phi(x_i)$ than with $\phi(x_i)$. That is to say, we can find the illumination condition in training dataset, which means that we can match the new gallery image under unknown illumination and we can approximate the illumination parameter from the training dataset. For verifying our assumption, we perform some experiments in Section 4 with popular face database, which includes various illumination conditions.

4 Experimental Results and Analysis

4.1 Facial Databases

For making experiments, we used the CMU PIE DB[13]. It contains 41,368 images of 68 subjects under 13 different poses, 43 different illumination conditions, and with 4 different expressions. 43 illumination variations are composed of 21 different flash directions with room light, 21 different flash directions without room light, and only room light without flash. Among this, we selected 1,428 facial images of $C27$ pose under 21 illumination changes without room light(like 3 images of first low in Fig. 2 (b)). Then we converted them to gray scale images and normalized as same size.

4.2 Pre-Image Synthesis

If a facial image under arbitrary illumination condition is given, we synthesize a new facial image, which is under same illumination with input image by proposed method. Fig. 3 shows the 12 examples of experiments. Input image(left column) is randomly selected in PIE database. It is used for synthesizing a new facial image of another person, who is also randomly selected. As mentioned in previous sections, we carried out several processes and obtained the experimental result(middle column). The original image(right column) is shown by selecting the facial image of ground truth, which we have already known. We aim that

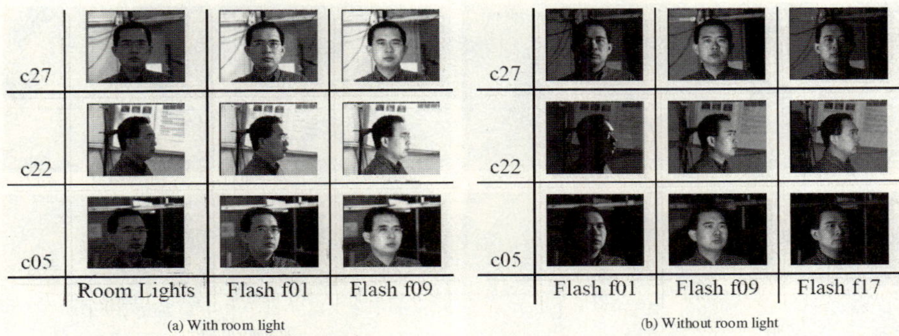

Fig. 2. Examples of facial images in CMU PIE Database [13]

the result is exactly same with the ground truth image. As shown in Fig. 3, two images almost resemble each other. However, in detailed view, there is little difference of shadow and reflectance. This may be caused by sleek surface. We could not consider this property. In order to compare two images, we measured the difference of pixel intensity. In other view, our SVDD-based method is called as non-linear combination of trained data using kernel trick. In this view, it is efficient way to compare linear combination method proposed by Moon et al.[8]. Table 1 shows the comparison with this method. As a result, the mean error of our proposed method is lower than one of theirs.

4.3 Performance in Face Recognition

In addition, our method is also useful in view-based face recognition. When recognizing a facial image, each training face is matched with input image. If two images were captured under different illumination condition, the recognition rate would be decreased. In case of this, we can repeat our approach for the illumination compensation of each training data to the direction of the illumination in input image.

In this strategy, we performed similar experiments with previous one. Firstly, we selected an input face under unknown illumination condition. Secondly, we synthesized each face by repeating all people in training set. Finally we recognized

Table 1. The results of face recognition with comparison

	Average of face recognition rate (%)	Average of image difference (grayscale)
Previous Method [8]	89	10.76
Proposed Method	94	6.73

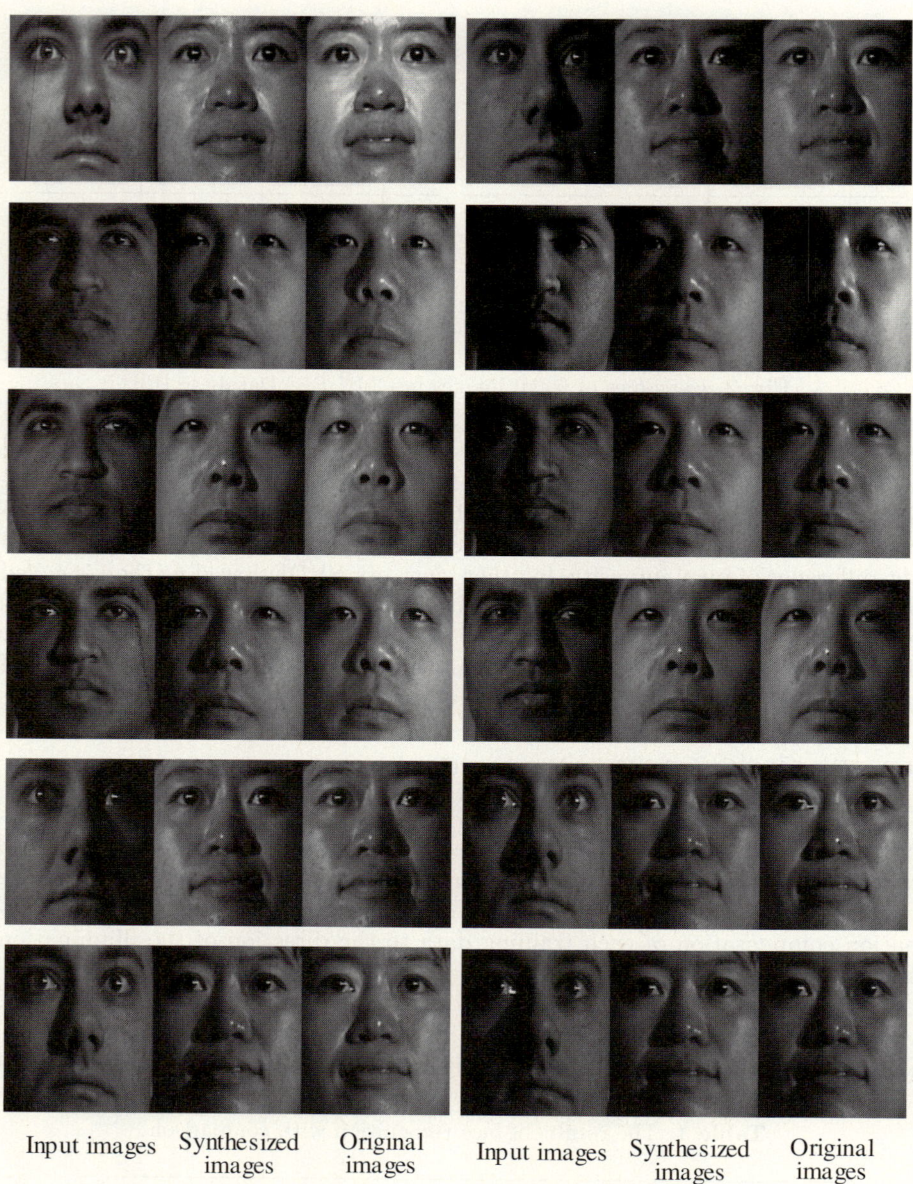

Fig. 3. Example images of synthesized results with CMU PIE database

an input person by matching it with all synthesized faces. We can identify a person by selecting the index, which has the minimum error. In this experiment, we perform this process 100 times. One hundred of arbitrary faces were randomly selected and we recognized them repeatedly. The result of this experiment is also compared with linear combination method [8] and is shown in Table 1. The experiment resulted in improvement of 5% recognition rate. As a result, our proposed method experimentally showed better performance, which is enough to draw the attraction in real application.

5 Conclusions

In this paper, we proposed a new method of synthesizing facial exemplars based on support vector data description and applied our approaches to illumination problem, which enables to recognize a face under arbitrary lighting condition. Our method is especially efficient in solving the limitation of view-based approaches. We first considered the SVDD problem for the data belonging to the trained facial images under various illuminations, and modelled the data region for each illumination as the ball resulting from the SVDD problem. Next, we impersonate an arbitrary illumination condition using feature vector projection onto the decision boundary of the SVDD ball. Finally, we combined facial images which are obtained from the pre-image of the projection, and built a facial image under compensated illumination. The applicability of the proposed method was illustrated via some experiments dealing with faces in popular facial databases. The experimental results showed that the facial images synthesized using the proposed method were quite similar to the original facial images, thus making it possible to recognize a person under various illuminations.

Acknowledgments

We would like to thank Prof. Takeo Kanade for his kind help and this work was supported by the Korea Research Foundation Grant funded by the Korean Government(MOEHRD)(KRF-2006-214-D00144).

References

1. Gross, R., Shi, J., Cohn, J.: Quo Vadis Face Recognition? In: Third Workshop on Empirical Evaluation Methods in Computer Vision (2001)
2. Zhao, W., Chellappa, R., Rosenfeld, A., Phillips, P.J.: Face Recognition: A Literature Survey. ACM Computing Surveys, 99–458 (2003)
3. Tan, X., Chen, S., Zhou, Z.-H., Zhang, F.: Face recognition from a single image per person: A survey. Pattern Recognition 39(9), 1725–1745 (2006)
4. Gross, R., Brajovic, V.: An Image Preprocessing Algorithm for Illumination Invariant Face Recognition. In: Kittler, J., Nixon, M.S. (eds.) AVBPA 2003. LNCS, vol. 2688, pp. 10–18. Springer, Heidelberg (2003)
5. Xie, X., Lam, K.-M.: An efficient method for face recognition under varying illumination. IEEE Int. Symp. on Circuits and Systems 4, 3841–3844 (2005)
6. Georghiades, A., Belhumeur, P., Kriegman, D.: From Few to Many: Illumination Cone Models for Face Recognition under Variable lighting and Pose. IEEE Transactions. on Pattern Analysis and Machine Intelligence 23(6), 643–660 (2001)

7. Zhou, S.K., Aggarwal, G., Chellappa, R., Jacobs, D.W.: Appearance Characterization of Linear Lambertian Objects, Generalized Photometric Stereo, and Illumination-Invariant Face Recognition. IEEE Transactions on Pattern Analysis and Machine Intelligence 29(2), 230–245 (2007)
8. Moon, S.-H., Lee, S.-W., Lee, S.-W.: Illumination Invariant Face Recognition Using Linear Combination of Face Exemplars. In: Kanade, T., Jain, A., Ratha, N.K. (eds.) AVBPA 2005. LNCS, vol. 3546, pp. 112–121. Springer, Heidelberg (2005)
9. Zhang, L., Samaras, D.: Face Recognition Under Variable Lighting using Harmonic Image Exemplars. IEEE Conference Computer Vision and Pattern Recognition 1, 19–25 (2003)
10. Park, J., Kang, D., Kim, J., Kwok, J.T., Tsang, I.W.: Pattern de-noising based on support vector data description. In: Proceedings of International Joint Conference on Neural Networks, Montreal, Canada, July 31-August 4, pp. 949–953 (2005)
11. Lee, S.-W., Park, J., Lee, S.-W.: Low Resolution Face Recognition Based on Support Vector Data Description. Pattern Recognition 39(9), 1809–1812 (2006)
12. Pentland, A., Moghaddam, B., Starner, T.: View-Based and Modular Eigenspaces for Face Recognition. In: IEEE Conf. Computer Vision and Pattern Recognition, pp. 84–91. IEEE Computer Society Press, Los Alamitos (1994)
13. Sim, T., Baker, S., Bsat, M.: The CMU Pose, Illumination, and Expression (PIE) Database of Human Faces. In: Proceedings of the IEEE International Conference on Automatic Face and Gesture Recognition, Washington, USA, pp. 53–58 (2002)

Keypoint Identification and Feature-Based 3D Face Recognition

Ajmal Mian, Mohammed Bennamoun, and Robyn Owens

School of Computer Science and Software Engineering,
The University of Western Australia,
35 Stirling Highway, Crawley, WA 6009, Australia
{ajmal,bennamou}@csse.uwa.edu.au, robyn.owens@uwa.edu.au

Abstract. We present a feature-based 3D face recognition algorithm and propose a keypoint identification technique which is repeatable and identifies keypoints where shape variation is high in 3D faces. Moreover, a unique 3D coordinate basis can be defined locally at each keypoint facilitating the extraction of highly descriptive pose invariant features. A feature is extracted by fitting a surface to the neighbourhood of a keypoint and sampling it on a uniform grid. Features from a probe and gallery face are projected to the PCA subspace and matched. Two graphs are constructed from the set of matching features of the probe and gallery face. The similarity between these graphs is used to determine the identity of the probe. The proposed algorithm was tested on the FRGC v2 data and achieved 93.5% identification and 97.4% verifiction rates.

1 Introduction

The human face is a socially acceptable and non-intrusive biometric. It requires minimal or no cooperation from the subject making it ideal for surveillance. However, machine recognition of faces is very challenging because the distinctiveness of facial biometrics is quite low compared to other biometrics [6]. Moreover, changes caused by expressions, illumination, pose, occlusions and facial makeup (e.g. beard) impose further challenges on accurate face recognition.

Zhao et al. [18] categorize face recognition algorithms as holistic, feature-based and hybrid. Holistic algorithms use global features (e.g. Eigenfaces [17]) of the complete face whereas feature-based algorithms use local features [7] or regions [11] of the face for recognition. Hybrid matching methods use a combination of global and local-features for recognition e.g. [4]. A limitation of holistic matching is that it requires accurate normalization of the faces according to pose, illumination and scale. Variations in these factors can affect the global features of the face leading to inaccuracies in the final recognition. Moreover, global features are also sensitive to facial expressions and occlusions. Feature-based matching algorithms have the advantage that they are robust to variations in pose, illumination, scale, expressions and occlusions.

Bowyer et al. [2] give a survey of 3D face recognition algorithms and argue that 3D face recognition has the potential to overcome the limitations of its

S.-W. Lee and S.Z. Li (Eds.): ICB 2007, LNCS 4642, pp. 163–171, 2007.

2D counterpart. However, there is a need for better algorithms which are more tolerant to the above mentioned variations. Many 3D face recognition approaches are based on the ICP algorithm [1] or its modifications because of two major advantages. Firstly, perfect normalization of the faces is not required as ICP iteratively corrects registration errors while matching. Secondly, a partial region can be matched with a complete face. The latter has been exploited to avoid facial expressions [11][14] and to handle pose variations [8]. On the downside, ICP is a computationally expensive algorithm and does not extract any feature from the face. This rules out any possibility of indexing to speed up the matching process. Unless another algorithm and/or modality is used to perform indexing or prior rejection of unlikely faces [12], ICP based algorithms must perform a brute force matching thereby making the recognition time linear to the gallery size. Selecting expression insensitive regions of the face for matching is a potentially useful approach to overcome the sensitivity of ICP to expressions. However, deciding upon such regions is a problem worth exploring as such regions may not only vary between different persons but between different expressions as well.

We propose a novel keypoint identification and feature extraction algorithm for 3D face recognition. The identification of keypoints is repeatable and allows for the extraction of highly descriptive 3D features. Each feature is extracted by fitting a surface to the neighbourhood of a keypoint and sampling it on a uniform grid. Multiple features are extracted from each gallery face and projected to a PCA subspace. During recognition, features are extracted at keypoints on the probe and projected to a similar PCA subspace before matching. The set of matching features from a probe and gallery face are individually meshed to form two graphs. A spatial constraint is used to remove false matches (nodes) and the remaining graph is used to calculate the similarity measure between the faces.

Preliminary results of our algorithm have been published [13]. However, a number of extensions have been done since then including keypoint identification, local 3D coordinate derivation from single keypoints, projection of the features to a subspace, use of a more sophisticated graph matching approach and results from experiments on the complete FRGC v2 data.

2 Keypoint Identification

The input to our algorithm is a point cloud of a face $\mathbf{F} = [x_i \; y_i \; z_i]^T$ (where $i = 1 \ldots n$) which is sampled at uniform intervals. At each sample point p, a local region is cropped from the face using a sphere of radius r_1 centered at p. The value of r_1 is a trade off between descriptiveness of the feature and its sensitivity to variations. The smaller the value of r_1, the less will be the sensitivity to variations but this will also decrease the descriptiveness of the feature.

Let $\mathbf{L} = [x_j \; y_j \; z_j]^T$ (where $i = 1 \ldots n_l$) be the points in the region cropped by the sphere of radius r_1 centered at p. The mean vector $\mathbf{m}$ and the covariance matrix $\mathbf{C}$ of $\mathbf{L}$ are given by

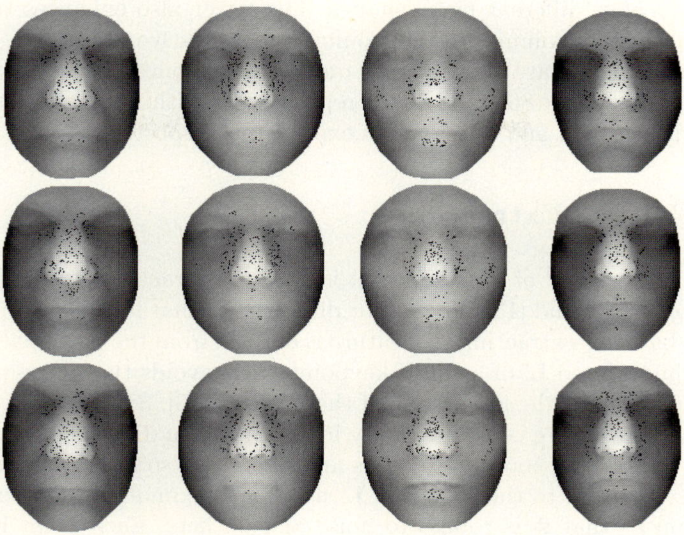

Fig. 1. Illustration of keypoint repeatability. Each column contains three range images of the same individual. Keypoints are repeatably identified for the same individual.

$$\mathbf{m} = \frac{1}{n_1} \sum_{j=1}^{n_1} \mathbf{L}_j \ , \quad \text{and} \tag{1}$$

$$\mathbf{C} = \frac{1}{n_1} \sum_{k=1}^{n_1} \mathbf{L}_j \mathbf{L}_j^T - \mathbf{m}\mathbf{m}^T \ , \tag{2}$$

where $\mathbf{L}_j$ is the jth column of $\mathbf{L}$. Performing PCA on the covariance matrix $\mathbf{C}$ gives the matrix $\mathbf{V}$ of eigenvectors such that Eqn. 3 is satisfied (where $\mathbf{D}$ is a diagonal matrix of the eigenvalues of $\mathbf{C}$). The matrix $\mathbf{L}$ can be aligned with its principal axes using Eqn. 4.

$$\mathbf{C}\mathbf{V} = \mathbf{D}\mathbf{V} \ , \tag{3}$$

$$\mathbf{L}' = \mathbf{V}(\mathbf{L} - \mathbf{m}). \tag{4}$$

$$\delta = \max(\mathbf{L}'_x) - \min(\mathbf{L}'_x) - (\max(\mathbf{L}'_y) - \min(\mathbf{L}'_y)) \tag{5}$$

In Eqn. 5, δ is the difference between the first two principal axes of the local region $\mathbf{L}'$ and $\mathbf{L}'_x$ is the vector of the x coordinates of $\mathbf{L}'$. If δ is greater than a threshold (i.e. $\delta \geq t_1$) p is selected as a keypoint. The total number of keypoints is determined by t_1. As the value of t_1 increases the total number of keypoints will decrease. The values of r_1 and t_1 are empirically chosen as $r_1 = 20mm$ and $t_1 = 2mm$. However, our algorithm is not sensitive to these parameters. Fig. 1 shows keypoints identified on different range images of four individuals. The keypoints are repeatably identified for a given individual but vary between individuals because they have different facial shapes. The latter also enhances recognition accuracy. In the first column, the keypoints cluster mostly on the nose. In column three, some keypoints are also detected on the cheek bones. Experiments showed that the keypoints have 86% and 75.6% repeatability within the sampling interval for faces with neutral and non-neutral expressions respectively.

3 3D Feature Extraction

The neighbourhood $\mathbf{L}'$ of each keypoint is used to extract a 3D feature which is an extension of [10] and [13]. The major difference is that in this paper, the local coordinate basis for extracting the feature is derived from the principal directions of the neighbourhood $\mathbf{L}'$ of a single keypoint. This avoids the C_2^n combinatorial problem [10] without the knowledge of the nose tip [13]. Since the keypoints are selected such that there is no ambiguity in the principal directions of the surface patch, the derived 3D coordinate bases are stable and so are the features.

A surface is fitted to the points in $\mathbf{L}'$ using approximation [3] as opposed to interpolation so that it is robust to noise and outliers. Each point in $\mathbf{L}'$ pulls the surface towards itself and a stiffness factor controls the flexibility of the surface. The surface is sampled on a uniform 20×20 lattice (see Fig. 2-a). In order to avoid the effects of boundaries, a larger region is cropped first using r_2 (where $r_2 > r_1$) and a surface is fitted to it. This surface is then sampled on a bigger lattice and only the central 20×20 samples covering the r_1 region are concatenated to form a vector of dimension 400.

A constant value of t_1 will result in different numbers of keypoints identified for each face and bias the recognition results in favor of faces with more features. Therefore, an upper limit of 200 is imposed on the total number of features per face. The feature vectors are projected to a subspace defined by the eigenvectors of their largest eigenvalues using PCA. Let $\mathcal{F} = [\mathbf{f}_1 \ldots \mathbf{f}_{200N}]$ (where N is the gallery size) be the $400 \times 200N$ matrix of all the feature vectors in the gallery. Each column of $\mathcal{F}$ contains a feature vector of dimension 400. The mean feature vector (Eqn. 6) is subtracted from all the feature vectors using Eqn. 7.

$$\overline{\mathbf{f}} = \frac{1}{200N} \sum_{i}^{200N} \mathbf{f}_i \tag{6}$$

$$\mathbf{f}'_i = \mathbf{f}_i - \overline{\mathbf{f}} \tag{7}$$

The mean subtracted feature matrix is given by Eqn. 8 and its covariance matrix by Eqn. 9 (where $\mathbf{C}$ is a 400×400 matrix). The eigenvalues and eigenvectors of $\mathbf{C}$ are calculated using Singular Value Decomposition (SVD) in Eqn. 10.

$$\mathcal{F}' = [\mathbf{f}'_1 \ldots \mathbf{f}'_{200N}] \tag{8}$$

$$\mathbf{C} = \mathcal{F}'(\mathcal{F}')^T \tag{9}$$

$$\mathbf{USV}^T = \mathbf{C} \ , \tag{10}$$

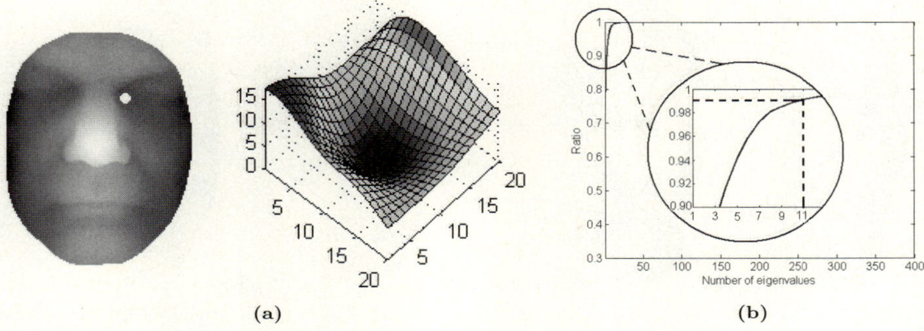

(a) (b)

Fig. 2. (a) A keypoint displayed (in white colour) on a 3D face and a local surface fitted to the neighbourhood of the keypoint using a 20×20 lattice. (b) A plot of the ratio ψ as a function of the number of eigenvalues k.

where $\mathbf{U}$ is a 400×400 matrix of the eigenvectors and $\mathbf{S}$ is a diagonal matrix of the eigenvalues, both sorted in decreasing order. The dimension of the PCA subspace is governed by the amount of required accuracy (fidelity) in the projected space. Plotting the ratio of the first k eigenvalues to the total eigenvalues (i.e. $\psi = \frac{\sum_{i=1}^{k} \lambda_i}{\sum_{i=1}^{400} \lambda_i}$, where λ_i is the ith eigenvalue) as a function of the number of eigenvalues k (Fig. 2-b) shows that 99% accuracy is reached at only $k = 11$. This means a compression ratio of $\frac{(400-11)}{400} = 97.3\%$ which is not surprising given that all human faces have a similar topological structure and are roughly symmetric on either side of the nose. The first k eigenvectors are taken as $\mathbf{U}_k = \mathbf{U}_i$ (where $i = 1 \ldots k$ and $\mathbf{U}_k$ is a $400 \times k$ matrix of the first k eigenvectors). The mean subtracted feature matrix is projected to the eigenspace

$$\mathcal{F}^{\lambda} = (\mathbf{U}_k)^T \mathcal{F}' \ , \tag{11}$$

where $\mathcal{F}^{\lambda}$ is a $k \times 200N$ matrix of the 3D feature vectors of the gallery faces. $\mathcal{F}^{\lambda}$ is normalized so that its variance along each of the k dimensions is equal

$$\mathcal{F}^{\lambda}_{rc} = \frac{\mathcal{F}^{\lambda}_{rc}}{\lambda_r} \quad \text{where } r = 1 \ldots k \text{ and } c = 1 \ldots 200N. \tag{12}$$

In Eqn. 12, r stands for the dimension or row number and c stands for the feature or column number. The feature vectors in $\mathcal{F}^{\lambda}$ (i.e. the columns) are normalized to unit magnitude and saved in a database along with $\overline{f}$ and $\mathbf{U}_k$ for online feature-based face recognition. The representation of gallery faces is quite compact as each face is represented by only 200 vectors of dimensionality 11.

4 Feature Matching

Indexing or hashing can speed up the matching process however, they are not the focus of this paper. Moreover, matching the probe with every gallery face results in many impostor scores useful for drawing the Receiver Operating Characteristic

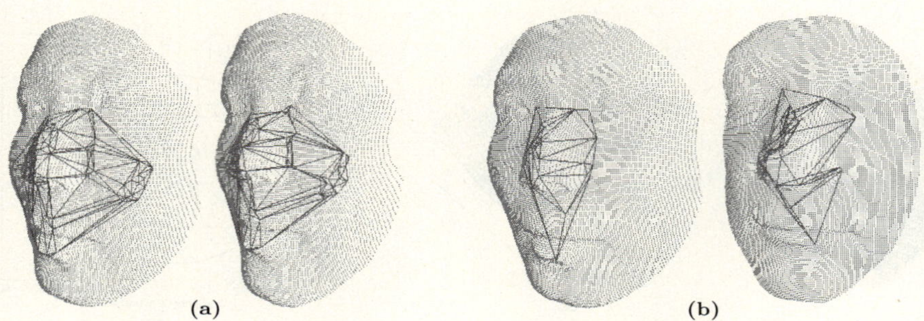

Fig. 3. (a) Correct match (b) Incorrect match

(ROC) curves. During recognition, features are extracted from the probe using the same parameters as the gallery. A probe feature vector $\mathbf{f}_p$ is first projected to the PCA subspace (Eqn. 13) and matched with a gallery feature (Eqn. 14).

$$\mathbf{f}_p^\lambda = (\mathbf{U}_k)^T(\mathbf{f}_p - \bar{\mathbf{f}}) \tag{13}$$

$$e = \cos^{-1}(\mathbf{f}_p^\lambda(\mathbf{f}_g^\lambda)^T) \tag{14}$$

The value e measures the matching error between the probe and gallery features ($\mathbf{f}_p^\lambda$ and $\mathbf{f}_g^\lambda$) in the PCA subspace. For a given probe feature, the feature from the gallery face that has the minimum error with it is taken as its match. Once all the features are matched, the list of matches is sorted according to e. If a gallery feature matches more than one probe feature, only the one with the minimum value of e is considered. This allows for only one-to-one matches and the total number of matches m is different for every probe-gallery pair.

The keypoints of the matching features on the probe are projected on the xy-plane, meshed using Delaunay triangulation and projected back to the 3D space resulting in a 3D graph. The edges of this graph are used to construct a graph from the corresponding nodes (keypoints) of the gallery face using the list of matches. If the matches are correct i.e. the matching pairs of features correspond to the same location on the probe and gallery face, the two graphs will be similar (Fig. 3). The similarity measure between the graphs is given by

$$\gamma = \frac{1}{n_\varepsilon}\sum_i^{n_\varepsilon}(\varepsilon_{pi} - \varepsilon_{gi}) , \tag{15}$$

where ε_{pi} and ε_{gi} are the lengths of the corresponding edges of the probe and gallery graphs respectively and n_ε is the total number of edges. Eqn. 15 is an efficient way of measuring the spatial error between the matching pairs of features. The measure γ is pose invariant because the edge lengths of the graphs remain constant under pose variation. Another similarity measure is the mean Euclidean distance d between the nodes of the two graphs after least squared error minimization.

The matching algorithm results in four measures of similarity between the two faces i.e. $\overline{e}$, the total number of matches m, γ, and d. Excluding m, all similarity measures have a negative polarity (i.e. a smaller value means a better similarity). A probe is matched with every gallery face resulting in four vectors $\mathbf{s}_q$ of similarity measures (where q corresponds to a similarity measure). Each vector is normalized on the scale of 0 to 1 using

$$\mathbf{s}'_q = \frac{\mathbf{s}_q - \min(\mathbf{s}_q)}{\max(\mathbf{s}_q - \min(\mathbf{s}_q)) - \min(\mathbf{s}_q - \min(\mathbf{s}_q))} , \tag{16}$$

where $\mathbf{s}'_q$ contains the normalized similarity measures. The elements of $\mathbf{s}'_m$ are subtracted from 1 in order to reverse their polarity. The overall similarity is calculated using a confidence weighted sum rule

$$\mathbf{s} = \kappa_e \mathbf{s}'_e + \kappa_m(1 - \mathbf{s}'_m) + \kappa_\gamma \mathbf{s}'_\gamma + \kappa_d \mathbf{s}'_d , \tag{17}$$

where κ_q is the confidence in a similarity measure which can be calculated offline from training data or dynamically during online recognition as $\kappa_q = \frac{\overline{s}_q - \min(\mathbf{s}_q)}{\overline{s}_q - \min_2(\mathbf{s}_q)}$ (where $\overline{s}_q$ is the mean value of $\mathbf{s}_q$ and the operator $\min_2(\mathbf{s}_q)$ produces the second minimum value of the vector $\mathbf{s}_q$). Note that κ_m is calculated from $1 - \mathbf{s}'_m$. The gallery face which has the minimum value in $\mathbf{s}$ is declared as the probe's identity.

5 Results and Analysis

The FRGC v2 [16] validation set comprises 4007 3D scans of 466 subjects along with their texture maps. We only used the 3D shape of the faces and selected one face per individual under neutral expression to make a gallery of 466. The remaining faces (4007 − 466) are treated as probes and divided into neutral expressions (1944) and non-neutral expressions (1597).

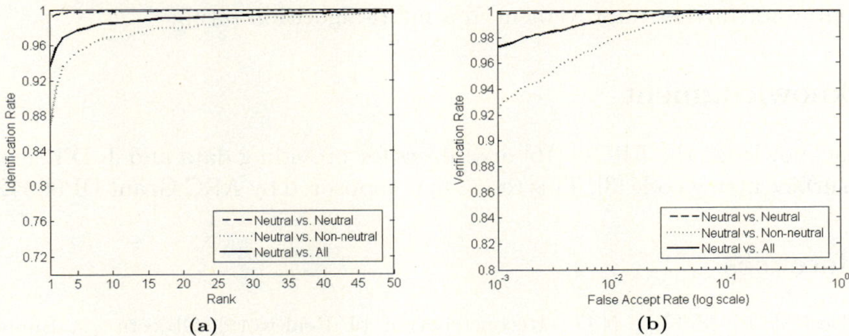

Fig. 4. (a) Identification results. The rank one identification rate for neutral vs. all is 93.5%. (b) ROC curves. The verification rate at 0.001 FAR for neutral vs. all is 97.4%.

Fig. 4-a shows our identification results. Our algorithm achieved rank one identification rates of 99.0% and 86.7% for probes with neutral and non-neutral expressions respectively. Under neutral expressions, only one probe is above rank 17 (100% recognition rate at rank 17). The identification rate drops under non-neutral expressions. However, it should be kept in mind that 3D face recognition is generally more sensitive to expressions. For example, the 3D face recognition rate of Lu et al. [8] dropped by 30%. In our case, the recognition rate drops by 12.3%. Moreover, the steep rise in the identification rate (i.e. 86.7% to 95%) from rank 1 to rank 5 indicates that the rank one identification rate will significantly improve by fusing other features e.g. global.

Fig. 4-b shows the ROC curves of our algorithm. At 0.001 FAR, we achieved verification rates of 99.9% and 92.7% respectively for probes with neutral and non-neutral expressions. In the neutral expressions case, a 100% verification rate is achieved at 0.01 FAR. It is not the aim of this paper to report the most accurate results on the FRGC v2 data and we believe that better results can be obtained by using a multi-algorithm approach. However, to give some idea of the performance of our algorithm, we compare our results to others. At 0.001 FAR we achieved a verification rate of 97.4% (neutral versus all) which can be compared to the results of Passalis et al. [15], Maurer et al. [9] and Huskën et al. [5] who achieved 85.1%, 86.5% and 89.5% verification rates respectively on the same dataset.

6 Conclusion

We presented a novel keypoint identification and feature extraction algorithm for 3D face recognition. These keypoints; (1) have 86% repeatability in the range images of the same individual, (2) vary between individuals, (3) are identified at locations where the shape variation is high, and (4) provide stable and repeatable local 3D coordinate frames for the computation of highly descriptive features. We also presented a graph based feature matching algorithm and reported experiments on the largest publicly available database of 3D faces. Our algorithm has an equal error rate (EER) of 0.75%(neutral vs. all) and has the potential for further improvement in a multi-algorithm setup.

Acknowledgment

We acknowledge the FRGC [16] organizers for providing data and J. D'Erico for the surface fitting code [3]. This research is sponsored by ARC Grant DP0664228.

References

1. Besl, P.J., McKay, N.D.: Reconstruction of Real-world Objects via Simultaneous Registration and Robust Combination of Multiple Range Images. IEEE TPAMI 14(2), 239–256 (1992)
2. Bowyer, K.W., Chang, K., Flynn, P.: A Survey Of Approaches and Challenges in 3D and Multi-modal 3D + 2D Face Recognition. CVIU 101, 1–15 (2006)

3. D'Erico, J.: Surface Fitting using Gridfit. MATLAB Central File Exchange (2006)
4. Huang, J., Heisele, B., Blanz, V.: Component-based Face Recognition with 3D Morphable Models. AVBPA (2003)
5. Huskën, M., Brauckmann, M., Gehlen, S., Malsburg, C.: Strategies and Benefits of Fusion of 2D and 3D Face Recognition. In: IEEE Workshop on FRGC Exp. (2005)
6. Jain, A.K., Ross, A., Prabhakar, S.: An Introduction to Biometric Recognition. IEEE TCSVT 14(1), 4–20 (2004)
7. Jones, M., Viola, P.: Face Recognition using Boosted Local Features. IEEE ICCV (2003)
8. Lu, X., Jain, A.K., Colbry, D.: Matching 2.5D Scans to 3D Models. IEEE TPAMI 28(1), 31–43 (2006)
9. Maurer, T., Guigonis, D., Maslov, I., Pesenti, B., Tsaregorodtsev, A., West, D., Medioni, G.: Performance of Geometrix ActiveID^{TM} 3D Face Recognition Engine on the FRGC Data. In: IEEE Workshop on FRGC Exp. (2005)
10. Mian, A.S., Bennamoun, M., Owens, R.A.: A Novel Representation and Feature Matching Algorithm for Automatic Pairwise Registration of Range Images. IJCV 66, 19–40 (2006)
11. Mian, A.S., Bennamoun, M., Owens, R.A.: 2D and 3D Multimodal Hybrid Face Recognition. ECCV 3, 344–355 (2006)
12. Mian, A.S., Bennamoun, M., Owens, R.A.: Automatic 3D Face Detection, Normalization and Recognition. 3DPVT (2006)
13. Mian, A.S., Bennamoun, M., Owens, R.A.: Face Recognition Using 2D and 3D Multimodal Local Features. ISVC, 860–870 (2006)
14. Mian, A.S., Bennamoun, M., Owens, R.A.: An Efficient Multimodal 2D-3D Hybrid Approach to Automatic Face Recognition. IEEE TPAMI 2007 (to appear)
15. Passalis, G., Kakadiaris, I., Theoharis, T., Tederici, G., Murtaza, N.: Evaluation of 3D Face Recognition in the Presence of Facial Expressions: An Annotated Deformable Model Approach. In: IEEE Workshop on FRGC Experiments. IEEE Computer Society Press, Los Alamitos (2005)
16. Phillips, P.J., Flynn, P.J., Scruggs, T., Bowyer, K., Chang, J., Hoffman, K., Marques, J., Min, J., Worek, W.: Overview of the Face Recognition Grand Challenge. IEEE CVPR (2005)
17. Turk, M., Pentland, A.: Eigenfaces for Recognition. JOCN 3 (1991)
18. Zhao, W., Chellappa, R., Phillips, P.J., Rosenfeld, A.: Face Recognition: A Literature Survey. ACM Computing Survey, 399–458 (2003)

Fusion of Near Infrared Face and Iris Biometrics*

Zhijian Zhang[1], Rui Wang[2], Ke Pan[1], Stan Z. Li[2], and Peiren Zhang[1]

[1] University of Science and Technology of China
Hefei 230026, China
[2] Center for Biometrics and Security Research &
National Laboratory of Pattern Recognition
Institute of Automation, Chinese Academy of Sciences, Beijing 100080, China
http://www.cbsr.ia.ac.cn

Abstract. In this paper, we present a method for fusing face and iris biometrics using single near infrared (NIR) image. Fusion of NIR face and iris modalities is a natural way of doing multi-model biometrics because they can be acquired in a single image. An NIR face image is taken using a high resolution NIR camera. Face and iris are segmented from the same NIR image. Face and iris features are then extracted from the segmented parts. Matching of face and iris is done using the respective features. The matching scores are fused using various rules. Experiments give promising results.

Keywords: NIR imaging, face, iris, multimodal biometrics, score fusion.

1 Introduction

Unimodal biometric systems perform person recognition based on a single source of biometric information. Face and iris recognition systems are of best choices. Face recognition is non-invasive and friendly; also, it is easy to get face images of good quality. Iris recognition is one of the most accurate biometrics. Unfortunately, both of them are often affected by a number of practical issues. The accuracy of face recognition is affected by illumination, pose, shelter and facial expression. In the case of iris recognition, the user must be cooperative to get iris images of good quality, because iris images must meet critical quality requirement. This may annoy the users.

Fusion of face and iris could overcome some of the limitations mentioned above and bring the following advantages [1]. 1) The total error rate (the false accept rate and the false reject rate) is known to go down [2]. 2) It reduces spoof attacks on the biometric system. Fusion of face of iris is a good method for liveness detection because of the difficulty in making fake iris images. 3) The population coverage of a multimodal biometric system is larger than that of

* The work presented in this paper was performed at CBSR during Zhijian Zhang and Ke Pan's visiting CBSR as visiting students.

S.-W. Lee and S.Z. Li (Eds.): ICB 2007, LNCS 4642, pp. 172–180, 2007.

a standalone biometric system. The use of the face recognizer can allow people with imperfect iris images to enroll, reducing the enrollment failure rate. Wang [2] used two different strategies for fusing iris and face classifiers. The first strategy was to compute either an unweighted or weighted sum and compare the result to a threshold. The second strategy was to treat the matching distances of face and iris classifiers as a two-dimensional feature vector and use a classifier to classify the vector to genuine or impostor. Byungjun Son [3] extracted features of face and iris by wavelet, and fused face and iris at feature level using reduced joint feature vector.

Two disadvantages exist in the conventional way of face+iris fusion. Firstly, face images are captured in the visible light (VL) spectrum. Lighting conditions influence the appearance of a face [4], and hence the accuracy of the face modality. Secondly, face images and iris images are captured using different imaging devices.

In this paper, we present a new method for fusion of face and iris biometrics, by taking advantages of the recently developed near infrared (NIR) face imaging and recognition [5]. NIR face and iris data are acquired using single high resolution camera with active frontal NIR lighting. This is not only a natural way for face and iris multimodal biometrics, because both modalities need active NIR modality, but also brings convenience to the user.

Face and iris regions are segmented from the same image, with sufficient details because of the high resolution. Face and iris biometric features are then extracted. They are matched against face and iris templates using the respective features. The matching scores are fused to give the final result. Experiments give promising results, with various fusion rules compared.

The rest of the paper is organized as follows: Section 2 introduces the image acquisition method and the algorithm structure for fusing face+iris biometrics using a single NIR face image. The database and experiments are given in section 3.

2 Face+Iris Multimodal Fusion

2.1 NIR Image Acquisition

The image resolution should be high enough to capture sufficient iris details. A typical iris image size is 320×280 pixels and the area of a face is 100 times larger than that of iris. So the resolution of the resulting image should be more than 9 megapixel pixels (320×280×100=8,960,000). Therefore, we choose to use a 10 megapixel CCD digital camera with up to 3648×2736 pixels. The camera is about 60-80 cm away from the subject.

To overcome influence of ambient lighting on face and to get iris patterns, active NIR LED lights of 850nm, mounted around the camera lens, are used to provide frontal lighting. We use a band pass optical filter on the camera lens to cut off visible light while allowing NIR light to pass. Figure 1 shows some examples of face images and segmented iris parts.

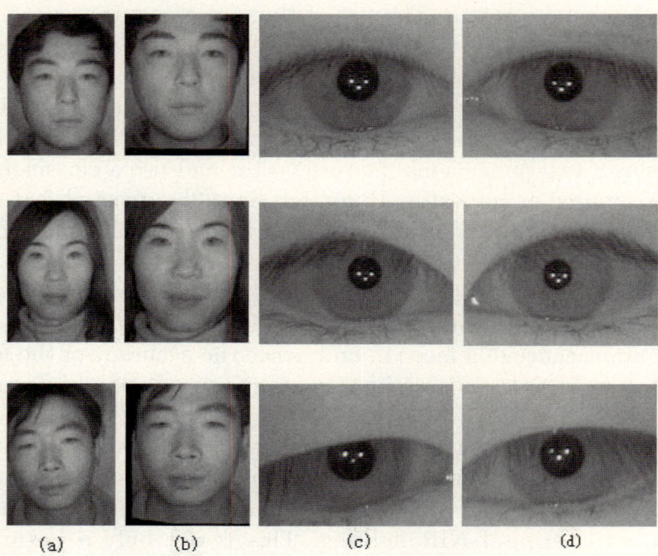

Fig. 1. High resolution NIR face images and corresponding face and iris images. (a) High resolution NIR face images. (b) NIR face image segmented from (a). (c) Left iris segmented from (a). (d) Right iris segmented from (a).

2.2 Face and Iris Recognition

We use the PCA [6] for face recognition. Suppose I_1, I_2, ..., I_n as a training set, its average face is defined by:

$$A = \frac{1}{S}\sum_{i=1}^{S} I_i \tag{1}$$

The margin between a face image and the average face is $Y_i = I_i - A$. Covariance matrix C is defined by:

$$C = \frac{1}{S}\sum_{i=1}^{S} Y_i \cdot Y_i^T \tag{2}$$

Let E^T be M maximum eigenvectors of C. Test image I_{test} projects to the face space as the algorithm:

$$W_{test} = E^T \cdot (I_{test} - A) \tag{3}$$

We use the well-known iris recognition algorithm of Daugman [7]. It comprises 4 steps. 1) It is necessary to localize precisely the inner and outer boundaries of the iris, and to detect and exclude eyelids if they intrude. 2) The portion of the image corresponding to the iris is translated to a normalized form, so that possible dilation of the pupil does not affect the system. 3) The feature extraction process is completed by the use of 2D Gabor wavelets to perform a multi-scale analysis of the iris. The information about local phase, coded with two bits corresponding to the signs of the real and imaginary parts, is obtained. The result is a 256-byte IrisCode. 4) Similarity scores are obtained by computing a Hamming Distance.

2.3 Score Level Fusion

There are two approaches for fusion at score level fusion. The first one is to formulate it as a classification problem. The second one is to treat it as a combination problem. The individual matching scores are combined to generate a single scalar score which is then compared to a threshold to make the final decision. To ensure a meaningful combination of scores, the scores must be transformed to a common domain. Normalization methods and combination approaches have been proposed in literatures [8,9].

Min-Max is a well-known normalization method:

$$n = \frac{s - \min(S)}{\max(S) - \min(S)} \tag{4}$$

Where, S is the score set composed of all scores for a matcher, $s \in S$, n is the normalized score, $\max(S)$ and $\min(S)$ specify the end points of S.

Two score level fusion methods, sum-rule (Eq. 5) and product rule (Eq. 6), are used in the work. Suppose f_i as the fused score for user i,

$$f_i = \sum_{m=1}^{M} n_i^m \tag{5}$$

$$f_i = \prod_{m=1}^{M} n_i^m \tag{6}$$

Where, n_i^m is the normalized score for matcher m applied to user i, $m = 1, 2, ..., M$, M is the number of matchers, $i = 1, 2, ..., I$, I is the number of individuals.

2.4 Summary of Algorithm

Figure 2 summarizes the structure of the algorithms of NIR face+iris biometric fusion using a single high resolution NIR face image:

1. Image Capturing: a high resolution NIR face image;
2. Face and eye localization: using a face and eye detection algorithm [10];
3. Segmenting irises from the face;
4. Normalizing the face and irises in given frames;
5. Extracting facial features using PCA [6];
6. Extracting iris features using Gabor [7];
7. Performing face and iris matching against respective templates using respective features;

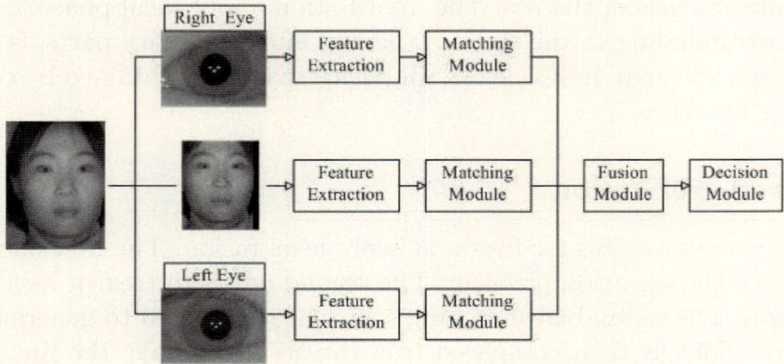

Fig. 2. Algorithm structure for fusing face+iris biometrics using a single NIR face image

8. Fusing the matching scores [8,9];
9. Comparing the fused score to a threshold to make the final decision.

The final matching scores of face and iris are normalized to [0,1] range using Min-Max normalization. A single scalar score is obtained using sum rule and product rule. The NIR face+Iris fusion may be done with different combinations: 1) fusion of face and left iris, 2) fusion of face and right iris, 3) fusion of face, left iris and right iris and 4) fusion of left iris and right iris.

3 Experiments

3.1 Database

A NIR face+iris database is built which contains 930 high resolution (2736×3648 pixels) NIR images. It includes 112 subjects of 55 females and 57 males, aged from 17 to 35, with 10 images for 76 subjects and 5 images for other 34 subjects. Some examples were shown in Figure 1.

The images in the database are divided into three parts, training set, test set 1 (a close set) and test set 2 (an open set). The training set includes 380 images (76 subjects, 5 images for each subject). The test set 1 includes 380 images (76 subjects, 5 images for each subject) with the same subjects as those of the training set. The test set 2 includes 170 images (34 subjects, 5 images for each subject) with totally different subjects from those of the training set. Test set 2 has more poor quality iris images than test set 1.

3.2 Results

Face and iris matching scores are obtained using the PCA and Gabor based methods. We use Min-Max to normalize the matching scores output from face/ iris verification. We use product rule and sum rule to combine the normalized scores.

Table 1. GAR(%) ($FAR = 0.001$, Min-Max Normalization)

	Test Set 1 Sum Rule	Test Set 1 Product Rule	Test Set 2 Sum Rule	Test Set 2 Product Rule
Face	97.35	97.35	83.31	83.31
Left	95.42	95.42	88.0	88.0
Right	95.0	95.0	86.33	86.33
Face+Left	99.36	99.39	97.24	97.34
Face+Right	98.65	99.49	92.63	94.17
Left+Right	97.64	98.0	93.29	93.80
Face+Left+Right	99.75	99.74	98.12	97.81

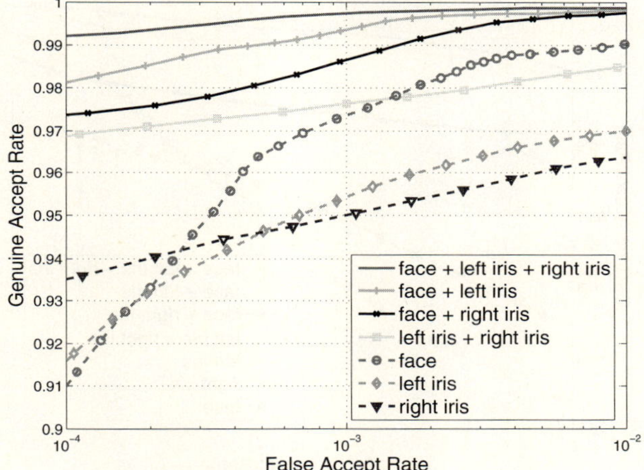

(a) Min-Max normalization and sum rule

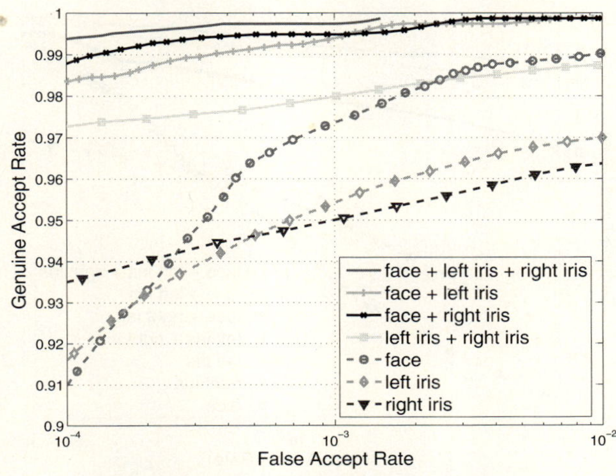

(b) Min-Max normalization and product rule

Fig. 3. ROC Curves for score level fusion of face and iris on test set 1 (close set)

Table 2. GAR(%) ($FAR = 0.0001$, Min-Max Normalization)

	Test Set 1 Sum Rule	Test Set 1 Product Rule	Test Set 2 Sum Rule	Test Set 2 Product Rule
Face	91.0	91.0	71.73	71.73
Left	91.60	91.60	84.47	84.47
Right	93.51	93.51	77.36	77.36
Face+Left	98.12	98.32	94.55	95.0
Face+Right	97.37	98.78	90.77	90.0
Left+Right	96.86	97.27	90.65	90.75
Face+Left+Right	99.21	99.38	95.30	95.88

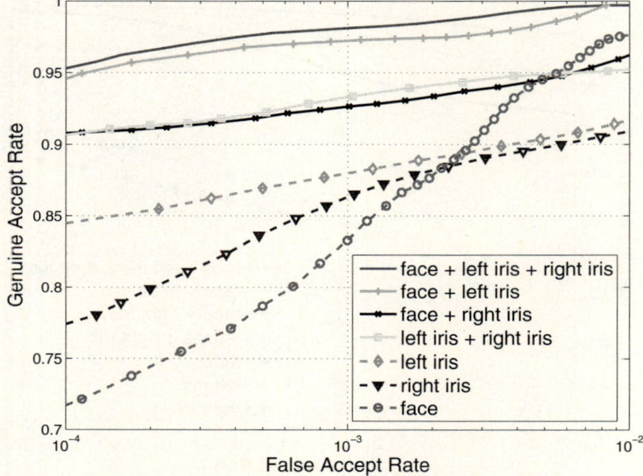

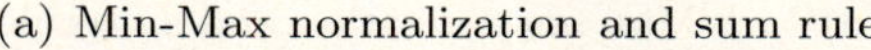

(a) Min-Max normalization and sum rule

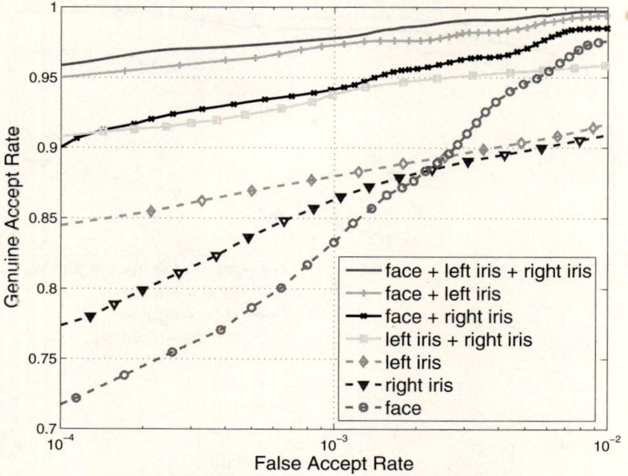

(b) Min-Max normalization and product rule

Fig. 4. ROC Curves for score level fusion of face and iris on test set 2 (open set)

Table 1 shows the genuine acceptance rate (GAR) when false acceptance rate (FAR) is at 0.001. Table 2 shows the GAR when FAR is at 0.0001. Figure 3 shows the ROC curves for score level fusion of face and iris obtained on test set 1. Figure 4 shows the ROC curves for score level fusion of face and iris obtained on test set 2.

3.3 Conclusions

Two conclusions may be drawn based on Figures 3 and 4, and Tables 1 and 2:

1) Fusion of NIR face and irises can improve the accuracy. In case of fusion of face and two irises, the genuine accept rate (GAR) increases from 97.35% (face biometric) to 99.75% on a close set and from 83.31% (face biometric) to 98.12% on an open set when false accept rate (FAR) is at 0.001. Fusion of multiple biometrics has a higher accuracy than fusion of multiple units of the same biometric.

2) Multimodal biometrics is a way to reduce the quality requirement of iris image. Some samples, such as the third image in Figure 1(c), fail the standalone iris classifier, but correctly recognized by the multimodal biometric system.

4 Summary and Future Work

In this work, we present a method for fusing NIR face and iris biometrics using single high resolution NIR face image. The image is taken with frontal active NIR illumination. This provides frontal NIR lighting for face image and iris pattern acquisition at the same time. Preliminary experiments shows that fusion of NIR face and iris biometrics can improve the accuracy.

We will be considering to integrate the two modalities in a better way to take advantages of both: (1) that NIR face biometric has a good accuracy, is fast and does not so stringent user cooperation, and (2) that iris biometric could have a higher accuracy, if the imaging is done properly, due to better separability of iris patterns. A careful design of integration of the NIR face and iris may lead to a system which has a high accuracy, and is fast, and easy to use.

Acknowledgments

This work was supported by the following funding resources: National Natural Science Foundation Project #60518002, National Science and Technology Supporting Platform Project #2006BAK08B06, National 863 Program Projects #2006AA01Z192 and #2006AA01Z193, Chinese Academy of Sciences 100 people project, and the AuthenMetric Collaboration Foundation.

References

1. Hong, L., Jain, A., Pankanti, S.: Can multibiometrics improve performance? In: Proceedings AutoID'99, pp. 947–950 (1999)
2. Wang, Y., Tan, T., Jain, A.K.: Combining face and iris biometrics for identity verification. In: Kittler, J., Nixon, M.S. (eds.) AVBPA 2003. LNCS, vol. 2688, pp. 805–813. Springer, Heidelberg (2003)

3. Son, B., Lee, Y.: Biometric authentication system using reduced joint feature vector of iris and face. In: Kanade, T., Jain, A., Ratha, N.K. (eds.) AVBPA 2005. LNCS, vol. 3546. Springer, Heidelberg (2005)
4. Moses, Y., Adini, Y., Ullman, S.: Face recognition: The problem of compensating for changes in illumination direction. In: Proceedings of the European Conference on Computer Vision, vol. A, pp. 286–296 (1994)
5. Li, S.Z., Chu, R., Liao, S., Zhang, L.: Illumination invariant face recognition using near-infrared images. IEEE Transactions on Pattern Analysis and Machine Intelligence 26 (2007)
6. Turk, M.A., Pentland, A.P.: Eigenfaces for recognition. Journal of Cognitive Neuroscience 3, 71–86 (1991)
7. Daugman, J.G.: High confidence visual recognition of persons by a test of statistical independence. IEEE Trans. Pattern Analysis and Machine Intelligence 15, 1148–1161 (1993)
8. Jain, A., Nandakumarand, K., Ross, A.: Score normalization in multimodal biometric systems. Pattern recognition 2005 (to appear)
9. Snelick, R., Uludag, U., Mink, A., Indovina, M., Jain, A.: Large scale evaluation of multimodal biometric authentication using state-of-the-art systems (2005)
10. Li, S.Z., Chu, R.F., Ao, M., Zhang, L., He, R.: Highly accurate and fast face recognition using near infrared images. In: Proceedings of IAPR International Conference on Biometric (ICB-2006), Hong Kong, pp. 151–158 (2006)

Multi-Eigenspace Learning for Video-Based Face Recognition

Liang Liu[1], Yunhong Wang[2], and Tieniu Tan[1]

[1]National Laboratory of Pattern Recognition
Institute of Automation, Chinese Academy of Sciences, Beijing, China
{lliu,tnt}@nlpr.ia.ac.cn
[2]School of Computer Science and Engineering
Beihang University, Beijing, China
yhwang@buaa.edu.cn

Abstract. In this paper, we propose a novel online learning method called Multi-Eigenspace Learning which can learn appearance models incrementally from a given video stream. For each subject, we try to learn a few eigenspace models using IPCA (Incremental Principal Component Analysis). In the process of Multi-Eigenspace Learning, each eigenspace generally contains more and more samples except one eigenspace which contains the least number of samples. Then, these learnt eigenspace models are used for video-based face recognition. Experimental results show that the proposed method can achieve high recognition rate.

Keywords: face recognition, online learning, incremental principal component analysis.

1 Introduction

For video-based face recognition, most state-of-the-art algorithms [1,2,5,9,10,12] can perform the recognition task in real time . However, the training process commonly runs off-line in a batch mode. Though several online learning algorithms were proposed recently, those algorithms generally need to perform online learning based on a pre-trained model. A pre-trained model is typically trained from a data set which is manually collected and labeled. The task of collecting and labeling data is usually tedious and boring. In addition, a pre-trained model may not be flexible enough to cope with various conditions online. Therefore, how to learn appearance models online without a pre-trained model is valuable to be considered.

Compared with batch training, there are several advantages to use online learning. First, it is convenient to add new training samples. Every time we add new samples, the computational complexity is roughly the same because we only need to update the models using new samples. Second, huge data sets can be easily handled by sequential processing. Third, online learning algorithms are suitable for real time online training. These properties are quite desirable for video-based face recognition.

S.-W. Lee and S.Z. Li (Eds.): ICB 2007, LNCS 4642, pp. 181–190, 2007.

In this paper, we propose an online learning algorithm which can learn appearance manifolds without a pre-trained model. Similar to [7], several eigenspace models are used to represent sub-manifolds. However, in our method, the eigenspace models are learnt completely online, while Lee and Kriegman's method [7] learnt appearance manifolds based on a pre-trained model.

The remainder of this paper is organized as follows. In Section 2, we will introduce some previous work on video-based face recognition. In Section 3, the proposed method will be described in detail. Some experimental results will be shown in Section 4. Finally, conclusions will be drawn in Section 5.

2 Previous Work

General reviews of recent face recognition literature can be found in [18,4]. Here, we only briefly review the literature which deals specifically with video-based face recognition.

In [17], Mutual Subspace Method (MSM) is proposed in which the similarity is defined by the angle between the input and the reference subspaces. Shakhnarovich *et al.* [12] defines the similarity as the KL divergence between the estimated density of two image sequences. Krüeger and Zhou [5] proposed an exemplar-based method which selects representative face images from training face videos. These representative face images are used for tracking and recognition. Liu and Chen [10] proposed to use adaptive Hidden Markov Models (HMM) which can learn temporal dynamics from each sequence. In [14] and [9], frame synchronization was used to align different sequences. They also exploit audio information in videos. In [1], a generic shape-illumination manifold is learnt off-line using Probabilistic PCA (PPCA) [15]. A generic framework for both tracking and recognition is proposed by Zhou *et al.* [19, 20]. They estimate the joint posterior probability distribution of motion vector and identity variable at each time instant and then propagate it to the next time instant.

Lee *et al.* [6] proposed a method using probabilistic appearance manifolds to model and recognize faces in video sequences. An appearance manifold is approximated by several eigenspaces and a transition matrix learnt from an image sequence. They also proposed an online learning algorithm for constructing a probabilistic appearance manifold [7]. In this online learning algorithm, an appearance model is incrementally learnt online using a prior generic model and successive frames from the video. Both the generic and individual appearances are represented as an appearance manifold that is approximated by several eigenspaces and the connectivity between them. One obvious limitation is that their method requires a generic prior model which should be learnt off-line.

In [8], an online learning method using eigenspace merging and splitting is proposed. For each subject, a fixed number of eigenspace models and a transition matrix are learnt to approximately construct the face appearance manifold. Then, these eigenspace models are used for video-based face recognition.

Different from our previous work [8], we avoid using eigenspace merging, eigenspace splitting and transition matrix. There are several reasons. First, eigenspace splitting may not be faithful to the original samples. Second, for eigenspace merging, two eigenspaces which correspond to different poses may be merged into one eigenspace. Third, the transition probability between two eigenspaces relies too much on the training samples. We also avoid setting a fixed number of eigenspace models to be learnt. Instead, we just set an upper bound of that number, which makes the process of learning more flexible.

3 Multi-Eigenspace Learning

In Section 3.1, we give a description of the eigenspace models to be learnt online. In Section 3.2, a framework of online appearance model learning method called Multi-Eigenspace Learning is presented. In our method, eigenspace update using IPCA (Incremental Principal Component Analysis) is a critical part and is discussed in Section 3.3. In Section 3.4, we discuss a desirable property of the algorithm of Multi-Eigenspace Learning.

3.1 Model Description

Given the training face video stream of each subject in the data set, we aim to construct up to K eigenspaces, $\Omega^{(1)}, \Omega^{(2)}, \cdots, \Omega^{(k)}$ ($k \leq K$, K is decided empirically), to approximately represent the appearance manifold of that subject. There are four parameters for each eigenspace [3]:

$$\Omega = (\overline{\mathbf{x}}, \mathbf{U}, \mathbf{\Lambda}, N), \tag{1}$$

where $\overline{\mathbf{x}}$ is the center of the eigenspace. $\mathbf{U}$ is a matrix whose columns are orthonormal bases of the eigenspace, namely eigenvectors. $\mathbf{\Lambda}$ is a diagonal matrix. Elements along the diagonal are variances for each principal axis, namely eigenvalues. They are arranged in descending order. N is the number of samples to construct the eigenspace.

How to learn these eigenspace models online is what we focus on in this paper. Our method will be described in Section 3.2.

3.2 The Algorithm of Multi-Eigenspace Learning

For each subject, suppose there are n frames which arrive sequentially. Initially, k is assigned as 1 and the center of $\Omega^{(1)}$ is assigned as the first frame. Then for each incoming frame $\mathbf{x}_t$, compute the distance between $\mathbf{x}_t$ and each eigenspace center. If the smallest distance is not greater than a given threshold, the corresponding eigenspace is updated using IPCA. Otherwise, a new eigenspace is established and its center is assigned as $\mathbf{x}_t$. If $k = K$, an eigenspace which is constructed from the least number of samples is discarded before the new eigenspace is established. Our algorithm is summarized as follows.

Algorithm 1. Multi-Eigenspace Learning
Input:
$\{\mathbf{x}_1, \mathbf{x}_2, \cdots, \mathbf{x}_n\}$: a consecutive face image sequence from a subject, where $\mathbf{x}_i$ is the feature vector extracted from the ith image. $(1 \leq i \leq n)$
K: upper limit of the number of eigenspaces. K can be decided empirically.
T: a threshold which can be decided empirically.

Output:
$\{\Omega^{(i)} | \Omega^{(i)} = (\overline{\mathbf{x}}^{(i)}, \mathbf{U}^{(i)}, \mathbf{\Lambda}^{(i)}, N^{(i)}), i = 1, \cdots, k, k \leq K\}$.

Method:
1. $k \leftarrow 1$
2. $\Omega^{(1)} \leftarrow (\mathbf{x}_1, \{\}, \{\}, 1)$
3. **for** $j \leftarrow 2$ to n
4. $\quad p^* \leftarrow \arg \min_{1 \leq p \leq k} d\left(\mathbf{x}_j, \Omega^{(p)}\right)$
5. $\quad$ **if** $d\left(\mathbf{x}_j, \Omega^{(p^*)}\right) \leq T$
6. $\qquad$ IPCA$(\Omega^{(p^*)}, \mathbf{x}_j)$
7. $\quad$ **else if** $k < K$
8. $\qquad k \leftarrow k + 1$
9. $\qquad \Omega^{(k)} \leftarrow (\mathbf{x}_j, \{\}, \{\}, 1)$
10. $\quad$ **else**
11. $\qquad p^* \leftarrow \arg \min_{1 \leq p \leq K} N^{(p)}$
12. $\qquad \Omega^{(p^*)} \leftarrow (\mathbf{x}_j, \{\}, \{\}, 1)$
13. $\quad$ **end if**
14. **end for**

In Line 4, $d\left(\mathbf{x}_j, \Omega^{(p)}\right)$ computes the l_1-distance between $\mathbf{x}_j$ and $\overline{\mathbf{x}}^{(p)}$. In Line 6, $\mathbf{x}_j$ is incorporated into $\Omega^{(p^*)}$ using IPCA. Generally, an eigenspace is more likely to be an outlier if it is constructed from fewer samples. In Lines 11-12, we remove an eigenspace which contains the least number of samples.

In Section 3.3, we will show how IPCA works without knowing both the original samples and the covariance matrix.

3.3 IPCA

In this section, we discuss more details about the computation of IPCA. An algorithm of IPCA was proposed by Hall *et al.* [3], but their method is complicated to some extent. A concise method is described as follows [8].

Algorithm 2. IPCA
Input:
$\Omega = (\overline{\mathbf{x}}, \mathbf{U}, \mathbf{\Lambda}, N)$: constructed from $\mathbf{x}_1, \mathbf{x}_2, \cdots, \mathbf{x}_N$.
$\mathbf{x}$: a new sample.

Output:
$\Omega' = (\overline{\mathbf{x}'}, \mathbf{U}', \mathbf{\Lambda}', N')$: constructed from $\mathbf{x}_1$, $\mathbf{x}_2$, $\cdots$,$\mathbf{x}_N$, $\mathbf{x}$.

Method:
1. $N' \leftarrow N + 1$.
2. $\alpha_1 \leftarrow N/N', \alpha_2 \leftarrow 1 - \alpha_1$.
3. $\overline{\mathbf{x}'} \leftarrow \alpha_1 \overline{\mathbf{x}} + \alpha_2 \mathbf{x}$.
4. Generate artificial data: $\mathbf{Y} \leftarrow \left[\sqrt{\alpha_1}\mathbf{U}\mathbf{\Lambda}^{1/2}, \sqrt{\alpha_1\alpha_2}(\overline{\mathbf{x}} - \mathbf{x})\right]$.
5. Compute the eigenvectors and eigenvalues of $\mathbf{Y}^T\mathbf{Y} : \mathbf{Y}^T\mathbf{Y} = \mathbf{V}\mathbf{\Lambda}'\mathbf{V}^T$.
6. $\mathbf{U}' \leftarrow \mathbf{Y}\mathbf{V}\mathbf{\Lambda}'^{-1/2}$.

This IPCA algorithm can be viewed as a special case of the algorithm of eigenspace merging [13]. For eigenspace merging, if one of the two eigenspaces to be merged has zero dimensions, the problem becomes IPCA.

In Step 5 and Step 6, it is enough to retain only a few relatively larger eigenvalues and corresponding eigenvectors.

3.4 A Desirable Property of Multi-Eigenspace Learning

Property (of Algorithm 1). *Suppose that after the iteration of $j = h$ ($h < n$), K eigenspace models are learnt and the ascending permutation of $N^{(1)}$, $N^{(2)}$, $\cdots$, $N^{(K)}$ is $N_{h1} \le N_{h2} \le \cdots \le N_{hK}$. Then for an arbitrary integer l subjected to $h < l \le n$, the following inequality holds.*

$$N_{hi} \le N_{li}, \;\; i = 2, 3, \cdots, K, \tag{2}$$

where $N_{l1} \le N_{l2} \le \cdots \le N_{lK}$ is the ascending permutation of $N^{(1)}$, $N^{(2)}$, $\cdots$, $N^{(K)}$ after the iteration of $j = l$.

Proof. To prove this property, we only need to prove that

$$N_{l-1,i} \le N_{li}, \;\; i = 2, 3, \cdots, K, \;\; h < l \le n. \tag{3}$$

Note that when $j \ge h$, $k = K$ holds. So the condition in Line 7 will be false. There are only the following two cases in the iteration of $j = l$.

Case 1: $d\left(\mathbf{x}_l, \Omega^{(p^*)}\right) \le T$. Line 6 is executed. So the update of $N^{(i)}$ ($i = 1$, $2, \cdots, K$) is as follows.

$$N_{li} \leftarrow \begin{cases} N_{l-1,i} + 1 & \text{when } i = p^*, \\ N_{l-1,i} & \text{otherwise.} \end{cases} \tag{4}$$

Case 2: $d\left(\mathbf{x}_l, \Omega^{(p^*)}\right) > T$. Lines 11-12 are executed. The update of $N^{(i)}$ ($i = 1, 2, \cdots, K$) is as follows.

$$N_{li} \leftarrow \begin{cases} 1 & \text{when } i = 1, \\ N_{l-1,i} & \text{otherwise.} \end{cases} \tag{5}$$

Obviously, (3) holds in both Case 1 and Case 2. From (3), we can get

$$N_{hi} \leq N_{h+1,i} \leq \cdots \leq N_{li}, \quad i = 2, 3, \cdots, K. \tag{6}$$

□

This property shows that after K eigenspaces are learnt, each eigenspace generally contains more and more samples except one eigenspace which contains the least number of samples. This is a desirable property for online learning.

Moreover, after K eigenspaces are learnt, the algorithm tends to establish new eigenspaces while discarding old eigenspaces which contain the least number of samples. This conforms with human experience.

4 Experimental Results

We conduct some experiments on a 36-subject face video data set which bears large pose variation collected by our lab. In this data set, there are 36 videos which correspond to 36 subjects respectively. These video sequences are captured indoors at 30 frames per second. The sequences contain large 2-D (in plane) and 3-D (out of plane) head rotation, with slight expression and illumination changes. In each video sequence, the number of frames ranges from 236 to 1270. The faces in the videos are cropped automatically using a boosted cascade face detector [16], or cropped manually when the detection results are not good enough. Then, all the cropped images are transformed into gray-level images and resized to a standard size of 20×20. Then a histogram equalization step is applied to eliminate the illumination impact to some extent. Some samples are shown in Figure 1.

We use the first half of each video sequence, ranging from 118 to 635 frames, for online learning. The second half of each video sequence is used for the recognition task. We do some experiments using the following two methods.

-**EMS + transition**, Eigenspace Merging and Splitting with consideration of transition matrix [8].

-**Multi-Eigenspace Learning**, the proposed method.

K, namely the number of eigenspace models, is a parameter which is difficult to optimize without experiments. Take this into consideration, we do experiments for $K = 6, 7, 8, 9$ respectively to evaluate the two methods. The test sets are constructed by randomly sampling from the second half of each video sequence for 10 times with each set containing 50 samples [2]. For each sample in the test

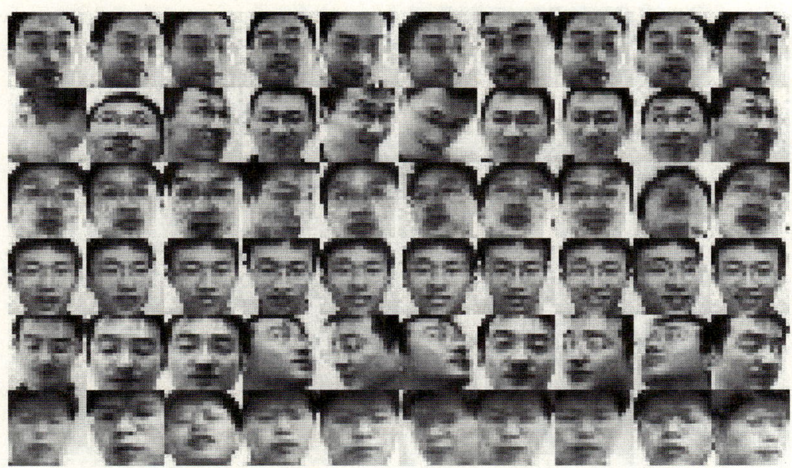

Fig. 1. Typical samples of the videos used in our experiments. The images in each row come from a different video sequence.

Table 1. Average recognition rates (%) of different methods when choosing $K = 6, 7, 8, 9$ respectively

Method \ K	6	7	8	9
EMS + transition [8]	90.0	91.9	96.4	91.4
Multi-Eigenspace Learning	97.5	96.7	98.1	96.4

set, we compute the likelihood probability of each eigenspace model and find the maximum to make a classification. The likelihood probability can be computed using the following formula [11]:

$$p(\mathbf{x}_t|\Omega^{(j)}) = \frac{\exp(-\frac{1}{2}\sum_{i=1}^{q}\frac{{y_i}^2}{\lambda_i})}{(2\pi)^{q/2}\prod_{i=1}^{q}{\lambda_i}^{1/2}} \cdot \frac{\exp(-\frac{\epsilon^2(\mathbf{x})}{2\rho})}{(2\pi\rho)^{(m-q)/2}}, \tag{7}$$

where q is the dimension of Eigenspace $\Omega^{(j)}$, and $[y_1, y_2, \cdots, y_q]^T$ is the projection from $\mathbf{x}_t$ to $\Omega^{(j)}$. $\epsilon^2(\mathbf{x})$ is the Euclidean distance from $\mathbf{x}_t$ to $\Omega^{(j)}$, and λ_i is the ith eigenvector in $\Omega^{(j)}$. m is the dimension of the original feature space. The parameter ρ is chosen as $0.3\lambda_q$ empirically.

For each test set, majority voting is used to make a final decision. The average recognition rates over all runs are shown in Table 1.

The results show that the proposed method outperforms EMS + transition. This conforms with the analysis at the last paragraph of Section 2. Figure 2 shows some eigenspace centers learnt using Multi-Eigenspace Learning when choosing $K = 8$.

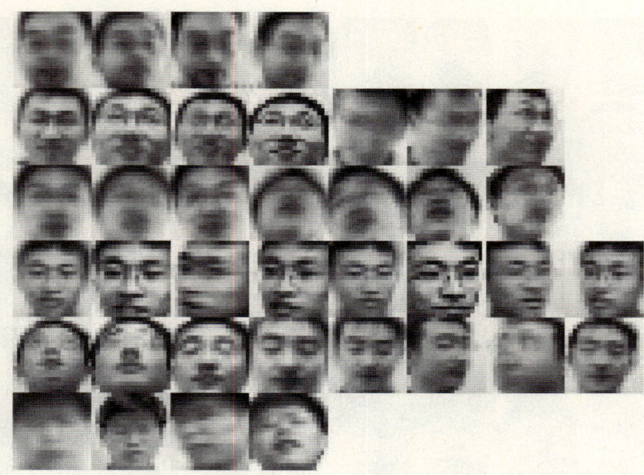

Fig. 2. Some eigenspace centers learnt using Multi-Eigenspace Learning when choosing $K = 8$.

We also implemented the Probabilistic Manifold online learning algorithm [7] for comparison. This algorithm starts with a generic manifold which is trained off-line in a batch mode. There are two steps in the online learning process. The first step is to find the pose manifold to which the current image belongs with the highest probability. The second step is to update the current appearance manifold using IPCA. The result from the first step is used to find a set of pre-training images that are expected to appear similar to the current subject in other poses. Then all of the other eigenspaces in the current appearance manifold are updated with synthetic images.

We use 15 of the 36 sequences for pre-training. The face images in the pre-training sequences are manually classified into 5 different pose clusters [7]. Then a 10-D pose subspace is computed from each cluster using PCA. The remain 21 video sequences are used for online learning and recognition. The first half of each sequence is used for online learning, and the second half is used for recognition. Our proposed algorithm also runs on these 21 sequences for comparison. The average recognition rates and the processing time are shown in Table 2. The recognition rate of Multi-Eigenspace Learning in Table 2 is different from that in Table 1. The reason is that the results in Table 2 are obtained from a 21-subject data set, while the results in Table 1 are obtained from a 36-subject data set.

In Table 2, we can see that our proposed algorithm gives higher recognition rate than that of Probabilistic Manifold algorithm [7], while the processing time is much shorter than the latter. One main reason is that the Probabilistic Manifold algorithm use only 5 pose manifolds which are not flexible enough to represent different poses. Moreover, updating eigenspaces with synthetic face images significantly increases the time complexity. In contrast, the proposed algorithm is more flexible to learn representative eigenspace models online.

Table 2. Comparison of the Probabilistic Manifold algorithm and our proposed algorithm. For Multi-Eigenspace Learning, we choose $K = 8$. Because Multi-Eigenspace Learning needs no pre-training, the corresponding blank is left empty.

Method	Probabilistic Manifold [7]	Multi-Eigenspace Learning
Recognition rates	92.4%	96.2%
Online learning	34.3s	7.1s
Pre-training	77.3s	-

5 Conclusions

In this paper we have presented a novel online appearance model learning algorithm for video-based face recognition. For each subject, we build several eigenspace models to approximately construct the face appearance manifold. The number of eigenspace models corresponding to each subject is variable. The eigenspace models are dynamically adjusted using IPCA. In the process of online learning, each eigenspace generally contains more and more samples except one eigenspace which contains the least number of samples. The learnt eigenspace models can be used for video-based face recognition. In our experiments, the average recognition rate can reach as high as 98.1%.

Acknowledgments. This work was supported by Program of New Century Excellent Talents in University, National Natural Science Foundation of China (No. 60575003, 60332010, 60335010, 60121302, 60275003, 69825105, 60605008), Joint Project supported by National Science Foundation of China and Royal Society of UK (60710059), Hi-Tech Research and Development Program of China (2006AA01Z133, 2006AA01Z193), the National Basic Research Program (Grant No.2004CB318110) and the Chinese Academy of Sciences.

References

1. Arandjelovie, O., Cipolla, R.: Face recognition from video using the generic shape-illumination manifold. In: Proc. European Conf. on Computer Vision, vol. 3594, pp. 27–40 (2006)
2. Fan, W., Yeung, D.-Y.: Face recognition with image sets using hierarchically extracted exemplars from appearance manifolds. In: Proceedings of the 7th International Conf. on Automatic Face and Gesture Recognition, pp. 177–182 (2006)
3. Hall, P.M., Marshall, D., Martin, R.R.: Incremental eigenanalysis for classification. In: The British Machine Vision Conference, pp. 286–295 (1998)
4. Kong, S.G., Heo, J., Abidi, B.R., Paik, J., Abidi, M.A.: Recent advances in visual and infrared face recognition - a review. Computer Vision and Image Understanding 97, 103–135 (2005)
5. Krueger, V., Zhou, S.: Exemplars-based face recognition from video. In: Proc. European Conf. on Computer Vision, vol. 4, pp. 732–746 (2002)

6. Lee, K.-C., Ho, J., Yang, M.-H., Kriegman, D.: Videobased face recognition using probabilistic appearance manifolds. In: proceedings of the CVPR, pp. 313–320 (2003)
7. Lee, K.-C., Kriegman, D.: Online learning of probabilistic appearance manifolds for video-based recognition and tracking. In: Proceedings of the CVPR, vol. 1, pp. 852–859 (2005)
8. Liu, L., Wang, Y., Tan, T.: Online appearance model learning for video-based face recognition. In: IEEE Computer Society Workshop on Biometrics. IEEE Computer Society Press, Los Alamitos (2007)
9. Liu, W., Li, Z., Tang, X.: Spatio-temporal embedding for statistical face recognition from video. In: Leonardis, A., Bischof, H., Pinz, A. (eds.) ECCV 2006. LNCS, vol. 3952, pp. 374–388. Springer, Heidelberg (2006)
10. Liu, X., Chen, T.: Video-based face recognition using adaptive hidden markov models. In: Proceedings of the CVPR, pp. 340–345 (2003)
11. Moghaddam, B., Pentland, A.: Probabilistic visual learning for object recognition. IEEE Transactions on Pattern Analysis and Machine Intelligence 19(7), 696–710 (1997)
12. Shakhnarovich, G., Fisher, J.W., Darrell, T.: Face recognition from long-term observations. In: Proc. European Conf. on Computer Vision, vol. 3, pp. 851–865 (2002)
13. Skarbek, W.: Merging subspace models for face recognition. In: Proceedings of the CAIP, pp. 606–613 (2003)
14. Tang, X., Li, Z.: Frame synchronization and multi-level subspace analysis for video based face recognition. In: Proceedings of the CVPR, pp. 902–907 (2004)
15. Tipping, M.E., Bishop, C.M.: Mixtures of probabilistic principal component analysers. Neural Computation 11(2), 443–482 (1999)
16. Viola, P., Jones, M.: Rapid object detection using a boosted cascade of simple features. In: Proceedings of the CVPR, vol. 1, pp. 511–518 (2001)
17. Yamaguchi, O., Fukui, K., ichi Maeda, K.: Face recognition using temporal image sequence. In: Proceedings of International Conf. on Automatic Face and Gesture Recognition, pp. 318–323 (1998)
18. Zhao, W., Chellappa, R., Phillips, P., Rosenfeld, A.: Face recognition: A literature survey. ACM Computing Surveys 35(4), 399–458 (2003)
19. Zhou, S., Krueger, V., Chellappa, R.: Probabilistic recognition of human faces from video. Computer Vision and Image Understanding 91, 214–245 (2003)
20. Zhou, S.K., Chellappa, R.: Probabilistic identity characterization for face recognition. In: Proceedings of the CVPR, vol. 2, pp. 805–812 (2004)

Error-Rate Based Biometrics Fusion

Kar-Ann Toh

Biometrics Engineering Research Center
School of Electrical & Electronic Engineering
Yonsei University, Seoul, Korea
katoh@yonsei.ac.kr

Abstract. This paper addresses the face verification problem by fusing visual and infra-red face verification systems. Unlike the conventional least squares error minimization approach which involves fitting of a learning model to data density and then perform a threshold process for error counting, this work directly formulates the required target error count rate in terms of design model parameters. A simple power series model is adopted as the fusion classifier and our experiments show promising results.

1 Introduction

Existing 2D face recognition systems are much hindered by external factors such as illumination, pose, expression and etc (see e.g. [1]). Apart from adopting complicated compensation means for illumination variations, fusion of the visual (VS) and infra-red (IR) images has been experimented ([2,3,4,5,6]). Different from these works, this paper focuses on identity verification based on fusion of matching scores from visual and infra-red face images, paying particular attention to effective and efficient fusion classifier design under difficult situations when fusing a moderately accurate system with a weak system.

Essentially, the task of identity verification can be considered as a pattern classification task since a comparison between two face images results in either a match (genuine-user) or a non-match (imposter) output. Apart from the statistical means, learning from examples constitutes a major paradigm in pattern classification (see e.g. [7,8]). Under this paradigm, a classifier is a map between the input feature space and the output hypothesis space. Although one usually does not have full access to the expected input-output spaces, a subset of this input-output space, which we called training set, is often available. Our work here belongs to the training based approach (see e.g.[9,10,11]) working at match score level.

We propose to use the total error counting rate instead of the data density fitting objective for supervised classifier learning. The error rate is a percentage count of misclassified samples and this poses difficulty to analyze it directly without imposing strong assumptions regarding the data distribution. However, utilizing a smooth functional approximation to the error counting objective, we are able to formulate a single-step solution to solve this problem. The solution

S.-W. Lee and S.Z. Li (Eds.): ICB 2007, LNCS 4642, pp. 191–200, 2007.

is found to belong to a particular setting of the weighted least squares solution having a class specific sample normalization. A simple power series model is found to be suitable in this classification application. The power series was not seen in biometrics fusion literature, perhaps, due to its non-compactness related to functional approximation.

The face images used in our experiments were captured under various illumination, pose and expression conditions. This gives rise to the visual face data showing relatively weak verification performance as compared to the infrared face data. Hence, the data set used demonstrates a particular difficult situation of fusing a moderately accurate biometric with a weak biometric since the weak biometric may deteriorate the fusion outcome.

2 An Error Counting Power Series Model

2.1 Power Series Model

Linear parametric models have been widely used due to their tractability in optimization and related analysis. The embedment of nonlinearities such as kernels and other basis functions into linear regression models has even widen their scope of applications (see e.g. [12,13,14]). Common choice of the basis functions includes radial basis function, polynomials, and sigmoid function [15]. Here, we consider a simple power series model as the basis function for fusion of visual and infra-red face score data.

Consider a l-dimensional input $\boldsymbol{x}$ and the following power series model:

$$g(\boldsymbol{\alpha}, \boldsymbol{x}) = \alpha_0 + \sum_{k=1}^{r} \sum_{j=1}^{l} \alpha_{k,j} x_j^k,$$

where $x_j, j = 1, ..., l$ are the biometric scores for fusion, α_0 and $\alpha_{k,j}$ are the weighting coefficients to be estimated. l and r correspond to input-dimension and order of system respectively. The total number of terms in this model can be expressed as $K = 1 + rl$. This model is different from the polynomial model in [16] ($K = 1 + r + l(2r - 1)$) since it has much smaller number of expansion terms.

The above power series model can be compactly written in vector form:

$$g(\boldsymbol{\alpha}, \boldsymbol{x}) = \sum_{k=0}^{K-1} \alpha_k p_k(\boldsymbol{x}) = \boldsymbol{p}(\boldsymbol{x})\boldsymbol{\alpha}, \quad (1)$$

where each $p_k(\boldsymbol{x})$ corresponds to a power basis expansion term, and collectively these power expansion terms form a row vector $\boldsymbol{p}(\boldsymbol{x}) = [1, p_1(\boldsymbol{x}), ..., p_{K-1}(\boldsymbol{x})]$. $\boldsymbol{\alpha} = [\alpha_0, \alpha_1, ..., \alpha_{K-1}]^T$ denotes the column parameter vector to be estimated.

When each element of $\boldsymbol{x} \in \mathbb{R}^l$ has a known label $y \in \{0, 1\}$ (e.g. '1' indicates a genuine-user and '0' indicates an imposter), we can form the learning data pairs $(\boldsymbol{x}_i, y_i)$ from $i = 1, 2, ..., m$ observations. The learning problem can then be *supervised*. Learning of the target labels (packed as $\mathbf{y} = [y_1, y_2, \cdots, y_m]^T$) is conventionally accomplished by minimizing a Sum of Squared-Errors criterion (SSE, the minimization process is also commonly called Least-Squares Error, LSE). To stabilize the solution for estimation, a weight decay regularization can be incorporated. The criterion function to be minimized thus becomes:

$$J(\boldsymbol{\alpha}) = \frac{1}{2}||\mathbf{y} - \mathbf{P}\boldsymbol{\alpha}||_2^2 + \frac{b}{2}||\boldsymbol{\alpha}||_2^2, \tag{2}$$

where b controls the weighting of regularization factor, $\mathbf{P} \in \mathbb{R}^{m \times K}$ packs the training features in matrix form, and $\|\cdot\|_2$ denotes the L_2-norm. The estimated training output is given by $\hat{\mathbf{y}} = \mathbf{P}\hat{\boldsymbol{\alpha}}$ where the solution for $\boldsymbol{\alpha}$ which minimizes J is

$$\text{LSE}: \qquad \hat{\boldsymbol{\alpha}} = (\mathbf{P}^T\mathbf{P} + b\mathbf{I})^{-1}\mathbf{P}^T\mathbf{y}, \tag{3}$$

with b being chosen to be a small value for stability and not introducing much bias. $\mathbf{I}$ is an identity matrix of similar dimension to $\mathbf{P}^T\mathbf{P}$.

For an unseen test data sample $\boldsymbol{x}_t$, a new power series vector $\boldsymbol{p}(\boldsymbol{x}_t)$ (row vector) can be generated. Prediction of the class label for this test data can be performed using the above learned $\hat{\boldsymbol{\alpha}}$ (i.e. $\hat{g}(\boldsymbol{x}_t) = \boldsymbol{p}(\boldsymbol{x}_t)\hat{\boldsymbol{\alpha}}$) and a threshold ($\tau$) process:

$$cls(\hat{g}(\boldsymbol{x}_t)) = \begin{cases} 1 & \text{if } \hat{g}(\boldsymbol{x}_t) \geqslant \tau \ , \\ 0 & \text{if } \hat{g}(\boldsymbol{x}_t) < \tau \ . \end{cases} \tag{4}$$

For multiple samples of test data, the multiple row vectors of $\boldsymbol{p}(\boldsymbol{x}_t)$ can be stacked to form a matrix $\mathbf{P}_t$ and predictions can be made collectively using $\mathbf{P}_t\hat{\boldsymbol{\alpha}}$.

2.2 Classification Error Rates

The above LSE formulation is a simple and effective method for classifier learning. However, LSE fits the training data according to the distribution density instead of the desired classification error, and this frequently results in overfitting. In this section, we introduce a deterministic error counting formulation to overcome this problem. We shall discuss a conventional method using nonlinear function approximation prior to presentation of a novel formulation which can be solved in a single step.

Consider the prediction and decision process in (4). For each operational setting of τ, a *False Acceptance Rate* (FAR) and a *False Rejection Rate* (FRR) can be defined. Without loss of generality, consider the case where the scores of genuine-users are distributed at higher values than those of imposters. By varying the threshold τ from $-\infty$ to $+\infty$ (or from 0 to 1 in a normalized case), the FRR shows an increasing trend while the FAR shows a decreasing trend, both with respect to this change of τ. Along the variation of threshold τ, there is a point (say, at τ^*) where the two curves (FAR and FRR) cross each other, and this point is called the *Equal Error Rate* (EER).

The *Total Error Rate* is defined as the sum of the False Acceptance and the False Rejection rates: TER = FAR + FRR. The EER mentioned above is frequently used as a performance index for biometric systems because at this particular operating point, the TER is frequently found to be near its minimum. This is particularly true when the genuine-user and imposter score distributions are normal. As such, the EER is frequently approximated by TER/2 at τ^* [17] and minimization of EER may be treated as minimization of the *minimum* TER. We shall minimize the empirical TER and observe its impact on the observed EER in this development.

Denote the genuine-user and imposter examples of variables $(\boldsymbol{x}, m)$ by superscripts + and − respectively, it is not difficult to see that the FAR and FRR are merely the averaged counts of decision scores falling within the opposite pattern categories:

$$\text{FAR} = \frac{1}{m^-}\sum_{j=1}^{m^-} 1_{g(\boldsymbol{x}_j^-)\geqslant\tau} \;, \tag{5}$$

$$\text{FRR} = \frac{1}{m^+}\sum_{i=1}^{m^+} 1_{g(\boldsymbol{x}_i^+)<\tau} \;, \tag{6}$$

where the term $1_{g(\boldsymbol{x})\geqslant\tau}$ ($1_{g(\boldsymbol{x})<\tau}$) corresponds to a '1' whenever $g(\boldsymbol{x}) \geqslant \tau$ ($g(\boldsymbol{x}) < \tau$), and '0' otherwise.

2.3 Solving the Error Counting Problem

To solve the TER problem from (5)-(6), an approximation to the non-differentiable counting or step function is often adopted. A natural choice to approximate the above step function is the sigmoid function [18] where the minimization problem becomes $\arg\min_{\boldsymbol{\alpha}} \text{TER}(\boldsymbol{\alpha})$:

$$\text{TER}(\boldsymbol{\alpha}) = \frac{1}{m^-}\sum_{j=1}^{m^-} \sigma(\epsilon(\boldsymbol{\alpha}, \boldsymbol{x}_j^-)) + \frac{1}{m^+}\sum_{i=1}^{m^+} \sigma(\varepsilon(\boldsymbol{\alpha}, \boldsymbol{x}_i^+)), \tag{7}$$

where

$$\sigma(x) = \frac{1}{1+e^{-\gamma x}}, \quad \gamma > 0 \;, \tag{8}$$

and $\epsilon(\boldsymbol{\alpha}, \boldsymbol{x}_j^-) = g(\boldsymbol{\alpha}, \boldsymbol{x}_j^-) - \tau$ for $j = 1, 2, ..., m^-$ and $\varepsilon(\boldsymbol{\alpha}, \boldsymbol{x}_i^+) = \tau - g(\boldsymbol{\alpha}, \boldsymbol{x}_i^+)$ for $i = 1, 2, ..., m^+$ are the error counts.

There are two problems associated with this approximation. The first problem is that the formulation is nonlinear with respect to the learning parameters. Although an iterative search can be employed for local solutions, different initializations may end up with different local solutions, hence incurring laborious trial and error efforts to select an appropriate setting. The second problem is that the objective function could be ill-conditioned due to the much local plateaus resulting from summing the flat regions of the sigmoid. A lot of search effort may be spent upon making little progress at locally flat regions.

Notice that the power series model is linear with respect to its parameters $\boldsymbol{\alpha}$. We then seek in this section a deterministic single-step solution from matching of the link-loss functional pair [19,20]. When we have all inputs normalized within $[0,1]$, the step functional can be approximated by centering a quadratic functional at the origin. With this idea in mind, the following regularized quadratic TER approximation is proposed:

$$\text{TER} = \frac{b}{2}\|\boldsymbol{\alpha}\|_2^2 + \frac{1}{2m^-}\sum_{j=1}^{m^-}\left[\epsilon(\boldsymbol{\alpha}, \boldsymbol{x}_j^-) + \eta\right]^2 + \frac{1}{2m^+}\sum_{i=1}^{m^+}\left[\varepsilon(\boldsymbol{\alpha}, \boldsymbol{x}_i^+) + \eta\right]^2. \quad (9)$$

where $\eta > 0$ and $\epsilon(\boldsymbol{\alpha}, \boldsymbol{x}_j^-) = \boldsymbol{p}(\boldsymbol{x}_j^-)\boldsymbol{\alpha} - \tau$, $\varepsilon(\boldsymbol{\alpha}, \boldsymbol{x}_i^+) = \tau - \boldsymbol{p}(\boldsymbol{x}_i^+)\boldsymbol{\alpha}$, for $j = 1, 2, ..., m^-$, $i = 1, 2, ..., m^+$.

Abbreviating the row power series vectors $\boldsymbol{p}_j = \boldsymbol{p}(\boldsymbol{x}_j^-) \in \mathbb{R}^K$ and $\boldsymbol{p}_i = \boldsymbol{p}(\boldsymbol{x}_i^+) \in \mathbb{R}^K$, the solution for $\boldsymbol{\alpha}$ which minimizes (9) can be written as

$$\boldsymbol{\alpha} = \left[b\mathbf{I} + \frac{1}{m^-}\sum_{j=1}^{m^-}\boldsymbol{p}_j^T\boldsymbol{p}_j + \frac{1}{m^+}\sum_{i=1}^{m^+}\boldsymbol{p}_i^T\boldsymbol{p}_i\right]^{-1}\left[\frac{(\tau-\eta)}{m^-}\sum_{j=1}^{m^-}\boldsymbol{p}_j^T + \frac{(\tau+\eta)}{m^+}\sum_{i=1}^{m^+}\boldsymbol{p}_i^T\right], \quad (10)$$

where $\mathbf{I}$ is an identity matrix of $K \times K$ size. The learned $\boldsymbol{\alpha}$ can then be used to predict new test samples in a similar manner as the procedure described in section 2.1.

Remark 1: Here we see that (10) consists of class-specific normalization of the input covariates, and this result can be considered as a specialized setting of the more generic weight least squares. It is noted that the solution given by (10) is deterministic and single-step without the need of initialization. This is a clear advantage over those conventional formulations such as (7) which require an iterative search. □

3 Face Verification

3.1 Visual Face Images

The visual face images used in this study were captured under various illumination and pose conditions using a Bumblebee CCD camera produced by Point Grey Research Inc. (see [6] for details). The resolution of the image used was 320×240 pixels. The top row of Fig. 1 shows some visual image samples for an identity under various illumination and pose conditions. In this work, we adopted the holistic approach using PCA since it is among the most common choices due to it simplicity and effectiveness. To compare similarity between two face images, the Euclidean distance was used for the first 100 eigenvalues [6].

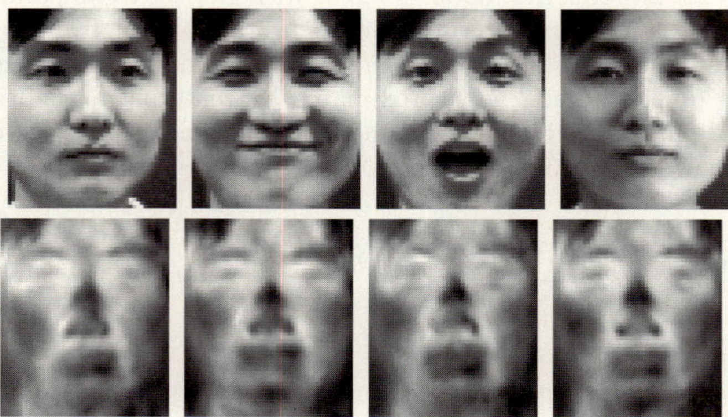

Fig. 1. Top row: visual face samples for an identity under different lighting, expression and pose conditions; **Bottom row**: infra-red face samples for the same identity under different lighting, expression and pose conditions

3.2 Infra-Red Face Images

The Infra-Red face images used in this study were captured using a ThermoVision S65 produced by FLIR Systems Inc. As in the visual face case, the images were captured under varying illumination and pose conditions with the resolution of the image being fixed at 320×240 pixels. The bottom row of Fig. 1 shows some infra-red image samples for the same identity under various conditions. Similar to the visual face, we adopted the holistic approach using PCA for the infra-red face. To compare similarity between two face images, the Euclidean distance was used for the first 100 eigenvalues [6].

In the following experiments, each data set corresponding to visual face (Face-VS) and infra-red face (Face-IR) verification consists of 96 identities, wherein each identity contains 10 image samples. For training and test purposes, each of these biometric data sets are partitioned into two equal sets consisting of $\mathcal{S}_{train}$ and $\mathcal{S}_{test}$, each with 96×5 samples. The genuine-user and the imposter match-scores are generated from these two sets by intra-identity and inter-identity matching among the image samples for each biometric. A total of 960 sample match-scores are thus available for the genuine-user class in each training set and test set for each biometric. As for the imposter scores, there are 114000 sample match-scores for the 96 identities. Since both face systems captured multiple images from the same person for each identity, the fusion constitutes a true multi-modal fusion.

3.3 Fusion of Face-VS and Face-IR scores

Based on the biometrics data described above, we perform fusion of the visual and infra-red face verification scores in the following experiments. Our main consideration is that ground applications encounter large variation of illumination conditions, and we believe that visual and infra-red images can complement each other. More importantly, these two modalities can be captured simultaneously and in a covert manner in practical scenarios.

In this experiment, we perform fusion experiments by combining the verification decisions from Face-VS and Face-IR where the images were captured simultaneously. Since the Face-VS has poor performance due to large variation of illumination conditions in the database, we shall observe the effects of fusing it with the much higher performed Face-IR. The following summarizes those fusion methods compared in our experiments:

i. Proposed PS-TER and PS-LSE: the proposed PS-TER (Power Series model trained by TER solution given by (10)) and PS-LSE (Power Series model trained by LSE solution given by (3)) are adopted for fusion of the above two face modalities. The power series are experimented with different model orders to observe the stability of test performance.
ii. Two simple SUM methods: the simple SUM rule was reported to be among the best fusion methods for multi-biometrics when the inputs are normalized appropriately (see e.g. [21]). For benchmarking purpose, we include in our experiments two important normalization methods namely the Min-Max and the robust hyperbolic tangent (*tanh*) method (see e.g. [21]) to precede the simple SUM rule.
iii. SVM adopting different kernels: in addition to the SUM rules, the Support Vector Machines adopting different kernels (polynomial and Radial Basis Function) are also included. This is to cater for nonlinear decision hypersurfaces as well as to benchmark with the well-acclaimed SVM in classification and biometrics fusion (see e.g. [22,23,12]). The SVMs are experimented with different model settings (polynomial order and Gaussian width) to observe the operational performance.

Performance evaluation: the EER shall be adopted as the performance comparison measure in all the forth coming experiments following [24]. There are also two reasons behind this choice of performance criterion: (i) it is a single value index which has a clear indication of high and low performances and this can be advantages to the use of ROC or DET where the curves for different algorithms may cross each other, and (ii) it is somewhat related to our optimization objective (minimization of TER).

Results:

Fig. 2 shows the average test EER performances for various model settings from two-fold validations. For SVM-Poly and PS model trained by LSE and TER, the model order varies for $r \in [1, 10]$. For SVM-Rbf, the kernel width (*gamma* parameter in [25]) varies in [0.1,1,...,10,100]. The DET plots for best performed settings of each method from the first-fold are shown in Fig. 3.

The results from Fig. 2(a) show that SVM-Rbf's performance deteriorates with small kernel widths (large *gamma* values). Both the fusion outputs from the SUM methods generated poorer performance than that from unimodal infra-red face.

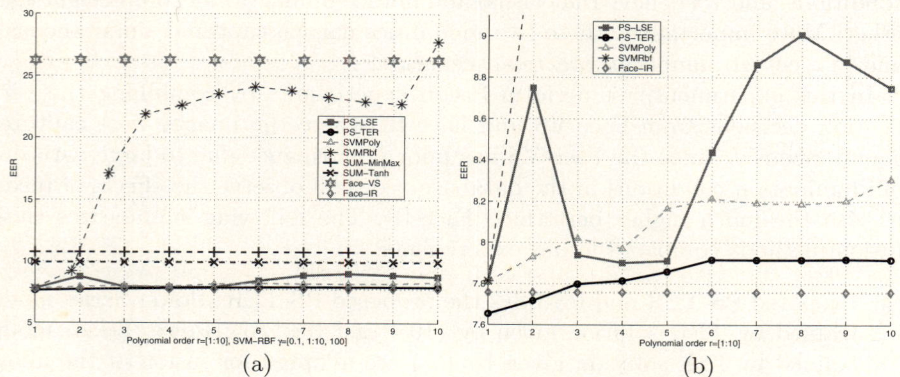

Fig. 2. (a) Average test EER values plotted over different classifier settings, (b) a zoom-in view

A zoom-in view of Fig. 2(a) in Fig. 2(b) shows superiority of PS-TER over PS-LSE for all power series order settings experimented. Two settings ($r = 1, 2$) of PS-TER show gain in fusion performance comparing to unimodal Face-IR (maximum improvement of 1.34% at $r = 1$, this can mean additional 1523 imposters being rejected based on the size of the database). For SVM-Poly and SVM-Rbf, no gain in performance is observed for all model settings.

The above results suggest that fusion of a moderate biometric with a weak one can have deteriorated performance when the fusion classifier is not well tuned. For the experimented data set, the proposed TER method shows good

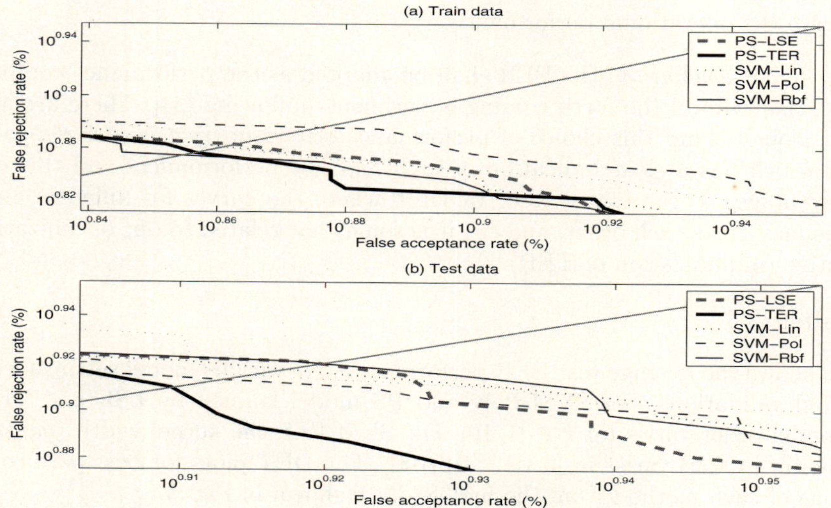

Fig. 3. Detection Error Tradeoff (DET) curves

generalization property with respect to different model tunings as compared to LSE and SVM. This shows that useful information gain can still be acquired from the weaker biometric with appropriate fusion classifier design.

4 Conclusion

In this paper, we proposed to minimize an error rate formulation for face recognition. Unlike conventional learning and threshold processes to arrive at a decision error count rate, the proposed method directly optimized the error count rate with respect to a power series model design. The identity verification was performed using both visual and infra-red face image cues which constitutes a difficult scenario of fusing a moderately accurate biometric to a weak one. Our experiments show stability of fusion results thereby illustrating useful information gain can still be acquired from a weak biometric in fusion.

Acknowledgements

The author would like to acknowledge Prof Anil. K. Jain (Michigan State University) for useful discussions regarding the research topic. The face data sets prepared by Mr Sangki Kim and Prof Sangyoun Lee are also acknowledged.

This work was supported by the Korea Science and Engineering Foundation (KOSEF) through the Biometrics Engineering Research Center (BERC) at Yonsei University.

References

1. Li, S.Z., Jain, A.K. (eds.): Handbook of Face Recognition. Springer, New York (2004)
2. Chen, X., Flynn, P.J., Bowyer, K.W.: IR and visible light face recognition. Computer Vision and Image Understanding 99(3), 332–358 (2005)
3. Kong, S., Heo, J., Abidi, B., Paik, J., Abidi, M.: Recent advances in visual and infrared face recognition–a review. Computer Vision and Image Understanding 97(1), 103–135 (2005)
4. Wilder, J., Phillips, P.J., Jiang, C., Wiener, S.: Comparison of visible and infrared imagery for face recognition. In: Proc. 2nd International Conference on Automatic Face and Gesture Recognition, pp. 182–187 (1996)
5. Socolinsky, D.A., Selinger, A., Neuheisel, J.D.: Face recognition with visible and thermal infrared imagery. Vision and Image Understanding 91(1-2), 72–114 (2003)
6. Kim, S.-K., Lee, H., Yu, S., Lee, S.: Robust face recognition by fusion of visual and infrared cues. In: Proceedings of the First IEEE Conference on Industrial Electronics and Applications, Singapore, May 2006, pp. 804–808 (2006)
7. Duda, R.O., Hart, P.E., Stork, D.G.: Pattern Classification, 2nd edn. John Wiley & Sons, Inc. New York (2001)
8. Schürmann, J.: Pattern Classification: A Unified View of Statistical and Neural Approaches. John Wiley & Sons, Inc. New York (1996)

9. Kittler, J., Messer, K.: Fusion of multiple experts in multimodal biometric personal identity verification systems. In: Proceedings of the 2002 12th IEEE Workshop on Neural Networks for Signal Processing, pp. 3–12 (2002)
10. Kuncheva, L.I., Bezdek, J.C., Duin, R.: Decision templates for multiple classifier design: An experimental comparison. Pattern Recognition 34(2), 299–314 (2001)
11. Huang, Y.S., Suen, C.Y.: A method of combining multiple experts for the recognition of unconstrained handwriten numerals. IEEE Trans. on Pattern Analysis and Machine Intelligence 17(1), 90–94 (1995)
12. Boser, B.E., Guyon, I.M., Vapnik, V.N.: A training algorithm for optimal margin classifier. In: Proceedings of the 5th ACM Workshop on Computational Learning Theory, Pittsburgh, PA, pp. 144–152 (1992)
13. Poggio, T., Girosi, F.: Networks for approximation and learning. Proceedings of the IEEE 78(9), 1481–1497 (1990)
14. Schölkopf, B., Smola, A.J.: Learning with Kernels: Support Vector Machines, Regularization, Optimization, and Beyond. MIT Press, Cambridge, MA (2002)
15. Toh, K.-A.: Training a ϕ-machine classifier using feature scaling-space. In: Proceedings of the 4th International IEEE Conference on Industrial Informatics, Singapore, August 2006, pp. 1334–1339 (2006)
16. Toh, K.-A., Tran, Q.-L., Srinivasan, D.: Benchmarking a reduced multivariate polynomial pattern classifier. IEEE Trans. Pattern Analysis and Machine Intelligence 26(6), 740–755 (2004)
17. Poh, N., Bengio, S.: How do correlation and variance of base-experts affect fusion in biometric authentication tasks? IEEE Trans. on Signal Processing 53(11), 4384–4396 (2005)
18. Toh, K.-A.: Learning from target knowledge approximation. In: Proceedings of the First IEEE Conference on Industrial Electronics and Applications, Singapore, May 2006, pp. 815–822 (2006)
19. Gordon, G.J.: Generalized^2 Linear^2 Models. In: Advances in Neural Information Processing Systems (NIPS 2002), Vancouver, British Columbia, Canada, December 2002, pp. 577–584 (2002)
20. McCullagh, P., Nelder, J.A.: Generalized Linear Models, 2nd edn. Chapman and Hall, London (1989)
21. Jain, A.K., Nandakumar, K., Ross, A.: Score normalization in multimodal biometric systems. Pattern Recognition 38, 2270–2285 (2005)
22. Ben-Yacoub, S., Abdeljaoued, Y., Mayoraz, E.: Fusion of face and speech data for person identity verification. IEEE Trans. on Neural Networks 10(5), 1065–1074 (1999)
23. Vapnik, V.N.: Statistical Learning Theory. Wiley-Interscience Pub. Chichester (1998)
24. Maio, D., Maltoni, D., Cappelli, R., Wayman, J.L., Jain, A.K.: FVC2000: Fingerprint verification competition. IEEE Trans. on Pattern Analysis and Machine Intelligence 24(3), 402–412 (2002)
25. Ma, J., Zhao, Y., Ahalt, S.: OSU SVM classifier Matlab toolbox (ver 3.00), the Ohio State University (2002), [http://eewww.eng.ohio-state.edu/~maj/osu_svm/]

Online Text-Independent Writer Identification Based on Stroke's Probability Distribution Function

Bangyu Li, Zhenan Sun, and Tieniu Tan

Center for Biometrics and Security Research, National Lab of Pattern Recognition, Institute of Automation, Chinese Academy of Science, Beijing, P.R. China
{byli,znsun,tnt}@nlpr.ia.ac.cn

Abstract. This paper introduces a novel method for online writer identification. Traditional methods make use of the distribution of directions in handwritten traces. The novelty of this paper comes from 1)We propose a text-independent writer identification that uses handwriting stroke's probability distribution function (SPDF) as writer features; 2)We extract four dynamic features to characterize writer individuality; 3)We develop new distance measurement and combine dynamic features in reducing the number of characters required for online text-independent writer identification. In particular, we performed comparative studies of different similarity measures in our experiments. Experiments were conducted on the NLPR handwriting database involving 55 persons. The results show that the new method can improve the identification accuracy and reduce the number of characters required.

Keywords: text-independent, writer identification, stroke's probability distribution function, dynamic features.

1 Introduction

Writer identification is the task of determining the writer of a sample handwriting [1]. Surveys covering work in automatic writer identification and signature verification until 1993 are given in [2][1]. Traditionally, research into writer identification has been focused on two streams: offline and online writer identification [3]. Scarce research results can be found in the online direction, in particular, personal identification using online Chinese handwriting. So far, two different kinds of methods find their ways in handwriting authentication: text-dependent way and text-independent way. Text-independent methods have prominent advantages over text-dependent cases in specific conditions. Text with the same content is not required for the training samples and the testing ones, and the natural handwriting in a wide range can be dealt with [4]. It is difficult for the imposter to imitate the handwriting of others. Therefore, text-independent methods have gained more and more attention in recent years.

Recently, a number of new approaches to writer identification have been proposed, such as those using connected-component contours and edge-based features [5], using dynamic features on strokes [6][7][8] or on hinge angles [9][10],

S.-W. Lee and S.Z. Li (Eds.): ICB 2007, LNCS 4642, pp. 201–210, 2007.

using texture feature[3] [11][12], using innovative binarised features [13], using moment feature [14], etc. Furthermore, some classical methods for character recognition are helpful, such as statistical character structure modeling [10], dynamic time warping (DTW) or cluster generative statistical dynamic time warping (CSDTW) [4] and so on. In these methods, dynamic or static features are widely adopted to discriminate the handwriting. They have been proved to be feasible, but some disadvantages still exist.

The proposed algorithm is implemented based on the strokes of the characters, for the Chinese characters are composed of multiple interlaced strokes in most cases. In this paper, with the information extracted from the strokes, a comprehensive analysis of the writing style is obtained. We propose a novel approach for online writer identification based on the stroke's probability distribution function.

The paper is structured as follows. The next section presents previous works and motivation. The dynamic features of strokes are extracted from handwriting in Section 3. In Section 4 we describe the writer identification algorithm with distance between histograms. The results of our experiments and discussion are presented in Section 5. Finally, in Section 6 we conclude the paper.

2 Previous Work and Motivation

2.1 Previous Work

We adopted the traditional framework of pattern recognition to our handwriting identification problem, as Fig. 1 shows [6].

On-line handwriting samples are obtained as a sequence of parameterized dots, inside which involves coordinates, relative time, pressure and pen inclination information. The raw data are tailored to fit in with the basic requirement

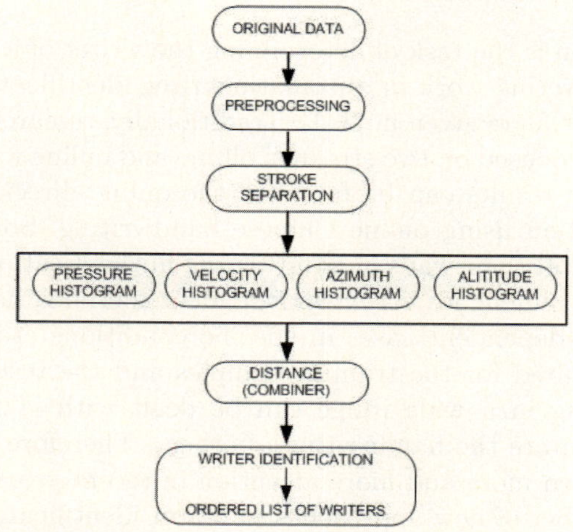

Fig. 1. Schematic diagram of the proposed algorithm

of subsequent process. Here only the fake writing movements are eliminated. Afterwards, the separation of strokes is implemented in three steps, namely 1) line separation, 2) connection separation and 3) stroke separation. The last step of preprocess is stroke type evaluation, where strokes are allocated to predefined stroke types. According to the structural constituents of the Chinese characters, 12 primary stroke types are selected, as Fig. 2 shows, and the arrow below each stroke indicates the writing direction of the stroke. Details may be found in [6].

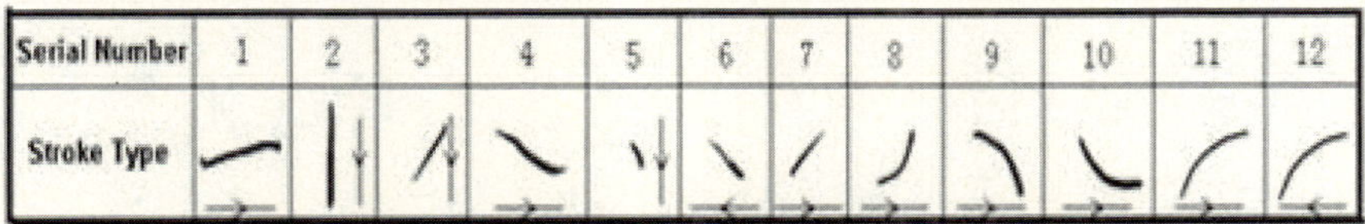

Fig. 2. The 12 Primary Stroke Types

2.2 Motivation

Online text independent writer identification usually requires the use of statistical features computed from a large quantity of data to avoid anomalies due to specific text. Our previous method builds Gaussian models that each model could be represented by its mean value and variance[6], which is lack of sufficient information to characterize dynamic attribute of strokes in handwriting.

We use the stroke's probability distribution function (SPDF) of four dynamic features to characterize writer individuality. The smallest units forming a Chinese character are strokes, and this method aims to capture more dynamic aspects of the writing behavior of an individual. Writing different Chinese characters will lead to the difference of strokes' statistical information and the emotional and physical state of writers will have influence on its dynamic features. However, this method uses statistical features of primary stroke types and four dynamic features are divided into small units that characterize more detailed writer individuality. The stroke's occurrence of PDF is a discriminatory feature among different writers. Moreover, the dynamic features can be computed very fast using histogram representation. So we decide to choose SPDF to model dynamic features.

3 Feature Extraction

The feature extraction procedure is described in this section. It has long been known from online handwriting research that the distribution of directions in handwritten traces, as a polar plot, yields useful information for writer identification [15][16][17].

We use probability distribution functions extracted from strokes in handwriting samples to characterize writer individuality in an online text-independent manner. The raw data collected from the tablet includes many fake strokes and noises, as Fig. 3(a) shows. After the preprocessing of wiping off fake strokes, the separation of strokes is implemented, as Fig. 3(b) shows. In our analysis, we will consider a number of features that we have designed (f1, f2, f3, f4) for writer identification. Strokes well allocated help to simplify further analysis; features are extracted from the main 12 types of strokes in our method. We select distribution of the pressure, the velocity, the altitude and azimuth of $i = 12$ primary stroke types for the representations of the writing gestures and movements. We

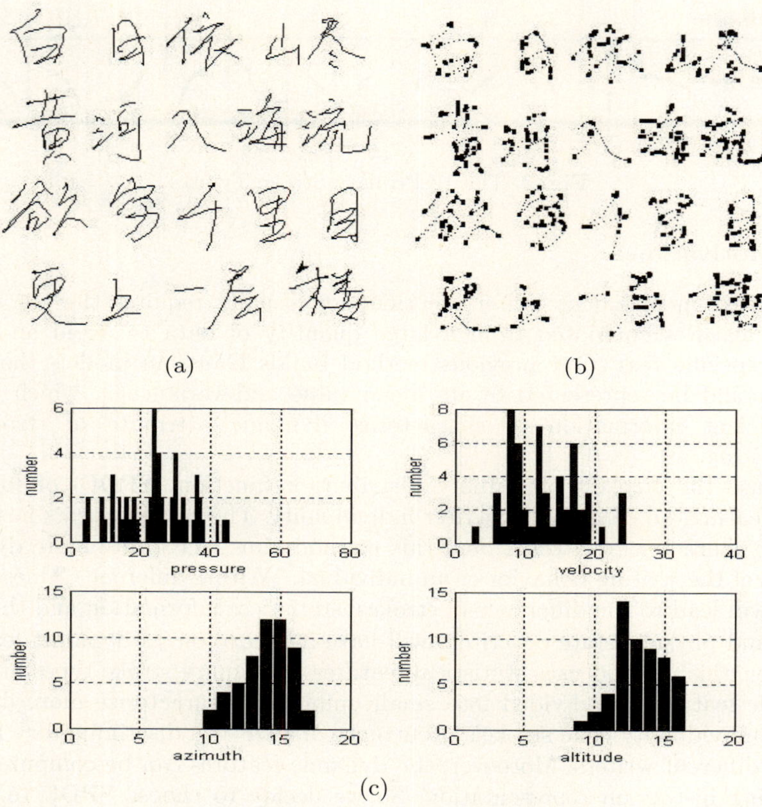

Fig. 3. (a)Original online text. (b)Stroke separation, where the black dots represent the starting and end points of a segment. (c)Pressure,velocity, azimuth and altitude histograms of Stroke type 1.

define four features (f1, f2, f3, f4) of stroke's probability distribution function. For pressure feature f1, the number of histogram bins spanning the interval 0-1024 was set $N = 64$ to through experimentation: 16/bin gives a sufficiently detailed and sufficiently robust description of handwriting to be used in writer identification. For velocity feature f2, by experiment, the number of histogram bins spanning the interval 0-300 was set to $N = 30$, so each bin has 10. The azimuth denotes the angle between the projection of the pen on the tablet and the vertical axis of the digital tablet, the altitude denotes the angle between the pen and its projection on the tablet, and synthesis of the two angles fixed the pen-grasping gesture of the writer. Because altitude ranges from 0^0 to 90^0 and azimuth ranges from 0^0 to 180^0, we choose 5^0 and 10^0 as a bin, respectively, as Figure 3(c) shows.

An overview of all the features used in our study is given in Table 1. In our analysis, we will consider four features based on strokes that we have designed and used for writer identification.

Table 1. Overview of the considered features

	Feature	Explanation	N dimensions
f1	$h_{1i}(A)$	Pressure-histogram	12*64
f1	$h_{2i}(A)$	Velocity-histogram	12*30
f3	$h_{3i}(A)$	Azimuth-histogram	12*18
f4	$h_{4i}(A)$	Altitude-histogram	12*18

4 Identification

Feature vectors of the testing data are extracted as well as the training data. The identification of writers based on given feature vectors is a typical recognition problem.

Writer identification is performed using nearest-neighbor classification in a "leave-one-out" strategy. For a query sample q, the distances to all the other samples $i \neq q$ are computed using a selected feature, and then all the samples are ordered in a sorted hit list with increasing distance to the query q. Ideally the first ranked sample should be the pair sample produced by the same writer. In our feature combination scheme, the five distances between any two handwritten samples is computed by weighted Sum-Rule of the dynamic features.

Most of the distance measures presented in the literature consider the overlap or intersection between two histograms as function of the distance value, but they do not take into account the similarity between the non-overlapping parts of the two histograms.

We choose new distances between histograms defined on a structure called signature, which is a lossless representation of histograms, the main advantage is that there is an important time-complexity reduction. Moreover, the type of the elements of the sets that the histograms represent are ordinal, nominal and modulo [18].

5 Experimental Results and Discussion

Our experiments are based on the NLPR handwriting database. In this database, samples are collected using a Wacom Intuos2 tablet. The tablet has 1024 levels of pressure sensitivity, and its maximum data rate is 200pps. 55 persons were required to write three different pages including approximately 600 Chinese characters altogether. The content of the handwriting is chosen by writers freely, so the database collected by this manner is text-independent handwriting database.

When we carry out the experiments with the method using dynamic features, two pages samples of each person are taken out for training and the other one (approximately 160 characters) is used for testing. We use x^2 distance, Euclidean distance and three distances [18] as a distance measure for SPDF features.

We are interested in a comparative performance analysis of the different features and in the improvements in performance obtained by combining multiple features. First we shall consider the individual features and then their combinations.

5.1 Performances of Individual Features

Fig. 4 gives the writer identification performance of the individual features considered in the present study. While there are important different in performance

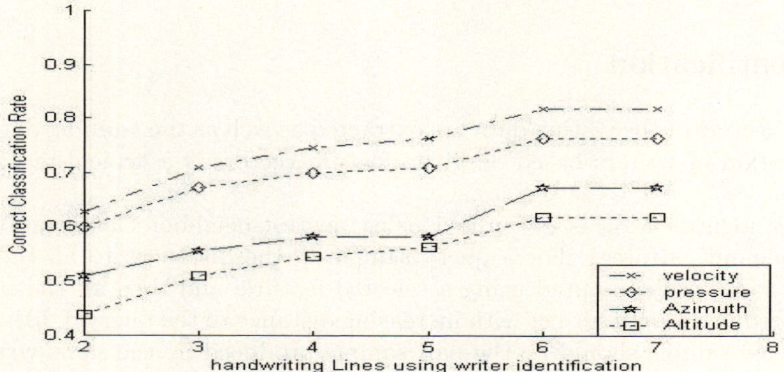

Fig. 4. The identification results for using individual feature

among the different features, the best performer is the velocity feature followed by the pressure feature. We select samples with 2 lines, 3 lines, 4 lines, 5 lines, 6 lines and 7 lines of characters for each time. The results are shown in Fig. 4.

5.2 Performances of Feature Combinations

The features considered in previous experiments capture different aspects of handwriting individuality, while our features are not completely orthogonal, combining multiple feature proves to be beneficial. In this paper, we use min-max rule for score normalization [19]. Given a set of matching scores $\{S_k\}$, $k = 1, 2, \cdots, n$, the normalized scores are given by

$$S_k^n = \frac{S_k - min}{max - min} \tag{1}$$

min and max are the minimum and maximum values estimated from $\{S_k\}$. The weighted sum rule is used to combine scores from each dynamic feature for text-independent writer identification. Let $\{S_1^j, S_2^j, \cdots, S_n^j\}$ be the matching scores for each dynamic feature, $j = 1, 2, \cdots, c$. Here, n is the number of samples, and c is the number of dynamic features. For the ith sample, the combined score can be computed as

$$S_i = \sum_{j=1}^{c} w^j * S_i^j \tag{2}$$

w^j is an indicator contribution coefficient defined as the confidence of each dynamic features. The confidence of each classifier is computed by the training result(the first experiment) as

$$w^j = \frac{FIR_j{}^{-1}}{\sum_{i=1}^{c} FIR_i{}^{-1}} \tag{3}$$

FIR is the False Identification Rate. Combination of dynamic features by five distances is performance in our method. We compare five distance in fusing features. The results are shown in Fig. 5.

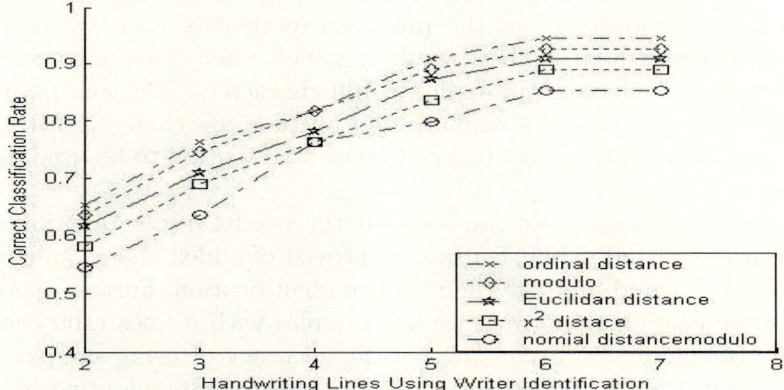

Fig. 5. The identification results for using feature combinations

For testing effectiveness of our method, we choose SVC 2004 database [20] and each signature as a stroke. The performance of feature combinations for writer identification on SVC 2004 database. We choose 40 writers and each writer has

Table 2. EER performance in our experiments

EER	Euclideanm dist	x^2dist	Nominal dist	Ordinal dist	Modulo dist
SVC database	11.4%	11.8%	15%	9.7%	10.4%

20 genuine signatures for our experiments, we apply feature combinations for writer identification, we can get results shown in Table 2.

The fourth set of experiments were performed to determine the effectiveness of feature extraction to classify handwritten data from strokes. Each stroke were extracted from one page (approx.8 lines) and the four dynamic features of each stroke was combined by the weighted sum rule. Table 3 shows the accuracy of each type of strokes. For other type of strokes, only 40% accuracy could be achieved, as the number of strokes extracted from handwriting is not so little that do contain much individuality information.

Table 3. Strokes Vs Accuracy

Type of Stroke	top-1 Accuracy	top-5 Accuracy
The horizontal(type 1)	70	92
The Verticcal(type 2)	68	90
The Left-falling Stroke(type 3)	60	73
The Right-falling Stroke(type 4)	63	74

5.3 Discussion

From experimental results we can find that: First, as Fig. 4 shows, it is important to observe that the feature f1 and f2 perform much better than the others, and the performance of the proposed method is also tested with increasing characters, where the best result is gained when the number of writing lines is beyond 6, including approximate 100 characters. The main reason for this result is that the range of azimuth and altitude are changing little in raw data, it is not sufficiently robust description of handwriting to be used in writer identification.

Second, as Fig. 5 shows, we can see that the results of combination are obviously better than individual feature. It proved our idea that combining the dynamic features could improve the result of identification. Further more, from the results, we can see that when we use samples with 6 lines (100 characters on average) of characters, it can achieve the accuracy of using samples with 7 lines (more than 120 characters on average) in experiments adopting individual dynamic features. The performance of ordinal distance is especially satisfactory. It shows that the combination method not only can improve the identification accuracy, but also reduces the amount of characters (lines) required in handwriting.

At last, as Table 2 shows, the ordinal distance performs better than the others. In SVC 2004 database, we find that distribution of pressure and velocity features can effectively describe the characteristics of the writer handwriting. The writer identification result is about 10% in terms of EER. The notable point is that the based on SPDF's feature can effectively describe the handwriting characteristics. and Table 3 shows, most of the shape primitive of Chinese character were straight lines. We can improve our accuracy as number of strokes increases, in future we can use straight lines to improve on the accuracy.

6 Conclusion

In this paper, we have proposed a novel method for online text-independent writer identification. In our method we not only adopt individual features based on SPDF for writer identification, but also choose feature combinations in some distance measures to improve identification accuracy. Experimental results show the dynamic features of strokes is a very stable personal characteristic and the most prominent attribute of online handwriting that reveals individual writing style and the dynamic features can be computed very fast using histogram representation with the additional advantage, the new method can improve the identification accuracy and reduce the number of characters required.

Acknowledgments. This work is funded by research grants from the National Basic Research Program (Grant No. 2004CB318110), the Natural Science Foundation of China (Grant No. 60335010, 60121302, 60275003, 60332010, 6982510560605008) and the Chinese Academy of Sciences.

References

1. Plamondon, R., Lorette, G.: Automatic signature verification and writer identification -the state of the art. Pattern Recognition, 107–131 (1989)
2. leclerc, F., Plamondon, R.: Automatic signature verification:the state of the art 1989-1993. International Journal of Pattern Recognition and Artificial Intelligence, 643–660 (1994)
3. Tan, T.N., Said, H., Baker, K.D.: Personal identification based on handwriting. Pattern Recognition, 149–160 (2000)
4. Bahlmann, C., Burkhardt, H.: The writer independent online handwriting recognition system frog on hand and cluster generative statistical dynamic time warping. IEEE Transactions on Pattern Analysis and Machine Intelligenc 1, 299–310 (2004)
5. Schomaker, L., Bulacu, M.: Automatic writer identification using connected-component contours and edge-based features of uppercase western script. IEEE Transactions on Pattern Analysis and Machine Intelligence 6, 787–798 (2004)
6. Wang, Y., Yu, K., Tan, T.: Writer identification using dynamic features. International Conference on Biometrics, 512–518 (July 2004)
7. Messerli, R., Marti, U.V., Bunke, H.: Writer identification using text line based features. In: Internal Conference on Document Anaysis and Recognition, pp. 101–105 (2001)
8. Schomaker, L.R.B., Plamondon, R.: The relation between pen force and pen-point kinematics in handwriting. Biological Cybernetics, 277–289 (1990)
9. Methasate, I., Sae-Tang, S.: On-line thai handwriting character recognition using stroke segmentation with hmm. In: International conference on Applied informatis-Artificial Intelligence and Applications, pp. 59–62 (2002)
10. Kim, I.-J., Kim, J.-H.: Statistical character structure modeling and its application to handwritten chinese character recognition. Biological Cybernetics, 1422–1436 (2003)
11. Wang, Y., Zhu, Y., Tan, T.: Biometric personal identification based on handwriting. International Conference on Pattern Recognition, 801–804 (2001)

12. Tan, T.N.: Texture feature extraction via cortical channel modeling. In: Proc.11th IAPR Inter. Conf. Pattern Recognition, pp. 607–610 (1992)
13. Leedham, G., Chachra, S.: Writer identification using innovative binarised features of handwritten numerals. In: Internal Conference on Document Anaysis and Recognition, pp. 413–417 (2003)
14. Mertzios, B.G., Tsirikolias, K.: Statistical pattern recognition using efficient two-dimensional moments with applications to character recognition. pattern recognition, 877–882 (1993)
15. maarse, F., Thomassen, A.: Produced and perceived writing slant:differences between up and down strokes. Acta psychologica 3, 131–147 (1983)
16. Schomaker, L., Maarse, F., Teulings, H.-L.: Automatic identification of writers. In: Human-computer interaction: Psychonomic aspects, pp. 353–360. Springer, Heidelberg (1988)
17. Crettez, J.-P.: A set of handwriting families:style recognition. In: Internal Conference on Document Anaysis and Recognition, pp. 489–494 (1995)
18. Serratosa, F., Sanfeliu, A.: Signatures versus histograms: Defintions, distances and algorithms. Pattern Recgnition, 921–934 (2006)
19. Jain, A.K., Nandakumar, K., Ross, A.: Score normalization in multimodal biometric systems. Pattern Recognition 12, 2270–2285 (2005)
20. Yeung, D.Y, Chang, H., Xiong, Y., George, S., Kashi, R., Matsumoto, T., Rigoll, G.: Svc 2004: First international signature verification competition. In: Zhang, D., Jain, A.K. (eds.) ICBA 2004. LNCS, vol. 3072, pp. 16–22. Springer, Heidelberg (2004)

Arm Swing Identification Method with Template Update for Long Term Stability

Kenji Matsuo[1], Fuminori Okumura[2], Masayuki Hashimoto[1], Shigeyuki Sakazawa[1], and Yoshinori Hatori[2]

[1] KDDI R&D Laboratories Inc.,
Ohara 2-1-15, Fujimino-shi, Saitama, 356-8502 Japan
matsuo@kddilabs.jp
[2] Tokyo Institute of Technology,
Nagatsuta 4259, Midori-ku, Yokohama-shi, 226-8502, Japan

Abstract. This paper proposes a novel method for biometric identification, based on arm swing motions with a template update in order to improve long term stability. In our previous work, we studied arm swing identification and proposed a basic method to realize a personal identification function on mobile terminals. The method compares the acceleration signals of arm swing motion as individual characteristics, with the tolerant similarity measurement between two arm swing motions via DP-matching, which enables users to unlock a mobile terminal simply by swinging it. However, the method has a problem with long term stability. In other words, the arm swing motions of identical individuals tend to fluctuate among every trial. Furthermore, the difference between the enrolled and trial motions increases over time. Therefore in this paper, we propose an update approach to the enrollment template for DP-matching to solve this problem. We employ an efficient adaptive update method using a minimum route determination algorithm in DP-matching. Identification experiments involving 12 persons over 6 weeks confirm the proposed method achieves a superior equal error rate of 4.0% than the conventional method, which has an equal error rate of 14.7%.

Keywords: behavior identification, template update, arm swing motion, cellular phone security, DP-matching.

1 Introduction

Recent mobile terminals, such as cellular phones, come equipped with various functionalities and require flexible means of authentication based on the nature of each function. Processing electronic payments on the phone requires highly secure authentication, while simple phone call functionality does not necessarily require such strict security. Current implementations of such devices employ a PIN code and/or fingerprint authentication. Although both methods can achieve a relatively high security level, the PIN code may often be annoying for users to enter, while biometrics involves a high risk in the case of theft of the registered fingerprint data, which is an unchangeable personal feature.

S.-W. Lee and S.Z. Li (Eds.): ICB 2007, LNCS 4642, pp. 211–221, 2007.

These days, human behaviors such as speech, signatures and gestures are employed for easy-to-use authentications [1]-[3]. As one of those research activities, we have proposed a new means of biometric identification, based on the similarity of arm swing motion [4]. Since arm swing motions are captured naturally through everyday behavior, they are suitable as a means of personal identification on mobile terminals, such as cellular phones. This method authenticates the genuine identity of individuals by comparing the acceleration signals acquired when they move their arms. The principles of differentiation are derived from the individual differences that exist in arm length, muscle strength, and the manner of swinging. Our method records arm swing motions on a serial basis and measures the similarity between two arm swing motions via DP-matching.

In general, behavior, including arm swing motion, is apt to fluctuate, since even identical individuals show slightly different behavior in every operation. Gaps from the enrollment template increase over time, since human muscles grow or decline and the swing pattern is forgotten unconsciously. Therefore, the behavior identifications need a template update to tolerate such long term fluctuations. Previously, the problems of long term fluctuations were studied for other biometrics identifications and Uludag et. al. proposed a fingerprint identification method using multiple templates to improve the discrimination accuracy [5]. They also proposed a template update procedure, in which a template set with discriminative characteristics is chosen from among several fingerprints acquired. However, this method requires computationally complex tasks to choose the best fingerprint, since similarity calculation between the new fingerprint data and all data in the templates, as well as the layered clustering calculation on a binary partition tree, is required. This method also requires considerable storage to hold the multiple templates. Kato et al. proposed an update method of an acoustic model for speech authentication using HMM [1]. The update method calculates the similarity for each trial and uses the new speech data for updating if the score exceeds a certain threshold. It also requires considerable storage for original speech data, in addition to the acoustic model, as well as vast computation for the reprocessing of models. Thus, it is difficult to perform these update processes on mobile terminals with limited CPU power and memory capacity.

In this paper, we propose a new approach to solve the fluctuations in arm swing identification occurring over time. The proposed method updates the enrollment template, using the minimum route of DP-matching to achieve long term stability. It does not require the original data used to create the template in previous operations, but merely requires the latest template and the new input data to update the template. Its performance was confirmed through identification experiments, carried out by 12 persons over a 6 week period.

2 Arm Swing Identification

Figure 1 shows the concept of the arm swing identification for cellular phones, which simplifies owner identification: This enables the owner to unlock his/her cellular phone by simply swinging it without any difficulty.

Fig. 1. Arm swing identification for cellular phone

However, it is difficult to acquire arm swing tracks precisely due to the accumulation of drift errors due to the noise of the motion sensor. Therefore, we proposed an identification method using an arm swing motion acquired by an acceleration sensor rather than a track [4]. The method represents the basic element of the method proposed in this paper and is thus described in detail in the following subsections.

2.1 Extraction of Acceleration Signals During the Motion Interval

All acceleration signals during the arm swing motion are obtained with a fixed sampling interval using an acceleration sensor. $\boldsymbol{a}[t]$ represents the 3 dimensional acceleration signals recorded at time t, while $a_x[t]$, $a_y[t]$, and $a_z[t]$ are the x, y, and z axis elements of $\boldsymbol{a}[t]$ respectively.

$$\boldsymbol{a}[t] = (a_x[t], a_y[t], a_z[t]) \tag{1}$$

The magnitude of acceleration signals $|\boldsymbol{a}[t]|$ is defined in the following equation:

$$|\boldsymbol{a}[t]| = \sqrt{a_x[t]^2 + a_y[t]^2 + a_z[t]^2} \tag{2}$$

Figure 2 shows the acceleration sensor and acceleration signals obtained when shaking up and down 5 times. The figure also shows the variance of a[t] in certain past samples. Although considerable variance is evident during arm swinging, this

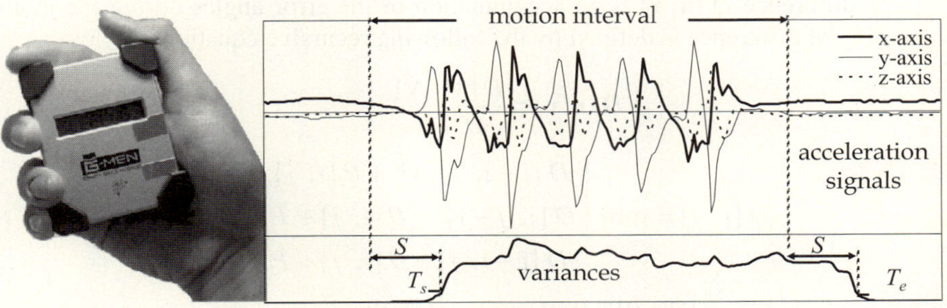

Fig. 2. Acceleration sensor and extraction of the motion interval

diminishes when the arms are kept still. Therefore, we judge the start and end of the significant motion based on this variance: If the variance in the previous S samples exceeds a threshold T_s, the starting point of S samples is judged to be the start of the motion, while if the variance falls below a threshold T_e, the starting point of S samples is judged to be the end of the motion. Extracted acceleration signals during the motion interval are recorded as the enrollment template $\boldsymbol{u}$ in the enrollment operation or input motion $\boldsymbol{v}$ in identification trials respectively.

2.2 Error Angle

The difference between the dual arm swing motions $\boldsymbol{u}$ and $\boldsymbol{v}$ is calculated based on the sum of the error angles. $\boldsymbol{u}$ $[i]$ is an acceleration vector in the enrollment template at the sampling time i (i =1, 2, …, M), while $\boldsymbol{v}$ $[j]$ is an acceleration vector in the input motion at sampling time j (j =1, 2, …, N). The error angle $\theta[i, j]$ is the inner angle between $\boldsymbol{u}$ $[i]$ and $\boldsymbol{v}$ $[j]$, as defined in the following:

$$\theta[i, j] = \arccos \frac{(\boldsymbol{u}[i], \boldsymbol{v}[j])}{|\boldsymbol{u}[i]||\boldsymbol{v}[j]|} \tag{3}$$

$$0 \leq \theta[i, j] \leq \pi \tag{4}$$

The value comes up to 0 when the directions of both acceleration vectors are identical. Conversely, the error angle increases when the directions differ. Although arm strengths often cause the amplitude of the acceleration signal to vary with every trial, the error angle is independent of the amplitude; hence the latter need not be taken into account [4].

2.3 DP-Matching Algorithm

As previously mentioned, arm swing motions tend to fluctuate, even in identical individuals, in terms of the positional shift, partial expansion and contraction, because the arm swing speed varies for each trial. Therefore, when evaluating the similarity between the enrollment template $\boldsymbol{u}$ and input motion $\boldsymbol{v}$, we use the difference D $(\boldsymbol{u}, \boldsymbol{v})$ with DP-matching, which is a measurement method with a high tolerance for gaps caused by such fluctuations.

The difference D $(\boldsymbol{u}, \boldsymbol{v})$ is an accumulation of the error angles during the motion interval. The difference is defined by the following recursive equations:

$$D(\boldsymbol{u}, \boldsymbol{v}) = \frac{D[M, N]}{M + N} \tag{5}$$

$$D[i, j] = \min \begin{Bmatrix} D[i-1, j-1] + \theta[i, j], \\ D[i, j-1] + \theta[i, j] + P, \\ D[i-1, j] + \theta[i, j] + P \end{Bmatrix} \tag{6}$$

$$D[0, 0] = 0, D[0, 1] = D[1, 0] = \infty \tag{7}$$

M and N represent the length of the enrollment template $\boldsymbol{u}$ and the input motion $\boldsymbol{v}$ respectively.

The algorithm is equivalent to searching for a minimum route, as shown in Figure 3, namely one where the difference among all the routes on the table is minimized. The indexes of the column and row correspond to the sampling times of ***u*** and ***v*** respectively, while the error angle $\theta[i, j]$ at points $[i, j]$ is measured from ***u*** $[i]$ and ***v*** $[j]$, and D (***u*** $[i]$, ***v***$[j]$) is calculated recursively. *P* is a toll penalty, which is imposed if a time-shifted sample is chosen when the temporal difference $D\ [i, j]$ is calculated. This makes it hard to choose samples of different times, while *P* is added when gaps are exceptionally permitted. The experiments mentioned later set $P = 0.2$. An example of a minimum route determined by DP-matching is illustrated in the form of bold lined blocks.

The smaller the measured difference D (***u***, ***v***), the more ***u*** and ***v*** resemble each other. Therefore, the threshold *T* is introduced for personal identification. If D (***u***, ***v***) falls below *T*, the person is accepted as a valid individual. Conversely, if D (***u***, ***v***) exceeds *T*, the person is rejected.

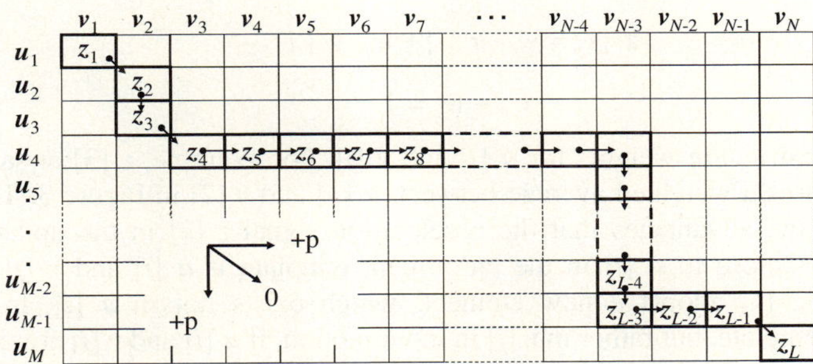

Fig. 3. DP-matching table. A minimum route is that illustrated by bold lined blocks.

3 Proposed Method

The basic arm swing authentication is relatively effective as reported in [4]. However the False Rejection Rate deteriorates over time, because the determination algorithm does not reflect the alteration of the arm swing. Therefore, this section proposes a method to update the enrollment template. The method does so using the minimum route, which is derived from DP-matching on the latest acceleration data determined as valid authentication. Figure 4 provides a conceptual explanation on the update process, using the distribution of templates in the arm swing motion space and its probability density for a person. ***u*** is the initial enrollment template, while the first and second updates create new templates, $\boldsymbol{u}_1$ and $\boldsymbol{u}_2$, respectively and the template becomes $\boldsymbol{u}_{\mathrm{End}}$ finally. During each update process, the updated template approaches the center of the distribution.

3.1 Template Update Using the Minimum Route in DP-Matching

Most pairs of acceleration vectors on the minimum route usually have a small error angle and high similarity. However the similarity of certain pairs decreases over time,

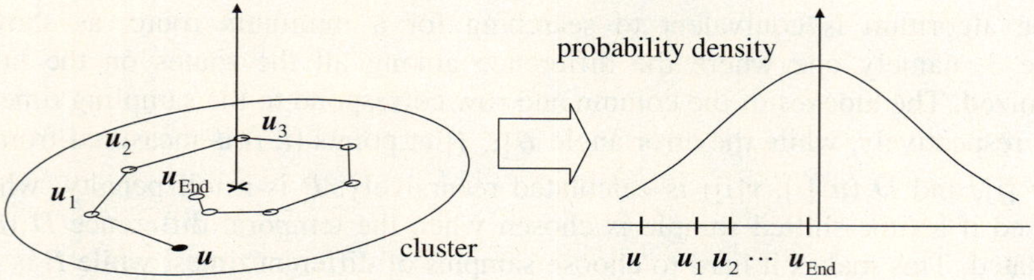

Fig. 4. Concept of the template update

even on the minimum route. The notation z indicates the update template generated from the current enrollment template $\boldsymbol{u}$ and an input motion $\boldsymbol{v}$. z $[k]$ at sampling time k (k =1, 2, …, L) in the updated template is calculated with the weighted average between the pair of acceleration vectors $\boldsymbol{u}$ $[i]$ and $\boldsymbol{v}$ $[j]$ on the minimum route, as defined in the following equations:

$$z\ [k] = w_u \cdot \boldsymbol{u}\ [i] + w_v \cdot \boldsymbol{v}\ [j] \tag{8}$$

$$w_u + w_v = 1 \tag{9}$$

Where, w_u and w_v are weights for $\boldsymbol{u}$ $[i]$ and $\boldsymbol{v}$ $[j]$. For example, z [3] at sampling time k = 3 comprises a weighted average between $\boldsymbol{u}$ [3] and $\boldsymbol{v}$ [2] in Figure 3. The weighted average has the advantages that the acceleration signal z $[k]$ in the updated template retains values close to $\boldsymbol{u}$ $[i]$ in the enrollment template if $\boldsymbol{u}$ $[i]$ and $\boldsymbol{v}$ $[j]$ are similar. Conversely, z $[k]$ adopts a new element, which exists not in $\boldsymbol{u}$ $[i]$, in the current enrollment template, but rather in $\boldsymbol{v}$ $[j]$ in input motion, if $\boldsymbol{u}$ $[i]$ and $\boldsymbol{v}$ $[j]$ are dissimilar.

However, the above simple update method always expands the length L of the updated motion series, because DP-matching inevitably finds the minimum route, where length L has the following relations: $L \geq \max(M, N)$. Therefore, we employ a normalization process to avoid expanding the length L. The length of the updated template is fitted to the average length, as calculated through previously identified trials.

3.2 Adaptive Update According to Adequacy Measurement

The simple update method may suffer from over-training caused by accidental movement during the arm swing, even if the trial is determined to be valid. Besides, with computational complexity in mind, unnecessary update operations should be avoided. If the latest minimum route in DP-matching is relatively similar to previous ones, there is little improvement in the enrollment template. Consequently, the use of an adaptive update algorithm is necessary in order to ensure the enrollment template remains effective and to reduce the number of unnecessary updates.

Figure 5 shows the adaptive update algorithm, where the threshold T defined in 2.3 is introduced for personal identification and two thresholds, T_l and T_h, are set to judge the necessity of an update. If a difference $D(\boldsymbol{u}, \boldsymbol{v})$ exists between T_l and T_h, the enrollment template is simply updated. The two thresholds T_l and T_h are determined from the following two criteria:

- Upper threshold T_h: If a considerable difference from the current enrollment template is apparent, such input motions might include many new elements, which are not contained in the current enrollment template. Renewal may actively incorporate those new elements into an updated template in this case. However, if the difference is excessive, input motions might include many accidental elements, which degrade the reliability of the updated template. Accordingly, the upper threshold T_h is applied to prevent the accidental elements from being reflected on the updated template.
- Lower threshold T_l: If the difference is very modest, such input motion is almost identical to the current enrollment template and there are no new elements which should be taken into account in the updated template. Therefore, the lower threshold T_l is equipped to prevent the increase in needless updates.

Thresholds T_l and T_h, having satisfied the above two criteria, can be determined based on the probability distribution of differences between the arm swing motions of identical individuals. Figure 6 shows an example of probability distribution actually generated from 7800 samples by 12 persons in a preliminary experiment. Both $\boldsymbol{u}$ and $\boldsymbol{v}$, used to calculate the difference D in Figure 6, are the arm swing motions of identical individuals. The pairs of T_l and T_h in later experiments are calculated based on the probability intervals of the difference distribution, such as 95%, 90%, and 80%.

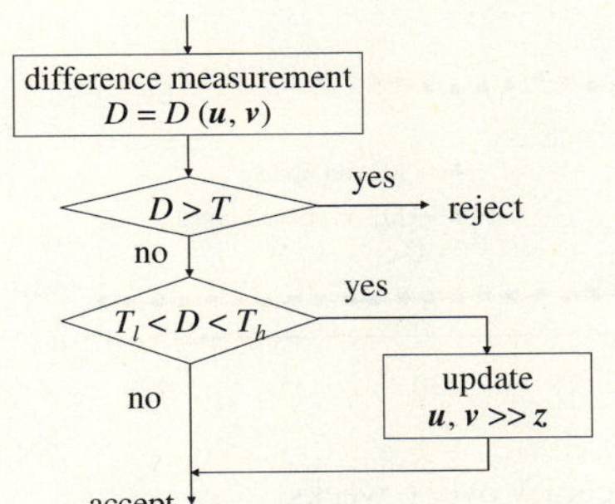

Fig. 5. Block diagram of adaptive update

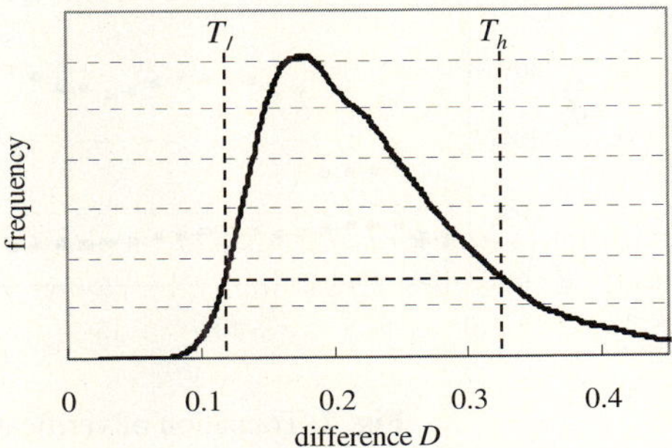

Fig. 6. Probability distribution of differences in identical people

4 Experimental Results and Discussions

Identification experiments involving 12 persons were conducted as personal verification for logging onto a PC. Each user swings his/her arm before using his/her own PC regularly and an acceleration sensor is connected to the PC via a USB cable. The sensor measures the acceleration signals with a range of 10G and sampling frequency of 100Hz. The extraction parameters S = 50, T_s = 1.0, and T_e = 0.2 are set according to the results of preliminary experiments. A total of 814 arm swing motions are accumulated over a 6 week period, as each individual tries 30 to 100 a day. All users write a star shape, namely a pentagram, during each trial, which all can achieve easily. Personal characteristics are also easily reflected in the star shape, making it a suitable pattern to evaluate malicious identification [6]. The following three methods, M1, M2, and M3, are defined for comparative evaluation as follows:

- M1 is the conventional method [4], whereby the enrollment template is not updated at all.
- M2 is the proposed method #1, which simply updates the enrollment template for every identified trial.
- M3 is the proposed method #2, which furnishes thresholds T_l and T_h to update the enrollment template adaptively.

4.1 Tolerances to the Long Term Fluctuations by Update

The transitions of False Rejection Rate: FRR were measured by M1 and M2 during the experimental period, where the threshold T for personal identification is fixed to 0.32 and the same value of 0.5 was used for both weights $\boldsymbol{w}_u$ and $\boldsymbol{w}_v$ of the weighted average. FRR is the rate of erroneous cases when the valid user is incorrectly rejected. 12 persons had participated in this experiment and Figure 7 shows the average of their results. The horizontal axis indicates the trial date counted from the beginning of experiment, while the vertical axis indicates the FRR in all trials until that day.

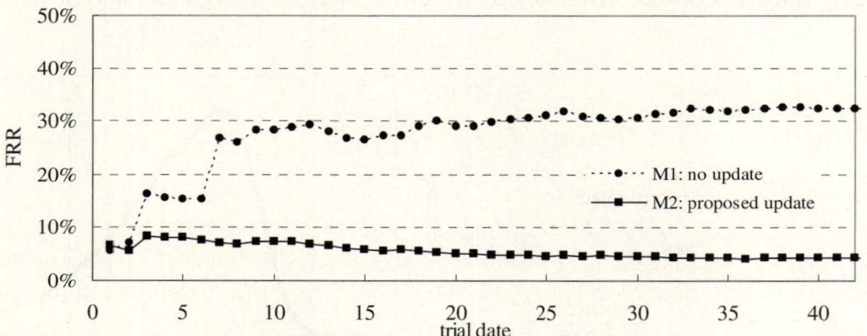

Fig. 7. Transition of verification accuracy over 6 weeks

Although the conventional method M1 maintains a low FRR of about 8% during the several initial days of the experiment, the FRR of M1 tends to rise over time; finally reaching 32.2%. This is probably due to the fact that the first enrollment template does not go with the latest arm swing motion. On the contrary, the proposed method M2 maintains a lower FRR than M1 from the beginning of the experiment and also achieves a preferable downward curve through the experiment. This result confirms that long term stability is achieved in the arm swing identification by M2, where the enrollment templates are simply updated for every identified trial.

Figure 8 shows the False Rejection Rate: FRR and False Acceptance Rate: FAR curves of M1 and M2. An enlarged graph around the cross point is also exhibited in Figure 8, while the performances of the methods are comparatively evaluated in terms of the Equivalent Error Rate: EER [6], which is the percentage when the FRR is equal to the FAR. M1 has an EER of 14.7%, while M2 achieves an EER of 4.7%. The above results confirm that the proposed update method improves the verification

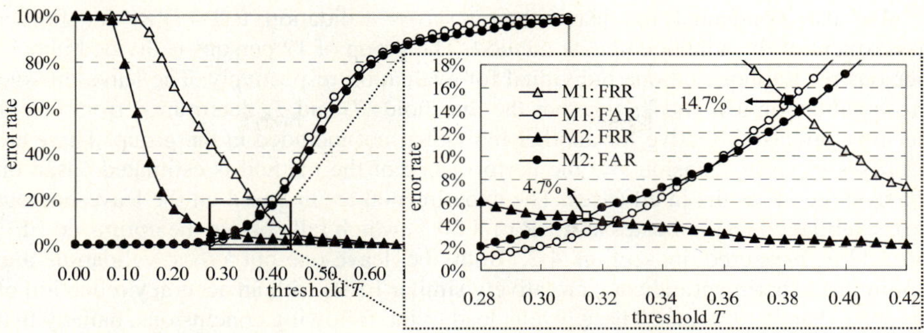

Fig. 8. FRR and FAR curve. The right graph shows an enlarged area around the cross point

accuracy of arm swing motion. However, Figure 8 also shows that FAR curves remain virtually unchanged between M1 and M2, although the FRR curve of M2 is considerably improved by updating. This is because the proposed update methods concentrate on reflecting the characteristics of the valid user so that new templates approach the center of distribution and the variance of his/her own probability distribution is reduced, as mentioned in the beginning of Section 3. Consequently, via the update, the rate of acceptance of the valid user increases and the FRR decreases, whereas FAR improvement is left for future work.

4.2 Effectiveness of the Adaptive Update

In this section, we investigate the effectiveness of M3, which has the adaptive update, as well as optimizing the thresholds T_l and T_h of M3. Table 1 shows certain pairs of thresholds T_l and T_h, determined based on the probability interval of the distribution on differences. The table also shows the M3's EER and the update frequency, which represents the ratio of occurrence of the update, when the threshold pairs are used.

M3 works most effectively, when $T_l = 0.095$ and $T_h = 0.369$, corresponding to a 90% interval of the probability distribution. Under these conditions, M3 achieves the best EER of 4.11%, which is improved by 0.6 points in comparison with the simple update method, M2. Furthermore, under these conditions, the update frequency of M3 is 83.2%, which is lower than that of M2 by 16.8 points. These results confirm that M3 significantly maintains its template effectively and reduces the number of needless updates.

Table 1. Probability interval and threshold for adaptive update. 0% is equivalent to the conventional method M1 and 100% is equivalent to the simple update method M2.

Probability interval	0%	20%	40%	60%	80%	90%	95%	100%
Threshold T_l	--	0.142	0.136	0.125	0.110	0.095	0.082	0
Threshold T_h	--	0.181	0.211	0.244	0.301	0.369	0.452	$+\infty$
EER	14.71	10.88	5.06	4.72	4.65	4.11	4.40	4.71
Cross point	0.382	0.358	0.320	0.318	0.315	0.308	0.310	0.233
Update frequency	0%	16.0%	34.3%	49.3%	68.0%	83.2%	92.3%	100%

We also conducted the leave-one-out cross validation test [7][8] for further assessment of the adaptive update method. The group of 12 persons is divided into 11 persons for training and one individual for evaluation respectively. The leave-one-out cross validation test checks whether the thresholds T_l and T_h, determined from the 11 persons, are also effective for another individual not included in the group. There are 12 cases of group division and the performance of the method is estimated based on the average of results in all cases. The experimental result based on the leave-one-out cross validation test indicates an EER of 4.30%, which falls below the optimized EER of 4.11% measured in section 4.2. Both the leave-one-out cross validation and optimized experiment indicate a relatively similar EER, with an accuracy reduction of no more than 0.19 points. These results lead to the following conclusions, namely that $T_l = 0.095$ and $T_h = 0.369$ prove to be the best thresholds in the adaptive update.

The EER performance of the proposed method is comparable to that of other identifications, based on human behaviors such as speech, signatures and gestures [1]-[3][9]. Their EER fall roughly 2 to 8% in the case of limited acquisition accuracy, for example, a small camera capturing images with insufficient illumination and so on, which represent typical circumstances facing mobile terminals.

4.3 Analysis of the Weighting Parameter Characteristics

Here, we also investigate the semi-optimal weights w_u and w_v for the weighted average. The thresholds in the adaptive update method M3 are fixed at $T_l = 0.095$ and $T_h = 0.369$, which achieves maximum efficiency in the previous experiment in section 4.2, while EER is also measured for each pair of weights w_u and w_v in Table 2. The pair of weights $w_u = 0.6$ and $w_v = 0.4$ achieves maximum efficiency, with an EER of 4.03% - results which lead to the following considerations. It is appropriate that the weighted average impose a slightly larger weight on the side of the enrollment template than that on the side of input motion. Appropriate weights prevent the original elements in the current enrollment template from being radically lost and also prevent the updated template from being degraded through accidentally input motion.

Table 2. Relations between the weighted average and EER

Weights (w_u / w_v)	1.0/0.0	0.8/0.2	0.7/0.3	<u>0.6/0.4</u>	0.5/0.5	0.4/0.6	0.3/0.7	0.0/1.0
EER	6.86	4.56	4.22	<u>4.03</u>	4.11	4.11	4.17	4.68
Cross point	0.351	0.310	0.310	0.310	0.308	0.310	0.308	0.315
Update frequency	94.5%	83.9%	82.4%	<u>82.2%</u>	83.2%	84.0%	84.9%	89.2%

5 Conclusion

This paper proposes a novel and stable human identification method based on arm swing motions. It also includes a common substantial problem, namely, an increase in the error rate over time like other human behavioral identifications. We introduce an adaptive update approach into the basic arm swing authentication method, and present a practical algorithm, using the DP-matching minimum route, to update the enrollment template. The algorithm can reflect a new tendency of motion while also preventing accidental movement from being learnt. Identification experiments show that EER decreases over time and reaches 4.0%. These preferable results are surely confirmed by the leave-one-out method and this performance is comparable to that of other identification, based on human behaviors such as speech, signatures and gestures. Although the proposed method requires an additional process to update a template, its computational complexity is executable on cellular phones. Moreover, our authentication method can be significantly improved when the arm swing motion is not limited to the star shape. Allowing an arbitrary arm swing for each individual contributes to decreasing FAR, meaning we can achieve much lower EER in the practical reformation. Thus, our method can achieve high accuracy in terms of operational adjustment and is quite suitable for authentication in mobile terminals with natural behavior.

Acknowledgments. The authors would like to thank Dr. Shigeyuki Akiba, Dr. Shuichi Matsumoto, Dr. Yasuyuki Nakajima, Dr. Atsushi Koike, of KDDI R&D Labs. and Dr. Akira Kubota of the Tokyo Institute of Technology, for their continuous support and encouragement.

References

1. Kato, T., Kawai, H.: A text-prompted speaker verification system implemented on a cellular phone and a mobile terminal. In: Proc. of ESCA ISCA, pp. 945–948 (2006)
2. Hangai, S., Yamanaka, S., Hamamoto, T.: On-line signature verification based on altitude and direction of pen movement. In: Proc. of IEEE ICME, vol. 1, pp. 489–492 (2000)
3. Patel, S.N., Pierce, J.S., Abowd, G.D.: A Gesture-based Authentication Scheme for Untrusted Public Terminal. In: Proc. of UIST, pp. 157–160 (2004)
4. Okumura, F., Kubota, A., Hatori, Y., Matsuo, K., Hashimoto, M., Koike, A.: A study on biometric identification based on arm sweep action with acceleration sensor. In: Proc. of IEEE ISPACS, pp. 219–222 (2006)
5. Uludag, U., Ross, A., Jain, A.K.: Biometric template selection and update: case study in fingerprints. Pattern Recognition 37(7), 1533–1542 (2004)
6. Mansfield, A.J., Wayman, J.L.: Best practices in testing and reporting performance of biometric devices version 2.01. NPL Report CMSC 14/02 (August 2002)
7. Shahraray, B., Anderson, D.J.: Optimal estimation of contour properties by cross-validated regularization. IEEE Trans. on PAMI 11(6), 600–610 (1989)
8. Krzanowski, W.J.: Cross-validation in principal component analysis. Biometrics 43, 575–584 (1987)
9. Jain, A.K., Bolle, R., Pankanti, S.: Biometrics: Personal identification in network society. Kluwer Academic Publishers, Dordrecht (1999)

Walker Recognition Without Gait Cycle Estimation

Daoliang Tan, Shiqi Yu, Kaiqi Huang, and Tieniu Tan

Center for Biometrics and Security Research,
National Laboratory of Pattern Recognition, Institute of Automation,
Chinese Academy of Sciences, Beijing, 100080, P.R. China
{dltan,sqyu,kqhuang,tnt}@nlpr.ia.ac.cn
http://www.cbsr.ia.ac.cn

Abstract. Most of gait recognition algorithms involve walking cycle estimation to accomplish signature matching. However, we may be plagued by two cycle-related issues when developing real-time gait-based walker recognition systems. One is accurate cycle evaluation, which is computation intensive, and the other is the inconvenient acquisition of long continuous sequences of gait patterns, which are essential to the estimation of gait cycles. These drive us to address the problem of distant walker recognition from another view toward gait, in the hope of detouring the step of gait cycle estimation. This paper proposes a new gait representation, called normalized dual-diagonal projections (NDDP), to characterize walker signatures and employs a normal distribution to approximately describe the variation of each subject's gait signatures in the statistical sense. We achieve the recognition of unknown gait features in a simplified Bayes framework after reducing the dimension of raw gait signatures based on linear subspace projections. Extensive experiments demonstrate that our method is effective and promising.

Keywords: Gait recognition, cycle estimation, PCA, LDA.

1 Introduction

To some extent, gait characterizes personal moving styles, e.g., walking, running, and jumping. There have been many efforts to perform gait-based walker recognition. In brief, the prior work pertaining to gait recognition generally takes three steps to identify walkers: 1) localize moving people in video or image sequences; 2) estimate gait cycles and pinpoint the walking phase; and 3) recognize unknown pedestrians based on the time-aligned features extracted from images.

But we are sometimes confronted with two unfavorable situations when developing real-time gait recognition systems. First, the accurate estimation of gait cycles often devours much computational resource and does not adapt well to the requirement of online recognition. Second, the inconvenient acquisition of continuous gait sequences of multiple cycles makes it impractical to evaluate gait cycles; gait motion can dramatically vary after a long time and is just approximately cyclic in the short term. The two facts plunge us into a dilemma

S.-W. Lee and S.Z. Li (Eds.): ICB 2007, LNCS 4642, pp. 222–231, 2007.

as to whether to proceed with the estimation of cycles of gait sequences or not. It is this dilemma that prompts us to reexamine gait recognition methods. This paper deals with the problem of walking people recognition at a distance. Rather than following the conventional route, we start from a statistical view on gait (just for recognition purpose), in the hope of bypassing the step of gait cycle estimation. From the perspective of security, this work is necessary.

The rest of this paper is as follows. Section 2 introduces related work. Then, we discuss technical details in Section 3 and justify our method in Section 4. Finally, Section 5 concludes this paper.

2 Related Work

Prior methods for gait recognition can be roughly clustered into two categories: the model-based category and the image appearance-based category. For example, Cunado et al. [3] used two inter-connected pendulums to model the kinematics of human legs and extracted magnitude and phase features in the frequency domain to differentiate subjects. Urtasun and Fua [12] further employed angle features in a 3D human physical model to describe the signatures of walking people. As opposed to the model-based methods, the work in [1,7,15] directly extracted different distance features from binary silhouette images for walker identification. Moreover, the research in [5,8,14] simplified the description of binary gait silhouettes within a cycle through averaging them and achieved satisfactory results. In particular, Sarkar et al. [10] established a baseline daytime gait database in an attempt to benchmark evaluation of gait recognition algorithms, and Tan et al. [11] created a large infrared night gait dataset in an effort to narrow the gap between daytime walker recognition and nighttime gait identification. However, it is still challenging to resolve the problems of how to balance the particularity of human structural models against the generality and how to extend the discriminative ability of appearance features across different harsh conditions.

The diligent efforts to shed light on cognitive principles deepen the insight into human perception of movement patterns. For instance, the body-inversion effect [9] showed that the perception of human body might be global. Surprisingly, a hemianopic patient AL [2] who lost the ability to recognize forms from motion could detect motion and distinguish static shape stimulus. Moreover, Downing et al. [4] figured out a region (EBA) in the lateral occipitotemporal cortex which focuses on the visual perception of appearance of human bodies (except face) and is not related to motion cues. Later, Jacobs and Pinto [6] showed that visual experience had a vital impact on identity perception, though disagreeing on the use of walking patterns for recognition. Meanwhile, Veeraraghavan et al. [13] concluded that shape cues play a more critical role in automatic gait recognition than those from motion. These findings reveal that the only use of global shape (or appearance) cues can achieve the human-recognition purpose; it seems that dynamic attributes are not suitable for discriminating walkers, since they are not reliable from the long-term perspective. This makes us rethink gait to form an alternative view on gait recognition.

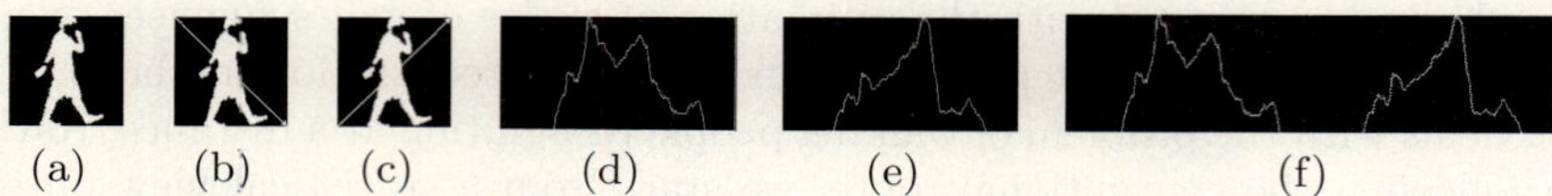

Fig. 1. NDDP illustration. (a) Normalized silhouette. (b) Positive diagonal direction. (c) Negative diagonal direction. (d) Curve for (b). (e) Curve for (c). (f) Curve concatenating (d) and (e).

3 Technical Details

In this paper, we consider human gait as a stochastic realization of one's static stances (or figures). It should be pointed out that we have employed this view for gait recognition in the form of equivalence constraints but did not provide extensive experiments to support this view. On the other hand, this paper uses this gait view in the Bayesian framework based on another gait representation, in the hope of justifying our view for gait recognition. Although this idea ignores the dynamic details in the human movement from the biomechanical point of view, it still grasps the more critical cues provided by human shapes for the recognition purpose. Assume that we have acquired human silhouettes. Then this paper will focus on gait representation, dimension reduction, and classification.

3.1 Gait Representation

This paper first normalizes each silhouette image to the same size of 32×32. Then, we project the size-normalized silhouette in the positive and negative diagonal directions, respectively. Meanwhile, it is easy to evaluate for each of the two directions a maximum value which indicates the maximal number of foreground pixels along that direction in this frame. Furthermore, the two maximums are used to normalize the respective projections. Finally, we concatenate the two normalized projections to represent human gait in the frame and refer to this representation as NDDP. It should be noted that a similar unnormalized diagonal representation is also able to describe human gait but is beyond the scope of this paper. Figure 1 illustrates the NDDP representation. The NDDP differs from [7] in that we are concerned with the relative number of foreground pixels in the dual diagonal directions whereas the authors in [7] are interested in the coarse number of foreground pixels in the single horizontal direction.

3.2 Dimension Reduction

We employ principal component analysis (PCA) and linear discriminant analysis (LDA) to achieve dimension reduction. The PCA projection matrix $U \in \mathbb{R}^{n \times d}$ can be derived from an intuitive, clear-cut geometric view. That is, we expect to search for a projection onto a subspace spanned by a group of orthonormal basis so that the transformed variables have as great the variance in each coordinate axis as possible—informative—and are implicitly uncorrelated. Suppose that U

has the form $U = [u_1 \dots u_d]$ and that we have found $j-1$ axes $(u_1, \dots, u_{j-1})$. Now the aim is to seek the j-th axis u_j $(j \leq d)$. This problem can be formulated as (1):

$$\max_{u_j \in \mathbb{R}^n} var(u_j^T x) \quad s.t. \ u_j^T u_j = 1, \ u_k^T u_j = 0 \quad (k = 1, 2, \cdots, j-1) \tag{1}$$

where $x \in \mathbb{R}^n$ is the initial NDDP vector. It is trivial to prove that the optimal $u_1, \dots, u_d$ should correspond to the top d largest eigenvalues of the covariance (or correlation) matrix of x. This paper chooses d to be the minimum number of components of x which at least account for the proportion 95% of the total variation of x. Additionally, the LDA projection V can be expressed as the problem (2):

$$\max_{V} \frac{tr(V^T S_B^Y V)}{tr(V^T S_W^Y V)} \tag{2}$$

where S_B^Y and S_W^Y are inter- and intra-class scatter matrices, respectively. It is easy to obtain that the columns of V constitute the generalized eigenvectors of S_B^Y and S_W^Y. Similarly, we consider a fraction 98% of the generalized "variation" in an attempt to further reduce the dimension of gait features. Finally, we can gain a composition $P = U^T V^T$ which directly projects x in the original space X to $y = Px$ in the dimension-reduced space Y.

3.3 Classification

Unlike the only mean description of gait sequences, we exploit a normal distribution $x^i \sim N(\mu_i, \Sigma_i)$, $i = 1, 2, \dots, n_c$, where n_c is the number of subjects in the gait database, to express the i-th person's gait signatures with regard to our gait view. Then the transformed vector y^i has the distribution $y^i \sim N(P\mu_i, P\Sigma_i P^T)$. Assume that x_t^s $(t = 1, 2, \dots, M)$ is the raw feature vector of an unknown gait sequence S at the time t. In theory, we can recognize the identity in a brute force manner—combining every identified result for the sequence of silhouettes. However, this strategy involves huge computational resource. Instead, this paper employs the average $\bar{x}^s$ of feature vectors x_t^s in S to describe the unknown gait sequence S for the computational simplicity. The next is to map $\bar{x}^s$ to $\bar{y}^s$ with the P. In addition, our method incorporates the second-order moment (covariance) into the distance measure in a quasi-Bayesian fashion: $d_i^* = (\bar{y}^u - P\mu_i)^T (P\Sigma_i P^T)^{-1} (\bar{y}^u - P\mu_i)$. Finally, the nearest distance rule is used to judge the identity of the unknown walker in the gait sequence S.

4 Experiments

In order to validate the proposed method, we perform walker-recognizing experiments on three gait databases in an increasing order of the number of subjects: CMU Mobo Database [1], USF-NIST Gait Database [10], and CASIA Infrared Night Gait Dataset [11]. Meanwhile, we employ cumulative match score (CMS)

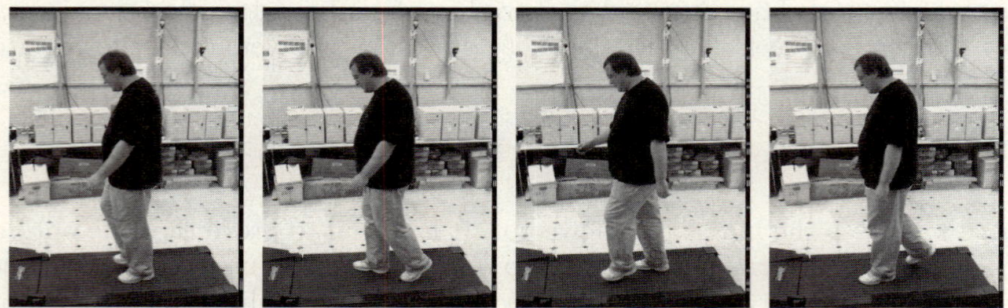

Fig. 2. Sample gait images in the CMU Mobo Gait Database

Table 1. Five Experiments on the CMU Mobo Gait Database

Exp.	Gallery	Probe	Remarks
A	Slow	Slow	Within-condition
B	Fast	Fast	Within-condition
C	Ball	Ball	Within-condition
D	Slow	Fast	Across-condition
E	Fast	Slow	Across-condition

[10] to assess recognition performance. Here the CMS value at rank k serves as an indicator of the fraction of probes whose leading k matches must include their real identities. In addition to the statistical estimation for Σ_i, our algorithm also replaces Σ_i with the global covariance matrix Σ estimated from training data for the computational convenience. We denote by D_G the distance measure which uses the plain estimates of Σ_i and by D_M the measure which utilizes the substitution of Σ for Σ_i. The following will give more experimental details.

4.1 CMU Mobo Gait Database

This database comprises gait sequences from 25 subjects and four kinds of walking patterns: slow walking, fast walking, slow walking at a certain slope, and slow walking with a ball. Figure 2 shows four sample gait images in the Mobo database. Five experiments designed for this database [7] are listed in Table 1. Table 2 presents the rank 1 performance of our approach and another two influential methods [7,13]. We can see from Table 2 that our method can produce near 100 percent recognition rate for the 25 subjects when the training and testing data share the same moving attributes, that across-condition recognition is more difficult than the recognition in the within-condition case, and that our approach outperforms [7] and is conservatively comparable to [13] just using a simple model, despite neglect of dynamic cues. Furthermore, Figure 3 depicts the CMS curves of our method on this database. The CMS values at least illustrate the potential of our approach in the identification mode.

Table 2. Comparison of the Rank 1 Performance on the Mobo Gait Database

	A	B	C	D	E
HMM[7]	72%	68%	92%	32%	56%
SC[13]	100%	100%	92%	80%	84%
Ours(D_G)	100%	100%	96%	88%	80%
Ours(D_M)	100%	100%	96%	88%	80%

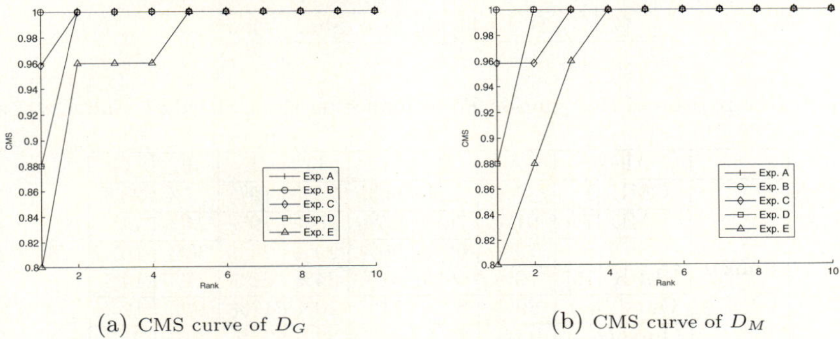

(a) CMS curve of D_G

(b) CMS curve of D_M

Fig. 3. CMS curves of our method on the CMU Mobo Gait Database

4.2 USF-NIST Gait Database

We use the precomputed silhouettes for the May-2001-No-Briefcase dataset in the USF-NIST Gait Database [10]. The dataset used includes 74 individuals and considers the conditions across viewpoint, footwear, and ground surface. Figure 4 displays four example images in the USF-NIST database. Table 3 lists seven challenging experiments [10] on this dataset. Moreover, Table 4 compares our method with some well-known approaches [1,7,10,15] in the literature.

Fig. 4. Sample gait images in the USF-NIST Gait Database

We can see from Table 4 that our model can produce a recognition rate close to 100 percent in the concurrent gait case (Exp. A) and that in the presence of disturbances on silhouette segmenting, the performance of our model begins to degrade as well as other algorithms' (this is an intrinsic flaw of appearance-based gait recognition algorithms). Moreover, our method is competitive with or comparable to the noted approaches on this gait database, in terms of both rank 1 and rank 5 values. In particular, our method has a much greater acceleration in

Table 3. Seven Challenging Experiments on the USF-NIST Gait Database

Exp.	Probe[1]	Difference
A	(G, A, L)[71]	View
B	(G, B, R)[41]	Shoe
C	(G, B, L)[41]	Shoe,View
D	(C, A, R)[70]	Surface
E	(C, B, R)[44]	Surface, Shoe
F	(C, A, L)[70]	Surface, View
G	(C, B, L)[44]	Surface, Shoe, View

Table 4. Comparison of Recognition Performance on the USF-NIST Gait Database

	Algo.	A	B	C	D	E	F	G
Rank 1	CMU [1]	87%	81%	66%	21%	19%	27%	23%
	UMD [7]	91%	76%	65%	25%	29%	24%	15%
	USF [10]	79%	66%	56%	29%	24%	30%	10%
	NLPR [15]	70%	59%	51%	34%	21%	27%	14%
	Ours(D_G)	99%	83%	71%	20%	17%	14%	12%
	Ours(D_M)	100%	83%	68%	32%	24%	30%	31%
Rank 5	CMU [1]	100%	90%	83%	59%	50%	53%	43%
	UMD [7]	100%	81%	76%	61%	39%	46%	33%
	USF [10]	96%	80%	76%	61%	24%	45%	33%
	NLPR [15]	93%	83%	71%	64%	45%	39%	26%
	Ours(D_G)	100%	90%	90%	82%	79%	76%	74%
	Ours(D_M)	100%	93%	93%	80%	83%	79%	74%

CMS values. These not only exemplify the promising usefulness of our approach and but also indirectly give an experimental support for that our view on gait recognition is to some extent reasonable.

4.3 CASIA Infrared Night Gait Dataset

The previous two databases pay more attention to daytime gait patterns. Hence this paper employs the CASIA Infrared Night Gait Dataset [11] to diversify the gait recognition experiments. This dataset consists of 153 subjects' night gait sequences and allows for four walking cases: normal walking, slow walking, fast walking, and normal walking with a bag. Figure 5 illustrates sample night gait in the CASIA dataset. Table 5 presents four experiments on this dataset [11]. It should be noted that we use the entire gait sequences in this data collection, rather than a fraction of the data. Figure 6 shows CMS curves of our method for ranks up to 20.

We can notice from Fig. 6 that Exp. A has the best performance (almost 100% recognition rates), due to the similarity in walking attributes between training and testing data. In addition, the changes in walking pace to some

[1] The value in the bracket indicates the number of subjects in the test.

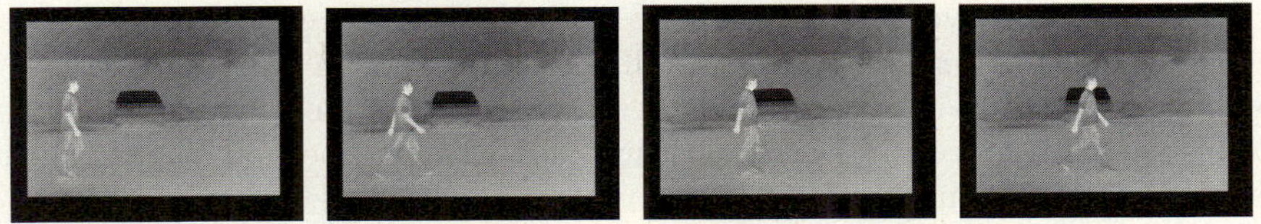

Fig. 5. Sample gait images in the CASIA Infrared Night Gait Dataset

Table 5. Four experiments on the CASIA Infrared Night Gait Dataset

Exp.	Gallery	Probe	#Gallery Seq.	#Probe Seq.
A	Normal	Normal	459	153
B	Normal	Fast	459	306
C	Normal	Slow	459	306
D	Normal	Bag	459	306

degree decline recognition accuracy largely because of the drastic departure of the means of feature vectors in some testing sequences from their corresponding training ones. Appearance variation can dramatically affect the precision of our recognition results; however, appearance-robust gait recognition is still not a well-resolved problem in the gait field. Nevertheless, the results favor the efficacy of our method with reference to the number of the subjects.

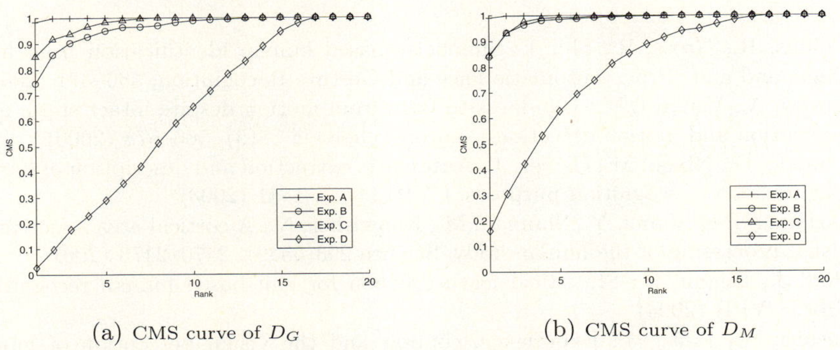

(a) CMS curve of D_G (b) CMS curve of D_M

Fig. 6. CMS curves of our method on the CASIA Night Gait Dataset

4.4 Discussions

In general, the measure d_i^* does not satisfy the distance definition and just serves as a simplified Bayesian classifier for the computational simplicity. Assuming that the prior distribution is uniform and that the volumes of eigenspaces of the subjects are equal (i.e., $|\Sigma_i|$ have the same value), we can obtain the D_G measure. Similarly, the much stronger assumption that all Σ_i are the same (homoscedastic) brings the D_M measure. The results indicate that both measures are sensible.

The aim of gait cycle estimation is to facilitate feature matching. As opposed to the conventional route, we make full use of features in static 2D shapes by combining the first- and second-order statistics to recognize walkers. A more promising scheme is to integrate posture cues into our method for recognition elaboration on a stance scale.

5 Conclusions

This paper has dealt with the problem of walker recognition in a simplified Bayesian framework. Experimental results show that our method is superior or comparable to the prior cycle-based algorithms. Our contribution is two-fold: One is that we propose the NDDP to characterize human gait patterns, and the other is that we explicitly incorporate second-order statistical cues into gait recognition and obtain an encouraging performance.

Acknowledgments. This work is funded by the National Natural Science Foundation of China (Grant No. 60605014, 60332010, and 60335010), the National Basic Research Program of China (Grant No. 2004CB318110), China International Science and Technology Cooperation (Grant No. 2004DFA06900), and the CASIA Innovation Fund for Young Scientists.

References

1. Collins, R., Gross, R., Shi, J.: Silhouette-based human identification from body shape and gait. Proc. Automatic Face and Gesture Recognition, 366–371 (2002)
2. Cowey, A., Vaina, L.M.: Blindness to form from motion despite intact static form perception and motion detection. Neuropsychologia 38(5), 566–578 (2000)
3. Cunado, D., Nixon, M., Carter, J.: Automatic extraction and description of human gait model for recognition purposes. CVIU 90(1), 1–41 (2003)
4. Downing, P.E., Jiang, Y., Shuman, M., Kanwisher, N.: A cortical area selective for visual processing of the human body. Science 293(5539), 2470–2473 (2001)
5. Han, J., Bhanu, B.: Statistical feature fusion for gait-based human recognition. Proc. CVPR (2004)
6. Jacobs, A., Pinto, J.: Experience, context and the visual perception of human movement. Journal of Experimental Psychology: Human Perception and Performance 30(5), 822–835 (2004)
7. Kale, A., Sundaresan, A., Rajagopalan, A., Cuntoor, N., RoyChowdhury, A., Krueger, V.: Identification of humans using gait. IEEE Trans. Image Processing 13(9), 1163–1173 (2004)
8. Liu, Z., Sarkar, S.: Simplest representation yet for gait recognition: Averaged silhouette. Proc. ICPR (2004)
9. Reed, C.L., Stone, V.E., Bozova, S., Tanaka, J.: The body-inversion effect. Psychological Science 14(4), 302–308 (2003)
10. Sarkar, S., Philips, P., Liu, Z., Vega, I., Grother, P., Bowyer, K.: The human gait challenge problem: data sets, performance and analysis. PAMI 27(2), 162–177 (2005)

11. Tan, D., Huang, K., Yu, S., Tan, T.: Efficient night gait recognition based on template matching. Proc. ICPR, 1000–1003 (2006)
12. Urtasun, R., Fua, P.: 3d tracking for gait characterization and recognition. Proc. Automatic Face and Gesture Recognition, 17–22 (2004)
13. Veeraraghavan, A., Roy-Chowdhury, A., Chellappa, R.: Matching shape sequences in video with applications in human movement analysis. PAMI 27(12), 1896–1909 (2005)
14. Veres, G., Gordon, L., Carter, J., Nixon, M.: What image information is important in silhouette-based gait recognition? In: Proc. CVPR (2004)
15. Wang, L., Tan, T., Hu, W., Ning, H.: Silhouette analysis-based gait recognition for human identification. PAMI 25(12), 1505–1518 (2003)

Comparison of Compression Algorithms' Impact on Iris Recognition Accuracy

Stefan Matschitsch[1], Martin Tschinder[1], and Andreas Uhl[1,2]

[1] School of Telematics & Network Engineering, Carinthia Tech Institute, Austria
[2] Department of Computer Sciences, Salzburg University, Austria
uhl@cosy.sbg.ac.at

Abstract. The impact of using different lossy compression algorithms on the matching accuracy of iris recognition systems is investigated. In particular, we relate rate-distortion performance as measured in PSNR to the matching scores as obtained by a concrete recognition system. JPEG2000 and SPIHT are correctly predicted by PSNR to be well suited compression algorithms to be employed in iris recognition systems. Fractal compression is identified to be least suited for the use in the investigated recognition system, although PSNR suggests JPEG to deliver worse recognition results in the case of low bitrates. PRVQ compression performs surprisingly well given the third rank in PSNR performance, resulting in the best matching scores in one scenario. Overall, applying compression algorithms is found to increase FNMR but does not impact FMR. Consequently, compression does not decrease the security of iris recognition systems, but "only" reduces user convenience.

1 Introduction

With the increasing usage of biometric systems the question arises naturally how to store and handle the acquired sensor data. In this context, the compression of these data may become imperative under certain circumstances due to the large amounts of data involved. Among other possibilities (e.g. like template storage on IC cards), compression technology may be used in two stages of the processing chain in classical biometric recognition:

1. **Storage of reference data**: In most template databases (where the reference data of the enrolled individuals is stored) only the extracted features required for the matching step are stored as opposed to retaining the originally acquired sensor data. However, in case the features should be replaced for some reason (e.g. when a superior or licence-free matching technique involving a different feature set becomes available), having stored only extracted features implies the requirement for all legitimate users for a re-enrollment, which can be expensive and is highly undesired since user-acceptance of the entire biometric system will suffer. Storing the original sensor data in addition to the features required for the current matching technique solves this problem. Of course, these data need to be stored in compressed (to save storage space) and encrypted (to protect privacy) form.

S.-W. Lee and S.Z. Li (Eds.): ICB 2007, LNCS 4642, pp. 232–241, 2007.

2. **Transmission of sample data after sensor data acquisition**: In distributed biometric systems, the data acquisition stage is often dislocated from the feature extraction and matching stage (this is true for the enrollment phase as well as for authentication). In such environments the sensor data have to be transferred via a network link to the respective location, often over wireless channels with low bandwidth and high latency. Therefore, a minimization of the amount of data to be transferred is highly desirable, which is achieved by compressing the data before transmission. An alternative solution would be to extract the features before transmission and to transfer feature data only – in many cases, feature extraction is more demanding as compared to compression which generates additional workload for the often mobile and low power acquisition devices.

Having found that compression of the raw sensor data can be advantageous in certain applications, we have to identify techniques suited to accomplish this task in an optimal manner. In order to maximize the benefit in terms of data reduction, lossy compression techniques have to be applied. However, the distortions introduced by compression artifacts may interfere with subsequent feature extraction and may degrade the matching results. In particular, FRR or FNMR will increase (since features of the data of legitimate users are extracted less accurately from compressed data) which in turn affects user convenience and general acceptance of the biometric system. In extreme cases, even FAR or FMR might be affected.

In this work, we will focus on the compression of iris images. Contrasting to the overwhelming majority of literature and studies in the field of compressing biometric sample data, we will not rely on assessing the resulting objective and subjective image quality after compression only, but we will apply a biometric iris recognition systems to the compressed sensor data to evaluate the effects of compression on recognition accuracy, in particular on the matching results of legitimate and illegitimate users.

In Section 2, we will review and discuss the available literature on biometric sample data compression with focus on iris data storage. Section 3 is the main part of this work where we first describe the employed image compression techniques, the used iris recognition system, and the data these algorithms are applied to. Subsequently we present and discuss our experimental results where we compare and rank the compression algorithms in use. Section 4 concludes the paper.

2 Iris Image Compression

The reason for focussing our investigations to iris recognition systems is that this biometric modality is claimed to be the most secure one exhibiting practically 0% FAR and low FRR. An interesting fact is that the iris recognition market is strongly dominated by Iridian Inc. based technology which is based on algorithms of J. Daugman [11]. The certainly most relevant standard for compressing iris image data is the recent ISO/IEC 19794-6 standard on Biometric Data Interchange Formats.

While the data formats specified by the ISO/IEC 19794 standard are fixed at present state, their impact on recognition accuracy as compared to other algorithms is not well documented. This is the scope of the current paper.

A vast amount of literature exists in which different compression algorithms are compared with respect to their rate-distortion performance on "usual" image data. It is worth noticing that also the evaluation of compression performance in biometric systems is surprisingly limited to PSNR or RMS-error computation and to psycho-visual studies in most investigations. Effects on actual matching rates or recognition accuracy are rarely documented. One of the few exceptions is found in [13] where image tiles containing fingerprint minutiae are compressed using PCA and wavelet transform and the effects on FAR of a specific recognition system are studied. In recent work [8], we have investigated the impact of JPEG, JPEG2000, SPIHT, PRVQ, and Fractal image compression on recognition accuracy of selected fingerprint and face recognition systems. [4] also relates JPEG, JPEG2000, and (WSQ) compression rates to recognition performance of some fingerprint and face recognition systems. Compression effects with respect to face recognition accuracy have been studied in dedicated papers as well: [6] investigates the impact of JPEG and JPEG2000 on the recognition results of 12 different face recognition techniques, and [7] employs varying bitrates using JPEG2000 to determine the trade-off points between recognition accuracy and compression rate.

ISO/IEC 19794-6 allows iris image data to be stored in lossy manner in the JPEG and JPEG2000 formats. Two types of iris image data are considered: rectilinear images (i.e. images of the entire eye) and polar images (which are basically the result of iris detection and segmentation), the latter much smaller in terms of storage requirement (e.g. 2kB vs. 25-30kB for rectilinear images). It is important to note that with this standardization it might become more attractive for companies to investigate alternatives to Iridian products due to the available common data format iris recognition systems can rely on.

Few studies are available on iris image compression and its impact on recognition performance. [10] applies JPEG2000 up to a compression rate of 20 to rectilinear image data (the CASIA database and a proprietary image collection is used) and investigates the effects on FAR and FRR of a 1-D version of the Daugman algorithm (the same system which is used in this study). [9] again uses JPEG2000 to compress polar iris images up to a compression rate of 80 and studies the impact on verification accuracy of three iris recognition systems (including the Daugman algorithm, the CASIA database is used). A more compact way of representing the Daugman IrisCode is discussed in [12], however, these results refer to template compression and are only valid for the techniques related to Iridian products.

In the subsequent experimental study we will apply a set of general purpose compression algorithms to rectangular iris image data and we will study their respective impact on the recognition accuracy of an iris template matching technique. Contrasting to the two studies reviewed before, we will not only rely on assessing JPEG2000 performance but will also investigate the performance of other schemes, e.g. like JPEG which is also covered by ISO/IEC 19794-6. Specifically, we will relate the rate-distortion performance of the compression schemes to the matching score of the recognition system applied to the compressed data. In this way, we are able to compare the compression schemes for their respective usefulness in the biometric context.

3 Experimental Study

3.1 Setting and Methods

Compression Algorithms. We use five different general purpose image compression algorithms: JPEG[1], JPEG2000[2], SPIHT[5], FRAC[14] and PRVQ[3]. Since the block-DCT based JPEG standard is a part of almost any image processing tool we do not give further reference on it. For the wavelet-based JPEG2000 standard we have used the JAVA reference implementation JJ2000[1]. SPIHT relies as well on the wavelet transform, but contrasting to JPEG2000 which exploits intra subband correlations only, SPIHT is a zero-tree based codec which exploits coefficient dependencies across subbands. We have employed the implementation as provided by the developers originally[2]. In addition to these described three transform-based compression algorithms we also use codebook-based schemes. Fractal image compression (FRAC) exploits self similarities within images (where the image itself may be interpreted as an internal codebook) and has been discussed controversially in the literature. We have employed an adaptive quadtree method implementation[3] based on Y. Fishers code. As the fifth algorithm a special flavour of vector quantization is used. PRVQ[4] performs a block-based prediction within the image to be compressed (similar to the intra-prediction mode in H.264), subsequently the residual image is compressed by a vector quantization strategy. [3] describes PRVQ and the used fractal compression variant in some detail. We apply each compression algorithm with 12 different bitrates distributed over the sensible operation range.

When applied to common images, JPEG2000 and SPIHT usually give the best results in terms of PSNR, closely followed by PRVQ. For high bitrates, JPEG provides fourth best results, whereas FRAC is superior to JPEG for medium and low bitrates. We expect the best results from JPEG2000, SPIHT and PRVQ, whereas JPEG and FRAC may not be able to represent the fine structure of the iris images with higher compression rates.

Iris Recognition System. The employed iris recognition system is Libor Masek's Matlab implementation[5] [15] of a 1-D version of the Daugman iris

[1] `http://jj2000.epfl.ch/`

[2] `http://www.cipr.rpi.edu/research/SPIHT/`

[3] `http://www.verrando.com/~verrando/pulcini/gp-ifs1.html`

[4] `http://www.ganesh.org/webcomp/images/`

[5] `http://www.csse.uwa.edu.au/~pk/studentprojects/libor/sourcecode.html`

recognition algorithm. First, this algorithm segments the eye image into the iris and the remainder of the image. After extracting the features if the iris (which are strongly quantized phase responses of complex 1-D Gabor filters in this case), considering translation, rotations and disturbed regions in the iris (a noise mask is generated), the algorithm outputs the similarity score by giving the hamming distance between two extracted templates. The range of the hamming distance reaches from zero (ideal matching of two iris images of the same person) to 0.5 (ideal mismatch between two iris images of different persons).

Sample Data. For all our experiments we considered images with 8-bit grayscale information per pixel from the CASIA[6] 1.0 iris image database (all images had been cropped and stored in a quadratic shape with a size of 280x280 pixels). We applied the experimental calculations on the images of the first 20 persons in the CASIA database using 7 iris images of each person. All employed compression software is able to handle this type of imagery, which is not true for color or non-squared images, and was applied on the raw rectangular image data and not on the extracted features. This has an important implication on the performance of the entire system. Whereas in the case of compressing polar iris images [9] only the iris texture information is affected, in the case of compressing rectangular image data also the iris detection and determination of the noise mask is potentially affected in addition to degrading texture information. Figure 1 shows an example of a JPEG2000 compressed (compression rate 96) iris image of one person, which was used in our calculations together with the extracted iris template data and the noise masks (template and noise mask have been scaled in y-direction by a factor of 4 for proper display).

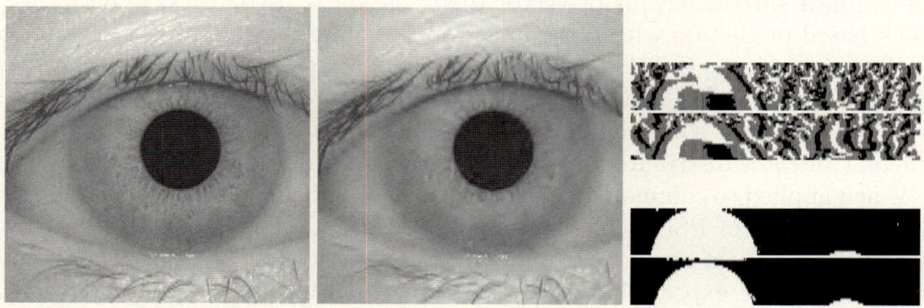

Fig. 1. Comparison of uncompressed/compressed iris image and the corresponding iris templates and noise masks

The differences in the templates are more significant as those in the noise masks which turn out to be very similar. Overall also iris detection is very robust to compression – all matching results shown in the following section have been generated without the software failing to detect the iris (results for compression

[6] `http://www.sinobiometrics.com`

rates where this happens have been omitted as found with fractal compression for example).

Compression can be used in various stages of the matching process. Either the stored reference data may be in compressed form, or the sample data acquired for verification may be compressed (e.g. for efficient transfer), or both. Therefore, we use two settings in our experiments: either both images are compressed and matched against each other or only one image is compressed in the matching stage. For investigating correct matches (matches from legitimate users enrolled in the database), we rely on 172800 generated images (i.e. for each of the 20 persons, we have 7 images resulting in 6! possible correct matches each; considering the 12 different compression rates we finally result in $20 \cdot 6! \cdot 12 = 172800$) for each compression technique. This is only true in the scenario with only 1 compressed image, for 2 compressed images this number is reduced due to symmetry reasons. For investigating matches between different persons (imposter matches), far more data is available.

3.2 Experimental Results

Figure 2 shows the averaged rate distortion comparison of the different compression algorithms applied to all iris images considered.

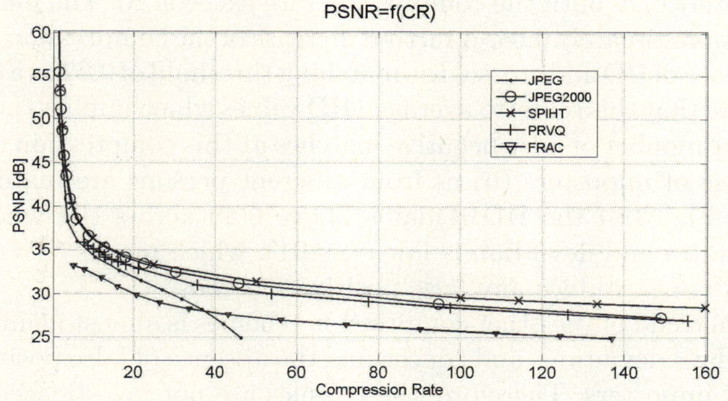

Fig. 2. Comparison of rate distortion of different compression algorithms

The highest average PSNR value is reached by JPEG2000 and SPIHT. PRVQ reaches PSNR values which are very close to those of JPEG2000 and SPIHT. JPEG and FRAC show the worst PSNR behaviour, which leads to the assumption that JPEG2000, SPIHT and PRVQ could be most suitable in iris recognition systems. Interestingly, FRAC outperforms JPEG for compression rates > 36. In the following, we investigate the impact of compression on the matching score (i.e. obtained hamming distance (HD)). The interval of $0.26 \leq HD \leq 0.35$ is discussed as the border between match and mismatch in iris recognition [11] – based on recommendations for the specific technique [10] used we choose $HD = 0.32$ as decision criterion between match and mismatch.

Fig. 3 shows the plot of the HD after applying the iris recognition algorithm to the JPEG compressed iris images. The x-axis shows the compression rates, whereas the y-axis shows the averaged hamming distance as well as the mean standard deviation of the HD.

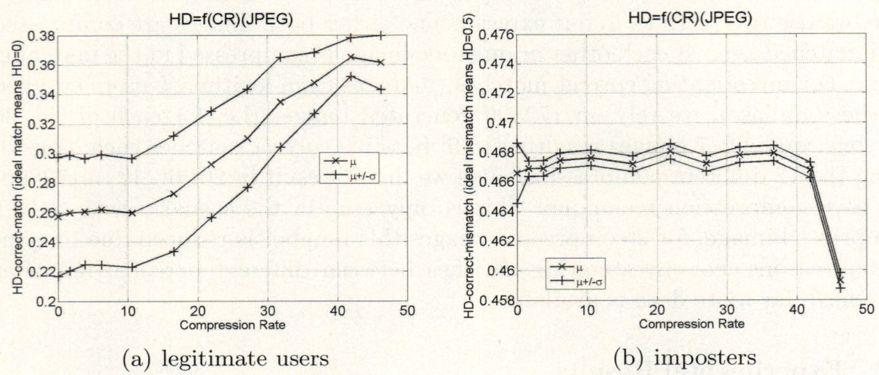

(a) legitimate users (b) imposters

Fig. 3. Impact of JPEG compression on iris recognition, 2 compressed images

In the case of legitimate users (Fig. 3.a), the mean value of the HD stays constant at approximately 0.26 until the compression rate exceeds 10. The mean standard deviation is approximately 0.04. A further increase of the compression rate leads to a steady increase of HD and crosses the matching threshold of 0.32 at a compression rate of 28. Note that this refers to averaged HD values which implies the occurrence of a significant number of false negative matches at this compression rate.

For the case of imposters (irises from different persons are matched against each other – Fig. 3.b) the HD remains above 0.45 across the whole range of compression rates and deviation is low (< 0.01), which means that JPEG compression does not introduce any false positive matches.

The general trend of the other compression schemes is almost identical with respect to standard deviations and concerning the absence of false positive matches in the case of imposters. Therefore, these issues are not investigated further. In the following, we compare the averaged HD values among the different compression techniques for the case of correct matches – legitimate users. Figs. 4(a) and 4(b) compare the scenarios with 1 and 2 compressed image(s).

The results indicate that PSNR is in most cases a good predictor for matching performance with compressed iris images. But there are some subtle differences between PSNR results and average HD matching scores. Even though PSNR values suggest FRAC to be superior to JPEG for compression rate > 36, there are no matching scores reported for FRAC in case of rate > 20. The reason is that for higher compression rates the iris detection process fails and no sensible results are obtained. As suggested by their respective PSNR values, JPEG2000, SPIHT, and PRVQ perform similarly crossing the 0.32 border at a compression rate of about 80 – 90. The superiority of those three compression

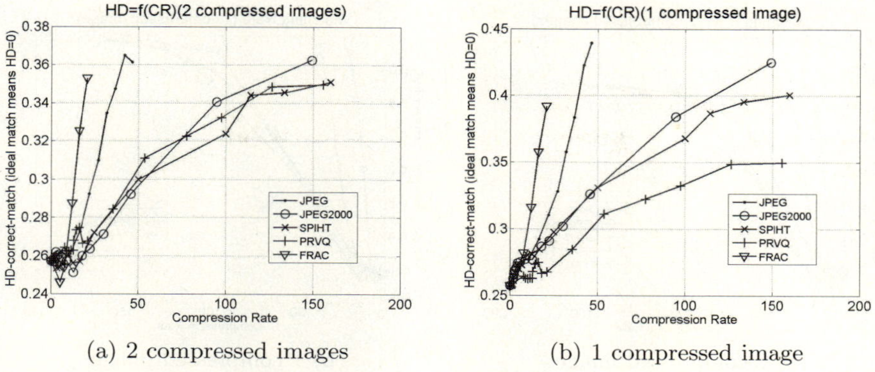

(a) 2 compressed images

(b) 1 compressed image

Fig. 4. Comparison of the HD for iris images for legitimate users

techniques over JPEG in terms of HD is even more significant as suggested by PSNR. When comparing the scenarios with 1 or 2 compressed image(s), it immediately gets clear that much lower HD scores are obtained in the 2 compressed images case. When considering the 1 compressed image case (Fig. 4(b)), only PRVQ shows matching scores similar to the 2 compressed images case, all other compression schemes perform worse. It is interesting that PRVQ is clearly the best algorithm is this scenario although only ranked third in terms of PSNR. Given the fact that lossy compression also acts as some sort of denoising, it is not surprising that the 2 compressed images scenario delivers lower HD values. The claim that compression up to a rate of 16 even improves the matching scores of not compressed images [9] can be supported at least for the 2 compressed images case.

In order to get rid of the standard deviation in the comparisons and to use a quantity often employed in the assessment of biometric system performance, we compute the false non-match rate (FNMR):

$$FNMR = \frac{\text{Number of (false) negative matches}}{\text{Number of legitimate users' matches}} \ . \qquad (1)$$

Figs. 5(a) and 5(b) compare the FNMR of different compression algorithms as a function of compression rate.

We notice similar behaviour as when comparing averaged HD values if we consider the ranking of the algorithms and when comparing the 1 and 2 compressed image(s) scenarios (the 2 compressed image scenario results in lower FNMR). Here, PRVQ is worse compared to JPEG2000 and SPIHT in the 2 compressed images case. This suggests the existence of more statistical outliers as for the other techniques leading to a higher number of false negative matches. Once again we would like to point out the performance difference between JPEG and JPEG2000: whereas JPEG reaches a FNMR of 50% at a compression rate of 20, JPEG2000 attains the same value at a compression rate of 40. However, for lower bitrates and more realistic FNMR values, the difference is not that pronounced but still significant.

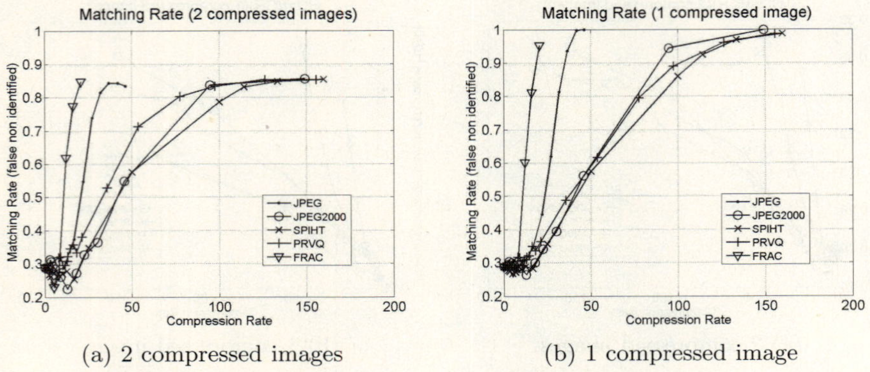

(a) 2 compressed images

(b) 1 compressed image

Fig. 5. FNMR with decision threshold at 0.32

Finally, we take a look on FMR. FMR is 0% in the case of 1 compressed image for all algorithms. In the case of the comparison of 2 compressed images, we found one false positive match at a compression rate of 130 with SPIHT – but this outlier is not a serious problem, because a compression rate of 130 is much too high for a realistic FNMR (see Figures 5(b) and 5(a)) and so an iris recognition system will never be operated at such high compression rates.

4 Conclusion and Future Work

JPEG2000, SPIHT, and PRVQ have been shown to be almost equally well suited for iris image compression. JPEG is significantly inferior to those techniques, especially when the bitrate decreases, the FNMR goes up dramatically fast. Fractal compression can be said to be non-suited at all for this application due to failing iris detection for compression rates > 20. Scenarios involving the compression of both images involved in the matching process turn out to deliver better matching scores and lower FNMR as compared to the case of compressing only 1 image. Therefore, in case compression is employed, both reference as well as sample data should be compressed. Overall, applying compression algorithms is found to increase FNMR but does not impact FMR. Consequently, compression does not decrease the security of iris recognition systems, but "only" reduces user convenience. Finally, it should be noted that the differences among the compression algorithms are relatively small with respect to recognition accuracy in a high quality environment with compression ratios < 10.

Acknowledgements

Most of the work described has been done in the scope of a semester project in the master program "Communication Engineering for IT" at CTI, Klagenfurt.

References

[1] Pennebaker, W., Mitchell, J.: JPEG – Still image compression standard. Van Nostrand Reinhold, New York (1993)

[2] Taubman, D., Marcellin, M.: JPEG2000 — Image Compression Fundamentals, Standards and Practice. Kluwer Academic Publishers, Dordrecht (2002)

[3] Jerabek, B., Schneider, P., Uhl, A.: Comparison of lossy image compression methods applied to photorealistic and graphical images using public domain sources. Tech. Rep. RIST++15/98, Research Institute for Softwaretechnology, University of Salzburg (1998)

[4] Funk, W., Arnold, M., Busch, C., Munde, A.: Evaluation of image compression algorithms for fingerprint and face recognition systems. In: Cole, J., Wolthusen, S. (eds.) Proceedings from the Sixth Annual IEEE Systems, Man and Cybernetics (SMC) Information Assurance Workshop, June 2006, pp. 72–78. IEEE Computer Society, Los Alamitos (2006)

[5] Said, A., Pearlman, W.A.: A new, fast, and efficient image codec based on set partitioning in hierarchical trees. IEEE Transactions on Circuits and Systems for Video Technology 6, 243–249 (1996)

[6] Delac, K., Grigic, M., Grigic, S.: Effects of JPEG and JPEG2000 compression on face recognition. In: Singh, S., Singh, M., Apte, C., Perner, P. (eds.) ICAPR 2005. LNCS, vol. 3687, pp. 136–145. Springer, Heidelberg (2005)

[7] McGarry, D., Arndt, C., McCabe, S., D'Amato, D.: Effects of compression and individual variability on face recognition performance. In: Biometric Technology for Human Identification. Proceedings of SPIE, vol. 5404, pp. 362–372 (August 2004)

[8] Mascher-Kampfer, A., Stögner, H., Uhl, A.: Comparison of Compression Algorithms' Impact on Fingerprint and Face Recognition Accuracy. In: Visual Computing and Image Processing VCIP 07. Proceedings of SPIE, vol. 6508, pp. 65080N-1–65050N-10 (January 2007)

[9] Rakshit, S., Monro, D.M.: Effects of Sampling and Compression on Human Iris Verification. In: Proceedings of the IEEE International Conference on Acustics, Speech, and Signal Processing ICASSP 2006. IEEE Signal Processing Society, pp. II-337–II-340 (July 2007)

[10] Ives, R.W., lBonney, B.L., Etter, D.M.: Effect of image compression on iris recognition. In: IMTC 2005 – Instrumentation and Measurement Technology Conference (May 2005)

[11] Daugman, J.: How iris recognition works. IEEE Transactions on Circiuts and Systems for Video Technology 14(1), 21–30 (2004)

[12] von Seelen, U.: IrisCode template compression and its effects on authentication performance. In: Biometrics Consortium Conference 2003 (September 2003)

[13] Beleznai, C., Ramoser, H., Wachmann, B., Birchbauer, J., Bischof, H., Kropatsch, W.: Memory-efficient fingerprint verification. In: Proceedings of the IEEE International Conference on Image Processing (ICIP'01), Thessaloniki, Greece, vol. 2, pp. 463–466 (October 2001)

[14] Fisher, Y. (ed.): Fractal Image Compression: Theory and Application. Springer, New York (1995)

[15] Masek, L., Kovesi, P.: MATLAB Source Code for a Biometric Identification System Based on Iris Patterns. The School of Computer Science and Software Engineering, The University of Western Australia (2003)

Standardization of Face Image Sample Quality*

Xiufeng Gao[1], Stan Z. Li[2], Rong Liu[2], and Peiren Zhang[1]

[1] University of Science and Technology of China
Hefei 230026, China
[2]Center for Biometrics and Security Research &
National Laboratory of Pattern Recognition
Institute of Automation, Chinese Academy of Sciences, Beijing 100080, China
http://www.cbsr.ia.ac.cn

Abstract. Performance of biometric systems is dependent on quality of acquired biometric samples. Poor sample quality is a main reason for matching errors in biometric systems and may be the main weakness of some implementations. In this paper, we present an approach for standardization of facial image quality, and develop facial symmetry based methods for its assessment by which facial asymmetries caused by non-frontal lighting and improper facial pose can be measured. Experimental results are provided to illustrate the concepts, definitions and effectiveness.

Keywords: Biometric sample quality, facial symmetry, local features, methodology, standardization.

1 Introduction

Sample quality has significant impact on accuracy of biometric recognition. Poor sample quality is a main reason for matching errors in biometric systems and may be the main weakness of some implementations. Automatic biometric image quality assessment may help improve system performance. It can be used to monitor image quality for different applications, capture devices, enrollment and recognition algorithms. The use of face image quality metrics to enhance the overall performance of the system is growing.

Fig. 1 shows a framework of a biometric recognition system using an image sample quality assessment component. Biometric images are preprocessed and their quality is evaluated. Only images with acceptable quality are received for recognition; others are discarded. Thus some of recognition errors can be avoided and matching time expense can be saved for a large biometric database. Also, in some security situation, quality assessment can give an alert when someone does not want to be recognized on purpose, for example, a criminal hiding himself. The quality value can be sent to recognition algorithm and helps to improve its accuracy. For example, the threshold can be decreased if an image's quality is low. In this way, low false reject rate (FRR) can be achieved.

* The original ideas presented in this paper belong to CBSR and the work was performed at CBSR.

S.-W. Lee and S.Z. Li (Eds.): ICB 2007, LNCS 4642, pp. 242–251, 2007.

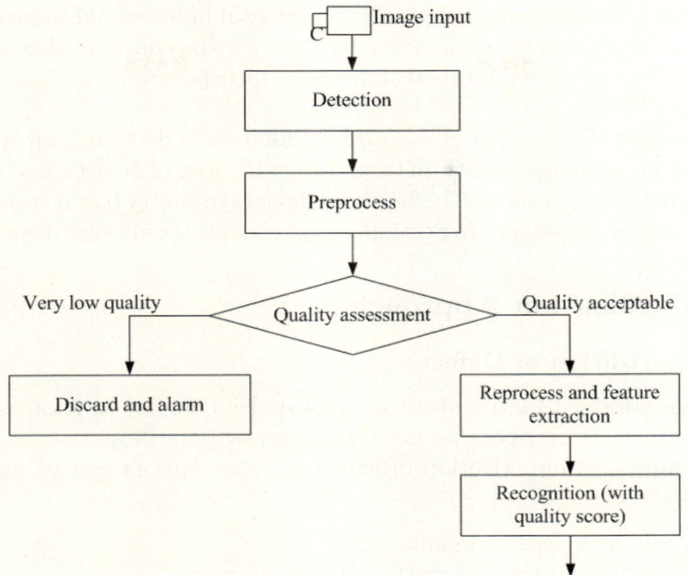

Fig. 1. A framework of biometric recognition using quality assessment

Standardization of quantitative face image quality score computation lays a basis for common interpretation of the quality scores. ISO/IEC WD 29794-1 [1] presents three approaches for calculating quantitative quality scores, namely "bottom-up", "top-down" and "combined". The presentation is based on the character, fidelity and utility concepts therein. ISO/IEC WD 29794-4 [2] emphasizes the use of annotated fingerprint corpus to standardize the score normalization. ISO-IEC WD [1,2] suggested the use of Quality Algorithm Identification (QAID), or Quality Percentile Rank upon standardization of a Quality Score Normalization (QSN) corpus. On the other hand, ISO/IEC standard WD 19794-5 [3] are also made to regulate enrollment of gallery faces for applications in E-passport, national ID, and driver license applications, aimed to achieve approximately frontal illumination and pose.

A number of research papers on biometric sample quality assessment are published in past years. Chen [4] proposed a wavelet-based quality measure for iris image which improveed the performance. Youmaran [5] introduced a definition of biometric information and proposed an algorithm to measure the changes in biometric sample quality resulting from image degradation. Most work on face image quality is based on general, face-nonspecific image properties, such as contrast, sharpness and illumination intensity etc [6]. These methods are not aimed to evaluate face quality degradation caused by non-frontal lighting and improper facial pose.

In this paper, we present an approach for standardization of facial image quality. Aspects of defects are categorized. A two-level quality score system, defect aspect level and overall level, is suggested. Then, we develop facial symmetry based methods for the assessment of facial image quality by proposing metrics measuring facial asymmetries caused by non-frontal lighting and improper facial pose. Experimental results are provided to illustrate the concepts, definitions and effectiveness. The proposed methods have been incorporated into SC37 standard working draft [7].

The remainder of this paper is organized as follows: In Section 2, an approach is presented for facial image quality, in terms of 4 categories of defects, and metrics of face image quality are proposed. In Section 3, facial symmetry based and other face quality metrics are presented. In Section 4, experimental results are demonstrated.

2 Standardization Approach

2.1 Categorization of Defects

A face image obtained from a static camera, video camera, or photo scanner is usually imperfect. It may contain defects caused by poor illumination, improper face positioning and imperfection of camera. These factors can be categorized into four aspects:

(1) Defects caused by environment
  - Deviation from the symmetric lighting
  - Uneven lighting on the face area
  - Extreme strong or weak illumination
  - Cluttered background

(2) Defects caused by camera conditions
  - Low resolution
  - Low contrast
  - High noise
  - Geometric distortion

(3) Defects caused by user's face conditions
  - Heavy facial wears, such as thick or dark glasses
  - Exaggerated expression
  - Closed eye(s)
  - Heavy makeup

(4) Defects caused by user-camera positioning
  - Deviation from frontal pose (yaw , tilt, in-plane rotation)
  - Too far (face too small) or too near (face too big)
  - Out of focus (low sharpness)
  - Partial occlusion of the face

2.2 Approach

The performance of an automated face recognition system is affected by the amount of defect or the degree of imperfection present in the face image. The knowledge of quality can be used to invoke appropriate processing algorithms, for example, some image enhancement or normalization algorithms prior to feature extraction, appropriate thresholds or matchers based on quality.

In this paper, we adopt the following approach for face sample quality standardization:

(1) Specifying possible defects of face biometric samples in categories. There can be several defect aspects in each category, some having been specified in Section 2.1.
(2) Defining a Face Quality Score (FQS), to be calculated by a Face Quality Assessment Algorithm (FQAA), to evaluate possible defect in each aspects.
(3) Mapping the raw FQS of each category to a normalized quality score using an annotated Quality Score Normalized Dataset (QSND) [1]. The category-normalized FQS indicates how good the sample is with respect to the considered category of quality.
(4) Mapping all the FQSs to an overall normalized quality score using the annotated QSND. This provides an overall evaluation of how good the sample is for biometric recognition.

An FQAA takes a face sample as its input and reports the associated quality score in some aspect. Essentially, at least one FQS should be defined for each category of defects, so that a tactic procedure can be deployed to deal with the problems.

A raw FQS should be normalized in order to achieve interoperability. This may be done by a quality score normalization procedure with a QSND [1]. In QSND, biometric samples are annotated with normalized quality scores. Such annotation may be partly derived from the results of controlled performance tests, and partly by manual labeling.

3 Face Quality Scores

In this section, we define FQSs based on facial symmetry, which evaluates degradation caused by non-frontal lighting and head pose by making use of face specific semantics; we also define FQSs based on the inter-eye distance and image characteristics, to evaluating.other user, camera and illumination conditions.

3.1 Facial Symmetry Based Quality Scores

The illumination and pose variations are two main issues that cause performance degradation for most existing systems [8]. Quality degradations caused by non-frontal lighting and facial pose may be assessed using facial symmetry. Fig. 2 gives intuitive illustrations of how illumination and pose affect the facial symmetry. Based on this, we propose the following facial symmetry based FQSs.

Facial Symmetry Analysis. The symmetry may be analyzed using some local image features, e.g., the raw image pixel values, or locally-filtered pixel values. When a local filter is chosen properly, it provides a better basis for computing facial symmetry[1]. The differences between image features at the corresponding

[1] Care must be taken that the filters used for the corresponding locations in the left and right halves should be appropriately mirrored.

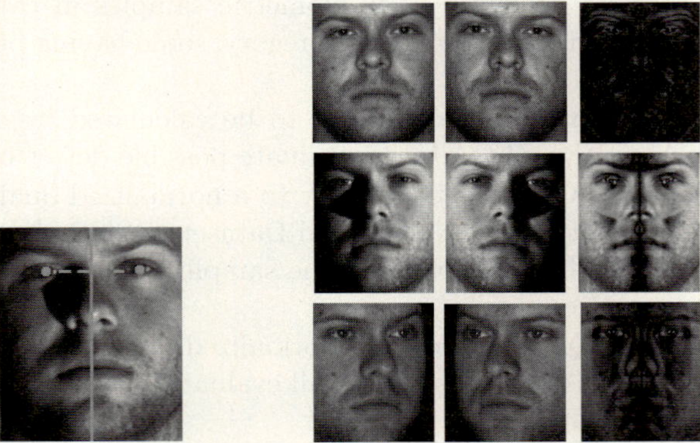

Fig. 2. Left: Division of a face into left and right half regions at the mid-line of the eyes. Right (columns 1-3): Original images, their mirror versions, and the corresponding left-right difference images.

left-right pixel locations provide local measures of asymmetry caused by non-frontal illumination or improper head pose. If the face image is strictly left-right symmetric, the differences should all be zero.

Because the histogram of a local feature may be a more descriptive feature than the local feature itself, we further propose to use the difference between corresponding histograms of local features as a local measure of asymmetry. Consider m local features produced by m local filters. Assume that the histogram of a local feature consists of n bins. Then the histogram at a location can be considered as a vector of $m \times n$ elements. A histogram difference between the ℓ-th pair of histograms left-right, H_ℓ^L and H_ℓ^R, can be calculated as follows

$$D_\ell = |H_\ell^L - H_\ell^R| \tag{1}$$

where $|\cdot|$ is some suitable form of histogram difference, e.g., city block distance (used in this paper), histogram intersection, cross-entropy, or Kullback-Leibler divergence. The larger the D_ℓ value is, the less the left-right symmetric of the face image is, and the lower the image quality is in some aspects for the subwindow at ℓ.

Lighting and Pose Asymmetries. Lighting symmetry should be measured based on illumination sensitive image properties. For example, Local Binary Pattern (LBP) [9] code is a local feature sensitive to illumination direction, and has been used for face recognition [10,11,12].

In this paper, we used an Adaboost learning algorithm to select the most effective subset from a large pool of LBP features [11,12], and use the local histograms of the selected LBP features as the basis for calculating facial asymmetry. A difference is derived between the corresponding left-right LBP histograms using Equ. 1. The larger the deviation, the larger the difference value, as will be seen in experiments.

This quality score is calculated as the sum of all the histogram differences as

$$Asymmetry(I) = \sum_{\ell=1}^{L} D_\ell \tag{2}$$

where L is the number of left-right histogram pairs. The larger $Asymmetry(I)$ is, the less frontal the lighting is for the face image I. This is used as a metric for evaluating the defect in the aspect of lighting direction.

Pose symmetry evaluation can be done based on pose-sensitive image features. In this paper, the same local LBP histogram features as used in lighting asymmetry are used for this purpose. The histogram distance are summed up to measure the pose asymmetry in the image. The larger the sum value, the more the face is deviated from the frontal pose, and the lower the image quality is in terms of pose symmetry.

The following summarizes an FQAA procedure for calculating facial symmetry based FQSs:

(1) Preprocess the cropped face image using appropriate algorithms;
(2) Perform local feature filtering using designated filters at designated locations;
(3) Calculate the difference between corresponding local feature histogram pairs;
(4) Calculate a suitable sum of the absolute values of the differences.

3.2 Other Face Quality Scores

User-Camera Distance. User-camera distance is recommended to be 1.2 - 2.5m in a typical photo studio and 0.7 - 1.0m in a typical photo booth (ISO/IEC 19794-5 AMD 1 [3]). The distance is inversely related the size of the face. Therefore, the inter-eye distance $Dist_{eye}$ can be used to estimate the quality score for whether the user is at a proper distance from the camera

$$Dist_{UserCam} = D(Dist_{eye}, Dist_0) \tag{3}$$

where $Dist_0$ is the average number of inter-eye pixels when the user is at the recommended distance and the image capture devise is at the recommended setting, and D is some function indicating deviation of $Dist_{eye}$ from $Dist_0$. Note, however, different individuals have different inter-eye distances, and therefor the use of this metric needs more consideration.

Illumination Strength. Let H_0 be the histogram of image under a standard illumination strength and H is the histogram of the image being assessed. H_0 provides a reference of standard illumination strength. In the case of very dark or very bright illumination, the distribution of the gray scale values is concentrated toward the lower or higher end of the histogram H. A quality score could be defined to be a distance between H_0 and the measured histogram H.

Contrast. Given an image I of size M by N, the image contrast may be calculated as the standard deviation of the pixel values:

$$Contrast_I = \sqrt{\frac{1}{MN}\sum_{x=0}^{M-1}\sum_{y=0}^{N-1}\left[I(x,y) - \frac{1}{MN}\sum_{x=0}^{M-1}\sum_{y=0}^{N-1} I(x,y)\right]^2} \tag{4}$$

It is suggested that the image $I(x, y)$ should not be normalized for this calculation in order to reflect the true situation.

Sharpness. The sharpness of a face image refers to the degree of clarity in both coarse and fine details in the face region. The quality value for sharpness can be calculated via image gradient

$$Shapeness_I = \sum_{x=1}^{M-2}\sum_{y=1}^{N-2} G(x,y) \tag{5}$$

where $G(x, y)$ is the value of gradient magnitude calculated in a neighborhood of (x, y).

4 Experiments

The following experiments examine on the facial asymmetry caused by non-frontal lighting and improper facial poses using the facial symmetry based methods presented in Section 3.1. Images of 10 persons are used from the Yale face database B [13].

4.1 Lighting Symmetry

Fig. 3 shows examples of LBP histogram differences (Equ. 1) for 3 face images of increasing deviation of lighting from the frontal direction. The differences are calculated between 2300 random pairs of LBP histograms, shown in horizontal axis. As can be seen, the larger the deviation, the larger the difference value.

Fig. 4 shows FQS (lighting asymmetry) values (Equ. 2 for the 10 persons (in horizontal axis) under the 5 illumination conditions (in 5 curves), where the values are normalized into the range [0,100]. For each of the 10 persons, 5 images, taken under 5 different illumination conditions, are used. The differences between 2300 pairs of corresponding histograms are calculated, and then summed according to Equ. 2. As can be seen, the larger the deviation from frontal lighting, the larger the overall asymmetry value.

4.2 Pose Symmetry

Fig. 5 shows FQS (pose asymmetric) values for 4 pose categories of the 10 people, calculated in the same way as in the lighting asymmetry. The Yale face database

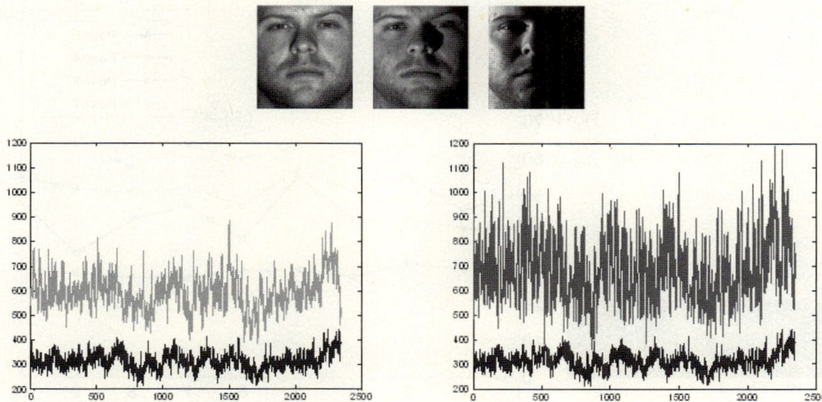

Fig. 3. Upper: 3 face images of increasing deviation of lighting from the frontal direction from left to right. Lower: histogram differences between 2300 pairs for the 1st and 2nd images (left) and for the 1st and 3rd images (right).

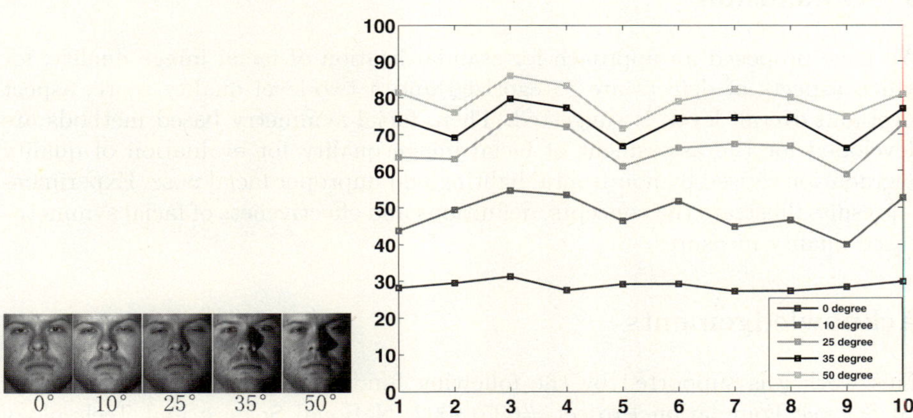

Fig. 4. Lighting FQS (lighting asymmetry) values. The 5 curves from bottom to top correspond to the face asymmetry values for the 5 light categories in the left from left to right.

B has 9 pose categories, examples being shown on the left of Fig. 5. Pose 0 is frontal (0 degree), poses 1, 2, 3, 4, and 5 are about 12 degrees from the camera optical axis, poses 6, 7, and 8 are about 24 degrees. Also note that poses 1, 2, 4, 5, 6, 8 have tilt variation. The images of poses 0, 4, 8, 7 are chosen for this experiment, and the corresponding FQSs are plotted on the right of the figure. As can be seen, the larger the deviation from frontal pose, the larger the overall asymmetry value.

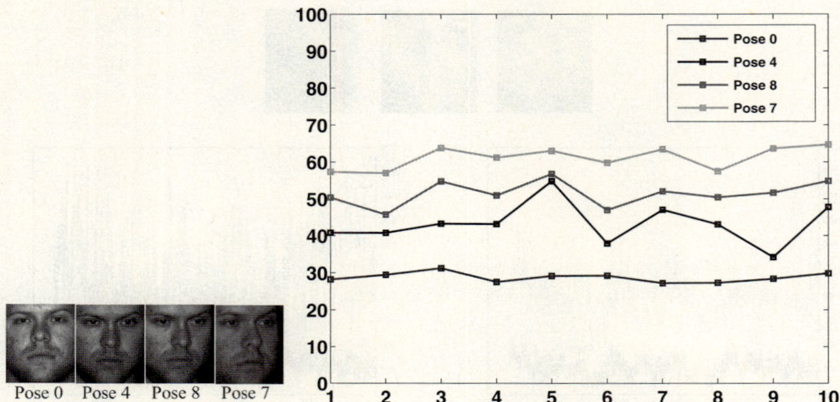

Fig. 5. Pose FQS (pose asymmetry) values. The 4 curves from bottom to top are calculated for poses 0, 4, 8, and 7.

5 Conclusion

We have proposed an approach for standardization of facial image quality, for which aspects of defects are categorized and a two-level quality score, aspect level and overall level, is suggested. Then, facial symmetry based methods are developed for the assessment of facial image quality for evaluation of quality degradation caused by non-frontal lighting and improper facial pose. Experimental results illustrate the concepts, definitions and effectiveness of facial symmetry based quality measures.

Acknowledgements

This work was supported by the following funding resources: National Natural Science Foundation Project #60518002, National Science and Technology Supporting Platform Project #2006BAK08B06, National 863 Program Projects #2006AA01Z192 and #2006AA01Z193, Chinese Academy of Sciences 100 people project, and the AuthenMetric Collaboration Foundation.

References

1. ISO/IEC JTC 1/SC 37 N 1477: Biometric Sample Quality Standard - Part 1: Framework (January 30, 2006)
2. ISO/IEC JTC 1/SC 37 N 1760: Biometric Sample Quality - Part 4: Fingerprint Sample Quality (August 21, 2006)
3. ISO/IEC JTC 1/SC 37 N 1511: Proposed Draft Amendment to ISO/IEC 19794-5 Face Image Data on Conditions for Taking Pictures (March 1, 2006)
4. Chen, Y., Dass, S.C., Jain, A.K.: Localized iris image quality using 2-d wavelets. In: Proc. of International Conference on Biometrics (ICB), pp. 373–381 (2006)

5. Youmaran, R., Adler, A.: Measuring biometric sample quality in terms of biometric information. In: Biometrics Consortium Conference (2006)
6. Brauckmann, M., Werner, M.: Technical report. In: Proceddings of NIST Biometric Quality Workshop (2006), at `http://www.itl.nist.gov/iad/894.03/quality/workshop/`
7. ISO/IEC JTC 1/SC 37 N 1477: Biometric Sample Quality - Part 5: Face Image Data Sample Quality(Working Draft for comment) (February 12, 2007)
8. Zhao, W., Chellappa, R., Phillips, P.J., Rosenfeld, A.: Face Recognition: A Literature Survey. ACM Computing Surveys 35(4), 399–458 (2003)
9. Ojala, T., Pietikainen, M., Maenpaa, M.: Multiresolution gray-scale and rotation invariant texture classification width local binary patterns. IEEE Transactions on Pattern Analysis and Machine Intelligence 24, 971–987 (2002)
10. Ahonen, T., Hadid, A., Pietikainen, M.: Face Description with Local Binary Patterns: Application to Face Recognition. IEEE Transactions on Pattern Analysis and Machine Intelligence 28(12), 2037–2041 (2006)
11. Zhang, G., Huang, X., Li, S.Z., Wang, Y., Wu, X.: Boosting local binary pattern (lbp)-based face recognition. In: Proc. Advances in Biometric Person Authentication: 5th Chinese Conference on Biometric Recognition, pp. 179–186 (2004)
12. Li, S.Z., Chu, R., Liao, S., Zhang, L.: Illumination invariant face recognition using near-infrared images. IEEE-PAMI 26, 627–639 (2007)
13. Georghiades, A.S., Belhumeur, P.N.: From few to many: Illumination cone models for face recognition under variable lighting and pose. IEEE Transactions on Pattern Analysis and Machine Intelligence 23(6), 643–660 (2001)

Blinking-Based Live Face Detection Using Conditional Random Fields

Lin Sun[1], Gang Pan[1,*], Zhaohui Wu[1], and Shihong Lao[2]

[1] Dept. of Computer Science, Zhejiang University, Hangzhou, P.R. China
Tel.:(86)571-8795-1647
{sunlin,gpan,wzh}@zju.edu.cn
[2] Sensing and Control Technology Laboratory, OMRON Corporation, Japan
lao@ari.ncl.omron.co.jp

Abstract. This paper presents a blinking-based liveness detection method for human face using Conditional Random Fields (CRFs). Our method only needs a web camera for capturing video clips. Blinking clue is a passive action and does not need the user to to any hint, such as speaking, face moving. We model blinking activity by CRFs, which accommodates long-range contextual dependencies among the observation sequence. The experimental results demonstrate that the proposed method is promising, and outperforms the cascaded Adaboost method and HMM method.

1 Introduction

Biometrics are emerging technologies that enable the authentication of an individual based on physiological or behavioral characteristics, which including faces, fingerprints, irises, voices, etc [1]. However, spoofing attack (or copy attack) is a serious threat for biometrics. Liveness detection in biometric systems can prevent spoofing attack, based on recognition of physiological activities as the sign of liveness.

Face recognition is one of the most useful biometrics and has many applications. However, the liveness detection in face recognition system has be little addressed. The vein map of the faces using ultra-violet cameras may be a secure method of identifying a live individual, but it needs additional expensive devices. It is a big challenge to detect live face from a web camera in face recognition system. A little work on live face detection has been done. Robert et al[2] used the multi-modal approaches against spoofing, which need voice recorder and user collaboration. Choudhary et al[3] used 3D depth information of a human head to detect live person. However, it is hard to estimate depth information when head is still. Li et al[4] proposed Fourier spectra to classify live faces and the faked images, but it strongly depends on the data quality. Kollreider et al[5] provided a method to determine liveness by applying optical flow to obtain the information of face motion. This kind of methods is vulnerable to photo motion, such as

* Corresponding author.

S.-W. Lee and S.Z. Li (Eds.): ICB 2007, LNCS 4642, pp. 252–260, 2007.

photo bending. Moriyama et al[6] proposed an eyeblink detection method based on the changes of mean intensity of the upper half and the lower half in eye region, usually the images of high quality are required.

Eye blinking is a spontaneous physiological behavior. The normal resting blink rate of a human being is 20 times per minute, with the average blink time lasting one quarter of a second[21]. Thus, eye blinking could be a very useful clue to identify a live face.

This paper focuses on using blinking clue for face liveness detection. We use CRFs to model blinking activities, for its accommodating long-range dependencies on the observation sequence [7]. We compare CRF model with cascaded AdaBoost [17], which is a discriminative model, and HMM, which is a generative model. The experiment results show that CRF model has better performance than the others.

2 Modelling Blinking Activities Using CRFs

Blinking is an action sequence that consists of two continuous sub-actions, from open to close and from close to open. Blinking activity could be sampled by web camera into an image sequence. The typical eye states in the images are *open*, *half-open* and *close*. Every state should not be considered independently for blinking recognition. It means that contextual dependencies in eye blinking sequence need to be considered when modelling blinking activities. It is hard to predict blinking activity at a particular time point using only the previous state and the current observation alone. Hidden Markov model (HMM)[13], which is a generative model, can't accommodate long-range dependencies on the observation sequence. Conditional random fields(CRFs) are probabilistic models for segmenting and labeling sequence data and mainly used in natural language processing for its accommodating long-range dependencies on the observation sequence [7,8,9].

We employ a linear chain structure of CRFs. It has discrete eye state label data $y_t \in \chi = \{1, 2, \ldots, c\}$, $t = 1 \ldots T$, and observation x_t. Half-open state is hard to define commonly over the different individuals, since the eye size of half-open state depends on the person eye appearance, for example, the open state of a small eye may look like the half-open state of a big eye. As for our blinking model, we use two state labels, C for close state and NC for non-close (include half-open and open), to label eye states. Observation data, which are features extracted from the image, will be discussed in next section. Graphical structure of our CRF-based blinking model is shown in Fig. 1. For notational compactness, we consider $Y = (y_1, y_2, \ldots, y_T)$ to be the label sequence, $X = (x_1, x_2, \ldots, x_T)$ to be the observation sequence.

Let $G = (V, E)$ be a graph and Y is indexed by the vertices of G. Then (Y, X) is called a *conditional random field*, when conditioned on X, the random variables X and Y obey the Markov property w.r.t. the graph:

$$p(y_v|X, Y_w, w \neq v) = p(y_v|X, Y_w, w \sim v), \tag{1}$$

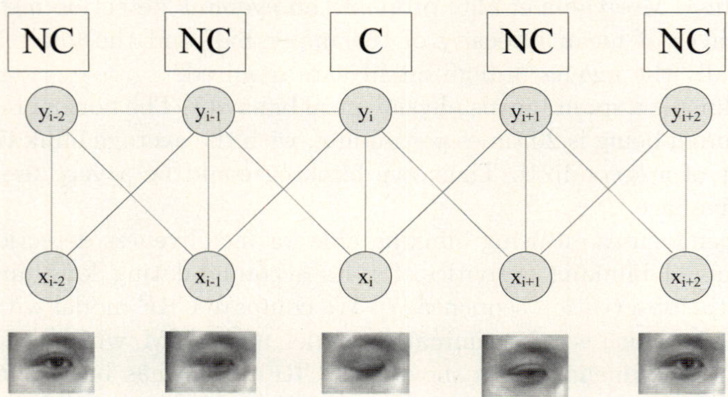

Fig. 1. Graphic structure of CRF-based blinking model. Here we show the model based on contexts of observation of size 3. Labels C and NC are for close state and non-close state respectively.

where $w \sim v$ means that w and v are neighbors in G. Using the Hammersley Clifford theorem [10], the joint distribution over the label sequence Y given observation X has the form:

$$p_\theta(Y|X) = \frac{1}{Z_\theta(X)} exp(\sum_{t=1}^{T} F(y_t, y_{t-1}, X)) \tag{2}$$

$$Z_\theta(X) = \sum_{Y} exp(\sum_{t=1}^{T} F_\theta(y_t, y_{t-1}, X)), \tag{3}$$

where $Z_\theta(X)$ is a normalized factor summing over all label sequences. Potential functions $F_\theta(y_t, y_{t-1}, X)$ is the sum of CRF features at time t:

$$F_\theta(y_t, y_{t-1}, X) = \sum_i \lambda_i f_i(y_t, y_{t-1}, X) + \sum_j \mu_j g_j(y_t, X), \tag{4}$$

with parameters $\theta = (\lambda_1, \lambda_2, \ldots; \mu_1, \mu_2, \ldots)$, to be estimated from training data. f_i and g_j are feature functions for inter-label and observation-label respectively. λ_i and μ_j are the feature weights associated with f_i and g_j. Feature functions f_i and g_j are based on conjunctions of simple rules. Inter-label feature functions f_j are:

$$f_i(y_t, y_{t-1}, X) = [y_t = l \wedge y_{t-1} = l'], \tag{5}$$

$l, l' \in \chi$. $[e]$ is equal to 1 if logical expression e is true, 0 otherwise. Given a temporal context window of size $2W+1$ around the current observation, observation-label feature functions g_j are:

$$g_j(y_t, X) = [y_t = l][D(x_{t-w}) = o], \tag{6}$$

$l \in \chi, o \in \tau$, $w \in [-W, W]$. τ is a set of discreted observation value. w is size of a context window around the current observation. $D(x_t) = \lceil x_t/H \rceil$, which is a function to convert float x_t into an integer. To compact the size of the discreted observation set τ, x_t is divided by H first, which is set to 6 in this paper.

CRFs could be trained by searching the set of weights $\theta = \{\lambda_1, \lambda_2, \ldots; \mu_1, \mu_2, \ldots\}$ to maximize the log-likelihood, L_θ, of a given training data set $D = \{Y^d, X^d\}_{d=1\ldots N}$

$$L_\theta = \sum_{d=1}^{N} log(p_\theta(Y^d|X^d)) = \sum_{d=1}^{N}(\sum_{t=1}^{T} F_\theta(y_t^d, y_{t-1}^d, X^d) - logZ_\theta(X^d)). \qquad (7)$$

Learning the model parameters leads to a convex problem with guaranteed global optimality. This optimization can be solved by a gradient ascent (BFGS) method[9], and inference can be performed efficiently using dynamic programming as HMM.

3 Observations in CRF-Based Blinking Model

Observation features can be selected variously according to different problems. For example, silhouette features are commonly used in human motion recognition [14,15,16]. Blinking activity is an action represented by the image sequence which consists of images with close and non-close state. Observation features that convey the eye state would be much helpful for the blinking model. We, integrating Adaboost algorithm [12], define the observation function as:

$$x_t(I) = \sum_{i=1}^{N}(log(1/\beta_i)h_i(I)), \qquad (8)$$

where $h(I, f, p, \theta)$ is a weak classifier which consists of a feature(f), a threshold(θ) and a polarity(p) indicating the direction of the inequality:

$$h(I, f, p, \theta) = \begin{cases} 1 & if \quad pf(I) < p\theta \\ 0 & otherwise \end{cases}. \qquad (9)$$

The parameter β_i and $h_i(I, f, p, \theta)$ can be obtained using Adaboost algorithm. In our implementation, the positive samples and negative samples are for open state and close state respectively. The over-complete haar-like features [11] are chosen as the feature(f). Some observation samples for the whole blinking activity are shown in Fig. 2.

4 Experiments

4.1 Database

In order to test our approach, we build a video database including blinking video clips and imposter video clips, which are captured by Logitech Pro5000, a

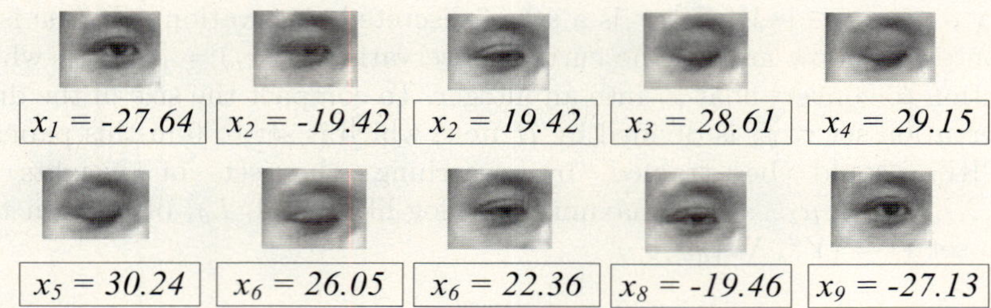

Fig. 2. The samples of observations in CRFs for an entire blinking activity. The observation value x_t of each frame is under the corresponding frame.

common web camera. There are totally 80 clips in blinking video database for 20 individuals, 4 clips for each individual: the first clip without glasses in frontal view, the second clip with thin rim glasses in frontal view, the third clip with black frame glasses in frontal view, and the last clip without glasses in upward view, shown in Fig. 4. Each video clip is about five seconds length with 30 fps and size of 320 × 240. The blinking number varies from 1 to 6 times in each clip. A typical blinking activity in our blinking videos is shown in Fig. 3. To test the ability against photo imposters, we also sampled 180 photo imposter video clips of 20 persons with various motions of photo, including rotating, folding and moving.

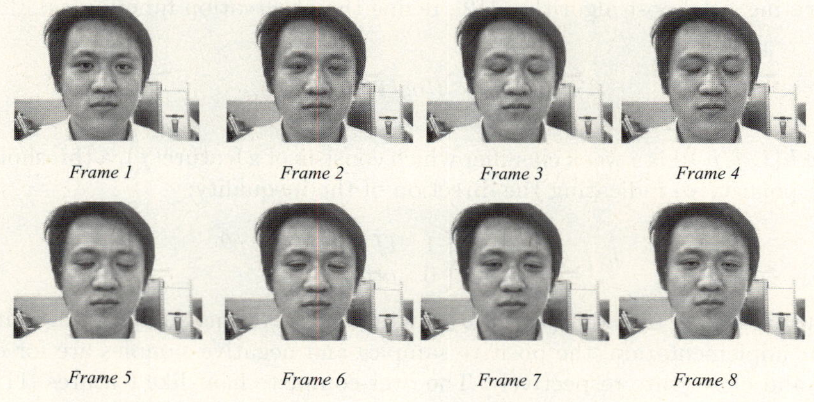

Fig. 3. A blinking example from blinking video database

4.2 CRF Training

State labels for CRF training, C and NC, are labeled manually. Observations calculating is base on the eye images that extracted from face images by OMRON Vision^{TM} software library and resized to 24 × 24 pixels. We have trained CRF that can model long-range dependencies between observations to various degrees.

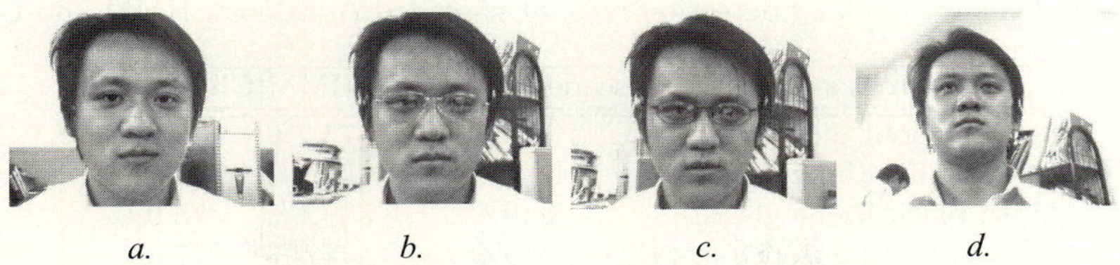

Fig. 4. Four styles in blinking video database. (a) Frontal + without glasses. (b) Frontal + thin rim glasses. (c) Frontal + black frame glasses. (d) Upward+without glasses.

Here window size $w = 2$ is chosen, meaning that we considered contexts of observations of size 5 centered at the current observation. Observation sequences and label sequences of five persons are used to estimate parameters of CRF.

The parameters β_i are obtained by AdaBoost, with 1016 labeled close eyes and 1200 open eyes, which are scaled to a base resolution of 24×24 pixels. Close eye samples are from CAS-PEAL-R1 face database [20] and Asian Face Image Database PF01 [19]. Open eye samples are from FERET face database [18]. The samples of close eye and open eye are shown in Fig. 5.

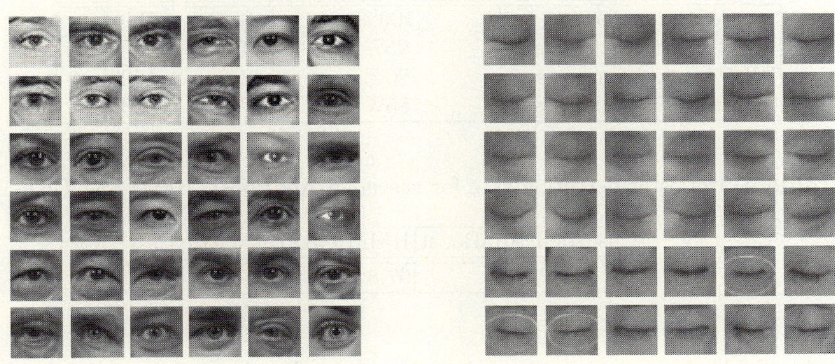

Fig. 5. Training samples for computing observation

4.3 Results

Using the blinking video database, we compare the CRF-based blinking detection with cascaded Adaboost and HMM approaches. Table 1 shows one eye blinking detected rate for the three methods. Table 2 shows two eyes' blinking detection rate, assuming that a blinking is detected if either left eye or right eye blinking is detected. Table 3 shows live face detection rate for the three models, assuming that live face is detected if there is one blinking of either left or right eye is detected in the clip. Table 1, 2 and 3 demonstrate that CRF-based approach outperforms the other two methods in blinking detection from Table 1 and 2 and also has less effect for glasses-wearing and upward view than the other two

Table 1. One-eye blinking detection rate for cascaded AdaBoost, HMM and CRF

Different styles	Cascaded AdaBoost	HMM	CRF($w = 2$)
Without glasses	96.5%	73.7%	98.2%
With thin rim glasses	60.0%	46.9%	68.5%
With black frame glasses	46.9%	39.1%	75.0%
Upward without glasses	52.5%	43.4%	77.0%

Table 2. Two-eye blinking detection rate for cascaded AdaBoost, HMM and CRF

Different styles	Cascaded AdaBoost	HMM	CRF($w = 2$)
Without glasses	98.2%	82.5%	100%
With thin rim glasses	80.0%	63.1%	84.6%
With black frame glasses	71.9%	50.0%	92.2%
Upward without glasses	62.3%	50.9%	100%

Table 3. Live face detection rate for cascaded AdaBoost, HMM and CRF

Different styles	Cascaded AdaBoost	HMM	CRF($w = 2$)
Without glasses	100%	100%	100%
With thin rim glasses	95%	95%	90%
With black frame glasses	80%	85%	100%
Upward without glasses	85%	95%	100%

Table 4. Imposter detection rate for cascaded AdaBoost, HMM and CRF

Cascaded AdaBoost	HMM	CRF($w = 2$)
95%	97.8%	98.3%

methods. Table 4 shows imposter detection rate for these three models tested by imposter video database.

5 Conclusions

This paper presented a CRF-based framework for face liveness detection using blinking clue. CRFs, which can accommodate arbitrary overlapping features of the observation as well as long-range contextual dependencies on observation sequence, are suitable for modeling blinking activities for liveness detection. The experimental results with cascaded AdaBoost, CRF and HMM show that CRF model significantly outperforms the other two models both in liveness detection and imposter detection.

Acknowledgements

This work is partly supported by NSF of China (60503019, 60525202), Key Program of NSF of China (60533040), Program for New Century Excellent Talents in University (NCET-04-0545) and a grant from OMRON corporation. The authors would be grateful to Mr. Yoshihisa Ijiri and Mr. Motoo Yamamoto for valuable discussions.

References

1. Jain, A., Bolle, R., Pankanti, S.: Personal Identification in Networked Society. Springer, Heidelberg (1999)
2. Robert, W.F., Ulrich, D.: BioID: A Multimodal Biometric Identification System. IEEE Computer 33(2), 64–68 (2000)
3. Choudhury, T., Clarkson, B., Jebara, T., Pentland, A.: Multimodal person recognition using unconstrained audio and video. In: Proc. 2nd Int. Conf. Audio-Video Based Person Authentication, pp. 176–181 (1999)
4. Li, J.W., Wang, Y.H., Tan, T.N., Jain, A.K.: Live Face Detection Based on the Analysis of Fourier Spectra. In: Proc. SPIE. Biometric Technology for Human Identification, vol. 5404, pp. 296–303 (2004)
5. Kollreider, K., Fronthaller, H., Bigun, J.: Evaluating liveness by face images and the structure tensor. AutoID (2005)
6. Moriyama, T., Kanade, T., Cohn, J.F., Xiao, J., Ambadar, Z., Gao, J., Imamura, H.: Automatic Recognition of Eye Blinking in Spontaneously Occurring Behavior. In: Proc. Int. Conf. on Pattern Recognition, vol. 4, pp. 78–81 (2002)
7. Lafferty, J., McCallum, A., Pereira, F.: Conditional Random Fields: Probabilistic Models for Segmenting and Labeling Sequence Data. In: Proc. 18th Int. Conf. Machine Learning, pp. 282–289 (2001)
8. Sha, F., Pereira, F.: Shallow Parsing with Conditional Random Fields. Proc. Human Language Technology, NAACL, 213–220 (2003)
9. McCallum, A.: Efficiently Inducing Features of Conditional Random Fields. Proc. 19th Uncertainty in Artificial Intelligence, 403–410 (2003)
10. Hammersley, J., Clifford, P.: Markov fields on finite graphs and lattices (Unpublished manuscript 1971)
11. Lienhart, R., Kuranov, A., Pisarevsky, V.: Empirical Analysis of Detection Cascades of Boosted Classifiers for Rapid Object Detection. In: Proc. 25th German Pattern Recognition Symposium, pp. 297–304 (2003)
12. Freund, Y., Schapire, R.E.: A decision-theoretic generalization of on-line learning and an application to boosting. Journal of Computer and System Sciences 55(1), 119–139 (1997)
13. Rabiner, L.: A tutorial on hidden markov models and selected applications in speech recognition. In: Proc. IEEE (1989)
14. Cristian, S., Kanaujia, A., Li, Z.G., Metaxas, D.: Conditional Models for Contextual Human Motion Recognition. In: Proc. Int. Conf. Computer Vision, pp. 1808–1815 (2005)
15. Bobick, A., Davis, J.: The recognition of human movement using temporal templates. In: Proc. IEEE Conf. Computer Vision and Pattern Recognition, pp. 928–934 (2001)

16. Gavrila, D.: The Visual Analysis of Human Movement: A Survey. Computer Vision and Image Understanding 73(1), 82–98 (1999)
17. Viola, P., Jones, M.J.: Rapid Object Detection using a Boosted Cascade of Simple Features. In: Proc. IEEE Conf. Computer Vision and Pattern Recognition, pp. 511–518 (2001)
18. Phillips, P.J., Moon, H., Rauss, P.J., Rizvi, S.: The FERET Evaluation Methodology for Face-Recognition Algorithms. IEEE Trans. Pattern Analysis and Machine Intelligence 22(10), 1090–1104 (2000)
19. Hyoja-Dong, Nam-Gu: Asian Face Image Database PF01. Technical Report, Pohang University of Science and Technology `http://nova.postech.ac.kr`
20. Zhang, X.H., Shan, S.G., Cao, B., Gao, W., Zhou, D.L., Zhao, D.B.: CAS-PEAL: A Large-Scale Chinese Face Database and Some Primary Evaluations. Journal of Computer-Aided Design and Computer Graphics 17(1), 9–17 (2005) (in Chinese)
21. Karson, C.N.: Spontaneous eye-blink rates and dopaminergic systems. Brain 106, 643–653 (1983)

Singular Points Analysis in Fingerprints Based on Topological Structure and Orientation Field

Jie Zhou[1], Jinwei Gu[1], and David Zhang[2]

[1] Department of Automation, Tsinghua University, Beijing 100084, China
jzhou@tsinghua.edu.cn
[2] Department of Computing, the Hong Kong Polytechnic University, Kowloon, Hong Kong

Abstract. As an important feature of fingerprints, singular points (including cores and deltas) not only represent the local ridge pattern characteristics, but also determine the topological structure (i.e. fingerprint type). In this paper, we have performed analysis for singular points in two aspects. (1) Based on the topology theory in 2D manifold, we deduced the relationship between cores and deltas in fingerprints. Specifically we proved that every completely captured fingerprint should have the same number of cores and deltas. We also proposed a flexible method to compute the Poincare Index for singular points. (2) We proposed a novel algorithm for singular point detection using global orientation field. After the initial detection with the widely-used Poincare Index method, the optimal singular points are selected to minimize the difference between the original orientation field and the model-based orientation field reconstructed from the singular points. The core-delta relation is used as a global constraint for final decision. Experimental results showed that our algorithm is rather accurate and robust.

1 Introduction

As a popular biometric feature, fingerprint is 2-dimensional oriented ridge-valley pattern captured from a finger by inked press, capacitive sensor, optical sensor, etc. Within each fingerprint, there are usually two kinds of singular points defined, i.e., *cores* and *deltas*, where the ridge orientation vanished or discontinued [1]. As an important topological feature for fingerprints, singular points can be used for fingerprint indexing [2], fingerprint alignment, orientation field modeling [3, 4], etc. In Fig. 1, singular points in different fingerprint types are provided.

Many previous works were proposed for singular point detection and analysis. Shu and Jain [5] used Partial Differential Equation modeling the local patterns for various kinds of singular points in general oriented texture images. For fingerprints, the Poincare Index is widely-used for singular points detection [2, 6, 7]. It is defined as the sum of the orientation change along a close circle around the points. Due to the noises in the real images, this local feature is not robust enough for detection. Tico et.al. [8] and Nilsson et.al.[9] used a multi-resolution approach to remove the spurious detections. Besides the above algorithms, there are also other approaches based on partitioning methods and heuristical rules for detection [10, 11].

S.-W. Lee and S.Z. Li (Eds.): ICB 2007, LNCS 4642, pp. 261–270, 2007.

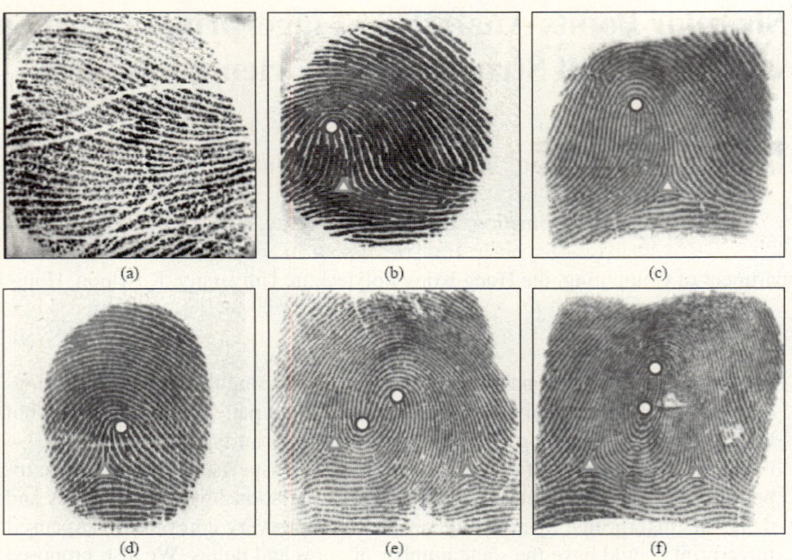

Fig. 1. Various types of fingerprints with the cores (circle) and the deltas (triangle) marked: (a) Plain Arch, (b) Tented Arch, (c) Left Loop, (d) Right Loop, (e) Twin Loop, and (f) Whorl

Basically all these works only utilized the local characteristics of singular points. However, only local information is not enough to discriminate the true singular points from spurious detections caused by creases, scars, smudges, damped prints, etc. In the orientation field, these spurious detections actually have nearly the same local patterns as the true ones. More global discriminative information should be incorporated for detection. One interesting work proposed by Perona [12] is orientation diffusion, which implicitly use the global constraint of the oriented texture during the dynamic diffusion process.

In this paper, we performed analysis of singular points based on topological structures and orientation field. It can be mainly summarized as the following two folds. (1) Based on the topology theory in 2D manifold, we deduced the relation between cores and deltas in fingerprints. Specifically we proved that every completely captured fingerprint should have the same number of cores and deltas. We also proposed a flexible method to compute the Poincare Index for singular points. Since the Poincare Index is independent with the integral paths if they are homotopic, we can adaptively select the path according to the confidence of the orientation values. (2) We proposed a novel algorithm for singular points detection using the orientation field. After the initial detection with the widely-used Poincare Index method, the optimal singular points are selected to minimize the difference between the original orientation field and the model-based orientation field reconstructed from the singular points. The core-delta relation is used as a global constraint for final decision. Experimental results showed that using both local feature and global information, our algorithm is rather accurate and robust for fingerprints with various qualities and types.

2 Topological Analysis for Fingerprint Structures

Given a continuous 2D vector field, $V(x, y)$, the Poincare Index for a path γ is defined as follows:

$$I(\gamma) = \frac{1}{2\pi} \int_{(x,y)\in\gamma} d\phi(x, y), \quad (1)$$

where $\phi(x, y) = \arg\{V(x, y)\} \in [0, 2\pi)$, being the angle of point $(x; y)$ on γ. The integral is performed counterclockwise. The Poincare Index is an integer if the path γ is closed. By computing I along a closed circle around a point P, we can define whether P is a singular point ($I \neq 0$) or not (I = 0). Refer [13, 14, 15] for more details.

Suppose V is defined in a region, Ω, with its exterior boundary, Γ_E, ψ and its interior boundary, Γ_I ψ, we denotes $\{\gamma_k\}$ as the singular points of V inside Ω by the circles around them. C is an arbitrary closed path inside Ω. There are two important properties about the Poincare Index formulated as follows:

Property 1. The Poincare Index of the boundary of a given region equals to the sum of the Poincare Indexes of the singular points inside this region, i.e.,

$$\sum I(\gamma_k) = I(\Gamma_E) - I(\Gamma_I) \quad (2)$$

Property 2. If two closed paths γ and δ are homotopic, then

$$I(\gamma) = I(\delta). \quad (3)$$

That is to say, if there is no other singular points between γ and δ, their Poincare Indexes are the same. In Fig. 2, we can easily see that $I(C) = I(\Gamma_E)$.

For oriented texture images, such as fingerprints and fluid flow, it is natural to establish the connection with 2D topology theory. By computing the orientation field, O, we can build a vector field $V = \cos 2O + i \sin 2O$ [4, 6], and apply the above definitions and properties on these images. The singular points in fingerprints are found to be consistent with the singular points defined in topology.

An interesting conclusion for fingerprints can be deduced based on Property 1. Since fingerprints do not have interior boundary Γ_I, and only have isolated singular points (cores and deltas) with known Poincare index (+1 for core and -1 for delta), Eqn(2) is written as

$$N_c - N_d = I(\Gamma_E), \quad (4)$$

where N_c is the number of the cores, N_d is the number of the deltas.

If a fingerprint is captured completely, it can be assumed that the left, right, bottom, and top boundaries are nearly horizontal (see Fig. 1). Although different type fingerprints can vary inside, this assumption still holds for their boundaries. For the path Γ_E consisting of this kind of boundaries, $I(\Gamma_E) = 0$, and then $N_c = N_d$. Therefore, we concluded that, *for each completely captured fingerprint, there are the same numbers of cores and deltas.*

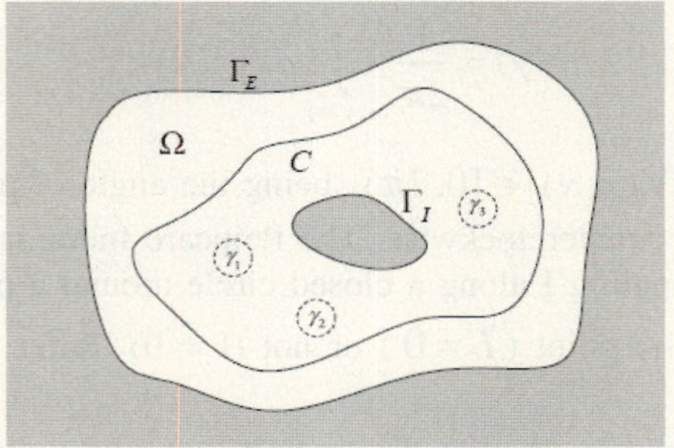

Fig. 2. Illustration of Poincare index

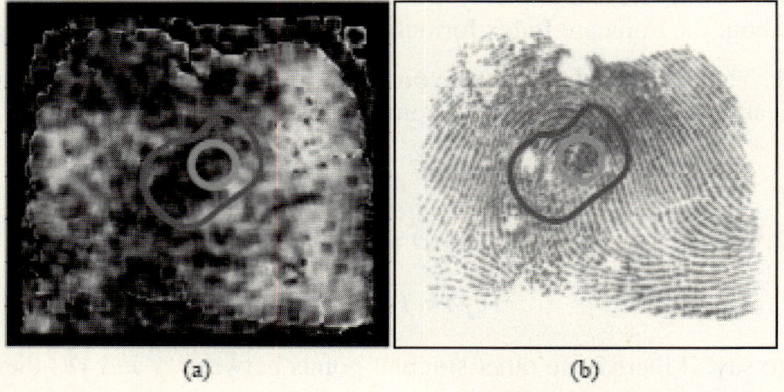

Fig. 3. Adaptively choose the integral path for the Poincare Index Computation based on the homotopic property. (a) The con_dence of the orientation field [16]. (b) The selected optimal path (red) where the confidence is high and the conventional circle (green). The selected path can give the correct Poincare Index (I = 1) while the circle cannot (I = 0).

As for **Property 2**, we know that the Poincare Index can be computed along any closed path as long as it is homotopic with the closed circle around the point (i.e., not including any new singular point). This allows us to adaptively choose the integral path, for example, the path where the orientation confidence is high. An example is shown in Fig. 3.

In real applications, many fingerprint images are not complete. In this case, the number of cores is not necessarily equal to the number of deltas. Nevertheless, Eqn(4) still presents us a global topological constraint for singular points. Suppose the effective region of the fingerprints is Ω, by computing $I(\partial\Omega)$, we can know that only finite combinations of the singular points are valid. In Table 1, we listed most of the possible combinations of singular points for fingerprints with the Poincare Index and the possible types (PA-plain arch, TA-tented arch, LL-left loop, RL-right loop, TL-twin loop).

Table 1. Combinations of singular points with the Poincare Index and possible types

$I(\partial\Omega)$	Core	Delta	Possible Types
0	0	0	PA
	1	1	LL, RL, TA
	2	2	TL, Whorl
1	1	0	LL, RL, TA
	2	1	TL, Whorl
2	2	0	TL, Whorl

In Fig. 4, we listed two fingerprints along with the corresponding $I(\partial\Omega)$ and the singular points. The results verified our conclusion about the topological constraint about the singular points.

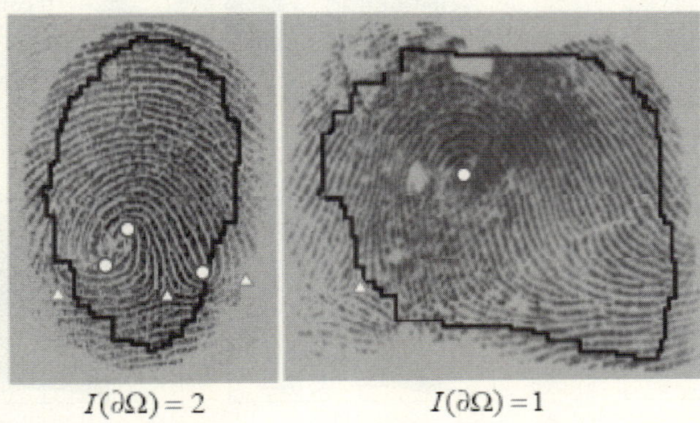

$I(\partial\Omega) = 2$ $I(\partial\Omega) = 1$

Fig. 4. Two examples for topological analysis of fingerprints. The blue curves are the boundary of the effective region. Circles are cores and triangles are deltas. The detected singular points are marked as red, while the singular points outside the boundary are marked with green.

3 Singular Points Detection Using Global Information

In this section, we proposed a novel algorithm for singular point detection using the global orientation field.

As known, singular points almost determine the global orientation field of fingerprints. In fact, there are several orientation field models related to singular points [3, 4, 19]. Our basic idea is to select the final optimal singular points by minimizing the difference between the original orientation field and the model-based orientation field reconstructed from the singular points. Specifically, each singular point detection is denoted by a triple, (x, y, t), with its positions and type (core/delta). All singular point candidates are in the set, $S = \{(x_i, y_i, t_i)\}_{i=1}^{M}$. The true singular points, s, is a subset of S. Denote the original orientation field with O_0, the reconstructed orientation field with $O(\Theta, s)$, where Θ is the model's parameter. The optimal singular points can be selected as:

$$s^* = \arg\min_{s \subseteq S} \left\| O_0 - O(\Theta, s) \right\|$$

where the difference function, $\|\cdot\|$, is defined as a averaged value of the absolute angular difference on all points of the fingerprint image.

Besides, the core-delta relation deduced in the above section can be used as a global constrain for the optimal singular points selection. By computing the global Poincare Index, we can remove some invalid combinations of singular points based on Table 1 and speed up the algorithm.

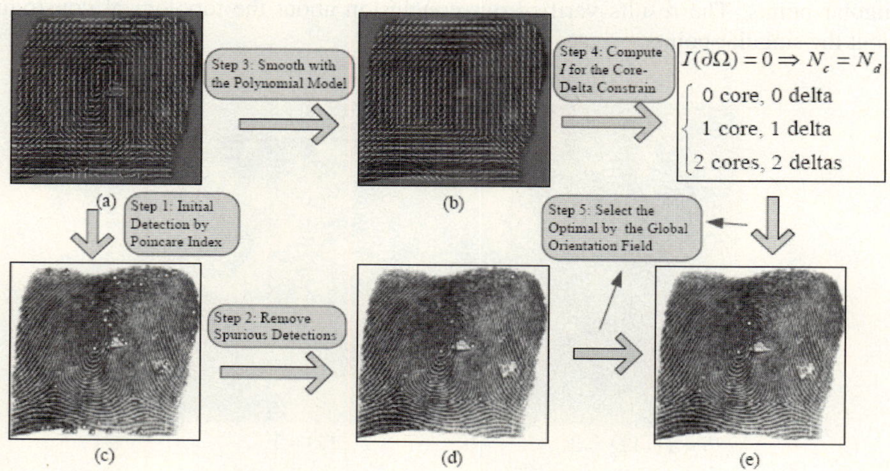

Fig. 5. Flowchart of our proposed detection method

Finally, we would like to emphasize that the widely-used Poincare Index method will not miss the true singular points as long as the process scale is low enough (i.e. small circle for computing), although it has lots of spurious detections. Actually this local method can detect the precise positions of the true singular points. This property guarantees our proposed method's robust and accurate performance after removing spurious detections. The flowchart of the proposed algorithm is shown in Fig. 5.

The original orientation field is computed by the hierarchical gradient-based method [17]. As for the model-based reconstructed orientation field, we choose the Zero-Pole model proposed by Sherlock and Monro in [3], considering both the model accuracy and the computational efficiency.

In this part, we propose to remove spurious points with a novel feature, *D*, which is a vector consisting the Differences of the ORIentation values along a Circle (DORIC) around the point. For a given point *P*, we uniformly sampled a set of points, $T_1, T_2, \cdots, T_L$, along a circle around it in anticlockwise direction. The feature can be formulated as:

$$D(P) = [\partial O_1, \partial O_2, \cdots, \partial O_L]^T$$

where O_i is the value of the orientation field, O at the point T_i, $\partial O_i = O_{i+1} - O_i$. Fig. 6 showed three typical texture patterns and their DORIC feature plotted as curves. Since the orientation field O is defined in $[0, \pi)$ instead of $[0, 2\pi)$, there will be a pulse for singular points (positive pulse for core, negative pulse for delta).

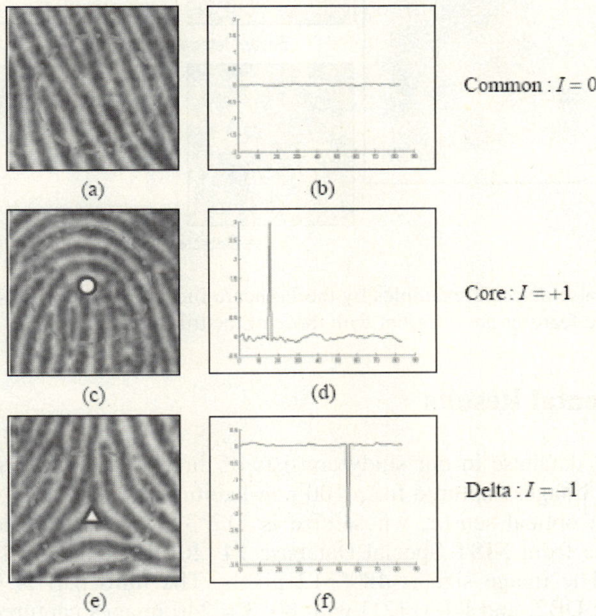

Fig. 6. Typical texture patterns and their DORIC features plotted as curves. There is a positive pulse for the core and a negative pulse for the delta.

This feature has strong relations with the Poincare Index defined in Eqn(1). Given a function $f(x)$ which equals to x when $|x| < \pi/2$, $\pi - x$ when $x > \pi/2$, and $\pi + x$ when $x < -\pi/2$, it can be proved that $I = \frac{1}{\pi}\sum_{i=1}^{L} f(\partial O_i)$. DORIC contains more discriminative information than the Poincare Index. Fig. 7 showed two examples from a poor-quality fingerprint, which are falsely detected as core and delta by the Poincare Index but have very different DORIC features compared with true ones in Fig. 6.

For each point with non-zero Poincare Index, we compute its DORIC feature. If there is exactly one pulse with the height nearly up to π, it is a valid candidate singular point; otherwise it will be removed from the candidate set S. In practice, multiple DORIC features are computed along a set of circles at different scales around the point P. Based on the votes from these multiple-scale DORIC features, we made the decision whether it should be removed from the candidate set S. The following experimental results proved that this feature can effectively remove spurious detections and can be computed very fast.

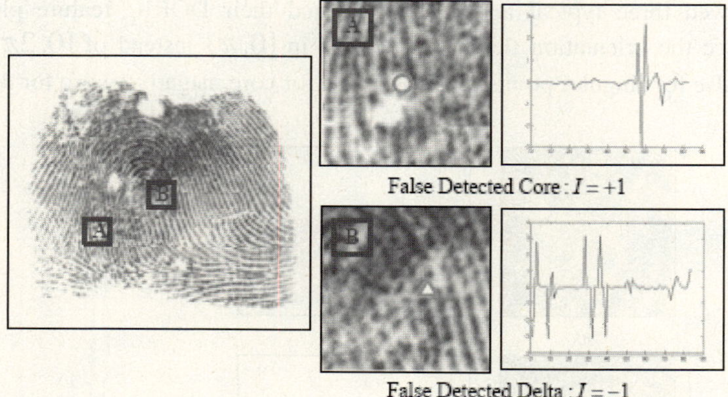

Fig. 7. Typical false detected examples by the Poincare Index, and their DORIC features plotted as curves. The features are different with those of the true singular points.

4 Experimental Results

The fingerprint database in our study consists of three parts. The first part contains 800 fingerprint images captured from 100 non-habituated cooperative subjects with a Digital Persona optical sensor, whose size is 512*320 pixels. The second part is a sample database from NIST Special Database 14 [20] that contains 40 inked fingerprint images. The image size is 480*512 pixels. The third part is from FVC2000 database (DB1, DB2, and DB3) [21] with 80*3 = 240 images captured by capacitive sensor and optical sensor. Thus there are total 1080 fingerprints in our database including various qualities and types.

In Fig. 8, we presented the detection results on some typical fingerprints which cover almost all the difficulties for singular point detection such as creases, scars, smudges, dryness, damped or blurred prints, etc. The first row showed the detected results with the widely-used Poincare Index method. The second row showed the results of our proposed method. Although we did not implement all of the previous methods using various heuristic rules or multiple resolutions, we would like to emphasize that, it is very hard to remove the spurious detections on these fingerprints without global constraints. With our method, the singular points are robustly detected and the positions are rather accurate.

To get the statistical performance of this algorithm, the singular points of these fingerprints are manually labeled by experts as the ground truth beforehand. The percentages for correct, missing, and false detection are provided in Table 2 (the position distance threshold is defined as 5 pixels). We found that for most of the missing cases, it is usually that one or two deltas are not detected. Since the cores (if available) can be correctly detected, the detection results are still good for applications.

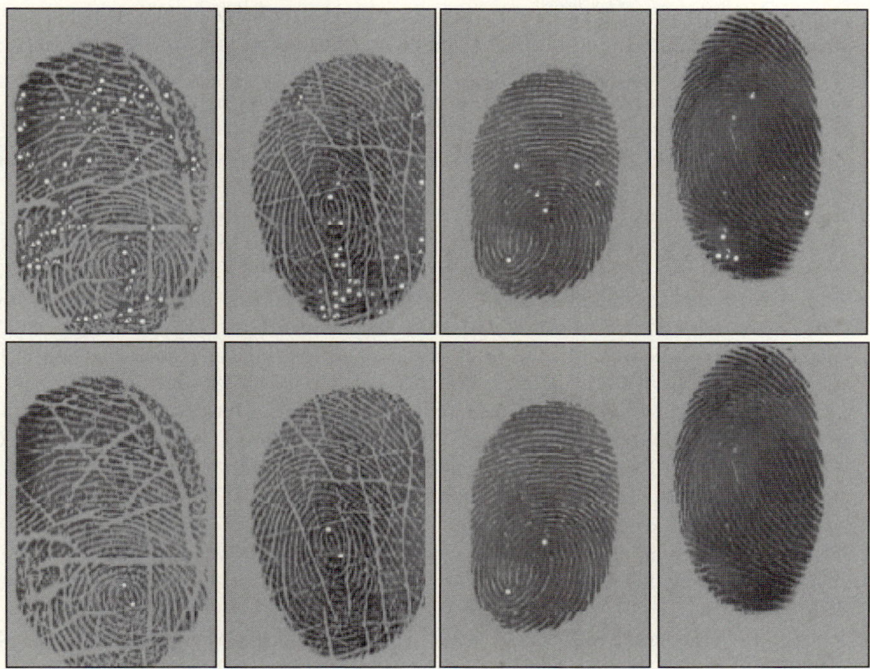

Fig. 8. Singular points detection results on various types of fingerprints. First row: results using widely-used Poincare Index method; second row: are based on our proposed method. These fingerprints cover most of the difficult situations for singular point detection: dryness, damped or blurred prints, and serious creases or scars.

Another advantage of our method is its real-time processing speed. It is currently implemented with Matlab and C on an AMD 2200Hz 512M PC computer without optimization. The average processing time for each fingerprint is around 0.10 sec.

Table 2. The performance of the proposed algorithm

	Correct	Missing	False Detection
Percentage	80.6%	14.6%	4.8%

Acknowledgement

The authors wish to acknowledge supports from Natural Science Foundation of China under grant 60205002 and 60332010. This research is also supported by National 863 Hi-Tech Development Program of China.

References

1. Maltoni, D., Maio, D., Jain, A.K., Probhaker, S.: Handbook of Fingerprint Recognition. Springer, New York (2003)
2. Karu, K., Jain, A.K.: Fingerprint classification. Pattern Recognition 17(3), 389–404 (1996)
3. Sherlock, B., Monro, D.: A model for interpreting fingerprint topology. Pattern Recognition 26(7), 1047–1055 (1993)
4. Gu, J., Zhou, J.: A novel model for orientation field of fingerprints. In: IEEE Int. Conf. on Computer Vision and Pattern Recognition, vol. 2, pp. 493–498 (June 2003)
5. Shu, C.F., Jain, R.C.: Vector field analysis for oriented patterns. IEEE Trans. on Pattern Analysis and Machine Intelligence 16(9), 946–950 (1994)
6. Bazen, A.M.: Systematic methods for the computation of the directional fields and singular points of fingerprints. IEEE Trans. on Pattern Analysis and Machine Intelligence 24(7), 905–919 (2002)
7. Jain, A.K., Prabhakar, S., Hong, L.: A multichannel approach to fingerprint classification. IEEE Trans. On Pattern Analysis and Machine Intelligence 21(4), 348–359 (1999)
8. Tico, M., Kuosmanen, P.: A multiresolution method for singular points detection in fingerprint images. In: IEEE Int. Conf. on ISCAS, vol. 4, pp. 183–186 (July 1999)
9. Nilsson, K., Bigun, J.: Complex filters applied to fingerprint images detecting prominent symmetry points used for alignment. In: Tistarelli, M., Bigun, J., Jain, A.K. (eds.) ECCV 2002. LNCS, vol. 2359, pp. 39–47. Springer, Heidelberg (2002)
10. Ramo, P., Tico, M., Onnia, V., Saarinen, J.: Optimized singular point detection algorithm for fingerprint images. In: IEEE Int. Conf. on ICIP, vol. 3(3), pp. 242–245 (October 2001)
11. Cappelli, R., Lumini, A., Maio, D., Maltoni, D.: Fingerprint classification by directional image partitioning. IEEE Trans. on Pattern Analysis and Machine Intelligence 21(5), 402–421 (1999)
12. Perona, P.: Orientation diffusions. IEEE Trans. On Image Processing 7(3), 457–467 (1998)
13. Fulton, W.: Algebraic Topology: A First Course. Springer, New York (1995)
14. Scheuermann, G.: Topological Vector Field Visualization with Clifford Algebra. PhD thesis (January 1999)
15. Scheuermann, G., Kruger, H., Menzel, M., Rockwood, A.P.: Visualizing nonlinear vector field topology. IEEE Trans. on Visualization and Computer Graphics 4(2), 109–116 (1998)
16. Kass, M., Witkin, A.: Analyzing oriented pattern. Computer Vision, Graphics and Image Processing 37, 362–397 (1987)
17. Jain, A.K., Hong, L.: On-line fingerprint verification. IEEE Trans. on Pattern Analysis and Machine Intelligence 19(4), 302–314 (1997)
18. Zhou, J., Gu, J.: A model-based method for the computation of fingerprints' orientation field. IEEE Trans. on Image Processing 13(6), 821–835 (2004)
19. Zhou, J., Gu, J.: Modeling orientation fields of fingerprints with rational complex functions. Pattern Recognition 37(2), 389–391 (2004)
20. Sample of nist special database 14: Nist mated fingerprint card pairs (mfcp2). Available at http://www.nist.gov/srd/nistsd14.htm
21. Maio, D., Maltoni, D., Cappelli, R., Wayman, J.L., Jain, A.K.: Fvc2000: Fingerprint verification competition. IEEE Trans. on Pattern Analysis and Machine Intelligence 24(3), 402–412 (2002)

Robust 3D Face Recognition from Expression Categorisation

Jamie Cook, Mark Cox, Vinod Chandran, and Sridha Sridharan

Speech, Audio, Image and Video Technology (SAIVT) Laboratory,
Queensland University of Technology, Brisbane, Queensland, 4000, Australia
jamie@ieee.org, {md.cox,v.chandran,s.sridharan}@qut.edu.au

Abstract. The task of Face Recognition is often cited as being complicated by the presence of lighting and expression variation. In this article a novel combination of facial expression categorisation and 3D Face Recognition is used to provide enhanced recognition performance. The use of 3D face data alleviates performance issues related to pose and illumination. Part-face decomposition is combined with a novel adaptive weighting scheme to increase robustness to expression variation. By using local features instead of a monolithic approach, this system configuration allows for expression variability to be modelled and aid in the fusion process. The system is tested on the Face Recognition Grand Challenge (FRGC) database, currently the largest available dataset of 3D faces. The sensitivity of the proposed approach is also evaluated in the presence of systematic error in the expression classification stage.

1 Introduction

Biometrics research has enjoyed a recent wave of increased interest fueled by a political climate demanding increased security. Face Recognition has the distinct advantage over other biometric modalities such as fingerprint, DNA and iris recognition, in that the acquisition stage is non-intrusive and can be achieved with readily available equipment. However widespread adoption of Face Recognition Technology (FRT) has been hindered by excessive sensitivity to 3 factors: pose, illumination and expression [1]. The use of 3D data has the potential to overcome issues relating to the first two factors and in this paper a novel system is demonstrated to alleviate performance degradation caused by the third.

Early work in 3D facial recognition emerged in the late 1980's but it wasn't until recently that substantial research databases have become available. The Face Recognition Grand Challenge (FRGC) [2] was created to address this issue and provides both a common dataset and experimental methodologies to enable accurate comparisons of different algorithms. A good summary of the current research in 3D and composite 2D-3D recognition is given in [3].

The task of expression classification is an interesting problem with the potential to further our understanding of inter-personal interaction and to enable sophisticated Human Machine Interfaces (HMI) [4]. There is considerable literature in the psychology community to suggest that in humans, recognition of

S.-W. Lee and S.Z. Li (Eds.): ICB 2007, LNCS 4642, pp. 271–280, 2007.

faces and expression comprehension occur in parallel with information fusion occuring subsequently.

Currently most automated face recognition systems provide robustness to expression variation by either a non-linear normalisation to remove expression [5] or by selecting features which are invariant to changes in expression. In [6], a 3D matching of faces is performed by defining three Regions Of Interest (ROI) around the nose which are deemed to be most stable in the presence of expression. These regions are matched between scans by means of the Iterative Closest Point (ICP) algorithm. Such an approach, however, doesn't make full use of the discriminable information that exists in the entire face. The explicit use of expression classification and categorisation to direct the operation of automated face recognition is a research area yet to be fully explored.

In 2002, Martinez [7] created 6 region and identity specific subspaces from face images in the AR database with the aim of alleviating the problems of occlusion and expression variation. The author posits that expressions do not manifest symmetrically on the human face and demonstrates that happy faces are better recognized by the left side while angry faces have better recognition from the right side. The author then uses a train set to define weights for each of three distinct expressions, which are used to modify the contribution from each of the 6 regions. Further testing on a test set with known expression showed improvements over an unweighted baseline when using weights appropriate to the currently displayed emotion.

In [8] an automated variant of this approach is detailed. A front end expression classification system is used to select from multiple classification systems. The authors posit the use of six expression categories, namely happiness, sadness, anger, fear, surprise and disgust. The core concept is demonstrated using a small database of 30 subjects and a "happy face" recognition system.

An important aspect which is not covered in either of the previous approaches is the so called "front end effect" [9]. This refers to the cascading effect of errors in the expression classification module (front end) to subsequent stages of the system. In the proposed approach, expression strength categorisation is combined with a part-face recognition system using an adaptive weighting scheme which is tolerant to expression misclassification. A discussion on automatic expression classification is given in Section 2 and details of the proposed system are presented in Section 3. Experimentation on the FRGC database and error analysis can be found in Section 4.

2 Expression Classification

Researchers in the field of facial expression and emotion analysis use the Facial Action Coding Scheme (FACS) as a method to encode the current state of the face as a combination of atomic facial actions. Subtlety of expression in the face is captured using an additional intensity parameter. After a face has been parameterised in this fashion, it can then be used to infer the underlying emotion or detect a particular facial expression [10].

For face recognition, comprehension of facial expression is of less use than a mapping of facial deformation. Such a mapping could allow the recognition algorithm to compensate for expression variation during the recognition process. The contribution of spatial regions exhibiting significant deformation can be adaptively de-emphasised while the contribution from portions of the face unaffected can be increased. Currently there exists no ground truth data for 3D face databases which provides a detailed annotation (FACS or other) of expression, and constructing such annotations is time consuming and expensive.

Instead, the manual annotations of the FRGC 3D data set by researchers at Geometrix [11] shall instead be used to demonstrate the proposed system. Each of the acquired images is allocated, based on the displayed expression, to one of the three classes: Neutral, Small (slight expression) and Large (highly expressive). A sample from each of the classes can be seen in Figure 1.

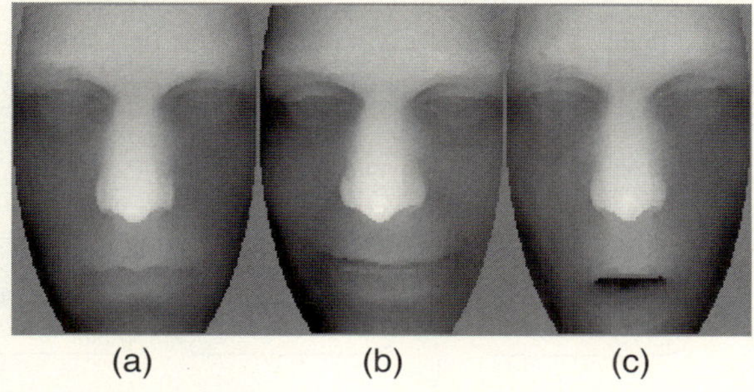

Fig. 1. Examples of FRGC 3D data for three classes of expression strength (a) Neutral (b) Small Expression and (c) Large Expression

The Geometrix annotations contain global rather than local deformation information, as such they can not be used to construct detailed mappings of which spatial regions to use in the recognition process. Instead, three generic weighting schemes shall be defined, correposponding to three classes of expression, details of this are given in Section 3.2. Given that knowledge of the expression displayed in the 3D scans being compared can be acquired, an appropriate weighting scheme can then be selected which emphasises regions that are more resilient to expression changes. It is expected that the extraction of FACS parameters would allow more detailed deformation maps to be constructed and hence allow more flexibilitiy in constructing weight vectors. Future work should utilise automated FACS annotations systems such as that detailed in [12].

3 Face Recognition

3.1 Part-Face Methodology

Face Verification techniques typically employ a monolithic representation of the face during recognition, however, approaches which decompose the face into sub-regions have shown considerable promise. Many authors [13,14] have shown superior performance by adopting a modular representation of the face provided that face localisation is performed accurately [14].

The recognition system used in the following experiments is an extension of previous work in component face recognition [15], a block diagram of the matching process is shown in Figure 2. In this approach face images are decomposed into multiple regions which are classified independently using subspace projection. PCA with a Mahalanobis Cosine distance metric was chosen due to the [-1,1] bounded nature of the output. Alternate subspaces projection methods such as Linear Discriminant Analysis (LDA) and Independent Component Analysis (ICA) are also equally applicable. Late fusion is then used to recombine the classifier scores into a single classification decision.

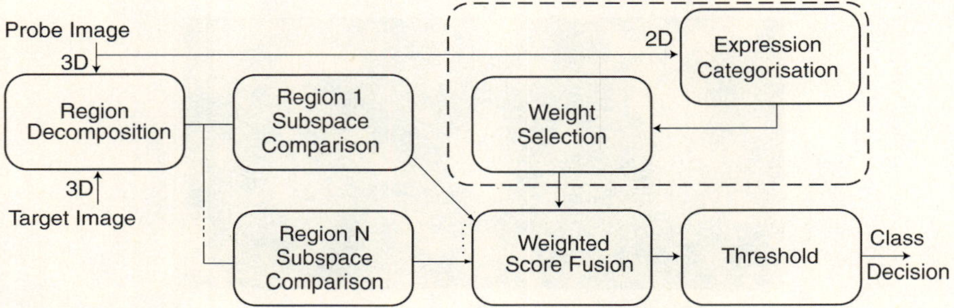

Fig. 2. Block Diagram of the proposed system (extension to previous work enclosed in dashed rectangle)

Regions decomposition is achieved by using a 32x32 pixel sliding window to extract a 13×13 grid of regions [demonstrated in Figure 3(a)]. The choice of window size is an important consideration for optimal performance and there is no single choice which will perform *best*. The selected window and step sizes were chosen so as to balance the conflicting needs to both accurately localise features and to encapsulate sufficient local information to enable discrimination.

3.2 Adaptive Weighting

Most existing recognition algorithms have satisfactory performance when the facial expression of gallery and probe images is similar. The goal then of expression classification in a Face Recognition context, should be to identify expression mismatch between the target and probe images and allow for graceful handling of such situations. *The novel contribution of this paper comes from the inclusion of the adaptive weighting scheme which modifies the behaviour of the fusion stage based on the detection of expression mismatch.*

Facial expression is a non-rigid distortion and as such can not be compensated for using standard global face normalisation techniques. When either the gallery

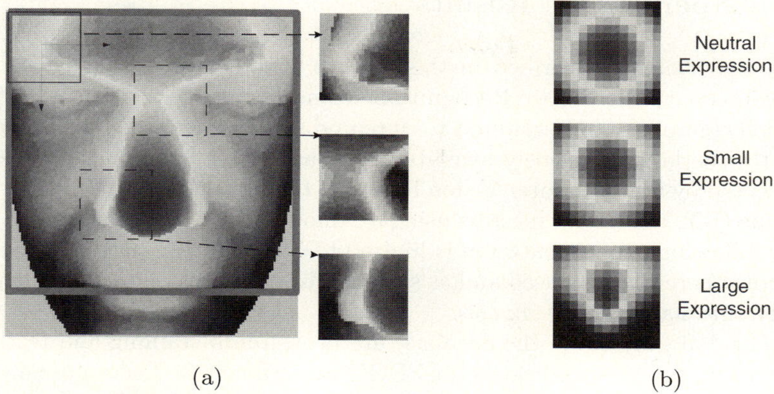

Fig. 3. (a) Example 3D face with 32x32 pixel sliding window with 8 pixel shift. (b) Three expression specific weighting functions which are selected based on the currently displayed expression for use in the weighted score fusion process.

or probe image contains significant expression the assumption of correspondence between the two images breaks down. However due to the physical characteristics of the human face, this break down is not uniform; for example the nose and cheek bone areas are less prone to expression distortion than the mouth region [6].

By identifying images in which expression mismatch is present, the decision process can place more emphasis on those regions which are least affected. By looking at the distortions on a region by region basis, this system configuration can scale to any number of facial expressions without requiring the use of expression specific recognition systems as in [8]. This also has the benefit over systems such as in [6], that when expression mismatch does not occur information from the entire face can be utilised.

Previous work has demonstrated that discriminative information in 3D faces is distributed towards the center of the face [15]. This corroborates the generally held belief of many researchers that the nose region is most invariant to expression variations [6,3]. The weighting models chosen for experimentation are therefore modeled using Gaussian Mixture Models which naturally emphasise the central regions. The three weighting schemes corresponding to expression categories are illustrated in Figure 3(b).

In the Neutral case, the model has a single mixture which encompases a significant portion of the face. In the case of mild expression, the model is shifted higher towards the nasal bridge, reducing the contribution of the lips and cheeks which are posited to be more variable under expression variation. Finally, for large expressions, the dominant mixture is tightened to further exclude the cheeks and mouth and a second mixture is added to retain contributions from the eyes and brow area. These weight vectors, w, are all then normalised such that $\sum w_i = 1$.

4 Experimental Results

The experiments described in this section were conducted using 3D data provided as part of the Face Recognition Grand Challenge [2]. The FRGC dataset, which contains 4007 registered texture and shape images of 466 subjects, is currently the largest publicly available database of 3D face images. The data was collected by the Computer Vision Research Laboratory at the University of Notre Dame (UND) over 3 semesters using a Minolta Vivid 900 range finder. Although the following experimentation is limited to 3D faces, the proposed methodology is not inherently 3D based and as such can be easily transposed to the processing of traditional intensity images.

The 466 subjects in the database are broken into training and testing groups according to the specification of FRGC Experiment 3. There are 943 images in the training set, and of the 4007 images in the test set 59% are captured with a neutral expression while the remainder are evenly distributed between mild and severe distortions [11]. These annotations are used in place of an automated system to demonstrate the efficacy of the proposed adaptive weighting scheme.

4.1 Baseline Results

In order to demonstrate the advantage of the proposed system a baseline is required for comparison. In keeping with previously published results, the standard monolithic PCA algorithm is used to provide a benchmark against which other researchers can measure. In Figure 4 Detection Error Tradeoff (DET) curves are presented for the monolithic system and for the corresponding part face approach utilising unweighted summation. These results compare a gallery of neutral faces against progressively more expressive probe sets. As can easily be seen, the inclusion of highly expressive faces significantly degrades the performance of both the monolithic and part face methods. The effects of expression however, do not affect all regions evenly, and the parts face approach is ideally suited to provide a mapping of how expression mismatch manifests as performance degradation. To visualise this, the performance of each individual face region is calculated using neutral gallery and probe sets. The resulting EER is then compared against the EER obtained using the same region with a highly expressive probe set.

The performance differential can then be measured as change in EER and this is reformed in Figure 5 into a viewable image. This demonstrates the non-linear nature of degradation effects caused by expression variation. As was postulated earlier, regions in the cheeks and around the corners of the mouth are the most effected by expression variation. In these regions the EER drops an average of around 14% for expressive faces compared to neutral faces. The upper portion of the face appears to be much more stable, in particular regions which encompass any significant portion of the nose appear to have a significantly greater resilience to these effects.

These results validate the significant de-emphasis of the cheek regions in the chosen weight vectors. They also add credence to the position that the upper part of the face contains discriminable information both in human recognition

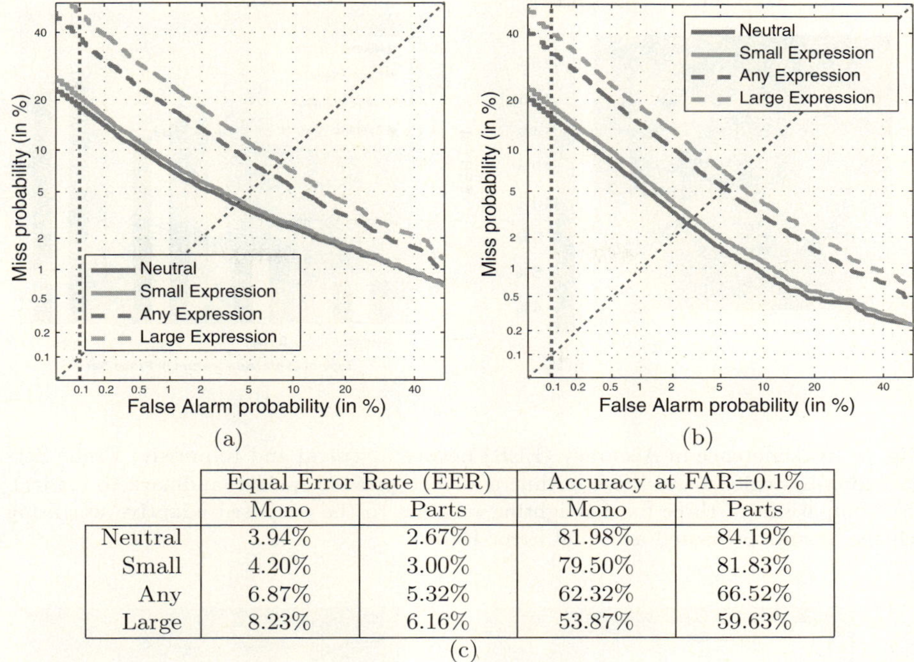

	Equal Error Rate (EER)		Accuracy at FAR=0.1%	
	Mono	Parts	Mono	Parts
Neutral	3.94%	2.67%	81.98%	84.19%
Small	4.20%	3.00%	79.50%	81.83%
Any	6.87%	5.32%	62.32%	66.52%
Large	8.23%	6.16%	53.87%	59.63%

Fig. 4. Baseline DET curves for (a) Monolithic PCA and (b) Part face PCA with unweighted summation. Four curves show performance for four levels of expression containined in the probe set. (c) Tabulated results from (a) and (b) are presented for the two indicated operating points (dashed red lines).

[16] and in automated systems [17]. In humans it is plausible that this extra weighting has been given to the upper portions of the face due to their stability in the presence of expression variation, given that such variations are encountered so often in everyday life.

4.2 Adaptive Weighting

Using the weight vectors defined in Section 3, the regions around the face are adaptively combined using the hand labeled expression data. These results, shown in Figure 5, show that the proposed method achieves the best performance across all expression categories. In the case of highly expressive faces the EER is only 5.37% compared against 6.16% for unweighted summation and 8.23% for the monolithic system. The use of hand labelled data makes this a best-case scenario, however it serves to demonstrate the performance that can be gained when using a reliable expression categorisation system.

In practice no system works at 100% accuracy and errors in the expression classification stage should not cause catastrophic failure of the system. In order to demonstrate the effects of misclassification, the two most serious types of error

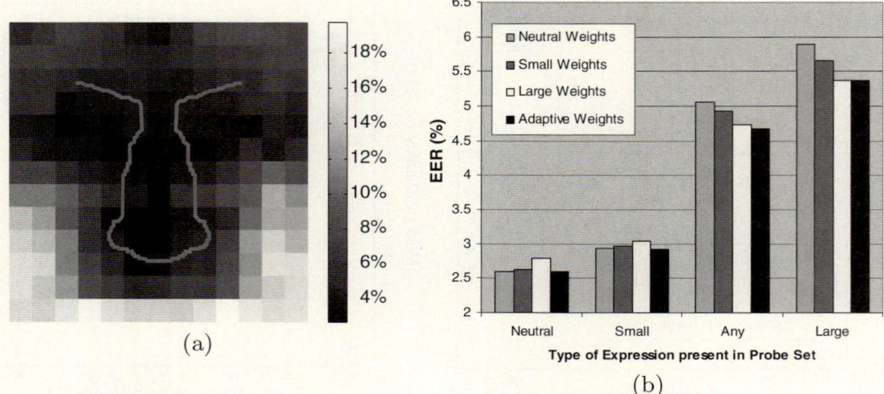

Fig. 5. (a) Difference in Accuracy (EER) between Neutral and Expressive Probe Sets on region-by-region basis (nose outline added to provide spatial landmark to reader). (b) Comparison of three fixed weighting schemes to the proposed adaptive weighting scheme, results presented as Equal Error Rates.

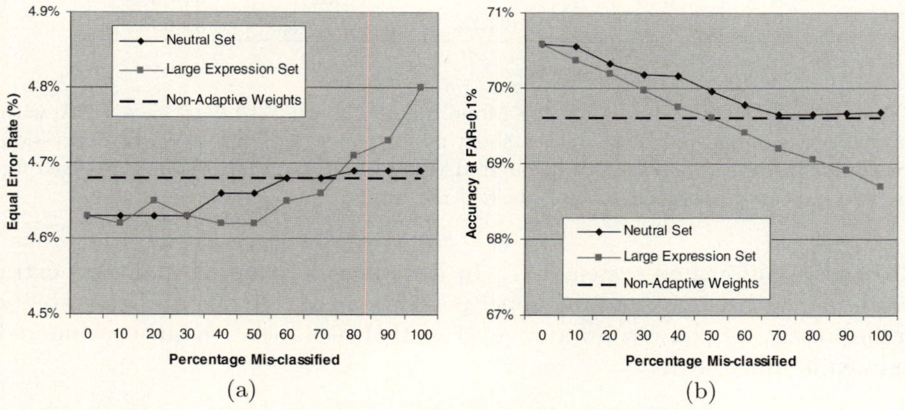

Fig. 6. Performance of adaptive weighting scheme as a function of introduced error in the indicated expression category. Results calculated using ROC III and expressed as (a) Equal Error Rate (b) Accuracy at a False Alarm Rate of 0.1%.

are considered: Neutral Expression misclassified as Large Expression and vice versa. Firstly system performance is evaluated while increasing the percentage of neutral images misclassified as expressive. The same process is then replicated to introduce errors to the set of images containing large expression. In this experiment performance is evaluated using the FRGC ROC III protocol, which incorporates time lapse of at least 1 semester between target and probe.

Results presented in Figure 6 show the EER and accuracy at a False Accept Rate (FAR) of 0.1% for both types of error. The non-adaptive weighting scheme, shown as a dashed black line in these plots, is the baseline achieved when using the 'Large' weight vector. This weight vector is chosen as the baseline because it is the most robust to expression variation and therefore the most logical choice when no knowledge of facial expression is assumed.

As can be expected, the mistaken use of a neutral weight vector when an expressive face is present gives the greatest degradation to recognition accuracy. The alternate type of error, i.e. using the "Large" weighting mask for neutral images, has a less significant impact upon performance. The robustness of the proposed system can be observed with performance improvements in the presence of up to 50% error of either variety.

5 Conclusion

In this paper a novel adaptive weighting scheme has been proposed which increases the robustness of parts based face recognition. The proposed system makes use of expression strength information to increase or decrease the contribution of regions susceptible to expression distortion. Testing is conducted using the 3D face component of the Face Recognition Grand Challenge dataset which is currently the largest publicly available. The resilience of the system to the "front end effect" is evaluated and shows robust performance in the presence of up to 50% error in the expression classification stage.

Acknowledgement

This research was supported by the Australian Research Council (ARC) through Discovery Grants Scheme, Grant DP0452676 and Linkage Grants Scheme, Grant LP0562101.

References

1. Zhao, W., Chellappa, R., Phillips, P., Rosenfeld, A.: Face recognition: A literature survey. ACM Computing Surveys (CSUR) 35(4), 399–458 (2003)
2. Phillips, P.J., Flynn, P.J., Scruggs, T., Bowyer, K.W., Chang, J., Hoffman, K., Marques, J., Min, J., Worek, W.: Overview of the Face Recognition Grand Challenge. In: CVPR '05: Proceedings of the 2005 IEEE Computer Society Conference on Computer Vision and Pattern Recognition (CVPR'05), Washington, DC, USA, vol. 1, pp. 947–954. IEEE Computer Society Press, Los Alamitos (2005)
3. Bowyer, K.W., Chang, K., Flynn, P.: A survey of approaches and challenges in 3D and multi-modal 3D + 2D face recognition. Computer Vision and Image Understanding 101(1), 1–15 (2006)
4. Pantic, M., Rothkrantz, L.: Toward an affect-sensitive multimodal human-computer interaction. Proceedings of the IEEE 91(9), 1370–1390 (2003)
5. Li, X., Mori, G., Zhang, H.: Expression-Invariant Face Recognition with Expression Classification. In: The 3rd Canadian Conference on Computer and Robot Vision (CRV'06), p. 77 (2006)

6. Chang, K.I., Bowyer, K., Flynn, P.: Adaptive rigid multi-region selection for handling expression variation in 3d face recognition. In: Computer Vision and Pattern Recognition, 2005 IEEE Computer Society Conference, vol. 3, p. 157. IEEE Computer Society Press, Los Alamitos (2005)
7. Martinez, A.: Recognizing imprecisely localized, partially occluded, andexpression variant faces from a single sample per class. Pattern Analysis and Machine Intelligence, IEEE Transactions 24(6), 748–763 (2002)
8. Li, C., Barreto, A.: An integrated 3D face-expression recognition approach. In: Acoustics, Speech and Signal Processing, 2006. ICASSP 2006 Proceedings. 2006 IEEE International Conference, vol. 3, pp. III-1132–III-1135. IEEE Computer Society Press, Los Alamitos (2006)
9. Lucey, S., Sridharan, S., Chandran, V.: Improved Facial-Feature Detection for AVSP via Unsupervised Clustering and Discriminant Analysis. EURASIP Journal on Applied Signal Processing 2003(3), 264–275 (2003)
10. Donato, G., Bartlett, M., Hager, J., Ekman, P., Sejnowski, T.: Classifying Facial Actions. Pattern Analysis and Machine Intelligence, IEEE Transactions 21(10), 974–989 (1999)
11. Maurer, T., Guigonis, D., Maslov, I., Pesenti, B., Tsaregorodtsev, A., West, D., Medioni, G.: Performance of Geometrix ActiveID^{TM}3D Face Recognition Engine on the FRGC Data. In: CVPR '05: Proceedings of the 2005 IEEE Computer Society Conference on Computer Vision and Pattern Recognition (CVPR'05), Washington, DC, USA, IEEE Computer Society Press, Los Alamitos (2005)
12. Bartlett, M., Littlewort, G., Frank, M., Lainscsek, C., Fasel, I., Movellan, J.: Recognizing facial expression: machine learning and application to spontaneous behavior. In: IEEE Computer Society Conference on Computer Vision and Pattern Recognition, 2005., vol. 2, pp. 568–573. IEEE Computer Society Press, Los Alamitos (2005)
13. Brunelli, R., Poggio, T.: Face Recognition: Features versus Templates. IEEE Trans. Pattern Anal. Mach. Intell. 15(10), 1042–1052 (1993)
14. Lucey, S., Chen, T.: Face recognition through mismatch driven representations of the face. In: Visual Surveillance and Performance Evaluation of Tracking and Surveillance, 2005. 2nd Joint IEEE International Workshop, pp. 193–199. IEEE Computer Society Press, Los Alamitos (2005)
15. Cook, J., Chandran, V., Fookes, C.: 3D Face Recognition using Log-Gabor Templates. British Machine Vision Conference (BMVC) (September 2006)
16. Shepherd, J., Davies, G., Ellis, H.: Studies of cue saliency. Perceiving and Remembering Faces, 105–131 (1981)
17. Gokberk, B., Akarun, L., Alpaydin, E.: Feature selection for pose invariant face recognition. In: Proceedings of the 16th International Conference on Pattern Recognition (2002)

Fingerprint Recognition Based on Combined Features

Yangyang Zhang, Xin Yang, Qi Su, and Jie Tian

Center for Biometrics and Security Research, Key Laboratory of Complex Systems and Intelligence Science, Institute of Automation, Chinese Academy of Sciences, Graduate School of the Chinese Academy of Sciences, P.O.Box 2728 Beijing 100080 China
tian@ieee.org, jie.tian@ia.ac.cn
http://www.fingerpass.net

Abstract. In this paper, we represent the fingerprint with a novel local feature descriptor, which is composed of minutia, the sample points on associated ridge and the adjacent orientation distribution. Then a novel fingerprint recognition method is proposed combining the orientation field and the local feature descriptor. We compare two descriptor lists from the input and template fingerprints to calculate a set of transformation vectors for fingerprint alignment. The similarity score is evaluated by fusing the orientation field and the local feature descriptor. The experiments have been conducted on three large-scale databases. The comparison results approve that our algorithm is more accurate and robust than previous methods based on the minutiae or ridge features, especially for those poor-quality and partial fingerprints.

Keywords: orientation field, local feature descriptor, fingerprint alignment, fusing, similarity score.

1 Introduction

Fingerprints are ridge patterns flowing on the surface of fingers, which have been increasingly used for individual identification in the civilian's daily life due to the uniqueness, permanence and universality. Previously researchers have proposed many kinds of fingerprint recognition algorithms. The most popular methods are based on point features (called minutiae), which extract minutiae sets from the input fingerprint and compare them with those from the template fingerprint to calculate the similarity score [1] [2]. The minutiae-based features are simple for storage and effective for comparison, but there are still some limits in fingerprint recognition. First, the accuracy of minutiae extraction relies on local quality of fingerprint. Second, minutiae cannot characterize the overall pattern of a fingerprint, and it is hard to further improve the performance. So researchers proposed other representations of fingerprints to resolve these problems, such as texture, ridge structure, orientation field and so on.

The ridge feature observes more information in the whole region of fingerprint and reinforces the individuality of fingerprint considerably. Tian et. al [3] constructed the minutia-simplex which contains a pair of minutiae with the associated local ridge information to estimate the parameters of affine transform and calculate the similarity

S.-W. Lee and S.Z. Li (Eds.): ICB 2007, LNCS 4642, pp. 281–289, 2007.

score. Feng et. al [10] established both the ridge correspondences and the minutia correspondences between two fingerprints. The method realized fingerprint verification after alignment by incrementally matching ridges and minutiae. Both of the algorithms survive the problem of the alignment inaccuracy, which influences their performance in some extent. Another kind of important features is orientation field in fingerprint processing. It describes the global structure of the fingerprint ridge pattern. Gu et. al [5] represented and verified the fingerprints combing both minutiae and model-based orientation field. The algorithm performs well on FVC2002 databases, but in reality it's difficult to estimate the global model for some partial fingerprints.

In this paper we represent the fingerprint with a novel local feature descriptor, which is composed of minutia, the sample points on associated ridge and the adjacent orientation distribution. A novel approach is introduced for fingerprint recognition by fusing the orientation field and the local feature descriptor. First, we align two fingerprints by the local feature descriptor and compute the transformation parameters including the translation and rotation. Second, we combine the local feature descriptor and orientation field feature in fingerprint matching. The comparison of orientation field can reduce the false accepted rate to accelerate the matching process. The similarity score is calculated based on combined features with the SUM rule, which is the most accurate in the experiments. We conduct a set of experiments on three large-scale databases and make comparisons with the state-of-the-arts. The results show that the fusion of local feature descriptor and orientation field can certainly obtain better fingerprint authentication performance than previous methods based on minutiae or ridge features.

The rest of the paper is organized as follows: Section 2 proposes the fingerprint representation with the local feature descriptor. Section 3 presents the method of alignment by using the local feature descriptor. Section 4 describes the process of fingerprint matching based on both the orientation field and the local feature descriptors. The experimental results for our algorithm are displayed in section 5 and Section 6 summarizes our researches.

2 Fingerprint Representation

We represent the fingerprint with a set of local feature descriptors, each of which consists of a minutia, the sample points on its associated ridge and the adjacent orientation distribution. The minutiae set denoted by $\{m^k = (x_m^k, y_m^k, \theta_m^k) | 1 \le k \le K\}$ are extracted from the thinned fingerprint image with the conventional methods, where m^k is the kth minutia, K is the number of minutiae, (x_m^k, y_m^k) and $\theta_m^k \in [0, \pi)$ are respectively the location and orientation for m^k. In this section, we mainly discuss how to construct the local feature descriptor for the minutiae of different types.

According to the traditional methods, minutiae are classified into two types: ridge termination and bifurcation. In practical it is rather difficult to distinguish them because of the noise and environment during fingerprint capture. The ridge ending is possibly mistaken as the bifurcation due to ridge conglutination, while the bifurcation may turn into the ending due to the broken ridge.

To solve this problem, we sample both the associated ridge and valley in a constant interval to express the ridge features in a common form. The ridge feature structure is constructed with the information of sample points assigned to minutia as shown in Fig. 1. We define the set of ridge structures $R = \{r^k\}_{k-1}^{K}$ in a fingerprint as follows:

$$r^k = \{\{x_{t,i}^k, y_{t,i}^k, len_{t,i}^k, \Delta\phi_{t,i}^k\}_{t=0,1}\}_{i=1}^{L_t^k}. \tag{1}$$

$$\Delta\phi_{t,i}^k = d(\theta_{t,i}^k, \theta_m^k) \tag{2}$$

$$d(\theta_1, \theta_2) = \begin{cases} \theta_1 - \theta_2 & \text{if } abs(\theta_1 - \theta_2) \leq \pi/2 \\ \theta_1 - \theta_2 - \pi & \text{if } (\theta_1 - \theta_2) > \pi/2 \\ \theta_1 - \theta_2 + \pi & \text{if } (\theta_1 - \theta_2) < -\pi/2 \end{cases} \tag{3}$$

where r^k is the local ridge structure belonging to the kth minutia. $t \in \{0, 1\}$ denotes the sampling type. When the sample points on the ridge for bifurcation or on the valley for ending, the value of t is set 0, otherwise, it's set 1. L_t^k denotes the number of sample points. $(x_{t,i}^k, y_{t,i}^k)$ are the coordinates of the sample points. $len_{t,i}^k, \theta_{t,i}^k$ are the distance and orientation from the kth minutia m^k to the ith sample point and $\theta_{t,i}^k \in [0, \pi)$. $d(\theta_1, \theta_2)$ is called the orientation distance taking the value in $[-\pi/2, \pi/2]$.The ridge and valley is traced until encountering another minutia or arriving the border of fingerprint. If the sampling number L_t^k is less than $lThr$ (In our experiments, $lThr = 3$), the associated ridge structure is considered false and discarded.

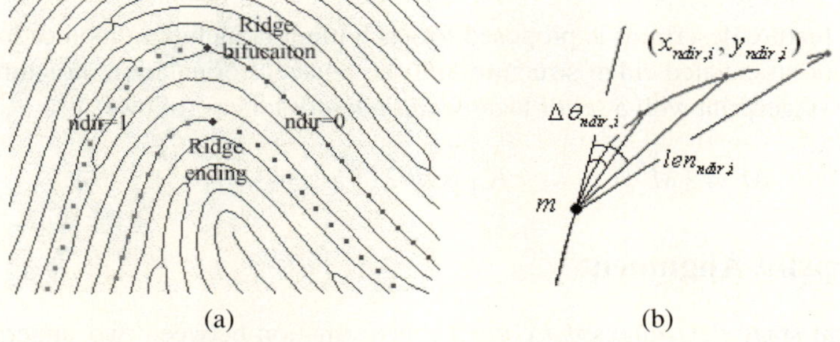

Fig. 1. (a) sampling ridges in two directions for two types of minutiae, (b) ridge structure in one direction for the minutia m

We also characterize each minutia with a structure that comprises information for the orientation field in a broad region around the minutia point. The structure comprises the sampling points equally distributed in a matrix pattern centered at each minutia as illustrated in Fig. 2. According to the sampling principle, the sampling interval v is selected as 2τ (τ is the average fingerprint ridge width) to obtain the best tradeoff between decreasing storage and preserving information.

We define the set of orientation structures $V = \{v_k\}_{k=1}^{K}$ in the fingerprint as follows:

$$v_k = \{(\Delta\varphi_{i,j}^k)_{j=-N_k}^{N_k}\}_{i=-N_k}^{N_k} \tag{4}$$

$$\Delta\varphi_{i,j}^{k} = d(\theta_{i,j}^{k}, \theta_{m}^{k}) \tag{5}$$

where K is the number of minutiae, $2N_k+1(1 \leq k \leq K)$ is the dimension of sampling matrix around the kth minutia and each sampling matrix consist of $(2N_k+1)*(2N_k+1)$ points $p_{i,j}^{k}(-N_k \leq i, j \leq N_k)$. $\theta_{i,j}^{k} \in [0, \pi)$ denote the orientation at each sample point.

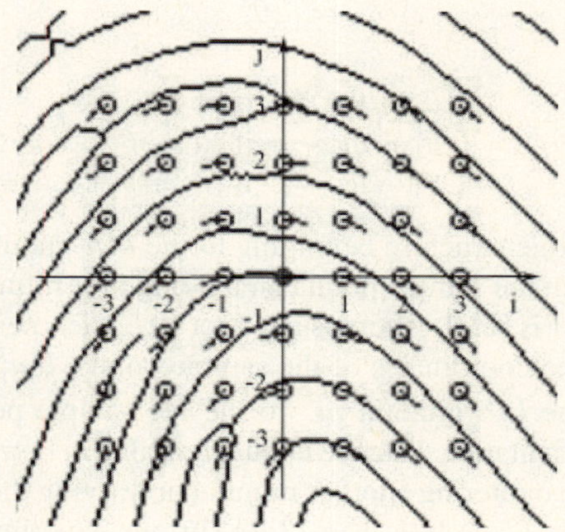

Fig. 2. The orientation distribution around a minutia (the red point), the circle denote the sample points $P_{i,j}$ ($N_k = 3$, v=16)

The local feature descriptor is proposed for each minutia including its location and orientation, the associated ridge structure and the adjacent orientation structure. We represent the fingerprint with a set of local feature descriptors as follows:

$$M = \{M^k | 1 \leq k \leq K\} \; and \; M^k = \{m^k, r^k, v^k\} \tag{6}$$

3 Fingerprint Alignment

The alignment stage determines the correct transformation between two fingerprints, which plays a crucial role in fingerprint recognition. In our approach, we realize the alignment by finding N most similar local feature descriptor pairs and calculating the corresponding transformation vectors as candidates. Compared with using the best one for alignment, the muti-candidates method is more robust to those incorrect and displaced descriptors.

A local similarity function between two descriptors $M^f = \{m^f, r^f, v^f\}$ and $M^t = \{m^f, r^f, v^f\}$ is defined as:

$$Sm(M^f, M^t) = Sr(r^f, r^t) * Sv(v^f, v^t) \tag{7}$$

where $Sr(r^f, r^t)$ and $Sv(v^f, v^t)$ denote the similarity of ridge and orientation structure.

In the local descriptor, $len_{t,i}^{k}$, $\Delta\phi_{t,i}^{k}$ and $\Delta\varphi_{t,i}^{k}$ describe the transformation-invariant relative features of M^k, while $(x_m^k, y_m^k, \theta_m^k)$, $\theta_{t,i}^{k}$ and $\theta_{i,j}^{k}$ represent the transformation-variant relative features. We utilize the transform-invariant parts of the local feature descriptor for their similarity calculation. The similarity functions of ridge and orientation structure are given in an exponential form [7]:

$$Sr(r^f, r^t) = \frac{1}{N_p} \sum_{p \in P} \exp\{-\frac{1}{\mu}(\alpha * |len_p^f - len_p^t| + (1-\alpha) * |\Delta\phi_p^f - \Delta\phi_p^t|)\} \quad (8)$$

$$Sv(v^f, v^t) = \frac{1}{N_q} \sum_{q \in Q} \exp\{-\frac{1}{\omega} * |\Delta\varphi_q^f - \Delta\varphi_q^t|\} \quad (9)$$

where $P = \{(t, i)\}$ denote the overlapped part of the sample points on the ridges. $Q = \{(i, j)\}$ indicate the overlapped part of the sample points of orientation field. N_p and N_q are the size of P and Q. $\alpha \in [0, 1]$ adjusts the scale difference between the distance and orientation. The values of μ, ω are empirically set in training.

Let $F = \{M^{fi}\}_{fi=1}^{Kf}$ and $T = \{M^{ti}\}_{ti=1}^{Kt}$ denote the descriptor sets detected from the input and template fingerprints. The similarity score is calculated between any pair of local feature descriptors M^{fi} and M^{ti}. A relative array C is established to store these index pairs (fi, ti) that satisfy $Sm(M^{ft}, M^{ti}) > SmThr$ ($SmThr$ is an experimental variant) in the decrease order of their similarity values.

We construct the alignment candidate set L to store the transformation vectors L^n between these descriptor pairs, which have the largest N similarity score $L = \{l_n\}_{n=1}^{N}$. For any pair of M^{fi} and M^{ti} in the candidate set, we average the difference of the position and orientation between two minutiae and the corresponding sample point pairs on the ridges to calculate their transformation vector which includes the translation and rotation parameters, $l^n = (dx, dy, d\theta)^T$:

$$d\theta = \frac{1}{N_p} \sum_{p \in P} \theta_p^t - \theta_p^f \quad (10)$$

$$\begin{bmatrix} dx \\ dy \end{bmatrix} = \frac{1}{N_p} \sum_{p \in P} (\begin{bmatrix} x_p^t \\ y_p^t \end{bmatrix} - R_{d\theta} * \begin{bmatrix} x_p^f \\ y_p^f \end{bmatrix}) \quad (11)$$

Where $R_{d\theta}$ is a $2 * 2$ operator of clockwise rotating with $d\theta$. P and N_p are defined in formula 8.

4 Fingerprint Matching

4.1 Matching Based on Orientation Field

In our approach the block orientation field is utilized to avoid misaligning two fingerprints, it measures the similarity of their global ridge patterns. For each transformation vector in the candidate set, we align the orientation fields extracted from the enhanced fingerprints, where the backgrounds have been excluded. The overlapped area A is partitioned into a lattice of blocks of size $n * n$ (n is decided by ridge frequency and fingerprint quality).

For each block B, let $g_s = (g_s^x, g_s^y)$ denotes the gradient intensity at each site s. We evaluate the local quality of the fingerprint by using the covariance matrix J and the normalized coherence measure $\widetilde{k} \in [0,1]$ in the block B as follows [8]:

$$J = \frac{1}{n^2} \sum_{s \in B} g_s g_s^T = \begin{bmatrix} j_{11} & j_{12} \\ j_{21} & j_{22} \end{bmatrix} \tag{12}$$

$$\widetilde{k} = \frac{j_{11}^2 - j_{22}^2 + 4j_{12}^2}{(j_{11} + j_{22})^2} \tag{13}$$

The similarity score of two orientation fields can be computed as the weighted average of the block-wise similarity measures:

$$So(O^f, O^t) = \frac{1}{\sum_{B \in A} \widetilde{k}_B^f * \widetilde{k}_B^t} \sum_{B \in A} S(B^f, B^t) * \widetilde{k}_B^f * \widetilde{k}_B^t \tag{14}$$

$$S(B^f, B^t) = \exp(-\frac{1}{v} * |d(\overline{\theta}_B^f, \overline{\theta}_B^t)|) \tag{15}$$

where $\overline{\theta}_B^f, \overline{\theta}_B^t$ are the average orientation in the block B of two fingerprints, $d(\overline{\theta}_B^f, \overline{\theta}_B^t)$ denotes the orientation distance as defined in the formula 3. v is experimentally selected based on the training results.

If $So(O^f, O^t) < SoThr$, the corresponding local descriptor pair is considered misaligned and discarded from the candidate set, which reduces the false accepted rate and accelerates the matching process. $SoThr$ is selected according to false reject rate (in our method at $FRR = 0.1\%$) in training.

4.2 Matching Based on Local Feature Descriptors

After refining the alignment candidates with the block orientation field, we apply each residual transformation vectors V^n in the candidate set V to the two descriptor sets F and T from the input and template fingerprints. The similarity score of fingerprints is evaluated based on local descriptor as the following stages:

- Initialize the set DP to store the corresponding matched descriptor pairs.
- Convert the descriptor set T in the template fingerprint into the aligned descriptor set T' with the transformation vector.
- Represent all the minutiae from the two sets F and T' in a polar coordinate system whose origin is set at the minutia in M^{fi}. Because of the non-linear deformation and the error in feature extracting, the corresponding minutiae from two fingerprints can't be exactly overlapped. If two minutiae fall in the same changeable tolerance box [8], which means, their Euclidean distance and orientation difference don't exceed the value δd and $\delta\theta$, two corresponding descriptors are considered as the matched pair. We delete those descriptor pairs that don't locate in the same tolerance box from the relative array C mentioned in section 3.
- Construct the set of matched descriptor pairs DP with the dynamic programming method. The descriptor pair (M^{fm}, M^{tm}) that has the largest similarity value is inserted to the set DP. All the pairs comprising the two descriptors are discarded from the array C. This step is repeated until the array is empty.

– Evaluate the global similarity score between all the matched descriptor pairs. Considering only the descriptors in the overlapped area after alignment, the similarity is computed as follows:

$$Sp(F,T) = \frac{1}{M} * \sum_{i=1}^{M} Sm(M^{fm[i]}, Sm(M^{tm[i]}) * \frac{(\sum_{i=1}^{M} Ns[i])^2}{Ns^f * Ns^t} \quad (16)$$

where M is the number of the matched descriptor pairs $(fm[i], tm[i])$. $Ns[i]$ is the number of the matched sample points in the ith descriptor pair. Ns^f and Ns^t respectively denote the number of all the sample points from the two descriptor sets F and T' in the overlapped area after fingerprint alignment.

4.3 Evaluating Combined Similarity Score

Fusing different features in matching stage can improve the fingerprint authentication performance. The detailed analysis on classifier fusion can be seen in the literatures [9] [10]. We combine the orientation field and local feature descriptors by different strategies in score level. The combined similarity score is evaluated in our approach using four different decision-level fusion rules as follows:

Max rule: $Score = \max(Sp, So)$
Min rule: $Score = \min(Sp, So)$
Product rule: $Score = Sp * So$

Sum rule: $Score = q * Sp + (1 - q) * So$, where $q \in [0, 1]$ adjusts the weight fractions between the similarity of orientation fields and local descriptors, it is selected based on the quality of fingerprints.

Table 1. Comparison of the performance on FVC2004 DB1

FVC2004 DB1	Only orientation-based	Only descriptors-based	Max	Min	Product	Sum
EER (%)	6.53	4.74	4.56	4.95	4.35	3.49
FMR100 (%)	17.33	11.97	10.42	11.72	9.71	6.21
FMR1000(%)	27.61	23.50	23.29	19.47	15.36	19.04
ZeroFMR(%)	38.43	28.97	28.97	23.45	19.93	24.61

We evaluate the set of combined similarity score according to each transformation vector in candidates. The maximum value is selected as the final matching score. Experimental results performed on DB1 of FVC2004 with four fusion rules are displayed in Table 1. It is obvious that the performance of the Sum rule is the best, while the performance of the Min rule is the worst. Hence, the Sum rule is selected in our algorithm to evaluate the combined similarity score between the template and input fingerprints.

5 Experimental Results

The experiments have been conducted on FVC2004 [11] and one database of our lab. Each database of FVC2004 consists of 800 fingerprint images (100 fingers 8 impressions per finger) captured at a resolution of about 500dpi. Databases emphasize on distortion, dry and wet fingerprints especially in DB1 and DB3 of FVC2004, which are more difficult than FVC2000/FVC2002. Therefore our algorithm is evaluated on DB1 and DB3 of FVC2004. We also establish the database to test the efficiency of our algorithm for poor-quality and partial fingerprints. The database comprises 1680 fingerprints (140 fingers 12 impressions per finger) acquired with an electric field sensor "Authentec 4000". The image size is 96*96 pixels at a resolution of 250 dpi. Due to the low resolution and small size of the sensor, the fingerprint ridges are blurry and the impressions from the same finger usually have small overlapped area. The fingerprints are collected from heterogeneous volunteers including manual workers and elderly people, so the majority of them suffer the influence from blur, scar, wetness or dryness.

The experiments are conducted on three databases (DB1, DB3 of FVC2004 and our established database). All the matching performance in this section is evaluated according to the experimental protocols in [12]. To approve the efficacy of the combined features, we display the performance of the ridge-based method [5] and the minutiae-based method [1] for comparison in Table 2. The results confirm that the combined features can significantly improve the performance of fingerprint matching, especially for the poor-quality and partial fingerprints.

Table 2. Comparison of performance between our algorithm and other matching methods

		EER(%)	FMR100(%)	FMR1000(%)	ZeroFMR(%)
DB1	Minutia-based	5.74	9.35	15.54	18.43
	Ridge-based	4.57	6.71	16.10	31.18
	Our algorithm	3.49	6.21	19.04	24.61
DB3	Minutia-based	2.78	4.47	8.40	11.86
	Ridge-based	2.11	3.04	8.75	16.86
	Our algorithm	1.31	1.61	4.29	9.15
Our established database	Minutia-based	6.55	10.89	17.54	39.18
	Ridge-based	5.01	5.51	8.28	30.69
	Our algorithm	3.33	4.47	19.39	33.54

6 Conclusion

In this paper we represent the fingerprint with a novel local feature descriptor, which is comprehensive and robustly holds the uniqueness of the fingerprint. We align the fingerprints using the descriptors and calculate a set of transform vectors as candidates. In matching process, the orientation field is used to avoid misaligning and to measure the similarity score of global ridge pattern. We also evaluate the similarity between the local descriptor sets from the input and template fingerprints. The two methods are fused with the Sum rule to obtain the final matching score. The experimental results demonstrate that our algorithm integrates the advantages of the local and global features and improves the algorithm performance and reliability.

Acknowledgments. This paper is supported by the Project of National Science Fund for Distinguished Young Scholars of China (No. 60225008), the Key Project of National Natural Science Foundation of China (No. 60332010 and 60575007), the Project for Young Scientists' Fund of National Natural Science Foundation of China (No.60303022), and the Project of Natural Science Foundation of Beijing (No.4052026).

References

1. Jain, A.K., Hong, L., Bolle, R.: On-Line Fingerprint Verification. IEEE Trans. Pattern Analysis and Machine Intelligence 19(4), 302–314 (1997)
2. Kovcs-Vajna, Z.M.: A Fingerprint Verification System Based on Triangular Matching and Dynamic Time Warping. IEEE Trans. Pattern Analysis and Machine Intelligence 22(11), 1266–1276 (2000)
3. Tian, J., He, Y.L., Chen, H., Yang, X.: A Fingerprint Identification Algorithm by Clustering Similarity. Science in China Ser. F Information Sciences 48(4), 437–451 (2005)
4. Feng, J.J., Ouyang, Z.Y., Cai, A.: Fingerprint Matching Using Ridges. Pattern Recognition 39, 2131–2140 (2006)
5. Gu, J.W., Zhou, J., Yang, C.Y.: Fingerprint Recognition by Combining Global Structure and Local Cues. IEEE Transaction on Image Processing 15(7), 1952–1964 (2006)
6. Tico, M., Kuosmanen, P.: Fingerprint Matching Using an Orientation-based Minutia Descriptor. IEEE Trans. on Pattern Analysis and Machine Intelligence 25(8), 1009–1014 (2003)
7. Chen, Y., Dass, S.C., Jain, A.K.: Fingerprint Quality Indices for Predicting Authentication Performance. In: Proc. of Audio- and Video-based Biometric Person Authentication (AVBPA), pp. 160–170. Rye Brook, NewYork (2005)
8. Luo, X.P., Tian, J.: Image Enhancement and Minutia Matching Algorithm in Automated Fingerprint Identification System. Journal of software 13 (2002)
9. Kittler, J., Hatef, M., Duin, P.W., Matas, J.: On combining classifiers. IEEE Trans. Pattern Analysis and Machine Intelligence 20(3), 226–239 (1998)
10. Ho, T.K., Hull, J.J., Srihari, S.N.: Decision combination in multiple classifier systems. IEEE Trans. Pattern Analysis and Machine Intelligence 16(1), 66–75 (1994)
11. `http://bias.csr.unibo.it/fvc2004/`
12. Maio, D., Maltoni, D., Cappelli, R., Wayman, J.L., Jain, A.K.: FVC2004: Third Fingerprint Verification Competition. In: Zhang, D., Jain, A.K. (eds.) ICBA 2004. LNCS, vol. 3072, pp. 1–7. Springer, Heidelberg (2004)

MQI Based Face Recognition Under Uneven Illumination

Yaoyao Zhang, Jie Tian, Xiaoguang He, and Xin Yang

Center for Biometrics and Security Research, Key Laboratory of Complex Systems and Intelligence Science, Institute of Automation, Chinese Academy of Sciences, P.O. Box 2728, Beijing, 100080, P.R. China
tian@ieee.org, jie.tian@ia.ac.cn

Abstract. Face recognition has been applied in many fields, while face recognition under uneven illumination is still an open problem. Our approach is based on Morphological Quotient Image (MQI) for illumination normalization, and Dynamic Morphological Quotient Image (DMQI) is proposed to improve the performance. Before applying MQI, singularity noise should be removed, and after MQI operation, an effective scheme is used to wipe off the grainy noise as postprocessing. Weighted normalized correlation is adopted to measure the similarity between two images. Experiments on Yale Face Database B show that the proposed MQI method has a good performance of face recognition under various light conditions. Moreover, its computational cost is very low.

Keywords: face recognition, illumination normalization, quotient image, morphological operation.

1 Introduction

Face recognition shows its importance nowadays, and more and more fields, such as intelligent human-computer interfaces and e-services, have been benefited from it [1]. Since the common and economical face recognition systems are based on face images captured in the visible light spectrum, the changes of environment light may do harm to the performance of the systems. Due to the uncertainty of light condition and the complexity of models, face recognition under uneven illumination gets more and more attention.

In recent years, many techniques have been proposed to solve such problem, among which quotient image method accounts for an important part. Quotient Image (QI) [2], first proposed by Shashua et al., is a novel means to address the illumination problem. It makes use of illumination invariant information, which is achieved by computing the ratio of a probe image and the linear combination of three known images under different light conditions, but the performance degrades if the main features between the test set and the bootstrap are misaligned. Quotient Illumination Relighting (QIR) [3] method gets the image of subject under canonical light condition by calculating the ratio between an arbitrary image and its quotient illumination. However, QIR relies on the assumption that the illumination of the current subject is

S.-W. Lee and S.Z. Li (Eds.): ICB 2007, LNCS 4642, pp. 290–298, 2007.

known in advance, while in most applications, such assumption can not be satisfied. H. Wang et al. brought out the conception of Self-Quotient Image (SQI) [4], and this method aims to estimate the light condition over the image by using Weighted Gaussian filter, but there may be some over-compensation regions when applying SQI. Total Variation based Quotient Image (TVQI) [5], developed by T. Chen et al., is an effective method for face recognition under different illumination. It is based on the estimation of light by solving an optimal problem, which is known as total variation function. However, because of its computational cost, it is not competent for real-time systems.

In this paper, we proposed a new face recognition method based on Morphological Quotient Image (MQI) [6]. It employs mathematical morphological theory and quotient image technique for illumination normalization. Such method obtains good test results on the publicly available face database, and the time consuming is very low. In despite of its low recognition error rates, the face recognition effect still can be further improved by choosing the size of templates for close operation dynamically, and adopting weighted normalized correlation as the measure of similarity. In addition, an effective scheme is brought out to wipe off the noise generated by division operation in the quotient image.

2 Morphological Quotient Image

Given an image I under certain light condition, we can represent it as the product of illumination L and the reflectance R [7], and in most cases, there may be some additional noise N. Such model can be expressed as follows:

$$I(i,j) = L(i,j)R(i,j) + N(i,j)\ . \tag{1}$$

Where we assume that illumination L is the smooth version of the original image with sharp edges, which shows the variation of the light intensity. Reflectance R, i.e. albedo, relies on the surface texture of the object, which is light free and stable for recognition. Additional noise N may do harm to the performance of face recognition algorithms, so it should be removed at first.

The method of Morphological Quotient Image (MQI) uses close operation, a kind of morphological approach, for light estimation. Close operator is a nonlinear operator, which is defined simply as a dilation followed by an erosion with the same structuring element. In general, dilation makes objects to expand or grow in size, while erosion causes objects to shrink. Therefore, with a suitable structuring element, close operation can preserve some particular patterns while attenuating others, and moreover, the original edges will not be blurred. Specially, when dealing with an image under uneven illumination, such morphological technique can be used to get a smooth version, and in such smooth image, the region with the points of the same gray value is believed to share the same light intensity. Fig.1 shows an example.

According to the model referred to above, reflectance R can be obtained simply as follows:

$$R(i,j)=\frac{I(i,j)-N(i,j)}{L(i,j)}=\frac{Denoise(I)}{Close(Denoise(I))} \quad (2)$$

We can denoise the image before applying close operation, and then compute the ratio of the gray values pixel by pixel before and after the image is morphological processed. The result is light free, so it can be used to face recognition. DMQI is proposed to dynamically choose the size of templates for close operation. Moreover, division operation may generate some grainy noise, especially in the dark regions, and such noise may do harm to face recognition. A simple and effective scheme is proposed to wipe the noise off as the postprocessing.

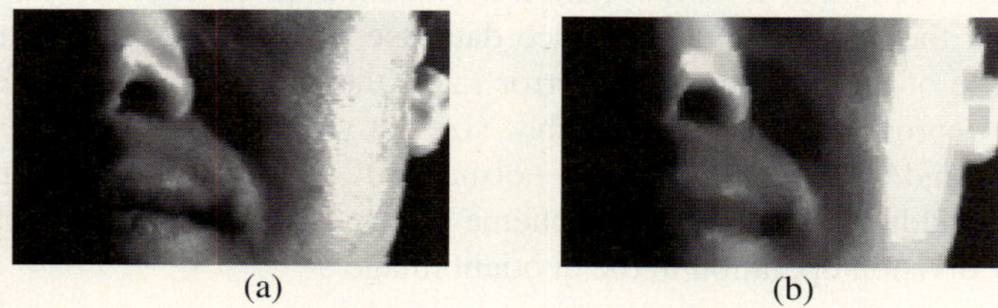

(a) (b)

Fig. 1. (a) The original image under uneven illumination. (b) The processed image after close operation.

2.1 DMQI

MQI choose $N*N$ template as the structuring elements, and the size N is the key parameter. With a large template, the close operation would focus on large scale features, but meanwhile has poor performance on local illumination compensation, especially in shadow. On the other hand, if the size is small, it results in good local illumination normalization, but simultaneously misses large scale features. In order to solve the problem, Dynamic Morphological Quotient Image (DMQI) is put forward to make the template size to be adaptive to the given image. The scheme of DMQI can be expressed as follows:

$$DClose(i,j)=\begin{cases} Close^{l}(i,j), & Close^{l}(i,j)>\alpha\cdot Close^{s}(i,j) \\ Close^{m}(i,j), & \alpha\cdot Close^{s}(i,j)>Close^{l}(i,j)>\beta\cdot Close^{s}(i,j) \\ Close^{s}(i,j), & \beta\cdot Close^{s}(i,j)>Close^{l}(i,j) \end{cases} . \quad (3)$$

Where α and β are the parameters of the feature scales, while $\alpha>\beta>1.0$. l, m, and s are the optional sizes of templates, while $l > m > s > 1$. If $Close^{l}(i,j)>\alpha\cdot Close^{s}(i,j)$, which shows that the result of large size template is very different from that of small one, the area around point (i, j) would be brow, eye, nose, mouth, or the boundary of light intensity changing, where the gray values of the pixels change significantly.

Therefore, large size template is chosen to keep features. If $\beta \cdot Close^{s}(i,j) > Close^{l}(i,j)$, which indicates that large template and small one have almost the same effect, the point (i, j) is in a smooth region, such as cheek and forehead, and the region is under even illumination. Gray values of the pixels in such areas have little changes. In this case, small size template is a good choice for the close operation.

2.2 Preprocessing

Denoising the image before applying MQI is necessary because noise can decrease the performance of the method, especially the singularity noise, which is defined as the points having the value to be the unique maximum or unique minimum of their neighbors' values. The denoising method can be expressed as follows:

$$Denoise(I(i,j)) = \begin{cases} \underset{(n,m)\in Neighbor(i,j)}{Maximum}(I(n,m)) & \forall (n,m)\in Neighbor(i,j), I(i,j) > I(n,m) \\ \underset{(n,m)\in Neighbor(i,j)}{Minimum}(I(n,m)) & \forall (n,m)\in Neighbor(i,j), I(i,j) < I(n,m) \\ I(i,j) & otherwise \end{cases} \quad (4)$$

Where Neighbor (i, j) means the 8-neighbor set of point (i, j). If the gray value of the current point is larger (smaller) than any of its 8-neighbor points, the point is given the value of maximum (minimum) of the gray values of all its 8 neighbors.

2.3 Postprocessing

Morphological Quotient Image method can be used to get the light free information of the objects, but in some regions, especially in shadows, grainy noise is generated with the operation. This is due to the division operation in the MQI model. Since the gray values of points in the dark region are very small compared to the points in the light region, division operation amplifies the original small gray value changes in the dark region, and such small changes are not the robust feature of the objects. Fig. 2 illustrates the generation of such noise. Image (d) shows that the gray values of the pixels on the line in image (c) fluctuate more significantly in the left part than that in the right part, and it is for the reason that the left part of original image is darker than the right part.

Removing the grainy noise is necessary since the noise does harm to face recognition. Here, by analyzing the main traits of such kind of noise, as well as the difference between the noise and useful texture information, a simple scheme is cast to wipe off the noise effectively and efficiently. For each point in the image, and all its 8-neighbor elements, we sort the 9 points in order according to their gray values, and check the value difference between neighbor ones. The point is considered to be noise if the values of neighbor differences are all small enough (except that all the neighbor differences are zero), and thus the point is given the value of the maximum of the 9 points. Otherwise, the point is thought to be the useful information and then keep its original value.

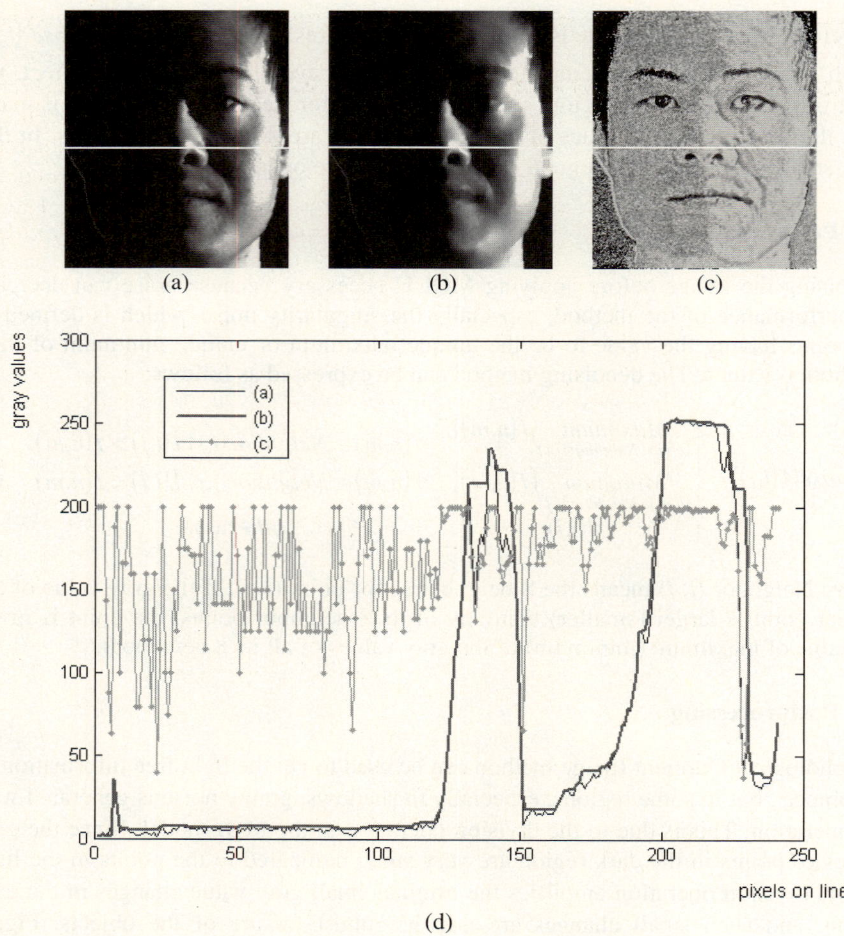

Fig. 2. (a) The original image. (b) The processed image after MQI operation. (c) The result of quotient image. All the three images have a line on them at the same position. (d) Changes of gray values of the pixels on the line of each image. Blue one refers to (a); red line refers to (b); green one refers to image (c).

3 Experiments

Face image is normalized according to the coordinates of eyes, and cropped to proper size in order that only the face region is used for recognition. It is first preprocessed to remove the singularity noise, and then morphological close operation is applied to the image. The ratio of the image before and after close operation is computed to get the light free information, and the grainy noise is wiped off as postprocessing. Face recognition is performed after face images are processed by MQI method.

Usually there are a large number of test images to be classified, while only a few images can be used as the training set; therefore, many sophisticated classifiers are not necessary, and nearest neighbor classifier is chosen to be used. Particularly, we can here have only one image in the gallery for each class. The distance between two images can be measured in various ways, for example, Euclidean Distance is the most common one, and here, we measure the dissimilarity of two images with normalized correlation, i.e. cosine of the angle between the two vectors, which is proved to be effective in this case. The similarity between two images can be computed as follows:

$$\Phi(I_i, I_t) = \cos(\angle\langle I_i, I_t\rangle) = \frac{I_i \cdot I_t}{\|I_i\|\|I_t\|} \quad . \tag{5}$$

Furthermore, not every local region of face plays the equal role on the effect of face recognition, and generally, some particular parts, such as brow, eye, nose and mouth, have most of the key features for identification. In addition, the face images to be classified have been normalized according to the coordinates of two eyes. That different local part of face has different weights value is more effective when measuring the similarity of two images. The weights are selected through experiment, not utilizing an actual optimization procedure, and thus they are probably not optimal. Fig. 3 shows an example. Compared to the method with equal weights, we get an improvement in the recognition rate.

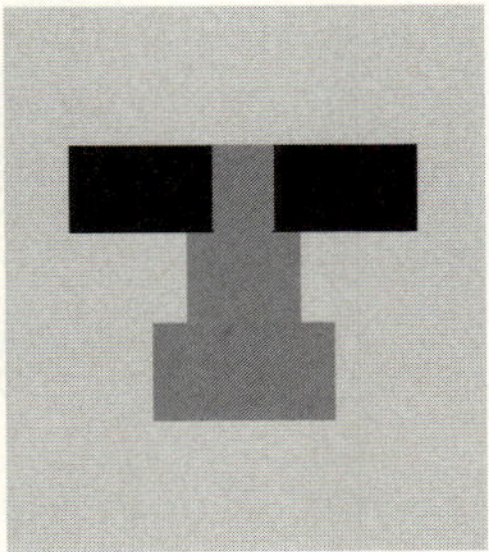

Fig. 3. An example of weight set over the face image. The darker the region is, the higher the weight value is.

The MQI method is tested on Yale Face database B, which includes 10 subjects, each with 64 frontal faces under different light conditions. In the 640 face images, there are no variations of pose, expression, age and so on. Those images are aligned according to the coordinates of eyes, and are cropped to size 281*241 in order that only the face region is used. All the 640 images are divided into five subsets according to the angle between the light source direction and the camera axis: Subset 1 (0° to 12°), Subset 2 (13° to 25°), Subset 3 (26° to 50°), Subset 4 (51° to 77°), and Subset 5 (above 78°), and each subset respectively has 70, 120, 120, 140, 190 face images. 7 corrupted images are discarded [8], and therefore there are totally 633 images left: Subset 1 to 5 respectively has 70, 118, 118, 138 and 189 images.

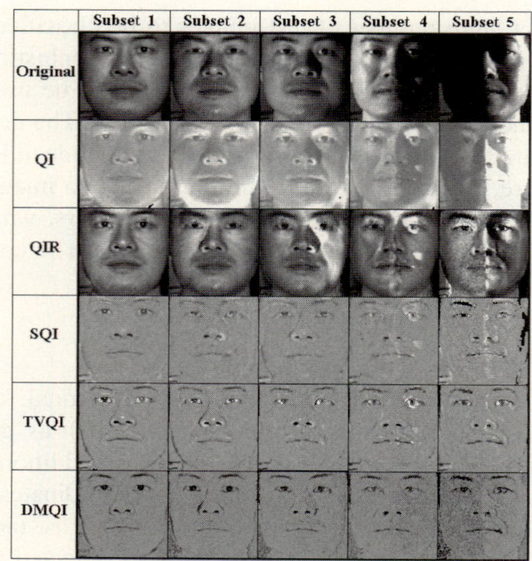

Fig. 4. Contrast of processed images after various quotient image operation

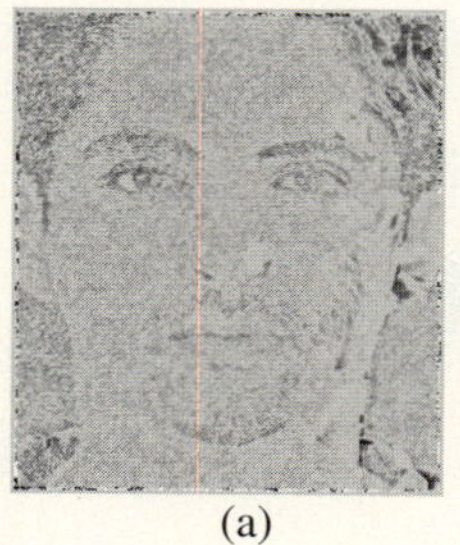

(a)

(b)

Fig. 5. (a) Face image with grainy noise. (b) Face image after being processed.

One of the advantages of MQI method is that only one image needed in the train set for each class, and here we choose the face images under frontal illumination as the templates, the other 623 images as the test samples. We first process the total 10 register images with MQI method, and then save them as templates. For each of the 623 test images, after being processed in the same way, we measure the similarities between the test image and each of the saved templates, and then decide the identity of test sample according to the nearest neighbor rule. Through experiment, The template size to be 7 is a proper selection, and in the case of adopting DMQI scheme, when parameters $\alpha=1.8$, $\beta=1.35$, size of template s = 5, m = 7, l = 9, the performance of illumination normalization is pretty good. Fig.4 shows the contrast of face images processed by several kinds of quotient methods, and these images are selected from the 5 subsets of Yale Face database respectively. We can see that the results of QI and QIR are not so competent as the other three, and in SQI, there exists some over-compensation regions, which shows additional dark blocks in appearance. TVQI and DMQI both have good performance visually on illumination normalization, while there seems to be more grainy noise generated by DMQI. Such grainy noise can be removed using the method referred to above as post processing, and experiments proved that the performance is quite good. Fig. 5 gives an example. Most of the noise is wiped off, and at the same time useful information are kept.

Table 1. RER Comparisons of various methods on Yale Face database B

Methods	Recognition Error Rate (%) vs. Illumination				
	Subset 1	Subset 2	Subset 3	Subset 4	Subset 5
Correlation[8]	N/A	0.0	23.3	73.6	N/A
Eigenface w/o 1st3 [8]	N/A	0.0	19.2	66.4	N/A
Linear Subspace [8]	N/A	0.0	0.0	15.0	N/A
Cones Cast [9]	N/A	0.0	0.0	10.0	37.0
QI	0.0	1.7	38.1	65.9	76.7
QIR	0.0	0.0	0.0	9.4	21.2
SQI	0.0	0.0	0.0	3.6	2.1
Relative Difference Space[10]	0.0	0.0	0.0	0.0	12.0
MQI	0.0	0.0	0.0	0.0	1.6
DMQI	0.0	0.0	0.0	0.0	1.1
DMQI + weighted normalized correlation	0.0	0.0	0.0	0.0	0.5
TVQI	0.0	0.0	0.0	0.0	0.0

Table 2. Comparison of computational complexity

	Computational complexity comparison		
Methods	MQI	DMQI	TVQI
Average processing time per image (Second)	0.09	0.21	12.89
Computational complexity	$O(n)$	$O(3 \cdot n)$	$O(l \cdot n^{3/2})$

Table 1 lists the Recognition Error Rates (RER) of different kinds of methods, including the QI schemes referred to above, and some classical techniques as well. It shows that Subset 5 gets the highest RER of all the subsets almost for all the methods, which is due to the acutest variation of the light condition, and therefore, it is most difficult to compensate illumination for the images. MQI outperforms most of the existing methods, and when choosing the size of template for close operation dynamically, DMQI gets lower RER. Moreover, the recognition performance improved when weighted normalized correlation is adopted to measure the similarity between two images.

RER of TVQI is lower than that of DMQI, but TVQI method is realized by solving an optimal problem, which needs a number of iterations to find the optimal solution. In other words, the time and resource consuming of TVQI is expensive, while MQI technique would be much faster, and is more competent to be used in real-time application. Table 2 shows the comparison of the computational complexity of MQI, DMQI and TVQI, where n is the pixel number of the whole image, and l is the time needed for each iteration for TVQI. Such data is calculated with the mean of the 633 images, and the evaluation is conducted on Dell 4700 with Pentium 4 CPU 2.80GHZ.

4 Conclusion

This paper is based on MQI, a new proposed method for illumination normalization. Morphological close operation and quotient computation are used to get light free information. The test on Yale Face Database B shows that it is very effective and efficient, and lower RER can be obtained when adopting DMQI and utilizing weighted nearest neighbor classifier. Moreover, an effective scheme is used to remove the noise generated by MQI as postprocessing.

References

1. Zhao, W., Chellappa, R., Rosenfeld, A., Phillips, P.: Face recognition: A literature survey. UMD CfAR Technical Report, CAR-TR-948 (2000)
2. Shashua, A., Riklin-Raviv, T.: The quotient image: Classbased re-rendering and recognition with varying illuminations. IEEE Transactions on Pattern Analysis and Machine Intelligence 23(2), 129–139 (2001)
3. Shan, S., Gao, W., Cao, B., Zhao, D.: Illumination normalization for robust face recognition against varying lighting conditions. In: Proc. of IEEE Workshop on AMFG, pp. 157–164. IEEE Computer Society Press, Los Alamitos (2003)
4. Wang, H., Li, S.Z., Wang, Y.: Generalized quotient image. In: IEEE International Conference on Computer Vision and Pattern Recognition. IEEE Computer Society Press, Los Alamitos (2004)
5. Chen, T., Yin, W., Zhou, X., Comaniciu, D., Huang, T.: Illumination Normalization for Face Recognition and Uneven Background Correction Using Total Variation Based Image Models. In: IEEE Computer Society Conference on Computer Vision and Pattern Recognition, vol. 2, pp. 532–539 (2005)
6. He, X., Jie, T., Wu, L., Zhang, Y., Yang, X.: Illumination Normalization with Morphological Quotient Image. Journal of Software 18(9) (2007)
7. Gross, R., Brajovie, V.: An Image Preprocessing Algorithm for Illumination Invariant Face Recognition. In: 4th International Conference on Audio and Video Based Biometric Person Authentication, pp. 10–18 (2003)
8. Georghiades, A., Belhumeur, P., Kriegman, D.: From Few to Many: Illumination Cone Models for Face Recognition under Variable Lighting and Pose. IEEE Trans. on Pattern Analysis and Machine Intelligence 23(6), 630–660 (2001)
9. Georghiades, A., Kriegman, D., Belhumeur, P.: Illumination Cones for Recognition under Variable Lighting: Faces. In: IEEE Computer Society Conference on Computer Vision and Pattern Recognition. IEEE Computer Society Press, Los Alamitos (1998)
10. He, X., Tian, J., He, Y., Yang, X.: Face Recognition with Relative Difference Space and SVM. In: Proce. of the 18th International Conference of Pattern Recognition, HongKong (August 2006)

Learning Kernel Subspace Classifier

Bailing Zhang[1], Hanseok Ko[2], and Yongsheng Gao[3]

[1] School of Computer Science and Mathematics
Victoria University, VIC 3011, Australia
bailing.zhang@vu.edu.au
[2] School of Electronics and Computer Engineering
Korea University, Seoul, 136-713, Korea
hsko@korea.ac.kr
[3] School of Engineering
Griffith University, QLD 4111, Australia
yongsheng.gao@griffith.edu.au

Abstract. Subspace classifiers are well-known in pattern recognition, which represent pattern classes by linear subspaces spanned by the class specific basis vectors through simple mathematical operations like SVD. Recently, kernel based subspace methods have been proposed to extend the functionalities by directly applying the Kernel Principal Component Analysis (KPCA). The projection variance in kernel space as applied in these earlier proposed kernel subspace methods, however, is not a trustworthy criteria for class discrimination and they simply fail in many recognition problems as we encountered in biometrics research. We address this issue by proposing a learning kernel subspace classifier which attempts to reconstruct data in input space through the kernel subspace projection. While the pre-image methods aiming at finding an approximate pre-image for each input by minimization of the reconstruction error in kernel space, we emphasize the problem of how to estimate a kernel subspace as a model for a specific class. Using the occluded face recognition as examples, our experimental results demonstrated the efficiency of the proposed method.

1 Introduction

Subspace classifier is a traditional pattern recognition method that has been broadly applied in signal processing and computer vision for performing various types of recognition. The essence of subspace classifier is classifying an unlabeld pattern based on its distance from different subspaces that represent known classes. One of the first subspace classification algorithms was CLASFIC (class feature information compression)[1], in which the basis vectors spanning the subspaces of each class are determined by a principal component analysis (PCA) of the patterns belonging to that class. The principal assumption behind subspace classifiers is that the vector distribution in each class lies in a lower-dimensional subspace of the original feature space and it is optimal from a reconstruction point of view. And the earlier subspace classifier has been extended in many

S.-W. Lee and S.Z. Li (Eds.): ICB 2007, LNCS 4642, pp. 299–308, 2007.

ways. For example, it was found a better performance could be gained if the subspaces are modified in an error-driven way, which was termed as Learning Subspace Method (LSM)[2].

Subspace classifiers are well suited for the classification problems with high dimensional input space. The best reconstruction property accompanized with the linear transformation offers an efficient way of handling missing pixels and occlusions that frequently appear in practices for many image recognition problems. The linear subspace methods, however, are limited in performance if non-linear features are involved. Furthermore, PCA encodes the data based on second order statistics and ignores higher-order dependencies, which may contain important discriminant information for recognition. As a solution, kernel representations can be introduced by projecting the input attributes into a high dimensional feature space, through which the complex nonlinear problems in the original space will more likely be formulated as near-linear ones [6,3,9].

In the past, several works have been reported on combining kernel method with subspace classifiers [4-5]. These earlier works, however, shared the same idea of applying the kernel principal component analysis (KPCA) and establishing the classifier based on the projection variance in kernel space. More specifically, the kernel trick is used to map each class of input data into their respective implicit feature space F and then PCA is performed in F to produce the nonlinear subspace of the corresponding class. A test data is then projected to all of the nonlinear subspaces and the projection variance in kernel space is used as classification criteria. Our extensive experiment on applying this idea to some face recognition problems, however, turned out that such a simple "kernel subspace" classifier does not work.

In addition to [4-5], the application of KPCA in pattern classification has also been extensively discussed in recent years. For example, KPCA de-noising and the pre-image problem [7-8] is very close to the kernel subspace classifier. For a given pattern, the pre-image algorithms attempt to find the reconstructed one in input space by minimizing the reconstruction error in kernel space F with gradient descent. Pre-image algorithms, however, do not measure the discrepancy between an input vector and its reconstruction in input space. This is more important in kernel subspace classifier as the reconstruction error in input space directly indicates the discrimination capability of a data class with its corresponding kernel subspace. We attempted to solve the problem by formulating the objective as best reconstructing input data from the kernel principal component projections and the new method is termed as *learning kernel subspace classifier*. On robust face recognition problems, our experiments showed its superiority over the pre-image algorithms and some complex occlusion robust face recognition methods.

2 Subspace Classifier

Assume that each of the data classes forms a lower-dimensional linear subspace distinct from the subspaces spanned by other data classes [1-2], then the subspace representing a class can be defined in terms of basis vectors spanning the subspace. And a testing data item is classified based on the lengths of its projections onto each of the subspaces or, alternatively, on the distances of the test vector from these subspaces.

Let $\mathbf{X} = (\mathbf{x}_1, ..., \mathbf{x}_\mathrm{N})$ be the training data matrix belongs to a class $\omega^{(c)}, c = 1, \cdots, C$, where $\mathbf{x}_\mathrm{i}$ is a training data vector. A set of orthonormal vectors $\mathbf{p}_\mathrm{i}$ can be obtained by, for example, the principal component analysis of the correlation matrix $\mathbf{X}^\mathrm{T}\mathbf{X}$, *i.e.*, $\mathbf{p}_\mathrm{i}^\mathrm{T}\mathbf{p}_\mathrm{j} = \delta_\mathrm{ij}$. The basis vectors $\mathbf{p}_\mathrm{i} \in \mathrm{R}^\mathrm{n}, \mathrm{i} = 1, \cdots, \mathrm{d}\ (\mathrm{d} < \mathrm{n})$, span a subspace for the class, which can be expressed as $L : L = L(\mathbf{p}_1, \cdots, \mathbf{p}_\mathrm{d})$. Denote P the matrix whose column vectors are $\mathbf{p}_\mathrm{i}$, $P = [\mathbf{p}_1, \cdots, \mathbf{p}_\mathrm{d}]$. When an unlabeled sample $\mathbf{x}$ is classified by the subspace classifier, the distance between $\mathbf{x}$ and each of the subspace is calculated by the projection $y = P^T\mathbf{x}$,. Then, $\mathbf{x}$ is classified to the class with the smallest distance. The distance between $\mathbf{x}$ and L is described as

$$d = ||\mathbf{x}||^2 - ||\mathrm{P}^\mathrm{T}\mathbf{x}||^2. \tag{1}$$

Since the first term is independent from the class, the discriminant function indicating the membership of $\mathbf{x}$ belonging to $\omega^{(c)}$, can be written as

$$f_\mathrm{c}(\mathbf{x}) = ||\mathrm{P}_\mathrm{c}^\mathrm{T}\mathbf{x}||^2, \qquad \mathrm{c} = 1, \cdots, \mathrm{C} \tag{2}$$

In training stage, the sum of the squared distances between the training samples and the subspace is minimized, *i.e.*, the reconstruction of $\mathbf{x}$

$$\hat{\mathbf{x}} = \sum_{i=1}^{m} y_i \mathbf{p}_\mathrm{i} = \sum_{i=1}^{\mathrm{m}} (\mathbf{x}^\mathrm{T}\mathbf{p}_\mathrm{i})\mathbf{p}_\mathrm{i} \tag{3}$$

will be minimized. This is also equivalent to the maximization of the projection variance in Eqn. (2) and the standard solution is the principal component analysis on the correlation matrix.

3 Kernel PCA and Kernel-Based Subspace Classifier

Subspace classifiers combined with kernel methods have been proposed in [4-5], which are all based on the direct application of Kernel Principal Component Analysis (KPCA) in feature space. KPCA maps all data samples to a higher-dimensional feature space via the so-called kernel trick and then finds the subspace in this transformed space through the PCA for each class separately.

Suppose a high dimensional feature space, F, is related to the input space by the (nonlinear) map $\mathbf{\Phi}(\mathbf{x}) : \mathrm{R}^\mathrm{n} \rightarrow \mathrm{F}$. The map $\mathbf{\Phi}$ and the space F are determined implicitly by the choice of a kernel function k, which computes the dot product between two input examples $\mathbf{x}$ and $\mathbf{y}$ mapped into F via

$$k(\mathbf{x}, \mathbf{y}) = \mathbf{\Phi}(\mathbf{x}) \cdot \mathbf{\Phi}(\mathbf{y}) \tag{4}$$

where $(\cdot)$ is the vector dot product in F. The most commonly used kernel is:

$$k(\mathbf{x}, \mathbf{y}) = \exp\left(-\frac{||\mathbf{x} - \mathbf{y}||}{2\sigma^2}\right) \quad (5)$$

where σ is the width of the kernel. And the space F is called a reproducing kernel Hilbert space (RKHS) generated by k [6]. The input space is then mapped to F in the way that a sample $\mathbf{v}$ is transformed to the kernel function centered on $\mathbf{v}$:

$$\mathbf{v} \rightarrow \mathrm{k}(\mathbf{x}, \mathbf{v})$$

For a set of N patterns $\mathbf{x}_\mathrm{i}$, $i = 1, 2, ...N$ in R^n, the $N \times N$ kernel matrix K can be formed:

$$K_{ij} = k(\mathbf{x}_\mathrm{i}, \mathbf{x}_\mathrm{j}) \quad (6)$$

The kernel matrix K should then be centralized with the result as the estimate of the covariance matrix of the new feature vector in F. Then the linear PCA is simply performed on it by finding a set of principal components in the span of vectors $\{\Phi(\mathbf{x})_\mathrm{r}\}$, which represents the principal axes in the kernel space.

Let $\alpha^k = [\alpha_1^k, \cdots, \alpha_N^k]^T$ be the normalized eigenvectors and $\lambda_1 \leq \cdots \leq \lambda_N$ be the eigenvalues of the matrix K such that $\lambda_k(\alpha^\mathrm{k}, \alpha^\mathrm{k}) = 1$ for all $k = 1, \ldots, N$ where $\lambda_p > 0$. It can be shown that the eigenvectors in F can be expressed as linear combinations of the mapped training samples:

$$\mathbf{v}_\mathrm{k} = \sum_{\mathrm{i}=1}^{\mathrm{N}} \alpha_\mathrm{i}^\mathrm{k} \Phi(\mathrm{x}_\mathrm{i}) \quad (7)$$

with known coefficients α_i^k. For a test data point $\mathbf{x}$ with image $\Phi(\mathbf{x})$ in kernel space, the projection of a mapped point $\Phi(\mathbf{x})$ on the eigenvector $\mathbf{v}_\mathrm{k}$ is therefore given by:

$$\beta_k = (\mathbf{v}_\mathrm{k}, \Phi(\mathbf{x})) = \sum_{\mathrm{i}=1}^{\mathrm{N}} \alpha_\mathrm{i}^\mathrm{k} \mathrm{k}(\mathbf{x}_\mathrm{i}, \mathbf{x}) \quad (8)$$

In RKHS, the conventional subspace classifier can be simply performed by replacing the inner product in Eqn (2) by the one from RKHS [6]. The discriminant function in RKHS can then be described as follows:

$$f_c(\mathbf{x}) = ||\sum_{\mathrm{k}=1}^{\mathrm{r}} \beta_\mathrm{k}||^2 = \sum_{\mathrm{k}=1}^{\mathrm{m}} \sum_{\mathrm{i}=1}^{\mathrm{N}} \alpha_\mathrm{i}^\mathrm{k} \mathrm{k}(\mathbf{x}_\mathrm{i}, \mathbf{x}), \quad (9)$$

where r is the number of principal components in F.

4 Learning Kernel Subspace Classifier in Input Space

The kernel subspace classifier based on Eqn (8) means performing PCA in F with optimal reconstruction of $\Phi(\mathbf{x})$ (the map of a test point $\mathbf{x}$ in F) based on its projections, i.e.,

$$\rho(\mathbf{x}) = ||\mathrm{P_r}\Phi(\mathbf{x}) - \Phi(\mathbf{x})||^2 \tag{10}$$

is minimized for a mapped test point with its projection onto the subspace spanned by the first r eigenvectors:

$$P_r\Phi(\mathbf{x}) = \sum_{\mathrm{k}=1}^{\mathrm{r}} \alpha_{\mathrm{k}}\mathbf{v}_{\mathrm{k}} \tag{11}$$

where P_r is the projection operator in F.

However, distance in Eqn (10) does not give the reconstruction of $\mathbf{x}$ in input space. Consequently, kernel subspace classifier based on Eq (9) or Eq. (10) can not work well, particularly for many classifications in biometrics where the small sample size (SSS) difficulties make the situation worse. For the KPCA to be efficient in data classification, the reconstructed pre-image of $\Phi(\mathbf{x})$ should be as close to $\mathbf{x}$ as possible, following the same principle of PCA.

The subject of data reconstruction has been discussed in the past with the name *data de-noising* or *pre-image* of KPCA [7-9]. That means, we are looking for an explicit vector $\mathbf{z} \in \mathrm{R^n}$ satisfying $\Phi(\mathbf{z}) = \mathrm{Pn}\Phi(\mathbf{x})$. In other words, pre-image concerns the best reconstruction of mapped data in the kernel space and the solution can be approximated by minimizing the squared distance $\rho(\mathbf{z})$ between the Φ-image of a vector $\mathbf{z}$ and the reconstructed pattern in F:

$$\rho(\mathbf{z}) = ||\Phi(\mathbf{z}) - \mathrm{P_n}\Phi(\mathbf{x})||^2 \tag{12}$$

For kernels satisfying $k(\mathbf{x},\mathbf{x}) = \text{const}, \forall\mathbf{x}$, an optimal $\mathbf{z}$ can be determined by an iterative update scheme as follows

$$\mathbf{z}_{\mathrm{t+1}} = \frac{\sum_{\mathrm{i=1}}^{\mathrm{N}} \gamma_{\mathrm{i}}\exp(-||\mathbf{z}_{\mathrm{t}} - \mathbf{x}_{\mathrm{i}}||^2/\mathrm{c})\mathbf{x}_{\mathrm{i}}}{\sum_{\mathrm{i=1}}^{\mathrm{N}} \gamma_{\mathrm{i}}\exp(-||\mathbf{z}_{\mathrm{t}} - \mathbf{x}_{\mathrm{i}}||^2/\mathrm{c})} \tag{13}$$

The popular kernel type which satisfies $k(x;x) = \text{const}$ are, *e.g.*, the RBF kernels. Though Eqn (13) seems applicable with the kernel subspace classifier paradigm, we will empirically prove in Section 5 that it does not work.

While pre-image of KPCA addresses the minimization of reconstruction error in kernel space F, we emphasize the data reconstruction in input space after the KPCA projection, as this will explicitly express the representation capability of the kernel subspace for the data class. We formulated the problem as *learning kernel subspace*, with the objective of minimization of reconstruction error for the input data. The objective can be simply solved based on the kernel principal component regression [3], which define the data reconstruction as a the following regression problem from kernel space:

$$\hat{\mathbf{x}} = \mathbf{\Phi}\xi + \epsilon \tag{14}$$

where $\mathbf{\Phi}$ is an matrix composed of vector $\Phi(\mathbf{x}_{\mathrm{i}})$, ξ is a vector of regression coefficients and ϵ is the error term. Performing PCA on $\mathbf{\Phi}^{\mathrm{T}}\mathbf{\Phi}$ will result in M eigenvalues $\{\lambda_j\}_{j=1}^{M}$ and corresponding eigenvectors $\{\mathbf{V}^{\mathrm{j}}\}_{\mathrm{j=1}}^{\mathrm{M}}$. The projection of the $\mathbf{\Phi}(\mathbf{x})$ onto the k-th principal components is given by Eqn (6). By projecting all the $\mathbf{\Phi}(\mathbf{x})$ onto the principal component, the above equation becomes

$$\hat{\mathbf{x}} = \mathbf{\Psi}\mathbf{w} + \epsilon \tag{15}$$

where $\mathbf{B} = \mathbf{\Phi}\mathbf{V}$ is an $(n \times M)$ matrix and $\mathbf{V}$ is an $(M \times M)$ matrix with $\mathbf{V}^{\mathrm{k}}$ as its $k-$th column. The least squares estimate of the coefficients $\mathbf{w}$ becomes:

$$\hat{\mathbf{w}} = (\mathbf{B}^{\mathrm{T}}\mathbf{B})^{-1}\mathbf{B}^{\mathrm{T}}\mathbf{x} = \mathbf{\Lambda}^{-1}\mathbf{B}^{\mathrm{T}}\mathbf{x} \tag{16}$$

where $\mathbf{\Lambda} = \mathrm{diag}(\lambda_1, \cdots, \lambda_{\mathrm{M}})$.

The proposed model (Eqn. (16)) has been discussed earlier by the author from the point of view of auto-associator model [18], which is a direct result of applying the kernel principal component regression [3]. The classification scheme has proved its efficiency in general face recognition problem [18] and in cancer classification [17]. Formulating the methodology in the framework of kernel subspace classifier not only justifies the model theoretically but also clarifies some confusions arose from recent works on kernelization of subspace classification.

In summary, the kernel subspace classifier model provides a description of the nonlinear relationships between input and features from the kernel space. The model building involves two operations. The first is the kernel operation which transforms an input pattern to a high-dimensional feature space. The second is the mapping of the feature space back to the input space. The proposed kernel subspace classifier proves satisfactory performance on some benchmarking robust face recognition problems, as explained in next section.

5 Experiments

5.1 Experiment with the AR faces

AR faces consist of frontal facial images of 135 subjects (76 male and 59 females), with 26 different images for each subjects. For each subject, the images were recorded in two different sessions separated by two weeks, each session consisting of 13 images. Each image is with 768×576 pixels.

Following the practice in [21, 12], we used the images of 50 subjects (the first 25 males and 25 females). In the pre-processing step, the original images were converted to gray scale, aligned by the eyes, resized, and cropped to size 104×85. In our experiment, the non-screaming and non-occluded images from both sessions were used for the training of each subject's kernel subspace classifier and the remaining occluded images by sunglasses and scarf and images of the screaming expression were used for testing. The first row of Fig. 1 gives examples of training images of the third subject from the AR database, while the second row of Fig 1 contains the test images for the same subject.

Recently, occlusion robust face recognition has attracted much attention and several algorithms have been published. In [15] a Selective Local Nonnegative Matrix Factorization (SL-LNMF) technique was proposed, which includes occlusion detection step and the selective LNMF-based recognition step. Paper

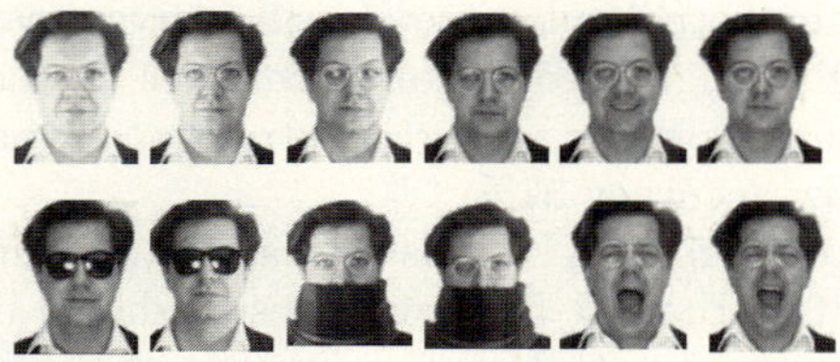

Fig. 1. Sample images from the AR database. First row: training images. Second row: test images with occlusion by sunglasses/scarf, and with screaming expression.

[13] proposed a *Face-ARG matching* scheme in which a line feature based Face-ARG model is used to describe face images. Based on robust estimation, [14] propounded a classification method that combines reconstructive and discriminative models. For brief, we term it as Reconstructive and Discriminative Subspace model (RDS). These published recognition performances on the AR face are compared in the Table 1. It is worthy to note that the experiment settings from these publications are not exactly same as us except the RDS in [14]. Therefore the comparison can only give an intuitive meaning.

Table 1. Comparison of the recognition accuracies

	RDS	IS-ICA	S-LNMF	Face-ARG	Pre-image	Kernel Subspace
sunglasses	84%	65%	90%	80.7%	50%	**92%**
scarf	93%	NA	92%	85.2%	13%	**51%**
scream	87%	NA	44%	66.7%	43%	**95%**

Figure 2 further explains the works of the proposed method. The first column displays the probe images from sunglasses/scarf occluded faces and the screaming face. The images from second column to sixth column are the first five best reconstructed images from the corresponding probe by applying the kernel subspace classifier. It can be observed that for sunglasses occluded face

Fig. 2. Reconstruction of probe images from the kernel subspace classifier. First column: probe images; Second column to sixth column are the first five best reconstructed images from the corresponding probe image.

and screaming face, the kernel subspace classifier gives reasonably good reconstructions, thus yielding high recognition accuracies as shown in Table 1. For the scarf occluded face, however, the reconstruction is pretty poor, which is consistent with the low accuracy 51%.

As the pre-image problem of KPCA is relevant to the kernel subspace classifier, we also applied it to the AR faces with result shown in Table 1. The poor performance is in agreement with the visualization of the reconstructed images from the three kind of probe face images, as illustrated in Fig. 3.

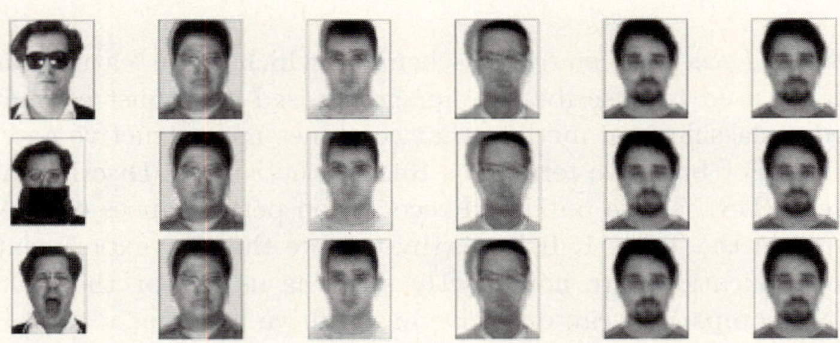

Fig. 3. Reconstruction of probe images from the pre-image algorithm Eqn. (13). First column: probe images; Second column to sixth column are the first five best reconstructed images from the corresponding probe image.

5.2 Experiment with the UPC Faces

In the second experiment, we used the UPC faces data provided by Universitat Politecnica de Catalunya [16], which was created for the purpose of testing the robustness of face recognition algorithms against strong occlusion, pose and illumination variations. This database includes a total of 18 persons with 27 pictures per person which correspond to different pose views. In our experiment, we chose 8 near-front images per person for training while used occluded images for testing, with occlusions from sunglasses or hands, as illustrated in the following Figure 4.

We tested the recognition performances on two different occlusions. The first is sunglasses occlusion which is similar to the AR face scenario. The second is occlusion by hand as shown in right of Fig. 4. The recognition accuracies from our proposed kernel subspace are 80% and 86% respectively. Figure 5 illustrated the corresponding reconstructed images from the two probe faces. As a comparison, the recognition accuracies from the pre-image algorithm are 43% and 47%, which shows again its unacceptability in kernel subspace classification.

Fig. 4. Left: training samples from the UPC data set; Right: some of the testing mages

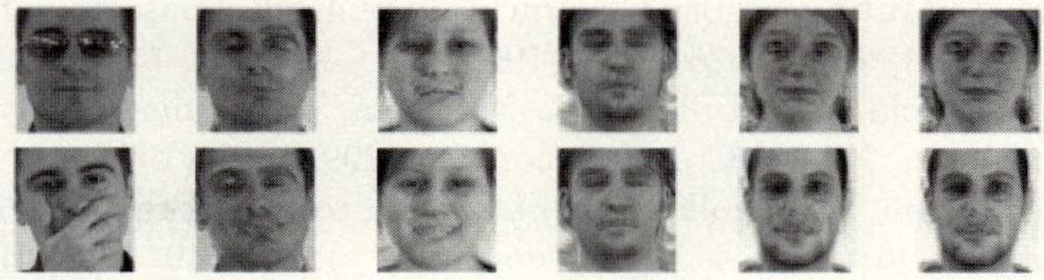

Fig. 5. First column: probe images; Second column to sixth column are the first five best reconstructed images from the corresponding probe

Table 2. Comparison of the recognition accuracies

	Pre-image	Kernel Subspace
sunglass	43%	**80%**
others	47%	**86%**

6 Conclusion

In this paper, a new kernel subspace classifier algorithm is proposed which is based on the KPCA image reconstruction in input space after the KPCA projection. With the objective of minimizing the reconstruction error in the input space, the least square regression is applied to map the KPCA projection from the implicit feature space to the input space. Our experiments on some occluded face recognition problems using the AR face and UPC face show very encouraging performance, which also compare favorably with some very complex occlusion robust face recognition methods proposed in recent years.

Acknowledgement

This research was supported by the MIC(Ministry of Information and Communication), Korea, Under the ITFSIP (IT Foreign Specialist Inviting Program) supervised by the IITA (Institute of Information Technology Assessment).

References

1. Oja, E.: Subspace Methods of Pattern Recognition. Research Studies Press, Letchworth and J.Wiley (1983)
2. Laaksonen, J., Oja, E.: Subspace Dimension Selection and Averaged Learning Subspace Method in Handwritten Digit Recognition. In: Vorbrüggen, J.C., von Seelen, W., Sendhoff, B. (eds.) Artificial Neural Networks - ICANN 96. LNCS, vol. 1112, pp. 227–232. Springer, Heidelberg (1996)
3. Rosipal, R., Girolami, M., Trejo, L., Cichocki, A.: Kernel PCA for Feature Extraction and De-Noising in Non-linear Regression. Neural Computing & Applications 10, 231–243 (2001)
4. Tsuda, K.: Subspace classifier in the Hilbert Space. Pattern Recognition Letters 20, 513–519 (1999)

5. Maeda, E., et al.: Multi-category Classification by Kernel based Nonlinear Subspace Method. ICASSP 1999 2, 1025–1028 (1999)
6. Scholkopf, B., Smola, A.: Muller K-R. Nonlinear component analysis as a kernel eigenvalue problem. Neural Computation 10, 1299–1319 (1998)
7. Bakir, G.H., Weston, J., Scholkopf, B.: Learning to Find Pre-Images. In: Advances in Neural Information Processing Systems, vol. 16, pp. 449–456. MIT Press, Cambridge, MA, USA (2004)
8. Mika, S., Scholkopf, B., Smola, A., Muller, K., Scholz, M., Ratsch, G.: Kernel PCA and De-Noising in Feature Spaces. In: Proc.1998 conference on Advances in neural information processing systems II, pp. 536–542. MIT Press, Cambridge, MA, USA (1998)
9. Scholkopf, B., Smola, A., Muller, K.: Kernel principal component analysis. In: Scholkopf, B., Burges, C.J.C., Smola, A.J. (eds.) Advances in Kernel Methods - SV Learning, pp. 327–352. MIT Press, Cambridge, MA. USA (1999)
10. Rosipal, R., Trejo, L.: Kernel Partial Least Squares Regression in Reproducing Kernel Hilbert Space. Journal of Machine Learning Research 2, 97–123 (2001)
11. Kim, J., Choi, J., Yi, J., Turk, M.: Effective Representation Using ICA for Face Recognition Robust to Local Distortion and Partial Occlusion. IEEE Trans. PAMI 27, 1977–1981 (2005)
12. Martinez, A., Kak, A.: PCA versus LDA. IEEE Trans. PAMI 23, 228–233 (2001)
13. Park, B., Lee, K., Lee, S.: Face Recognition Using Face-ARG Matching. IEEE Trans. PAMI 27, 1982–1988 (2005)
14. Fidler, S., Skocaj, D., Leonardis, A.: Combining Reconstructive and Discriminative Subspace Methods for Robust Classification and Regression by Subsampling. IEEE Trans. PAMI 28, 337–350 (2006)
15. Oh, H., Lee, K., Lee, S.: Occlusion invariant face recognition using selective LNMF basis images. In: Narayanan, P.J., Nayar, S.K., Shum, H.-Y. (eds.) ACCV 2006. LNCS, vol. 3851, pp. 120–129. Springer, Heidelberg (2006)
16. UPC Face Database: `http://gps-tsc.upc.es/GTAV`
17. Zhang, B.: Cancer Classification by Kernel Principal Component Self-regression. In: Australian Conf. on Artificial Intelligence 2006, Horbat, Australia, pp. 719–728 (2006)
18. Zhang, B.: Kernel Auto-associator from Kernel Principal Component Autoregression with Application to Face Recognition. In: Proc. Int'l Conf. Comput. Inte. for Modeling, Control & Automation (CIMCA) 2005, Vienna, pp. 15–19 (2005)

A New Approach to Fake Finger Detection Based on Skin Elasticity Analysis

Jia Jia, Lianhong Cai, Kaifu Zhang, and Dawei Chen

Key Laboratory of Pervasive Computing (Tsinghua University), Ministry of Education
Beijing 100084, P.R. China
jiajia@mails.tsinghua.edu.cn,
clh-dcs@tsinghua.edu.cn,
zkf03@mails.tsinghua.edu.cn,
RunningOn9@gmail.com

Abstract. This work introduces a new approach to fake finger detection, based on the analysis of human skin elasticity. When a user puts a finger on the scanner surface, a sequence of fingerprint images which describes the finger deformation process is captured. Then two features which represent the skin elasticity are extracted from the image sequence: 1) the correlation coefficient of the fingerprint area and the signal intensity; 2) the standard deviation of the fingerprint area extension in x and y axes. Finally the Fisher Linear Discriminant is used to discriminate the finger skin from other materials such as gelatin. The experiments carried out on a dataset of real and fake fingers show that the proposed approach and features are effective in fake finger detection.

1 Introduction

Fingerprint authentication (verification/identification) is one of the most important biometric technologies [1]. A fingerprint is the pattern of ridges and valleys (furrows) on the surface of the finger. As the fingerprint of a person is unique and immutable, the automatic fingerprint authentication system can be widely used in both anti-criminal and civilian applications. However, the security of fingerprint scanners has been questioned. Previous studies have shown that fingerprint scanners can be fooled with artificial fingerprints, i.e. copies of real fingerprints [2, 3]. Some approaches have been recently presented to deal with the above problem which is often referred to as "fake finger detection", i.e. the discrimination of a fake fingerprint from real ones [4, 5, 6]. Some of them use extra hardware to acquire life signs such as epidermis temperature, pulse oximetry, blood pressure and electric resistance [2, 5, 7]. Unfortunately, due to the inherent variability of such characteristics, the performance achieved by most of these methods is not satisfactory [6]. Furthermore, the equipments are usually expensive. Another fake finger detection method has been recently proposed in [8]. The user is required to move the finger once it touches the scanner surface, and a sequence of DistortionCodes [9] is captured from the fingerprint frames acquired during the finger movement and further analyzed to determine the nature of the finger. However, the way how the images are acquired is not user friendly.

S.-W. Lee and S.Z. Li (Eds.): ICB 2007, LNCS 4642, pp. 309–318, 2007.

This paper introduces a novel approach which is based on the elasticity analysis of human skin. When a user puts a finger on the scanner surface as normal fingerprint authentication system required, a sequence of fingerprint images which describes the finger deformation process is captured (explained by Fig. 1). Two features representing the skin elasticity are extracted from the image sequence. As fake finger detection is actually a two-class classification problem, the Fisher Linear Discriminant [10] is finally used to label the feature vectors with "real" or "fake".

Fig. 1. A sequence of fingerprint images which describes the deformation of a real finger

The proposed approach has the following advantages: 1) the sequence of fingerprint images used for fake finger detection is also used for fingerprint authentication. The whole sequence is used for fake finger detection while one or more of them can be used for fingerprint authentication. It's an effective way to prevent the attacker from using artificial fingerprint and real fingerprint for fake finger detection and authentication steps respectively; 2) the way how the image sequences are acquired is user friendly. The approach requires no extra hardware or special finger movement. The experiments carried out on a dataset of real and fake fingers show that the proposed approach and features are effective in fake finger detection.

The rest of this paper is organized as follows. Section 2 introduces the related work. And section 3 describes the proposed approach in detail. In section 4, we give the experimental results and discussion. Finally, we wrap up with the conclusions and future work in section 5.

2 Related Work

Fake finger detection in a fingerprint authentication system means the capability for the system to detect, during enrollment and authentication, whether the fingerprint presented is alive or not [11]. Fake finger detection can be performed either at the fingerprint acquisition stage, or at the fingerprint processing stage [12].

There are essentially three different ways to introduce liveness detection into a biometric system [5]:

- Using extra hardware to acquire life signs [3, 6, 13]. In this way, the liveness detection takes place at the acquisition stage.
- Using the information already captured by the system to detect life signs [7, 8, 14]. In this way, the liveness detection takes place at the processing stage.
- Using liveness information inherent to the biometric [15].

The first way introduces a few other problems: 1) it is expensive; 2) it is bulky; and 3) it could still be possible to present the artificial fingerprint to the fingerprint scanner and the real fingerprint of the intruder to the hardware that detects liveness. Also, in some cases it is still possible to fool the additional hardware with a wafer-thin artificial fingerprint. The second method does not have these disadvantages, except maybe that it is a bit more complicated to extract the life signs using no additional hardware. Furthermore, special finger movement is usually required to acquire life signs in this kind of methods. The third method is not applicable to fingerprint recognition. Other biometric systems including face recognition, gait recognition, etc. use this however. These technologies are not widely implemented and still need to be validated as reliable biometric identifiers [11, 15].

The proposed approach performs fake finger detection at the image processing stage. We adopt the second way which uses the information already captured by the system to detect life signs. No special finger movement is required in our approach.

3 A New Approach to Fake Finger Detection

When a user puts a finger on the scanner surface, our scanner captures a sequence of fingerprint images at a certain frame rate. For example, when the frame rate is 20 fps (frames per second) and the capturing duration is 1.5s, the image number of every sequence is 30. The image sequence is used for fake finger detection. One or more of them can be used for fingerprint authentication. Let $\{F_1, F_2, \ldots\ldots, Fn\}$ be the sequence of n images. For each image sequence, we compute two features:(1) the correlation coefficient of the fingerprint area and the average signal intensity; (2) the standard deviation of the fingerprint area extension in x and y axes. Finally the Fisher Linear Discriminant is used to determining the final "real" or "fake" results.

In order to show the ability of the presented two features in discriminating fake fingers from real ones, we used one-way analysis of variance□ANOVA□and Multiple Comparison Method to do the statistical tests on the dataset of real and fake fingers. As the material humidity has great effects on the elasticity of fake fingers and the signal intensity of gray-level image, we collected 4 different data groups in ANOVA and Multiple Comparison tests:

- R Real finger group (Real): 30 real fingers;
- Wet gelatin fake finger group (Wet): 47 gelatin fake fingers with high humidity;
- Medium gelatin fake finger group (Medium): 47 gelatin fake fingers with normal humidity;
- Dry gelatin fake finger group (Dry): 47 gelatin fake fingers with low humidity.

We used capacitive scanner Veridicom FPS200 to record the image sequences. For each finger, only one image sequence was recorded. The humidity of different groups of fake fingers compared with real ones is shown in Table 1.

Table 1. The humidity of fake fingers compared with real ones

	Wet gelatin	Medium gelatin	Dry gelatin
Humidity	>> Real	Approximately = Real	< Real

3.1 Computing the Correlation Coefficient of Fingerprint Area and Signal Intensity

For a sequence $\{F_i\,(i=1, 2,\ldots\ldots, n)\}$, the following steps are performed on each frame $F_i\,(i=1, 2,\ldots\ldots, n)$:

Extracting the fingerprint area: let $S_i\,(i=1, 2,\ldots\ldots, n)$ represents the fingerprint area of $F_i\,(i=1, 2,\ldots\ldots, n)$. We first divide F_i into blocks of size $w\times w$ (16×16). The variance of each block is computed by Eq.1.

$$VAR = \frac{1}{w^2}\sum_{i=0}^{w-1}\sum_{j=0}^{w-1}(I(i,j) - M)^2,\quad M = \frac{1}{w^2}\sum_{i=0}^{w-1}\sum_{j=0}^{w-1}I(i,j) \tag{1}$$

where $I(i, j)$ represents the intensity (0-255) of the pixel at the ith row and jth column in one block. M represents the mean value of the block intensity. The fingerprint area S_i is obtained by Eq.2.

$$S_i = N_i \times w \times w \tag{2}$$

where N_i is the number of blocks whose VAR is greater than a certain threshold.

Computing the average signal intensity of the fingerprint area: the average signal intensity $AvgInt_i\,(i=1, 2,\ldots\ldots, n)$ of the fingerprint area is computed by Eq.3.

$$AvgInt_i = \sum_{I(x,y)>\varepsilon} I(x,y)/S_i \tag{3}$$

where $I(x, y)$ is the intensity of the pixel in fingerprint area of F_i.$\varepsilon$is a threshold which is used to separate the pixels in fingerprint area from the ones in background.

Let $Corr$ represents the correlation coefficient of the fingerprint area $\boldsymbol{S}=\{S_i\}$ $(i=1,2,\ldots\ldots, n)$ and the signal intensity $\boldsymbol{AvgInt}=\{AvgInt_i\}(i=1,2,\ldots\ldots, n)$. The $Corr$ is obtained by Eq.4.

$$Corr(\boldsymbol{S},\boldsymbol{AvgInt}) = \frac{Cov(\boldsymbol{S},\boldsymbol{AvgInt})}{\sqrt{D(\boldsymbol{S})\times D(\boldsymbol{AvgInt})}} \tag{4}$$

where $Cov(\boldsymbol{X}, \boldsymbol{Y})$ is the covariance of $\boldsymbol{X}$ and $\boldsymbol{Y}$, and $D(\boldsymbol{X})$ is the squared deviation of $\boldsymbol{X}$.

The signal intensity captured by a capacitive sensor is effected by to two factors: the pressing pressure and the humidity of finger skin (or other materials). For a real finger, with the increase of pressure, the fingerprint area S and the signal intensity $AvgInt$ increases both, which means they have a positive correlation. Fig. 2 shows the relation of S and $AvgInt$ of a real finger and a gelatin finger. For real finger, with the increase of fingerprint area from 3.5 to 5.5 ($\times 10^4$), the average intensity monotonically increases from 100 to 170. But for fake finger, with the increase of fingerprint area, the average intensity presents a random fluctuation, which means they have no obvious correlation.

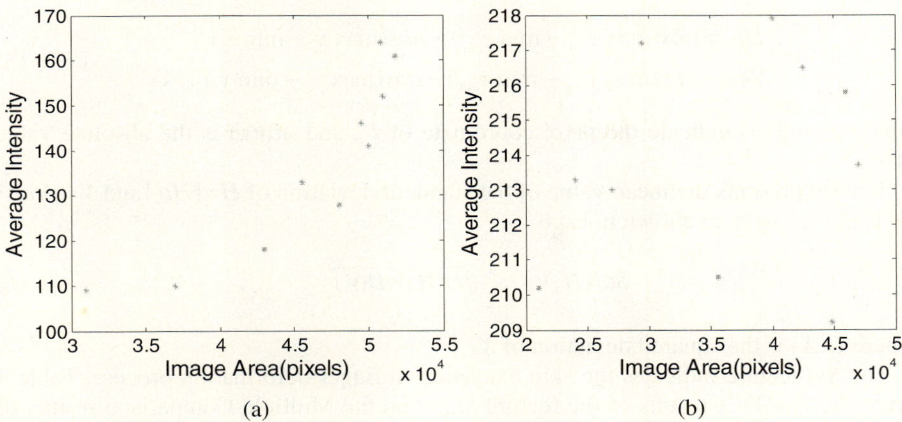

Fig. 2. The average intensity as a function of the fingerprint area. (a) a real finger, (b) a gelatin finger.

Table 2 gives the ANOVA results of the feature *Corr*. The Multiple Comparison results of *Corr* are shown in Fig.3(a). The p value of ANOVA is 2.77e-008, which indicates that this feature is effective in discriminating samples of different groups. The Multiple Comparison results shows that although the humidity of the finger skin (or other materials) can affect the image signal intensity, the *Corr* value can still clearly separate the real finger group from other three fake finger groups.

Table 2. ANOVA Table of feature *Corr*

ANOVA Table			
Source[1]	Groups	Error	Total
SS	15.1235	22.6909	37.8144
d.f.	3	74	77
MS	5.0412	0.30663	
F	16.4403		
p>F	2.77e-008		

3.2 Computing the Standard Deviation of Fingerprint Area Extension in x and y Axes

For each frame F_i and its next frame F_{i+1} in a image sequence $\{F_i\ (i=1, 2,\ldots\ldots, n)\}$, we compute the fingerprint area extension Ho_i (i=1, 2,……, n-1) in x axis and Ver_i (i=1, 2,……, n-1) in y axis, shown in Eq.5.

[1] The notations in ANOVA: 1. SS: Sum of Squares; 2. d.f.: degrees of freedom; 3. MS: Mean Square; 4. F ratio = (found variation of the group averages)/ (expected variation of the group averages); 5. p: probability.

$$Ho_i = abs(\max x_{i+1} - \min x_{i+1}) - abs(\max x_i - \min x_i)$$
$$Ver_i = abs(\max y_{i+1} - \min y_{i+1}) - abs(\max y_i - \min y_i) \quad (5)$$

where x_i and y_i indicate the pixel coordinate of F_i, and $abs(x)$ is the absolute value of x.

Let *Std* presents the mean value of the standard deviation of $\boldsymbol{H}=\{Ho_i\}$and $\boldsymbol{V}=\{Ver_i\}$ (i=1,2,……, n-1), as shown in Eq.6.

$$Std(\boldsymbol{H},\boldsymbol{V}) = \frac{1}{2}\sqrt{D(\boldsymbol{H}) \times D(\boldsymbol{V})} \quad (6)$$

where $D(\boldsymbol{X})$ is the squared deviation of $\boldsymbol{X}$.

The *Std* feature indicates the skin extension in finger deformation process. Table 3 gives the ANOVA results of the feature *Std*. And the Multiple Comparison results of *Std* are shown in Fig.3(b). The p value of ANOVA is 0.0062, which indicates this *Std* feature can discriminate fake fingers from real ones for most cases. But it has a lower discriminating ability than feature *Corr*. The Multiple Comparison results shows that the *Std* feature can clearly separate the real finger group from medium/dry fake finger groups, while it still has limitation in discriminating the real finger group and the wet fake finger group.

Table 3. ANOVA Table of feature *Std*

ANOVA Table			
Source	Groups	Error	Total
SS	351.88	1946.27	2298.14
d.f.	3	74	77
MS	117.292	26.301	
F	4.46		
p>F	0.0062		

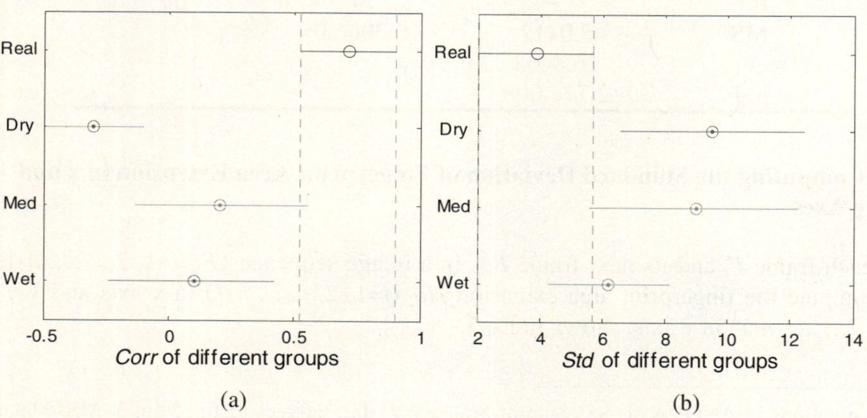

Fig. 3. The Multiple Comparison results in four different groups. (a)feature Corr, (b)feature Std.

3.3 Determining Results by the Fisher Linear Discriminant

We define a 2-tuple vector V=(*Corr*, *Std*) to describe the elasticity features of each sequence. Where *Corr* is the correlation coefficient of the fingerprint area $\boldsymbol{S}=\{S_i\}$ (i=1,2,……, n) and the average signal intensity $\boldsymbol{AvgInt}=\{AvgInt_i\}(i=1,2,\ldots\ldots,n)$; *Std* is the mean value of the standard squares of $\boldsymbol{H}=\{Ho_i\}$and $\boldsymbol{V}=\{Ver_i\}$ (i=1,2,……, n-1).

As fake finger detection is actually a two-class classification problem, the Fisher Linear Discriminant is chosen as the classifier. The Fisher Linear Discriminant is a classification method that projects high-dimensional data onto a line and performs classification in this one-dimensional space. The projection maximizes the distance between the means of the two groups while minimizing the variance within each group. The decision function of the Fisher Linear Discriminant is explained by Eq.7.

$$\begin{aligned} Group(\boldsymbol{X}) &= \text{real finger} \quad \text{for } \boldsymbol{W} \times \boldsymbol{X} + b >= c \\ &= \text{fake finger} \quad \text{for } \boldsymbol{W} \times \boldsymbol{X} + b < c \end{aligned} \tag{7}$$

where b is a constant, c is the threshold and W is the regression coefficients matrix.

The flowchart of our fake finger detection approach is shown as Fig. 4. This paper focuses on the parts with gray-background.

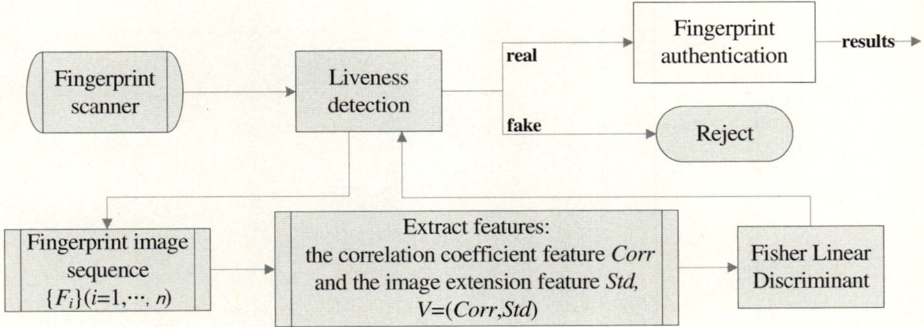

Fig. 4. A flowchart showing different phases of our approach

4 Experiments and Discussion

In this section we describe some experiments to evaluate the presented fake fingerprint detection approach.

4.1 Datasets

In order to evaluate the proposed approach, a dataset of image sequences was collected. The dataset was acquired from 15 volunteers, all of whom were graduates of the Computer Science and Technology Department, Tsinghua University. For real fingerprints, two fingers were collected from each volunteer; ten image sequences were recorded for each real finger. For fake fingerprints, 47 fake fingers were manufactured, all of which were made of gelatin and had medium humidity; ten image sequences were recorded for each fake finger. The total number of the image sequences is 770. And the image sequences were acquired using the capacitive fingerprint scanner "Veridicom Fps200", which produces 250×300 fingerprint images at 500 DPI.

Table 4. The information of dataset

	Different fingers/ Image sequences	Sensors	Image size	Resolution
Real fingerprint	30/300	capacitive sensor	250×300	500 dpi
Fake fingerprint	47/470	capacitive sensor	250×300	500 dpi

4.2 Measures

Let FAR (False Accept Rate) be the proportion of fake fingers that are incorrectly accepted, and FRR (False Reject Rate) be the proportion of real fingers that are incorrectly rejected. The EER (that is the value such that FRR =FAR) is reported as a performance indicator. Note that FAR and FRR do not include verification/identification errors. The configuration of the running computer is Pentium 2.60 GHz, 1.00GB.

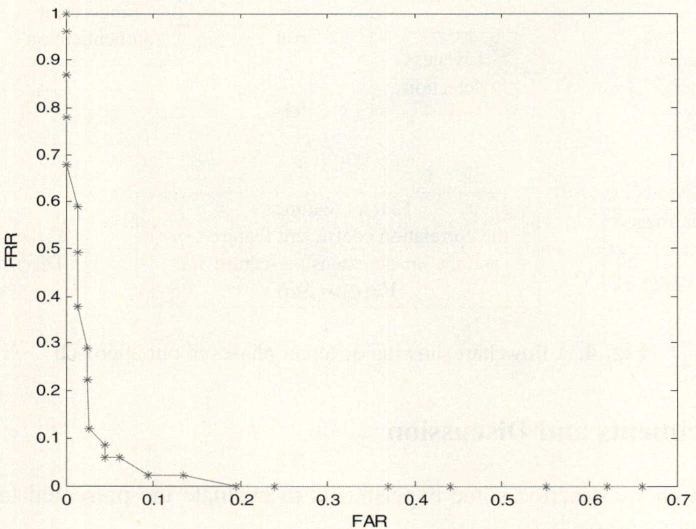

Fig. 5. The FRR as a function of FAR of the proposed approach

Table 5. The experimental result for fake finger detection of different systems

	Fake finger detection by odor analysis	Fake finger detection based on skin distortion	Our approach
EER	7.48%	4.90%	4.78%

4.3 Experimental Results and Discussion

For each fingerprint image sequence, we extracted the features and used the Fisher Linear Discriminant to determine the final results. In our experiments, the dataset was divided into two parts: a set (400 sequences, from 15 real fingers and 25 fake fingers) used for training the classification models; and a test set (370 sequences, from the other 15 real fingers and 22 fake fingers) used to measure the performance. We change the threshold parameter of the Fisher Linear Discriminant ($\boldsymbol{W} \times \boldsymbol{X} + b > c$, changed c) to get the FRR as a function of FAR. The experimental result is shown in Fig.5. And the EER of the proposed approach measured in the above described experimentation was 4.78%. The experimental results strongly suggest that the presented features and approach are effective in discriminating fake fingers from real ones. Although it is not fair to compare our approach with other fake finger detection systems due to the difference in experimental datasets, we also list the experimental results of three different systems in Table 5. The first system uses extra hardware to capture the odor signal to discriminate the finger skin odor from that of other materials [6]. The second system requires user to move the finger once it touches the scanner surface; and uses a sequence of DistortionCodes to determine the nature of the finger [8]. Obviously it is impossible for our approach to use the same datasets with the other two systems.

5 Conclusion

Our main contributions to fake finger detection are: 1) proposing a software-based fake finger detection approach. The approach uses a user friendly way to acquire a sequence of fingerprint images for each finger. The features are extracted from the image sequences and further analyzed by Fisher Linear Discriminant to determine the nature of the finger; 2) proposing two features representing the skin elasticity: the correlation coefficient of the fingerprint area and the average image signal intensity, and the standard deviation of the fingerprint area extension in x and y axes. The features have strong ability in discriminating the fake fingers from real ones. The experimental results show that the proposed features and approach are effective in fake finger detection.

Future work may include: acquiring a larger dataset to evaluate the performance of the proposed approach, and investigating more features that represent the skin elasticity.

Acknowledgements

This research was supported by China National Natural Science Foundation (60433030, 60418012), and the Special Funds for Major State Basic Research Program of China (973 Program) (No. 2006CB303101). And we would like to thank reviewers for their kindly review and helpful comments for this paper.

References

1. Newham, E.: The Biometric Report. SJB Services, New York (1995)
2. Matsumoto, T., Matsumoto, H., Yamada, K., Hoshino, S.: Impact of Artificial "Gummy" Fingers on Fingerprint Systems. In: Proceeding of SPIE, Optical Security and Counterfeit Deterrence Techniques IV, vol. 4677, pp. 275–289 (2002)
3. Putte, T.v.D., Keuning, J.: Biometrical Fingerprint Recognition: Don't Get Your Fingers Burned. In: Proceeding of IFIP TC8/WG8.8 Fourth Working Conference on Smart Card Research and Advanced Applications, pp. 289–303 (2000)
4. Derakhshani, R., Schuckers, S.A.C., Hornak, L., O'Gorman, L.: Determination of Vitality from a Non-invasive Biomedical Measurement for Use in Fingerprint Scanners. Pattern Recognition 36(2), 383–396 (2003)
5. Schuckers, S.A.C.: Spoofing and Anti-spoofing Measures. Information Security Technical Report 7(4), 56–62 (2002)
6. Baldisserra, D., Franco, A., Maio, D., Maltoni, D.: Fake Fingerprint Detection by Odor Analysis. In: Zhang, D., Jain, A.K. (eds.) Advances in Biometrics. LNCS, vol. 3832, pp. 265–272. Springer, Heidelberg (2005)
7. Parthasaradhi, S.T.V., Derakhshani, R., Hornak, L.A., Schuckers, S.A.C.: Time-Series Detection of Perspiration as a Liveness Test in Fingerprint Devices. IEEE Transactions on Systems, Man, and Cybernetics-Part C:Applications and Reviews 35(3) (2005)
8. Antonelli, A., Cappelli, R., Maio, D., Maltoni, D.: A New Approach to Fake Finger Detection Based on Skin Distortion. In: Zhang, D., Jain, A.K. (eds.) Advances in Biometrics. LNCS, vol. 3832, pp. 221–228. Springer, Heidelberg (2005)
9. Cappelli, R., Maio, D., Maltoni, D.: Modeling Plastic Distortion in Fingerprint Images. In: Singh, S., Murshed, N., Kropatsch, W.G. (eds.) ICAPR 2001. LNCS, vol. 2013, pp. 369–376. Springer, Heidelberg (2001)
10. Fisher, R.A.: The Use of Multiple Measurements in Taxonomic Problems. Annals of Eugenics 7(partII), 179–188 (1936)
11. Sandstrom, M.: Liveness Detection in Fingerprint Recognition Systems. Master thesis (2004), http://www.ep.liu.se/exjobb/isy/2004/3557/exjobb.pdf
12. International Biometric Group: Optical-silicon-ultrasound. White paper (2004), Available at http://www.biometricgroup.com/reports/public/reports/finger-scan optsilult.html
13. Lapsley, P.D., Lee, J.A., Pare Jr., D.F., Hoffman, N.: Anti-fraud biometric sensor that accurately detects blood flow. SmartTouch, LLC., US Patent #5737439 (April 1998)
14. Maltoni, D., Maio, D., Jain, A.K., Prabhakar, S.: Handbook of Fingerprint Recognition. Springer, New York (2003)
15. Woodward Jr., J.D., Orlands, N.M., Higgins, P.T.: Biometrics: Identity assurance in the information age. McGraw-Hill/Osborne, Berkeley, California, USA (2003)

An Algorithm for Biometric Authentication Based on the Model of Non–Stationary Random Processes

Vladimir B. Balakirsky, Anahit R. Ghazaryan, and A.J. Han Vinck

Institute for Experimental Mathematics, Ellernstr. 29, 45326 Essen, Germany
v_b_balakirsky@rambler.ru, a_ghazaryan@rambler.ru, vinck@iem.uni-due.de

Abstract. We present a biometric authentication algorithm with 3 possible outputs: accept the claimed identity, reject the claimed identity, and no answer. The algorithm is based on the model of non–stationary random processes and transformations of realizations of the processes to q-ary vectors whose components are uniformly distributed over the set $\{0, \ldots, q-1\}$, where q is fixed. An application of the algorithm brings the false acceptance and the false rejection rates that do not depend on the probability distribution over the templates space and exponentially decrease with the number of independent biometric parameters available to an observer.

1 Introduction

There are many situations where an object is characterized by some list of parameters of different nature. Examples include biometric measurements when the list can consist of the height of the person, the color of hairs, the weight, etc. [1]. These parameters are written in a vector and stored in a database under the name of the person. The claimed identity of a person is then checked by comparison of the vector consisting of results of his measurements and the corresponding vector fetched from the database. The difficulties of organizing such a procedure are caused by the fact that independent measurements of the same parameter of a person usually bring different results. Therefore one has to develop criteria that specify contributions of non-equal components of two vectors to the binary decision: the claimed identity should be either accepted or rejected.

By the point that components of two vectors under considerations are measured in different units, one has to find an artificial space where results of two measurements can be compared. We develop mathematical model of non-stationary random processes assuming that components are outcomes of random experiments with specified probability density functions (PDF's). Different components are assumed to be independent. The PDF also determines the probability distribution function (PD) whose value belongs to the interval $[0, 1]$ for any PDF. This observation allows us to unify parameters: the value of each parameter is considered as the argument of the corresponding PD and it is replaced by the value of function.

S.-W. Lee and S.Z. Li (Eds.): ICB 2007, LNCS 4642, pp. 319–327, 2007.

Our analysis of the approach above is presented via evaluation of the false acceptance and the false rejection rates, where the false acceptance rate is the probability that the claimed identity is accepted while people are different, and the false rejection rate is the probability that the claimed identity is not accepted while parameters are measured for the same person. The basic result is the point that our approach guarantees these rates to be exponentially decreasing functions with the number of parameters under certain conditions. Furthermore, we prove a universal estimate on the false rejection rate that does not depend on the PDF's of parameters.

2 Statement of the Problem and a General Authentication Algorithm

We will use notation of probability theory where capital letters denote random variables and random processes.

Let $\mathbf{X} = (X^{(1)}, \ldots, X^{(n)})$ and $\mathbf{Y} = (Y^{(1)}, \ldots, Y^{(n)})$ be random processes, where $(X^{(1)}, Y^{(1)}), \ldots, (X^{(n)}, Y^{(n)})$ are independent pairs of random variables. Suppose that the PDF's of random variables $X^{(t)}$ and $Y^{(t)}$ be given as functions $f_{\mathrm{x}}^{(t)}$ and $f_{\mathrm{y}}^{(t)}$ in such a way that the PD's

$$F_{\mathrm{x}}^{(t)}(x) \triangleq \int_{-\infty}^{x} f_{\mathrm{x}}^{(t)}(x')dx', \;\; F_{\mathrm{x}}^{(t)}(y) \triangleq \int_{-\infty}^{y} f_{\mathrm{y}}^{(t)}(y')dy'$$

are strictly increasing functions over the set R. This property will be indicated as $F_{\mathrm{x}}^{(t)}, F_{\mathrm{y}}^{(t)} \in \mathcal{F}$, where $F_{\mathrm{x}}^{(t)} = (F_{\mathrm{x}}^{(t)}(x), x \in \mathsf{R})$ and $F_{\mathrm{y}}^{(t)} = (F_{\mathrm{y}}^{(t)}(y), y \in \mathsf{R})$.

Let $f_{\mathrm{y|x}}^{(t)}(y|x), x, y \in \mathsf{R}$, be introduced as a kernel of the integral transformation

$$\int_{\mathsf{R}} f_{\mathrm{x}}^{(t)}(x) f_{\mathrm{y|x}}^{(t)}(y|x)dx = f_{\mathrm{y}}^{(t)}(y), \;\; \text{for all } y \in \mathsf{R}, \tag{1}$$

and let

$$F_{\mathrm{y|x}}^{(t)}(y|x) \triangleq \int_{-\infty}^{y} f_{\mathrm{y|x}}^{(t)}(y'|x)dy', \;\; y \in \mathsf{R},$$

denote the conditional PD for all $x \in \mathsf{R}$.

Suppose that $\mathbf{x} = (x^{(1)}, \ldots, x^{(n)}) \in \mathsf{R}^n$ and $\mathbf{y} = (y^{(1)}, \ldots, y^{(n)}) \in \mathsf{R}^n$ are realizations of the processes $\mathbf{X}$ and $\mathbf{Y}$. Denote

$$\begin{aligned} &\Big(f_{\mathrm{x}}(\mathbf{x}), f_{\mathrm{y}}(\mathbf{y}), f_{\mathrm{y|x}}(\mathbf{y}|\mathbf{x}) \Big) \\ &\triangleq \Big(\prod_{t=1}^{n} f_{\mathrm{x}}^{(t)}(x^{(t)}), \; \prod_{t=1}^{n} f_{\mathrm{y}}^{(t)}(y^{(t)}), \; \prod_{t=1}^{n} f_{\mathrm{y|x}}^{(t)}(y^{(t)}|x^{(t)}) \Big), \end{aligned} \tag{2}$$

and formulate two problems.

I: Is it true that $\mathbf{x}$ and $\mathbf{y}$ are realizations of independent processes and the value of the joint PDF is expressed as $f_{\mathrm{x}}(\mathbf{x}) f_{\mathrm{y}}(\mathbf{y})$? The question corresponds to the case when the vector $\mathbf{x}$ contains biometrics of a person from the database, and the vector $\mathbf{y}$ contains biometrics of a person chosen at random.

D: Is it true that $\mathbf{x}$ and $\mathbf{y}$ are realizations of dependent processes and the value of the joint PDF is expressed as $f_{\mathrm{x}}(\mathbf{x})f_{\mathrm{y}|\mathrm{x}}(\mathbf{y}|\mathbf{x})$? The question corresponds to the case when the vector $\mathbf{y}$ contains a noisy version of biometrics $\mathbf{x}$ of some person from the database.

General solutions to the **I/D** problems can be specified by sets $\mathcal{I}, \mathcal{D} \subset \mathsf{R}^n \times \mathsf{R}^n$. The answers are positive if $(\mathbf{x}, \mathbf{y}) \in \mathcal{I}$ and $(\mathbf{x}, \mathbf{y}) \in \mathcal{D}$ in the **I** and the **D** problem, respectively. The peculiarities of our situation as compared to the situation considered in the hypotheses testing direction [2] are caused by the fact that sets $\mathcal{I}$ and $\mathcal{D}$ have to be disjoint. In other words, these sets cannot be assigned independently, and an algorithm for testing the independence in the **I** problem depends on the specification of the dependency in the **D** problem. However, one can overcome these difficulties if the "no answer" output is allowed in the case when $(\mathbf{x}, \mathbf{y}) \in \mathcal{I} \bigcap \mathcal{D}$. We accept such an assumption and translate it to a general authentication algorithm as follows. *Given the claim that* $\mathbf{x}$ *and* $\mathbf{y}$ *describe biometrics of the same person, assign two sets,* $\mathcal{I}, \mathcal{D} \subset \mathsf{R}^n \times \mathsf{R}^n$, *and denote*

$$\overline{\mathcal{I}} \triangleq (\mathsf{R}^n \times \mathsf{R}^n) \backslash \mathcal{I}, \ \ \overline{\mathcal{D}} \triangleq (\mathsf{R}^n \times \mathsf{R}^n) \backslash \mathcal{D}. \tag{3}$$

Set

$$\text{Decision} = \begin{cases} \text{“accept the claim”}, & \textit{if } (\mathbf{x}, \mathbf{y}) \in \overline{\mathcal{I}} \bigcap \mathcal{D}, \\ \text{“no answer”}, & \textit{if } (\mathbf{x}, \mathbf{y}) \in \mathcal{I} \bigcap \mathcal{D}, \\ \text{“reject the claim”}, & \textit{if } (\mathbf{x}, \mathbf{y}) \in \overline{\mathcal{D}}. \end{cases} \tag{4}$$

Notice that the acceptance and the rejection decisions in (4) are non-symmetric, since we reject the identity if $(\mathbf{x}, \mathbf{y}) \in \{\mathcal{I} \bigcap \overline{\mathcal{D}}, \overline{\mathcal{I}} \bigcap \overline{\mathcal{D}}\}$.

If only the **I** problem is considered, then it can be viewed as testing of hypotheses $f = f_{\mathrm{x,y}}$ or $f \neq f_{\mathrm{x,y}}$, and the performance of an **I** algorithm is characterized by the error probability

$$\Pi_{\mathrm{i}}(\mathcal{I}) \triangleq \int_{\mathsf{R}^n \times \mathsf{R}^n} f_{\mathrm{x}}(\mathbf{x}) f_{\mathrm{y}}(\mathbf{y}) \chi\{(\mathbf{x}, \mathbf{y}) \notin \mathcal{I}\} d\mathbf{x} d\mathbf{y}, \tag{5}$$

where χ denotes the indicator function: $\chi\{S\} = 1$ if the statement S is true and $\chi\{S\} = 0$ otherwise. Similarly, if only the **D** problem is considered, then it can be viewed as testing of hypotheses $f = f_{\mathrm{x,y|x}}$ or $f \neq f_{\mathrm{x,y|x}}$, and the performance of a **D** algorithm is characterized by the error probability

$$\Pi_{\mathrm{d}}(\mathcal{D}) \triangleq \int_{\mathsf{R}^n \times \mathsf{R}^n} f_{\mathrm{x}}(\mathbf{x}) f_{\mathrm{y}|\mathrm{x}}(\mathbf{y}|\mathbf{x}) \chi\{(\mathbf{x}, \mathbf{y}) \notin \mathcal{D}\} d\mathbf{x} d\mathbf{y}. \tag{6}$$

Certainly, assignments $\mathcal{I}, \mathcal{D} = \mathsf{R}^n \times \mathsf{R}^n$ bring the probabilities $\Pi_{\mathrm{i}}(\mathcal{I})$ and $\Pi_{\mathrm{d}}(\mathcal{D})$ equal to zero. However, combining the **I** and the **D** problems impose three hypotheses: 1) $f = f_{\mathrm{x,y}}$; 2) $f = f_{\mathrm{x,y|x}}$; 3) $f \neq f_{\mathrm{x,y}}$ and $f \neq f_{\mathrm{x,y|x}}$. Then the performance is also characterized by the probabilities

$$\Pi_{\mathrm{id}}(\mathcal{D}) \triangleq \int_{\mathsf{R}^n \times \mathsf{R}^n} f_{\mathrm{x}}(\mathbf{x}) f_{\mathrm{y}}(\mathbf{y}) \chi\{(\mathbf{x}, \mathbf{y}) \in \mathcal{D}\} d\mathbf{x} d\mathbf{y}, \tag{7}$$

$$\Pi_{\mathrm{di}}(\mathcal{I}) \triangleq \int_{\mathsf{R}^n \times \mathsf{R}^n} f_{\mathrm{x}}(\mathbf{x}) f_{\mathrm{y}|\mathrm{x}}(\mathbf{y}|\mathbf{x}) \chi\{(\mathbf{x}, \mathbf{y}) \in \mathcal{I}\} d\mathbf{x} d\mathbf{y}. \tag{8}$$

Roughly speaking, we want all four probabilities to be small. For example, the problem can be formulated as follows: *given the PDF's satisfying (1), (2), construct sets $\mathcal{I}$, $\mathcal{D}$ in such a way that*

$$\max\Big\{ \Pi_{\rm i}(\mathcal{I}), \Pi_{\rm d}(\mathcal{D}), \Pi_{\rm id}(\mathcal{D}), \Pi_{\rm di}(\mathcal{I}) \Big\} \to \min. \tag{9}$$

We will present a specific construction of the sets $\mathcal{I}$, $\mathcal{D}$ that are parameterized by non-negative numbers δ_0 and δ_1. *Independently of the PDF's, the probabilities $\Pi_{\rm i}(\mathcal{I})$ and $\Pi_{\rm d}(\mathcal{D})$ are expressed through δ_0, δ_1, and auxiliary integer q, and they exponentially decrease with the number of observations n.* Notice also that the same value of $\Pi_{\rm i}(\mathcal{I})$ and $\Pi_{\rm d}(\mathcal{D})$ can be obtained for different parameters δ_0 and δ_1. These parameters have to be assigned to minimize $\Pi_{\rm id}(\mathcal{D})$ and $\Pi_{\rm di}(\mathcal{I})$. The result of optimization depends on the PDF's under considerations.

3 The ξ Transformations of Random Variables and the Conditional Distortions Between Biometric Vectors

Suppose that X is a continuous random variables with the PD $F \in \mathcal{F}$ and let q be a fixed positive integer. Denote $\mathcal{Q} \triangleq \{0, \ldots, q-1\}$ and

$$\mathcal{Q}^{(n)} \triangleq \bigcup_{c=0}^{n(q-1)} \{c/(nq)\}.$$

Introduce the $\xi_{\rm x}$, $\xi_{\rm y}$, and $\xi_{\rm y|x}$ transformations in the following way. For all $x, y \in \mathsf{R}$, let

$$\xi_{\rm x}(x) = \lfloor qF_{\rm x}(x) \rfloor, \;\; \xi_{\rm y}(y) = \lfloor qF_{\rm y}(y) \rfloor, \;\; \xi_{\rm y|x}(y|x) = \lfloor qF_{\rm y|x}(y|x) \rfloor, \tag{10}$$

where $\lfloor z \rfloor$ denotes the integer part of $z \in \mathsf{R}$.

The $\xi_{\rm x}$ transformation is illustrated in Fig. 1. Notice that equalities (10) determine a uniform distribution over the set $\mathcal{Q}$:

$$\Pr\{\xi_{\rm x}(X) = i\} = \int_{F_{\rm x}^{-1}(i/q)}^{F_{\rm x}^{-1}((i+1)/q)} f_{\rm x}(x)dx = 1/q, \;\; i \in \mathcal{Q}. \tag{11}$$

Furthermore, for all $x \in \mathsf{R}$,

$$\Pr\{\xi_{\rm y|x}(Y|x) = j\} = \int_{F_{\rm y|x}^{-1}(j/q|x)}^{F_{\rm y|x}^{-1}((j+1)/q|x)} f_{\rm y|x}(y|x)dy = 1/q, \;\; j \in \mathcal{Q}. \tag{12}$$

Let us apply transformations (10) to components of the processes $\mathbf{X}$ and $\mathbf{Y}$ by substituting $(F_{\rm x}, F_{\rm y}, F_{\rm y|x}(x)) = (F_{\rm x}^{(t)}, F_{\rm y}^{(t)}, F_{\rm y|x}^{(t)}(x^{(t)}))$, $t = 1, \ldots, n$. Set

$$\Delta_{\rm i}(x^{(t)}, y^{(t)}) \triangleq \frac{|\,\xi_{\rm x}(x^{(t)}) - \xi_{\rm y}(y^{(t)})\,|}{q}, \tag{13}$$

$$\Delta_{\rm d}(x^{(t)}, y^{(t)}) \triangleq \frac{|\,\xi_{\rm x}(x^{(t)}) - \xi_{\rm y|x}(y^{(t)}|x^{(t)})\,|}{q}, \tag{14}$$

and define

$$\Delta_{\rm i}(\mathbf{x},\mathbf{y}) \triangleq \sum_{t=1}^{n} \Delta_{\rm i}(x^{(t)},y^{(t)}), \quad \Delta_{\rm d}(\mathbf{x},\mathbf{y}) \triangleq \sum_{t=1}^{n} \Delta_{\rm d}(x^{(t)},y^{(t)})$$

as the conditional distortions between $\mathbf{x}$ and $\mathbf{y}$.

Introduce the $(\Delta|\xi)$-authentication algorithm as follows. *Fix two thresholds, δ_0 and δ_1. Given the claim that $\mathbf{x}$ and $\mathbf{y}$ describe biometrics of the same person, compute $\Delta_{\rm i}(\mathbf{x},\mathbf{y})$, $\Delta_{\rm d}(\mathbf{x},\mathbf{y})$, and denote*

$$\mathcal{I} \triangleq \Big\{ (\mathbf{x},\mathbf{y}) \in \mathsf{R}^n \times \mathsf{R}^n : \Delta_{\rm i}(\mathbf{x},\mathbf{y}) \in (n\delta_0, n\delta_1) \Big\}, \tag{15}$$

$$\mathcal{D} \triangleq \Big\{ (\mathbf{x},\mathbf{y}) \in \mathsf{R}^n \times \mathsf{R}^n : \Delta_{\rm d}(\mathbf{x},\mathbf{y}) \in (n\delta_0, n\delta_1) \Big\}. \tag{16}$$

Follow rules (4), where sets $\overline{\mathcal{I}}, \overline{\mathcal{D}}$ are defined in (3).

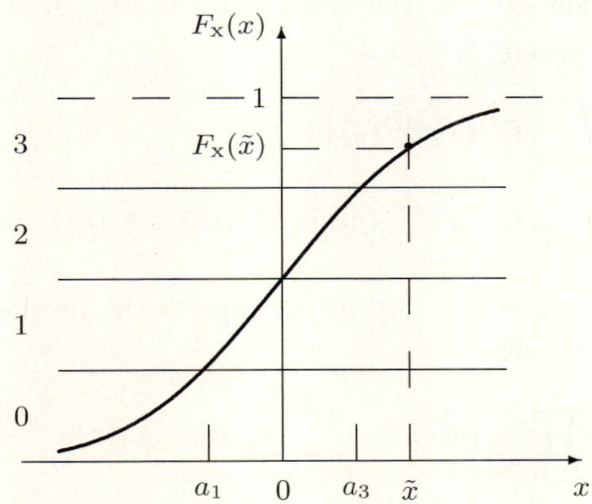

Fig. 1. Example of the transformation $\tilde{x} \to \xi_{\rm X}(\tilde{x}) = 3$ for $q = 4$, where $a_1 = F_{\rm X}^{-1}(1/4)$ and $a_3 = F_{\rm X}^{-1}(3/4)$

4 Performance of the $(\Delta|\xi)$-algorithm

Given a PD over the set $\mathcal{Q}^{(1)}$ specified by some vector $\mathbf{p} = (p_0, \ldots, p_{q-1})$, introduce the generating function

$$G_{\mathbf{p}}(w) \triangleq \sum_{c=0}^{q-1} p_c w^c,$$

where w is a formal variable, and express the n-th power of the polynomial $G_{\mathbf{p}}(w)$ as

$$\Big(G_{\mathbf{p}}(w)\Big)^n = \sum_{\delta \in \mathcal{Q}^{(n)}} \Psi_{\mathbf{p}}(\delta) w^{nq\delta}.$$

The equalities (11), (12) immediately bring the following universal statement (the claimed performance does not depend on the PDF's under considerations).

Proposition 1. *Let* $\boldsymbol{\beta} = (\beta_0, \ldots, \beta_{q-1})$ *be the vector having components*

$$\beta_c \triangleq \frac{1}{q^2}\left|\left\{ i,j \in \mathcal{Q} : |i-j| = c \right\}\right| = \frac{q-c}{q^2} \cdot \begin{cases} 1, \text{ if } c = 0, \\ 2, \text{ if } c \in \{1, \ldots, q-1\}. \end{cases}$$

If the sets $\mathcal{I}$ *and* $\mathcal{D}$ *are defined by (15), (16), then, for all* $(F_{\rm x}^{(1)}, \ldots, F_{\rm x}^{(n)})$, $(F_{\rm y}^{(1)}, \ldots, F_{\rm y}^{(n)})$, $(F_{\rm y|x}^{(1)}(x^{(1)}), \ldots, F_{\rm y|x}^{(n)}(x^{(n)})) \in \mathcal{F}^n$,

$$\Pi_{\rm i}(\mathcal{I}) = \Pi_{\rm d}(\mathcal{D}) = \sum_{\delta \in \mathcal{Q}^{(n)} \cap (\delta_0, \delta_1)} \Psi_{\boldsymbol{\beta}}(\delta), \tag{17}$$

where the probabilities $\Pi_{\rm i}(\mathcal{I})$ *and* $\Pi_{\rm d}(\mathcal{D})$ *are defined in (5), (6).*

Results of the analysis of the probabilities $\Pi_{\rm id}(\mathcal{D})$ and $\Pi_{\rm di}(\mathcal{I})$ are less universal in a sense that they depend on the specific PDF's. For all $t = 1, \ldots, n$, introduce two PD's over the set $\mathcal{Q}^{(1)}$ by the vectors $\boldsymbol{\beta}_{\rm id}^{(t)} = (\beta_{{\rm id},0}^{(t)}, \ldots, \beta_{{\rm id},q-1}^{(t)})$ and $\boldsymbol{\beta}_{\rm di}^{(t)} = (\beta_{{\rm di},0}^{(t)}, \ldots, \beta_{{\rm di},q-1}^{(t)})$, where

$$\beta_{{\rm id},c}^{(t)} = \int_{\mathsf{R}\times\mathsf{R}} f_{\rm x}^{(t)}(x) f_{\rm y}^{(t)}(y) \chi\{\, |\, \xi_{\rm x}(x) - \xi_{\rm y|x}(y|x)\,| = c\,\} dx dy,$$

$$\beta_{{\rm di},c}^{(t)} = \int_{\mathsf{R}\times\mathsf{R}} f_{\rm x}^{(t)}(x) f_{\rm y|x}^{(t)}(y|x) \chi\{\, |\, \xi_{\rm x}(x) - \xi_{\rm y}(y)\,| = c\,\} dx dy.$$

For $\mathbf{p}^{(t)} = \boldsymbol{\beta}_{\rm id}^{(t)}, \boldsymbol{\beta}_{\rm di}^{(t)}$, $t = 1, \ldots, n$, let us express the product of n polynomials $G_{\mathbf{p}^{(1)}}(w), \ldots, G_{\mathbf{p}^{(n)}}(w)$ as

$$\prod_{t=1}^{n} G_{\mathbf{p}^{(t)}}(w) = \sum_{\delta \in \mathcal{Q}^{(n)}} \Psi_{\mathbf{p}^{(1)}, \ldots, \mathbf{p}^{(n)}}(\delta) w^{nq\delta}.$$

Proposition 2. *If the sets* $\mathcal{I}$ *and* $\mathcal{D}$ *are defined by (15), (16), then, for all* $(F_{\rm x}^{(1)}, \ldots, F_{\rm x}^{(n)})$, $(F_{\rm y}^{(1)}, \ldots, F_{\rm y}^{(n)})$, $(F_{\rm y|x}^{(1)}(x^{(1)}), \ldots, F_{\rm y|x}^{(n)}(x^{(n)})) \in \mathcal{F}^n$,

$$\Pi_{\rm id}(\mathcal{D}) = \sum_{\delta \in \mathcal{Q}^{(n)} \cap (\delta_0, \delta_1)} \Psi_{\boldsymbol{\beta}_{\rm id}^{(1)}, \ldots, \boldsymbol{\beta}_{\rm id}^{(n)}}(\delta),$$

$$\Pi_{\rm di}(\mathcal{I}) = \sum_{\delta \in \mathcal{Q}^{(n)} \cap (\delta_0, \delta_1)} \Psi_{\boldsymbol{\beta}_{\rm di}^{(1)}, \ldots, \boldsymbol{\beta}_{\rm di}^{(n)}}(\delta),$$

where the probabilities $\Pi_{\rm id}(\mathcal{D})$ *and* $\Pi_{\rm di}(\mathcal{I})$ *are defined in (7), (8). In particular, if* $\boldsymbol{\beta}_{\rm id}^{(t)} = \boldsymbol{\beta}_{\rm id}$ *and* $\boldsymbol{\beta}_{\rm di}^{(t)} = \boldsymbol{\beta}_{\rm di}$ *for all* $t = 1, \ldots, n$, *then*

$$\Pi_{\rm id}(\mathcal{D}) = \sum_{\delta \in \mathcal{Q}^{(n)} \cap (\delta_0, \delta_1)} \Psi_{\boldsymbol{\beta}_{\rm id}}(\delta), \tag{18}$$

$$\Pi_{\rm di}(\mathcal{I}) = \sum_{\delta \in \mathcal{Q}^{(n)} \cap (\delta_0, \delta_1)} \Psi_{\boldsymbol{\beta}_{\rm di}}(\delta). \tag{19}$$

5 Numerical Illustrations

Let $(\mathrm{g}_{m,\sigma^2}(x), x \in \mathsf{R})$ denote a Gaussian PDF with the mean m and the variance σ^2. We also write $\mathrm{g}_{\sigma^2}(x) \overset{\triangle}{=} \mathrm{g}_{\sigma^2}(x|0)$ and denote the corresponding Gaussian PD by $(\mathrm{G}_{\sigma^2}(x), x \in \mathsf{R})$. Suppose that $q = 4$ and that

$$\left(f_{\mathrm{x}}^{(t)}(x), f_{\mathrm{y}}^{(t)}(y), f_{\mathrm{y|x}}^{(t)}(y|x) \right) = \left(\mathrm{g}_2(x), \mathrm{g}_{2.5}(y), \mathrm{g}_{x,0.5}(y) \right) \tag{20}$$

for all $t = 1, \ldots, n$.

Notice that

$$\begin{aligned}
(\mathrm{G}_2^{-1}(1/4), \mathrm{G}_2^{-1}(2/4), \mathrm{G}_2^{-1}(3/4)) &= (-0.954, 0, +0.954),\\
(\mathrm{G}_{2.5}^{-1}(1/4), \mathrm{G}_{2.5}^{-1}(2/4), \mathrm{G}_{2.5}^{-1}(3/4)) &= (-1.066, 0, +1.066),\\
(\mathrm{G}_{0.5}^{-1}(1/4), \mathrm{G}_{0.5}^{-1}(2/4), \mathrm{G}_{0.5}^{-1}(3/4)) &= (-0.477, 0, +0.477).
\end{aligned}$$

To solve the **I** problem we map the t-th components of the vectors $\mathbf{x}$ and $\mathbf{y}$ to the q-ary elements according to the rules:

$$\xi_{\mathrm{x}}(x^{(t)}) = \begin{cases} 0, \text{ if } x^{(t)} \le -0.954,\\ 1, \text{ if } x^{(t)} \in (-0.954, 0],\\ 2, \text{ if } x^{(t)} \in (0, +0.954),\\ 3, \text{ if } x^{(t)} \ge +0.954, \end{cases} \tag{21}$$

$$\xi_{\mathrm{y}}(y^{(t)}) = \begin{cases} 0, \text{ if } y^{(t)} \le -1.066,\\ 1, \text{ if } y^{(t)} \in (-1.066, 0],\\ 2, \text{ if } y^{(t)} \in (0, +1.066),\\ 3, \text{ if } y^{(t)} \ge +1.066. \end{cases} \tag{22}$$

To solve the **D** problem we map the t-th component of the vector $\mathbf{x}$ to the q-ary element according to (21) and replace (22) with the rule:

$$\xi_{\mathrm{y|x}}(y^{(t)}|x^{(t)}) = \begin{cases} 0, \text{ if } y^{(t)} - x^{(t)} \le -0.477,\\ 1, \text{ if } y^{(t)} - x^{(t)} \in (-0.477, 0],\\ 2, \text{ if } y^{(t)} - x^{(t)} \in (0, +0.477),\\ 3, \text{ if } y^{(t)} - x^{(t)} \ge +0.477. \end{cases}$$

The constructed q-ary vectors are then used to determine the values of the conditional distortions and their comparisons with the thresholds.

One can check that, for any vector $\mathbf{p}$ specifying a PD on the set $\mathcal{Q}^{(1)}$, the PD $(\Psi_{\mathbf{p}}(\delta), \delta \in \mathcal{Q}^{(n)})$ simulates the binomial distribution over the set $\mathcal{Q}^{(n)}$ with the mean

$$\delta(\mathbf{p}) \overset{\triangle}{=} \sum_{c=0}^{q-1} (c/q) p_c.$$

These PD's determine the performance of the $\Delta|\xi$-algorithm according to (17) and (18), (19). An example for $(n, q) = (32, 4)$ and the PDF's defined by (20) is shown in Fig.2 where we also illustrate possible assignments of parameters δ_0

and δ_1 under the conditions $\Pi_{\rm id}(\mathcal{D}) \approx \Pi_{\rm i}(\mathcal{I})$ and $\Pi_{\rm di}(\mathcal{I}) \approx \Pi_{\rm d}(\mathcal{D})$. Notice that in this case,

$$\boldsymbol{\beta}_{\rm id} = (0.666, 0.320, 0.013, 0.000),$$
$$\boldsymbol{\beta} = (0.250, 0.375, 0.250, 0.125),$$
$$\boldsymbol{\beta}_{\rm di} = (0.094, 0.222, 0.288, 0.396)$$

and $(\delta(\boldsymbol{\beta}_{\rm id}), \delta(\boldsymbol{\beta}), \delta(\boldsymbol{\beta}_{\rm di})) = (0.188, 0.312, 0.498)$. As a result one can reliably distinguish between hypotheses under consideration.

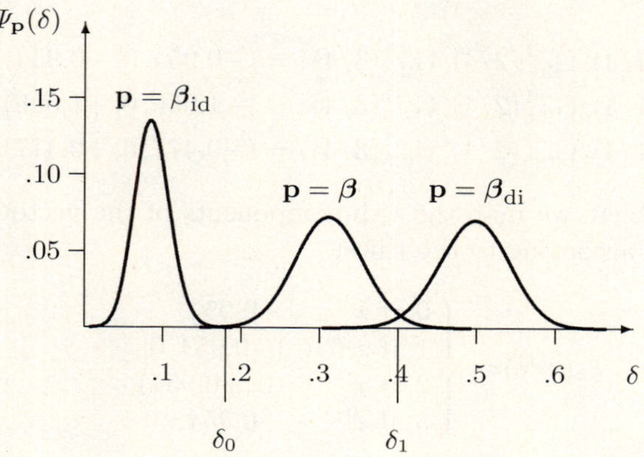

Fig. 2. The probabilities $\Psi_{\mathbf{p}}(\delta)$ for $(n, q) = (32, 4)$; the PDF's are defined in (20)

6 Conclusion

Let us summarize the main ideas included into our analysis.

1. Suppose that the data consist of the height of a person, h (in centimeters), and the weight, w (in kilograms). If realizations of the noise of measurements are independent, then the conditional probability of a certain pair of parameters for a person P is expressed as

$$\Pr\{(\hat{\rm H}, \hat{\rm W}) = (\hat{\rm h}, \hat{\rm w}) \,|\, ({\rm H_P}, {\rm W_P}) = ({\rm h_P}, {\rm w_P})\}$$
$$= \Pr_{\rm h}\{{\rm Noise_h}(\hat{\rm h} - {\rm h_P})\} \Pr_{\rm w}\{{\rm Noise_w}(\hat{\rm w} - {\rm w_P})\}.$$

Notice that the product above combines contributions of parameters measured in different units over a probabilistic space. The conditional probability under consideration can be used for testing the given dependency: if it is greater than a certain threshold, then we accept the claim that the outcome of measurements correspond to person P. However, we are also interested in testing the independence of the input and the output parameters. In this case, the algorithm, which is based on the computation of the product

$$\Pr\{(\hat{\rm H}, \hat{\rm W}) = (\hat{\rm h}, \hat{\rm w})\} = \Pr_{\rm h}\{\hat{\rm h}\} \Pr_{\rm w}\{\hat{\rm w}\}$$

and comparison it with the threshold fails (for example, the marginal probability distributions of parameters can be uniform).

2. Suppose that there are 3 hypotheses about person P. Namely, we assume that

$$\mathrm{P} \in \{\mathrm{A}, \mathrm{B}, \text{neither A nor B}\}.$$

Having received the observations, an algorithm has to check whether they belong to the decision regions of A or B. Thus, these decision regions have to be disjoint, i.e., the decision about the person A cannot be made without taking into account the person B and *vise versa.* Furthermore, the conditional probabilities for "neither A nor B" are not defined. In the biometric authentication problem we have only parameters of a fixed person involved. Nevertheless, since we also want to evaluate the false acceptance rate, the scheme above is relevant: "person A" is the joint probability distribution $f_{\mathbf{x}}(\mathbf{x})f_{\mathbf{y}}(\mathbf{y})$, "person B" is the joint probability distribution $f_{\mathbf{x}}(\mathbf{x})f_{\mathbf{y}|\mathbf{x}}(\mathbf{y}|\mathbf{x})$. The space where the decision regions are constructed is the probabilistic space.

3. The basic step of our approach to solving the authentication problem uses the constructions of pseudo-random generators. Let F^* be an arbitrary function satisfying the constraints: (a) F^* is defined over the interval I where a random variable X can take values; (b) $F^*(x) \in [0,1]$ for all $x \in I$; (c) F^* is a strictly increasing function over I. Thus, F^* is a PD of some random variable X^* and if $z \in (0,1)$, then the equation $z = F^*(x)$ has a unique solution for $x \in I$. Furthermore, if $F^* = F$, where F is the PD of the random variable X, then $F(X)$ is a random variable uniformly distributed over the $[0,1]$ interval. As a result, if our hypotheses about probability distributions of components of the vectors $\mathbf{x}$ and $\mathbf{y}$ are correct, then one of the distortion functions, Δ_{i} or Δ_{d}, is distributed according to the vector $\boldsymbol{\beta}$, which is completely determined by the parameter q.

4. The feature of biometric authentication is making the decisions by investigation of samples of small sizes. Our technique allows us to carry out such an analysis, since all probabilities under consideration are expressed exactly using the generating functions of discrete random variables. An introduction of the parameter q in the ξ transformation also brings data compression.

5. Notice that optimization over possible assignments of the distortion functions Δ_{i} and Δ_{d} introduced in (13), (14) is possible and it results in the improvement of the performance, when (9) is understood as a criterion. In particular, if the absolute values of the differences at the right-hand sides of (13), (14) are taken to the power α, then the optimum assignment is $\alpha \approx 1.7$ for the example given in the previous section.

References

1. Bolle, R.M., Connell, J.H., Pankanti, S., Ratha, N.K., Senior, A.W.: Guide to Biometrics. Springer, New York (2004)
2. Kullback, S.: Information Theory and Statistics. Dover, New York (1968)

Identity Verification by Using Handprint

Hao Ying, Tan Tieniu, Sun Zhenan, and Han Yufei

National Laboratory of Pattern Recognition,
Institute of Automation, Chinese Academy of Sciences, China
{yhao,tnt,znsun,yfhan}@nlpr.ia.ac.cn

Abstract. In recent years, palmprint based personal identification has been extensively explored by researchers. The success of this technology has demonstrated that the inner part of palm skin is capable of distinguishing one person from another in case that proper representation is utilized. However, earlier work mainly focused on scenarios where the position and pose of hands are constrained by pegs or plates. In contrast, our purpose is to design and implement a system which is capable of recognizing an individual once he/she naturally stretches his/her hand in front of the camera. Since human hand is an articulated object, it is important to filter out geometry variations. This paper presents and compares two hand texture based personal identification methods, which are called hand-print verification in this paper to denote the idea of utilizing whole hand skin image for recognition. In one of the method, hand articulation is eliminated in a well-defined way and then the hand is treated as a whole for feature extraction, while in the other method, features are extracted in different parts of the hand, and final decision is made in a matching score level fusion manner. Experimental results for both methods are presented and compared.

Keywords: Biometrics, Verification, Identification, Ordinal Representation, Texture Analysis, Handprint.

1 Introduction

In our increasingly digitalized and connected society, personal impact expands from several meters to millions of miles. We all have a high probability of making conversation, communicating, sending email or even making business with people who connect with us from remote places via cable. In such an environment, identity is becoming more and more ambiguous. Determined criminals might threaten our life in dozens of ways, ranging from minor financial loss to personal safety. Biometrics has emerged as a novel way to establish identity by analyzing physical or behaviorial traits which have been recognized to be intrinsic to each person. Although palmprint recognition is a relatively young member of the Biometric family, its growth is considerably fast. Different approaches have been proposed. In our opinion, there are three categories of features that have been explored in the literature:

S.-W. Lee and S.Z. Li (Eds.): ICB 2007, LNCS 4642, pp. 328–337, 2007.

- *structural features*, referring to line features, such as principal lines, wrinkles and even ridges,
- *appearance based features*, exploiting global texture by using linear subspace methods,
- *texture features*, adopting local textual information.

However, the above mentioned feature extraction schemes are all proposed for the scenarios where the position and/or pose of hands are constrained with pegs or plates, for example, scanner and dedicated device are most commonly adopted for palm image acquisition. What we want to do is to set free of the users from theses constraints by designing and implementing a system which is capable of recognizing an individual once he/she naturally stretches his/her hand in front of the camera. This is a much more difficult task compared with those in previous literature. For example, at least the following issues have to be considered:

- *Localization.* How to detect the presence of human hands? How to decide the precise orientation, location and scale of hands?
- *Hand pose evaluation.* How to evaluate hand images so that only hands with proper pose are selected for feature extraction?
- *Preprocessing.* How to process hand images so that ROIs (Region of Interest) are exactly located and hand articulation is eliminated?
- *Feature extraction.* How to make use of or modify previously successful feature extraction schemes?

Among the three categories of features, texture based approach is reported to be most powerful in distinguishing people. Representative work of this category [2], [5], [3] and [6], has been reporting better and better performance. These approaches share a common characteristics: a simple feature is extracted at each local region and a mesh containing one feature at each grid is utilized to provide a much more distinctive representation. Despite the success of this representation scheme, there is a major disadvantage: it does not contain a built-in mechanism to deal with partial skin deformation, such as the effect caused by stretching and scrunching, in which case the inner part of the palm changed considerably. In this paper, we seek to eliminate the variation of hand poses in preprocessing stage.

The texture of inner hand skin is affected by complex mechanism involved with hand bones, muscles and skin status, which make it difficult to model. However, if the anatomically meaningful points can be extracted from hand image, it is possible to compensate for the above mentioned non-linear deformation at preprocessing stage.

Besides palmprint, researchers have shown that finger surface regions also convey distinctive information[7], which motivates us to extend the concept of palmprint to a larger one: handprint, which denotes the idea of utilizing the whole hand skin image for recognition. Similar idea has been proposed in [8], where the authors present a method which utilizes grayscale distribution variance as features to describe non-normalized hands, which is inevitably sensitive to hand pose variations and illumination changes.

2 Proposed Methods

We proposed two strategies to achieve the goal, one is a holistic method and the other is a fusion based method. The holistic method treats the hand as a whole and it is composed of the following steps:

1. A set of landmarks is defined and extracted by contour geometry as well as skin texture to provide geometrical information of hands;
2. The geometrical variation is filtered out by image warping;
3. Binary textual features are extracted to represent handprint;
4. Hamming distance is adopted to measure the similarity of two features.

While in fusion based method, feature extraction and matching are performed in a part by part manner, where a hand is partitioned to six parts, namely, palm region and five fingers. The matching results on different parts are finally combined at matching score level to make the final verification decision.

2.1 Hand Landmark Localization

Hand shapes, and hand contours accordingly, may change whenever hands move, rotate or hand pose varies. In order to analyze the hand texture as a whole, the shape variation must be somehow filtered out. One solution to this problem is to find out a representation of the hand shape and then transform this representation to a translation-, rotation- and pose-free one. A sparse landmark based approach can obviously meet this goal.

For hand images captured indoors under constrained environment, high quality hand contour can be easily obtained by any adaptive global thresholding algorithm followed by a boundary tracking method. By summing up all pixel values along the four thresholded image boundaries, the wrist position can be immediately recognized as the side that produces maximal sum value. After that, the middle of wrist is selected as reference point and distance from each contour point to the reference point is calculated, thus producing a one-dimensional profile. The five local maximums and four local minimums of this profile obviously correspond to finger tips and finger roots respectively. Then the starting point of thumb and index as well as end point of little finger are detected and fingers are separated by adopting the preprocessing method proposed by Xiong et. al.[4].

After the above process, 12 landmarks are detected. Although these landmarks are capable of characterizing hand shape coarsely, they do not meet the requirement of capturing hand shape variation.

Observation on hand images demonstrates that the pixel values near knuckle region are normally lower than other parts of fingers. This property makes it possible to extract knuckles and use them as landmarks. Fig. 1 shows the process of knuckle detection. Firstly, each separated finger image is rotated so that its principal axis becomes 90 degree. After that, histogram equalization is adopted to normalize contrast and enhance details. The mean pixel value along each horizontal line is then calculated and a one-dimensional signal is produced. The two local minimal points correspond to two knuckles of that finger, as illustrated in Fig. 1(c). The thumb knuckle normally locate near the middle of the whole finger while knuckles of other fingers usually lie close to $\frac{1}{3}$ and $\frac{2}{3}$ percent of the fingers. The above prior knowledge can be easily implemented in the localization process.

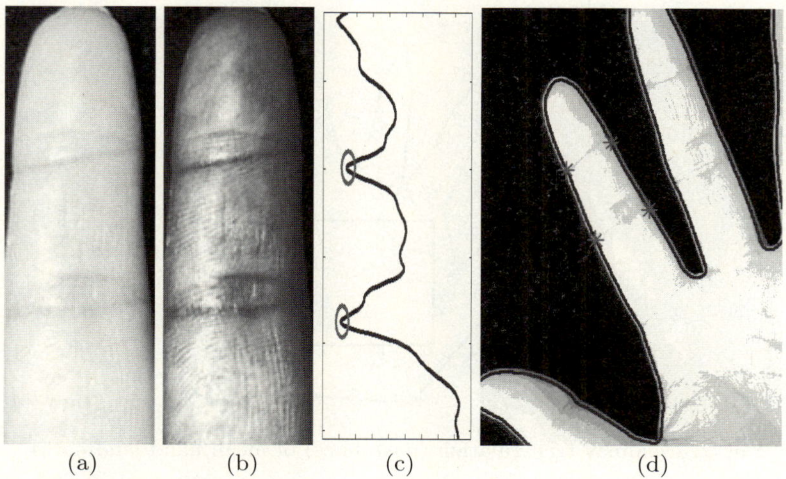

(a) (b) (c) (d)

Fig. 1. Knuckle detection: (a) original finger image; (b)finger image after histogram equalization; (c) horizontal profile of (b) with the circles indicating the local minimums, and (d) detected knuckle landmarks(stars) labeled on original hand image

The wrist beginning and ending point play important roles in defining the region of hand. However, they are much more subtle than other landmarks and more difficult to extract automatically, so we manually label them out.

The mean difference between proposed landmarks used here and those of Yörük et. al.[1] lies in that all the landmarks that we used here have straightforward anatomical meaning. This enables us to map one representation to another while minimizing the risk of introducing geometrical artifacts to hand shape.

2.2 Holistic Method

Image warping is an image processing method which moves image pixels from one spatial configurations to another. Digital image warping has benefited dramatically from several fields, ranging from early work in remote sensing to recent developments in computer graphics [9]. Basically, image warping involves two operations, namely mapping and resampling, where mapping defines destination for each source pixel and resampling decides the contribution of neighboring pixel values to the current one. Since the contour of each hand is defined by a set of landmarks, $\{\mathbf{x}_1, \mathbf{x}_2, \ldots, \mathbf{x}_n\}$, the simplest way to perform warping is to assume that the mapping function is locally linear.

The Delaunay triangulation is a collection of lines that connect each point to its nearest neighbors, where the 'empty circle' property is satisfied: no points are contained in any triangle's circumscribed circle. The Delaunay triangulation of the mean hand contour is given in Fig. 2, where the convex hull of the hand is partitioned to a set of non-overlapping triangles.

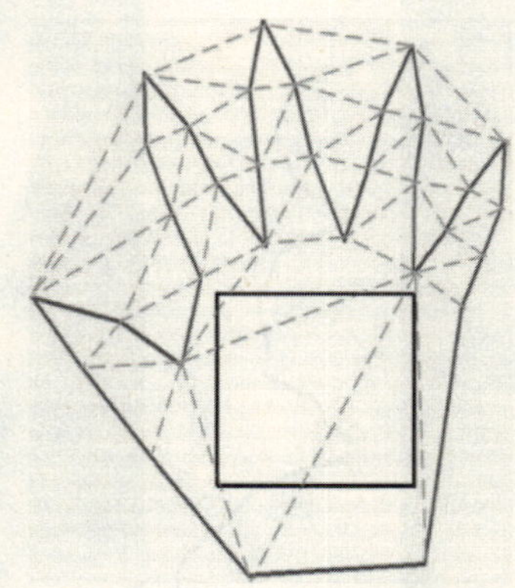

Fig. 2. Delaunay triangulation (dash lines) of mean hand landmarks

The warping is therefore implemented by transforming the triangles from one point set $\mathbf{P}$ to another point set $\mathbf{P}'$. Since each triangle pair provides 3 pairs of correspondence, an affine transformation consisting of scaling, translation, rotation and shearing, can be uniquely decided. Suppose that $\mathbf{x}_1$, $\mathbf{x}_2$, $\mathbf{x}_3$ denote the three vertices of a certain triangle TR, and $\mathbf{x}'_1$, $\mathbf{x}'_2$, $\mathbf{x}'_3$ denote vertices of the target triangle TR'. Suppose that $\mathbf{x}$ lies in triangle TR, it can be represented as:

$$\mathbf{x} = \alpha\mathbf{x}_1 + \beta\mathbf{x}_2 + (1 - \alpha - \beta)\mathbf{x}_3 \tag{1}$$

then its target point satisfies:

$$\mathbf{x}' = \alpha\mathbf{x}'_1 + \beta\mathbf{x}'_2 + (1 - \alpha - \beta)\mathbf{x}'_3 \tag{2}$$

Therefore, each point in TR can be mapped to the target triangle TR', which indicates that each hand can be mapped to the target one. In case that in-depth rotation of hand occurs or parts of hand are deformed by finger movement, this process helps to decrease intra-class differences.

2.3 Fusion Based Method

To deal with articulation of complex objects, a more flexible approach is to detect its constituent yet distinctive parts and combine cues from these parts to recognize objects. Motivated by this approach, we partition the hand into six meaningful parts: palm region and five finger regions. A rectangle region that covers approximately 80% percent of each finger is selected and resized to the average size of that finger. Palm region is denoted in Fig. 2 by the square of bold line.

Fig. 3 demonstrated the results of the above two methods, where the first row denotes four original hand images, the second row shows corresponding warping result and the last row indicates the segmented parts of each hand. Notice that anatomically meaningful regions are mapped to the same target region no matter what pose, location and angle it has on original images, which is obviously preferable in case of deformation. Since inter-finger regions are also processed in warping-based method, artifacts are introduced, especially when the inter-finger distances are small on original images, see Fig. 3(b)(f) and (d)(h) for examples. However, these artifacts do not propagate to feature-level representation, because we only extract feature within hand skin regions as indicated in Fig. 3(e)-(h).

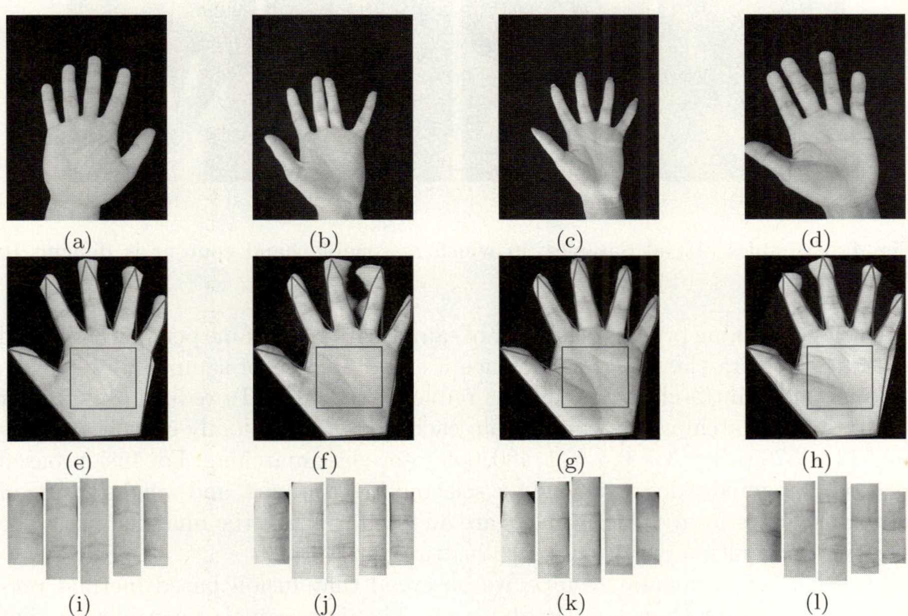

Fig. 3. Image warping result: the first row shows four sample original hand images; the second row denotes corresponding warping results, where the lines denote the mean shape obtained by averaging all samples and squares indicate the palm regions; and the last row demonstrates the segmented fingers of each hand

In low resolution hand skin images, there exist numerous randomly distributed negative lines. In our earlier work, we have demonstrated that *Orthogonal Line Ordinal Features* (OLOF) is capable of establishing stable and powerful representation for palmprint[6]. Due to the similarity of skin of palm and that of fingers, it is reasonable to adopt the same feature here for both of the two methods. The similarity of features is measured by Hamming distance.

3 Experimental Results

Experiments were conducted on a popular database, namely the UST hand image database[11]. It contains 5,660 hand images captured from 287 subjects, i. e. 10 images per hand. In the experiments, each hand is considered to be one class, thus the total number of classes is 574. UST Database distinguishes itself from PolyU Palmprint Database and CASIA Palmprint Database (which is captured in our laboratory) in that the whole hand is imaged, which makes it more suitable for our proposed method. However, in some of the images, such as those shown in Fig. 4, it is very difficult to extract precise hand contour or locate landmarks, we manually remove these samples, finally producing a database of 5,497 samples.

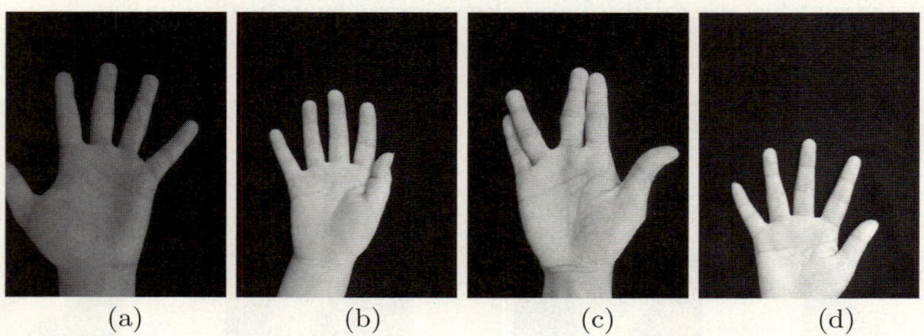

(a) (b) (c) (d)

Fig. 4. Examples of bad Samples, in which reasonable hand contour is difficult to extract

During matching process, each pair of samples from the same person is matched to form the intra-class matching. Since a small portion of samples is removed, the number of intra-class matching is reduced to 25,830. To reduce the number of inter-class matching, 3 samples from each class are randomly chosen, producing $574 \times 573 \times 3 \times 3 \times 0.5 = 1,480,059$ inter-class matching. For fusion based method, a manually decided weight is selected for each part, and weighted sum of matching scores from different parts are adopted to make the final decision. The resulting recognition performance is illustrated in Fig. 5.

From the experimental results, we observed that fusion based method performs much better than holistic approach. This is reasonable considering that holistic method is actually a straight-forward feature level fusion scheme in that features from palm region and fingers are spatially arranged to form a higher dimension feature. However, the flexibility of fine tuning preprocessing error during matching stage, which is implemented in fusion based method by matching several horizontally or vertically switched features, is sacrificed.

The matching performance of different fingers indicates that index and middle are most reliable for matching, while thumb and little are worst among five fingers. The underlying reason for them is a little different. The feature vector for little finger is much smaller, therefore the overall discriminant power is low. However, thumb suffers most from hand pose change, in consequence, its recognition performance is sensitive to pose change and landmark localization noise.

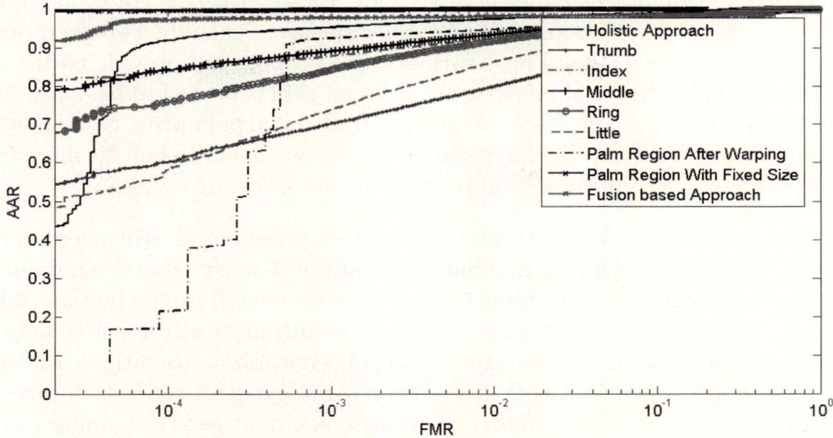

Fig. 5. Receiver Operation Characteristic Curve of proposed methods

In Fig. 5, the curve labeled with palmprint with fixed size corresponds to the matching result by locating a predefined size palm region from the hand image. The performance of fusion based method is a little lower than this non-warping version approach. Although there is no improvement regarding recognition rate, our proposed methods do better in practical case where the scale of hands changes. Notice that the palm region based method by its own does not perform well, there are several reasons for this observation:

- While normalizing scale change, the warping process decreases the distinctiveness of hand itself. Notice that during image warping process, principal lines, and knuckles tend to be mapped to the similar region in the target images. What's more, right hand images are flipped horizontally. The consequence is that the discriminating power of warped images tends to degrade comparing with those in the literature, where a fixed size palm regions are usually selected. However, in our application scenario, a fixed size palmprint region of interest is obviously impossible because the distance between hand and camera varies.
- Non-perfect landmark localization. The precision of landmark localization is essential to warping. Visual inspection of warped images indicates that a mis-localization of 10 pixels will cause a large region of texture to stretch, which introduces negative effect to recognition performance.

4 Conclusion and Discussion

Our ultimate purpose is to develop a system which is capable of recognizing an individual once he (or she) naturally stretch his (or her) hand in front of camera. To achieve this goal, a pose-, scale-, translation-, and rotation- invariant image preprocessing and matching scheme is critical. The work presented in this paper serves as the first step towards this goal.

The contribution of this paper is three folds. Firstly, the concept of handprint is proposed, which explores larger hand inner surface; Secondly, two preprocessing schemes to deal with hand pose variation are proposed to provide better user experience; Finally, textural information of finger skin is proved to be distinctive.

Although the performance is not as good as traditional palmprint-based method at current stage, there is still a large space for improvement. To benefit more from the proposed scheme, efforts should be made in the following issues:

- *Automatic landmark localization.* Human involvement is still necessary in wrist localization. During manual localization of wrist, global hand shape, underlying bone structure and texture cues all contribute to human judgement, which implies that wrist can not be automatically located only by contour information. In the light of this observation, automatic wrist localization may be realized with a two-step strategy: first coarsely locate the wrist using shape and geometry cues such as curvature, then refine the results with textual analysis approach.
- *Better hand texture warping method.* When the thumb moves from and to the palm, the region from thumb root to wrist changed dramatically. Since this movement is caused by complex mechanism which involves in many bones and muscles, it is almost impossible to fully compensate for the deformation. Similar phenomena can be observed when the fingers moves relative to each other but the deformation is less significant. Better warping method which better reflects the nature of hand skin variation may help to improve the recognition performance. Although the possibility of improvement exists, we still have to keep in mind that capturing local variations composed of occlusions, foreshortening and shadowing caused by fine scale geometry change of human skin can not be tackled only by image warping, which essentially provides no more information than the original image[10].

Acknowledgments. This work is funded by research grants from the National Basic Research Pro- gram (Grant No. 2004CB318110), the Natural Science Foundation of China (Grant No. 60335010, 60121302, 60275003, 60332010, 6982510560605008) and the Chinese Academy of Sciences.

References

1. Yörük, E., Dutağaci, H., Sankur, B.: Hand Biometrics. Image and Vision Comptuting 24, 483–497 (2006)
2. Kumar, A., Shen, H.C.: Palmprint Identification using PalmCodes. In: Intl. Conf. Image and Graphics. IEEE, Los Alamitos (2004)
3. Kong, A.W.-K., Zhang, D.: Competitive Coding Scheme for Palmprint Verification. In: Intl. Conf. on Pattern Recognition, vol. 1, pp. 520–523 (2004)
4. Xiong, W., Toh, K.-A., Yau, W.-Y., Jiang, X.: Model-guided Deformable Hand Shape Recognition Without Positioning Aids. Patern Recognition 38, 1651–1664 (2005)
5. Kong, A.W.-K., Zhang, D.: Feature Level Fusion for Effective Palmprint Authentication. In: Intl. Conf. Biometric Authentication (2004)

6. Sun, Z., Tan, T., Wang, Y., Li, S.Z.: Ordinal Palmprint Recognition for Personal Identification. Proc. of Computer Vision and Patrern Reccognitin (2005)
7. Ribaric, S., Fratric, I.: A Biometrics Identification System Based on Eigenpalm and Eigenfinger Features. IEEE Trans. on Pattern Analysis and Machine Intelligence 27(11), 1698–1709 (2005)
8. Wu, J., Qiu, Z.: A Hierarchical Palmprint Identification Method Using Hand Geometry and Grayscale Distribution Features. In: Intl. Conf. on Pattern Recognition, vol. 4, pp. 409–412 (2005)
9. Wolberg, G.: Digital Image Warping. IEEE Computer Society Press, Los Alamitos (1990)
10. Cula, G.O.G., Dana, K.J.: Skin Texture Modeling. Intl. Journal of Computer Vision 12(1) (2005)
11. UST Hand Image Database: `http://visgraph.cs.ust.hk/biometrics/Visgraph_web/index.html`
12. PolyU Palmprint Database: `http://www.comp.polyu.edu.hk/~biometrics/`

Reducing the Effect of Noise on Human Contour in Gait Recognition

Shiqi Yu, Daoliang Tan, Kaiqi Huang, and Tieniu Tan

National Laboratory of Pattern Recognition,
Institute of Automation, Chinese Academy of Sciences,
P.O. Box 2728, Beijing, 100080, China
{sqyu,dltan,kqhuang,tnt}@nlpr.ia.ac.cn

Abstract. Gait can be easily acquired at a distance, so it has become a popular biometric especially in intelligent visual surveillance. In gait-based human identification there are many factors that may degrade the performance, and noise on human contours is a significant one because to extract contours perfectly is a hard problem especially in a complex background. The contours extracted from video sequences are often polluted by noise. To improve the performance, we have to reduce the effect of noise. Different from the methods which use dynamic time warping (DTW) in previous work to match sequences in the time domain, a DTW-based contour similarity measure in the spatial domain is proposed to reduce the effect of noise. The experiments on a large gait database show the effectiveness of the proposed method.

1 Introduction

Gait has recently received an increasing interest from researchers. Gait is an attractive biometric feature for human identification at a distance because it is non-contact, non-invasive and can be easily acquired at a distance in contrast with other biometrics. Now gait has been considered as a suitable biometric for human identification in visual surveillance.

Many gait recognition methods have been developed in recent years, and most of them can be explicitly classified into two main categories: model-based approaches and appearance-based approaches. Model-based approaches [1,2,3] generally aim to recover gait features, such as stride dimensions, limb lengths and kinematics of joint angles, by model matching in each frame of a walking sequence. Appearance-based approaches [4,5] usually use the silhouettes as a whole to analyze dynamic features of motion bodies, so these methods are efficient and simple, and most of existing gait recognition approaches belong to this category.

The human contour, outline of the sihouette, is popular [5,6,7,8] in appearance-based gait recognition. A contour is more compact than its corresponding silhouette because only the points on the shape outline are considered. The shortcoming of contours is that they are more sensitive to noise than silhouettes. Dynamic time warping (DTW) is a common technique for matching time-varying signals. It has been used for matching sequences in the time domain [9,10,11,12]. We use DTW in the spatial domain and

S.-W. Lee and S.Z. Li (Eds.): ICB 2007, LNCS 4642, pp. 338–346, 2007.

proposed two contour similarity measures to make contour-based gait recognition algorithms robust to noise. Experiments were carried out on a large gait database, CASIA Gait Database (Dataset B) [13], which contains 124 subjects. The experimental results show that the proposed method can greatly improve the performance.

The remainder of this paper is organized as follows. Section 2 briefly introduces the contour extraction and representation, and Section 3 describes the effect of noise on contours. The proposed similarity measures are presented in Section 4. Experiments and results are shown in Section 5. Section 6 concludes the paper.

2 Human Contour Extraction

If video sequences are captured by fixed cameras, human silhouettes can be extracted by background subtraction and thresholding. A human contour, outline of a body, can be easily obtained from a human silhouette by a border following algorithm based on connectivity. The contour can be further viewed as being in the complex plane [7]. Each point on the contour can be represented by a complex number:

$$p_i = x_i + j \cdot y_i, (i = 1, 2, \cdots, N) \tag{1}$$

where N is the number of points on the contour. An equal number of points are used to express each contour. And each contour are counterclockwise unwrapped from the top point of the contour to turn it into a complex vector:

$$\boldsymbol{s} = [p_1, p_2, \cdots, p_N]^T. \tag{2}$$

Here, walking direction is normalized based on gait symmetry in the side view.

Suppose a video sequence contains C gait cycles, then the sequence can be divided into C short sequences using the method mentioned in [14] and each one contains a gait cycle. To reduce the influence of the walking speed, contours in a gait cycle are interpolated to the same number T. The C gait cycles in a video sequence $\mathbb{S}$ are shown as follows:

$$\begin{aligned} \boldsymbol{S}_1 &= [\boldsymbol{s}_1, \quad \boldsymbol{s}_2, \quad \cdots, \boldsymbol{s}_T \ ] \\ \boldsymbol{S}_2 &= [\boldsymbol{s}_{T+1}, \quad \boldsymbol{s}_{T+2}, \quad \cdots, \boldsymbol{s}_{2T} \ ] \\ &\cdots \\ \boldsymbol{S}_C &= [\boldsymbol{s}_{(C-1)T+1}, \boldsymbol{s}_{(C-1)T+2}, \cdots, \boldsymbol{s}_{CT} \ ] \end{aligned} \tag{3}$$

where $\boldsymbol{s}_i$ is a contour as illustrated in Equation 2, and $\boldsymbol{S}_c$ is a $N \times T$ matrix which represent a gait cycle.

The frames in a gait cycle are aligned to make the stance with the greatest width be the first frame of the cycle. Some stances from a gait cycle are shown in Fig. 1.

Fig. 1. Stances from a gait cycle

3 The Effect of Noise on Contours

To segment the human body is a hard problem especially in a complex background. The extracted silhouettes and contours may be affected by noise. Fig. 2.(a) shows a silhouette with noise where a portion is lost, and Fig. 2.(b) shows the corresponding ground-true silhouette. The following formula is used to measure the difference between a feature and its corresponding ground-truth feature.

$$\rho = \frac{|\mathbf{f} - \mathbf{f}_{gt}|}{|\mathbf{f}_{gt}|} \quad (4)$$

where $\mathbf{f}$ is the feature vector and $\mathbf{f}_{gt}$ is the ground-truth feature vector. The ρ value between the two silhouettes (Fig. 2(a) and (b)) is 1.8%. This means that 1.8% of the human silhouette area is different.

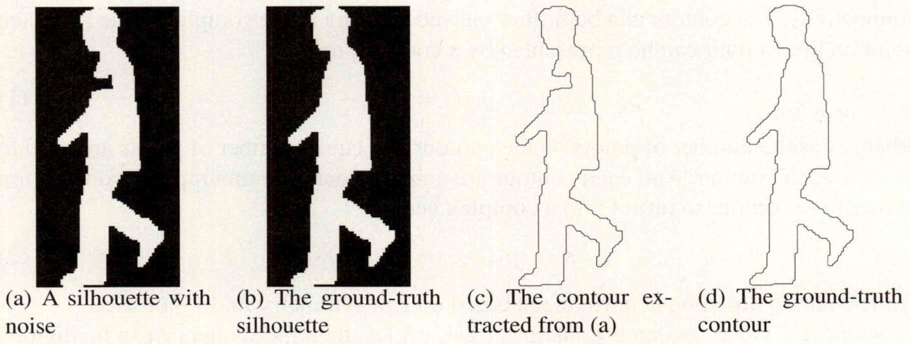

(a) A silhouette with noise (b) The ground-truth silhouette (c) The contour extracted from (a) (d) The ground-truth contour

Fig. 2. Silhouette with noise and the ground-truth one

Fig. 2(c) and (d) are the contours extracted from Fig. 2(a) and (b), respectively. We use the formula in Equation 2 to represent contours. The difference ratio, ρ, between the two contours is 7.6%, and it is over 4 times greater than the ρ value of silhouettes. It means that noise has a greater effect on contours than on silhouettes. This is consistent with one's intuition.

To improve contour-based methods, one solution is to improve human detection and segmentation algorithms. But it is not easy to segment human body perfectly from background especially in a complex outdoor scene. Another solution is to improve the similarity measure for contours. In the following section, we propose two DTW-based contour similarity measures.

4 Algorithm Overview

To improve the robustness of contour to noise, one straightforward idea is to match contours first before computing the similarity. If each of the body components, such as head, hands and feet, can be correctly matched between two human body contours, the effect of noise should be greatly reduced. Dynamic time warping is used in our proposed method to match two contours.

4.1 Dynamic Time Warping

Dynamic time warping (DTW) [15] is an algorithm for measuring the similarity between two series, which may vary in time or speed, and has been widely used in speech processing, gesture recognition [16], etc. DTW can find an optimal match between two given series P and Q. Suppose the length of P and Q are n and m, respectively:

$$P = [p_1, p_2, \cdots, p_m]^T \tag{5}$$

$$Q = [q_1, q_2, \cdots, q_n]^T. \tag{6}$$

To find the best alignment of the two series, an $m \times n$ matrix D, namely a cost matrix, is created. The element $d(i, j)$ of the matrix D is the distance between p_i and q_j:

$$d(i, j) = dist(p_i, q_j) \tag{7}$$

where $dist$ can be the Euclidean distance or other kinds of distances. In our experiments, the Euclidean distance was used.

A warp path W can be constructed as shown in Fig. 3 and expressed in the following way:

$$W = [w_1, w_2, \cdots, w_K] \qquad \max(m, n) \leq K \leq m + n \tag{8}$$

where K is the length of the warp path, and the kth element of W, w_k, is $\langle i, j \rangle$ which means the ith element of P corresponds with the jth one of Q.

To ensure every element of the two series to be used in the warp path, the warp path must start at the beginning of each series at $w_1 = \langle 1, 1 \rangle$ and finish at the end of both series at $w_K = \langle m, n \rangle$. Another constraint on the warp path is the two neighbor steps must be adjacent cells (including diagonally adjacent cells). Given $w_k = \langle i, j \rangle$, $w_{k+1} = \langle i', j' \rangle$ must satisfy $i' - i \leq 1$ and $j' - j \leq 1$.

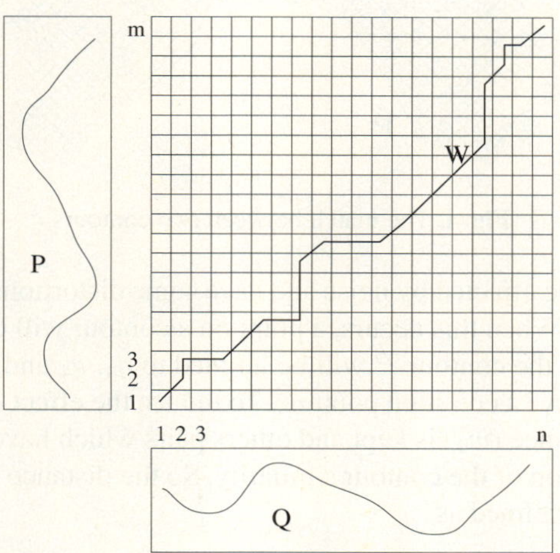

Fig. 3. An example of dynamic time warping

The optimal warp path is the minimum-distance one, where the distance of a warp path is

$$L = \sum_{k=1}^{K} d(i_k, j_k) = \sum_{k=1}^{K} d(w_k) \tag{9}$$

and $w_k = \langle i_k, j_k \rangle$ is the kth matched pair of the two series. This optimal path can be found very efficiently using dynamic programming [17].

4.2 Contour Similarity Measures

Since an optimal match can be found through DTW, using the average path distance of L to measure the similarity between two contours is a matter of course. The average distance between two contours P and Q is

$$\bar{L}(P, Q) = \frac{1}{K} \sum_{k=1}^{K} d(w_k) \tag{10}$$

where $W = [w_1, w_2, \cdots, w_K]$ is the optimal match between the contours P and Q.

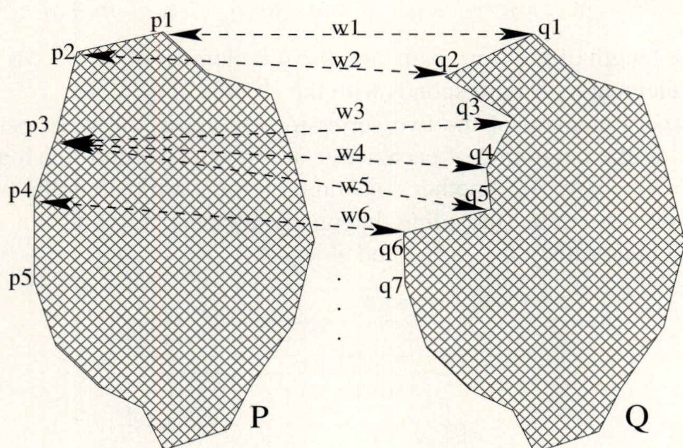

Fig. 4. The match between two contours

The contours can be affected by noise and have some distortions (q_3, q_4 and q_5 on the contour Q in Fig. 4). When this occurs, a point on a contour will be aligned to multiple points. That is, p_3 on the contour P will be aligned to q_3, q_4 and q_5 on the contour Q, and w_3, w_4 and w_5 have a common point p_3. To reduce the effect of noise, only the pair with the shortest distance (w_4) is kept and others pairs which have a common point are discarded in calculation of the contour similarity. So the distance between the contours P and Q can also be defined as

$$\mathbb{L}(P, Q) = \frac{1}{K'} \sum_{k \in \mathbb{K}} d(w_k) \tag{11}$$

where K' is the number of elements in $\mathbb{K}$, $\mathbb{K}$ is a subset of $\{1, 2, \cdots, K\}$, and the pairs with a common point are removed and only the one with the shortest distance is kept.

Now we have two similarity measures: the traditional DTW average distance $\bar{L}$ and the improved DTW average distance $\bar{\mathbb{L}}$.

4.3 Video Sequence Similarity Measures

Suppose that there are two gait sequences $\boldsymbol{S}^G$ and $\boldsymbol{S}^P$, with sequence $\boldsymbol{S}^G$ from the gallery set (the training set), and sequence $\boldsymbol{S}^P$ from the probe set (the test set). The two sequences can be divided ino several gait cycles as illustrated in Equation 3. The distance between the two sequences is

$$\begin{gathered} SeqDist(\boldsymbol{S}^G, \boldsymbol{S}^P) = \min_{i,j}(CycleDist(\boldsymbol{S}_i^G, \boldsymbol{S}_j^P)) \\ i \in \{1, 2, \cdots, C^G\}, j \in \{1, 2, \cdots, C^P\} \end{gathered} \tag{12}$$

where $\boldsymbol{S}_i^G$ is the ith gait cycle in the sequence $\boldsymbol{S}^G$, and $\boldsymbol{S}_j^P$ is the jth gait cycle in the sequence $\boldsymbol{S}^P$. The distance between these two gait cycles can be:

$$CycleDist(\boldsymbol{S}_i^G, \boldsymbol{S}_j^P) = \frac{1}{T}\sum_{t=1}^{T} \bar{L}(\boldsymbol{s}_t^G, \boldsymbol{s}_t^P) \tag{13}$$

or

$$CycleDist(\boldsymbol{S}_i^G, \boldsymbol{S}_j^P) = \frac{1}{T}\sum_{t=1}^{T} \bar{\mathbb{L}}(\boldsymbol{s}_t^G, \boldsymbol{s}_t^P) \tag{14}$$

where $\boldsymbol{s}_t^G$ is the tth contour in the gait cycle $\boldsymbol{S}_i^G$, and $\boldsymbol{s}_t^P$ is the tth contour in the gait cycle $\boldsymbol{S}_j^P$.

5 Experimental Results

The proposed method was tested on CASIA Gait Database (Dataset B) [13] which contains 124 subjects (93 males and 31 females) captured from 11 views. One experiment was carried out for each view. There are six sequences for each subject at each view. The first four sequences were put into the gallery set, and the last two were put into the probe set as in [13]. Each sequence in the probe set was compared with all sequences in the gallery set using the DTW distance in Equation 12. Besides the DTW distance, the Euclidean distance was also involved for performance comparison.

Because the focus here is the contour similarity measure, a simple and most commonly used classifier, nearest neighbor classifier, was used in the experiments. The correct classification rates (CCRs) are listed in Table 1. We can find from Table 1 that the DTW-based measures greatly improve the recognition rate of gait recognition. The improve DTW-based measure, $\bar{\mathbb{L}}$, which achieves the highest CCR. The average CCR by the Euclidean distance is only 67.7%. The KFD method in [18] obtained better results than the Euclidean distance, but the average CCR is just 2.6% higher than that by the Euclidean distance. The improvement by the KFD method is not as great as the DTW-based methods achieved.

Table 1. CCRs by different methods(%)

Method	0°	18°	36°	54°	72°	90°	108°	126°	144°	162°	180°	Average
Improved DTW($\mathbb{L}$)	93.5	84.7	85.9	80.2	83.9	83.5	73.0	80.6	89.9	90.7	92.7	85.3
Trad. DTW($\bar{L}$)	91.1	81.9	83.1	79.4	81.0	81.0	70.6	80.6	88.7	86.7	90.3	83.1
Euclidean Dist.	60.5	51.2	63.3	67.3	72.2	71.4	63.3	72.6	79.0	77.8	66.1	67.7
KFD in [18]	71.8	49.2	72.6	69.4	77.8	75.0	69.8	71.4	71.0	77.8	67.7	70.3

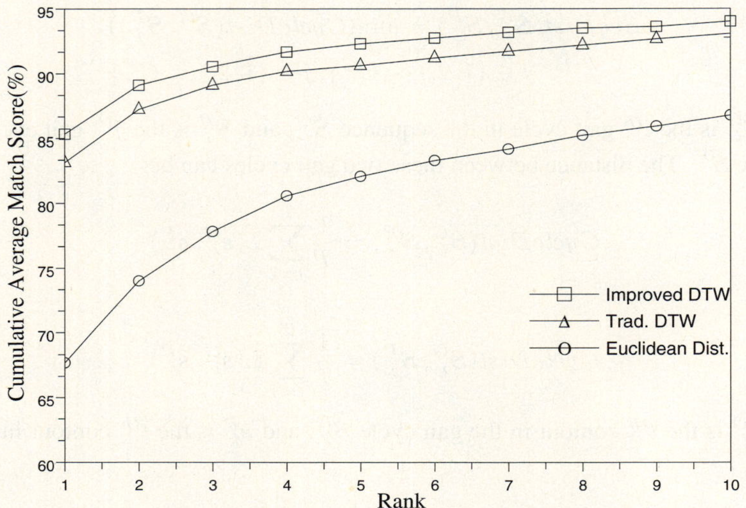

Fig. 5. Cumulative Average match scores of three different measures

Cumulative match scores (CMS) are also used to evaluate the performance of proposed methods. The match scores in Fig. 5 are the average match scores of 11 views from rank 1 to 10. From Fig. 5, we can draw similar conclusions to that from Table 1.

Although the DTW-based contour similarity measures are simple methods, they greatly improve the robustness to noise. The experiments discover their potential in gait recognition and show contour matching is effective in reducing the impact of noise.

6 Conclusions and Future Work

We have presented two novel contour similarity measures for gait recognition. DTW is used to match the points on two contours before computing their similarity. The similarity between two contours is computed based on their optimal match. Experiments on a large gait database show that the DTW-based measures are superior to direct contour comparison and even some other feature extraction methods. Although the proposed method is simple and straightforward, it indicates a principle that contour matching can reduce the effect of noise.

In future we will design more sophisticated similarity measures to make the algorithm more robust to noise and even some other variations. Some other advanced classifiers, such as SVM and AdaBoost, will also be investigated.

Acknowledgements

This work is partially supported by National Natural Science Foundation of China (Grant No. 60332010 and 60335010), the National Basic Research Program of China (Grant No. 2004CB318100) and China International Science and Technology Cooperation (Grant No. 2004DFA06900).

References

1. Johnson, A.Y., Bobick, A.F.: A multi-view method for gait recognition using static body parameters. In: Proc. of 3rd International Conference on Audio and Video Based Biometric Person Authentication, Halmstad, Sweden, pp. 301–311 (June 2001)
2. Wang, L., Ning, H., Tan, T., Hu, W.: Fusion of static and dynamic body biometrics for gait recognition. IEEE Transactions on Circuits and Systems for Video Technology 14(2), 149–158 (2004)
3. Yam, C.Y., Nixon, M.S., Carter, J.N.: On the relationship of human walking and running: automatic person identification by gait. In: Proc. of International Conference on Pattern Recognition, Quebec,Canada, pp. 287–290 (2002)
4. Mowbray, S.D., Nixon, M.S.: Automatic gait recognition via fourier descriptors of deformable objects. In: Proc. of 4th International Conference on Audio- and Video-based Biometric Person Authentication, Guildford, UK, pp. 566–573 (June 2003)
5. Wang, L., Tan, T., Ning, H., Hu, W.: Silhouette analysis-based gait recognition for human identification. IEEE Transactions on Pattern Analysis and Machine Intelligence 25(12), 1505–1518 (2003)
6. Niyogi, S.A., Adelson, E.H.: Analyzing and recognizing walking figures in xyt. In: CVPR, pp. 469–474. IEEE Computer Society Press, Los Alamitos (1994)
7. Yu, S., Wang, L., Hu, W., Tan, T.: Gait analysis for human identification in frequency domain. In: Proc. of the 3rd International Conference on Image and Graphics, Hong Kong, China, pp. 282–285 (December 2004)
8. Lam, T.H.W., Lee, R.S.T.: Human identification by using the motion and static characteristic of gait. In: ICPR, pp. 996–999. IEEE Computer Society Press, Los Alamitos (2006)
9. Cuntoor, N., Kale, A., Chellappa, R.: Combining multiple evidences for gait recognition. In: Proc. of the International Conference on Acoustics Speech and Signal Processing, Hong Kong (cancelled), April 6-10, 2003, vol. III, pp. 113–116 (2003)
10. Boulgouris, N.V., Plataniotis, K.N., Hatzinakos, D.: Gait recognition using dynamic time warping. In: Proc. of the 6'th IEEE workshop on multimedia signal processing, BC, Canada, pp. 263–266. IEEE Computer Society Press, Los Alamitos (2004)
11. Pandey, N., Abdulla, W., Salcic, Z.: Human identification using vector quantisation technique. In: Proceedings of the Eighth International Symposium on Signal Processing and Its Applications, Sydney, Australia, pp. 671–674 (August 2005)
12. Veeraraghavan, A., Member, S., Roy-Chowdhury, A.K., Chellappa, R.: Matching shape sequences in video with applications in human movement analysis. IEEE Transactions on Pattern Analysis and Machine Intelligence 27(12), 1896–1909 (2005)

13. Yu, S., Tan, D., Tan, T.: A framework for evaluating the effect of view angle, clothing and carrying condition on gait recognition. In: Proc. of the 18'th International Conference on Pattern Recognition (ICPR06), Hong Kong, China, pp. 441–444 (August 2006)
14. Sarkar, S., Phillips, P.J., Liu, Z., Vega, I.R., Grother, P., Bowyer, k.W.: The humanid gait challenge problem: Data sets, performance, and analysis. IEEE Transactions on Pattern Analysis and Machine Intelligence 27(2), 162–177 (2005)
15. Kruskal, L.: The symmetric time-warping problem: From continuous to discrete. In: Sankoff, D., Kruskal, J.B. (eds.) Time Warps, String Edits, and Macromolecules: The Theory and Practice of Sequence Comparison. Addison-Wesley, Reading (1983)
16. Veeraraghavan, A., Chellappa, R., Roy-Chowdhury, A.K.: The function space of an activity. In: Proceedings of the 2006 IEEE Computer Society Conference on Computer Vision and Pattern Recognition (CVPR'06), New York, USA, pp. 959–968. IEEE Computer Society Press, Los Alamitos (2006)
17. Keogh, E.J., Pazzani, M.J.: Derivative dynamic time warping. In: Proc. of the First SIAM International Conference on Data Mining, Chicago, USA, pp. 285–289 (April 2001)
18. Yu, S., Tan, D., Tan, T.: Modelling the effect of view angle variation on appearance-based gait recognition. In: Proc. of the 7'th Asian Conference on Computer Vision, Hyderabad, India, pp. 807–816 (January 2006)

Partitioning Gait Cycles Adaptive to Fluctuating Periods and Bad Silhouettes

Jianyi Liu and Nanning Zheng

Institute of AI & Robotics, Xi'an Jiaotong University, P.R. China
jyliu@aiar.xjtu.edu.cn

Abstract. Period detection and cycle partitioning are always the very beginning for most gait recognition algorithms. Badly segmented silhouettes and random fluctuations in walking speed are two of the main problems for this basic but important issue. In this paper, we propose a method of cycle partitioning that is adaptive to silhouette quality and speed fluctuations. To do that, autocorrelation on sliding window is proposed to quantify the silhouette quality into "trusted zones" and "uncertain zones". Prior period estimation and observation of fluctuations are incorporated to obtain more precise cycle detection. One criterion based on the difference of Common Phase Frames (CPF) is proposed to evaluate the precision of detection. In experiment, our method was compared with the traditional autocorrelation method using sequences from the USF gait database. The results showed the improved cycle partitioning performance of the proposed method.

1 Introduction

As a young branch of biometrics, human gait has raised much attention in recent years. It has great potential in individual identification and video surveillance areas. Research in this field includes gait modeling [11], gait feature analysis [13], gait recognition based on model [4,8,12,13] or appearance [2,7,9,10], silhouette extraction and refinement [8,10], and semantic gait analysis etc.

Periodicity is one of the important characteristics of gait out of other biometrics. Precise period estimation is always the very beginning of any gait recognition algorithm. The autocorrelation-based methods [1,5] are a simple but common way to compute period from the foreground sum of silhouettes. Sinusoidal signal was used in [3] to fit such foreground sum curve so that the period was ready to be read. In [4], minima of the sum signal were detected and used as the separating points of cycles. [2] investigated and quantified the impacts of 4 different walking speeds (0.7, 1.0, 1.3, 1.6 m/s) upon gait recognition performance, and proposed method to normalize gait features across varying period lengths. [6] estimated the stride length and cadence by assuming a linear characteristic of them under multiple walking speeds.

S.-W. Lee and S.Z. Li (Eds.): ICB 2007, LNCS 4642, pp. 347–355, 2007.

The major problems of gait cycle detection lie in two aspects: badly segmented silhouettes and varying walking speeds. The first problem is mainly caused by complex background. Pre-filtering [4,5] is usually applied to de-noise the foreground sum signal prior to analysis. However, local signals with severe noise are hard to remedy through this global filtering. The second problem is varying speed, which has been paid less attention in literature up to now. Some works [2,6] analyzed gait at several discrete speeds. Instead, we aim to study fluctuating walking speed, which means the speed varies randomly around an approximate constant. This reflects the real status of walking behavior.

In this article, systematical study on periodicity and cycle detection of silhouette-based gait sequences is performed: we proposed the concept as well as a prototype approach of Silhouette Quality Quantification (SQQ) using autocorrelation on sliding window. Based on the binary estimation of sequence quality along frame number, "trusted zones" and "uncertain zones" were separated. Cycle detection adaptive to fluctuating speed and silhouette quality were implemented by incorporating the prior estimation and observations in each zone. In addition, a criterion based on the mean difference of Common Phase Frames (CPF) was proposed to quantitatively evaluate the cycle partitioning precision.

Our method contributes on robust period detection even with very bad silhouette parts, and can detect the time-variation cycles of gait sequence with subtle fluctuation in walking speed. Comparing with the fixed period detection in traditional approaches, our method results in more precise cycle partitioning that is beneficial for any further gait analysis task.

2 Fixed Period Detection

Most of the approaches towards gait recognition detect gait cycles using foreground sum signal $S(n)=\sum_{x,y} I(x,y,n)$, $n=0\cdots N-1$, from all N silhouette images $I(x,y,n)$. This signal is usually very noisy due to complex background so that pre-processing is required. In [4], an adaptive filter was applied prior to the calculation of gait cycles. In general, Gaussian filter [7] is a usual way to smooth the raw sum signal.

Given filtered foreground sum signal, the fixed period detection method works based on the autocorrelation function of $S(n)$, denoted as $A_S(n)$. Its peaks n^+ can be located by judgements of $A_S(n^+)-A_S(n^+-1)>0$ and $A_S(n^+ +1)-A_S(n^+)\le 0$. The x-coordinate of the second peak will tell the half gait period (e.g. from one double support stance to the next), denoted as prd. For simplicity, we use prd as the period value in the following.

However, the fixed period value can't precisely partition a gait sequence with fluctuating walking speed which is ordinary for normal walking. Besides, this method is also vulnerable from silhouettes with low quality.

3 Adaptive Period Detection

3.1 Silhouette Quality Quantification

In outdoor environment, complex backgrounds make the background subtraction task difficult and produce "polluted" silhouettes, which obviously will affect the performance of appearance-based gait recognition algorithms. Therefore, methods for refining the silhouettes were proposed [8]. However, in most of the literature considering silhouette quality, the means for evaluating it still remains unsettled. We introduce a quantitative method in this paper addressing this issue.

It is easy to notice that a "clean" silhouette sequence will produce a smooth $S(n)$ curve with clear periodicity, while a "polluted" one will show a chaos $S(n)$ with vague periodicity. So $S(n)$ is a direct embodiment of silhouette quality. Because bad silhouettes often occur consecutively in real case, we study the quality of sub-sequence of $S(n)$ rather than single frame. Let $Si(n)$ denote the *i*-th fragment of $S(n)$. It starts from the *i*-th frame of the sequence and has a length of *W*. We can use *sliding window* to define such a fragment: $Si(n) = S(n+i)R_W(n)$. Here $R_W(n)$ denotes the rectangle window function which has unit values for $n = 0 \cdots W-1$ and zero elsewhere.

Using the same approach described in section 2, $Si(n)$ can also produce its own autocorrelation function $A_{Si}(n)$ and period value prd_i. For walking sequence with approximately constant speed, a widely different local period prd_i apart from holistic period prd can tell a bad fragment. We use the normalized difference between these two period values as part of our fragment quality metric:

$$Q_x(i) = 1 - \frac{|prd_i - prd|}{prd} \tag{1}$$

Another characteristic of bad fragments is their vague periodicity as mentioned above. We use the normalized difference between the heights of the first and the second peaks of $A_{Si}(n)$ to measure the periodicity here:

$$Q_y(i) = 1 - \frac{|A_{Si}(0) - A_{Si}(prd_i)|}{A_{Si}(0)} = \frac{A_{Si}(prd_i)}{A_{Si}(0)} \tag{2}$$

In fact, Q_x and Q_y are respectively derived from the horizontal and the vertical observations of the autocorrelation curve $A_{Si}(n)$. The final estimation of silhouette quality on fragment *i* is defined as the product of them:

$$\mathcal{Q}(i) = Q_x(i) \cdot Q_y(i) \tag{3}$$

3.2 Adaptive Cycle Partitioning

For robust and precise cycle partitioning, we start with the fixed period value *prd* obtained in section 2. It serves as the prior knowledge of our period estimation and needs to be refined.

For simplicity, binary silhouette quality is used below. We binarize the $\mathcal{Q}(i)$ according to a predefined threshold *th*, thus dividing the whole $S(i)$ into "trusted zones" (with $\mathcal{Q}(i) \geq th$) and "uncertain zones" (with $\mathcal{Q}(i) < th$). $S(i)$ within the latter one is erased to decrease the impact coming from bad silhouettes:

$$S'(i) = \begin{cases} G(S(i)), & \mathcal{Q}(i) \geq th \\ 0, & \mathcal{Q}(i) < th \end{cases}, \quad i = 0 \cdots N-1 \tag{4}$$

Here, Gaussian filter $G(\cdot)$ is applied upon $S(i)$ to smooth it.

In [3], a sinusoidal wave signal was used to fit the periodical foreground sum signal so that cycles of the sequence were available. Here we use a similar way and a saw wave signal $saw(n)$, $n = 0 \cdots N-1$ is used. Its initial period is set to *prd*. We perturb its period and phase to find its optimal fitness with $S'(i)$ by searching the max normalized cross-correlation of them. In the obtained $saw'(n)$, each peak is ready to tell a partitioning position.

Since the fragments of $S(i)$ within $\mathcal{Q}(i) < th$ is "uncertain" and thus erased, partitioning within such zones can only rely on the prior knowledge coming from the peaks on $saw'(n)$. In the "trusted zones" however, the observation from $S'(i)$ is also available. So for each prior peak position i on $saw'(n)$, we search $S'(i)$ within its δ neighbor region to find the posterior peak n^* as depicted in (5). All these n^* act as the partitioning points in the "trusted zones".

$$n^* = \underset{n \in [i-\delta, i+\delta]}{\arg\max}\, S'(n) \tag{5}$$

The adaptive period detection described above can partition the cycles according to the prior rough estimation for silhouettes with bad quality, and can adjust them according to the observation from fluctuating cycle lengths for good silhouettes. So compared to the fixed period method, our method can partition the gait cycles more precisely.

3.3 Evaluation Method

For perfectly partitioned cycles with perfect silhouettes, all frames with the same relative offset from the start of each cycle should appear with salient similarity. Based on this idea, we built up our evaluation criterion for cycle partitioning.

Let n^j denote the start frame number of any cycle j which occupies a phase increment of 2π. Then the frame number on phase φ ($0 \le \varphi < 2\pi$) in cycle j can be computed by $n^j + round\left(\left(n^{j+1} - n^j\right) \cdot \varphi / 2\pi\right)$. The operator $round(\cdot)$ is applied here to acquire integer value. We name all such frames on the same phase of every cycle Common Phase Frames (CPF), and their frame numbers constitute set N^φ. The intention of defining CPF is to evaluate the precision of cycle partitioning according to their similarity. To do that, we firstly compute the average image of all CPFs on any phase φ:

$$\overline{I}^\varphi(x,y) = \frac{1}{\left|N^\varphi\right|} \sum_{n \in N^\varphi} I(x,y,n) \tag{6}$$

Here, $\left|N^\varphi\right|$ means the number of elements in set N^φ. Similar definition as $\overline{I}^\varphi$ has also been used by Gait Energy Image (GEI) [9]. In our evaluation criterion, the similarity of CPFs is measured through their mean error from $\overline{I}^\varphi$:

$$err^\varphi = \frac{1}{\left|N^\varphi\right|} \sum_{n \in N^\varphi} \sum_{x,y} \left| I(x,y,n) - \overline{I}^\varphi(x,y) \right| \tag{7}$$

In general, more precise partitioning of cycles should result in greater similarity of CPFs, that is, smaller err^φ.

4 Experiments

The gait sequences used in our experiments comes from the USF gait database [10]. The videos in it were captured in outdoor environment with complex background and varying illumination, so many silhouettes with low quality were produced. We randomly selected 5 sequences from the gallery set to test our method.

4.1 Silhouette Quality

In Fig. 1, the foreground sum signals $S(n)$ derived from two different silhouette sequences are plotted in (a) and (d). The "polluted" silhouette fragments present weak periodicity comparing to the "clean" fragments. This is the basis of our Silhouette Quality Quantification (SQQ) criterion. The quality curves $\mathcal{Q}(i)$ of (a) and (d) are showed in (b) and (e) respectively. These SQQ results present similar judgments with our subjective observations. After binarization, their respective binary silhouette quality estimations are plotted in (c) and (f). The threshold *th* is empirically set to 0.7 based on the characteristic of the data used in this paper. The "uncertain zones" labeled with 0 are clearly distinguishable from the "trusted zones" labeled with 1.

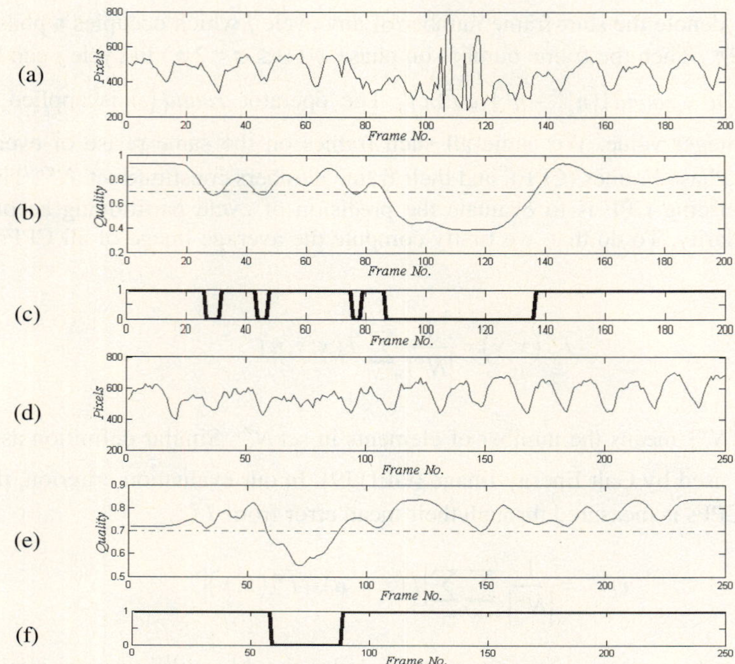

Fig. 1. Two examples of Silhouette Quality Quantification (SQQ). (a) and (d) are foreground sum signals $S(n)$ from two of our test sequences. (b) and (e) are their SQQ curves $\mathcal{Q}(i)$. (c) and (f) are their corresponding binarized results.

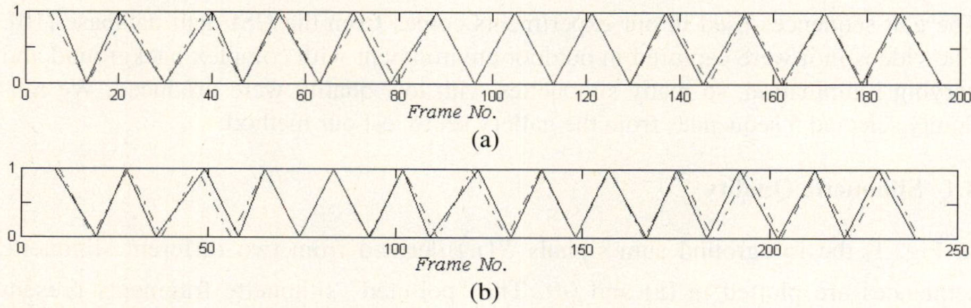

Fig. 2. Comparison of fixed cycle detection and adaptive cycle detection. (a) and (b) are from the same sequences as (a) and (d) in Fig. 1. Adaptive cycle detection is denoted by saw wave signals with solid line, while the fixed period results use the dashed line.

4.2 Cycle Partitioning

In Fig. 2, two examples of cycle detection results are denoted through saw waves. We use the same sequences as in section 4.1. The fixed period detections are plotted with dashed line, while the same sequences with adaptive cycle detection are plotted with solid line for comparison. Note that in the "uncertain zones", they overlap with each other, because only prior period value can be exploited here. However, in the "trusted zones", using neighbor region width of $\delta = 2$, the prior positions of peaks have been updated by more precise observations according to (5). Same approach has also been applied to search valleys of the saw waves. The results show the characteristic of speed fluctuations in normal walking.

Table 1. The err^{φ} of CPFs are used to evaluate the precision of partitioning

	Phase	*Seq.1*	*Seq.2*	*Seq.3*	*Seq.4*	*Seq.5*	*Total mean*
Adaptive cycles	0	6.70	5.42	7.47	3.19	5.61	
	$\pi/2$	8.51	8.72	11.60	5.57	7.86	
	π	9.12	8.98	9.84	4.83	7.59	
	$3\pi/2$	7.49	7.79	8.75	3.45	4.25	
	mean	**7.96**	**7.73**	**9.42**	**4.26**	**6.33**	**7.14**
Fixed cycles	0	7.64	6.48	8.02	3.16	5.97	
	$\pi/2$	10.56	8.28	12.37	6.06	5.83	
	π	10.10	9.13	11.59	4.50	8.31	
	$3\pi/2$	8.52	7.70	8.28	5.12	4.09	
	mean	**9.21**	**7.90**	**10.07**	**4.71**	**6.05**	**7.59**

Table 1 has compared the two methods introduced in this paper. CPFs on 4 different phases ($\varphi = 0, \pi/2, \pi, 3\pi/2$) from one of our test sequences are extracted and computed for evaluation of partitioning precision using the mean error criterion as (7). The proposed adaptive partitioning method outperforms the fixed period partitioning as a whole. Fig. 3 shows the CPFs produced by both methods. The results from our method (enclosed by rounded rectangles) show more consistency comparing to those from the fixed period detection.

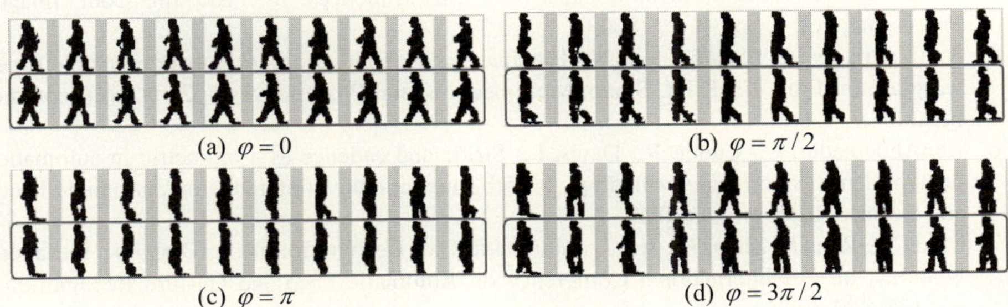

Fig. 3. Eamples of CPFs on 4 phases from one of our test sequences. For each phase, the first row shows CPFs coming from the fixed period detection, while the second row enclosed by rounded rectangle corresponds to CPFs coming from the adaptive cycle detection.

5 Conclusion and Future Works

In this paper, gait cycle partitioning was systematically studied, considering bad silhouette quality and fluctuating walking speed. The fixed period detection result was used as the prior estimation, which was further refined by the observation of fluctuations in the "trusted zones" to obtain more precise cycle partitioning. To do that, criteria for quantifying silhouette quality and evaluating cycle precision were proposed. The experiment results showed improved performance on partitioning precision of our method comparing with the fixed period approach.

Precision period detection is with no doubt essential to gait recognition task. Further more, the detection result of subtle fluctuations in walking speed can also provide beneficial cues for semantic and affective gait analysis. For instance, hesitating wandering will present totally different fluctuating features on walking speed compared to consistently striding. This will be our research interest next.

Acknowledgements. This work was supported by the National Science Foundation of China (Grant No. 60405004) and the National High-Tech Research and Development Plan of China (Grant No.20060101Z1059).

References

1. Boulgouris, N.V., Hatzinakos, D., Plataniotis, K.N.: Gait recognition: a challenging signal processing technology for biometric identification. IEEE Signal Processing Magazine 22(6), 78–90 (2005)
2. Tanawongsuwan, R., Bobick, A.: Modelling the Effects of Walking Speed on Appearance-Based Gait Recognition. In: IEEE Computer Society Conference on Computer Vision and Pattern Recognition, pp. 783–790 (2004)
3. Little, J., Boyd, J.: Recognizing people by their gait: The shape of motion. Videre, Int. J. Computer Vision 14(6), 83–105 (1998)
4. Sundaresan, A., Roy Chowdhury, A.K., Chellappa, R.: A hidden Markov model based framework for recognition of humans from gait sequences. In: Proc. Int. Conf. Image Processing, vol. 2, pp. 14–17 (2003)
5. Boulgouris, N.V., Plataniotis, K.N., Hatzinakos, D.: Gait recognition using dynamic time warping. In: Proc. IEEE Int. Symp. Multimedia Signal Processing, pp. 263–266 (September 2004)
6. BenAbdelkader, C., Cutler, R., Davis, L.: Stride and cadence as a biometric in automatic person identification and verification. In: 5th International Conference on Automatic Face and Gesture Recognition (2002)
7. Chai, Y., Ren, J., Zhao, R., Jia, J.: Automatic Gait Recognition using Dynamic Variance Features. In: 7th International Conference on Automatic Face and Gesture Recognition, pp. 475–480 (2006)
8. Lee, L., Dalley, G., Tieu, K.: Learning pedestrian models for silhouette refinement. In: Proc. of Ninth IEEE International Conference on Computer Vision, pp. 663–670 (2003)
9. Han, J., Bhanu, B.: Individual Recognition Using Gait Energy Image. IEEE Trans. on Pattern Analysis and Machine Intelligence 28(2), 316–322 (2006)

10. Sarkar, S., Phillips, P.J., Liu, Z., Vega, I.R., Grother, P., Bowyer, K.W.: The Humanid Gait Challenge Problem: Data Sets, Performance, and Analysis. IEEE Trans. on Pattern Analysis and Machine Intelligence 27(2), 162–177 (2005)
11. Lu, H., Plataniotis, K.N., Venetsanopoulos, A.N.: A Layered Deformable Model for Gait Analysis. In: Proc. IEEE Int. Conf. on Automatic Face and Gesture Recognition, pp. 249–256 (2006)
12. Wang, L., Tan, T., Ning, H., Hu, W.: Fusion of Static and Dynamic Body Biometrics for Gait Recognition. IEEE Trans. on Circuits and Systems for Video Technology 14(I2), 149–158 (2004)
13. Wagg, D.K., Nixon, M.S.: On Automated Model-based Extraction and Analysis of Gait. In: 6th International Conference on Automatic Face and Gesture Recognition, pp. 11–16 (2004)

Repudiation Detection in Handwritten Documents

Sachin Gupta and Anoop M. Namboodiri

International Institute of Information Technology, Hyderabad, India
sachin_g@students.iiit.ac.in, anoop@iiit.ac.in

Abstract. Forensic document verification presents a different and interesting set of challenges as opposed to traditional writer identification and verification tasks using natural handwriting. The handwritten data presented to a forensic examiner is often deliberately altered, in addition to being limited in quantity. Specifically, the alterations can be either forged, where one imitates another person's handwriting; or repudiated, where one deliberately distorts his handwriting in order to avoid identification. In this paper, we present a framework to detect repudiation in forensic documents, where we only have one pair of documents to arrive at a decision. The approach generates a statistically significant confidence score from matching two documents, which can be used to screen the documents that are passed on to an expert examiner. The approach can be extended for detection of forgeries as well.

1 Introduction

In forensic science, the primary role of handwriting analysis is in Questioned Document Examination (QDE) [1,2]. Determining the authorship of a document is the main task in QDE, where one has to decide whether a pair of documents, the *questioned document* (one whose origin is unknown) and the *reference document* (one whose origin might be known), were written by the same writer or not. However, due to the circumstances under which the documents are generated, there is a motivation for the writer to deliberately alter his natural handwriting to avoid detection. We refer to this problem as *handwriting repudiation*, as the purpose of distortion is to deny someone's involvement in the case (repudiation [3]).

The problem of detection of repudiation in QDE is different from that of traditional writer identification and verification tasks. Writer identification is the problem of identifying the writer of a document as one of the enrolled candidates. In writer verification, the writer claims an identity and we need to verify the claim. In both identification and verification problems, writer need to be enrolled into the system before hand. However, in the case of forensic documents, we only have a single questioned document, and a reference sample collected from the suspect, which in turn might not be natural. The two problems that arise here are:

- *Forgery Detection*: The problem is identical to that of verification, except that there is an additional suspicion that the writer could be an impersonator.
- *Repudiation Detection*: Given two samples of handwriting (both could be deliberately distorted), verify the claim that they are from different writers.

S.-W. Lee and S.Z. Li (Eds.): ICB 2007, LNCS 4642, pp. 356–365, 2007.

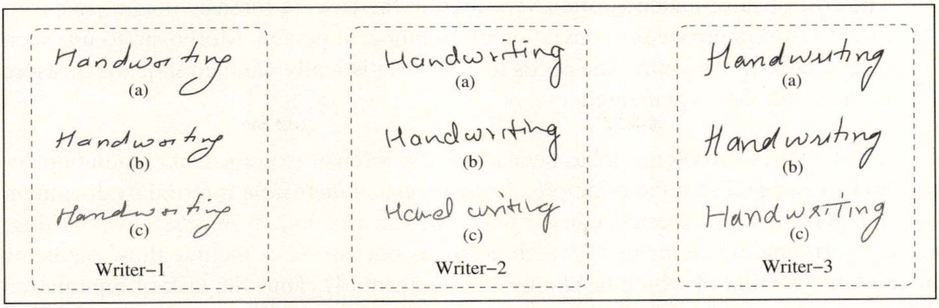

Fig. 1. (a) and (b) show natural handwriting samples from 3 writers, and (c) shows the repudiated samples from the writers

Note that in both identification and verification tasks, the users are assumed to be cooperative, and one could build statistical models for each writer from their natural handwriting. However, in the case of forgery, the questioned document need not be natural, and in repudiation, both the questioned document and the reference document could be distorted. Moreover, we have to assume that the writer is non-cooperative. Figure 1 shows examples of words from two writers in their natural form, as well as when they distort their handwriting for repudiation.

In this paper, we primarily deal with the problem of repudiation in handwritten documents. We propose a generic framework for automated analysis of handwritten documents to flag suspicious cases of repudiation.

1.1 Automatic Detection of Repudiation

Extraction of writer information from handwriting is more challenging as compared to verification based on physical biometrics traits, due to the large intra-class variation (between handwriting samples of the same person), and the large inter-class similarity (same words being written by different people). Moreover, the handwriting of a writer may also be affected by the nature of the pen, writing surface, and writers mental state. In addition, the problem of forensic document analysis is particularly difficult due to the additional problems posed by repudiation:

- During repudiation, a writer tries to change his handwriting style to be different from that of his natural handwriting. This introduces a large amount of intra-class variability that the system has to handle. Moreover, the writer need to be assumed to be non-cooperative, unlike in forgery, where the person who is being forged will be cooperative and will provide his natural handwriting in the required manner and amount.
- The content of the handwriting that is available in QDE is not in our control, and is often small in quantity. This prevents us from using the less frequent statistical properties of the handwriting for the purpose of verification of the claims.

– The cost of false match is often very high in the case of forensic documents, as it might result in erroneous conviction of an innocent person. Moreover, to use such an evidence in the court, one needs to give a statistically valid confidence measure in the result that is generated.

In spite of all these problems, it has been shown by forensic experts, that repudiation detection is possible. From the principle of *exclusion* and *inclusion*, inferred by document examiners from their experience in the field, one can't exclude from one's own writing, those discriminating elements of which he/she is not aware, or include those elements of another's writing of which he/she is not cognizant [4]. Thus the task of repudiation detection comes down to finding the discriminating elements of which, the writer is not aware of. We propose a framework (see Figure 2) that exploits the statistical similarity between lower level feature distributions in two documents to detect possible cases of repudiation. One needs to add a line of caution here that many of the clues that are used by forensic experts comes from external sources (such as background of the suspect, examination of paper material, etc.) and are not available to an automatic writer verification system. Hence any such system can only be used as an aid to a forensic expert, and not a replacement.

The prior work in this area primarily concentrates on the problems of natural handwritten documents.Comprehensive survey of work untill 1989 has been given in [5]. Based on previous research in the field, we can categorize it as text independent vs text dependent, identification vs verification, and online vs offline handwriting. One major class of text independent methods consider handwriting as texture and use various texture analysis methods, such as multi resolution gabor filter [6]. Another class of text independent methods consider handwriting as a psychomotor process and human being as a perpetual motion genertor. Schomacker et al. [7], presented a method based on density functions of lower level features extracted from connected components in handwritten images for writer identification. However, this approach requires a large amount of handwritten data to model the writer, which is not available in the case of QDE.

Macro features (such as grey level distributions, grey level threshold, contour connectivity, contour slope and slant of characters) and micro features (such as, gradient, structural and concavity) [8] are popular for writer identification and verification with natural handwriting. Such features are possible candidates for repudiation detection as well. However, in the case of QDE, as the data available is limited, it is difficult to calculate the distributions of such features, robustly.

Velocity based approaches, like FIR response of Fourier coefficients of velocity [9] and pen pressure based approaches [10] have also been tried in context of online documents. However, in the case of repudiation detection, the questioned document might not be online. Hence, features based only on velocity or pen pressure can not be used. Approaches that uses text line based features with HMM [11] to statistically model handwriting of a writer, also extract high level features and thus is not appropriate for QDE.

The work proposed by Srihari et al. [12], for writer verification using statistical inference can be used to calculate the significance of distance between a given pair of documents. In case of forgery, most of the work is done in physical biometrics [13] as

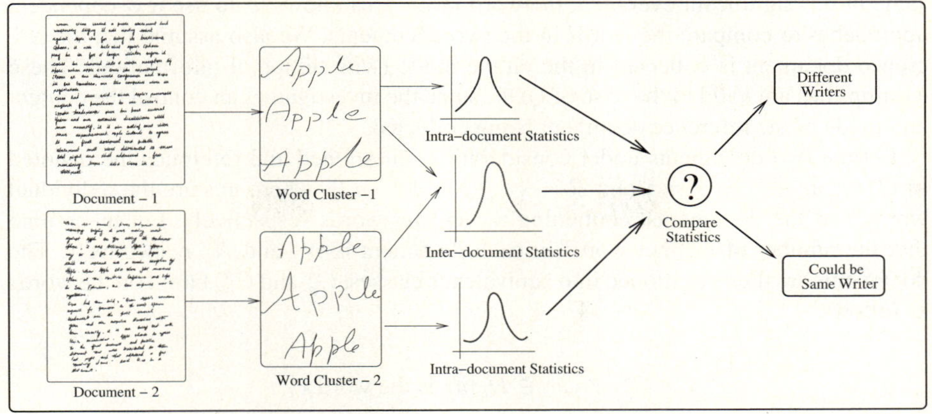

Fig. 2. Framework for detecting repudiation from handwriting

well as signature verification [14]. We are not aware of any work done on repudiation of handwritten documents till date. The approaches used for identification and verification can not be directly applied to repudiation, owing to the additional constraints involved. Moreover, all of the above approaches used for generic writer verification and identification extract discriminative elements of handwriting that can be used to discriminate between writers, while in repudiation detection, the major goal is to detect the underlying similarity between documents.

The remainder of this paper is organized as follows. The overall framework used in our solution is presented in Section 2. In Section 2.2, we will discuss implementation details with feature vector extraction. The experimental results and discussions are presented in section 3, followed by the conclusions and future work.

2 A Framework for Repudiation Detection

This section describes a generic framework for repudiation detection for questioned document examination. The primary goals of the framework are:

1. To develop a statistically significant matching score between two documents, without any additional information in the form of training data.
2. Utilize the online information that could be obtained from the reference document to improve the matching.
3. Allow the inclusion of additional features that might be extracted from the handwriting to enhance the results. This would also mean, we should not make specific assumptions about the distributions of the features, in the framework.
4. Allow the user to specify a confidence threshold, beyond which, the system will pass the documents for expert examination.

We also make the certain assumptions in our approach. The primary assumption is that the content of the questioned document and the reference document are either the same or has significant overlap at the word level. This allows us to use text-dependent approaches to compare the words in the two documents. We also assume that the reference document is collected in the online mode (with temporal information). These assumptions are valid in the case of QDE, since the investigator can control the content and mode of the reference document being collected.

Let the two documents under consideration, questioned and reference, be denoted as $Q = \{w_i; i = 1 \cdots n_q\}$ and $R = \{w_j; j = 1 \cdots n_r\}$, where w_is are the individual words and the documents, containing n_q and n_r words respectively. Let us assume that the number of distinct words in each document is N_q and N_r respectively. The documents are then partitioned into equivalence classes, C_q^k and C_r^k, based on the words as follows:

$$C_q^k = \{w_i \in D_q | w_i \text{ is the word } k\}$$
$$D_q = \bigcup_{k=1}^{N_q} C_q^k \tag{1}$$

This partitioning can be done using recognition-based or ink-matching based techniques. We then compute the correspondence between the sets in C_q and C_r, based on the words they denote. Note that we have assumed that there is a significant overlap between the sets, and hence some of the sets will match. Once again, we can find the correspondence based on recognition results or ink matching. Without loss of generality, we assume that the corresponding sets are C_q^k and C_r^k, $k = 1 \cdots K$.

To compute the similarity between the two documents, we first define a distance measure between two corresponding words, w_i and w_j, $d(w_i, w_j)$. This distance could be based on any set of features that are extracted from the words. We compute two distributions from these distances: i) p_w, the *within document distance distribution*; from the distances of corresponding words within the same document, and ii) p_b, the *between document distance distribution*; from the distances of corresponding words, one each from Q and R.

We now pose the computation of similarity between the two documents as that of testing the hypothesis, whether the two distributions, p_w, and p_b, come from the same population or not. The distance between the two distributions could be used in deciding, whether the two documents come from the same writer or not. We now look into the details of the distance measures and their statistical significance.

2.1 Detecting Repudiation and Forgery

One of the major problem in the case of verification by matching, is to assign a significance or confidence to the distance measure, computed between two documents. Traditionally, this is done based on a threshold, which in turn is calculated from training data. In the case of forensic documents, where training data is not available, we cannot rely on a threshold, which might be different for different writers. Hence we use a hypothesis testing based approach that computes the significance of the decision, taken at a particular level of confidence. It provides us with a formal means for verifying whether the two sample distributions, p_w and p_b come from the same population or not. We start with the assumption that the two documents are indeed from the same writer and test the validity of this hypothesis. If the hypothesis is rejected with sufficient confidence, we can eliminate the suspect from consideration. The two-class hypothesis testing problem for forensic documents can be posed as:

$$\begin{aligned} H_0 &= \text{Documents written by same writer} \\ H_1 &= \text{Documents written by different writers,} \end{aligned} \tag{2}$$

where H_0 is referred to as the null hypothesis, and H_1, the alternate hypothesis.

Several approaches have been used to compute the similarity between two distributions, the most popular of which are the Kullback-Leibler(KL) divergence or Kolmogorov-Smirnov(KS) test. Kullback-Leibler divergence or relative entropy measures the natural distance between a true probability distribution, P, and an arbitrary distribution, Q. For probability distributions P and Q of discrete variables, the KL divergence (or informally KL distance) of Q from P is given by:

$$\begin{aligned} D_{KL}(P||Q) &= \textstyle\sum_i P(i) \log \frac{P(i)}{Q(i)}; \text{ and} \\ P_{KL} &= e^{-\xi D_{KL}}, \end{aligned} \tag{3}$$

where P_{KL} gives the probability that the samples of the two distributions are drawn from the same population. Kullback Leibler distance essentially calculates divergence between distributions, and is not a distance metric, as it is neither symmetric nor satisfies triangle inequality. On the other hand, KS test determines whether whether an underlying probability distribution differs from a hypothesized distribution, based on finite samples. The KS-test also has the advantage of not making assumptions about the distribution of data and hence is non parametric. The two parameter KS-test is sensitive to differences in both location and shape of the empirical cumulative distribution functions of the two samples. KS test computes a simple distance measure, given by:

$$D_{KS}(P||Q) = \max_i |P(i) - Q(i)|, \tag{4}$$

where P and Q are the cumulative probability distribution functions and $P(i)$ and $Q(i)$ are corresponding probability values. The distance D_{KS} is, hence, the maximum absolute difference of cumulative probability on all potential values of i. The probability of similarity between two distributions is then calculated by:

$$\begin{aligned} P_{KS} &= Q_{KS}(\sqrt{N_e} + 0.12 + (\frac{0.11}{\sqrt{N_e}})D_{KS}) \\ Q_{KS}(\lambda) &= 2\sum_{j=1}^{\infty}(-1)^{j-1}e^{-2j^2\lambda^2} | Q_{KS}(0) = 1, Q_{KS}(\infty) = 0, \end{aligned} \tag{5}$$

where $N_e = N_1 N_2 (N_1 + N_2)^{-1}$ is effective number of data points (N_1 and N_2 are number of data points in two distributions respectively). The major limitation of the KS test is that it is more sensitive near the center of the distribution than at the tails. In this paper, we have used the KS test in all the experiments. A distance metric based on a combination of KL test and KS test explained in [15], and can be used to get some improvement in the results.

The formulation of the comparison using hypothesis test, makes an implicit assumption that any two documents from the same writer will have identical distribution of features. However, this is not true due to two factors: i) natural handwriting of two documents from a writer tends to be different due to environmental and physical conditions of the writer, and ii) in case of repudiation and forgery, the writer deliberately introduces some variations even if appropriate features are extracted. Hence we modify the hypothesis test result by looking at the confidence level of the result, and choosing a threshold, α, on the confidence to decide if we should involve an expert or not.

2.2 Comparison of Words

In case of repudiated documents, the extraction of appropriate features play an important role in deciding whether we can effectively deal with deliberate distortions of handwritten data. Based on the level of details, the discriminating features of handwriting can be divided as macro level or high level features and micro level or low level features. High level features, such as alignment, slope, slant of line and words can be altered with relative ease, as the person is quite aware of these features and thus can be changed forcefully. However, lower-level features such as shape and size of primitive curves and connection between these curves can not be changed easily, as the person is habituated to write these primitive curves over a long period of time.

Although the primitive curves are used in computing the distance measure, we use words as the basic units of comparison. The words are natural units of writing and contain both primitive curves as well as their interconnections. Another major reason for choosing words as our comparison unit is that the same character is written quite differently (with respect to shape and size) within different words and this will introduce large intra class variations at character level. Individual words are segmented and clustered into clusters of same words using automatic clustering and segmentation methods. Simple features such as lower and upper profiles of the word are used to partition the documents into clusters of same words. Errors in data clustering and segmentation can be removed manually, as in case of forensic documents, manual intervention is possible as volume of data is small.

The distance between a pair of words is calculated using low-level features such as shape and size of the constituent primitive curves [16]. The primitive curves from the words are extracted by dividing the handwritten data at certain critical points in the pen trace. The critical points are often defined as the points of maximum curvature in the pen trace. However, computation of these critical points is error-prone in offline documents. We utilize the possibility of collecting online reference data to alleviate this problem. For online handwriting (reference document), the dominant points are defined based on the maximum and minimum velocity points. These dominant points form a robust basis for extraction of primitive curves. Although, the velocity of handwriting can change with change in environmental conditions, or be changed deliberately; it is observed that the critical points of velocity remains the same. Figure 3 shows the primitive extraction and comparison process, where two words (*apple*) written by the same person from both

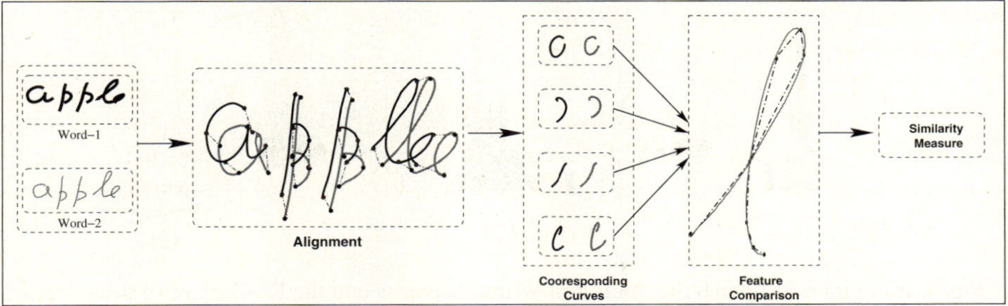

Fig. 3. Comparison between two words '*apple*'

natural and repudiated handwriting are compared. The primitive curves are defined as the portion of curves between three consecutive minimum velocity points on the stroke. Note that in case both documents are offline, critical points can be calculated using curvature, or can be computed by matching the curves to the corresponding online word.

Distance between a pair of words is calculated using a dynamic time warping based matching process. Each word is represented as a feature matrix of size $m \times n$, where, m is the number of curves in a word, and n is size of features extracted from each curve. Curves are represented using their curvature, size of connecting vectors, and higher order moments to capture the relative velocity and shape. Euclidian distance is used to calculate distance between two primitive curves. The method used is relatively simple, and could be replaced with a more comprehensive distance measure that uses various properties that are extracted from the curves.

3 Experimental Results and Analysis

The data used in our experiments was collected from 23 different writers. Each writer was asked to write three pages on A5 sized sheets in his/her own natural handwriting. In addition, three pages of data was collected from each writer, while trying to masquerade his/her handwriting style. The data was collected using iball take-note, which collects the data in both on-line and off-line forms. The data is then segmented into words and clustered into groups of same words.

As noted before, the actual significance of the distance between two documents cannot be used directly as it is based on the assumption that two documents from a writer will have identical distributions of features. Hence, a threshold on the confidence of the decision need to be identified, below which, we use the services of an expert. To present the capabilities of the system, we plot the ROC curve of the system by varying the threshold. Figure 4 shows ROC curve and the corresponding distributions of within-writer and between-writer distance distributions. The document pairs that are written by same person is considered as genuine documents. Note that this includes repudiated documents from the same writer. The genuine accept rate is the rate of acceptance (or matching) of documents that are written by same person and false accept rate is percentage of documents that are considered as matching, when they actually belong to different writers. ROC curve shows that about 82% of documents which belong

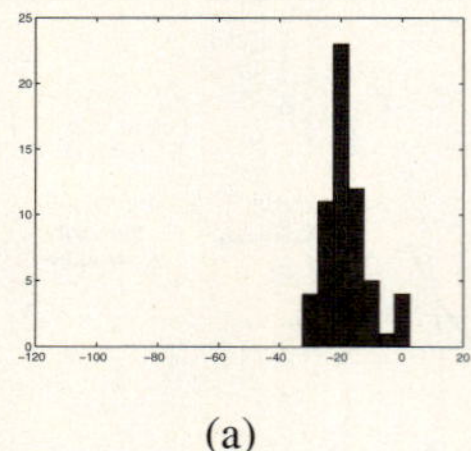

(a)

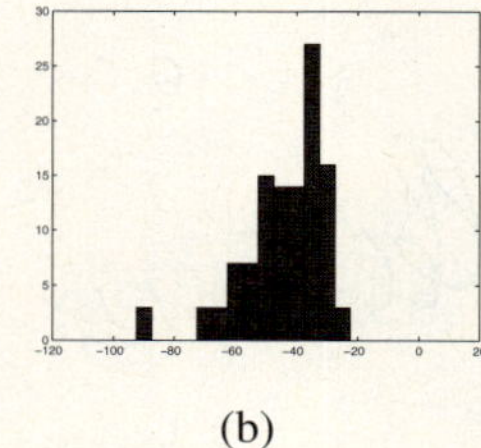

(b)

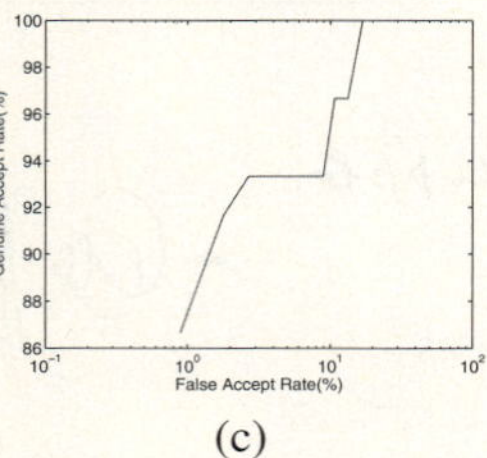

(c)

Fig. 4. Histogram of Inter-writer and Intra-writer distances and the ROC curve of the system

to different writers are rejected, while keeping the genuine acceptance rate at 100%. As discussed before, this step is considered as the preliminary step for the document screening before it goes to expert, and hence we need to operate at a point, where the automatic decisions made by the system should be highly accurate. All the documents, which are not rejected can be processed further by handwriting expert.

An alternate way of presenting the results of matching a particular document pair to an expert is on the traditional nine-point scale. Forensic experts use this scale to indicate the level of match between two documents under consideration. The scale consists of: *identification*, *strong probability of identification*, *probable*, *indications*, *no conclusion*, *indications did not*, *probably did not*, *strong probability did not* and *elimination*. We can present a similar result based on the densities in the corresponding histograms in figure 4. However, due to the bias introduced by hypothesis testing (tests are done under the assumption that null hypothesis is true), the results will be confined to the values of *no conclusion*, *indications did not*, *probably did not*, *strong probability did not* and *elimination*, in the case of repudiation.

4 Conclusions and Future Work

We have introduced the problem of repudiation in handwritten documents, which is particularly relevant for forensic document examination. A statistical model for automatic repudiation (and forgery) detection, which uses the statistical significance of the distance between two distributions, is presented. Preliminary results support the validity of the model. Such an automated system can act either as a screening mechanism for questioned documents, or could provide additional insights to an expert examiner of the documents.

Preliminary investigations into the use of the model for detecting forgeries seem to be promising. However, we need to conduct extensive experiments using expert forgeries to make conclusive statements on the effectiveness. One can also experiment with a variety of features to compute the distance between two words, in order to improve the matching results.

References

1. Morris, R.: Forensic Handwriting Identification: Fundamental concepts and principles. Academic Press, London (2000)
2. Srihari, S., Huang, C., Srinivasan, H., Shah, V.: Biometric and Forensic Aspects of Digital Document Processing. In: Digital Document Processing, pp. 379–405. Springer, London (2007)

3. Fogarolo, L.: Questioned document examination using graphology (2007), http://www.graphology.it/forensic/
4. Huber, R., Headrick, A.: Handwriting Identification: Facts and Fundamentals. CRC Press, Boca Roton (1999)
5. Plamondon, R., Lorette, G.: Automatic signature identification and writer verification - the state of the art. Pattern Recognition 22(2), 107–131 (1989)
6. He, Z., Tang, Y.: Chinese handwriting based writer identification by texture analysis. In: Proceedings of International Conference on Machine Learning and Cybernetics, Shanghai, vol. 6, pp. 3488–3491 (2004)
7. Schomaker, L., Bulacu, M.: Text-independent writer identification and verification using textural and allographic features. IEEE Transactions on Patterh Analysus and Machine Intelligence, Special Issue - Biometrics: Progress and Directions 29(4), 701–717 (2007)
8. Tomai, C., Zhang, B., Srihari, S.: Discriminatory power of handwritten words for writer recognition. In: Proceedings of Int'l conf. of Pattern Recognition, Cambridge, UK, vol. 2, pp. 638–641 (2004)
9. Thumwarin, P., Matsuura, T.: On-line writer recognition for thai based on velocity of barycenter of pen-point movement. In: Proceedings of IEEE Int'l conf. of Image Processing, Singapore, pp. 889–892. IEEE Computer Society Press, Los Alamitos (2004)
10. Yu, K., Wang, Y., Tan, T.: Writer identification using dynamic features. In: Proceedings of Int'l conf. on Biometric Authentication, Hong Kong, China, pp. 512–518 (2004)
11. Schlapbach, A., Bunke, H.: A writer identification and verification system using hmm based recognizers. Pattern Analysis & Applications 10(1), 33–43 (2007)
12. Srihari, S., Bandi, K., Beal, M.: A statistical model for writer verification. In: Proceedings of the Int'l. conf. of Document Analysis and Research, Seoul, Korea, pp. 1105–1109 (2005)
13. Jain, A.K., Ross, A., Prabhakar, S.: An introduction to biometric recognition. IEEE Transactions on Circuits and Systems for Video Technology. Special Issue on Image- and Video-Based Biometrics 14(1), 4–20 (2004)
14. Jain, A.K., Griess, F., Connell, S.D.: On-line signature verification. Pattern Recognition 35(12), 2963–2972 (2002)
15. Press, W., Flannery, B., Teukolsky, S., Vetterling, W.: Numerical Recepies in C: The Art of Scientific Computing. Cambridge University Press, Cambridge (1992)
16. Namboodiri, A.M., Gupta, S.: Text independent writer identification from online handwriting. In: Proceedings of Int'l workshop of Frontier in Handwriting Recognition, La Baule, Centre de Congreee Atlantia, France, pp. 23–26 (2006)

A New Forgery Scenario Based on Regaining Dynamics of Signature

Jean Hennebert, Renato Loeffel, Andreas Humm, and Rolf Ingold

Université de Fribourg, Boulevard de Pérolles 90, 1700 Fribourg, Switzerland

Abstract. We present in this paper a new forgery scenario for dynamic signature verification systems. In this scenario, we assume that the forger has got access to a static version of the genuine signature, is using a dedicated software to automatically recover dynamics of the signature and is using these regained signatures to break the verification system. We also show that automated procedures can be built to regain signature dynamics, making some simple assumptions on how signatures are performed. We finally report on the evaluation of these procedures on the MCYT-100 signature database on which regained versions of the signatures are generated. This set of regained signatures is used to evaluate the rejection performance of a baseline dynamic signature verification system. Results show that the regained forgeries generate much more false acceptation in comparison to the random and low-force forgeries available in the MCYT-100 database. These results clearly show that such kind of forgery attacks can potentially represent a critical security breach for signature verification systems.

1 Introduction

One of the main advantage of biometric systems lies in the fact that the user does not have anymore to remember passwords or keep all his different access keys. Another important advantage lies in the difficulty to steal, imitate or generate genuine biometrics data, leading to enhanced security. The work described in this paper is challenging this last statement in the framework of dynamic signature verification systems.

Many signature verification systems have been developed in the past [1] [2]. Signature verification has the advantage of a very high user acceptance because people are used to sign in their daily life. Signature verification systems are said to be static (off-line) or dynamic (on-line). Static verification systems use a static digitalized image of the signature. Dynamic signature verification (DSV) systems use the dynamics of the signature including coordinates, pressure and sometimes angle of the pen as a function of time. Thanks to the extra information included in the time evolution of these features, dynamic systems are usually ranked as more accurate and more difficult to attack than static verification systems.

Signature verification systems are evaluated by analyzing their accuracy to accept genuine signatures and to reject forgeries. When considering forgeries, four categories can be defined from the lowest level of attack to the highest (as presented in [3] [4], and extended in [5]).

S.-W. Lee and S.Z. Li (Eds.): ICB 2007, LNCS 4642, pp. 366–375, 2007.

– **Random forgeries**. These forgeries are simulated by using signature samples from other users as input to a specific user model. This category actually does not denote intentional forgeries, but rather accidental accesses by non-malicious users.
– **Blind forgeries**. These forgeries are signature samples generated by intentional impostors having access to a descriptive or textual knowledge of the original signature.
– **Low-force forgeries**. The impostor has here access to a visual static image of the original signature. There are then two ways to generate the forgeries. In the first way, the forger can use a blueprint to help himself copy the signature, leading to low-force **blueprint** forgeries. In the second way, the forger can train to imitate the signature, with or without a blueprint, for a limited or unlimited amount of time. The forger then generate the imitated signature, without the help of the blueprint and potentially after some time after training, leading to low-force **trained** forgeries. The so-called skilled forgeries provided with the MCYT-100 database [6] correspond here to low-force trained forgeries.
– **Brute-force forgeries**. The forger has access to a visual static image and to the whole writing process, therefore including the handwriting dynamics. The forger can analyze the writing process in the presence of the original writer or through a video-recording or also through a captured on-line version of the genuine signature. This last case is realized when genuine signature data can be intercepted, for example when the user is accessing the DSV system. In a similar way as in the previous category, the forger can then generate two types of forgeries. Brute-force **blueprint** forgeries are generated by projecting on the acquisition area a real-time pointer that the forger then needs to follow. Brute-force **trained** forgeries are produced by the forger after a training period where he or she can use dedicated tools to analyze and train to reproduce the genuine signature. In [4] [3] and [5], tools for training to perform brute-force forgeries are presented.

We report in this article on a new type of signature forgeries that we call **regained forgeries**. The forgery scenario makes three assumptions. First, the forger has got access to one or more versions of a static genuine signature. This assumption is reasonable as it is nowadays usual for us to provide static signatures to third-parties. For example, we are signing credit card receipt almost on a daily basis. Second, the forger is using a dedicated software that automatically allows to analyse the static version of the signature and to *regain* one or more versions of its dynamics. Third, the forger has a way to stream the regained dynamic version into the verification system. This can be done if, for example, the forger has access to the acquisition tablet[1].

Our primary objective in this work is therefore to assess if a procedure can be put in place to automatically compute reliable estimates of signature

[1] Alternatively to the third assumption, the forger could also train himself to imitate the recovered dynamics in a similar way as for the brute-force forgery scenario described earlier.

dynamics starting from a static version of it. A secondary objective is to measure the impact of such forgeries on a state-of-the-art DSV systems. Finally, if such forgeries reveals efficient in breaking DSV systems, the open question is how can we improve DSV systems to diminish the potential risk of such forgeries.

Section 2 introduces the procedure that was crafted to automatically compute sequence of strokes. In Section 3, we present the procedure used to estimate local pen speed. In section 4, the procedure used to estimate the pen pressure is described. In Section 5, experiments performed using the regain procedure are reported using the MCYT-100 database. Finally, conclusions are drawn in the last section.

2 Problem Description

Our objective is to design a procedure to regain the dynamics of a signature given its static representation. Figure 1 illustrates the regain procedure with, on the right-hand part of the figure, a typical example of the signature information that needs to be recovered. A dynamic signature sample is actually a time sequence of points that includes the (x/y) coordinates and the pressure of the pen measured at a given frequency, typically 100 Hz. The time sequence may also include the pen azimuth and elevation angles that are provided with some high-end graphical tablets. In this paper, we focus on the recovery of pen coordinates and pressure. The recovery of pen angles is not addressed.

More formally, the regain procedure is defining a mapping

$$I \overset{regain}{\longrightarrow} (\ x,\ y,\ p\ )(\ t\ ) \tag{1}$$

where I is a scanned version of the signature, $x(t)$ and $y(t)$ correspond to the pen trajectory and $p(t)$ is the evolution of the pen pressure. As these information are sampled at a regular time interval, the distance between each point also defines the instantaneous pen speed that also needs to be recovered. The gray block areas in Figure 1 corresponds to the so-called *pens-up* that appear in the signal when the hand jumps from one stroke to another. These pens-up are usually recorded by the acquisition device provided that the pen remains in a

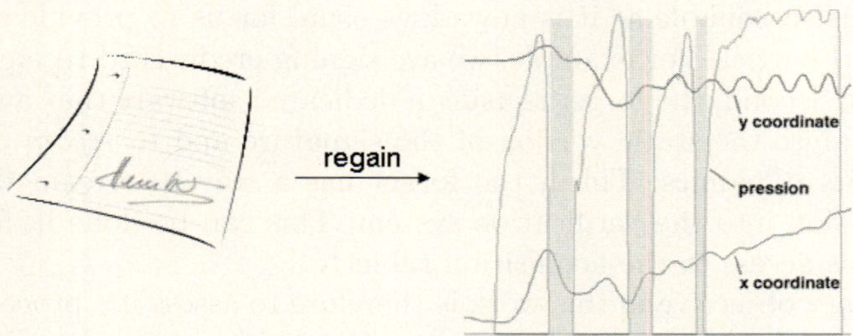

Fig. 1. The regain procedure aims at estimating pen dynamics by analyzing a static version of a signature

given range above the tablet. The corresponding samples have then zero pressure values and valid coordinates[2]. Obviously, such pens-up sequences are not visible in the static version and will therefore need to be re-created.

Of course, the regain mapping of equation 1 has no unique solution as we have no information about the ordering of coordinates and evolution of pressure. The only thing we know for sure is that the the coordinates of the signature pixel in the image must appear at some point of the dynamic signature. On the other hand, not all the solutions are equally probable if we can make some assumptions on how signatures are produced by humans.

3 Regaining the Drawing Order

Our first objective is here to build a procedure that will reorder the set of visible signature points in the input image. In other words, this operation needs to discover, for each black pixel $I(x, y)$ of the image, its corresponding time index i to re-create an ordered sequence $O = [(x_1, y_1), \ldots, (x_i, y_i), \ldots, (x_N, y_N)]$. We propose a procedure in three steps: segments detection, segments merging and segments ordering.

3.1 Segments Detection

In this step, we exploit the fact that adjacent signature points of the input image are drawn in consecutive order. The order of the pixels can be determined using a simple neighborhood function applied to each pixel. In the example of Fig. 2, 5 segments are detected. The segments extremities are defined either when the neighborhood function returns no more pixels (for example left hand side of segment 1 in 2(b), or when it returns more than one pixel (crossing points of segments 1, 2 and 3 in 2(b). At this stage, we have a set of K segments S_k that are composed of ordered sets of pixels. We do not know yet if the pixels are ordered in the right direction in a given segment, but at least, an order is existing.

3.2 Segments Merging

In order to reduce further the number of segments, we apply a continuity criterion to detect segments that can be merged together. This criterion simply states that whenever a crossing point is reached, it is very likely that the drawing will continue in a similar direction. We propose to use the following continuity measure:

$$c(S_k, S_l) = \begin{cases} 0.1 * \cos(\alpha) \text{ if } \alpha < \frac{\Pi}{2} \\ \left(\frac{2*\alpha}{\Pi} - 1\right)^2 \text{ if } \frac{\Pi}{2} \leq \alpha \leq \Pi \end{cases} \quad (2)$$

[2] Some devices may not record such pens-up but we assume for our approach that they need to be also recovered by the regain procedure.

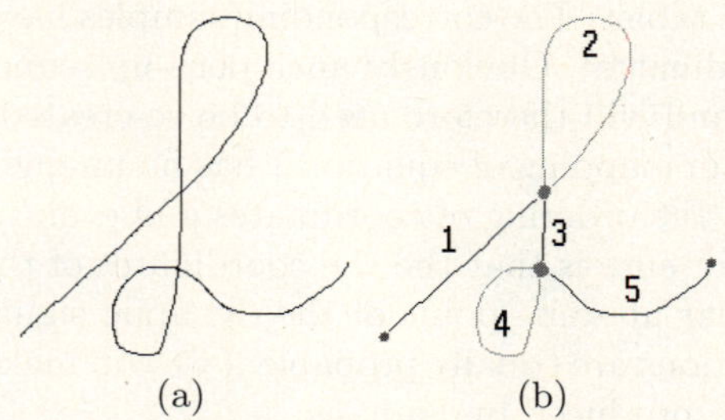

Fig. 2. (a) Static signature image. (b) The signature after segment detection.

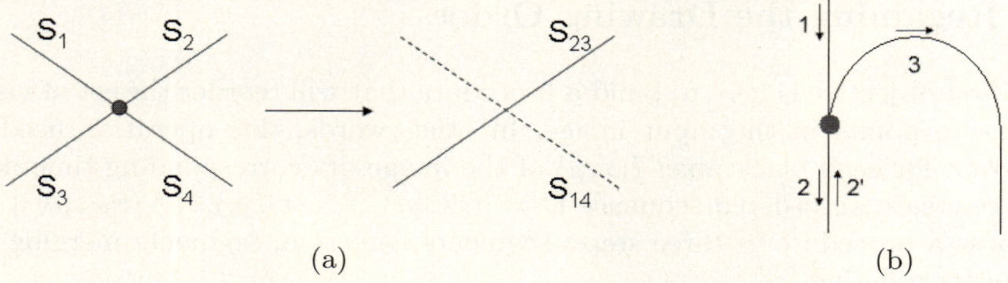

Fig. 3. (a) Procedure to merge segments. According to the computation of the continuity measure, segments S_1 and S_4 are merged, as well as segments S_2 and S_3. (b) Special case of a crossing point having 3 incoming segments.

where α denotes the angle between segment S_k and S_l. The angle α is estimated from the two straight lines tangent of both segments at the crossing point. The closer the angle to 180 degrees, the more likely both segments are the continuation of each other. As illustrated on Fig. 3(a), the continuity measure c is computed for each crossing point of the signature, i.e. where segment extremities are coinciding. The decision to merge two segments S_k and S_l into a unique one is then taken if the value $c(S_k, S_l)$ higher than a given threshold.

A special treatment is performed in the case of crossing points with 3 incoming segments, such as illustrated on Fig. 3(b). In this example, the values of $c(S_1, S_2)$ and $c(S_2, S_3)$ are above the merging threshold but no decision can be taken as the number of segment is odd. In such case, it is likely that the segment that is common in the best two values of the continuity measure is actually double traced by the user (S_2 in our example). In this case, our procedure artificially duplicates the concerned segment S_2 into a new segment S_2' where the pixel order is reversed. The merging procedure can then continue.

3.3 Segments Ordering

The reduced set of segments needs now to be ordered. We have to determine the most likely sequence of segments but also the ordering direction of pixels within each segment. Our proposal is here to compute a likelihood measure for a given sequence by taking into account some reasonable assumptions on the signature production process. We can then compute this likelihood measure for all possible sequence of segments and elect the best one. The procedure also allows to elect the n best sequences of segments if required. Assuming a sequence of segments $(S_1, \ldots, S_K)$, the likelihood of the sequence is computed with

$$L(S_1, \ldots, S_K) = is(S_1)sd(S_K) \prod_{i=1}^{K-1} em(S_i, S_{i+1})wd(S_i, S_{i+1})sd(S_i) \quad (3)$$

where we have the following contributing terms:

Energy minimization. This term is introduced according to the assumption that humans are minimizing the energy spent while producing signatures. If the ending point of one segment is close to the starting point of another, then it is likely that these segments follow each other:

$$em(S_i, S_j) = \max\{1 - \sigma d(S_i, S_j), 0\} \quad (4)$$

where $d(S_i, S_j)$ is the euclidian distance between the ending point of S_i and the starting point of S_j and σ is a parameter used to control the severity of the energy criterion. In our configuration, σ has been experimentally set by visually analyzing the output of the system.

Writing direction. In western civilizations it is common to write from left to right and from the top to the bottom. More likelihood is then given to consecutive segments that are ordered according to this rule:

$$wd(S_i, S_j) = 0.5 + 0.5\cos(\alpha - \frac{\Pi}{4.0}) \quad (5)$$

where α denotes the angle between the horizontal axis and the direction vector formed by the ending point of S_i and starting point of S_j.

Intra segment direction. We assume here that segments drawn from left to right and from top to bottom are more likely:

$$sd(S_i) = 0.5 + 0.5\cos(\beta + \frac{\Pi}{4.0})d(S_i) \quad (6)$$

where $d(S_i)$ is the distance between the starting point and the ending point of segment S_i and β the angle of the vector defined by these points.

Initial segment. Segments that are close to the origin of the coordinate system are more likely:

$$is(S_1) = 0.5 + 0.5\max\left(1 - \frac{d(S_1, o)}{d(S, o)}, -1\right) \quad (7)$$

where $d(S_1, o)$ represents the distance between the starting point of segment S_1 and the origin and $d(S, o)$ is the average distance between all segment starting points and the origin.

3.4 Invisible Segment Recovery

In this step we estimate the invisible sequences of point that are recorded between a pen-up and a pen-down. We have chosen to implement a simple linear interpolation between the pen-up and the pen-down. This is rather an inaccurate estimation, but as the amount of invisible points is much lower than for visible points, this estimation is probably sufficient as a first approach. A possible improvement would be to implement an non linear interpolation that preserves realistic values of the inertia of the pen.

4 Velocity Recovery

Thanks to the previous steps, we now have a unique segment composed of a likely ordered sequence of visible and invisible signature points. The next step is to simulate back the 100 Hz sampling procedure of the tablet, taking into account the effect of the velocity of the pen that may vary between each point. We analyzed the velocity information of several dynamic signatures and we could make the following observations. First, we observed that the speed of the pen remains relatively stable but presents local variations. When observing these local variations, we noticed that the longer and the straighter the segments, the faster they were drawn. The velocity recovery procedure that we propose here is directly inspired from these observation.

We first estimate the average speed of the regained signature looking up the speech value in a table that was built by inspecting 50 signatures taken from the MCYT database. The table stores the average speed values according to the spatial length of the signature. The number of signature points recovered as explained in the previous sections allows us to compute the spatial length of the signature from which we can look up the average speed from the table.

In a second step, the sequence of points of the static signature is divided into smaller sub-sequences S_k that are delimited by regions of abrupt change of direction. An instantaneous speed $s_l(S_k)$ is associated to each of these sub-sequences according to

$$s_l(S_k) = s_a f_l(S_k) f_s(S_k) \tag{8}$$

where s_a is the average speed, $f_l(S_k)$ is a multiplying factor which is dependent to the length of segment S_k and where $f_s(S_k)$ is a factor which is dependent to the straightness of the segment S_k. Without entering into too many details, we implemented these factors with sigmoid-like functions where the parameters were tuned to provide realistic values of the instantaneous speed. The sequence of signature points can then be non-linearly downsampled according to the instantaneous speed values and a natural evolution of the pen velocity can be recovered.

5 Regaining the Pressure

The last value that needs to be recovered for our purpose is the pressure value. We used here a very simple step function where every visible signature point obtains a pressure value that corresponds to the maximum pressure value and where invisible points obtain a pressure value of 0. This is a rather crude approximation of the actual pressure value, but sufficient in a first approach. We could easily refine this procedure by ramping up and down the passage from invisible to visible points or by introducing a correlation between the speed and the pressure. However, we leave this for future work.

6 Database, DSV System Description and Experiments

Experiments have been done with online signatures of the public MCYT-100 database [6]. This mono-session database contains signatures of 100 users. For each user, 25 genuine signatures and 25 low-force trained forgeries are available[3]. These forgeries are produced by 5 other users by observing the static images and training to copy them. We used the 50 first signatures of the database as development data on which the different parameters of the regain procedure were tuned. The 50 last signatures of the database were used for the evaluation. As static versions of signatures are not available in MCYT, we generated static signature images from the dynamic data. This procedure may be considered as optimistic as the static versions of signatures are not including additional noise or distortion coming from a scanning procedure. However, we can reasonably assume that an intentional impostor could easily arrive to similar image quality by using widely available image processing tools to thin the segments and to remove noise from a scanned signature.

We have chosen to measure the impact of our regained signatures on a state-of-the-art DSV system based on local feature extraction and Gaussian Mixture Models (GMMs). The system and the evaluation procedure is here very much similar to what is described in [7]. For the feature extraction, x, y, pressure, trajectory tangent angles $\left(\arctan \frac{\dot{y}(t)}{\dot{x}(t)}\right)$ and instantaneous displacements $\left(\sqrt{\dot{x}(t)^2 + \dot{y}(t)^2}\right)$ are used. The features are mean and standard deviation normalized on a per signature basis. For the modelling with GMMs, we make the hypothesis that the features are uncorrelated so that diagonal covariance matrices can be used. We normalize the client score using a world model trained by pooling the data of many other users. The training of the client and world models is here performed with the Expectation-Maximization (EM) algorithm [8]. The client and world model are trained independently by applying iteratively the EM procedure until convergence is reached, typically after few iterations. In our setting, we apply a simple binary splitting procedure to increase the number of gaussian mixtures to the predefined value. For each user, we trained a GMM composed of 64 Gaussian mixtures using the data of 5 signatures taken out from the 25 available genuine signatures. Additionally to the user models, we trained a world model comprising 1250 genuine signatures taken from the first 50 users.

For each users, the remaining 20 signatures were used for genuine tests. We performed three different types of forgeries: random, low-force and regained.

[3] These forgeries are named as *skilled* forgeries in the distribution of the database.

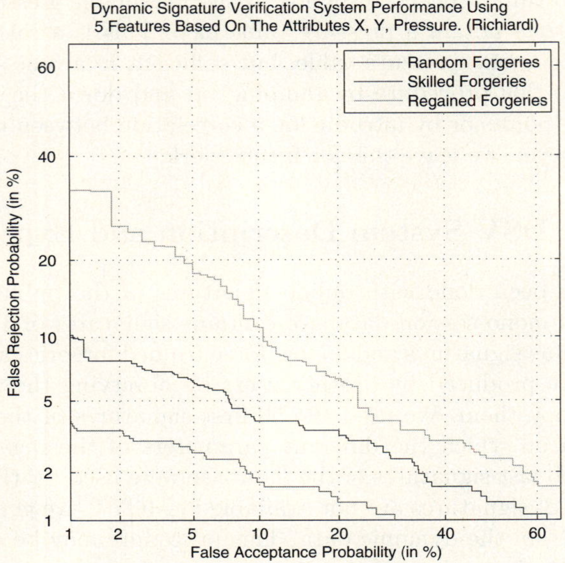

Fig. 4. Evaluation of regained forgeries on the MCYT-100 database

Random forgeries were performed using one genuine signature randomly selected from each remaining user. The low-force forgeries are performed using the 25 so-called *skilled* forgery signatures supplied with the MCYT database. For the regained forgeries, we took the 5 most probable signature versions found during the regain process. If less versions were available only these were considered. From the 50 signatures composing our test suite, 4 signatures could not be regained with our procedure. The number of segments after the segment merging step described in section 3.2 was simply too high to allow for the computation of the best segment ordering. Fig. 4 shows the detection performance curve for the tree types of forgeries. We can see that regained forgeries are significantly degrading the performance in comparison to random and skilled forgeries. The equal error rate jumps from about 6% for skilled forgeries to more than 10% for regained forgeries.

7 Conclusions and Future Work

We have introduced a new forgery scenario where it is assumed that the forger has got access to a static version of a genuine signature to attack a dynamic verification system. We have shown that automated procedures can be proposed to regain signature dynamics, making some simple assumptions on how signatures are produced by humans. We have finally evaluated these procedures on the MCYT-100 signature database on which regained versions of signatures are successfully generated. This set of regained signatures is used to evaluate the rejection performance of a state-of-the-art dynamic signature verification system.

Results show that the regained forgeries generate much more false acceptation in comparison to the random and low-force forgeries. These results clearly show that such kind of regained forgery attacks can potentially represent a critical security breach for signature verification systems. In potential future work, we would like to investigate more refined recovery procedures, attempting to model more closely the signature production process of humans. Also, an important area of research would be to investigate how DSV systems can be improved in order to diminish the potential risks of such regained forgeries.

Acknowledgments. This work was supported by the EU BioSecure NoE (6th Framework - IST-2002-507634). and by the University of Fribourg.

References

1. Plamondon, R., Lorette, G.: Automatic signature verification and writer identification - the state of the art. Pattern Recognition 22(2), 107–131 (1989)
2. Leclerc, F., Plamondon, R.: Automatic signature verification: the state of the art–1989-1993. Int'l J. Pattern Recog. and Artificial Intelligence 8(3), 643–660 (1994)
3. Vielhauer, C.: Biometric User Authentication for IT Security. Springer, Heidelberg (2006)
4. Zoebisch, F., Vielhauer, C.: A test tool to support brut-force online and offline signature forgery tests on mobile devices. In: Proc. of the IEEE Int'l Conf. on Multimedia and Expo 2003 (ICME), Baltimore, USA, vol. 3, pp. 225–228 (2006)
5. Wahl, A., Hennebert, J., H, A., Ingold, R.: Generation and evaluation of brute-force signature forgeries. In: Gunsel, B., Jain, A.K., Tekalp, A.M., Sankur, B. (eds.) MRCS 2006. LNCS, vol. 4105, pp. 2–9. Springer, Heidelberg (2006)
6. Ortega-Garcia, J., et al.: Mcyt baseline corpus: a bimodal biometric database. IEE Proc.-Vis. Image Signal Process. 150(6), 395–401 (2003)
7. Richiardi, J., Drygajlo, A.: GMMs for on-line signature verification. In: Proc. 2003 ACM SIGMM workshop on Biometrics methods and applic., pp. 115–122. ACM Press, New York (2003)
8. Dempster, A., Laird, N., D.B., R.: Maximum likelihood from incomplete data via the em algorithm. Journal of Royal Statistical Society 39(1), 1–38 (1977)

Curvewise DET Confidence Regions and Pointwise EER Confidence Intervals Using Radial Sweep Methodology

Michael E. Schuckers[1], Yordan Minev[1], and Andy Adler[2]

[1] Department of Mathematics, Computer Science and Statistics
St. Lawrence University, Canton, NY USA
[2] Department of Systems and Computer Engineering
Carleton University, Ottawa, ON Canada

Abstract. One methodology for evaluating the matching performance of biometric authentication systems is the detection error tradeoff (DET) curve. The DET curve graphically illustrates the relationship between false rejects and false accepts when varying a threshold across a genuine and an imposter match score distributions. This paper makes two contributions to the literature on the matching performance evaluation of biometric identification or bioauthentication systems. First, we create curvewise DET confidence regions using radial sweep methods. Second we use this same methodology to create pointwise confidence intervals for the equal error rate (EER). The EER is the rate at which the false accept rate and the false reject rate are identical. We utilize resampling or bootstrap methods to estimate the variability in both the DET and the EER. Our radial sweep is based on converting the false reject and false accept errors to polar coordinates. Application is made of these methods to data from three different biometric modalities and we discuss the results of these applications.

1 Introduction

Biometric identification is the process of matching an individual's physical or behavioural traits to a stored version of those same traits. Measuring how well a bioauthentication process matches these traits is an important facet of the overall performance of the system in which it is embedded. The focus of this article will be the statistical estimation of the matching performance of these bioauthentication systems. In this context genuine users are generally those that the system should accept and imposters are those that the system should reject. An effective biometrics authentication system evaluates a given match score as a genuine or an imposter match score with a minimal error. There are two possible error rates that can occur. The proportion of imposter match scores which are accepted from the system is called the False Accept Rate (FAR). The proportion of genuine match scores which are rejected by the system is called the False Reject Rate (FRR). Some authors prefer the use of false match and false non-match rate. For generality here we will use FAR and FRR. See Mansfield and Wayman

S.-W. Lee and S.Z. Li (Eds.): ICB 2007, LNCS 4642, pp. 376–385, 2007.

[1] for a discussion of the differences. Our interest focuses on the representation of the tradeoff between these two curves known as the DET. The DET curve evaluates the matching performance of a biometric system. One factor that is often overlooked in the use of DET's is that the curves are sample estimates of a population DET and, thus, there is variability in the estimated curves. This paper quantifies this variability and builds confidence regions for the population DET curve based upon the observed sample.

There is a good deal of literature on DET's or their equivalent the receiver operating characteristic curve (ROC) beginning with the work of Green and Swets [2]. In this paper we will concentrate on the DET; however, the methods described here apply directly to the ROC. An ROC is a plot of the FAR against the true accept rate (TAR) — TAR = 1 - FRR — while we use a DET that is a plot of the FAR against the FRR. (Some authors, e.g. Poh *et al* [3] transform the FAR and FRR to achieve a DET.) A good deal has been written about the ROC in a variety of contexts. See, e.g. Zhou *et al* [4] or Hernández-Orallo *et al* [5] . Macskassy *et al* [6] compared three methods that have been proposed for ROC confidence bands. These include: a simultaneous joint confidence region and a fixed width approach both due to Campbell [7], a Working-Hotelling band technique due to Ma and Hall [8]. The simultaneous joint confidence approach converts confidence rectangles at various points along the ROC to create a joint region. The fixed width approach creates a region of single width in a direction determined by number of observations used to calculate each FAR and TAR. Working-Hotelling bands are based upon confidence regions for a regression line. Based upon its performance in their evaluation, Macskassy *et al* recommend the fixed width approach. The drawback of this methodology for bioauthentication applications is that it produces large regions near the ends of the ROC or DET which is often the area of interest for such applications. Recall that larger intervals imply less knowledge about an estimate. Recently, Poh *et al* [9] suggested a new DET confidence methodology based upon the radial sweep methodology of Adler and Schuckers [10]. However, this methodology is a pointwise approach to confidence unlike the curvewise approach described by Macskassy *et al* [6]. The difference between them is that a curvewise approach aims to capture the entire DET curve while a pointwise approach only provides confidence about a single point and thus neglects the correlation between points along the curve. This is often referred to as the multiple comparison problem. We will utilize the pointwise approach to make a confidence interval for the EER since it is appropriate for a single point; however, we take the curvewise approach for DET estimation. Finally, we mention the work by Dass *et al* [11] to create a confidence region for FRR's given a range of values for FAR. This approach is essentially univariate rather than the bivariate approach taken here.

The approach we propose in this paper is a new curvewise method for creating a confidence region for the DET as a function of both the FAR and FRR based on a radial sweep methodology. By curvewise in this context we mean that our confidence will be based upon the entire curve rather than on each individual point. This yields a wider confidence interval – due to the correlation between points on the curve – but one that is more accurate for variability of the entire curve. This approach, described below, transforms each curve from the (FAR, FRR) space to polar coordinates, (radius, angle). By using a polar representation of the error rate data we can create regions that are appropriate for inference about both the FAR and FRR simultaneously. Adler and Schuckers [10] originally used this approach to average across several DET's to create a composite DET. We extend their work to create a curvewise confidence region. In addition, this methodology has variable width which allows for smaller intervals as the DET curves approach the axes. This is a distinct advantage over the fixed width approach advocated by Macskassy *et al* [6]. These regions — where the FAR and FRR approach unity — are often the focus of biometric authentication applications and threshold settings. Having created such a confidence region, one gains a better understanding of the variability in the system and the location of the population DET based upon the sample selected. Further, it is possible to derive using a pointwise confidence interval for the equal error rate (EER) as a carryover of the work done to create the DET region. The rest of this article is organized in the following way. Section 2 discusses the calculation of a DET and the conversion to polar coordinates. Our approach for making a confidence region for a DET is given in Section 3. This section also describes the methodology for creating an EER confidence interval. We apply our inferential estimation approach to data from three biometric modalities: face, fingerprint and hand geometry in Section 4. These data comes from the paper by Ross and Jain [12]. Section 5 discusses these results and their possible extensions.

2 DET Curve Estimation

We begin by outlining the methodology for estimating a DET curve. For the purposes here, we assume that we have a population of *genuine* and *imposter* matching scores from a biometric system. Further we assume that these scores represent a sample of an ongoing process which we would like to evaluate. The distributions of match scores, t, are denoted by $g(t)$ and $f(t)$ for the genuine and imposters distributions respectively. From these distributions, a DET, R, is plotted as the false accept rate (FAR) on the *x-axis* against the false reject rate (FRR) on the *y-axis*, by varying a threshold τ, and calculating

$$FAR(\tau) = \int_{\tau}^{\infty} f(x)dx \quad \text{and} \quad FRR(\tau) = \int_{-\infty}^{\tau} g(y)dy. \tag{1}$$

If $f(t)$ and $g(t)$ are known then R can be calculated based upon Equation (1) by varying τ. In general this is rarely the case and these distributions must be estimated. In that case we can calculate, $\hat{R}$ based upon an approximation of $f(t)$ and $g(t)$.

$$F\hat{A}R(\tau) = \int_{\tau}^{\infty} \hat{f}(x)dx = \frac{\sum_x I(x > \tau)}{\sum_x I(x \in \mathbb{R})} \quad \text{and} \tag{2}$$

$$F\hat{R}R(\tau) = \int_{-\infty}^{\tau} \hat{g}(y)dy = \frac{\sum_y I(y \leq \tau)}{\sum_y I(y \in \mathbb{R})} \tag{3}$$

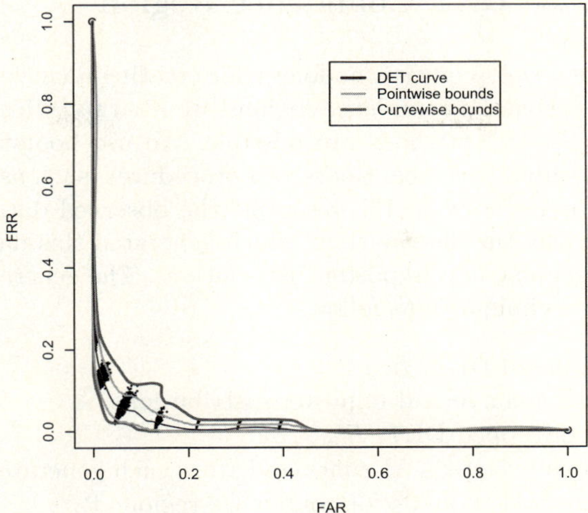

Fig. 1. 95% confidence region for DET of Facial Recognition System

where $I()$ represents an indictor function and x and y are observed scores from imposter and genuine distributions, respectively . As with R, $\hat{R}$ is computed by calculating $F\hat{A}R$ and $F\hat{R}R$ for various values of τ. In this way the sample DET curve summarizes the authentication performance of the biometric system on the sample on which it is calculated. The FAR and FRR calculations above are based on a criterion of accept if a match score is greater than τ. An alternative formulation can easily be made for other decisions. Thus, we will treat this DET, $\hat{R}$ as an estimate of the population DET, R.

Having calculated a DET, either sample or population, We next convert the coordinates of the curve from rectangular to polar coordinates. Then our DET curve over a range of values Θ is $R = \{(r_\theta, \theta) : \theta \in \Theta = (\theta_L, \theta_U)\}$ and θ_L and θ_U represent lower and upper values for the range of the radial angles. In practice we sweep across a range of T θ's using a discrete list of values $\Theta^* = (\theta_L, \theta_L + \delta, \theta_L + 2\delta, \ldots, \theta_L + (T-2)\delta, \theta_U)$ where $\Theta = (\theta_L, \theta_U)$ is given. Then we can write $\hat{R} = \{(\hat{r}_\theta, \theta) : \theta \in \Theta^*\}$ One important issue in radial sweeping is the location of the radial center, (c_x, c_y). Because we would like the confidence region to not depend on which error rate is on which axis and in order to have a confidence interval for the EER as a derived outcome for our data, we limited possible center points $c_x = c_y = c$ for some specified constant c. (See Figure 1 from [10] for a graphical representation of the conversion to polar coordinates.) It is immediately clear that choosing a center along the $FAR = FRR$ line results in an average curve that is independent of the selection of axes. Once we have determined the origin of the polar coordinate system, we can convert the coordinates of every point on the DET curve, R, to polar coordinates. We next turn our attention to deriving a confidence region for the DET, R.

3 A Curvewise DET Confidence Region

In this section, we develop our methodology for creating a curvewise DET confidence region. To derive the confidence regions, we need to estimate the variance of $\hat{r}_\theta$ for each θ. Several methods are possible. We use bootstrap methods to approximate this radial variance. Bootstrap procedures, such as those proposed by Poh *et al* [9] or Bolle *et al* [13], resample the observed data to estimate in a non-parametric way the distributions which generated this data. Here, we resample both the genuine and imposter distributions. The general outline for our confidence region technique is as follows:

1. Calculate estimated DET, $\hat{R}$.
2. Bootstrap both genuine and imposter distributions.
3. Calculate bootstrapped DET, $R^\dagger$.
4. Repeat previous two steps M times and store each generated DET.
5. Determine curvewise bounds for confidence region, $\Re$.

Let $R^\dagger = \{(r^\dagger_{m\theta}, \theta) : \theta \in \Theta^*\}$ be the mth bootstrapped DET $m = 1, \ldots, M$ for some large number M. $r^\dagger_{m\theta}$ represents the radial length for the mth bootstrapped DET at the angle θ. Next we find the adjusted standard deviation of $r_{m\theta}$'s at each θ in Θ^* by taking the square root of the variance plus a slight adjustment, ϵ. We will denote this by $s_{\hat{r}_\theta} = \sqrt{var(r^\dagger_\theta)} + \epsilon$. This adjustment is made to ensure that some variability is present in the confidence region when no radial variability is present in the bootstrapped replications.

We define the DET confidence region $\Re$ as the region bounded by a spline of $r_{L,\theta}$'s, the lower limits for the region at angle θ, and a spline of $r_{U,\theta}$'s, the upper limits for the region at angle θ for each $\theta \in \Theta^*$. We want that region to have the property that $P(R \in \Re) = 1 - \alpha$ where $1 - \alpha$ is the confidence level. We say the population DET, R, is captured by the $(1-\alpha)100\%$ ROC confidence region and denote it by $R \in \Re$ if $r_{L,\theta} \leq r_\theta \leq r_{U,\theta}$ for all $\theta \in \Theta^*$. In order to determine the DET confidence region, $\Re$, we need to create a region that captures the entire curve R with probability $(1 - \alpha)$. The pointwise approach of Poh *et al* [9], is to take the $\alpha/2^\times 100th$ and $(1 - \alpha/2) \times 100^{th}$ percentiles of the $r^\dagger$'s at each θ. As mentioned above, this ignores the correlation between radii at different values of θ, particularly neighboring values of θ in Θ^*. Consequently it fails to yield a confidence region with $P(R \in \Re) = 1 - \alpha$.

Several options exist for finding an DET confidence region, $\Re$, that meets our criteria. We prefer an approach that uses a different width at each θ to match the variability in the data. To achieve this systematically we build our DET region by connecting the endpoints $(\hat{r}_\theta + \eta_L s_{r_\theta}, \hat{r}_\theta + \eta_U s_{r_\theta})$ at each $\theta \in \Theta^*$ where η_L and η_U represent lower and upper constants, respectively, that yield the desired $(1 - \alpha) \times 100\%$ confidence level. Below we describe the process for determining η_L and η_U. First, we calculate a standardized residual, $e_{m\theta}$ for each $r_{m\theta}$,

$$e_{m\theta} = \frac{r_{m\theta} - \hat{r}_\theta}{s_{\hat{r}_\theta}}. \tag{4}$$

This residual tells us how far each bootstrapped radius, $\hat{r}_\theta$, is from the estimated DET, $\hat{R}$ as measured by the variability, s_{r_θ} at each θ. Next, the maximum absolute standardized residual, ω_m, for the mth DET curve is calculated. This value, ω_m, tells us the furthest amount that each bootstrapped curve is from the the estimated DET, $\hat{R}$. We do this in order to determine the largest standardized valued needed to have $(1-\alpha)100\%$ of the bootstrapped curves within the DET region, $\Re$. We define ω_m to be:

$$\omega_m = \begin{cases} \min_\theta(e_{m\theta}) \text{ if } \mid \min_\theta(e_{m\theta}) \mid < \mid \max_\theta(e_{m\theta}) \mid \\ \max_\theta(e_{m\theta}) \text{ if } \mid \min_\theta(e_{m\theta}) \mid \geq \mid \max_\theta(e_{m\theta}) \mid . \end{cases} \tag{5}$$

Once we have all M ω_m's we find the $\alpha/2^{th}$ and the $1-\alpha/2^{th}$ percentiles of the ω_m's and they become η_L and η_U respectively. Note that the ω_m's can take both positive and negative values. In fact, in our experience it is likely that η_L will be negative. Having found η_L and η_U we then build our confidence region $\Re$, as the region bounded by the splines created by connecting the upper endpoints, $\hat{r_\theta}+\eta_U s_{\hat{r}_\theta}$, and the splines created by connecting the lower endpoints, $\hat{r_\theta}+\eta_L s_{\hat{r}_\theta}$.

4 Application and Results

In this section we apply the methodology proposed above to three different biometric modalities. These are facial recognition, fingerprints and a hand geometry. These data is described in Ross and Jain [12]. We briefly summarize them here. Biometric captures were taken from 50 individuals. Ten genuine comparisons were made for each individual and five imposter comparisons were made for each cross- comparison pair. All cross-comparison pairs were run. Thus, there were $10 \times 50 = 500$ genuine comparisons and $50 \times 49 \times 5 = 12250$ imposter comparisons. For these regions we followed Adler and Schuckers [10] in establishing the radial center at $(c = 1, c = 1)$. This value was chosen because the radial angles from this center point seem match the typical curvature of a DET curve and, hence, are more likely to be perpendicular to such curves. Note that it is possible to use this methodology to create regions strictly for the FAR or FRR like those proposed by Dass *et al* [11] by allowing the coordinate of the polar center for the error rate of interest to become very small i.e. $(0, -C)$ for some larger number C. We selected T, the number of angles in Θ^*, to be 1000 so that there were 1000 different angles, θ's, used to create our confidence region. Due to our choice of $c = 1$, θ_L was π and θ_U was $3\pi/2$. We adjusted the radial variance by $\epsilon = 2\bar{n}^{-2}$ where $\bar{n}$ is the average number of comparisons between the genuine and imposter samples. For the data here that is $\bar{n} = 6375$. The use of this ϵ is meant to approximate the use of the $+2/+4$ adjustment suggested by Agresti and Coull [14]. Finally it is worth noting that, in practice, we truncate the final DET confidence region by limiting it to values in the range of $(0, 1) \times (0, 1)$. In some cases the confidence region included negative values because of the width of $\Re$ due to the calculation of η_L and η_U. Note also that since η_L and η_U are global values in the sense that they have to hold for all θ that they do not necessarily reflect the variability at a particular θ. We use 95% for the confidence level in

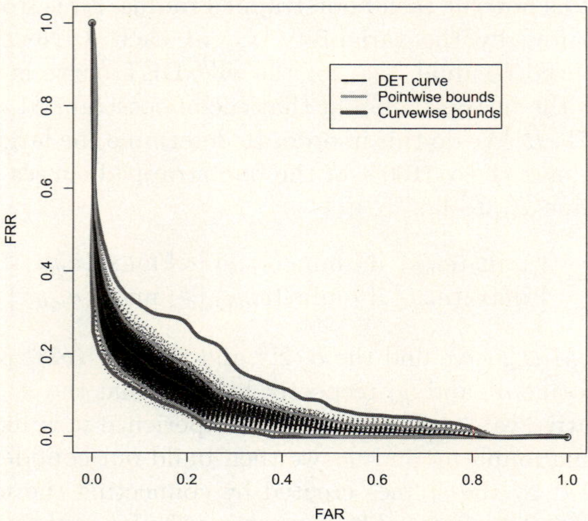

Fig. 2. 95% confidence region for DET of a Hand Geometry System

these applications. Figures 1, 2, 3 contain the DET curves and the derived 95% confidence regions for each of these curves. In these figures the center line is the estimated DET, $\hat{R}$, the next pair of lines moving outward are the pointwise confidence bounds and the last pair of lines are the curvewise confidence bounds which define the confidence region, $\Re$. The lighter dashed lines represent the $M = 1000$ bootstrapped DET's. Table 1 gives a summary of the percentage of ROC curves that are inside each of these bounds.

The confidence region for the facial recognition system and the hand geometry classifier tend to both be symmetric around the EER while the fingerprint region tends to diminish quickly along the FRR axis and very slowly along the FAR axis. The latter effect is due to the larger variability in bootstrapped DET's in that region. This can be seen by the dashed lines, each being a bootstrapped DET, in Figure 3. Thus the DET confidence region accurately reflects the variability in the sample data.

One byproduct of this methodology is that we can derive a confidence interval for the EER. As mentioned above this quantity is a one that is often reported as an overall measure of performance for a biometric classifier. As with other sample measures, there is a need to quantify the variability in such estimates.

Table 1. Percent of bootstrapped ROC curves inside the bounds of 95% confidence regions

Modality	Pointwise Region	Curvewise Region
Face	64.5%	95.0%
Hand Geometry	62.5%	94.9%
Fingerprint	81.2%	95.0%

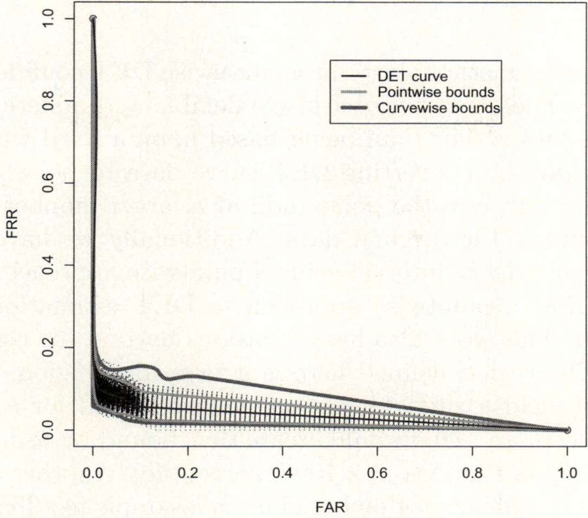

Fig. 3. 95% confidence region for the DET of a Fingerprint System

Table 2. Pointwise 95% EER confidence intervals for three modalities

Modality	Lower Bound	Equal Error Rate	Upper Bound
Face	0.0384	0.0575	0.0847
Hand Geometry	0.1168	0.1494	0.1810
Fingerprint	0.0430	0.0715	0.0972

To that end, it is possible to create an approximate $(1-\alpha)100\%$ confidence interval for the EER from the bootstrapped DET's. Since the EER is found at a single θ, there is no need to worry about the multiple comparisons problem outlined above. Consequently, we can simply find the $\alpha/2^{th}$ percentile and the $1-\alpha/2^{th}$ percentile for the appropriate radius. (In the case when T, the number of angles, is an even number, an approximation can be calculated by taking the average of the two appropriate endpoints.) Table 2 contains 95% confidence intervals for the EER's of the three classifiers described above. Note that the EER for the facial recognition system here is the lowest; however, there is a great deal of variability in that estimate. The width of the error rate is approximately 4.75%. The hand geometry system has the highest estimated EER and the upper bound on that EER is approximately 18%. Given that we are dealing with non-Gaussian distributions it is not a surprise that the confidence regions are asymmetric. It is perhaps surprising that the facial recognition system outperforms the fingerprint system in this particular application; however, the larger overlap in these two distributions suggests that their EER's are not significantly different.

5 Discussion

This paper proposes a methodology for a curvewise DET confidence region. The region and the methods that created it are flexible and adhere to the variability in the sample data rather than being based upon a fixed width. We achieve this confidence region by converting DET curve data to polar coordinates and calculating the variability in the polar radii at a larger number of angles based upon bootstrapping of the original data. Additionally we have shown how to produce an EER confidence interval using a pointwise approach. It is clear from the results here that a pointwise approach to DET estimation yields regions that are too small. This work also has extensions beyond the confidence regions described here. The region defined here is a two-sided region. A one-sided region which would yield a single upper confidence bound for a DET would be straightforward to create. (One would create that bound by using $\hat{r} + \eta s_{r_\theta}$ where η would be based upon the $(1-\alpha) \times 100^{th}$ percentile). Another extension would be to compare the confidence region based upon a sample to a hypothesized DET curve. This would allow the acceptance or rejection of that hypothesized curve based upon whether or not the curve fell within the confidence region. Dass *et al* [11] tests a hypothesized curve with their univariate error rate approach. Likewise a corresponding approach could be taken for testing of an EER. Lastly, we note that all of this work has been done on axes defined by the FAR and FRR. There are equivalent confidence regions for any one-to-one transformations of the axes and these regions will have the same properties as the confidence regions described here.

Acknowledgements. This work is supported by NSF grants CNS-0325640 and CNS-0520990 (Dr. Schuckers) which is cooperatively funded by the National Science Foundation and the United States Department of Homeland Security and by NSERC Canada (Dr. Adler).

References

1. Mansfield, T., Wayman, J.L.: Best practices in testing and reporting performance of biometric devices (2002), on the web at `www.cesg.gov.uk/site/ast/biometrics/media/BestPractice.pdf`
2. Green, D.M., Swets, J.A.: Signal Detection Theory and Psychophysics. John Wiley & Sons, Chichester (1966)
3. Poh, N., Bengio, S.: Database, protocol and tools for evaluating score-level fusion algorithms in biometric authentication. Pattern Recognition Journal (2005)
4. Zhou, X.-H., McClish, D.K., Obuchowski, N.A.: Statistical Methods in Diagnostic Medicine. John Wiley & Sons, Chichester (2002)
5. Hernández-Orallo, J., Ferri, C., Lachiche, N., Flach, P.A. (eds.): ROC Analysis in Artificial Intelligence, 1st Int. Workshop, ROCAI-2004, Valencia, Spain (2004)
6. Macskassy, S.A., Provost, F.J., Rosset, S.: Roc confidence bands: an empirical evaluation. In: De Raedt, L., Wrobel, S. (eds.) ICML, pp. 537–544. ACM, New York (2005)

7. Campbell, G.: Advance in statistical methodology for the evaluation of diagnostic and laboratory tests. Statistics in Medicine 13, 499–508 (1994)
8. Ma, G., Hall, W.J.: Confidence bands for receiver operating characteristics curves. Medical Decision Making 13, 191–197 (1993)
9. Poh, N., Martin, A., Bengio, S.: Performance generalization in biometric authentication using joint user-specific and sample bootstraps. IEEE Transactions on Pattern Analysis and Machine Intelligence (to appear)
10. Adler, A., Schuckers, M.E.: Calculation of a composite DET curve. In: Kanade, T., Jain, A., Ratha, N.K. (eds.) AVBPA 2005. LNCS, vol. 3546, pp. 279–288. Springer, Heidelberg (2005)
11. Dass, S.C., Zhu, Y., Jain, A.K.: Validating a biometric authentication system: Sample size requirements. IEEE Transactions on Pattern Analysis and Machine Intelligence 28(1), 19–30 (2007)
12. Ross, A., Jain, A.K.: Information fusion in biometrics. Pattern Recognition Letters 24(13), 2115–2125 (2003)
13. Bolle, R.M., Ratha, N.K., Pankanti, S.: Error analysis of pattern recognition systems – the subsets bootstrap. Computer Vision and Image Understanding 93, 1–33 (2004)
14. Agresti, A., Coull, B.A.: Approximate is better than "exact" for interval estimation of binomial proportions. The American Statistician 52(2), 119–126 (1998)

Bayesian Hill-Climbing Attack and Its Application to Signature Verification

Javier Galbally, Julian Fierrez, and Javier Ortega-Garcia

Biometric Recognition Group–ATVS, EPS, Universidad Autonoma de Madrid,
C/ Francisco Tomas y Valiente 11, 28049 Madrid, Spain
{javier.galbally,julian.fierrez,javier.ortega}@uam.es

Abstract. A general hill-climbing attack algorithm based on Bayesian adaption is presented. The approach uses the scores provided by the matcher to adapt a global distribution computed from a development set of users, to the local specificities of the client being attacked. The proposed attack is evaluated on a competitive feature-based signature verification system over the 330 users of the MCYT database. The results show a very high efficiency of the hill-climbing algorithm, which successfully bypassed the system for over 95% of the attacks.

1 Introduction

Due to the advantages that biometric security systems present over traditional security approaches [1], they are currently being introduced in many applications, including: access control, sensitive data protection, on-line tracking systems, etc. However, in spite of these advantages they are not free from external attacks which can decrease their level of security. Thus, it is of utmost importance to analyze the vulnerabilities of biometric systems, in order to find their limitations and to develop useful countermeasures for foreseeable attacks.

Attacks on biometric systems can be broadly divided into: *i) direct attacks*, which are carried out at the sensor level using synthetic traits (e.g., printed iris images, gummy fingers); and *ii) indirect attacks*, which are carried out against the inner modules of the application and, therefore, the attacker needs to have some information about the system operation (e.g., matcher used, storage format). Ratha *et al.* in [2] made a more exhaustive analysis of the vulnerable points of biometric systems, identifying 8 types of possible attacks. The first point corresponded to direct attacks and the remaining seven were included in the indirect attacks group.

There are several works that study the robustness of biometric systems, specially finger- and iris-based, against direct attacks, including [3,4,5]. Some efforts have also been made in the study of indirect attacks to biometric systems. Most of these works use some type of variant of the hill-climbing algorithm [6]. Some examples include an indirect attack to a face-based system in [7], and to a PC and Match-on-Card minutiae-based fingerprint verification systems in [8] and [9], respectively. These attacks, which belong to types 2 or 4 of the classification

S.-W. Lee and S.Z. Li (Eds.): ICB 2007, LNCS 4642, pp. 386–395, 2007.

reported by Ratha *et al.* [2], take advantage of the score given by the matcher to iteratively change a synthetically created template until the similarity score exceeds a fixed decision threshold and the access to the system is granted. These hill-climbing approaches are all highly dependent of the technology used, only being usable for very specific type of matchers.

In the present work, a general hill-climbing algorithm based on Bayesian adaptation [10] is presented. The contribution of this new approach lies in the fact that it can be applied to any system working with fixed length feature vectors. The proposed attack uses the scores provided by the matcher to adapt a global distribution computed from a development set of users, to the local specificities of the client being attacked. We then present a case study where the attack is tested on a feature-based signature verification system using the 330 subjects of the MCYT database [11]. In the experiments the attack showed remarkable performance, being able to bypass over 95% of the accounts attacked for the best configuration of the algorithm found. Furthermore, the hill-climbing approach was faster than a brute-force attack in two of the three operating points of the system evaluated.

The paper is structured as follows. The general hill-climbing algorithm is described in Sect. 2, while the case study in signature verification is reported in Sect. 3. In Sect. 3.1 we present the attacked system, and the database and experimental protocol followed are described in Sect 3.2. The results are detailed in Sect. 3.3. Conclusions are finally drawn in Sect. 4.

2 Bayesian Hill-Climbing Algorithm

Consider the problem of finding a K-dimensional vector $\mathbf{y}$ which, compared to an unknown template $\mathcal{C}$ (in our case related to a specific client), produces a similarity score bigger than a certain threshold δ, according to some matching function J, i.e.: $J(\mathcal{C}, \mathbf{y}) > \delta$. The template can be another K-dimensional vector or a generative model of K-dimensional vectors. Consider a statistical model G (K-variate Gaussian with mean $\boldsymbol{\mu}_G$ and diagonal covariance matrix $\boldsymbol{\Sigma}_G$, with $\boldsymbol{\sigma}_G^2 = \text{diag}(\boldsymbol{\Sigma}_G)$), in our case related to a background set of users, overlapping to some extent with $\mathcal{C}$. Let us assume that we have access to the evaluation of the matching function $J(\mathcal{C}, \mathbf{y})$ for several trials of $\mathbf{y}$. The problem can be solved by adapting the global distribution G to the local specificities of template $\mathcal{C}$, through the following iterative strategy:

1. Take N samples ($\mathbf{y}_i$) of the global distribution G, and compute the similarity scores $J(\mathcal{C}, \mathbf{y}_i)$, with $i = 1, \ldots, N$.
2. Select the M points (with $M < N$) which have generated higher scores.
3. Compute the local distribution $L(\boldsymbol{\mu}_L, \boldsymbol{\sigma}_L)$, also K-variate Gaussian, based on the M selected points.
4. Compute an adapted distribution $A(\boldsymbol{\mu}_A, \boldsymbol{\sigma}_A)$, also K-variate Gaussian, which trades off the general knowledge provided by $G(\boldsymbol{\mu}_G, \boldsymbol{\sigma}_G)$ and the local information given by $L(\boldsymbol{\mu}_L, \boldsymbol{\sigma}_L)$. This is achieved by adapting the sufficient statistics as follows:

$$\boldsymbol{\mu}_A = \alpha\boldsymbol{\mu}_L + (1-\alpha)\boldsymbol{\mu}_G \tag{1}$$

$$\boldsymbol{\sigma}_A^2 = \alpha(\boldsymbol{\sigma}_L^2 + \boldsymbol{\mu}_L^2) + (1-\alpha)(\boldsymbol{\sigma}_G^2 + \boldsymbol{\mu}_G^2) - \boldsymbol{\mu}_A^2 \tag{2}$$

5. Redefine $G = A$ and return to step 1.

In Eq. (1) and (2), $\boldsymbol{\mu}^2$ is defined as $\boldsymbol{\mu}^2 = \text{diag}(\boldsymbol{\mu}\boldsymbol{\mu}^T)$, and α is an adaptation coefficient in the range [0,1]. The algorithm finishes either when one of the N similarity scores computed in step 2 exceeds the given threshold δ, or when the maximum number of iterations is reached.

In the above algorithm there are two key concepts not to be confused, namely: *i)* number of *iterations* (n_{it}), which refers to the number of times that the statistical distribution G is adapted, and *ii)* number of *comparisons* (n_{comp}), which denotes the total number of matchings carried out through the algorithm. Both numbers are related through the parameter N, being $n_{comp} = N \cdot n_{it}$.

3 Case Study: Attacking a Feature-Based On-Line Signature Verification System

3.1 Signature Verification System

The proposed Bayesian hill-climbing algorithm is used to attack a feature-based on-line signature verification system. The signatures are parameterized using the set of features described in [12]. In that work, a set of 100 global features was proposed, and the individual features were ranked according to their individual discriminant power. A good operating point for the systems tested was found when using the first 40 parameters. In the present contribution we use this 40-feature representation of the signatures, normalizing each of them to the range [0,1] using the tanh-estimators described in [13]:

$$p_k^{'} = \frac{1}{2}\left\{\tanh\left(0.01\left(\frac{p_k - \mu_{p_k}}{\sigma_{p_k}}\right)\right) + 1\right\}, \tag{3}$$

where p_k is the kth parameter, $p_k^{'}$ denotes the normalized parameter, and μ_{p_k} and σ_{p_k} are respectively the estimated mean and standard deviation of the parameter under consideration.

The similarity scores are computed using the Mahalanobis distance between the input vector and a statistical model of the attacked client $\mathcal{C}$ using a number of training signatures (5 in our experiments). Thus,

$$J(\mathcal{C}, \mathbf{y}) = \frac{1}{\left((\mathbf{y} - \boldsymbol{\mu}^{\mathcal{C}})^T (\boldsymbol{\Sigma}^{\mathcal{C}})^{-1} (\mathbf{y} - \boldsymbol{\mu}^{\mathcal{C}})\right)^{1/2}}, \tag{4}$$

where $\boldsymbol{\mu}^{\mathcal{C}}$ and $\boldsymbol{\Sigma}^{\mathcal{C}}$ are the mean vector and covariance matrix obtained from the training signatures, and $\mathbf{y}$ is the 40-feature vector used to attack the system.

3.2 Database and Experimental Protocol

The experiments were carried out on the MCYT signature database [11], comprising 330 users. The database was acquired in 4 different sites with 5 time-spaced capture sets. Every client was asked to sign 5 times in each set, and to carry out 5 skilled forgeries of one of his precedent donors, thus capturing a total 25 genuine signatures and 25 skilled forgeries per user.

The database is divided into a training (used to estimate the initial K-variate distribution G) and a test set (containing the user's accounts being attacked), which are afterwards swapped (two-fold cross-validation). The training set initially comprises the genuine signatures of the odd users in the database and the test set the genuine signatures of the even users. This way, the donors captured in the 4 sites are homogenously distributed over the two sets.

For each user, five different genuine models are computed using one training signature from each acquisition set, this way the temporal variability of the signing process is taken into account. With this approach, a total $330 \times 5 = 1,650$ accounts are attacked (825 in each of the two-fold cross-validation process).

In order to set the threshold δ, where we consider that the attack has been successful, the False Acceptance (FA) and False Rejection (FR) curves of the system are computed. In the case of considering skilled forgeries, each of the 5 estimated models of every user are matched with the remaining 20 genuine signatures ($5 \times 20 \times 330 = 33,000$ genuine scores), while the impostor scores are generated comparing the 5 statistical models to all the 25 skilled forgeries of every user ($5 \times 25 \times 330 = 41,250$ skilled impostor scores). In the case of random forgeries (i.e., impostors try to access other's accounts using their own signature), genuine scores are computed as above, while the set of impostor scores is generated matching the 5 user models with one signature of the remaining donors, making a total of $5 \times 330 \times 329 = 542,850$ random impostor scores. The FA and FR curves both for skilled (left) and random (right) forgeries are depicted in Fig. 1, together with three different realistic operating points used in the attacks experiments(FR=20%, FR=30%, and FR=40%). The similarity scores were normalized following the criterion described in Eq. (3).

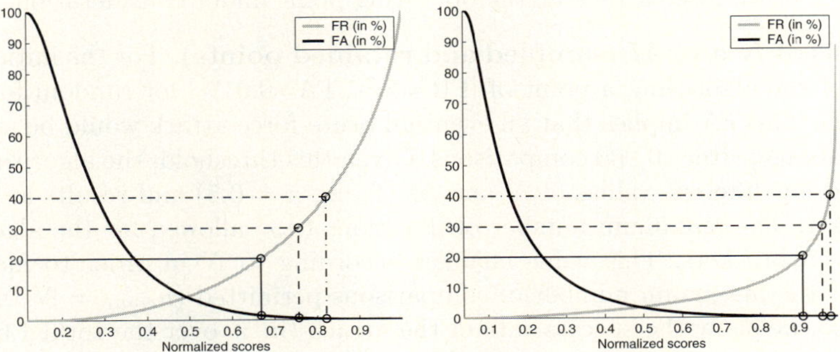

Fig. 1. FA and FR curves for skilled (left) and random (right) forgeries

Table 1. Success rate (in %) of the hill-climbing attack for increasing values of N (number of sampled points) and M (best ranked points). The maximum number of iterations allowed is given in brackets. The success rate (in %) appears in plain text, while the average number of iterations needed to break an account appears in **bold**.

		N				
		10 (2500)	25 (1000)	50 (500)	100 (250)	200 (125)
M	3	5.03 **24,082**	68.18 **11,292**	78.78 **9,725**	86.78 **10,611**	84.00 **14,406**
	5	2.72 **24,404**	71.27 **10,713**	85.57 **7,957**	92.00 **8,752**	91.09 **12,587**
	10		38.18 **17,598**	84.18 **8,609**	92.78 **8,602**	92.06 **12,261**
	25			41.33 **17,972**	89.57 **10,857**	91.63 **13,633**
	50				51.45 **18,909**	83.15 **16,660**
	100					39.39 **22,502**

3.3 Results

The goal of the experiments is to study the effect of varying the three parameters of the algorithm (N, M, and α), on the number of broken accounts, while minimizing the average number of comparisons (n_{comp}) needed to reach the fixed threshold δ. As described in Sect. 2, the above mentioned parameters denote: N the number of sampled points of the adapted distribution at a given iteration, M the number of top ranked samples used at each iteration to adapt the global distribution, and α is an adaptation coefficient.

Although the proposed hill-climbing algorithm and a brute-force attack are not fully comparable (for example, the resources required differ greatly as an efficient brute-force attack needs a database of thousands of signatures), in the experiments we compare n_{comp} with the number of matchings necessary for a successful brute-force attack at the operating point under consideration.

Analysis of N and M (sampled and retained points). For the initial evaluation of the algorithm, a point of [FR=30%, FA=0.01%] for random forgeries was fixed. This FA implies that an eventual brute-force attack would be successful, in average, after 10,000 comparisons. Given this threshold, the algorithm was executed for different values of N and M (fixing $\alpha = 0.5$) and results are given in Table 1. The maximum number of iterations (n_{it}) allowed for the algorithm appears in brackets. This value changes according to N in order to maintain constant the maximum number of comparisons permitted ($n_{comp} = N \cdot n_{it}$). In plain text we show the success rate of the attack (in % over the total 1,650 accounts tested), while the average number of comparisons needed for a successful attack is represented in **bold**.

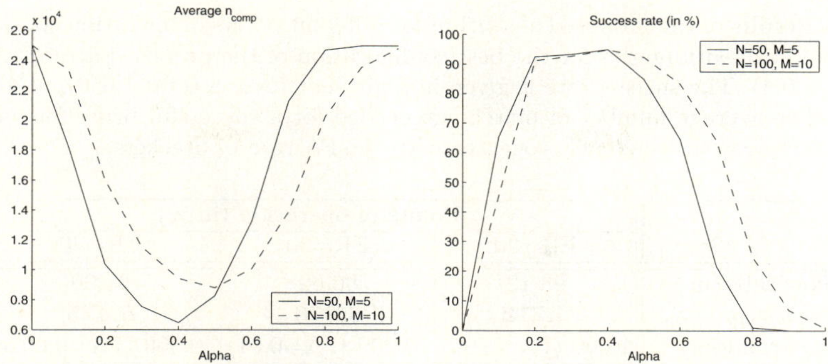

Fig. 2. Impact of α (adaptation coefficient) on the average number of comparisons needed for a successful attack (left), and on the success rate (right)

An analysis of the results given in Table 1 shows that for $N \gg M$, the points selected to estimate the local distribution are too specific and thus, the success rate of the attacks degrades slightly with respect to the best trade-off combination ($N \approx M$). On the other hand, if $N \simeq M$, the local distribution computed is too general, and the attack success rate is significantly reduced. The same effect is observed for the average number of comparisons (n_{comp}).

In this case, two good configurations of the parameters $[N,M]$ can be extracted from Table 1, namely: *i*) [50,5], and *ii*) [100,10]. For these two points, the number of accounts broken is close to the total attacked, 85.57% and 92.78% respectively, while n_{comp} reaches a minimum (7,957 and 8,602, respectively) which is lower than the expected number of matchings required for a successful brute-force attack based on random forgeries (10,000 in average).

Analysis of α (adaptation coefficient). For the two best configurations found, the effect of varying α on the performance of the attack is studied sweeping its value from 0 (only the global distribution G is taken into account), to 1 (only the local distribution L affects the adaptation stage). The results are depicted in Fig. 2 where we show the evolution of n_{comp} (left), and the success rate (right), for increasing values of α and for the two configurations mentioned above.

It can be observed that for the point [50,5], the maximum number of accounts broken, and the minimum number of comparisons needed is reached for $\alpha = 0.4$ and both (maximum and minimum) are respectively greater and lower than those achieved with the values [100,10]. Thus, the best configuration of our algorithm is obtained for the values $[N,M,\alpha]$=[50,5,0.4], which leads to 1,594 broken accounts (out of the 1,650 tested), and an average number of comparisons for a successful attack of 6,076, which represents almost half of the attempts required by a brute-force attack based on random forgeries. This value of α indicates that, for the best performance of the attack, the global and local distributions should be given approximately the same importance.

Table 2. Results of the proposed algorithm for different points of operation considering random and skilled forgeries for the best configuration of the proposed attack (N=50, M=5, $\alpha = 0.4$). The success rate is given in plain text (over a total 1,650), and n_{comp} in **bold**. The average number of matchings needed for a successful brute-force attack (n_{bf}) is also given for reference, together with the FA rate in brackets.

	Points of operation (in %)		
	FR=20	FR=30	FR=40
Success rate (in %)	98.12	96.60	94.90
n_{comp}	**5,712**	**6,076**	**6,475**
n_{bf} (random)	2,000 (FA=0.05)	10,000 (FA=0.01)	40,000 (FA=0.0025)
n_{bf} (skilled)	70 (FA=1.42)	180 (FA=0.55)	475 (FA=0.21)

Analysis of different operating points. Using the best configuration found, the algorithm was evaluated in two additional operating points of the system, namely (random forgeries): *i)* FR=20%, FA=0.05% (which implies a 2,000 attempt random brute-force attack), and *ii)* FR=40%, FA=0.0025%, where a random brute-force attack would need in average 40,000 matches before gaining access to the system. Results are given in Table 2 where the success rate over the total 1,650 accounts appears in plain text , and the average number of comparisons required by the bayesian hill-climbing attack in **bold**.

Smaller values of the FA rate imply a bigger value of the threshold δ to be reached by the algorithm, which causes a rise in the average number of iterations required for a successful attack. Compared to brute-force attacks, this increase of the number of iterations is significantly lower, which entails that the hill-climbing algorithm is clearly better than brute-force for FR rates over 25% and less effective for smaller values of the FR rate. Even though for some operating points the attacking strategy described in the present contribution is slower than a brute-force attack, it has to be emphasized that this latter approach would require, for instance in FR=20%, a database of 2,000 different signatures, which is not straightforward.

As described in Sect. 3.2 the genuine scores for the skilled forgeries case are computed the same way as in the random approach, therefore the FR rates remain unaltered. This means that the threshold δ to be reached by the hill-climbing algorithm is the same in both cases (comparing the proposed hill-climbing to either random or skilled brute-force attack), thus, the performance measures (success rate and number of comparisons n_{comp}) do not change. Only the FA values have to be recomputed and, as a result, the number of comparisons required by a successful skilled brute-force attack also change, being in the skilled forgery case: 70 for FR=20%, 180 for FR=30%, and 475 for FR=40%. These are significantly smaller than the average number of iterations needed by the hill-climbing algorithm, however, it has to be taken into account that in this case, for instance in FR=30%, we would need 180 different *skilled forgeries* of the same signer to access the system.

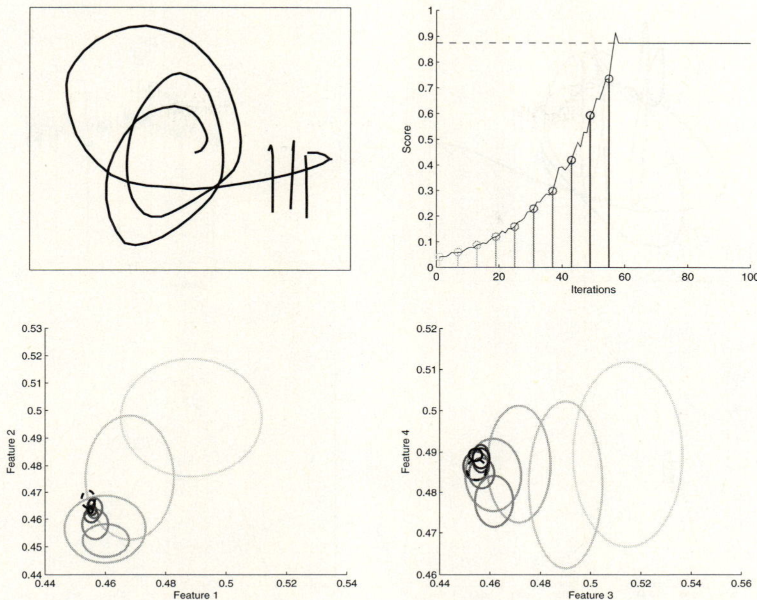

Fig. 3. Example execution of a successful attack, showing a sample signature of the attacked model (top left), evolution of the best score through the iterations (top right) with the threshold δ marked with a dashed line, and progress of the adapted distribution for the first two parameters (bottom left) and for the third and fourth parameters (bottom right). Lighter gray denotes a previous iteration, and the dashed ellipse the target model.

Graphical examples. Two example executions of the attack, at the FR=30% operating point and using the best algorithm configuration (N=50, M=5, α=0.4), are shown in Fig. 3 (successful attack) and Fig. 4 (unsuccessful attack).

In Fig. 3 a signature which was successfully attacked in very few iterations (57), is depicted. The evolution of the best similarity score through all the iterations is shown in the top right plot, where we can see how the threshold δ (dashed line) is quickly reached. In the bottom row we show the evolution followed by the two dimensional Gaussian distributions of the first two parameters (left), and of the parameters 3 and 4 (right). A lighter color denotes a previous iteration (corresponding to the highlighted points of the top right plot) and the dashed ellipse is the target distribution of the attacked model. It can be observed that the adapted distribution rapidly converges towards the objective model.

A sample signature of one of the few models which was not bypassed with the proposed algorithm is given in Fig. 4. The curves depicted are analog to the those plotted in Fig 3. The curves in the bottom row are zoomed versions of the squares shown in the pictures above, in order to show how in this case the adapted distribution does not converge towards the target model (dashed).

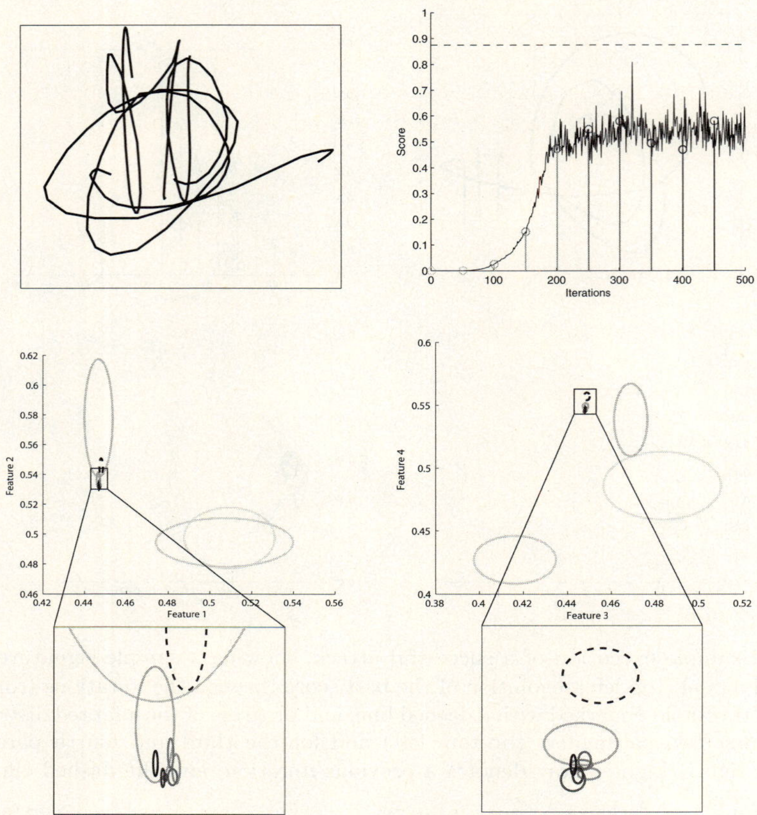

Fig. 4. Example execution of an unsuccessful attack. The images shown are analogue to those reported in Fig. 3. The bottom pictures are enlarged versions of the squares depicted in the above images.

4 Conclusions

A hill-climbing attack algorithm based on Bayesian adaptation was presented and evaluated on a feature-based signature verification system over a database of 330 users. The experiments showed a very high efficiency of the hill-climbing algorithm, reaching a success rate for the attacks of over 95% for the best algorithm configuration found.

The performance of the hill-climbing attack was directly compared to that of a brute-force attack. The algorithm described in the present contribution needed less number of matchings than the brute-force approach in two out of the three operating points evaluated when considering random forgeries. Worth noting that the resources required by both approaches are not comparable. In order to perform an efficient brute-force attack, the attacker must have a database of more than a thousand real different templates, while the hill-climbing approach does not need real templates to be successful.

It has to be emphasized that the proposed algorithm is not thought for a specific matching strategy, and can be applied for the evaluation of the vulnerabilities of any biometric system based on fixed length templates.

Acknowledgements

J. G. is supported by a FPU Fellowship from Spanish MEC and J. F. is supported by a Marie Curie Fellowship from the European Commission. This work was supported by Spanish MEC under project TEC2006-13141-C03-03 and the European NoE Biosecure.

References

1. Jain, A.K., Ross, A., Pankanti, S.: Biometrics: a tool for information security. IEEE Trans. on Information Forensics and Security 1, 125–143 (2006)
2. Ratha, N., Connell, J., Bolle, R.: An analysis of minutiae matching strength. In: Proc. AVBPA, pp. 223–228 (2001)
3. van der Putte, T., Keuning, J.: Biometrical fingerprint recognition: don't get your fingers burned. In: Proc. IFIP, pp. 289–303 (2000)
4. Galbally, J., Fierrez, J., et al.: On the vulnerability of fingerprint verification systems to fake fingerprint attacks. In: Proc. IEEE of ICCST, pp. 130–136. IEEE Computer Society Press, Los Alamitos (2006)
5. Pacut, A., Czajka, A.: Aliveness detection for iris biometrics. In: Proc. ICCST, pp. 122–129 (2006)
6. Soutar, C.: Biometric system security, `http://www.bioscrypt.com/assets/security_soutar.pdf`
7. Adler, A.: Sample images can be independently restored from face recognition templates. In: Proc. CCECE, vol. 2, pp. 1163–1166 (2003)
8. Uludag, U., Jain, A.K.: Attacks on biometric systems: a case study in fingerprints. In: Proc. SPIE, vol. 5306, pp. 622–633 (2004)
9. Martinez-Diaz, M., Fierrez, J., et al.: Hill-climbing and brute force attacks on biometric systems: a case study in match-on-card fingerprint verification. In: Proc. IEEE of ICCST., pp. 151–159. IEEE Computer Society Press, Los Alamitos (2006)
10. Duda, R.O., Hart, P.E., Stork, D.G.: Pattern Classification. Wiley, Chichester (2001)
11. Ortega-Garcia, J., Fierrez-Aguilar, J., et al.: MCYT baseline corpus: a bimodal biometric database. IEE Proc. Vis. Image Signal Process. 150, 395–401 (2003)
12. Fierrez-Aguilar, J., Nanni, L., et al.: An on-line signature verification system based on fusion of local and global information. In: Kanade, T., Jain, A., Ratha, N.K. (eds.) AVBPA 2005. LNCS, vol. 3546. Springer, Heidelberg (2005)
13. Jain, A.K., Nandakumar, K., Ross, A.: Score normalization in multimodal biometric systems. Pattern Recognition 38, 2270–2285 (2005)

Wolf Attack Probability: A New Security Measure in Biometric Authentication Systems

Masashi Une[1], Akira Otsuka[2], and Hideki Imai[2,3]

[1] Center for Information Technology Studies (CITECS), Institute for Monetary and Economic Studies (IMES), Bank of Japan, 2-1-1, Nihonbashi-Hongokucho, Chuo, Tokyo 103-8660, Japan
masashi-une@boj.or.jp

[2] Research Center for Information Security (RCIS), National Institute of Advanced Industrial Science and Technology (AIST), Akihabara-Daibiru Room 1102, 1-18-13, Sotokanda, Chiyoda, Tokyo 101-0021, Japan
a-otsuka@aist.go.jp

[3] Faculty of Science and Engineering, Chuo University, 1-13-27, Kasuga, Bunkyo, Tokyo 112-8551, Japan

Abstract. This paper will propose a wolf attack probability (WAP) as a new measure for evaluating security of biometric authentication systems. The wolf attack is an attempt to impersonate a victim by feeding "wolves" into the system to be attacked. The "wolf" means an input value which can be falsely accepted as a match with multiple templates. WAP is defined as a maximum success probability of the wolf attack with one wolf sample. In this paper, we give a rigorous definition of the new security measure which gives strengh estimation of an individual biometric authentication system against impersonation attacks. We show that if one reestimates using our WAP measure, a typical fingerprint algorithm is turned out to be much weaker than theoretically estimated by Ratha et al. Moreover, we apply the wolf attack to a finger-vein-pattern matching algorithm. Surprisingly, we show that there exists an extremely strong wolf which falsely matches all templates for any threshold values.

1 Introduction

A biometric authentication system automatically authenticates an individual by using physiological and/or behavioral characteristics. Recently, the use of biometric authentication systems has spread in various services such as the immigration control at an airport, financial transactions at an ATM (automated tellers machine) terminal, the access control for a mobile phone, and so on. This trend has made it more important to exactly evaluate the security of biometric authetication systems.

In order to conduct the security evaluation, it is necessary to identify threats and vulnerabilities regarding the biometrics. General threats and vulnerabilities common to biometric authentication systems have already been clarified in

S.-W. Lee and S.Z. Li (Eds.): ICB 2007, LNCS 4642, pp. 396–406, 2007.

many literatures. The committee draft of ISO/IEC 19792 describes three threats and eleven vulnerabilities [1]. With regard to the threats, the draft includes "intentional impersonation," "unexpected high FAR (false acceptance rate)," and "creating backdoor." Focusing on the intentional impersonation, the following three attacks have been widely discussed so far: a brute-force attack, a zero-effort attack, and an artifact attack. The artifact attack is that an attacker presents the victim's biometric characteristic by using some artifacts[2]. Although a security measure against the zero-effort attack has been established as FAR, no measures are commonly accepted by the industry against the brute-force attack and the artifact attack.

With regard to the brute-force attack, Ratha et al.[3] estimates its success probability in a fingerprint-minutiae matching algorithm. We will call the success probability a "minutiae collision probability (MCP)." However, MCP of Ratha et al. is computed under the following condition: the attacker presents an input value that consists of the same number of minutiae as that of all templates to be compared with. Therefore, MCP of Ratha et al. does not give the exact success probability of the brute-force attack. In order to do so, we have to compute MCP in such a way to take all possible input values into account.

The brute-force attack is supposed to be carried out under the situation that an attacker blindly selects an input value to be presented to a biometric authentication system. However, if we assume that the attacker has some information on the internal algorithms employed in the system, we have to pay attention to an attack with a smarter choice of a sample, "wolf." The draft of ISO/IEC 19792 defines the wolf as a biometric sample that shows high similarity to most of the templates[1]. If the attacker successfully found the wolf, he could impersonate the victim with a higher probability than MCP by presenting the wolf.

In this paper, we call such an attack a "wolf attack," and propose a "wolf attack probability (WAP)" as a maximum success probability of the wolf attack with one wolf sample. WAP is considered to be the upper bound of the success probability of attacks that are carried out without knowledge of a victim's biometric sample. Therefore, WAP can be used as a security measure to evaluate the lower bound of a security level in an individual biometric authentication system.

We show that WAP is extremely larger than the theoretical estimation of MCP by Ratha et al. in the fingerprint-minutiae matching algorithm. Ratha et al. computed MCP under the condition that the number of minutiae in the input value N_q is identical to that of minutiae in the template N_r. Especially, they discussed MCP for $N_q = N_r = 40$. On the other hand, WAP is given as the maximum of MCP where $N_q = 400$ and $N_r = 40$. For example, while Ratha et al. obtained $MCP = 2^{-80}$ for threshold $m = 25$, we show that $WAP = 2^{-21}$. In this case, we can understand that the wolf attack gains the attack complexity of about 2^{59}.

Moreover, we will apply the wolf attack to a finger-vein-pattern matching alorithm proposed by [4]. Surprisingly, we show that there exists the wolf which falsely matches any templates for any threshold values. Especially, we call such a wolf a "universal wolf." This result implies that it is necessary to evaluate an impact of the wolf attack on a matching algorithm by applying the wolf attack and obtaining WAP.

This paper continues as follows. Section 2 will obtain exact MCP on the basis of [3]. By using MCP, we will search for an input value that maximizes the probability of a false match with a given template, and show that the maximized probability is extremely larger than MCP of Ratha et al. Section 3 will define the wolf attack and WAP. Section 4 will describe FAR and discuss its limitation as a security measure for the wolf attack. Section 5 will show a result of applying the wolf attack to the finger-vein-pattern matching alorithm proposed by [4]. Section 6 will summarize our results and show future research topics.

2 Brute-Force Attack in a Fingerprint-Minutiae Matching Algorithm

2.1 Minutiae Collision Probability by Ratha et al.

Ratha et al.[3] discusses a typical fingerprint-minutiae matching algorithm in which the number of matched minutiae between an input value and a template reflects the degree of the match. The feature of a minutia consists of its location (x, y) and the ridge direction d. If the number of paired minutiae whose locations and ridge directions are equal to or more than a threshold value m, the input value is accepted as a match with the corresponding template.

In such a matching algorithm, Ratha et al. discussed the security level against the brute-force attack. Assuming that the attacker presents an input value consisting of forged minutiae whose locations and ridge directions are randomly selected, Ratha et al. attempted to compute the probability that the input value falsely matches a given template in both a location and a ridge direction. We call the probability a "minutiae collision probability (MCP)." In general, the definition of MCP is given as follows.

Definition 1. *Let S_{N_q} and T_{N_r} be a set of input values consisting of N_q minutiae and a set of templates consisting of N_r minutiae, respectively. Let match be a function that has two inputs $s(\in S_{N_q})$ and $t(\in T_{N_r})$ and an output of "accept" or "reject" as the result of the match under a predetermined threshold. For given N_q and N_r,*

$$MCP \stackrel{\triangle}{=} \underset{s \in S_{N_q}}{Ave} \underset{t \in T_{N_r}}{Ave} Pr[match(s,t) = accept] \tag{1}$$

where Pr[X] and Ave Y denote a probability of the occurrence of phenomenon X and a mean of Y, respectively.

In [3], MCP is discussed under the condition of $N_q = N_r$. This condition means that the number of minutiae in the input value is identical to that of the template. As a result, MCP_R, which denotes conditional MCP computed by Ratha et al., is defined as follows.

Definition 2. *For a given $N_p(= N_q = N_r)$,*

$$MCP_R \triangleq \underset{s \in S_{N_p}}{Ave} \; \underset{t \in T_{N_p}}{Ave} \; Pr[match(s,t) = accept]. \tag{2}$$

The difference between MCP and MCP_R is whether the condition of $N_q = N_r$ is applied or not.

On the basis of the definition of MCP_R, Ratha et al. employs the following p_{hi} as a probability that a minutia selected randomly is included in the template:

$$p_{hi} = \frac{N_p}{(K - N_p + 1) \times d} \tag{3}$$

where K denotes the number of possible minutiae locations. This value p_{hi} indicates a probability that after $N_p - 1$ minutiae fail to match, the N_pth minutia matches. Therefore, p_{hi} is the conservative approximation of the probability.

As a result, Ratha et al. obtained MCP_R as follows:

$$MCP_R = \sum_{t=m}^{N_p} \binom{N_p}{t} (p_{hi})^t (1 - p_{hi})^{N_p - t}. \tag{4}$$

2.2 Computing MCP

Let us consider the condition of $N_q = N_r$ in MCP_R. With regard to this condition, Ratha et al. describes as follows: "Note that brute force attacks with N_q excessively large (close to the value K) would be easy to detect and reject out of hand." This claim may be correct when considering not only the security level of the matching algorithm itself but also some additional countermeasures that reduce the strength of the brute-force attack. However, in order to focus on the security level of the algorithm itself as an objective to be evaluated, we should at first discuss MCP without putting any conditions on N_q and N_r.

To handle with the various values of N_q and N_r, we will give the exact probability of MCP instead of the approximation used by Ratha et al.

Let us compute MCP instead of MCP_R. At first, we obtain probability P_N that $N(\geq m)$ of N_q minutiae in an input value match with regard to their locations. Then, we obtain probability P'_N that $t(\geq m)$ of the N minutiae match with regard to their ridge directions. As a result, MCP is expressed as follows:

$$MCP = \sum_{N=m}^{N_r} (P_N \times P'_N). \tag{5}$$

P_N and P'_N are expressed as follows.

$$P_N = \frac{\binom{N_q}{N}\binom{K - N_q}{N_r - N}}{\binom{K}{N_r}}. \tag{6}$$

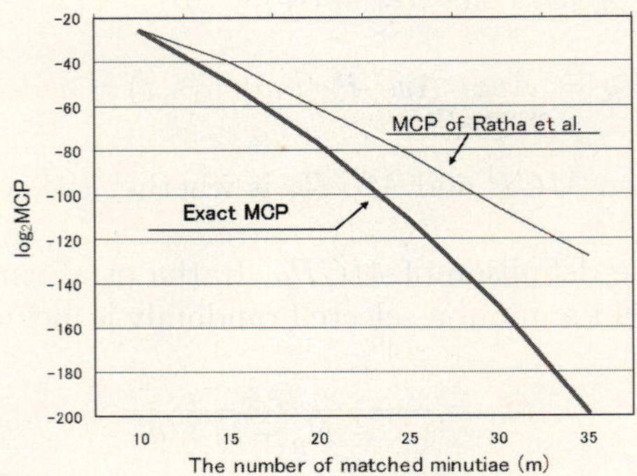

Fig. 1. Comparison between MCP and MCP_R for $N_q = N_r = 40$

$$P'_N = \sum_{t=m}^{N} \binom{N}{t} \left(\frac{1}{d}\right)^t \left(1 - \frac{1}{d}\right)^{N-t} . \tag{7}$$

2.3 Comparison Between MCP and MCP_R

Let us calculate concrete values of MCP and MCP_R by using equations (4)-(7). Basically, we employ the following parameters used by Ratha et al.

- The size of an input value $S = 300 \times 300$ pixels.
- A ridge plus valley spread $T = 15$ pixels.
- The total number of possible minutiae sites $(K = S/(T^2)) = 20 \times 20 = 400$.
- The number of orientations allowed for the ridge angle at a minutia point $d = 4$.
- The minimum number of corresponding minutiae in an input value and template, i.e., a threshold value $m = 10, 15, 20, 25, 30, 35$.

At first, let us compare exact MCP with MCP_R for $N_q = N_r = 40$ (see fig.1). Figure 1 indicates that MCP_R is larger than MCP. For example, while MCP_R is about 2^{-80} for $m = 25$, MCP is about 2^{-111}. As mentioned above, Ratha et al. approximated the success probability of the brute-force attack in the conservative manner, thus they slightly overestimated the strength of the brute-force attack.

Next, let us calculate MCP for any N_q and m. N_r is fixed as 40 as previous. The result is shown in fig. 2. As expected by Ratha et al., figure 2 indicates that the input values of $N_q = 400$ make MCP maximized for any m. In case of $m = 25$, MCP is maximized as about 2^{-21} for $N_q = 400$ and as about 2^{-111} for $N_q = 40$, respectively. It turns out that the attacks using the fingerprints with 400 minutiae extremely gains the attack complexity of about 2^{90} in comparison with the attacks using the fingerprints with only 40 minutiae.

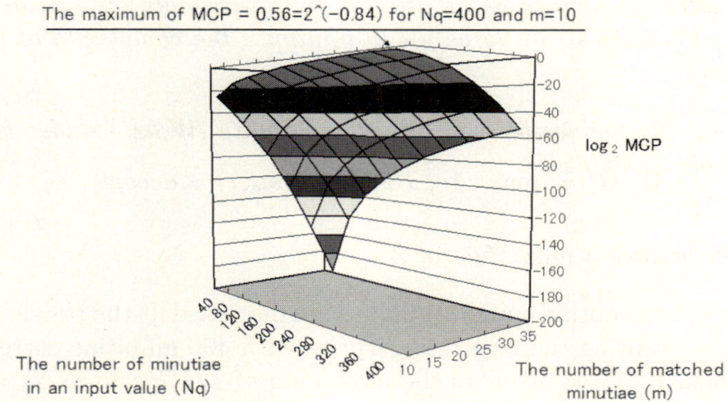

Fig. 2. MCP for $N_r = 40$

3 Wolf Attack and Wolf Attack Probability

A phenomenon that a special input value causes an extremely high success probability of the false match has been recognized mainly in the field of the speaker recognition[5]. Such an input value is called a *wolf*. As shown in [1], it has been common that the wolf means a biometric sample, not a synthesised one.

However, considering the case of input values with 400 minutiae described at the previous section, we should assume that an attacker may successfully find the special input value not only from a group of biometric samples but also from that of non-biometric samples. Moreover, we also have to pay attention to the fact that some biometric authentication systems falsely accept non-biometric samples presented by artifacts [2]. When one wants to evaluate the security of a certain biometric authentication system, we should take it into account that the attacker successfully finds some special input value, "wolf," and may present it by using some artifacts.

We define the wolf as follows.

Definition 3. *Let S_A be a group of all possible input values including ones taken from artifacts. Let T_h be a group of templates taken from all human samples. A wolf is defined as an input value $s_w \in S_A$ such that $match(s_w, t) = accept$ for multiple templates $t \in T_h$ under a predetermined threshold.*

We call an input value, s_w, is "p-wolf," if the matching probability of the input value s_w is given by $p = Ave_{t \in T_h} Pr[match(s_w, t) = accept]$ under a predetermined threshold. Especially, we call *1*-wolf a "universal wolf," which falsely matches any templates with probability $p = 1$.

We also define the wolf attack and the wolf attack probability as follows.

Definition 4. *Assume that the following two conditions are satisfied. The one is that the attacker has no information of a biometric sample of a victim to be impersonated. The other is that the attacker has complete information of a matching algorithm in the biometric authentication system to be attacked.*

The wolf attack is defined as an attempt to impersonate the victim in such a way to present p-wolves with large p's to minimize the complexity of the impersonation attack.

Definition 5. *We define the wolf attack probability (WAP) under a predetermined threshold as follows:*

$$WAP = \max_{s_w \in S_A} \underset{t \in T_h}{Ave}\, Pr[match(s_w, t) = accept] \tag{8}$$

where max Z *denotes a maximum of* Z.

In the fingerprint-minutiae matching algorithm discussed at the previous section, the attack of presenting the forged fingerprint with 400 minutiae corresponds to the wolf attack. WAP is given as the maximum of MCP where $N_q = 400$ and $N_r = 40$. As shown in fig. 2, WAP depends on the threshold m. In case of $m = 10$, WAP is maximized as about $2^{-0.8}$.

Next, we will discuss the lower bound on the number of wolves to be presented in order to make any templates falsely matched under a given WAP.

Theorem 1. *Given a biometric authentication system with wolf attack probability* WAP*, suppose there exists an attacker who has a set of wolves* $\{s_{w_1}, s_{w_2}, \ldots, s_{w_l}\}$ *which covers the whole group of templates* T_h*. Then, the following equation holds:*

$$l \geq \frac{1}{WAP}. \tag{9}$$

Proof. Let $T_h^{w_i}$ be a group of templates falsely matched by s_{w_i} for $i = 1, 2, \ldots, l$. Since both $T_h = (T_h^{w_1} \cup T_h^{w_2} \cup \cdots \cup T_h^{w_l})$ and $|T_h^{w_i}|/|T_h| \leq WAP$ hold,

$$|T_h| = |T_h^{w_1} \cup T_h^{w_2} \cup \cdots \cup T_h^{w_l}| \leq \sum_{i=1}^{l} |T_h^{w_i}| \leq l \times |T_h| \times WAP. \tag{10}$$

Therefore, $l \geq 1/WAP$. □

The equality, $l = 1/WAP$, holds, when the following conditions are satisfied. The first is $T_h^{w_i} \cap T_h^{w_j} = \emptyset$ for all $i \neq j$. The second is $|T_h^{w_i}|/|T_h| = WAP$ for all i.

Even though the attacker has a set of the wolves that covers all of the templates, the number of attempts required for falsely matches with any templates are lower bounded by $1/WAP$. Thus, WAP gives a good security measure for evaluating an individual biometric authentication system against general impersonation attacks considering the existence of wolves.

4 Is *FAR* Suitable for the Security Measure Regarding the Wolf Attack?

In the previous section, we defined the wolf attack and WAP, and explained why we had to pay attention to them. Then, let us discuss whether or not FAR

is suitable for the evaluation of a security level against the wolf attack, instead of WAP.

By using the terms of the definition of the wolf attack, we can define FAR as follows.

Definition 6. *Let $S_h(\subset S_A)$ be a group of input values taken from all human samples. Let T_h be a group of templates taken from all human samples. FAR is defined under a predetermined threshold as the following probability:*

$$FAR \stackrel{\triangle}{=} \underset{s \in S_h}{Ave} \underset{t \in T_h}{Ave} Pr[match(s,t) = accept]. \quad (11)$$

Note that FAR is defined by using both biometric samples and templates from S_h and T_h, respectively. If both $S_h = S_{N_q}$ and $T_h = T_{N_r}$ hold in the fingerprint-minutiae matching algorithm, FAR is equal to MCP.

With regard to a relationship between FAR and WAP, we can obtain the following lemma.

Lemma 1. *$FAR \leq WAP$.*

Proof. Trivial. □

As discussed later, some biometric authentication system may have strong wolves, and in the extreme case the system may contain a universal wolf, hence $WAP = 1 \gg FAR$. If only FAR is given as the impersonation measure for a biometric authentication system, such a strong wolf is not explicitly indicated in the specification of the system.

5 Applying the Wolf Attack to a Finger-Vein-Pattern Matching Algorithm

We will demonstrate how to search for the wolf and obtain WAP by applying to a finger-vein-pattern matching algorithm proposed by [4]. This algorithm is similar to an iris-pattern matching algorithm proposed by Daugman[6][1].

5.1 Overview of the Algorithm to Be Analyzed

Let us briefly introduce an overview of the algorithm proposed by [4]. A finger vein pattern, which is a binarized image of 240×180 pixels, is extracted from an infrared image of the finger. In generating an input value to the matching algorithm from the binarized image, spatial reduction and relabeling of pixels are performed.

In the spatial reduction, the binarized image is reduced to one third of its original size in x and y dimensions. In this process, the binarized image is divided into $4,800$ windows of 3×3 pixels, and a mean of the grayscale of each window

[1] Daugman has proposed a new iris-pattern matching algorithm slightly different from that of [6] in his recent paper[7].

is calculated. The grayscale of each pixel in the reduced image is assigned with the mean.

In the relabeling of the reduced image, which is used as the input value, each pixel in the reduced image is classified into the following three: a vein region, a background region and an ambiguous region. Pixels whose grayscales are between 171 and 255 are labeled as the vein region. Pixels whose grayscales are between 0 and 84 are labeled as the background region. The other pixels are labeled as the umbiguous region. Then, grayscales of pixels in background, ambiguous and vein regions are reassigned with 0, 128 and 255, respectively.

The input value is matched with the corresponding template. The differentiation between the input value and the template is represented by a "mismatch ratio (R_m)." R_m is defined as follows.

Definition 7. *Let an input value and a template be*

$$I = \{x_{i,j} | x_{i,j} \in \{0, 128, 255\}, i = 1, 2, \ldots, 80, j = 1, 2, \ldots, 60\}, and \quad (12)$$

$$T = \{y_{i,j} | y_{i,j} \in \{0, 128, 255\}, i = 1, 2, \ldots, 80, j = 1, 2, \ldots, 60\}, \quad (13)$$

respectively. $x_{i,j}$ *and* $y_{i,j}$ *denote grayscales of pixels at* (i, j) *in the input value and the template, respectively.* $x_{i,j} = 0, 128$ *and* 255 *indicate that a pixel at* (i, j) *in* I *belongs to background, ambiguous and vein regions, respectively.* $y_{i,j} = 0, 128$ *and* 255 *indicate that a pixel at* (i, j) *in* T *belongs to background, ambiguous and vein regions, respectively.*

R_m *is defined as follows:*

$$R_m = \frac{|\{x_{i,j} || x_{i,j} - y_{i,j}| = 255\}|}{|\{x_{i,j} | x_{i,j} = 255\}| + |\{y_{i,j} | y_{i,j} = 255\}|}. \quad (14)$$

If R_m is equal to or less than the predetermined threshold, the input value is decided to match the template[1].

5.2 Searching a Universal Wolf

We show that there exists a universal wolf in the finger-vein-pattern matching algorithm as follows.

Lemma 2. *There exists a universal wolf* s_{uw} *in the finger-vein-pattern matching algorithm[4].*

Proof. In order to prove this lemma, it is sufficient to show one example of s_{uw} that causes $R_m = 0$ for any templates.

From the definition of R_m, it is clear that if all of pixels in the input value belong to the ambiguous region, $R_m = 0$ holds. Namely, if $x_{i,j} = 128$ for all (i, j) in s_{uw}, $|\{x_{i,j} || x_{i,j} - y_{i,j}| = 255\}| = 0$ holds because there exists no $y_{i,j}$ such that $|128 - y_{i,j}| = 255$. Then, the following equation holds for any templates:

$$R_m = \frac{0}{0 + |\{y_{i,j} | y_{i,j} = 255\}|} = 0. \quad (15)$$

[1] [4] does not describe how to compute R_m if both a denominator and a numerator of R_m become zero. In this paper, we regard such R_m as zero.

Thus, an input value in which all pixels belong to the ambiguous region is one example of s_{uw}. □

We put emphasis on that the universal wolf exists in their "matching algorithm" only. Moreover, we add that we have not found a universal wolf for the whole biometric authentication system described in [4] including their probabilistic feature extraction process. In the real evaluation of WAP on an individual biometric authentication system, we need to analyze the feature extraction algorithm altogether.

6 Concluding Remarks

In this paper, we proposed the wolf attack and the wolf attack probability (WAP). We showed that WAP is extremely larger than the success probability which Ratha et al. estimated with regard to the brute-force attack in the fingerprint-minutiae matching algorithm. We also found the universal wolf in the finger-vein-pattern matching algorithm [4]. The universal wolf is an input value that falsely matches any templates for any threshold values.

We have proposed to evaluate the security level against the wolf attack by computing WAP. Assuming that the attacker attempts to impersonate a victim without the knowledge of the victim's biometric sample, WAP gives the lower bound of the security level satisfied by a biometric authentication system.

One of future research topics is to apply the wolf attack to the other matching algorithms. Such research results are useful in comparing the algorithms from the viewpoint of the security against the impersonation attack. Furthermore, one may think of "provable security" in the sense of non-existence of strong p-wolf for any $p > k_0$, with some security parameter k_0. It is an open problem to show a construction of provably-secure biometric authentication systems in the above sense.

Acknowledgement

This study has been sponsored by the Ministry of Economy, Trade and Industry, Japan (METI) under contract, New-generation Information Security R&D Program.

References

1. International Organization for Standardization (ISO), International Electrotechnical Commission (IEC): ISO/IEC CD 19792: Information technology – Security techniques – Security evaluation of biometrics (2006)
2. Matsumoto, T., Matsumoto, H., Yamada, K., Hoshino, S.: Impact of Artificial 'Gummy' Fingers on Fingerprint Systems. In: Optical Security and Counterfeit Deterrence Techniques IV, Proc. SPIE, vol. 4677, pp. 275–289 (2002)

3. Ratha, N.K., Connell, J.H., Bolle, R.M.: Enhancing security and privacy in biometrics-based authentication systems. IBM Syst. J. 40, 614–634 (2001)
4. Miura, N., Nagasaka, A., Miyatake, M.: Feature Extraction of Finger Vein Patterns Based on Iterative Line Tracking and its Application to Personal Identification. IEICE Trans. Inf. & Syst. (Japanese Edition) J-86-D-II, 678–687 (2003)
5. Doddington, G., Liggett, W., Martin, A., Przybocki, M., Reynolds, D.: SHEEP, GOATS, LAMBS and WOLVES: A Statistical Analysis of Speaker Performance in the NIST 1998 Speaker Recognition Evaluation. In: Proc. ICSLP, vol. 98, pp. 1351–1354 (1998)
6. Daugman, J.: How Iris Recognition Works. IEEE Trans. Circuits and Syst. Video Technology 14, 21–30 (2004)
7. Daugman, J.: Probing the Uniqueness and Randomness of IrisCodes: Results From 200 Billion Iris Pair Comparisons. Proc. IEEE 94, 1927–1935 (2006)

Evaluating the Biometric Sample Quality of Handwritten Signatures

Sascha Müller[1] and Olaf Henniger[2]

[1] Technische Universität Darmstadt, Darmstadt, Germany
mueller@sec.informatik.tu-darmstadt.de
[2] Fraunhofer Institute for Secure Information Technology, Darmstadt, Germany
henniger@sit.fraunhofer.de

Abstract. This paper addresses the problem of evaluating the quality of handwritten signatures used for biometric authentication. It is shown that some signature samples yield significantly worse performance than other samples from the same person. Thus, the importance of good reference samples is emphasized. We also give some examples of features that are related to the signature stability and show that these have no influence on the actual utility of the sample in a comparison environment.

1 Introduction

Not all biometric samples are equally well suited for the automated recognition of the persons from whom they are acquired. For example, one fingerprint sample may contain a very low number of utilisable minutiae, making biometric recognition difficult, while another one may contain more distinctive features and be better suited. In the case of handwritten signatures – which are widely accepted for authenticating purposes – this is specifically an issue since the stability of a signature varies greatly between individuals.

The question raises how useful an acquired biometric sample will be in a comparison environment. This can be expressed by a quality score that is assigned to that sample. The quality score of a genuine biometric sample is a quantitative expression of the predicted utility of the sample for telling genuine and forged samples apart. It can be used, for instance, for deciding whether a repetition of the data acquisition is necessary or for weighting results in multi-biometric systems.

Fields that can hold biometric sample quality scores have been introduced into the headers of several biometric data structures [1,2,3]. If a biometric sample quality score is reported, valid values are integers between 1 and 100. Values in the range 1–25 are supposed to indicate unacceptable quality, in the range 26–50 marginal quality, in the range 51–75 adequate quality, and in the range 76–100 excellent quality.

Quality assessment algorithms have been developed mainly for image samples such as fingerprint samples [4], but there are also proprietary algorithms in use for assessing the complexity of handwritten signature samples during the enrollment process. How to objectively assess biometric sample quality, such that

S.-W. Lee and S.Z. Li (Eds.): ICB 2007, LNCS 4642, pp. 407–414, 2007.

quality assessment algorithms of different suppliers would result in consistent sample quality scores is the topic of ongoing research activities. Results may enter the standardization process [5].

There are two approaches to evaluating the quality of a biometric sample [6]:

A-posteriori approach. Assessing the quality of a genuine biometric sample a posteriori means evaluating the utility of the sample by comparing it with the other samples from a database.

A-priori approach. Assessing biometric sample quality a priori means predicting the utility of the sample without comparing it with other samples from a database.

In order that the a-priori quality score of a biometric sample can be used as a predictor of the utility of that sample, the a-priori quality score must be assigned in such a way that it correlates with the a-posteriori quality score. This paper investigates the problem of quality evaluation in the case of handwritten signatures captured using a graphic tablet.

The quality of a biometric sample depends on the comparison algorithm used. So, a decision had to be taken on the comparison algorithm. In order to obtain results that are representative for practical scenarios of handwritten signature verification, we decided to apply the widely used comparison algorithm Dynamic Time Warping (DTW), which can be considered among the best approaches for online signature verification [7,8]. The algorithm determines the "distance" between two time series as a measure for their dissimilarity. As a common optimization a Sakoe/Chiba band [9] has been implemented, the width of which is set automatically to 10% of the length of the longer of the two time series that are to be compared.

A-posteriori biometric sample quality also depends on the database used for comparison. A publicly available subset of the database [10] has been used that consists of signature samples of 100 persons. For each person, there are 25 genuine samples and 25 skilled forgeries. Using skilled forgeries is important to estimate the resistance of the samples against forgery. In addition to the X and Y coordinates, each sample point record includes a numeric value representing the associated pen pressure.

The remainder of the paper is organized as follows: Section 2 deals with the a-posteriori assessment of the quality of handwritten signatures. Section 3 considers the a-priori quality assessment. Section 4 summarizes the results and gives an outlook.

2 A-Posteriori Quality Assessment

2.1 Obtaining Quality Scores From Comparison Results

Using the genuine sample to be assessed as biometric reference, its distance to the other genuine signatures of the same person and to the forgeries can be determined. Each of the 250 genuine signature samples has been compared both to the other 24 genuine samples of the same person and to the 25 forgery attempts. All distance values resulting from these comparisons have been recorded.

Two measures have been chosen to express the quality of a signature sample:

1. The sample equal error rate (sEER) that is achieved when comparing a sample with the corresponding genuine and forged samples. The lower it is, the better suited is the sample for keeping genuine and forged samples apart.
2. The mean value μ of the distances of the sample to the other genuine samples. This measure depends only on the signature's stability. The lower it is, the more similar is the sample to the other genuine samples.

The mean value is strongly correlated to the standard deviation σ of the distances of the sample to the other genuine samples (correlation coefficient 0.8), which can therefore be used for signature stability considerations, too.

2.2 Results

The overall EER of the comparison algorithm over all reference samples is 4.82%, but it could be improved, as will be shown: Fig. 1 visualizes the sEER's of the signatures of the persons 60 to 79. Note, for instance, the outlier that occurs in the second sample of person 71. Using this sample as reference template causes an sEER that is significantly higher than the average sEER of the other genuine samples of the same person (3.57%). Visual inspection of the sample in question does not show any obvious aberration, and the mean value μ of the distances of this sample to the other genuine samples is only marginally worse than that of the other samples (cf. Fig. 2). Outliers like this occur very often, so care has to be taken when choosing a reference sample during enrollment.

When all samples with an sEER of 20% or higher are prohibited as biometric reference – less than 4.5% of all authentic signatures fall into this category – then the overall EER lessens to 3.54%. Taking out the worst tenth of all signatures further reduces the overall EER to 2.71%. However, such strict requirements would make it impossible for some persons to use the biometric system at all because all of their samples would be rejected. A strong impact of outliers on the overall performance of biometric systems has been observed before for other systems [4].

A similar phenomenon, though less extreme, can be seen in the mean values of the distances of a sample to the other genuine samples (Fig. 2). Obviously, large distance values have a conspicuous impact on the sEER. For instance, the mean values of distances of genuine signatures of person 78 range from 41 to 114.[1] Accordingly, the sEER ranges from acceptable values to unusable ones of more than 80% (as seen in Fig. 1). This is plausible because the stability influences the sEER.[2] These results clearly show the importance of using a good (i.e., similar to other genuine signatures) reference signature. If the reference signature is one of the outliers, the recognition performance is bad even for the best possible threshold.

[1] These values are distances returned by the DTW algorithm, and thus depend on specific implementation details. In the implementation used for our research, the distances range from 0 for identical samples to about 250 for incomparable ones.

[2] In our tests, a correlation coefficient of 0.55 has been observed between the mean μ of the distances of genuine signatures and the sEER.

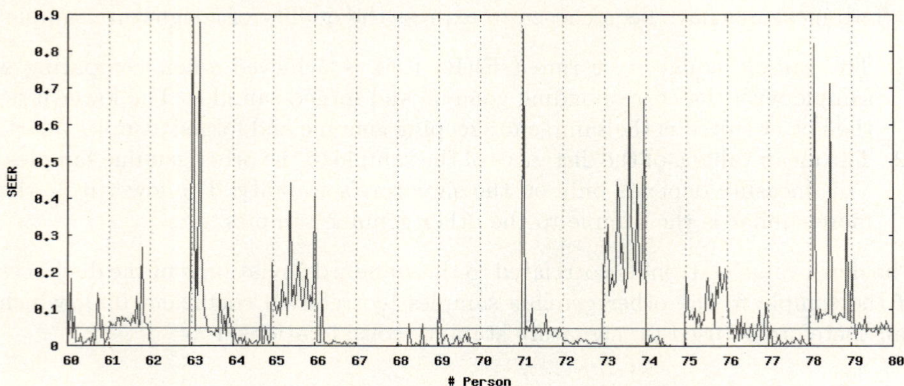

Fig. 1. sEER's of the genuine signatures of the persons 60–79

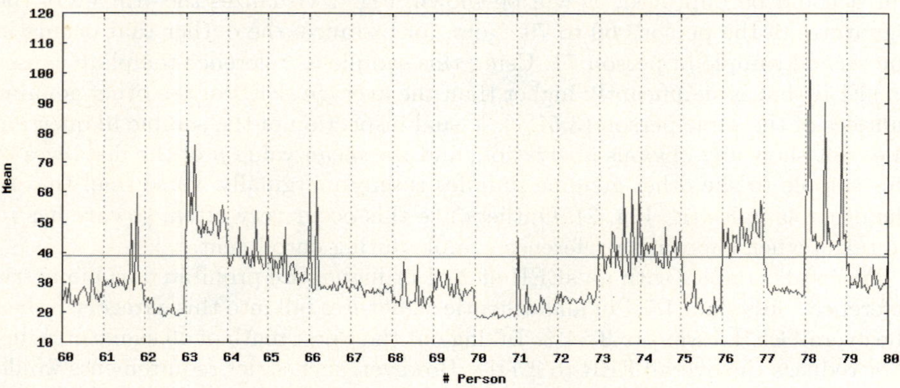

Fig. 2. Mean values μ of the distances of the genuine signatures of the persons 60–79

3 A-Priori Quality Assessment

3.1 Examined Features

In order to find correlations between global signature features and the a posteriori signature quality, the Pearson product-moment correlation coefficient was used to compare the distributions of the recorded quality measures (cf. Section 2) with certain features of the associated signature samples. Since only linear relationships can be detected this way, all features were also plotted and analyzed by visual inspection.

In the past a lot of global signature features have been considered for the analysis of signatures. [11], for example, uses a feature vector of 100 global features for this purpose. We selected a set of 12 global features that we considered obvious candidates for quality considerations and easy to extract from a given signature sample. All of the following global features were examined:

1. Length in the writing plane
2. Ratio of length to area
3. Average writing speed
4. Maximum writing speed
5. Average pen pressure in pen down strokes
6. Average acceleration
7. Maximum acceleration
8. Average absolute value of curvature
9. Number of pen down strokes
10. Number of extrema of x channel
11. Number of extrema of y channel
12. Ratio of width to height

3.2 Results

For lack of space, only a few representative results are given in detail, as well as a summary of all results. In most cases the correlation coefficients were very low, especially when looking at the sEER. Still, visual inspection allowed some interesting discoveries. For example, there is no linear correlation between the sEER and the maximum acceleration (coefficient -0.029), but it can be seen in the plot (not given here) that all signatures that lead to very bad sEER (40% or higher) have very low maximum acceleration.

Some of the following examples have stronger correlations:

Number of pen-down strokes. With a correlation coefficient of -0.463, a slight inverse linear correlation can be assumed between the number of pen-down strokes of a signature sample and the mean value of the distances of the signature to the other genuine samples of the same person. This tells us that signatures with more pen-down strokes tend to be more stable than signatures consisting of only a few strokes. This can also be verified by examining Fig. 3a.

The connection between the number of pen-down strokes and the equal error rate (Fig. 3b) is a lot weaker, the correlation coefficient being only -0.223. This means, for the success of a forgery attempt it does not matter much of how many pen-down strokes the original signature consists.

Average writing speed. The correlation coefficient of the average writing speed and the mean value μ of distances of genuine signatures is 0.797 – the highest value obtained in all tests. Surprisingly, the correlation with the sEER amounts to only 0.130, meaning that there is no linear relationship. Obviously, slower signatures are more stable, but easier to forge. Fig. 4 shows the plots.

Average absolute value of curvature. The idea here is to measure the "shakiness" of the handwriting. The curvature is the difference of the gradients of adjacent sample points. Since gradient values can be very big, the tilt angle was used instead, which is $\arctan(\frac{dy}{dx})$. If $dx = 0$, some small value ϵ was used instead. This is reasonable because $\arctan(\frac{1}{\epsilon}) \approx \frac{1}{2}\pi = \arctan(\infty)$. As the plot (Fig. 5) shows, this feature is neither correlated with sEER nor with μ. Also, the correlation coefficients are very small (-0.223, resp. -0.144).

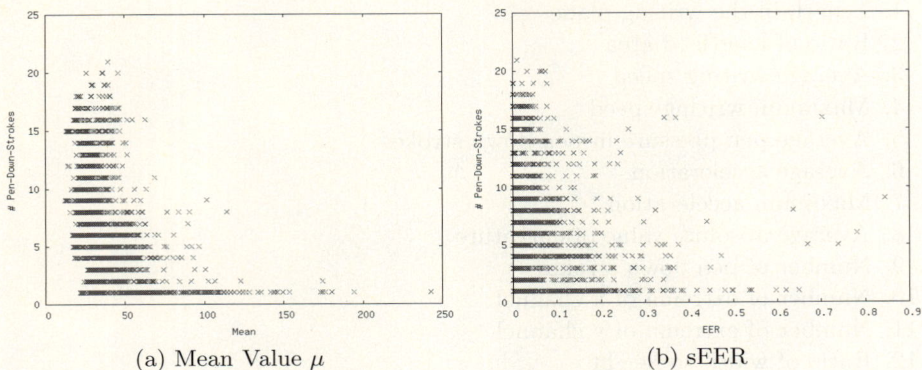

(a) Mean Value μ (b) sEER

Fig. 3. Correlation between number of pen-down strokes and a-posteriori quality

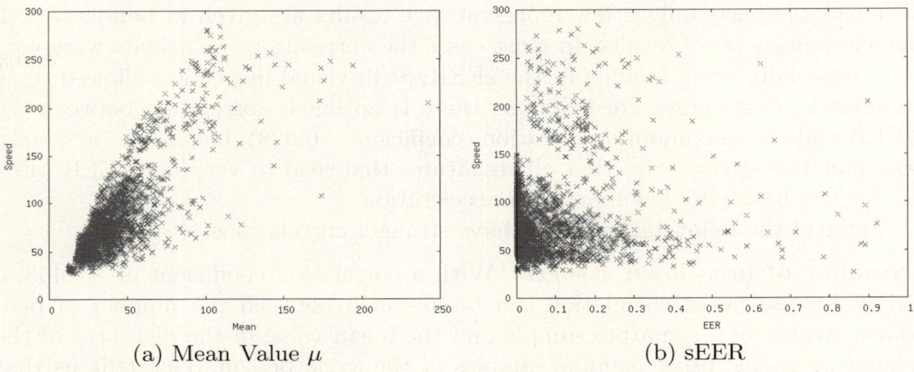

(a) Mean Value μ (b) sEER

Fig. 4. Correlation between average writing speed and a-posteriori quality

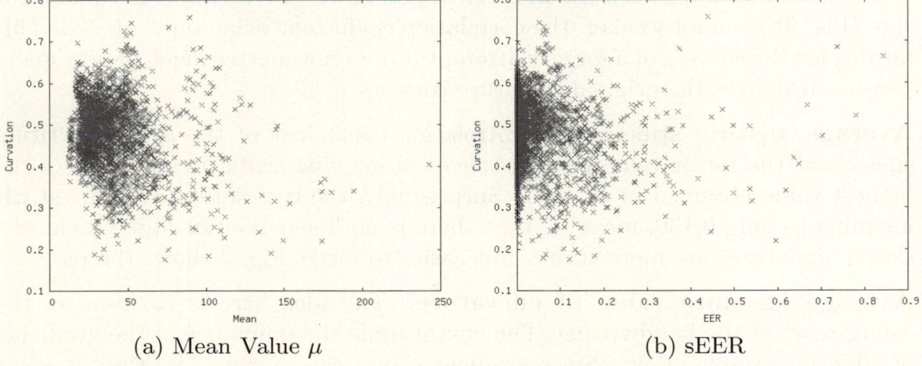

(a) Mean Value μ (b) sEER

Fig. 5. Correlation between average absolute value of curvature and a-posteriori quality

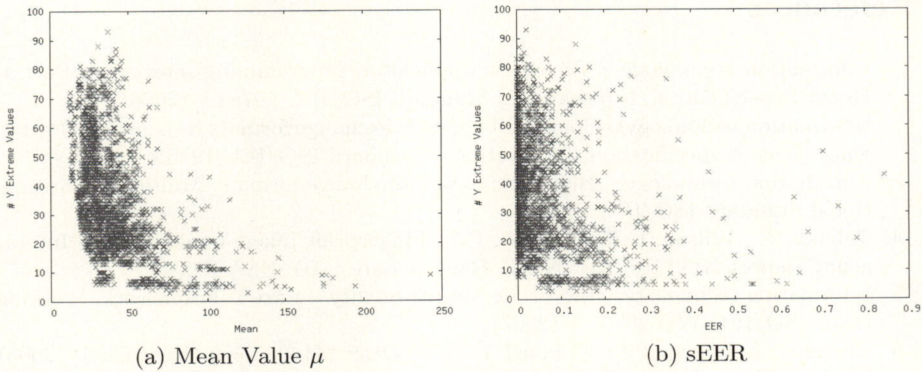

(a) Mean Value μ (b) sEER

Fig. 6. Correlation between number of Y extrema and a-posteriori quality

Number of extrema of Y channel. This is another example of a nonlinear relationship that can be seen in the plot (Fig. 6). The correlation coefficient when relating the number of extrema to the mean μ is -0.453, and – as with all examined features – the correlation coefficient with the sEER is quite low (-0.249).

4 Summary and Outlook

Our research confirmed the widespread view that the evaluation of biometric sample quality is a difficult problem. Among the a-priori signature features that have been tested for correlation with the chosen a-posteriori quality measures, there are some that allow a faint prediction of a signature's stability, but none that allow a prediction of a signature's forgeability. Stronger correlations with a-posteriori quality measures may be found by looking at feature vectors instead of individual features as in [4]. This is future work.

This paper investigated the influence of the character (the inherent features) of a biometric sample on its utility. There is also an influence of a sample's fidelity on its utility that should be investigated. The influence of fidelity can be observed by using samples captured with different sensors and sampling rates. Although the influence of different capture devices has been observed before [12], its implications on quality considerations is an open question and will also be the subject of future research.

Acknowledgments

The authors are grateful to J. Ortega-Garcia and J. Fiérrez-Aguilar for making a subcorpus of the MCYT database available for research purposes.

References

1. Information technology – Biometric application programming interface – Part 1: BioAPI specification. International Standard ISO/IEC 19784-1 (2006)
2. Information technology – Common biometric exchange formats framework – Part 1: Data element specification. International Standard ISO/IEC 19785-1 (2006)
3. Information technology – Biometric data interchange formats. Multi-Part International Standard ISO/IEC 19794
4. Tabassi, E., Wilson, C.R., Watson, C.I.: Fingerprint image quality. NIST Interagency Report NISTIR 7151, NIST, Gaithersburg, MD, USA (2004)
5. Information technology – Biometric sample quality – Part 1: Framework. Working Draft ISO/IEC WD 29794-1 (2007)
6. Biometric sample quality standard. INCITS Draft M1/05-0306 (Revision 4) (2005)
7. Kholmatov, A., Yanikoglu, B.A.: Identity authentication using improved online signature verification method. Pattern Recognition Letters 26(15), 2400–2408 (2005)
8. Yeung, D.-Y., Chang, H., Xiong, Y., George, S., Kashi, R., Matsumoto, T., Rigoll, G.: SVC2004: First international signature verification competition. In: Zhang, D., Jain, A.K. (eds.) ICBA 2004. LNCS, vol. 3072, pp. 16–22. Springer, Heidelberg (2004)
9. Sakoe, H., Chiba, S.: Dynamic programming algorithm optimization for spoken word recognition. IEEE Transactions on acoustics, speech and signal processing 26(1), 1–2 (1978)
10. Ortega-Garcia, J., Fiérrez-Aguilar, J., Simon, D., Gonzalez, J., Faundez-Zanuy, M., Espinosa, V., Satue, A., Hernaez, I., Igarza, J.-J., Vivaracho, C., Escudero, D., Moro, Q.-I.: MCYT baseline corpus: a bimodal biometric database. IEE Proceedings Visual Image Processing 150(6), 395–401 (2003)
11. Fiérrez-Aguilar, J., Nanni, L., Lopez-Peñalba, J., Ortega-Garcia, J., Maltoni, D.: An on-line signature verification system based on fusion of local and global information. In: Kanade, T., Jain, A., Ratha, N.K. (eds.) AVBPA 2005. LNCS, vol. 3546, pp. 523–532. Springer, Heidelberg (2005)
12. Elliot, S.J.: A Comparison of On-Line Dynamic Signature Trait Variables Across Different Computing Devices. PhD thesis, Purdue University (2001)

Outdoor Face Recognition Using Enhanced Near Infrared Imaging

Dong Yi, Rong Liu, RuFeng Chu, Rui Wang, Dong Liu, and Stan Z. Li

Center for Biometrics and Security Research &
National Laboratory of Pattern Recognition,
Institute of Automation, Chinese Academy of Sciences, Beijing 100080, China
http://www.cbsr.ia.ac.cn

Abstract. In this paper, we present a robust and accurate system for outdoor (as well as indoor) face recognition, based on a recently developed enhanced near-infrared (ENIR) imaging device. Using a narrow band NIR laser generator instead of LED lights for active frontal illumination, the ENIR device can provide face images of good quality even under sunlight. Experiments show that the ENIR system performs similarly to the existing NIR system when used indoors, but outperforms it significantly outdoors especially under sunlight.

Keywords: Face recognition, near-infrared (NIR), imaging device, illumination, outdoor, statistical learning.

1 Introduction

Over the past few years, face recognition has more and more applications in our daily life such as access control, surveillance, information safety, human-machine interaction and multimedia communication. However, for practical face recognition systems, the effect of variation in the lighting conditions is one of the most challenging problems [1]. As report in FRVT2002, the variation of outdoor lighting has a drastic affect on performance of face recognition system [2]. For the best systems, verification performance drops from 95% to 54% going indoors to outdoors.

To solve this difficult problem caused by variant lighting conditions, many approaches have been proposed. They can be divided into three categories. The first category includes those methods based on Lambertian model, which is too simply to describe the real face surface under various illuminations. Illumination Cone methods [3], quotient image based approaches [4,5] belong to this category. Although these methods have achieved a degree of success in some face database such as Yale and CMU PIE, they need a large volume of training data under various illumination conditions. Another technique is using 3D data obtained from a laser scanner and 3D vision method [6]. Because the shape of 3D face is not affected by environmental lighting, such systems can obtain reasonable performance. The disadvantages are the increased cost, slowed speed and fussy pretreatment. The last category is using different imaging sensors in invisible

S.-W. Lee and S.Z. Li (Eds.): ICB 2007, LNCS 4642, pp. 415–423, 2007.

spectral bands which can reduce the affection of ambient light. Thermal or far infrared imagery systems have advantages for detecting disguise faces, but they are subject to environment temperature, emotions and health conditions. In particular, infrared (IR) imaging sensor has become an area of growing interest [7]. Near-infrared (NIR) image based techniques have been developed to achieve highly accurate face recognition for indoor applications under varying lighting conditions [8,9].

In this paper, we present a system for face recognition outdoor even in sunlight. Firstly, an enhanced near-infrared (ENIR) face imaging device is presented for outdoor face recognition. Then, algorithms are described for face detection and recognition in ENIR images. After that, an ENIR face recognition system is built. Experimental results show that the system performs slightly better than the existing NIR system [8,9] while both are significantly better than visible light image based systems. In outdoor sunlight, the ENIR system can achieve relatively high recognition rate while NIR and visible light (VIS) systems cannot function properly.

The rest of the paper is organized as follows: Section 2 describes the design of the imaging hardware and presents an analysis of characteristics and amicability of resulting images for subsequent face processing. Section 3 discuses the face/eye detection and face recognition algorithms. Section 4 evaluates the system, including acquisition of testing database and comparison between VIS, NIR, ENIR systems. We will conclude in section 5.

2 Enhanced NIR Imaging

The existing NIR based imaging hardware described in [8,9] can produce face images of good quality for face recognition under indoor lighting. But outdoors, the environmental lighting contains much stronger NIR component, especially under sunlight. Under such circumstances, the existing NIR imaging cannot produce face images of proper quality.

The goal of making an ENIR hardware is to get rid of influence of strong NIR component under the outdoor sunlight. Like the NIR imaging device in [8,9], we still use active light source mounted on the camera to provide frontal lighting and use filter to reduce environmental lighting. But to improve outdoor performance of the face recognition system, we make some revision on the basis of the NIR solution. The active light source must meet the following conditions: (1) In order to produce images of good quality, the strength of active light source must be stronger $1.5 - 2.5$ times than the strength of the sunlight. (2) The strength of active light source can not be too strong to disturb human eyes. (3) The resulting face images should be affected as little as possible when minimizing the sunlight.

Our solution uses the following strategies [10]:

1. Use a narrow band NIR laser generator, instead of LED, to provide active lighting;
2. Use very short exposure time (50ns), synchronized with the laser light;

3. Use a narrow band pass optical filter on the camera lens to cut off visible light and sunlight while allowing NIR light to pass. The center frequency of optical filter is 808nm as same as the laser generator and bandwith of the optical filter is 16nm.
4. Apply a differentiation between two successive frames. The first frame is captured by illuminating the subject's face with an active light source and the second is captured by turning this light source off. The differentiation operation can successfully eliminate NIR component in the static ambient light and sunlight [11].

As a result, this ENIR imaging hardware not only provides appropriate active frontal lighting but also minimizes ambient light as well as outdoor sunlight.

Fig. 1 shows the ENIR imaging device and some images captured when the active light source on/off and the finally output of the ENIR camera under the sunlight. From the third image in Fig. 1, we can see that ENIR imaging hardware can work properly under the sunlight. While active NIR illumination has been widely used in surveillance, face detection and face recognition [12,13,11], the novelty of our hardware is to combine a strong active NIR light and differentiation technique together.

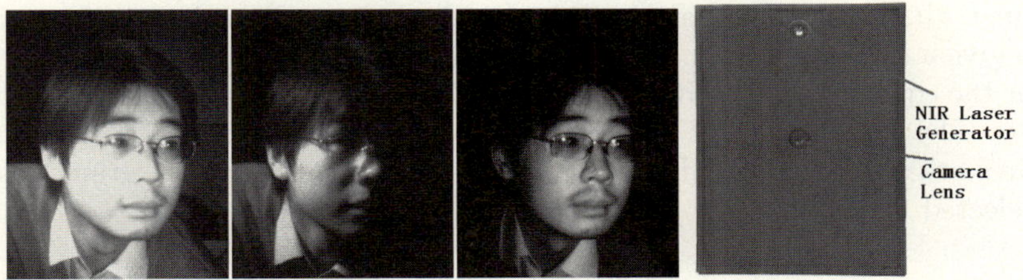

Fig. 1. From left to right: (a) Face image under mixture of sunlight and NIR light, (b) face image under sunlight only, (c) face image difference (a)-(b), (d) the ENIR imaging device

3 Face/Eye Detection and Face Recognition

In this system, face and eye detection is performed using an AdaBoost learning algorithm with an extended Haar feature [14]. A cascade form classifier is learned from face and non-face training data. For face detection, an example is a 20×20 image, containing a face or non-face pattern. Face detection in NIR or ENIR images is relatively easier than in VIS images, because the background of NIR or ENIR images is nearly black. On the contrary, detection of eyes in NIR or ENIR images is more challenging than in normal VIS images due to likely specular reflections on eyeglasses, eyelid occlusion, which happens among people in some ethnic groups and senior people and eye closing due to blinking are among other problems. Eye detection in these situations cannot be done by using a simple eye detector. To tackle the difficulties, a coarse to fine, easy to complex architecture is used to overcome the problem and achieve very high performance, see [9] for details.

For face recognition, we use statistical learning method based on AdaBoost [9] to build the classifier. Given a training set of local binary pattern (LBP) features [15] of faces subject to image noises, slight pose changes, and alignment errors, such a learning method performs a transform to the find most discriminative features and thereby builds a strong classifier. Because AdaBoost is usually used to solve two-class problem, we convert the multi-class problem to many two-class problems using intra-person and extra-person divergence [16]. Using AdaBoost learning, we select a number of most discriminative LBP histogram features to combine to a strong classifier. The procedure learns a sequence of k weak classifiers, and linearly combines them into a stronger classifier as follow :

$$H(x) = \text{sign}\left(\sum_{t=1}^{T} \alpha_t h_t(x)\right).$$

In the test phase, the selected LBP features of two face images are matched, one for template face image and one for test face image. Some distance are taken between these two set of face images. And then each distance is input to weak classifier $h_t(x)$. At last, weak decisions are linearly combined with the weights α_t to give a final decision.

For the equality, VIS, NIR and ENIR systems all use the algorithms above for face/eye detection and face recognition. For VIS system, 2346 LBP histogram features are selected. For NIR and ENIR system, 1024 LBP histogram features are selected.

4 System Evaluation

4.1 Database

The purpose is to evaluate the ENIR face recognition system and compare it to a VIS and an NIR systems [8,9]. The classifier for each system is trained by 12000 face images containing 200 persons. A independent database of 20 persons was built for testing. The subjects were asked to face to our camera, about 50-100cm to the device, presenting neutral and smile expressions. 10 face images were taken for each person, using 3 types of imaging devices (VIS, NIR and ENIR), for each of the following different lighting conditions:

1. normal indoor frontal lighting,
2. normal indoor non-frontal lighting,
3. strong indoor frontal lighting,
4. strong indoor non-frontal lighting,
5. outdoor frontal sunlight,
6. outdoor side sunlight, and
7. outdoor back sunlight.

The strong indoor frontal lighting was produced using a tungsten-halogen lamp made by Mingzhu Livastore Industrial Co.,Ltd. The lamp has a color temperature of 2500-3000K, and spectral property as in Fig.2. It was 1000W in power, placed at 3.5-4 meters away from the subject. The lamp contained a range of NIR composition and was powerful, thus well simulated the sunlight for indoor testing.

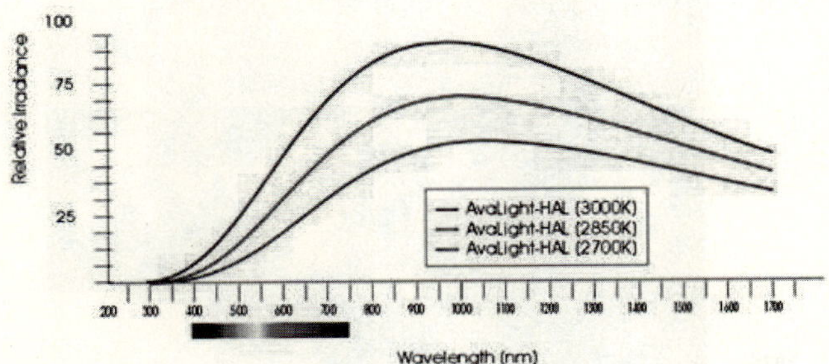

Fig. 2. Spectral property of the tungsten-halogen lamp

The VIS and NIR cameras are saturated easily by sunlight, and so the database does not include VIS and NIR images outdoor. The number of VIS face images in this database is 4 (indoor conditions) $\times 20$ (people) $\times 10$ (images) $= 800$ and we have the same amount of NIR face images. The amount of ENIR faces is $800 + 3$ (outdoor conditions) $\times 20$ (people) $\times 10$ (images) $= 1400$. The resolution of VIS, NIR and ENIR cameras are all 640×480.

Fig. 3 shows some face image examples from the database. We can see that VIS face images were unstable to the direction and strength of lighting, NIR images were less unstable, and ENIR images were most stable to changes under various lighting condition.

4.2 Performance

The 3 systems (VIS, NIR and ENIR) were run in fully automatically for face detection, alignment and matching. Table 1 shows the face and eye detection rate of VIS, NIR and ENIR systems under different lighting conditions, where the "×" signs denote no performance measures due to unacceptable drop in performance. From the table, we see that the eye detection rate in VIS images dropped under halogen lamp light but not in a dreadful way; however, the eye detection rate in NIR images dropped acutely under the strong indoor non-frontal lighting because the detector was trained using frontal NIR light only. As expected, the ENIR system has consistently good performance except under outdoor frontal sunlight; we are investigating the reasons.

The database was divided into 2 sets, the gallery set and the probe set. The face images under normal indoor frontal lighting were used as the gallery images

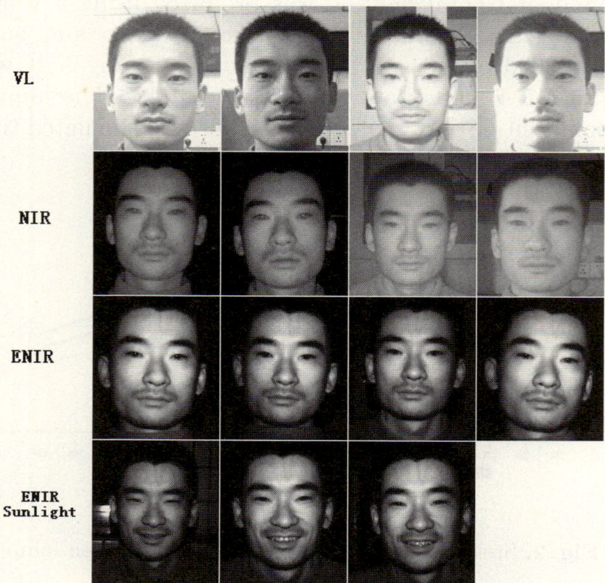

Fig. 3. Example face images in test database. Row 1-3: VIS, NIR and ENIR images under 4 indoor lighting conditions. Row 4: ENIR images outdoor.

Table 1. Face and eye detection rates under 7 lighting conditions

	VIS		NIR		ENIR	
	Face	Eye	Face	Eye	Face	Eye
Normal indoor frontal	100%	94.3%	100%	99.8%	100%	99.4%
Normal indoor non-frontal	100%	92%	100%	99.5%	100%	97.2%
Strong indoor frontal	100%	87.4%	100%	85.5%	100%	93.6%
Strong indoor non-frontal	100%	91.6%	91.6%	38.4%	100%	98.5%
Outdoor frontal sunlight	×	×	×	×	100%	75.5%
Outdoor side sunlight	×	×	×	×	100%	96.6%
Outdoor back sunlight	×	×	×	×	100%	95.5%

and the other images were used as probe images. Two protocols were used to compare the three systems:

1. For indoor images taken under 4 lighting conditions: comparing recognition rates of all the 3 systems.
2. For outdoor images taken under 3 lighting conditions: evaluating recognition rates of the ENIR system only, while the other 2 systems could not function to a satisfactory extent.

Fig. 4 shows the ROC curves for the tests. The performance of the ENIR system was significantly higher than the other systems for all conditions. In

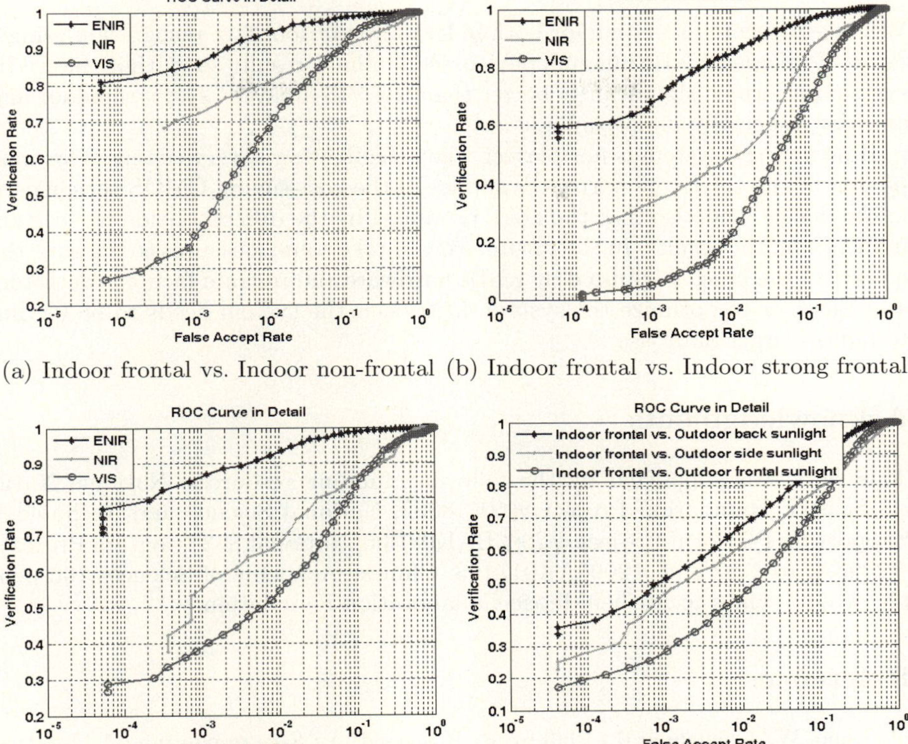

(a) Indoor frontal vs. Indoor non-frontal (b) Indoor frontal vs. Indoor strong frontal

(c) Indoor frontal vs. Indoor strong non-frontal (d) ENIR system under outdoor sunlight

Fig. 4. ROC curves for the test data sets

Fig. 4(b), the performance of VIS and NIR systems dropped significantly under strong frontal halogen lamp light, whereas the ENIR system still has relatively high verification rate (VR = 69% when FAR = 0.001 and VR = 85% when FAR = 0.01). Similarly in Fig. 4(c), the impact of strong frontal lighting was greater than that of strong non-frontal lighting. Fig. 4(d) shows the results of the ENIR system under outdoor sunlight in three different directions. The verification accuracy was the highest (VR = 50% when FAR = 0.001 and VR = 69% when FAR = 0.01) when the sunlight was from the back direction, and was the worst for frontal sunlight.

As a rough comparison: for the best face recognition systems in FRVT 2002, the recognition rate for faces captured outdoors, at a FAR of 0.01, was 50% [2]. Hence, we conclude that overall, the ENIR system performed significantly better the VIS and NIR systems.

5 Conclusion

We have presented a system for both indoor and outdoor face recognition using a newly developed ENIR imaging device. Preliminary results show that the ENIR system performed significantly better than the VIS and NIR systems indoor and outdoor, especially under sunlight.

However, the system is not perfect when the lighting is very strong. This may be due to the relatively narrow dynamics of the cost-saving CMOS sensor used in the device, and also that the noise produced by the differentiation has certain influence on the results. In the future, we will take some measures to improve the quality of the images acquired by ENIR hardware and re-train face/eye detectors and classifier to optimize the system. Moreover, the system needs to be further tested on larger database.

Acknowledgments

This work was supported by the following funding resources: National Natural Science Foundation Project #60518002, National Science and Technology Supporting Platform Project #2006BAK08B06, National 863 Program Projects #2006AA01Z192 and #2006AA01Z193, Chinese Academy of Sciences 100 people project, and the AuthenMetric Collaboration Foundation.

References

1. Zhao, W., Chellappa, R., Phillips, P., Rosenfeld, A.: Face recognition: A literature survey. In: ACM Computing Surveys, pp. 399–458. ACM Press, New York (2003)
2. NIST: Face Recognition Vendor Tests (FRVT) (http://www.frvt.org)
3. Georghiades, A.S., Belhumeur, P.N., Kriegman, D.J.: From few to many: Illumination cone models for face recognition under variable lighting and pose. IEEE Transactions on Pattern Analysis and Machine Intelligence 23(6), 643–660 (2001)
4. Shashua, A., Raviv, T.R.: The quotient image: Class based re-rendering and recognition with varying illuminations. IEEE Transactions on Pattern Analysis and Machine Intelligence 23(2), 129–139 (2001)
5. Wang, H.T., Li, S.Z., Wang, Y.S.: Generalized quotient image. In: Proceedings of IEEE Computer Society Conference on Computer Vision and Pattern Recognition, pp. 498–505. IEEE Computer Society Press, Los Alamitos (2004)
6. Bowyer, K.W., Chang, Flynn, P.J.: A survey of 3D and multi-modal 3d+2d face recognition. In: Proceedings of International Conference Pattern Recognition, pp. 358–361 (2004)
7. Kong, S.G., Heo, J., Abidi, B., Paik, J., Abidi, M.: Recent advances in visual and infrared face recognition - A review. Computer Vision and Image Understanding 97(1), 103–135 (2005)
8. Li, S.Z., et al.: AuthenMetric F1: A Highly Accurate and Fast Face Recognition System. In: ICCV2005 - Demos (2005)
9. Li, S.Z., Chu, R., Liao, S., Zhang, L.: Illumination invariant face recognition using near-infrared images. IEEE Transactions on Pattern Analysis and Machine Intelligence 26 (Special issue on Biometrics: Progress and Directions) (2007)

10. AuthenMetric and CASIA: An Image Acquisition Aparatus, and Method and System for Its applications in Face Recognition. Patent Application No.200710062725.3 (2007)
11. Hizem, W., Krichen, E., Ni, Y., Dorizzi, B., Garcia-Salicetti, S.: Specific sensors for face recognition. In: Proceedings of IAPR International Conference on Biometric, vol. 3832, pp. 47–54 (2006)
12. Dowdall, J., Pavlidis, I., Bebis, G.: Face detection in the near-IR spectrum. Image and Vision Computing 21, 565–578 (2003)
13. Zou, X., Kittler, J., Messer, K.: Ambient illumination variation removal by active near-ir imaging. In: Proceedings of IAPR International Conference on Biometric, pp. 19–25 (2006)
14. Li, S.Z., Zhang, Z.Q.: FloatBoost learning and statistical face detection. IEEE Transactions on Pattern Analysis and Machine Intelligence 26(9), 1112–1123 (2004)
15. Ahonen, T., Hadid, A., Pietikainen, M.: Face recognition with local binary patterns. In: Proceedings of the European Conference on Computer Vision, Prague, Czech, pp. 469–481 (2004)
16. Moghaddam, B., Nastar, C., Pentland, A.: A Bayesian similarity measure for direct image matching. Media Lab Tech Report No.393, MIT (1996)

Latent Identity Variables: Biometric Matching Without Explicit Identity Estimation

Simon J.D. Prince[1], Jania Aghajanian[1],
Umar Mohammed[1], and Maneesh Sahani[2]

[1] Computer Science
[2] Gatsby Unit, University College London, UK
{s.prince,j.aghajanian,u.mohammed}@cs.ucl.ac.uk,maneesh@gatsby.ucl.ac.uk
http://www.cs.ucl.ac.uk/staff/s.prince

Abstract. We present a new approach to biometrics that makes probabilistic inferences about matching without ever estimating an identity "template". The biometric data is considered to have been created by a noisy generative process. This process consists of (i) a deterministic component, which depends entirely on an underlying representation of identity and (ii) a stochastic component which accounts for the fact that two biometric samples from the same person are not identical. In recognition, we make inferences about whether the underlying identity representation is the same *without ever estimating it*. Instead we treat identity as fundamentally uncertain and consider all possible values in our decision. We demonstrate these ideas with toy examples from face recognition. We compare our approach to the class-conditional viewpoint.

Keywords: Biometrics, Face Recognition, Bayesian Methods.

1 Introduction

Typical biometric systems have the following structure[3]: features are extracted from a biometric sample to form a biometric template. This represents the discriminative aspects of the sample such as face texture, fingerprint minutiae or iris pattern. In order to compare two templates, a score is calculated representing the similarity of the two templates. This is often based on a distance metric in feature space (e.g.[10]). In face identification we search for the gallery image with maximum similarity to a probe image. In face verification, we impose a threshold, T on the similarity: if the two biometric samples are not sufficiently similar we infer that they came from different individuals.

Although this approach has yielded much success, it has several drawbacks. First, most algorithms of this type cannot provide an estimate of certainty on the final decision. In real systems, we might wish to defer decision making and gather more data if we are not confident. Second, there is no principled way to deal with multiple gallery and/or probe observations from the same individual. Third, there is no easy way to incorporate prior information about the relative likelihood of different matching hypotheses. For example, the time of day

S.-W. Lee and S.Z. Li (Eds.): ICB 2007, LNCS 4642, pp. 424–434, 2007.

or location might change the likelihood of different individuals being present. Fourth, it is not obvious how to construct non-uniform similarity metrics that address the fact that different regions of the feature space may be differently discriminable. Fifth, it is hard to incorporate the possibility of errors in the preprocessing into the decision metric. For example, in fingerprint recognition, the preprocessing algorithm might misclassify minutiae, or in face recognition the face features might be mis-localized. If this process is not modelled, erroneous matching decisions will result. Finally, these algorithms struggle in the presence of nuisance variables which change the appearance of observations. For example, in face recognition, pose and illumination changes reduce matching performance.

The emphasis in these approaches is on extracting a template which is essentially a representation of identity. In this paper, we pose the following philosophical question: *is it necessary to estimate identity to make inferences about whether biometric samples match?*

In recent work in face recognition, we have introduced a new framework for biometric matching[9]. We treat the data as having been generated from a smaller number of underlying variables. Some of these variables are pure representations of identity (i.e. signal), whereas others may represent irrelevant extrinsic factors such as capture conditions. The generative process also contains stochastic elements, which explain why the measured biometric data varies, even when the identity of the individual and the capture conditions are identical. In recognition, we pose the question: what is the likelihood that the underlying identity variables that explain two biometric samples were the same? We estimate this likelihood *regardless* of the actual values of these variables and the other contributing factors. This approach has proven extremely successful when applied to face recognition across pose[9].

The goal of this paper is to introduce this approach to the wider biometric community. In Sections 2 and 3 we present a simple tutorial example in the domain of face recognition and give examples of both identification and verification. In Section 4 we discuss more sophisticated examples of this approach. In Section 5 we discuss how the advantageous features of our approach might be applied to other biometrics. Finally, in Section 6 we describe how our approach can be rationalized with a class-conditional viewpoint.

2 Latent Identity Variable Models

Underpinning our approach is the attempt to explain variation in biometric data with a structured model. Imagine that we have J measurements from each of I individuals in a training database. We denote the j'th measurement of the i'th individual as $\mathbf{x}_{ij}$. In the simplest case we will consider models of the form

$$\mathbf{x}_{ij} = g(\mathbf{h}_i, \theta) + \epsilon_{ij}. \tag{1}$$

The term $\mathbf{h}_i$ is known as a latent identity variable (LIV). This is a pure representation of identity which contains no noise or nuisance factors and hence only depends on the individual i, not the instance, j. The data $\mathbf{x}_{ij}$ are modelled as being generated by the operation of some function g(.) on the LIV plus additive Gaussian noise ϵ_{ij} with diagonal covariance Σ. The function $g(.)$ depends on some fixed parameters θ.

The two terms of the model divide the data into signal and noise components. The first (signal) term is deterministic in that it depends only on the identity of the individual. The second (noise) term is stochastic and explains why each measurement of the same individual differs. The term 'latent' (or equivalently 'hidden') indicates that although the identity variable $\mathbf{h}_i$ explains some of the observed data variation, it cannot be directly measured: since generation is noisy, we can never know exactly what value it takes for a given observation $\mathbf{x}_{ij}$. The best that we can do is to make probabilistic statements about its likely values.

3 Single Feature Model

In order to make these ideas concrete, we will provide a very simple example. We will consider the generative model:

$$x_{ij} = \mu + fh_i + \epsilon_{ij} \tag{2}$$

where x_{ij} is a single scalar biometric measurement (e.g. height) from the j'th measurement of the i'th training individual. This is explained by a signal term $\mu + fh_i$ which is a function $g(.)$ of the latent identity variable h_i and a noise term ϵ_{ij} which is Gaussian with mean 0 and with variance σ^2. We can alternatively write the model in terms of conditional probability:

$$Pr(x_{ij}|h_i, \mu, f, \Sigma) = \mathcal{G}_{x_{ij}}\left[\mu + fh_i, \sigma^2\right] \tag{3}$$

$$Pr(h_i) = \mathcal{G}_{h_i}\left[0, 1\right]. \tag{4}$$

where $\mathcal{G}_a[b, c]$ represents a Gaussian distribution in a, with mean b and (co)-variance c. In order to complete the model, we have also defined a prior distribution over the latent identity variable, h_i. This is defined to be Gaussian with zero mean and unity variance. There are two phases to using the LIV model:

- **Learning:** in the learning phase, we learn the parameters μ, f, σ from a training set of data $x_{1...I,1...J}$.
- **Recognition:** in the recognition phase, we use this model to infer whether test data originates from the same person.

3.1 Learning

In learning, we want to find the values of the parameters $\Theta = \{\mu, f, \sigma\}$ under which the training data is most likely. This would be easy if we knew the identity variables h_i, but unfortunately these are unknown as well. Likewise, it would be easy to estimate the identity variables h_i if we already knew the parameters $\Theta = \{\mu, f, \sigma\}$. Fortunately, there is a well-established solution to this "chicken and egg" problem: we use the Expectation Maximization (EM) algorithm[4] to alternately estimate the two sets of parameters in such a way that guarantees the likelihood of the data will increase at each stage (see Appendix A).

3.2 Recognition

In recognition we do not know the relationship between different individuals I and the data vectors. We denote the k'th hypothesized relationship a "model", $\mathcal{M}_k$. We can calculate the likelihood of the data given a model $\mathcal{M}$ using:

$$Pr(X|\Theta,\mathcal{M}) = \prod_{i=1}^{I}\int\prod_{j=1}^{N_I} Pr(x_{ij},h_i|\Theta)d\mathbf{h}_i \tag{5}$$

In this expression we calculate the total likelihood of all of the data X for model $\mathcal{M}$ by (i) writing the joint likelihood of the observed and hidden variables and (ii) marginalizing (integrating out) the unknown hidden variables. Finally, we compare these models using Bayes' rule:

$$Pr(\mathcal{M}_k|X) = \frac{Pr(\mathbf{x}|\mathcal{M}_k)Pr(\mathcal{M}_k)}{\sum_{l=0}^{N} Pr(\mathbf{x}|\mathcal{M}_l)Pr(\mathcal{M}_l)} \tag{6}$$

We include priors $Pr(\mathcal{M}_k)$ which allow us to incorporate our prior expectations as to which measurements belong together. To illustrate these ideas we will give two concrete examples: Identification and Verification.

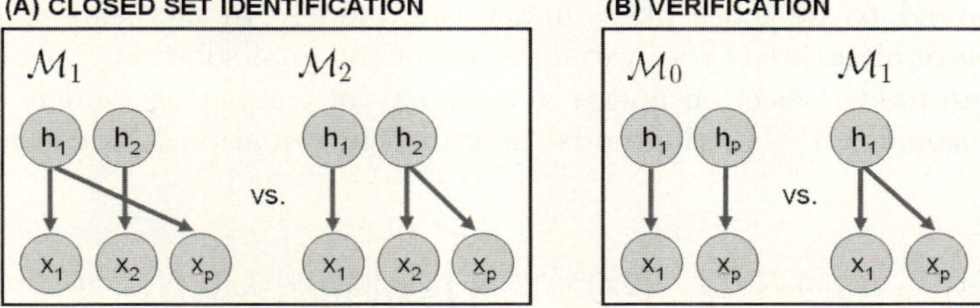

Fig. 1. Relationship between latent identity variables (top) and measurements (bottom) for identification (A) and verification tasks (B). Recognition is framed as comparing models $\mathcal{M}_k$ of the data. Each model represents a different relationship between the observed measurements x and the latent identity variables h. If two measurements come from the same individual then the underlying identity variable is the same.

(A) Identification: Consider identification with two data points in the gallery x_1, x_2 and a probe data point x_p. In model $\mathcal{M}_1$ the probe data matches the first gallery data, and in model $\mathcal{M}_2$, the probe matches the second gallery data. The first gallery data x_1 and the probe data x_p are both explained by identity variable h_1. The second gallery data has its own latent identity variable h_2. Conversely, in model $\mathcal{M}_2$, the probe face matches the second gallery face and so these share an identity variable h_2 (see Figure 1A). We write the likelihood of the first model as:

$$\begin{aligned} Pr(x_{1,2,p}|\mathcal{M}_1) &= \int Pr(x_1,x_p,h_1)dh_1 \int Pr(x_2,h_2)dh_2 \\ &= \int Pr(x_1|h_1)Pr(x_p|h_1)Pr(h_1)dh_1 \int Pr(x_2|h_2)Pr(h_2)dh_2 \end{aligned} \tag{7}$$

where in the second line, we have written the joint probabilities as conditional probabilities. Notice that all of the terms in the second line were defined in Equations 3 and 4. Similarly, the likelihood for model $\mathcal{M}_2$ can be written:

$$Pr(x_{1,2,p}|\mathcal{M}_2) = \int Pr(x_1|h_1)Pr(h_1)dh_1 \int Pr(x_2|h_2)Pr(x_p|h_2)Pr(h_2)dh_2 \quad (8)$$

(B) Verification: In verification we have two biometric data measurements x_1 and x_p, and we would like to say whether these belong to different people (model $\mathcal{M}_0$) or the same person (model $\mathcal{M}_1$). In model $\mathcal{M}_0$ the measurements x_1 and x_p do not match, so each has its own identity variable (h_1 and h_p). In model $\mathcal{M}_1$ the measurements match and are both explained by one identity variable h_1 (see Figure 1B). The likelihoods can be written:

$$Pr(x_{1,p}|\mathcal{M}_0) = \int Pr(x_1|h_1)Pr(h_1)dh_1 \int Pr(x_p|h_p)Pr(h_p)dh_p \quad (9)$$

$$Pr(x_{1,p}|\mathcal{M}_1) = \int Pr(x_1|h_1)Pr(x_p|h_1)Pr(h_1)dh_1 \quad (10)$$

One might be concerned about this comparison: there are more underlying identity variables h in model $\mathcal{M}_0$ than there are in model $\mathcal{M}_1$, so surely the data is bound to be more likely under this model? In fact this is not true since we have integrated these variables out of the final solution. This is known as Bayesian model selection and is a valid way of comparing models of different dimensionality[7]. For the model described in Equation 2, it can be shown that:

$$\int Pr(x_{1\ldots N}, h) = N\sigma^2 f^{-2}(2\pi)^{-D_h/2} \prod_{i=1}^{N} \mathcal{G}_{\hat{x}_i}[0, \sigma^2]/\mathcal{G}_y[0, N\sigma^{-2}f^2 + 1] \quad (11)$$

where $y = f\sigma^{-2}\sum \hat{x}_i$ and $\hat{x}_i = x_i - \mu$. Note that we don't estimate the underlying identity representation. Instead we ask: were two biometric samples generated from the same underlying identity, *regardless* of what that identity was?

3.3 Face Recognition Example: Independent Pixel Model

To validate these ideas, we present a face recognition example using the XM2VTS database[12]. We spatially register each RGB image, resize to 70×70 pixels and vectorise the pixel contents, to form training data vectors $\mathbf{x}_{ij}$, each of dimension $d = 70 \times 70 \times 3 = 14700$. We describe the generation process as:

$$\mathbf{x}_{ij} = \mu + \mathbf{F}\mathbf{h}_i + \epsilon_{ij} \quad (12)$$

where $\mathbf{F}$ is a diagonal $d \times d$ matrix, μ is a vector representing the mean face and ϵ_{ij} is a multivariate Gaussian variable representing noise with diagonal

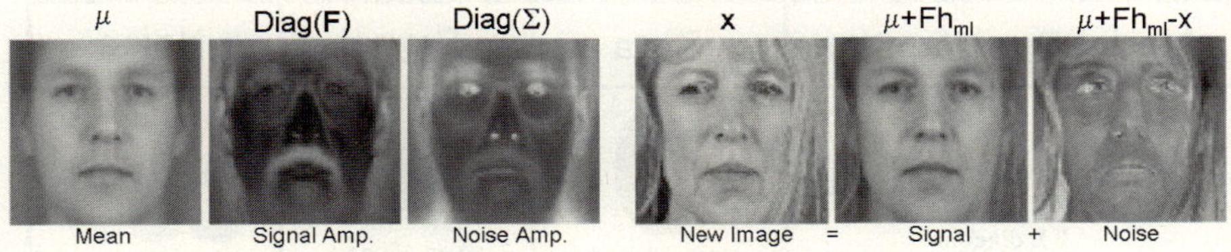

Fig. 2. Results from the "Independent Pixels" face recognition model. The first three panels indicate the results of the learning phase, $\Theta = \{\mu, f, s\}$. The fourth panel is a new face, which has been decomposed into the signal (panel 5) and noise (panel 6) components. Note that this is only the most likely decomposition. In our recognition metric, all possible decompositions are taken into account.

covariance Σ. As before, we assume a Gaussian prior over the latent identity variable $\mathbf{h}_i$ with zero mean and identity covariance. This model is a multivariate version of Equation 2 where each pixel is treated as independent. We train this model with 4 examples each of 160 people, using 10 iterations of the EM algorithm. We then performed face identification and verification experiments with 100 pairs of images that were not part of the training data.

In Figure 2 we show the results of the learning process, and for a new image, the most likely apportioning of signal and noise. For this toy model, recognition performance was 60%. In the next section, we present a series of increasingly sophisticated LIV models. In Section 5 we discuss other aspects of generative models which might be applied to biometric data.

4 A Family of Abstract LIV Models

In Figure 3 we present a series of more sophisticated abstract Latent Identity Variable models. We use the term abstract to denote the fact that they do not encompass any information that is specific to the biometric domain. The "Factor Analyzer" model permits linear correlations between the measurements, but maintains an independent noise model. In face recognition, this is similar to the eigenfaces approach[10]. The "Probabilistic Linear Discriminant Analyzer" model also models correlations in the noise. Here, there is a second latent variable ν_{ij}, which is not associated with identity, which must also be integrated out of the final formulation.

The "Mixture of Gaussians" model is particularly interesting in that the representation of the signal is entirely discrete: the signal is described as being one of L canonical data points μ_l. Here, the identity vector l_i simply describes which of these canonical examples we are seeing. An example of this type of model is explored for the case of face recognition in Figure 4A. Combining the previously discussed models leads naturally to the "Mixture of Factor Analyzers" and

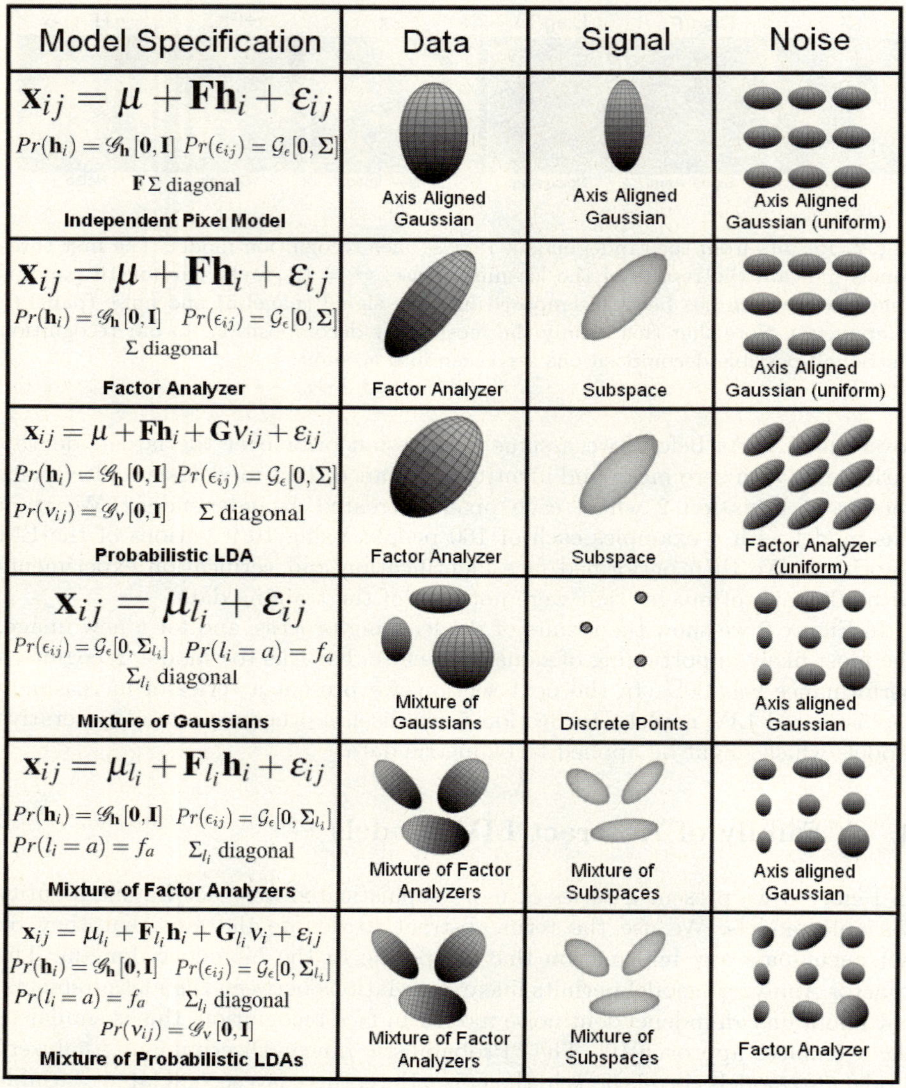

Model Specification	Data	Signal	Noise
$\mathbf{x}_{ij} = \mu + \mathbf{F}\mathbf{h}_i + \varepsilon_{ij}$ $Pr(\mathbf{h}_i) = \mathcal{G}_{\mathbf{h}}[\mathbf{0},\mathbf{I}]$ $Pr(\epsilon_{ij}) = \mathcal{G}_{\epsilon}[0,\Sigma]$ $\mathbf{F}\,\Sigma$ diagonal **Independent Pixel Model**	Axis Aligned Gaussian	Axis Aligned Gaussian	Axis Aligned Gaussian (uniform)
$\mathbf{x}_{ij} = \mu + \mathbf{F}\mathbf{h}_i + \varepsilon_{ij}$ $Pr(\mathbf{h}_i) = \mathcal{G}_{\mathbf{h}}[\mathbf{0},\mathbf{I}]$ $Pr(\epsilon_{ij}) = \mathcal{G}_{\epsilon}[0,\Sigma]$ Σ diagonal **Factor Analyzer**	Factor Analyzer	Subspace	Axis Aligned Gaussian (uniform)
$\mathbf{x}_{ij} = \mu + \mathbf{F}\mathbf{h}_i + \mathbf{G}v_{ij} + \varepsilon_{ij}$ $Pr(\mathbf{h}_i) = \mathcal{G}_{\mathbf{h}}[\mathbf{0},\mathbf{I}]$ $Pr(\epsilon_{ij}) = \mathcal{G}_{\epsilon}[0,\Sigma]$ $Pr(v_{ij}) = \mathcal{G}_{v}[\mathbf{0},\mathbf{I}]$ Σ diagonal **Probabilistic LDA**	Factor Analyzer	Subspace	Factor Analyzer (uniform)
$\mathbf{x}_{ij} = \mu_{l_i} + \varepsilon_{ij}$ $Pr(\epsilon_{ij}) = \mathcal{G}_{\epsilon}[0,\Sigma_{l_i}]$ $Pr(l_i = a) = f_a$ Σ_{l_i} diagonal **Mixture of Gaussians**	Mixture of Gaussians	Discrete Points	Axis aligned Gaussian
$\mathbf{x}_{ij} = \mu_{l_i} + \mathbf{F}_{l_i}\mathbf{h}_i + \varepsilon_{ij}$ $Pr(\mathbf{h}_i) = \mathcal{G}_{\mathbf{h}}[\mathbf{0},\mathbf{I}]$ $Pr(\epsilon_{ij}) = \mathcal{G}_{\epsilon}[0,\Sigma_{l_i}]$ $Pr(l_i = a) = f_a$ Σ_{l_i} diagonal **Mixture of Factor Analyzers**	Mixture of Factor Analyzers	Mixture of Subspaces	Axis aligned Gaussian
$\mathbf{x}_{ij} = \mu_{l_i} + \mathbf{F}_{l_i}\mathbf{h}_i + \mathbf{G}_{l_i}v_i + \varepsilon_{ij}$ $Pr(\mathbf{h}_i) = \mathcal{G}_{\mathbf{h}}[\mathbf{0},\mathbf{I}]$ $Pr(\epsilon_{ij}) = \mathcal{G}_{\epsilon}[0,\Sigma_{l_i}]$ $Pr(l_i = a) = f_a$ Σ_{l_i} diagonal $Pr(v_{ij}) = \mathcal{G}_{v}[\mathbf{0},\mathbf{I}]$ **Mixture of Probabilistic LDAs**	Mixture of Factor Analyzers	Mixture of Subspaces	Factor Analyzer

Fig. 3. Examples from the family of linear additive Latent Identity Variable models. Each row represents a different model, as defined by the first column. The second column depicts the probability model for the data as a whole. This is composed of the signal component (third column), which provides information about identity and the noise component (fourth column) which does not.

"Mixture of Probabilistic LDAs" models. The latter can potentially describe an arbitrary signal distribution, combined with an arbitrary noise distribution that varies with the position in data space.

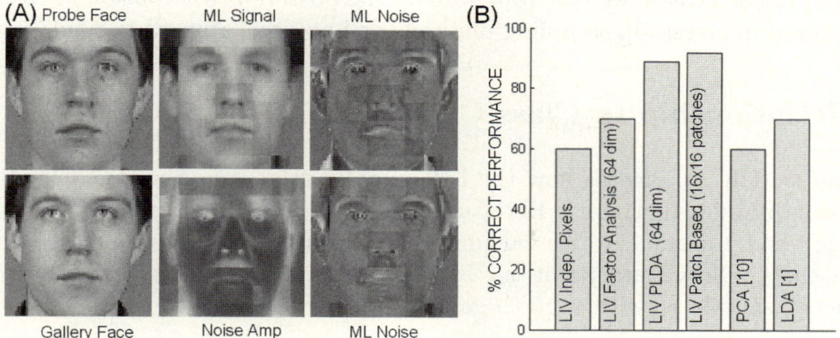

Fig. 4. (A) Results of "Mixture of Gaussians" model. Faces are represented as a regular grid of patches. Each patch is taken from a library with a finite discrete set of 16 possibilities. Hence the identity variable holds a set of indices to the library. The top-center panel shows the approximation that explains the probe and gallery images best (signal). The right panel shows the residual noise component. (B) Empirical comparison for several LIV models and two well-known methods for face identification with 100 XM2VTS images. Task is difficult as (i) training and gallery sets are not overlapping (ii) there is no attempt to compensate for photometric variation (iii) registration is poor (iv) images were captured in different recording sessions.

5 Strengths of Generative Modelling Approach

Domain Specific Information: up until now, all of the models used have been very general. However, it is quite possible to incorporate domain specific information about how the measurements were generated. For example, in face recognition, we might explicitly describe the lighting and 3D projection process as in[2]. Similarly, in fingerprint analysis, we could model the smudging and printing process, and in iris recognition we might model image blurring.

Missing Data: generative models can handle missing data, by including a binary latent variable encoding the presence or absence of a feature. This could be used in fingerprint recognition where minutiae may be missed or misclassified.

Invariance to transformations: many biometrics require spatial registration of data before comparison. This registration is prone to error. By treating the transformation parameters as hidden variables (i.e. as fundamentally uncertain), we can make the system invariant to these transformations and robust in cases where the transformation parameters are ambiguous.

Multiple Appearances: generative models can also describe situations in which the same underlying identity created quite different looking observations[9]. For example, fingerprint data differ depending on the type of scanner used to collect it, and face images may differ depending on the expression.

In all the models from Section 4, the integral in the recognition step can be calculated exactly. However, this may not be true for complex domain specific models. In such cases, we can approximate the posterior distribution for $\mathbf{h}$ using variational inference[6], sampling methods or Laplace's approximation[7].

6 Relationship to Class Conditional Viewpoint

In this section, we discuss how the LIV method relates to a more conventional class-conditional viewpoint. Here, each gallery data point induces a density $Pr(x_p|x_i,\mathcal{M}_i)$ around it. We calculate the probability of seeing probe data x_p given each gallery data point x_i. If $\mathcal{M}_i$ is the model that groups the probe biometric sample x_p with the i'th gallery biometric sample x_i then

$$
\begin{aligned}
Pr(X|\mathcal{M}_i) &= \prod_{k\neq i} Pr(x_k|\Theta,\mathcal{M}_i)Pr(x_i,x_p|\Theta,\mathcal{M}_i) \\
&= \prod_{k\neq i} Pr(x_k|\Theta)Pr(x_i|\Theta,\mathcal{M}_i)Pr(x_p|x_i,\Theta,\mathcal{M}_i) \\
&= \prod_{k} Pr(x_k|\Theta)Pr(x_p|x_i,\Theta,\mathcal{M}_i)
\end{aligned} \tag{13}
$$

The integral over, h_i is then buried in the conditional $Pr(x_p|x_i,\Theta,\mathcal{M}_i)$:

$$
\begin{aligned}
Pr(x_p|x_i,\Theta,M_i) &= \int Pr(x_p|h_i,\Theta)Pr(h_i|x_i,\Theta)dh_i \\
&= \frac{1}{Pr(x_i|\Theta)}\int Pr(x_p|h_i,\Theta)Pr(x_i|h_i,\Theta)Pr(h_i|\Theta)dh_i
\end{aligned} \tag{14}
$$

which recovers the form that we originally used. This viewpoint is closely related to Bayesian one shot learning[5]. The training process can be thought of as implicitly learning a prior over face data and combines with the gallery data x_i to build a class conditional probability distribution for the gallery individual.

7 Discussion

In this paper, we have discussed a new approach to biometric matching. We model observed data as being the result of a generative process, in which some of the component variables are pure representations of identity (latent identity variables). We learn the parameters of this model from training data. In recognition, we calculate the probability that the probe and gallery data were generated from the same underlying identity regardless of what that identity was.

There are several advantages to our formulation. (i) It provides valid posterior probability over possible hypotheses in both verification and identification scenarios. (ii) There is no need to set arbitrary parameters as all components can be learnt. (iii) In our method it is easy to compare biometric data captured in quite different circumstances. (iv) We can easily incorporate prior information about possible data hypotheses. (v) It is easy to incorporate domain specific information about the generation process. (vi) There is a clear way to deal with multiple gallery and/or probe data belonging to the same person.

Our method compares favorably to other decision algorithms. Distance based methods (e.g.[10]) cannot always easily be adapted to have these advantages. Decision based on frequentist statistical principles do not provide a method to incorporate prior information. Previous probabilistic approaches (e.g.[11,?]) have been focussed on either identification or verification tasks, but cannot easily handle both.

References

1. Belhumeur, P.N., Hespanha, J., Kriegman, D.J.: Eigenfaces vs. Fisherfaces: Recognition Using Class Specific Linear Projection. PAMI 19, 711–720 (1997)
2. Blanz, V., Romdhani, S., Vetter, T.: Face identification across different poses and illumination with a 3D morphable model. In: ICFGR, pp. 202–207 (2002)
3. Bolle, R.M., Connell, J.H., Pankathi, S., Ratha, N.K., Senior, A.W.: Guide to Biometrics. Springer, New York (2004)
4. Dempster, A.P., Laird, N.M., Rubin, D.B.: Maximum likelihood for incomplete data via the EM algorithm. Proc. Roy. Stat. Soc. B 39, 1–38 (1977)
5. Fei-Fei, L., Fergus, R., Perona, P.: A Bayesian approach to unsupervised one-shot learning of object categories. In: CVPR, pp. 1134–1141 (2003)
6. Jordan, M.I., Ghahramani, Z., Jaakola, T.S., Saul, L.K.: An introduction to variational methods for graphical models. In: Jordan, M.I. (ed.) Learning in Graphical Models (1998)
7. MacKay, D.: Information theory, inference, and learning algorithms. Cam. U. Press, Cambridge (2003)
8. Moghaddam, B., Jebra, T., Pentland, A.: Bayesian face recognition. Pattern Recognition 3, 1771–1782 (2000)
9. Prince, S.J.D., Elder, J.H.: Tied factor analysis for face recognition across large pose changes. In: BMVC, vol. 3, pp. 889–898 (2006)
10. Turk, M., Pentland, A.P.: Face recognition Using eigenfaces. In: CVPR, pp. 586–591 (1991)
11. Zhou, S.K., Chellappa, R.: Probabilistic Identity characterization for face recognition. In: CVPR, vol. 2, pp. 805–812 (2004)
12. `http://www.ee.surrey.ac.uk/Research/VSSP/xm2vtsdb/`

Appendix A: Learning LIV Models

In the expectation step (or E-Step) we fix Θ and find the posterior distribution over the hidden identity variables h_i. In the maximization step (or M-Step) we re-estimate $\Theta = \{\mu, f, \sigma\}$ given the distribution calculated in the E-Step.

E-Step: In the E-Step, we use Bayes' rule to calculate the posterior distribution of the latent identity variables h_i given the data x_{ij}:

$$Pr(h_i|x_{i,1\ldots J}, \Theta) = \frac{\prod_{j=1}^{J} Pr(x_{ij}|h_i, \Theta) Pr(h_i)}{\int \prod_{j=1}^{J} Pr(x_{ij}|h_i, \Theta) Pr(h_i) dh_i} \tag{15}$$

where we have assumed that all of the data samples for each person were independent. Notice that all of the terms in this equation were defined in our original description of the generative model in Equations 3 and 4. For this particular model, substituting in and rearranging gives:

$$Pr(h_i|x_{i,1\ldots J},\Theta) = \mathcal{G}_{h_i}\left[\frac{f}{Jf^2+\sigma^2}\sum_{j=1}^{J}(x_{ij}-\mu), \frac{\sigma^2}{Jf^2+\sigma^2}\right] \tag{16}$$

M-Step: In the M-Step we update our current estimate of the parameters by optimizing the following expression:

$$Q(\Theta_t,\Theta_{t-1}) = \sum_{i,j=1}^{I,J} E_{h_i}\left[\log[Pr(\mathbf{x}_{ij}|\mathbf{h}_i)Pr(\mathbf{h}_i)]\right] \tag{17}$$

where t is the iteration index and for this model:

$$E_{h_i}\left[\log[Pr(\mathbf{x}_{ij}|\mathbf{h}_i)Pr(\mathbf{h}_i)]\right] = \kappa - 0.5\log|\sigma^2| - E_{h_i}\left[\left(\frac{x_{ij}-\mu-fh_i}{2\sigma^2}\right)^2\right] \tag{18}$$

where κ is an unimportant constant. We maximize this with respect to μ,f and σ by taking derivatives and setting the resulting expressions to zero.

2^N Discretisation of BioPhasor in Cancellable Biometrics

Andrew Beng Jin Teoh[1], Kar-Ann Toh[1], and Wai Kuan Yip[2]

[1] Biometrics Engineering Research Center (BERC)
Yonsei University, Seoul, South Korea
{bjteoh,katoh}@ieee.org
[2] Faculty of Information Science and Technology (FIST)
Multimedia University,
Jalan Ayer Keroh Lama, 75450 Melaka, Malaysia
wkyip@mmu.edu.my

Abstract. BioPhasor was introduced as a form of cancellable biometrics which integrates a set of user-specific random numbers (RN) with biometric features. This BioPhasor was shown to fulfil diversity, reusability and performance requirements in cancellable biometrics formulation. In this paper, we reformulate and enhance the BioPhasor in terms of verification performance and security, through a 2^N stage discretisation process. The formulation is experimented under two scenarios (legitimate and stolen RN) using 2400 FERET face images. Apart from the experiments, desired properties such as one-way transformation and diversity are also examined.

Keywords: BioPhasor, Cancellable biometrics, 2^N stage discretisation, Face Biometrics.

1 Introduction

When a biometric is compromised, it is compromised forever because it cannot be changed. Cancellable biometrics has thus been proposed, whereby a biometric image is distorted in a repeatable but non-reversible manner before template generation. If the cancellable template is compromised, it can be disposed of. The distortion characteristics can then be changed, and the same biometric is mapped to a new template for subsequent use. There are four principal criteria to be fulfilled before a cancellable biometric template can be considered useful [1]:

i. Diversity: No same cancellable template can be used in two different applications.
ii. Reusability: Straightforward revocation and reissue in the event of compromise.
iii. One-way transformation: Non-invertibility of template computation to prevent recovery of biometric data.
iv. Performance: The formulation should not deteriorate the recognition performance.

Ratha et al [2] was the first to concretise the idea of cancellable biometrics. They sketched an idea regarding an intentional distortion of a biometric signal based on a chosen transform function. The biometric signal was distorted in a similar fashion at

S.-W. Lee and S.Z. Li (Eds.): ICB 2007, LNCS 4642, pp. 435–444, 2007.

each presentation, that is, during enrolment and for every subsequent authentication. With this approach, every instance of enrolment can use a different transform function thus rendering cross-matching impossible. Furthermore, if one variant of the biometric templates is compromised, then the transformation can simply be changed to create a new variant for re-enrolment. Since then, many constructs have been proposed [3].

In this paper, we focus only on the constructs which combine external factors such as tokenized random data with biometrics. Soutar et al [4] proposed a cancellable biometrics which was generated from fingerprints using optical computing techniques. The templates consisted of correlation patterns derived from training images, which are subsequently mixed with random data to generate identification codes. However, the scheme was not explained in a satisfactory manner regarding the cryptographic security aspects of the transformations where no related results can be found. Teoh et al. [5] introduced a cancellable biometrics/key, known as BioHash, via inner product between randomized token and biometric data. This method is advantageous in comparison to that of Soutar et al since the transformation is a one-way process. However, the verification performance degraded when the genuine token was stolen and used by an imposter to claim as the genuine user (stolen-token scenario). This violated the performance criterion. Savvides et al. [6] proposed a cancellable biometrics scheme which encrypted the training images by synthesizing a correlation filter for biometrics authentication. They demonstrated that convolving the training images with any random convolution kernel prior to building the biometric filter does not change the resulting correlation output peak-to-sidelobe ratios, thus preserving the authentication performance. Despite that, the security can be jeopardized via a deterministic deconvolution with a known random kernel, thus against the criterion of non-invertibility. Recently, BioPhasor was proposed as a non-linear extension of BioHash [7]. The BioPhasor was shown to fulfil diversity, reusability and performance criteria. However, Bio-Phasor's non-invertible property is unknown. In this paper, we present an enhanced version of BioPhasor which incorporates a 2^N discretisation, thereby offering a better verification performance, particularly in generic stolen-token scenario as well as fulfilling diversity and one-way transformation properties.

2 Brief Introduction of BioPhasor

BioPhasor is originally described as follow:

(a) Feature Extraction. A feature extraction technique is used to extract the biometric feature. The biometric feature is represented in a vector form, $\boldsymbol{x} \in \Re^n$, with n denoting the feature length of $\boldsymbol{x}$.

(b) Use token to generate a set of pseudo-random vectors, $\{\boldsymbol{r}_i \in \Re^n \mid i = 1,\dots,m\}$ which is distributed according to $\mathcal{N}(0, 1)$ and apply the Gram-Schmidt process to transform the basis $\{\boldsymbol{r}_i \in \Re^n \mid i = 1,\dots,m\}$ into an orthonormal set of $\boldsymbol{r}$, $\{\boldsymbol{r}_{\perp i} \in \Re^n \mid i = 1,\dots,m\}$.

(c) Mix $\boldsymbol{x}$ with $\boldsymbol{r}_{\perp i}$ repeatedly to form a set of complex vectors, $\{z_i=\boldsymbol{x}+\boldsymbol{r}_{\perp i}\,\mathrm{j}\in C^n \mid i=1,...,m\}$, where j=√-1, and then calculate the complex argument of each element in z_i, where z_i={arg($\tilde{z}_k$)| k=1,…,n}, ie. $\{\arg(\tilde{z}_k)\in\Re \mid k=1,...,n\}$.

(d) Average the complex arguments, $\left\{\alpha_l = \frac{1}{n}\sum_{k=1}^{n}\arg(z_k)\in\Re^m \mid l=1,...,m\right\}$ where $-\pi \le \alpha_j \le \pi$ and $m \le n$.

In general, the BioPhasor formulation can be rewritten as

$$\alpha_j = \frac{1}{n}\sum_{i=1}^{n}\tan^{-1}(x_i / r_{ij}),\, j = 1,\ldots,m,\ m<n \text{ and } r \neq 0 \tag{1}$$

For the sake of simplicity and security concern of not to reveal the actual value of α_j, a quantization is carried out. Since α_j is a principle value, it makes sense to divide the complex plane into two sectors to convert α_j into a single bit as follows: $b_i = \begin{cases} 0 & \text{if} \quad 0 \le \alpha_i < \pi \\ 1 & \text{if} \quad -\pi < \alpha_i \le 0 \end{cases}$ where $i = 1,...,m$. For implementation purpose, the BioPhasor template can be stored in a central database during enrolment. During the verification stage, the extracted feature image is mixed with the genuine token (*legitimate-token scenario*) and the resulting BioPhasor template is compared with the enrolled template by using Hamming distance (the difference in the number of bits). One should note that this cancellable biometrics approach, of mixing the user-specific pseudo-random number with the biometric features, has the drawback when an impostor B steals the pseudo-random numbers of A and tries to verify as A. We call this a *stolen-token scenario*.

3 2^N Stage Discretisation

The quantization of BioPhasor may bring to performance degradation due to information lost. In the original algorithm, complex plane can be further divided into 2^q sectors and thus q bits can be assigned per sector. This enables an algorithm to render a more refined feature representation, $\boldsymbol{b}^q$ = { b_k^q |k = 1,…,m, q=1, 2, 3,…} with higher number of bits per user and thus higher accuracy [5]. However, a direct extension of the scheme is still confined to the accuracy level that can be achieved by equation (1).

To increase the stability of the resulting bitstrings, we propose to transform the BioPhasor feature set $\boldsymbol{\alpha}$ ={α_i |i=1,…, m} (computed using equation (1)) such that each transformed feature is discernible to separate the genuine user from potential impostor users. Specifically, we transform α_i from the real into the index space and convert the resultant indices to Gray code. We assume that α_i is distributed according to normal distribution, $\alpha_i \sim \mathcal{N}(0, \pi^2/9)$ and the element values fall within twice of user-dependent standard deviation from the mean value. The feature element space is next divided into 2^N segments by adjusting the user-dependent standard deviation, σ_{ij}. The $\alpha_i \sim \mathcal{N}(0, \pi^2/9)$

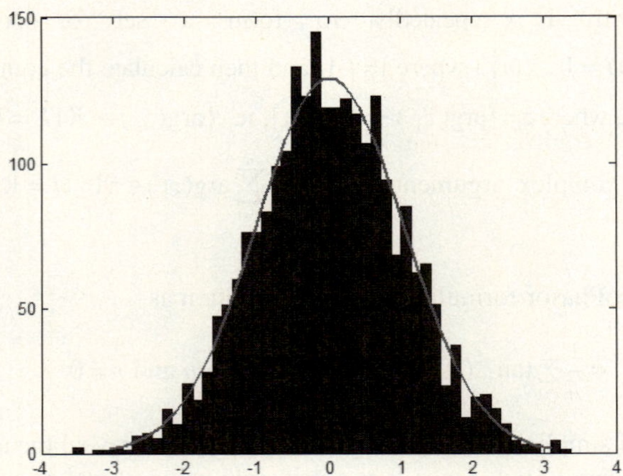

Fig. 1. Distribution of α_i is close to $\mathcal{N}(0, \pi^2/9)$. The red line represents $\mathcal{N}(0, \pi^2/9)$.

assumption is verified by using the 2400 samples of $\boldsymbol{\alpha}$ which shall be described in section 4. This leads to a distribution of $\left\{ \overline{\alpha}^k = \frac{1}{m}\sum_{i=1}^{m} \alpha_i^k \mid k = 1,...,2400 \right\}$ with mean and standard deviation being $0.0001 \approx 0$ and 3.21 respectively. As shown in Fig. 1, the histogram distribution closely approaches $\mathcal{N}(0, \pi^2/9)$.

Our implementation is outlined below:

a) At enrolment, we compute the standard deviation of α_i of user j, $\sigma_{ij} = \sqrt{\left(\sum_{k=1}^{p} (\alpha_{ijk} - \overline{\alpha}_{ij})^2\right) / p}$, $i = 1, \ldots, m$ where p is the number of training samples and $\overline{\alpha}_{ij}$ is the mean of α_{ij}.

b) For a user j, the feature space is divided into 2^N segments with range $[L\ R]$ and the segment width, w which varies according to $w = \arg\min_N \left(\left| \frac{R - L}{2^N} - 2\sigma_{ij} \right| \right)$ for feature element i of user j. In this case, L and R are the right and left boundaries of entire feature space and they take the values $-\pi$ and π, respectively, due to the observation that $\alpha_i \sim \mathcal{N}(0, \pi^2/9)$. The number of bits in each segment, n_i can be determined by enumerating a set of N values, $\psi_j = \left\{ \left| \frac{R - L}{2^N} - 2\sigma_{ij} \right|, i = 1,...,m \text{ and } N = 1,...,c \right\}$ where n_i is the smallest N value in set ψ. Alternatively, $n_i = N_{\min(\psi_j)}$ where $\psi_j = \left\{ \left| 2^{1-N} - 2\sigma_{ij} \right|, i = 1,...,m \text{ and } N = 1,...,c \right\}$. In this paper, c is arbitrarily set to 10 to avoid too many bits being used for a single representation.

c) At verification, the *genuine segment index* α_i of user j can be obtained from $d_i = \left\lfloor \left(\frac{\alpha_i - L}{R-L}\right) 2^{n_i} \right\rfloor$ or $d_i = \left\lfloor ((\alpha_i + \pi)/\pi) 2^{n_i - 1} \right\rfloor$ and its binary representation of α_i is rendered by Gray Coding, b_i = gray(d_i).

With the above procedure, a BioPhasor with length $\gamma = \sum_{i=1}^{m} n_i$ can be generated by cascading all Gray encoded indices of genuine segments from the m-dimensional $\boldsymbol{\alpha}$. Our 2^N discretisation functions as an error correction mechanism to further reduce the real-valued BioPhasor which combined vector to bit strings. Discretising each value in the combined vector forces closely located values to be replaced by a single index integer, which indirectly correct the fuzziness within the biometric data.

4 Performance Evaluations

In this paper, the proposed method is evaluated using face images from FERET database [8]. EigenFace [9] is adopted as the feature extractor and the Euclidean distance is used for matching. For the eigenbasis training, we use 400 images ie. 40 subjects with 10 images per identity, from ORL Face Database (http://www.uk.research.att.com/facedatabase.html). In the experiments using FERET database, we randomly selected a subset of 400 subjects, each having 6 essentially normalised frontal images with variations in pose, ie. within ±25 degree of angles, scale and illuminations. We randomly select 2 images from each subject to be the training samples and the others for testing purposes. However, 2 samples per subject are too few to estimate reliable statistics for 2^N discretisation (see step (a) in section 3), we employ the method proposed by [10] to derive multiple samples from 2 images. We perform geometric transforms, such as translation, rotation in plane, scale variance etc. and gray-scale transforms, such as simulative directional lighting, man-made noise etc. Then, we carry out FERET geometrical, lighting normalization [8] and BioPhasoring on the training (synthesized) and testing images. As such, we generated 20 training samples. We randomly select p (≥10) BioPhasor templates for 2^N discretisation and we repeat the same process 20 times for each run and the results are averaged to reduce the statistical frustration caused by the varying random numbers.

To generate the impostor distribution, the first template of each subject is matched against the first template of all other subjects, and the same matching process was repeated for subsequent templates, leading to (400x399)/2 x 4 = 319,200 impostor attempts. For the genuine distribution, each template of each subject is matched against all other templates of the same subject, leading to 2,400 ((3x4)/2 attempts of each subject x 400). For the stolen-token scenario, we consider the worst case where the impostors always manage to obtain the genuine token. In other words, only one set of pseudo-random numbers is mixed with all face features and the matching is performed according to the impostor match described above. In this paper, pca, bioh, biop, biop2N denote EigenFace, BioHash [5], BioPhasor [7] and 2^N discretised BioPhasor, respectively. Note that the feature length of pca, n= 150 is used while m= 100 is applied for BioHash and BioPhasor and evaluated using p= 10, 15 and 20 training samples for 2^N discretised BioPhasor. The performance will be evaluated using Equal Error Rate (EER) and Receiver Operating Curve (ROC).

Table 1 shows the performance comparisons of pca, bioh, biop and biop2N. It is clearly shown that bioh, biop and biop2N in legitimate token case significantly outperform pca, as what we had expected to see in all user-specific token mixing algorithms [5][7]. However, we are more interested in the stolen-token scenario which is generic in real world applications. From the experiments, the length of biop2N that we obtained is the range [210 290] and we take an average of 250 by appending zeros within those lesser than 250 and discard those which are longer.

Table 1 and ROC in Fig. 2 show that BioHash is the poorest compares to original PCA, BioPhasor and 2^N discretised BioPhasor in the stolen-token scenario. The 2^N discretised BioPhasor achieves the best performance especially in the case with large

Table 1. Performance comparisons of pca, bioh, biop and biop2N (both legitimate and stolen-token scenarios)

EER(%)	**pca**	**bioh**	**biop**	**biop2N (*p*=10)**	**biop2N (*p*=15)**	**biop2N (*p*=20)**
Genuine-token	15.63	0.01	0	0	0	0
Stolen-token	-	16.21	14.91	6.21	4.81	2.11

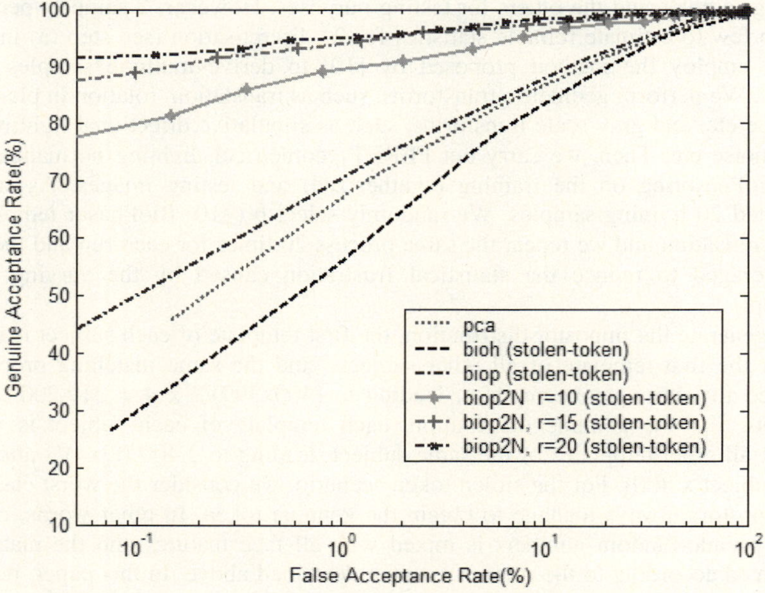

Fig. 2. ROC for performance comparisons in stolen-token scenario

number of training samples. The significant performance improvement observation indicates the potential generic discrimination capability of the BioPhasor based 2^N formulation. This phenomenon shall be explored in our subsequent works.

5 Diversity Property

Next we examine the diversity property of 2^N discretised BioPhasor by evaluating whether the random numbers, $\boldsymbol{r}_A$ mixed 2^N discretised template and the $\boldsymbol{r}_B$ mixed 2^N discretised template (with similar face identity) are correlated with each other. In other words, we wish to avoid the old template from falling into the region of acceptance of the refreshed template. In this case, the evaluation is exactly the same as the imposter distribution generation which has been discussed, but different $\boldsymbol{r}$ is used to mix with the same face feature and 2^N discretisation with training samples, p=20 is applied. According to [1], the comparisons of two truly uncorrelated binary bitstrings with length γ can be interpreted as a binomial distribution which have the functional form $f(x)=\dfrac{\gamma!}{\lambda!(\gamma-\lambda)!}0.5^{\gamma}$, with expectation π=0.5 and standard deviation $\dfrac{0.5}{\sqrt{\gamma}}$ where $x = \lambda/\gamma$, is the fraction of bits that happen to agree when two uncorrelated bitstrings are compared.

As shown in Fig. 3, the imposter distribution closely resemblance the theoretical fractional Binomial distribution where π=0.5 and standard deviation is $0.5/\sqrt{250}$ = 0.0316. This implies that the refreshed 2^N discretised BioPhasor has almost no

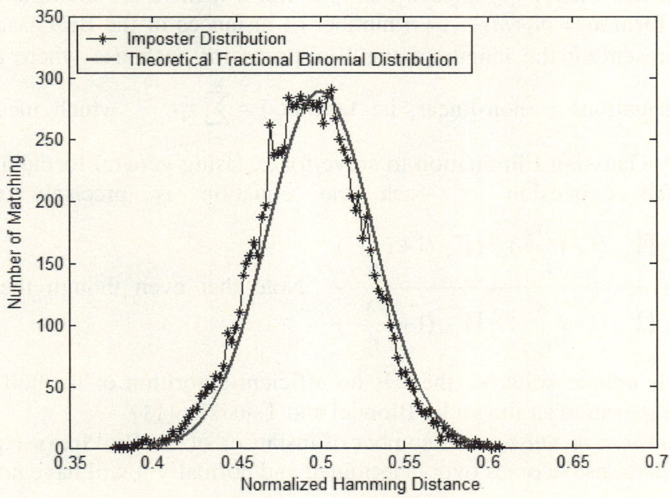

Fig. 3. 2^N discretised BioPhasor Diversity Distribution

correlation with 2^N discretised BioPhasor, and hence random number refreshment is equivalent to issuing the user a new template.

6 One-Way Transformation Property

BioPhasor is essentially designed for cancellable biometrics and its security concern such as whether it is one-way transformation is crucial. An examination of the one-way transformation property of 2^N stage discretised BioPhasor lies in two important dispositions: (1) irreversible random extraction of biometrics information via BioPhasor, and (2) transformation from real-valued biometric features to index space. The overall effect of these two steps is a one-way transformation of the real-space biometric vector into binary-space hashes without compromising the biometrics itself. We proceed to show the security proofs of the proposed scheme.

Proposition 1: Factoring out biometric feature, $\boldsymbol{x}$ from $\boldsymbol{\alpha}$, given random vector $\boldsymbol{r}$, is an intractable problem, even if $\boldsymbol{r}$ is known and is used multiple number of times.

Proof: Consider the scenario when $\boldsymbol{r}$ is used once and, α_i and $\boldsymbol{r}$ are known. The BioPhasor elements, $\alpha_j = \frac{1}{n}\sum_{i=1}^{n}\tan^{-1}\frac{x_i}{r_{i,j}} = \frac{1}{n}\sum_{i=1}^{n}(\frac{\pi}{2} - \tan^{-1}\frac{r_{i,j}}{x_i})$ form m system of equations where $\boldsymbol{r}_i \perp \boldsymbol{r}_j$ for $i \neq j$ and $\boldsymbol{r}_i \neq \boldsymbol{r}_j$. Since there are n number of unknowns and only $m<n$ number of equations, the system of equations has infinite number of solutions and hence, $\boldsymbol{x}$ is not recoverable in polynomial time. Therefore, factoring $\boldsymbol{x}$ out from $\boldsymbol{\alpha}$ and $\boldsymbol{r}$ is an intractable problem if $\boldsymbol{r}$ is known and used once.

Next consider when $\boldsymbol{r}$ is replaced multiple times. If there are multiple tokens $\boldsymbol{r}$, $\boldsymbol{r}'$, $\boldsymbol{r}''$, we can form $m = m_1+m_2+\ldots= n$ number of instances of the BioPhasor equations with m_i representing the length of the BioPhasor for each use where $\boldsymbol{r}_i \neq \boldsymbol{r}_j$. The system of equations is non-linear, i.e. $\tan(n\alpha_j) = \sum_{i=1}^{n} x_i r_{i,j}^{-1}$ which means that we cannot apply Gaussian Elimination to solve for $\boldsymbol{x}$. Using general formula for tangent addition, the expansion of each the equation is precisely defined as $\tan(n\alpha_k) = i\frac{\Pi_{j=1}^{n}(1-i\frac{x_j}{r_{k,j}}) - \Pi_{j=1}^{n}(1+i\frac{x_j}{r_{k,j}})}{\Pi_{j=1}^{n}(1-i\frac{x_j}{r_{k,j}}) + \Pi_{j=1}^{n}(1+i\frac{x_j}{r_{k,j}})}$. Note that even though the system of equations has unique solution, there is no efficient algorithm or method for solving this non-linear system as shown by Blondel and Tsitsiklis [11].

If there are $m = m_1+m_2+\ldots> n$ number of instances of the BioPhasor equations, the system of equations becomes over determined and normally it will have no solution. □

Note that BioPhasor mixing has higher security compared to BioHashing method. This is because of the $\tan^{-1}(.)$ function which converts the mixing formula to a non-linear operation.

Proposition 2: The vector $\boldsymbol{a}$ cannot be recovered exactly from 2^N discretised vector $\boldsymbol{d}$.

Proof: Let the 2^N discretisation be defined as $f:(-\pi,\pi)^m \rightarrow Z_{2^N}^m$ (discretisation) and $f \circ g$ where $g: Z_{2^N}^m \rightarrow \{0,1\}^\gamma$ (binarisation and Gray encoding) with $m < \gamma$. Since range(g) ≠ domain(f), hence $g \circ f$ is not possible. Since f is a transformation from real to index space, information will be lost. In particular, the continuous to discrete entropy lost is $\log(2^{n_i})$ based on individual segment size n_i as mentioned in Joy and Thomas [12]. Hence the 2^N stage discretisation is irreversible. □

The overall effect of 2^N discretised BioPHasor is a one-way transformation of the real-space biometric feature into binary-space hashes based on the product principle of Shannon [12], which stated the systematic cascading of different types of ciphers in single cryptosystems will increase the cipher strength provided that the product ciphers are associative but not commutative. We let the BioPhasor mixing be defined as h: $\Re^n \times \Re^n \rightarrow (-\pi, \pi)^m$ and let 2^N discretisation be k: $(-\pi, \pi)^m \rightarrow \{0, 1\}^\gamma$ with $m < \gamma$. Clearly $h \circ k$ is associative but not commutative since the domain and range cannot be interchanged. Since h and k are non-invertible and due to the product principle, $h \circ k$ is a one-way transformation.

7 Conclusion

In this paper, we proposed an extension of BioPhasor which incorporates a 2^N discretisation instead of using simple quantization scheme. From our experimental results on FERET dataset, the 2^N discretised BioPhasor survives the simulated stolen-token attacks. Consequently, the 2^N discretised BioPhasor could function as an effective cancellable biometrics technique to protect the privacy of biometric data without compromising the recognition performance in the event of compromised token. We also showed that 2^N discretised BioPhasor fulfils two other crucial requirements for a cancellable biometrics formulation, namely the diversity and non-invertible properties.

Acknowledgement

This work was supported by the Korea Science and Engineering Foundation (KOSEF) through the Biometrics Engineering Research Center (BERC) at Yonsei University.

References

[1] Andrew Teoh, B.J., Goh, A., David Ngo, C.L.: Random Multispace Quantisation as an Analytic Mechanism for BioHashing of Biometric and Random Identity Inputs. IEEE Transactions on Pattern Analysis and Machine Intelligence 28(12), 1892–1901 (2006)

[2] Ratha, N., Connell, J., Bolle, R.: Enhancing security and privacy in biometrics-based authentication systems. IBM Syst. J. 40(3), 614–634 (2001)

[3] Uludag, U., Pankanti, S., Prabhakar, S., Jain, A.K.: Biometric Cryptosystems: Issues and Challenges. Proceedings of the IEEE 92(6), 948–960 (2004)

[4] Soutar, C., Roberge, D., Stoianov, A.R., Gilroy, Vijaya Kumar, B.V.K.: Biometrics Encryption. In: Nichols, R.K. (ed.) ICSA Guide to Cryptography, pp. 649–675. McGraw-Hill, New York (1999)

[5] Andrew, B.J., David Ngo, C.L.: Cancelablle Biometrics Featuring With Tokenised Random Number. Pattern Recognition Letter 26(10), 1454–1460 (2005)

[6] Savvides, M., Vijaya Kumar, B.V.K., Khosla, P.K.: Cancelable Biometrics Filters for Face Recognition. Int. Conf. of Pattern Recognition 3, 922–925 (2004)

[7] Andrew Teoh, B., David Ngo, C.: Cancellable Biometrics Realization through BioPhasoring. In: 9th IEEE International Conference on Control, Automation, Robotics and Vision, ICARCV 2006, pp. 201–205 (2006)

[8] Phillips, P., Moon, H., Rauss, P., Rizvi, S.: The FERET Database and Evaluation Methodology for Face Recognition Algorithms. In: Proc. IEEE Conf on Computer Vision and Pattern Recognition, pp. 137–143. IEEE Computer Society Press, Los Alamitos (1997)

[9] Turk, M., Pentland, A.: Eigenfaces for Recognition. Journal of Cognitive Neuroscience 13(1), 71–86 (1991)

[10] Shan, S., Cao, B., Gao, W., Zhao, D.: Extended Fisherface for face recognition from a single example image per person. Proc. IEEE Int. Symp. Circ. Syst. 2, 81–84 (2002)

[11] Blondel, V.D., Tsitsiklis, J.N.: A Survey of Computational Complexity Results in Systems and Control. Automatica 36(9), 1249–1274 (2000)

[12] Joy, T.M., Thomas, J.A.: Elements of Information Theory, 2nd edn. John Wiley & Sons Inc., Chichester (1991)

Probabilistic Random Projections and Speaker Verification

Chong Lee Ying and Andrew Teoh Beng Jin

Faculty of Information Science and Technology (FIST), Multimedia University,
Jalan Ayer Keroh Lama, 75450 Melaka, Malaysia
lychong@mmu.edu.my
Biometrics Engineering Research Center (BERC), Yonsei University, Seoul, South Korea
bjteoh@ieee.org

Abstract. Biometrics is susceptible to non-revocable and privacy invasion problems. Multiple Random Projections (MRP) was introduced as one of the cancellable biometrics approaches in face recognition to tackle these issues. However, this technique is applicable only to 1D fixed length biometric feature vector but failed in varying size feature, such as speech biometrics. Besides, simple matching metric that used in MRP unable to offer a satisfactory verification performance. In this paper, we propose a variant of MRP, coined as Probabilistic Random Projections (PRP) in text-independent speaker verification. The PRP represents speech feature in 2D matrix format and speaker modeling is implemented through Gaussian Mixture Model. The formulation is experimented under two scenarios (legitimate and stolen token) using YOHO speech database. Besides that, desired properties such as one-way transformation and diversity are also examined.

Keywords: Speaker verification, Cancellable biometrics, Probabilistic Random Projections.

1 Introduction

Although biometrics is a powerful tool against repudiation and has been widely deployed in various security systems, the biometric characteristics are largely immutable, resulting in permanent biometric compromise. Cancellable biometrics was introduced by Ratha et al. [1] in storing a transformed version of the biometric template and provides higher privacy level by allowing multiple templates to be associated with the same biometric data. This helps to promote non-linkability of user's data stored across various databases. Basically, a good cancellable biometrics formulation must fulfill the following requirements:

1. Diversity: The same cancellable template cannot be used in two different applications.
2. Reusability: Straightforward revocation and reissue in the event of compromise.
3. Non-invertibility of template computation to prevent recovery of biometrics.
4. Performance: The cancellable biometric template should not deteriorate the recognition performance.

S.-W. Lee and S.Z. Li (Eds.): ICB 2007, LNCS 4642, pp. 445–454, 2007.

The details survey of various cancellable biometrics constructs can be found in [2]. In this paper, we focus only on the constructs which combine external factors such as tokenized random data with biometrics. Soutar et al. [3] first proposed a cancellable biometrics generated from fingerprints using optical computing techniques. The idea is to create identification codes, which are completely independent to the biometric data and can be easily modified and updated in the future. The templates consisted of correlation patterns derived from training images, which are subsequently mixed with random data to generate identification codes. However, the scheme was not explained in a satisfactory manner regarding the cryptographic security aspects of the transformations where no related results can be found. Teoh et al. [4] introduced a cancelable biometrics/key via inner product between randomized token and biometric data with quantization. This method is advantageous in comparison to that of Soutar et al since the transformation is a one-way process. Unfortunately, their formulation suffered from the scenario when the genuine token was stolen and used by the imposter to claim as the genuine user (stolen-token scenario). In this case, the recognition performance becomes poorer. This against the fourth criteria of cancellable biometrics.

Savvides et al. [5] proposed a cancellable biometrics scheme which encrypted the training images by synthesizing a correlation filter for biometric authentication. They demonstrated that convolving the training images with any random convolution kernel prior to building the biometric filter does not change the resulting correlation output peak-to-sidelobe ratios, thus preserving the authentication performance. Despite of that, the security will be jeopardized via a deterministic deconvolution with a known random kernel. Chong et al. [6] presented a work by utilizing multi-space random mapping to formulate a dual-factor speaker recognition system which combines speaker biometrics and user-specific token, but no report was given on the performance in stolen-token scenario. Note that Soutar et al. and Savvides et al. applied a set of common random numbers for all users whereas Teoh et al. and Chong et al. are using user-specific random numbers. The former aimed to conceal the biometrics data whereas the later utilized token's randomness for performance enhancement.

Recently, Teoh et al. [7] introduced the Random Multispace Quantization (RMQ), as an analytic mechanism for BioHash in face recognition, where the process is carried out by the non-invertible random projection of biometric feature and quantization. RMQ can be revoked through the pseudo-random numbers (PRN) replacement so that a new template can be generated instantly. When RMQ does not involve the quantization process, the formulation is named as Multiple Random Projections (MRP) [9]. Performance of MRP is improved through the projection from feature domain to a class-specified random subspace. Thus, the intra-class variations are preserved and enhance the inter-class variations. They inferred that the recognition performance is retained as sole biometrics performance in stolen-token scenario. This is accomplished through the choice of dissimilarity metric - normalized dot product that governs the statistic preservation transformation.

In this paper, we extend the MRP for speaker verification by using the 2D Principle Component Analysis Gaussian Mixture Model (2DPCA-GMM) [8] in speaker modeling instead of using normalized dot product. We name this method as Probabilistic Random Projections (PRP). Specifically, we remove the limitation of MRP, which is applicable only to fixed length 1D feature vectors. This is important because speech feature is varied in size due to the recording time length and it is normally represented in 2D matrix format. Beside that, we show that probabilistic treatment of MRP still survives in stolen-token scenario, subjected to certain condition. We also examine the diversity property of PRP.

This paper is organized as followed: Section 2 presents the brief introduction of Multispace Random Projections. Section 3 explains the Probabilistic Random Projections method. The experimental results and discussion are given in Section 4. The conclusion and future works are provided in Section 5.

2 Brief Reviews of Multispace Random Projections (MRP)

Multiple Random Projections (MRP) comprises two stages: (a) feature extraction and (b) random projections. In feature extraction stage, the individual's 1D feature vector, $\mathbf{x} \in \Re^{d}$, with length d is extracted. The feature vector is then projected onto a random subspace, $\mathbf{R} \in \Re^{mxd}$, $m<d$ through $\mathbf{y}= (1/\sqrt{m})\, \mathbf{Rx} \in \Re^{m}$. $\mathbf{R}$ is generated from the external sources such as pseudo-random numbers (PRN). During verification, the feature vector is mixed with genuine PRN and the resulting vector is compared with the enrolled template by using the normalized dot product.

Since MRP performs on user-specific basis; in the real world application, we should consider two different scenarios:

1. Legitimate Token: When the genuine **x** is concealed with **R**, which is generated by his specific PRN.
2. Stolen Token: in which an imposter has access genuine **R** and used by the imposter to claim as the genuine user.

We summarize the performance behavior of above two scenarios by using the genuine-imposter distribution as shown in Fig. 1.

In general, the accuracy of the biometrics system is determined by how much overlapping there is between the two distributions - genuine and imposter distributions. The larger of overlapping of two distributions, the poorer of system will be and vice versa. For the MRP in all scenarios, it shows that the statistical properties – mean and standard deviation of *genuine distribution* are preserved just like in the feature vector level (original system without random projection). On the other hand, imposter distribution is peaked at 1 and the standard deviation is equal to $1/\sqrt{m}$ in scenario 1 (Legitimate Token) by using normalized dot-product as matcher. This echoes that the clear separation of the genuine-imposter distribution can be attained, and hence near to zero error rate if m is sufficiently large as depicted in Fig. 1. However, in the second scenario, the inter-class variation shall revert to its original state in feature vector level and hence the performance is retained like before random projection is performed when $m<d$.

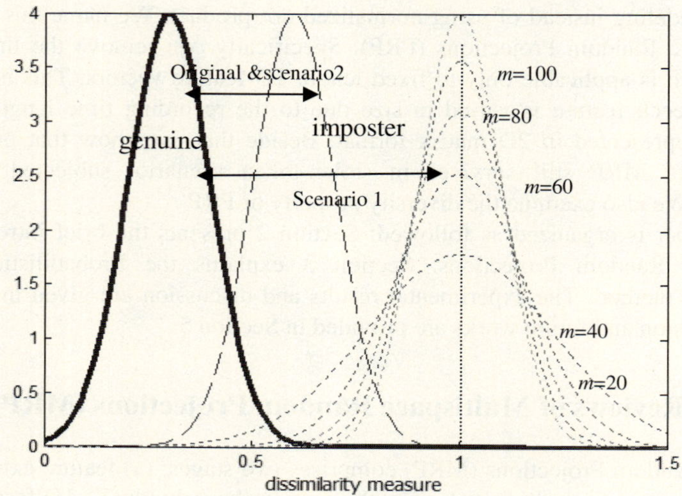

Fig. 1. Genuine-Imposter distributions for MRP

3 Probabilistic Random Projections

Probabilistic Random Projections (PRP) consists of three stages: (a) feature extraction (b) random projection (c) probabilistic modeling. The block diagram of Probabilistic Random Projections in speaker verification system is shown in Fig. 2.

The individual's feature matrix, $\mathbf{X} \in \Re^{qxr}$ is first extracted from the preprocessed framed speech signal through Linear Predictive Coding [10], where q represents the order of feature coefficient and r represents the frame number. Note that r is varied according to the recording length. Then, 2D Principal Component Analysis is used to compress **X,** hence, $\mathbf{W} \in \Re^{pxr}$ where $p \leq q$.

The 2D-PCA feature, **W** is further projected onto a random subspace as determined from an externally derived PRN, $\mathbf{R} \in \Re^{mxp}$, where $m \leq p$. The user-specific random-projected vector, $\mathbf{Y} \in \Re^{mxr}$ is obtained through the random projection process which is defined as:

$$\mathbf{Y} = \mathbf{RW} \tag{1}$$

The non-invertible property of **Y** can be assessed by referring the equation (1). **Y** can be regarded as a set of underdetermined systems of linear equations (more unknowns than equations). Therefore, it is impossible to find the exact values of all the elements in **W** by solving an underdetermined linear equation system in $\mathbf{Y} = \kappa\mathbf{RW}$ if $m<p$, based on the premise that the possible solutions are infinite.

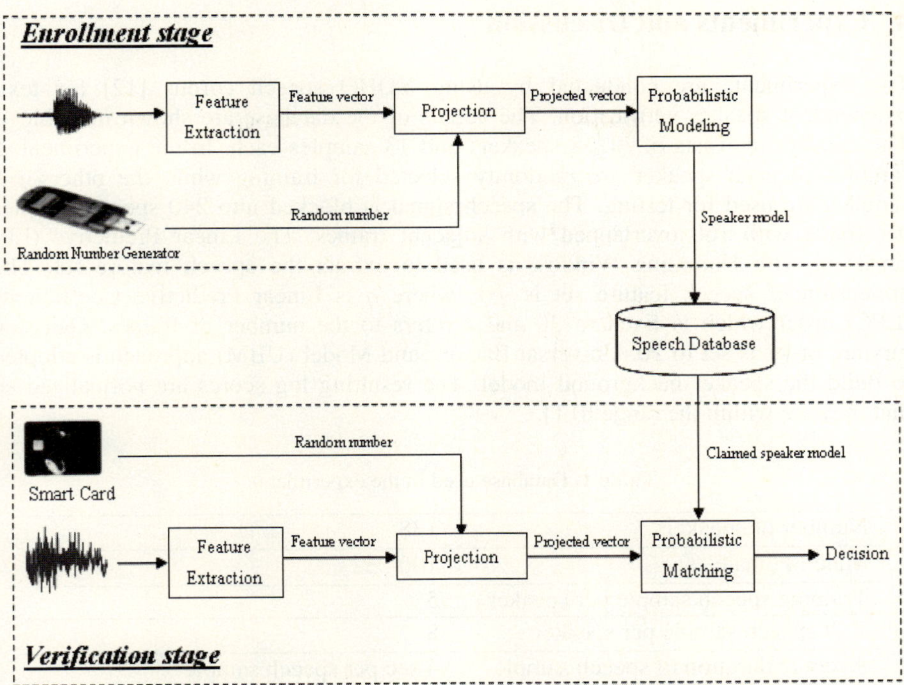

Fig. 2. Block diagram of Probabilistic Random Projections in speaker verification system

In the probabilistic modeling stage, the random-projected vector **Y** is fed into a Gaussian Mixture Model (GMM) [11] to construct a probabilistic speaker model. The speaker model produced by each speaker, λ is located in different random subspace. The Gaussian mixture density is computed by a weighted sum of M component densities defined as $p(\mathbf{Y} \mid \lambda) = \sum_{k=1}^{M} m_k b_k(\mathbf{Y})$, where M is the Gaussians mixture order. Mixture weights for Gaussian are represented by m_k, which satisfy the constraints $\sum_{k=1}^{M} m_k = 1$ and $b_k(\bullet)$, is a Gaussian function $\mathcal{N}(\boldsymbol{\mu}_k, \Sigma_k)$ with mean vector $\boldsymbol{\mu}_k$ and covariance, Σ_k. Each speaker is parameterized by its mixture weights, mean vectors and covariance matrices as $\lambda_k = \{m_k, \boldsymbol{\mu}_k, \Sigma_k\}$. GMM is vital to resolve the varying matrix size problem in 2D-PCA features that is not possible to be handled by simple metric used in [7].

During verification, the claimed speaker will present his speech biometrics and personal PRN. The feature extracted from the test sample will be projected to the user-specific random subspace generated from the personal PRN sequence from the claimed speaker. This new random-projected feature is then input into GMM for probabilistic matching. A likelihood ratio test is used to produce a match score. If match score is larger than the decision threshold, the claimed speaker is accepted as a true user and otherwise. As PRP is inherited from the MRP formulation, we shall consider two performance scenarios that mentioned in section 2.

4 Experiments and Discussion

The experiments are conducted by using YOHO speech corpus [12] for text-independent speaker verification. The details of the database are shown in Table 1. The database consists of i=138 speakers and 13 samples each. In the experiment, 5 samples of each speaker are randomly selected for training while the others j=8 samples are used for testing. The speech signal is blocked into 240 speech samples per frame with 160 overlapped with adjacent frames. The Linear Predictive (LP) cepstrum with Hamming Window is used to extract the speech feature set. The dimension of speech feature set is qxr, where q is Linear Predictive Coefficients (LPC) order which is fixed to 30 and r refers to the number of frames. Gaussian mixture order is set to 20. Universal Background Model (UBM) approach is adopted to build the speaker background model. The resulting log scores are normalized so that they are within the range [0 1].

Table 1. Database used in the experiments

Number of speakers	138
Male : Female	106 : 32
Training speech sample per speaker	5
Test speech sample per speaker	8
Average duration of speech sample	4 sec per speech sample
Sampling frequency	8kHz

The system performance will be evaluated by using False Accept Rate (FAR), False Reject Rate (FRR) and Equal Error Rate (EER). The EER is obtained when the FAR and the FRR are equal. FRR is the rate in which the system incorrectly rejects a valid verification attempt and FAR is the rate in which the system wrongly accepts an invalid attempt.

For the imposter distribution in the FAR calculation, the first speech feature in the test set is fed into the speaker model, λ of all other speakers, and the same process is repeated for subsequent speech feature. Thus, it yields a total of 151248 (ix(i-1)xj) imposter probabilistic scores. For the genuine speaker distribution in the FRR test, each speech feature is fed into their corresponding speaker model, λ leading to 1104 (ixj) genuine probabilistic scores. We repeat the same process 20 times and the results are averaged to reduce the statistical frustration caused by the different random numbers.

We fix 2D PCA row dimension, p=30. In this paper, PRP-m and PRPs-m denotes PRP in genuine-token and stolen-token scenarios, respectively with various $m \leq p$ row dimensions (5, 10, 15, 20, 25, 27, 29 and 30). Table 2 shows the performance comparisons of 2DPCA-GMM, PRP-m, PRPs-m for various m. It is clearly shown that the PRP significantly outperforms the original method (2DPCA-GMM in this context). PRP attains zero EER when m increases beyond m=10, as what we expected to see in all user-specific token mixing algorithms [4][7].

For the stolen-token case, we take the worst scenario where the imposters always manage to steal the genuine token. In other words, only one set of PRN is applied to all speech samples and the feeding is done according to the imposter match described above. In Table 2, we observe the degraded performance of PRPs-*m* as compared to PRP-*m*. However, PRPs-*m* with EER=5.96% (*m*=29) and EER=6.43 % (*m*=27) are close to 2DPCA-GMM with EER=5.78% when *m* is slightly less than *p*. In other words, PRPs-*m* reverts the system to its original state when $m \approx p$. From Table 3, it is showed that the imposter distribution of mean and variance (0.5640 and 0.0110) for PRPs-*m* are close to the 2DPCA-GMM with mean and variance (0.5628 and 0.0118), when *m*=29. Similar result has been seen in the genuine distribution where the mean and variance (0.7880 and 0.0055) of PRPs-*m* are close to the mean and variance of 2DPCA-GMM (0.7937 and 0.0057), when *m*=29. This indicates that the preservation of genuine-imposter distribution is valid when $m \approx p$. By setting the *m* slightly less than *p*, the performance will be retained and this does not jeopardize the condition of non-invertibility. Similar result is also presented in MRP [7] which utilizes the normalized dot-product as the matching metric. In PRP, we employ the probabilistic score, which is derived from GMM. Although different matching techniques are employed, both methods lead to preservation of the intra-class variations (genuine distribution) as well as inter-class variations (imposter distribution). It is also depicted in Fig. 3 where the separation of the genuine-imposter class distribution for 2DPCA-GMM and PRPs-*m* are almost identical.

To fulfill the diversity requirement of cancellable biometrics, we examine whether the PRP with PRN A and PRP with PRN B (both with same speech feature) are associated. This can be done by using Pairwise Independent Test. We mix the same speech feature with different PRN and the scores generation procedure is followed

Table 2. Performance comparison for 2DPCA-GMM, PPR-*m*, PRPs-*m*

	m	FAR(%)	FRR(%)	EER(%)
2DPCA-GMM	-	5.76	5.79	5.78
PRP-*m*	5	1.65	1.63	1.64
	10	0.03	0	0.02
	15	0	0	0
	20	0	0	0
	25	0	0	0
	27	0	0	0
	29	0	0	0
	30	0	0	0
PRPs-*m*	5	15.89	15.94	15.92
	10	12.85	12.95	12.90
	15	10.33	10.41	10.37
	20	8.76	9.10	8.93
	25	7.80	8.11	7.96
	27	6.12	6.73	6.43
	29	5.81	6.11	5.96
	30	5.69	5.70	5.70

Table 3. Statistic measurement for 2DPCA-GMM and PRPs-*m* (stolen-token scenario)

	m	μ_g	μ_i	σ_g^2	σ_i^2
2DPCA-GMM	-	0.7937	0.5628	0.0057	0.0118
PRPs-*m*	5	0.8205	0.7054	0.0031	0.0066
	10	0.7700	0.5794	0.0054	0.0105
	15	0.7784	0.5674	0.0055	0.0110
	20	0.8002	0.5842	0.0051	0.0107
	25	0.7895	0.5680	0.0054	0.0109
	27	0.7787	0.5736	0.0053	0.0109
	29	0.7880	0.5640	0.0055	0.0110
	30	0.7964	0.5620	0.0058	0.0121

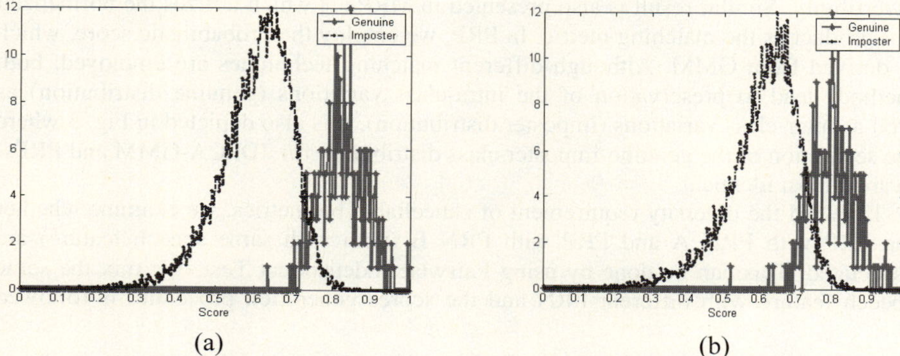

Fig. 3. Genuine and Imposter class distribution for (a) 2DPCA-GMM and (b) PRPs-27 (Probabilistic scores were normalized to [0-1] for better visualization purpose)

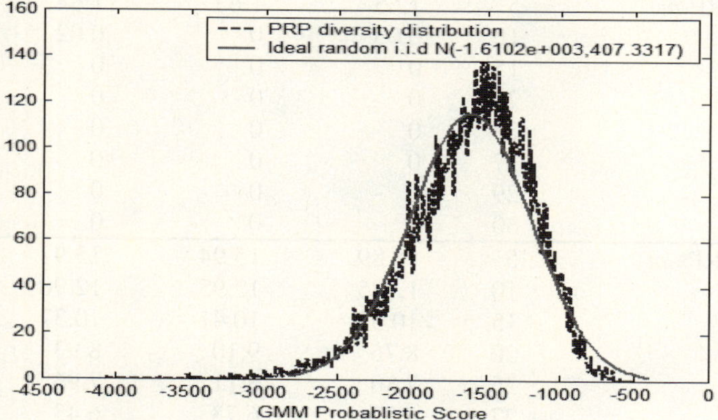

Fig. 4. Pairwise Independent Test of PRP

exactly by the imposter scores collection as described above. As shown in Fig. 4, the mean and standard deviation of collected scores are -1483.4 and 373.1, respectively. As the histogram closely approaches the independent and identically distributed (i.i.d) random variables drawn from Gaussian distribution, $\mathcal{N}$(-1610.2, 407.3), we can conclude that the PRP is pairwise independent. This implies that the refreshed PRP has almost no correlation with old PRP, and hence random number refreshment is equivalent to issue a new template for the user.

From the above findings, we observed that PRP fulfills the requirement of cancellable biometrics in term of performance, even in stolen-token scenario whereby the performance is retained as at feature vector level. In practical usage, we should set the system threshold *t*, which is used to decide the acceptance/rejection of the users according to the feature vector level performance (or stolen-token performance profile), instead of other scenarios. Nevertheless, recall that our results are important contribution to preserving the privacy of the speech feature and enable the enrolled template to be replaced in the event of template compromise.

5 Conclusions and Future Works

In this paper, we proposed a cancellable biometrics formulation, coined as Probabilistic Random Projections (PRP) which extends the MRP by employing the 2D Principal Component Analysis Gaussian Mixture Model. The PRP represents the speech feature in the 2D matrix format and hence, removes the limitation of MRP, which is only applicable to 1D fixed length feature vector. Besides that, the probabilistic modeling leads to better performance in speaker verification. The projection is non-invertible. The irrevocable and non-replacement issue of biometrics can be solved through the PRN replacement once the biometric template is compromised. Experiments showed that PRP survives in stolen-token attacks when the random subspace dimension is near to the original feature dimension. Thus, PRP functions well without compromising the verification performance in the event of compromised token. We also showed that PRP fulfilled another important property of cancellable biometrics, ie. diversity property. Our future work will be focusing on the theoretical justification on why the statistical preservation transformation can be achieved through the probabilistic scores that derived from GMM.

Acknowledgement

This work was supported by the Korea Science and Engineering Foundation (KOSEF) through the Biometrics Engineering Research Center (BERC) at Yonsei University.

References

1. Ratha, N., Connell, J., Bolle, R.M.: Enhancing Security and Privacy in Biometrics-based Authentication Systems. IBM Syst. J. 40, 614–634 (2001)
2. Uludag, U., Pankanti, S., Prabhakar, S., Jain, A.K.: Biometric Cryptosystems: Issues and Challenges. Proc. IEEE 92, 948–960 (2004)

3. Soutar, C., Roberge, D., Stoianov, A.R., Gilroy, Vijaya Kumar, B.V.K.: Biometrics Encryption. In: Nichols, R.K (ed.) ICSA Guide to Cryptography, pp. 649–675. McGraw-Hill, New York (1999)
4. Teoh, B.J.A., Ngo, C.L.D., Goh, A.: Personalised Cryptographic Key Generation Based on FaceHashing. Computers and Security J. 23, 606–614 (2004)
5. Savvides, M., Vijava Kumar, B.V.K., Khosla, P.K.: Cancelable Biometrics Filters for Face Recognition. Int. Conf. of Pattern Recognition 3, 922–925 (2004)
6. Chong, T.Y., Teoh, B.J.A., Ngo, C.L.D., Goh, M.: Multi-Space Random Mapping for Speaker Identification. IEICE Electron. Express 2, 226–231 (2005)
7. Teoh, B.J.A., Ngo, C.L.D., Goh, A.: Random Multispace Quantisation as an Analytic Mechanism for BioHashing of Biometric and Random Identity Inputs. IEEE Transactions on Pattern Analysis and Machine Intelligence 28(12), 1892–1901 (2006)
8. Chong, L.Y., Teoh, B.J.A., Khor, S.E.: 2D CLAFIC Subspace Technique in Probabilistic Speaker Verification. In: Fifth IEEE Workshop on Automatic Identification Advanced Technologies. IEEE Computer Society Press, Los Alamitos (2007)
9. Teoh, B.J.A., Chong, T.Y.: Cancellable Biometrics Realization with Multispace Random Projections. Accepted to publish in IEEE Transactions SMC Part B (2007)
10. Makhoul, J.: Linear Prediction: A tutorial review. Proc. IEEE 63, 561–580 (1975)
11. Reynolds, D.A.: Speaker Verification using Adapted Gaussian Mixture Models. Digital Signal Processing 10, 19–41 (2000)
12. Higgins, A.: YOHO Speaker Verification. In: Speech Research Symposium (1990)

On Improving Interoperability of Fingerprint Recognition Using Resolution Compensation Based on Sensor Evaluation

Jihyeon Jang[1], Stephen J. Elliott[2], and Hakil Kim[1]

[1] Graduate School of Information Technology & Telecommunication, Inha University
jhjang@vision.inha.ac.kr, hikim@inha.ac.kr
[2] Department of Industrial Technology, Purdue University
elliott@purdue.edu

Abstract. The purpose of this paper is the development of a compensation algorithm by which the interoperability of fingerprint recognition can be improved among various different fingerprint sensors. In order to compensate for the different characteristics of fingerprint sensors, an initial evaluation of the sensors using both the ink-stamped method and the flat artificial finger pattern method was undertaken. Then the resulted image resolution was incorporated to the compensation algorithms. This paper proposes Common resolution method and Relative resolution method for compensating different resolutions of fingerprint images captured by disparate sensors. Both methods can be applied to image-level and minutia-level. This paper shows the results of the minutiae-level compensation. The Minutiae format adhered to the standard format established by ISO/IEC JTC1/SC37. In order to compensate the direction of minutiae in minutia-level, Unit vector method is proposed. The fingerprint database used in the performance evaluation is part of KFRIA-DB (Korea Fingerprint Recognition Interoperability Alliance Database) collected by the authors and supported by KFRIA. Before compensation, the average EER was 8.62% and improved to 5.37% by the relative resolution compensation and to 6.37% by the common resolution compensation. This paper will make a significant contribution to interoperability in the system integration using different sensors.

1 Introduction

After the 9/11 terror incident, the major applications of biometrics have been shifted from personal identity authentication replacing passwords or tokens, towards national ID programs such as border control, e-passport, and seafarer's ID. Fingerprint is the main modality in biometrics due to its high accuracy and low cost. Unlike the other biometric modalities, however, there are many fingerprint sensors on the market, with various sensing mechanisms, such as optical, semiconductor, ultrasonic, thermal, polymer, TFT, and so on. Figure 1 presents various commercial fingerprint sensors and corresponding images of the same finger. Different sensor modules produce fingerprint images of different characteristics and fingerprint features of different types, which prevent them from being interoperable.

S.-W. Lee and S.Z. Li (Eds.): ICB 2007, LNCS 4642, pp. 455–463, 2007.

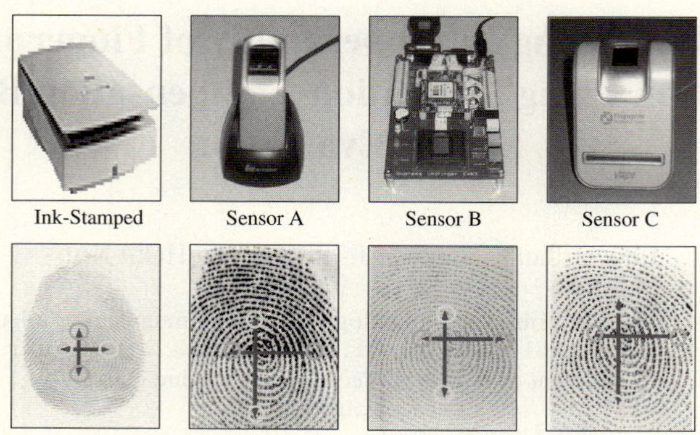

Fig. 1. Images of the different sensors on the same minutiae pairs

In order to analyze the characteristics of the different sensors presented in Figure 1, the actual horizontal and vertical resolutions of each fingerprint sensor are measured by comparing the pixel distances of a pair of the same minutiae between the ink-stamped and scanned image by a 500 dpi flat-bed scanner and the live-scanned image by each fingerprint sensor [1-2]. Table 1 summarizes the horizontal, vertical resolutions and the aspect ratio of the three fingerprint sensors used in this study. It should be noted that there are considerable amounts of differences between the actual resolutions and the vendor-provided specifications.

Recently, ISO/IEC JTC1/SC37 has been establishing the biometric standards for interoperability among disparate sensor modules as well as different modalities [3]. Interoperability between these different sensors can be examined from three points of view; the interface, data format, and algorithm. CBEFF [4] and BioAPI [5] are standards to provide interoperability of the interface between a sensor module and an application, while the standard data formats [6-9] are intended to furnish the interoperability among various fingerprint sensor modules. From the algorithm point of view, the interoperability is achieved by development of sensor-independent features that are invariable from sensor characteristics: resolution, image size, aspect ratio, and distortion. A ridge-counting algorithm [10-14] is a good example of the interoperability in algorithm level. In addition, various activities on interoperability test are underway [15-16].

The purpose of this study is to compensate the fingerprint template resolution and distortion before matching, in order to increase the fingerprint recognition rate

Table 1. Comparison of sensor characteristics

Item / Sensor	Sensor Image (# of Pixels)		Measured Resolution		Vendor Resolution	Aspect Ratio
	Hor.	Ver.	Hor.	Vor.		
A (500dpi Optical)	136	160	483	497	500	0.971
B (500dpi Capacitive)	138	170	490	529	500	0.926
C (460dpi Optical)	121	141	429	437	460	0.981

between the different sensor systems. The following section describes the proposed method for compensating the resolution and distortion of disparate fingerprint images.

2 Compensation Algorithms

Figure 2 depicts the overall compensation scheme in the image level as well as template level, using 500dpi common resolution or relative resolution method. Various compensation processes between an enrolled sample and a test sample can be implemented, such as template-template, template-image, and image-image.

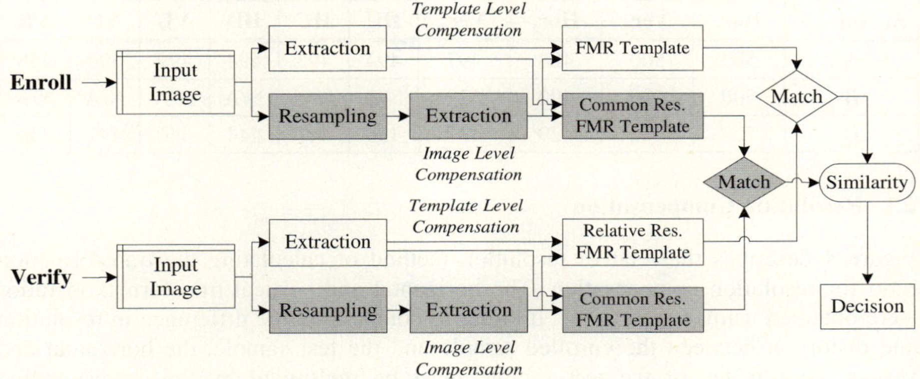

Fig. 2. Overall Compensation Scheme

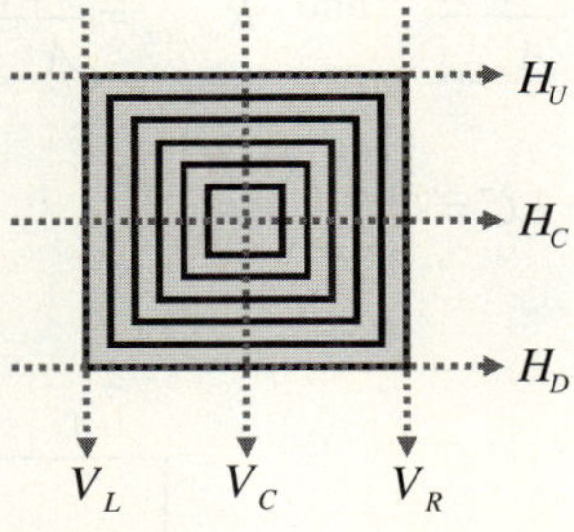

Fig. 3. Specification of flat artificial finger pattern

The resolution and distortion of each sensor should be provided prior to compensation. Figure 3 is the specification of Flat Artificial Finger Pattern which was to measure the actual resolution and distortion of the sensors. The flat artificial finger pattern was made using the pattern mold with silicon and the resolution information of each sensor is measured along six directions: H_U (horizontal upper), H_C (horizontal center), H_D (horizontal down), V_L (vertical left), V_C (vertical center), and V_R (vertical right).

In order to compensate for the different characteristics of fingerprint sensors, an evaluation of the sensors was undertaken using both the ink-stamped method and the flat artificial finger pattern method. The resulting image resolution was then incorporated to the compensation algorithms. Table 2 compares the sensor evaluation results with the manufacturer's sensor specifications.

Table 2. DPI Results of the Fingerprint Sensor Evaluation

Items / Sensor	DPI									
	Vendor Spec.		Ink-Stamped		Flat Artificial					
	Hor.	Ver.	Hor.	Ver.	HU	HC	HD	VL	VC	VR
A	500	500	483	497	494	495	494	499	499	498
B	500	500	490	529	N/A	N/A	N/A	N/A	N/A	N/A
C	723	460	429	437	436	441	444	440	441	440

2.1 Resolution Compensation

Figure 4 describes the relative resolution method of calculating the transformation ratio for resolution compensation. The horizontal and vertical transformation ratios were obtained using equation (1). In order to compensate the difference in resolution and distortion between the enrolled sample and the test sample, the horizontal and vertical coordinates of the test sample must be multiplied by the corresponding transformation ratio. Equation (2) defines the location compensation, LC.

$$R_{x-dpi} = \frac{B_{x-dpi}}{A_{x-dpi}} \quad \text{and} \quad R_{y-dpi} = \frac{B_{y-dpi}}{A_{y-dpi}} \tag{1}$$

$$LC = \begin{cases} x' = x \times R_{x-dpi} \\ y' = y \times R_{y-dpi} \end{cases} \tag{2}$$

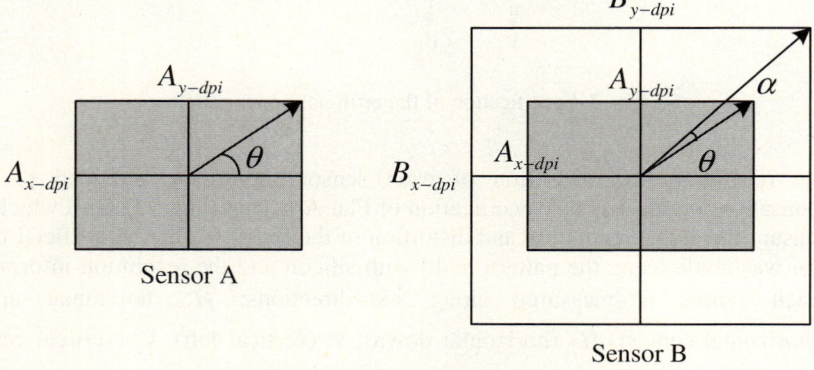

Fig. 4. Relative resolution method

Likewise, both the enrolled sample and the test sample can be converted to the same resolution of 500dpi with the aspect ratio equal to 1. This common resolution method is presented in equations (3).

$$R_{x-dpi} = \frac{500}{A_{x-dpi}} \quad \text{and} \quad R_{y-dpi} = \frac{500}{A_{y-dpi}} \tag{3}$$

2.2 Minutiae Direction Compensation

Given a template sample, instead of converting the coordinates of all the pixels as in Relative and Common resolution methods, only the positions and angles of minutia can be converted using the Unit vector method described in Figure 5, where the new position of a minutiae is computed by equation (2) and the new angle is obtained by equation (4).

$$\theta' = \tan^{-1}\frac{b'}{a'} = \tan^{-1}\left(\frac{R_{y-dpi}}{R_{x-dpi}} \cdot \tan\theta\right) \tag{4}$$

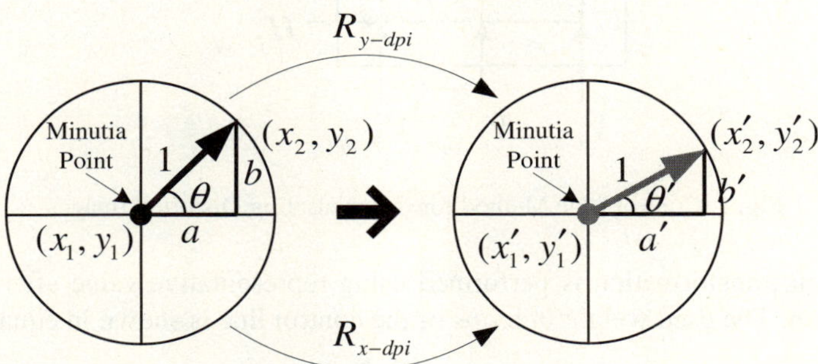

Fig. 5. Unit vector method for compensating minutiae direction

2.3 Distortion Compensation

The proposed approach employs the control line method in order to compensate the sensor distortion. Figure 6 presents the parameter of a single control line. When the position of the control line from before compensation $r-s$ to after compensation $r'-s'$ is obtained, the displacement of each pixel can be obtained by considering the length of the control line and the distance to the control line from the pixel.

Figure 7 presents the measuring method of resolutions along each direction, using the Flat Artificial Finger Pattern. After the six control lines for compensation is defined with initial values of 1/4 and 1/2 of the image width and height, the average resolution is modeled to be equal to the position and length of the initial control lines. If any resolution differs from the average resolution should compensate longer than the initial and vice versa.

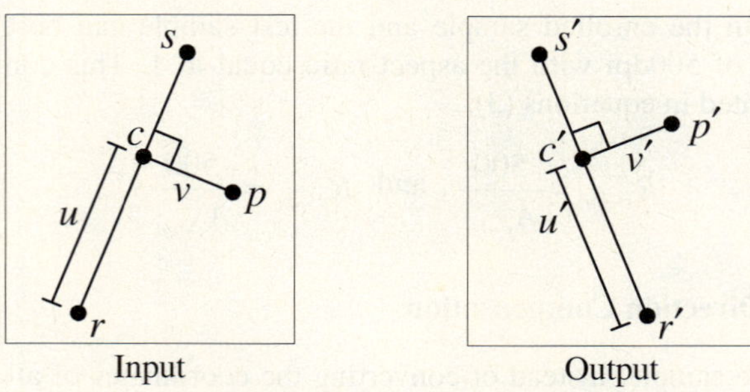

Fig. 6. Control Line Parameter

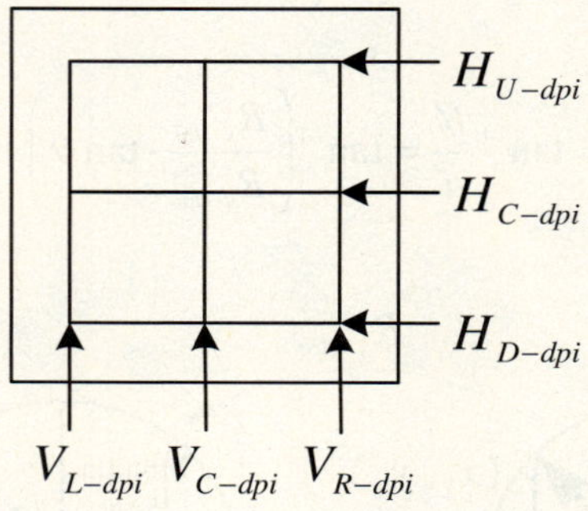

Fig. 7. Control Line Method for Compensating Distorted Images

Resolution transformation is performed using representative value after distortion compensation. The used weight in terms of the control line is shown in equation (5).

$$w = \left(\frac{l^c}{(a+d)} \right)^b \tag{5}$$

where, $a =$ Adherence Constant of the control line
$b =$ Concentration of the strength of the control line
$c =$ Importance of the length of the control line
$d =$ Distance between control line and pixel

The distance d is defined by equation (6). Therefore, the compensation of the transformation is achieved by considering the distance of the points, in order to use the segment feature: far points have small influence in the computation, and near points have a great amount of influence. The number of control lines is six. Final transformation is shown in equation (7) [17].

$$d = \begin{cases} |v| & 0 < u < 1 \\ \|\mathbf{p} - \mathbf{r}\| & u < 0 \\ \|\mathbf{p} - \mathbf{s}\| & u > 1 \end{cases} \tag{6}$$

$$\mathbf{p}' = T(\mathbf{p}) = \mathbf{p} + \frac{\sum_{i=1}^{n} w_i \Delta \mathbf{p}_i}{\sum_{i=1}^{n} w_i}, \quad \Delta \mathbf{p}_i = T_i(\mathbf{p}) - \mathbf{p} \tag{7}$$

where, $i =$ Control Line Index, $w =$ Weight
$\mathbf{p} =$ Considering Pixel
$\mathbf{p}' =$ Target Pixel
$T_i(\mathbf{p}) =$ Transformation Result on *i-th* Control Line
$T(\mathbf{p}) =$ Total Transformation Result

3 Experimental Results

The database used in this test is part of KFRIA-DB (Korea Fingerprint Recognition Interoperability Alliance Database) collected by INHA University and supported by KFRIA in Korea [18]. As presented in Table 3, the KFRIA-DB was collected in order to evaluate interoperable fingerprint recognition systems. The database consists of images acquired from 3 sensors and 344 people. Six fingers were used to obtain images exclusive of ring and little finger for 5 visits offering 5 impressions per visit. Therefore, the total database size comes to 154,800 images. The operator recorded the temperature and humidity during the acquisition period. In addition, the age distribution, which refers to the National Statistical Office, is considered.

The experiments were executed with compensated templates of 3 sensors and corresponding 3 different algorithms. Table 4 shows the results of the performance evaluation in terms of EER comparing between before and after the compensation.

Table 3. Database Specification on KFRIA-DB

Item	Description	
Organization	INHA University	
Modality	Fingerprint	
Purpose	For the Development and Evaluation of Interoperable Algorithm between Disparate Fingerprint Sensors	
Target Sensor	Optical	Sensor A, Sensor C
	Capacitive	Sensor B
Corpus	344 persons (Male:Female = 134:210, Age :10 ~ 70) 154,800 fingerprint images (5 times visiting * 5 impressions * 6 fingers * 3 sensors * 344 persons)	
Environment	Indoor Office Environment (Temperature 23~30°, Humidity 51~75%)	
Period	2005.7 ~ 2005.9	

Table 4. Results of the Performance Evaluation on the Interoperability

EER (%)	**Before Compensation**			**Relative Resolution Compensation**			**Common Resolution Compensation**			**Relative + Distortion Compensation**			**Common + Distortion Compensation**		
Enroll \ Test	**A**	**B**	**C**	**A**	**B**	**C**	**A**	**B**	**C**	**A**	**B**	**C**	**A**	**B**	**C**
Sensor A	2.14	15.61	17.72		5.16	8.89		7.67	12.92		5.16	8.89		7.67	12.92
Sensor B	4.05	1.07	3.65	4.08		3.42	3.49		3.49	4.08		3.42	3.49		3.49
Sensor C	7.31	3.40	1.72	7.26	3.40		7.26	3.40		7.26	3.41		7.26	3.40	

The average EER was 8.62% before compensation and improved to 5.37% by the relative resolution compensation, to 6.37% by the common resolution compensation. The relative resolution method produced better performance than the common resolution method because the common compensation error was accumulated by compensating both of the enrolled sample and the matched sample to 500 dpi with the unity aspect ratio.

4 Conclusions

The purpose of this paper is the development of a compensation algorithm by which the interoperability of fingerprint recognition can be improved among various fingerprint sensors. This paper proposed a *Common resolution method* and *Relative resolution method* for compensating different resolutions of fingerprint images captured by disparate sensors. Both methods were applied to image-level and minutia-level. While the common resolution method converts both an enrolled sample and a matched sample to 500 dpi samples, the relative resolution method converts the resolution of a matched sample to that of an enrolled sample. In order to compensate the direction of minutiae in minutia-level, *Unit vector method* was proposed. Various compensation schemes were implemented between an enrolled sample and a matched sample, such as template-template, template-image, and image-image.

Future works include the evaluation of the effectiveness of the resolution and distortion compensation process in an overall fingerprint recognition system with disparate sensors and development of deformation compensation methods against fingerprint elasticity. Development of a sensor independent feature vector and interoperable algorithms, compliant with CBEFF, BioAPI will also be investigated.

Acknowledgments. This work was supported in part by the Korea Small and Medium Business Administration through Fingerprint Recognition Interoperability Alliance (FRIA) at INHA University.

References

[1] Lee, B.G., Nam, J.W., Kim, H.I.: Evaluation Methodology for Fingerprint Sensors using Image. In: CISC2005, vol. 15(1), pp. 9–12 (June 2005)

[2] Nam, J.W., Kim, H.I.: Evaluation of Fingerprint Sensors using Confidence Interval. In: CISC2005, vol. 15(2), pp. 527–530 (December 2005)

[3] Text of CD 19795-4, Biometric Performance Testing and Reporting - Part 4: Performance and Interoperability Testing of Interchange Formats.

[4] http://www.itl.nist.gov/div895/isis/bc/cbeff/CBEFF%20Data%20Elements.htm

[5] http://www.bioapi.org/

[6] ISO/IEC JTC1/SC37 N927, Text of FDIS 19794-4, Biometric Data Interchange Formats - Part 4: Finger Image Data.

[7] ISO/IEC JTC1/SC37 N1488, Text of FDIS 19794-3, Biometric Data Interchange Formats - Part 3: Finger Pattern Spectral Data.

[8] ISO/IEC JTC1/SC37 N1567, Text of FDIS 19794-8, Biometric Data Interchange Formats - Part 8: Finger Pattern Skeletal Data

[9] ISO/IEC JTC1/SC37 N945, Text of FDIS 19794-2, Biometric Data Interchange Formats - Part 2: Finger Minutiae Data.

[10] Bolle, R.M., Colville, S.E., Pankanti, S.U.: System and method for determining ridge counts in fingerprint image processing. U.S. Patent No. 6266433 (July 2001)

[11] Kovacs-Vajna, Z.M.: A Fingerprint Verification System Based on Triangular Matching and Dynamic Time Warping. IEEE Transactions on Pattern Analysis and Machine Intelligence 22(11) (November 2000)

[12] Germain, R.S., Califano, A., Colville, S.: Fingerprint Matching Using Transformation Parameter Clustering. IEEE Computational Science & Engineering (1997)

[13] Ratha, N.K., Pandit, V.D., Bolle, R.M., Vaish, V.: Robust Fingerprint Authentication Using Local Structural Similarity. In: Proc. Workshop on Applications of Computer Vision, pp. 29–34 (December 4-6, 2000)

[14] Yi, E., Jun, S., Ryu, C., Kim, H.: A Cross-Matching System for Various Types of Fingerprint Scanner. In: Proc. The 4th International Workshop on Information Security Information (2003)

[15] http://www.ilo.org

[16] http://fingerprint.nist.gov/minex04/

[17] Gomes, J., Darsa, L., Costa, B., Velho, L.: Warping and Morphing of Graphical Object. Morgan Kaufmann, San Francisco (1999)

[18] http://www.fria.or.kr/

Demographic Classification with Local Binary Patterns

Zhiguang Yang and Haizhou Ai

Department of Computer Science and Technology,
Tsinghua University, Beijing 100084, China
ahz@mail.tsinghua.edu.cn

Abstract. LBP (Local Binary Pattern) as an image operator is used to extract LBPH (LBP histogram) features for texture description. In this paper, we present a novel method to use LBPH feature in ordinary binary classification problem. Given a restricted local patch, the Chi square distance between the extracted LBPH and a reference histogram is used as a measure of confidence belonging to the reference class, and an optimal reference histogram is obtained by iteratively optimization; real AdaBoost algorithm is used to learn a sequence of best local features iteratively and combine them into a strong classifier. The experiments on age, gender and ethnicity classification demonstrate its effectiveness.

Keywords: real AdaBoost, LBPH, demographic classification.

1 Introduction

LBP operator was introduced by Ojala in 1996 [14] for texture classification, later it was used for face recognition [1], facial expression recognition [2] and so on. In the early stage, the image is divided into several equal sized windows and represented as the combination of LBPH features from all windows; the classification methods can be nearest neighbors [1] [14] or linear programming [2]. Later, the LBPH features with various sizes and locations are used as weak classifiers, from which JS Boosting is used to learn a strong face recognition classifier by Huang et al [6]. In this paper, we use LBP histogram for demographic classification, which is age, gender and ethnicity classification, by face texture. Age is classified into three periods: child, youth and oldness; ethnicity is classified into Asian and non-Asian. We treat demographic classification as an ordinary binary classification problem, regarding age as a composition of two binary classifications. Our method is integrated with face detection [5] to form an automatic system.

Human face represents a variety of information, such as identity, age, gender, ethnicity, expression and so on. Specifically for one person, gender and ethnicity always remain the same as his or her identity does, while his or her age changes. As a result, it is reasonable that age classification is even harder. Recent works on demographic classification can be divided into two main approaches. One is pattern classification by face texture, such as decision tree [3], SVM [4][9],

S.-W. Lee and S.Z. Li (Eds.): ICB 2007, LNCS 4642, pp. 464–473, 2007.

real AdaBoost [15] and so on; the other focuses on both shape and texture information, such as dealing with 2D shape and wrinkled texture in [7] and 3D structure in [8]. In this paper, we treat LBPH as a distribution description of given local texture patch, and partition the feature domain of Chi square distance between this histogram and a reference histogram to form a LUT (look up table) based weak classifier. Within the set of all promising local patches, real AdaBoost is used to select the best ones and construct a strong classifier.

This paper is organized as follows: the following section describes the LBP histogram feature, real AdaBoost algorithm and the organization of age classification; the experiment on a large snapshot image database is shown in section 3; and section 4 gives the conclusion finally.

2 Demographic Classification

We combine face detection [5] and our demographic classification algorithm into an automatic system. After face detection, we detect six facial feature points, four eye corners and two mouth corners; and normalize the face texture by affine transformation based on the correspondence between the six points and the frontal template shape. In the normalized face texture, real AdaBoost selects a sequence of local LBPH features, and combines them into a strong binary classifier. The gender, ethnicity and age classifiers are trained respectively.

2.1 LBPH Feature

Basic LBP operator [14] is a computational efficient operator. Taking each pixel as a threshold, the operator transferred its 3×3 neighborhood into a 8-bit binary code, as shown in Fig.1(a). Later in [10], LBP operator is extended that an arbitrary number of bilinear interpolated pixels on a circle with arbitrary size are used as neighbor pixels, instead of its 3×3 neighborhood, as shown in the Fig.1(b).

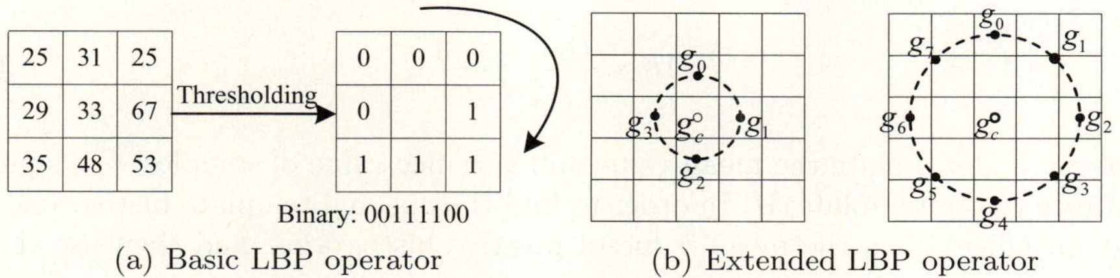

(a) Basic LBP operator (b) Extended LBP operator

Fig. 1. LBP operators

Another extension in [10] to the basic LBP operator is the so called *uniform* LBP that is found to be the fundamental property of local image texture. A LBP is called uniform if there are no more than two 0/1 or 1/0 bitwise transitions in its binary code, being considered as a circular code. The extended LBP operator is donated as $LBP^{u2}_{P,R}$, where P is the number of bilinear interpolated pixels, R is the radius of the neighbor circle and $u2$ stands for uniform criterion.

It is reported in [10] that, the contribution of uniform pattern to $LBP^{u2}_{8,1}$ and $LBP^{u2}_{16,2}$ is about 87.2% and 70.7% respectively. That is to say, the uniform patterns take a majority percentage of all patterns. As a result, each uniform pattern is given a unique label and all other minorities are given a mutual label in histogram calculation. In this paper, $LBP^{u2}_{8,2}$ is used, and all the LBP feature value is quantified into $[1, 59]$ by uniform criterion.

Given a local texture patch, LBPH is used to summarize all pixels (except pixels on the border of the image) with each pixel represented by the quantified LBP label.

2.2 Construct a Weak Classifier

Suppose S and M are two different histograms, the Chi square distance can be defined as:

$$\chi^2(S, M) = \sum_{i=1}^{n} \frac{(S_i - M_i)^2}{S_i + M_i}, \tag{1}$$

where n is the number of elements in the histogram ($n = 59$ in this paper).

Chi square distance is an effective measurement of similarity between a pair of histograms, hence it is suitable for nearest neighbor [10] and intra/extra based classification [6]. However, find a pair of similar samples doesn't make sense in most binary classification problem.

In this section, we want to find an optimal template histogram M as the reference template for every positive or negative sample to calculate a Chi square distance for ordering. With the hypothesis of Gaussian distribution of positive and negative samples respectively, the template M is expected to be near to one cluster and far from the other, in order that positive and negative samples can be discriminated successfully by Chi square distance.

Via Chi square distance, the separability of each LBPH feature could be measured as Fisher's discriminant ratio:

$$FDR = \frac{(\mu_+ - \mu_-)^2}{\sigma_+^2 + \sigma_-^2}, \tag{2}$$

where μ and σ donate the mean value and variance value of samples' Chi square distance to the template M. In order to find the optimal template histogram, we first initialize M as the mean value of positive histograms, and then use steep decent method to find an optimal solution.

Given sample set $S = (h_1, y_1), \ldots, (h_m, y_m)$, where h_i is the LBPH feature, and $y_i = \pm 1$ is the class label. μ_y and σ_y of positive and negative samples illustrated by $y = 1$ and $y = -1$ respectively can be written as:

$$\mu_y = \frac{1}{N_y} \sum_{k=1, y_k = y}^{m} \chi^2(h_k, M), \tag{3}$$

$$\sigma_y^2 = \frac{1}{N_y} \sum_{k=1, y_k = y}^{m} (\chi^2(h_k, M) - \mu_y)^2. \tag{4}$$

For the n-elements template histogram, whose items sum up to 1, the previous $n-1$ items are supposed to be independent, and their partial derivative of μ_y and σ_y can be written as:

$$\frac{\partial \mu_y}{\partial M_i} = \frac{1}{N_y} \sum_{k=1, y_k = y}^{m} \frac{-4h_k^2(k)}{(h_k(i) + M_i)^2} + 1, \tag{5}$$

$$\frac{\partial \sigma_y^2}{\partial M_i} = \frac{2}{N_y} \sum_{k=1, y_k = y}^{m} (\chi^2(h_k, M) - \mu_y)(\frac{-4h_k^2(k)}{(h_k(i) + M_i)^2} + 1 - \frac{\partial \mu_y}{\partial M_i}). \tag{6}$$

As a result, the gradient of Fisher discriminate ratio can be calculated as follow

$$\frac{\partial FDR}{\partial M_i} = \frac{2(\mu_+ - \mu_-)}{\sigma_+ + \sigma_-}(\frac{\partial \mu_+}{\partial M_i} - \frac{\partial \mu_-}{\partial M_i}) - \frac{(\mu_+ - \mu_-)^2}{(\sigma_+ + \sigma_-)^2}(\frac{\partial \sigma_+^2}{\partial M_i} + \frac{\partial \sigma_-^2}{\partial M_i}). \tag{7}$$

By this means, an optimal M could be found by iterative search, and it is used as the reference template for the given local texture patch. We divide the main feature domain of Chi square distance from training samples to the reference template into 32 bins, and Fig.2 gives an example distribution of samples' Chi square distance to the reference histogram, which meets the prior hypothesis of Gaussian distribution well.

With respect to training samples' distribution on the Chi square distance, a LUT based weak classifier is used. Its output on each domain can be defined as:

$$\forall h \in H_i, f(h) = \frac{1}{2}(\frac{W_+^i + \varepsilon}{W_-^i + \varepsilon}), i = 1, \ldots, 32, \tag{8}$$

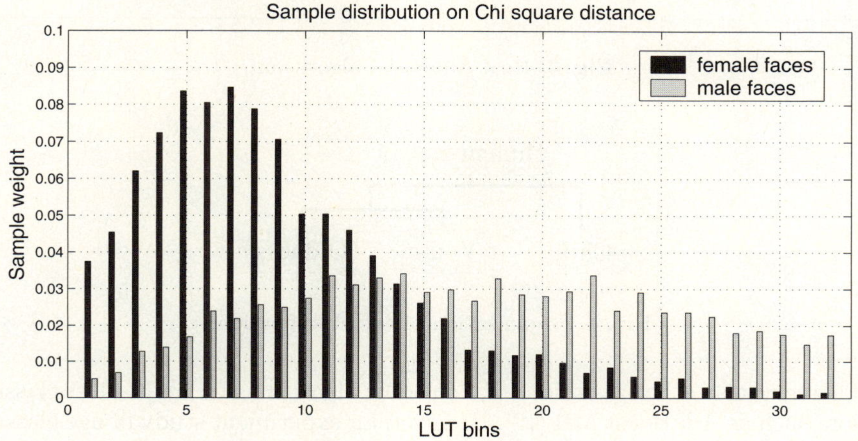

Fig. 2. Sample distribution on Chi square distance

where W_i is the sum weight of samples H_i on the i-th domain and ε is a small positive constant.

2.3 Real AdaBoost Learning

Real AdaBoost [12] is a statistical learning algorithm by maximizing classification margin iteratively. In each iteration t, one weak classifier is selected from a large hypothesis space; after the final iteration T, all the selected weak classifiers are combined together to construct a strong classifier. The training algorithm is shown in Fig. 3.

Given Training sample set $S = \{(x_1, y_1), \ldots, (x_m, y_m)\}$ where x_i is the face sample, $y_i = \pm 1$ is the class label. All promising local texture LBPH features L.
Initialize Sample weight $w_1(i) = \frac{1}{2N_{y_i}}$, $i = 1, \ldots, m$
Prepare Find a reference template histogram for each LBPH feature
For $t = 1, \ldots, T$

1. Under distribution w_t, select a weak classifier f_t to minimize the factor

$$Z = \sum_{j=1}^{32} \sqrt{W_+^j W_-^j}.$$

2. Update the weights:

$$w_{t+1}(i) = w_t(i) \frac{exp(-y_i f_t(x_i))}{U_t}, i = 1, \ldots, m,$$

where U_t is a normalization factor so that w_{t+1} is a p.d.f.

Output The final strong classifier: $F(x) = sign(\sum_{t=1}^{T} f_t(x) - b)$,where b is a threshold whose default is 0. And the confidence of the classifier is defined as $\sum_{t=1}^{T} f_t(x) - b$.

Fig. 3. Real AdaBoost algorithm

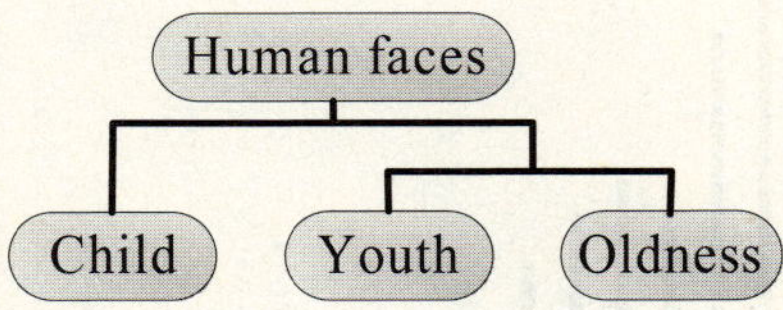

Fig. 4. Organization of age classification

There are also other variations of AdaBoost algorithms for multi-class classification, such as AdaBoost.MH [12]. However, an experiment study of age classification shows that, the three age periods don't share the same optimal separable features and the difficulty of classification differs as well. Child is the easiest to be discriminated, and the second one is oldness. As a result, a binary tree structure is used for age classification. That is, the first node is used to classify child and adult, the second one is used to discriminate old people from youth, as shown in Fig. 4.

3 Experimental Result

We carry out experiment on three different databases: FERET[11], PIE[13] and a snapshot database. All frontal images in FERET which account for 1196 individuals and 3540 images are used, and 68 individuals with 696 good illumination frontal PIE images are also used; the snapshot image database contains 9000 Chinese snapshot images. The three databases contain three kinds of expression, with glasses or without.

We use the snapshot database for five-fold cross validation on age and gender classification, FERET and PIE are used for independent database testing. When we do experiment on ethnicity classification, FERET and snapshot images are merged for cross validation, and PIE is left for testing.

All the faces are normalized automatically as described in section 2. To show the effectiveness of our approaches, the experimental result of the method (represented as LBPH* hereinafter) that takes the mean histogram of positive samples as the reference template histogram is also given in the three sub-sections for comparison. Meanwhile, Real AdaBoost with Haar like features is also used for comparison.

3.1 Gender Classification

There are 4696 male and 3737 female faces in the snapshot images (children are not used for gender classification), they are always upright and neutral without full beard or strange hairstyle. In each round of five fold cross validation experiment, 80% faces were used for training, and the others were used for testing. Besides cross validation, we also use all the snapshot images for training, and FERET and PIE database for testing. For a comparison, we additionally implement RBF-kernel SVM with ensemble face textures, in which PCA coefficients with 95% energy are used for dimension reduction. Tab.1 lists the experiment result of gender classification on cross validation and independent database verification.

SVM leads in the cross validation experiment, but is poor in generalization ability, as it suffers from improper representation by eigenvectos generated from independent database. LBPH is comparable to Haar like feature in the cross validation experiment, and slightly better in independent verification. Meanwhile, they are all much better than LBPH* feature.

3.2 Ethnicity Classification

In the experiment of ethnicity classification, snapshot database and FERET database are merged, that results in 11680 Asian characters and 1016 non-Asian

Table 1. Experiment result (error rate) on gender classification

	Cross validation	FERET	PIE
SVM	3.18%	19.4%	24.2%
Real AdaBoost(Haar)	3.58%	8%	12.3%
Real AdaBoost(LBPH*)	6.52%	11.9%	16.8%
Real AdaBoost(LBPH)	3.68%	6.7%	8.9%

characters. In each round of cross validation, a 80% number of characters were used for training, and the rest were used for testing, although some characters have more than one images in the integrated database. Tab.2 gives the comparison result of multiple methods on cross validation and independent database verification.

Table 2. Experiment result (error rate) on ethnicity classification

	Cross validation	PIE
Real AdaBoost(Haar)	2.98%	7.9%
Real AdaBoost(LBPH*)	7.11%	14.6%
Real AdaBoost(LBPH)	3.01%	6.8%

LBPH feature is again confirmed to be comparable to Haar like feature in the cross validation experiment, and slightly better in independent verification.

3.3 Age Classification

There are 567 children, 6951 youth and 1482 oldness in the snapshot images. We first train a children classifier to separate children from adult people, and then train an oldness classifier to separate oldness from youth. FERET and PIE databases are also used for testing. The experiment results are shown in Tab. 3.

Table 3. Experiment result (error rate) on age classification

	Cross validation	FERET	PIE
Real AdaBoost(Haar)	10.8%	20.6%	23.3%
Real AdaBoost(LBPH*)	8.18%	18.9%	20.4%
Real AdaBoost(LBPH)	6.82%	7.88%	12.5%

The result corresponds with the above two experiments, and the result of LBPH is better than that of Haar like feature in cross validation and independent verification.

The result shown in the above three sub experiments proves effectiveness of LBPH feature. Via iterative optimization, LBPH makes much better result than LBPH*, and maintains a good generalization ability as well. The LBPH feature is confirmed to be comparable to the Haar like feature in gender and

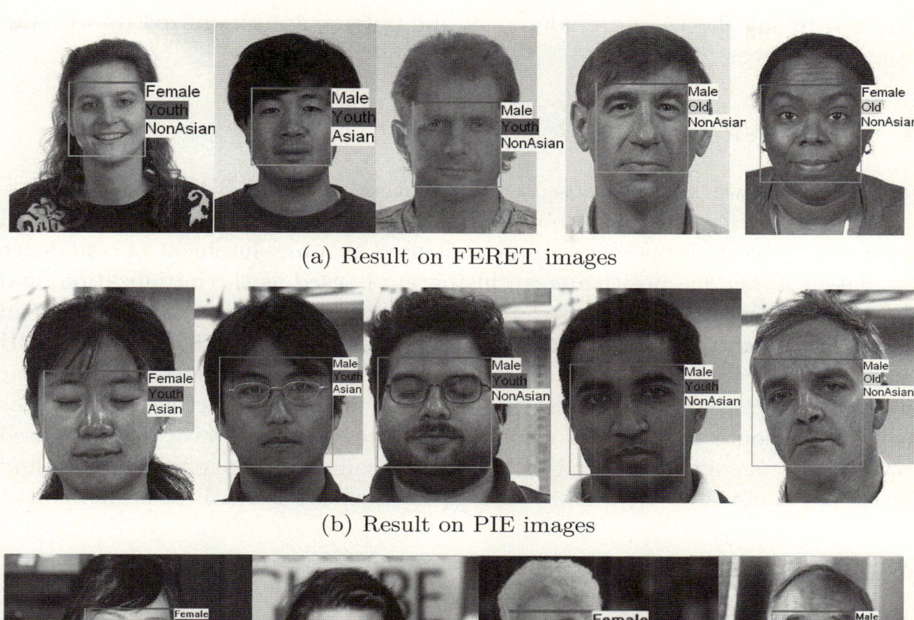

(a) Result on FERET images

(b) Result on PIE images

(c) Result on www images

Fig. 5. LBP operators

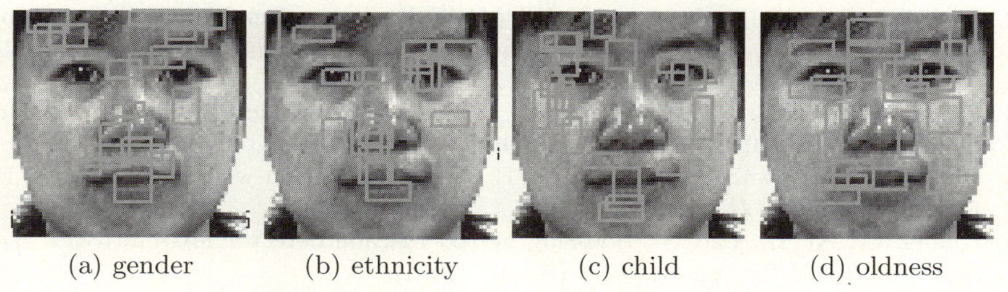

(a) gender (b) ethnicity (c) child (d) oldness

Fig. 6. Example of boosted weak demographic classifiers

ethnicity classification, and much better in age classification. Meanwhile, each classifier used above is composed of less than 100 weak classifiers, which can be used for realtime demographic classification. Fig.5 gives some demographic classification results, and Fig.6 shows the first 20 boosted weak classifiers by three experiments respectively. As a semantic explanation, male faces are distinguished by the areas of pronounced brow bossing and longer philtrum; non-Asian faces are characterized by deeper eyehole, different shapes of nose and lip; children are featured by fat cheeks and tender skin; and oldness are recognized by wrinkles in multiple areas.

4 Conclusion

In this paper, we have proposed a new method to use LBPH feature for ordinary binary classification problems. For each LBPH feature, a sample's Chi Square distance to a reference template is used as a measurement of confidence for classification; the positive mean histogram is used as the initialization, and the steep decent method is used to find an optimal reference template. Real AdaBoost is used to train a strong classifier by composing a sequence of LBPH features. The experiments on gender, ethnicity and age classification prove our method's effectiveness. However, there is some work to be further studied. For example, it could be better if color image instead of gray level image is used for ethnicity classification. And LBP operator could be more effective if we find better parameters, or use a more efficient face texture normalization method.

Acknowledgments

This work is supported in part by National Science Foundation of China under grant No.60332010, No.60673107.

References

1. Ahonen, T., Hadid, A., Pietikainen, M.: Face recognition with local binary patterns. In: Pajdla, T., Matas, J(G.) (eds.) ECCV 2004. LNCS, vol. 3021, pp. 469–481. Springer, Heidelberg (2004)
2. Feng, X., Cui, J., Pietikainen, M., Hadid, A.: Real time facial expression recognition using local binary patterns and linear programming. In: MICAI, pp. 328–336 (November 2005)
3. Gutta, S., Wechsler, H., Phillips, P.J.: Gender and ethnic classification of face images. In: FG, pp. 194–199 (April 1998)
4. Hosoi, S., Takikawa, E., Kawade, M.: Ethnicity estimation with facial images. In: FGR, pp. 195–200 (May 2004)
5. Huang, C., Ai, H., Lao, S.: Boosting nested cascade detector for multi-view face detection. In: ICPR, pp. 415–418 (August 2004)
6. Huang, X., Li, S.Z., Wang, Y.: Jensen-shannon boosting learning for object recognition. In: CVPR, pp. 144–149 (June 2005)
7. Kwon, Y.H., da Vitoria Lobo, N.: Age classification from facial images. Computer Vision and Image Understanding 74(1), 1–21 (1999)
8. Lu, X., Chen, H., Jain, A.K.: Multimodal facial gender and ethnicity identification. In: ICB, pp. 554–561 (January 2006)
9. Moghaddam, B., Yang, M.-H.: Learning gender with support faces. IEEE Trans. Pattern Anal. Mach. Intell. 24(5), 707–711 (2002)
10. Ojala, T., Pietikainen, M., Maenpaa, M.: Multiresolution gray-scale and rotation invariant texture classification with local binary patterns. IEEE Trans. Pattern Anal. Mach. Intell. 24(7), 971–987 (2002)

11. Phillips, P., Moon, H., Rizvi, S.A., Rauss, P.J.: The feret evaluation methodology for face-recognition algorithms. IEEE Trans. PAMI 22(10), 1090–1104 (2000)
12. Schapire, R.E., Singer, Y.: Improved boosting algorithms using confidence-rated predictions. Machine Learning 37(3), 297–336 (1999)
13. Sim, T., Baker, S., Bsat, M.: The cmu pose, illumination, and expression (pie) database. In: FGR, pp. 53–58 (May 2002)
14. Ojala, T., Pietikainen, M., Harwood, D.: A comparative study of texture measures with classification based on feature distribution. Pattern Recognition 29(1), 51–59 (1996)
15. Wu, B., Ai, H., Huang, C.: Lut-based adaboost for gender classification. In: AVBPA, pp. 104–110 (June 2003)

Distance Measures for Gabor Jets-Based Face Authentication: A Comparative Evaluation

Daniel González-Jiménez[1], Manuele Bicego[2], J.W.H. Tangelder[3], B.A.M Schouten[3], Onkar Ambekar[3], José Luis Alba-Castro[1], Enrico Grosso[2], and Massimo Tistarelli[4]

[1] TSC Department, University of Vigo, Vigo (Spain)
{danisub,jalba}@gts.tsc.uvigo.es
[2] DEIR - University of Sassari, Sassari (Italy)
{bicego,grosso}@uniss.it
[3] CWI, Amsterdam (The Netherlands)
{J.W.H.Tangelder,B.A.M.Schouten,Onkar.Ambekar}@cwi.nl
[4] DAP - University of Sassari, Alghero (Italy)
tista@uniss.it

Abstract. Local Gabor features (jets) have been widely used in face recognition systems. Once the sets of jets have been extracted from the two faces to be compared, a proper measure of similarity (or distance) between corresponding features should be chosen. For instance, in the well known Elastic Bunch Graph Matching (EBGM) approach and other Gabor-based face recognition systems, the cosine distance was used as a measure. In this paper, we provide an empirical evaluation of seven distance measures for comparison, using a recently introduced face recognition system, based on Shape Driven Gabor Jets (SDGJ). Moreover we evaluate different normalization factors that are used to pre-process the jets. Experimental results on the BANCA database suggest that the concrete type of normalization applied to jets is a critical factor, and that some combinations of *normalization* + *distance* achieve better performance than the classical cosine measure for jet comparison.

1 Introduction

Face analysis and recognition is an important and active research area [15], whose interest has increased in recent years for both theoretical and application-driven motivations. Among the huge amount of approaches presented in this context, a wide group is based on the extraction of a particular class of features from points on the face, automatically or manually found. Different features have been proposed, like DCT [11], Local Binary Patterns [13], SIFT [12,10] and others, showing different characteristics, in terms of robustness, ease of computation, computational requirements etc. In this context, Gabor features received great attention, and several methods for face recognition using these features have been proposed (see [1,2,3,4] among others — and [5] for a recent survey). One of the most important algorithms falling in that category is the Elastic Bunch Graph Matching (EBGM) approach proposed by Wiskott et al. [1]. In

S.-W. Lee and S.Z. Li (Eds.): ICB 2007, LNCS 4642, pp. 474–483, 2007.

this technique, Gabor responses (jets) are extracted from a set of (the so-called) fiducial points, located at specific face regions (eyes, tip of the nose, mouth...). On the other hand, a recently proposed method in [4] focuses on the selection of an *own* set of points and features for a given client by exploiting facial structure (Shape-Driven Gabor Jets or SDGJ). Although both approaches used cosine distance in order to compare corresponding features, this choice is not motivated, neither with a theoretical nor with an experimental evaluation. To the best of our knowledge, the only evaluation of distances for Gabor jet comparison was performed in [14], where the authors concluded that Manhattan (or city block) distance outperformed both cosine and euclidean distances. However, it is not explicitely described, neither in [14] nor in other research papers dealing with Gabor jets-based face recognition systems, whether jets have been previously normalized or not. In this paper we propose a more extensive evaluation, comparing seven different distances for measuring similarities between Gabor jets, as well as assessing the impact of the concrete normalization method that is applied to jets before comparison. Finally, three different resolutions of input images are tested in order to provide a more complete set of results.

The paper is organized as follows. Section 2 briefly introduces the Shape-driven Gabor Jets (SDGJ) algorithm: Section 2.1 describes the set of Gabor filters used for feature extraction, and Section 2.2 presents the algorithm used to map points between two faces. The different distances involved in the comparison are introduced in Section 3. Experimental results are given in Section 4. Finally, conclusions and future research lines are drawn in Section 5.

2 Shape-Driven Gabor Jets (SDGJ)

In this approach [4], the selection of points is accomplished by exploiting shape information. Lines depicting face structure are extracted by means of a ridges and valleys detector [6], leading to a binary representation that sketches the face. In order to select a set of points from this sketch, a dense rectangular grid ($n_x \times n_y$ nodes) is applied onto the face image and each grid node is moved towards its nearest line of the sketch. Finally, a set of points $\mathcal{P} = \{\boldsymbol{p_1}, \boldsymbol{p_2}, \ldots, \boldsymbol{p_n}\}$, with $n = n_x \times n_y$ are obtained. This set of points samples the original sketch, as it can be seen in figure 1.

2.1 Extracting Textural Information

A set of 40 Gabor filters $\{\psi_m\}_{m=1,2,\ldots,40}$, with the same configuration as in [1], is used to extract textural information. These filters are convolution kernels in the shape of plane waves restricted by a Gaussian envelope, as it is shown next:

$$\psi_m(\boldsymbol{x}) = \frac{\|\boldsymbol{k}_m\|^2}{\sigma^2} exp\left(\frac{-\|\boldsymbol{k}_m\|^2 \|\boldsymbol{x}\|^2}{2\sigma^2}\right)\left[exp(i \cdot \boldsymbol{k}_m \boldsymbol{x}) - exp\left(\frac{-\sigma^2}{2}\right)\right] \quad (1)$$

Fig. 1. Left: Original rectangular dense grid. Center: Valleys and ridges sketch. Right: Grid adjusted to the sketch.

Fig. 2. Real part of the set of 40 (8 orientations × 5 scales) Gabor filters used in this paper

where $\boldsymbol{k}_m$ contains information about scale and orientation, and the same standard deviation $\sigma = 2\pi$ is used in both directions for the Gaussian envelope. Figure 2 shows the real part of the 40 Gabor filters used in this paper.

The region surrounding a pixel in the image is encoded by the convolution of the image patch with these filters, and the set of responses is called a jet, $\mathcal{J}$. So, a jet is a vector with 40 complex coefficients, and it provides information about an specific region of the image. At each shape-driven point $\boldsymbol{p_i} = [x_i, y_i]^T$, we get the following feature vector:

$$\{\mathcal{J}_{\boldsymbol{p}_i}\}_m = \sum_x \sum_y I(x,y)\psi_m(x_i - x, y_i - y) \qquad (2)$$

where $\{\mathcal{J}_{\boldsymbol{p}_i}\}_m$ stands for the m-th coefficient of the feature vector extracted from $\boldsymbol{p}_i$. So, for a given face with a set of points $\mathcal{P} = \{\boldsymbol{p_1}, \boldsymbol{p_2}, \ldots, \boldsymbol{p_n}\}$, we get n Gabor jets $\mathcal{R} = \{\mathcal{J}_{\boldsymbol{p}_1}, \mathcal{J}_{\boldsymbol{p}_2}, \ldots, \mathcal{J}_{\boldsymbol{p}_n}\}$.

2.2 Mapping Corresponding Features

Suppose that shape information has been extracted from two images, $\mathcal{F}_1$ and $\mathcal{F}_2$. Let $\mathcal{S}_1$ and $\mathcal{S}_2$ be the sketches for these incoming images, and let $\mathcal{P} = \{\boldsymbol{p_1}, \boldsymbol{p_2}, \ldots, \boldsymbol{p_n}\}$ be the set of points for $\mathcal{S}_1$, and $\mathcal{Q} = \{\boldsymbol{q_1}, \boldsymbol{q_2}, \ldots, \boldsymbol{q_n}\}$ the set of points for $\mathcal{S}_2$. In the SDGJ approach, there does not exist any a priori correspondence between points nor features (i.e. there is no label indicating which pair of points are matched). So, in order to compare jets from both faces, the authors of [4] make use of a point matching algorithm based on shape contexts [7], obtaining a function ξ that maps each point from $\mathcal{P}$ to a point within $\mathcal{Q}$:

$$\xi(i) : \boldsymbol{p_i} \Longrightarrow \boldsymbol{q}_{\xi(i)} \tag{3}$$

with an associated cost denoted by $C_{\boldsymbol{p}_i \boldsymbol{q}_{\xi(i)}}$ [4]. Finally, the feature vector from $\mathcal{F}_1$, $\mathcal{J}_{\boldsymbol{p}_i}$, will be compared to $\mathcal{J}_{\boldsymbol{q}_{\xi(i)}}$, extracted from $\mathcal{F}_2$.

3 Distance Between Faces

Let $\mathcal{R}_1 = \{\mathcal{J}_{\boldsymbol{p}_1}, \mathcal{J}_{\boldsymbol{p}_2}, \ldots, \mathcal{J}_{\boldsymbol{p}_n}\}$ be the set of jets calculated for $\mathcal{F}_1$ and $\mathcal{R}_2 = \{\mathcal{J}_{\boldsymbol{q}_1}, \mathcal{J}_{\boldsymbol{q}_2}, \ldots, \mathcal{J}_{\boldsymbol{q}_n}\}$ the set of jets extracted from $\mathcal{F}_2$. Before computing distances, each jet $\mathcal{J}$ is processed as follows:

1. Each complex coefficient is replaced by its modulus, obtaining $\mathcal{J}'$.
2. The obtained vector can be either normalized (to have unit L_1 or L_2 norm for instance) or not. Although some of the distances that will be introduced next, such as cosine distance, are invariant to these normalizations, some of them are not, and it seems that the concrete type of normalization applied to jets could be a critical point. In this paper, the three possibilities described above (no normalization, L_1 normalization and L_2 normalization) will be evaluated. Hence, given a vector, $\mathcal{J}'$, comprising the moduli of jet coefficients, we divide it by a normalization factor α given by:
   - No normalization: $\alpha = 1$.
   - L_1 normalization: $\alpha = \sum_i |\mathcal{J}'_i|$.
   - L_2 normalization: $\alpha = \sqrt{\sum_i (\mathcal{J}'_i)^2}$.

We will denote the resulting vector by $\boldsymbol{J}$ ($\boldsymbol{J} = \mathcal{J}'/\alpha$) and, for the sake of simplicity, we will maintain the name of jet. The distance function between the two faces, $\mathcal{DF}(\mathcal{F}_1, \mathcal{F}_2)$ is given by:

$$\mathcal{DF}(\mathcal{F}_1, \mathcal{F}_2) = \Upsilon_{i=1}^{n} \left\{ \mathcal{D}\left(\boldsymbol{J}_{\boldsymbol{p}_i}, \boldsymbol{J}_{\boldsymbol{q}_{\xi(i)}}\right) \right\} \tag{4}$$

where $\mathcal{D}\left(\boldsymbol{J}_{\boldsymbol{p}_i}, \boldsymbol{J}_{\boldsymbol{q}_{\xi(i)}}\right)$ represents the distance used to compare corresponding jets, and $\Upsilon_{i=1}^{n}\{\ldots\}$ stands for a generic combination rule of the n local distances $\mathcal{D}\left(\boldsymbol{J}_{\boldsymbol{p}_1}, \boldsymbol{J}_{\boldsymbol{q}_{\xi(1)}}\right), \ldots, \mathcal{D}\left(\boldsymbol{J}_{\boldsymbol{p}_n}, \boldsymbol{J}_{\boldsymbol{q}_{\xi(n)}}\right)$. In the EBGM approach [1] and other

Gabor-based face recognition systems, it is proposed to use a normalized dot product to compare jets. In this work, we assess the performance of the system varying $\mathcal{D}(\ldots)$, i.e. we compare the following distances:

1. Cosine distance (negated normalized dot product as used in [1]).

$$\mathcal{D}(X,Y) = -\cos(X,Y) = -\frac{\sum_{i=1}^{n} x_i y_i}{\sqrt{\sum_{i=1}^{n} x_i^2 \sum_{i=1}^{n} y_i^2}} \tag{5}$$

2. Manhattan distance (L_1 metrics or city block distance)

$$\mathcal{D}(X,Y) = L_1(X,Y) = \sum_{i=1}^{n} |x_i - y_i| \tag{6}$$

3. Squared Euclidean Distance (sum of squared errors-SSE)

$$\mathcal{D}(X,Y) = \mathrm{SSE}(X,Y) = \sum_{i=1}^{n} (x_i - y_i)^2 \tag{7}$$

4. Chi square distance

$$\mathcal{D}(X,Y) = \chi^2(X,Y) = \sum_{i=1}^{n} \frac{(x_i - y_i)^2}{x_i + y_i} \tag{8}$$

5. Modified Manhattan distance

$$\mathcal{D}(X,Y) = \frac{\sum_{i=1}^{n} |x_i - y_i|}{\sum_{i=1}^{n} |x_i| \sum_{i=1}^{n} |y_i|} \tag{9}$$

6. Correlation-based distance

$$\mathcal{D}(X,Y) = -\frac{n\sum_{i=1}^{n} x_i y_i - \sum_{i=1}^{n} x_i \sum_{i=1}^{n} y_i}{\sqrt{\left(n\sum_{i=1}^{n} x_i^2 - \left(\sum_{i=1}^{n} x_i\right)^2\right)\left(n\sum_{i=1}^{n} y_i^2 - \left(\sum_{i=1}^{n} y_i\right)^2\right)}} \tag{10}$$

7. Canberra distance

$$\mathcal{D}(X,Y) = \sum_{i=1}^{n} \frac{|x_i - y_i|}{|x_i| + |y_i|} \tag{11}$$

In the definition of all presented distances (equation (5) to equation (11)), n stands for the length of the vector, i.e. $n = 40$. It is easy to see that both cosine and correlation-based distances are invariant to α, i.e. the type of normalization (L_1, L_2 or no normalization at all) applied to jets does not change the result. It is also straightforward to realize that the Modified Manhattan distance is equivalent to the Manhattan distance when jets are normalized to have unit L_1 norm.

4 Face Authentication on the BANCA Database

4.1 Database and Experimental Setup

We have used the english part of the BANCA database on protocol Matched Controlled (MC) to test the different measures. For this database, face and voice were recorded using both high and low quality microphones and cameras. The subjects were captured in three different scenarios: controlled, degraded and adverse over 12 different sessions spanning three months. This subset of the BANCA database (english part) consists of 52 people, half men and half women.

In order to propose an experimental protocol, it is necessary to define a *development* set, on which the system can be adjusted by setting thresholds, etc. and an *evaluation* set, where the system performance can be assessed. For this reason, two disjoint subsets were created, namely $G1$ and $G2$, each one with 26 people (13 men and 13 women). So, when $G1$ is used as development set, $G2$ is used for evaluation and vice versa.

In the experiments carried out, three specific operating conditions corresponding to three different values of the Cost Ratio, $R = FAR/FRR$, namely $R = 0.1$, $R = 1$, $R = 10$ have been considered. Assuming equal a priori probabilities of genuine clients and impostor, these situations correspond to three quite distinct cases:

- $R = 0.1$, FAR is an order of magnitude less harmful than FRR,
- $R = 1$, FAR and FRR are equally harmful,
- $R = 10$, FAR is an order of magnitude more harmful than FRR.

The so-called Weighted Error Rate (WER) given by:

$$WER(R) = \frac{FRR + R \cdot FAR}{1 + R} \tag{12}$$

was calculated for the test data of groups $G1$ and $G2$ at the three different values of R. The average WER was reported as final performance measure.

4.2 Results

In order to provide a more complete set of results, we repeated the experiments using images at 3 different resolutions (55×51, 150×115 and 220×200 pixel images). We used the median rule to fuse the n local distances, i.e. $\Upsilon_{i=1}^{n} \{\ldots\} \equiv$ median. Moreover, in protocol MC there are 5 training images to build the client model. Whenever a test image claims a given identity, this

test face is compared to each of the 5 training images. Hence, we get 5 scores which are combined (using again the median rule) to obtain the final score ready for authentication. Tables 1, 2 and 3 show the obtained results changing the normalization factor (α) applied to jets (no normalization, L_1 normalization and L_2 normalization respectively). If no normalization is applied to jets, the best performing distance is cosine. The remaining choices achieve significantly

Table 1. Average WER (%) using several distance measures $\mathcal{D}\left(\boldsymbol{J}_{\boldsymbol{p}_i}, \boldsymbol{J}_{\boldsymbol{q}_{\xi(i)}}\right)$ to compare jets and different resolution of input images (jets are *not* normalized)

$\mathcal{D}\left(\boldsymbol{J}_{\boldsymbol{p}_i}, \boldsymbol{J}_{\boldsymbol{q}_{\xi(i)}}\right)$	Input Image Resolution 55 × 51	 150 × 115	 220 × 200
Cosine	**5.13**	**4.64**	**3.40**
Manhattan	8.54	10.56	13.16
SSE	8.45	9.45	12.60
χ^2	6.53	7.53	10.28
Modified Manhattan	8.18	9.71	12.72
Correlation	6.70	7.01	5.45
Canberra	6.10	5.05	5.11

Table 2. Average WER (%) using several distance measures $\mathcal{D}\left(\boldsymbol{J}_{\boldsymbol{p}_i}, \boldsymbol{J}_{\boldsymbol{q}_{\xi(i)}}\right)$ to compare jets and different resolution of input images (jets are normalized to have unit L_1 norm)

$\mathcal{D}\left(\boldsymbol{J}_{\boldsymbol{p}_i}, \boldsymbol{J}_{\boldsymbol{q}_{\xi(i)}}\right)$	Input Image Resolution 55 × 51	 150 × 115	 220 × 200
Cosine	5.13	4.64	3.40
Manhattan	5.28	3.73	**2.90**
SSE	**4.49**	**3.53**	3.17
χ^2	5.33	4.03	3.01
Modified Manhattan	5.28	3.73	**2.90**
Correlation	6.70	7.01	5.45
Canberra	5.26	3.84	3.63

Table 3. Average WER (%) using several distance measures $\mathcal{D}\left(\boldsymbol{J}_{\boldsymbol{p}_i}, \boldsymbol{J}_{\boldsymbol{q}_{\xi(i)}}\right)$ to compare jets and different resolution of input images (jets are normalized to have unit L_2 norm)

$\mathcal{D}\left(\boldsymbol{J}_{\boldsymbol{p}_i}, \boldsymbol{J}_{\boldsymbol{q}_{\xi(i)}}\right)$	Input Image Resolution 55 × 51	 150 × 115	 220 × 200
Cosine	5.13	4.64	3.40
Manhattan	5.93	6.20	4.68
SSE	5.14	4.61	3.42
χ^2	5.60	5.29	3.80
Modified Manhattan	**4.75**	**3.10**	**3.34**
Correlation	6.70	7.01	5.45
Canberra	5.07	3.69	3.88

worse results for all resolutions (except Canberra distance, with similar performance). In the EBGM approach [1], the authors did not apply any normalization to jets (at least, they did not state it explicitely) and these results may support their choice of the cosine distance for jet comparison. However, the use of L_1 and L_2 normalization factors (tables 2 and 3) leads to completely different conclusions. Cosine is outperformed by other distances such as SSE or Modified Manhattan distance (MMD). If we compare the results obtained, for instance, with the MMD varying the normalization factor, we see that impressive improvements are obtained with the use of L_1 and L_2 normalization factors (WER decreases from 12.72% to 3.34–2.90% using 220×200 pixel images). Hence, we conclude that the concrete type of normalization that is applied to jets is, in fact, a critical point. In [14], the authors observed that the Manhattan distance outperformed cosine after identification experiments. According to our results, Manhattan outperforms cosine when L_1 normalization is used. Although the authors of [14] do not describe whether they have normalized their jets or not, we have obtained results supporting their finding. As stated in Section 3, both cosine and correlation-based distances are invariant to the tested normalization factors, and this is reflected in the obtained results. It is also interesting to note that, in general terms, error rates decrease (or stays approximately equal) as long as the resolution of input images grows. A clear exception occurs when testing Manhattan, SSE, χ^2 and Modified Manhattan distances without normalization. Further research is needed in order to better understand this behavior.

Other results on BANCA. The CSU Face Identification Evaluation System (`http://www.cs.colostate.edu/evalfacerec/index.html`), including several face recognition techniques such as PCA and PCA+LDA, was tested on the BANCA database using protocol MC to provide baseline results for the ICBA 2004 face authentication contest [9]. These baseline performances can be found in `http://www.ee.surrey.ac.uk/banca/icba2004/csuresults.html`. The lowest average WER's using PCA and PCA+LDA were 9.71% and 6.25% respectively. On the other hand, the best performance in this competition (with manual face localization) was achieved by the Université Catholique de Louvain with an average WER of 1.95%.

5 Conclusions and Further Research

In this work, we have proposed an empirical evaluation of different combinations of normalization and distance measures for Gabor jet comparison. The SDGJ algorithm was tested on the BANCA database with 3 input image resolutions, 3 distinct normalization factors and 7 distance measures to compare jets. It has been shown that:

- The performance of a given distance strongly depends on the concrete preprocessing applied to jets.
- When no normalization ($\alpha = 1$) is used, the cosine distance outperforms the remaining ones. Although the authors of [1] did not explicitely state whether they have normalized their jets or not, this result would support their choice.

– The use of L_1 and L_2 normalization factors lead to completely different results, turning out that other distances, such as SSE or MMD, achieve better performance than the cosine measure.

Although we have shown that there exist better choices than cosine distance for Gabor jet comparison, no theoretical reasons supporting this fact have been provided. Recently [16], it has been demonstrated that Gabor coefficients can be accurately modeled using Generalized Gaussian Distributions (GGD's) and this finding opens new possibilities in terms of selecting optimal ways to compare jets from a theoretical point of view.

No discriminant analysis of jet coefficients has been applied, i.e. we have considered that all coefficients have the same discriminative power. Thus, the next step will be to select the most important Gabor jet coefficients according to their classification ability, a selection that should depend on the concrete facial region we are analyzing. Moreover, the function $\Upsilon_{i=1}^{n}\{\ldots\}$ used to combine the n local distances should weigh the different jet contributions according to the discriminative power of the facial regions from where they are extracted.

Acknowledgments

Part of this work was performed during the visit of Daniel González-Jiménez and Manuele Bicego to the CWI, in the framework of the Biosecure Network of Excellence mobility program.

References

1. Wiskott, L., Fellous, J.M., Kruger, N., von der Malsburg, C.: Face Recognition by Elastic Bunch Graph Matching. IEEE Transactions on PAMI 19(7), 775–779 (1997)
2. Duc, B., Fischer, S., Bigun, J.: Face Authentication with Gabor Information on Deformable Graphs. IEEE Transactions on Image Processing 8(4), 504–516 (1999)
3. Smeraldi, F., Bigun, J.: Retinal Vision applied to Facial Features Detection and Face Authentication. Pattern Recognition Letters 23(4), 463–475 (2002)
4. González-Jiménez, D., Alba-Castro, J.L.: Shape Contexts and Gabor Features for Face Description and Authentication. In: Proceedings IEEE ICIP 2005, pp. 962–965 (2005)
5. Shen, L., Bai, L.: A review on Gabor wavelets for Face Recognition. Pattern Analysis and Applications 9, 273–292 (2006)
6. López, A.M., Lumbreras, F., Serrat, J., Villanueva, J.J.: Evaluation of Methods for Ridge and Valley Detection. IEEE Transactions on PAMI 21(4), 327–335 (1999)
7. Belongie, S., Malik, J., Puzicha, J.: Shape Matching and Object Recognition Using Shape Contexts. IEEE Transactions on PAMI 24(24), 509–522 (2002)
8. Bailly-Bailliere, E., et al.: The BANCA Database and Evaluation Protocol. In: Kittler, J., Nixon, M.S. (eds.) AVBPA 2003. LNCS, vol. 2688, pp. 625–638. Springer, Heidelberg (2003)
9. Messer, K., et al.: Face Authentication Test on the BANCA Database. In: Zhang, D., Jain, A.K. (eds.) ICBA 2004. LNCS, vol. 3072, pp. 8–15. Springer, Heidelberg (2004)

10. Bicego, M., Lagorio, A., Grosso, E., Tistarelli, M.: On the Use of SIFT Features for Face Authentication. In: Proc. of IEEE CVPR Workshop on Biometrics, p. 35 (2006)
11. Kohir, V.V., Desai, U.B.: Face Recognition Using DCT-HMM Approach. In: Proc. Workshop on Advances in Facial Image Analysis and Recognition Technology (AFI-ART), Freiburg, Germany (1998)
12. Lowe, D.G.: Distinctive Image Features from Scale-Invariant Keypoints. Int. Journal of Computer Vision 60(2), 91–110 (2004)
13. Ahonen, T., Hadid, A., Pietikainen, M.: Face description with local binary patterns: Application to face recognition. IEEE Transactions on Pattern Analysis and Machine Intelligence 28(12), 2037–2041.
14. Jiao, F., Gao, W., Shan, S.: A Face Recognition Method Based on Local Feature Analysis. In: ACCV 2002, Melbourne, Australia, pp. 188–192 (2002)
15. Zhao, W., Chellappa, R., Phillips, P.J., Rosenfeld, A.: Face Recognition: A Literature Survey. ACM Computing Surveys 35, 399–458 (2003)
16. González-Jiménez, D., Pérez-González, F., Comesaña-Alfaro, P., Pérez-Freire, L., Alba-Castro, J.L.: Modeling Gabor Coefficients Via Generalized Gaussian Distributions for Face Recognition. In: IEEE International Conference on Image Processing 2007 (accepted)

Fingerprint Matching with an Evolutionary Approach

W. Sheng, G. Howells, K. Harmer, M.C. Fairhurst, and F. Deravi

Department of Electronics,
University of Kent, Canterbury,
Kent, CT2 7NT, United Kingdom
{W.Sheng,K.Harmer,W.G.J.Howells,M.C.Fairhurst,
F.Deravi}@kent.ac.uk

Abstract. Minutiae point pattern matching is probably the most common approach to fingerprint verification. Although many minutiae point pattern matching algorithms have been proposed, reliable automatic fingerprint verification remains a challenging problem, both with respect to recovering the optimal alignment as well as to the construction of adequate matching function. In this paper, we develop an evolutionary approach for fingerprint matching by combining the use of the global search functionality of a genetic algorithm with a local improvement operator to search for the optimal global alignment between two minutiae sets. Further, we define a reliable matching function for fitness computation. The proposed approach was evaluated on two public domain collections of fingerprint images and compared with previous work. Experimental results show that our approach is reliable and practical for fingerprint verification, and outperforms the traditional genetic algorithm based method.

Keywords: Fingerprints, matching/verification, alignment, minutiae, genetic algorithms.

1 Introduction

Fingerprints are graphical ridge and valley patterns on the tips of human fingers. Owing to their uniqueness and permanence, the use of fingerprints is considered to be one of the most reliable methods of personal verification. Fingerprints are today among the most popularly used biometric modality in automatic verification systems. Due to the continuing needs of law enforcement and interest from the developers of civilian applications, automated fingerprint verification systems are becoming increasingly widespread and are being extensively researched by the pattern recognition and image processing communities. Although fingerprints possess much discriminatory information, and although significant progress in automating the verification process has been made, reliable automatic fingerprint verification is still a challenging problem [4].

The uniqueness of fingerprints has been well established [22], and can be determined by the overall pattern of ridges and valleys as well as the local ridge discontinuities termed "minutiae". It is widely believed that the minutiae are the most discriminating and reliable features [17, 29] present in the fingerprints. For this reason, they are the most important and common features used in automatic fingerprint verification systems. The two prominent types of minutiae commonly used in automatic fingerprint verification are ridge ending and ridge bifurcation. The representation of a fingerprint pattern thus comprises all detected ridge endings and ridge bifurcations in a so called *minutiae set*.

S.-W. Lee and S.Z. Li (Eds.): ICB 2007, LNCS 4642, pp. 484–492, 2007.

By representing the minutiae set as a point pattern, the fingerprint verification problem can be viewed as a minutiae point pattern matching problem. Suppose a minutiae template set P is composed of m points, $P = \{p_1, p_2, \ldots, p_m\}$, and a query minutiae set Q is composed of N points, $Q = \{q_1, q_2, \ldots, q_n\}$. Each minutia is usually described by parameters (x, y, α), where (x, y) are the pixel coordinates of the minutia with respect to the image frame and α is the orientation of the minutia, which is defined as the angle that the ridge associated with the minutia makes with the horizontal axis [17]. Typically, ridge orientations are restricted to the range $[0, \pi)$, so that directions θ and $\theta+\pi$ have the same orientation. It should be noted that most minutiae representation schemes do not distinguish endings from bifurcations since the type of a minutia can be easily interchanged by acquisition noise or pressure differences during acquisition. However, the orientation remains the same when this occurs. The alignment between a template and a query minutiae set can be simplified as an affine transformation $G(t_x, t_y, \theta, s)$ composed of four parameters: t_x, t_y, θ, and s, where t_x and t_y are the translations along the x and y directions, respectively, θ is the rotation angle and s is a scaling factor. Thus, the transformation $F(q_i) = (x_i', y_i', \alpha_i')$ of a minutia $q_i = (x_i, y_i, \alpha_i)$ can be written as follows:

$$\begin{bmatrix} x_i' \\ y_i' \\ \alpha_i' \end{bmatrix} = s \begin{bmatrix} \cos\theta & -\sin\theta & 0 \\ \sin\theta & \cos\theta & 0 \\ 0 & 0 & 1/s \end{bmatrix} \begin{bmatrix} x_i \\ y_i \\ \alpha_i \end{bmatrix} + \begin{bmatrix} t_x \\ t_y \\ \theta \end{bmatrix}.$$

The fingerprint verification process can then be defined as the problem of finding the transformation between the template and query minutiae sets which can optimize a given matching function.

Due to the large number of possible translations, rotations and scalings, finding the best alignment between two point patterns is an extremely difficult problem. A number of algorithms [5, 9, 10, 12, 13, 14, 15, 23, 25, 26] have been proposed in the literature. A common technique for these algorithms is to use local features associated with minutiae and/or their spatial properties to reduce the exponential number of search paths. These methods typically recover the transformation by choosing a reference minutia or minutia group (in which minutiae are close to each other) from the template and the query fingerprint, respectively. The two sets of minutiae are then aligned according to local structures of the two references. We refer to these methods as single reference based approaches. This approach can guarantee satisfactory alignments of regions adjacent to the reference minutia or minutia group. However, alignments of regions far away from the reference minutia or minutia group are usually not so satisfactory. This is largely because the alignment which tends to be found is locally strong, yet poor in areas distant to the local structure it has matched. Naturally, researchers have explored the use of a size-changeable bounding box [10, 12, 13].

Another alternative approach is to find a transformation in order to globally align two sets of minutiae. This approach tends to evenly align two sets of minutiae and thus one can use a size-fixed bounding box to identify corresponding minutiae. Zhu et al. [28] have proposed a method which aligns two sets of minutiae based on multiple pairs of reference minutiae. This method depends highly on the initialization of the minutiae pairs. Since the global alignment is a computationally intractable problem, naturally inspired evolutionary optimization algorithms have recently been a source of interest for minutiae point pattern matching [16, 24]. Tan and Bhanu [24] proposed the use of a traditional genetic algorithm [11] for fingerprint matching. Le et al. [16] employed the technique of fuzzy evolutionary programming to match two sets of minutiae. These methods try to identify the optimal or near optimal global alignment between two minutiae sets and their experimental results are promising. However, they may take a large amount of time to converge, mainly because these methods employ either the simple evolutionary algorithm or its variants, which may not be well suited to fine-tuning search in complex search spaces.

In this paper, we develop a novel evolution based algorithm for fingerprint matching that follows the scheme of global minutiae alignment. In contrast to previous methods, our proposed algorithm hybridizes a genetic algorithm (GA) with a local improvement operator. Further, we define a reliable and discriminating matching function for fitness computation by combining the globally matched minutiae pairs with the result of the minutiae's local feature similarity based on the product rule.

2 Evolution Based Algorithm for Fingerprint Matching

In this section, we present the details of our proposed algorithm, which combines the use of a global search via a genetic algorithm (GA) with a local improvement operator to search for the optimal global matching between two minutiae sets. Abstractly, the proposed algorithm (called EAFM) consists of selecting parents for reproduction, performing a modified arithmetic crossover with the parents, applying mutation to the offspring, running a local improvement operator on each offspring, and carrying out a competition replacement. The evolution is terminated when one of the following two stopping criteria is met: 1) the fitness value of the best individual has not changed for N generations or 2) the fitness value of the best individual exceeds a certain threshold value, which means the two fingerprints are verified as from the same finger. The output of the algorithm is the best solution encountered during the evolution. The algorithm may be expressed concisely as follows with the subsequent sections elaborating on the individual component phases:

Step 1. Randomly initialize P sets of chromosomes, which encode alignment configurations, based on a real-parameter representation (see Section 2.1).

Step 2. Calculate the fitness value according to the method described in Section 2.4 for each individual chromosome in the initial population.

Step 3. Repeat the following sub-steps (a) to (e) until a stopping criterion is met.

- a) Select the pairing individuals based on the k-fold tournament selection method [8]. This procedure is repeated until $P/2$ parent pairs are selected.
- b) Generate intermediate offspring by applying a modified arithmetic crossover and then perform Gaussian mutation on the offspring (see Section 2.2).
- c) Run the local improvement operator on the offspring and update the offspring (see Section 2.3).
- d) Calculate the fitness value for each of the offspring according to the method described in Section 2.4.
- e) Create a new generation of size P from the best individual of the previous generation and the best offspring that resulted from crossover, mutation and local improvement operations.

Step 4. Provide the alignment configuration for the terminal population individual with the best fitness.

Algorithm 1. An evolution based algorithm for fingerprint matching

2.1 Representation and Initialization

Our representation for the individual chromosome consists of a vector of four real numbers, where the first two positions represent translations along the x and y directions respectively, the next position represents the rotation angle, and the last position represents the scaling factor. Each individual in the population is constructed by random assignment of a real number to each of the attributes of the solution. The initial values are constrained to be in the range of the attribute to which they are assigned (determined empirically from the experimental data sets) but are otherwise random.

2.2 Crossover and Mutation

Crossover is a probabilistic process that exchanges information between a pair of parents to generate two offspring. The arithmetic crossover technique [8] has been used as the reproduction operator in the EAFM. Traditional arithmetic crossover linearly combines two parent chromosomes to produce two new offspring according to the following equations:

$$Offspring1 = a * Parent1 + (1-a) * Parent2, \quad (1)$$

$$Offspring2 = (1-a) * Parent1 + a * Parent2, \quad (2)$$

where $a \in [0,1)$ is a random weighting factor. In our approach, we apply either equation (1) or (2) randomly to produce only one single offspring. This helps to save time in processing the other similar offspring. The crossover is performed on each paired parent.

After crossover, a low probability of Gaussian mutation is applied to the offspring. Gaussian mutation adds a unit Gaussian-distributed random value to the chosen attribute value. The new attribute value is clipped if it falls outside of the lower or upper bounds of that attribute.

2.3 Local Improvement Operation

GAs are able to escape from local optima by means of crossover and mutation operators. However, they are not well suited for fine-tuning structures which are close to optimal solutions [8], and this results in their exhibiting a large execution time. To improve the time efficiency, incorporation of local improvement operators into the regeneration step of GAs, which called hybrid GAs, is essential. Hybrid GAs have been shown to be very effective for many combinatorial optimization problems [1, 4, 18, 21, 27]. In this subsection we present the local improvement operator to effectively design a hybrid GA for minutiae point pattern matching.

The local improvement operator is inspired by the iterated closest point (ICP) algorithm [3]. The ICP is a widely used heuristic for the alignment of 3D geometric models. It utilizes the *nearest-neighbour* relationship to assign a binary correspondence at each step. This estimate of the correspondence is then used to refine the transformation, and vice versa. This iterative scheme is known to converge fast [6]. However, it is sensitive to its initial rotations and translations, and susceptible to local optima. Its performance degenerates quickly with outliers (point features exist in one point-set that have no corresponding points in the other), which is common in fingerprint minutiae point pattern matching problem.

In order to improve the computational efficiency, we design a local improvement operator based on one iteration of the ICP to fine-tune new offspring during each generation, after the regeneration step. This operator is summarized below:

Step 1. Extract the transformation information encoded in the individual solution. Apply the transformation to the query minutiae set.
Step 2. Compute the closest point pairs between the two minutiae sets by estimating the Euclidean distance between the minutiae coordinates. Collect corresponding pairs if they satisfy the following geometric constraints: 1) the Euclidean distance does not exceed a certain value Δd and 2) the angular difference between their directions is less than a certain tolerance $\Delta\theta$ (see Section 4.2 for setting of the parameters Δd and $\Delta\theta$). To avoid a minutia being doubly used for pairing, we mark the minutiae that have already been paired.
Step 3. Compute the new transformation, in the sense of minimizing the sum of squared Euclidean distance error among the collected corresponding pairs.
Step 4. Update the individual solution with the new transformation.

Algorithm 2. A local improvement operator

2.4 Fitness Computation

The fitness of an individual indicates the degree of suitability of the solution it represents. Here, we introduce a local feature similarity to define a reliable and discriminating matching function to compute the fitness of individual solutions. The minutiae local feature proposed by Tico and Kuosmanen [25] has been used for designing such a matching function. In [25], each minutia defines a local structure, which is called a *minutia descriptor*. The minutia descriptor comprises information about the orientation field sampled in a circular pattern in a broad region around the minutia point. The circular pattern consists of L concentric circles of radii r_l, ($1 \le l \le L$), each one comprising K_l sampling points $p_{k,l}$, ($1 \le k \le K_l$), equally distributed along its circumference. Let $a = \{\alpha_{k,l}\}$ and $b = \{\beta_{k,l}\}$ be two minutia descriptors. The similarity function between a and b is defined as:

$$S(a,b) = (1/K)\sum_{l=1}^{L}\sum_{k=1}^{K_l}\exp(-16 * \Lambda(\alpha_{k,l}, \beta_{k,l})), \quad (3)$$

where $K = \sum_{l=1}^{L} K_l$, $\alpha_{k,l}$ and $\beta_{k,l}$ are the local ridge orientations estimated at $p_{k,l}$ for descriptors a and b, respectively, and $\Lambda(\alpha_{k,l}, \beta_{k,l})$ is the orientation distance between angles, which takes values between 0 and 1.

The minutia descriptors contain useful discriminatory information. Additionally, they can tolerate some deformation since they are formed from only a small area of the fingerprint. Thus, the similarity of minutia descriptors can be used to increase the reliability of the matching between two minutiae sets. Further, to make the matching function more discriminatory, we combine the globally matched minutiae pairs with the result of the minutiae's local feature similarity based on the product rule. Now the matching function can be defined as:

$$fitness = \frac{1}{n}\sum_{i=1}^{n} S(a_i, b_i) \times \frac{2n}{(q+t)}, \tag{4}$$

where t and q are the number of minutiae located inside the intersection of the two fingerprint images for template and query respectively. The number of matched pairs, n, is identified using the same geometric constraints as those described in Section 2.4.

For each individual, the transformation encoded within it is first extracted, then subsequently we apply the transformation onto the query minutiae set Q to obtain the set Q' comprising the transformed minutiae set. Given the minutiae sets P and Q', the number of matched minutiae, n, is first computed. If n is less than a threshold F_n, then let the fitness of the individual be f=-1/n ($1 \leq n \leq F_n$) or f=-1 (n=0). In this case, it makes no sense to evaluate the matching function. Otherwise, the fitness of the individual is defined according to equation (4), so that maximization of the fitness is equivalent to finding the maximum number of matched minutiae points with the maximum average local feature similarity.

3 Data Sets and Parameter Settings

In this section, we describe the data sets used in the experiments. This is followed by a description of the implementation parameter settings for the proposed algorithm. Two public domain collections of fingerprint images, labeled DB_1 and DB_3, proposed in [32] as part of the FVC2002 Fingerprint Verification Competition were used in the experiments. The fingerprint images were captured using fingerprint scanners and contain a wide variety of fingerprint image qualities. Each of the two data collections comprises 800 fingerprint images captured at a resolution of 500dpi, from 100 fingers (eight impressions per finger). The minutiae information of the data sets is derived using the method described in [7].

The EAFM has a few parameters which need to be set. These include the GA parameters, the ranges used for population initialization and several thresholds. The values of GA parameters and ranges are determined experimentally on the above data sets. To establish these values, all other variables were held constant with only the one to be established changing, and five runs were completed for a wide range of values in each case. The results from each of the five runs were averaged and the best average was selected. Both the matching accuracy and efficiency of results were used in determining the values of variables. The crossover and mutation probabilities are set to be 0.9 and 0.02 respectively. Generally, we have found that a crossover rate of 0.8-0.95 with a mutation rate of 0.01-0.05 offer best results. The order of tournament selection controls how quickly a population is “taken over” by dominant individuals in the population [2]. We used a tournament order of three. The number of generations, N, used to terminate the evolution and the population size, p, are set to be 5 and 20, respectively. A larger value of either p or N may lead to a longer running time, however, with no significant improvement of the matching performance. The ranges of the rotation angle, scaling factor, translations along the x and y directions are set to be [-0.6, 0.6], [0.9, 1.1], [-150, 150] and [-150, 150], respectively. The threshold of F_n for fitness computation is set to be four. The minutiae matching threshold values of Δd and $\Delta\theta$ are set as 15 and 0.195, respectively, which were established in [22] for fingerprint images scanned at 500dpi resolution.

4 Experimental Results

In this section, we evaluate the EAFM and compare its performance with a traditional GA based fingerprint matching method described in [24]. All the results reported in this section were obtained with simulations on a PC with an Intel^{TM} Pentium^{TM} 4 running under WindowsXP Professional.

Before discussing the comparative results, we first briefly describe the method to be compared. The GA based fingerprint matching method was recently proposed by Tan and Bhanu [24]. In this method, a GA with the traditional roulette wheel selection, uniform crossover, and binary flip mutation was used with a binary code representation, which represents alignment parameters, for fingerprint matching. The fitness function is based on the local properties of each minutia-triplet.

We mainly concern the performance with respect to matching accuracy and efficiency. Therefore, we report the Equal Error Rate (EER) and average matching time estimated using the experimental protocol proposed in [19]. The EER, which is commonly used to summarize the accuracy of a matching system [20], is defined as the error rate where the system's false match rate equals its false non-match rate. Table 1 lists the results of the EER values and average matching time of the two methods over the two data sets introduced above.

Table 1. EERs and average matching times estimated on DB_1 and DB_3 for the two methods (EAFM and Tan et al.'s method)

Methods	DB_1		DB_3	
	EER (%)	**Average matching time (s)**	**EER (%)**	**Average matching time (s)**
EAFM	1.1	2.91	3.6	3.07
Tan et al.'s method [24]	1.5	6.74	4.2	7.26

The results in Table 1 show that the EAFM is a reliable and practical matching algorithm. Compared with Tan et al.'s method, the EAFM is able to achieve lower error rate in both data sets. The EER of Tan et al.'s method turns out to be 1.5% and 4.2%, while our algorithm returns about 1.1% and 3.6% on DB_1 and DB_3, respectively. Further, matching operations of our algorithm are faster than the Tan et al.'s method. For example, Tan et al.'s method needs 6.74 second on DB_1 while our method takes about 2.91 second on average. The improvement of matching efficiency of our proposed algorithm is mainly due to the use of local improvement operation.

5 Conclusion

In this paper, we have reported on the design and implementation of a novel evolution based algorithm for fingerprint matching which seeks to identify the optimal global matching between two minutiae sets. A GA based evolution with local improvement hybridization is at the heart of the proposed algorithm. This has been developed with the particular goal of improving the efficiency of identifying optimal, or near optimal, global matching between two fingerprint minutiae sets. Another key aspect of the proposed algorithm is the use of a reliable matching function for fitness computation. The experimental results confirm that the EAFM is a reliable and practical matching algorithm. The algorithm can achieve accurate matching results faster than the traditional GA based global fingerprint matching method.

References

Areibi, S., Yang, Z.: Effective memetic algorithms for VLSI design automation = genetic algorithms + local search + multi-level clustering. Evolutionary Computation 12(3), 327–353 (2004)

Bäck, T., Kursawe, F.: Evolutionary algorithms for fuzzy logic: A brief overview. Proc. Information Processing and Management of Uncertainty in Knowledge-Based Systems, 659–664 (1994)

Besl, P.J., McKay, N.D.: A method for registration of 3D shapes. IEEE Trans. Pattern Anal. and Machine Intell. 14, 239–256 (1992)

Branke, J., Middendorf, M., Schneider, F.: Improved heuristics and a genetic algorithm for finding short supersequences. OR Spektrum 20(1), 39–45 (1998)

Chen, X., Tian, J., Yang, X.: A new algorithm for distorted fingerprints matching based on normalized fuzzy similarity measure. IEEE Transactions on Image Processing 15(3), 767–776 (2006)

Chui, H., Rangarajan, A.: A new point matching algorithm for nonrigid registration. Comput. Vision and Image Und. 89, 114–141 (2003)

Garris, M.D., McCabe, R.M., Watson, C.I., Wilson, C.L.: User's guide to NIST fingerprint image software (NFIS). NISTIR 6813, National Institute of Standards and Technology, Gaithersburg, MD (2001)

Goldberg, E.: Genetic Algorithms in Search, Optimization, and Machine Learning. Addison-Wesley, Reading, Mass (1989)

He, Y., Tian, J., Li, L., Chen, H., Yang, X.: Fingerprint matching based on global comprehensive similarity. IEEE Transactions on Pattern Analysis and Machine Intelligence 28(6), 850–862 (2006)

He, Y., Tian, J., Luo, X., Zhang, T.: Image enhancement and minutiae matching in fingerprint verification. Pattern Recognition Letters 24, 1349–1360 (2003)

Holland, J.H.: Adaptation in Natural and Artificial Systems. University of Michigan Press, Ann Arbor (1975)

Jain, K., Hong, L., Bolle, R.: On-line fingerprint verification. IEEE Transactions on Pattern Analysis and Machine Intelligence 19(4), 302–314 (1997)

Jain, K., Hong, L., Pankanti, S., Bolle, R.: An identity-authentication system using fingerprints. Proc. IEEE 85(9), 1365–1388 (1997)

Jea, T.Y., Govindaraju, V.: A minutia-based partial fingerprint recognition system. Pattern Recognition 38, 1672–1684 (2004)

Jiang, X., Yau, W.: Fingerprint minutiae matching based on the local and global structures. In: Proc. 15th International Conference on Pattern Recognition, pp. 1038–1041 (2000)

Le, T.V., Cheung, K.Y., Nguyen, M.H.: A fingerprint recognizer using fuzzy evolutionary programming. In: Proc. of 34th International Conference on System Sciences (2001)

Lee, H.C., Gaensslen, R.E.: Advances in Fingerprint Technology. Elsevier, New York (1991)

Li, F., Morgan, R., Williams, D.: Hybrid genetic approaches to ramping rate constrained dynamic economic dispatch. Electric Power Systems Research 43(2), 97–103 (1997)

Maio, D., Maltoni, R., Cappelli, J., Wayman, L., Jain, A.K.: FVC2002: second fingerprint verification competition. In: Proc. International Conference on Pattern Recognition, pp. 811–814 (2002)

Maltoni, D., Maio, D., Jain, A.K., Prabhakar, S.: Handbook of Fingerprint Recognition. Springer, Heidelberg (2003)

Merz, P., Freisleben, B.: Memetic algorithms and the fitness landscape of the graph bipartitioning problem. LNCS, pp. 765–774 (1998)

Pankanti, S., Prabhakar, S., Jain, A.K.: On the individuality of fingerprints. IEEE Trans. Patt. Anal. Mach. Intell. 24(8), 1010–1025 (2002)

Qi, J., Shi, Z., Zhao, X., Wang, Y.: A robust fingerprint matching method. In: 7th IEEE Workshops on Application of Computer Vision, pp. 105–110 (2005)

Tan, X., Bhanu, B.: Fingerprint matching by genetic algorithms. Pattern Recognition 39(3), 465–477 (2006)

Tico, M., Kuosmanen, P.: Fingerprint matching using an orientation-based minutia descriptor. IEEE Transactions on Pattern Analysis and Machine Intelligence 25(8), 1009–1014 (2003)

Tong, X., Huang, J., Tang, X., Shi, D.: Fingerprint minutiae matching using the adjacent feature vector. Pattern Recognition Letters 26(9), 1337–1345 (2005)

Whitley, D.: Modeling hybrid genetic algorithms. In: Winter, G., Periaux, J., Galan, M., Cuesta, P. (eds.) Genetic Algorithms in Engineering and Computer Science, pp. 191–201. John Wiley, Chichester (1995)

Zhu, J., Yin, P., Zhang, G.M.: Fingerprint matching based on global alignment of multiple reference minutiae. Pattern Recognition 38(10), 1685–1694 (2005)

The Science of Fingerprints: Classification and Uses. Federal Bureau of Investigation, Washington, DC (1984)

Stability Analysis of Constrained Nonlinear Phase Portrait Models of Fingerprint Orientation Images

Jun Li[1], Wei-Yun Yau[2], Jiangang Wang[2], and Wee Ser[1]

[1] CSP, School of EEE, Nanyang Technological University, 639798, Singapore,
{junl,ewser}@ntu.edu.sg

[2] Institute for Infocomm Research, 21 Heng Mui Keng Terrace, 119613, Singapore
{wyyau,jgwang}@i2r.a-star.edu.sg

Abstract. Model based methods to compute the fingerprint orientation images were considered more robust and accurate than the gradient based methods as model based methods considered not only the local regions but also the global orientations. This paper presented the stability analysis of the constrained nonlinear phase portrait models of fingerprint orientation images. Thereafter, the constrained nonlinear phase portrait models were revised according to the stability analysis so that they were able to avoid the potential errors due to the stability. Experimental results were presented to demonstrate the revised algorithm.

Keywords: Fingerprint, Orientation Models, Stability Analysis.

1 Introduction

In recent decades, automatic fingerprint identification system has attracted significant interest among the scientific research community. Though large amount of effort has been made in both the academic and industrial communities, there are still unsolved problems. Noisy image processing and large scale database processing are two typical problems.

Fingerprint images consist of oriented texture. Therefore the orientation information plays a very important role in fingerprint processing. Moreover, the orientation of the fingerprint follows a certain structure that is not random. Such oriented structure provides a possibility to recover the orientation information in fingerprints corrupted by noise, even for a large noise patch which cannot be solved by the traditional gradient based methods. Accurate reconstruction of the orientations is useful for fingerprint filtering, segmentation, classification and recognition.

The orientation can be obtained using gradient based method [1] as shown in Eqn. 1:

$$\theta(x_i, y_i) = \frac{1}{2}\arctan\left(\frac{\sum 2G_xG_y}{\sum(G_x^2 - G_y^2)}\right) + \frac{\pi}{2} \tag{1}$$

where G_x and G_y is the gradient vectors along the x and y components respectively computed in the window region centered at (x_i, y_i).

S.-W. Lee and S.Z. Li (Eds.): ICB 2007, LNCS 4642, pp. 493–502, 2007.

This gradient based method has an assumption that there is a single dominant orientation. Otherwise, the result will not be meaningful. This assumption implies that if a fingerprint orientation has been corrupted by noise, a trustworthy orientation cannot be estimated. To overcome the noisy influence, a low pass filter is generally adopted. While a low pass filter focuses on a local region, it is not able to solve the large patch of noise.

Besides the gradient based methods, the model based methods have been proposed to improve the estimation of the orientation image [2,3,4,5,6]. Model based methods were motivated by the fact that the fingerprint ridges flow with a certain regularity except for the limited number of singular regions. Therefore, mathematical description of such orientation field can be achieved. The most attractive feature of the orientation model is that it has capability to give a global constraint to each point in an orientation image. When reconstructing one orientation in an orientation image, all the other orientations will show their contribution. Thus, these methods are able to overcome the limitation of filter-based methods, which only considers the nearby orientations.

Several model-based methods have been proposed in the literature. we coarsely divide the model based method into two categories: Zero-Pole based method and phase portrait based methods.

A: Zero-Pole Model Based Methods

In 1993, Sherlock *et al.* presented an approach to model the fingerprint orientation topology [2]. The basic mathematical description of this model is given in Eqn 2.

$$O_m(z) = O_0 + \frac{1}{2}\Sigma_{l=1}^{L} arg(z - z_{c_l}) - \Sigma_{k=1}^{K} arg(z - z_{d_k}) \tag{2}$$

where z_{c_l} and z_{d_k} are the core point positions and delta point positions respectively; z is the position of an arbitrary point; O_0 is an initial or background orientation; O_m is the orientation at z; K and L are the numbers of delta points and core points respectively.

The zero-pole model provides not a quantitative but a qualitative analysis of the fingerprint orientation as it cannot differentiate two orientation fields with the same singular points. It also cannot model the fingerprint without any singular points.

In 1996, Vizcaya *et al.* revised the zero-pole model to a nonlinear orientation model [3]. Eqn. 3 describes this model in a mathematical form.

$$O_m(z) = O_0 + \frac{1}{2}\Sigma_{l=1}^{L} g_{c_l}(arg(z - z_{c_l})) - \Sigma_{k=1}^{K} g_{d_k}(arg(z - z_{d_k})) \tag{3}$$

The difference between Eqn. 2 and Eqn. 3 is the addition of the nonlinear function g. g is some family of nonlinear functions that preserve the singularity at the given point. Essentially, g is decided by the mean-square orientation error between the actual orientation estimated from the fingerprint images and the orientation provided by the zero-pole model.

Zhou and Gu [4] presented another complex model as shown in Eqn. 4 in 2004, which was also based on the zero-pole model while the high order rational function $f(z)$ is used as the nonlinear correction instead.

$$O_m = \frac{1}{2} arg \left[f(z) \frac{\prod_{l=1}^{L}(z - z_{c_l})}{\prod_{k=1}^{K}(z - z_{d_k})} \right] \tag{4}$$

Zero-pole based methods have capability to recover the fingerprint orientation. While these methods encounter a problem in actual usage that they require all the singular points appearing in the image. This is not always true, especially for small sensors used for commercial purpose.

B: Phase Portrait Based Methods

Zero-pole based methods focus on obtaining the local orientation patterns near the singular point regions followed by a series of nonlinear functions to correct the global patterns. Unlike these methods, phase portrait based methods focus on obtaining the global orientation patterns first. A correction will be given to compensate the local errors near the singular points if necessary. Thus the model will not depend on the existence of the singular points.

Gu, Zhou and Zhang [5] proposed a combination model which consists of a polynomial model[1] as in Eqn. 5 and a point charge model as in Eqn. 6. The phase portrait model is used to approximate the global orientation image and the point charge model is used to correct the orientation images formed by the phase portrait model near singular points. This combination model gives better estimation of the orientation compared to the other previous models.

$$\cos(2\theta') = \Sigma_{i=0}^{n} \Sigma_{j=0}^{i} a_{(i-j)j} x^{i-j} y^j \tag{5a}$$

$$\sin(2\theta') = \Sigma_{i=0}^{n} \Sigma_{j=0}^{i} b_{(i-j)j} x^{i-j} y^j \tag{5b}$$

$$PC_c = \begin{cases} \frac{y-y_0}{r}Q - i\frac{x-x_0}{r}Q & \text{r} \leq \text{R} \\ 0 & \text{r} > \text{R} \end{cases}, PC_d = \begin{cases} -\frac{y-y_0}{r}Q - i\frac{x-x_0}{r}Q & \text{r} \leq \text{R} \\ 0 & \text{r} > \text{R} \end{cases} \tag{6}$$

where Q represents the strength of the singular points and R denotes the radius of the region which the point charge model can affect.

The combination model empirically determines r which depends on the difference between the original orientation and the phase portrait model reconstructed orientation. Furthermore, the combination model may fail where the large patch of noise appears in the image.

In 2006, Li *et al.* proposed a constrained nonlinear phase portrait model. Compared with Gu *et al.* approach, Li *et al.* used the 1st order phase portrait model to describe the local orientation pattern near the singular points instead

[1] In their paper, two polynomial models are used. Here we call two polynomial models as phase portrait according to the convention in ordinary differential equations.

of point charge model. More importantly, Li *et al.* used the 1st order phase portrait as the constraint of the high order phase portrait model which was used to describe the global orientation pattern. Thus no ad-hoc parameters are necessary to combine the different models. Moreover, the 1st order phase portrait model is able to predict the orientation when a large patch of noise appears.

In this paper, we'll give the stability analysis of the constrained nonlinear phase portrait model. According to the stability analysis, we provide the theoretical background why and how to improve the constrained nonlinear phase portrait model.

This paper is organized as follows: section 2 briefly introduces the constrained nonlinear phase portrait model, following the section 3 : stability analysis. In section 4, experimental results are provided. Section 5 concludes the paper.

2 Constrained Nonlinear Phase Portrait Model

The constrained nonlinear phase portrait model is composed of two parts: (1) the 1st order phase portrait model as given by Eqn. 7 to represent the local pattern near the singular points; (2) the high order phase portrait model to represent the global patterns as given by Eqn. 8.

$$dx = m * x + n * y \tag{7a}$$

$$dy = c * x + d * y \tag{7b}$$

where $\{c, d, m, n\}$ are the first order coefficients, dx, dy are the x,y components of the orientation image.

$$\begin{aligned}\cos(2\theta') =& \Sigma_{i=0}^{n}\Sigma_{j=0}^{i}a_{(i-j)j}(x-x_s)^{i-j}(y-y_s)^j \\ =& \Sigma_{i=0}^{n}\Sigma_{j=0}^{i}a_{(i-j)j}(-x)_s^{i-j}(-y)_s^j + \Sigma_{i=0}^{n}\Sigma_{j=0}^{i}a_{(i-j)j}(i-j)(-y)_s^j x \\ &+ \Sigma_{i=0}^{n}\Sigma_{j=0}^{i}a_{(i-j)j}j(-x)_s^{i-j}y + O_1(x^p y^q) \qquad p+q \geq 2\end{aligned} \tag{8a}$$

$$\begin{aligned}\sin(2\theta') =& \sum_{i=0}^{n}\Sigma_{j=0}^{i}b_{(i-j)j}(x-x_s)^{i-j}(y-y_s)^j \\ =& \Sigma_{i=0}^{n}\Sigma_{j=0}^{i}b_{(i-j)j}(-x)_s^{i-j}(-y)_s^j + \Sigma_{i=0}^{n}\Sigma_{j=0}^{i}b_{(i-j)j}(i-j)(-y)_s^j x \\ &+ \Sigma_{i=0}^{n}\Sigma_{j=0}^{i}b_{(i-j)j}j(-x)_s^{i-j}y + O_2(x^p y^q) \qquad p+q \geq 2\end{aligned} \tag{8b}$$

where $\{a_{ij}\}$ and $\{b_{ij}\}$ are the coefficients; O_1 and O_2 are the high order items.

$$\begin{cases}\Sigma_{i,j}a_{(i-j)j}(-x_s)^{i-j}(-y_s)^j = 0 \\ \Sigma_{i,j}a_{(i-j)j}(i-j)(-y_s)^j = m \\ \Sigma_{i,j}a_{(i-j)j}j(-x_s)^{i-j} = n\end{cases} \quad \begin{cases}\Sigma_{i,j}b_{(i-j)j}(-x_s)^{i-j}(-y_s)^j = 0 \\ \Sigma_{i,j}b_{(i-j)j}(i-j)(-y_s)^j = c \\ \Sigma_{i,j}b_{(i-j)j}j(-x_s)^{i-j} = d\end{cases} \tag{9}$$

where $\{x_s, y_s\}$ represent the position of a singular point.

According to the linearization theorem stated in [7]: "*Let the non-linear system has a simple singular point at* $\boldsymbol{x} = 0$. *Then in a neighborhood of the origin the phase portraits of the system and its linearization are qualitatively equivalent.*

Here a singular point at the origin of a non-linear system is said to be simple if its linearized system is simple", since the singular point in fingerprints has its own complete behavior and can be considered as the simple singular point, the nonlinear phase portrait model can be linearized at the singular point. Therefore, we have the following constraints for $\{a_{ij}, b_{ij}\}$ and $\{m, n, c, d\}$ as Eqn. 9.

Incorporating the constraints of the 1st order phase portrait with local descriptions of the high order phase portrait gives the constrained high order phase portrait model. Thus the proposed model incorporates the best of both the local and global descriptions, which can describe the global orientation image but still preserves an accurate local description near the singular points.

3 Solution of Coefficients and Stability Analysis

The solution of the coefficients $\{a_{ij}\}$ and $\{b_{ij}\}$ are obtained from the x and y components separately. Thus the stability analysis is also done on each component separately. To understand the stability of the solution for either $\{a_{ij}\}$ or $\{b_{ij}\}$, the following analysis takes the $\{a_{ij}\}$ as the example. The x component can be represented by its corresponding coefficients $\{a_{(n-m)m}\}$ as shown in Eqn. 10:

$$dx(x_i, y_j) = \Sigma_{n=0}^{N} \Sigma_{m=0}^{n} a_{(n-m)m} x_i^{n-m} y_j^m \tag{10}$$

where N represents its order.

Rewrite it in a matrix form as follows:

$$\mathbf{DX} = \mathbf{XY} \cdot \mathbf{A} \tag{11}$$

where $\mathbf{A} = \begin{bmatrix} a_{00} \; a_{10} \; a_{01} \; \cdots \; a_{(n-m)m} \; \cdots \; a_{0N} \end{bmatrix}^T$,

$$\mathbf{DX} = \begin{bmatrix} \cos(2\theta(x_1, y_1)) \\ \cos(2\theta(x_1, y_2)) \\ \vdots \\ \cos(2\theta(x_I, y_J)) \end{bmatrix} \quad \mathbf{XY} = \begin{bmatrix} 1 \; x_1 \; y_1 \; \cdots \; x_1^{n-m} y_1^m \; \cdots \; y_1^N \\ 1 \; x_1 \; y_2 \; \cdots \; x_1^{n-m} y_2^m \; \cdots \; y_2^N \\ \vdots \; \vdots \; \vdots \; \vdots \qquad \ddots \qquad \vdots \\ 1 \; x_I \; y_J \; \cdots \; x_I^{n-m} y_J^m \; \cdots \; y_J^N \end{bmatrix} \tag{12}$$

The constraints in Eqn. 9 have its matrix form as shown in Eqn. 13:

$$\mathbf{L} \cdot \mathbf{A} = \mathbf{H} \tag{13}$$

where $\mathbf{H} = \begin{bmatrix} 0 \; m \; n \end{bmatrix}^T$ and

$$\mathbf{L} = \begin{bmatrix} 1 \ldots (-x)_s^{i-j}(-y_s^j) \ldots (-y)_s^N \\ 0 \ldots \; (i-j)(-y)_s^j \; \ldots \; 0 \\ 0 \ldots \; j(-x)_s^{i-j} \; \ldots \; N \end{bmatrix} \tag{14}$$

Hence the constrained nonlinear phase portrait model can be viewed as the weighted linear least square problem with linear equality constraints, as stated in the following Eqn. 15:

$$\min_{A \in B} \|\mathbf{W}(\mathbf{XY} \cdot \mathbf{A} - \mathbf{DX})\|_2, \qquad B = \{\mathbf{A} | \mathbf{L} \cdot \mathbf{A} = \mathbf{H}\} \tag{15}$$

where $\|\cdot\|_2$ is the norm, **W** represents the weights which generally are represented by the corresponding coherence.

If the constrained matrix **L** has full row rank: $rank(\mathbf{L}) = p$, the least square problem has the unique solution, which has been proven by Eldèn [8]:

$$\mathbf{A} = \mathbf{L}_{I\cdot W\cdot XY^{+}} \cdot \mathbf{H} + (\mathbf{W}\cdot\mathbf{XY}\cdot\mathbf{P_0})^{+}\cdot\mathbf{W}\cdot\ \mathbf{DX} \tag{16}$$

where $(\cdot)^{+}$ represents the pseudo inverse of a matrix, $\mathbf{L}^{+}_{\mathbf{I\cdot W\cdot\ XY}} = (\mathbf{I}-(\mathbf{W}\cdot\ \mathbf{XY}\cdot\mathbf{P_0})^{+}\cdot \mathbf{W}\cdot\ \mathbf{XY})\cdot\mathbf{L}^{+}$, and $\mathbf{P_0} = \mathbf{I}-\mathbf{L}^{+}\cdot\mathbf{L}$.

Now let us consider the perturbation problem defined in Eqn. 17:

$$\min_{A\in\tilde{B}} \|\tilde{\mathbf{W}}\cdot\tilde{\mathbf{XY}}\cdot\mathbf{A}-\tilde{\mathbf{W}}\cdot\tilde{\mathbf{DX}}\|, \quad \tilde{B}=\{\mathbf{A}|\tilde{\mathbf{L}}\cdot\mathbf{A}=\tilde{\mathbf{H}}\} \tag{17}$$

where

$$\begin{aligned}\tilde{\mathbf{XY}} &= \mathbf{XY}+\Delta XY\mathbf{E}_{XY}\\ \tilde{\mathbf{DX}} &= \mathbf{DX}+\Delta DX\mathbf{E}_{DX}\\ \tilde{\mathbf{L}} &= \mathbf{L}+\Delta L\mathbf{E}_{L}\\ \tilde{\mathbf{H}} &= \mathbf{H}+\Delta H\mathbf{E}_{H}\\ \tilde{\mathbf{W}} &= \mathbf{W}+\Delta W\mathbf{E}_{W}\end{aligned} \tag{18}$$

and $\|\mathbf{E}_{XY}\| = \|\mathbf{E}_{DX}\| = \|\mathbf{E}_{L}\| = \|\mathbf{E}_{H}\| = \|\mathbf{E}_{W}\| = 1$ and ΔXY, ΔL, ΔDX, ΔH, $\Delta W \geq 0$.

In this study, the matrix **XY** and **L** are combination of the coordinates of the points (x, y), so we have $\Delta XY = 0$ and $\Delta L = 0$.

According to the perturbation theory for the least square problem with linear equality constraints developed by Eldèn in [8], the estimation errors $\Delta\mathbf{A} = \tilde{\mathbf{A}}-\mathbf{A}$ can be expressed as Eqn. 19:

$$\begin{aligned}\|\Delta\mathbf{A}\| \leq \|(\mathbf{XY}\cdot\mathbf{P_0})^{+}\|\ \|\mathbf{W}^{+}\|\|\mathbf{DX}-\mathbf{XY}\cdot\mathbf{A}\|\Delta\mathbf{W}\\ +\|(\mathbf{XY}\cdot\mathbf{P_0})^{+}\|\Delta DX+\|\mathbf{L}_{I,XY}\|\Delta H\end{aligned} \tag{19}$$

The relative error can be estimated using Eqn. 20:

$$\begin{aligned}\frac{\Delta\mathbf{A}}{\mathbf{A}} \leq & \frac{\Delta\mathbf{DX}}{\mathbf{DX}}\cdot\kappa_{\mathbf{L}}(\mathbf{XY})\frac{\|\mathbf{DX}\|}{\|\mathbf{XY}\|\|\mathbf{A}\|}+\frac{\Delta\mathbf{H}}{\mathbf{H}}\cdot\kappa^{\mathbf{XY}}(\mathbf{L})\frac{\|\mathbf{H}\|}{\|\mathbf{L}\|\|\mathbf{A}\|}\\ &+\frac{\Delta\mathbf{W}}{\mathbf{W}}\kappa_{\mathbf{W}}\kappa_{\mathbf{L}}(\mathbf{XY})\frac{\Delta\mathbf{DX}}{\mathbf{DX}}\end{aligned} \tag{20}$$

where

$$\kappa_L(\mathbf{XY}) = \|\mathbf{XY}\|\cdot\|(\mathbf{XY}\cdot\mathbf{P_0})^{+}\| \tag{21a}$$

$$\kappa^{XY}(\mathbf{L}) = \|\mathbf{L}\|\cdot\|\mathbf{L}^{+}_{\mathbf{I\cdot XY}}\| \tag{21b}$$

$$\kappa_W = \|\mathbf{W}\|\|\mathbf{W}^{+}\| \tag{21c}$$

We may justify the stability of estimated coefficients **A** according to the constrained condition numbers $\kappa_L(\mathbf{XY})$, $\kappa^{XY}(\mathbf{L})$ and κ_W defined in Eqn. 21 (a & b &c) and its relative error bound according to $\frac{\Delta\mathbf{A}}{\mathbf{A}}$ defined in Eqn. 20.

From Eqn. 20, the estimation error of coefficients comes from two cases:

1. Ill conditioned matrix **L**, which means that **L** tends to be singular, it will result in a large $\kappa^{XY}(\mathbf{L})$. Therefore in this case, the estimated error of the coefficients **A** may be large.
2. Noise. If the perturbation of the original orientation is large, which is always indicated by the small coherence value, this will cause large κ_W, ΔDX and ΔW. Therefore the estimated error of coefficients **A** will be large as well.

The solution for the 2nd case generally required the image enhancement and noisy reduction, which is out of the scope of this paper. In this paper, we only focus on the first case.

Robustness in Cases of Two Singular Points Close to One Another

The constraints that will be added to the nonlinear phase portrait shall abide by the linearization theorem. Therefore in fingerprints the two singular points should be well separated so that each singular point exhibits a simple behavior that can be described by the first order phase portrait.

The computation of the orientation uses the pixel values in a block of size $h \times w$ (typically 8×8 or 16×16). Thus the orientation image has a smaller size. In some loop (or tented arch) cases, the core point and the delta point are close to each other in the orientation image. Therefore the singular point region cannot be viewed as a simple singular point. They will interact with each other such that the first order phase portrait description fail near the singular regions. Therefore the perturbation ΔH of **H** computed from the first order phase portrait is quite large. Moreover, it will cause a smaller (x_s, y_s). Let us consider the constraints matrix in Eqn. 14. If (x_s, y_s) is small, the elements in the first row will be smaller than the elements in the other rows. This will cause the condition number $\kappa^{XY}(\mathbf{L})$ large, which means the **L** tends to be singular. With large $\kappa^{XY}(\mathbf{L})$ and ΔH, the estimated error of the coefficients **A** will be large. In Fig. 1 we show a fingerprint with two close singular points. Its reconstructed orientation using the 1st order phase portrait as constraints near singular points is shown in Fig. 1 (a). It fails to precisely reconstruct the orientation at the singular point region.

In order to model the orientation in these cases, we consider the functions 22:

$$\begin{aligned} dx &= x \times (x - x_d) + y \times (y - y_d) \\ dy &= -x \times (y - y_d) + y \times (x - x_d) \end{aligned} \tag{22}$$

and the orientation reconstructed using these functions is shown in Fig. 1(c).

From Fig. 1(c), we can observe the loop orientation behavior where the core and the delta are close to each other. The solutions to the Eqns. 22 are $(x = 0, y = 0)$ and $(x = x_d, y = y_d)$. Supposing the core is at the origin and the delta is at (x_d, y_d), we can coarsely reconstruct the loop orientation with constraints of two close singular points by Eqn. 22. Compared with the constraints matrix H, we don't use the 1st order phase portrait to describe the singular point orientation pattern but keep the orientation of the singular points 0. In this way, we keep the singularity of those points but no strong constraints added to cause the constraints matrix H unstable.

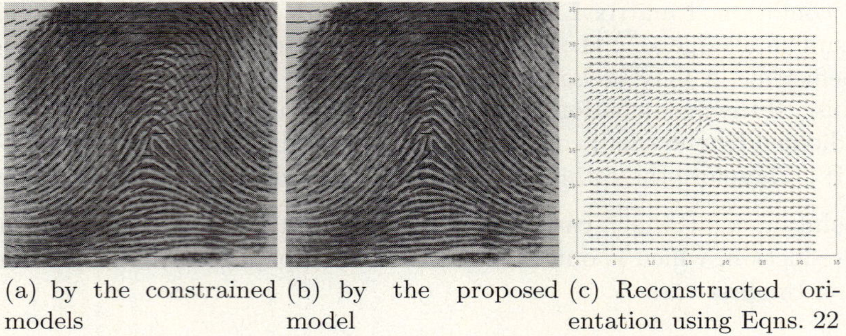

(a) by the constrained models (b) by the proposed model (c) Reconstructed orientation using Eqns. 22

Fig. 1. Reconstruction orientation of fingerprint with two close singular points

In order to obtain the more precise reconstructed orientation, we incorporate polynomial functions to Eqn. 22 as in Eqn. 23:

$$\begin{aligned} dx &= (x \times (x - x_d) + y \times (y - y_d)) \times (\Sigma_{n=0}^{N} \Sigma_{m=0}^{n} a_{(n-m)m} x^{n-m} y^m) \\ dy &= (-x \times (y - y_d) + y \times (x - x_d)) \times (\Sigma_{n=0}^{N} \Sigma_{m=0}^{n} b_{(n-m)m} x^{n-m} y^m) \end{aligned} \tag{23}$$

$\{\Sigma_{n=0}^{N} \Sigma_{m=0}^{n} b_{(n-m)m} x^{n-m} y^m\}$

where the items $\{\Sigma_{n=0}^{N} \Sigma_{m=0}^{n} a_{(n-m)m} x^{n-m} y^m\}$ and $\{\Sigma_{n=0}^{N} \Sigma_{m=0}^{n} b_{(n-m)m} x^{n-m} y^m\}$ are used to correct the overall orientation patterns other than singular point regions. In Fig. 1 (b), we show an example of the reconstructed orientation using the constraints in Eqn. 23.

4 Experiments

The proposed method aims to improve the stability of constrained nonlinear phase portrait model when there are two singular points close to each other. In order to verify the accuracy of the proposed method, we select 38 images from the NIST Database 4. The size of the image is 512 × 480. The block size for the orientation estimation is 16 × 16 pixels. In all these 38 images, there are at least two singular points close to each other (Here we set the distance between the two close singular points in 3 blocks as the close singular points according to the empirical test, which make the constrained nonlinear phase portrait model unstable). In order to reduce the effect of noise, all these 38 images have clear ridge-valley structure.

As the errors always occur at the singular point region, the difference between the original orientations and the reconstructed orientations is defined only around the singular point region (here 14×14 blocks are taken) as Eqn. 24 shows.

$$Dis(O_o, O_M) = \frac{1}{N} \sum_{O \in \Omega} |O_o - O_M| \tag{24}$$

where O_o and O_M are the original orientation and the reconstructed orientation respectively; Ω is the area around the singular points; N is the amount of the orientation in the region Ω.

Table 1. The experimental results

	Constrained model	The proposed model
Dis	18.18°	9.94°

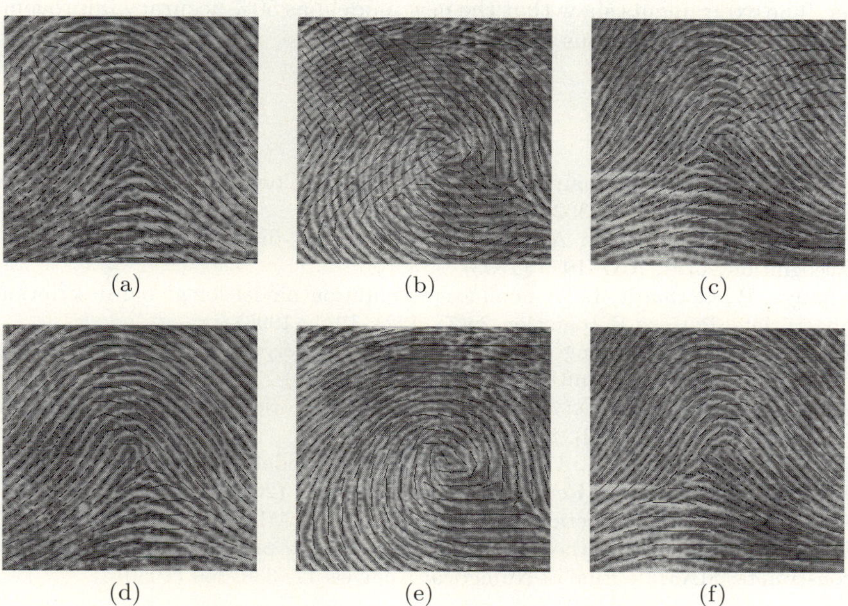

Fig. 2. Comparisons of reconstructed orientation of fingerprint with two close singular points. The first row shows the reconstructed orientation by the constrained nonlinear phase portrait model; the second row by the proposed method.

Table 1 shows the experimental results. The *Dis* between the original orientation and the orientation reconstructed by the constrained nonlinear phase portrait model is 18.18° while the *Dis* between the original orientation and the orientation reconstructed by the proposed method is 9.94°, which has 50% improvement.

More examples are illustrated in Fig. 2. Due to the instability of the constrained matrix when the two singular points are close to each other, the reconstructed orientation becomes unpredictable. In Fig. 2 (a, b & c), the reconstructed orientations have obvious errors. Such errors have been corrected using the proposed method as shown in Fig. 2 (d, e & f).

5 Conclusion

The effectiveness of the constrained nonlinear phase portrait model has been shown by the experimental results in our early paper [6]. However, errors do occur, especially when the two singular points are close to each other. The analysis in this paper showed that the solution will malfunction in such case. Consequently, we propose a new model to deal with such case. The new model has only one constraint which keeps the singularity at the singular points and abandons the 1st order phase portrait constraints as it is hard to obtain the correct 1st order phase portrait description when the two singular points are close to each other. The experiments show that the new model has 50% accuracy improvement compared with the previous model.

References

1. Kass, M., Witkin, A.: Analyzing oriented patterns. Computer Vision Graphics and Image Processing 37(3), 362–385 (1987)
2. Sherlock, B., Monro, D.: A model for interpreting fingerprint topology. Pattern Recognition 26(7), 1047–1055 (1993)
3. Vizcaya, P., Gerhardt, L.: A nonlinear orientation model for global description of fingerprints. Pattern Recognition 29(7), 1221–1231 (1996)
4. Zhou, J., Gu, J.: Modeling orientation fields of fingerprints with rational complex functions. Pattern Recognition 37(2), 389–391 (2004)
5. Zhou, J., Gu, J., Zhang, D.: A combination model for orientation field of fingerprints. Pattern Recognition 37(3), 543–553 (2004)
6. Li, J., Yau, W., Wang, H.: Constrained nonlinear models of fingerprint orientations with prediction. Pattern Recognition 39(1), 102–114 (2006)
7. Arnold, V.I.: An Introduction to Analysis, 2nd edn. MIT Press, Cambridge (1973)
8. Eldèn, L.: Perturbation theory for the least squares problem with linear equality constraints. SIAM Journal of Numerical Analysis 17, 338–350 (1980)

Effectiveness of Pen Pressure, Azimuth, and Altitude Features for Online Signature Verification

Daigo Muramatsu[1] and Takashi Matsumoto[2]

[1] Department of Electrical and Mechanical Engineering, Seikei University, 3-3-1 Kichijoji-kitamachi, Musashino-shi, Tokyo 180-8633, Japan
muramatsu@st.seikei.ac.jp

[2] Department of Electrical Engineering and Bioscience, Waseda University, 3-4-1 Okubo, Shinjuku-ku, Tokyo 169-8555, Japan
takashi@mse.waseda.ac.jp

Abstract. Many algorithms for online signature verification using multiple features have been proposed. Recently it has been argued that pen pressure, azimuth, and altitude can cause instability and deteriorate the performance. Algorithms without pen pressure and inclination features outperformed with them in SVC2004. However, we previously found that these features improved the performance in evaluations using our private database. The effectiveness of the features thus depended on the algorithm. Therefore, we re-evaluated our algorithm using the same database as used in SVC2004 and discuss the effectiveness of pen pressure, azimuth and altitude. Experimental results show that even though these features are not so effective when they are used by themselves, they improved the performance when used in combination with other features. When pen pressure and inclination features were considered, an EER of 3.61% was achieved, compared to an EER of 5.79% when these features were not used.

Keywords: Online signature verification, Pen pressure, Pen azimuth, Pen altitude, Fusion, SVC2004.

1 Introduction

Recently, the renewed interest in biometric authentication has resulted in its application to many situations. Several biometric authentication methods have been proposed and studied; however, no perfect method currently exists. The suitability of the method depends on the situation, as well as the required security level. Online signature verification is a promising candidate as an authentication method for several reasons. First, handwritten signatures are widely accepted as the authentication method in many countries for various purposes, such as authorizing credit card and banking transactions and signing agreements and legal documents.

S.-W. Lee and S.Z. Li (Eds.): ICB 2007, LNCS 4642, pp. 503–512, 2007.

Second, because online signature verification can incorporate dynamic information about the handwritten signature, it can often achieve higher performance than static signatures[1]. Moreover, since it is difficult to extract dynamic information from a static signature, it is more difficult to forge. Finally, a person can modify his or her signature if it is stolen. This is a notable feature because physiological biometrics such as fingerprints or irises cannot be modified or renewed. Therefore, online signature verification is a promising candidate as an authentication method. However, online signature verification is not perfect, and it is important to develop algorithms that can achieve high performance.

Many algorithms have been proposed for online signature verification, using multiple features acquired using various types of devices. Some special devices[2]–[4] and techniques[5] for doing so have been proposed; however, popular devices for online signature verification are tablets (graphic tablets), Tablet PCs, and PDAs. The features that can be obtained depend on the type of device; for example, only pen position and pen up/down information are available using PDAs, whereas pen pressure features are also available when using Tablet PCs. Moreover, some tablets can acquire pen inclination information, like pen altitude and azimuth. Some public databases for online signature verification, for example, BIOMET[6], MCYT[7], and SVC[8], were prepared using data captured from tablets. Thus, information about pen position, pen pressure, pen altitude, and pen azimuth is available[1] Researchers who use these databases generally use all of the information in the database[9]–[14]. However, it has argued that using the pressure, azimuth, and altitude can cause instability and deteriorate the performance [8][15]-[17].

The First International Signature Verification Competition (SVC) was held in 2004; there were two tasks in the competition, Task 1 and Task 2. Participants could use pen position, pressure, azimuth, and altitude in Task 2, though only pen position and pen up/down information were available in Task 1. The results of Task 1 outperformed those of Task 2[8]. As a result, some researchers have stopped using pen pressure,[15], pen altitude, and pen azimuth[16] or have expressed concern about using pen inclination features[17]. On the other hand, some researchers have proposed algorithms taking account of pen inclination features and reported improved performance[18]–[20]. We also reported improved performance using pen pressure and inclination features[14]. However, the databases used by researchers for evaluation were not same. Thus, we evaluated an algorithm using the same database as that used in SVC2004 and report the results in this paper.

We performed several experiments, and the results show that our algorithm could improve the performance from an equal error rate (EER) of 5.79% to 3.61% for user-dependent threshold parameters, and from 12.67 % to 10.15 % for a global threshold parameter by using pen pressure, altitude, and azimuth features. Thus, the effectiveness of using these features depends on the type of algorithm.

---

[1] Information about pen pressure, pen altitude, and pen azimuth were not made available in Task 1 of the SVC database.

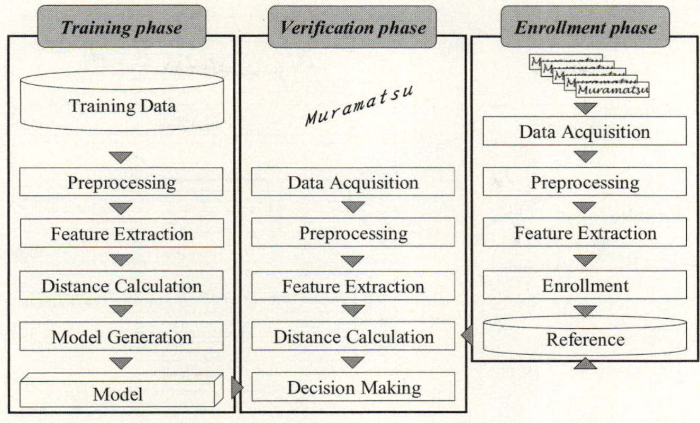

Fig. 1. Overall algorithm

2 The Algorithm

Figure 1 depicts our algorithm for online signature verification. There are three phases in the algorithm:

(i) Training phase

Signatures for training are provided in the training phase. After preprocessing and feature extraction, multiple distances between the training signatures are calculated. Parameters of a fusion model are estimated by using the distances from the training signatures.

(ii) Enrollment phase

In the enrollment phase, candidates of reference signatures are provided, together with the identity of the users (signers). After preprocessing and feature extraction, reference signatures are selected.

(iii) Verification phase

In the verification phase, a signature under question, with a claimed identity, is provided. After preprocessing and feature extraction, multiple distances between the signature under question and the reference signatures are calculated. Then, these multiple distances are combined in the fusion model and a decision is made.

The training, enrollment, and verification phases involve all or some of the following stages: (a) data acquisition, (b) pre-processing, (c) feature extraction, (d) enrollment, (e) similarity/distance calculation, (f) model generation, and (g) decision making. The boundaries between the stages are not rigid; therefore, one stage can be included in another stage. Only the feature extraction, distance calculation, and decision making stages are explained in this paper. Details of our signature verification algorithm were given in reference[11] and reference[14].

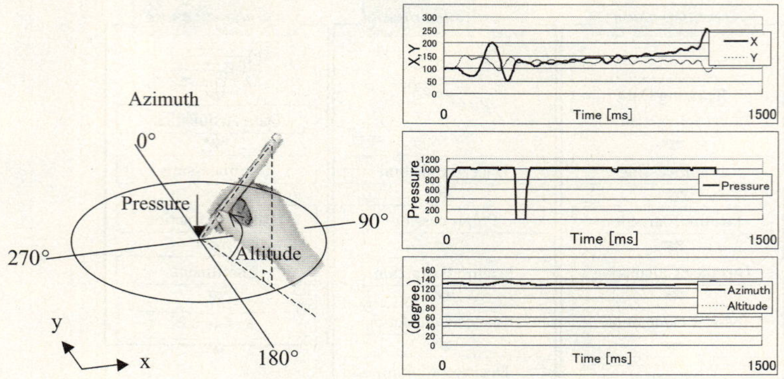

Fig. 2. Data from the tablet

Fig. 3. Top: Trajectories of x and y pen positions. Middle: Trajectory of pen pressure. Bottom: Trajectories of azimuth and altitude.

2.1 Feature Extraction

Raw data from the tablet consists of five-dimensional time-series data:

$$Signature = (x(j), y(j), p(j), \psi(j), \phi(j)) \qquad (1)$$
$$j = 1, 2, ..., J$$

Here, $(x(j), y(j))$ is the pen position; $p(j)$, the pen pressure; $\psi(j)$, the azimuth; and $\phi(j)$, the altitude of the pen at time j (depicted in Figs. 2 and 3).
The following features are extracted from the raw data.

$$X(j) = \frac{x(j) - x_g}{x_{max} - x_{min}} \qquad (2)$$

$$Y(j) = \frac{y(j) - y_g}{y_{max} - y_{min}} \qquad (3)$$

$$|V|(j) = \sqrt{V_x^2(j) + V_y^2(j)} \qquad (4)$$

$$\theta_V(j) = \tan^{-1}\frac{V_y(j)}{V_x(j)} \qquad (5)$$

$$where \quad V_x(j) = X(j+1) - X(j), V_y(j) = Y(j+1) - Y(j)$$

where (x_g, y_g) is the centroid of the signature, and x_{min}, y_{min} and x_{max}, y_{max} are the minimum and maximum values of $x(j), y(j)$. In addition to the above features, pen pressure $p(j)$, azimuth $\psi(j)$, and altitude $\phi(j)$ are used as features. Although other features proposed in reference[16][21]-[23] can be useful, our goal is to discuss the effectiveness of pen pressure, azimuth, and altitude. Thus, we use only seven features in this paper.

2.2 Distance Calculation

Our approach calculates multiple distances from multiple features using dynamic programming. The distance of each feature was calculated independently. Thus, the distance vector between two signatures, $Rsig$ and Sig, is

$$Dist(Rsig, Sig) = (D_X, D_Y, D_{|V|}, D_{\theta_V}, D_p, D_\psi, D_\phi). \quad (6)$$

2.3 Decision Making

Our fusion model calculates the following score:

$$Score(Sig; ID) = \sum_{m=1}^{M} f(X(Rsig_{ID_m}, Sig), Mean_{ID}; \Theta), \quad (7)$$

where M is a number of reference signatures and X is the input vector to the fusion model, described by

$$\begin{aligned} X\ (\ & Rsig_{ID_m}, Sig) \\ &= \left(\frac{D_1(Rsig_{ID_m}, Sig)}{Z_1 T_m}, .., \frac{D_i(Rsig_{ID_m}, Sig)}{Z_i T_m}, .., \frac{D_N(Rsig_{ID_m}, Sig)}{Z_N T_m}\right). \end{aligned} \quad (8)$$

Here, D_i is a distance calculated with the i_{th} feature, T_m is the duration of the reference signature, Z_i is a normalization constant calculated from a training dataset, and N is a dimension of input vector X. $Mean_{ID}$ is a mean vector defined by

$$Mean_{ID} = (mean_1^{ID}, .., mean_i^{ID}, .., mean_N^{ID}) \quad (9)$$

$$mean_i^{ID} = \frac{1}{M^2} \sum_{m=1}^{M} \sum_{n=1}^{M} \frac{D_i(Rsig_{ID_m}, Rsig_{ID_n})}{Z_i T_m}, \quad (10)$$

and Θ is a parameter set for the fusion model estimated from the training dataset.

A final decision is made by the following rule:

$$\text{Signature is} \begin{cases} \text{Accept if } Score(Sig; ID) \geq Threshold(c) \\ \text{Reject if } Score(Sig; ID) < Threshold(c) \end{cases} \quad (11)$$

where c is a parameter for adjusting the threshold value.

3 Experiments

Two experiments are described in this paper:

(i) Experiment 1: Performance evaluation of each distance from a feature; and
(ii) Experiment 2: Performance evaluation of fusion models that combine different distances.

The following three databases were used for evaluating the performance:

BIOMET

This database was collected by Garcia-Salicetti et al.[6]. From this database, signatures for 61 persons were used in our experiments. For each person, five genuine signatures were used as reference signatures, and ten genuine signatures from a second session and twelve skillfully forged signatures were used for evaluation. This database was used for training the parameters of the fusion model in Experiment 2 and was used for evaluation only in Experiment1.

MCYT

This database was collected by Ortega-Garcia et al.[7]. Signatures from 100 persons were used for evaluation in our experiments. For each person, five genuine signatures were used as reference signatures, and twenty genuine signatures and twenty-five skillfully forged signatures were used for evaluation.

SVC

This database was collected by Yeung et al.[8] and was used for the First International Signature Verification Competition. This database is formed of two databases for task 1 and task 2. In task 2, pen position, pressure, and inclination features are available, whereas in task 1, only pen position and pen up/down features are available. Five genuine signatures randomly selected from a first session were used as reference signatures, and ten genuine signatures from a second session and twenty skillfully forged signatures were used for evaluation in one experiment. We considered ten combinations of five genuine signatures as reference signatures, and performed ten experiments while changing only the reference signatures. These were the same conditions as in the competition and the study described in reference[24].

3.1 Experiment 1

The three public databases described above, BIOMET, MCYT, and SVC (task 1 and task 2), were used to evaluate the performance. To evaluate the effectiveness of each feature, a one-dimensional distance score was calculated:

$$D'(Sig; ID, i) = \frac{1}{M} \sum_{m=1}^{M} \frac{D_i(Rsig_{ID_m}, Sig)}{T_m}. \tag{12}$$

Table 1. EER for each distance measure (global threshold parameter)

No.	Feature	MCYT	BIOMET	SVC (task 1)	SVC (task 2)
1	X	10.5	9.39	24.1	22.6
2	Y	7.7	9.54	17.8	20.2
3	$\lvert V\rvert$	7.2	7.32	16.9	16.9
4	θ_V	7.8	6.57	16.1	17.6
7	P	16.1	23.24	-	24.6
8	ψ	23.3	21.41	-	31.6
9	ϕ	27.0	24.58	-	32.2

Then, a decision was made based on

$$Signature = \begin{cases} Accept\ if\ D'(Sig; ID, i) < Threshold_{D_i}(c) \\ Reject\ if\ D'(Sig; ID.i) \geq Threshold_{D_i}(c) \end{cases} . \qquad (13)$$

The experimental results are summarized in Table 1. The pen altitude and azimuth did not produce good results; pressure was better than both altitude and azimuth but was worse than pen position and velocity features.

3.2 Experiment2

The BIOMET database was used for training the fusion model parameters, and the MCYT and SVC (task 1 and task 2) databases were used for evaluation.

Table 2. EER of fusion model

Threshold	User-dependent			Global		
Feature set	MCYT	SVC (task 1)	SVC (task 2)	MCYT	SVC (task 1)	SVC (task 2)
Setting 1	3.05	7.46	10.7	6.30	15.04	15.38
Setting 2	2.23	4.74	5.79	4.91	11.67	12.67
Setting 3	1.75	-	5.45	3.93	-	10.35
Setting 4	1.89	-	4.57	4.32	-	11.58
Setting 5	2.29	-	4.32	4.50	-	11.52
Setting 6	1.50	-	4.56	3.52	-	10.38
Setting 7	1.75	-	4.30	3.58	-	10.38
Setting 8	2.00	-	3.53	4.44	-	10.69
Setting 9	1.57	-	3.61	3.72	-	10.15

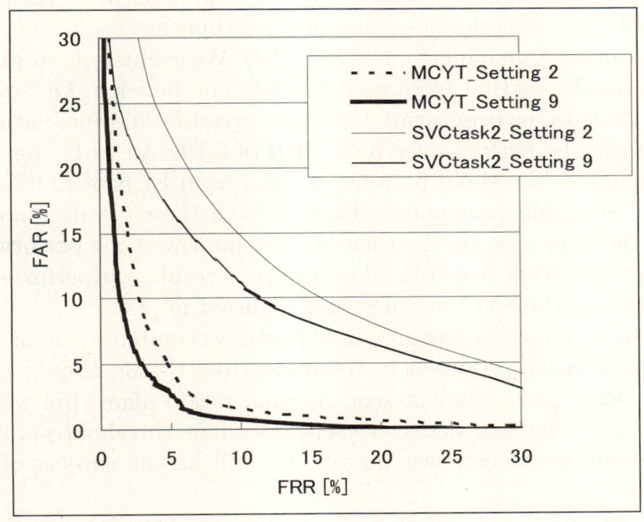

Fig. 4. Error trade-off curves of fusion model for MCYT and SVC (task 2) databases

The following combinations of distances were evaluated:

Setting 1: $Dist = (D_X, D_Y)$
Setting 2: $Dist = (D_X, D_Y, D_{|V|}, D_{\theta_V})$
Setting 3: $Dist = (D_X, D_Y, D_{|V|}, D_{\theta_V}, D_P)$
Setting 4: $Dist = (D_X, D_Y, D_{|V|}, D_{\theta_V}, D_\psi)$
Setting 5: $Dist = (D_X, D_Y, D_{|V|}, D_{\theta_V}, D_\phi)$
Setting 6: $Dist = (D_X, D_Y, D_{|V|}, D_{\theta_V}, D_P, D_\psi)$
Setting 7: $Dist = (D_X, D_Y, D_{|V|}, D_{\theta_V}, D_P, D_\phi)$
Setting 8: $Dist = (D_X, D_Y, D_{|V|}, D_{\theta_V}, D_\psi, D_\phi)$
Setting 9: $Dist = (D_X, D_Y, D_{|V|}, D_{\theta_V}, D_P, D_\psi, D_\phi)$

Equal error rates were obtained with both user-dependent threshold parameters and a global threshold parameter (results summarized in Table 2). EER was calculated using the methods of Fingerprint Verification Competition (FVC)[25]. Figure4 shows the error trade-off curve of Setting 2 and Setting 9 for the MCYT and SVC (task 2) databases with a global threshold parameter. An error trade-off curve shows the relation between false rejection rate (FRR) and false acceptance rate (FAR). Judging from the results of Settings 2, 3, 4, and 5, pen pressure, azimuth, and altitude features contributed to improved performance.

4 Conclusion

We evaluated our online signature verification algorithm using the BIOMET, MCYT, and SVC public databases. It has recently been argued that pen pressure, azimuth, and altitude can cause instability and deteriorate the performance of online signature verification, because an algorithm that used only pen position features won a previous competition (SVC2004). We evaluated our algorithm using the same databases that were used for that competition. Our experimental results show that, by incorporating both pen pressure and inclination features, we could improve the performance from EER of 5.79% to 3.61% for SVC task 2 with user-dependent threshold parameters, and from EER of 12.67% to 10.15% with a global threshold parameter . Even though these features are not so effective when they are used by themselves, they improved the performance when used together with other features. Moreover, our results outperformed the best result published on the SVC website[2] and reported in [24].

We only evaluated a few features in this study; combinations of many more features, such as those proposed in references[16][21]-[23], should improve the performance. Also, more efficient score normalization algorithm will be necessary because the difference between user-dependent threshold parameters and a global threshold parameter was large. This will be the subject of our future work.

---

[2] http://www.cs.ust.hk/svc2004/results-EER2.html

Acknowledgements

The authors are grateful to J. Ortega-Garcia and J. Fierrez-Aguilar of Universidad Politecnica de Madrid, Madrid, Spain, and to B. Dorizzi and S. Garcia-Salicetti of Institut National Des Telecommunications, Evry, France for providing us with the databases. The authors would also like to thank D.Y. Yeung for advice on the evaluation method used in SVC2004. This work was supported by Grants-in-Aid for Scientific Research from Ministry of Education, Culture, Sports, Science and Technology.

References

1. Plamondon, R., Lorette, G.: Automatic signature verification and writer identification - The state of the art. Pattern Recognition 22(2), 101–131 (1989)
2. Martens, R., Claesen, L.: Incorporating local consistency information into the on-line signature verification process. IJDAR 1(2), 110–115 (1998)
3. Shimizu, H., Kiyono, S., Motoki, T., Gao, W.: An electrical pen for signature verification using a two-dimensional optical angle sensor. Sensor and Actuators A111, 211–216 (2004)
4. Hook, C., Kempf, J., Scharfenberg, G.: A Novel digitizing pen for the analysis of pen pressure and inclination in handwriting biometrics. In: Maltoni, D., Jain, A.K. (eds.) BioAW 2004. LNCS, vol. 3087, pp. 283–294. Springer, Heidelberg (2004)
5. Munich, M.E., Perona, P.: Visual identification by signature tracking. IEEE Trans. Pattern Anal. and Machine Intell. 25(2), 200–217 (2003)
6. Garcia-Salicetti, S., Beumier, C., Chollet, G., Dorizzi, B., Leroux-Les Jardins, J., Lunter, J., Ni, Y., Petrovska-Delacretaz, D.: BIOMET: a multimodal person authentication database including face, voice, fingerprint, hand and signature modalities. In: Kittler, J., Nixon, M.S. (eds.) AVBPA 2003. LNCS, vol. 2688, pp. 845–853. Springer, Heidelberg (2003)
7. Ortega-Garcia, J., Fierrez-Aguilar, J., Simon, D., Gonzalez, J., Faundez-Zanuy, M., Espinosa, V., Satue, A., Hernaez, I., Igarza, J.-J., Vivaracho, C., Escudero, D., Moro, Q.-I.: MCYT baseline corpus: a bimodal biometric database. IEE Proceedings Vision, Image and Signal Processing 150(6), 395–401 (2003)
8. Yeung, D.-Y., Chang, H., Xiong, Y., George, S., Kashi, R., Matsumoto, T., Rigoll, G.: SVC. First international signature verification competition. In: Zhang, D., Jain, A.K. (eds.) ICBA 2004. LNCS, vol. 3072, pp. 16–22. Springer, Heidelberg (2004)
9. Ortega-Garcia, J., Fierrez-Aguilar, J., Martin-Rello, J., Gonzalez-Rodriguez, J.: Complete signal modeling and score normalization for function-based dynamic signature verification. In: Kittler, J., Nixon, M.S. (eds.) AVBPA 2003. LNCS, vol. 2688, pp. 658–667. Springer, Heidelberg (2003)
10. Van Ly, B., Garcia-Salicetti, S., Dorizzi, B.: Fusion of HMM's likelihood and viterbi path for on-line signature verification. In: Maltoni, D., Jain, A.K. (eds.) BioAW 2004. LNCS, vol. 3087, pp. 318–331. Springer, Heidelberg (2004)
11. Hongo, Y., Muramatsu, D., Matsumoto, T.: Modification on intersession variability in on-line signature verifier. In: Kanade, T., Jain, A., Ratha, N.K. (eds.) AVBPA 2005. LNCS, vol. 3546, pp. 455–463. Springer, Heidelberg (2005)
12. Muramatsu, D., Kondo, M., Sasaki, M., Tachibana, S., Matsumoto, T.: A Markov chain Monte Carlo algorithm for bayesian dynamic signature verification. IEEE Trans. Information Forensics and Security 1(1), 22–34 (2006)

13. Marcos Faundez-Zanuy, M.: On-line signature recognition based on VQ-DTW. Pattern Recognition 40, 981–992 (2007)
14. Muramatsu, D., Matsumoto, T.: Online signature verification using user generic fusion model. IEICE Trans. J90-D(2), 450–459 (2007)
15. Kholmatov, A., Yanikoglu, B.: Identity authentication using improved online signature verification method. Pattern Recognition Letters 26(15), 2400–2408 (2005)
16. Fierrez-Aguilar, J., Nannil, L., Lopez-Peñalba, J., Ortega-Garcia, J., Maltoni, D.: An on-line signature verification system based on fusion of local and global information. In: Kanade, T., Jain, A., Ratha, N.K. (eds.) AVBPA 2005. LNCS, vol. 3546, pp. 523–532. Springer, Heidelberg (2005)
17. Lei, H., Govindaraju, V.: A comparative study on the consistency of features in online signature verification. Pattern Recognition Letters 26(15), 2483–2489 (2005)
18. Taguchi, H., Kiriyama, K., Tanaka, E., Fujii, K.: On-line recognition of handwritten signature by feature extraction of the pen movements. IEICE Trans. J71-D(5), 830–840 (1988) (Japanese)
19. Komiya, Y., Ohishi, T., Matsumoto, T.: A pen input on-line signature verifier integration position, pressure and inclination trajectories. IEICE Trans. INF. & SYST. E84-D(7), 833–838 (2001)
20. Hangai, S., Yamanaka, S., Hanamoto, T.: On-line signature verification based on altitude and direction of pen movement. In: Proc. ICME 2000, vol. 1, pp. 489–492 (2000)
21. Lee, L.L., Berger, T., Aviczer, E.: Reliable on-line human signature verification systems. IEEE Trans. Pattern Anal. and Machine Intell. 18(6), 643–647 (1996)
22. Nalwa, V.S.: Automatic on-line signature verification. Proc. IEEE 85(2), 215–239 (1997)
23. Jain, A.K., Griess, F.D., Connell, S.D.: On-line signature verification. Pattern Recognition 35(12), 2963–2972 (2002)
24. Fierrez-Aguilar, J., Krawczyk, S., Ortega-Garcia, J., Jain, A.K.: Fusion of local and regional approaches for on-line signature verification. In: Li, S.Z., Sun, Z., Tan, T., Pankanti, S., Chollet, G., Zhang, D. (eds.) IWBRS 2005. LNCS, vol. 3781, pp. 188–196. Springer, Heidelberg (2005)
25. Maio, D., Maltoni, D., Cappelli, R., Wayman, J.L., Jain, A.K.: FVC2000: Fingerprint verification competition. IEEE Trans. on Pattern Anal. Machine Intell. 24(3), 402–412 (2003)

Tracking and Recognition of Multiple Faces at Distances

Rong Liu, Xiufeng Gao, Rufeng Chu, Xiangxin Zhu, and Stan Z. Li

Center for Biometrics and Security Research & National Laboratory of Pattern Recognition
Institute of Automation, Chinese Academy of Sciences
95 Zhongguancun Donglu Beijing 100080, China

Abstract. Many applications require tracking and recognition of multiple faces at distances, such as in video surveillance. Such a task, dealing with non-cooperative objects is more challenging than handling a single face and than tackling a cooperative user. The difficulties include mutual occlusions of multiple faces and arbitrary head poses. In this paper, we present a method for solving the problems and a real-time system implementation. An appearance model updating mechanism is developed via Gaussian Mixture Models to deal with tracking under head rotation and mutual occlusion. Face recognition based on video sequence is then performed to get the identity information. Through fusing the tracking and recognition information, the performance of them are both improved. A real-time system for multi-face tracking and recognition at distances is presented. The system can track multiple faces under head rotations, and deal with total occlusion effectively regardless of the motion trajectory. It is also able to recognize multi-persons simultaneously. Experimental results demonstrate promising performance of the system.

1 Introduction

Many applications need the system to have the ability to track and recognize faces at a distance, for example, in intelligent video surveillance. In such settings, the system should be able to keep track of the faces when the people are not facing to the camera. In addition, mutual occlusions may occur as multiple faces move and interact one another, and then some faces may disappear for several frames due to total occlusion. Moreover, the head poses of the persons in the scene are very free. As a result, tracking and recognition of multiple faces at distances is a challenging task.

While there is an abundant literature on face tracking in video sequences, not much is focus on developing a system for the above mentioned problem. To handle the head rotation, Chen and Kee [3] train a head detector based on head shapes. However, the high false ratio of this head detector leads it can't be used directly as a face detector in video surveillance. Yang and Li [5] present a system which can track varying poses. Due to them only use the face detection results to update the tracker, it is not very stable when the person turns back from the camera. Multi-features are also fused together to keep more stable face tracking [4,7], such as contour, color and motion information. To develop a real-time system, however, the computation complexity is generally high.

To handle the total occlusion, Niu et al [6] use Kalman filter to predict the motion trajectory. The defect is it can not endure too free motions. Lerdsudwichai et al [8] use

S.-W. Lee and S.Z. Li (Eds.): ICB 2007, LNCS 4642, pp. 513–522, 2007.

color histogram to build the upper body model to recover the person after occlusion. It is easy to be failure, when the occluded person reappears with her/his face turning away from the camera.

Based on face tracking, the sequence information of each face can be easily obtained. Taking advantage of these video sequences, face recognition can be more accurate through Video-based recognition method. There are some works related to it. Zhao and Chellappa et al [1] analyze the advantages of face recognition based on video. McKenna and Gong et al [9] model face eigenspace in video data via principal component analysis. Probability vote approach is then used to fuse the sequence information. Krueger and Zhou et al [10] take advantage of the temporal information to improve the recognition performance. These recognition methods are initially developed to recognize one person in video sequence. In addition, how to fuse the temporal and identity information for recognizing multi-faces is still a problem. In [2], two cameras, a static and a PTZ, work cooperatively. The static camera is used to take image sequences for face tracking, and the PTZ camera is used to take images for face recognition. In this

(a)

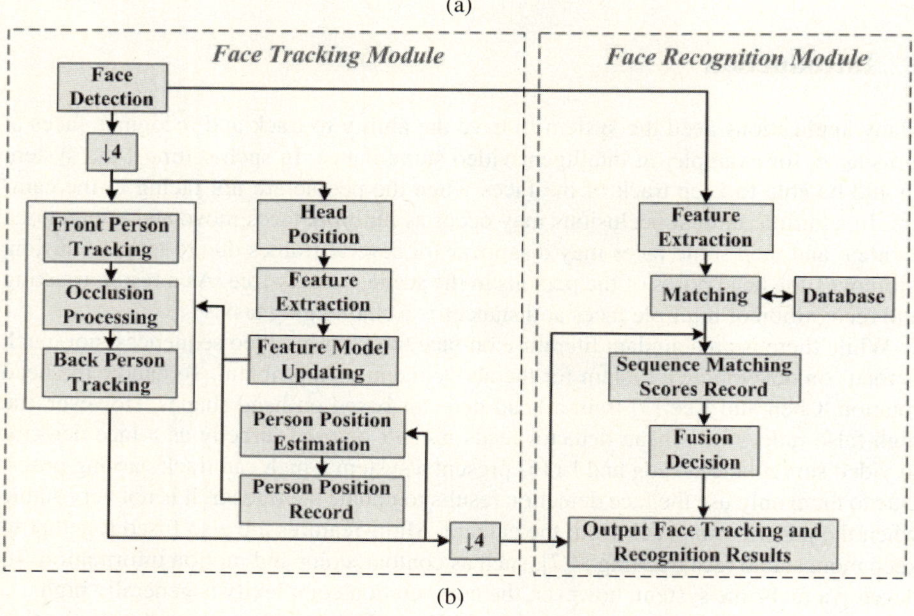

(b)

Fig. 1. The system: (a) environment setting, and (b) diagram

way, the system is supplied with high quality images for face recognition since the PTZ camera can be adjusted to focus on the face to be recognized. However, that system can only recognize a single face in the scene.

In this paper, we develop a method and a system for tracking multiple faces at distances (see Fig. 1). The method involves a face tacking module and a face recognition module. In the face tracking module, Two GMMs are used to represent the appearance of each person. One is applied to the head appearance to keep head tracking. The other is applied to that of the upper body to deal with occlusions. These two models are updated online.

In the face recognition module, a face recognition engine, which is learned from a classifier based on a Local Binary Pattern (LBP) representation [13] using AdaBoost learning [14], is used to obtain identity matching scores for each frame. These matching scores are computed over time to obtain a score sequence. The matching scores are fused and used to associate the tracked persons in consecutive frames, as well as to provide face recognition results. When the fused scores are below a given threshold, the system will consider the corresponding persons as unenrolled ones.

Based on the two modules introduced above, a real-time system for multiple faces tracking and recognition at distances is built. The system can track multiple faces under head rotations, and deal with total occlusion effectively regardless of the motion trajectory. It is also able to recognize multi-persons simultaneously.

The remainder of this paper is organized as follows: Section 2 develops an updating mechanism for appearance model based on Gaussian Mixture Models to deal with tracking under head rotation and mutual occlusion. Section 3 describes the recognition method used in the system. Section 4 describes how to fuse the tracking and recognition information to improve the performance of the system. Section 5 presents experimental results.

2 Face Tracking Method

In this section, we describe the tracking module for handling head rotation and total occlusion. Feature modeling and online model updating are two important components in object tracking. Two GMMs are learned to model the colors of the head and upper body of each tracked people, one for tackling head rotation and the other for handling total occlusion. An online GMM updating mechanism is incorporated.

2.1 GMM and Online Updating

A GMM with K component densities at time t can be modeled as follow:

$$P(X_t|Y) = \sum_{k=1}^{K} w_{k,t} \cdot N(X_t, \mu_{k,t}, \Sigma_{k,t}) \quad (1)$$

where X_t denotes the appearances of the person in the video sequence and Y denotes the tracked person. $N(X_t, \mu_{k,t}, \Sigma_{k,t})$ denotes the k-th Gaussian component with mean vector $\mu_{k,t}$ and covariance matrix $\Sigma_{k,t}$. $w_{k,t}$ is the corresponding weight. The appearance information is the head colors when the GMM model is applied to head tracking. It describes the colors of the upper body when the GMM is used to deal with occlusion.

During track process, new color information of tracked person can be obtained in each frame. Let x_{t+1} be the color information of tracked person Y obtained at time $t+1$. It can be modeled as

$$P(x_{t+1}|Y) = \sum_{k=1}^{K'} w'_{k,t+1} \cdot N(x_{t+1}, \mu'_{k,t+1}, \Sigma'_{k,t+1}) \tag{2}$$

Due to the occlusion or the interference of background, more color components are needed to describe the model $p(x_{t+1}|Y)$. So the K' in Equ. 2 is always larger than the K in Equ. 1.

$p(x_{t+1}|Y)$ is used to update $p(X_t|Y)$ into $p(X_{t+1}|Y)$. However, some components of the distribution should not be used for the update, such as those belonging to occluding objects and the background. The distribution distances between these and each component of old model $p(X_t|Y)$ are usually great. The components of $p(x_{t+1}|Y)$, which have big Mahalanobis distances to $p(X_t|Y)$, are dropped in the updating process. Only those components of $p(x_{t+1}|Y)$, which have small Mahalanobis distances to $p(X_t|Y)$, are used to update $p(X_t|Y)$. The updating formulae are as follows:

$$w_{k,t+1} = \frac{w_{k,t} + \sum_{i=1}^{K'} I_{i,k} w'_{i,t+1}}{1 + \sum_{i=1}^{K'} I_{i,k} w'_{i,t+1}} \tag{3}$$

$$\mu_{k,t+1} = \frac{w_{k,t}\mu_{k,t} + \sum_{i=1}^{K'} I_{i,k} w'_{i,t+1}\mu'_{i,t+1}}{w_{k,t} + \sum_{i=1}^{K'} I_{i,k} w'_{i,t+1}} \tag{4}$$

$$\Sigma_{k,t+1} = \frac{w_{k,t}\left[\Sigma_{k,t} + (\mu_{k,t+1} - \mu_{k,t})(\mu_{k,t+1} - \mu_{k,t})^T\right] + \sum_{i=1}^{K'} I_{i,k} w'_{i,t+1} B_i^{(k)}}{w_{k,t} + \sum_{i=1}^{K'} I_{i,k} \cdot w'_{i,t+1}} \tag{5}$$

where $B_i = \left[\Sigma'_{i,t+1} + (\mu_{k,t+1} - \mu'_{i,t+1})(\mu_{k,t+1} - \mu'_{i,t+1})^T\right]$, $I_{i,k}$ is an indicator. $I_{i,k} = 1$, if the i-th component of $P(x_{t+1}|Y)$ is matched to the k-th component of $P(X_t|Y)$. Otherwise, it is equal to zero.

The process of head rotation can be considered as a process of color distribution change in tracking. In this process, the online update method presented above plays two roles: (1) Accepts the matched color model to update the former one. It can maintain the adaptability of the feature model. (2) Prevents the unmatched color model from participating in the updating process. It keeps the validity of the feature model.

After the feature model is obtained at current time, we can construct a weight map for mean shift tracking based on the GMM. To reduce effect of background, the ratio of the head appearance model to the one of background is used to construct the weight map [5]. This treatment is proved effective.

2.2 Handle the Total Occlusion

Fig. 2 shows the area used for handling occlusion. This area is modeled to compare with the upper body models which is built by GMM and updated by the method presented in section 2.1. The person whose upper body model is less matched to the occlusion area is considered as the back person. The Chi-square (χ^2) statistic is used to measure the distinction between the models.

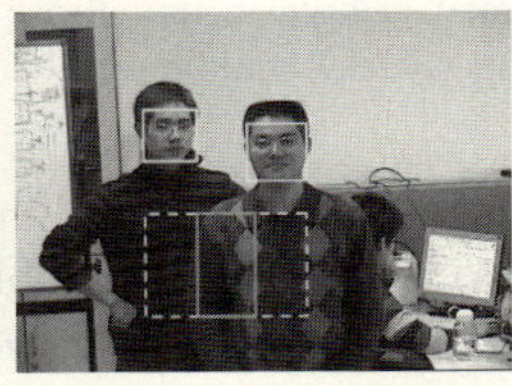

Fig. 2. Each upper body area, which is shown in dashed rectangle, is obtained relative to the face position. The intersection area of the upper body areas is considered as the area of occlusion (green rectangle).

When occlusion occurs, the information of the front person keeps intact. Therefore the position of her/him can be considered as prior knowledge using the general tracking method. Under the tracking of the front person, the weight of the area which is consistent to the moving direction is enhanced. After obtaining the position of the front face, the weight map of the back person is reconstructed. In this map, the weight in the head area of the front person is reduced. As a result, the tracking of the back person will not be affected by the front person (see Fig. 3).

In Fig. 3, the position relationship is estimated in frame 159, and then the weight adjustment for the back person is done in the next frames until the occlusion ends.

3 Face Recognition Method

The face recognition engine is learned from a classifier based on a Local Binary Pattern (LBP) representation [13] using AdaBoost learning [14].

Recently, Local Binary Patterns(LBP) is introduced as a powerful local descriptor for microfeatures of images [13]. The LBP operator labels the pixels of an image by thresholding the 3×3-neighborhood of each pixel with the center value and considering the result as a binary number (or called LBP codes). In our work, a histogram of the base LBP codes is computed over a local region centered at each pixel, and it is considered as a set of individual features. Given a training set of LBP histogram features of faces subjected to image noises, slight pose changes and alignment errors, the AdaBoost learning

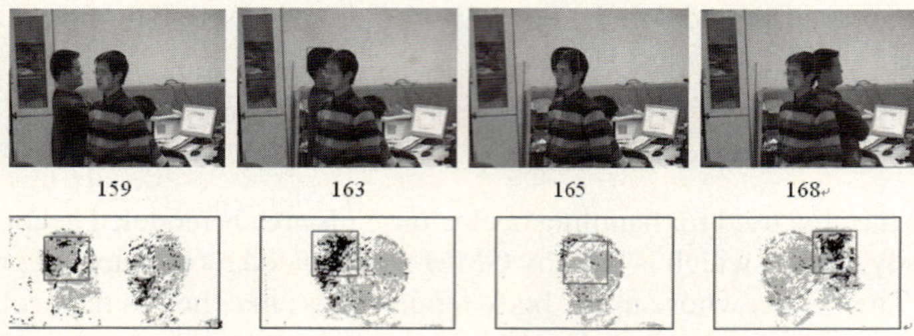

Fig. 3. Face tracking under total occlusion: frames in video sequence (upper), and weight maps for tracking (lower). The red rectangle shows the head position of the back person obtained by tracking mechnism. In the weight map, weight in the ellipse area is reduced. The weights are divided into three levels: high weights (black), middle weights (gray) and low weights (white).

method can find the most discriminative features and thereby build a strong classifier. Due to AdaBoost is usually used to solve two-class problem, we convert the multi-class problem to many two-class problems using intra-person and extra-person divergence [15].

The recognition engine described above performs one-to-many matching and outputs a matching score for each person in a database. The person's identity is determined based on a fused matching score, which is the average of several consecutive matching scores. The fused score is compared with a threshold, then a decision is made to obtain the person's identity referenced in the face database, or label him/her as unenrolled.

4 Fusing the Tracking and Recognition Information

Two types of IDs are maintained in a track list for tracking and recognition of each face: the TID (Tracking ID) and the RID (Recognition ID). The TID associates a face in different frames, whereas the RID identifies a face referenced in the database. The TID is obtained from the tracking module, whereas the RID is obtained as the result of the aforementioned face recognition decision.

After the TID and the RID are both obtained, they are bonded together, and putted into a track list. For face tracking, the use of RIDs makes face association in different frames as 1-1 matching problem. For recognition, TIDs are used as index for face identity. The tracked person is deleted from the list after the person leaves the scene.

The process of fusing tracking and recognition information is shown in Fig. 4. Using the track list, we can obtain a TID-indexed face and a RID-indexed face for each tracked person. Then a 1-1 matching is made between both of them. If they are matched, we accept the tracking result and the corresponding identity information. Otherwise, we reduce the weight of this face area, and track it again. Through this process, the performance of tracking and recognition are both improved.

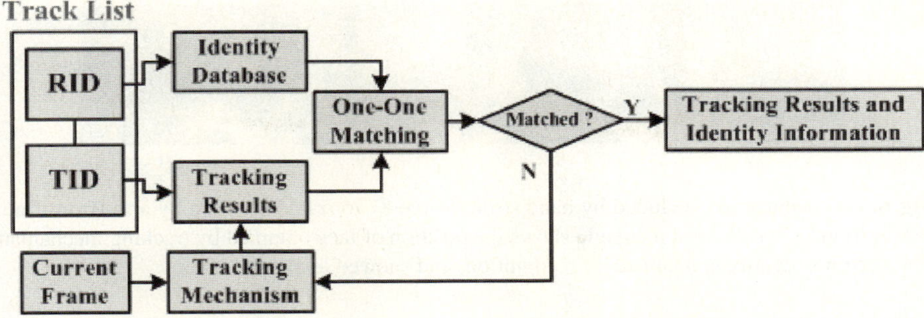

Fig. 4. The diagram of using TID and RID to fuse tracking and recognition information

5 Experimental Results

The system is implemented on a standard PC (Pentium IV at 3.0GHz). The video image size is 640x480 (24 bits per pixel) captured by IKEGAWA SN-600H-22 at 25fps and it is down-sampled to 320x240 for face tracking (while face recognition is performed on the resolution of 640x480). The RGB color space is down-sampled to 20x20x20 bins for building the color distribution of the object. The face is cropped to the size of 120. The tracking mechanism is initialized by multi-view face detector [11]. An ellipse model matching method [4] is used to find the head region from the position of detected face. The system works at about 10 fps. The following presents experiments for face tracking and face recognition.

The system was tested with significant head rotations in-plane and out of plane, large scale changes, multiple persons, nonlinear fast moving and total occlusion. We deliberately selected clips taken under difficult conditions, especially those with rotation and occlusion. Fig. 5- 7 present the results.

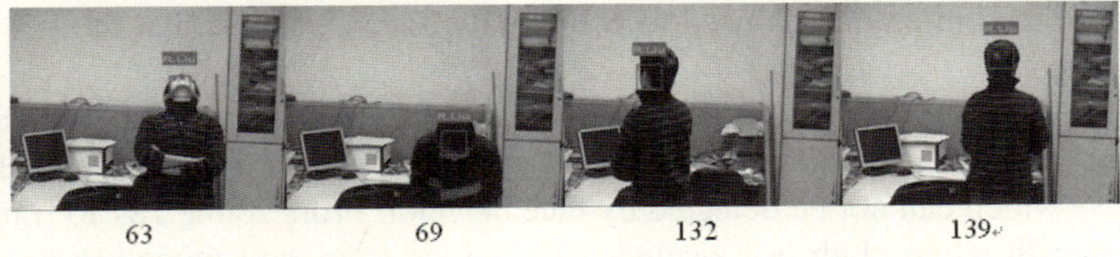

Fig. 5. Several typical head poses: looking up (frame 63), looking down (frame 69), turning about (frame 132) and turning back (frame 139). The red rectangle shows the position of head obtained by tracking mechanism. The person's identity is obtained by recognition, and showed above face.

In Fig. 5, the person looked up at frame 63; looked down at frame 69; turned about at frame 132; turned back at frame 139. These were the most challenge poses when tracking under head rotation. The high performance of the system to handle head rotations is shown in this experiment.

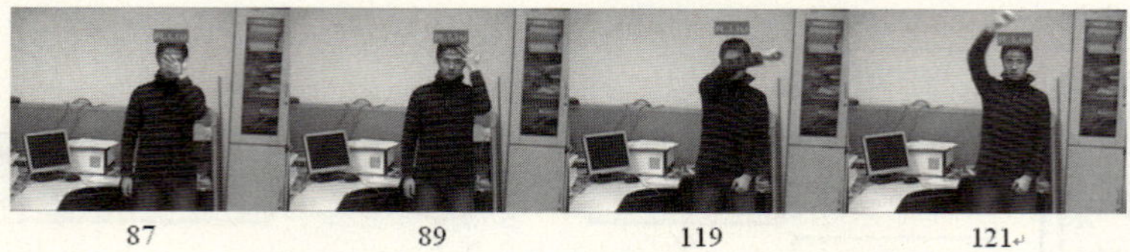

Fig. 6. Part occlusions: occluded by hand (from frame 87 to frame 89), and by arm (from frame 119 to frame 121). The red rectangle shows the position of face obtained by tracking mechanism. The person's identity is obtained by recognition, and showed above face.

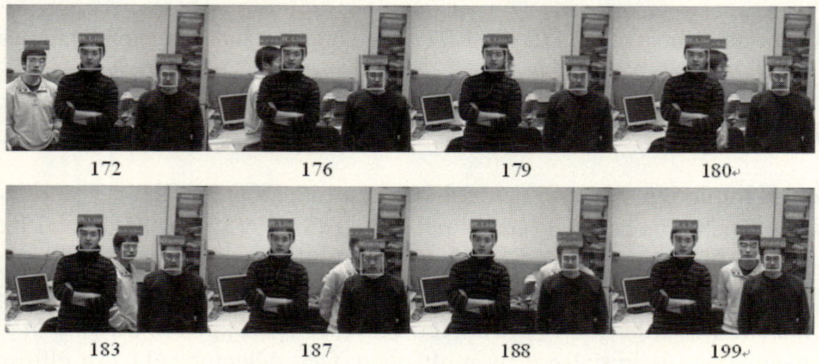

Fig. 7. Multi-person demos. There are three persons in the scene. The person with white cloth is first occluded from frame 176 to frame 180, and then from frame 187 to frame 199. The rectangles show the positions of faces. The identity of each person is obtained by recognition, and showed above each face.

In Fig. 6, the person was occluded by hand from frame 87 to frame 89, and by arm from frame 119 to frame 121. For a tracking method based on color feature, occluded by the object with the similar color is a great challenge. In this experiment, the hand which is of the skin color was used to occlude the face. It shows that the system can robustly handle part occlusions.

In Fig. 7, the person with white cloth was first occluded by the person with red cloth from frame 176 to frame 180. When the total occlusion ends, the back person also kept profile pose which can not be detected by face detector. From frame 187 to frame 189, the person with white cloth was occluded for a long time, and moved to the inverse direction after occlusion ends. These instances are hard to be handled in a single face tracking system. It shows that the system can robustly handle total occlusions.

The recognition performance of the system was tested in a indoor environment. In the face recognition process, the system were done in the form of one-to-many matching in each frame and fusion decision based on the matching scores of past frames, with the following protocol: fifty people were enrolled as clients, with twenty templates per person recorded. Images of the fifty clients were not included in the training set. The enrolled population was mostly composed of Chinese people with a few Caucasians and Negroes. Five people participated as the regular imposters (not enrolled) and some visitors were requested to participate as irregular imposters.

These participants entered the scene of the system several times for test. It provided statistics of correct recognition rate, correct rejection rate and average recognition time. Some client people deliberately challenged the system by exaggerated expressions, turning back to the camera or occluding part of the face with a hand so that the system did not recognize them. We counted these as invalid. Only those tests which were reported having problems getting recognized were counted as false rejections. On the other hand, the imposters were encouraged to challenge the system to get false acceptances.

After near seven hundred tests, the system has demonstrated excellent accuracy, speed, usability, and stability. The correct recognition rate is above 99%. The correct rejection rate is above 97%. the ART (Average Recognition Time) is below 2 seconds. Hence, we can conclude that the system achieves high-performance of recognition.

6 Conclusion

This paper presented a method for tracking and recognition multiple faces at distances, and its real-time system implementation. The method employs several tracking strategies for reliable face tracking and further enhance it by making use of face identity information. The system can track multiple faces under head rotations, and deal with total occlusion effectively regardless of the motion trajectory. It is also able to recognize multiple persons simultaneously and the recognition performance is demonstrated accuracy, speed, usability, and stability.In the future, we will extend the work to tackle a more challenging problem, that of more reliable face recognition at distances, by taking advantages of the present tracking system and developing a face recognition module optimized for the surveillance ID task.

Acknowledgements

This work was supported by the following funding resources: National Natural Science Foundation Project #60518002, National Science and Technology Supporting Platform Project #2006BAK08B06, National 863 Program Projects #2006AA01Z192 and #2006AA01Z193, Chinese Academy of Sciences 100 people project, and the AuthenMetric Collaboration Foundation.

References

1. Zhao, W., Chellappa, R., Phillips, P., Rosenfeld, A.: Face recognition: a literature survey. ACM Computing Surveys 35, 399–458 (2003)
2. Prince, S., Elder, J., Hou, Y., Sizinstev, M., Olevskiy, E.: Towards face recognition at a distance. In: Proc. IET Conference on Security (2006)
3. Chen, M.L., Kee, S.: Head tracking with shape modeling and detection. Computer and Robot Vision, 483–488 (2005)
4. Birchfield, S.: Elliptical head tracking using intensity gradients and color histograms. Computer Vision and Pattern Recognition, 232–237 (1998)

5. Yang, T., Li, S.Z., Pan, Q., Li, J., Zhao, C.: Reliable and fast tracking of faces under varying pose. Automatic Face and Gesture Recognition, 421–426 (2006)
6. Niu, W., Jiao, L., Han, D., Wang, Y.F.: Real-time multiperson tracking in video surveillance. AInformation, Communications and Signal Processing, 1144–1148 (2003)
7. Jin, Y.G., Mokhtarian, F.: Towards robust head tracking by particles. Image Processing (2005)
8. Lerdsudwichai, C., Abdel-Mottaleb, M., Ansari, A.: Tracking multiple people with recovery from partial and total occlusion. Pattern Recognition 38, 1059–1070 (2005)
9. McKenna, S.J., Gong, S., Raja, Y.: Face recognition in dynamic scenes. British Machine Vision (1997)
10. Krueger, V., Zhou, S.: Examplar-based face recogntion from video. Automatic Face and Gesture Recognition (2002)
11. Li, S.Z., Zhu, V., Zhang, L., Blake, Z.Q., Zhang, A., Shum, H.J.: Statistical learning of multiview face detection. In: European Conference on Computer Vision, Copenhagen, Denmark (2002)
12. Li, S.Z., Chu, R.F., Liao, S.C., Zhang, L.: Illumination Invariant Face Recognition Using Near-infrared Images. IEEE transaction on Pattern Analysis and Machine Intelligence, April 2007 (to appear)
13. Ahonen, T., Hadid, A., Pietikainen, M.: Face Description with Local Binary Patterns: Application to Face Recognition. IEEE transaction on Pattern Analysis and Machine Intelligence 28, 2037–2041 (2006)
14. Viola, P., Jones, M.: Robust Real-time Object Detection. International Journal of Computer Vision 57, 137–154 (2004)
15. VioMoghaddam, B., Nastar, C., Pentland, A.: A Bayesian similarity measure for direct image matching. Media Lab Tech. Report No. 393, vol. 57, MIT (1996)

Face Matching Between Near Infrared and Visible Light Images

Dong Yi, Rong Liu, RuFeng Chu, Zhen Lei, and Stan Z. Li

Center for Biometrics Security Research & National Laboratory of Pattern Recognition
Institute of Automation, Chinese Academy of Sciences, Beijing 100080, China
http://www.cbsr.ia.ac.cn

Abstract. In many applications, such as E-Passport and driver's license, the *enrollment* of face templates is done using visible light (VIS) face images. Such images are normally acquired in controlled environment where the lighting is approximately frontal. However, *Authentication* is done in variable lighting conditions. Matching of faces in VIS images taken in different lighting conditions is still a big challenge. A recent development in near infrared (NIR) image based face recognition [1] has well overcome the difficulty arising from lighting changes. However, it requires that enrollment face images be acquired using NIR as well.

In this paper, we present a new problem, that of matching a face in an NIR image against one in a VIS images, and propose a solution to it. The work is aimed to develop a new solution for meeting the accuracy requirement of face-based biometric recognition, by taking advantages of the recent NIR face technology while allowing the use of existing VIS face photos as gallery templates. Face recognition is done by matching an NIR probe face against a VIS gallery face. Based on an analysis of properties of NIR and VIS face images, we propose a learning-based approach for the different modality matching. A mechanism of correlation between NIR and VIS faces is learned from NIR→VIS face pairs, and the learned correlation is used to evaluate similarity between an NIR face and a VIS face. We provide preliminary results of NIR→VIS face matching for recognition under different illumination conditions. The results demonstrate advantages of NIR→VIS matching over VIS→VIS matching.

Keywords: Face Recognition, Near Infrared (NIR), Visible Light (VIS) Images, Dimension Reduction, Canonical Correlation Analysis (CCA).

1 Introduction

This work is developed for *cooperative user applications*, such as E-passport, machine readable traveling document (MRTD), ATM ,and driver's license. In such applications, a user is required to cooperate with the camera to have his/her face image captured properly, in order to be permitted for some access. However, even in such applications, face recognition is compromised by environmental illumination changes. Much effort has been made to model and correct illumination changes on faces in visible light (VIS) images, eg [2,3,4]; however, this challenge remains unsolved problems due to formidable difficulties, especially uncontrolled illumination directions [5].

S.-W. Lee and S.Z. Li (Eds.): ICB 2007, LNCS 4642, pp. 523–530, 2007.

As a recent advance, the use of active near infrared (NIR) imaging provides an effective approach to solving the illumination problem. Face images are acquired with frontal lighting using active NIR lights mounted coaxal to the camera. This active NIR imaging method provides a good basis for face recognition regardless of environmental lighting. When incorporated with effective algorithms and system work, it leads to truly illumination invariant face recognition and excellent results for indoor, cooperative user applications [6,1].

However, the exiting NIR based face recognition method [1] requires that the face templates of *enrollment* be also created from NIR face images, in addition to the use of NIR images for *authentication*. However, in many applications, templates of users were produced from VIS images taken in the visible light spectrum, such as passport and driver license photos. The ICAO (International Civil Aviation Organization) and ISO/IEC standards [7] have made recommendations for taking VIS photos.

In this work, we propose a new problem for face biometric, that of matching a face in an NIR image taken on authentication against a face in a VIS images taken on enrollment. This is for those applications where the use of VIS face images on enrollment is administratively required, such as E-passport and driver's license; the use of NIR face images on authentication is to take advantages of NIR face imaging in the latest NIR face recognition technology to combat illumination variations.

A solution to this new problem is to extract facial feature templates in the NIR and VIS face images, respectively, and then match them against each other. However, a straightforward matching between the two types of templates is not effective mainly because of different spectral properties in the two types of images, in addition to differences in the lighting conditions.

Therefore, we propose a more effective method for solving this new problem. We adopt a learning approach: Given that NIR→VIS image pairs of subjects are available for training, a canonical correlation analysis (CCA) [8] based correlation mechanism is learned from corresponding NIR→VIS face images for the NIR→VIS face matching. Here, the CCA learning is performed between features in linear discriminant analysis (LDA) subspaces, rather than between images. This leads to better classification performance. We provide preliminary results for NIR→VIS matching based face recognition. The results confirms advantages of NIR→VIS matching over VIS→VIS matching under varying illumination conditions.

2 NIR Vs. VIS Images

We assume that enrollment is done using VIS images in controlled environment where the lighting is nearly frontal, following the Standard [7], whereas the authentication is done using NIR images in environment of arbitrary lighting but with active frontal NIR illumination [1]. Fig.1 shows example VIS and NIR face images taken in the two conditions. In the following, we give an analysis of these images.

According to the Lambertian reflectance model, an image $I(x,y)$ under a point light source is formed according to the following

$$I(x,y) = \rho(x,y)\mathbf{n}(x,y)\mathbf{s} \tag{1}$$

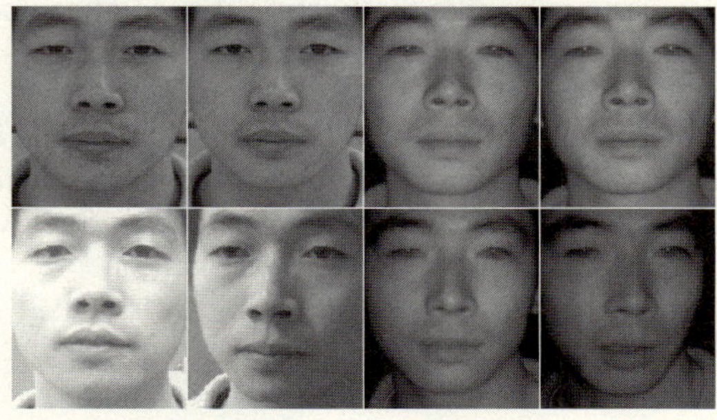

Fig. 1. Face image examples. Row 1: VIS face images (two on the left) taken on enrollment with frontal lighting and pose, and two NIR face images (two on the right) taken at the same time. Row 2: Two VIS image (left) and two NIR face images taken on authentication with lighting and pose variations.

where $\rho(x,y)$ is the albedo at point (x,y), $\mathbf{n} = (n_x, n_y, n_z)$ is the surface normal (a unit row vector) in the 3D space, and $\mathbf{s} = (s_x, s_y, s_z)^T$ is the lighting direction (a column vector, with magnitude). The albedo $\rho(x,y)$ function reflects the photometric properties, such as facial skin and hairs, and $\mathbf{n}(x,y)$ is the geometric shape (2.5 map) of the surface.

The product of $\rho(x,y)\mathbf{n}(x,y)$ is the intrinsic property of the face at a fixed imaging viewpoint, and is the only thing needed for face detection and recognition. Assume $\mathbf{s} = \kappa \mathbf{s}^0$, where κ is a multiplying constant due to the strength of the lighting, and $\mathbf{s}^0 = (s_x^0, s_y^0, s_z^0)^T$ is a unit column vector of the lighting direction. Equ.1 can be expressed as

$$I(x,y) = \kappa \rho(x,y)\mathbf{n}(x,y)\mathbf{s}^0 \tag{2}$$

We see that the face image changes as the lighting direction changes, given albedo $\rho(x,y)$ and 3D shape $\mathbf{n}(x,y)$ fixed.

The photo taking Standards [7] suggest to use controlled lighting for face enrollment. The suggested lighting consists of mainly a frontal light, a little above the eyes (biased toward y direction), and some other auxiliary lights symmetric left-right. For cooperative users standing in front of camera, the overall lighting direction may be approximated by $\mathbf{s}^0 = (0, S_y^0, S_z^0)^T$ where $S_y^0 \ll S_z^0$ and S_y^0 is nonzero due to slight lift of the lighting above the eyes. Given these, the Lambertian equation can be written as

$$I(x,y) = \kappa \rho(x,y) \left[S_y^0 n_y(x,y) + S_z^0 n_z(x,y) \right] \tag{3}$$

where $n_y(x,y)$ and $n_z(x,y)$ are the y and z components of the surface normal.

On authentication, the NIR images are taken by a camera with active NIR lighting. The active NIR lights, mounted on the camera panel, is from the frontal direction, *i.e.* $\mathbf{s}^0 = (0,0,1)^T$. An NIR image is depicted by

$$I(x,y) = \kappa \rho(x,y) n_z(x,y) \tag{4}$$

Assuming VIS and NIR images are both taken in (nearly) frontal lighting, then both may be modeled by Equ.(4). However, the albedo $\rho(x,y)$ is different for the two imaging processes due to different spectral properties of the facial surface in VIS and NIR spectra. Moreover, the assumption that the lighting is a point source and is from the frontal direction is an approximation. These cause matching from NIR to VIS a more challenging problem than the pure NIR to NIR matching [1].

In comparison, in the traditional VIS to VIS face matching, the images on enrollment and authentication are of homogeneous type. The main difficulties there are due to significant variation in lighting direction, *i.e.* $\mathbf{s}$ in Equ.(1). Such variation has been causing formidable difficulties for VIS→VIS face recognition.

3 Matching by Multivariate Correlation

Critical to the success of matching between NIR face and VIS face is the formulation of a correlation score for the evaluation of matches. The present method learns such a score function from a set of training examples. Let $\{(\mathbf{X}_1,\mathbf{Y}_1),\cdots,(\mathbf{X}_K,\mathbf{Y}_K)\}$ be a training set of K examples where $\mathbf{X}_k$ (NIR) and $\mathbf{Y}_k$ (VIS) are cropped NIR→VIS face pairs $W \times H$ pixels. These face images are aligned by the same fixed eye coordinates, and properly preprocessed to be zero mean and of unit length. Assume that these faces come from L subjects, denoted $\{C_1,C_2,\cdots,C_L\}$ where C_ℓ consists of subscripts $k \in \{1,\cdots,K\}$ of the training examples $(\mathbf{X}_k,\mathbf{Y}_k)$ belonging to subject ℓ.

The most naive method for NIR→VIS matching would be to compare the images $\mathbf{X}_k$ and $\mathbf{Y}_k$ directly. A better way could be to formulate the problem as correlational regression between $\mathbf{X}$ to $\mathbf{Y}$. However, it is difficult to learn a regression between image pairs directly to achieve a reasonable performance, because of different properties of $\mathbf{X}$ and $\mathbf{Y}$, the high dimensionality $W \times H$, and the insufficient sample size K.

Therefore, we propose the following three steps for the NIR→VIS face matching :

1. Transform $\mathbf{X}$ and $\mathbf{Y}$, respectively, into features spaces of lower dimensionality, as $\mathbf{X} \to \mathbf{X}' = \mathbf{P}_X(\mathbf{X})$ and $\mathbf{Y} \to \mathbf{Y}' = \mathbf{P}_Y(\mathbf{Y})$, where $\mathbf{P}_X$ and $\mathbf{P}_Y$ are dimension reductions for images $\mathbf{X}$ and $\mathbf{Y}$, respectively.
2. Perform multivariate regression between features in the reduced feature spaces, so that the corresponding feature vectors $(\mathbf{X}'_k,\mathbf{Y}'_k)$ are best correlated.
3. Evaluate the similarity between two types of features based on the feature regression using some correlation score.

In this paper, we will use baseline feature extraction and dimension reduction methods of PCA and LDA [9], and baseline correlational regression methods of CCA [8]. The process is further described below.

In the first step, two projection matrices $\mathbf{P}_X$ and $\mathbf{P}_Y$ are learned from the NIR images $\{\mathbf{X}_k\}$ and VIS images $\{\mathbf{Y}_k\}$, respectively, to reduce the dimensionality from $W \times H$ to two much smaller numbers. For PCA, the projections are learned based on total scatter matrices of $\{\mathbf{X}_k\}$ and $\{\mathbf{Y}_k\}$. For LDA, they are based on the intra-class and extra-class scatter matrices of the two image sets, where class labels of C_ℓ are used in the calculation.

In the second step, CCA is used to compute best correlational regression between the two sets of corresponding feature vectors $(\mathbf{X}',\mathbf{Y}')$. CCA here finds two linear projection matrices $\mathbf{W}_X = [\mathbf{w}_X^1,\mathbf{w}_X^2,\cdots,\mathbf{w}_X^d]$ and $\mathbf{W}_Y = [\mathbf{w}_Y^1,\mathbf{w}_Y^2,\cdots,\mathbf{w}_Y^d]$ from $\{(\mathbf{X}'_k,\mathbf{Y}'_k)\}$ (d is the dimension of CCA subspaces), such that $\mathbf{x} = \mathbf{w}_X^{i\ T}\mathbf{X}'$ and $\mathbf{y} = \mathbf{w}_Y^{i\ T}\mathbf{Y}$ are most correlated. This is done by maximizing the following correlation

$$\rho(\mathbf{w}_X, \mathbf{w}_Y) = \frac{E[\mathbf{x}\mathbf{y}^T]}{\sqrt{E[\|\mathbf{x}\|^2]E[\|\mathbf{y}\|^2]}} = \frac{\mathbf{w}_X^T \mathbf{C}_{XY}\mathbf{w}_Y}{\sqrt{\mathbf{w}_X^T \mathbf{C}_{XX}\mathbf{w}_X \mathbf{w}_Y^T \mathbf{C}_{YY}\mathbf{w}_Y}} \tag{5}$$

where $\mathbf{C}_{XY}$, $\mathbf{C}_{XX}$ and $\mathbf{C}_{YY}$ are the correlation matrices computed from the training features $\{(\mathbf{X}'_k, \mathbf{Y}'_k)\}$. This problem can be converted to the following generalized eigen problem:

$$\mathbf{A}\mathbf{w} = \lambda \mathbf{B}\mathbf{w}, \tag{6}$$

where

$$\mathbf{A} = \begin{pmatrix} 0 & \mathbf{C}_{XY} \\ \mathbf{C}_{YX} & 0 \end{pmatrix}, \mathbf{B} = \begin{pmatrix} \mathbf{C}_{XX} & 0 \\ 0 & \mathbf{C}_{YY} \end{pmatrix}, \mathbf{w} = \begin{pmatrix} \mathbf{w}_X \\ \mathbf{w}_Y \end{pmatrix}.$$

The solution $\mathbf{w}_X$ and $\mathbf{w}_Y$ can be found using singular value decomposition [9].

The third step evaluates correlation between $\mathbf{X}$ and $\mathbf{Y}$ in the learned subspaces. Features $\mathbf{X}'$ and $\mathbf{Y}'$ are extracted from $\mathbf{X}$ and $\mathbf{Y}$ using PCA or LDA projection learned in step 1. They are projected into the CCA subspaces as $\mathbf{x}$ and $\mathbf{y}$ using $\mathbf{w}_X$ and $\mathbf{w}_Y$ found in step 2. The correlation between $\mathbf{x}$ and $\mathbf{y}$, namely $\mathbf{x} \cdot \mathbf{y}/(\|\mathbf{x}\|\|\mathbf{y}\|)$, is calculated as the matching score.

CCA has been used for face recognition [10,11]. There, both probe and gallery face templates are extracted from VIS images. Two other interesting related papers are [12,13]. There, CCA-based methods are proposed for estimating face depth maps from color face images [12] and for generating NIR face images from RGB images [13]. Those are good examples of CCA based face analysis and synthesis. This paper explores another type of application of CCA, that for matching different face modalities.

4 Experiments

The experiments were aimed to evaluate the proposed NIR→VIS face matching method, as opposed to the conventional method of VIS→VIS matching. The following 6 algorithms were evaluated:

1. NIR→VIS / LDA+CCA;
2. NIR→VIS / PCA+CCA;
3. VIS→VIS / LDA+CCA;
4. VIS→VIS / PCA+CCA;
5. VIS→VIS / LDA;
6. VIS→VIS / LDA;

Methods using CCA directly on images without using LDA or PCA dimension reduction was not evaluated due to the memory limitation. We assumed that it was similar to the NIR→VIS / PCA+CCA and VIS→VIS / PCA+CCA algorithms. The VIS→VIS / PCA and VIS→VIS / LDA algorithms without CCA were included to provide baseline performances of the conventional algorithms. Note that pure PCA and LDA without CCA are inappropriate for NIR→VIS matching since NIR and VIS are images of different properties.

4.1 Data Description

A database of NIR and VIS face images of 200 persons was collected for the training and testing of the proposed method. The images were taken in 2 sessions, an enrollment session and an authentication session.

The enrollment session was with normal frontal lighting and frontal pose. For the enrollment session, 20 VIS face images were taken for each person, using a VIS camera, which was to simulate passport photos. We name this set as $\mathbf{VIS}_{\text{frt}}$, where the subscript $_{\text{frt}}$ stands for frontal lighting and pose. $\mathbf{VIS}_{\text{frt}}$ corresponds to Y in (X,Y) in the aforementioned formulations.

The authentication session was carried out with varying illuminations and slightly varying pose. 20 VIS face images were taken for each person using a VIS camera, and 20 NIR images were taken in the same condition. This was to simulate the situation of on-site person authentication. We name these sets as $\mathbf{VIS}_{\text{var}}$ and $\mathbf{NIR}_{\text{var}}$, where the subscript $_{\text{var}}$ stands for varying lighting and pose. Either $\mathbf{NIR}_{\text{var}}$ or $\mathbf{VIS}_{\text{var}}$ corresponds to $\{\mathbf{X}\}$.

The faces were detected in the images, and then aligned with eye positions and cropped into 120×142 pixels using automatic programs. The detection and alignment results were of acceptable quality. Some example face images were shown in Fig. 1.

5 data sets were constructed from the database, each comprising all the 200 persons:

1. Training set for NIR→VIS matching – $\{\mathbf{X}\}$ consisting of 10 samples per person from $\mathbf{NIR}_{\text{var}}$, and $\{\mathbf{Y}\}$ consisting of 10 samples per person from $\mathbf{VIS}_{\text{frt}}$;
2. Training set for VIS→VIS matching – $\{\mathbf{X}\}$ consisting of 10 samples per person from $\mathbf{VIS}_{\text{var}}$, and $\{\mathbf{Y}\}$ consisting of 10 samples per person from $\mathbf{VIS}_{\text{frt}}$;
3. Gallery set – consisting of the other 10 samples per person from $\mathbf{VIS}_{\text{frt}}$;
4. Probe set for NIR→VIS matching – consisting of the other 10 samples from $\mathbf{NIR}_{\text{var}}$;
5. Probe set for VIS→VIS matching – consisting of the other 10 samples from $\mathbf{VIS}_{\text{var}}$.

Data sets (1), (3) and (4) were for evaluating NIR→VIS matching, whereas (2), (3) and (5) were for VIS→VIS matching. Note that the gallery and probe sets did not include any of the training data.

4.2 Results

The training of the model was performed as follows: For algorithms 1-4, PCA and LDA projection matrices are computed from the $\{\mathbf{X}\}$ and $\{\mathbf{Y}\}$ parts of the training set, respectively. For algorithms 5-6, PCA and LDA projection matrices are computed from the $\{\mathbf{Y}\}$ parts of the training set, respectively. The projection reduces the dimensionality from 120×142 to 199. CCA projections further reduce the 199 to 100 dimensions. Figure 2 shows the final ROC curves for the 6 algorithms. The ranking of the 6 algorithms in terms of verification rates at FAR=0.001 and 0.0001 as 1, 2, 3, 5, 4, and 6, Algorithm 1 giving the highest verification rate of all.

Table 1 provides verification rates at FAR=0.1% and 0.01%. Note that the verification rate of algorithm 1, the best of the NIR→VIS matching algorithms, is about 11% higher than algorithm 3, the best of the VIS→VIS algorithms. This was owing to the fact the NIR imaging is more stable than VIS imaging under various illuminations.

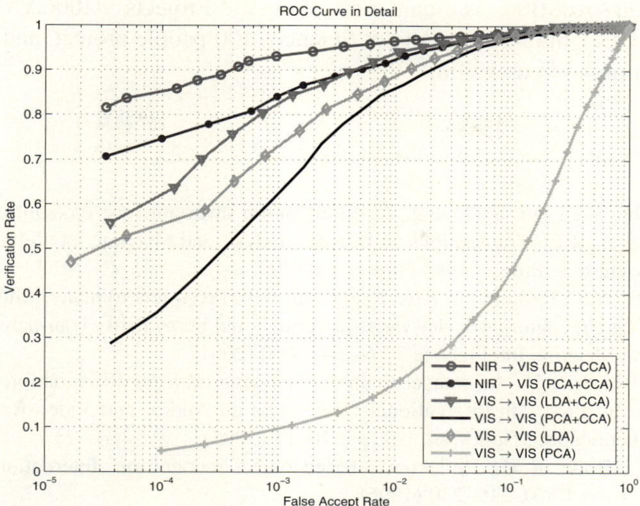

Fig. 2. ROC curves for the 6 algorithms

Table 1. Comparison of verification rates for the 6 algorithms

Algorithm	1	2	3	4	5	6
FAR=0.1%	93.1%	84.1%	82.1%	62.4%	73.3%	9.8%
FAR=0.01%	85.5%	75.5%	61.5%	37.2%	54.3%	4.9%

5 Summary and Conclusions

Face matching from NIR to VIS images is a new problem in biometrics. Taking advantages of the recently developed NIR-based face recognition technology, the problem is presented as a new approach towards accurate face recognition in practical applications. The preliminary results show that NIR→VIS matching is more advantageous than VIS→VIS matching for biometric authentication in environments of varying illumination. The success would have a positive impact on biometric applications such as E-Passport and drivers license.

Currently, we are using CCA for matching faces in different types of images. However, the CCA learning can be prone to over-fitting when the training data size is small, which has been reported elsewhere. The future work include developing better learning methods for object matching in different types of images (such as NIR vs. VIS), performing training and testing using larger data sets, and evaluating the performance under various conditions.

Acknowledgments

This work was supported by the following funding resources: National Natural Science Foundation Project #60518002, National Science and Technology Supporting Platform

Project #2006BAK08B06, National 863 Program Projects #2006AA01Z192 and #2006AA01Z193, Chinese Academy of Sciences 100 people project, and the AuthenMetric Collaboration Foundation.

References

1. Li, S.Z., Chu, R., Liao, S., Zhang, L.: Illumination invariant face recognition using near-infrared images. IEEE Transactions on Pattern Analysis and Machine Intelligence 26(Special issue on Biometrics: Progress and Directions) (2007)
2. Georghiades, A.S., Belhumeur, P.N., Kriegman, D.J.: From few to many: Illumination cone models for face recognition under variable lighting and pose. IEEE Transactions on Pattern Analysis and Machine Intelligence 23(6), 643–660 (2001)
3. Gross, R., Brajovic, V.: An image preprocessing algorithm for illumination invariant face recognition. In: Proc. 4th International Conference on Audio- and Video-Based Biometric Person Authentication, Guildford, UK, pp. 10–18 (2003)
4. Nayar, S.K., Bolle, R.M.: Reflectance based object recognition. International Journal of Computer Vision 17(3), 219–240 (1996)
5. Adini, Y., Moses, Y., Ullman, S.: Face recognition: The problem of compensating for changes in illumination direction. IEEE Transactions on Pattern Analysis and Machine Intelligence 19(7), 721–732 (1997)
6. Li, S.Z.: and His Face Team: AuthenMetric F1: A Highly Accurate and Fast Face Recognition System. In: ICCV2005 - Demos (2005)
7. ISO/IEC JTC 1/SC 37: Proposed Draft Amendment to ISO/IEC 19794-5 Face Image Data on Conditions for Taking Pictures. ISO/IEC 19794-5:2005/PDAM 1 (2006)
8. Hotelling, H.: Relations between two sets of variates. Biometrika 28, 321–377 (1936)
9. Fukunaga, K.: Introduction to statistical pattern recognition, 2nd edn. Academic Press, Boston (1990)
10. Sun, Q., Heng, P., Zhong, J., Xia, D., Huang, D., Zhang, X., Huang, G.: Face recognition based on generalized canonical correlation analysis. In: Huang, D.-S., Zhang, X.-P., Huang, G.-B. (eds.) ICIC 2005. LNCS, vol. 3645. Springer, Heidelberg (2005)
11. He, Y., Zhao, L., Zou, C., Lipo, W., Ke, C., Soon, O.Y.: Face recognition based on pca/kpca plus cca. In: Proceedings of International Conference on Advances in Natural Computation, Changsha, China. Springer, Heidelberg (2005)
12. Reiter, M., Donner, R., Georg, L., Horst, B.: 3D and infrared face reconstruction from RGB data using canonical correlation analysis. In: Proceedings of International Conference on Pattern Recognition (2006)
13. Reiter, M., Donner, R., Georg, L., Horst, B.: Predicting near infrared face texture from color face images using canonical correlation analysis. In: Proceedings of the Workshop of the Austrian Association for Pattern Recognition (2006)

User Classification for Keystroke Dynamics Authentication

Sylvain Hocquet, Jean-Yves Ramel, and Hubert Cardot

Université François Rabelais de Tours,
Laboratoire d'Informatique (EA 2101),
64 Avenue Jean Portalis, 37200 TOURS, France
{sylvain.hocquet,jean-yves.ramel,hubert.cardot}@univ-tours.fr

Abstract. In this paper, we propose a method to realize a classification of keystroke dynamics users before performing user authentication. The objective is to set automatically the individual parameters of the classification method for each class of users. Features are extracted from each user learning set, and then a clustering algorithm divides the user set in clusters. A set of parameters is estimated for each cluster. Authentication is then realized in a two steps process. First the users are associated to a cluster and second, the parameters of this cluster are used during the authentication step. This two steps process provides better results than system using global settings.

Keywords: keystroke dynamics, clustering, parameters adaptation.

1 Introduction

Since a few years, the need of more security for every day life has greatly increased. The biometric is a promising solution to answer this challenge. Biometric divides itself in two fields: the physical biometric and the behavioral biometric. The physical biometric methods (fingerprint, hand recognition...) are usually more accurate compared to methods based on the study of behavior (signature, voice, gait…). However, the behavioral methods are easier to implement, and better accepted by users. The problem of this kind of methods is the great variability in the user behaviors. In the case of an authentication problem, this variability implies difficulties for the setting of thresholds used by the system to separate authentic users from impostors. Most of the times, the parameters and thresholds are the same for all the users. This choice results in a great disparity of performances between users. The variability of some user profiles implies to accept impostors and at the opposite side, for some users with specific practice, all attempts including authentic ones are refused. Therefore, the automatic determination of the threshold for each user seems to be a solution to solve this problem. This paper first describes briefly classical methods used in keystroke dynamics. Next, our clustering algorithm is detailed and results are discussed in conclusion.

2 Keystroke Dynamics

Keystroke dynamics is the field of biometrics that studies the way a user interacts with a keyboard. To extract data from the striking of a user, the times between

S.-W. Lee and S.Z. Li (Eds.): ICB 2007, LNCS 4642, pp. 531–539, 2007.

keyboard events are used. One commercial application exist [1]. Keyboard events are the pressure and the release of a key. For a couple of successive keys, several different times are extracted:

- P-P (Press - Press) : time between two key pressures (T2-T1)
- P-R (Press - Release) : time between the pressure on a key and his release (T3-T1 and T4-T2)
- R-P (Release - Press) : time between the release of a key and the press on the next key (T3-T2)
- R-R (Release - Release) : time between the release of two successive keys (T4-T3)

For a sequence of strokes, the system extracts a feature vector for each type of time; to finally obtain vectors of four features (PP, PR, RP, and RR). The first test to differentiate people using the keystroke dynamics were carried out by Gaines et al. [2] in 1980. These first results were encouraging but inapplicable in real cases because of the low number of involved people and because of the length of the text used for the authentication. In the five last years, many studies took place on this subject, a summary of many of them is presented in [3] and a more recent review has been conducted in [4]. In this study, we restrict our investigations to the authentication or identity verification problem. Our goal is to compare a new observation with feature vector associated to only one profile and then to decide if the observation is from the same user or not. Therefore, we are limited to only a few observations from the user in the learning process. In addition, no impostor's data are available. A great variability of methods has been applied to solve this problem using similarity measure [5], one class support vector machine and genetic algorithm [6], hidden markov model [7], neural network [8]…

3 The Proposed Methods

To prove the performances of such systems, we have chosen to use a fusion of three different methods to decide if a new observation is corresponding or not to a given user. We have chosen these methods for their fair good performance, the low volume of data needed for training, and their easy implementation. The first one is an adaptation of a statistical method and uses the average and the standard deviation of each feature. The second is based on a measure of disorder between the different feature vectors, and the third one uses the concept of time discretization.

3.1 The Statistical Method

This method uses statistical measures extracted from the keystroke dynamics; that is to say the average and standard deviation of the different acquired times are computed. User profile is composed of the ten logins acquired during enrollment process. The profile contains the average and standard deviation of all times extracted from the striking sequences. To compute a score on an n length feature vector, with t_i

the ith time and μi, σ_i the associated average and standard deviation stored in the profile, the method use:

$$score_{statiscal} = 1 - \frac{1}{n}\sum_{i=1}^{n} e^{-\frac{|t_i - \mu_i|}{\sigma_i}}$$

3.2 Method Based on a Measure of Disorder

The second method studies the variation between the time ranks in the profile and in the tested sequences. This is corresponding in fact to the measurement of disorder between two vectors. To measure the difference between the ranks of the times, the times of each observation are reordered from the longest to the shortest. The information store in the profile for each time is the average rank computed according to the logins in the training set. To compute the distance the sum of the ranks difference in the profile and in the observation is used. With r_i^O the rank of time *i* in the observation and r_i^P the average rank of time *i* in the profile, *n* the number of times, the formula to compute a score is:

$$score_{disorder} = \frac{\sum_{i=1}^{n}(r_i^P - r_i^O)}{n*(n-1)}$$

3.3 Time Discretization Method

The third method uses a time discretization. Each time is put into a class according to its duration. To compare an observation with a profile, the difference between the indexes of the interval was chosen. The intervals are fixed for each class of times (for example between 0 and 30 ms for the 5th class). The class of each time *i* in the profile c_i^p are compared with the one in the tested sequences c_i^o Then the score is computed with:

$$score_{discretization} = \frac{1}{n}\sum_{i=1}^{n}\left|c_i^p - c_i^o\right|$$

3.4 Fusion of the Three Methods

Each one of the scores provided by these three methods must be normalized. Then, the fusion of the three results is computed by combining the scores. Previous experiments using fusion in biometric have shown that good results are obtained with a sum rule [9] and a z-score [10] normalization. To manage the differences of performances of the three methods, fusion weights (w_i) are associated to each of score from our method. So the final score becomes:

$$Final\ score(FSC) = \Sigma_i w_i * score_i$$

To normalize the final score, the sum of the weights has to be equal to 1, so only two weights must be estimated.

4 The User Classification Step

4.1 Parameters Personalization

Each classification method applied to an authentication problem needs in most cases a few parameters to be set in order to give the similarity score. In addition, a threshold is needed to take the final decision of authentication. All these parameters are often chosen according to all users after several experiments. However, such methods can cause some problems in one class problem, especially in the case of the behavioural biometrics. For example, if the threshold is the same for all the users, it can result in a great disparity of performances between users. To estimate these parameters for each user according to information present in their profile, a set of information can be extracted for each user from the set of ten sequences in their profile. This information includes:

- The length of one sequence, in characters (1 feature)
- The average, standard deviation, maximum and minimum of the times from the four extracted time vectors (PP, RP RR, PR) (4*4 features)
- The average and standard deviation of the total duration of the striking sequences (2 features)
- The average, standard deviation maximum and minimum of the three scores computed on the learning sequences by our three methods. In order to compute these scores, the leave-one-out method is used; nine sequences are included in the profile and the score is computed with the last one. The process is repeated with the other combinations of sequences.(3*4 features)

Finally, 31 features can be used, to characterize a profile containing ten learning sequences. In a previous work [11] we have decided to simplify the problem by making classes of users based on the proximity of their optimum parameters. So a set of parameters is no more associated to one user but to a class of users. The construction of the classes is made by auto associative methods and clustering algorithm on the optimum parameters found by using a private base. We obtain a good clustering result with a number of clusters equal to four. We finally use SVMs to compute the class of a new user. These SVMs were trained with the set of features extracted from user profiles.

In the following, we present a different approach; we tried to make classes using only the feature extracted from the user profile. Adequate parameters are then computed for each class. At the enrollment step, the class of the user is determined. The class whose center is near the user profile according to Euclidian distance is chosen. The parameters of this class will be used during the authentication process. Our first tests show that a clustering realized only on users training set give bad results. We observed that keystroke features evolve along the time. Therefore, we decide to continually recreate the classifiers with the last ten authentic sequences.

Therefore, users have not a single profile, but a profile for each acquisition they made after the enrollment.

4.2 Data Analysis

The clustering algorithm working on the 31 features extracted on the user profile may have difficulties to learn on this high dimensional space. So we decided to reduce the dimension of this space. It is impossible to a priori know wich features will best characterize a user. Therefore, data analysis methods are available to simplify the representation space. The method, we have used is a principal component analysis (PCA) [12]. The values of the first ten eigenvalues obtained after a PCA on the 31 features is presented in Table 1.

Table 1. Eigen values

Order	value	Cumulate value	% of inertia
1	8.6	8.6	38
2	4.2	12.8	56
3	2.7	15.6	68
4	2.3	17.9	78
5	1.3	19.3	84
6	0.9	20.2	88
7	0.6	20.9	90
8	0.5	21.4	93
9	0.4	21.8	95
10	0.3	22.1	96

The first five values are explaining more than 80 % of the inertia of the system. So we decided to keep only the first five factorial axes to represent a user profile.

A major advantage of factorial analysis is to represent on a small dimension, data that are defined in a high dimension space. On Figure 1, the first factorial plan is drawn. This plan explained only 56% of the initial inertia, but this is a fine first approximation. Each user profile is represented by a point. We can easily see on this figure, the division of user population into three apparent classes. One class contains the majority of users; we suppose these users will share common parameters. The other two classes regroup users with different behaviours and may need specific set of parameters. Our test has showed us, that this number of class still valid in the five dimensional spaces we have chosen.

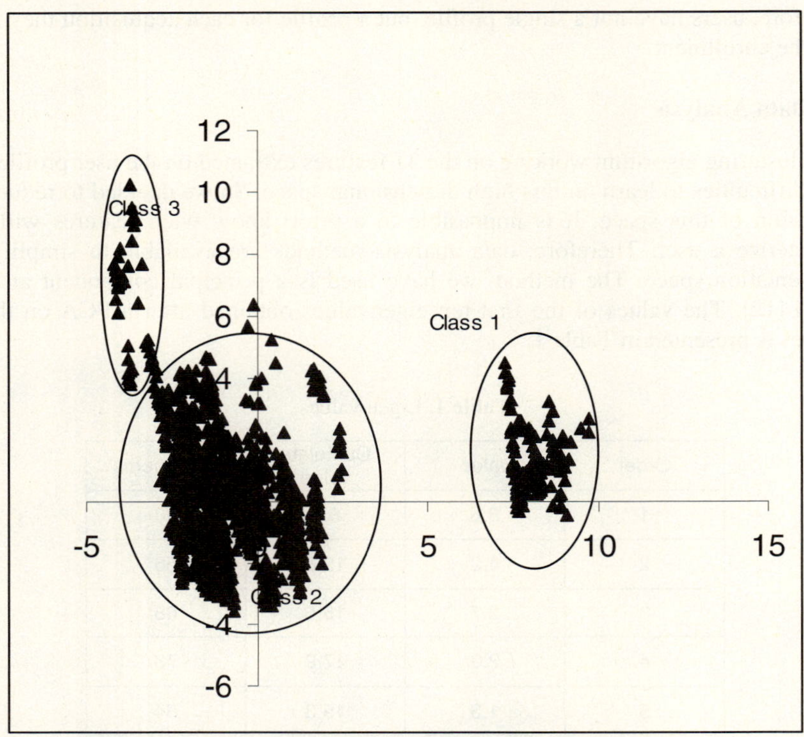

Fig. 1. First factorial plan and clustering on the feature extracted from user profile

The k-means algorithm is used to make clustering starting from the coordinates of the point on the first two axes, with k set to three. This simple algorithm gives a good classification using a low dimension space. The k-means with k equal to three will be used in the rest of our works, to create the class with the five retained values.

4.3 Computation of the Required Parameters

Our classification method required three parameters:

- A security threshold: this threshold needs to be determined according to the variability of the user profile. If the user has a stable profile, the security level can be high so the threshold has to be decrease. If the user profile has a lot of variation, the threshold must be increased to relax the security and allow him to authenticate itself.
- Two-fusion weights: these weights determinate the most accurate feature for a user

For each of our three classes the three parameters are computed by minimizing the sum of the FRR and FAR. The space of parameters is explored during an exhaustive search.

Table 2. Description of classes

	threshold	The weight of statistical method	The weight of disorder method	number of profiles in the classes
class 1	0.9	0.10	0.3	340
class 2	1	0	0.5	1322
class 3	1.2	0.2	0.4	156

Table 2 presents the characteristics of the three classes. The largest class is the class two. This class is characterized by an average threshold, and by the dual utilization of the disorder measure method and time discretization method, rather than the statistical method.

The class one regroups users with a low threshold. This class may contain profiles characterized by their stability. This class has the lowest weights for the disorder measure method.

The class three seems to represents users with great variations in the profiles as the threshold is high.

To verify such affirmation, we have proceeded to several experiments described in the following section.

5 Experiments and Results

Our private database is composed of 38 users. The keystroke sequences are corresponding to user names and passwords with different lengths (between 8 and 30 characters for the total length of the sequences). The data base is also containing impostor's attacks for each user. Each user has provided between 20 and 110 logins sequences and some people have been asked to try to reproduce some sequences between 20 and 100 times.

The different methods proposed to adapt the parameters (the security threshold and the fusion weights) for each user have been evaluated by using the leave one out method. We estimated the parameters of one user with a tool trained on all the other users.

Implementation of real life applications should also integrated our private database. This database will be considered as a training set and is supposed to be representative of the different classes of users. Results provided by a such application are presented in table 3.

Table 3 shows important improvements compared to the use of global parameters. Performances are improved for all the classes. The obtained error rates are very good for a keystroke dynamics method. However, these error rates hide the fact that the

Table 3. Results of user classification

	FAR% Global Parameter	FRR% Global Parameter	FAR %	FRR%
class 1	0	0.1	0	0
class 2	1.8	5.8	2.8	3.3
class 3	0	1.9	0	1.9
Total	1.8	5.3	1.7	2.1

error is computed on all profiles of a class. It tends to minimize the influence of low performance users, who has catastrophic results. We have identified three of this type of users in our base (EER>30%), they have given only a few sequences (between 20 and 40) so their influence is small. If we compute the average of the EER computed on each user we obtain 4.5%, corresponding to a fair performance.

This value points an other problem of our method: probably, because of the few numbers of problematic users, we are unable to achieve our second objective which was identifying them before the authentication with our clustering methods.

6 Conclusion

The works presented in this paper shows that the keystroke dynamics can be used to perform authentication or identification in real case applications (with an EER around 5%). Adaptation of thresholds and parameters of the system according to user behaviour is a promising way for improving the performances of keystroke dynamics. In addition, the combination of classifiers by adding a fusion step in the system architecture also improves performances. Our experiment shows important improvements even with simple classifiers. Our works on parameters adaptation and classification of user show also interesting results and other improvements remain possible. The authentication of problematic users is still a problem. Therefore, the keystroke dynamics is beginning reaching maturity even if, in real applications, a series of problems can occur: For example, how the systems will react when the keyboard changed? This problem is also present in other biometric systems. It can probably explain why behavioural biometric remains rather marginal in commercial applications.

References

1. Biopassword: Biopassword, http://www.biopassword.com
2. Gaines, R.S., al.: Authentication by Keystroke Timing: Some Preliminary Results. Rand Corporation (1980)
3. Ilonen, J.: Keystroke dynamics. In: Advanced Topics in Information Processing (2003)
4. Peacock, A., Ke, X., Wilkerson, M.: Typing Patterns: A Key to User Identification. IEEE: Security & Privacy Magazine 02(5), 40–47 (2004)
5. Monrose, F., Rubin, A.D.: Keystroke dynamics as a biometric for authentication. Future Generation Computer Systems 16(4), 351–359 (2000)
6. Yu, E., Cho, S.: Keystroke dynamics identity verification–its problems and practical solutions. Computers and Security 23(5), 428–440 (2004)
7. Chen, W., Chang, W.: Applying Hidden Markov Models to Keystroke Pattern Analysis for Password Verification. In: IEEE International Conference on Information Reuse and Integration, pp. 467–474. IEEE Computer Society Press, Los Alamitos (2004)
8. Revett, K., al.: Authenticating computer access based on keystroke dynamics using a probabilistic neural network. DSI - Sistemas de Computação e Comunicações, 2006 (to appear)
9. Kittler, J., al.: On Combining Classifiers. IEEE Transactions on Pattern Analysis and Machine Intelligence 20(3), 226–239 (1998)
10. Jain, A.K., Nandakumar, K., Ross, A.: Score Normalization in Multimodal Biometric Systems. Pattern Recognition 38(12), 2270–2285 (2004)
11. Hocquet, S., Ramel, J.-Y., Cardot, H.: Estimation of User Specific Parameters in One-class Problems. In: 18th International Conference on Pattern Recognition, Hong Kong, pp. 449–452 (2006)
12. Jolliffe, I.T.: Principal Component Analysis. Springer, Heidelberg (1990)

Statistical Texture Analysis-Based Approach for Fake Iris Detection Using Support Vector Machines

Xiaofu He, Shujuan An, and Pengfei Shi

Institute of Image Processing and Pattern Recognition,
Shanghai Jiao Tong University, Shanghai, 200240, China
{xfhe,sj_an,pfshi}@sjtu.edu.cn

Abstract. This paper presents a novel statistical texture analysis based method for detecting fake iris. Four distinctive features based on gray level co-occurrence matrices (GLCM) and properties of statistical intensity values of image pixels are used. A support vector machine (SVM) is selected to characterize the distribution boundary, for it has good classification performance in high dimensional space. The proposed approach is privacy friendly and does not require additional hardware. The experimental results indicate the new approach to be a very promising technique for making iris recognition systems more robust against fake-iris-based spoofing attempts.

1 Introduction

Biometrics systems offer great benefits with respect to other authentication techniques, in particular, they are often more user friendly and can guarantee the physical presence of the user[1-2]. Iris recognition is one of the most reliable biometric technologies in terms of identification and verification performance. It mainly uses iris pattern to recognize and distinguish individuals since the pattern variability among different persons is enormous. In addition, as an internal (yet externally visible) organ of the eye, the iris is well protected from the environment and stable over time [3-9]. Whereas, it is important to understand that, as any other authentication technique, iris recognition is not totally spoof-proof. The main potential threats for iris-based systems are [10-12]: 1) Eye image:Screen image,Photograph,Paper print,Video signal; 2)Artificial eye:Glass/plastic etc; 3) Natural eye(user):Forced use; 4) Capture/replay attacks: Eye image, IrisCode template; 5) Natural eye(impostor): Eye removed from body, Printed contact lens. Recently, the feasibility of the last type of attack has been reported by some researchers [10-14]: they showed that it is actually possible to spoof some iris recognition systems with well-made iris color lens. Therefore, it is important to detect the fake iris as much as possible before subsequent iris recognition.

In previous research, Daugman introduced the method of using FFT (Fast Fourier Transform) in order to check the printed iris pattern [10-12]. His method detects the high frequency spectral magnitude in the frequency domain, which can be shown distinctly and periodically from the print iris pattern because of the characteristics of the periodic dot printing. However, if the input counterfeit iris is defocused and blurred purposely, the counterfeit iris may be accepted as live one. Some iris camera

S.-W. Lee and S.Z. Li (Eds.): ICB 2007, LNCS 4642, pp. 540–546, 2007.

manufacturer also proposed counterfeit iris detection method by using the method of turning on/off illuminator and checking the specular reflection on a cornea. Whereas, such method can be easily spoofed by using the printed iris image with cutting off the printed pupil region and seeing through by attacker's eye, which can make corneal specular reflection [13]. Lee et al. [14] proposed a new method of detecting fake iris attack based on the Purkinje image by using collimated IR-LED (Infra-Red Light Emitting Diode). Especially, they calculated the theoretical positions and distances between the Purkinje images based on the human eye model. However, this method requires additional hardware and need the user's full cooperation. To some extent, this interactive mode demands cooperation of the user who needs to be trained in advance and will eventually increase the time of iris recognition.

In this paper, we propose a new statistical texture analysis based method for detecting fake iris. Four distinctive features based on co-occurrence matrix and properties of statistical intensity values of image pixels are used. A support vector machine (SVM) is used to characterize the distribution boundary, for it has good classification performance in high dimensional space and it is originally developed for two-class problems. The proposed approach is privacy friendly and does not require additional hardware. The remainder of this paper is organized as follows: the proposed method is described in section 2. Section 3 reports experiments and results. Section 4 concludes this paper.

2 Proposed Approach

2.1 Preprocessing

In our experiments, we find that the outer portion of the color contact lens (corresponding to regions closer to outer circle) provides the most useful texture information for fake iris detection since this section of the fake iris is insensitive to the pupil dilation. In addition, the iris maybe corrupted by the occlusion of eyelashes and eyelids, it is necessary to exclude them as much as possible. Therefore, we extract features only in the lower half part of the iris pattern (called region of interest, ROI), i.e we minimize the influence of eyelashes and eyelids by abandoning up half part of the iris pattern.

As mentioned above, useful iris information distributes in the outer portion of the color contact lens. We have found empirically that ROI is usually concentric with the outer circle of iris and the radius of the ROI areas is restricted in a certain range. We therefore detect outer circle to acquire the most discriminating iris features. Outer boundary is detected using Hough transform together with the improved Canny edge detector [15-17], shown in Fig. 1(a). After outer boundary detection, ROI is estimated according to the radius r_{ROI} empirically, as seen in Fig.1(b). In order to achieve invariance to translation and scale, the ROI is further normalized to a rectangular block of a fixed size $W \times H$ by anti-clockwise unwrapping the iris ring, as shown in Fig. 1(c).

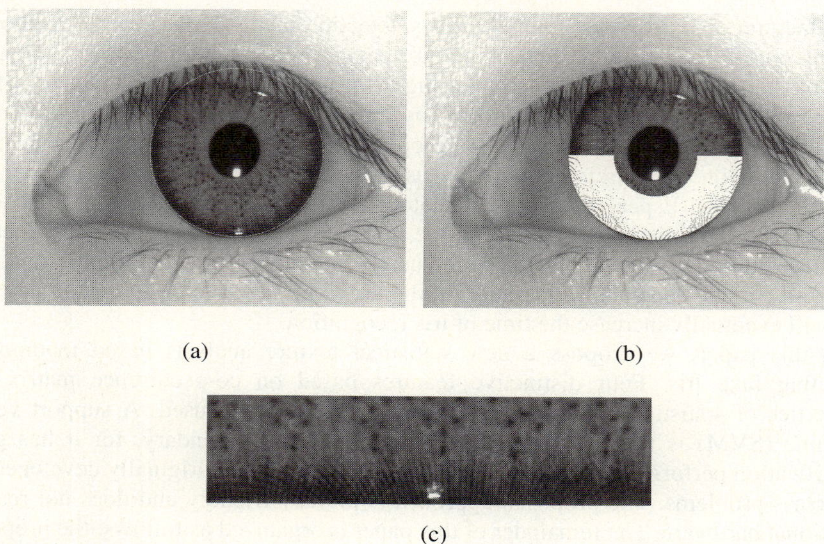

Fig. 1. Preprocessing. (a) Source color contact lens image and outer boundary detection result. (b) The normalization region used for fake detection. (c) Normalized image.

2.2 Feature Vector

The gray level co-occurrence matrices (GLCM) based analysis [18] is one of the most prominent approaches used to extract textural features. Each element $P(i, j)$ of the GLCM represents the relative frequency with which two neighboring pixels separated by a distance of certain columns and certain lines occur, one with gray tone i and the other with gray tone j. Such matrices of gray-level spatial-dependence frequencies are a function of the angular relationship between the neighboring resolution cells as well as function of the distance between them. It is common practice to utilize four well-known properties, i.e, contrast, correlation, angular second moment (is also known as energy) and homogeneity, of a GLCM as the co-occurrence matrix-based features. Although the approach was proposed more than 30 years ago, the properties still remain amongst the most popular and the most discriminative types of texture features [19-20].

In this study, two well-known properties of the GLCM, i.e contrast con and angular second moment asm are utilized for creating feature vector. In addition, the mean m and standard deviation σ_1 value of the intensity values of image pixels are also used for feature value. These four feature values are defined as following:

$$m = \frac{1}{W \times H} \sum_{x=1}^{H} \sum_{y=1}^{W} I(x, y) \tag{1}$$

$$\sigma_1 = \sqrt{\frac{1}{W \times H} \sum_{x=1}^{H} \sum_{y=1}^{W} (I(x,y) - m)^2} \tag{2}$$

$$con = \sum_{i=1}^{N} \sum_{j=1}^{N} (i-j)^2 P(i,j) \tag{3}$$

$$asm = \sum_{i=1}^{N} \sum_{j=1}^{N} P(i,j)^2 \tag{4}$$

Where I denotes the normalized iris image, W is the width of the normalized iris image, H is the height of the normalized iris image. P is the co-occurrence matrix, N denotes the dimension of the co-occurrence matrix.

Therefore, these feature values are arranged to form a four dimensional feature vector.

$$V = [m, \sigma_1, con, asm]^T \tag{5}$$

2.3 Classification

After feature extraction, ROI is represented as a feature vector of length four. The features extracted are used for classification by SVM [21] that appear to be a good candidate because of their ability to transform the learning task to the quadratic programming problem in high-dimensional spaces. In addition, SVM is originally developed for two-class problems.

In this paper, radial basis functions (RBF) kernel function is used as,

$$K(x, x_i) = \exp\{-\frac{|\mathrm{x} - x_i|^2}{{\sigma_2}^2}\} \tag{6}$$

where, x_i comprises the input features, and σ_2 is the standard deviation of the RBF kernel, which is three in our experiments.

The input to the SVM texture classifier comes from a feature vector of length four. This reduces the size of the feature vector and results in an improved generalization performance and classification speed. The sign of the SVM output then represents the class of the iris. For training, +1 was assigned to the live iris class and -1 to the fake iris class. As such, if the SVM output for an input pattern is positive, it is classified as live iris.

3 Experimental Results

In this work, experiment is performed in order to evaluate the performance of the proposed method, which is implemented using Matlab 7.0 on an Intel Pentium IV 3.0G processor PC with 512MB memory. We manually collect 2000 live iris images, 250 contact color lens images. 1000 live iris images and 150 contact lens images are used for training and the rest for testing. The positive samples (the live iris images) come from the SJTU iris database version 3.0 (Iris database of Shanghai Jiao Tong University, version 3.0) which is created by using contactless iris capture device. The negative samples (the color contact lens image, bought at market) come from those images that captured at one session. The size of eye images is 640×480. The radius r_{ROI} of the ROI is 70. The size of each normalized iris image is 90×360. The iris feature vector consists of a feature vector of length four. Samples of the live and fake iris are shown in Fig. 2.

The main drawback of the GLCM approach is the large computer resources required. For example, for an 8-bit image (256 gray level), the co-occurrence matrix has 65536 elements. The number of gray levels determines the size of the GLCM. To reduce this problem, the number of gray levels is set to 8 gray levels when scaling the grayscale values in image. The parameters of RBF kernel function are set: upper bound is 10, standard deviation is 3. The correct classification rate is 100%. The average execution time for feature extraction and classification (for testing) is 31.3ms and 14.7 ms respectively. The results indicate that the proposed scheme should be feasible in practical applications.

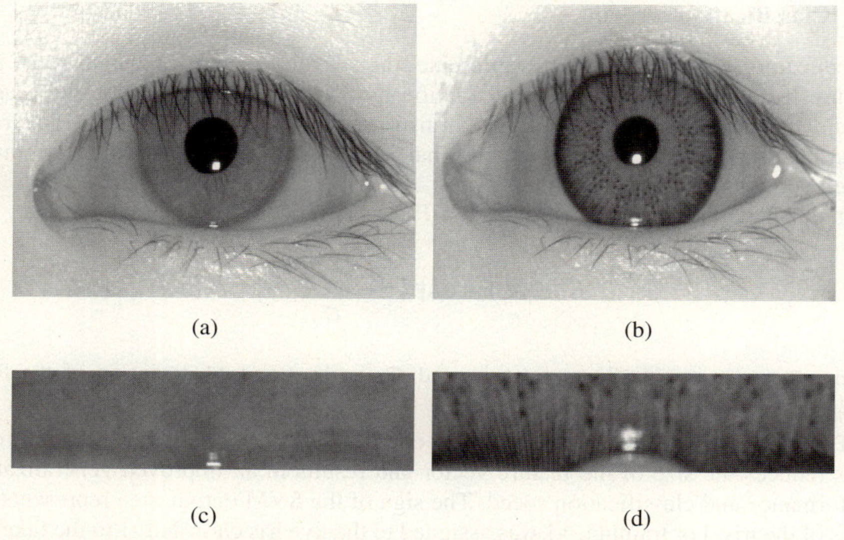

Fig.2. The test examples of live and fake iris. (a) Live eye. (b) Live eye with a color contact lens. (c) Normalized image of ROI of the live eye. (d) Normalized image of ROI of the live eye with a color contact lens.

4 Conclusion

In this paper, we have presented an efficient fake iris detection method based on statistical texture analysis. Four feature values, i.e the mean and standard deviation value of the intensity values of image pixels, contrast and angular second moment of the GLCM, are used for creating feature vector. We choose SVM to characterize the distribution boundary, for it has good classification performance in high dimensional space. Experimental results have illustrated the encouraging performance of the current method in accuracy and speed. The correct classification rate was 100%. The average execution time for feature extraction and classification is 31.3ms and 14.7 ms respectively using Matlab 7.0 on an Intel Pentium IV 3.0G processor PC with 512MB memory.

In the future work, we will extend the fake iris database and conduct experiments on a large number of iris databases in various environments for the proposed method to be more stable and reliable.

Acknowledgements

The authors would like to thank Mr. Eui Chul Lee (Dept. of Computer Science, Sangmyung University) for his helpful discussions. They also thank the anonymous referees for their constructive comments. This work is funded by the National Natural Science Foundation (No.60427002) and the National 863 Program of China (Grant No. 2006AA01Z119).

References

1. Jain, A.K., Bolle, R.M., Pankanti, S. (eds.): Biometrics: Personal Identification in Networked Society. Kluwer, Norwell, MA (1999)
2. Zhang, D.: AutomatedBiometrics: Technologies andSystems. Kluwer, Norwell, MA (2000)
3. Daugman, J.: High confidence visual recognition of persons by a test of statistical independence. IEEE Trans. Pattern Anal. Mach. Intell. 15(11), 1148–1161 (1993)
4. Daugman, J.: The importance of being random: Statistical principles of iris recognition. Pattern Recognition 36(2), 279–291 (2003)
5. Daugman, J.: How iris recognition works. IEEE Trans. on Circuits and Systems for Video Technology 14(1), 21–30 (2004)
6. Wildes, R.P.: Iris recognition: An emerging biometric technology. Proc. IEEE 85(9), 1348–1363 (1997)
7. Ma, L., Tan, T., Wang, Y., Zhang, D.: Personal identification based on iris texture analysis. IEEE Trans. Pattern Anal. Mach. Intell. 25(12), 1519–1533 (2003)
8. Sun, Z., Wang, Y., Tan, T., Cui, J.: Improving iris recognition accuracy via cascaded classifiers. IEEE Trans. on Systems, Man and Cybernetics, Part C 35(3), 435–441 (2005)
9. Park, K.R., Kim, J.: A real-time focusing algorithm for iris recognition camera. IEEE Trans. on Systems, Man and Cybernetics, Part C 35(3), 441–444 (2005)
10. Daugman, J.: Recognizing Persons by their Iris Patterns: Countermeasures against Subterfuge. In: Jain, et al. (eds.) Biometrics. Personal Identification in a Networked Society, pp. 103–121 (1999)
11. Daugman, J.: Demodulation by complex-valued wavelets for stochastic pattern recognition. International Journal of Wavelets, Multiresolution,and Information Processing 1(1), 1–17 (2003)
12. Daugman, J.: Iris Recognition and Anti-Spoofing Countermeasures. In: 7th International Biometrics Conference, London (2004)
13. http://www.heise.de/ct/english/02/11/114/

14. Lee, E.C., Park, K.R., Kim, J.: Fake iris detection by using purkinje image. In: Zhang, D., Jain, A.K. (eds.) Advances in Biometrics. LNCS, vol. 3832, pp. 397–403. Springer, Heidelberg (2005)
15. He, X., Shi, P.: A Novel Iris Segmentation method for Hand-held Capture Device. In: Singh, S., Singh, M., Apte, C., Perner, P. (eds.) ICAPR 2005. LNCS, vol. 3687, pp. 479–485. Springer, Heidelberg (2005)
16. Fleck, M.M.: Some defects in finite-difference edge finders. IEEE Transactions on Pattern Analysis and Machine Intelligence 14(3), 337–345 (1992)
17. Canny, J.: A Computational Approach to Edge Detection. IEEE Transaction on Pattern Analysis and Machine Intelligence 8, 679–714 (1986)
18. Haralick, R.M., Shanmugam, K., Dinstein, I.: Textural features for image classification. IEEE Trans. Syst. Man Cybern. 3(6), 610–621 (1973)
19. Soares, J.V., Renno, C.D., Formaggio, A.R., etc.: An investigation of the selection of texture features for crop discrimination using SAR imagery. Remote Sensing of Environment 59(2), 234–247 (1997)
20. Walker, R.F., Jackway, P.T., Longstaff, D.: Genetic algorithm optimization of adaptive multi-scale GLCM features. Int. J. Pattern Recognition Artif. Intell. 17(1), 17–39 (2003)
21. Burges, C.J.C.: A tutorial on support vector machines for pattern recognition. Data Mining Knowledge Discovery 2, 955–974 (1998)

A Novel Null Space-Based Kernel Discriminant Analysis for Face Recognition

Tuo Zhao[1], Zhizheng Liang[1], David Zhang[2], and Yahui Liu[1]

[1] Harbin Institute of Technology
tourzhao@gmail.com
[2] Hongkong Polytechnic University

Abstract. The symmetrical decomposition is a powerful method to extract features for image recognition. It reveals the significant discriminative information from the mirror image of symmetrical objects. In this paper, a novel null space kernel discriminant method based on the symmetrical method with a weighted fusion strategy is proposed for face recognition. It can effectively enhance the recognition performance and shares the advantages of Null-space, kernel and symmetrical methods. The experiment results on ORL database and FERET database demonstrate that the proposed method is effective and outperforms some existing subspace methods.

Keywords: symmetrical decomposition, symmetrical null-space based kernel LDA, weighted fusion strategy, face recognition.

1 Introduction

Linear Discriminant Analysis (LDA) is a popular method in extracting features, and it has been successfully applied to many fields. In general, the objective of LDA is to seek a linear projection from the image space to a low dimensional space by maximizing the between-class scatter and minimizing the within-class scatter simultaneously. It is shown that LDA is better than PCA especially under illumination variation [1]. In [2], Zhao also favorably supported this point under the FERET testing framework. However, in many practical applications of LDA, when the number of the samples is much smaller than the dimension of the sample space, it results in the small size sample (SSS) problem [3]. During the past several decades, many methods have been proposed to deal with this problem. Belhumeur [1] used PCA to reduce the dimension of the samples to an intermediate dimension and then Fisher LDA is used to extract the features. However, the Fisher LDA only uses the regularized space of the within-class scatter matrix. Considering this point, Yu [4] proposed Direct LDA. In their method, they projected all the samples directly by removing the null space of between-class scatter matrix. Chen [5] made a more crucial modification. That is, they firstly projected all the samples onto the null space of within-class scatter matrix before doing DLDA and proposed a more powerful Null-space Based LDA (NLDA).

Although the methods mentioned above have proved to be efficient for face recognition, they are still linear techniques in nature. Hence they are inadequate to

S.-W. Lee and S.Z. Li (Eds.): ICB 2007, LNCS 4642, pp. 547–556, 2007.

describe the complexity of real face images because of illumination, facial expression and pose variations. To deal with this problem, kernel methods including Kernel PCA (KPCA) and Kernel LDA [6, 7] are proposed. The idea of kernel methods is to map all the data by a non-linear function into the feature space and then to perform some operations in this space.

In recent years, some researchers introduced the symmetric idea in face recognition. Yang [8] presented a symmetrical principal component analysis (SPCA) algorithm according to the symmetry of human faces. Their method can reduce the sensitivities to outliers. In this paper, we propose a symmetrical null space-based kernel LDA method, which can simultaneously provide the advantages of kernel, symmetrical and Null-space methods.

The rest of this paper is organized as follows. Section 2 reviews the related work on Kernel Fisher and its variants. Section 3 proposes our method. The experimental results are shown in section 4. Section 5 gives discussion and conclusions.

2 Related Work

2.1 Fundamentals

In Kernel methods, the *input space* R^n firstly is mapped into the *feature space* F by a non-linear mapping ϕ, denoted as:

$$\phi : R^n \to F, x \mapsto \phi(x). \tag{1}$$

Kernel Fisher Discriminant is to solve the problem of LDA in the feature space F by a set of nonlinear discriminant vectors in *input space*. By maximizing the following Fisher criterion:

$$J^{\phi}(\varphi) = \frac{|\varphi^T S_b^{\phi} \varphi|}{|\varphi^T S_t^{\phi} \varphi|}, \tag{2}$$

where S_b^{ϕ} and S_t^{ϕ} are defined as below:

$$S_b^{\phi} = \frac{1}{M} \sum_{i=1}^{c} l_i (m_i^{\phi} - m^{\phi})(m_i^{\phi} - m^{\phi})^T, \tag{3}$$

$$S_t^{\phi} = \frac{1}{M} \sum_{i=1}^{M} (\phi(x_i) - m^{\phi})(\phi(x_i) - m^{\phi})^T, \tag{4}$$

where $x_1, x_2, ..., x_M$ is a set of M training samples in *input space*, l_i is the number of training samples of class i and satisfies $\sum_{i=1}^{c} l_i = M$, m_i^{ϕ} is the mean vector of the mapped training samples of class i, and m^{ϕ} is the mean vector across all mapped training samples.

2.2 Kernel Fisher and Its Variant (KFD and NKLDA)

Actually, we can obtain the discriminant vectors with the respect to the Fisher criterion by computing the Eigenvalue problem as $S_b^\phi \varphi = \lambda S_t^\phi \varphi$. In theory, any solution $\varphi \in F$ must lie in the span of all samples in F, so we can view φ as a linear combination of $\phi(x_i)$:

$$\varphi = \sum_{j=1}^{M} a_j \phi(x_j) = Q\alpha \,, \tag{5}$$

where $Q = [\phi(x_1), \phi(x_2), ..., \phi(x_M)]$ and $\alpha = (a_1, a_2, ..., a_M)^T$.

The matrix K is defined as

$$K = \tilde{K} - 1_M \tilde{K} - \tilde{K} 1_M + 1_M \tilde{K} 1_M \,. \tag{6}$$

Here $1_M = (1/M)_{M \times M}$, $\tilde{K} = Q^T Q$ is an $M \times M$ matrix and its elements are

$$\tilde{K}_{ij} = \phi(x_i)^T \phi(x_j) = (\phi(x_i) \cdot \phi(x_j)) = k(x_i, y_j) \tag{7}$$

corresponding to a given nonlinear mapping ϕ and, the new sample vector by kernel tricks, $K(x_i)$, is defined as a column of K:

$$K(x_i) = [k(x_1, x_i), k(x_2, x_i), ..., k(x_M, x_i)]^T \,. \tag{8}$$

Substituting Eq.(5) into Eq.(2) gives

$$J^K(\alpha) = \frac{|\alpha^T K_b \alpha|}{|\alpha^T K_t \alpha|} \,, \tag{9}$$

where the new between-class scatter matrix K_b and total scatter matrix K_t are

$$K_b = \frac{1}{M} \sum_{i=1}^{c} l_i (m_i - m)(m_i - m)^T \,, \tag{10}$$

$$K_t = \frac{1}{M} \sum_{i=1}^{M} (K(x_i) - m)(K(x_i) - m)^T \,, \tag{11}$$

where m_i is the mean vector of all $K(x_j)$ belonging to class i, and m is the mean vector of all $K(x_j)$. Eq.(9) is a standard Fisher equation and we obtain the final discriminant vectors by:

$$X_i = \alpha \cdot K(x_i) \,. \tag{12}$$

Liu [8] developed kernel null space method. The between class scatter matrix K_b is projected onto the null space of new within-class scatter matrix K_w. That is, the null space of K_w in the mapping space is firstly calculated as

$$Y^T K_w Y = 0, \tag{13}$$

where Y consists of the eigenvectors with zero eigenvalues and $Y^T Y = I$. Then we obtain

$$\tilde{K}_b = Y^T K_b Y. \tag{14}$$

Furthermore, the eigenvectors U of $\tilde{K}_b$ with the first several largest eigenvalues are selected to form the transformation matrix

$$X_i = U^T Y^T K(x_i). \tag{15}$$

3 Symmetrical Null-Space Based Kernel LDA (SNKLDA)

3.1 Symmetrical Ideas

For any function f, it can be written as $f = f_e + f_o$, in which $f_e = (f + f_m)/2$ and $f_o = (f - f_m)/2$. Here f_m is the symmetrical counterpart of f. f_e and f_o are, respectively, described by a linear combination of a set of even or odd symmetrical basis functions. Thus, any function can be linearly reconstructed by the two basis functions, one even symmetrical and another odd symmetrical. This is the even-odd decomposition principle. We can apply this principle to face images and define symmetry to be the horizontal mirror symmetry with the vertical midline of the image as its axis. According to the odd-even decomposition theory, x_i can be decomposed as $x_i = x_{ei} + x_{oi}$ with $x_{ei} = (x_i + x_{mi})/2$ denoting the odd symmetrical image, and $x_{ei} = (x_i - x_{mi})/2$ denoting the odd symmetrical image, where x_{mi} is the mirror image of x_i. Based on this, symmetrical methods perform classification on two new symmetrical image sets, and then combine the features of odd and even images as the final features.

3.2 Our Proposed Method

Theorem: For any polynomial kernel function ϕ and any two vectors x_a and x_b, if $< x_a, x_b >= 0$, there exits a relationship: $\phi(x_a + x_b) = \phi(x_a) + \phi(x_b)$

Proof: Because $\phi(x)$ is a polynomial function, $\phi(x)$ can be written as $\phi(x) = \sum_{i=0}^{N} a_i x^i$, and similarly $\phi(x_a + x_b) = \sum_{i=0}^{N} a_i (x_a + x_b)^i$. Since $< x_a, x_b >= 0$,

$$\begin{aligned}\phi(x_a + x_b) &= \sum_{i=0}^{N} a_i (x_a + x_b)^i \\ &= \sum_{i=0}^{N} \beta_i^0 a_i x_a^i + \ldots + \sum_{i=0}^{N} \beta_i^j a_i x_a^j x_b^{i-j} + \ldots + \sum_{i=0}^{N} \beta_i^i a_i x_b^i\end{aligned}$$

$$= \sum_{i=0}^{N} a_i x_a^i + \sum_{i=0}^{N} a_i x_b^i$$
$$= \phi(x_a) + \phi(x_b)$$

where β is the coefficients of a linear combination.

So for new training samples in the feature space, the following equation holds

$$\begin{aligned} K_{ij} &= < \phi(x_i), \phi(x_j) > \\ &= < \phi(x_{oi} + x_{ei}), \phi(x_{oj} + x_{ej}) > \\ &= < \phi(x_{oi}) + \phi(x_{ei}), \phi(x_{oi}) + \phi(x_{ej}) > \\ &= < \phi(x_{oi}), \phi(x_{oj}) > + < \phi(x_{oi}), \phi(x_{ej}) > + < \phi(x_{ei}), \phi(x_{oj}) > + < \phi(x_{ei}), \phi(x_{ej}) > . \end{aligned} \tag{16}$$

Since the polynomial kernel $K_{ij} = < \phi(x_i), \phi(x_j) > = (< x_i, x_j > +1)^d$ is adopted for the symmetrical decomposition. Then we obtain:

$$\begin{aligned} < \phi(x_{oi}), \phi(x_{ej}) > &= (< x_{oi}, x_{ej} > +1)^d = (0+1)^d = 1 , \\ < \phi(x_{ei}), \phi(x_{oj}) > &= (< x_{ei}, x_{oj} > +1)^d = (0+1)^d = 1 . \end{aligned} \tag{17}$$

Thus, it means that $k(x_{oi}, x_{ej})$ and $k(x_{ei}, x_{oj})$ do not contain the valid discriminant information. In [10], Lu et al. discussed the orthogonally of Kernel Symmetrical PCA in the original space and used the polynomial kernel in their experiments. But we find that in the feature space the inner product of $\phi(x_o)$ and $\phi(x_e)$ are constant when the polynomial kernel is applied. Therefore, when a symmetrical method adopts the polynomial kernel, it still only considers the principal components of even and odd symmetrical images, not considering the correlative components between even and odd symmetrical images. Therefore, when the Kernel Symmetrical PCA method adopts the polynomial kernel, we can decompose the sample set into two new sets. Then we can perform classification on even and odd images by combing their features.

Since NKLDA is more effective than KPCA in solving small size sample problem [6]. In the following, we combine it with symmetrical ideas in discriminant analysis to improve the classification performance. To this end, we propose SNKLDA. The proposed method utilizes the symmetrical properties to do NKLDA in both the even and odd space and it shares the advantages of two methods in some sense.

In the following, we describe the proposed method.

We firstly convert the training samples into two training sets $\{x_{ei}\}_{1\le i\le M}$ and $\{x_{oi}\}_{1\le i\le M}$. Then we project the new sample set in the feature space by the kernel trick. That is, we can obtain the following new kernel training sets:

$$\begin{aligned} K_e(x_{ei}) &= (k(x_{e1}, x_{ei}), k(x_{e2}, x_{ei}), \ldots, k(x_{eM}, x_{ei}))^T, 1 \le i \le M , \\ K_o(x_{oi}) &= (k(x_{o1}, x_{oi}), k(x_{o2}, x_{oi}), \ldots, k(x_{oM}, x_{oi}))^T, 1 \le i \le M . \end{aligned} \tag{18}$$

Then we calculate class mean, total mean, the between-class scatter matrix and the within-class scatter matrix of each new kernel training set as follows:

$$m_{ej} = \sum_{j \in c} K(x_{ej}) / M, m_e = \sum_{j \in c} m_{ej} / c, \; m_{oj} = \sum_{j \in c} K(x_{oj}) / M, m_o = \sum_{j \in c} m_{o_j} / c, \tag{19}$$

$$\begin{aligned} K_{we} &= \sum_{j=1}^{c} \sum_{i \in C_j} (K(x_{ei}) - m_{ej})(K(x_{ei}) - m_{ej})^T, \\ K_{wo} &= \sum_{j=1}^{c} \sum_{i \in C_j} (K(x_{oi}) - m_{oj})(K(x_{oi}) - m_{oj})^T, \end{aligned} \tag{20}$$

$$K_{be} = \sum_{i \in C_j} (m_{ej} - m_e)(m_{ej} - m_e)^T, \; K_{bo} = \sum_{i \in C_j} (m_{oj} - m_o)(m_{oj} - m_o)^T. \tag{21}$$

Based on the above steps, we perform feature extraction in both the odd and even spaces. That is, we extract the null space Y_e of K_{we} and Y_o of K_{wo} such that

$$Y_e^T K_{we} Y_e = 0, \; Y_o^T K_{wo} Y_o = 0. \tag{22}$$

Subsequently, the between class scatter matrix K_{be} and K_{bo} are projected onto the null space of K_{we} and K_{wo}

$$\tilde{K}_{be} = Y_e^T K_{be} Y_e, \; \tilde{K}_{bo} = Y_o^T K_{bo} Y_o. \tag{23}$$

Furthermore, the eigenvectors U_e of $\tilde{K}_{be}$ and U_o of $\tilde{K}_{bo}$ with the first several largest eigenvalues are selected to form the transformation matrix

$$X_e = U_e^T Y_e^T K_e(x_e), \; X_o = U_o^T Y_o^T K_o(x_o). \tag{24}$$

It is obvious that we get two sets of features from Eq. (24). It is necessary to use these features for classification. Note that in the previous symmetrical methods, the features are usually directly combined as the final features [9, 10]. Different from the previous methods, we assign different weights to fuse the features in the odd and even spaces to improve the classification performance. The final features are defined as

$$\begin{aligned} X_{fuse}(x) &= [w_e X_e(x), w_o X_o(x)], \\ w_o &= \left(\frac{R_o}{R_e + R_o} \right)^t, w_e = \left(\frac{R_e}{R_e + R_o} \right)^t \end{aligned} \tag{25}$$

where w_o and w_e are fused weights, R_e and R_o are the correct recognition rates with even features and odd respectively, and $t = 0, 1, 2$ in our experiment. To reduce the computational complexity of weight training, we compute the weights on a small set of samples.

4 Experimental Results

In order to compare the performance of SKNLDA with other methods, the experiments are performed on two popular face databases: ORL database and FERET database. All the following experiments share the same steps. The image data are preprocessed including histogram equalization, normalization. For the sake of simplicity, we choose the Nearest Neighbor as the classifier and the polynomial kernel function is selected as $k(x, y) = (1 + < x, y >)^d$ with degree $d = 2$. In addition, we select $c-1$ and $N-1$ as the finial dimensions in Fisher LDA and KSPCA.

4.1 Experiments on ORL Database

There are 10 different images for each subject in ORL face database composed of 40 distinct subjects. All the subjects are in up-right, frontal position. The size of each face image is downsampled to 46×56. Fig.1 shows all 10 images of the first person after histogram equalization.

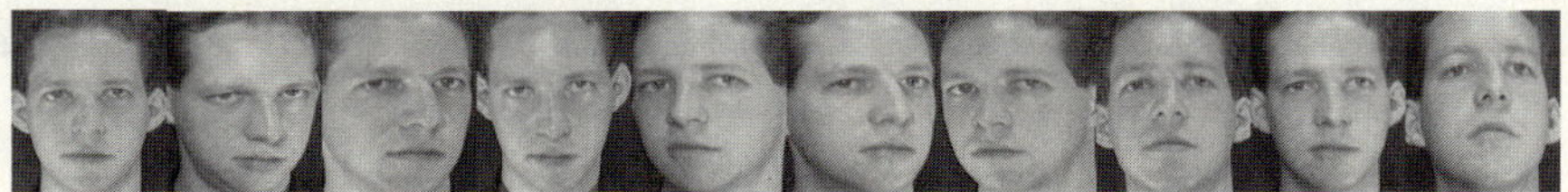

Fig. 1. Samples from the first person in ORL Database

In this set of experiments, the first 10 subjects in the database are selected to determine the weights: In order to reduce variation, we random select 2 images from each subject as training samples and the others are testing samples. The results are the average of 20 runs. We obtain even CRR 96.44% and odd CRR: 59.00%. Table 1 shows the performance of SNKLDA under different t.

Table 1. The performance of SNKLDA under different t on ORL database

K	$t=0$	$t=1$	$t=2$
2	85.39	86.44	86.33
3	91.35	92.03	91.88
4	94.52	94.82	94.75

Table 2. The experiment results on ORL database

K	*Fisher*	*NLDA*	*NKLDA*	*KSPCA*	*SNKLDA*
2	75.72	85.26	84.13	84.22	86.44
3	86.31	91.06	91.02	89.78	92.03
4	91.40	94.18	94.42	92.99	94.82

Then we compare SNKLDA with some methods in the case of different numbers of training samples. The number of training samples per subject, *k*, varies from 2 to 4. In each round, *k* images are randomly selected from the database for training and the remaining images of the same subject are used for testing. For each *k*, 50 tests are performed and the final results are averaged over 50 runs. Table 2 shows the CRR (%) and we can see that the performance of SNKLDA is better than other methods.

4.2 Experiments on FERET Database

In order to further test the capability of the proposed method, experiments are made on the dataset with more subjects such as the FERET database. In the experiments, we select a subset including 200 subjects respectively from FERET database with 11 upright, frontal-view images of each subject. The face images on this database involve much more variations in lighting, view and expressions. The size of face images is downsampled to 50×60. Fig.2 shows all 11 images of the first person after histogram equalization.

Fig. 2. Samples from the first person in FERET Database after histogram equalization

In this set of experiments, the first 40 subjects in the database are selected to determine the weights. In order to reduce variation, we random select 2 images from each subject as training samples and the others are testing samples. The results are the average of 20 runs. We obtain even CRR 80.81% and odd CRR: 20.56%. Table 3 shows the performance of SNKLDA under different t.

Table 3. The performance of SNKLDA under different t on ORL database

K	$t=0$	$t=1$	$t=2$
2	66.70	68.07	67.99
3	73.21	74.67	74.64
4	77.42	78.34	78.27

Table 4. The experiment results on ORL database

K	***Fisher***	***NLDA***	***NKLDA***	***KSPCA***	***SNKLDA***
2	31.20	60.00	62.25	56.94	68.07
3	55.64	64.60	68.47	63.88	74.67
4	68.16	68.81	74.00	67.93	78.34

The number of samples in each class, *k*, varies from 2 to 4. For each *k*, 100 tests are performed and the final results are averaged over 100 runs. Table 4 shows the experimental results and we can see SNKLDA outperforms all the other subspace methods in all the cases.

5 Discussions and Conclusions

From the above two experiments we can find that SNKLDA is better than all the other methods. It may come from the fact that the SNKLDA method has the advantages of

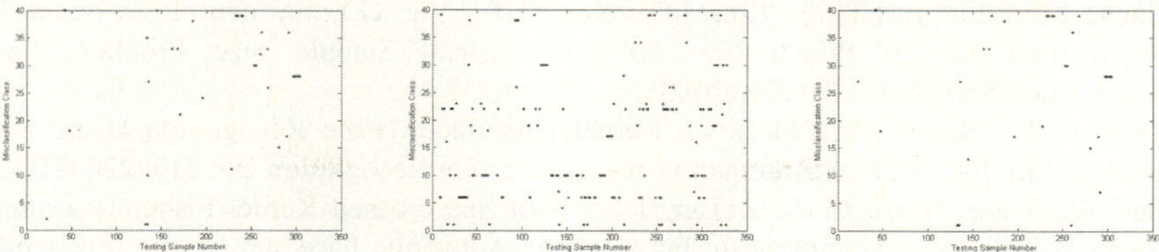

Fig. 3. Misclassification in even (L), odd (M) and full space with weighted strategy(R) on ORL

the NKLDA method in the small sample size problem. Although SNKLDA has twice computational complexity of NKLDA due to the symmetrical decomposition, the symmetry decomposition contributes to about 5% increases on FERET. In the above experiments the number of the subspace dimension is $(c-1)\times 2$ which is much lower than PCA method in the symmetrical methods.

It should be noted that extracting complementary discriminative information and the fusion strategy are also important for symmetrical methods. From the experiment we can see our weighted strategy is better than directly combination. In addition, from Fig. 3, we note that the two spaces are not complementary enough to increase the recognition rate greatly by the basic fusion strategy. The misclassified samples in the even space are usually also misclassified in the odd space. Hence how to efficiently use the complementary information in two spaces deserves the further research.

In all, the main contributions of this paper are briefly summarized as follows: (a) Proposed SNKLDA method that can provide better performance than other methods; (b) Proposed weighted strategy for even and odd features and revealed the bottleneck of the symmetrical method ;(d) pointed out that the SKPCA method in the polynomial kernel still only considers the principal components of even and odd symmetrical images, not considering the correlative components between even and odd symmetrical images. However, considering the problems in the above discussion, there still has some wok to do in the near future. That is, we will pay much more attention to the following two aspects: (1) Fusion strategy: a more powerful fusion strategy should be used to maximize the utilization of the complementary information; (2) Kernel function: a novel kernel function should be used to avoid the orthogonality of even and odd features to generate a mixed space for classification.

References

1. Belhumeur, P.N., Hespanha, J.P., Kiregman, D.J.: Eigenfaces vs. Fisherfaces: Recognition Using Class Specific Linear Projection. IEEE Trans. on PAMI. 19(7), 711–720 (1997)
2. Zhao, W., Chellappa, R., Philips, P.J.: Subspace Linear Discriminant Analysis for Face Recognition. Tech Report CAR-TR-914 Center for Automation Research, University of Maryland (1999)
3. Fukunaga, K.: Introduction to Statistical Pattern Recognition. Academic Press, London (1990)
4. Yu, H., Yang, J.: A Direct LDA algorithm for High-dimensional Data with Application to Face Recognition. Pattern Recognition 34(10), 2067–2070 (2001)

5. Chen, L.F., Liao, H.Y.M., Lin, J.C., Ko, M.T., Yu, G.J.: A new LDA-based Face Recognition System Which Can Solve the Small Sample Size Problem. Pattern Recognition 33(10), 1713–1726 (2000)
6. Yang, M.H.: Kernel Eigenfaces vs. Kernel Fisherfaces: Face Recognition Using Kernel Methods. In: Int. Conf. on Automatic Face and Gesture Recognition, pp. 215–220 (2002)
7. Liu, W., Wang, Y.H., Li, S.Z., Tan, T.N.: Null Space-based Kernel Fisher Discriminant Analysis for Face Recognition. In: Int. Conf. on Automatic Face and Gesture Recognition, pp. 369–374 (2004)
8. Yang, Q., Ding, X.: Symmetrical PCA in Face Recognition. In: IEEE Int. Conf. on Image Processing, pp. 97–100 (2002)
9. Lu, C., Zhang, C., Zhang, T., Zhang, W.: Kernel Based Symmetrical Principal Component Analysis for Face Classification. Nerucomputing 70(4-6), 904–911 (2007)

Appendix

Let a sample vector be $x=\{x_1, x_2, ..., x_{n-1}, x_n\}$ and its mirror vector be $x_m=\{x_n, x_{n-1}, ..., x_2, x_1\}$, and another sample vector be $y=\{y_1, y_2, ..., y_{n-1}, y_n\}$ and its mirror vector be $y_m=\{y_n, y_{n-1}, ..., y_2, y_1\}$. Then by symmetrical decomposition, we obtain

$$x_e=\frac{x+x_m}{2}=\{\frac{x_1+x_n}{2},\frac{x_2+x_{n-1}}{2},...,\frac{x_{n-1}+x_2}{2},\frac{x_n+x_1}{2}\}, \quad (A.1)$$

$$x_o=\frac{x-x_m}{2}=\{\frac{x_1-x_n}{2},\frac{x_2-x_{n-1}}{2},...,\frac{x_{n-1}-x_2}{2},\frac{x_n-x_1}{2}\}, \quad (A.2)$$

$$y_e=\frac{y+y_m}{2}=\{\frac{y_1+y_n}{2},\frac{y_2+y_{n-1}}{2},...,\frac{y_{n-1}+y_2}{2},\frac{y_n+y_1}{2}\}, \quad (A.3)$$

$$y_o=\frac{y-y_m}{2}=\{\frac{y_1-y_n}{2},\frac{y_2-y_{n-1}}{2},...,\frac{y_{n-1}-y_2}{2},\frac{y_n-y_1}{2}\}. \quad (A.4)$$

The inner product is

$$<x_e, y_o>=((\frac{x_1+y_n}{2})(\frac{x_1-y_n}{2})+...+(\frac{x_n+y_1}{2})(\frac{x_n-y_1}{2})). \quad (A.5)$$

It is obvious that $(\frac{x_i+y_{n-i}}{2})(\frac{x_i-y_{n-i}}{2})+(\frac{x_{n-i}+y_i}{2})(\frac{x_{n-i}-y_i}{2})=(\frac{x_i+y_{n-i}}{2})(\frac{x_i-y_{n-i}}{2})+$ $(-(\frac{x_{n-i}+y_i}{2})(\frac{x_i-y_{n-i}}{2}))=0$, so

$$<x_e, y_o>=0. \quad (A.6)$$

In the similar way, we prove

$$<x_o, y_e>=0. \quad (A.7)$$

Changeable Face Representations Suitable for Human Recognition

Hyunggu Lee, Chulhan Lee, Jeung-Yoon Choi, Jongsun Kim, and Jaihie Kim

School of Electrical and Electronic Engineering, Yonsei University,
Biometrics Engineering Research Center (BERC), Republic of Korea
{lindakim,devices,jychoi,kjongss,jhkim}@yonsei.ac.kr

Abstract. In order to resolve non-revocability of biometrics, changeable biometrics has been recently introduced. Changeable biometrics transforms an original biometric template into a changeable template in a non-invertible manner. The transformed changeable template does not reveal the original biometric template, so that secure concealment of biometric data is possible using a changeable transformation. Changeable biometrics has been applied to face recognition, and there are several changeable face recognition methods. However, previous changeable face transformations cannot provide face images that can be recognized by humans. Hence, 'human inspection', a particular property of face biometrics, cannot be provided by previous changeable face biometric methods.

In this paper, we propose a face image synthesis method which allows human inspection of changeable face templates. The proposed face synthesis method is based on subspace modeling of face space, and the face space is obtained by projection method such as principle component analysis (PCA) or independent component analysis (ICA). The face space is modeled by fuzzy C-means clustering and *partition-based PCA*. Using the proposed method, human-recognizable faces can be synthesized while providing inter-class discrimination and intra-class similarity.

Keywords: changeable face biometrics, non-invertibility, human inspection, face image synthesis, *partition-based PCA*.

1 Introduction

The human face is a key biometric characteristic for human recognition of personal identity. Current face recognition algorithms can handle large amounts of face biometric data very quickly. However, face recognition algorithms are not perfect. In many cases, face recognition algorithms are not as good as human inspection. Hence, the human ability of face recognition is still an important factor in recognition of a human face. Additionally, there are some examples where the human ability to recognize faces is an important issue, such as human inspection of the pictures of faces in a driver's license or a passport. In an ideal face recognition system, images of users are stored in a trusted database, and in that case, human inspection is possible using the face images of the database.

S.-W. Lee and S.Z. Li (Eds.): ICB 2007, LNCS 4642, pp. 557–565, 2007.

However, storing user's face images can cause privacy violations. In order to resolve this problem, changeable biometrics has been introduced [1].

Ratha et al. [1] proposed a changeable face synthesis method based on morphing. Synthesizing face images by morphing allows human inspection. However, the original face image can be reconstructed when an attacker learns the morphing function. Besides the method of Ratha et al., there are several methods for generating changeable face biometrics [2][3][4]. A common point of these methods is that they cannot provide for human inspection.

Boult [2] proposed a transformation method for face recognition, in which a face feature is transformed via scaling and translation. Using robust distance measure, the transformed feature can provide improved performance, and the original biometric data cannot be inverted from their encrypted data, which is cryptographically secure. However, as mentioned, this transform does not allow human inspection.

Savvides et al. [3] proposed changeable biometrics for face recognition that uses minimum average correlation energy (MACE) filters and random kernels. However, the original face image can be recovered via deconvolution if the random kernel is known. Moreover, because the face is convolved with a random kernel, their method cannot provide for human inspection.

Teoh et al. [4] proposed a new authentication approach called BioHashing which combines user-specific tokenized random vectors with biometric feature vectors to generate a biometric code. The inner product between biometric feature vectors and a set of orthonormal random vectors are calculated and a biometric code is generated by using a predefined threshold. By thresholding, the original biometric can not be recovered from the biometric code. Again, however, their method does not provide for human inspection.

In this paper, we propose a subspace based changeable face synthesis method which allows human recognition of the generated faces. The organization of the paper is as follows. Section 2 briefly describes the method for generating changeable coefficient vectors from face images and our motivation for recognizable face synthesis. In Section 3, the subspace modeling and range fitting methods for face synthesis follow. Finally, results of our face synthesis and future work are discussed in Section 4 and Section 5, respectively.

2 Changeable Coefficient Vector Generation

A changeable face template can be generated by combining PCA and ICA coefficient vectors [5]. Two different face feature coefficient vectors, $\mathbf{P}$ and $\mathbf{I}$ are extracted from an input face image using PCA and ICA, and the two coefficient vectors are normalized as follows.

$$\begin{aligned}\mathbf{p} &= \mathbf{P}/\left|\mathbf{P}\right| = [\mathbf{p}_1, \mathbf{p}_2, \mathbf{p}_3, ..., \mathbf{p}_N],\\ \mathbf{i} &= \mathbf{I}/\left|\mathbf{I}\right| = [\mathbf{i}_1, \mathbf{i}_2, \mathbf{i}_3, ..., \mathbf{i}_N].\end{aligned} \tag{1}$$

Then, the two normalized feature coefficient vectors, $\mathbf{p}$ and $\mathbf{i}$ are scrambled using two permutation matrices.

$$\mathbf{p}^s = \mathbf{S}_{ID}^{PCA}(\mathbf{p}), \quad \mathbf{i}^s = \mathbf{S}_{ID}^{ICA}(\mathbf{i}). \tag{2}$$

The permutation matrices, $\mathbf{S}_{ID}^{PCA}$ and $\mathbf{S}_{ID}^{ICA}$ are generated by a random number generator whose seed is the user's personal ID. Finally, a changeable face coefficient vector $\mathbf{c}$ is generated by addition of the scrambled coefficient vectors,

$$\mathbf{c} = \mathbf{p}^s + \mathbf{i}^s. \tag{3}$$

Even if an attacker knows the changeable face coefficient vector $\mathbf{c}$ and the scrambling rule, the original PCA or ICA coefficient vector can not be recovered because the changeable coefficient vector is generated by addition. Moreover, due to scrambling and addition, the changeable coefficient vector is not the same as either the PCA or the ICA coefficient vector, so that the changeable coefficient vector cannot represent a human-like image when the changeable coefficient vector is reprojected onto either the PCA or ICA basis. Fig. 1 shows some reprojected images using the PCA and ICA coefficient vectors and using the changeable coefficient vector. Fig. 1 (b) and (c) show reconstruction images using the original subspace coefficient vectors and corresponding subspace basis. Reconstructed images are rather degraded because we do not use the full number of basis vectors. The changeable coefficient vector can be directly reprojected using the PCA or ICA basis. Since the changeable coefficient vector differs from either the PCA or ICA coefficient vector, the reprojected images in Fig. 1 (d) and (e) cannot be recognized as human. Hence humans cannot inspect the resulting changeable face templates as to whether it is similar or not to a corresponding template in the database.

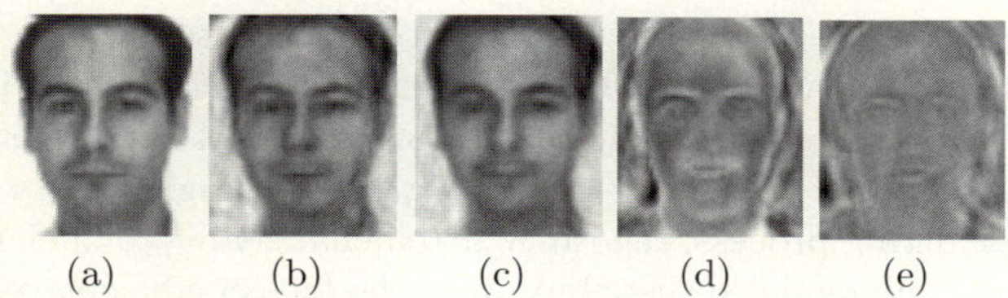

Fig. 1. Face generation using changeable coefficient vector (a): input face image, (b): reconstruction using the PCA coefficient vector, (c): reconstruction using the ICA coefficient vector, (d): reprojected image using changeable coefficient vector with the PCA basis, (e): reprojected image using changeable coefficient vector with the ICA basis

From the above discussion, it is clear that the changeable face template cannot yield a human face image. In fact, because the original face image cannot be stored in changeable biometrics, there is no specific face image that is associated with the changeable template. However, for human inspection, a new face image ought to be synthesized, and that synthesized face image should be generated from a changeable face template. In this paper, we propose a face synthesis method which can generate a new face image using a changeable coefficient vector from a modeled face subspace. In the following sections, the proposed face synthesis method is described more specifically.

3 Subspace Based Face Synthesis

The proposed face image synthesis method is founded on face space modeling on a subspace such as the PCA or ICA coefficient vector space. As a subspace distribution modeling method, *partition-based PCA* follows fuzzy C-means clustering [6]. As shown in Fig. 2 (a) and (b), grouping is carried out by the clustering method, then PCA is applied to each cluster. Hereafter, this type of approach will be called '*partition-based PCA*'. However, due to differences of the modeled

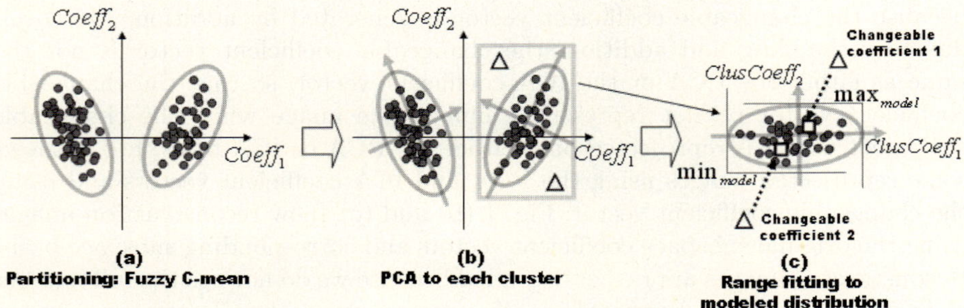

Fig. 2. Conceptual picture of face subspace modeling and range fitting for changeable coefficient vector (a): subspace is partitioned using clustering, (b): PCA is applied to each cluster, (c): range of changeable coefficient vector is fitted into range of coefficient vector of *partition-based PCA*

distributions between the face coefficient vector and the changeable coefficient vector, the changeable coefficient vector should be fitted within the modeled distribution of the face coefficient vector when synthesizing a face image. Before range fitting, the changeable coefficient vector is located outside of the modeled distribution of the face coefficient vector, e.g., the triangle points in Fig. 2 (c). After the range fitting process, the range fitted changeable coefficient vectors are located inside of the modeled distribution of the face coefficient vector, e.g., the square points in Fig. 2 (c). Because the face subspace coefficient vector, which exists inside of the modeled distribution of face coefficient vector, does represent a real face image, the range fitted changeable coefficient vector can also represent a face image that allows human inspection. Detail of the distribution modeling of face coefficient vector and the range fitting of the changeable coefficient vector into the distribution of the face coefficient vector will be covered in below.

3.1 Face Distribution Modeling on the Subspace

We use fuzzy C-means (FCM) method for subspace modeling, which is a soft clustering method. In order to update cluster prototypes, the overall information of data points are utilized with a weight which specifies the responsibility to cluster prototypes [6]. After partitions are obtained from clustering, PCA is applied to each cluster. Local PCA [7] is a method similar to *partition-based*

PCA. which iteratively updates partitions and PCA basis of the partitions using the reconstruction error. However, in our experiments, in order to utilize the local structure of initial clusters (FCM result), we use *partition-based PCA* as a non iterative version of local PCA.

3.2 Local Surface Determination and Face Synthesis

After FCM clustering, PCA is applied to each cluster in the subspace. Because PCA captures maximum variation of the distribution, the local surface of each subspace can be determined from the *partition-based PCA* components. For the k th cluster of the subspace, $\mathbf{p}^i_{cluster\_k}$ is the ith element of *partition-based PCA* coefficient vector $\mathbf{p}_{cluster\_k}$. For face synthesis, $\mathbf{p}^i_{cluster\_k}$ should be restricted with an upper and a lower limit, which can be selected using the mean $\mathbf{m}^i_{cluster\_k}$ and standard deviation $\sigma^i_{cluster\_k}$ of $\mathbf{p}^i_{cluster\_k}$.

$$\begin{aligned} &\min{}^i_{Cluster\_k} \leq \mathbf{p}^i_{Cluster\_k} \leq \max{}^i_{Cluster\_k}, \\ &where \begin{pmatrix} \min{}^i_{Cluster\_k} = \mathbf{m}^i_{Cluster\_k} - \alpha\sigma^i_{Cluster\_k} \\ \max{}^i_{Cluster\_k} = \mathbf{m}^i_{Cluster\_k} + \alpha\sigma^i_{Cluster\_k}. \end{pmatrix} \end{aligned} \tag{4}$$

As a result, the local surface of the kth cluster can be determined by $\min^i_{cluster\_k}$ and $\max^i_{cluster\_k}$ of $\mathbf{p}^i_{cluster\_k}$ with scale factor α which controls the width of the modeled local surface. For face synthesis, *partition-based PCA* coefficient vector $\mathbf{p}_{cluster\_k}$ should be selected within the local surface of the kth cluster. The selected $\mathbf{p}_{cluster\_k}$ is associated with one synthesized face in the corresponding subspace, and face images can be generated as follows. The synthesized face coefficient vector λ_{syn} is the result of reprojecting $\mathbf{p}_{cluster\_k}$ into the corresponding *partition-based PCA* basis $\mathbf{\Phi}_{cluster\_k}$.

$$\lambda_{syn} = \mathbf{\Phi}_{cluster\_k}\mathbf{p}_{cluster\_k}. \tag{5}$$

After the synthesized face coefficient vector λ_{syn} is obtained, the synthesized face image $\mathbf{x}_{syn}$ can be generated by reprojection with the corresponding subspace basis $\mathbf{\Psi}$.

$$\mathbf{x}_{syn} = \mathbf{\Psi}\lambda_{syn}. \tag{6}$$

Hence, a face image can be synthesized using $\mathbf{p}_{cluster\_k}$. However, a changeable face image is synthesized from a changeable coefficient vector $\mathbf{c}$. Therefore, the changeable coefficient vector $\mathbf{c}$ should be converted accordingly. The conversion of $\mathbf{c}$ is done by range fitting; the range fitted changeable coefficient vector is $\mathbf{y}_{cluster\_k}$. To do this, the range of the changeable coefficient vector should be determined. After range determination, the changeable coefficient vector is fitted within the distribution of *partition-based PCA* coefficient vector $\mathbf{p}_{cluster\_k}$. Then $\mathbf{y}_{cluster\_k}$ is able to represent a face image that is recognizable by a human using reprojection as follows:

$$\mathbf{x}_{syn} = \mathbf{\Psi}\mathbf{\Phi}_{cluster\_k}\mathbf{y}_{cluster\_k}. \tag{7}$$

3.3 Determining the Range of the Changeable Coefficient Vector

Because a changeable coefficient vector is a mixed feature of two different subspace coefficient vectors (PCA and ICA), the distribution of the changeable coefficient vector is unrelated to the original two subspace coefficient vectors. However, if we assume that the original two coefficient vectors are statistically independent, then because the changeable coefficient vector $\mathbf{c}$ is no more than the addition of PCA and ICA coefficient vectors, the range of $\mathbf{c}$ can be determined from the ranges of the PCA and ICA coefficient vectors. The range of $\mathbf{p}_i$, the ith element of PCA coefficient vector $\mathbf{p}$, can be obtained from the training data, which exists between a lower limit $\min^i_{pca}$ and upper limit $\max^i_{pca}$. In a similar way, the range of $\mathbf{i}_i$, the ith element of ICA coefficient vector $\mathbf{i}$, can be obtained. Because the scrambling rule, i.e., $\mathbf{S}^{PCA}_{ID}$ and $\mathbf{S}^{ICA}_{ID}$, are stored for changeable coefficient vector generation, they can also be used for range determination of the changeable coefficient vector. Hence, scrambling can be ignored for notational simplification. Then, $\mathbf{c}_i$ becomes an addition of $\mathbf{p}_i$ and $\mathbf{i}_i$. Using the independence assumption between $\mathbf{p}_i$ and $\mathbf{i}_i$, the range of $\mathbf{c}_i$, ith element of changeable coefficient vector $\mathbf{c}$, can be inferred by examining the range of $\mathbf{p}_i$ and $\mathbf{i}_i$ as follows:

$$\begin{aligned} &\min^i_c \le \mathbf{c}_i \le \max^i_c, \\ &\mathit{where} \begin{pmatrix} \min^i_c = \min^i_{pca} + \min^i_{ica} \\ \max^i_c = \max^i_{pca} + \max^i_{ica} \end{pmatrix}. \end{aligned} \tag{8}$$

3.4 Range Fitting of Changeable Coefficient Vector into *partition-based PCA* Coefficient Vector

The range of the changeable coefficient vector is then fitted into the range of the *partition-based PCA* coefficient vector. Using the ranges as determined in previous subsection, the changeable coefficient vector $\mathbf{c}$ is converted to be in the range of *partition-based PCA* coefficient vector $\mathbf{p}_{cluster\_k}$. Because there is no restrictions on selection of cluster partition k, k can be selected freely for each person, and the converted coefficient vector is represented by $\mathbf{y}_{cluster\_k}$.

$$\begin{aligned} \mathbf{y}^i_{Cluster\_k} = &\left(\frac{\mathbf{c}_i - \min^i_c}{\max^i_c - \min^i_c}\right) \times (\max^i_{Cluster\_k} - \min^i_{Cluster\_k}) \\ &+ \min^i_{Cluster\_k}. \end{aligned} \tag{9}$$

As a result, the synthesized face image $\mathbf{x}_{syn}$ can be reprojected from $\mathbf{y}_{cluster\_k}$ using the corresponding basis of *partition-based PCA* and the basis of the subspace.

$$\mathbf{x}_{syn} = \mathbf{\Psi}\mathbf{\Phi}_{cluster\_k}\mathbf{y}_{cluster\_k}. \tag{10}$$

4 Experiment and Result

In our experiment, 492 frontal facial images from the AR database [8] are used. Images with occlusion and illumination changes are excluded, for a total of 6 different images per subject. The dimension of PCA and ICA spaces is set to 100. For face space modeling, FCM is applied to the face coefficient vector space. In our experiments, two distinct clusters are formed for each coefficient vector space. When generating a changeable coefficient vector, different scrambling rules are applied to each person. Performance can be evaluated in two aspects. One is the EER using the generated changeable coefficient vector $\mathbf{c}$, and the other is the EER using the range fitted coefficient vector $\mathbf{y}_{cluster\_k}$. The EER of the changeable coefficient vector $\mathbf{c}$ can be used to evaluate the performance of the changeable face recognition system, and the EER of the range fitted coefficient vector $\mathbf{y}_{cluster\_k}$ can be used for quantitative evaluation of human inspectibility. As Table 1 shows, due to different scrambling of changeable coefficient vectors for each person, the EER of the changeable coefficient vector is very low. The EER of $\mathbf{y}_{cluster\_k}$ fitted to ICA clusters is similar to the EER using ICA coefficient vectors, and the EER of $\mathbf{y}_{cluster\_k}$ fitted to PCA clusters is similar to the EER using PCA coefficient vectors. This result is due to the range fitting process. During range fitting, whatever the value of the changeable coefficient vector $\mathbf{c}$, the range fitted coefficient vector $\mathbf{y}_{cluster\_k}$ is located within the local surface of the modeled subspace cluster. Hence, EER of the range fitted coefficient vector is similar to the EER of the corresponding subspace coefficient vector. This implies that inter-class discrimination and intra-class similarity of the original input faces is preserved in the synthesized changeable faces.

Table 1. Performance of changeable coefficient vector and *partition-based PCA* coefficient vectors of modeled clusters

PCA coefficient vector	ICA coefficient vector	Changeable coefficient vector	Range fitted coefficient vector - ICA cluster	Range fitted coefficient vector - PCA cluster
15.03%	12.6%	0.02%	13.83%	14.88%

Fig. 3 shows the result of changeable face image synthesis. Because two clusters are formed for each subspace, two types of face images can be synthesized from each subspace. Fig. 3 (d) and (e) show synthesized face images from ICA clusters, and Fig. 3 (h) and (i) show synthesized images from PCA clusters. In both subspaces, using changeable coefficient vectors, synthesized images from different clusters show distinct characteristics, such as gender. Using the proposed face synthesis method, we can represent any person as a different person of either gender. From Fig. 3, we can discern the distinctiveness of the synthesized face image for each person. Hence, the above result shows inter-class discrimination of the proposed face synthesis method. However, synthesized faces from the same person's images should show similarity between synthesized faces. This intra-class similarity can be shown in Fig. 4. Input faces of Fig. 4 (a) contain expressional variation. Fig. 4 (b) is a result of synthesized images from ICA cluster 1, and Fig 4 (c) is a result of synthesized images from ICA cluster 2. For

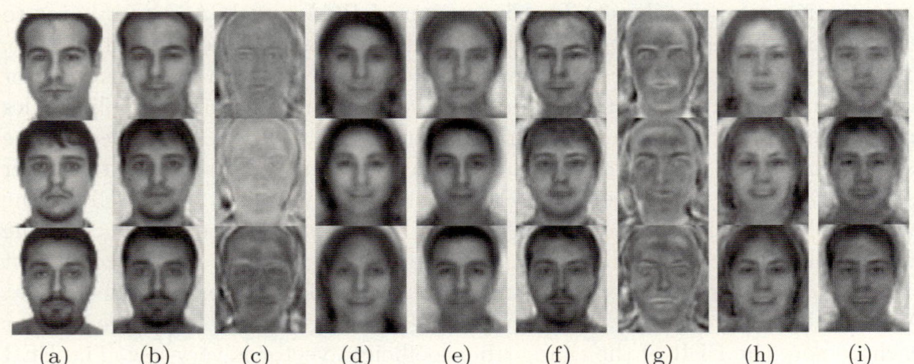

(a) (b) (c) (d) (e) (f) (g) (h) (i)

Fig. 3. Synthesized changeable faces (a):input image, (b):reconstructed image by ICA basis, (c):direct reprojection of changeable coefficient vector using ICA basis, (d):synthesized image from cluster 1 of ICA, (e):synthesized image from cluster 2 of ICA, (f):reconstructed image by PCA basis, (g): direct reprojection of changeable coefficient vector using PCA basis , (h):synthesized image from cluster 1 of PCA, (i):synthesized image from cluster 2 of PCA

Fig. 4 (b) and (c), because images of the same row are synthesized from the same person's input images, images within a row are similar each other. However, images of different rows are synthesized from images of different person, and any two images between two different rows are not similar. From Fig. 3 and Fig. 4, it can be shown that synthesized face images can be used to substitute the original face image. In other words, with respect to inspectability, the proposed face synthesis method shows intra-class similarity while providing inter-class discrimination. The similarity between the EER using the original subspace coefficient vector and the EER using the changeable coefficient vector of Table 1 supports the above results.

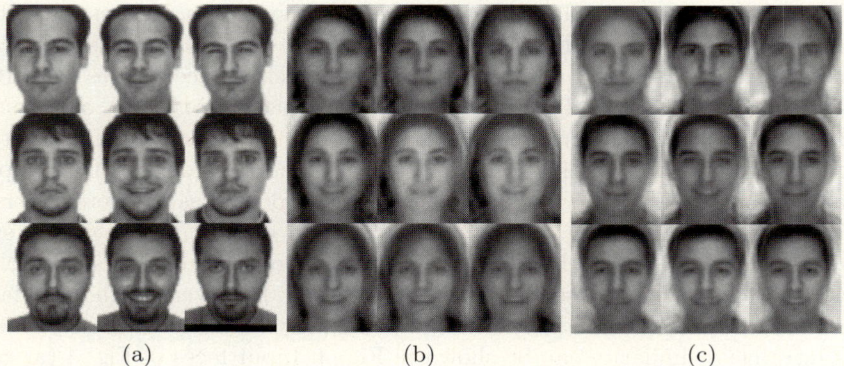

(a) (b) (c)

Fig. 4. Synthesized changeable faces of two ICA clusters (a): input faces, (b): synthesized faces from ICA cluster 1, (c): synthesized faces from ICA cluster 2

5 Conclusion and Future Works

The proposed face synthesis method for changeable face biometrics can generate face images which allow human recognition. The quality of the synthesized face image depends on the accuracy of the subspace modeling method and the compactness of the subspace. From the point of view of human inspectability, face image synthesis using ICA cluster modeling is better than PCA cluster modeling. The quality of the synthesized face image also can be improved by using a more accurate subspace modeling method. In this work, face subspace modeling is accomplished by a simple clustering method (FCM) and *partition based PCA*. However, the face subspace can be modeled by more accurate clustering methods such as Gaussian Mixture Models (GMM) or Gustafson-Kessel clustering, etc. In future works, such subspace modeling methods may be tested for changeable face synthesis.

Acknowledgements

This work was supported by the Korea Science and Engineering Foundation (KOSEF) through the Biometrics Engineering Research Center (BERC) at Yonsei University

References

1. Ratha, N.K., Connell, J.H., Bolle, R.M.: Enhancing security and privacy in biometrics-based authentication systems. IBM Systems Journal. 40, 614–634 (2001)
2. Boult, T.: Robust Distance Measures for Face-recognition supporting revocable biometrics token. In: 7th International Conference Automatic Face and Gesture Recognition, pp. 560–566 (2006)
3. Savvides, M., Vijaya Kumar, B.V.K., Khosla, P.K.: Cancelable Biometric Filters for Face Recognition. In: Proc. of the 17th International Conference on Pattern Recognition (ICPR 2004), vol. 3, pp. 922–925 (2004)
4. Teoh, A.B.J., Ngo, D.C.L., Goh, A.: BioHashing: two factor authentication featuring fingerprint data and tokenised random number. Pattern Recognition 37, 2245–2255 (2004)
5. Jeong, M.Y., Lee, C.H., Kim, J.S., Choi, J.Y., Toh, K.A., Kim, J.H.: Changeable biometrics for appearance based face recognition. In: The Biometric Consortium Conference, Baltimore convention center, Baltimore, MD, USA, September 19th-21th, 2006 (2006)
6. Bezdek, J.C.: Pattern Recognition with Fuzzy Objective Function Algorithms. Plenum Press, New York (1981)
7. Kambhatla, N., Leen, T.K.: Dimension Reduction by Local Principal Component Analysis. Neural Computation 9, 1493–1516 (1997)
8. Martinez, A.M., Benavente, R.: The AR Face Database. CVC Technical Report. #24 (1998)

"3D Face": Biometric Template Protection for 3D Face Recognition

E.J.C. Kelkboom , B. Gökberk, T.A.M. Kevenaar, A.H.M. Akkermans, and M. van der Veen

Philips Research, High-Tech Campus 34, 5656AE, Eindhoven
{emile.kelkboom,berk.gokberk,tom.kevenaar,ton.h.akkermans, michiel.van.der.veen}@philips.com

Abstract. In this paper we apply template protection to an authentication system based on 3D face data in order to protect the privacy of its users. We use the template protection system based on the helper data system (HDS). The experimental results performed on the FRGC v2.0 database demonstrate that the performance of the protected system is of the same order as the performance of the unprotected system. The protected system has a performance of a FAR $\approx$ 0.19% and a FRR $\approx$ 16% with a security level of 35 bits.

Keywords: Template protection, privacy protection, helper data system (HDS), 3D face recognition.

1 Introduction

Biometrics is used to recognize people for identification or verification purposes. It is expected that in the near future, biometrics will play an increasing role in many security applications. Today the market is dominated by fingerprint recognition, but for the near future market studies predict that face recognition technologies will also play an important role. This is driven by initiatives like the ePassport for which the ICAO standardized the face as being one of the modalities to be used for verification purposes. Following these trends, recently the European Project "3D Face"[1] was initiated. The principal goals of this project are to (i) improve the performance of classical face recognition techniques by extending it to 3D, (ii) integrate privacy protection technology to safeguard the biometric information and (iii) deploy the secure face recognition system at several international airports for the purpose of employee access control.

In this paper we concentrate on the privacy protection for 3D face recognition. In any biometric system, the storage of biometric information, also called biometric template, may be a privacy risk. To mitigate these risks, we see in recent literature different theoretical methods of privacy protection, e.g. *fuzzy commitment* [2], *fuzzy vault* [3], *cancelable biometrics* [4], *fuzzy extractors* [5], and the *helper data system* (HDS) [6,7]. The general goal of these systems is to (i) prevent *identity theft*, (ii) introduce *versatility*, and (iii) prevent *cross matching*. Also several attempts were made to integrate these techniques in practical systems for face [8] or fingerprint [9].

S.-W. Lee and S.Z. Li (Eds.): ICB 2007, LNCS 4642, pp. 566–573, 2007.

In our work we make use of the HDS template protection approach in the verification setting. We use a 3D face feature extraction algorithm that is based on the maximum and minimum principal curvature directions. The aim is to have at least the same verification performance in the protected case as in the unprotected case.

The remainder of the paper is organized as follows. In Section 2, we present a brief description of the feature extraction algorithm followed by the introduction of the HDS template protection system in Section 3. The results are given in Section 4 followed by the conclusions in Section 5.

2 3D Face Feature Extraction

In this work, we use a shape-based 3D face recognizer [10]. It has two main steps: 1) the alignment of faces, and 2) the extraction of surface features from 3D facial data. In the alignment step, each face is registered to a generic face model (GFM) and the central facial region is cropped. The GFM is computed by averaging correctly aligned images from a training set. After the alignment step, we can assume that all faces are transformed in such a way that they best fit the GFM, and have the same position in the common coordinate system.

After alignment, the facial surface is divided into 174 local regions. For each region, the maximum and minimum principal curvature direction are computed. Each of the two directions is presented by the azimuthal and the polar angle in the spherical coordinate system. Combining all the regions leads to a feature vector with $174 \times 2 \times 2 = 696$ entries. For matching two feature vectors, the distance is computed using the L_1 or the L_2 norm.

3 The Template Protection System: Helper Data System

The helper data system (HDS) is shown in Figure 1. It consists of the training, enrollment and verification stages. The inputs to all stages are real-valued feature vectors defined as, $\boldsymbol{z} \in \Re^k$, $\boldsymbol{x} \in \Re^k$ and $\boldsymbol{y} \in \Re^k$, respectively (k is the number of components of the feature vector). The feature vectors are derived from the 3D face image by the feature extraction algorithm described in Section 2. In each stage, users may have multiple images and therefore multiple feature vectors, which are defined as

$$\begin{array}{lll} (\boldsymbol{z}_{i,j})_t, \; i = 1,\ldots,N_T; & j = 1,\ldots,M_{T_i}; & t = 1,\ldots,k, \\ (\boldsymbol{x}_{i,j})_t, \; i = 1,\ldots,N; & j = 1,\ldots,M_{E_i}; & t = 1,\ldots,k, \\ (\boldsymbol{y}_{i,j})_t, \; i = 1,\ldots,N; & j = 1,\ldots,M_{V_i}; & t = 1,\ldots,k, \end{array} \tag{1}$$

where N_T is the number of users in the training stage with user i having M_{T_i} images, and N is the number of users in the enrollment and verification stage with user i having M_{E_i} images in the enrollment and M_{V_i} images in the verification stage. The notation $(\boldsymbol{x}_{i,j})_t$ indicates the t-th component of vector $\boldsymbol{x}_{i,j}$.

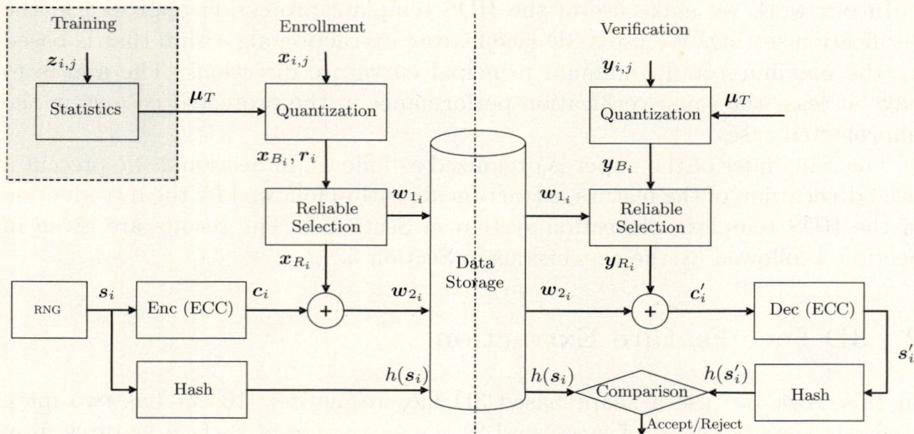

Fig. 1. The HDS template protection system; the enrollment (*left*), and verification stage (*right*). This figure is adapted from [8,9].

3.1 Training Stage

For template protection, binary feature vectors (binary strings) must be derived from the real-valued feature vectors. This is done by quantizing the feature vector with respect to a single threshold vector. In the training stage, this quantization threshold vector is calculated from the feature vectors of the training population $z_{i,j}$. As threshold vector, we use the mean of the feature vectors defined as

$$\mu_T = \frac{1}{\sum_{i=1}^{N_T} M_{T_i}} \sum_{i=1}^{N_T} \sum_{j=1}^{M_{T_i}} z_{i,j}. \tag{2}$$

3.2 Enrollment Stage

In the enrollment stage, each user i has M_{E_i} feature vectors $x_{i,j}$. In the *Quantization* block, the real-valued feature vectors are quantized into binary feature vectors x_{B_i} using the following equation

$$(x_{B_i})_t = \begin{cases} 0, & \text{if } (\mu_i)_t < (\mu_T)_t \\ 1, & \text{if } (\mu_i)_t \geq (\mu_T)_t \end{cases}, \text{with } (\mu_i)_t = \frac{1}{M_{E_i}} \sum_{j=1}^{M_{E_i}} (x_{i,j})_t, \tag{3}$$

such that $(\mu_i)_t$ is the mean of component t of the feature vectors of user i. The reliability $(r_i)_t$ of each component $(x_{B_i})_t$ is calculated as the ratio

$$(r_i)_t = \frac{|(\mu_T)_t - (\mu_i)_t|}{(\sigma_i)_t}, \text{with } (\sigma_i)_t = \sqrt{\frac{1}{M_{E_i} - 1} \sum_{j=1}^{M_{E_i}} ((x_{i,j})_t - (\mu_i)_t)^2} \tag{4}$$

such that $(\sigma_i)_t$ is the standard deviation of component t of the feature vectors of user i. In the single image enrollment scenario, $M_{E_i} = 1$, we define $(\sigma_i)_t = 1$.

Also, a secret $\boldsymbol{s}_i$ of L_S bits is randomly generated by the *Random Number Generator* (*RNG*) block. The security level of the system is higher at larger secret lengths L_S. A codeword $\boldsymbol{c}_i$ of an error correcting code with L_C bits is obtained by encoding $\boldsymbol{s}_i$ in the *ENC* block. In our case we use the "Bose, Ray-Chaudhuri, Hocquenghem" (BCH) Error Correction Code (ECC) [11]. For the BCH code, the codeword length is equal to $L_C = 2^n - 1$, where n is a natural number. The most common codeword lengths for our application are 127, 255, and 511 bits and can be freely chosen as long as it is smaller than or equal to the feature vector length k. Examples of some BCH parameter combinations are given in Table 1. In the *Reliable Component* block, the reliable binary string $\boldsymbol{x}_{R_i}$ is created by cropping the binary feature vector $\boldsymbol{x}_{B_i}$ to the same length as the codeword by selecting the L_C components having the largest reliability $(\boldsymbol{r}_i)_t$. The indices of the L_C most reliable components are collected in the public helper data $\boldsymbol{w}_{1_i}$. Hereafter, the reliable binary feature vector $\boldsymbol{x}_{R_i}$ is bitwise XOR-ed with codeword $\boldsymbol{c}_i$. This XOR operation leads to the second helper data $\boldsymbol{w}_{2_i}$. The third and last helper data is the hashed value of secret $\boldsymbol{s}_i$, indicated as $h(\boldsymbol{s}_i)$. The cryptographic hash function can be considered as a one-way function which makes it computationally hard to retrieve the secret $\boldsymbol{s}_i$ from its hashed value $h(\boldsymbol{s}_i)$. The protected template corresponds to the three helper data denoted as: $[X]_i = \{h(\boldsymbol{s}_i), \boldsymbol{w}_{1_i}, \boldsymbol{w}_{2_i}\}$. The protected template can be considered as public and reveals only a minimum amount of information of $\boldsymbol{s}_i$ and $\boldsymbol{x}_{i,j}$. Therefore it can be easily stored on a less secure local data storage device or on a centralized database, depicted here as the *Data Storage*.

Table 1. Some examples of BCH parameter combinations

Codeword (L_C)	Secret (L_S)	Correctable bits (η)	BER $= \eta/L_C$
127	36	15	11.8%
	64	10	7.9%
255	37	45	17.7%
	63	30	11.8%
511	31	109	21.3%
	67	87	17.0%

3.3 Verification Stage

In the verification stage, a single feature vector $\boldsymbol{y}_{i,j}$ is used. As in classical biometric systems, this feature vector is compared to the reference data stored in the system. In the current setup, $\boldsymbol{y}_{i,j}$ is compared to the protected template $[X]_i$ derived in the enrollment stage using a dedicated matching method as follows. In the *Quantization block*, the binary feature vector $\boldsymbol{y}_{B_i}$ is obtained by quantizing $\boldsymbol{y}_{i,j}$ using Eq. 3, where $(\boldsymbol{\mu}_i)_t$ is replaced by $(\boldsymbol{y}_{i,j})_t$. The same threshold $\boldsymbol{\mu}_T$ is used as in the enrollment stage. In the *Reliable Component* block, the helper data

$\boldsymbol{w}_{1_i}$ is used to select components in $\boldsymbol{y}_{B_i}$ to obtain $\boldsymbol{y}_{R_i}$. The recovered codeword $\boldsymbol{c}'_i$ is the output of the XOR operation between the helper data $\boldsymbol{w}_{2_i}$ and $\boldsymbol{y}_{R_i}$. Next, this codeword is decoded to recover the (candidate) secret $\boldsymbol{s}'_i$, which is hashed into $h(\boldsymbol{s}'_i)$. In the *Comparison* block, $h(\boldsymbol{s}'_i)$ is matched bitwise with $h(\boldsymbol{s}_i)$ as obtained from the protected template $[X]_i$. If the hashes are bitwise exact the user is accepted, otherwise rejected. We have a match only if the following is true

$$\begin{gathered} h(\boldsymbol{s}_i) = h(\boldsymbol{s}'_i) \text{ iff } \boldsymbol{s}_i = \boldsymbol{s}'_i \text{ iff} \\ ||\boldsymbol{c}_i \oplus \boldsymbol{c}'_i||_1 = ||(\boldsymbol{x}_{R_i} \oplus \boldsymbol{w}_{2_i}) \oplus (\boldsymbol{w}_{2_i} \oplus \boldsymbol{y}_{R_i})||_1 = ||\boldsymbol{x}_{R_i} \oplus \boldsymbol{y}_{R_i}||_1 \leq \eta \end{gathered} \tag{5}$$

where η is the number of bits the ECC can correct and $||\boldsymbol{x}_{R_i} \oplus \boldsymbol{y}_{R_i}||_1$ is the hamming distance (HD) between $\boldsymbol{x}_{R_i}$ and $\boldsymbol{y}_{R_i}$. This means that the number of bit differences between $\boldsymbol{x}_{R_i}$ and $\boldsymbol{y}_{R_i}$ should be equal or less than η for a match.

4 Verification Performance Results

To analyze the verification performance of the system, we use the FRGC v2.0 database [12], which has 465 subjects having between 1 or 22 3D face images with a total of 4007 images. The 1st version, FRGC v1.0, is used to derive the GFM in the feature extraction algorithm. When applying our feature extraction algorithm to the FRGC images, we obtain feature vectors with $k = 696$ (see Section 2). Our verification performance test is complex, because the template protection system uses multiple enrollment images. The test protocol we use is elaborated next followed by the verification performance results.

4.1 Test Protocol

We first divide the FRGC v2.0 database into a training and a test set. The training set is used to obtain the quantization threshold $\boldsymbol{\mu}_T$, while the test set is used to analyze the verification performance. The optimal number of enrollment images, N_{enrol}, is not known and has to be verified. Its range is set to [1, 10], and two images of each subject are used in the verification stage. In the FRGC v2.0 database, subjects have varying numbers of 3D face images. In order to have the same subjects in each test, only the subjects having at least 12 images are selected for the test set, while the rest is used as the training set. This results into a test set containing 145 subjects with a total of 2347 images. For each N_{enrol} and codeword length {127, 255, 511} case, 20 verification runs are performed. Each run consists of randomly selecting $(N_{enrol} + 2)$ images of each subject and performing experiments for the $\binom{N_{enrol}+2}{N_{enrol}}$ possible combination of dividing the selected images into N_{enrol} enrollment images and two verification images. The results are averaged over all combinations and runs.

We evaluate the verification performance for both the protected and the unprotected case. For the template protection system, we evaluate its performance by studying the reliable binary feature vectors $\boldsymbol{x}_{R_i}$ and $\boldsymbol{y}_{R_i}$ and assuming a hamming distance classifier given as

$$HD = ||\boldsymbol{x}_{R_i} \oplus \boldsymbol{y}_{R_i}||_1. \tag{6}$$

The verification performance test is performed for feature lengths of 127, 255, and 511 bits, corresponding to possible codeword lengths of the ECC code. We also look at the verification performance of the full binary feature vectors $\boldsymbol{x}_{B_i}$ and $\boldsymbol{y}_{B_i}$, indicated as the "696" bits case. For the unprotected case, we use the real-valued feature vectors $\boldsymbol{x}_{i,j}$ and $\boldsymbol{y}_{i,j}$ and the L_1 and the L_2 norm as distance measure.

4.2 Performance Results: Protected and Unprotected Templates

Figure 2(a) shows the Equal Error Rate (EER) at different choices of N_{enrol}. It is clear that N_{enrol} has influence on the performance and we observe that at 7 or more images the performance stabilizes. For the real-valued (unprotected) case the EER is around 7.2%, while for binary (protected) case the EER is between 3-4%. This shows that in this case our binarization method itself leads to a significant performance improvement. We assume that the performance gain is achieved due to the filtering property of the binarization method on the real-valued feature vectors. The influence of N_{enrol} on the False Acceptance Rate

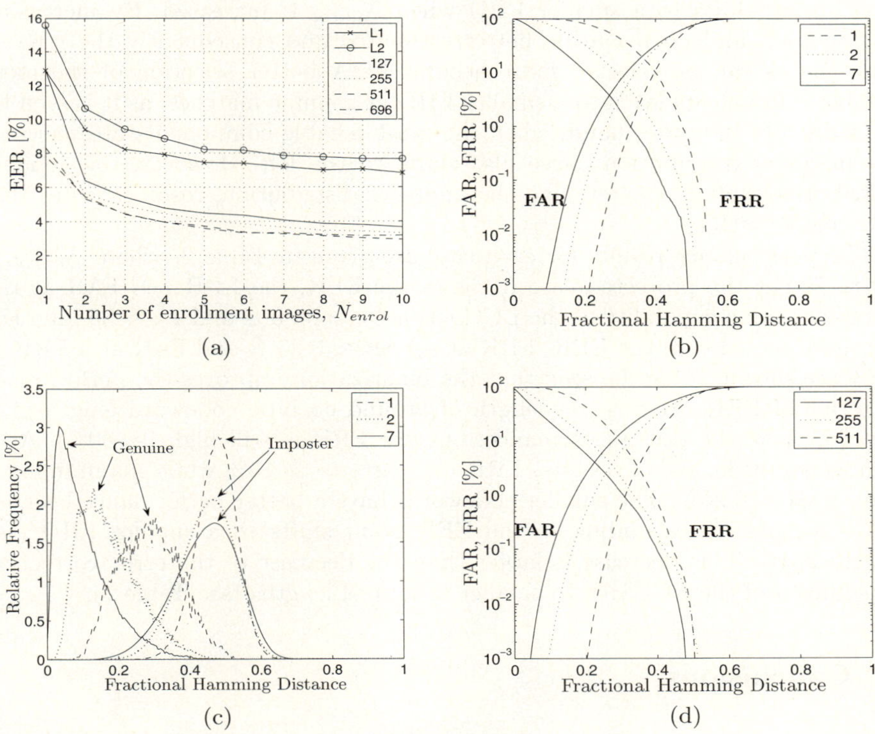

Fig. 2. At different N_{enrol} values (a) shows the EER for each case, (b) the FAR and FRR curves for the 255 bits case, and (c) gives the genuine and imposter distribution. For different codeword lengths, (d) gives the FAR and FRR curves.

Table 2. Verification performance for the protected (reliable binary feature vectors) and unprotected (real-valued and full binary feature vectors). N_{enrol} is set to 7.

Protected Templates				Unprotected Templates			
case	EER	FAR, FRR @ $L_S \approx 65$	FAR, FRR @ $L_S \approx 35$	case	EER	FRR @ FAR $\approx$ 0.25%	FAR @ FRR $\approx$ 2.5%
127	4.1	0.023%, 30.0%	0.18%, 17.7%	Binary "696"	3.3%	14.9%	4.7%
255	3.7	0.007%, 32.8%	0.19%, 15.6%	Real, L_1	7.2%	25.3%	25.2%
511	3.2	$\approx$ 0%, 58.5%	$\approx$0%, 36.8%	Real, L_2	7.8%	28.3%	27.5%

(FAR) and False Rejection Rate (FRR) curves is shown in Figures 2(b) for the 255 bits case and is representative for the other cases. It can be seen that with a larger N_{enrol}, both the EER and the corresponding threshold value, given as the Fractional Hamming Distance (FHD), decreases. FHD is defined as the hamming distance divided by the feature vector length. The EER threshold value also stabilizes at a N_{enrol} larger than 7.

The shift of the EER threshold can be explained with Figure 2(c). The genuine distribution shifts to a smaller FHD when N_{enrol} is increased. By increasing N_{enrol}, $(\sigma_i)_t$ and $(\boldsymbol{\mu}_i)_t$ can be better estimated and consequently the reliable components can be selected more accurately. A better selection of the most reliable components leads to a smaller FHD at genuine matches, as it is seen by the shift. On the other hand, when the most reliable components are selected, the imposter distribution curve also shifts to the left. However, the genuine distribution shift is greater than the imposter distribution, resulting in a EER at a smaller FHD.

The performance results for each case are given in Table 2, where N_{enrol} is set to 7. For the protected case it shows the EER, the FRR and FAR at the error correction capability of the ECC when $L_S \approx 65$ bits and $L_S \approx 35$ bits. For the unprotected case the EER, FRR at a FAR $\approx$ 0.25%, and FAR at a FRR $\approx$ 2.5% are shown. It can be seen that the binarization improves the performance in terms of EER. At a secret length of around 65 bits, codeword lengths 127 and 255 have the best performance, but the FRR is still high ($\approx$ 30%). At a smaller secret length of 35 bits, FRR decreases to $\approx$ 15% while maintaining a good FAR $\approx$ 0.20%. The smaller codewords have a better performance because the threshold corresponding to the EER point shifts to a smaller FHD (see Figure 2(d)). This decrease is larger than the decrease of the error correcting capabilities of the ECC due to smaller codeword lengths (see Table 1).

5 Conclusions

In this work, we successfully combined the HDS template protection system with a 3D face recognition system. The verification performance of the protected templates is of the same order as the performance of the unprotected, real-valued, templates. In order to achieve this improvement we proposed a special binarization method, which uses multiple enrollment images. In a HDS template protection system, the choice of the operating point is limited by the number of bits the ECC can correct. Using multiple images and varying the number of binary features (corresponding to the codeword length of the ECC) the operating point can be brought closer to the EER point. We obtained the best verification performances at a codeword length of 255 bits with a FAR $\approx$ 0.19% and a FRR $\approx$ 16% at 35 bits of security. This is better than the FAR = 0.25% and FRR $\approx$ 26% performance of the real-valued case.

It is expected that if the performance of the real-valued feature vectors is improved, it will further improve the performance of the protected templates. Furthermore, the verification performance of the protected templates can be enhanced with a more robust binarization algorithm. If the resulting binary templates are more robust, the EER will be achieved at a lower fractional Hamming distance. This will give the template protection system the flexibility to choose different operating points, leading to a more secure or a more convenient system.

References

1. 3DFace: (`http://www.3dface.org/home/welcome`)
2. Juels, A., Wattenberg, M.: A fuzzy commitment scheme. In: 6th ACM Conference on Computer and Communications Security, pp. 28–36. ACM Press, New York (1999)
3. Juels, A., Sudan, M.: A fuzzy vault scheme. In: Proc. of the 2002 International Symposium on Information Theory (ISIT 2002), Lausanne (2002)
4. Ratha, N.K., Connell, J.H., Bolle, R.M.: Enhancing security and privacy in biometrics-based authentication systems. IBM Systems Journal 40, 614–634 (2001)
5. Dodis, Y., Reyzin, L., Smith, A.: Fuzzy extractors: How to generate strong secret keys from biometrics and other noisy data. In: Cachin, C., Camenisch, J.L. (eds.) EUROCRYPT 2004. LNCS, vol. 3027, pp. 532–540. Springer, Heidelberg (2004)
6. Verbitskiy, E., Tuyls, P., Denteneer, D., Linnartz, J.P.: Reliable biometric authentication with privacy protection. In: Proc. of the 24th Symp. on Inf. Theory in the Benelux, Veldhoven, The Netherlands, pp. 125–132 (2003)
7. Linnartz, J.-P., Tuyls, P.: New shielding functions to enhance privacy and prevent misuse of biometric templates. In: 4th Int. Conf. on AVBPA (2003)
8. Kevenaar, T.A.M., Schrijen, G.-J., Akkermans, A.H.M., van der Veen, M., Zou, F.: Face recognition with renewable and privacy preserving binary templates. In: 4th IEEE workshop on AutoID, Buffalo, New York, USA, pp. 21–26. IEEE Computer Society Press, Los Alamitos (2005)
9. Tuyls, P., Akkermans, A.H.M., Kevenaar, T.A.M., Schrijnen, G.J., Bazen, A.M., Veldhuis, R.N.J.: Pratical biometric authentication with template protection. In: 5th International Conference, AVBPA, Rye Brook, New York (2005)
10. Gökberk, B., Irfanoglu, M.O., Akarun, L.: 3D shape-based face representation and feature extraction for face recognition. Image and Vision Computing 24, 857–869 (2006)
11. Purser, M.: Introduction to Error-Correcting Codes. Artech House, Boston (1995)
12. Phillips, P.J., Flynn, P.J., Scruggs, T., Bowyer, K.W., Chang, J., Hoffman, K., Marques, J., Min, J., Worek, W.: Overview of the face recognition grand challenge. In: IEEE CVPR, vol. 2, pp. 454–461. IEEE Computer Society Press, Los Alamitos (2005)

Quantitative Evaluation of Normalization Techniques of Matching Scores in Multimodal Biometric Systems

Y.N. Singh and P. Gupta

Department of Computer Science and Engineering,
Indian Institute of Technology Kanpur, Kanpur-208016, India
singhyn@iitk.ac.in
pg@iitk.ac.in

Abstract. This paper attempts to make an quantitative evaluation of available normalization techniques of matching scores in multimodal biometric systems. Two new normalization techniques Four Segments Piecewise Linear (FSPL) and Linear Tanh Linear (LTL) have been proposed in this paper. FSPL normalization techniques divides the region of genuine and impostor scores into four segments and maps each segment using piecewise linear function while LTL normalization techniques maps the non-overlap region of genuine and impostor score distributions to a constant function and overlap region using tanh estimator. The effectiveness of each technique is shown using EER and ROC curves on IITK database of having more than 600 people on following characteristics: face, fingerprint, and offline-signature. The proposed normalization techniques perform better and particularly, LTL normalization is efficient and robust.

1 Introduction

In the recent years biometric becomes popular due to automated identification of people based on their distinct physiological and/or behavioral characteristics [1]. Most of the practical biometric systems are *unimodal* (e.g., rely on the evidence of any single biometric information). Unimodal systems are usually, cost-efficient but may not achieve the desired performance because of, noisy data, non-universality, lack of uniqueness of the biometric trait, and spoofing attacks [2]. The performance of the biometric system can be improved by combining of multiple biometric characteristics. These systems are referred as *multimodal* biometric systems [3]. In multimodal biometric systems fusion at matching score level is commonly preferred because matching scores are easily available and contains a sufficient information to make decision about legitimate user and impostor.

Assume that $O_k^G = \{r_{k_1}^G, r_{k_2}^G, \ldots, r_{k_N}^G\}$ is the set of genuine scores of N individuals and $O_k^I = \{r_{k_1}^I, r_{k_2}^I, \ldots, r_{k_n}^I\}$ is the set of impostor scores of those individuals where, $n = NX(N-1)$ for characteristic k. The complete set of matching scores is denoted as O_k where, $O_k = O_k^G \cup O_k^I$ and $|O_k^G \cup O_k^I| = N + n$.

S.-W. Lee and S.Z. Li (Eds.): ICB 2007, LNCS 4642, pp. 574–583, 2007.

Prior to combine the matching scores of different characteristics, scores are preprocessed and to make them homogeneous. The dissimilarity score (r'_{k_i}) of user i for characteristic k can be converted into similarity score in the common numerical range, let it be [0, 1] using the formula, $r_{k_i} = \frac{max(O_k^G, O_k^I) - r'_{k_i}}{max(O_k^G, O_k^I) - min(O_k^G, O_k^I)}$. Alternatively, if the raw scores are found in the range $[min(O_k), max(O_k)]$, then they are converted to similarity scores by simply subtracting them from $max(O_k)$ (e.g., $max(O_k) - r'_{k_i}$). In the rest of the paper the symbol r_{k_i} is used for similarity score of user i for characteristic k. Further, matching scores of different characteristics need not to be on same numerical scale. Using normalization technique scores of different characteristics are transformed to a common numerical scale. In this paper matching scores of face and fingerprint characteristics are obtained using Haar wavelet [4] and minutiae based technique [5], respecively while global and local features are used to compute the matching scores for offline-signature [6].

The rest of the paper is organized as follows: Section 2 presents the related work in the area of normalization techniques of matching score in multimodal biometric systems. Section 3 proposes two new normalization techniques of matching scores that improve the system performance. The performance of normalization techniques is evaluated using different fusion strategies. Normalization and fusion at matching score level are discussed in Section 4. Experimental results are given in Section 5. Finally, conclusions are presented in the last Section.

2 Related Work

Normalization of matching scores in the multimodal biometric systems is an important issue that leads to system performance. In [7] experiments on a database of 100 users for face, fingerprint and hand-geometry characteristics indicate that the performances of min-max, z-score, and tanh normalizations are found to be better than others. Also, min-max and z-score normalization techniques are sensitive to outliers. Hence, there is a need for a robust and efficient normalization procedure like the tanh normalization. A comprehensive study on normalization-fusion, permutations has been done in [8] where Snelick *et al.*, have proposed an adaptive normalization technique of matching scores. This technique is computationally intensive and suffered with parameters overhead.

Score Normalization

Score normalization refers to transformation of scores obtain from different matchers into a common numerical range. A number of normalization techniques such as min-max, z-score, double sigmoid, tanh, piecewise linear, adaptive normalization along with their evaluation are well studied in [7] and [8]. Assume n_{k_i} be the normalized score corresponding to the similarity score r_{k_i}.

Min-Max (MM) - MM normalization transforms the raw scores of O_k in the range of [0, 1] using,

$$n_{k_i} = \frac{r_{k_i} - min(O_k^G, O_k^I)}{max(O_k^G, O_k^I) - min(O_k^G, O_k^I)}$$

Z-Score (ZS) - ZS normalization transforms the scores to a distribution with mean 0 and standard deviation 1. Let μ_{O_k}, δ_{O_k} be the mean and standard deviation of the set O_k then ZS represents the distance between raw score r_{k_i} and μ_{O_k} in units of δ_{O_k} as,

$$n_{k_i} = \frac{r_{k_i} - \mu_{O_k}}{\delta_{O_k}}$$

Since μ_{O_k}, δ_{O_k} are sensitive to outliers, therefore z-score is not robust. Statistically using Grubbs' test [9] one can identify outliers and evaluate the performance of ZS.

Double-Sigmoid (DS) - DS normalization transforms the scores into the range of [0, 1] using,

$$n_{k_i} = \begin{cases} \frac{1}{1+exp\left(-2\left(\frac{r_{k_i}-t_k}{t_{k_L}}\right)\right)} & \text{if } r_{k_i} < t_k, \\ \frac{1}{1+exp\left(-2\left(\frac{r_{k_i}-t_k}{t_{k_R}}\right)\right)} & \text{otherwise.} \end{cases}$$

where t_k is the reference point chosen some value falling in the region of genuine and impostor scores and the parameters t_{k_L} and t_{k_R} are chosen as, $t_{k_L} = t_k - min(O_k^G)$ and $t_{k_R} = max(O_k^I) - t_k$. DS exhibits a linear characteristic of scores in the overlap region of interval $[t_k - t_{k_L}, t_{k_R} - t_k]$ and nonlinear characteristic beyond to that.

Tanh - Tanh normalization is based on tanh estimator [10]. It maps the raw scores of O_k in the range of [0, 1] as,

$$n_{k_i} = 0.5 * \left[tanh\left\{0.01 * \left(\frac{r_{k_i} - \mu_{O_k^G}}{\sigma_{O_k^G}}\right)\right\} + 1\right]$$

where, $\mu_{O_k^G}$ and $\sigma_{O_k^G}$ are the mean and standard deviation of the genuine matching scores of characteristic k, respectively.

Piecewise-Linear (PL) - Piecewise linear (PL) normalization technique transforms the scores of O_k in the range of [0, 1]. The normalization function of PL maps the raw scores using piecewise linear function as,

$$n_{k_i} = \begin{cases} 0 & \text{if } r_{k_i} \leq min(O_k^G), \\ 1 & \text{if } r_{k_i} \geq max(O_k^I), \\ \frac{r_{k_i} - min(O_k^G)}{max(O_k^I) - min(O_k^G)} & \text{otherwise.} \end{cases}$$

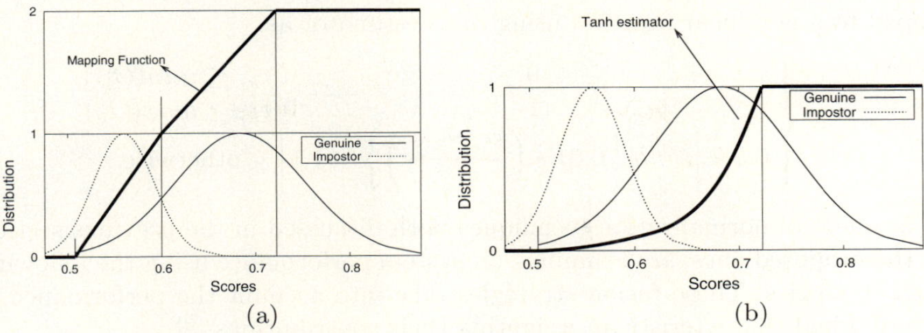

Fig. 1. Proposed Score Normalization Techniques (a) Four Segments Piecewise Linear (FSPL) (b) Linear Tanh Linear (LTL)

3 Proposed Score Normalization Techniques

This section proposes two new matching score normalization techniques: *Four-Segments-Piecewise-Linear* (FSPL) and *Linear-Tanh-Linear* (LTL) normalization, using quantitative combination of multiple normalization techniques. FSPL and LTL techniques take advantages of the characteristics resulted from the piecewise linear function and the tanh estimator for the separability of genuine and impostor scores distributions and robustness, respectively.

3.1 Four-Segments-Piecewise-Linear (FSPL)

FSPL normalization technique divides the regions of impostor and genuine scores into four segments and map each segment using piecewise linear functions (Fig. 1(a)). A reference point t_k is chosen in between the overlapping region of O_k^G and O_k^I. The scores between two extremities of the overlap region are mapped using two linear functions separately in range of [0, 1] and of [1, 2] towards left and right of t_k, respectively as,

$$n_{k_i} = \begin{cases} 0 & \text{if } r_{k_i} \leq min(O_k^G), \\ \frac{r_{k_i} - min(O_k^G)}{t_k - min(O_k^G)} & \text{if } min(O_k^G) < r_{k_i} \leq t_k, \\ 1 + \frac{r_{k_i} - t_k}{max(O_k^I) - t_k} & \text{if } t_k < r_{k_i} \leq max(O_k^I), \\ 2 & \text{if } r_{k_i} > max(O_k^I). \end{cases}$$

3.2 Linear-Tanh-Linear (LTL)

LTL normalization technique takes the advantage of the characteristic resulted from *tanh* estimator. Normalization function of LTL maps the non overlap region of impostor scores to a constant value 0 and non overlap region of genuine scores to a constant value 1 (Fig. 1(b)). The overlapped region between O_k^I and O_k^G is mapped to a nonlinear function using *tanh* estimator as,

$$n_{k_i} = \begin{cases} 0 & \text{if } r_{k_i} \leq min(O_k^G), \\ 1 & \text{if } r_{k_i} \geq max(O_k^I), \\ 0.5 * \left[tanh \left\{ 0.01 * \left(\frac{r_{k_i} - \mu_{O_k^G}}{\delta_{O_k^G}} \right) \right\} + 1.5 \right] & \text{otherwise.} \end{cases}$$

The effect of normalization techniques both discussed in the previous section and the proposed ones, are examined on system performance using the following fusion strategies. These fusion strategies take into account the performance of the individual characteristic in weighting their contributions [8].

I. Fusion Strategy A. *(Assignment of Weights based on EER)*
This fusion strategy assigns the weight to each characteristic based on their equal error rate (EER). Weights for more accurate characteristics are higher than those of less accurate characteristic. Thus, the weights are inversely proportional to the corresponding errors. Let e_k be the EER to characteristic k, then weight w_k associated to characteristic k can be computed by,

$$w_k = \left(\sum_{k=1}^{t} \frac{1}{e_k} \right)^{-1} * \frac{1}{e_k} \tag{1}$$

II. Fusion Strategy B. *(Assignment of Weights based on Score Distributions)*
Here weights are assigned to individual characteristic based on their impostor and genuine scores distributions. The means of these distribution are defined by $\mu_{O_k^I}$ and $\mu_{O_k^G}$ respectively, and standard deviations by $\sigma_{O_k^I}$ and $\sigma_{O_k^I}$ respectively. A parameter d_k [11] is used as a measure of the separation of these two distributions for characteristic k as,

$$d_k = \frac{\mu_{O_k^G} - \mu_{O_k^I}}{\sqrt{\left(\sigma_{O_k^G}\right)^2 + \left(\sigma_{O_k^I}\right)^2}}$$

If d_k is small, overlap region of two distributions is more, and if d_k is large, overlap region of two distributions is less. Therefore, weights are assigned to each characteristic proportional to this parameter as,

$$w_k = \left(\sum_{k=1}^{t} d_k \right)^{-1} * d_k \tag{2}$$

For both fusion strategies, $0 \leq w_k \leq 1$, $(\forall k)$; $\sum_{k=1}^{t} w_k = 1$ and the fused score f_i for user i is computed as,

$$f_i = \sum_{k=1}^{t} w_k * n_{k_i}; (\forall i)$$

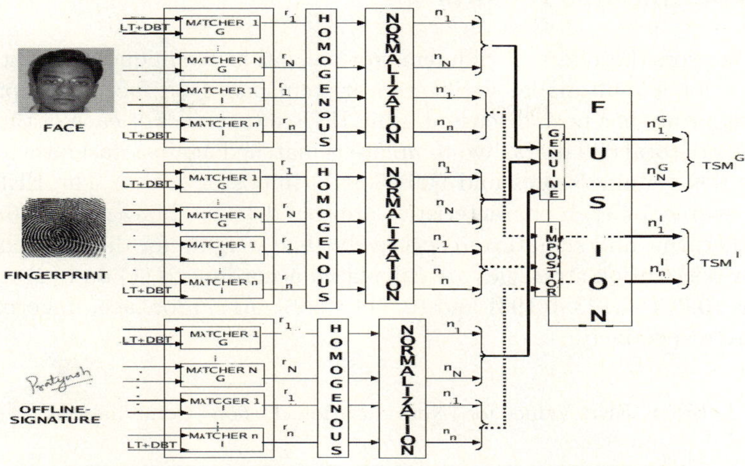

Fig. 2. Block Diagram of Multimodal System

4 System Description

Block diagram of the multimodal biometric verification system based on the fusion of face, fingerprint and signature information at matching score level is shows in Fig. 2. For each characteristic k, first N matchers generate genuine scores $\{r^G_{k_1}, r^G_{k_2}, \ldots, r^G_{k_N}\}$ using the matching of live-template to the template of the same individual stored in the database. Next n matchers generate impostor scores $\{r^I_{k_1}, r^I_{k_2}, \ldots, r^I_{k_n}\}$ using matching of live-template to the template of other individual stored in the database. Prior to transformation of scores to a common numerical range matching scores of different characteristics must be homogeneous. In the normalization phase scores obtained from different matchers (genuine and impostor) are scaled to a common numerical range. Finally to obtain the fused scores, genuine and impostor scores of each characteristic are combined separately using the weighted fusion strategies as follows,

$$(n_1, n_2, \ldots, n_N)^G = \sum_{k=1}^{t} w_k * (n_{k_1}, n_{k_2}, \ldots, n_{k_N})^G$$

and

$$(n_1, n_2, \ldots, n_n)^I = \sum_{k=1}^{t} w_k * (n_{k_1}, n_{k_2}, \ldots, n_{k_n})^I ;$$

The fused matching scores $(n_1, n_2, \ldots, n_N)^G \cup (n_1, n_2, \ldots, n_n)^I$ are commonly referred as *total similarity measures (TSM)* of the biometric system. The performance of different normalization techniques for each fusion method is studied against EER values, number of false rejections for subjects and Receiver Operating Characteristics (ROC) curves.

5 Experimental Results

In this section the effect of different normalization techniques on system performance for a multimodal verification system based on face, fingerprint and offline-signature has been discussed using IITK database. For each of these characteristics of total 609 users, live-template is matched against database template, yielding 609 genuine scores and 609 (609x1) impostor scores. The EER values for raw scores for each characteristics are found to be 2.03%, 9.86%, 6.25% for face, fingerprint and signature respectively. The weights for different characteristics for both fusion strategies are calculated according to (1) and (2) which are found as (0.684, 0.123, 0.193) and (0.530, 0.297, 0.177) for face, fingerprint and signature respectively.

Table 1. EER Values for (Normalization, Fusion) Combinations (%)

Normalizations	*Fusion Strategy A*	*Fusion Strategy B*
MM	1.07	0.75
ZS	0.74	0.58
DS	0.77	1.08
Tanh	0.91	0.48
PL	1.08	0.91
FSPL	0.71	0.45
LTL	**0.42**	**0.38**

Table 1 shows the EER values against different normalization techniques under two fusion strategies. The best one is the lowest EER value in the individual column. As seen in Table 1, the proposed new normalization technique LTL leads to better performance of EER values 0.42% and 0.38% than any other normalization techniques under fusion strategy A and B, respectively. These two near EER values also lead to conclude that the performance of LTL normalization is least dependent upon the distribution of matching scores. The effect of

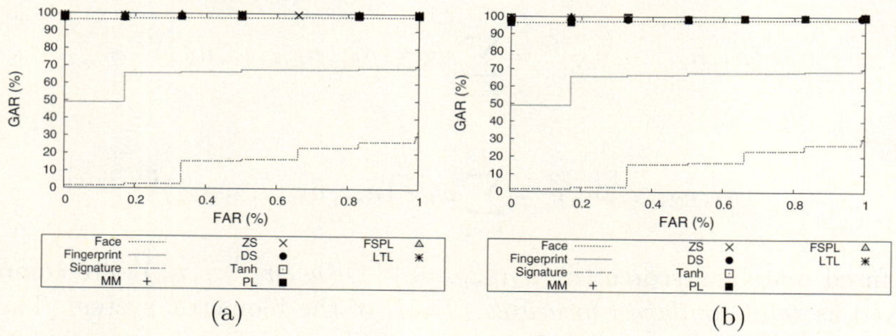

Fig. 3. Effect of Different Normalization Techniques on System Performance (a) Fusion Strategy A and (b) Fusion Strategy B

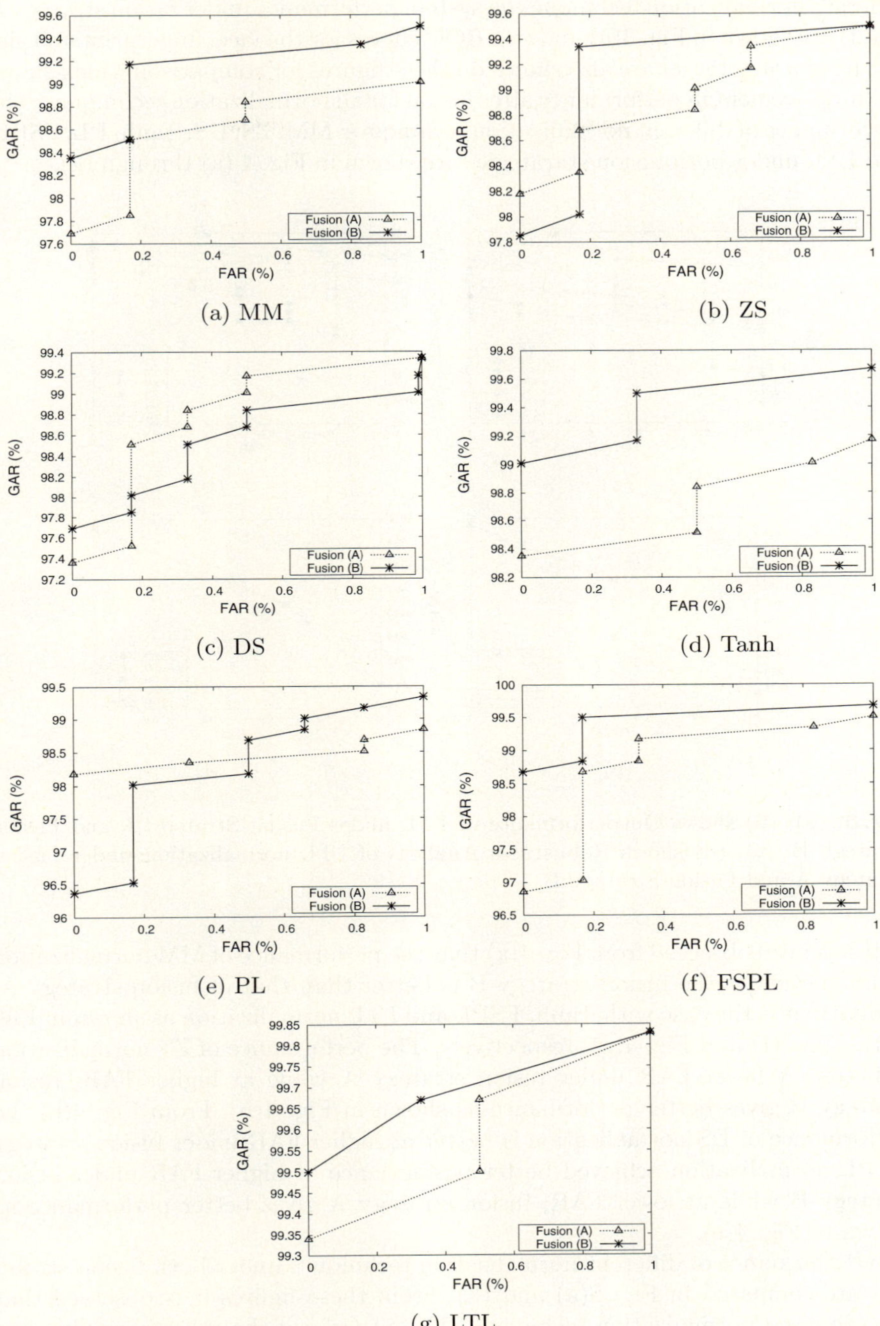

Fig. 4. Performance of Different Normalization Techniques under Fusion Strategy A and B

different normalization techniques on system performance under fusion strategy A and B are shown in Fig. 3(a) and (b). ROC curves for the face, fingerprint and signature characteristics are also shown on these figures for comparison which shows the improvement in performance after fusion for all normalization techniques. The performance of different normalization techniques: MM, ZS, DS, Tanh, PL, FSPL, and LTL under both fusion starategies are shown in Fig. 4 (a) through (g).

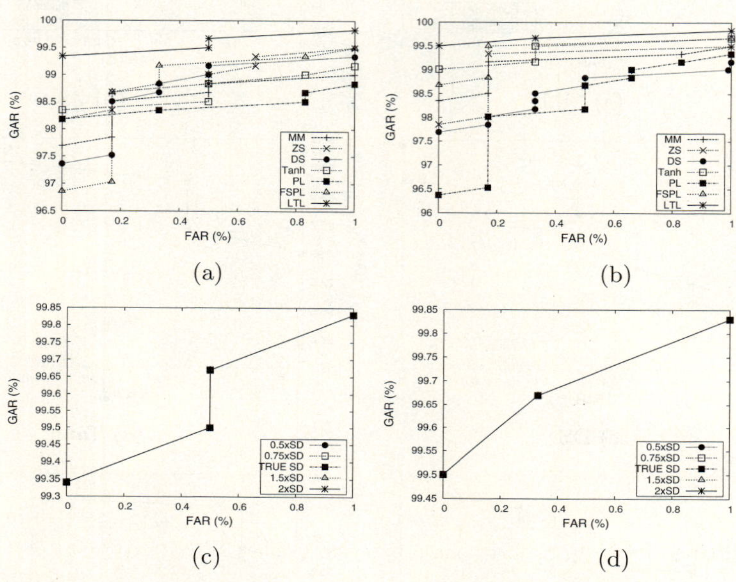

Fig. 5. (a), (b) shows Outperformance of LTL under Fusion Strategy A and Fusion Strategy B. (c), (d) shows Robustness Analysis of LTL normalization under Fusion Strategy A and Fusion Strategy B.

It has been observed from Fig. 4(a) that the performance of MM normalization technique under the fusion strategy B is better than that of fusion strategy A. Similarly it is the case with Tanh, FSPL and LTL normalization as shown in Fig. 4(d), Fig. 4(f) and Fig. 4(g), respectively. The performance of ZS normalization is better at lower FAR under fusion strategy A while at higher FAR, fusion strategy B gives better performance as shown in Fig. 4(b). From Fig. 4(c) the performance of DS normalization is better at higher FAR under fusion strategy A. PL normalization achieved better performance at higher FAR under fusion strategy B while at lower FAR, fusion strategy A gives better performance as shown in Fig. 4(e).

wPerformance of different normalization techniques under both fusion strategies are compared in Fig. 5(a) and (b). From these figures it is observed that the proposed normalization technique LTL outperform the other normalization techniques under both fusion strategies at lower FAR as well as at higher FAR.

The performance of another proposed normalization technique FSPL is better at higher FAR under both fusion strategies. Robustness behavior of the proposed normalization technique LTL is analyzed under fusion strategy A and fusion strategy B that are respectively shown in Fig. 5(c) and (d). From these figures it is found that the performance of the biometric system is completely invariant to the change in standard deviation (SD) of matching scores. In other words, LTL normalization is insensitive towards outliers and hence, it is a robust matching scores normalization technique.

6 Conclusion

This paper deals with the effect of normalization techniques of matching scores on the performance of multimodal biometric systems using face, fingerprint and offline-signature. The experimental results, obtained on a biometric database of IITK of more than 600 individuals, show that the proposed normalization technique Linear-Tanh-Linear (LTL) is *efficient* and *robust.* The performance of Four-Segments-Piecewise-Linear (FSPL) normalization technique is better at low FAR. This analysis of normalization techniques of matching scores suggests that an exhaustive testing of score normalization is needed to evaluate the performance of any multimodal biometric system.

References

1. Jain, A.K., Ross, A.: Information Fusion in Biometrics. Pattern Recognition Letters, Special Issues on Multimodal Biometrics, 2115–2125 (2003)
2. Snelick, R., Indovina, M., Yen, J., Mink, A.: Multimodal Biometrics: Issues in Design and Testing. In: ICMI'03, Canada, pp. 68–72 (2003)
3. Jain, A.K., Ross, A.: Learning User Specific Parameters in a Multimodal Biometric Systems. In: Proc. Inter. Conf. on Image Processing (ICIP), pp. 57–60 (2002)
4. Hassanien, A.E., Ali, J.M.: An Iris Recognition System to Enhance E-security Environment Based on Wavelet Theory. AMO 5(2), 93–104 (2003)
5. Raymond Thai: Fingerprint Image Enhancement and Minutiae Extraction. Technical Report, The University of Western Australia (2003)
6. Ismail, M.A., Gad, S.: Off-line Arabic Signature Recognition and Verification. Pattern Recognition 33, 1727–1740 (2000)
7. Jain, A.K., Nandakumara, K., Ross, A.: Score Normalization in Multimodal Biometric Systems. Pattern Recognition 38, 2270–2285 (2005)
8. Snelick, R., Uludag, U., Mink, A., Indovina, M., Jain, A.K.: Large-Scale Evaluation of Multimodal Biometric Authentication Using State-of-the-Art Systems. IEEE Trans. on PAMI 27(3), 450–455 (2005)
9. Grubbs, F.E.: Procedures for Detecting Outlying Observations in Samples. Technometrics 11(1), 121 (1969)
10. Hampel, F.R., Ronchetti, E.M., Rousseeuw, P.J., Stahel, W.A.: Robust Statistics: The Approach Based on Influence Functions. Wiley, New York (2005)
11. Bolle, R.M., Pankanti, S., Ratha, N.K.: Evaluation Techniques for Biometrics-Based Authentication Systems (FRR). In: Proc. of 15th International Conference Pattern Recognition, vol. 2, pp. 831–837 (2000)

Keystroke Dynamics in a General Setting

Rajkumar Janakiraman and Terence Sim

School of Computing, National University of Singapore, Singapore 117543
{rajkumar,tsim}@comp.nus.edu.sg

Abstract. It is well known that Keystroke Dynamics can be used as a biometric to authenticate users. But most work to date use fixed strings, such as userid or password. In this paper, we study the feasibility of using Keystroke Dynamics as a biometric in a more general setting, where users go about their normal daily activities of emailing, web surfing, and so on. We design two classifiers that appropriate for one-time and continuous authentication. We also propose a new Goodness Measure to compute the quality of a word used for Keystroke Dynamics. From our experiments we find that, surprisingly, non-English words are better suited for identification than English words.

Keywords: Keystroke dynamics, biometrics.

1 Introduction

Keystroke Dynamics is increasingly being used as a biometric for user authentication, no doubt because keyboards are common input devices, being readily found on computers, telephones, ATM machines, etc. By Keystroke Dynamics we mean the temporal typing pattern (the way you type), rather than the content typed (what you type). Most of the research into Keystroke Dynamics, however, is done on fixed-text input, otherwise called *password hardening* [3,4,6,10], rather than on free text. Typically, keystroke authentication is performed during user-login on a pre-determined string, such as the userid or password. This seems to us to be somewhat limiting, considering that most people continue to use the keyboard well beyond user-login. It would certainly be more useful if Keystroke Dynamics can handle free text as well as fixed text.

In our literature search, we note that S.J. Shepherd [1] was perhaps the first to explore using Keystroke Dynamics for continuous authentication, using the rate of typing. The system authenticated the user based only on the mean and standard deviation of the Held Times and the Interkey Times, irrespective of the key being pressed. Although it worked for a user population of four, the accuracy of the system is likely decrease as the number of users increase. There is no guarantee that these features are sufficiently discriminative. Indeed, our experiments conducted with a larger pool of 22 users confirm this.

Recent works of Villani et al., Rao et al., and Leggett et al. [7,8,9], conducted studies on keystroke verification on fixed text as well as free text. The users were asked to type a pre-determined text of a few hundred keystrokes (much longer

S.-W. Lee and S.Z. Li (Eds.): ICB 2007, LNCS 4642, pp. 584–593, 2007.

than the usual userid and password), and a text of a few hundred keystrokes of their own choice in the keystroke capture application. This data is then used for training and testing of their verification systems. The general conclusion from their studies is that Keystroke Dynamics works better on fixed text than on free text. We remark that these researchers all used Held Times and Interkey Times (of up to three consecutive keystrokes) as features, and did not consider the actual words being typed. We believe this is the cause of their poor performance. Our work in this paper suggests that Held Times and Interkey Times do indeed depend on the words typed. That is, the timings for 'THE' is different for 'FOR'. By using word-specific Held and Interkey Times, we are able to achieve greater accuracy. In other words, we are using fixed strings within free text for the purpose of discrimination. We show that many fixed strings qualify as good candidates, and this allows us to verify the user as soon as any of these strings are typed.

Can a sample of keystroke data identify a user without any constraints on language or application? In other words, we wish to identify a person without any constraint on what he or she types. The person is not required to input a pre-determined text. Can Keystroke Dynamics still be used in such a general setting? In this paper, we attempt to answer this question. The answer will help in the design of *continuous authentication* systems [5], in which the system continuously checks for the presence of the authorized user after initial login. In such a scenario, it is impractical to demand the user to repeatedly type her userid or any other pre-determined text. Instead, the system has to utilize the typing patterns present in free text for authentication.

Perhaps the work closest to ours is that of Gunetti and Picardi [12], in which clever features were devised (along with suitable distance metrics) for free-text authentication. More precisely, Gunetti and Picardi avoided using the usual digraph and trigraph latencies directly as features. Instead, they used the latencies only to determine the relative ordering of different digraphs, and devised a distance metric to measure the difference between two orderings of digraphs, without regard to the absolute timings. The authors reported a False Accept Rate (FAR) of 0.0456% at a False Reject Rate (FRR)[1] of 4.0%, which, although worse than their fixed-text system, is state of the art for free-text systems.

We begin by analyzing the keystrokes of users as they go about their normal daily activities of emailing, web surfing, etc. We then look for patterns that can be used as a biometric. Such a pattern has to be discriminative, and at the same time common (universal) across all users (because the pattern cannot be used on people who do not type it). Also, for practical purposes, we should not have to wait too long for such a pattern to appear. The pattern should be readily available. We discover that, indeed, discriminative, universal and available patterns do exist even when the typing is unconstrained. Moreover, non-English words are better suited for this task. As far as we can tell, we are the first to investigate the problem of Keystroke Dynamics in a general setting. Our paper makes the following contributions:

---

[1] In the keystroke dynamics literature, FRR and FAR are also known as the False Alarm Rate and the Imposter Pass Rate, respectively.

1. We propose a new Goodness Measure to assess a keystroke pattern based on its discriminability, universality, and availability.
2. We show that Keystroke Dynamics can be used as a biometric even in a general setting.
3. We show that, surprisingly, some non-English words have a higher Goodness Measure than English words.
4. We propose two classifiers that are suitable for one-time and continuous keystroke authentication.

2 Basic Concepts

In this section we explain the basic terminology used in this paper. Fig. 1 shows a typical keystroke stream, collected from a user. Each arrow indicates a keyevent - the down facing arrow indicates a key being depressed, the upward facing arrow indicates the key being released. A pair of keyevents, a press and a release of the same key, form a keystroke.

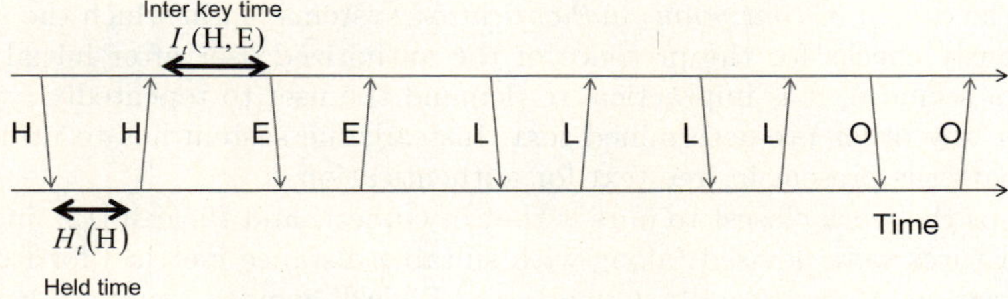

Fig. 1. Typical keystroke data. Each upward and downward pointing arrow indicates a keyevent.

2.1 Definitions

Held Time (H_t). We define Held Time as the time (in milliseconds) between a key press and a key release of the same key. Fig. 1 shows how the Held Time of the key 'H' is determined. Note that Held Time is strictly greater than zero.

Interkey Time (I_t). This is defined as the time in milliseconds between two consecutive keystrokes. In Fig. 1, I_t(H,E) is the time between the key release of 'H' and key press of 'E'. Interkey Times can be negative, i.e. the second key is depressed before the first key is released.

Sequence. We define Sequence as a list of consecutive keystrokes. For example 'HELLO' in the Fig. 1 is a Sequence. A Sequence can be of any length, the minimum being two. In this example, the Sequence is a valid English word, but this need not be the case. Thus, 'HEL', 'LLO' are also valid Sequences from the same keystroke stream in Fig. 1.

Feature Vector (F_t). This is a vector of the Held Times followed by the Interkey Times of a Sequence. For the Sequence 'THE', its feature vector is:

$$F_t(\mathrm{THE}) = \left[H_t(\mathrm{T}) \;\; H_t(\mathrm{H}) \;\; H_t(\mathrm{E}) \;\; I_t(\mathrm{T,H}) \;\; I_t(\mathrm{H,E}) \right]^\top \tag{1}$$

For a Sequence of length n, the length of the feature vector will be $2n - 1$.

2.2 Histogram ($\mathbf{Hist_{seq}}$)

From the samples of the Sequence appearing in the keystroke data, we estimate the probability density function (pdf) for each element in the feature vector F_t. This information is stored as a normalized histogram for the Sequence, which in turn will be used for classification.

We choose to represent the pdf as a histogram rather than as the parameters of a multidimensional Gaussian pdf because we observe that the data are rarely normally distributed. It is well known that a histogram with a fixed bin size is able to represent any pdf more accurately than a single Gaussian distribution.

Given two pdfs h_i, h_j, how similar are they? This may be measured using the Bhattacharyya distance or the Kullback-Leibler divergence [11]. We prefer the Bhattacharyya distance [11] because of its symmetry:

$$Dist_B(h_i, h_j) = \int \sqrt{h_i(\mathbf{x}) h_j(\mathbf{x})} d\mathbf{x} \tag{2}$$

This distance is always between 0 and 1, with 1 meaning that the two pdfs overlap perfectly, and 0 meaning that the pdfs do not overlap at all. Since our pdfs are discretized as histograms, the actual computation of Equation (2) is performed by first multiplying the corresponding bins of the two histograms, taking the positive square root of the products, and then summing over all the bins. We will use the Bhattacharyya distance in Classifier B (see Section 2.3).

2.3 Classifier

Classifier A is designed to identify a person from a single instance of a Sequence appearing in the keystroke data. The identity of the person is given by

$$\arg \max_{person} P(\mathrm{person} \mid \mathrm{seq}) \tag{3}$$

where,

$$P(\mathrm{person} \mid \mathrm{seq}) = \prod_{f \in F_t} P(\mathrm{Hist}_{seq}^{person} \mid f) \tag{4}$$

Here we are making the Naïve Bayes assumption, i.e. the elements of the Feature Vector F_t are statistically independent. Classifier A is useful for applications where authentication is required immediately without any delay; for example, in a login module that prompts the user to type a system-generated string (such a string is different each time, to guard against replay attacks).

Classifier B is designed to identify a person from multiple instances of the same Sequence appearing in the keystroke data. Here we first build a histogram ($Hist_{in}$) from the input keystroke stream and then compare it with the learned histogram ($Hist_{seq}$) using the Bhattacharyya distance. The identity of the person is given by

$$\arg\max_{person} Dist_B(\text{Hist}_{seq}, \text{Hist}_{in}) \qquad (5)$$

Again, we make the Naïve Bayes assumption. Classifier B is useful for applications which can afford to wait and collect enough keystrokes (thereby accumulating more evidence) before authentication.

3 Experiments

All our experiments are based on keystroke data collected from 22 users over a period of two weeks. The users are staff or students from our department, with different typing abilities. Some are trained typists, in that they had undergone typing classes and could type without looking at the keyboard. Others are untrained typists, but are still familiar with the keyboard as they have used it for many years. The users are of Chinese, Indian or European origin, and all are fluent in English.

Unlike most other studies, the data we collected were not controlled by any means. Keystrokes were logged as users went about their daily work of using email, surfing the web, creating documents, and so on. The collected data from individual users ranged from 30,000 keyevents to 2 million keyevents. In total 9.5 million keyevents were recorded. The PCs used belonged to each individual user, that is, they were not shared machines nor public access computers. Most PCs had keyboards with the Dell™ US layout, although a few users used their own non-Dell laptops. Each user used the same keyboard throughout the data collection, and thus the problem of different keyboards affecting their typing speed did not arise.

To collect keystrokes, we wrote a data collector program in Visual C. This was basically a System Wide Keyboard and Mouse hook, which collects keyboard and mouse events regardless of the application. The data collector was installed in the user's machine running Microsoft Windows XP™ . When activated the program collects all the keyevents and the mouseevents along with the timestamp and name of the application receiving the event. To protect the privacy of the users, each userid and machine id were hashed to a unique number. Also, a shortcut key was provided so that the user can switch it off while typing sensitive information such as passwords or pin numbers.

Table 1. The ten most frequently used English words, in descending order of frequency

THE, OF, AND, A, TO, IN, IS, YOU, THAT, IT

3.1 Results I - For Sequences That Are English Words

Classifier A and Classifier B were run on selected Sequences from the keystroke data that are English words. The words are selected from a Corpus [2] of most frequently appearing English words, see Table 1. The user data was split into 10 bins and 10-fold-cross-validation was conducted with both classifiers. The presented results are the mean and the standard deviation of the classification accuracy from the cross-validation. Accuracy is computed as a number (probability) between 0 and 1.

From Tables 2 and 3 it is evident that the Classifier B outperforms Classifier A. But we should note that Classifier A uses only one instance of the Sequence for identification, whereas Classifier B uses multiple instances for a combined result. Classifier A will be suitable for applications like Continuous Authentication [5] which needs to authenticate a user immediately upon receiving a biometric sample. Note that Table 2 shows the accuracy for identification tasks (multiclass classification) rather than for verification (two-class classification with a claimed identity). We can in principle get even better performance for verification by choosing a sequence that works best for each person, i.e., since we know the identity of the person being verified, we can sacrifice universality for discriminability.

Table 2. Performance of Classifier A - English Words

Sequence	Mean of Accuracy	Std. dev. of Accuracy
FOR	0.0598	0.1224
TO	0.0838	0.1841
THE	0.0562	0.1504
YOU	0.0512	0.0733
IS	0.0538	0.0432
IN	0.0573	0.0669
AND	0.0878	0.2682
OF	0.0991	0.2809

Classifier B can be aptly called a post-login identifier, as it needs significant amount of keystroke data to identify the person. The identification accuracy is very high, but the price to pay is the large number of samples required. Although it might not be suitable for Continuous Verification, it can used as a forensic tool to identify the person after data collection. In our experiments, we also observed that the accuracy of Classifier B increases with the number of samples. We surmise that this is due to better estimation of the histogram.

3.2 Results II - For Non-English Sequences

In order to perform keystroke identification in a general setting, we cannot depend only on English words. Almost all users, even native English speakers, type abbreviated words every so often. For example, 'tmr' is frequently used to

Table 3. Performance of Classifier B - English Words

Sequence	Mean of Accuracy	Std. dev. of Accuracy
FOR	0.7955	0.2319
TO	0.9455	0.1184
THE	0.8409	0.2443
YOU	0.7364	0.2985
IS	0.9591	0.0796
IN	1.0000	0.0000
AND	0.8318	0.2191
OF	0.8000	0.1927

mean 'tomorrow'. In this age of short text messaging, such abbreviations are increasingly common. In fact, by regarding such words as coming from a foreign language, it is clear that our approach can be applied to other languages as well.

Running Classifier B on non-English Sequences produces Table 4. Generally the accuracies for non-English Sequences are higher than that for English words. Although the corpus listed 'THE' as the most frequently used word in English, it was no longer the case when non-English Sequences are considered.

4 Goodness Measure

Given that we are allowing non-English text, we can no longer rely on the Corpus to guide us in selecting useful sequences. How then do we select a Sequence for identification? We will need to look for them from the training data. According to Jain [13], a good biometric ought to satisfy seven criteria: Universality, Uniqueness, Permanance, Collectability, Performance, Acceptability, Circumvention. Of these, we only need to consider the first two, because the others have to do with technology, or user perception. Universality (commonality) means the biometric should be measurable across all users. Uniqueness (individuality) has to do with its discriminative power. From these two criteria, we derive a new *Goodness Measure* to measure the quality of a Sequence based on the criteria of accuracy, availablity and universality. First, a few definitions.

1. **Universality** (U)**.** A Sequence is not useful for identification unless it is commonly used by users. For English text, the Corpus lists 'THE' as frequently occuring because every person uses it. We define universality as,

$$U = \frac{\text{No. of Users having this Sequence in their keystrokes}}{\text{Total No. of users}} \tag{6}$$

2. **Accuracy** (A)**.** The classification accuracy of the Sequence. Note that $0 \leq A \leq 1$. Accuracy is a measure of how discriminative a Sequence is, i.e. its uniqueness.

3. **Expectancy** (E). Unlike other kinds of biometrics, keystroke dynamics requires the system to wait until the user enters the required text. A particular string may be Universal, but the user may not type it frequently, thus keeping the system waiting for a long time. To capture this notion, we define the Expectancy of a Sequence to be the average number of keystrokes until an instance of the Sequence appears in the text. Intuitively, this measures how readily available the Sequence is. At best, the Sequence could appear on every keystroke (E=1); at worst, it might never appear in the text ($E = \infty$). For example, in the keystroke stream, 'TO BE OR NOT TO BE', $E(\text{'TO'}) = \frac{18}{2} = 9$ and $E(\text{'THE'}) = \infty$.

With the above definitions, we can now define Goodness Measure of a Sequence, G_m as follows:

$$G_m = \begin{cases} 0 & \text{if } E = \infty \\ \frac{U \times A}{E} & \text{otherwise} \end{cases} \tag{7}$$

Ideally, if all the factors are at their best (A=1,E=1,U=1), G_m will equal 1. In the Worst case (A=0 or E=∞ or U=0), G_m will equal 0. When E = 1, Equation (7) reduces to the special case,

$$G_m = U \times A \tag{8}$$

which may be interpreted as the Goodness Measure for a fixed-text keystroke identification system. Thus, our Goodness Measure is also applicable for traditional fixed-text systems.

Table 4 shows the Goodness Measure of a number of English and non-English sequences. The table is sorted by Accuracy, but a quick glance reveals that Accuracy does not mean a high G_m score. For example, the Sequence 'NE' (row four) has a high Accuracy but a low G_m score. The reason is its long Expectancy: one has to wait, on the average, over 400 keystrokes before this Sequence appears. For applications that require immediate authentication, 'NE' is a poor choice.

Table 4 also shows that the best performing English words (those that appear in Table 3) rank below non-English Sequences, both in terms of Accuracy and G_m score. Surprisingly, the Sequence 'THE' (third row from the bottowm) has a long Expectancy and is not Universal. This yields a low G_m score. We surmise that this counter-intuitive observation is because the subjects in our experiments did not write in complete, grammatical English. This, in turn, probably reflects the informal way English prose is used in everyday communication, rather than an indictment of the subjects' poor command of the language. Finally, the table also highlights the fact that Expectancy is the dominant criteria affecting G_m score. Many Sequences with approximately equal Accuracy and Universality scores differ greatly in their G_m scores because of different Expectancy values. For Keyboard Dynamics in a free-text setting, waiting for a long Expectancy Sequence limits how quickly the system can authenticate. Sequences with short Expectancy are more useful in this regard.

Table 4. Performance of Classifier B - non-English sequences

Sequence	Accuracy	Expectancy	Universality	G_m
AN	1.0000	113	1	0.008866
IN	1.0000	125	1	0.007986
NG	0.9955	150	1	0.006636
NE	0.9909	407	1	0.002433
LE	0.9864	294	1	0.003360
RE	0.9818	218	1	0.004498
TI	0.9818	324	1	0.003030
HE	0.9773	157	1	0.006226
EN	0.9773	207	1	0.004722
MA	0.9773	383	1	0.002549
ER	0.9727	245	1	0.003977
OU	0.9682	317	1	0.003051
IT	0.9682	339	1	0.002857
ING	0.9682	345	1	0.002802
AI	0.9636	312	1	0.003083
⋮	⋮	⋮	⋮	⋮
TO	0.9455	411	1	0.002298
THE	0.8409	350	0.95	0.002296
AND	0.8318	814	1	0.001022
FOR	0.7955	1062	1	0.000749

5 Conclusion and Future Work

In this paper, we presented a technique to identify a person based on Keystroke Dynamics in a general setting. This generalizes traditional fixed-text Keystroke Dynamics to free-text systems. Essentially, we identify a person based on a common list of fixed strings which we discover from analyzing users' keystroke logs. Our technique can also be used for verification, in which case each user can have his/her own list of strings.

We also found that non-English Sequences were more accurate than English words. This is useful because the prevalence of new communication technologies, such as instant messaging, online chat, text messaging, etc., means that users increasingly use informal English (containing abbreviations and even new words) when composing messages. This is true even for native English speakers. To guide our selection of good non-English words to use, we proposed a novel Goodness Measure based on well-studied properties that all biometrics ought to possess.

In the future, we would like to conduct the experiments on a larger pool of users to see if our results hold up. Also, we intend to investigate the effect of different keyboards on a person's typing speed, and how we may mitigate against this. Finally, it would be interesting to see if keystroke dynamics can distinguish between trained and untrained typists.

References

1. Shepherd, S.J.: Continuous authentication by analysis of keyboard typing characteristics. In: IEEE Conf. on Security and Detection, European Convention, pp. 111–114. IEEE Computer Society Press, Los Alamitos (1995)
2. Fry, E.B., Kress, J.E., Fountoukidis, D.L.: The Reading Teachers Book of Lists, 3rd edn.
3. Monrose, F., Reiter, M.K., Wetzel, S.: Password hardening based on keystroke dynamics. In: Proceedings of the 6th ACM Conference on Computer and Communications Security. ACM Press, New York (1999)
4. Rodrigues, R.N., Yared, G.F.G., Costa, C.R.D., Yabu Uti, J.B.T., Violaro, F., Ling, L.L.: Biometric Access Control Through Numerical Keyboards Based on Keystroke Dynamics. In: International Conference of Biometrics, pp. 640–646 (2006)
5. Kumar, S., Sim, T., Janakiraman, R., Zhang, S.: Using Continuous Biometric Verification to Protect Interactive Login Sessions. In: ACSAC, pp. 441–450 (2005)
6. Joyce, R., Gupta, G.: Identity authentication based on keystroke latencies. In: Communications of the ACM, vol. 33(2), pp. 168–176. ACM Press, New York (1990)
7. Villani, M., Tappert, C., Ngo, G., Simone, J., St. Fort, H., Cha, S.: Keystroke Biometric Recognition Studies on Long-Text Input under Ideal and Application-Oriented Conditions. In: Proceedings of the 2006 Conference on Computer Vision and Pattern Recognition Workshop, p. 39. IEEE Computer Society, Washington (2006)
8. Rao, B.: Continuous Keystroke Biometric System M.S. thesis, Media Arts and Technology, UCSB (2005)
9. Leggett, J., Williams, G., Usnick, M., Longnecker, M.: Dynamic identity verification via keystroke characteristics. Int. J. Man-Mach. Stud. 35(6), 859–870 (1991)
10. Obaidat, M.S., Sadoun, B.: Keystroke Dynamics Based Authentication. Ch. 10, Textbook (1998), `http://web.cse.msu.edu/~cse891/Sect601/textbook/10.pdf`
11. Duda, R., Hart, P., Stork, D.: Pattern Classification, 2nd edn. John Wiley and Sons, Chichester (2000)
12. Gunetti, D., Picardi, C.: Keystroke analysis of free text. ACM Transactions Information Systems Security 8(3), 312–347 (2005)
13. Jain, A.K.: Biometric recognition: how do I know who you are? In: Proceedings of the 12th IEEE Signal Processing and Communications Applications Conference. IEEE Computer Society Press, Los Alamitos (2004)

A New Approach to Signature-Based Authentication

Georgi Gluhchev[1], Mladen Savov[1], Ognian Boumbarov[2], and Diana Vasileva[2]

[1] Institute of Information Technologies, 2, Acad. G. Bonchev Str., Sofia 1113, Bulgaria
gluhchev@iinf.bas.bg, ihaiha99@abv.bg
[2] Faculty of Communication Technologies, Technical University,
8, Kl. Ohridski, 1000 Sofia, Bulgaria
olb@tu-sofia.bg, diana@engineer.bg

Abstract. A new signature based authentication approach is described, where signing clips are analyzed. Using an web-camera a series of frames is acquired that allows investigating the dynamics of the complex "hand-pen". For this a set of features of the hand, the pen and their mutual disposition at the time of signing is derived. Classification and verification decision-making rule based on the Mahalanobis distance has been used. A class-related feature weighting is proposed for the improvement of accuracy. A Gaussian-based model for the description of skin color is suggested. The preliminary experimental results have confirmed the reliability of the approach.

Keywords: Signature, Authentication, Biometrics, Feature weight, Classification error, Color modeling.

1 Introduction

The signature has been and is still used as a principal mean for person authentication. This is due to the comparative stability of the graph and of the movement dynamics stemming from the stereotype built in the years.

Until now two approaches to signature authentication have been brought to life called *off-line* and *on-line*. The development of the *off-line* methods started in 70-ies of the last century [11,12]. They are based on the evaluation of sophisticated static features describing the signature's graph [3,6,7,9,10]. Unfortunately, the graph can be imitated skillfully within the range of the admissible variations of the individual. This makes the identification methods using *off-line* analysis of the signature not quite reliable.

To speed up the authentication and increase the reliability *on-line* analysis has been introduced, where a pressure sensitive graphic tablet is used, thus giving the possibility for the analysis of the graph, dynamics and pressure simultaneously [4,8]. Since it is difficult to imitate dynamics, it is believed that this approach will be more resistant to forgeries. However, the non-standard way of signing may involve deviations in the signature parameters and may cause an increase in the error.

While the two above-mentioned approaches encompass the signature graphics, dynamics and pressure, there is one more aspect of the writing process that may contribute to the authentication problem solution. This concerns the hand position and parameters, pen orientation and its relevant position to the hand during the signing,

S.-W. Lee and S.Z. Li (Eds.): ICB 2007, LNCS 4642, pp. 594–603, 2007.

i.e. the behavior of the complex "hand-pen". This aspect is described in the paper and some preliminary results are reported. To the best of our knowledge, such an investigation, where interconnected parameters of different character, reflecting the individuality of the signing subject, has not been carried out.

The paper is organized in the following way: in section 2 some preprocessing and segmentation steps are presented; section 3 describes feature extraction; section 4 introduces the authentication rule; in section 5 experimental results are presented; in section 6 some problems are discussed and the possibilities for further extension of the approach are outlined.

2 Pre-processing and Segmentation

The approach is based on the processing of images of a signing hand. For this the following scenario is used: the hand enters the field of a web-camera mounted above the desk, does signing and leaves the field after that. Thus, a video-clip is obtained and saved. Depending on the signature length, the series of images can contain between 100 and 200 frames.

2.1 Image Pre-processing

The image processing consists of several steps: detection of the signature end points, hand-pen extraction and evaluation of features related to the hand parameters and hand-pen dynamics.

2.2 Detection of the Signature's Start and End Points

The procedure for detection of the signature's start and end points was described in detail in [15]. The absolute difference between the frames and an empty reference frame is used for this. When the hand enters the view field of the camera this difference will rise sharply, then will oscillate about some constant value and will diminish with the hand's outdrawing, so a graph with steep slope at the beginning and at the end of the signing will be produced (Fig. 1). Calculating the values of the gradient of the graph provides an easy determination of the "plateau" and so of the beginning and the end of the signature.

The experiments carried out in [15] have shown satisfying precision in the localization of the signature. Variations of about 2 frames have been observed.

At this initial step the signature duration d as a number of frames can be obtained and used further as an identification feature.

2.3 Object Detection

The complex "hand-pen" is the object that we are interested in. Because of the almost uniform background a fixed threshold could be applied for the object's detection. To evaluate it, a few frames, say K, are recorded in the absence of any object. For every two consecutive empty frames (k, k+1) the maximal absolute difference $E^{k,k+1}$ of the values of the three color components is evaluated:

$$E^{k,k+1} = \max | E^{k+1}(i, j) - E^{k}(i, j) |, \qquad (1)$$

where $E^{k}(i, j)$ is the color components vector at pixel (i, j) in the k-th image (k = 1, 2, …, K-1) and K is the number of the frames in the series.

The maximal difference

$$E = \max_{k} E^{k,k+1} \qquad (2)$$

is further used as a threshold for the object detection in the image sequence. After this operation, some "salt and pepper"- type noise could remain in the image (Fig.2b), but it could be easily removed using morphological or heuristic techniques.

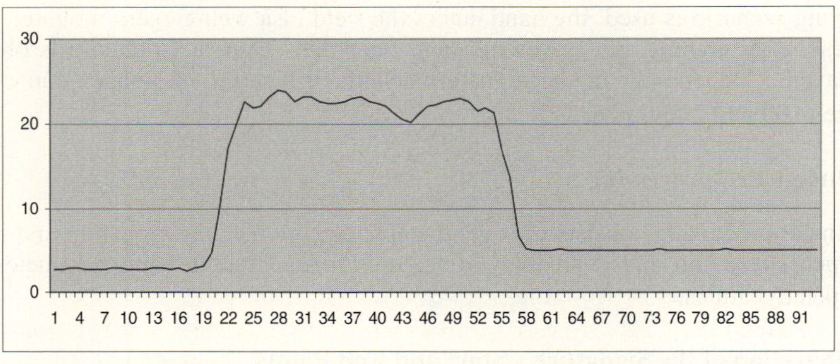

Fig. 1. Graph of the absolute differences. The horizontal axis represents the frame numbers, differences are alongside the vertical axis.

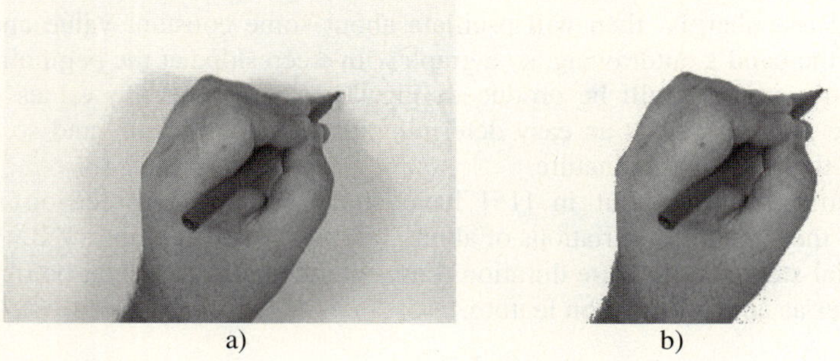

Fig. 2. a) Original image; b) background subtracted

2.4 Hand – Pen Segmentation

For the analysis of the hand and pen movement, a separation of the two elements is required. To facilitate the task, a blue color pen is used which makes good contrast with the predominant skin color (red with blue and green tinges) and the background which is a sheet of white paper. The use of the "red/blue" relation in the pixels leads to a good separation of the hand from the pen (Fig. 3).

3 "Hand-Pen" System Features Extraction

The essential authentication features include hand characteristics and movement, pen position and the mutual hand-pen disposition.

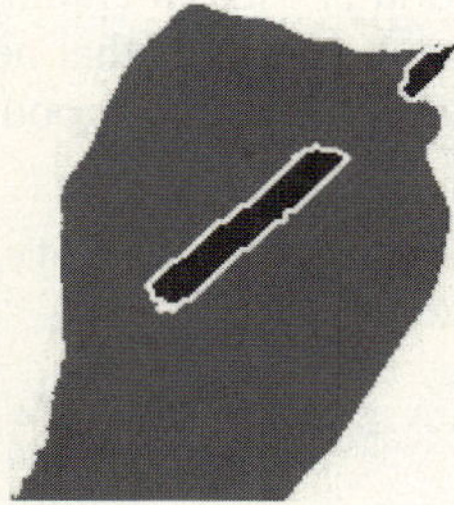

Fig. 3. Separation of the pen from the hand

3.1 Hand Features

Hand color and hand geometry are biometrics parameters specific for the individual and can contribute to the authentication.

Hand color. The hand color will speed up the search and increase the accuracy provided a large data-base of individuals of different races has to be searched for. To achieve this, models of the skin color of different races have to be generated. This requires a proper color space of minimal dimension to be selected, on the one hand, and the color components to be separated from the intensity, on the other hand. The YCbCr space is one of the possibilities studied in the literature that satisfies these requirements [2,5]. It is obtained from the RGB space using the non-linear transformation

$$\begin{aligned} Y &= 0.299R + 0.587G + 0.114B \\ Cb &= B - Y \\ Cr &= R - Y \end{aligned} \tag{3}$$

The first component *Y* reprisents the light intensity, i.e. it produces a gray-level image, while Cb and Cr are not influenced by the intensity change.

To describe the distribution of the skin color components, Gaussian function is usually used. Since the parameter distribution depends on the race, a Gaussian mixture model (GMM) is expected to be more adequate for an overall skin color presentation. The distribution density function of the mixture is defined as

$$p(x \mid \Theta) = \sum_{i=1}^{M} P(i)p(x \mid i, \Theta) \tag{4}$$

where P(i) is the prior probability of the *i*-th race, and $p(x \mid i, \Theta)$ is its density function. The parameter Θ consists of mean values and co-variances that have to be estimated from the experimental data. The Expectation Maximization proved to be a suitable technique for the evaluation of Θ in case of mixed models [1].

To demonstrate the possibility of GMM to distinguish between the races, a mixed distribution is shown in Fig. 4. For the evaluation of its parameters a data base created at the Technical University in Sofia is used, including 50 images of individuals from the white, black and yellow races. It is visible that nevertheless the three race-related areas overlap, it is possible to obtain a relatively good separation between them.

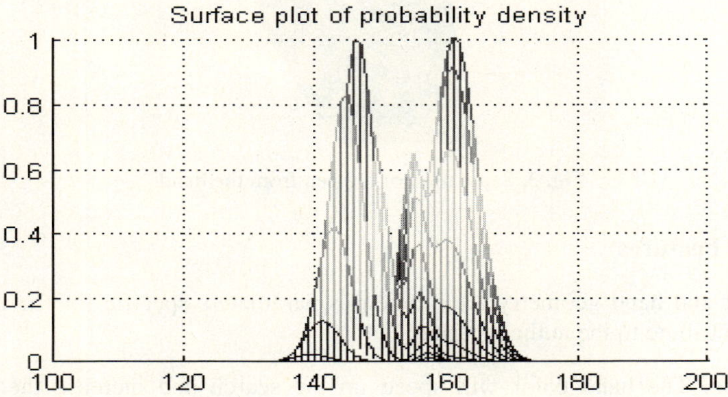

Fig. 4. Projection of a mixture of Gaussian distributions of white, black and yellow skin color. The horizontal axis represents the value of C_b, the probability density is alongside the vertical axis.

More sophisticated approach may use color properties of different parts of the hand, thus characterizing the individual more accurately.

Hand position and geometry. The main geometric features of the hand and its position during signing could be evaluated from its upper contour $\mathcal{K}$, scanning the image column by column and taking the coordinates (x, y) of the first pixel from the hand (x is the column number and y is the row number in the frame). The hand shape will be different for different persons because it depends on the size of the hand, on the way it holds the pen and on its movements while signing.

Hand position. The slope angle α of the line l: y = ax + b, which approximates $\mathcal{K}$ the best way in the sense of minimal mean-square distance, could be used as a general characteristic of the hand position. For that the line parameters a and b are evaluated minimizing the sum:

$$S = \sum_{x=0}^{M-1} [y - (ax + b)]^2 \tag{5}$$

where $(x, y) \in \mathcal{K}$ and M is the number of the contour points.

Geometric features. The geometric features are extracted using the characteristic points of the hand contour. End points and points of curvature larger than a predefined threshold are assumed as "characteristic". Different techniques could be used for curvature evaluation. To simplify the calculations, we have used the following formula

$$c = \frac{\left|\overline{PP_{-q}}\right| + \left|\overline{PP_{+q}}\right|}{\left|\overline{P_{-q}P_{+q}}\right|}, \tag{6}$$

where P denotes the current point, and P_{-q} and P_{+q} are the points remote q points far from P in both directions. Different geometric parameters of the obtained polygon like perimeter, area or distances from its centre to specific points could be measured.

Pen position. The pen position is described by the angle γ of its tilt towards the plane and the angle β of its projection in the plane. Since the pen length l is fixed, the first angle is determined by the ratio of the projection length l' to l. To determine β and l', we have to determine the major axis of the pen. For this its centre (C_x, C_y) is evaluated averaging the x and y coordinates of the pixels from the pen. After that the eigen values λ_1 and λ_2 of the characteristic equation

$$\left|\Sigma - \lambda I\right| = 0, \tag{7}$$

where Σ is a co-variance matrix and I is the unitary matrix is solved. β is evaluated according to the formula

$$\beta = \operatorname{arctg}\left(\frac{cov_{11} - \lambda_1}{cov_{12}}\right), \quad (\lambda_1 \geq \lambda_2) \tag{8}$$

To determine the angle γ, a straight line of angle β is drawn through the center and the distance l' between the utmost pixels from the pen coinciding with the straight line is evaluated. γ is obtained from the equation

$$\gamma = \arccos(l'/l). \tag{9}$$

Hand-pen relative position. The mutual position of the hand and pen is described using the following parameters:

a) The difference $\delta = \alpha - \beta$

b) The distances between the pen center and hand contour. For this a straight line perpendicular to the pen's longitudinal axis and passing through the center is used. The distances $r_1(C, H_1)$ and $r_2(C, H_2)$ between the two cross-points H_1 and H_2 of that line and contour are evaluated (Fig. 5).

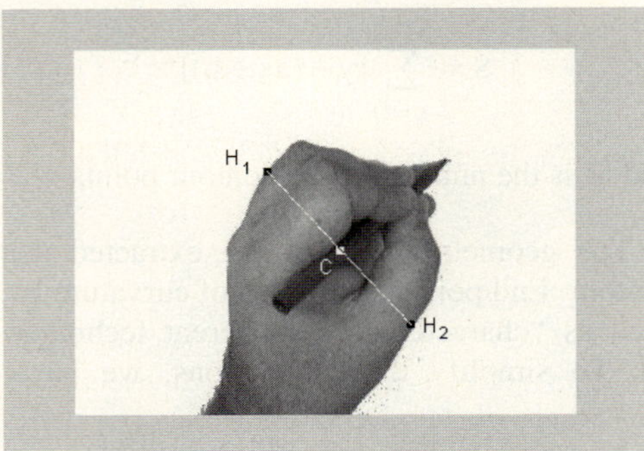

Fig. 5. Distances between the pen and hand contour

4 Authentication

The described in **3** set of features is measured for every individual whose signing has to be recognized. The mean value vectors $\mathbf{m}_i$ and covariance matrices $\mathbf{S}_i$ are evaluated and used as parameters of the squared Mahalanobis distance

$$R_i(x) = (x - m_i)^t S_i^{-1}(x - m_i) \tag{10}$$

between the current signing **x** and the i-th individual from the data base (i = 1,2,…,N).

There are two aspects of the authentication problem: classification and verification. While the classification problem is aimed at the assignment of a class-label to an unknown sample, the verification is aimed at the confirmation of the claimed class-label. This difference is further used to show how the verification accuracy could be improved.

Formula (10) treats all the features equally. However, in real cases the contribution of the features may not be equal. It is more reasonable to accept that different features will have different classification value for different individuals. Therefore, it makes sense to try to evaluate feature weights for each class separately and use them as weight factors for distance evaluation. This means evaluation of class-dependent values of the features.

In this paper we show that such a class-based evaluation of feature significance is possible and may improve the decision-making. The claim is that not only the feature values characterize the individual, but also the weights of the features are specific for him.

4.1 Feature Weighting

The accuracy of the classification is usually evaluated in terms of correct and wrong answers. This suggests using the function φ = Tp - Fp as a measure of accuracy, where Tp is the number of the true-positive answers and Fp is the number of the false-positive ones for a particular class. The goal is to find the maximal value of φ as a function of the feature weights t_{ij} for every class i and every feature j. Since there is no analytical relationship between the weights and the classification rate the only way to optimize φ consists in varying the weights t_{ij}. A good practical scheme for this was suggested by the theory of experiment planning [14]. The gradient for the surface φ is evaluated and the search goes in its direction until a maximal value of φ is obtained.

5 Experimental Results

To test the described approach, 14 volunteers have taken parts in the experiments. 10 signatures have been acquired from each of them in different days and at different time of the day. In this study the following 8 features have been measured and used for the evaluation of $\mathbf{m}_i$ and $\mathbf{S}_i$: 1) signature length d as a number of frames, 2) hand slope α, 3) pen projection angle β, 4) pen slope γ, 5) difference $\delta = \alpha - \beta$, 6) ratio r_1 / r_2 of the distances between the pen centre and hand contour, 7) perimeter p of the polygon defined by the characteristic points of the upper hand contour, and 8) area of the polygon. The feature "skin colour" was not used because all the volunteers were from the same race.

5.1 Verification

Using the Matlab random number generator 1000 signatures have been simulated for every individual. Assuming independent features the Mahalanobis distance was evaluated according to the formula

$$R_{ik} = \sum_{j=1}^{8} t_{ij}(f_{kj} - m_i)^2 / \sigma_i^2 \tag{11}$$

Moving in the gradient direction the best values of t_{ij} in terms of maximal classification rate have been determined.

The verification results are shown in Table 1. Some individuals (Nos 3, 8, 9, 11 and 14) are not included in the table because an absolute score of 100% was achieved for them. The first three rows include the values of Tp, Fp and φ in case of weights equal to 1. For the next rows the above described scheme was applied. It is seen that there is an improvement of the classifier performance for all the individuals, except No 10, where no effect is observed. The most significant improvement is obtained at Nos 2 and 7. Thus, an average accuracy φ = 99.9% was achieved after the modification of the weights, compared to the initial accuracy of 99.6%. The highest rate of false-positive Fp = 0.4% was observed at the individual No 1. The best reduction in Fp was obtained for No 2, where the accuracy increased from 99.2% to 100%.

It was interesting to see how the evaluated weights would affect the results if applied to a classification problem. Using again 1000 simulations per class and the evaluated weight factors for the classes no significant changes have been observed. Almost the same average accuracy was achieved resulting in 0.02% increase in Tp and 0.04% decrease in Fp. Therefore, for the classification problem there is may be no need to evaluate class-dependent feature weight factors.

Table 1. Experimental results

weights	score	1	2	4	5	6	7	10	12	13
initial values	*Tp*	999	999	997	996	994	990	998	1000	999
	Fp	6	17	0	1	2	0	1	1	0
	φ_i	993	982	997	995	992	990	997	999	999
new values	*Tp*	999	1000	998	999	998	999	998	1000	1000
	Fp	4	1	0	0	0	0	1	0	0
	φ_f	995	999	998	999	998	999	997	1000	1000
	$\varphi_f - \varphi_i$	2	17	1	4	6	9	0	1	1

6 Conclusion

A new signature based authentication approach that takes into account the dynamics of the complex "hand-pen" is suggested. It allows evaluating specific parameters of the hand and pen and their mutual position. While the acquired source information allows for the extraction of many features of different nature, only a small number of global features and a simple classification rule have been used in the investigation. Nevertheless, the obtained tentative results aimed at the illustration of the approach, have shown quite satisfactory results. The assumption that the use of class-specific feature weights will improve the overall accuracy in case of verification has proven to be correct. The intuitive explanation of this is that if a sample does not belong to a particular class its features will not be properly weighted when a distance to that class will be measured and, as a result, larger distance value will be obtained.

The future work will be aimed at the thorough analysis of the parameter dynamics. Also, the acquisition of more experimental data will be of primary importance.

A possible extension of the approach may include different alternatives like: using a tablet instead of paper or capturing signature after signing and processing it in *off-line* mode. Thus, more accurate dynamic and/or static information will be obtained.

Acknowledgments. The investigation was supported by BioSecure Network of Excellence of the 6th European Framework Program, contract No 507634, and the Ministry of Education and Sciences in Bulgaria, contract No 1302/2003.

References

1. Bouguila, N., Ziou, D.: Dirichlet-based probability model applied to human skin detection. In: Proc. Int. Conf. ASSP'04, vol. V, pp. 521–524 (2004)
2. Boumbarov, O., Vassileva, D., Muratovski, K.: Face extraction using 2D color histograms. In: XL Int. Scientific Conf. on Information, Communication and Energy Systems and Technologies (ICEST'2005), Nis, Serbia and Montenegro, vol. 1, pp. 334–337 (2005)
3. Fang, B., Leung, C.H., Tang, Y.Y., Kwok, P.C.K., Tse, K.W., Wong, Y.K.: Off-line signature verification with generated training samples. IEE Proc. Vis. Image Signal Process 149(2), 85–90 (2002)
4. Fink, G., Wienecke, M., Sagerer, G.: Video-Based On-Line Handwriting Recognition. In: Proc. Int. Conf. on Document Analysis and Recognition, pp. 226–230. IEEE, Los Alamitos (2001)

5. Fu, Z., Yang, J., Hu, W., Tan, T.: Mixture clustering using multidimensional histograms for skin detection. In: Proc. of the 17th Int. Conf. on Pattern Recognition (ICPR'04), pp. 549–552 (2004)
6. Hairong, L., Wenyuan, W., Chong, W., Quing, Z.: Off-line Chinese signature verification based on support vector machines. Pattern Recognition Letters 26, 2390–2399 (2005)
7. Ismail, M.A., Gad, S.: Off-line arabic signature recognition and verification. Pattern Recognition 33, 1727–1740 (2000)
8. Jain, A.K., Griess, F.D., Connell, S.D.: On-Line Signature Verification. Pattern Recognition 35(12), 2963–2972 (2002)
9. Ka, H., Yan, H.: Off-line signature verification based on geometric feature extraction and neural network classification. Pattern Recognition 30(1), 9–17 (1996)
10. Kai, H., Yan, H.: Off-line signature verification using structural feature correspondence. Pattern Recognition 35, 2467–2477 (2002)
11. Kuckuk, W., Rieger, B., Steinke, K.: Automatic Writer Recognition. In: Proc. of Carnahan Conf. on Crime Countermeasures, Kentuky, pp. 57–64 (1979)
12. Lantzman, R.: Cybernetics and forensic handwriting investigation, Nauka, Moscow (1968)
13. Munich, M.E., Perona, P.: Camera-Based ID Verification by Signature Tracking. In: Burkhardt, H.-J., Neumann, B. (eds.) ECCV 1998. LNCS, vol. 1406, pp. 782–796. Springer, Heidelberg (1998)
14. Nalimov, V.V., Chernova, N.A.: Statistical Methods in Experiment Planning, Nauka, Moskow (1965)
15. Savov, M., Gluhchev, G.: Automated Signature Detection from Hand Movement. In: Proc. of CompSysTech'04, Rousse, Bulgaria, pp. III.A.3-1–III.A.3-6 (2004)

Biometric Fuzzy Extractors Made Practical: A Proposal Based on FingerCodes*

Valérie Viet Triem Tong[1], Hervé Sibert[2], Jérémy Lecœur[3], and Marc Girault[4]

[1] Supelec, Campus de Rennes, Avenue de la Boulaie F-35576 Cesson-Sévigné Cedex, France
[2] NXP Semiconductors, 9 rue Maurice Trintignant, F-72081 Le Mans Cedex 9, France
[3] Irisa-Inria, Campus de Beaulieu, F-35042 Rennes Cedex
[4] France Telecom Research and Development, 42 rue des Coutures, BP6243, F-14066 Caen Cedex 4, France

Abstract. Recent techniques based on error-correction enable the derivation of a secret key for the (varying) measured biometric data. Such techniques are opening the way towards broader uses of biometrics for security, beyond identification. In this paper, we propose a method based on fingerprints to associate, and further retrieve, a committed value which can be used as a secret for security applications. Unlike previous work, this method uses a stable and ordered representation of biometric data, which makes it of practical use.

1 Introduction

Biometric authentication refers to verifying physiological or behavioral features such as voiceprint, fingerprint or iris scan [9,2]. From personal device unlock to e-passports, biometry-based authentication schemes have spread into our lives. Such schemes usually run as follows: the user presents his current biometric data, and the verifier checks if the measured data match the biometric reference data acquired during the enrollment.

Biometric data have several properties which make them natural candidates for security applications: they are hard to forge, they are unique to each person, and they are a good source of entropy. However, they also have several drawbacks which slow down their adoption: one cannot change his biometric data, biometric data are often easy to steal, and acquisition of biometric data is subject to variations.

As the measured data can vary, they cannot be directly used as a password or as a cryptographic secret. Moreover, they have to be sent across a possibly insecure network for matching against reference data stored in a database, whose loss would be disastrous. Several research directions address these concerns. First, recent schemes avoid the storage of the whole reference data. Second, new techniques based on error-correction enable the derivation of a constant secret key

* Most of the research work that this article stems from was carried out by the authors at France Telecom Research and Development in Caen (France).

S.-W. Lee and S.Z. Li (Eds.): ICB 2007, LNCS 4642, pp. 604–613, 2007.

from the (varying) measured biometric data. Such techniques can also naturally address the biometric data storage problem.

Still, stolen biometric data are stolen for life. Unlike a cryptographic key, they cannot be updated or destroyed. To solve this last problem, it remains to be able to use biometric data to retrieve a secret value linked to each user, instead of them directly as a secret. Few such proposals have been made, but they are not practical. In this paper, we propose a practical method based on fingerprints to associate, and further retrieve, a committed value which can be used as a secret for security applications.

1.1 Related Works

The fact that storing biometric reference data should be avoided for distant authentication system is commonly accepted, as mentioned by Jain *et al.* in [16]. In an attempt to do so [8], Jain and Uludag propose to use watermarking to secure the transmission of biometric data across a network. However, they still use a biometric database.

In [11], Juels and Wattenberg present the first *crypto-biometric system* called *fuzzy commitment*, in which a cryptographic key is decommitted using biometric data. *Fuzziness* means that a value close to the original (under some suitable metrics) is sufficient to extract the committed value. The scheme is based on the use of error-correcting codes, and runs as follows. Let $C \subset \{0,1\}^n$ a set of codewords for a suitable error-correcting code. The user chooses a secret codeword $c \in C$, the decommitment key is the enrolled fingerprint x and the commitment is the pair $(c - x, \mathcal{H}(c))$, where $\mathcal{H}$ is a one-way function. When a user tries to decommit a pair $(c - x, \mathcal{H}(c))$ using a decommitment key x', he attempts to decode $c - x + x'$ to the closest codeword c'. Decommitment is successful if $\mathcal{H}(c') = \mathcal{H}(c)$, which means the user has retrieved his secret c. In this scheme, the key x is built from a fingerprint, as a set of minutiae positions. This yields two shortcomings. First, it does not allow modifications of x, such as re-ordering, and addition/deletion of an element in x, although such modifications are frequent in real life. Second, the security proof of this scheme holds only if x is uniformly distributed, which is not the case in reality.

In order to overcome these drawbacks, Juels and Sudan propose a *fuzzy vault* scheme [10]. This scheme may be thought of as an order-invariant version of the fuzzy commitment scheme, obtained by using a generalization of Reed-Solomon codes in which they think of a codeword as an evaluation of a polynomial over a set of points. The idea is to encode a secret s as a polynomial p of degree d using the Reed-Solomon encoding scheme. The codeword consists of a set of pairs $R_1 = \{(x, p(x)\}_{1 \leq i \leq n}$, where the x-coordinates represent the position of minutiae in the reference fingerprint. A set R_2 of *chaff* points that are not on p is added to R_1 to form the *vault* V. To rebuild the codeword using the Reed-Solomon decoding scheme, the user needs $d+1$ pairs $(x, y) \in R_1$ from the original n points. The method has been successfully tested by Uludag and Jain with the IBM-GTDB database [15]. However, the fuzzy vault has one main drawback, which is its restricted use. Indeed, if the polynomial p is compromised, then the fingerprint itself is, as all the other minutiae in the fingerprint are the points on p in the vault V. Thus, if this method was used for different applications, with different vaults each time, as the x-coordinates correspond to the minutiae, disclosure of different vaults for the same user would reveal his minutiae.

Next, Clancy *et al.* considered a practical implementation of the fuzzy vault in a secure smartcard [4]. Their experimentation showed that a sufficient security level for the fuzzy vault cannot be obtained with real-life parameters. They thus defined a modified scheme called the *fingerprint vault*, and proposed a way to find the optimal vault parameters.

However, the choice of chaff points also yields uniformity problems, that can be exploited by an attacker to distinguish between chaff points and real points in the vault. Chang and Li have analyzed this problem [3] in a general setting. They show that, since secret points are not uniformly distributed, the proper way of choosing chaff point is far from being trivial, and there is no known non-trivial bound on the entropy loss.

1.2 Contents of the Paper

In this paper, we propose a new method to associate, and further retrieve, a committed value using a fingerprint. Our method is based on a special fingerprint data representation measure called FingerCode [14]. The committed value is rebuilt from the FingerCode biometric data and public data we call **FingerKey**. The committed value cannot be recovered from the public data, and we show that no illegitimate user is able to forge it. Moreover, using the FingerCode, we avoid the minutiae set modifications concerns. At last, our method does not require storage of any biometric reference, and therefore, when the committed value is used as a (seed for generation of a) secret key in a secure cryptographic protocol, an attacker cannot learn the biometric data.

The paper is organized as follows: after the introduction, we present the tools we use and, more particularly, error-correcting codes, the FingerCode definition and its extraction method in Section 2. In Section 3, we describe our construction and give our experimental results. In Section 4, we give some advice on possible applications and security parameters. At last, we give directions for future work and we conclude.

2 Preliminaries

2.1 Error-Correcting Codes

Like the *fuzzy* schemes of Juels *et al.*, our scheme relies on using error-correcting codes. We refer the reader to [12,13] for more details on error-correcting codes.

The goal of error-correcting codes is to prevent loss of information during the transmission of a message over a noisy channel by adding redundancy to the original message m to form a message m', which is transmitted instead of m. If some bits are corrupted during the transmission, it remains possible for the receiver to reconstruct m', and therefore m. In our scheme, the noise is the result of the use of different measures of the fingerprint.

More formally, an error-correction code over a message space $M = \{0,1\}^k$ consists of a set of codewords $C \subset \{0,1\}^n$ $(n > k)$ associated with a coding function denoted by `encode`, and a decoding function denoted by `decode`, such that `encode`$: M \to C$ injects messages into the set of codewords and `decode`$: \{0,1\}^n \to C \cup \emptyset$ maps an n-bits string to the nearest codeword if the string does not have too many errors, otherwise it outputs $\emptyset$.

We recall that the Hamming distance between binary strings is the number of bit locations where they differ. The *distance* Δ of a code is the minimum Hamming distance between its codewords. Therefore, to be properly decoded, a string must have at most $\frac{\Delta-1}{2}$ errors. In the sequel, we have chosen to use Reed-Solomon codes for their correction power.

2.2 FingerCode

Our purpose is to retrieve constant secret data from a varying measures of biometric data. This measure should have be reasonably stable, which means slight modifications of the acquisition should result in a low distance from the reference. Therefore, we cannot use a minutiae-based matching method.

We propose to use a texture-based method, called *FingerCode*, which is stable in size, and founded on the localization of the morphological centre of the fingertip and the use of a well-known pattern analysis method to characterize a fingerprint. It was introduced by Jain and Prabhakar in [14,6]. A FingerCode is a 640-component vector of numbers that range from 0 to 7, which is ordered and stable in size. The matching is then handled by a simple Euclidean distance. Here is a summary of this method.

Using Bazen and Guerez method [1], an estimation of the block orientation field is computed. Using this orientation, a very simple curvature estimator can be designed for each pixel. The maximum value of this estimator is the morphological center that we are searching. We extract a circular region of interest around this point in which we consider 5 concentric bands and 16 angular portions making a total of 80 sectors. The width of the band is related to the image resolution, e.g. for a 500-dpi image, the band is 20-pixels wide. Although we avoid the problem of translation and rotation of the image by using the morphological center and a circular area, we still have to handle the finger pressure differences. Hence, we normalize the image to given values of mean and variance.

If normalization is performed on the entire image at once, then the intensity variations due to the finger pressure difference remain. Therefore, it is necessary to normalize separately each sector of the image, in order to obtain an image where the average intensity at a local scale is about the same as that of the whole image.

Ridges and valleys can be characterized by their local frequency and orientation. So, by using a properly tuned Gabor filter, we can remove noise and catch this piece of information. An even symmetric Gabor filter has the following general form in the spatial domain:

$$G(x,y,f,\theta) = \exp\left\{-\frac{1}{2}\left[\frac{x'^2}{\delta_x^2} + \frac{y'^2}{\delta_y^2}\right]\right\} \times \cos(2\pi \times f \times x')$$
$$x' = x\sin\theta + y\cos\theta$$
$$y' = x\cos\theta - y\sin\theta$$

where f is the frequency of the sinusoidal plane along direction t from the x-axis, and δ_x and δ_y are the space constants of the Gaussian envelope along the corresponding axis. The filtering in the spatial domain is performed with a 19×19 mask in 8 directions from 0 to $157,5\,^\circ$, resulting in 8 filtered images of the region of interest.

Finally, we compute the FingerCode as the average absolute deviation from the mean (AAD) of each sector of each image. The feature vector is organized as follows: values from 0 to 79 correspond to the $0\,^\circ$ filter, the 80 following values to the $22,5\,^\circ$ filter and so on. In these 80 values, the 16 first are the innermost band values, the first one being the top sector and the other values corresponding to the sectors counted clockwise. The matching is based on Euclidean distance between FingerCodes. We also use cyclic rotation of the FingerCode, up to 2 steps, to handle rotations up to $45\,^\circ$.

3 Our Construction

The idea behind our proposal is to use the FingerCode, which offers ordered and stable biometric data, in the fuzzy commitment scheme [11], in order to avoid minutiae-related drawbacks. However, the FingerCode has a too high FRR rate to be used directly as the decommitment key: error-correction would never be efficient enough to recognize a legitimate user. Therefore, our scheme slightly differs from the fuzzy commitment. It consists of a fuzzy extractor and of a secure sketch according to the definitions of Dodis *et al.* [5]. In our construction, the secret is represented as a word of $d+1$ letters, which correspond to the $d+1$ integer coefficients of a polynomial $p \in \mathbb{Z}[X]$ of degree d.

The registration step consists in extracting public data called *FingerKey* from the pair (F, p), where F is a FingerCode. To this end, n points of p are randomly chosen, with $n > d$, and we hide these points using n stable subparts of the FingerCode like in the fuzzy commitment scheme. To retrieve the secret polynomial p, we use the usual decoding procedure for each point. If at least $d+1$ points can be decommitted, then p is obtained by Lagrange interpolation.

3.1 Encoding

The encoding part, or *fuzzy extractor* as defined in [5], is a set of fuzzy commitments where the committed values are points of on a secret polynomial. First, the system chooses a secret polynomial p of degree d (for instance, using a bijection between a secret key chosen by user U and the polynomials space), and n random points $p_0 \ldots p_{n-1}$ on this polynomial ($n > d$). These points are represented by $l-bit$ strings, and encoded with an encoding function $\mathcal{RS}$-encode which outputs n codewords $c_0, \ldots, c_{n-1} \in \{0,1\}^{l+e}$. In our experimentation,

$\mathcal{RS}$-encode is the encoding function for Reed-Solomon codes. The FingerCode F_U of the user is then divided into n parts $F_U = f_0||\ldots||f_{n-1}$. The system then computes $\{\delta_i = c_i - f_i, 0 \le i \le n-1\}$. The FingerKey K_{F_U} for user U consists of the set of pairs $(\delta_i, \mathcal{H}(c_i))$ where $\mathcal{H}$ is a one-way function and $0 \le i \le n-1$. This algorithm is described in Figure 1. The FingerKey is then made public for future reference, and may be stored in a server or in a user's smartcard.

Inputs	polynomial p of degree d integer n with $n > d$ family $(p_i)_{0\le i\le n}$ of randomly chosen points of p FingerCode $F_U = f_0\|\|\ldots\|\|f_{n-1}$
Outputs	FingerKey K_{F_U}
Algorithm	$K_{F_U} \leftarrow \emptyset$ For i going from 0 to $n-1$ do | $c_i \leftarrow \mathcal{RS}\texttt{-encode}(x_i, p(xi))$ | $\delta_i \leftarrow c_i - f_i$ | $K_{F_U} \leftarrow K_{F_U}\|\|(\delta_i, \mathcal{H}(c_i))$ Return K_{F_U}

Fig. 1. Encoding algorithm: FingerKey extractor for user U

3.2 Decoding

In order to retrieve his secret, user U has his FingerCode $F'_U = f'_0||\ldots||f'_n$ measured by the system. The system looks up the FingerKey K_{F_U} for U, and uses the $\mathcal{RS}$-decoding function to compute, for each value $\delta_i + f'_i$, the closest codeword c'_i. In our experimentation, as we use the Reed Solomon code for encoding, we use the Reed Solomon decoding function $\mathcal{RS}$-decoding. If equality $\mathcal{H}(c_i) = \mathcal{H}(c'_i)$ holds, then, the decommitment of the codeword is successful. If at least $d+1$ values f'_i $(i \le 0 \le n)$ yield a successful decommitment, the user is able to rebuild p using Lagrange interpolation. The user is thus authenticated as U if he succeeds in decommitting at least $d+1$ points and thus rebuild the secret polynomial p. The system can then rebuild the user-chosen secret. The algorithm is given in detail in Figure 2.

3.3 Experimentation

We have experimented this method on a fingerprint database containing 1000 pictures. In a first attempt, we used FingerCode values rounded to the nearest integer. It turned out that the FingerCode differed too much from the original value to be corrected by error-correction. We then changed our rounding method as follows: values from 0 to 2 were replaced by 0, those from 2 to 4 were replaced by 1, and the others (from 4 to 7) were replaced by 2. Thus, we used transformed FingerCodes whose vector components values were 0, 1 or 2, which yields 3^{640}

Inputs	degree d of the committed polynomial integer n with $n > d$ User FingerCode $F'_U = f'_0 \| \| \dots \| \| f'_{n-1}$ FingerKey for user U $K_{F'_U} = (\delta_0, \mathcal{H}(c_0)) \| \| \dots \| \| (\delta_{n-1}, \mathcal{H}(c_{n-1}))$
Outputs	polynomial p or Failure

Algorithm	$P \leftarrow \emptyset$
	For i going from 0 to $n-1$ do
	    $c'_i \leftarrow \mathcal{RS}$-decode$(\delta_i + f'_i)$
	    If $\mathcal{H}(c_i) = \mathcal{H}(c'_i)$
	        $P \leftarrow P \cup \{c_i\}$
	If $\|P\| > d$,
	    $p \leftarrow$ Lagrange Interpolation of elements in P
	    Return p
	otherwise return Failure.

Fig. 2. Decoding algorithm: Secure sketch for a user pretending to be U

possible values for an entire FingerCode. We divided each FingerCode into sixteen parts, used the Reed-Solomon code $RS(2^5, 10)$ defined by his generator polynomial $X^6 + X^5 + 1$, and we chose secrets as being polynomials of degree 8. Then, no FingerCode coming from a fingerprint of another user could lead to a successful decommitment. For a FingerCode coming from another fingerprint of the legitimate user, the decommitment success rate was more than 60%.

As our system is more flexible than the standard procedure and as it allows the regeneration of a user-chosen secret, with public data(FingerKey), we may have expected worse results than standard matching. However, using the standard FingerCode matching on the same picture database, we obtained a FRR of 78% for a FAR of 0, 1%. Therefore, it appears that splitting the FingerCode into several parts and using our construction allows for better results than the standard FingerCode matching. In the literature, better results are given for usual FingerCode matching: Prabhakar obtains a 19,32% FRR for a 0,1% FAR. Therefore, it is likely that our results can also be improved, and, using FingerCode enhancements (picture optimization...), we can reasonably expect results for our construction similar to those obtained for standard FingerCode matching.

4 Applications and Security

4.1 Security

The scheme we have presented enables users to retrieve a committed secret, without biometric data storage. Just like other biometric systems, our system should be used in a safe manner. Indeed, measuring biometric data and then using these data to impersonate the legitimate user is still possible. Retrieving a user's secret is always possible given his FingerKey and a measure of his

FingerCode. Nevertheless, the concealment property ensures that retrieving the secret is unfeasible given the FingerKey only.

More formally, the security of the scheme relies on three properties:

1. an attacker who knows only a published **FingerKey** cannot retrieve the biometric data which it was computed from,
2. *(concealment)* an attacker who knows only a published **FingerKey** cannot retrieve the corresponding secret polynomial p,
3. an attacker who knows both a published **FingerKey** and the polynomial p cannot retrieve the corresponding biometric data.

First, let us notice that retrieving the secret polynomial p from the biometric data (FingerCode) associated with a **FingerKey** is straightforward. Property 1 arises from the security of the *fuzzy commitment* scheme [11]. We will show how it extends to Property 3. In the following Theorem, we show that the computational complexity of retrieving p is at least equal to the computational complexity of the inversion of the hash function used. Therefore, Property 2 holds as long as inverting the hash function is not computationally feasible.

Theorem 1. *Suppose that an attacker knows the value K_F of a* **FingerKey** *, and that he has access neither to the biometric data of the user corresponding to K_F, nor to a view of an execution of the scheme.*

Consider the following parameters of our system: ℓ is the length of the FingerCode subcomponents f_i, n is the number of FingerCode subcomponents, Δ is the distance of the error-correcting code used, L is the output length of the one-way function $\mathcal{H}$, d is the degree of the secret polynomial p, and $\mathcal{C}(\mathcal{H})$ the complexity of inverting $\mathcal{H}$ for a random input.

Given the FingerKey K_F, the complexity of retrieving p is equal to

$$\min(2^L, (d+1) * \mathcal{C}(\mathcal{H}), (d+1) * \frac{2^\ell}{\binom{\ell}{\frac{\Delta-1}{2}}}).$$

Sketch of the proof. We suppose p is chosen in a set whose cardinality is beyond exhaustive search. In order to retrieve p, the attacker has to find $d+1$ points on p. As he knows only the FingerKey K_F, this means he has to find $d+1$ elements in $\{c_i \in C\}_{1 \leq i \leq n}$. As p is independent from the FingerCode, the values δ_i do not reveal any information about the c_i's. Therefore, the attacker has either to revert $\mathcal{H}$, or to find at least $d+1$ values f such that $\mathcal{H}(RS - decode(\delta_i + f)) = \mathcal{H}(c_i)$ for different i's.

In order to find some f such that the distance between c_i and $\delta_i + f$ is at most $\frac{\Delta-1}{2}$, the attacker has to try an average of $\frac{2^\ell}{\binom{\ell}{\frac{\Delta-1}{2}}}$ values, and to test each value by computing $\mathcal{H}(RS - decode(\delta_i + f))$ for a given i. Trying several i's simultaneously would just multiply the complexity by the number of i's targeted, thus it does not reduce the global complexity of the attack, which is thus $(d+1) * \frac{2^\ell}{\binom{\ell}{\frac{\Delta-1}{2}}}$.

If the attacker chooses to revert $\mathcal{H}$, there should be no algorithm better than brute force for a proper choice of $\mathcal{H}$, so the complexity of inversion of $\mathcal{H}$ would be 2^L. In the case when there exists an algorithm better than exhaustive search to invert $\mathcal{H}$, the complexity of the attack is at most $(d+1) * \mathcal{C}(\mathcal{H})$. □

The idea behind the proof is that, as all the values $c_i - f_i$ are given, and that knowing the c_i's yields p, the gap between Properties 1 and 2 lies in the given values $\mathcal{H}(c_i)$.

At last, Property 3 holds thanks to the fact that the choice of the points on the polynomial is random. Hence, providing p does not give information on the c_i's, the knowledge of which is equivalent to knowing the biometric data.

Any implementation of the system should ensure that the FingerCode is not stored, and the user should only present his fingerprint to a trusted device. If this is not the case, then, the system could still be secure if the FingerKeys of the user are stored in a user-owned device. For instance, a FingerKey may be stored in a smartcard, which would, on input of the FingerCode value, regenerate the user's secret and perform cryptographic operations using this secret internally.

4.2 Applications

Our system addresses two usual drawbacks of biometrics: it enables the regeneration of constant data, and it also allows to change these data in case of loss or theft.

This system enables applications beyond the reach of usual biometric identification. For instance, the regenerated value can be used as the seed for obtaining a constant RSA keypair (or any other cryptographic key), used for applications such as digital signature, or encryption/decryption. Moreover, a user can choose different secrets for different applications, and also change every secret that would be compromised. Therefore, this system also offers scalability, and decreases the risks linked to the theft of private data.

5 Conclusion

We have presented a system in which no biometric data has to be stored, and the current biometric data is used to decommit a secret value. This enables the regeneration of several secret values used for various applications for each user. By reducing the need for transmission of biometric data, our system also reduces the risks of biometric data theft. This proposal is the first to combine error-correcting codes with stable and ordered biometric templates. Our experiments, based on the FingerCode, provide encouraging results. We now wish to improve our results by finding more suitable biometric measures. Hybrid methods that mix minutia and texture features, as introduced in as in [7], provide more stable biometric measures than the one we have used. One promising research direction is thus to adapt such methods to our construction, in order to improve our experimental results.

References

1. Bazen, A.M., Guerez, H.: Directional field computation for fingerprints based on the principal component analysis of local gradients. In: Proc. of 11th annual Workshop on Circuits, Systems and Signal Processing, 2000 (2000)
2. Bolle, R., Pankanti, S.: Biometrics, Personal Identification in Networked Society: Personal Identification in Networked Society. Kluwer Academic Publishers, Norwell, MA, USA (1998)
3. Chang, E.-C., Li, Q.: Hiding secret points amidst chaff. In: Vaudenay, S. (ed.) EUROCRYPT 2006. LNCS, vol. 4004, pp. 59–72. Springer, Heidelberg (2006)
4. Clancy, T.C., Kiyavash, N., Lin, D.J.: Secure smartcardbased fingerprint authentication. In: WBMA '03: Proceedings of the 2003 ACM SIGMM workshop on Biometrics methods and applications, pp. 45–52. ACM Press, New York (2003)
5. Dodis, Y., Reyzin, L., Smith, A.: Fuzzy extractors: How to generate strong keys from biometrics and other noisy data. In: Cachin, C., Camenisch, J.L. (eds.) EUROCRYPT 2004. LNCS, vol. 3027, pp. 523–540. Springer, Heidelberg (2004)
6. Jain, A., Prabhakar, S., Hong, L., Pankanti, S.: Filterbank-based fingerprint matching. In: Proc. of IEEE Transactions on Image Processing, vol. 9(5), pp. 846–859. IEEE Computer Society Press, Los Alamitos (2000)
7. Jain, A., Ross, A., Prabhakar, S.: Fingerprint matching using minutiae and texture features. In: Proc. of International Conference on Image Processing (ICIP), Thessaloniki, Greece, pp. 282–285 (October 2001)
8. Jain, A., Uludag, U.: Hiding biometric data. IEEE Transactions on Pattern Analysis and Machine Intelligence (2003)
9. Jain, A.K., Maltoni, D.: Handbook of Fingerprint Recognition. Springer, New York (2003)
10. Juels, A., Sudan, M.: A fuzzy vault scheme. In: Proceedings of IEEE International Symposium on Information Theory, 2002. IEEE Computer Society Press, Los Alamitos (2002)
11. Juels, A., Wattenberg, M.: A fuzzy commitment scheme. In: CCS '99: Proceedings of the 6th ACM conference on Computer and communications security, pp. 28–36. ACM Press, New York (1999)
12. MacWilliams, F.J., Sloane, N.J.A.: The Theory of Error-Correcting Codes, North-Holland (1977)
13. MacWilliams, F.J., Sloane, N.J.A.: The Theory of Error-Correcting Codes, Part II, North-Holland (1977)
14. Prabhakar, S.: Fingerprint Classification and Matching Using a Filterbank. PhD thesis
15. Uludag, U., Jain, A.K.: Fuzzy fingerprint vault. In: Proc. Workshop: Biometrics: Challenges Arising from Theory to Practice, pp. 13–16 (2004)
16. Uludag, U., Pankanti, S., Prabhakar, S., Jain, A.: Biometric cryptosystems: Issues and challenges (2004)

On the Use of Log-Likelihood Ratio Based Model-Specific Score Normalisation in Biometric Authentication

Norman Poh and Josef Kittler

CVSSP, University of Surrey, Guildford, GU2 7XH, Surrey, UK
normanpoh@ieee.org, j.kittler@surrey.ac.uk

Abstract. It has been shown that the authentication performance of a biometric system is dependent on the models/templates specific to a user. As a result, some users may be more easily recognised or impersonated than others. We propose a *model-specific* (or user-specific) likelihood based score normalisation procedure that can reduce this dependency. While in its original form, such an approach is not feasible due to the paucity of data, especially of the genuine users, we stabilise the estimates of local model parameters with help of the user-independent (hence global) parameters. The proposed approach is shown to perform better than the existing known score normalisation procedures, e.g., the Z-, F- and EER-norms, in the majority of experiments carried out on the XM2VTS database . While these existing procedures are *linear* functions, the proposed likelihood based approach is *quadratic* but its complexity is further limited by a set of constraints balancing the contributions of the local and the global parameters, which are crucial to guarantee good generalisation performance.

1 Introduction

An automatic biometric authentication system works by first building a model or template for each user. During the operational phase, the system compares a scanned biometric sample with the registered model to decide whether an identity claim is authentic or fake. Typically, the underlying class-conditional probability distributions of scores have a strong user dependent component, modulated by within model variations. This component determines how easy or difficult it is to recognise an individual and how successfully he or she can be impersonated. The practical implication of this is that some user models (and consequently the users they represent) are systematically better (or worse) in authentication performance than others. The essence of these different situations has been popularized by the so called Doddington's zoo, with each of them characterized by a different animal name such as lamb, sheep, wolf or goat [1]. A sheep is a person who can be easily recognized; a goat is a person who is particularly difficult to be recognized; a lamb is a person who is easy to imitate; and a wolf is a person who is particularly successful at imitating others.

In the literature, there are two ways to exploit the Doddington'zoo effect to improve the system performance by using model-specific threshold and by model-specific score normalisation. The term *client-specific* is more commonly used than *model-specific*.

S.-W. Lee and S.Z. Li (Eds.): ICB 2007, LNCS 4642, pp. 614–624, 2007.

However, we prefer the latter because the source of variability is the model and *not* the user (or client). For instance, if one constructs two biometric models to represent the same person, these two models may exhibit different performance.

In model-specific thresholding, one employs a different decision threshold for each user, e.g. [2,3,4,5]. The model-specific threshold can be a function of a *global* decision threshold [6,7,8]. In model-specific score normalisation, one uses a one-to-one mapping function such that after this process, only a global threshold is needed. Examples of existing methods are Z-, D- (for Distance), T- (for Test), EER- (for Equal Error Rate) and more recently, F-Norms (for F-ratio). According to [9,10], Z-Norm [10] is impostor-centric, i.e, normalisation is carried out with respect to the impostor distributions calculated "offline" by using additional data. T-Norm [10] is also impostor-centric and its normalisation is a function of a given utterance calculated "online" by using additional cohort impostor models. D-Norm [11] is neither client- nor impostor-centric; it is specific to the Gaussian mixture model (GMM) architecture and is based on Kullback-Leibler distance between two GMM models. EER-norm [9] is client-impostor centric. In [5], a client-centric version of Z-Norm was proposed. However, this technique requires as many as five client accesses. As a consequence of promoting user-friendliness, one does not have many client-specific biometric samples. F-norm [12] is client-impostor centric; it is designed to cope with learning using as few as one sample per client (apart from those used to build the model).

In this paper, we propose a model-specific log-likelihood ratio (MS-LLR) based model-specific score normalisation procedure. While the existing Z-, D- and T-norms are linear functions, the proposed MS-LLR procedure is quadratic. Note that directly estimating the model-specific class-conditional score distributions is difficult because the number of samples available for each user is often very small. As a result, the estimated parameters of the distributions are very unreliable and this leads to unsatisfactory generalisation. We overcome this problem by adapting the model-specific (hence local) parameters from the model-independent (hence global) parameters. An important assumption in MS-LLR is that the class conditional score distributions are Gaussian. When this assumption is likely to be violated, we first transform the scores to exhibit distribution that is closer to Gaussian. The rationale is as follows: if the global (user-independent) class conditional score distributions are obviously violating the Gaussian, e.g., highly skewed, one cannot expect that the MS-LLR will be Gaussian.

When we applied the MS-LLR procedure to the individual systems in the XM2VTS score-level fusion benchmark database [13], almost all the systems showed *systematic improvement* over the baseline and more than half of them were better than the existing normalisation procedures in terms of *a posteriori* equal error rate (EER). The overall result is that better generalisation performance is obtained in terms of DET curve and of expected performance curve (EPC) where *a priori* threshold is used. This means that improvement is likely over various operating thresholds.

2 Methodology

Let y be the output score of a biometric system and $p(y|j, k)$ be its model-specific class-conditional score distribution, where $j \in \{1, \dots, J\}$ is a model identity and there are J models. k is the class label which can be client (genuine user) or impostor, i.e., $k \in \{\mathtt{C}, \mathtt{I}\}$. A score normalisation procedure based on the log-likelihood ratio framework can be realised as follow:

$$y^{norm} = \Psi_j(y) = \log \frac{p(y|j, \mathtt{C})}{p(y|j, \mathtt{I})} \tag{1}$$

We will assume that $p(y|j,k)$ is a Gaussian, i.e., $p(y|j,k) = \mathcal{N}\left(\mu_j^k, (\sigma_j^k)^2\right)$, where μ_j^k and σ_j^k are the class conditional mean and standard deviation of user j for $k = \{\mathtt{C}, \mathtt{I}\}$. We refer to μ_j^k and σ_j^k as *user-specific statistics*. In this case, $\Psi_j(y)$ can be written as:

$$\Psi_j(y) = \frac{1}{2(\sigma_j^{\mathtt{C}})^2}(y - \mu_j^{\mathtt{C}})^2 - \frac{1}{2(\sigma_j^{\mathtt{I}})^2}(y - \mu_j^{\mathtt{I}})^2 + \log \frac{\sigma_j^{\mathtt{C}}}{\sigma_j^{\mathtt{I}}}, \tag{2}$$

Being an LLR, such a user-specific normalization procedure is optimal (i.e., results in the lowest Bayes error) when

1. the parameters μ_j^k, σ_j^k for $k \in \{\mathtt{C}, \mathtt{I}\}$ and for all j are estimated correctly.
2. the class-conditional scores can be described by the first and second order statistics.

The first condition is unlikely to be fulfilled in practice because there is always lack of user-specific training data. For instance, one has only two or three genuine scores to estimate $p(y|j, \mathtt{C})$ but may have more simulated impostor scores, e.g., in the order of hundreds, to estimate $p(y|j, \mathtt{I})$. As a result, in its original form, (2) is not a practical solution. The second condition can be fulfilled by converting any score such that the resulting score distribution confirms better to a Gaussian distribution.

In Section 2.1, we present the Z-norm and its variants (D- and T-norms). Other existing score normalisation procedures will also be discussed. In Section 2.2, we will show how to estimate robustly the parameters in (2) in order to fulfill the first condition. We then deal with the second condition in Section 2.3.

2.1 Some Existing Score Normalisation Procedures

Three types of score normalisation will be briefly discussed here. They are Z-, EER- and F-norms.

Z-norm [2] takes the form.:

$$y_j^Z = \frac{y - \mu_j^{\mathtt{I}}}{\sigma_j^{\mathtt{I}}}. \tag{3}$$

Z-norm is *impostor* centric because it relies only on the impostor distribution. In fact, it can be verified that after applying Z-norm, the resulting expected value of the impostor scores will be zero across all the models j. The net effect is that applying a global threshold to Z-normalised scores will give better performance than doing so with the baseline unprocessed scores.

An alternative procedure that is *client-impostor* centric is called the EER-norm [9]. It has the following two variants:

$$y^{TI1} = y - \Delta_j^{theo} \tag{4}$$

$$y^{TI2} = y - \Delta_j^{emp} \tag{5}$$

where $\Delta_j^{theo} = \frac{\mu_j^I \sigma_j^C + \mu_j^C \sigma_j^I}{\sigma_j^I + \sigma_j^C}$ is a threshold found as a result of assuming that the class-conditional distributions, $p(y|j,k)$ for both k, are Gaussian and Δ_j^{emp} is found empirically. In reality, the empirical version (5) cannot be used when only one or two user-specific genuine scores are available[1]. Another study conducted in [14] used a rather heuristic approach to estimate the user-specific threshold. This normalization is defined as:

$$y^{mid} = y - \underbrace{\frac{\mu_j^I + \mu_j^C}{2}} \qquad (6)$$

The rest of the approaches in [14] can be seen as an approximation to this one. The under-braced term is consistent with the term Δ_j^{theo} in (4) when one assumes that $\sigma_j^C = \sigma_j^I = 1$.

A significantly different normalisation procedure than the above two is called F-norm [12]. It is designed to project scores into another score space where the expected client and impostor scores will be the same, i.e., one for client and zero for impostor, across all J models. Therefore, F-norm is also client-impostor centric. This transformation is:

$$y_j^F = \frac{y - \mu_j^I}{\gamma \mu_j^C + (1-\gamma)\mu^C - \mu_j^I}. \qquad (7)$$

where γ has to be tuned. Two sensible default values are 0 when μ_j^C cannot be estimated because no data exists and at least 0.5 when there is only a single user-specific sample. γ thus accounts for the degree of reliability of μ_j^C and should be close to 1 when abundant genuine samples are available. In all our experiments, $\gamma = 0.5$ is used when using F-norm.

In order to illustrate why the above procedures may work, we carried out an experiment on the XM2VTS database (to be discussed in Section 3). This involved training the parameters of the above score normalisation procedures on a development (training) set and applied it to an evaluation (test) set. We then plotted the model-specific class conditional distribution of the *normalised* scores, $p(y^{norm}|j,k)$, for all j's and the two k's. The distributions are shown in Figure 1. Since there are 200 users in the experiment, each sub-figure shows 200 Gaussian fits on the impostor distributions (the left cluster) and another 200 on the client distributions (right cluster). The normalisation procedures were trained on the development set and were applied on the evaluation set. The figures shown here are the *normalised score distributions* on the evaluation set. Prior to any normalisation, in (a), the model-specific class conditional score distributions are very different from one model to another. In (b), the impostor score distributions are aligned to centre close to zero. In (c), the impostor distributions centre around zero whereas the client distributions centre around one. Shown in (d) is the proposed MS-LLR score normalisation (to be discussed). Its resulting optimal decision boundary is located close to zero. This is a behaviour similar to EER (which was not shown here due to bad generalisation). Since the distributions in (b), (c) and (d) are better aligned than (a), improvement is expected.

[1] In our experiments, due to too few user-specific genuine scores, (4) results in poorer performance than the baseline systems without normalisation. Following this observation, the performance of EER-norm and its variants will not be reported in the paper.

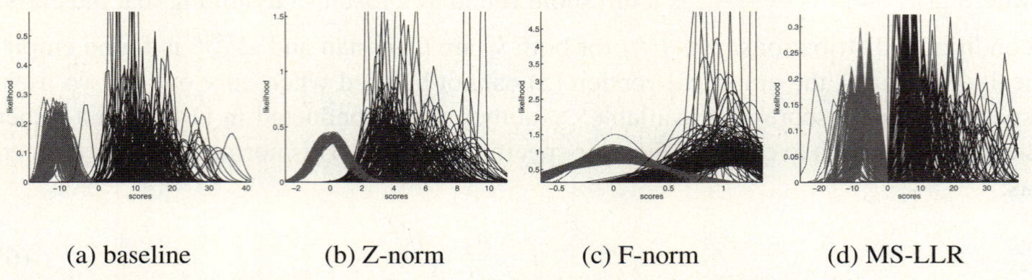

(a) baseline (b) Z-norm (c) F-norm (d) MS-LLR

Fig. 1. Model-specific distributions $p(y^{norm}|j,k)$ for (a) the baseline system, (b) Z-norm, (c) F-norm and (d) our proposed MS-LLR using one of the 13 XM2VTS systems

2.2 User-Specific Parameter Adaptation

In order to make (2) practical enough as a score normalisation procedure, we propose to use the following *adapted* parameters:

$$\mu^k_{adapt,j} = \gamma^k_1 \mu^k_j + (1-\gamma^k_1)\mu^k \tag{8}$$

$$(\sigma^k_{adapt,j})^2 = \gamma^k_2 (\sigma^k_j)^2 + (1-\gamma^k_2)(\sigma^k)^2 \tag{9}$$

where γ^k_1 weighs the first moment and γ^k_2 weighs the second moment of the model-specific class-conditional scores. γ^k_t thus provides an *explicit* control of contribution of the user-specific information against the user-independent information. Note that while (8) is found by the maximum *a posteriori* adaptation [15], (9) is not; (9) is motivated by parameter regularisation as in [16] where, in the context of classification, one can adjust between the solution of a linear discriminative analysis and that of a quadratic discriminative analysis.

We used a specific set of γ^k_t values as follows:

$$\gamma^{\mathrm{I}}_1 = 1, \gamma^{\mathrm{I}}_2 = 1, \gamma^{\mathrm{C}}_1 = 0.5, \gamma^{\mathrm{C}}_2 = 0 \tag{10}$$

The rationale for using the first two constraints in (10) is that the model-specific statistics μ^{I}_j and σ^{I}_j can be estimated reliably since a sufficiently large number of simulated impostor scores can be made available by using a development population of users. The rationale of the third (10) and fourth constraints is exactly the opposite of the first two, i.e., due to the lack of user-specific genuine scores, the statistics μ^{C}_j and σ^{C}_j cannot be estimated reliably. Furthermore, between these two parameters, the second order moment (σ^{C}_j) is more affected than its first order counterpart (μ^{C}_j). As a result, if one were to fine tune γ^k_t, the most likely one should be γ^{C}_j. Our preliminary experiments on the XM2VTS database (to be discussed in Section 3) show that the value of γ^{C}_j obtained by the cross-validation procedure is not necessarily optimal. Furthermore, in the case of having only one observed genuine training score, cross-validation is impossible. For this reason, we used the default $\gamma^{\mathrm{C}}_j = 0.5$ in all our experiments. This hyper-parameter plays the same role as that of γ in the F-norm in (7). Although the F-norm and the proposed MS-LLR are somewhat similar, MS-LLR is a direct implementation of (1) whereas the

F-norm, as well as other normalisation procedures surveyed in Section 2.1, are, at best, approximations to (2).

In brief, the proposed MS-LLR is based on (2) whose model-specific statistics are obtained via adaptation, i.e., (8) and (9). To further constrain the model, we suggest to use (10). When only one genuine samples is available, we recommend $\gamma_j^{\mathtt{C}} = 0.5$. However, when more user-specific genuine samples are available, $\gamma_j^{\mathtt{C}} > 0.5$ generalises probably better.

2.3 Improving the Estimate of Parametric Distribution By Score Transformation

All the existing procedures mentioned in Section 2.1, as well as our proposed one based on LLR, i.e., (2), strongly rely on the Gaussian assumption on $p(y|j,k)$. There are two solutions to this limitation. Firstly, if the physical characteristic of scores is known, the associated theoretical distribution can be used so that one replaces the Gaussian assumption with the theoretical one in order to estimate $p(y|j,k)$. Unfortunately, very often, the true distribution is not known and/or there is always not enough data to estimate $p(y|j,k)$, especially for the case $k = \mathtt{C}$.

Secondly, one can improve the parametric estimation of $p(y|j,k)$ by using an order preserving transformation that is applied globally (independent of any user). When the output score is bounded in $[a,b]$, the following transformation can be used [17]:

$$y' = \log\left(\frac{y-a}{b-y}\right) \tag{11}$$

For example, if y is the probability of being a client given an observed biometric sample x, i.e., $y = P(\mathtt{C}|x)$, then $a = 0$ and $b = 1$. The above transformation becomes:

$$\begin{aligned} y' &= \log\left(\frac{y}{1-y}\right) = \log\left(\frac{P(\mathtt{C}|x)}{P(\mathtt{I}|x)}\right) \\ &= \log\left(\frac{p(x|\mathtt{C})}{p(x|\mathtt{I})}\right) + \log\left(\frac{P(\mathtt{C})}{P(\mathtt{I})}\right) \\ &= \underbrace{\log\left(\frac{p(x|\mathtt{C})}{p(x|I)}\right)} + const \end{aligned} \tag{12}$$

The function $\log\left(\frac{y}{1-y}\right)$ is actually an inverse of a sigmoid (or logistic) function. The underbraced term is called a log-likelihood ratio (LLR). Therefore, y' can be seen as a shifted version of LLR. When the output score is not bounded, in our experience, we do not need to apply any transformation because assuming $p(y|j,k)$ to be Gaussian is often adequate. We believe that the Gaussian distribution exhibits such a good behaviour because it effectively approximates the *true* distribution using its first two moments. It should be emphasized here that the order preserving transformation discussed here does not guarantee that the resulting score distribution to be Gaussian. In fact, this is not the goal because $p(y|k)$ is in fact a mixture $p(y|j,k)$ for all j's by definition. Conversely, if $p(y|k)$ is higly skewed, one cannot expect that $p(y|j,k)$ to be Gaussian.

3 Database, Evaluation and Results

The publicly available[2] XM2VTS benchmark database for score-level fusion [13] is used. The systems used in the experiments are shown in the first column of Table 1. For each data set, there are two sets of scores, i.e., the *development* and the *evaluation* sets. The development set is used *uniquely* to train the parameters of a given score normalisation procedure, including the threshold (bias) parameter, whereas the evaluation set is used uniquely to evaluate the generalisation performance. The fusion protocols were designed to be compatible with the originally defined Lausanne Protocols [18] (LPs). In order to train a user-specific procedure, three user-specific genuine scores are available per client for LP1 whereas only two are available for LP2.

Table 1. Absolute performance for the *a posteriori* selected threshold calculated on the evaluation (test) score set of the 11 XM2VTS systems as well as two whose outputs are post-processed according to the techniques described in Section 2.3

no.	system (modality, feature, classifier)	*a posteriori* EER (%) baseline	Z-norm	F-norm	MS-LLR
1	(F,DCTs,GMM)	4.22	4.04	∗ 3.57	3.79
2	(F,DCTb,GMM)	1.82	1.92	∗ 1.43	1.65
3	(S,LFCC,GMM)	1.15	1.34	0.68	∗ 0.44
4	(S,PAC,GMM)	6.62	4.96	4.63	∗ 4.37
5	(S,SSC,GMM)	4.53	2.57	2.33	∗ 2.03
6	(F,DCTs,MLP)	3.53	3.28	3.14	∗ 2.89
7	(F,DCTs,iMLP)	3.53	3.18	3.19	∗ 2.70
8	(F,DCTb,MLP)	6.61	6.32	6.53	∗ 6.31
9	(F,DCTb,iMLP)	6.61	∗ 6.35	6.84	6.77
10	(F,DCTb,GMM) †	∗ 0.55	0.97	0.79	0.78
11	(S,LFCC,GMM)	1.37	0.99	0.58	∗ 0.48
12	(S,PAC,GMM)	5.39	∗ 4.65	5.28	5.07
13	(S,SSC,GMM)	3.33	∗ 2.20	2.60	2.32

Note: Rows 1–9 are from LP1 where 3 genuine samples per client are used for training; whereas rows 10–13 are from LP2 where only two are available for training. ∗ denotes the smallest EER in a row. †: We verified that for this system, the scores between the development and evaluation sets are somewhat different, thus resulting in poor estimation of the parameters of the score normalisation procedures.

The most commonly used performance visualising tool in the literature is the Decision Error Trade-off (DET) curve [19]. It has been pointed out [20] that two DET curves resulting from two systems are not comparable because such comparison does not take into account how the thresholds are selected. It was argued [20] that such threshold should be chosen *a priori* as well, based on a given criterion. This is because when a biometric system is operational, the threshold parameter has to be fixed *a priori*. As a result, the Expected Performance Curve (EPC) [20] was proposed and the following criterion is used:

[2] Accessible at http://www.idiap.ch/~norman/fusion

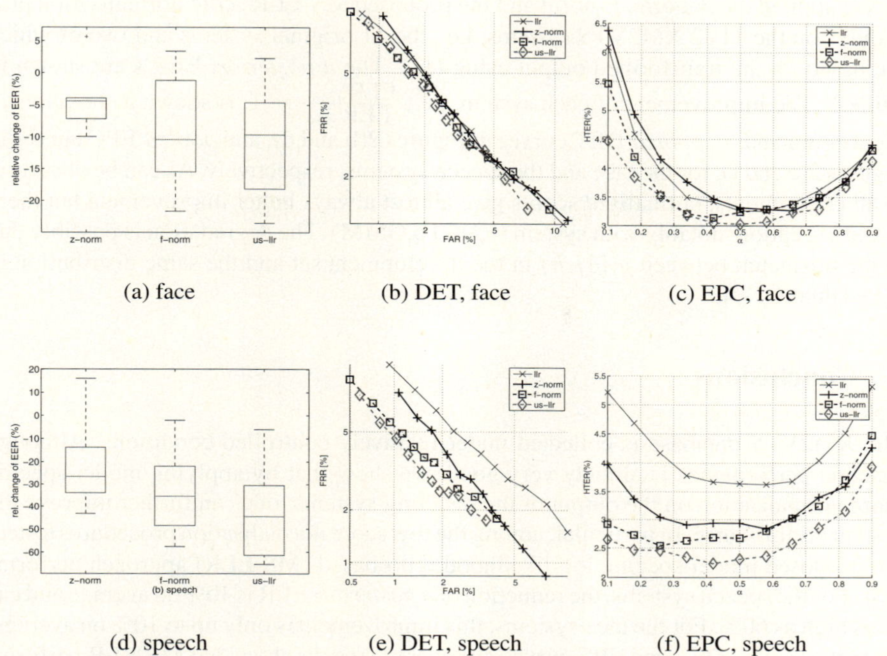

(a) face (b) DET, face (c) EPC, face

(d) speech (e) DET, speech (f) EPC, speech

Fig. 2. Performance of the baseline, Z-norm, F-norm and MS-LLR score normalisation procedures on the 11+2 XM2VTS systems in terms of the distribution of relative change of *a posteriori* EERs for (a) the face and (d) the speech systems shown here in boxplots; in *pooled* DET curves (b and e); and in *pooled* EPC curves (c and f). A box in a boxplot contains the first and the third quantile of relative change of *a posteriori* EERs. The dashed lines ending with horizontal lines show the 95% confidence of the data. Outliers are plotted with "+". The statistics in (a–c) are obtained from the 7 face systems shown in Table 1 whereas those in (d–f) are obtained from the remaining 6 speech systems.

$$\mathrm{WER}_\alpha(\Delta) = \alpha \mathrm{FAR}(\Delta) + (1-\alpha)\mathrm{FRR}(\Delta), \tag{13}$$

where $\alpha \in [0, 1]$ balances FAR and FRR.

An EPC is constructed as follows: for various values of α in (13) between 0 and 1, select the optimal threshold Δ on the development (training) set, apply it on the evaluation (test) set and compute the half total error rate (HTER) on the evaluation set. HTER is the average of false acceptance rate (FAR) and false rejection rate (FRR). This HTER (in the Y-axis) is then plotted with respect to α (in the X-axis). The EPC curve can be interpreted similarly to the DET curve, i.e., the lower the curve, the better the generalisation performance. In this study, the *pooled* version of EPC is used to visualise the performance. This is a convenient way to compare methods on several data sets by viewing only a single curve per method. This is done by calculating the *global* FAR and FRR over a set of experiments for *each* of the α values. The pooled EPC curve and its implementation can be found in [13].

We applied the Z-norm, F-norm and the proposed MS-LLR score normalisation procedures on the 11+2 XM2VTS systems, i.e., the 11 original systems and two of which are based on the transformed output using (11). The *a posteriori* EER's are shown in Table 1. The improvement of each system, i.e., $\frac{\text{EER}_{norm}}{\text{EER}_{orig}} - 1$, is shown as boxplots in Figures 2(a and c), *pooled* DET curves in Figures 2(b and d), and *pooled* EPC curves in Figures 2(c and f), for the face and the speech systems, respectively. As can be observed, in all experiments, normalised scores give almost always better improvement but there is one exception, notably with system (F,DCTb,GMM). The degradation is possibly due to the mismatch between $p(y|j,k)$ in the development set and the same distribution in the evaluation set.

4 Conclusions

The XM2VTS database is collected under relatively controlled conditions. Although baseline performance is already very good, we show that by applying model-specific score normalisation on the output of the resulting systems, one can further improve the system performance. In particular, among the few score normalisation procedures tested, our proposed model-specific log-likelihood ratio-based (MS-LLR) approach performs best . For the speech systems, the reduction of *a posteriori* EER is 40% on average and can be as high as 60%. For the face systems, this improvement is only up to 10% on average. From the *pooled* DET and EPC curves, the average results show that MS-LLR performs best; this is followed by F-norm and Z-norm. The EER-norm performs worse than the baseline systems due to overfitting on the development set. This is because only two or three genuine samples are available. Nevertheless, for the F-norm and the proposed MS-LLR, thanks to parameter adaptation, the additional genuine scores are fully exploited. This is contrary to the Z-norm which does not make use of such information.

We conjecture that the proposed MS-LLR works best because it combines the following strategies: the general LLR framework shown in (1), the Gaussian assumption on the model-specific class conditional score distribution and the constraints in (10).

We also observe that when there is a mismatch between the development and the evaluation sets, e.g., due to different noise factors to which a biometric system is vulnerable, the model-specific class conditional distributions will change. As a result, without taking this change into account, any model-specific score normalisation may fail. This calls for predicting this change in order to take the effect of Doddington's zoo fully into account. An interesting observation is that the speech systems improve much better than the face systems. Finding out why is beyond the scope of this paper and it will be the subject of future investigation.

Another potential research direction is to combine the system outputs *after* applying model-specific score normalisation. Fusion at this level can be intramodal, i.e., involving a single biometric modality, or multimodal, i.e., involving more than one biometric modalities. Since we have already observed somewhat systematic improvement of performance after the score normalisation process, further improvement is to be expected when these outputs are used in the context of fusion. This subject is currently being investigated.

Acknowledgment

This work was supported partially by the prospective researcher fellowship PBEL2-114330 of the Swiss National Science Foundation, by the BioSecure project (www.biosecure.info) and by the Engineering and Physical Sciences Research Council (EPSRC) Research Grant GR/S46543. This publication only reflects the authors' view.

References

1. Doddington, G., Liggett, W., Martin, A., Przybocki, M., Reynolds, D.: Sheep, Goats, Lambs and Woves: A Statistical Analysis of Speaker Performance in the NIST 1998 Speaker Recognition Evaluation. In: Int'l Conf. Spoken Language Processing (ICSLP), Sydney (1998)
2. Furui, S.: Cepstral Analysis for Automatic Speaker Verification. IEEE Trans. Acoustic, Speech and Audio Processing / IEEE Trans. on Signal Processing 29(2), 254–272 (1981)
3. Pierrot, J.-B.: Elaboration et Validation d'Approaches en Vérification du Locuteur, Ph.D. thesis, ENST, Paris (September 1998)
4. Chen, K.: Towards Better Making a Decision in Speaker Verification. Pattern Recognition 36(2), 329–346 (2003)
5. Saeta, J.R., Hernando, J.: On the Use of Score Pruning in Speaker Verification for Speaker Dependent Threshold Estimation. In: The Speaker and Language Recognition Workshop (Odyssey), Toledo, pp. 215–218 (2004)
6. Jonsson, K., Kittler, J., Li, Y.P., Matas, J.: Support vector machines for face authentication. Image and Vision Computing 20, 269–275 (2002)
7. Lindberg, J., Koolwaaij, J.W., Hutter, H.-P., Genoud, D., Blomberg, M., Pierrot, J.-B., Bimbot, F.: Techniques for a priori Decision Threshold Estimation in Speaker Verification. In: Proc. of the Workshop R̈econnaissance du Locuteur et ses Applications Commerciales et Criminalistiques(̈RLA2C), Avignon, pp. 89–92 (1998)
8. Genoud, D.: Reconnaissance et Transformation de Locuteur, Ph.D. thesis, Ecole Polythechnique Fédérale de Lausanne (EPFL), Switzerland (1998)
9. Fierrez-Aguilar, J., Ortega-Garcia, J., Gonzalez-Rodriguez, J.: Target Dependent Score Normalisation Techniques and Their Application to Signature Verification. In: Zhang, D., Jain, A.K. (eds.) ICBA 2004. LNCS, vol. 3072, pp. 498–504. Springer, Heidelberg (2004)
10. Auckenthaler, R., Carey, M., Lloyd-Thomas, H.: Score Normalization for Text-Independant Speaker Verification Systems. Digital Signal Processing (DSP) Journal 10, 42–54 (2000)
11. Ben, M., Blouet, R., Bimbot, F.: A Monte-Carlo Method For Score Normalization in Automatic Speaker Verification Using Kullback-Leibler Distances. In: Proc. Int. Conf. Acoustics, Speech and Signal Processing (ICASSP), Orlando, vol. 1, pp. 689–692 (2002)
12. Poh, N., Bengio, S.: F-ratio Client-Dependent Normalisation on Biometric Authentication Tasks. In: IEEE Int'l Conf. Acoustics, Speech, and Signal Processing (ICASSP), Philadelphia, pp. 721–724 (2005)
13. Poh, N., Bengio, S.: Database, Protocol and Tools for Evaluating Score-Level Fusion Algorithms in Biometric Authentication. Pattern Recognition 39(2), 223–233 (2005)
14. Toh, K.-A., Jiang, X., Yau, W.-Y.: Exploiting Global and Local Decision for Multimodal Biometrics Verification. IEEE Trans. on Signal Processing 52(10), 3059–3072 (2004)
15. Gauvain, J.L., Lee, C.-H.: Maximum a Posteriori Estimation for Multivariate Gaussian Mixture Obervation of Markov Chains. IEEE Tran. Speech Audio Processing 2, 290–298 (1994)
16. Friedman, J.: Regularized discriminant analysis. J. American Statiscal Association 84, 165–175 (1989)

17. Dass, S.C., Zhu, Y., Jain, A.K.: Validating a biometric authentication system: Sample size requirements. IEEE Trans. Pattern Analysis and Machine Intelligence 28(12), 1302–1319 (2006)
18. Matas, J., Hamouz, M., Jonsson, K., Kittler, J., Li, Y., Kotropoulos, C., Tefas, A., Pitas, I., Tan, T., Yan, H., Smeraldi, F., Begun, J., Capdevielle, N., Gerstner, W., Ben-Yacoub, S., Abdeljaoued, Y., Mayoraz, E.: Comparison of Face Verification Results on the XM2VTS Database. In: Proc. 15th Int'l Conf. Pattern Recognition, Barcelona, vol. 4, pp. 858–863 (2000)
19. Martin, A., Doddington, G., Kamm, T., Ordowsk, M., Przybocki, M.: The DET Curve in Assessment of Detection Task Performance. In: Proc. Eurospeech'97, Rhodes, pp. 1895–1898 (1997)
20. Bengio, S., Mariéthoz, J.: The Expected Performance Curve: a New Assessment Measure for Person Authentication. In: The Speaker and Language Recognition Workshop (Odyssey), Toledo, pp. 279–284 (2004)

Predicting Biometric Authentication System Performance Across Different Application Conditions: A Bootstrap Enhanced Parametric Approach

Norman Poh and Josef Kittler

CVSSP, University of Surrey, Guildford, GU2 7XH, Surrey, UK
normanpoh@ieee.org, j.kittler@surrey.ac.uk

Abstract. The performance of a biometric authentication system is dependent on the choice of users and the application scenario represented by the evaluation database. As a result, the system performance under different application scenarios, e.g., from cooperative user to non-cooperative scenario, from well controlled to uncontrolled one, etc, can be very different. The current solution is to build a database containing as many application scenarios as possible for the purpose of the evaluation. We propose an alternative evaluation methodology that can reuse existing databases, hence can potentially reduce the amount of data needed. This methodology relies on a novel technique that projects the distribution of scores from one operating condition to another. We argue that this can be accomplished efficiently only by modeling the genuine user and impostor score distributions for each user parametrically. The parameters of these model-specific class conditional (MSCC) distributions are found by maximum likelihood estimation. The projection from one operating condition to another is modelled by a regression function between the two conditions in the MSCC parameter space. The regression functions are trained from a small set of users and are then applied to a large database. The implication is that one only needs a small set of users with data reflecting both the reference and mismatched conditions. In both conditions, it is required that the two data sets be drawn from a population with similar demographic characteristics. The regression model is used to predict the performance for a large set of users under the mismatched condition.

1 Introduction

The performance of a biometric system involves a biometric database with multiple records of N users. In a typical experimental evaluation, the records of a reference user are compared with the remaining users, hence resulting in impostor match scores. The comparisons among records of the same reference user result in genuine user (or referred to as "client") match scores. By sweeping through all possible decision threshold values given these two sets of class conditional match scores, one obtains the system performance in terms of pairs of false acceptance (FAR) and false rejection (FRR) rates, respectively. Consequently, the measured performance is inevitably database- and protocol-dependent. For instance, running the same matching algorithm on a single database but with two different protocols (or ways of partitioning the training and test

S.-W. Lee and S.Z. Li (Eds.): ICB 2007, LNCS 4642, pp. 625–635, 2007.

data) may result in two correlated but nevertheless slightly different performance measures. A good example is the XM2VTS database and its two Lausanne protocols. As a result, if one algorithm outperforms another, one cannot be certain that the same relative performance is repeatable when a different set of users is involved. The same concern about the preservation of relative performance applies to changes in application scenarios, e.g., from a controlled to uncontrolled ones, and from cooperative to non-cooperative users. These changes will result in *variability* of the measured performance.

The goal of this paper is to propose a statistical model that can capture the above factors of variability such that given a small set of development (training) data where samples acquired during the reference and mismatched conditions are present, one can apply the model to predict the performance on an evaluation (test) data set composed of samples collected in the mismatched condition only. We use the term *mismatched* condition as the one that is significantly different *relative* to the reference one. In this work, we assume that the population of users in both the development and the evaluation sets are drawn from a *common* demographic population. This itself is a difficult problem because given this common demographic population, one still has to deal with the other three sources of variability.

The novelty of this study is to propose an evaluation methodology as well as a statistical model developed for that purpose to avoid collecting more data (although more data is always better) but instead to put more emphasis on *predicting the performance* under various operating conditions based only on the development data set. The proposed methodology can thus significantly reduce the cost of data collection.

This contrasts with the conventional evaluation methodology which is inherently demanding in terms of the amount of data required, e.g., the BANCA [1] and FERET [2] evaluations. Furthermore, given limited resources in data collection, one has to trade-off the amount of data (users) against the number of application scenarios available.

Preliminary experiments on 195 experiments carried out on the BANCA database show that predicting the performance from the reference to the mismatched condition is possible even when the performance associated with these two conditions were assessed on two *separate* populations of users.

2 Towards Generalising Biometric Performance

In order to model the change of score distribution, we will need a statistical model that can effectively model the score distribution *within* a given operating condition. We opt to build a model known as the *model-specific class conditional* (MSCC) distributions. If there are J users, there will be $2 \times J$ MSCC distributions since each user has two class conditional scores, one reflecting genuine match scores and the other impostor match scores. An MSCC distribution represents a statistical summary of class-conditional scores specific to each user. In essence, it captures the sample variability but conditioned on the class label. Then, in order to capture the change from a reference operating condition to a mismatched one, we need a *projection function* that can map a set of MSCC distributions to another set. One reasonable assumption that is used here is that the effect of the mismatch, as observed given only the scores, is the *same*

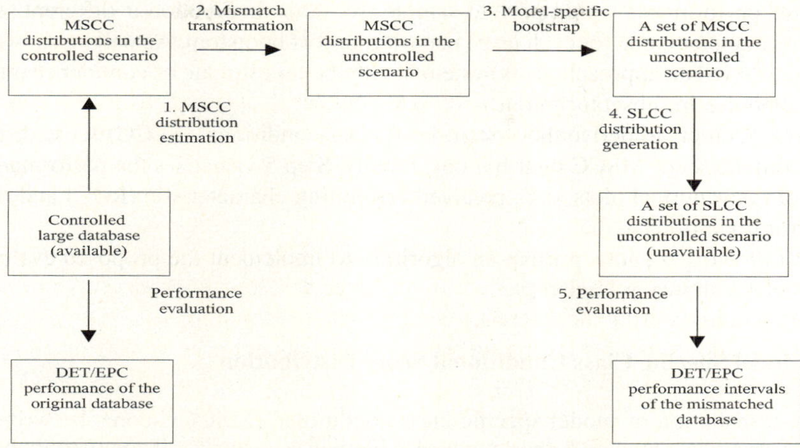

Fig. 1. A procedure to predict performance as well as its associated confidence intervals based on MFCC distributions under mismatched application scenario and user composition. Since the MSCC parameters under mismatched situation can only be estimated probabilistically, we propose a slightly different version of model-specific bootstrap which also referred to as the bootstrap subset technique [3].

across all the user models of the same group, i.e., the users are drawn from the common demographic population. (e.g., bankers or construction workers, but not both).

Figure 1 outlines an algorithm to train and infer the proposed statistical model. In Step 1, the parameters of the MSCC distributions are estimated via the maximum likelihood principle. In Step 2, the projection function between the set of MSCC distributions corresponding to the reference operating condition and the mismatched one is modeled via regression. The projection function has to be learnt from the smaller data set containing biometric samples recorded in both types of conditions. The transformation is then applied to a larger data set recorded in the reference operating condition. Thanks to this projection, the MSCC distributions of the mismatched condition becomes available, while, avoiding the need of actually collecting the same amount of data set for the mismatched condition.

In Step 3, we derive the confidence interval around the predicted performance. The state-of-the-art technique to do so in biometric experiments is known as the *bootstrap subset* technique [3]. This technique is different from the conventional bootstrap because it does not draw the score samples directly but draws the user models acquired for the database. In our context, this technique draws with replacement the user models associated with *a pair of* MSCC distributions in each round of the bootstrapping process. The bootstrap subset technique assumes that the parameters of the MSCC distributions are known. We propose a Bayesian approach which defines a distribution over each of the MSCC parameters. In order to estimate confidence intervals around the predicted performance we propose to sample from this distribution J different sets of MSCC parameters (one for each user) in each round of bootstrap. As will be shown, the proposed Bayesian approach gives systematically better estimate of confidence interval than the bootstrap subset technique.

Step 4 attempts to derive the system-level class-conditional (SLCC) score distributions from the set of MSCC distributions. Finally, Step 5 visualises the performance in terms of conventional plots, e.g., receiver's operating characteristic (ROC) and detection error trade-off (DET).

The following sections present an algorithm to implement the proposed evaluation methodology shown in Figure 1.

2.1 Model Specific Class Conditional Score Distribution

Let the distribution of model-specific class-conditional (MSCC) scores be written as $p(y|k, j, m)$ where $y \in \mathbb{R}$ is the output of a biometric system, j is the user index and $j \in [1, \ldots, J]$ and m is the m-th model/template belonging to user j. Without loss of generality, $p(y|k)$ can be described by:

$$p(y|k) = \sum_j \underbrace{\sum_m p(y|k, j, m)P(m|j, k)}\, P(j|k) \tag{1}$$

$$p(y|k) = \sum_j p(y|k, j)P(j|k) \tag{2}$$

where $p(y|k, j, m)$ is the density of y conditioned on the user index j, true class label k and the m-th model (a discrete variable) specific to user j; $P(m|j, k)$ specifies how probable it is that m is used (when $k = C$) or abused (when $k = I$); and, $P(j|k)$ specifies how probable it is that user j uses the system or persons impersonating him/her abuses his identity. All the data sets we deal with have only one model/template per user, i.e., $m = 1$. As a result, (1) and (2) are identical. The false acceptance rate (FAR) and false rejection rate (FRR) are defined as a function of the global decision threshold $\Delta \in [-\infty, \infty]$ in the following ways:

$$\text{FAR}(\Delta) = 1 - \Psi_I(\Delta) \tag{3}$$

$$\text{FRR}(\Delta) = \Psi_C(\Delta), \tag{4}$$

where Ψ_k is the cumulative density function (*cdf*) of $p(y|k)$, i.e.,

$$\Psi_k(\Delta) = p(y \leq \Delta|k) = \int_{-\infty}^{\Delta} p(y|k)dy \tag{5}$$

In this study, we assume that $p(y|k, j)$ (or more precisely $p(y|k, j, m = 1)$) is Gaussian, i.e.,

$$p(y|k, j) = \mathcal{N}(\mu_j^k, (\sigma_j^k)^2), \tag{6}$$

where, μ_j^k and $(\sigma_j^k)^2$ are respectively the mean and the variance of the underlying scores. When the true score distribution is known, it should be used. However, as is often the case, due to the paucity of user-specific data, especially the genuine user match

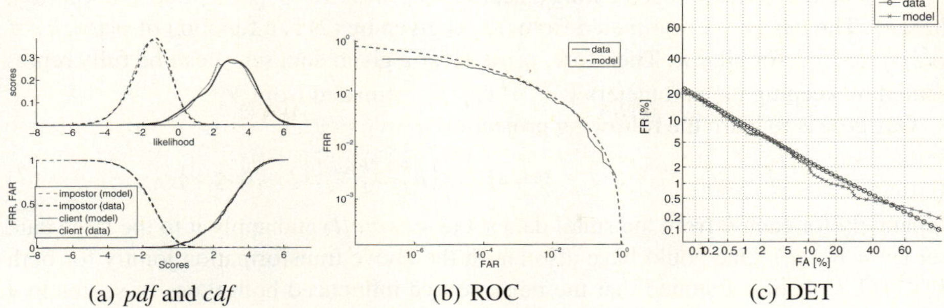

(a) *pdf* and *cdf* (b) ROC (c) DET

Fig. 2. (a) Comparison between the *pdf*s (top) and *cdf*s (bottom) estimated from the model and the data; the same comparison when visualised using (b) ROC in log-log scales and (c) DET (in normal deviate scales). In order to estimate the *pdf*s in the top figure of (a), the kernel density (Parzen window) method was used with a Gaussian kernel; the *cdf*s of the data used for visualising the ROC curve are based on (5).

Table 1. The partition of the data sets. The first row and first column should read "the score set $\mathcal{Y}^C_{small}$ is available".

Data set size	reference		degraded	
	Genuine (C)	impostor (I)	Genuine (C)	impostor (I)
small	available	available	available	available
large	available	available	not available	not available

scores, one may not be able to estimate the parameters of the distribution reliably. As a result, a practical solution may be to approximate the true distribution with a simpler one, e.g., using only the first two order of moments as represented by a Gaussian distribution.

Figure 2 compares the class-conditional score distribution estimated from the data with the one estimated from the model. Referring back to Figure 1, Step 1 is an application of (1); Step 4 of (5) and Step 5 of (3) and (4), respectively.

2.2 Estimation of Score Distribution Projection Function

In this section, we develop the projection function from the score distribution of the reference operating condition to a mismatched one. Suppose that for a small number of user models, we have access to both their reference and degraded class-conditional scores, i.e., $\{\mathcal{Y}^k_{small}|Q\}$ for $Q \in \{\text{ref}, \text{deg}\}$ (for reference and degraded, respectively) and $k \in \{C, I\}$. For another set with a much larger number of user models, we have only access to their data captured in the reference condition, $\{\mathcal{Y}^k_{large}|Q = \text{ref}, \forall_k\}$ and we wish to predict the density of the degraded scores $\{\mathcal{Y}^k_{large}|Q = \text{deg}, \forall_k\}$ which we do not have access to. Table 1 summarises the availability of scores data. In our experimental setting, $\{\mathcal{Y}^k_{large}|Q = \text{deg}, \forall_k\}$ serves as the ground-truth (or *test*) data whereas the other six data sets are considered as the *training* data in the usual sense.

Let y be the variable representing a score in $\mathcal{Y}_s^k$ where $k \in \{C, I\}$ and $s \in \{small, large\}$. The *pdf* $p(y|k)$ estimated from $\mathcal{Y}_s^k$ as given by (2) is a function of $p(y|j,k) \equiv \mathcal{N}(\mu_j^k, (\sigma_j^k)^2)$ for all j, k. Therefore, $p(y|k)$ (for a given data set s) can be fully represented by keeping the parameters $\{\mu_j^k, \sigma_j^k|\forall_j, s\}$ estimated from $\mathcal{Y}_s^k$.

Our goal is to learn the following projection

$$f : \{\mu_j^k, \sigma_j^k|\forall_j, Q = \text{ref, s}\} \rightarrow \{\mu_j^k, \sigma_j^k|\forall_j, Q = \text{deg}, s\} \quad (7)$$

separately for each k from the small data set ($s = small$) and apply it to the large data set ($s = large$). One could have also learnt the above transformation jointly for both $k \in \{C, I\}$ if one assumed that the noise source influenced both types of scores in a similar way. Our preliminary experiments show that this is, in general, not the case. For instance, degraded biometric features affect the magnitude of the genuine scores much more than that of the impostor scores. For this reason, it is sensible to model the transformation functions for each class of access claims separately. This is done in two steps for each of the two parameters separately:

$$f_\mu : \{\mu_j^k|\forall_j, Q = \text{ref}, s\} \rightarrow \{\mu_j^k|\forall_j, Q = \text{deg}, s\} \quad (8)$$

$$f_\sigma : \{\sigma_j^k|\forall_j, Q = \text{ref}, s\} \rightarrow \{\sigma_j^k|\forall_j, Q = \text{deg}, s\} \quad (9)$$

where f_{param} is a polynomial regression function for $param \in \{\mu, \sigma\}$. Note that in (9), the function is defined on the standard deviation and not on the variance because noise is likely to be amplified in the latter case. This observation was supported by our preliminary experiments (not shown here). We have also considered modeling the joint density of $\{\mu_j^k, \sigma_j^k|\forall_j\}$ and found that their correlation is extremely weak across the 195 experiments taken from the BANCA database (to be described in Section 3), i.e., on average -0.4 for the impostor class and 0 for the genuine user (client) class. This means that the two Gaussian parameters are unlikely to depend on each other and there is no additional advantage to model them jointly. These two regression functions give us the predicted degraded Gaussian parameters – $\hat{\mu}_j^k$ and $\hat{\sigma}_j^k$ – given the Gaussian parameters of the reference condition–μ_j^k and σ_j^k.

The polynomial coefficients are obtained by minimising the mean squared error between the predicted and the true values of the larger data set given the values of the smaller data set. We used Matlab's `polyfit` function for this purpose. As a by-product, the function also provides a 95% confidence around the predicted mean value, which corresponds to the variance of the prediction, i.e., $Var[f_\mu(\mu_j^k)]$ for the mean parameter and $Var[f_\sigma(\sigma_j^k)]$ for the standard deviation parameter. These two by-products will be used in Section 2.3.

In our preliminary experiments, the degree of polynomial was tuned using a two-fold cross validation procedure. However, due to the small number of samples (in fact the number of users) used, which is 26, using a quadratic function or even of higher order does not necessarily generalise better than a linear function. Following the Occam's Razor principle, we used only a linear function for (8) and (9), respectively.

Examples of fitted regression functions for each f_μ and f_σ conditioned on each class k are shown in Figure 3(a). The four regression functions aim collectively to predict a DET curve in degraded condition given the MSCC parameters of the reference condition. Figure 3(b) shows both the reference and predicted degraded DET curves. Two

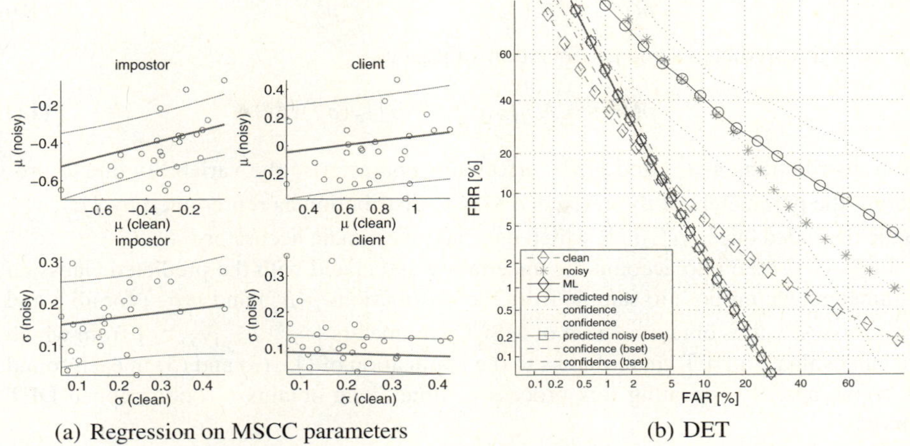

(a) Regression on MSCC parameters (b) DET

Fig. 3. One of 195 BANCA experiments showing the regression fits to project the MSCC parameters under the reference condition to those under the degraded conditions. Note that there is also user composition mismatch because the reference and degraded data come from two disjoint sets of users (the g1 and g2 sets according to the BANCA protocols). Four regression fits are shown in (a) for each of the client and impostor classes and for each of the two Gaussian parameters (mean and standard deviation). The regression lines together with their respective 95% confidence intervals were estimated on the development set whereas the data points (each obtained from a user model) were obtained from the evaluation set. Figure (b) shows the DET curves (plotted with '○') along with its upper and lower confidence bounds (dotted lines) as compared to the original reference ('◇') and degraded ('∗') DET curves. The 95% confidence intervals around the predicted degraded DET curves were estimated by 100 bootstraps as described in Section 2.3 (not the bootstrap subset technique). In each bootstrap (which aims to produce a DET curve), we sampled the predicted MSCC parameters given the reference MSCC parameters from the four regression models assuming Gaussian distribution.

procedures were used to derive the predicted degraded DET curves, thus resulting in two predicted degraded curves as well as their corresponding confidence intervals. They will be described in Section 2.3.

2.3 Bootstraps Under Probabilistic MSCC Parameters: A Bayesian Approach

This section deals with the case where the MSCC parameters can only be estimated probabilistically, e.g., when applying (7) which attempts to project from the reference MSCC parameters to the degraded ones, the exact degraded MSCC parameters are unknown. This is in contrast to the bootstrap subset technique which assumes that the MSCC parameters can be estimated deterministically (which corresponds to the usual maximum likelihood solution).

Let $\hat{\mu}_j^k = f_\mu(\mu_j^k)$ be the predicted mean parameter given the reference mean parameter μ_j^k via the regression function f_μ. The predicted standard deviation is defined similarly, i.e., $\hat{\sigma}_j^k = f_\sigma(\sigma_j^k)$. We assume that the predicted mean value is normally distributed, i.e.,

$$p(\hat{\mu}_j^k) = \mathcal{N}(f_\mu(\mu_j^k), Var[f_\mu(\mu_j^k)]), \tag{10}$$

and so is the predicted standard deviation value, i.e.,

$$p(\hat{\sigma}_j^k) = \mathcal{N}(f_\sigma(\sigma_j^k), Var[f_\sigma(\sigma_j^k)]). \tag{11}$$

Both distributions $p(\hat{\mu}_j^k)$ and $p(\hat{\sigma}_j^k)$ effectively characterise the variability due to projecting the parameters of the reference MSCC distribution as represented by $\{\mu_j^k, \sigma_j^k\}$ to the degraded ones $\{\hat{\mu}_j^k, \hat{\sigma}_j^k\}$, which one cannot estimate accurately.

In order to take into account the uncertainty associated with the predicted Gaussian parameters, we propose to sample from the distributions $p(\hat{\mu}_j^k)$ and $p(\hat{\sigma}_j^k)$ for all j and both classes k, thus obtaining a set of MSCC parameters $\{v_{\mu_j}{}^k, v_{\sigma_j}{}^k|\forall_j, \forall_k\}$ from which we can evaluate a DET curve thanks to the application of (1), (3) and (5) in each round of bootstraps. By repeating this process U times, one obtains U bootstrapped DET curves.

We give a brief account here how to obtain the expected DET curve and its corresponding 95% confidence intervals given the U bootstrapped DET curves. This technique was described in [4]. First, we project a DET curve into polar coordinates (r, θ), i.e., radius and DET angle, such that $\theta = 0$ degree is parallel to FRR=0 in normal deviate scale and $\theta = 90$ degree is parallel to FAR=0. To obtain $\alpha \times 100\%$ confidence, given the set of bootstrapped DET curves in polar coordinates, we estimate the upper and lower bounds:

$$\frac{1-\alpha}{2} \le \Psi_\theta(r) \le \frac{1+\alpha}{2},$$

where $\Psi_\theta(r)$ is the empirical *cdf* of the radius r observed from the U bootstrapped curves for a given θ. Note that each bootstrapped curve cuts through θ exactly once. The lower, upper and median DET curves are given by setting r to be $\frac{1-\alpha}{2}$, $\frac{1+\alpha}{2}$, and $\frac{1}{2}$, respectively. By back-projecting these three curves from the polar coordinates to the DET plane, one obtains the expected DET curve as well as its associated confidence region at the desired $\alpha \times 100\%$ level of confidence. This technique was described in [4].

A large U is necessary in order to guarantee stable results. Our preliminary experiments show that $U > 40$ is fine. We used $U = 100$ throughout the experiments. Our initial experiments show that the most probable DET curve derived this way generalises much better compared to plotting a DET directly from the predicted MSCC parameters, i.e., $\{\hat{\mu}_j^k, \hat{\sigma}_j^k|\forall_{j,k}\}$ because by using these parameters, one does not take the uncertainty of the prediction into consideration. Our preliminary experiments, as shown for instance in Figure 3(b), suggest that in order to generalise to a different user population and under a mismatched situation, it is better to sample from (10) and (11) for each user and for each class k in each round of bootstraps than to use the bootstrap subset procedure with the predicted MSCC parameters.

3 Database, Performance Evaluation and Results

We chose the BANCA database for our experiments for the following reasons:

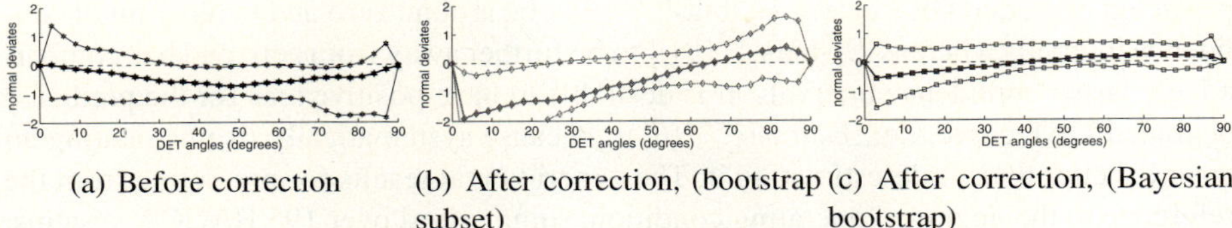

(a) Before correction (b) After correction, (bootstrap subset) (c) After correction, (Bayesian bootstrap)

Fig. 4. Comparison of DET bias due to noise and user composition mismatches on 195 BANCA systems under degraded (Ud) conditions as compared to the reference (Mc) conditions. Each of the three figures here presents the distribution of 195 DET radius bias for all $\theta \in [0, 90]$ degrees. The upper and lower confidence intervals represent 90% of the data. Prior to bias correction, in (a), the DET bias is large and is systematic (none zero bias estimate); in (b), after bias correction using the predicted MSCC parameters, i.e., following the bootstrap subset technique, the DET radius bias is still large and non-zero; in (c), after bias correction using the Bayesian bootstrap approach, the bias is significantly reduced and is close to zero – indicating the effectiveness of the regression functions in projecting the MSCC parameters from the reference to both the degraded (Ud) conditions. An example of the actual DET curve was shown in Figure 3(b). Similar results were obtained when the experiments were repeated to predict the performance on the adverse (Ua) conditions instead of the degraded (Ud) conditions (not shown here).

(a) **Availability of mismatched conditions:** It has three application scenarios: controlled, degraded and adverse operating conditions.
(b) **Different sets of user:** It comes with a defined set of protocols that has two partitions of gender-balanced users, called g1 and g2. This allows us to benchmark the quality of performance prediction by training the projection function on g1 and testing it on g2. In each data set, there are only 26 users. 3 genuine scores are available per user; and 4 for the impostor scores to estimate $p(y|j, k, m = 1)$.
(c) **Availability of many systems:** Being a benchmark database, 195 face and speech verification systems have been assessed on this database. These systems were obtained from "ftp://ftp.idiap.ch/pub/bengio/banca/banca_scores" as well as from [5].

In order to assess the quality of predicted DET curve, we consider three DET curves: two derived experimentally using the reference and the degraded data, and one based on the MSCC models (i.e., the predicted degraded curve from the reference data). These three curves can be expressed by $r_u^{ref}(\theta)$, $r_u^{deg}(\theta)$ and $r_u^{pdeg}(\theta)$ ($pdeg$ for predicted degraded curve), respectively, in polar coordinates for convenience with $\theta \in [0, \frac{\pi}{2}]$. In order to quantify the merit of the proposed approach, we define the bias of the reference and the predicted degraded curves, with respect to the ground-truth degraded DET curve as follows:

$$\text{bias}_u^{ref}(\theta) = r_u^{ref}(\theta) - r_u^{deg}(\theta) \tag{12}$$

and

$$\text{bias}_u^{pdeg}(\theta) = r_u^{pdeg}(\theta) - r_u^{deg}(\theta), \tag{13}$$

where u is one of the 195 data sets. By performing $U = 195$ independent experiments, we can then estimate the density $p(\text{bias}_u^{data}(\theta))$ for each of the θ values for $data \in \{ref, pdeg\}$ condition) separately. We expect that the expected bias due to the predicted degraded DET curve, $E_u[\text{bias}_u^{pdeg}(\theta))]$ be around zero and to have small confidence intervals whereas $E_u[\text{bias}_u^{ref}(\theta))]$ to be further away from zero and has comparatively larger confidence intervals. It is desirable to have positive bias for the predicted degraded DET curve, i.e., $E_u[\text{bias}_u^{pdeg}(\theta))]$, because systematically overestimating an error is better than underestimating it. The experimental results for predicting from the reference to the degraded operating condition, summarised over 195 BANCA systems, are shown in Figure 4.

4 Conclusions

While prior work has been reported on the effect of the sample and user variability, e.g., [6,3], to the best of our knowledge, none could be used to predict the biometric performance under mismatched conditions. As a result, the conventional methodology in biometric evaluation has always relied on collecting more data and one had to decide on a trade-off between the amount of data and the number of application scenarios available. We propose an evaluation methodology along with an algorithm that does not rely on a large quantity of data. Instead, it attempts to predict the performance under the mismatched condition by adequately modeling the score distribution and then projecting the distribution into one that matches the target mismatched condition for a given target population of users. Generalisation to different population of users (but of the *same* demographic characteristic) can be inferred from the resulting confidence interval. As a result, significantly fewer data is needed for biometric evaluation and existing databases can be reused to predict the performance behaviour of a system.

Our on-going work attempts to remove the Gaussian assumption made regarding the MSCC distribution. One important assumption about the current choice of regression algorithm (polyfit) used as the projection function is that the variance of the error terms is constant. A complete non-parametric modelling of the pair of MSCC parameters would have been more desirable. This issue is also being investigated. Finally, more comprehensive experiments, notably as to how well each predicted DET curve performs, will also be conducted.

Acknowledgment

This work was supported partially by the prospective researcher fellowship PBEL2-114330 of the Swiss National Science Foundation, by the BioSecure project (www.biosecure.info) and by Engineering and Physical Sciences Research Council (EPSRC) Research Grant GR/S46543. This publication only reflects the authors' view.

References

1. Bailly-Baillière, E., Bengio, S., Bimbot, F., Hamouz, M., Kittler, J., Mariéthoz, J., Matas, J., Messer, K., Popovici, V., Porée, F., Ruiz, B., Thiran, J.-P.: The BANCA Database and Evaluation Protocol. In: Kittler, J., Nixon, M.S. (eds.) AVBPA 2003. LNCS, vol. 2688. Springer, Heidelberg (2003)

2. Phillips, P.J., Rauss, P.J., Moon, H., Rizvi, S.: The FERET Evaluation Methodology for Face Recognition Algorithms. IEEE Trans. Pattern Recognition and Machine Intelligence 22(10), 1090–1104 (2000)
3. Bolle, R.M., Ratha, N.K., Pankanti, S.: Error Analysis of Pattern Recognition Systems: the Subsets Bootstrap. Computer Vision and Image Understanding 93(1), 1–33 (2004)
4. Poh, N., Martin, A., Bengio, S.: Performance Generalization in Biometric Authentication Using Joint User-Specific and Sample Bootstraps, IDIAP-RR 60, IDIAP, Martigny. IEEE Trans. Pattern Analysis and Machine Intelligence 2005 (to appear)
5. Cardinaux, F., Sanderson, C., Bengio, S.: User Authentication via Adapted Statistical Models of Face Images. IEEE Trans. on Signal Processing 54(1), 361–373 (2006)
6. Doddington, G., Liggett, W., Martin, A., Przybocki, M., Reynolds, D.: Sheep, Goats, Lambs and Woves: A Statistical Analysis of Speaker Performance in the NIST 1998 Speaker Recognition Evaluation. In: Int'l Conf. Spoken Language Processing (ICSLP), Sydney (1998)

Selection of Distinguish Points for Class Distribution Preserving Transform for Biometric Template Protection

Yi C. Feng and Pong C. Yuen

Department of Computer Science
Hong Kong Baptist University
{ycfeng, pcyuen}@comp.hkbu.edu.hk

Abstract. This paper addresses the biometric template security issue. Follow out previous work on class distribution transform, the proposed scheme selects the distinguish points automatically. By considering the geometric relationship with the biometric templates, the proposed scheme transforms a real-value biometric template to a binary string such that the class distribution is preserved and proved mathematically. The binary string is then further encoded using BCH and hashing method to ensure that the template protecting algorithm is non-invertible. Two face databases, namely ORL and FERET, are selected for evaluation and LDA is used for creating the original template. Experimental results show that by integrating the proposed scheme into the LDA (original) algorithm, the system performance can be further improved by 1.1% and 4%, in terms of equal error rate, on ORL and FERET databases respectively. The results show that the proposed scheme not only can preserve the original template discriminant power, but also improve the performance if the original template is not fully optimized.

Keywords: Biometric template security, face recognition, one-way transform, class distribution preserving.

1 Introduction

Biometric recognition is a reliable, robust and convenient way for person authentication [1,2,4]. With the growing use of biometrics, there is a rising concern about the security and privacy of the biometric template itself. Recent studies have shown that "hill climbing attacks" [5] on a biometric system are able to recover the biometric templates. As a result, templates have to be stored in an encrypted form to protect them. The matching step needs to be performed in encrypted domain because the decrypted templates are insecure. Different biometric template protection algorithms have been proposed in the last few years and can be categorized into two approaches.

The first approach is the cancelable template proposed by Ratha et al. [2] in 2001. The basic idea is that the system only uses a cancelable template, which is transformed by the original template using a one-way function. Therefore,

S.-W. Lee and S.Z. Li (Eds.): ICB 2007, LNCS 4642, pp. 636–645, 2007.

if the cancelable template is lost or stolen, the system may reset and re-issue another cancelable template using different set of parameters of the one-way function. In their recent study on cancelable biometric for fingerprint [3], the use of distortion function caused the FAR to increase by about 5% for a given FRR. While the invertibility of their transform is low, the discriminability of their cancelable template is not known. No analysis of invertibility vs. discriminability was reported in [3].

The second approach combined cryptographic methods with the biometric system, known as biometric cryptosystem. This approach consists of two stages [10]. First, the biometric template is transformed into a string. The second step generates a cryptographic key from the string using cryptographic technique. Some methods such as fuzzy commitment scheme [7] and fuzzy vault scheme [8,9], have been proposed for the second step. However, direct applying error correcting coding can only handle relatively small intra-class variations. In order to handle a relative large variation such as face template, Ngo et al. [10] proposed a new algorithm for the first step. They employed random projection and other appearance-based dimension reduction methods (PCA, LDA) to further extract the features. After that, a bit string is obtained using a thresholding technique. However, it is not clear whether the algorithm preserves the original template discriminability. Along this line, Feng and Yuen [11] proposed a new conceptual model called Class Distribution Preserving (CDP) Transform. A new scheme was proposed using a set of "distinguish point" and distance measurement. The "distinguish point" set is randomly generated, which will increase the randomness of the representation. A tri-state representation is proposed to overcome the distortion in transform, but the tri-state bit is hard to estimate.

In this paper, based on the concept of CDP transform, a new scheme is proposed to transform a real value biometric template into a bit string. In the proposed scheme, the set of "distinguish point" will be selected and the estimation of the tri-state bit is not required. The rest of the paper is organized as follows. Section 2 will give a review on the class distribution preserving transform. Section 3 will present our new proposed scheme while the experimental results will be reported in Section 4. Finally, Section 5 will give the conclusion.

2 Class Distribution Preserving Transform

The basic idea of class distribution preserving (CDP) transform [11] can be illustrated using Fig. 1. Consider a two class problem with class Ω_1 (data represented by "cross") and Ω_2 (data point represented by "circle"). Given distinguish points say B_1 and B_2, for any real value feature vector (biometric template) V in d-dimensional space, it can be transformed into a k-dimensional ($k = 2$ in this case) tri-state bit string $[b_1, b_2]$, where

$$b_i = \begin{cases} 0 & : \quad d(B_i, V) < th_i - \frac{r}{2} \\ \phi & : \quad th_i - \frac{r}{2} \le d(B_i, V) \le th_i + \frac{r}{2} \\ 1 & : \quad d(B_i, V) > th_i + \frac{r}{2} \end{cases} \tag{1}$$

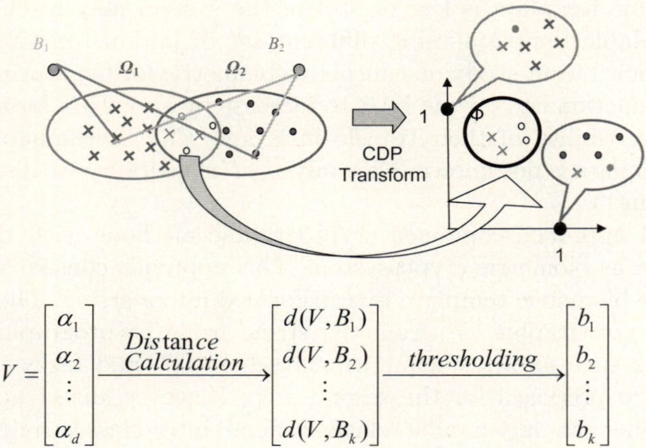

Fig. 1. Illustration for the Class Distribution Preserving Transform

Although the scheme in [11] works, there are rooms for improvement. First, all distinguish points are randomly generated and therefore, may not be able to generate a set of optimal bit string. Second, the number of distinguish points depends on the number of class which may introduce a complexity burden when the class number is large. Finally, it is hard to estimate the parameter "r" in calculating the tri-state ϕ.

3 Our Proposed Scheme

The block diagram of the proposed system is shown in Fig. 2. It consists of enrollment and authentication phases. The template protection algorithm consists of three blocks, namely class distribution preserving transform, error correction coding and hashing. The error correction coding and hashing steps are used to ensure that the protecting algorithm is non-invertible. This paper mainly focuses on the class distribution preserving transform.

The proposed scheme follows the concept of class distribution preserving (CDP) transform [11], but removes the limitations in our previous work [11]. This paper makes two major changes. First, instead of follow the scheme in [11] for biometric identification system (one to many), the new scheme is designed for authentication system (one to one). In practice, most of the biometric systems perform authentication, such as border control in Hong Kong and China. Second, the distinguish point set is determined so as to preserve the class distribution after transformation. Details of our scheme are discussed as follows.

3.1 CDP Transform for Authentication System

Assume there are c classes $C_T = \{\Omega_1, \Omega_2 \ldots \Omega_c\}$ with the cluster centers $\{M_1, M_2 \ldots M_c\}$ respectively. For each class Ω_o, let r_o be the largest distance any two

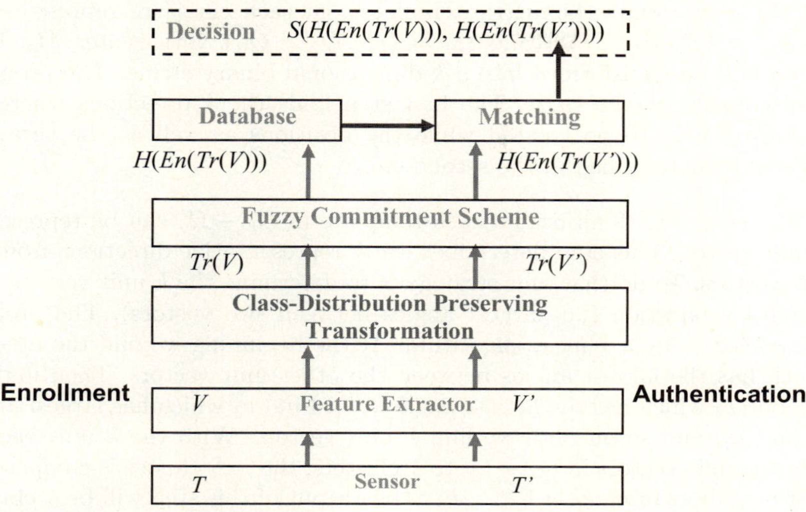

Fig. 2. Block diagram of the proposed system

data points in Ω_o, For authentication system, we only need to solve a two-class problem. Therefore, in determining the distinguish point set for class Ω_o, we only need to consider the class Ω_o, and $C_T - \Omega_o = \{x \in C_T | x \notin \Omega_o\}$. So the problem is defined as follows. Given a data point (biometric template) V, we would like to find a transformation T which has the following two CDP properties, where d_1 and d_2 are distance functions in input and transformed space respectively and t_o is the threshold in the transformed domain.

– Property One

  If $d_1(V, M_o) < r_o$, then $d_2(T(V), T(M_o)) \leq t_o$

  This property shows that if V belongs to class Ω_o, after transformation, V also belongs to the same class.

– Property Two

  If $d_1(V, M_o) > r_o$, then $d_2(T(V), T(M_o)) > t_o$

  This property shows that if V does not belong to class Ω_o, after transformation, V will also not belong to the class Ω_o.

3.2 Determining Distinguish Points and Thresholds

In order to develop the CDP transformation for authentication system as discussed in Section 3.1, we need to determine the set of k distinguish points $\{B_1, B_2 \ldots B_k\}$ and the responding thresholds $\{th_1, th_2 \ldots th_k\}$ for each class. For simplicity, we will represent them in pairs $\{B_1, th_1\}$.

Let the data points (biometric templates) in each class are represented as $CT - \Omega_o = \{P_1, P_2 \dots P_m\}$ and $\Omega_o = \{Q_1, Q_2 \dots Q_n\}$ with center M_o. Each template will be transformed into a k-dimensional binary string. The proposed method consists of two steps. The first step finds the k directions where the distinguish points to be located while the positions as well as the threshold values will be determined in the second step.

Step 1. Using M_o as an origin, each template in $C_T - \Omega_o$ can be represented by a unit vector. This step determines the k representative directions from the m unit vectors. To do that, our strategy is to determine the k unit vectors with the largest separation (i.e. largest angles between two vectors). The problem can be solved using a k-mean algorithm: At the beginning we find the first one v_1 which has the largest angles between the other unit vectors. Then find the second one v_2 which has the largest angle to v_1. Find v_3 which has largest angles to v_1 and v_2, and so on until we find k unit vectors. With the k unit vectors, classify the unit vectors in $C_T - \Omega_o$ to k clusters, the i-th cluster is composed of nearest neighbors of v_i. $(i = 1, 2 \dots k)$. The output of this step will be k clusters $\{G_1, G_2, \dots G_k\}$ in which $\{v_1, v_2 \dots v_k\}$ are a set of k unit vectors (from M_o).

Step 2. This step determines the exact positions of distinguish points in each direction (unit vector). The position of the i-th distinguish point along the direction of v_i can be written as $B_i = M_o + a_i v_i$, where a_i is a real value (parameter) and controls the position of B_i along v_i. The threshold th_i for the point B_i is then equal to $th_i = |a_i - r_o|$. Therefore, what we need to do is to estimate a_i.

The value of a_i can be positive or negative. $a_i < 0$ means that $B_i M_o$ is with the same direction of v_i and $th_i = |B_i M_o| + r_o$. If $a_i > 0$, $B_i M_o$ is in the opposite direction of v_i and $th_i = |B_i M_o| - r_o$. Here we give a definition of a_i as $a_i = \pm(2 + e_i)d$, $(i = 1, 2 \dots k)$.

The parameter d here is the largest value of $|P_j M_o|$, $(j = 1, 2 \dots m)$ and $e_i (i = 1, 2 \dots k)$ here is random generated value between range $[0, 2]$. The rationale in determining the a_i will be discussed in next section.

3.3 Proof of the CDP Properties

Before discussing the proof, let's consider two scenarios in which a distinguish point is located in two positions with respect to a data point outside the class Ω_o as shown in Fig. 2.

Scenario One. Considering a distinguish point $\{B_i, th_i\}$ where B_i and P_j are located in the opposite direction with respect to Ω_o with center M_o as Fig. 3. In this case, $th_i = |B_i M_o| + r_o$. For any data point P_j in group G_i (after clustering in step 1) and $Q_s (s = 1, 2 \dots n)$ in Ω_o, if θ_j is the angle between direction $B_i M_o$ and $M_o P_j$, then $\cos\theta_j > r_o / |P_j M_o|$.

The distance between the distinguish point B_i and P_j, Q_s, M_o can be written as

$$\begin{aligned} |B_iP_j| &\geq |B_iM_o| + |P_jM_o|\cos\theta_j > |B_iM_o| + r_o = th_i; \\ |B_iQ_s| &\leq |B_iM_o| + |Q_sM_o| \leq |B_iM_o| + r_o = th_i; \\ |B_iM_o| &< |B_iM_o| + r_o = th_i. \end{aligned} \tag{2}$$

That means, $|B_iP_j| > th_i$, $|B_iM_o| \leq th_i$ and $|B_iQ_s| \leq th_i$. So, using B_i as a distinguish point, the point P_j, Q_s and M_o are then transformed into bit $b_i(P_j) = 1$, $b_i(M_o) = 0$, $b_i(Q_s) = 0$. That means, data points within the class Ω_i will be transformed into same bit value while data points outside the class Ω_o will be transformed into opposite value.

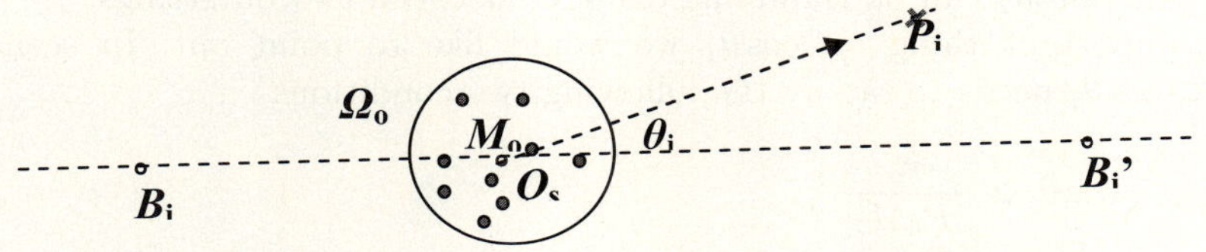

Fig. 3. Distinguish one point from M_o with pair B_i, th_i

Scenario Two. In this scenario, B_i' (with threshold th_i') and P_j are located in the same direction with respect to Ω_o with center M_o as Fig. 3. In this case, $th_i = |B_iM_o| - r_o$. Then the angle between direction $B_i'M_o$ and M_oP_j, θ_j, will satisfy

$$\cos\theta_j > \frac{|P_jM_o|}{2|B_i'M_o|} + \frac{r_o}{|P_jM_o|} - \frac{r_o^2}{2|B_i'M_o| \cdot |P_jM_o|} \tag{3}$$

and

$$|B_j'M_o| > 2|P_jM_o|. \tag{4}$$

The distance between the distinguish point B_i' and P_j, Q_s, M_o can be written as

$$\begin{aligned} |B_i'Q_s| &\geq |B_i'M_o| - |Q_sM_o| \geq |B_i'M_o| - r_o = th_i; \\ |B_i'M_o| &> |B_i'M_o| - r_o = th_i; \\ |B_i'P_j|^2 &= |B_i'M_o|^2 + |P_jM_o|^2 - 2\cos\theta_j \cdot |B_i'M_o| \cdot |P_jM_o| \\ &< |B_i'M_o|^2 + |P_jM_o|^2 - |P_jM_o|^2 - 2r_o|B_i'M_o| + r_o^2 \\ &= |B_i'M_o|^2 - 2r_o|B_i'M_o| + r_o^2 = th_i'^2. \end{aligned} \tag{5}$$

That means $|B_i'P_j| \leq th_i'$, $|B_i'M_o|, |B_i'Q_s| > th_i'$. So, using B_i' as a distinguish point, the point P_j, Q_s and M_o are then transformed into bit $b_i(P_j) = 0, b_i(M_o) = 1, b_i(Q_s) = 1$. That means, data points within the class Ω_o will be transformed into same bit value while data points outside the class Ω_o will be transformed into opposite value.

So far, we have shown that under the above two scenarios, the transformed bit of any feature vector Q in class Ω_o will be the same with M_o, and the transformed bit of any feature vector V in group G_i will be different from M_o. Using the same argument as above, consider all k pairs $\{B_1, th_1\}, \{B_2, th_2\} \ldots \{B_k, th_k\}$, the transformed bit string of any feature vector Q in class Ω_o will be the same with M_o. And there is at least one bit in the transformed bit string of any feature vector V out of class Ω_o which is different from M_o. (Because V should belong to one group G_i and the corresponding pair $\{B_i, th_i\}$ will contribute a different bit from M_o.) Therefore, we can prove that

If V belongs to Ω_o, $d_2(T(V), T(M_o)) = 0$;
If V dose'nt belong to Ω_o, $d_2(T(V), T(M_o)) > 0$.

The function d_2 can be Hamming distance between two bit strings.

One important thing on $\cos\theta_j$ we would like to point out. In scenarios 1 and 2, $\cos\theta_j$ needs to satisfy the following two conditions

$$\begin{aligned} \cos\theta_j &> \frac{r_o}{|P_jM_o|} \\ \cos\theta_j &> \frac{|P_jM_o|}{2|B_i'M_o|} + \frac{r_o}{|P_jM_o|} - \frac{r_o^2}{2|B_i'M_o| \cdot |P_jM_o|} \end{aligned} \tag{6}$$

And hence,

$$\begin{aligned} &\frac{r_o}{|P_jM_o|} < 1 \\ &\frac{|P_jM_o|}{2|B_i'M_o|} + \frac{r_o}{|P_jM_o|} - \frac{r_o^2}{2|B_i'M_o| \cdot |P_jM_o|} < 1 \end{aligned} \tag{7}$$

Because P_j is out of class Ω_o, i.e., $|P_jM_o| > r_o$, thus $r_o/|P_jM_o| < 1$. With the given condition that $|B_i'M_o| \geq 2|P_jM_o|$ in scenario 2, we have

$$\frac{|P_jM_o|}{2|B_i'M_o|} + \frac{r_o}{|P_jM_o|} - \frac{r_o^2}{2|B_i'M_o| \cdot |P_jM_o|} < \frac{1}{4} + \frac{r_o}{|P_jM_o|} - \frac{1}{4}\left(\frac{r_o}{|P_jM_o|}\right)^2 < 1. \tag{8}$$

(Because $r_o < |P_jM_o|$.)

To satisfy the requirement $|B_i'M_o| \geq 2|P_jM_o|$ in scenario 2, we give the definition of $a_i = \pm(2 + e_i)d$ in Section 3.2. With it, $|B_i'M_o| = |a_i| = (2 + e_i)d \geq 2d \geq 2|P_jM_o|$. The parameter e_i is used to increase the randomness of the generated pairs of distinguish points and thresholds because they do contain some information of the class Ω_o.

4 Experiment Results

Two experiments on ORL and FERET face databases are performed to evaluate our proposed scheme. The ORL database consists of 40 individuals, 10 images per individual while FERET database consists of 250 individuals, 4 images per individual. The experiments are conducted based on the block diagram in Fig. 2 in which the Fisherface [12] algorithm (feature extractor) is used to construct the original template while the matching is performed in hashed domain to ensure that the template protection algorithm is non-invertible.

Since the database size is relatively small, leave-one-out method is employed to conduct the experiments. The average error/accuracy is recorded. The results are plotted in Fig. 4 and 5 with different number of distinguish points (k). Fig. 4 and 5 show the ROC curves (with label "CDP") on ORL and FERET databases respectively. It can be shown that the performance increases when the number of distinguish points increase. The performance of the Fisherface algorithm with nearest neighbor classifier are also recorded and plotted in Fig. 4 and 5 (label as "original"). It can be shown that the proposed scheme outperforms original Fisherface algorithm while the biometric template is protected.

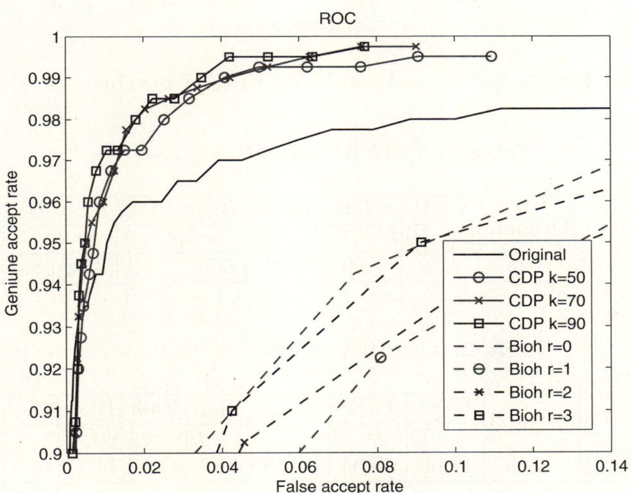

Fig. 4. Experiment results on ORL database

To compare with the existing algorithm, the bio-hashing scheme proposed by Ngo et al. [10] is selected because this algorithm also follows the biometric hardening approach. Same experiments setting are used for bio-hashing algorithm and the results are plotted in Fig. 4 and 5 with label "bioh". Parameter r here means the variation σ related to transform of ϕ in the bio-hashing algorithm. It can be seen that our proposed outperforms bio-hashing algorithm as well.

The equal error rates (ERR) of each curve are recorded and tabulated in Tab. 1 and 2. Comparing with the original template, the proposed method improves the performance at 1.1% and 4% on ORL and FERET databases respectively, while it is about 4.6% and 1.3% in comparing with the bio-hashing scheme.

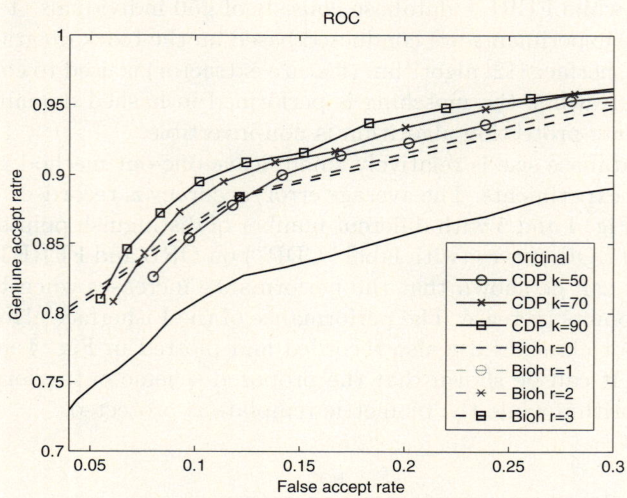

Fig. 5. Experiment results on FERET database

Table 1. The ERR on ORL database

	Original	CDP	CDP	CDP	Bioh	Bioh	Bioh	Bioh
		$k = 50$	$k = 70$	$k = 90$	$r = 0$	$r = 1$	$r = 2$	$r = 3$
ERR(%)	3.43	2.30	1.90	1.89	6.59	7.92	7.72	6.86

Table 2. The ERR on FERET database

	Original	CDP	CDP	CDP	Bioh	Bioh	Bioh	Bioh
		$k = 50$	$k = 70$	$k = 90$	$r = 0$	$r = 1$	$r = 2$	$r = 3$
ERR(%)	16.03	12.00	10.94	10.39	11.7	11.87	11.87	11.87

5 Conclusions

A new scheme for the class preserving transform has been developed and reported in this paper. The scheme is designed for the authentication system and determines the distinguish point set automatically so that after transformation, the inter-class and intra-class data distribution are preserved. Two face databases, namely ORL and FERET, are selected for evaluation and LDA is used for creating the original template. Two face databases, namely ORL and FERET, are selected for evaluation and LDA is used for creating the original template. Experimental results show that by integrating the proposed scheme into the LDA (original) algorithm, the system performance can be further improved by 1.1% and 4%, in terms of equal error rate, on ORL and FERET databases respectively.

The results show that the proposed scheme not only can preserve the original template discriminant power, but also improve the performance if the original template is not fully optimized.

Acknowledgments. This project is partially supported by the Faculty Research Grant of Hong Kong Baptist University.

References

1. Uludag, U., Pankanti, S., Prabhakar, S., Jain, A.K.: Biometric cryptosystems: issues and challenges. Proceedings of the IEEE 92(6), 948–960 (2004)
2. Ratha, N., Connell, J., Bolle, R.: Enhancing security and privacy in biometric-based authentication systems. IBM Systems Journal 40(3), 614–634 (2001)
3. Ratha, N., Connell, J., Bolle, R., Chikkerur, S.: Cancelable biometrics: A case study in Fingerprints. In: Proceedings of International Conference on Pattern Recognition (2006)
4. Jain, A.K., Ross, A., Pankanti, S.: Biometrics: A Tool for Information Security. IEEE Transactions on Information Forensics and Security 1(2), 125–143 (2006)
5. Adler, A.: Images can be regenerated from quantized biometric match score data. In: Proceedings of Canadian conference of Electrical and Computer Engineering, pp. 469–472 (2004)
6. Boult, T.: Robust distance measures for face-recognition supporting revocable biometric tokens. In: Proceeding of International Conference on Automatic Face and Gesture recognition (2006)
7. Juels, A., Wattenberg, M.: A fuzzy commitment scheme. In: Sixth ACM Conf. on Comp. and Comm. Security, pp. 28–36 (1999)
8. Juels, A., Sudan, M.: A Fuzzy Vault Scheme. In: IEEE International Symposium on Information Theory. IEEE Computer Society Press, Los Alamitos (2002)
9. Clancy, T.C., Kiyavash, N., Lin, D.J.: Secure smartcard-based fingerprint authentication. In: Proc. ACMSIGMM 2003 Multimedia, Biometrics Methods and Applications Workshop, pp. 45–52 (2003)
10. Ngo, D.C.L., Teoh, A.B.J., Goh, A.: Biometric Hash: High-Confidence Face Recognition. IEEE transactions on circuits and systems for video technology 16(6) (2006)
11. Feng, Y.C., Yuen, P.C.: Class-Distribution Preserving Transform for Face Biometric Data Security. In: Proceedings of IEEE International Conference on Acoustics, Speech, and Signal Processing (ICASSP) 2007 (in press)
12. Belhumeur, P.N., Hespanha, J.P., Kriegman, D.J.: Eigenfaces vs. fisherfaces: Recognition using class specific linear projection. IEEE Trans. on PAMI 19(7), 711–720 (1997)
13. Goh, A., Ngo, D.C.L.: Computation of cryptographic keys from face biometrics. In: Proc. 7th IFIP TC6/TC11 Conf. Commun. Multimedia Security, vol. 22, pp. 1–13 (2003)

Minimizing Spatial Deformation Method for Online Signature Matching

Bin Li[1], Kuanquan Wang[1], and David Zhang[2]

[1] Department of Computer Science and Technology, Harbin Institute of Technology
Harbin, China
{lbn,wangkq}@hit.edu.cn
[2] Department of Computing, The Hong Kong Polytechnic University
Kowloon, Hong Kong, SAR
csdzhang@comp.polyu.edu.hk

Abstract. Elastic matching is an important algorithm for online signature verification. Most of elastic matching algorithms are based on dynamic time warping(DTW). In this paper, we propose a new points matching algorithm for online signature verification. After resampling a signature with equidistant spacing, we describe the resampling point by its (3+1) demesional((3+1)D) information: 3D spatial information (x-axis, y-axis, time) and a feature vector. A soft-assign matrix and two special restrictions are introduced for recording the correspondence between two signatures. With a deterministic annealing framework, the mapping between two sets of (3+1)D signature points is achieved by minimizing the warping energy of the thin-plate spline(TPS). Experimental results demonstrate that the proposed algorithm outperforms the DTW-based matching algorithms.

Keywords: Signature verification, (3+1)D information, warping energy, thin-plate spline, deterministic annealing.

1 Introduction

The methods of online signature verification can be generally classified into two categories: function-based and parameter-based. Elastic matching algorithm is widely applied to parameter-based online signature verification, since the number of points(or strokes) is not consistent between any two signatures. For the past two decades, Dynamic time warping(DTW) has become a major algorithm for online signature verification. For example, A. Jain presented a DTW-based string matching algorithm which gives a penalty for the matching of two point sets with large differences in their number[1]. H. Feng proposed an alterant DTW algorithm named as extreme points warping(EPW) for online signature verification [2]. By accumulating the local distances of points, DTW is used to find the best matching path, in terms of the least global cost, between an input signal and a template. However, the spatial positional relation of the signature point is not considered in DTW-based elastic matching algorithm. Actually, this relation is very important for matching and verifying. For the correspondence of two pure 2D (or 3D) spatial point

S.-W. Lee and S.Z. Li (Eds.): ICB 2007, LNCS 4642, pp. 646–652, 2007.

sets, H. Chui presented a point matching algorithm based on soft-assign and TPS[3]. It is also not satisfied to online signature points matching, since local features of the signature point are not considered.

In this paper, considering the spatial information and local features of a signature point, we describe a signature point by its (3+1)D information: 3D spatial information (x-axis, y-axis, time) and a feature vector. Based on minimizing the warping energy(WE) of thin-plate spline(TPS) mapping, an elastic matching algorithm is proposed for the matching of two (3+1)D signature point sets.

2 (3+1)D Description of the Signature Point

With a fixed sampling frequency, a signature can be captured and described by a series of points $\{(x_i, y_i, t_i), i = 1,2,...,M\}$, where x_i, y_i and t_i is the x-, y- and time-coordinates of ith signature point. In order to evaluate our algorithm with DTW, we use the same preprocessing and feature extraction with Jain's [1]. After smoothing and normalizing, we resample the signature with equidistant spacing in x-y plane. The original time information is directly kept down for each resampling point. The resampling signature can be defined as a point set

$$\{p_i = (x_i, y_i, t_i), i = 1,..., N\}, \tag{1}$$

where p_i is a resampling point and N is the number of resampling points.

Jain evaluated 11 local features in his experiments and achieved the best result when selecting the feature set consisting of the features δx , δy , $\sin\alpha$, $\cos\alpha$, and the absolute speed v between two resampling points. The feature computation is described in Fig. 1. In this paper, we construct a feature vector for each signature point by these 5 local features. The feature vector is named as a feature dimension opposite to 3D spatial information of the point.

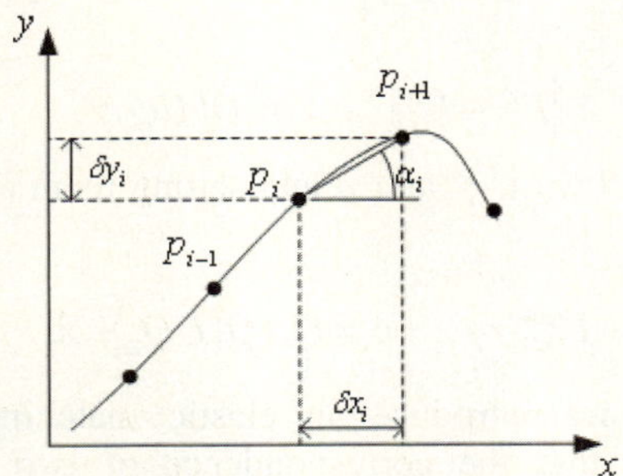

Fig. 1. Feature description of a resampling point

By combining the 3D spatial information and the feature vector, a signature S can be defined as:

$$S = \{((x_i, y_i, t_i), F_i), i = 1,..., N\},\ F_i = (\delta x_i, \delta y_i, \sin\alpha_i, \cos\alpha_i, v_i), \tag{2}$$

where F_i is a feature vector, and N is the number of resampling points.

3 Description of Elastic Matching Algorithm

Assume we have two point sets S^a and S^b with known correspondence, which include 3D spatial homogeneous coordinates sets P^a and P^b, and feature vector sets F^a and F^b. The 3D spatial TPS mapping function $f: P^b \to P^a$ can be defined as following:

$$f(P^b) = P^b \cdot d + U \cdot c, \tag{3}$$

where d is a 4×4 affine transformation matrix and c is a $N\times4$ non-affine coefficient matrix, U is the $N\times N$ 3D TPS kernel matrix consisting of $u_{ij} = -\left\|p_i^b - p_j^b\right\|$.

Considering the distance of feature vector sets F^a and F^b, we can obtain the TPS mapping function f by minimizing the following warping energy function:

$$E_{TPS}(d,c) = \left\|P^a - P^b d - Uc\right\|^2 + \lambda_1\left\|F^a - F^b\right\|^2 + \lambda_2 \mathrm{trace}\left(c^T U c\right). \tag{4}$$

The QR decomposition and the least-squares solution are used to solve parameters d and c [4]. With the QR decomposition, we decompose P^b into $N\times4$ orthonormal matrix Q_1, $N\times(N-4)$ orthonormal matrix Q_2 and 4×4 upper triangular R. With the permutation of $c = Q_2\gamma$, the Eq.4 can be transformed to

$$\begin{aligned} E_{TPS}(d,\gamma) = &\left\|Q_2^T P^a - Q_2^T U Q_2 \gamma\right\|^2 + \left\|Q_1^T P^a - Rd - Q_1^T U Q_2 \gamma\right\|^2 \\ &+ \lambda_1\left\|F^a - F^b\right\|^2 + \lambda_2 \gamma^T Q_2^T U Q_2 \gamma. \end{aligned} \tag{5}$$

By differentiating Eq. 5 w.r.t. γ and d and setting them to zeros, d and c can be calculated by:

$$d = R^{-1} Q_1^T (P^a - U Q_2 r), \quad c = Q_2 (Q_2^T U Q_2 + \lambda_2 I)^{-1} Q_2^T P^a. \tag{6}$$

Actually, the reason we introduce an elastic matching algorithm for online signature verification is that the correspondence of two signature point sets is unknown. Now we explain our elastic matching algorithm as follows.

Set S^a and S^b are two point sets with unknown correspondence whose point numbers are K and N respectively. A $K\times N$ soft-assign matrix M consisting of $m_{ij} \in [0,1]$ is introduced to record the correspondence between S^a and S^b. Intuitively, the larger m_{ij} is, the bigger the possibility of point s_i^a corresponding to

s_j^b is. An extra row and column are given to ensure that the accumulation of each row or column holds to 1, i.e. $\sum_{i=1}^{K+1} m_{ij} = 1, \forall \ \ j \in \{1,...,N\}$, $\sum_{j=1}^{N+1} m_{ij} = 1, \forall \ \ i \in \{1,...,K\}$.

For the feature vector, we define a distance matrix D^F consisting of $d_{ij} = \left\| F_i^a - F_j^b \right\|$, where $\|\bullet\|$ is the Euclidean distance, to record feature distances between each pair of points in S^a and S^b.

With the definitions of soft-assign matrix M and distance matrix D^F, the TPS warping energy function (Eq.5) is redefined by following:

$$E_{TPS}(M,d,c) = \sum_{i=1}^{K}\sum_{j=1}^{N} m_{ij}\left(\left\|P_i^a - P_j^b d - U\left(P_j^b\right)c\right\|^2 + \lambda_1 d_{ij}^{\ 2}\right) \\ + \lambda_2 trace(c^T Uc) + T\sum_{i=1}^{K}\sum_{j=1}^{N} m_{ij}\log m_{ij}\,. \tag{7}$$

The first term and the second term are related to the energy of affine transformation and non-affine warping respectively. The third term is a entropy barrier function that ensures the positivity of matrix M. In order to make the soft-assign matrix M evolving to a binary-assign matrix which will include the final best matching path, a determinate annealing framework is introduced. With a annealing rate R^{anneal}, the temperature parameter T, the controlling parameters λ_1 and λ_2 will be gradually reduced by $T = T^{init} R^{\text{anneal}}$, $\lambda_1 = \lambda_1^{init} R^{\text{anneal}}$ and $\lambda_2 = \lambda_2^{init} R^{\text{anneal}}$.

The algorithm is described as follows:

<u>Step 1</u> Initialize parameters M, d, c, λ_1^{init}, λ_2^{init} and T^{init}.

<u>Step 2</u> Fixing the TPS mapping parameters d and c, the equation $\partial E_{TPS} / \partial M = 0$ is solved to achieve a new soft-assign matrix whose element can be calculated by

$$m'_{ij} = \exp\left(-\left(\sum_{i=1}^{K}\sum_{j=1}^{N} m_{ij}\left(\left\|P_i^a - P_j^b d - U\left(P_j^b\right)c\right\|^2 + \lambda_1 d_{ij}^{\ 2}\right)\right)\Big/ T\right). \tag{8}$$

We normalize m'_{ij} across all rows and all columns, and update the soft-assign matrix M.

<u>Step 3</u> With the updated soft-assign matrix M, we calculate the 3D spatial coordinates of each corresponding point by $P_i^a \leftarrow \sum_{i=1}^{K} m_{ij} P_i^a$ and then recalculate d and c by Eq.6.

Step 4 Decrease T, λ_1 and λ_2, repeat *step 2* and *step 3* alternately until the algorithm converges. In our algorithm, the terminational condition of the convergence is $T \le T_{final}$.

Step 5 The soft-assign matrix M is regressed to a binary-assign matrix. When the algorithm has converged, we search each row and column of the soft-assign matrix M for the maximum element, mark this element as 1 and the others as 0. If the maximum is the *i*th element of the extra row or column, that means the point corresponding to the *i*th column or row is a mismatching point and will be eliminated.

In particular, there are two restrictions for the regression of soft-assign matrix M to ensure the strict monotonicity and one-to-one mapping.

(1) Strict monotonicity:

$$m_{ij} = 0, \quad \forall \begin{cases} 1 \le i \le i_0 - 1, j_0 + 1 \le j \le N, \\ or \quad i_0 + 1 \le i \le K, 1 \le j \le j_0 - 1 \end{cases}, \tag{9}$$

where $m_{i_0 j_0} = 1, \quad i_0 \in \{1,...,K\}, j_0 \in \{1,...,N\}$.

(2) One-to-one mapping:

If both m_{ij_1} and m_{ij_2} which belong to *i*th row of M are equal to the maximum of *i*th row, then

$$\begin{cases} m_{ij_1} = 1, m_{ij_2} = 0, & if \quad d_{ij_1} \le d_{ij_2} \\ m_{ij_1} = 0, m_{ij_2} = 1, & else \end{cases}, \tag{10}$$

where $d_{ij_1}, d_{ij_2} \in D^F, i \in \{1,...,K\}, j_1, j_2 \in \{1,...,N\}$.

The restriction for each column is the same.

Fig. 2 shows the elastic matching results that a template signature is compared with a genuine signature and a forgery.

4 Experimental Results

A digital tablet with 100Hz sampling frequency was used for capturing the signatures. Over a period of 4 months, 102 Chinese volunteers took part in the data acquisition. Each writer was asked to write his/her signature 10 times. 1020 genuine signatures are collected in our database. About the forgery, 6 forgers were asked to imitate 5 signatures for each genuine signer, after they observed both the shape and the dynamic writing process of genuine signatures. Total 1530 signatures in our experimental database are used to evaluate our algorithm.

In our experiments, the annealing rate is set to 0.6 and parameters λ_1^{init} and λ_2^{init} are set to 1. The initial value of T is set to a value which is isometric with the largest square distance, which also contains the maximum of feature distance matrix D^F, for

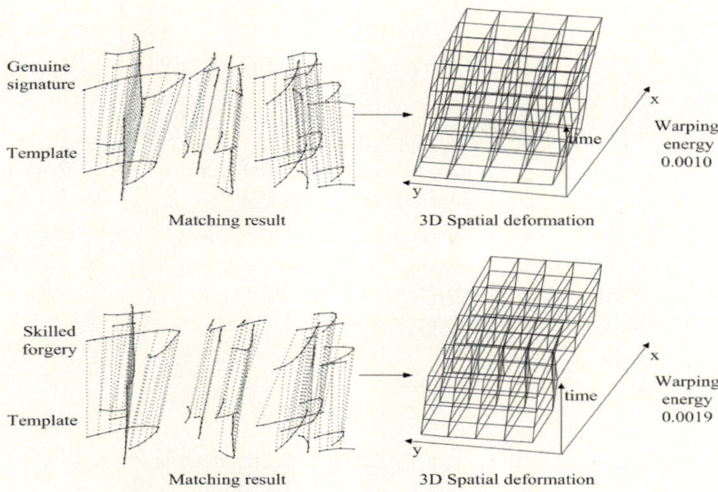

Fig. 2. Flexible matching based on TPS mapping

all possible pairs of points. The soft-assign matrix M is initialized to a $K \times N$ matrix in which each element is set to $1/\arg\max(K,N)$, and the outlier row and column are set to $1/(100 \times \arg\max(K,N))$. d and c is initialized to a unit matrix and a zero matrix respectively. After about 7~8 times iteration, the proposed algorithm can converge at a good matching results.

In order to evaluate the proposed algorithm, with same database set, Jain's algorithm is implemented [1]. Based on the same preprocessing and feature extraction, Jain used DTW for elastic matching. For each signer, 3 and 5 genuine signatures are used in training, 5 samples of the rest genuine signatures and 5 skilled forgeries are used for testing. Table 1 gives the experimental comparison between Jain's DTW-based algorithm and the proposed algorithm. From Table 1, we can see that the verification performance using only the warping energy(WE) is already a little better than Jain's DTW-based algorithm. Combining WE and the Euclidean distance of local features(ED-F), the (3+1)D algorithm can achieve better results than Jain's. The best result of our algorithm yields an equal error rate of 1.9% for 5 references. The error tradeoff curves for the comparison are shown in Figure 3.

Table 1. Comparison between Jain's and the proposed algorithm for 3 and 5 references

Reference number	Jain's DTW-based	(3+1)D:WE	(3+1)D:ED-F	(3+1)D
3	EER=5.3%	EER=4.3%	EER=8.3%	EER=3.4%
5	EER=3%	EER=2.8%	EER=5.8%	**EER=1.9%**

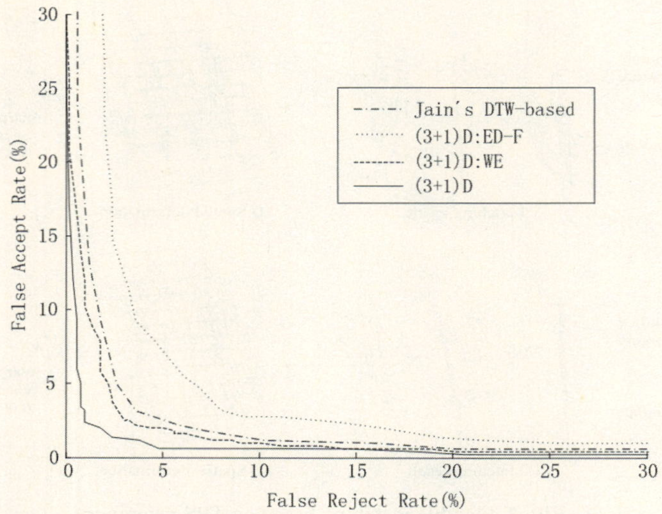

Fig. 3. Error tradeoff curves for the comparison between Jain's and the proposed algorithm

References

1. Jain, A.K., Griess, F.D., Connell, S.D.: Online Signature Verification. Pattern Recognition 35(2), 2963–2972 (2002)
2. Feng, H., Wah, C.C.: Online Signature Verification Using a New Extreme Points Warping Technique. Pattern Recognition Letters 24(16), 2943–2951 (2003)
3. Chui, H., Rangarajan, A.: A New Algorithm for Non-rigid Point Matching. In: IEEE Conf. on Computer Vision and Pattern Recognition, pp. 2044–2051. IEEE Computer Society Press, Los Alamitos (2000)
4. Wahba, G.: Spline Models for Observational Data. Society for Industrial and Applied Mathematics, PA (1990)

Pan-Tilt-Zoom Based Iris Image Capturing System for Unconstrained User Environments at a Distance

Sowon Yoon[1], Kwanghyuk Bae[1], Kang Ryoung Park[2], and Jaihie Kim[1]

[1] School of Electrical and Electronic Engineering, Yonsei University, Biometrics Engineering Research Center (BERC), Republic of Korea
{swyoon,paero,jhkim}@yonsei.ac.kr
[2] Division of Digital Media Technology, Sangmyung University, Hongji-Dong, Jongro-Ku, Seoul, Republic of Korea, Biometrics Engineering Research Center (BERC)
parkgr@smu.ac.kr

Abstract. This paper proposes a novel iris image capturing system using a pan-tilt-zoom camera for unconstrained user environments at a distance. To provide wide operating range, we are trying to develop iris image acquisition system using pan-tilt-zoom camera. This paper verifies that iris recognition is possible when iris images are captured with zoom lens at a distance from camera. Iris images are collected by changing the distance from camera to user, zoom factor to maintain face size in an image, and focus lens position. And they are assessed by Hamming distance. Experimental results show that iris images captured at a distance of 1.5–3 m from camera can be verified as genuine and proposed system has 5–10 cm depth of field. This means that users have freedom of position as 1.5 m and natural movement of a standing user can be covered.

Keywords: Iris image capturing system, pan-tilt-zoom camera, depth of field, depth of focus, operating range.

1 Introduction

According to [1], [2], the ideal biometric characteristic has five qualities: robustness, distinctiveness, availability, accessibility, and acceptability. Robustness means unchanging on an individual overtime and repeatable to use. Distinctiveness refers to the existence of wide differences in the pattern among the population. Availability means that the entire population should ideally have this measure in multiples. Accessibility means that features are easily presented to an imaging sensor. Acceptability refers that people do not object to having the measurement taken from them and perceive as non-intrusive.

Iris recognition technology satisfies three of above qualities: robustness, distinctiveness, availability [2], [3], [4], [9]. Robustness is satisfied by the fact that the iris is protected behind eye structures such as eyelid and cornea, and the features of the iris, their placement, size, shape and orientation remain stable and fixed from about one year of age throughout life [3]. Distinctiveness is satisfied by the fact that the iris pattern has 200 or more independent degrees of freedom. It implies that the probability of two different irises agreeing by chance in more than 70% of their phase sequence is about one in 7 billion [4]. Availability is satisfied by the fact that every

S.-W. Lee and S.Z. Li (Eds.): ICB 2007, LNCS 4642, pp. 653–662, 2007.

person has two distinctive irises. These three qualities are recently shown in J. Daugman's paper [9]. In this paper, he probes uniqueness and randomness of the templates for identifying each iris from a database of 632,500 iris images.

Despite these desirable characteristics, iris recognition system is not as popular as other biometric systems such as fingerprint and face. For most of the current iris recognition systems, users try to put their eyes in a certain range because they offer very small operating range [6]. This yields low accessibility and acceptability. Accessibility is low because of two reasons. First, they have low throughput because clear iris images are hard to obtain due to small operating range. Second, the systems require many conditions such as well-trained operator, a cooperative user, adjusted equipment and well-controlled lighting conditions [2]. Acceptability is also low because of three reasons. First, users try to put their eyes in operating range several times, so that capturing in-focus iris images takes much time [5]. Second, once their eyes come into operating range they have to stay still. Third, users keep their eyes close to the camera. These make users uncomfortable. In other words, constraints on position and motion of users in a small operating range drop accessibility for in-focus image acquisition of the iris as well as acceptability for user convenience.

There are several efforts to improve accessibility and acceptability of iris recognition system: Sarnoff Corporation and Mitsubishi Corporation. They all try to improve acceptability by recognizing iris at a distance over 1 m in common. According to [13], the iris image can be captured at even 10 m distance between user and camera using a telescope and infrared camera.

Sarnoff Corporation suggests a portal system for iris recognition [6]. Their system takes pictures continuously with high resolution camera while a user passes through the portal at a normal walking pace. This system can capture average 1.5 in-focus iris images. They increase accessibility by high throughput (20 subjects/min) and acceptability by the fact that users just walk through the portal. However, there are three disadvantages of their system. First, their system is not useful for the disabled, children, and tall people because the height of capture volume (20 cm width × 37 cm height × 10cm depth) is small to cover height variation. Second, users should be very cooperative; eyes wide open, look straight ahead, walk at a moderate pace, and try to be recognized. Third, there are many specular reflections in iris images and glasses can corrupt the iris image seriously because 8 illuminators close to the user are used.

Mistubishi Corporation proposes an iris image capturing system using a video camera with wide-field-of-view lens, a high resolution digital still camera with narrow-field-of-view lens and a pan-tilt unit [7]. Wide-field-of-view video camera detects a face and pan-tilt unit rotates to the direction which narrow-field-of-view camera can capture the full face image with high resolution. And then the iris region crops from the face image for recognition. Their system improves acceptability by providing wide operating range using pan-tilt unit and a camera with high resolution and big sized CCD sensor. But three disadvantages remain. Since they use a fixed focal lens for narrow-field-of-view camera, the depth of operating range is limited. And it needs two-camera calibration. Also, users have to stay very still.

This paper proposes a novel iris image acquisition system for unconstrained user environments using a pan-tilt-zoom camera at a distance. To achieve acceptability for user convenience, proposed system offers wide operating range which can cope with height variation and positioning with a camera. Wide width and height of operating range are achieved by pan-tilt unit and wide depth is obtained by zoom lens. This system can work with relatively less user cooperation and few equipments. Illuminators do not make few specular reflections in the iris and glasses because two near-infrared illuminators are used at a distance. Thus proposed system does not make serious problem on users who wear glasses.

Overall procedure for capturing the iris image is following. In zoom-out state, user's face is detected. After the face is zoomed in until it fills entire image, high resolution iris image is obtained from the face image. To capture the iris stably in unconstrained user environments, obtaining iris image from full face image is advantageous for catching up the user's movement. If the iris is fully zoomed, small movement at a distance of over 1 m makes the iris disappeared in the camera view.

In this paper, we introduce overall system configuration and algorithms used. And we probe the feasibility of acquired iris images taken at a distance of 1.5–3 m between user and camera with adjusting zoom factor to fit the face to whole image. We show accessibility by measuring depth of focus. Because wide depth of focus means that focusing on the iris is easy, as a result, we can get in-focus iris images readily. And we show acceptability that operating range in depth is guaranteed as 1.5m and natural movement of a standing user is acceptable because depth of field is 5–10 cm in whole operating range.

The practical system based on pan-tilt-zoom camera with a light stripe projection is proposed in [14]. This system detects the horizontal position of the user by light stripe projection. It reduces search range of the user's face from 2D to 1D and obtains the distance between camera and user's face, so that the initial zoom and focus lens positions are determined. Therefore operating time for searching face, zooming and focusing is greatly reduced.

2 System Configuration

Proposed system is designed for providing wide operating range: 1 m width × 1 m height × 1 m depth at a distance of 1.5–2.5 m. The entire concept of proposed system is shown in Fig. 1. By panning and tilting the width and height of operating range are expanded even if actual field of view of a camera is limited. To cover height variation of about 1 m at a distance of 1.5 m, tilt range should be ±18.43°. To obtain the iris image robustly allowing user's small movement, zooming into the face instead of the iris is required. While the iris can be missed easily in the state of zooming into the iris, it can remain in the image in the state of zooming into the face under the user's movement. To get iris image with over 150 pixels for its diameter which is medium or high quality [8] from the full face image, the width of CCD camera should be over 1,950 pixels. The depth of operating range is enlarged by zooming. For acquiring iris images with enough size for recognition, according to simple lens equation, required focal lengths at a distance of 1.5 m and 2.5 m are 149.87 mm and 249.78 mm, respectively. Two illuminators of 830 nm are used here. When illuminated with near-infrared light in the 700–900 nm band, even dark brown irises reveal rich texture [9].

Fig. 2 shows proposed system configuration: 4 mega-pixel CCD camera, a zoom lens with focal length of 70–300 mm, a pan-tilt unit with pan angle of 360 ° and tilt angle of ±45° and two near-infrared illuminators. To control zoom and focus, stepping motors are used.

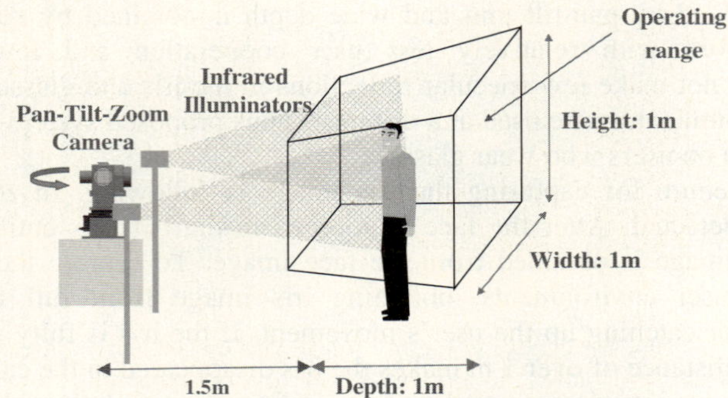

Fig. 1. Concept of proposed system: width and height of operating range are determined by angle of view of camera and angle of pan-tilt unit; depth of operating range is determined by zoom lens

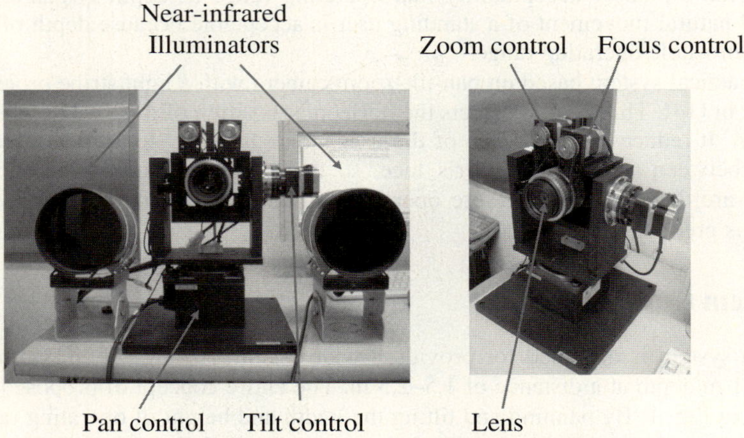

Fig. 2. System configuration: mega-pixel camera, zoom lens, control units for pan, tilt, zoom and focus, and two near-infrared illuminators

The overall procedure for iris image acquisition is following. First, the user's face is detected in zoom-out state using face detector based on AdaBoost algorithm by Viola and Jones [11], which is fast, accurate and robust. Fig. 3(a) shows face detection result in zoom-out state. To be fast and remove unnecessary details which often cause false detection due to high resolution, image size is reduced by 1/100. To evaluate face detection rate of near-infrared images, new database is collected under near-infrared illuminators. It consists of 540 images from 35 persons (19 persons with glasses and 16 persons without glasses). Each person takes pictures at 10 different positions in camera angle shown in Fig. 4 (left). Users with glasses take pictures once

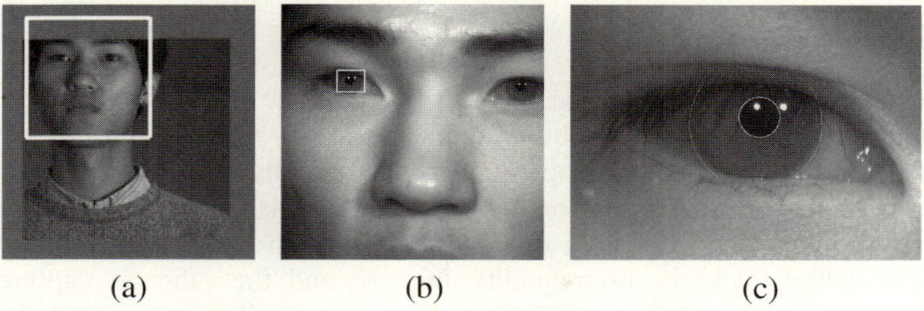

Fig. 3. Overall procedure for capturing the iris image at a distance. (a) Face detection in wide angle view, (b) iris detection after zooming in the full face, (c) iris localization.

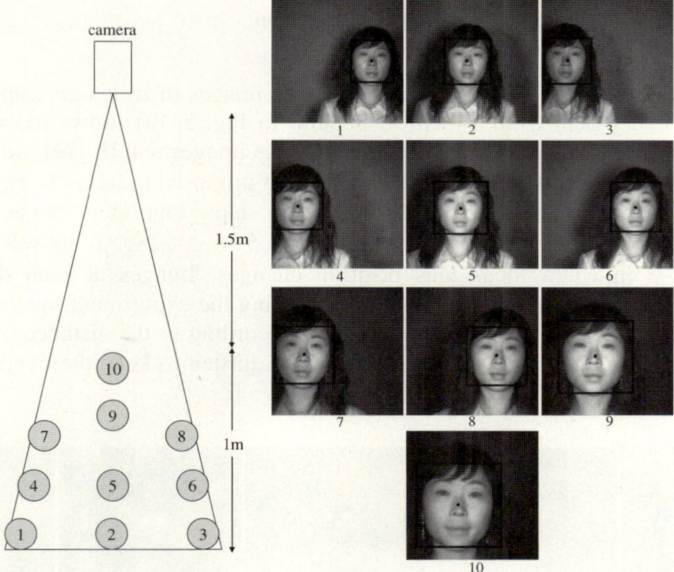

Fig. 4. Positions that face database is collected under near-infrared illuminators (left) and detection results at each position (right). The detection rate in this range is 98.7%.

more without glasses. Fig. 4 (right) shows face detection results at each position. Detection rate is 98.7%. Second, pan and tilt control are performed to place the face in the center of the image. And zoom control to fill the entire image with the user's face is done. Third, iris detection by template matching returns the location and size of the iris. For computational efficiency, search area for template matching is limited on upper half region of the resized image. The result is shown in Fig. 3(b). Fourth, iris localization is required to extract iris pattern. Iris boundary extraction is by circular edge detector [10]. Finally, focus assessments [10], [12] can be performed for capturing in-focus iris image by controlling focus lens movement.

3 Experimental Results

Experiments are designed to probe the feasibility of the iris images captured from proposed system and show accessibility and acceptability of the system by measuring depth of focus, depth of field, and operating range of depth.

In iris recognition, a criterion for image quality of iris can be Hamming distance between two images of same iris: one is acquired from the camera system for iris enrollment, which captures high quality images, and the other is captured from proposed system. If a Hamming distance between enrolled image and the image captured from this system is lower than the threshold, we can say the quality of captured image is good enough to be recognized.

In this paper, the experiment is performed under following two assumptions:

(1) User agrees to iris recognition with cooperation.
(2) User's face appears in zoom-out state.

The procedure of experiment is following. Iris images of user were captured at the distance of every 5cm from 140cm to 300cm. In Fig. 5, (a) shows iris image from enrollment system which acquires high quality iris images and (b)–(e) are iris images captured at different distances from the camera of proposed system. At each distance, focus lens position varied from -1000 to 1000 steps. One step moves focus lens position as 1/47000 of full focus range from 1.5 to ∞. Fig. 6 shows iris images captured at 2 m when focus lens position changes. Images at each distance are collected from totally defocused to in-focus. During the experiment, magnification of face was maintained by changing zoom factor according to the distance. And camera parameters such as gain and shutter speed were adjusted to keep the overall intensity of the images manually.

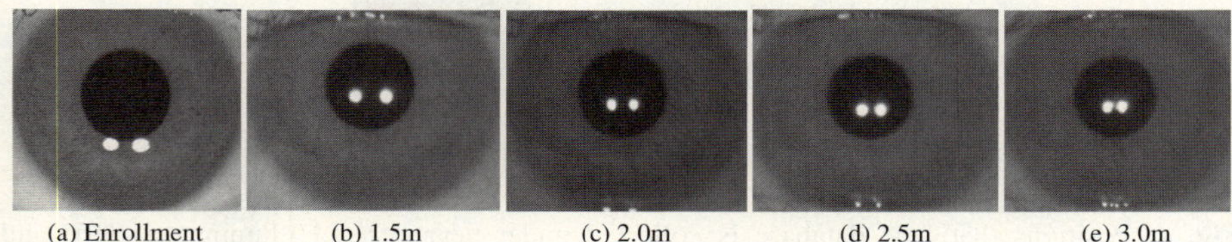

(a) Enrollment (b) 1.5m (c) 2.0m (d) 2.5m (e) 3.0m

Fig. 5. (a) Enrolled image from enrollment device and (b) iris images captured at different distances

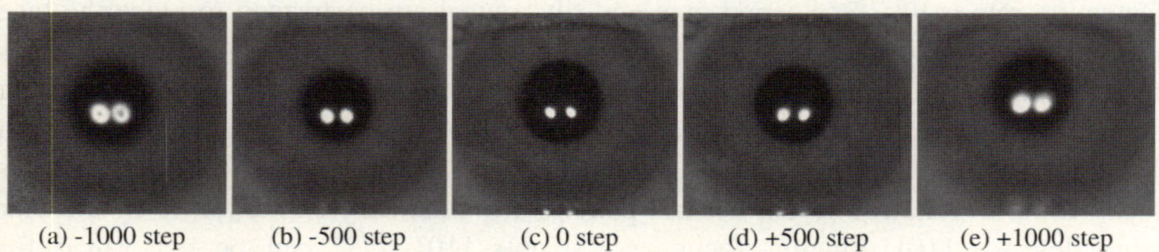

(a) -1000 step (b) -500 step (c) 0 step (d) +500 step (e) +1000 step

Fig. 6. Iris images captured by changing focus lens position at 2 m

Depth of focus is obtained at each distance. Depth of focus is related to the question: 'do we need delicate focusing algorithm?' It can be one of the measurements for accessibility, because wide depth of focus means that focusing on iris is easy.

Depth of field means permissible range for the depth variation of user position at fixed focus lens position. It means acceptability for depth variation. By this, we can prove that proposed system is feasible in a practical situation that a user stands in front of the system. Even if a user tries to stand still for recognition, there exists variation of the position. The variations of width and height are not critical because we capture the full face, thus the iris still remains in the image despite small movement. The variation of depth, however, may be critical because the iris may be out of focus. Depth of field is related to this question: 'is it robust for natural movement of a standing user?'

Depth of operating range is determined by the range that proposed system can capture the iris images which can be recognized. It means acceptability for depth position. Users can stand anywhere in the operating range. We use Gabor wavelet algorithm for creating iris templates which has threshold around 0.32. This threshold is usual in Gabor wavelet [10].

Fig. 7 shows Hamming distance of captured images changing focus lens position at 2 m. As the position of focus lens is changed, defocus images and in-focus images are obtained. Among them, images with lower Hamming distance than threshold can be recognized. The range of focus lens position with lower Hamming distance than threshold is depth of focus.

Depth of focus at each distance is presented in Fig. 8. Range between maximum focus lens position (line with cross) and minimum focus lens position (line with point) means available focus lens position at a certain user distance. Inside that range, depth of field and depth of focus can be measured. At a certain distance, variable range of

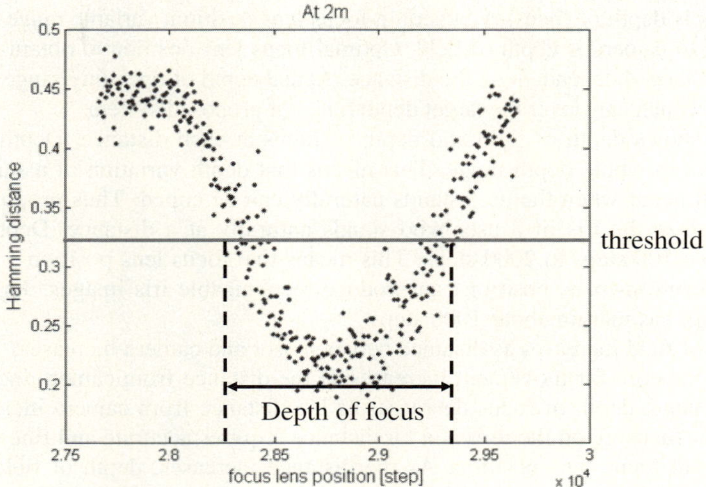

Fig. 7. Hamming distance of iris images captured from proposed system when focus lens position is changed at 2 m and depth of focus

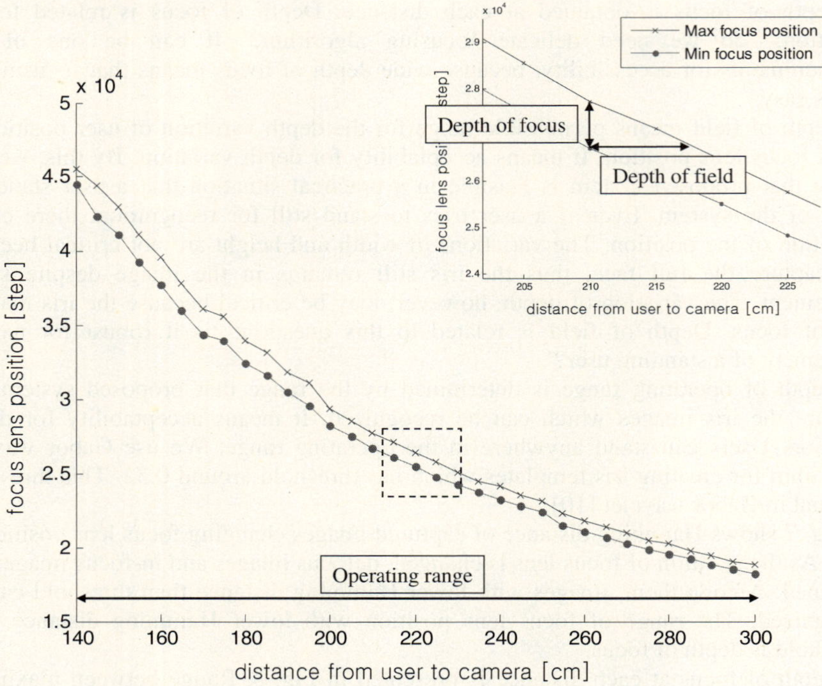

Fig. 8. Depth of focus, depth of field and operating range of proposed system; upper right figure is the enlarged dotted rectangle region of original figure. Line with cross is maximum focus lens position and line with point is minimum focus lens position at each distance.

focus lens is depth of focus. At a certain focus lens position, variable range of distance from user to camera is depth of field. Optimal focus lens position to obtain an in-focus image is changed dependent on the distance. Actual depth of operating range is from 1.4 m to 3 m, which can cover the target depth range of proposed system.

Fig. 9 shows depth of field and depth of focus at each distance. Depth of field is 4.5–9.5 cm in whole depth range. This means that depth variation of a standing user which can occur when the user stands naturally can be coped. Thus proposed system can recognize the iris of a user who stands naturally at a distance. Depth of focus varies from 500 steps to 2000 steps. This means that focus lens position within depth of focus from in-focus position can produce recognizable iris images. That is, focus lens control has margin about 1000 steps.

Depth of field increases as distance between user and camera increases. This means that user freedom for movement increases as the distance from camera increases. On the other hand, depth of focus decreases as the distance from camera increases. This means that focusing on the user at a far distance requires accurate and fine searches to find optimal focus lens position. As the distance increases, depth of field increases and we can get high user acceptability. However, focusing is getting difficult because depth of focus decreases. And power of illuminator drops rapidly. Thus we need to adjust camera parameters such as shutter speed and gain automatically.

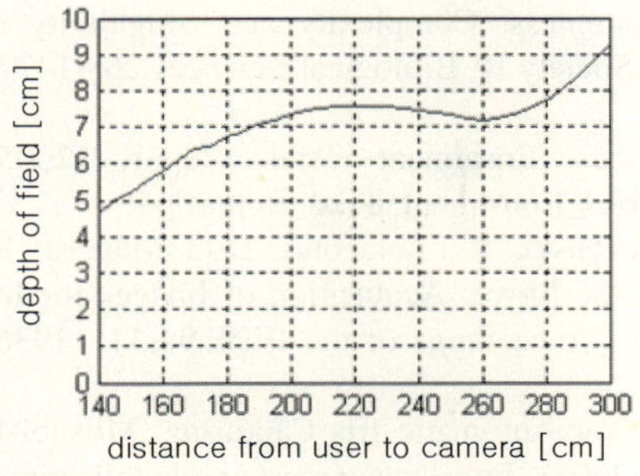

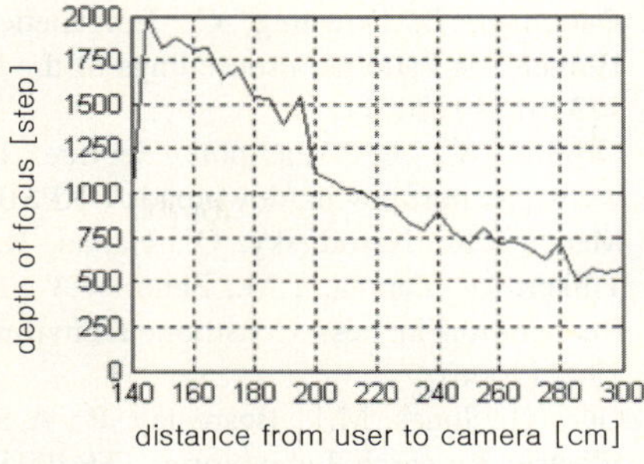

Fig. 9. Depth of field (left) and depth of focus (right) with respect to the distance from user and camera

4 Conclusions and Future Works

In this paper, pan-tilt-zoom based iris image acquisition system is proposed. To achieve acceptability for user convenience, this system is designed for wide operating range, 1 m width × 1 m height × 1 m depth at a distance of 1.5–2.5 m, using pan-tilt-zoom camera. To capture iris image stably at a distance of 1.5–2.5 m, zooming into the face size is advantageous because zooming into iris can lose the iris easily by small movement. Face detection, pan-tilt-zoom control and iris localization are performed to get iris image at a distance. Also, we probe the feasibility of acquired iris images at various distances and at various focus lens positions using Hamming distance. Actual depth of operating range is 1.5–3 m, which is larger than the target distance 1.5–2.5 m. Depth of field is 5–9.5 cm, which can cover natural movement of a standing user. That is, proposed system can be used with less user's cooperation and improve acceptability. Depth of focus is 500–2000 steps for whole area. This makes focusing on the iris facilitate and increases accessibility.

Focusing on the iris based on above experimental results will be performed in the future. We still have problems when a user moves rapidly or panning and tilting are fast, because they cause motion blur. And toward more unconstrained environment, pan-tilt-zoom control will be developed by estimating user's movement in more moderate method.

Acknowledgments. This work was supported by the Korea Science and Engineering Foundation (KOSEF) through the Biometrics Engineering Research Center (BERC) at Yonsei University.

References

1. Wayman, J., Jain, A., Maltoni, D., Maio, D. (eds.): Biometric Systems: Technology, Design and Performance Evaluation. Springer, London (2005)
2. Wayman, J.L.: Fundamentals of Biometric Authentication Technologies. International Journal of Image and Graphics 1(1), 93–113 (2001)
3. Williams, G.O.: Iris Recognition Technology. Aerospace and Electronic Systems Magazine 12(4), 23–29 (1997)

4. Daugman, J., Downing, C.: Epigenetic Randomness, Complexity and Singularity of Human Iris Patterns. Proceedings of the Royal Society B: Biological Sciences 268(1477), 1737–1740 (2001)
5. Origin, A.: UK Passport Service Biometrics Enrolment Trial. Report (2005), www.passport.gov.uk/downloads/UKPSBiometrics_Enrolment_Trial_Report.pdf
6. Matey, J.R., Naroditsky, O., Hanna, K., Kolczynski, R., Loiacono, D.J., Mangru, S., Tinker, M., Zappia, T.M., Zhao, W.Y.: Iris on the Move: Acquisition of Images for Iris Recognition in Less Constrained Environments. Proceedings of the IEEE 94(11), 1936–1947 (2006)
7. Guo, G., Jones, M.J., Beardsley, P.: A System for Automatic Iris Capturing. Mitsubishi Electric Research Laboratories, TR2005-044 (2005), http://www.merl.com/publications/TR2005-044/
8. ANSI INCITS 379-2004.
9. Daugman, J.: Probing the Uniqueness and Randomness of IrisCodes: Results From 200 Billion Iris Pair Comparisons. Proceedings of the IEEE 94(11), 1927–1935 (2006)
10. Daugman, J.: How Iris Recognition Works. IEEE Transactions on Circuits and Systems for Video Technology 14(1), 21–30 (2004)
11. Viola, P., Jones, M.J.: Robust Real-Time Face Detection. International Journal of Computer Vision 57(2), 137–154 (2004)
12. Kang, B.J., Park, K.R.: A Study on Iris Image Restoration. In: Kanade, T., Jain, A., Ratha, N.K. (eds.) AVBPA 2005. LNCS, vol. 3546, pp. 31–40. Springer, Heidelberg (2005)
13. Fancourt, C., Bogoni, L., Hanna, K., Guo, Y., Wildes, R., Takahashi, N., Jain, U.: Iris Recognition at a Distance. In: Kanade, T., Jain, A., Ratha, N.K. (eds.) AVBPA 2005. LNCS, vol. 3546, pp. 1–13. Springer, Heidelberg (2005)
14. Yoon, S., Jung, H.G., Suhr, J.K., Kim, J.: Non-intrusive Iris Image Capturing System Using Light Stripe Projection and Pan-Tilt-Zoom Camera. In: IEEE Computer Society Workshop on Biometrics, accepted for publication (2007)

Fingerprint Matching with Minutiae Quality Score

Jiansheng Chen, Fai Chan, and Yiu-Sang Moon

Department of Computer Science and Engineering
The Chinese University of Hong Kong, Shatin, N.T., Hong Kong
{jschen,fchan,ysmoon}@cse.cuhk.edu.hk

Abstract. The accuracy of minutiae based fingerprint matching relies much on the minutiae extraction process. However, during minutiae extraction, false minutiae may be extracted due to bad fingerprint image quality. One commonly used solution to this problem is to filter out the false minutiae using minutiae quality scores. However, as indicated by the fingerprint matching results, the reliabilities of the existing minutiae scoring algorithms in discriminating genuine and false minutiae are significantly lower than that of the fingerprint matching process. To study the actual difficulties in minutiae filtering, we have conducted extensive experiments to compare two minutiae quality scoring algorithms. Then, four fingerprint matching strategies using minutiae quality scores were employed to investigate how the minutiae quality scores can affect fingerprint matching accuracy. Our results show that only proper combinations of minutiae quality scoring algorithms and fingerprint matching strategies can achieve improvement in fingerprint matching accuracy.

Keywords: Fingerprint verification, Fingerprint minutiae quality.

1 Introduction

Fingerprint verification is widely used in our daily life for security purposes. The performance of fingerprint verification systems depends a lot on the fingerprint image quality. Due to predictable factors such as thin ridges, scars as well as unpredictable factors such as dry/wet fingers, moving fingers, fingerprint images are sometimes of low quality. This may harm the reliability of fingerprint authentication systems by the extraction of false minutiae.

One possible solution to this problem is to adopt a post processing step, called minutiae filtering, to remove falsely extracted minutiae in fingerprint authentication systems. One recent work is D.H. Kim's algorithm [1] which is based on skeletons of binarized and thinned fingerprint ridges. To extend the applicability of this algorithm, we have modified it to support ridges extracted by Direct Gray Scale algorithm, which is relatively more computationally efficient when compared to the Binarization and Thinning approach. The results showed that our extension to this algorithm can distinguish false minutiae from genuine minutiae with accuracy comparable to or even better than the original algorithm. Then, we implemented a novel minutiae quality scoring scheme using minutiae image correlation [2]. The inspiration of this method comes from the study of fingerprint ridges correlation for fingerprint

S.-W. Lee and S.Z. Li (Eds.): ICB 2007, LNCS 4642, pp. 663–672, 2007.

verification [3]. Experimental results show that the accuracy for distinguishing false minutiae from genuine minutiae is comparable to Kim's method.

We further investigate the effects of different strategies for embedding the minutiae quality scores into minutiae matching schemes. Intuitively, fingerprint minutiae quality scores can help in improving verification accuracy. However, the accuracy in automatic differentiation of genuine or false minutiae is significantly lower than that in fingerprint verification. The effect of using minutiae quality scores for improving verification accuracy through eliminating low quality minutiae may not be satisfactory. Therefore, the problem of making use of the less reliable information (the minutiae quality scores) to help a reliable task (fingerprint matching) is worthwhile to study. In this paper, four minutiae matching strategies were proposed to evaluate the performance of embedding the two proposed minutiae quality scoring algorithms in fingerprint verification systems. We show that only proper combinations of minutiae quality scoring algorithms and fingerprint matching schemes can practically improve fingerprint matching accuracy.

The organization of this paper is as follows. Section 2 introduces two fingerprint quality scoring algorithms used in this paper. The four matching schemes are presented in Section 3. Experimental results and analysis are described in Section 4. Section 5 is a conclusion.

2 Minutiae Quality Scoring

2.1 Minutiae Quality Scoring Based on Local Ridge Pattern (LRP) [1]

A fingerprint consists of ridges and valleys. Based on ridge patterns, we can extract minutiae, which are some special ridge line patterns. According to [1], regular minutiae consist of linked neighboring ridges that have been developed in particular direction and distance in parallel. Such features were employed to distinguish whether an extracted minutia is genuine or not [1], [4]. These ideas were then implemented in the Local Ridge Pattern (LRP) algorithm in [1].

Minutiae quality scores produced by the LRP algorithm are calculated based on statistical data of inter-ridge distance around the genuine and false minutiae. This algorithm is proposed to evaluate minutiae scores based on neighboring ridge information of minutiae detected by Binarization and Thinning approach.

Although the LRP algorithm is originally designed for ridge skeletons extracted using the Binarization and Thinning algorithm, the approximate ridge skeletons called walked map produced by Direct Gray Scale algorithm [5] may be more desirable in some cases because of its high computational efficiency. We, therefore, extend the this algorithm by using direct gray scale images as input and investigate the consistency of ridge information around a minutia in direct gray scale images instead of binarized and thinned images.

From Fig. 1b, we can notice that ridge skeletons extracted by Binarization and Thinning are more stable and regular, and thus ridge information around minutiae is more reliable and suitable for Kim's LRP algorithm. However, the ridge skeletons from extracted from direct gray scale images by "walking" along the ridges show significant dithering. The ridge skeletons showed in Fig. 1c is relatively less reliable in presenting the real fingerprint ridges.

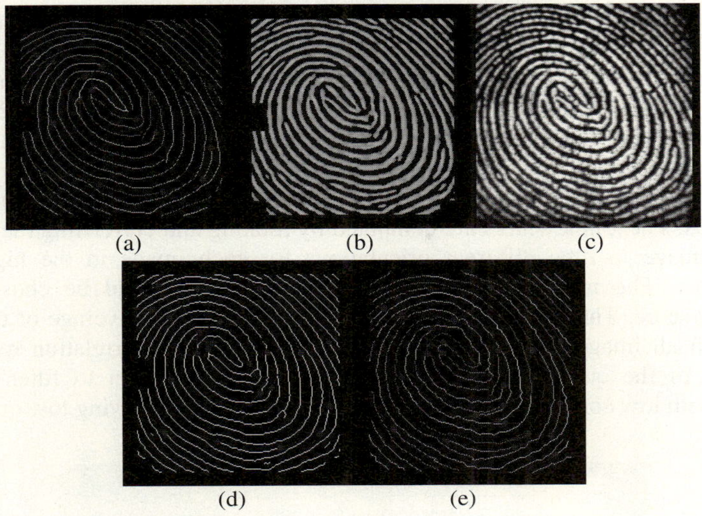

Fig. 1. (a) Original Fingerprint, (b) Ridge skeletons extracted by Binarization and Thinning algorithm, (c) Ridge skeletons extracted by Direct Gray Scale algorithm, (d) Enhanced fingerprint image using Gabor filters, (e) Ridges extracted by Direct Gray Scale algorithm after Gabor filter based fingerprint image enhancement

Considering such a difficulty, fingerprint image enhancement step for achieving more regular ridges is necessary for improving the ridge skeleton quality in the direct gray scale walked map. Among existing techniques applicable to fingerprint image enhancement, the Gabor filter based method reported by Hong et al [6] has been proven as an effective way to improve the accuracy of ridge and minutiae extraction of fingerprint images. Thus, we have applied an efficient Gabor filtering algorithm proposed in [7] before minutiae extraction and minutiae quality evaluation.

According to Fig. 1e, the ridge skeletons extracted after image enhancement is even more regular than that from the Binarization and Thinning algorithm. Therefore, the enhanced direct gray scale images are suitable for performing LRP algorithm to evaluate minutiae quality. Then the minutiae quality scores are calculated on the walked map of the enhanced fingerprint image using the LRP algorithm.

2.2 Minutiae Quality Scoring Based on Correlation with High Quality Minutiae Images (QMC)

We applied the LRP algorithm to our FP-383 database [8] and found that around 30% of the minutiae cannot be assigned with legal quality scores. Parts of these minutiae are located near the edges or core point of the fingerprint images so that inter-ridge parameters cannot be found for minutiae quality scoring because of incomplete ridge information or dramatic ridge direction changes. In order to overcome this problem, we have adopted an image correlation based approach (QMC) to address the minutiae quality scoring. The inspiration of this approach comes from the fact that correlation of fingerprints perform satisfactorily in certain matching tasks [2], [3].

Firstly a set of high quality minutiae images, which contain clear ridge patterns, was selected manually. For a given minutia, its quality score can be calculated by correlating the local image around this minutia with the high quality minutiae images selected. In the implementation of the QMC algorithm as shown in Fig. 2, we have extracted minutiae images in circular shapes. This would cause less deviation when rotating and aligning candidate minutiae images with the high quality minutiae images. After image scaling, we can extract the minutiae images with approximately equal radius. Then, nine scores are computed by rotating and correlating the candidate minutiae image to nine different orientations for each image in the high quality minutiae set. The maximum score of nine orientations would be chosen as the correlation score. The quality score of a minutia is simply the average of correlation scores with all images inside the set. Finally, by using the correlation result as an estimation of the quality of a minutia, a threshold can be set to filter out those minutiae with low correlation scores, or minutiae classified as having low qualities.

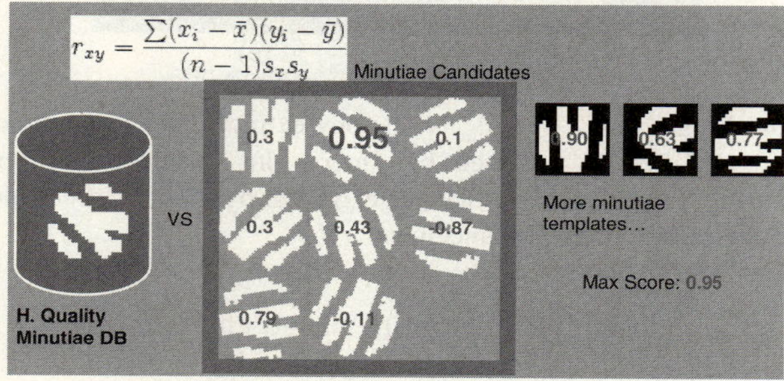

Fig. 2. Correlation method in evaluating fingerprint minutiae quality

3 Fingerprint Matching Schemes Using Minutiae Quality Scores

Many minutiae matching algorithms have been proposed [9], [10], [11]. To achieve optimum matching of different fingerprint minutiae patterns, some of these algorithms use complicated methods to shift, rotate or even deform the minutiae patterns. Nevertheless, the focus of our work is to study how the minutiae quality scores can affect the fingerprint matching accuracy. Therefore, we propose four relatively more straightforward minutiae matching strategies into which minutiae quality scores can be embedded in intuitive ways.

3.1 Basic Fingerprint Matcher (BFM)

In Basic Fingerprint Matcher (BFM), every minutia from two fingerprints will be stored in two lists accordingly. At each time, a minutia will be selected from each list. These two minutiae are the candidates to form a candidate pair. For the candidate to be matched, preliminarily, they should have a tolerable difference for the following three parameters, distance and orientation of the minutiae with respect to the core point and also the direction of the minutiae [12]. At the same time, both of their quality scores should exceed an acceptable threshold. If any one of them has a quality score less than the threshold, they will not be regarded as a matched pair.

If they satisfy the matching criterion described above, the two minutiae are matched. Then, the matching score of the two fingerprints will be increased by one and both minutiae candidates will be removed from the candidate lists. The whole process continues until one of the lists becomes empty. If more than 80% of total minutiae of two fingerprints are matched, the two fingerprints are said to be matched.

3.2 Best-Pair-Come-First Fingerprint Matcher (BPM)

This algorithm is basically a variation of BFM. The use of minutiae quality scores in this algorithm is similar to that of BFM. However, unlike the basic matcher, instead of finding a first matched pair, Best-Pair-Come-First algorithm aims at finding the best matched pair from all possible minutiae pairs. It is based on a belief that first matched minutiae pairs are not always the correct matched pairs. After it first finds a match pair similar to BFM, instead of removing them from the candidate lists, it would continue to match all other possible pairs until the pair with the highest matching score (the best matched pair) for that minutia is found. The matching process will be continued for all other minutiae.

3.3 Score Filtering Before Fingerprint Matching (SFBM)

Intuitively, high quality minutiae pairs should contribute more to the fingerprint matching score. However, in the previous two matching strategies, low quality minutiae pairs contribute equally to the fingerprint matching score. Furthermore, for low quality minutiae, their parameters may be seriously affected by image noises. Thus, it is expected for fingerprint matching to be more reliable if some of these uncertainties could be eliminated. Therefore, so as not to match minutiae with uncertain or low quality, minutiae with low quality scores will be removed before matching in BFM.

3.4 Minutiae Quality Averaging (MQA)

As we have mentioned before, around 30% of minutiae can not be scored using the LRP algorithm. However, such minutiae cannot be simply ignored as it will cause fingerprint features loss. Besides, some minutiae may have extremely low quality scores due to image noises, which is unfavorable to minutiae quality evaluation. Under the assumption that the minutiae quality within a small fingerprint area should be consistent, the quality scores of minutiae which cannot be scored or have extremely low quality scores can be approximated by averaging the quality scores of their neighboring minutiae

In this matcher, if a minutia is un-scored or having an extreme low quality score, a list of neighboring minutiae of this particular minutia will be generated within a searching radius. The quality score of each neighboring minutia will be accumulated when it is within an acceptable range. The final quality score of that minutia will be the average of all accumulated scores. After that, the minutiae will be matched as explained in BFM.

4 Experiments and Discussions

The purposes of the experiments are 1) to evaluate the discriminative power of the modified LRP and the correlation based method in evaluating the minutiae quality, 2) to investigate the effect of minutiae quality scores to the accuracy of fingerprint verification. In our experiments, we used the FP-383 database [8] which contains 1149 fingerprints from 383 users. The whole database has been manually marked with minutiae. We treat all the 14000 manually marked minutiae as the ground true minutiae, or genuine minutiae. Then we applied the minutiae extraction program proposed in [8] to FP-383. Among all the program extracted minutiae, the 8000 minutiae which cannot be corresponded to any genuine minutiae are considered as false minutiae.

4.1 Minutiae Quality Evaluation Schemes

The first part of the experiments is to test the effectiveness of the modified LRP algorithm and QMC algorithm in discriminating genuine and false minutiae. We first employed the Binarization and Thinning algorithm and the Direct Gray Scale algorithm to extract the minutiae for every fingerprint in the database. We then compared the program extracted minutiae to the genuine minutiae set. If a program extracted minutia is located within a certain distance from a genuine minutia, then, this particular program extracted minutia is said to be genuine, otherwise, it is a false minutia.

For each program extracted minutia, its quality score was calculated using the modified LRP algorithm and QMC algorithm respectively. The minutiae scores are normalized to the range from 0 to 100. Then, the cumulative probability density function (CDF) for minutiae scores of genuine and false minutiae could be obtained as shown in Fig. 3 and 4.

According to Fig. 3a, our LRP implementation with direct gray scale images achieves an error rate of 25%, which it is slightly lower than that of the original's one achieved using binarized and thinned images (29% error rate). Although the ridges appear less smooth in the direct gray scale images, the inter-ridge distances around minutiae does not deviate much because of enhancement of fingerprint images by Gabor filters.

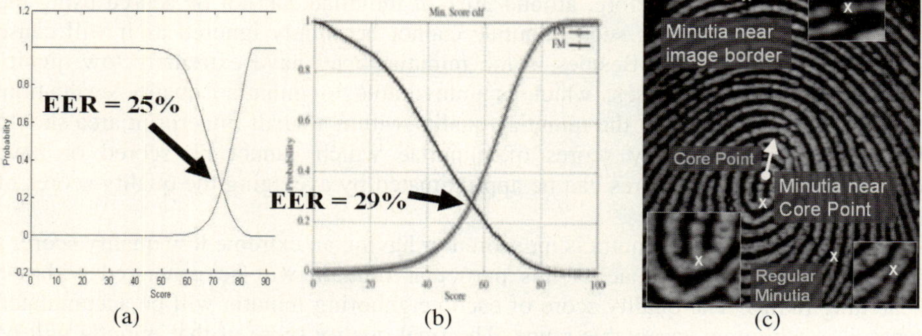

Fig. 3. CDF of Minutiae Quality Score of LRP for the genuine minutiae and false minutiae using a) walked map b) thinned image [1]. c) Examples of un-scored and scored minutiae images.

In the original LRP algorithm, 30% of minutiae are left un-scored either because they are too close to the image borders, where ridge patterns are incomplement; or because they are near to the core points, where ridge directions change dramatically, as shown in Fig. 3c. These un-scored minutiae greatly degrade the performance of distinguishing genuine and false minutiae. In our Direct Gray Scale supported LRP algorithm, Gabor filters smooth the ridge skeletons and dramatic direction changing ridges. This has caused around 40% of the un-scored minutiae in the original LRP algorithm to be scored. Thus, increase the accuracy to distinguish genuine and false minutiae.

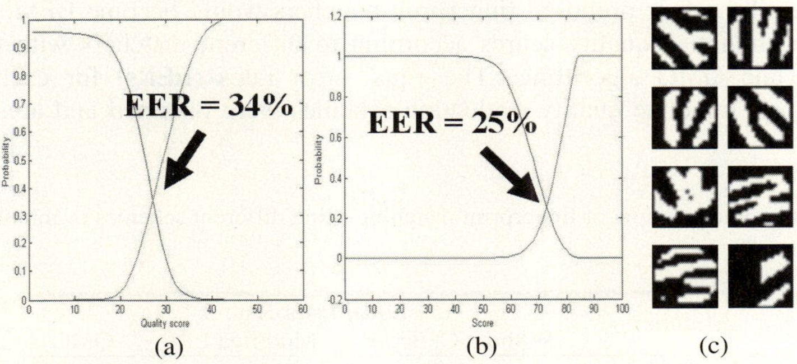

Fig. 4. CDF of Minutiae Quality Score of (a) QMC, (b) LRP with walked map, for the genuine minutiae and false minutiae. (c) Examples of high (Upper 4 images) and low (Lower 4 images) quality minutiae.

Then we applied the correlation based minutiae quality evaluation method (QMC) to the FP-383 database. The experiment steps are similar to that of the first experiment introduced above. According to Fig. 4a, the minutiae quality evaluation accuracy using QMC algorithm is generally lower than the modified LRP algorithm. The result is predictable since the templates selected cannot include all the cases of possible high quality minutiae. Moreover, correlation cannot completely reflect how alike two minutiae images are, considering incorrect alignment of two images could significantly biased the correlation result. To overcome this problem, we may compute the orientation for each minutia and then align them accordingly. This is left for further improvement of our algorithm.

Besides, the minutiae discriminative power of the modified LRP algorithm cannot be accurately described by Fig. 4b. This is because in Fig. 4b, only the 70% minutiae which can be scored are taken into account. In other words, it may not be fair to say that the modified LRP algorithm actually outperforms the QMC algorithm in distinguishing genuine and false minutiae. As mentioned before, both LRP and QMC algorithms have their own characteristics in distinguishing genuine and false minutiae. The LRP method, based on analyzing the detail ridge patterns around a minutia, is more suitable for calculating the minutiae scores for high quality fingerprint images. The fundamental assumptions of LRP are a) the ridge skeletons can be reliably extracted, b) the ridges skeletons are regular enough for extracting parameters such as the inter ridge distances. Nevertheless, the correlation based method basically has no assumption on the target fingerprint image, and therefore is more universal.

4.2 Using Minutiae Quality Scores in Fingerprint Matching

The second part of the experiments is to investigate the effect of minutiae quality scores on the accuracy of fingerprint verification. The experiments were performed in two steps. First, one-to-one fingerprint verification was performed directly on all fingerprints in the FP-383 database without consideration of minutiae quality scores. Therefore, all the four proposed fingerprint matchers would become BFM. Then, we applied the minutiae quality scores according to different matchers with the modified LRP and QMC algorithms. The equal error rates (EERs) for each matcher with different minutiae quality evaluation schemes were obtained and are shown in Table 1.

Table 1. Experiment results of fingerprint matching using different schemes of minutiae quality evaluation

Matchers	Equal Error Rate %		
	Without Q. Score	Modified LRP	QMC
BFM	4.3 %	3.8 %	**3.2 %**
BPM	4.3 %	3.7 %	**3.2 %**
SFBM	4.3 %	20.0 %	**4.0 %**
MQA	4.3 %	3.5 %	**3.1 %**

Generally speaking, the verification performance is improved after minutiae quality scores are considered. Also, according to Table 1, the correlation based method (QMC) outperforms the modified local ridge pattern method (LRP). This is because the QMC algorithm is able to assign a quality score to each minutia, while the LRP algorithm can only score minutiae with regular and clear local ridge patterns.

The degradation of the LRP algorithm due to matching strategies is even obvious in those matcher that perform quality score filtering before matching (SFBM). An extremely high EER of 20% is reported under such a strategy. The phenomenon can be attributed by the drawback of LRP algorithm - no quality score would be assigned to minutiae with incomplete neighborhood ridge information. Therefore, many minutiae, which are actually high quality minutiae, near core point and the borders of the image, are brutally filtered out. Besides, a suitable threshold is hard to obtain in order to prevent high quality minutiae from being filtered out, since the minutiae quality evaluation can only achieve 70% accuracy according to Fig. 3. Therefore, there exist many cases that only a few qualified minutiae left after minutiae filtering with the modified LRP algorithm, resulting in poor matching performance.

On the other hand, experimental results show that the correlation based method do improve the verification accuracy in SFBM. However, the EER of SFBM with QMC is slightly higher than other matchers. The threshold to classify genuine and false minutiae is again hard to define because of the close minutiae quality score distribution for two genuine and false minutiae. Therefore, a small deviation of the quality threshold could decrease the accuracy of minutiae quality evaluation noticeably.

Satisfactory results were achieved for the basic matcher (BFM) under both the modified LRP and the QMC algorithm as shown in Table 1. Again, un-scored minutiae count for the higher EER of LRP as compared to that of the QMC. Similar results were achieved in BPM. One possible reason that the verification performance under BPM is not obviously better than that under BFM is that matching score of minutiae pairs are not taken into account. The BPM strategy simply counts the number of matched minutiae pairs from two fingerprints just as BFM does. The major difference between BPM and BFM is that the minutiae correspondences are declared in different order. Taking the minutiae matching scores into account while calculating the fingerprint matching scores, may help to improve the verification accuracy of BPM.

Both LPR and QMC algorithms achieved satisfactory results in MQA. It is foreseeable as extremely low quality minutiae are smoothed to prevent extreme quality scores. However, the main concern of this algorithm is that it is applicable only to the dense minutiae regions. Therefore, there might be some room for improving MQA by studying the minutiae distribution of a fingerprint.

After analyzing the experimental results, we find that minutiae quality evaluation does not always improve fingerprint verification accuracy. The result greatly depends on the choice of fingerprint matching schemes. Therefore, before applying minutiae quality information into fingerprint matching, we should study the quality evaluation schemes and matching strategies carefully. And in our case, we achieve an optimal result by using "Minutiae Quality Averaging" scheme under the correlation based minutiae quality scoring algorithm.

5 Conclusion

In this paper, we successfully extended a minutiae quality scoring algorithm LRP to the more efficient Direct Gray Scale method for minutiae extraction. Also, we have implemented a new quality scoring algorithm based on correlation of minutiae images in order to avoid un-scored minutiae problem in LRP. The idea comes from the use of image correlation in fingerprint matching. Its accuracy is comparable to LRP despite the tremendous efforts needed to build a high quality minutiae database.

To evaluate our method for minutiae scoring, we apply the minutiae quality scores to four fingerprint matching schemes. Since we are interested in relationship between the minutiae quality scoring algorithms and different matching schemes, four straightforward matching schemes were adopted in the experiments.

From the results, we showed that the best combination comes from using the QMC minutiae quality evaluation scheme and the MQA fingerprint matcher. We believe that fingerprint matching scheme is strongly correlated to its quality scoring algorithm in terms of verification accuracy. Further study on this problem can probably be conducted using a more complicated fingerprint matchers like the triangular matching scheme [13].

Acknowledgements. This work was partially supported by the Hong Kong Research Grants Council Project 2150449, "Palmprint authentication using time series".

References

1. Kim, D.H.: Minutiae Quality Scoring and Filtering Using a Neighboring Ridge Structural Analysis on a Thinned Fingerprint Image. In: Kanade, T., Jain, A., Ratha, N.K. (eds.) AVBPA 2005. LNCS, vol. 3546, p. 674. Springer, Heidelberg (2005)
2. Krishnan, N., Fred, A.L., Padmapriya, S.: A Novel Technique for Fingerprint Feature Extraction Using Fixed Size Templates. In: IEEE INDICON Conf., India, pp. 371–374 (2005)
3. Bhanu, B., Tan, X.: Learned templates for feature extraction in fingerprint images. In: Proc. of CVPR, vol. 2, pp. 591–596 (2001)
4. Jiang, X., Yau, W.Y.: Fingerprint minutiae matching based on the local and global structures. In: Proc. of 15th ICPR, vol. 2, pp. 1038–1041 (2000)
5. Maio, D., Maltoni, D.: Direct gray-scale minutiae detection in fingerprints. IEEE Trans. on PAMI 19(1), 27–40 (1997)
6. Lin, H., Wan, Y., Jain, A.: Fingerprint image enhancement: algorithm and performance evaluation. IEEE Trans. on PAMI 20(8), 777 (1998)
7. Chen, J.S., Moon, Y.S., Fong, K.F.: Efficient Fingerprint Image Enhancement for Mobile Embedded Systems. In: Maltoni, D., Jain, A.K. (eds.) BioAW 2004. LNCS, vol. 3087. Springer, Heidelberg (2004)
8. Chan, K.C., Moon, Y.S., Cheng, P.S.: Fast Fingerprint Verification using Sub-regions of Fingerprint Images. IEEE Trans. on Circuits and Systems for Video Technology 14(1), 95–101 (2004)
9. Jain, A., Ross, A., Prabhakar, S.: Fingerprint matching using minutiae and texture features. In: Proc. IEEE Int'l Conf. on Image Processing (ICIP), Greece, pp. 282–285 (October 2001)
10. Bebis, G., Deaconu, T., Georgiopoulos, M.: Fingerprint Identification Using Delaunay Triangulation. In: International Conf. on Information Intelligence and Systems, p. 452 (1999)
11. Ross, A., Dass, S., Jain, A.: A deformable model for fingerprint matching. Pattern Recognition 38(1), 95–103 (2005)
12. Luo, X.P., Tian, J., Wu, Y.: A Minutiae Matching Algorithm in Fingerprint Verification. Proc. of 15th ICPR 4, 4833 (2000)
13. Kovács-Vajna, Z.M.: A Fingerprint Verification System Based on Triangular Matching and Dynamic Time Warping. IEEE Trans. on PAMI 22(11), 1266–1276 (2000)

Uniprojective Features for Gait Recognition

Daoliang Tan, Kaiqi Huang, Shiqi Yu, and Tieniu Tan

Center for Biometrics and Security Research,
National Laboratory of Pattern Recognition, Institute of Automation,
Chinese Academy of Sciences, Beijing, P.R. China, 100080
{dltan,kqhuang,sqyu,tnt}@nlpr.ia.ac.cn
http://www.cbsr.ia.ac.cn

Abstract. Recent studies have shown that shape cues should dominate gait recognition. This motivates us to perform gait recognition through shape features in 2D human silhouettes. In this paper, we propose six simple projective features to describe human gait and compare eight kinds of projective features to figure out which projective directions are important to walker recognition. First, we normalize each original human silhouette into a square form. Inspired by the pure horizontal and vertical projections used in the frieze gait patterns, we explore the positive and negative diagonal projections with or without normalizing silhouette projections and obtain six new uniprojective features to characterize walking gait. Then this paper applies principal component analysis (PCA) to reduce the dimension of raw gait features. Finally, we recognize unknown gait sequences using the Mahalanobis-distance-based nearest neighbor rule. Experimental results show that the horizontal and diagonal projections have more discriminative clues for the side-view gait recognition and that the projective normalization generally can improve the robustness of projective features against the noise in human silhouettes.

Keywords: Gait recognition, projective features, PCA.

1 Introduction

In a broad sense, gait means the moving style on bodies and involves dynamic and static features. Cutting and Kozlowski [3] found out from their cognitive experiments that gait can be used to recognize the identity of walking people. It is this psychological finding that inspires many computer vision researchers to pursue gait-based walker recognition.

There has thus far been a body of work in the gait recognition field. For example, Cunado et al. [2] described the motion of human legs using a model of two connected pendulums and distinguished walkers using the Fourier transform coefficients of the thigh movement in the low frequency band. Later, Urtasun and Fua [9] built on a 3D model to characterize the physical structure of human bodies and recognized unknown gait patterns with the help of a vector of 84 angles in the 3D model. By contrast, Liu et al. [5] used projective frieze patterns to represent gait signatures. In addition, Kale et al. [4] encoded human silhouette

S.-W. Lee and S.Z. Li (Eds.): ICB 2007, LNCS 4642, pp. 673–682, 2007.

gait into a group of distances in the horizontal direction. Furthermore, Wang et al. [11] employed contour-to-centroid distances to depict human figures (shapes). In particular, Veeraraghavan et al. [10] revealed that shape clues dominate gait recognition in comparison with dynamic features. On the other hand, it seems that dynamic features are susceptible to behavioral changes from the long-term point of view.

The success of shape features in gait recognition, together with the simplicity and robustness of projective frieze patterns [5], motivates us to recognize walking people through projective features in 2D human silhouettes. In this paper, we propose six projection-based features to describe human gait and compare them with frieze features to figure out which of the projective directions are important to walker recognition.

The rest of this paper is organized as follows. Section 2 introduces our method. Then, In Section 3, we examine the method on three well-known gait databases. Finally, Section 4 concludes this paper.

2 Method

Since current gait databases [1,7,8] provide segmented silhouettes apart from raw video sequences, this paper will focus on gait representation, dimension reduction, and identity recognition. First of all, we normalize each human silhouette image into a square form of 32×32 shown in Fig. 1. Then we project the normalized silhouette in four directions: horizontal ($\rightarrow$), vertical ($\downarrow$), positive diagonal ($\searrow$), and negative diagonal ($\nearrow$); we use the vector of projective values in each projection direction to represent human gait. Furthermore, we apply principal component analysis (PCA) to reduce the dimension of the original feature vector. Finally, we exploit the simple nearest neighbor rule to classify the identity of unknown gait.

2.1 Gait Representation

We can obtain eight projective representations, two of which are the same as the frieze features [5], with or without projection normalization. More specifically, given a normalized silhouette, we can evaluate for each projective direction a maximum indicating the largest number of foreground pixels in that direction and choose whether to normalize the projection by the maximum or not. In addition, this paper uses the symbols H, V, PD, and ND to denote the $\rightarrow$, $\downarrow$, $\searrow$, and $\nearrow$ projections without normalization, respectively; the normalized projections are expressed as the star versions: H*, V*, PD*, and ND*. Figure 1 illustrates the eight projective features in the form of curves.

2.2 Dimension Reduction

The aim of this step is to reduce the redundancy in the projective feature vector $x \in \mathcal{R}^n$ for the benefit of lower computational complexity. Moreover, since the distance measure used involves the second-order covariance matrix, it naturally

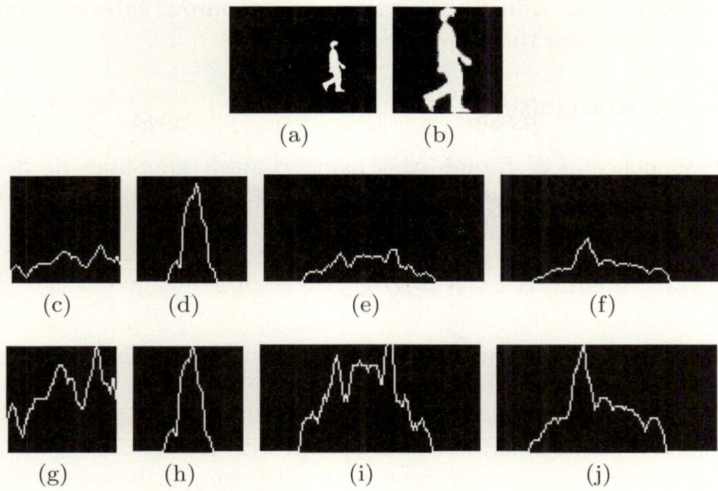

Fig. 1. Illustration of eight projective gait features. (a) Initial silhouette. (b) Normalized silhouette. (c) H. (d) V. (e) PD. (f) ND. (g) H*. (h) V*. (i) PD*. (j) ND*.

seems more favorable to perform this operation in return for the lower-order covariance matrix.

More precisely, we take advantage of PCA to accomplish this aim, since PCA has an analytical form and small computational burden. This paper presents the derivation of the PCA-transformation matrix $W \in \mathcal{R}^{n \times d}$ from the variance maximization criterion. Assume that W can be written as $W = [w_1 \ldots w_d]$ and we have known $k-1$ columns $(w_1, \ldots, w_{k-1},\ k \leq d)$. The next is to determine the remaining $d-k+1$ columns $(w_k, \ldots, w_d)$. We can concisely formulate this problem as (1):

$$\max_{w_k \in \mathcal{R}^n} var(w_k^T x) \quad s.t.\ w_k^T w_k = 1,\ w_k^T w_l = 0 \quad (l = 1, \cdots, k-1) \tag{1}$$

where k ranges from 2 to d. Furthermore, we can reduce the constrained optimization problem (1) to the unconstrained one (2) by introducing Lagrange multipliers:

$$\min f(w_k, \lambda_1, \ldots, \lambda_k) = -w_k^T C_x w_k + \lambda_k (w_k^T w_k - 1) + \sum_{l=1}^{k-1} \lambda_l w_k^T w_l \tag{2}$$

where C_x is the covariance matrix of the vector x and λ_l $(l = 1, 2, \ldots, k)$ is the Lagrange multiplier. Differentiating $f(w_k, \lambda_1, \ldots, \lambda_k)$ with respect to w_k and λ_l $(l = 1, 2, \ldots, k)$ to be zero yields that the optimal w_k and λ_k compose an eigenpair of C_x, with λ_k being the k-th largest eigenvalue of C_x. Thus the mapping W belongs to the column-orthogonal matrices (i.e., $W^T W = I$) and has as its columns $w_1, w_2, \ldots, w_d$. In this paper, we make d be the minimum number of components of x needed to explain at least a fraction 95% of the total variation of x [6]. Finally, we can project x onto a subspace spanned by the columns of W using the mapping $y = W^T x$.

2.3 Identity Recognition

For a gait sequence of N frames, this paper coarsely simplifies its description using the average feature vector $\bar{y}$ shown in Eq. (3):

$$\bar{y} = \frac{1}{N} \sum_{t=1}^{N} W^T x_t \tag{3}$$

where x_t is an original feature vector in the sequence at time t. Moreover, we employ the Mahalanobis distance to evaluate the similarity measure, since the Mahalanobis measure generally can produce a better and more robust performance in our extensive experiments, compared with the L_1, L_2, and L_∞ metric. Finally, this paper classifies the identity of unknown gait based on the nearest neighbor rule.

3 Experiments

In order to figure out which projective features or directions are important to gait recognition, we compare the performance of the eight projective features on three important gait databases: CMU Mobo Database [1], USF-NIST Gait Database [7], and CASIA Infrared Night Gait Dataset [8]. In addition, cumulative match scores (CMS) are used to quantitatively assess the recognition performance. Here the CMS value α corresponding to rank r indicates a fraction $100 \cdot \alpha\%$ of probes whose top r matches must include the real identity matches. The following will give more experimental details.

3.1 CMU Mobo Gait Database

This database consists of gait sequences—captured in an indoor scenario—from a small number of 25 subjects and records four walking conditions: slow walking, fast walking, slow walking at a certain slope, and slow walking with a ball. Figure 2 displays unnormalized sample silhouette images in the Mobo database. We carry out two types of experiments based on the side-view gait sequences in this database: within-condition tests, where the training and testing data has the same walking attribute, and across-condition tests, where the training and testing data has different walking attributes. More specifically, in the within-condition cases, this paper employs the first half part of each subject's sequence to be the training data and the remaining half sequence to be the testing data, whereas we exploit the whole sequences of each subject for training or testing in the across-condition cases [4].

Furthermore, Table 1 presents five experiments proposed by Kale et al. [4] on this database, and Table 2 compares the rank 1 performance (correct recognition

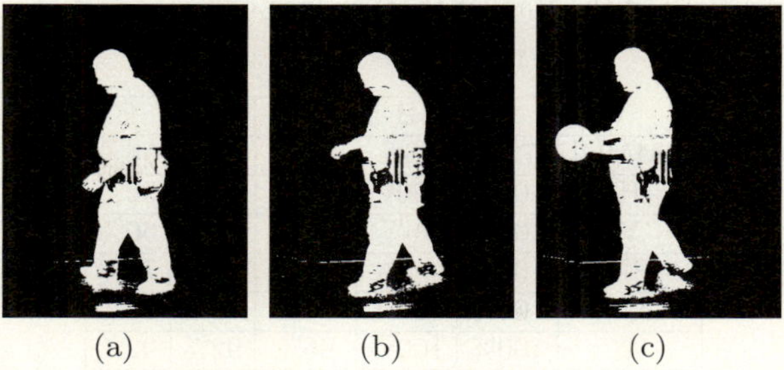

(a) (b) (c)

Fig. 2. Sample silhouette images in the CMU Mobo Database. (a) Fast walking. (b) Slow walking. (c) Slow walking with a ball.

Table 1. Five Experiments on the CMU Mobo Gait Database

Exp.	Gallery	Probe	Type
A	Slow	Slow	Within-condition
B	Fast	Fast	Within-condition
C	Ball	Ball	Within-condition
D	Slow	Fast	Across-condition
E	Fast	Slow	Across-condition

rates) of the eight projective features and the baseline method [4]. It can be seen from Table 2 that the V and V^* representations are inferior to other six projective features but comparable to the baseline method in terms of the recognition accuracy, though our method depends not on an HMM to simulate the temporal relations in the gait movement. Moreover, Figure 3 depicts the CMS curves of the eight projective gait features in the five experiments and illustrates the fast convergence of the CMS values toward the unity. In addition, the recognition in the across-condition case poses a much greater challenge than in the within-condition case owing to the variation in walking attributes. Finally, both Table 2 and Fig. 3 show that the horizontal and positive diagonal directions have more important discriminating clues.

3.2 USF-NIST Gait Database

After considering the issues about storage capacity and computational time, we make direct use of the precomputed silhouettes for the May-2001-No-Briefcase data of a moderate size in the USF-NIST Gait Database [7]. Figure 4 displays four noisy sample walker silhouettes in this database. The gait collection used in this paper includes 74 individuals and has such factors as view (left and right), footwear (two types of shoes), and ground surface (concrete and grass). Sarkar et al. [7] designed seven challenging recognition experiments shown in Table 3 for this data collection so as to benchmark the assessment of gait recognition algorithms.

Table 2. A Comparison of the Rank 1 Performance of nine gait features on the Mobo Gait Database

	A	B	C	D	E
HMM[4]	72%	68%	92%	32%	56%
H	100%	100%	96%	96%	92%
V	100%	96%	92%	44%	60%
PD	100%	96%	100%	92%	72%
ND	100%	100%	96%	72%	60%
H*	100%	100%	96%	92%	92%
V*	92%	88%	88%	32%	48%
PD*	100%	96%	96%	80%	80%
ND*	100%	100%	96%	72%	60%

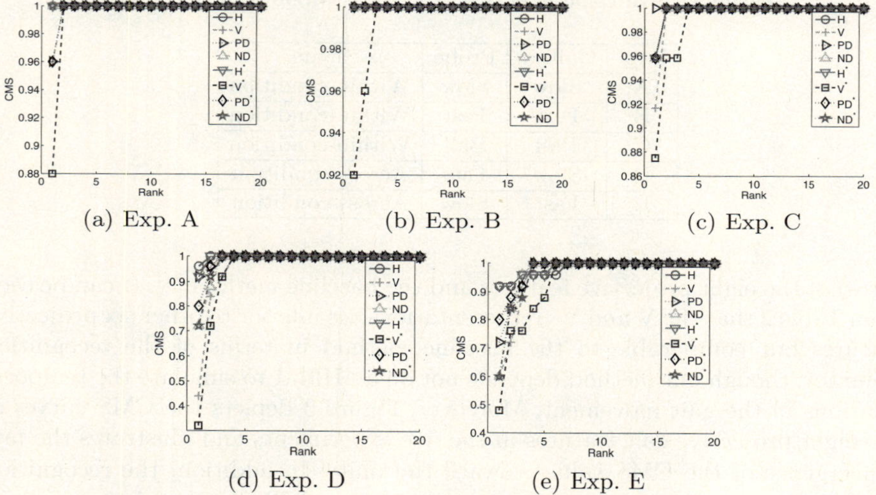

(a) Exp. A (b) Exp. B (c) Exp. C

(d) Exp. D (e) Exp. E

Fig. 3. CMS curves on the CMU Mobo Database

Figure 5 compares the CMS performance of the eight projective features and the baseline algorithm [7] denoted by BL in the legends. We can draw four points from Fig. 5. First, the projective features except for V and V* have the better recognition rates (CMS at rank 1) than BL in Exps. A, B, and C. Second, the recognition rate of BL is superior to the eight features in Exps. D, E, and F and to the → and ↓ projective features in Exp. G. Third, the normalized features are more robust against the segmenting noise (due to surface changes) than the unnormalized features in Exps. D, E, F, and G. Last but not least, the eight gait features exhibit more rapid CMS rises than the BL method.

As far as recognition results from this database are concerned, it appears that view variation has the weakest impact and ground surface types have

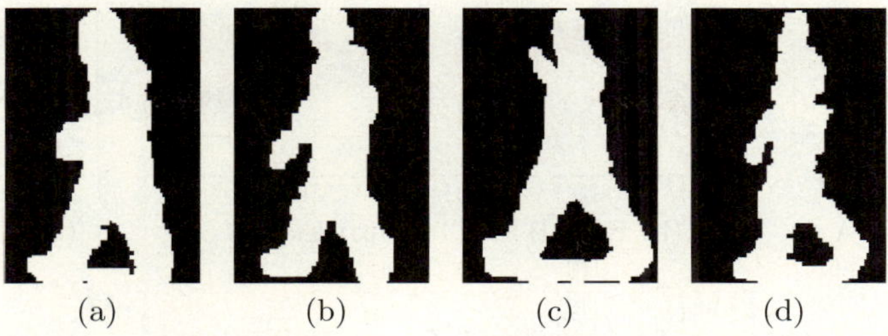

Fig. 4. Sample silhouette images from the USF-NIST Gait Database. (a) Left view on the grass surface. (b) Right view on the grass surface. (c) Left view on the concrete surface. (d) Right view on the concrete surface.

Table 3. Seven Experiments on the USF-NIST Gait Database

Exp.	Probe	Difference
A	(G, A, L)	View
B	(G, B, R)	Shoe
C	(G, B, L)	Shoe,View
D	(C, A, R)	Surface
E	(C, B, R)	Surface, Shoe
F	(C, A, L)	Surface, View
G	(C, B, L)	Surface, Shoe, View

the strongest impact on appearance-based gait recognition algorithms. The real reason for the vital effect of ground surface is, in our opinion, that surface type changes can induce great silhouette variation originating from inconsistent segmentation errors. It is this drastic silhouette changes that take the responsibility for the decline in the precision of recognition results.

3.3 CASIA Infrared Night Gait Dataset

This dataset comprises the night gait sequences of 153 subjects and takes into account four classes of walking patterns: normal walking, slow walking, fast walking, and normal walking with a bag. Each subject has ten sequences of his or her own gait: four sequences for the normal walking case and two sequences for each of the other walking cases. Figure 6 shows some unnormalized binary profile images of one person within this dataset. Furthermore, Table 4 lists four experiments on this gait dataset: we use the set of the first two normal-walking sequences of each person as the training data and the remaining sequences as the testing data. More precisely, Exp. A is concerned with the recognition performance of different projective features in the normal walking case. The purpose of Exps. B and C is to examine the effect of walking paces on recognition accuracy. Finally, the focus of Exp. D is on the degree to which appearance variation affects the gait-recognizing performance.

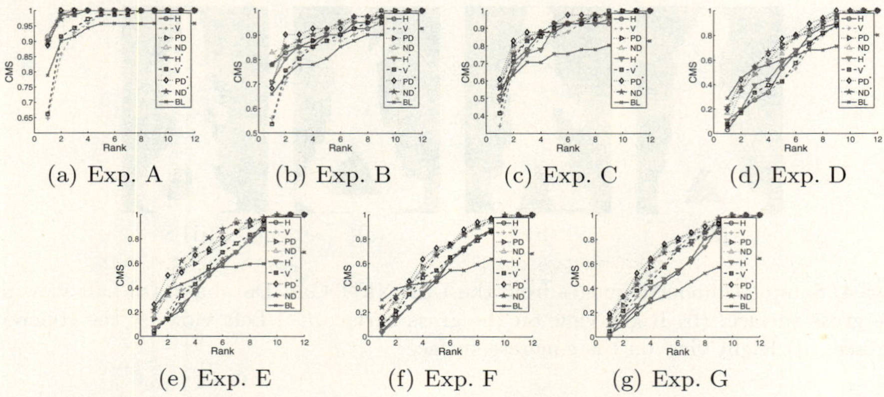

(a) Exp. A (b) Exp. B (c) Exp. C (d) Exp. D

(e) Exp. E (f) Exp. F (g) Exp. G

Fig. 5. CMS curves on the USF-NIST Gait Database

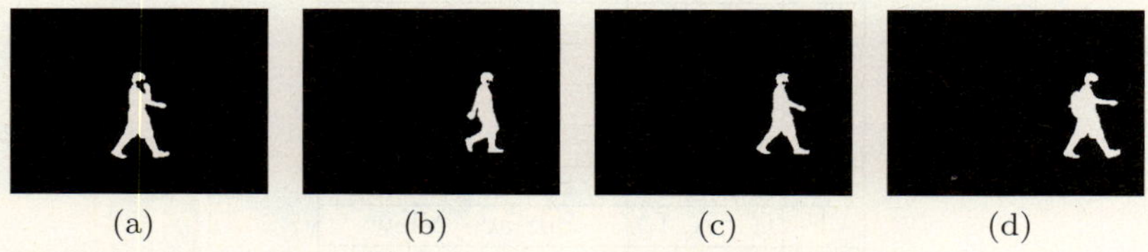

(a) (b) (c) (d)

Fig. 6. Sample silhouette images in the CASIA Night Gait Dataset. (a) Normal walking. (b) Fast walking. (c) Slow walking. (d) Normal walking with a bag.

Figure 7 delineates the CMS values in response to the rank ranging from 1 to 20. We can notice from Fig. 7 that the normalization step in projecting human silhouettes generally can improve recognition performance. Additionally, the $\rightarrow$, $\searrow$, and $\nearrow$ projections can produce more useful features than the $\downarrow$ one. Furthermore, the changes in walking attributes more or less affect the recognition accuracy due to the chain-linked appearance variation. In general, the projective gait features other than the $\downarrow$ one can yield acceptable recognition performance, in view of the large number of subjects in this gait dataset. In particular, the $\rightarrow$ features can give the best performance in the four experiments on this dataset.

3.4 Discussions

As far as the current experimental results are concerned, it seems that the $\rightarrow$, $\searrow$, and $\nearrow$ features have more discriminative clues for the side-view gait, but this does not mean that the $\downarrow$ features play a less important role in gait recognition. In fact, we found out in other experiments (omitted here) that the $\downarrow$ projections can bring good recognition performance for the frontal-view gait. In a word, there does not exist one projective feature or direction winning all the contests.

In addition, the 30° view difference [7] may be not large enough to cause great changes in appearance features and further to deteriorate recognition accuracy, according to the recent multiview gait recognition experiments by Yu et al. [12].

Table 4. Four experiments on the CASIA Infrared Night Gait Dataset

Exp.	Gallery	Probe	#Gallery Seq.	#Probe Seq.
A	Normal	Normal	306	306
B	Normal	Fast	306	306
C	Normal	Slow	306	306
D	Normal	Bag	306	306

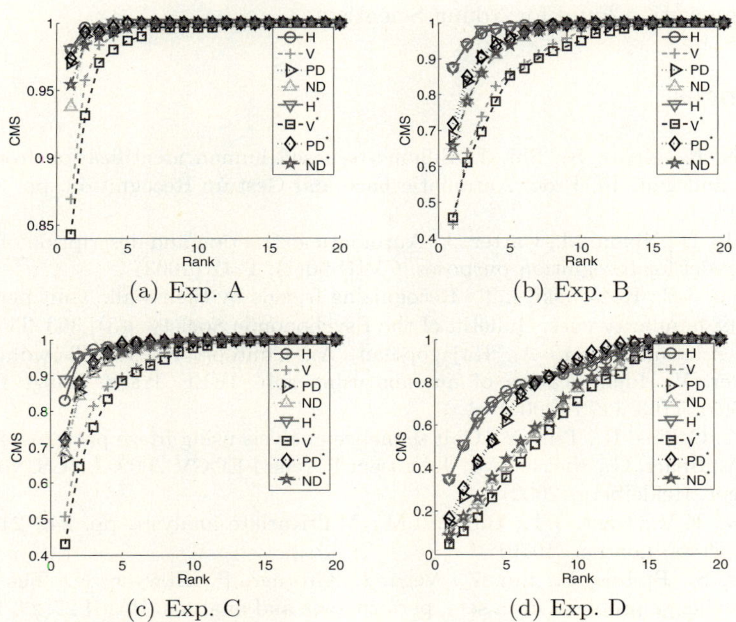

(a) Exp. A (b) Exp. B

(c) Exp. C (d) Exp. D

Fig. 7. CMS curves on the CASIA Night Gait Dataset

It is thoughtless to conclude just based on current results that surface types are more crucial than view to appearance-based gait recognition. The general point is, in our eyes, that care should be taken of those factors which have an important effect on silhouette generation.

4 Conclusions

This paper has discussed the performance of eight uniprojetive shape features for gait recognition. Experimental results show that the horizontal and diagonal projections play a more critical role in the recognition performance than the vertical projection for the side-view walking gait recognition. In addition, the projection normalization can further enhance the robustness of the projective features against the noise in human silhouettes in terms of the correct recognition accuracy. Our contribution lies in the five promising uniprojective features for gait recognition. A natural idea will be to combine these uniprojective features and make full use of their respective advantages. We will look into this issue in our future work.

Acknowledgments. This work is funded by the National Natural Science Foundation of China (Grant No. 60605014, 60332010, and 60335010), the National Basic Research Program of China (Grant No. 2004CB318110), China International Science and Technology Cooperation (Grant No. 2004DFA06900), and the CASIA Innovation Fund for Young Scientists.

References

1. Collins, R., Gross, R., Shi, J.: Silhouette-based human identification from body shape and gait. In: Proc. Automatic Face and Gesture Recognition, pp. 366–371 (2002)
2. Cunado, D., Nixon, M., Carter, J.: Automatic extraction and description of human gait model for recognition purposes. CVIU 90(1), 1–41 (2003)
3. Cutting, J.E., Kozlowski, L.T.: Recognizing friends by their walk: Gait perception without familarity cues. Bulletin of the Psychonomic Society 9(5), 353–356 (1977)
4. Kale, A., Sundaresan, A., Rajagopalan, A., Cuntoor, N., RoyChowdhury, A., Krueger, V.: Identification of humans using gait. IEEE Trans. Image Processing 13(9), 1163–1173 (2004)
5. Liu, Y., Collins, R., Tsin, Y.: Gait sequence analysis using frieze patterns. In: Heyden, A., Sparr, G., Nielsen, M., Johansen, P. (eds.) ECCV 2002. LNCS, vol. 2351, Springer, Heidelberg (2002)
6. Mardia, K.V., Kent, J.T., Bibby, J.M.: Multivariate analysis, pp. 242–243. Academic Press, London (1979)
7. Sarkar, S., Philips, P., Liu, Z., Vega, I., Grother, P., Bowyer, K.: The human gait challenge problem: data sets, performance and analysis. PAMI 27(2), 162–177 (2005)
8. Tan, D., Huang, K., Yu, S., Tan, T.: Efficient night gait recognition based on template matching. In: Proc. ICPR, pp. 1000–1003 (2006)
9. Urtasun, R., Fua, P.: 3d tracking for gait characterization and recognition. In: Proc. Automatic Face and Gesture Recognition, pp. 17–22 (2004)
10. Veeraraghavan, A., Roy-Chowdhury, A., Chellappa, R.: Matching shape sequences in video with applications in human movement analysis. PAMI 27(12), 1896–1909 (2005)
11. Wang, L., Tan, T., Hu, W., Ning, H.: Silhouette analysis-based gait recognition for human identification. PAMI 25(12), 1505–1518 (2003)
12. Yu, S., Tan, D., Tan, T.: Modelling the effect of view angle variation on appearance-based gait recognition. In: Narayanan, P.J., Nayar, S.K., Shum, H.-Y. (eds.) ACCV 2006. LNCS, vol. 3851, pp. 807–816. Springer, Heidelberg (2006)

Cascade MR-ASM for Locating Facial Feature Points

Sicong Zhang, Lifang Wu*, and Ying Wang

School of Electronic Information and control Engineering
Beijing University of Technology, Beijing, China, 100022
Tel.: 8610-67396151,
{apatroit,lfwu}@bjut.edu.cn,

Abstract. Accurate and robust location of feature point is a difficult and challenging issue in face recognition. In this paper we propose a new approach of using a cascade of Multi-Resolution Active Shape Models (C-MR-ASM) to locate facial feature points. In our approach, more than one MR-ASMs are obtained from different subsets of training set automatically, and these MR-ASMs are integrated in a cascade to locate facial feature points. Experimental results show that our algorithm is more accurate than traditional MR-ASM. The contribution of this paper includes: 1, unlike traditional MR-ASM, the training set is divided into several subsets automatically based on the principle a trained model should describe all the samples in training set accurately. 2, we propose the new cascade framework, which integrates all the subset MR-ASM.

1 Introduction

Accurate and robust location of feature point is a difficult and *challenging* issue in face recognition. Cootes et al. proposed a Multi-Resolution Active Shape Models (MR-ASM) algorithm [1], which could extract specified shape efficiently and accurately.

Because of the robustness of MR-ASM, a lot of improved algorithms have been proposed. MR-ASM is a statistic model of shape variation, and so the accuracy of estimated distribution of training samples will determine the location result. Traditional improvements of MR-ASM focus on estimating and simulating the probability distribution [2,3,4]. In fact, due to the complicated variation of training samples, it is almost impossible that the training set conform to certain clustering property. It is therefore difficult to estimate and simulate the distribution of training samples accurately [6].

In this paper, we propose an algorithm that can easily avoid this problem. Firstly, the training set is divided into several subsets automatically based on the principle that a trained model should describe all the samples in training set accurately. Then each subset is used to train a subset MR-ASM. At last, all subset MR-ASMs can represent all the samples in training set more accurately than one single model.. To locate facial

* Corresponding author.

S.-W. Lee and S.Z. Li (Eds.): ICB 2007, LNCS 4642, pp. 683–691, 2007.

feature points, all the trained subset MR-ASMs are organized in cascade, so that a face image can be represented using the most suitable model.

Our algorithm comprises two stages: training of subset MR-ASMs and location of facial feature points using cascade MR-ASMs. We first describe our procedure to obtain a subset MR-ASM at the training stage. Firstly, we use the whole training set to train a model. We then use this model to fit the training samples: we pick a subset of training samples that can be accurately represented using the trained model. This subset of training samples is then used to train a new model. The above procedure is repeated until a model is obtained that can accurately enough (at a certain precision) represent all the samples in the subset under consideration. This model is model 1 and the corresponding subset is subset 1. The whole training set excluding subset1 is used as the new training set. By repeating the above procedure, model 2 and subset 2, model 3 and subset 3,…can be obtained in sequence. When the number of samples in all the subsets is more than 97.5% of the whole training set, about 2.5% reminder training samples are trained to get the final MR-ASM （MR-ASM l） .

To locate feature points, all trained models are organized in a cascade. For an input image, the first model is used to fit it. If the texture of matched LMPs （LandMark Points） doesn't satisfy texture distribution of the training set, the second model is used, …… The procedure will continue until the texture of LMPs matched by a model satisfy the distribution of training set, the location of feature points will be obtained by the output of the model. If there is not a model (from MR-ASM 1 to MR-ASM l-1) by which the texture of output LMPs satisfy the distribution of training set, the face image will be fitted using the final model (MR-ASM l), and its output will be the location of feature points.

The following parts of this paper are organized as follows: In section 2, the training of MR-ASMs is described. In Section 3, the location of facial feature points using cascade MR-ASMs is described in details. Then experimental results are presented in section 4. Finaly, the paper is concluded in section 5.

2 Training of MR-ASMs

In our work, 98 feature points in a face image are used as landmark points (LMPs), as shown in Fig. 1.

2.1 Training Texture at Each LMP

Training texture is to extract the gray level feature in the neighbours of each LMP. The neighbour of a LMP is a rectangle area, whose long side is parallel to the normal of the LMP, as shown in Fig. 2.

The gray level of pixels inside the neighbour of the ith LMP is extracted one by one at the same order from inner face to outside, which forms a vector of gray level g_i. Two statistics mean g_i and covariance matrix Σ_i of vector of gray level g_i of all the training samples are computed respectively.

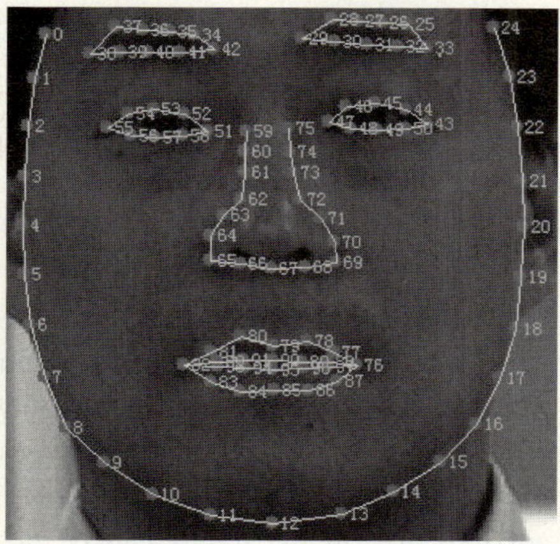

Fig. 1. Shape model in our work

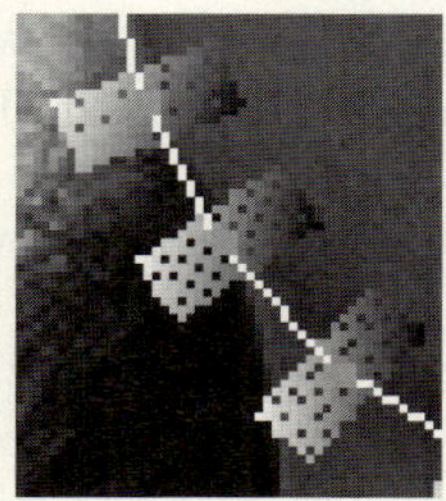

Fig. 2. Neighbour of LMPs

2.2 Training a MR-ASM

Training a MR-ASM comprises five steps [1]: 1.Labeling the training set (as Showing in Fig.2). 2. Extracting gray profile at every landmark point. 3. Aligning training set ASM. 4. Computing the statistics of aligned training set by PCA. 5. Repeat from step 1 to step 4 at each resolution level.

After these five steps, any shape X_i can be expressed as:

$$X_i = \overline{X} + P \bullet b \tag{1}$$

Where, $\overline{X}$ is the mean ASM of training set, eigenvectors P represents the most important t modes of variation, b is the vector of coefficients.

2.3 Training Subset MR-ASMs

With the traditional methods estimating and simulating the probability distribution of training set were the focus. One would expect to find one or a set of perfect description to represent the whole distribution. However in fact, it is very difficult to estimate and simulate the distribution of the whole training set [6].

Cootes et al [7] proposed a different way to solve this problem. They sorted training set into several subsets manually by the angle of the head. Samples of each subset are used to train a MR-ASM. The collection of these trained MR-ASMs as a whole represent the faces from a wide range of angles. We push Cootes's idea further in this work.

With traditional methods one model is obtained from the training set. In fact, however, due to the complicated variation of samples in training set, it is difficult to represent all training samples accurately in the training set using one model. The naïve explanation for this phenomenon is that it is difficult to observe all of the things clearly from one perspective. On the contrary if we observe different subsets of things from different angles, it is possible that all the things can be observed clearly overall. Cootes's idea is based on the above naïve understanding, where the subsets were created manually [7]. However Cootes' approach is somewhat subjective and it is difficult to justify the subsets produced. In our work, the subsets are obtained automatically, based on the principle that a trained model should describe all the training samples accurately.

The framework of our algorithm is shown as follows:

Suppose, the whole training set is N_0, the number of samples in N_0 is $Number_{N_0}$. The sequence of subset MR-ASMs is represented as L_i, $i = 0, 1, 2, ...k-1$. Let $i = 0$.

1. Suppose that there are two subsets $SP = N_i$, $SN = \{\Phi\}$,From the training set SP, we can get a trained model $M_{i,0}$ by the steps in Section 2.2, and let $j = 0$

2. Using model $M_{i,j}$ to locate the LMPs of all the samples in subset SP. Computing the displacement from labeled LMPs for every samples and the average displacement $\overline{E_{i,j}}$ in subset SP.

3. If $\overline{E_{i,j}} < C_{th}$,

It means that the model $M_{i,j}$ can represent all the samples in sebset SP, go to step5.

Otherwise,

Remove all the samples in which the average displacement of LMPs is bigger than $\overline{E_{i,j}}$ from subset SP , and insert them into subset SN .

4. Let $j = j+1$, using the training set SP , we can train a model $M_{i,j}$, go to step 2.

5. do the following operation:

$L_i = M_{i,j},\ i = i+1,\ N_i = SN$

Count the number $Number_{SN}$ of samples in SN .

If $Number_{SN} \leq 0.025 Number_{N_0}$

It means that at least 97.5% training samples have been used,, the loop should be stopped. go to step 6.

Otherwise go to step 1.

6. From subset SN , we can train a model L_{k-1}.

7. Ordering the sequence of models L_i, $i = 0,1,2,...k-1$ by the number of samples in the corresponding subset SP, so that models at the front can represent more common variation in training set.

3 Location of the Facial Feature Points

In our approach the sequence of subset MR-ASMs are organized in a cascade, as shown in Fig. 3.

The fitting result is tested using the square of Mahalanobis distance:

$$M_{dist} = \sum_{i=1}^{n} (g_i - \overline{g_i})^T \Sigma_i^{-1} (g_i - \overline{g_i}) \tag{2}$$

Where, g_i is the vector of gray level at the ith LMP, $\overline{g_i}$ is the trained mean of gray level at the corresponding LMP. Σ_i^{-1} is the inverse of covariance matrix of the corresponding LMP.

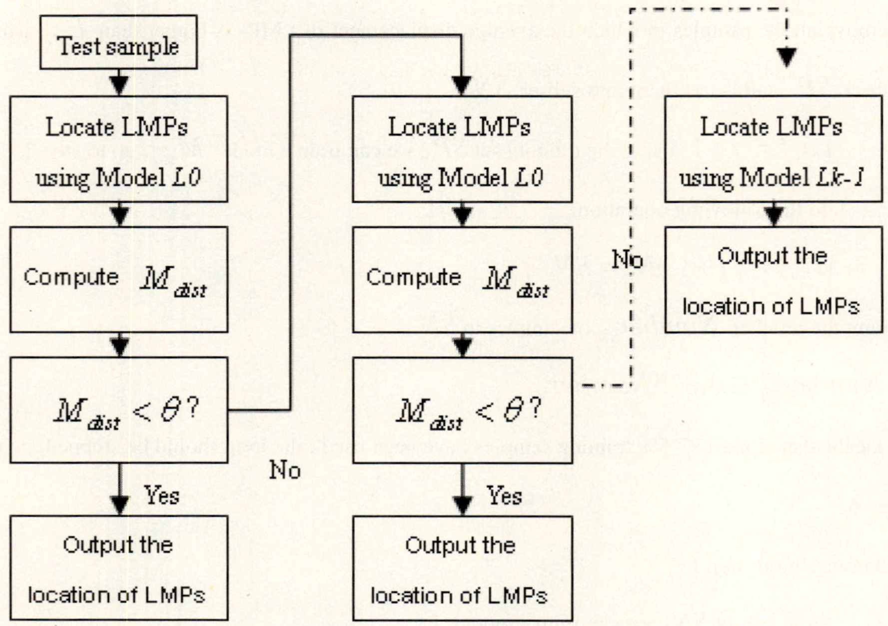

Fig. 3. The framework of feature point location

4 Experimental Results

The CMU-PIE face database is used to test the accuracy of our algorithm. A total of 153 face images of 17 people (each person uses 3 different images under 3 expressions) are chosen as training set. 36 unseen face images from the same 17 people are used as the test set. The size of images is 640×480 pixels. The average distance between two eyes is 90 pixels.

The PCA thresholds are set to 95% for every MR-ASM locators. Three gray levels are used in the MR-ASM algorithm. The length of gray profile at each LMP is set to 11 pixels. The number of searching positions is three in the both normal directions of face contour.

In the experiment, we trained five locators to compose the cascade location system. Details are shown in table 1.

Table 1. The cascade locator training information

Locator No.	Training sample selected	Location error for whole face	Location error for F.S.O.	Location error for chin
1	32	3.53	3.04	4.93
2	26	4.02	3.36	5.96
3	31	8.32	5.98	15.1
4	24	5.86	5.25	7.65
5	40	10.52	7.65	18.89

Where F.S.O. means five sense organs. Location error is measured in pixel.

Table 2 shows the first two shape parameters of each locator. It presents the main shape variation trend of each automatically selected subset of the train set.

Table 2. The shape parameters of the cascade locators

Locator No.	-3std	0	+3std	-3std	0	+3std
1	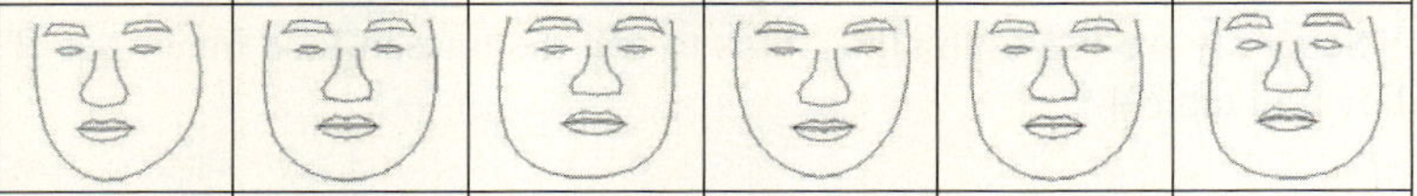					
2	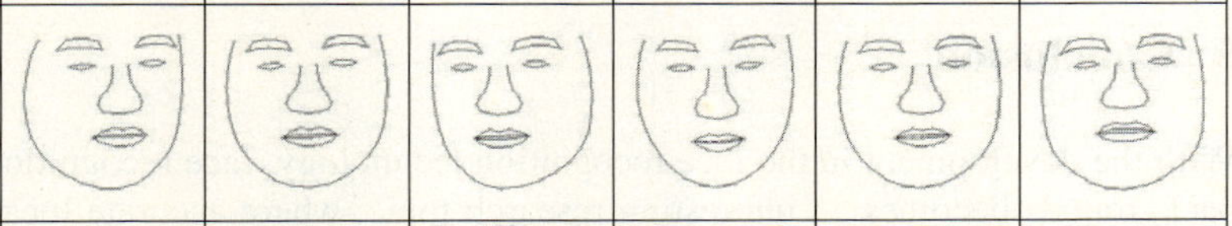					
3	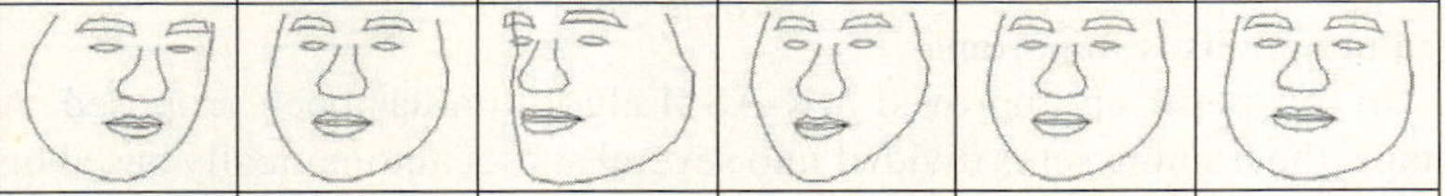					
4	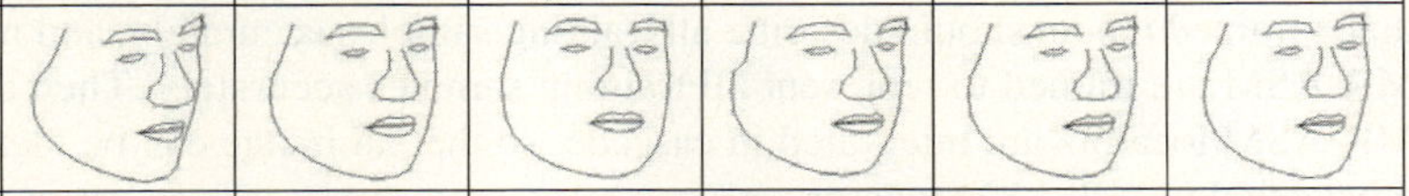					
5	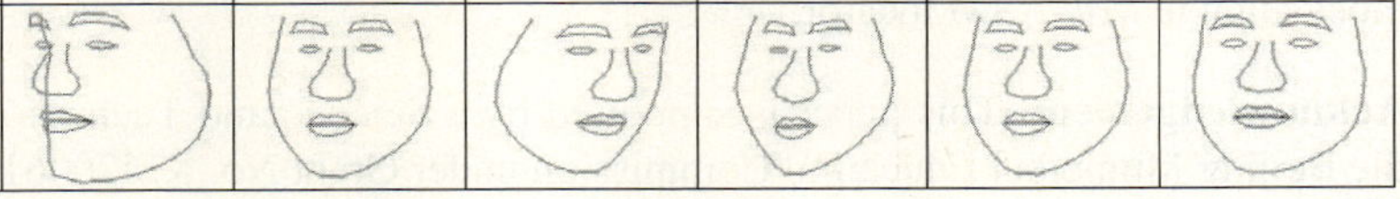					

The second to the fourth coloumns correspond to the first parameter. The fifth to the seventh coloumns correspond to the second parameter. It can be seen that different locators represent different variations of face shape.

We first compared the performance of testing the whole train set between our algorithm and traditional MR-ASM. The results are shown in table 3.

Table 3. The results compared with traditional MR-ASM for train set

	Face (pxl.)	F.S.O. (pxl.)	Cheek contour (pxl.)
MR-ASM	9.3	6.6	16.6
Our algorithm	4.98	4.00	7.32
Improvement	46.5%	39.4%	55.9%

It can be seen that, for all testing subjects, our algorithm is much more accurate than traditional MR-ASM. Further more, because of the less influence of background, the location results of eye, mouth, nose and eyebrow for both algorithms are the best. For the same reason, as to the feature points of cheek contour, both results are the worst.

Table 4. The results compared with traditional MR-ASM for testing set

	Face (pxl.)	F.S.O. (pxl.)	Cheek contour (pxl.)
MR-ASM	6.42	5.15	10.12
Our algorithm	5.53	4.65	8.11
Improvement	13.9%	9.7%	19.9%

Secondly we use both algorithms to test the unseen face image set. The results are shown in table 4.

5 Conclusion

With the development in the face recognition technology, face recognition in complex backgrounds becomes an interesting research topic, where accurate location of facial feature points is important.

In this paper an improved MR-ASM algorithm has been proposed. At the training stage, the training set is divided into several subset automatically based on the principle that a trained model should describe all training samples accurately, and more than one MR-ASM are trained to represent all training samples accurately. Then all the trained MR-ASM locators are integrated in cascade, so that an image can be identified by the most suitable MR-ASM locator.

Acknowledgement. This paper is supported by a Science and Technology project of the Beijing Municipal Education Commission under Grant No. KM200610005011 and an Academic Human Resources Development project of the Institutions of Higher Learning Under the Jurisdiction of Beijing Municipality (PHR-IHLB).

References

1. Cootes, T.F., et al.: Multi-Resolution Search with Active Shape Models. In: Pattern Recognition 1994 Conference A: Computer Vision & Image Processing Proceedings of the 12th IAPR International Conference, 9-13 October 1994, vol. 1, pp. 610–612 (1994)
2. Hu, C., Chang, Y., Feris, R., Turk, M.: Manifold Based Analysis of Facial Expression. In: Computer Vision and Pattern Recognition Workshop, 2004 Conference, 27-02 June 2004, p. 81 (2004)
3. Rogers, M., Graham, J.: Robust Active Shape Model Search for Medical Image Analysis. Medical Image Understanding and Analysis, 81–84 (August 2002)
4. Romdhani, S., Psarrou, A., Gong, S.: Learning A Single Active Face Shape Model across Views, Recognition, Analysis, and Tracking of Faces and Gestures in Real-Time Systems, 1999. In: Proceedings. International Workshop, 26-27 September 1999, pp. 31–38 (1999)
5. Viola, P., Jones, M.: Rapid Object Detection using a Boosted Cascade of Simple Features. In: Computer Vision and Pattern Recognition, 2001. CVPR 2001. Proceedings of the 2001 IEEE Computer Society Conference, vol. 1, pp. 511–518 (2001)

6. Cootes, T.F., Taylor, C., Wolfson, J.: Statistical Models of Appearance for Computer Vision. Image Analysis Unit, Imaging Science and Biomedical Engineering, University of Manchester. http://www.medicine.manchester.ac.uk/isbe/
7. Cootes, T., Walker, K., Taylor, C.: View-based active appearance model. In: Proceedings, International Conference on Automatic Face and Gesture Recognition. Automatic Face and Gesture Recognition, 2000. Proceedings. Fourth IEEE International Conference, 28-30 March 2000, pp. 227–232. IEEE Computer Society Press, Los Alamitos (2000)

Reconstructing a Whole Face Image from a Partially Damaged or Occluded Image by Multiple Matching

Bon-Woo Hwang[1] and Seong-Whan Lee[2]

[1] The Robotics Institute, Carnegie Mellon University,
5000 Forbes Ave., Pittsburgh, PA 15213, USA
bwhwang@cs.cmu.edu
[2] Center for Artificial Vision Research, Korea University,
Anam-dong, Seongbuk-gu, Seoul 136-713, Korea
swlee@image.korea.ac.kr

Abstract. The problem we address in this paper is, given a facial image that is partially occluded or damaged by noise, to reconstruct a whole face. A key process for the reconstruction is to obtain the correspondences between the input image and the reference face. We present a method that matches an input image with multiple example images that are generated from a morphable face model. From the matched feature points, shape and texture of the full face are inferred by the non-iterative data completion algorithm. Compared with single matching with the particular "reference face", this multiple matching method increases the robustness of the matching. The experimental results of applying the algorithm to face images that are contaminated by Gaussian noise and those which are partially occluded show that the reconstructed faces are plausible and similar to the original ones.

Keywords: Face reconstruction, morphable face model, SIFT feature, data completion.

1 Introduction

Reconstructing a whole face from partially damaged facial image due to occlusion or sensor noise can improve the performance of face recognition and authentication applications. Most of previous methods proposed for the purpose take advantage of the fact that face images have a certain statistical structure of shape and texture representable by a lower dimensional subspace, and that therefore once the subspace coefficients are recovered from the input (even partially impaired) the whole face can be reconstructed. The two most popular representations are the Eigenface [4][12] and a morphable model [2][3][5][6][7]; the major difference between the two is whether shape and texture are represented jointly or separately.

The most critical process of the reconstruction is to precisely align the input image to the reference image coordinates so that the subspace coefficients can be computed. The task is not trivial since the input is assumed to be partially damaged. Everson and Sirovich [4], Jones and Poggio [7] established the correspondence of the input face with the iteration of the stochastic gradient procedure. Hwang et al. proposed a

S.-W. Lee and S.Z. Li (Eds.): ICB 2007, LNCS 4642, pp. 692–701, 2007.

method for reconstructing 2D shape and texture from correspondence of a set of 2D point without iteration procedure [5][6]. Blanz et al. presented a method for inferring missing coordinates from sparse 2D or 3D feature coordinates [3]. These matching methods have limitations in that reconstruction of damaged region was obtained as only a side-effect in iterative optimization process [2][7] or in that feature points required for reconstruction should be labeled by hand [3][5][6].

In order to obtain the correspondence between the input facial image and the reference face image without human intervention, the stable and effective algorithms for extracting, describing and matching feature points are required. Matching should be robust to illumination change, noise and deformation within a single object category. One can consider use of Scale Invariant Feature Transform (SIFT) [10]. The SIFT features are invariant to image scale and rotation, and robust to affine distortion, illumination, and additive image noise. In addition to object recognition [8][9][11] in general, SIFT feature matching has been also used for face authentication [1]. However, this algorithm is applied to matching between facial images for two different persons, the number of matched feature points is typically 5 to 15 even if pose, facial expression and illumination conditions are almost identical. For the purpose of face reconstruction, the input and the reference must be matched densely.

In this paper, we present an algorithm to precisely and densely align the input partially damaged image with the reference face coordinates by extending the number of matched feature points between them. We use the morphable face model [2] for shape and texture representation of faces. An input image and the reference images are matched by using a set of example images that are generated from a morphable face model. From the matched feature points, full shape and texture for the input face are inferred from by the non-iterative data completion algorithm. We can reconstruct a facial image similar to original one even from damaged one by Gaussian noise and occluded one by an object.

2 Face Reconstruction

2.1 Face Reconstruction Procedure

If the input face matches with the single reference face, due to the large difference of appearances between the input face and the reference face, only a small number of keypoints can be matched. We prepare multiple example images that are generated from a morphable face model and store the correspondence between the generated example images and the reference face image. If the input facial image is given, the multiple matching results between the input facial image and all the example images are combined into a dense matching between the input facial image and the reference face image.

The entire procedure for reconstructing a facial image consists of 6 steps, categorized into on-line and off-line processes(Fig. 1). In the reconstruction procedure, forward and backward warping mean deformation of a texture onto each face with a shape and deformation of input face onto the defined reference face with a shape [13].

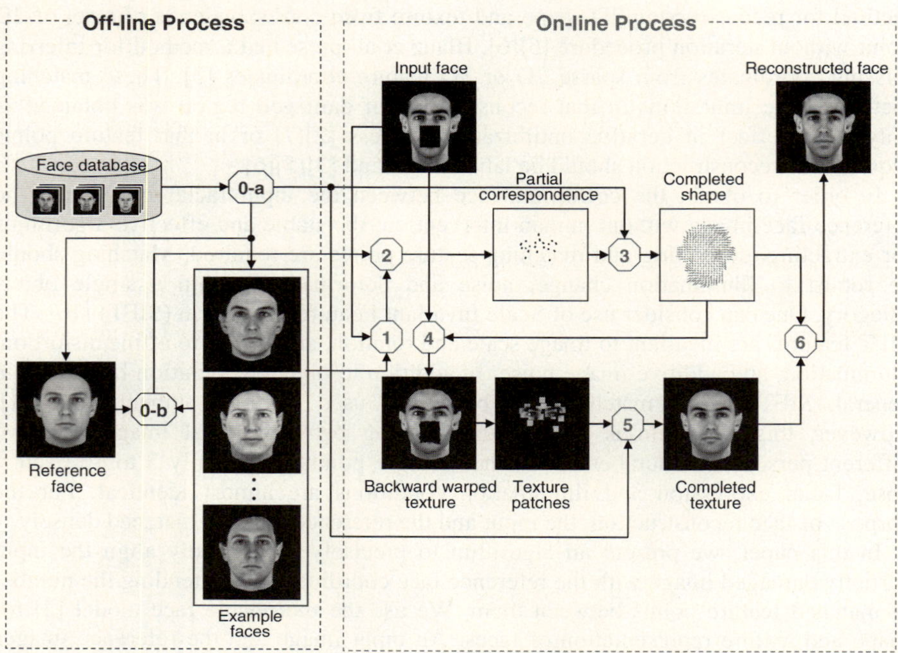

Fig. 1. Face reconstruction procedure: off-line(steps 0-a and 0-b) and on-line(steps 1 to 6) processes

- **Step 0-a:** a) Develop a morphable face model from a face database in which all facial images have dense correspondence with a defined reference face; and b) Synthesize multiple example faces by forward warping textures with shapes. Shape and texture are obtained by generating random coefficients with multivariate Gaussian distribution in the morphable face model.
- **Step 0-b:** a) Obtain SIFT descriptors at keypoints from the example faces by the SIFT algorithm; and b) Compute the corresponding points on the reference face to keypoints on the example face by triangle mesh interpolation from the shape of example face.
- **Step 1:** a) Obtain SIFT descriptors at keypoints from an input face by using the SIFT algorithm; and b) Match the SIFT descriptor of the input face with those of multiple example faces.
- **Step 2:** Obtain the correspondence between the input face and the reference face only in an internal face mask using correspondences among the input face, example faces and the reference face in Step 0-b. The internal face mask includes only main facial components such as eyebrows, eyes, a nose and a mouth and is defined on the reference face.

- **Step 3:** Complete shape from partial correspondence at the matched keypoints by using the data completion algorithm which will be described in section 2.3. The shape eigenvectors $\mathbf{S}$ in the morphable face model are exploited in this step.
- **Step 4:** a) Warp the input face to texture with the completed shape; and b) Extract $n \times n$ texture patch at each keypoint point of reference face from the backward warped texture. Other regions of the backward warped texture are masked.
- **Step 5:** Complete texture from texture patches at the matched keypoints by using the data completion algorithm which is used for shape completion. The texture eigenvectors $\mathbf{T}$ in the morphable face model are also exploited in this step.
- **Step 6:** a) Warp the completed texture with the completed shape only for the inside region defined by the internal face mask. This step results in a reconstructed facial region containing eyebrows, eyes, a nose and a mouth; b) Overlay the reconstructed facial region on the input face to evaluate the reconstruction results.

Steps 0-a and 0-b are performed as an off-line process to prepare: (1) a morphable face model for completing shape and texture; (2) SIFT descriptors of example faces for multiple matching with those of an input face; and (3) correspondence between reference face and the example face. Contrarily, steps 1 to 6 are performed as an on-line process after an input face is given.

2.2 Preparing Multiple Reference Image

By employing Gaussian random coefficients with multivariate normal distribution on the morphable face model (Step 0-a), we can generate facial images as many as required for getting enough number of keypoints matched with those for an input face. In this study, 1,000 example faces are synthesized to match with input face. SIFT descriptors of each example face are obtained at keypoints by using the SIFT algorithm and stored separately (Step 0-b). Next, the correspondence between point on the reference and a keypoint on the example face is computed by using the known shape for the example face and triangle mesh interpolation algorithm. This correspondence is saved into a "keypoint lookup table".

2.3 Matching

If an input face is given for the reconstruction, the SIFT descriptors at keypoints are obtained and matched with those of multiple example faces by using SIFT matching algorithm (Step 1). This on-line multiple matching allows getting point on the reference face corresponding to a keypoint on the input face using the "keypoint lookup table". If a keypoint on the input face corresponds to that on the example face, the counter for corresponding point of reference increases. The counter for each keypoint on the reference face is accumulated for all example face to select the best matched point on the reference face. A single point on the reference face may have several corresponding points on the input face because the input face is matched with multiple example faces. By selecting the point with the largest value, accurate correspondence can be obtained. If the second largest value for the keypoint is greater than the given threshold multiplied by the largest one, this keypoint is rejected similar to Lowe's SIFT matching strategy for the stability of the matched keypoints(Step 2) [11].

It is assumed that the input faces are roughly aligned and normalized by translation, rotation and scale by a face detector. Therefore, if the distance of a matched keypoint in common image coordinate is larger than the given threshold, this is excluded from the list of the matched keypoints. After eliminating the incorrect keypoints, we estimate three parameters, translation, rotation and scale, for the input face by minimizing L2-norm of difference vector of matched points' coordinates. The input face is normalized by using the estimated parameters.

Fig. 2 shows matching between an input face and the reference face by matching the input face with the synthesized multiple example faces. The blue and red dots in Fig. 2 represent the position of SIFT keypoints. The correspondences from keypoints(blue dots) on the example face to points on the reference face are represented by blue dashed arrows and the correspondence from keypoints(red dots) on the input face to those on the example face are represented by red solid arrows. In our experiments, more than 30 keypoints are finally matched between the input face and the reference face even if an input face is damaged by a virtual object(about 10% of face region) or Gaussian noise(standard deviation of 20). These are enough to reconstruct a quite plausible face (Fig. 3)

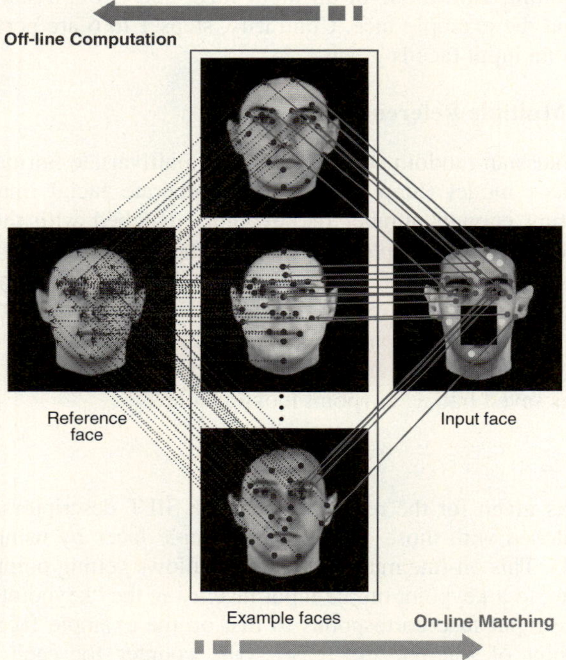

Fig. 2. Indirect matching between the reference face and an input face by using example faces

2.4 Reconstruction

By using defined reference face and pixelwise correspondences between given facial images and the reference face, facial images can be separated into shape and texture[13]. With the shape S and the texture T separated from the facial image, we fit a multivariate normal distribution to a data set of faces. This is based on the mean of shape, $\overline{S}$ and that of texture $\overline{T}$, covariance matrices $\sum_S$ and $\sum_T$ computed over the differences of the shape and texture:

$$X^S = S - \overline{S}\,,\ X^T = T - \overline{T} \tag{1}$$

By Principal Component Analysis(PCA), a basis transformation is performed to an orthogonal coordinate system formed by eigenvectors S_i and T_i of the covariance matrices, $\sum_S$ and $\sum_T$ on our data set of m faces.

$$S = \overline{S} + \sum_{i=1}^{m-1} c_i^S S_i,\ T = \overline{T} + \sum_{i=1}^{m-1} c_i^T T_i, \tag{2}$$

where $C = (c_1, c_1, \cdots, c_{m-1}) \in \Re^{m-1}$. σ_i^S and σ_i^T are standard deviations within the shape and texture along the eigenvectors S_i and T_i. The dimension of the space spanned by S_i and T_i is at most $m-1$.

To reconstruct a facial image from the obtained correspondence at SIFT keypoints, we can apply two methods: (1) shape and texture reconstruction method using a set of 2D point coordinates[5] and (2) the 3D extended and regularized method[3] of the method (1). In this paper, the latter method is selected due to the robustness and the stability of reconstruction.

The barycentric shape vector X^S is defined by the set of the scaled eigenvector $\sigma_i S_i$ and coefficients c_i :

$$X^S = \sum_{i=1}^{m-1} c_i \sigma_i S_i = \mathbf{S} \cdot diag(\sigma_i) C \tag{3}$$

The data selection matrix, $\mathbf{P}: \Re^n \rightarrow \Re^p$ is also defined for representing shape corresponding to the keypoints on an input face. p is the number of matched keypoints. $\mathbf{P}$ is a linear mapping that select a subset of components from an entire vector. Using the data selection matrix $\mathbf{P}$, partial shape vector, F corresponding to the keypoints is represented by

$$F = \mathbf{P}S - \mathbf{P}\overline{S} = \mathbf{P}X \tag{4}$$

The reduced version of the scaled eigenvectors, $\mathbf{Q}$ is also defined as:

$$\mathbf{Q} = \mathbf{PS}diag(\sigma_i) \in \Re^{p \times (m-1)} \tag{5}$$

According to the number of keypoints, p and the number of eigenvectors, solution of Equation (4) may be not unique. In order to find optimal coefficients for linear combination of the basis vectors, we minimize the cost function, E, which is given as:

$$C^* = \arg\min_C E(C), \qquad E(C) = \|\mathbf{Q}C - F\|^2 + \kappa \cdot \|C\|^2 \tag{6}$$

where $\kappa \geq 0$ is a regularization factor. This regularization factor derived from a statistical approach provides the stability and robustness to noise by controlling the tradeoff between fitting accuracy and plausibility[3].

The optimal solution C^* is obtained by Singular Value Decomposition $\mathbf{Q} = \mathbf{UWV}^T$ with diagonal matrix $\mathbf{W} = diag(w_i)$ [3].

$$C^* = \mathbf{V} diag\left(\frac{w_i}{w_i^2 + \kappa}\right)\mathbf{U}^T F \tag{7}$$

The completed shape can be obtained from (1) and (3):

$$S = \overline{S} + S \cdot diag\ (\sigma_i)\mathbf{V}\, diag\left(\frac{w_i}{w_i^2 + \kappa}\right)\mathbf{U}^T F \tag{8}$$

From Equation (8), we can get the complete correspondence for all pixels. Similarly, we can reconstruct complete texture T. From the complete shape and texture, facial image can be synthesized by forward warping.

2.5 Summary of the Process

If an input facial image is given, the partial correspondences between the input face and the reference face are obtained by using multiple matching and a "keypoint lookup table". The partial correspondences are completed to full shape by the data complete algorithm. From the input face image and the completed shape, the backward warped texture is generated and extract texture patch at each keypoint from the texture. The completed texture from texture patches is obtained by using the same data completion algorithm which is used for shape completion. The completed texture is warped with the completed shape to the reconstructed facial image.

3 Experimental Results

3.1 Face Database

Two hundred of 2D faces were used to test and validate the proposed method. These images were rendered with only ambient light using a database of three-dimensional head models recorded with a laser scanner (CyberwareTM) [2][13]. The resolution was 256 by 256 pixels and the color images were converted to 8-bit gray level images. One hundred of facial images in the database were randomly selected to generate a morphable face model by PCA. The other 100 images were used to test our reconstruction algorithm. The test sets were strictly separated from training tests in our experiments.

3.2 Face Reconstruction

If a facial image is given, facial image are reconstructed by the on-line procedure described in section 2.1. Fig. 3 shows the reconstructed examples for two persons.

The facial images for each person are reconstructed from an original face, a damaged face by Gaussian noise and an occluded face by a virtual object, respectively. The damaged faces by Gaussian noise are generated by adding the Gaussian noise with standard deviation of 20 to the original image. The size of the virtual object is 60×60 pixels(about 10% of internal face region) and its position is restricted to the inside of the face in order to occlude facial components such as eyes, a nose and a mouth. Although input faces are damaged by Gaussian noise(left , center in each face group) or occluded by virtual objects(left, bottom), the reconstruction results(right, middle and right, bottom) from them are very similar to original faces(left, top) or the reconstructed faces(right, top) from original faces.

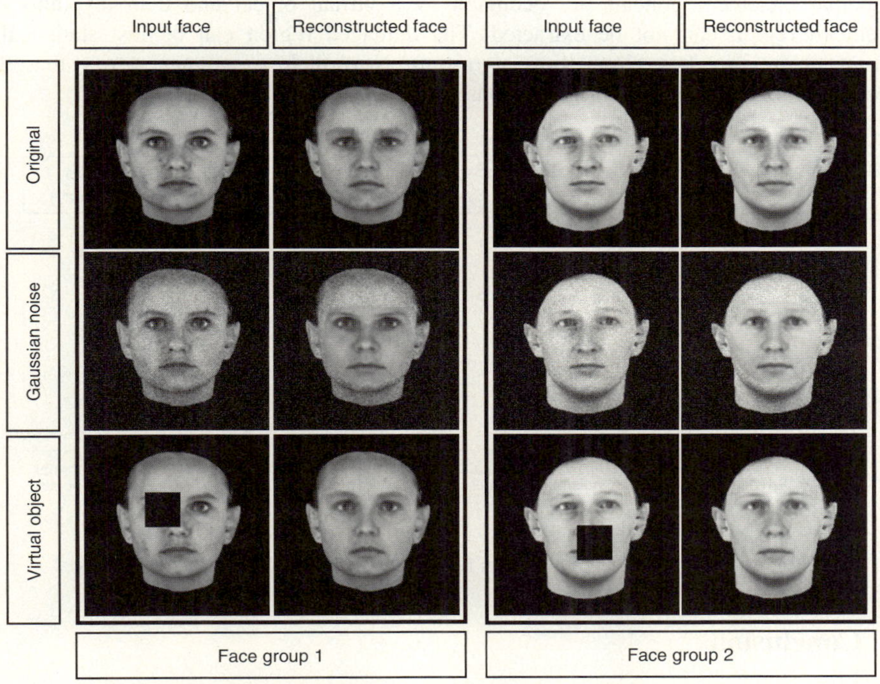

Fig. 3. Examples of input faces and reconstructed faces

Fig. 4 shows the mean reconstruction errors for shapes, textures and synthesized images. Horizontal axis of each graph indicates the type of input for reconstruction face except PCA projection. In the case of PCA projection, we get the projected shape and texture for test faces to the shape and texture eigenvector space, $\mathbf{S}$ and $\mathbf{T}$, and the synthesized image from the projected shape and texture by forward warping. Vertical axes of the graphs are the mean displacement error per pixel and the mean intensity error per pixel (for an 8 bit gray scale image), respectively. Err_S_x and Err_S_y in Fig. 4a imply the x-directional and the y-directional mean displacement error for shape, respectively. Err_T and Err_I in Fig. 4b imply the mean intensity errors for texture and image, respectively.

The case of PCA projection naturally shows the minimum errors in the graphs because they contain the errors occurred by only PCA projection. The reconstruction errors in a damaged face by Gaussian noise do not increase much due to the stability of SIFT descriptor and the robustness of our indirect matching algorithm using the SIFT descriptors. The differences in the reconstruction errors from an original face and a damaged face by Gaussian noise are 0.03(x-direction) and -0.02(y-direction) for shape, 2.25 for texture, and 1.48 for image while the reconstructions from an original face and an occluded face by virtual object causes the differences in the error by 0.08(x-direction) and 0.05(y-direction) for shape, 3.26 for texture and 3.60 for image. This reveals that the errors of occluded faces by a virtual object tend to be relatively higher than the errors of damaged faces by Gaussian noise. The possible reasons for this result are that the principal facial components are occluded by a virtual object and that keypoints on occluded region can not be extracted. The damaged region can be just statistically estimated by the data completion algorithm. Nevertheless, we can verify that the occluded face regions are plausibly reconstructed by the proposed method(Fig. 3).

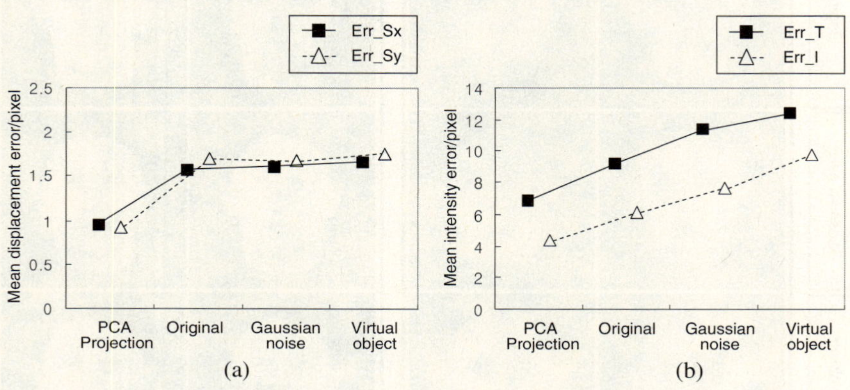

Fig. 4. Mean reconstruction errors for shape, texture and synthesized images

4 Conclusion

This paper present an automatic algorithm to align the input partially damaged image with the reference face by extending the number of matched feature points between them. It has been a challenge for many researchers to obtain the correspondences between two faces when one face of them is damaged by an objects or sensor noise. The proposed matching technique provides the enough number of the matched feature points and the accurate correspondence between an input face and the defined reference face by matching the input face with multiple example faces synthesized by the morphable face model. From the matched feature points, full shape and texture for the input face are inferred by the non-iterative data completion algorithm. The proposed methods were tested and evaluated in three types of test sets: original faces, damaged faces by Gaussian noise and occluded faces by a virtual object. The experimental results showed that the reconstructed faces are plausible and similar to original faces.

Our approach will be tested for facial images including real objects such as sunglasses, a gauze mask and hands, and camera sensor noise. In addition, face reconstruction in various pose, facial expression and illumination condition is also considered as future works. We expect that the proposed method be applied to various practical applications such as face recognition and authentication system.

Acknowledgments. This work was supported by the Korea Research Foundation Grant(KRF-2005-000-10384-0). We would like to thank Prof. Takeo Kanade for his helpful discussions and advices. In addition, we also thank the Max-Planck-Institute for providing the MPI Face Database.

References

1. Bicego, M., Lagorio, A., Grosso, E., Tistarelli, M.: On the Use of SIFT Features for Face Authentication. In: Proc. of IEEE Conference on Computer Vision and Pattern Recognition Workshops, June 2006, p. 35 (2006)
2. Blanz, V., Vetter, T.: Morphable Model for the Synthesis of 3D Faces. In: Proc. of SIGGRAPH '99, Los Angeles, USA, August 1999, pp. 187–194 (1999)
3. Blanz, V., Mehl, A., Vetter, T., Seidel, H.-P.: A Statistical Method for Robust 3D Surface Reconstruction from Sparse Data. In: Proc. of International Symposium on 3D Data Processing, Visualization and Transmission, Thessaloniki, Greece, September 2004, pp. 293–300 (2004)
4. Everson, R., Sirovich, L.: The Karhunen-Loeve Transform for Incomplete Data. Journal of the Optical Society of America A. 12(8), 1657–1664 (1995)
5. Hwang, B.-W., Blanz, V., Vetter, T., Song, H.-H., Lee, S.-W.: Face Reconstruction from a Small Number of Feature Points. In: Proc. of International Conference on Pattern Recognition, Barcelona, Spain, September 2000, vol. 2, pp. 842–845 (2000)
6. Hwang, B.-W., Lee, S.-W.: Reconstruction of Partially Damaged Face Images Based on a Morphable Face Model. IEEE Transaction on Pattern Analysis and Machine Intelligence 25(3), 365–372 (2003)
7. Jones, M.J., Poggio, T.: Multidimensional Morphable Models: A Framework for Representing and Matching Object Classes. International Journal of Computer Vision 29(2), 107–131 (1998)
8. Lowe, D.G.: Object Recognition from Local Scale-Invariant Features. In: Proc. of International Conference on Computer Vision, Corfu, Greece, September 1999, pp. 1150–1157 (1999)
9. Lowe, D.G.: Local Feature View Clustering for 3D Object Recognition. In: Proc. of IEEE Conference on Computer Vision and Pattern Recognition, Hawaii, USA, December 2001, pp. 682–688 (2001)
10. Lowe, D.G.: Distinctive Image Features from Scale-Invariant Keypoints. International Journal of Computer Vision 60(2), 91–110 (2004)
11. Mikolajczyk, K., Schmid, C.: A Performance Evaluation of Local Descriptors. IEEE Transactions on Pattern Analysis and Machine Intelligence 27(10), 1615–1630 (2005)
12. Turk, M., Pentland, A.: Eigenfaces for Recognition. Journal of Cognitive Neuroscience 3(1), 71–86 (1991)
13. Vetter, T., Troje, N.E.: Separation of Texture and Shape in Images of Faces for Image Coding and Synthesis. Journal of the Optical Society of America A 14(9), 2152–2161 (1997)

Robust Hiding of Fingerprint-Biometric Data into Audio Signals

Muhammad Khurram Khan[1,2], Ling Xie[2], and Jiashu Zhang[2]

[1] Research Group for Biometrics & Security Engineering,
Bahria University, Dept. of Computer Science & Engineering,
13- National Stadium Road, Karachi, Pakistan
khurram.khan@scientist.com
[2] Sichuan Key Lab of Signal & Information Processing,
Southwest Jiaotong University, Chengdu 610031, China

Abstract. This paper presents a novel fingerprint-biometric template protection scheme, in which templates are concealed into audio signals. Fingerprint templates are encrypted by chaotic encryption and then hid into the chaotically selected random sampling points of the host audio signal by a new non-uniform discrete Fourier transform (NDFT)-based data hiding method. The template extraction process is completely blind and does not require original audio signal, thus the extraction depends on the secret key. Experimental results show that the proposed scheme is robust against common signal processing attacks and achieves higher verification accuracy.

1 Introduction

With the recent advances of internet, the security and privacy issues in authentication systems have raised an important research concern. Applications such as electronic banking, e-commerce, m-commerce, ATM, and smart cards etc. require high attention of data security either data is stored in the database/token, or flow over the network. The implementation of automatic, robust, and secure person identification has become a hot research topic [1]. Traditional ID, PIN, and password-based authentication systems have been widely used for long time to authenticate a claimed identity [2]. The knowledge-based [password or personal identification number (PIN)] and token-based [ID card] identification systems are not secure enough, because passwords can be guessed or hacked, and ID cards can be stolen or lost. Only the citizens of USA loss more than 450 million dollars per annum because of credit card fraud [2].

The drawbacks of traditional identification systems have drawn attention towards secure and unique authentication method, in which biometrics has shown itself an emerging cutting edge identification and authentication technology. Biometric refers to identifying a person on the basis of his physiological or behavioral characteristics [1-4]. It includes fingerprint, hand geometry, palm print, voice, face, and iris recognition etc [3]. Among all the biometrics e.g., fingerprint, iris, face, hand geometry, retina, signature, keystroke dynamics, etc; fingerprint-based authentication is the most mature, proven, and widely used technique around the world [4].

S.-W. Lee and S.Z. Li (Eds.): ICB 2007, LNCS 4642, pp. 702–712, 2007.

Biometric indicators have an advantage over traditional security identification methods, because these inherent attributes cannot be easily shared and every person has unique biometric-attributes [5]. Biometric is of interest in any area where it is important to verify and authenticate the true identity of an individual. Biometric technologies are gaining more attraction because of secure authentication methods for user access, e-commerce, remote authentication, and access control. Biometric provides uniqueness, but the dilemma is that it is not secret and has some risks of being hacked, modified, and reused [6,7]. The integrity of biometric templates/data become more critical whenever it is sent over the network, so there is a need to protect biometric data from different attacks. The reliability and user acceptance of a biometric system depends on the effectiveness and the security of the system against intruders, unauthorized modification, and misuse [6-9]. A biometric-based verification system works properly only if the verifier system can guarantee that the templates come from the valid and legitimate user at the time of enrollment [8]. Although, there is a lot of work done in the pattern recognition and matching of biometric systems, unfortunately only few papers adhere to the security issues inherent with them. To promote worldwide implementation of biometric techniques, an increased security and secrecy of its data are necessary [6].

1.1 Related Work

Recently some techniques based on encryption, watermarking, and data hiding are proposed for the security and secrecy of biometric templates or data. Among the published techniques for biometric encryption, first, Davida et al. [10] proposed a study on the feasibility of protecting the privacy of a user's biometric data on an insecure storage device. They suggest that providing additional privacy for the biometric data may provide stronger user acceptance. In their second work [10], they utilize the error correction codes and explain their role in the cryptographically secure biometric authentication scheme. They save the error correcting codes in the database, which leaks some information of user's biometric template, thus makes their system vulnerable. To enhance Davida's work, Soutar et al. [12,13] proposed an optical correlation-based fingerprint system, which binds a cryptographic key with the user's fingerprint images at the time of biometric enrollment. The cryptographic key is then retrieved only upon a successful identification. Later on, Andy [14] presented a scheme that appears to show vulnerabilities in Soutar et al.'s system. Andy's system extracts the secret code by applying hill-climbing attack on the enrolled image, which is then used to decrypt that code. Tuyls et al. [15-17] have also presented good work on the protection of biometric templates by quantizing secret extraction from significant components of the biometric traits. But, their system has less practicality and is sensitive to invariance, as mentioned in [18]. Uludag et al. [18] presented a comprehensive analysis on the biometric cryptosystems issues and challenges, and compared the performances of the biometric security pitfalls. This is a nice study on the security issues of the biometric systems.

On the other hand, digital watermarking and data hiding is also explored to secure the biometric data. At the beginning, Yeung-Pankanti [19] researched and presented the effects of watermarking fingerprint images on the overall system recognition and retrieval accuracy using an invisible fragile watermarking scheme for image verification applications on a fingerprint identification system. Yeung-Pankanti identified that using watermarking in the fingerprint images can provide a value-added protection and security, as well as copyright notification capability, to the fingerprint data collection processes and its usage. Their technique checks the watermark in the fingerprint images and verifies their integrity. Their scheme is useful before performing the identification, because system can check the fragile watermark embedded in the fingerprint images, but unfortunately it scheme can not be used for the secure transmission of biometrics over insecure network or communication channel.

In 2000, Sonia [20] investigated on a local average method where an executable compares block-by-block local average of the transmitted and the received image over the network. But this method does not provide or elaborate detailed experiments on the watermarked image, and Sonia did not give any signal or image processing attacks on her method during the transmission.

In 2002, Gunsel et al. [7] proposed two spatial domain-watermarking schemes. Their first scheme utilizes an image adaptive strength adjustment technique to make low visibility of embedded watermark, while their second method uses feature adaptive watermarking technique and is applicable before feature extraction. The pitfall of their system is that they did not perform encryption of watermarking data, so their method is susceptible to attack in case if an adversary extracts biometric template from the transmitted image over insecure network.

Recently, Jain-Uludag [6] published two application scenarios based on amplitude modulation watermarking method for hiding biometric data. Their first application is based on steganography, while another is embedding the facial data in fingerprint images. Their both applications embed the biometric template without performing encryption so it could also have the risk of biometric data copy attack [9] incase if an adversary is able to extract it from the transmitted host image. In addition, Jain-Uludag did not perform experiments for different kinds of noises and attacks on their method, so it is difficult to measure the performance of their system under different conditions over the network.

The problems of biometric template security raise concerns with the wide spread proliferation and deployment of biometric systems both commercially and in government applications, especially when its data flow in the air. So by keeping security and secrecy issues in concern for the template security enhancement, in this paper, we present a novel chaos and NDFT (Nonuniform Discrete Fourier Transform)-based biometric data hiding technique in the audio signals. For the experiments, we use fingerprint-biometric as a reference biometric because of its large-scale utilization in commonly used biometric-based authentication systems [1,4]. Fingerprint templates are encrypted by chaotic encryption, encoded by BCH codes, modulated by chaotic parameter modulation (CPM) scheme, and then hid by chaotically selected random frequency points in the original audio signal. Encryption and modulation of fingerprint templates, and chaotically selected hiding frequency points using secret key ensure the robustness against steganalysis attack [21]. Furthermore, proposed method is blind-hiding method and does not require original audio signal for the fingerprint template extraction at the server end. Experimental and simulation results show that the presented scheme: (i) accomplishes perceptual transparency, after template hiding, by exploiting the masking effects of the human auditory system (HAS), (ii) shows robustness against attacks, (iii) secure by using secret keys, (iv) and efficient in speed and hidden-template decoding performance.

2 Proposed Scheme

2.1 Template Generation and Encryption

Our proposed scheme is depicted in Figure 1. Fig. 1(a) delineates the fingerprint template hiding method, and Fig. 1(b) shows the template extraction process at the server end.

The presented scheme starts with capturing fingerprint images from the sensor. In the proposed scheme, fingerprint images are preprocessed by the image processing and pattern recognition algorithms. Fingerprint features are extracted by the Gabor filter bank-based technique [4]. The extracted feature vector is composed of both the global and local characteristics of ridges and valleys of fingerprint image. The extracted fingerprint-biometric feature vector $x \in R^M$ is reduced down to a set of single bits $b \in \{0,1\}^N$ where, N is length of the bit string; in actual it is the template size of the extracted fingerprint [4].

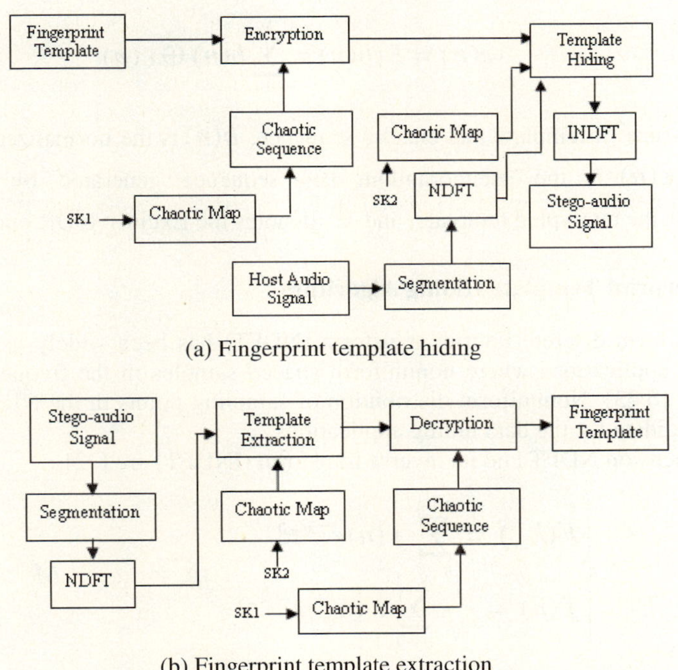

(a) Fingerprint template hiding

(b) Fingerprint template extraction

Fig. 1. Proposed fingerprint template hiding scheme

After feature extraction, fingerprint-biometric template is encrypted by chaotic encryption method. For the encryption, we employed skew tent map, which is a piecewise-linear Markov chaotic map that shows superiority against the some widely used pseudorandom sequences and have controllable correlation properties [5].

$$s(x)=\begin{cases}\frac{1}{a}x, & 0\le x\le a\\ \frac{1}{a-1}x+\frac{1}{1-a}, & a\le x\le 1\end{cases} \tag{1}$$

where, $a\in(0,1)$ and used as the encryption/decryption-key of fingerprint template. The sequence generated by Tent map is composed of real numbers, so the output sequence of equation (1) is quantized into binary stream by the following threshold:

$$c(n)=\begin{cases}1, & x_n\ge 0.5\\ 0, & x_n<0.5\end{cases} \tag{2}$$

The normalized sequence is $c(n)\in\{0,1\}$. We use XOR operation to encrypt the fingerprint template, and the encrypted template is obtained by:

$$e(n)=E(b(n)=\sum_{n=1}^{N}b(n)\oplus c(n) \tag{3}$$

where N is size of template and chaotic sequence, $b(n)$ is the normalized fingerprint template, $c(n)$ is the pseudorandom key sequence generated by Tent map, $E(b(n))$ is the encrypted template, and $\oplus$ denotes the Exclusive-OR operation.

2.2 Fingerprint Template Hiding Algorithm

The nonuniform discrete Fourier transform (NDFT) has been widely used in signal processing applications where nonuniform spaced samples in the frequency domain are needed [6,23]. Nonuniform distribution of sampling points in the NDFT makes it a good candidate for the data hiding applications.

One dimension NDFT and its inverse transform (INDFT) are [22]:

$$\begin{cases}F(k_m)=\sum_{n=0}^{N-1}f(n)e^{-jk_mn}\\ f(n)=\frac{1}{N}\sum_{n=0}^{N-1}F(k_m)e^{-jk_mn}\end{cases},\ \mathrm{m}=1,\cdots,M \tag{4}$$

Where, k_m may choose any real number and M expresses the number of sampling points.

NDFT of N points can be represented by arbitrary N points on unit circle in the Z-plane [6]. It can be expressed by:

$$X(z_k) = \sum_{n=0}^{N-1} x(n) z_k^{-n}, \quad \mathrm{k} = 0,1,\ldots \mathrm{N-1} \tag{5}$$

Where, z_0, z_1,...z_{N-1} are arbitrary N different points in the Z-plane. Equation (5) can be further represented in matrix form by:

$$X = Dx \tag{6}$$

$$X = \begin{bmatrix} X(z_0) \\ X(z_1) \\ \vdots \\ X(z_{N-1}) \end{bmatrix}, \quad x = \begin{bmatrix} x(0) \\ x(1) \\ \vdots \\ x(N-1) \end{bmatrix}, \quad D = \begin{bmatrix} 1 & z_0^{-1} & z_0^{-2} & \cdots & z_0^{-(N-1)} \\ 1 & z_1^{-1} & z_1^{-2} & \cdots & z_1^{-(N-1)} \\ \vdots & \vdots & \vdots & \ddots & \vdots \\ 1 & z_{N-1}^{-1} & z_{N-1}^{-2} & \cdots & z_{N-1}^{-(N-1)} \end{bmatrix},$$

where, Matrix D is Vandemone matrix and entirely determined by N points z_k, $(k = 1,2,..., N-1)$. Expression of matrix D can be shown as:

$$\det(D) = \prod_{i \neq j, i > j} (z_i^{-1} - z_j^{-1}) \tag{7}$$

where, D is nonsingular, so INDFT (inverse NDFT) exists and is unique, that is: $x = D^{-1}X$.

2.2.1 Embedding Details

The original audio signal has the sampling frequency of 44.1 KHZ and the quantization ratio is 16 bits. The amplitude of the original audio signal is 0~65535 (2^{16}-1). The total length of the samples is 4096.

The details of embedding biometric data are as follows:

(1). To embed the data in the NDFT domain, first we segment the host/cover original audio signal into 8 samples per segment. For each segment, a frequency point in the selectable frequency range is chosen by the secret key to carry on NDFT transform, which keeps privacy of embedding position. We use Logistic map to generate the specific frequency chosen rule.

$$x_{n+1} = g(x_n) = \mu x_n (1 - x_n) \tag{8}$$

where, $n = 1,2,3,...$ is the map iteration index and μ is the parameter value. For $3.57 < \mu \leq 4.0$, the generated real number sequence is non-periodic, non-convergent, and very sensitive to its initial value [3].

(2). After segmenting and choosing the frequency points, we quantize the frequency coefficient to embed the template. The quantization rule is as follows:

For the coefficient $f(k)$ to be embedded, the modulus and residual are $m = \lfloor | f(k) | / \Delta \rfloor$, $r = | f(k) | - m \times \Delta$. Where, m is the modulus, r is the residual, and Δ is the quantization step.

$$| f(k)^w | = \begin{cases} \dfrac{\Delta}{2} & WW(k) = 1 \\ \dfrac{3\Delta}{2} & WW(k) = 0 \end{cases} \qquad m = 0 \tag{9}$$

$$| f(k)^w | = \begin{cases} \begin{cases} 2k\Delta + \frac{1}{2}\Delta & if\ m = 2k \\ 2k\Delta + \frac{1}{2}\Delta & if\ m = 2k+1\ and\ | r | \le \frac{1}{2}\Delta \\ 2k\Delta + 2\Delta + \frac{1}{2}\Delta & if\ m = 2k+1\ and\ | r | > \frac{1}{2}\Delta \end{cases} & WW(k) = 1 \\ \begin{cases} (2k+1)\Delta + \frac{1}{2}\Delta & if\ m = 2k+1 \\ 2k\Delta - \frac{1}{2}\Delta & if\ m = 2k\ and\ | r | \le \frac{1}{2}\Delta \\ (2k+1)\Delta + \frac{1}{2}\Delta & if\ m = 2k\ and\ | r | > \frac{1}{2}\Delta \end{cases} & WW(k) = 0 \end{cases} \qquad m \ne 0$$

where, $| f(k)^w |$ are the stego-coefficients, which contain the fingerprint template.

During the embedding process, two aspects should be paid more attention:

(2a). To guarantee embedded coefficients are also real number by way of INDFT manipulation, the embedding data is implemented under positive symmetric condition similar to DFT-based embedding method. That is: on the chosen frequency point, let $X(k) = X^*(N-k)$. The positive symmetric condition is defined as:

$$| X(k) | \leftarrow | X(k) | + \varepsilon \tag{10}$$

$$| X(N-k) | \leftarrow | X(N-k) | + \varepsilon \tag{11}$$

(2b). Choosing quantization step Δ: The quantization step $\Delta = 5120$ is used in the proposed scheme. This quantization value ensures the robustness of the algorithm and sensitivity to audible that is an important issue in human auditory system (HAS).

At the end of embedding fingerprint template, we carry out INDFT of the stego-coefficients to get the stego-audio signal. Now this stego-audio signal, which hides fingerprint template, can be securely transmitted to authentication server for the identification of a person.

2.3 Fingerprint Template Extraction and Verification

At the authentication server end, we perform NDFT on the stego-signal to extract the fingerprint template. Extracting data does not need original audio signal, because template/data is embedded by quantizing NDFT amplitude coefficients. The process of extracting hidden data is the inverse of the embedding process; the detailed steps are as follows:

(a) Perform segmentation of the received audio signal;
(b) Carry out NDFT on segmented stego-audio signal by secret key;
(c) Extract fingerprint template by quantization rule in the chosen frequency point;

After performing extraction, the biometric template is decrypted by the same method as described in subsection 2.1. At the end, we perform verification of the extracted fingerprint template, $t'(n)$, against the pre-stored template database by the following equation:

$$M = \frac{1}{N}\sum_{i=1}^{N} t'(n) \oplus t(n) \qquad (12)$$

where, N is the size of the fingerprint template, $t(n)$ is original fingerprint template stored in the database, while $t'(n)$ is an extracted template from the stego-audio signal.

3 Experimental Results and Discussions

Experiments are conducted on the public domain fingerprint images dataset, DB3, FVC2004 that contains a total of 120 fingers and 12 impressions per finger (1440 impressions) using 30 volunteers. The size of fingerprint images is 300×480 pixels captured at a resolution of 512 dpi.

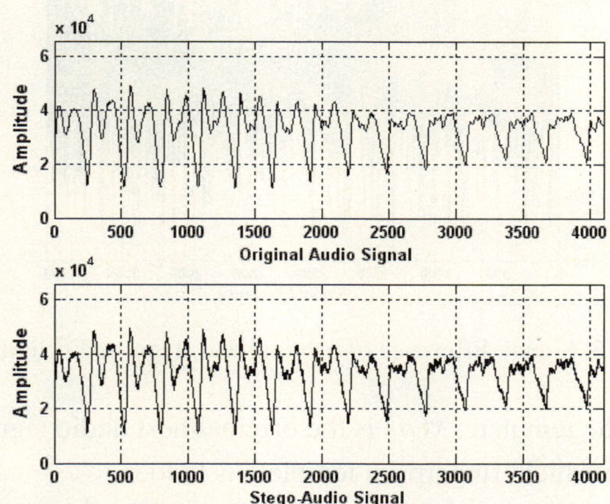

Fig. 2. Original audio signal without fingerprint template and Stego-audio signal with hidden fingerprint template

To evaluate the performance of the proposed scheme, in terms of robustness and inaudibility, we performed a set of experiments including Gaussian noise, low pass filtering, Mp3 compression, re-sampling, and re-quantization on the stego-transmitted signal that contains hidden biometric-fingerprint template. The original audio signal and stego-audio signal containing hidden biometric-fingerprint template are depicted in figure 2, and their signal difference is shown in figure 3.

Presented system shows 100% fingerprint template decoding accuracy without any attacks as shown in Table 1. We evaluated the performance of our system by calculating Signal-to-Noise Ratio (SNR), Mean Squared Error (MSE), and Bit Error Rate (BER), and their mathematical formulae are shown in equations (13) to (15), respectively.

$$SNR(dB) = 10\log_{10} \frac{\sum_{i=0}^{N-1} x^2(n)}{\sum_{i=0}^{M-1} [x(n) - y(n)]^2} \tag{13}$$

$$MSE = \frac{1}{N} \sum_{i=0}^{M-1} [x(n) - y(n)]^2 \tag{14}$$

$$BER = \frac{1}{N} \sum_{i=0}^{N-1} x(n) \oplus y(n) \tag{15}$$

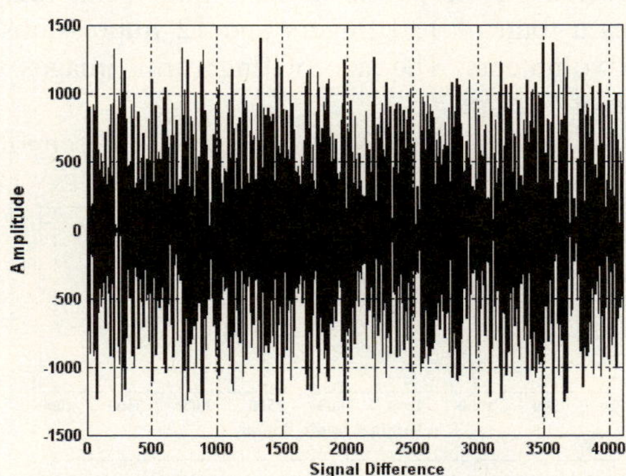

Fig. 3. Signal difference of original and stego-audio signals

where, N is size of the template, $x(n)$ is the original/host audio signal and $y(n)$ is the stego-audio signal in which, fingerprint template is hidden.

Hence, it is apparent from the experimental results that the proposed system is an ideal candidate for secure transmission of biometric templates over insecure communication network. Moreover, it achieves an outstanding decoding performance, even under different kinds of attacks which could be possible during the transmission.

Table 1. Experimental Results

Attack	SNR (dB)	MSE	BER	Accuracy (%)
No Attack	34.9622	3.4076e-004	0	100
Gaussian Noise	32.7750	5.6386e-004	0.0059	99.41
Low-pass Filtering	34.8085	3.5304e-004	0.0020	99.80
128K Mp3 Compression	34.5605	3.7379e-004	0.0000	100
Re-Sampling	34.8861	3.4679e-004	0.0020	99.80
Re-Quantization	34.8991	3.4575e-004	0.0000	100

4 Conclusion

We have presented a novel covert-transmission scheme of biometric-fingerprint templates, in which audio signal hid templates as container to protect from attacks and kept secret the existence of fingerprint templates from the communication eavesdropping. We used chaos and NDFT-based template hiding scheme and proved that biometric template in audio signal could not affect the identification performance of the biometric recognition system. In addition, we performed a series of experiments to evaluate the performance of the system and the experimental results have shown that the proposed system is robust against noises and attacks, and achieves better verification accuracy. Our future work would focus on hiding different type of biometrics templates e.g. face, iris etc; into audio signal to evaluate the robustness of our system.

Acknowledgements

This project is supported by 'Sichuan Youth Science and Technology Funds' under grant number: 03ZQ026-033 and ‘Southwest Jiaotong University Doctors Innovation Funds 2005’.

References

1. Anil, K.J., Prabhakar, S., Hong, L., Pankanti, S.: Filterbank-based fingerprint matching. IEEE Transactions On Image Processing 9, 846–859 (2000)
2. Anil, K.J., Pankanti, S., Bolle, R.: Biometrics: Personal Identification in Networked Society. Kluwer, USA (1999)
3. Khan, M.K., Jiashu, Z., Lei, T.: Chaotic secure content-based hidden transmission of biometrics templates. In: Chaos, Solitons, and Fractals, vol. 32(5), pp. 1749–1759. Elsevier Science, Amsterdam (2007)
4. Anil, K.J., Prabhakar, S., Hong, L.: A multichannel approach to fingerprint classification. IEEE Transactions on Pattern Analysis and Machine Intelligence 21, 348–359 (1999)
5. Daugman, J.: High confidence visual recognition of persons by a test of statistical independence. IEEE Transactions on Pattern Analysis and Machine Intelligence 15, 1148–1161 (1999)
6. Anil, K.J., Umut, U.: Hiding biometric data. IEEE Transactions on Pattern Analysis and Machine Intelligence 25, 1494–1498 (2003)

7. Gunsel, B., Umut, U., Tekalp, A.M.: Robust watermarking of fingerprint images. In: Pattern Recognition, vol. 35, pp. 2739–2747. Elsevier Science Ltd., Amsterdam (2002)
8. Khan, M.K., Jiashu, Z., Lei, T.: Protecting biometric data for personal identification. In: Li, S.Z., Lai, J.-H., Tan, T., Feng, G.-C., Wang, Y. (eds.) SINOBIOMETRICS 2004. LNCS, vol. 3338, pp. 629–638. Springer, Heidelberg (2004)
9. Ratha, N., Connell, J., Bolle, R.: Enhancing security and privacy in biometrics-based authentication systems. IBM System Journal 40, 614–634 (2001)
10. Davida, G.I., Frankel, Y., Matt, B.J.: On enabling secure applications through online biometric identification. In: IEEE Symposium on Security and Privacy, pp. 148–157 (1998)
11. Davida, G.I., Frankel, Y., Matt, B.J., Peralta, R.: On the relation of error correction and cryptography to an offline biometric based identification scheme. In: Proc. Workshop Coding and Cryptography, pp. 129–138 (1999)
12. Soutar, C., Roberge, D., Stojanov, S.A., Gilroy, R., Vijaya Kumar, B.V.K.: Biometric encryption using image processing. In: Proc. SPIE, Optical Security and Counterfeit Deterrence Techniques II, vol. 3314, pp. 178–188 (1998)
13. Soutar, C., Roberge, D., Stojanov, S.A, Gilroy, R., Vijaya Kumar, B.V.K.: Biometric encryption, enrollment and verification procedures. In: Proc. SPIE, Optical Pattern Recognition IX, vol. 3386, pp. 24–35 (1998)
14. Andy, A.: Vulnerabilities in biometric encryption systems. In: Kanade, T., Jain, A., Ratha, N.K. (eds.) AVBPA 2005. LNCS, vol. 3546. Springer, Heidelberg (2005)
15. Linnartz, J.P., Tuyls, P.: New shielding functions to enhance privacy and prevent misuse of biometric templates. In: Proc. of the 4th Int. Conf. on Audio and Video Based Biometric Person Authentication, UK, pp. 393–402 (2004)
16. Verbitskiy, E., Tuyls, P., Denteneer, D., Linnartz, J.P.: Reliable biometric authentication with privacy protection. In: Proc. of the 24th Symposium on Inf. Theory, pp. 125–132 (2003)
17. Tuyls, P., Gosling, J.: Capacity and examples of template-protecting biometric authentication systems. In: Maltoni, D., Jain, A.K. (eds.) BioAW 2004. LNCS, vol. 3087, pp. 158–170. Springer, Heidelberg (2004)
18. Uludag, U., Pankanti, S., Prabhakar, S., Jain, A.K.: Biometric cryptosystems: issues and challenges. Proceedings of the IEEE 92, 948–960 (2004)
19. Yeung, M.M., Pankanti, S.: Verification watermarks on fingerprint recognition and retrieval. Journal of Electronic Imaging 9, 468–476 (2000)
20. Sonia, J.: Digital watermarking techniques: a case study in fingerprints and faces. In: Proc. Indian Conference on Computer Vision, Graphics, and Image Processing, pp. 139–144 (2000)
21. Andrew, D.K.: Steganalysis of LSB matching in grayscale images. IEEE Signal Processing Letters 12, 441–444 (2005)
22. Bagchi, S., Mitra, S.K.: The Nonuniform Discrete Fourier Transform and its application in filter design. IEEE Trans. on Circuits and System: Analog and Digital Signal Processing 43, 422–433 (1996)
23. Ling, X., Jiashu, Z., Hong-Jie, H.: NDFT-based Audio Watermarking Scheme with High Security. In: IEEE ICPR, vol. 4, pp. 270–273 (2006)

Correlation-Based Fingerprint Matching with Orientation Field Alignment

Almudena Lindoso, Luis Entrena, Judith Liu-Jimenez, and Enrique San Millan

University Carlos III of Madrid, Electronic Technology Department, Butarque 15, 28911 Leganes, Madrid, Spain
{alindoso,entrena,jliu,quique}@ing.uc3m.es

Abstract. Correlation-based techniques are a promising approach to fingerprint matching for the new generation of high resolution and touchless fingerprint sensors, since they can match ridge shapes, breaks, etc. However, a major drawback of these techniques is the high computational effort required. In this paper a coarse alignment step is proposed which reduces the amount of correlations that should be performed. Contrarily to other alignment approaches based on minutiae or core location, the alignment is based on the orientation field estimations. Also the orientation coherence is used to identify the best areas for correlation. The accuracy of the approach is demonstrated by experimental results with an FVC2000 fingerprint database. The approach is also very well suited for hardware acceleration due to the regularity of the used operations.

1 Introduction

Fingerprints are widely used in recognition of a person's identity because of its proven uniqueness, stability and universality. Characteristic fingerprint features are generally categorized into three levels [1]. Level 1 features, or patterns, are the macro details of the fingerprint such as ridge flow and pattern type (loop, arch, etc.). Level 2 features are the minutiae, such as ridge bifurcations and endings. Level 3 features include all dimensional attributes of the ridge such as ridge width, shape, pores, incipient ridges, breaks, creases, scars, and other permanent details.

Most commercial Automated Fingerprint Identification Systems (AFIS) are based on Level 1 and Level 2 features. This is because the extraction of Level 3 features requires high resolution images, in the order of 1000 pixels per inch (ppi). However, Level 3 features are also claimed to be permanent, immutable and unique according to the forensic experts, and can provide discriminatory information for human identification. With the advent of high resolution fingerprint sensors and "touch-less" sensors that eliminate skin deformation, such as those introduced by TBS, Inc [2], recognition considering Level 3 features becomes feasible. However, many of the existing fingerprint matching techniques cannot take full advantage of these new sensors since they barely consider Level 3 features.

This work focuses on correlation-based fingerprint matching. Correlation uses the gray level information of the fingerprint image since a gray-level fingerprint contains

S.-W. Lee and S.Z. Li (Eds.): ICB 2007, LNCS 4642, pp. 713–721, 2007.

much richer, discriminatory information than only the minutiae locations. Correlation-based techniques can take into account Level 3 features as well as other fingerprint features. As a matter of fact, these methods have been used successfully for fingerprint matching with conventional sensors, as demonstrated in the last two fingerprint verification competitions (FVC) [3], [4].

Approaches to correlation-based fingerprint matching have already been proposed [5], [10]. Among the most important aspects of these techniques are the selection of appropriate areas of the fingerprint image for correlation and the computational effort required to consider translation and rotation between the fingerprint images. In order to take into account displacement and rotation, Ouyang et al. propose the use of a local Fourier-Mellin Descriptor (FMD) [6]. However, since the center of relative rotation between two compared fingerprints is unknown, the local FMD has to be extracted for a large number of center locations. Other works correlate ridge feature maps to align and match fingerprint images [7], but do not consider rotation yet.

In this paper we propose techniques that reduce the correlation effort and minimize the effect of deformation by focusing on high-quality and distinctive fingerprint image regions. To this purpose, we introduce a coarse alignment step based on the correlation of the orientation fields of the fingerprints. The alignment dramatically reduces the correlation search space and is further refined at the final correlation step. Due to the lack of high resolution (1000 ppi) fingerprint databases available in the public domain, experimental results have been conducted with a low resolution database (FVC 2000 DB2). Finally, in order to deal with the high computational requirements of correlation techniques, we propose the use of hardware acceleration techniques. As correlation computations are highly regular, they are much more suitable for hardware acceleration than other approaches [8].

The remaining sections of this paper are organized as follows: Section 2 formulates correlation-based fingerprint matching, Section 3 summarizes the fingerprint preprocessing steps, Section 4 describes the matching algorithm including the alignment and correlation region selection approaches, Section 5 analyses the use of hardware acceleration, Section 6 presents the experimental results and finally Section 7 presents the conclusions.

2 Correlation-Based Fingerprint Matching

Cross-correlation, or simply correlation, is a measurement of image similarity. In order to compensate variations of brightness, contrast, ridge thickness, etc. that affect the correlation of fingerprint images, the Zero Mean Normalized Cross Correlation (ZNCC) can be used [11]. ZNCC is defined by the expression:

$$ZNCC\ (x,y,\alpha)=\frac{CC(T-\overline{T},I(x,y,\alpha)-\overline{I}(x,y,\alpha))}{\left\|T-\overline{T}\right\|\cdot\left\|I(x,y,\alpha)-\overline{I}(x,y,\alpha)\right\|} \tag{1}$$

where CC is the cross-correlation, T is the template image and I(x, y, α) is the input image shifted by x and y pixels in vertical and horizontal directions, respectively, and rotated by an angle α.

As an alternative, the cross-correlation required to compute ZNCC can be obtained by multiplication in the Fourier domain, using the following formula:

$$CC(T,I) = F^{-1}(F^{*}(T) * F(I)) \tag{2}$$

3 Image Preprocessing

Correlation-based matching requires good image quality because the matching is performed directly with gray-level fingerprint images. Figure 1 summarizes the preprocessing that has been used in our approach, which is based in [9]. The main steps are: normalization, low frequency noise filtering, orientation field estimation and frequency estimation with their respective coherences, Gabor filtering and finally equalization.

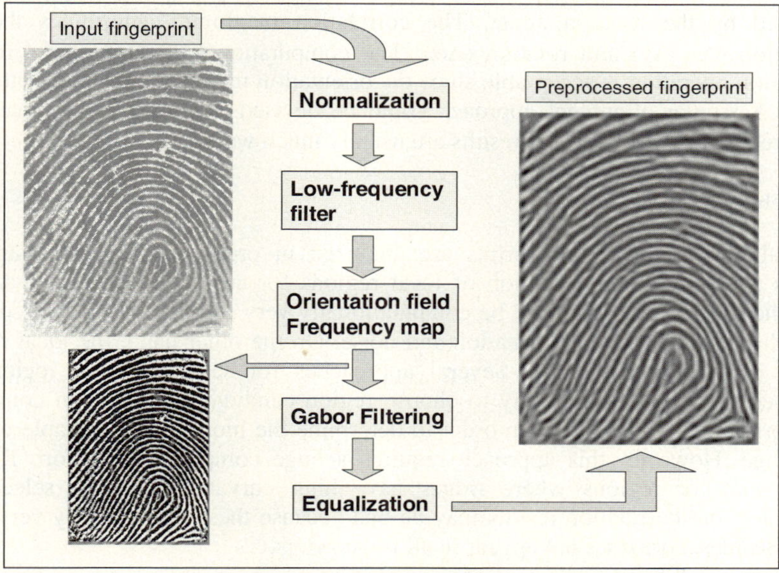

Fig. 1. Preprocessing

4 Fingerprint Matching

In the proposed algorithm matching is divided in three steps: image alignment, selection of correlation regions and correlation-based matching.

4.1 Coarse Alignment

The purpose of the alignment step is to estimate the translation and rotation between input and template images. This step allows reducing dramatically the amount of correlations that should be performed. On the other hand, only a coarse alignment is needed since it will be refined later on in the correlation step.

Most approaches for alignment use features extracted from the images, such as minutiae or core locations [10], [14]. In order to avoid extracting these features, we propose a new approach based on the correlation of the orientation fields computed in the preprocessing step. More precisely, we compute the correlation of the sine and the cosine of the estimated orientation angle weighted by the coherence (Coh(θ)) as the input image is translated by (x, y) pixels and rotated by an angle α with respect to the template image:

$$CC_{\sin}(x, y, \alpha) = CC(\sin(2\theta_T) * Coh(\theta_T), \sin(2\theta_I^{x,y,\alpha}) * Coh(\theta_I^{x,y,\alpha})) \quad (3)$$

$$(\Delta x, \Delta y, \Delta\alpha) = \max_{x,y,\alpha}(CC_{\sin}(x, y, \alpha) + CC_{\cos}(x, y, \alpha)) / CC_{Coh}(x, y, \alpha) \quad (4)$$

Note that as the orientation field is rotated, the orientation angle $\theta_I^{x,y,\alpha}$ must be corrected by the rotation angle. The correlation maximum determines the best translation (Δx, Δy) and rotation (Δα). The computational effort required for this correlation operation is acceptable since the orientation map is much smaller than the image. A similar alignment approach could be devised based on the estimation of ridge frequency. However, the results are usually much worse.

4.2 Selection of Regions

After alignment, both fingerprints are analyzed in order to determine candidate regions for correlation. Selection of local regions for correlation is required, since using the entire fingerprint will be computationally very expensive and will correlate badly due to fingerprint deformation and noise. On the other hand, the local regions should be highly distinctive. Several approaches for selecting local regions are discussed in [5]. A typical way to choose region candidates consists in computing auto-correlation of the image in order to determine the more distinguishable parts of the image. However, this approach requires a huge computational effort. Regions around core or regions where ridges have high curvature may be selected as candidates, but correlation results may be bad because these are typically very noisy areas. Besides, core does not appear in all fingerprints.

Our approach for the selection of regions is based on image quality and fingerprint overlapping. The quality of the images is an important factor in the search of region candidates for correlation computation. If the region candidate chosen corresponds to a bad quality area in any of the fingerprints, then the verification will fail. To this purpose we use the coherence of the orientation field as a measure of quality [12]. In particular, the multiplication of the coherence of input and template fingerprints is our basic criterion to select region candidates. This computation is only considered for the overlapping areas of both fingerprints, which can be computed thanks to the relative translation and rotation estimated in the alignment step. Notwithstanding, this approach can lead to select regions without enough distinction. To avoid this problem, an average filter is applied to the coherence map, thus allowing the selection of regions with lower coherence as long as they have high coherence neighbours. This correction increases the chances to select distinctive regions located in good quality areas of the image.

It must be pointed out that if two samples of the same finger are excessively rotated or translated, insufficient overlapping may occur because the images could show non-coincident parts of the same finger. In addition, the overlapping areas may have low quality. In such a case, the matching is attempted with the overlapping portion of the selected region, but the chances the verification fails increase.

4.3 Matching

Finally, in the matching step the input region candidates are correlated with the template using ZNCC formula described in section 2. An area, called search area, corresponding to the input region but a little larger is chosen in the template image to perform the correlation. Figure 2 illustrates the region selection process and the main matching steps. Matching is done considering translation and rotation of the input region over the search area. Thanks to the previous alignment step, translation and rotation can be performed at a fine scale within a reduced searching space. In particular, 12 rotations are considered, 6 clockwise and 6 counterclockwise with an angle step of 2º.

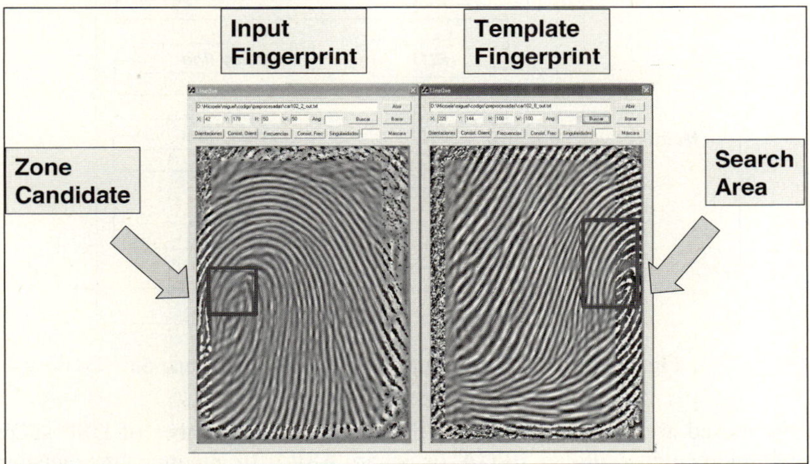

Fig. 2. Region selection and matching steps

5 Hardware Acceleration

The proposed fingerprint verification approach relies basically in correlation computations, which are used for the alignment and the matching steps. As correlation computations are highly regular, they are much more suitable for hardware acceleration than other approaches.

Recent results presented in [8] demonstrate that correlation can be accelerated using a FPGA by more than 600 times with respect to a modern PC. This result is obtained by taking advantage of specialized digital signal processing hardware modules, known as DSP slices [16], which are available in modern FPGAs.

The hardware architecture designed to accelerate correlation computations is summarized in Fig. 3. The architecture follows equation (1) to compute CC as a series of multiply-accumulate (MAC) operations. This approach adapts easily to a variety of correlation sizes, as required for the alingment and the matching steps. The input fingerprint image is stored in the input memory. The template fingerprint image is stored in the input registers of the DSP slices. DSP slices are organized in a matrix, where each slice computes a MAC and passes the result to next slice in the same row. In other words, each row is organized as a systolic array that computes a row correlation. The correlation matrix results from the addition of n consecutive row correlations R(i), i=0,…,n-1. A delay line is inserted after the last slice in every row in order that the result R(i) reaches the first slice in the next row at the required time to be added up. With this approach, a single data is read from the input memory at every clock cycle, which is supplied to the first slice in each row. At the output of the last row, a correlation result is obtained at every clock cycle for the possible displacements of the input image with respect to the template image.

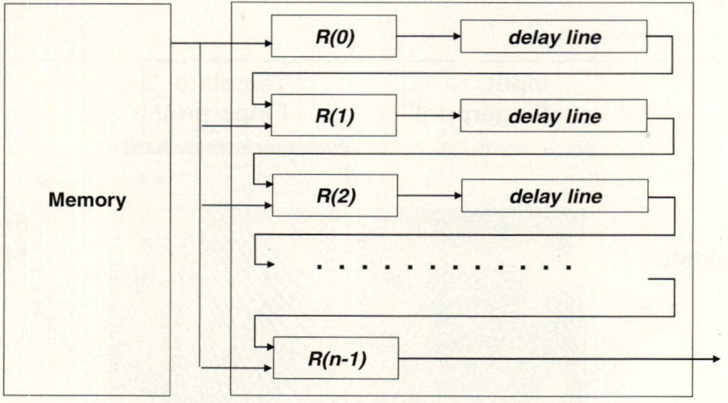

Fig. 3. Hardware architecture for correlation computation

The proposed architecture can be easily scaled to any number of DSP slices and can be implemented with an FPGA or in an ASIC. In practice, the acceleration requirements for real time applications are usually moderate and can be achieved with a low cost FPGA or application-specific hardware in a cost effective manner.

6 Experimental Results

The proposed algorithm has been tested with FVC 2000 2 A [13] data base. This database consists of 100 different fingers, with 8 samples per finger, giving a total of 800 fingerprints. The image size is 256x364 pixels. For the computation of the orientation field, fingerprint images are divided into blocks of size 64x64. The resulting orientation field has blocks of size 18x24. Initially, several number of correlation regions were considered, but after analyzing the results obtained, the number of regions was set to three. After some preliminary experiments, the size of the region was set to 50x50 pixels and the search area to 100x100 pixels.

The tests have been conducted considering the FVC premises [15]. To determine the FMR (False Match Rate) curve, the first sample of each finger has been matched against the first sample of all fingers. To determine the FNMR (False Non Match Rate), all the samples of each finger have been matched among themselves. In our case, symmetric matches have been considered in the results because the proposed algorithm is not symmetric.

The ROC (Receiving Operating Curve) obtained for the proposed algorithm is shown in Figure 4. The EER (Equal Error Rate) achieved is 9 %.

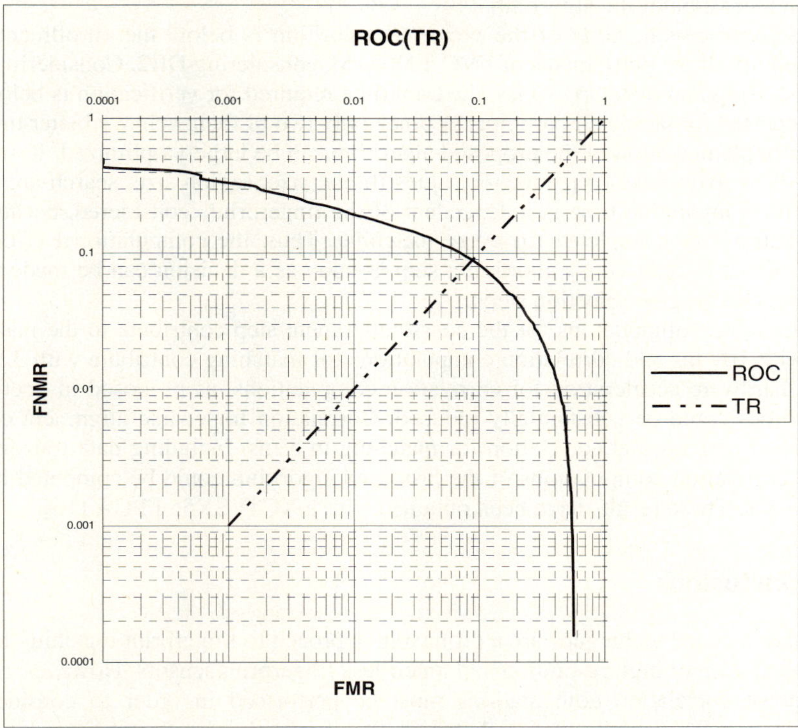

Fig. 4. ROC curve in logarithmic scale of the proposed algorithm tested with FVC 2000 2 A data Base, FNMR (False Non-Match Rate), FMR (False Match Rate) TR (Correlation Threshold)

The FVC 2000 participants [13] were 11 and their EER range from 0.61 % to 46.15 %, for the considered database (DB2). Comparing our results with the participants' results, the EER of the proposed algorithm is below the EER achieved by five of the participants and above the EER achieved by 6 of the participants.

Most of the false matches were due to very bad quality images or insufficient overlapping between the images. These cases can be solved with additional pre-processing steps and particularly, with slightly higher resolution images. With the image size used in the experiments, the correlation regions contain a significant portion of the image. This sometimes prevents avoiding low quality areas or using fully overlapped correlation areas of the required size. Also, these cases can be detected at the preprocessing step or later by setting thresholds in the alignment and correlation steps. In a practical application, the verification should be rejected if the image quality is bad or the overlapping is not sufficient, asking the user for a new fingerprint sample. However, this option has not been used in our tests.

The time required to complete the computation for each single verification is 1.15 seconds, divided in 0.25 seconds for preprocessing and 0.9 seconds for matching. This time has been measured with a PC Pentium IV 3 GHz with 2 GB of RAM for a C implementation of the algorithm.

The preprocessing time of the proposed algorithm is below the enrollment time reported for all the participants of FVC 2000 [15], considering DB2. Considering both preprocessing and matching times, the total time required for verification is below the time reported for nearly all participants, since only two of them achieve better times.

The implementation of the proposed algorithm can be largely optimized. It must be noted that, given a set of parameter values (block size, region size, search area size, etc.), the computation time is independent of the fingerprints considered, because all computations are completed for every matching. Thus, the computational effort can be significantly reduced by aborting a step as soon as a decision can be made in the alignment and region selection steps.

Correlation computations for the coarse alignment step contribute to the matching time with 109 ms and correlation computations for matching contribute with 320 ms. Using hardware acceleration for correlation computations, as proposed in Section 5, these times could be substantially reduced. Correlation for coarse alignment can be completed in 1 ms and correlation for matching in 8 ms. Including data transfer, the whole correlation computations of the proposed algorithm could be computed in less than 14 ms. These results have been obtained with a XC4VSX55 FPGA [16].

7 Conclusions

Correlation-based techniques are a promising approach to fingerprint matching for the new generation of high resolution and touch-less fingerprint sensors. However, a large number of correlation computations must be performed in order to consider the possible translation and rotation between the fingerprint images. In this paper, a coarse alignment step based on the correlation of the orientation fields of the fingerprints has been proposed. This alignment dramatically reduces the correlation search space and is further refined at the final correlation step. The orientation field coherence is used to weight the contribution of the orientation estimations to the alignment and to select appropriate regions for correlation.

The experiments presented in this paper demonstrate that this approach produces acceptable results with low resolution sensors. It can be expected that the matching accuracy will improve with high resolution and touchless fingerprint sensors, as these sensors will be able to show Level 3 features and to reduce deformation.

In the past, one of the main drawbacks of correlation-based fingerprint matching approaches was the high computational effort required. With the proposed approach the computational effort has been reduced to an effort comparable to other techniques. Moreover, since this approach relies basically on correlation computations it is very suitable for hardware acceleration in order to reduce the verification time. To this purpose, a hardware acceleration architecture has also been proposed that is able to reduce the computational effort required by correlation by two orders of magnitude.

References

1. Jain, A., Chen, Y., Demitrius, M.: Pores and Ridges: Fingerprint Matching using Level 3 Features. In: Proc. 18th Int'l Conf. on Pattern Recognition (ICPR'06), vol. 4, pp. 477–480 (2006)
2. Parziale, G., Diaz-Santana, E.: The Surround Imager: A Multicamera Touchless Device to Acquire 3D Rolled-Equivalent Fingerprints. In: Zhang, D., Jain, A.K. (eds.) Advances in Biometrics. LNCS, vol. 3832, pp. 244–250. Springer, Heidelberg (2005)
3. Maio, D., Maltoni, D., Cappelli, R., Wayman, J.L., Jain, A.K.: FVC 2002: Second Fingerprint Verification Competition. In: 16th Proc. Int. Conf. on Pattern Recognition, vol. 3, pp. 811–814 (2002)
4. Maio, D., Maltoni, D., Cappelli, R., Wayman, J.L., Jain, A.K.: FVC 2004: Third Fingerprint Verification Competition. In: Proc. Int. Conf. on Biometric Authentication (2004)
5. Bazen, A.M., Verwaaijen, G.T.B., Gerez, S.H., Veelenturf, L.P.J., van der Zwaang, B.J.: A Correlation-Based Fingerprint Verification System. In: Proc. Workshop on Circuits, Systems and Signal Processing (ProRISC), pp. 205–213 (2000)
6. Ouyang, Z., Feng, J., Su, F., Cai, A.: Fingerprint Matching with Rotation-Descriptor Texture Features. In: Proc. 18th Int'l Conf. on Pattern Recognition (ICPR'06), vol. 4, pp. 417–420 (2006)
7. Ross, A., Reisman, J., Jain, A.: Fingerprint Matching using Feature Space Correlation. In: Tistarelli, M., Bigun, J., Jain, A.K. (eds.) ECCV 2002. LNCS, vol. 2359, pp. 48–57. Springer, Heidelberg (2002)
8. Lindoso, A., Entrena, L., Ongil-Lopez, C., Liu, J.: Correlation-based fingerprint matching using FPGAs. In: Proc. Int. conf. on Field Programmable Technology, FPT, pp. 87–94 (2005)
9. Hong, L., Wan, Y., Jain, A.: Fingerprint image enhancement: algorithm and performance evaluation. IEEE Transactions on Pattern Analysis and Machine Intelligence 20(8), 777–789 (1998)
10. Maltoni, D., Maio, D., Jain, A.K., Prabhakar, S.: Handbook of Fingerprint Recognition. Springer, New York (2003)
11. Crouzil, A., Massip-Pailhes, L., Castan, S.: A New Correlation Criterion Based on Gradient Fields Similarity. In: Proc. 13th Int. Conf. on Pattern Recognition, pp. 632–636 (1996)
12. Lim, E., Toh, K.A., Suganthan, P.N., Jiang, X., Yan, W.Y.: Fingerprint quality analysis. In: Proceedings on International Conference on Image Processing, pp. 1241–1244. IEEE, Los Alamitos (2004)
13. Maio, D., Maltoni, D., Cappelli, R., Wayman, J.L., Jain, A.K.: FVC2000: Fingerprint Verification Competition. IEEE Transactions on Pattern Analysis Machine Intelligence 24(3), 402–412 (2002)
14. Park, C.H., Oh, S.K., Kwak, D.M., Kim, B.S., Song, Y.C., Park, K.H.: A new reference point detection algorithm based on orientation patron labelling in fingerprint images. In: Perales, F.J., Campilho, A., Pérez, N., Sanfeliu, A. (eds.) IbPRIA 2003. LNCS, vol. 2652, pp. 697–703. Springer, Heidelberg (2003)
15. Wayman, J., Jain, A., Maltoni, D., Maio, D.: Biometric Systems, Technology, Design and Performance Evaluation. Springer, London (2005)
16. Virtex-4 Family Overview (2004), www.xilinx.com, Xilinx Inc.

Vitality Detection from Fingerprint Images: A Critical Survey

Pietro Coli, Gian Luca Marcialis, and Fabio Roli

University of Cagliari – Department of Electrical and Electronic Engineering
Piazza d'Armi – 09123 Cagliari (Italy)
{pietro.coli,marcialis,roli}@diee.unica.it

Abstract. Although fingerprint verification systems reached a high degree of accuracy, it has been recently shown that they can be circumvented by "fake fingers", namely, fingerprint images coming from stamps reproducing an user fingerprint, which is processed as an "alive" one. Several methods have been proposed for facing with this problem, but the issue is far from a final solution. Since the problem is relevant both for the academic and the industrial communities, in this paper, we present a critical review of current approaches to fingerprint vitality detection in order to analyze the state–of–the art and the related open issues.

1 Introduction

In the last years, fingerprint verification systems for personal identity recognition reached a high degree of accuracy [1]. Fingerprints can be reasonably considered the biometric for which academic and industrial research achieved the highest level of maturity. In fact, many capture devices have been implemented with powerful software development kits for acquiring, processing and matching fingerprint images. The reason of this success is mainly due to the most claimed characteristic of fingerprints: their uniqueness [2]. In other words, it is claimed that fingerprints are unique from person to person, and the probability to find two similar fingerprints characterized, for example., by minutiae is very low [2].

However, recent works pointed out that the current fingerprint capture devices can be deceived by submitting a "fake fingerprint" made up of gelatine or liquid silicon [3]. This fake finger can be obtained by person coercion (the so-called "consensual" method) or by latent fingerprints [3]. The first method is the most simple, as it requires that the person put his finger on a plasticine-like material. The next step is to drip over this mould some liquid silicon. After its solidification, a fake stamp reproducing the fingerprint of the client can be used for deceiving the acquisition sensor, which processes that as an "alive" fingerprint. An example of "live" and "fake" fingerprint images fabricated by the consensual method and acquired with an optical sensor is given in Figure 2. Obviously, reproducing a fingerprint is not so easy as it may appear, because high quality stamps are necessary for a successful logon on a system protected with a fingerprint authentication module. On the other hand, the issue exists, as it was pointed out in [3].

S.-W. Lee and S.Z. Li (Eds.): ICB 2007, LNCS 4642, pp. 722–731, 2007.

Since fingerprints can be reproduced, this has a dramatic impact on the main property which made them so popular and appealing for security applications: their uniqueness. The state-of-the-art literature addresses this crucial problem as follows: is the finger on the acquisition sensor alive or "fake" ? In order to handle this problem, several methods to detect the fingerprint vitality (or "liveness") have been proposed, and this research field is still very active. A first subdivision of the state-of-the-art approaches can be made by observing that vitality is detected by extracting vitality measures from the finger, as the heartbeat or the blood pressure (hardware-based approaches), or from the fingerprint image(s) directly (software-based approaches).

As, to our knowledge, no previous paper reviewed critically the state-of-the-art of fingerprint vitality detection methods, in this paper, we propose a taxonomy of current methods (Section 2) and discuss and compare some key features of previous works, such as the material used for fingerprint reproduction and the data sets used (Section 3). In section 4, we analyze and compare the detection performances reported in the literature. Some conclusions are drawn in Section 5.

2 Fingerprint Vitality Detection: A Taxonomy of Existing Methods

A possible taxonomy of fingerprint vitality detection methods is proposed in Figure 1. Roughly, existing approaches can be subdivided in "hardware-based" and "software-based". The first ones try to detect the vitality of the fingertip put on the sensor by additional hardware able to measure, for example, blood pressure [4], heartbeat [5], fingertip odor [6], or skin impedance [7]. These approaches are obviously expensive as they require additional hardware and can be strongly invasive: for example, measuring person's blood pressure is invasive as it can be used for other reasons that for simply detecting the vitality of his fingertip [8]. Moreover, in certain cases a clever imitator can circumvent these vitality detection methods.

Therefore, making the image processing module more "intelligent", that is, making it able to detect if a fake finger has been submitted is an interesting alternative to the hardware-based approaches. Several approaches aimed to extract vitality features from the fingerprint images directly have been recently proposed [9-15]. The general rationale behind these approaches is that some peculiarities of "live fingerprints" cannot be hold in artificial reproductions, and they can be detected by a more or less complex analysis of fingerprint images. The related vitality detection approaches can be named "software-based".

In this survey, we focus on the software-based approaches. Therefore, in the taxonomy of Figure 1, the leave associated to hardware-based approaches is not expanded further.

According to the taxonomy of Figure 1, the initial subdivision of the software-based approaches is based on the kind of features used. If the features extracted derive from the analysis of multiple frames of the same image, captured while the subject puts his fingertip on the acquisition surface at certain time periods (e.g., at 0 sec and at 5 sec), the related methods are named "dynamic" (as they use dynamic features).

On the other hand, if features are extracted from a single fingerprint impression or the comparison of different impressions, the methods are named "static"(as they use static features).

Referring to the leaves of the taxonomy in Figure 1, they describe software-based approaches as functions of the physical principle they exploit: the perspiration, the elastic distortion phenomena, and the intrinsic structure of fingerprints (morphological approaches).

According to the proposed taxonomy, in the following sections, we review the vitality detection methods proposed in the scientific literature.

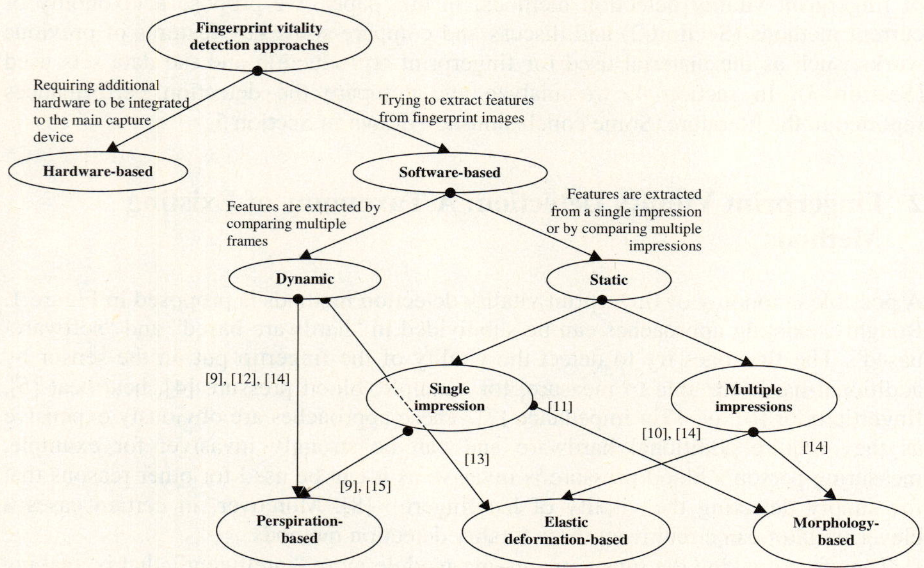

Fig. 1. The proposed taxonomy of fingerprint vitality detection methods. Labels of the edges in the form [*] are the number of the related Reference.

2.1 Static Methods

2.1.1 Static Methods Using a Single Impression

Following the path of the tree in Figure 1 from the static methods-junction, we first consider methods which exploit single impression. These can be classified into two further classes: perspiration and morphology based. About the former we have selected two main works as [15] and [9]. Both study the perspiration phenomenon with two transforms, [15] with wavelet space, [9] with Fourier space. Tan and Schuckers [15] showed how it is possible to clearly distinguish a live from a fake finger by wavelet transform. The rationale of this method is the analysis of the particular shape of the finger surface. In live fingers, in order to guarantee the physiological thermo-regulation, there are many little chinks named "pores" scattered along the center of the ridges. Because of this characteristic the acquired image of a finger shows a non-regular shape of the ridges. Generally the path of the ridges is irregular and, if the resolution of the device is high enough, it is possible to observe these pseudo-periodic conformations at the center of the ridges. With the fabrication step of an artificial finger it is possible to lose these micro-details and consequently the correspondent acquired image is more regular in the ridge shape. The authors propose to analyze this feature with a wavelet decomposition. In particular, the image is enhanced and converted into a mono-dimensional signal as the gray level profile extracted in correspondence of the center of the ridges. A wavelet decomposition of this signal is applied with a five-levels multiresolution scheme: The standard deviation, the mean value for each wavelet coefficient and from the original and the last approximation signals are computed. The obtained 14 parameters are considered as a feature-vector for the next classification stage.

The concept of detecting liveness from the skin perspiration analysis of the pores has been already proposed in [9]. In particular, the authors uses one static feature, named *SM*, based on the Fast Fourier Transform of the fingerprint skeleton converted into a mono-dimensional signal. The rationale is that for a live finger it is possible to notice clearly the regular periodicity due to the pores on the ridges. On the contrary this regularity is not evident for spoof fingerprint signals.

Carrying on with single impression-static methods, another work is noticeable to mention. Unlike the previous works, this applies a liveness detection studying the morphology of the fingerprint images. So, referring to Figure 1, the branch ending to morphologic based method is related to the work by Moon et al. [11].

The study is based on a different method with a contrasting argument. Looking at the finger surface with an high resolution Digital Single Lens Reflex camera, they observe that the surface of a fake finger is much coarser then that of a live finger. The main characteristic of this work is that an high resolution sensor is necessary for successfully capturing this difference (1000 dpi, whilst current sensors exhibit 500 dpi on average). Moreover, this approach does not work with the entire image, too large because of its resolution, but with subsamples of a fixed size. For extracting this feature, the residual noise returned from a denoising-process applied to the original sub-images is considered. The standard deviation of this noise is then computed to highlight the difference between live and fake coarseness.

2.1.2 Static Methods Using Multiple Impressions

Whilst the previous studies search a liveness indication from intrinsic properties of a single impression, there are other static features based on multiple impressions: in this case the liveness is derived from a comparison between a reference template image and the input image. This methods are represented in Figure 1 with two branches starting from the "Multi-impressions" node: one indicates method based on elastic-deformation features, the other indicates ones based on morphologic features. Ref [10] falls within the first category. Given a genuine query-template pair of fingerprints, the entity of elastic distortion between the two sets of extracted minutiae is measured by a thin-plate spline model. The idea is that live and spoof fingerprints show different elasticity response repeating the acquisitions.

The experimental investigation of Coli et al. [14] considers both the elastic-deformation based method and the morphology-based one. The elastic deformation is evaluated by computing the averaged sum of all the distances among the matched minutiae of input and template fingerprints. The different elastic response of a live finger or an artificial stamp is linked with the spread of this mean value. The other static multi-impression measure is based on morphologic investigation. The feature that makes use of the ridge width is based on the idea that during the creation of fingerprint replica, there is an unavoidable modification of the thickness of the ridges: first when the user put his finger on the cast material, next when the stamp is created with liquid silicone.

2.2 Dynamic Methods

Dynamic methods for vitality detection relies on the analysis of different image frames acquired during an interval while the user put his finger on the scanner.

As it is schematized in Figure 1 there are two types of dynamic methods: one based on the perspiration phenomenon, the other on the elastic response of the skin.

The same properties of the skin used for a static measure in [9, 11] is exploited with dynamic analysis based on the first approach [9]: the pores scattered on the fingertip surface are the source of the perspiration process. When the finger is in contact with the surface of the scanner, the skin gets wetter because of an increasing of sweat amount. This physiological phenomenon can be recorded by acquiring sequential frames during a fixed interval of few seconds. The variation of the wetness of the fingertip skin reflects on a variation of the gray-level profile of the acquired images. In order to evaluate this feature, the fingerprint skeleton of the image at 0 and 5 seconds is converted into a couple of mono-dimensional signals (*C1, C2*). Several statistical measures are proposed on the basis of the obtained signals. In particular [9], *DM1* (*Total swing ratio*), *DM2* (*Min/Max growth ratio*), *DM3* (*Last-First fingerprint signal difference mean*), *DM4* (*Percentage change of standard deviation*).

By considering that Ref. [12] draws up a more complete vitality analysis on different technology of fingerprint scanner, it has been necessary to introduce some modifications to the original method. The dynamic of the device can produce a saturated signal for excessive amount of wetness, in such situation the feature *DM2* lost its original efficacy. In order to avoid this drawback two new features named *DM5* (*Dry saturation percentage change*) and *DM6* (*Wet saturation percentage change*) are elaborated. With a selection of these measures, Coli et al. [14] applies a liveness detection on their extended database.

As the previous works can be considered an extension of the static perspiration measures, the work of Antonelli et Al. [13] adopts a dynamic procedure in order to perform a liveness detection based on elastic deformation. The user holding his finger on the scanner surface is invited to apply a rotation of the fingertip. The movement of the fingertip on the surface induces an elastic tension to the whole surface and consequently an elastic deformation depending on the level of elasticity of the skin, for live finger, or of the artificial material for the spoof stamp. A dynamic acquisition extracts a sequence of images at high frame rate (> 20 fps). The authors named "distortion-code" the feature-vector encoding the elastic distortion from the current frame to the next one, obtained computation of the optical flows that estimates the variation in the time of the rotating images.

3 Previous Works: Fabrication Process of Fake Stamps and Data Sets Used

We believe that a critical review of previous works on fingerprint vitality detection should analyze: (i) the different materials employed for fake stamps and the methods used for creating them; (ii) the characteristics of the data sets used for the vitality detection experiments.

Table 1 deals with Item (i) for the methods we reviewed in Section 2. Item (i) is important because the response of a certain fingerprint scanner varies with the material adopted (e.g., gelatine or silicon). Secondly, the intrinsic quality of the stamp depends on the material for the cast and the method followed for its creation. With regard to the mould materials, all those employed are able to deceive an optical sensor, as pointed out in [3]. On the other hand, using the silicone material is not effective for capacitive sensors, probably due to the different electrical properties of this material with respect to the skin.

Table 1. Software-based methods for fingerprint vitality detection and materials and methods used for stamp fabrication

Reference	Scanner	Method	Cast material	Mould material
[9]	Capacitive	Consensual	Rubber	Play-Doh
[10]	Not specified	Consensual	Gum	Gelatine
[11]	Digital cam.	Consensual	Not specified	Gelatine Plastic clav.
[13]	Optical	Consensual	Not specified	Silicone, Gelatine, Latex
[12]	Optical Electro-optical Capacitive	Consensual	Dental impression	Play-Doh
[14]	Optical	Consensual	Plasticine	Silicone
[15]	Optical Electro-optical Capacitive	Consensual	Not specified	Play-Doh Gelatine

In table 1 it is worth noting that all the approaches at the state-of-the-art used the consensual method for creating the stamp. This method consists in three steps: (1) the user put his finger on a mould material: the pattern of the fingerprint image negative is reproduced in a mould; (2) the cast material (e.g. liquid silicon with a catalyst) is dripped over the mould: the liquid covers the negative fingerprint; (3) after some hours the solidification of the rubber is completed and the cast can be removed from the mould; (4) the rest of the mould is cleaned off from the surface of the cast. This method exploits the subject cooperation whilst other approaches, e.g., the ones that produce a fake stamp from latent fingerprints, are more complex and requires more expert knowledge [3]. Moreover, the quality of stamps is intrinsically lower than that obtained with the consensual method. The consensual method is used for obtaining high quality stamps, in order to create a severe performance test for vitality detection.

It is, in fact, easy to see that fraudulent attacks using high quality stamps are much more difficult to detect, while attacks with low quality stamps can be, in many cases, detected also without using a vitality detection module (the fake impression is rejected as an impostor impression).

However, it should be noted that several variables are involved in the fraudulent access process, in particular: (1) the initial pressure of the subject on the cast; (2) the mould material dripped over the cast; (3) the contact of the stamp on the acquisition surface. These variables concur to alter the shape of the reproduced fingerprint and, in some cases, these alterations strongly impact on the final quality of the obtained image. Figure 2 shows some examples of fake fingerprint images where it can be easily observed the different visual quality. It is worth noting that no previous work has devoted much attention to this issue. However, in our opinion, it is important because adding a fake fingerprint detector obviously impacts on the false rejection rate of the system, that is, the rate of genuine rejected due to misclassified live fingerprints. Fake fingerprint images of poor quality, as those showed in Figure 2(a, c), could be easily rejected without employing a fake detector. It is worth noting that this problem arises independently on the position of the fake detection module into the processing chain (e.g. if the fake detection is done before or after the verification stage).

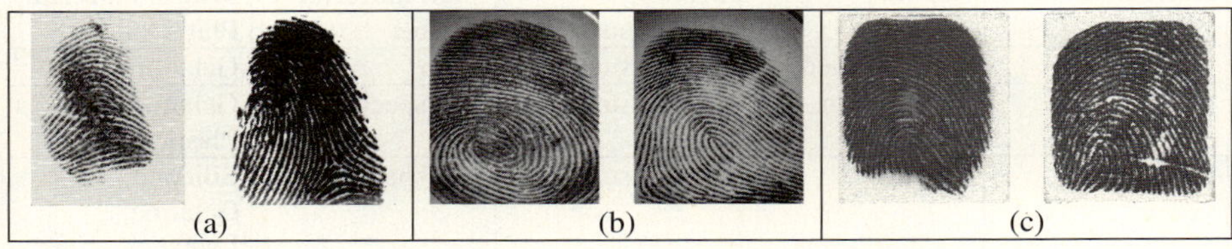

Fig. 2. Examples of fake fingerprint images from Ref. [9] (a), Ref. [14] (b), Ref. [11] (c)

The second item we raised in this Section concerns the characteristics of the data set used for the vitality detection experiments. Table 2 points out the most important characteristics of the data sets used in previous works. The second column reports the number of different fake fingerprints (subjects), the third the number of impressions for each fingerprint, the fourth the number of image frames acquired. The fifth column points out if the subjects used for producing stamps are the same used as clients, namely, if the data set contains both fake and live fingerprint images for each individual.

Information reported in Table 2 is useful to analyze: (1) the sample size of data sets for fake detection rate evaluation; (2) the protocol adopted in experiments.

With regard to item (1), it is worth noting that it requires several resources in terms of volunteers, time, and personnel devoted to stamp fabrication. In particular, volunteers must be trained to appropriately press their finger on the mould material, and a visual analysis of the stamp is necessary in order to obtain good quality images. In order to produce an acceptable stamp, many trials are required. Since the solidification of the mould material can require several hours, this impacts on the number of fake stamps produced per time unit. As a consequence, reported experimental results can be affected by the small sample size of the used data set. This could cause a not reliable estimation of the detection performance.

Table 2. Some key characteristics of the data set used for vitality detection experiments in previous works

Reference	No. fakes	No. impressions	No. frames	Correspondence with clients ?
[9]	18	1	2	NO
[10]	32	10	0	YES
[11]	24	1	0	NO
[13]	12	5	20	NO
[12]	33	1	2	NO
[14]	28	2	2	YES
[15]	80	1	0	NO

The differences about the above item (2), i.e., the differences of the characteristics of the data sets, are pointed out by the fifth column of Table 2. The term "correspondence with client" means that for each fake image, there is the correspondent live image. This impacts on the experimental protocol used and the final goal of the experimentation. In particular, works for which this correspondence is absent are aimed to point out that the proposed feature(s) can allow to distinguish a fake image from an alive one. Accordingly, they do not require the presence of related clients. On the other hand, they do not allow evaluating the penetration rate of the stamps in a verification system, that is, to assess the rate of fake fingerprints which would be accepted as live fingerprints.

In some cases (Table 2, third and sixth rows), a certain number of live and fake fingerprint frames/impressions is captured from the same subject. This is due to the characteristic of the measure, which requires the comparison of the input impression with the related template client (e.g. elastic distortion or morphological measures [10, 14] which require an additional minutiae extraction step), and also to the possibility of evaluating the relationship between fake detection rate and verification performance. In this case the protocol adopted is a little more complex, because the fake detection features can be extracted only by the comparison phase. As an example, the protocol adopted in [14] is made up of the following steps:

- the second impression has been considered as the template of the fingerprint stored in the system database. The minutiae-points were manually detected in order to avoid errors due to the minutiae detection algorithm;
- the first and the second frame of the first impression have been considered as the images provided by the system during an access attempt. Only attempts related to fingerprints of the same subject were considered ("genuine" attempts by live and fake fingers). Even for these images the minutiae-points were manually detected.

4 Previous Works: Vitality Detection Performances

Table 3 reports a preliminary comparison of previous works in terms of overall miss-detection (classification) rate, that is, the average between the rate of "live" fingerprints wrongly classified as fake ones and viceversa.

Due to several problems, as the differences in terms of sensors used, data set size, protocol, and classifiers, it is difficult to fairly compare these values. As an example, the work by Antonelli et al. [13] uses a threshold-based classifier based on the mono-dimensional distribution of live and fake classes. This distribution has been computed by the Euclidean distance between template and input distortion codes. The threshold has been tuned on the "equal error rate" value. This value is obviously different from the overall error rate usually considered for evaluating the performance of vitality detection systems.

Moreover, the strong variations in error rates even when using similar approaches (e.g. see [10] and [14], or [9] and [12]) suggest that a common experimental protocol is necessary in order to avoid the difficulty in interpreting reported results.

Finally, an average error rate of 3-5% even in small data sets makes these systems quite unacceptable for a real integration in current fingerprint verification systems, due to their impact on the false rejection rates (i.e. wrongly rejected clients) which could increase. As an example, the best fingerprint verification system at the 2004 edition of Fingerprint Verification Competition exhibited a 2% equal error rate on average. [16]

Table 3. Vitality detection performance reported in previous works

Reference	Classification method	Error rate
[9]	Back-propagation neural network	0%
[10]	Support Vector Machine	18%
[11]	Threshold	0%
[13]	Threshold	5% (equal error rate)
[12]	Neural Network, Threshold, Linear Discriminant Analysis	6% (capacitive sensor) 3% (electro-optical sensor) 2% (optical sensor)
[14]	k-NN Classifier	6%
[15]	Classification Tree	5% (capacitive sensor) 13% (optical sensor)

5 Conclusions

Fingerprint vitality detection has become a crucial issue in personal verification systems using this biometric.

In this paper, we critically reviewed the main approaches to fingerprint vitality detection proposed in these years. To the best of our knowledge, this is the first survey about fake fingerprint detection methods. In particular, we proposed a possible taxonomy for summarizing the current state-of-the-art and also examined the scientific literature from other point of views, as the materials employed for producing fake stamps and the data sets used for experiments. Finally, we reported the detection rates of previous works in order to trace a preliminary comparison among the current approaches.

Our future work will analyze further the state of the art and will also perform a fair experimental comparison by adopting an appropriate data set aimed to highlight pros and cons of the state-of-the-art methods for fingerprint vitality detection.

References

[1] Maltoni, D., Maio, D., Jain, A.K., Prabhakar, S. (eds.): Handbook of fingerprint recognition. Springer, Heidelberg (2003)

[2] Bolle, R.M., Connell, J.H., Ratha, N.K.: Biometric perils and patches. Pattern Recognition 35(12), 2727–2738 (2002)

[3] Matsumoto, T., Matsumoto, H., Yamada, K., Hoshino, H.: Impact of artificial 'gummy' fingers on fingerprint systems. In: Proceedings of SPIE, vol. 4677 (2002)

[4] Lapsley, P., Less, J., Pare, D., Hoffman, N.: Anti-Fraud Biometric Sensor that Accurately Detects Blood Flow, SmartTouch, LLC, US Patent #5,737,439 (1998)

[5] Biel, L., Pettersson, O., Philipson, L., Wide, P.: ECG analysis: A new approach in human identification. IEEE Transactions on Instrumentation and Measurement 50(3), 808–812 (2001)

[6] Baldissera, D., Franco, A., Maio, D., Maltoni, D.: Fake Fingerprint Detection by Odor Analysis. In: proceedings International Conference on Biometric Authentication (ICBA06), Hong Kong (January 2006)

[7] Osten, D., Carim, H.M., Arneson, M.R., Blan, B.L.: Biometric, Personal Authentication System, U.S. Patent #5 719 950 (February 17, 1998)

[8] Jain, A.K., Bolle, R., Pankanti, S. (eds.): BIOMETRICS: Personal Identification in Networked society. Kluwer Academic Publishers, Dordrecht (1999)

[9] Derakhshani, R., Schuckers, S., Hornak, L., O'Gorman, L.: Determination of vitality from a non-invasive biomedical measurement for use in fingerprint scanners. Pattern Recognition 36(2), 383–396 (2003)

[10] Chen, Y., Jain, A.K., Dass, S.: Fingerprint deformation for spoof detection. In: Biometric Symposium, Cristal City, VA (2005)

[11] Moon, Y.S., Chen, J.S., Chan, K.C., So, K., Wool, K.C.: Wavelet based fingerprint liveness detection. Electronics Letters 41(20), 1112–1113 (2005)

[12] Parthasaradhi, S., Derakhshani, R., Hornak, L., Schuckers, S.: Time-series detection of perspiration as a vitality test in fingerprint devices. IEEE Trans. On Systems, Man and Cybernetics, Part C 35(3), 335–343 (2005)

[13] Antonelli, A., Cappelli, R., Maio, D., Maltoni, D.: Fake Finger Detection by Skin Distortion Analysis. IEEE Transactions on Information Forensics and Security 1(3), 360–373 (2006)

[14] Coli, P., Marcialis, G.L., Roli, F.: Analysis and selection of feature for the fingerprint vitality detection. In: SSPR/SPR 2006, pp. 907–915 (2006)

[15] Tan, B., Schuckers, S.: Liveness detection for fingerprint scanners based on the statistics of wavelet signal processing. In: Conference on Computer Vision Pattern Recognition Workshop (CVPRW'06) (2006)

[16] Maio, D., Maltoni, D., Cappelli, R., Wayman, J.L., Jain, A.K.: FVC2004: Third Fingerprint Verification Competition. In: Zhang, D., Jain, A.K. (eds.) ICBA 2004. LNCS, vol. 3072, pp. 1–7. Springer, Heidelberg (2004)

Optimum Detection of Multiplicative-Multibit Watermarking for Fingerprint Images

Khalil Zebbiche, Fouad Khelifi, and Ahmed Bouridane

School of Electronics, Electrical Engineering and Computer Science,
Queen's University Belfast
BT7 1NN Belfast, UK
{kzebbiche01,fkhelifi01,A.Bouridane}@qub.ac.uk

Abstract. Watermarking is an attractive technique which can be used to ensure the security and the integrity of fingerprint images. This paper addresses the problem of optimum detection of multibit, multiplicative watermarks embedded within Generalized Gaussian distribution features in Discrete Wavelet Transform of fingerprint images. The structure of the proposed detector has been derived using the maximum-likelihood approach and the Neyman-Pearson criterion. The parameters of the Generalized Gaussian distribution are directly estimated from the watermarked image, which makes the detector more suitable for real applications. The performance of the detector is tested by taking into account the different quality of fingerprint images and different attacks. The results obtained are very attractive and the watermark can be detected with low detection error. Also, the results reveal that the proposed detector is more suitable for fingerprint images with good visual quality.

Keywords: Fingerprint images, multibit watermarking, multiplicative rule, maximum-likelihood.

1 Introduction

Fingerprint-based authentication systems are the most advanced and accepted techniques of the biometric technologies. They have been used in law enforcement agencies and have been progressively automated over the last years. With the recent developments in fingerprint sensing, an increasing number of non-criminal applications are either using or actively considering using fingerprint-based identification. However, biometric-based systems, in general, and fingerprint-based systems, in particular, may risk several threats. Ratha et *al.* [1] describe eight basic sources of possible attacks on biometric systems. In addition Schneir [2] identifies many other types of abuses. Watermarking, which is one of the possible techniques that may be used, has been introduced to increase the security and the integrity of fingerprint data [3]-[7].

One of the most important stages in watermarking is the detection stage, which aims to decide whether a given watermark has been inserted within an image or not. This can be seen as a hypothesis testing in that the system has to decide the alternative hypothesis (the image is watermarked) and the null hypothesis (the image is not

S.-W. Lee and S.Z. Li (Eds.): ICB 2007, LNCS 4642, pp. 732–741, 2007.

watermarked). In binary hypothesis testing two kinds of errors can occur: accepting the alternative hypothesis, when the null hypothesis is correct and accepting the null hypothesis when the alternative hypothesis is true. The first error is often called false alarm error and the second error is usually called missed detection error.

The problem of watermarking detection has been investigated by many researchers; however, the most of these works consider the case of one-bit watermarking. The problem of assessing the presence of a multibit watermark is more difficult than the one-bit watermark because the information bits embedded are unknown for the detector. Hernandez et *al.* [8] derived an optimum detection strategy for additive watermarking rule, which cannot be used when another embedding rule is used. Barni et *al.* [9] proposed a structure of an optimum multibit detector for multiplicative watermarks embedded in Weibull distribution features.

In this paper, we propose an optimum detector of a multibit, multiplicative watermark embedded in the DWT coefficients of fingerprint images. The structure of the proposed detector is derived using a maximum-likelihood (ML) method based on Bayes' decision theory, whereby the decision threshold is obtained using the Neyman-Pearson criterion. A Generalized Gaussian Probability Density Function (PDF) is used to model the statistical behavior of the coefficients. The performance of the proposed decoder is examined through a number of experiments using real fingerprint images with different quality.

The rest of the paper is organized as follows: Section 2 shows how the watermark sequence is hidden into the DWT coefficients. Section 3 explains the derivation of the decision rule based on ML method while the derivation of the decision threshold is presented is Section 4. The experimental results are provided in Section 5. The conclusion is presented in Section 6.

2 Embedding Stage

The watermark is embedded into the DWT subbands coefficients. Let $b=\{b_1...b_{Nb}\}$ be the information bit sequence to be hidden (assuming value +1 for bit 1 and -1 for bit 0) and $m=\{m_1m_2...m_{Nb}\}$ a pseudo-random set uniformly distributed in [-1, 1], which is generated using a secret key *K*. The information bits *b* are hidden as follows: (i) the DWT subband coefficients used to carry the watermark are partitioned into N_b non-overlapping blocks $\{B_i\text{: } 1 \leq i \leq N_b\}$. (ii) the watermark sequence *m* is split into N_b non-overlap chunks $\{M_i\text{: } 1 \leq i \leq N_b\}$ so that, each block B_k and each chunk M_k will be used to carry one in information bit. (iii) each chunk M_k is multiplied by +1 or -1 according to the information bit b_k to get an amplitude-modulated watermark. Finally, the watermark is embedded using the multiplicative rule, given by:

$$y_{B_k} = \left(1 + \gamma M_k b_k\right) x_{B_k} \tag{1}$$

where $x_{B_k} = \{x_{1B_k} x_{2B_k} \cdots x_{NB_k}\}$ and $y_{B_k} = \{y_{1B_k} y_{2B_k} \cdots y_{NB_k}\}$ are the DWT coefficients of an original image and the associated watermarked image belonging to the block B_k, respectively. γ is a positive scalar value used to control the strength of the watermark. The larger the strength, the more robust is the watermark but the visual quality of the image may be affected. So, it is important to set γ to a value which maximizes the robustness while keeping the visual quality unaltered.

3 Maximum-Likelihood Detection

Since the exact information bit sequence is unknown for the detector for blind watermarking, multibit detection is more difficult than the one-bit case. However, an optimum detector for multibit watermark can be derived following the same approach for the one-bit watermark described in [10], [11]. The watermark is detected using ML based on Bayes' decision theory, whereby the decision threshold is derived using the Neyman-Pearson criterion which aim to minimize the missed detection probability for a fixed false alarm rate. According to this approach, the problem is formulated as a statistical hypothesis testing. Two hypotheses can be established as follows:

H_0: Coefficients are marked by a spreading sequence *m*, modulated by one of the 2^{Nb} possible bit sequence *b*.
H_1: Coefficients are marked with another possible sequence *m'*, including the null sequence, where $m' \neq m$.

The likelihood ratio, denoted by $l(y)$, is defined as:

$$l(y) = f_Y(y|m) / f_Y(y|m'). \tag{2}$$

where $f_Y(y|m)$ and $f_Y(y|m')$ represent the PDF of *y* conditioned to the presence of the sequence *m* and *m'*, respectively. In fact, it has been proved in [10] that for reasonably small value of the strength γ, the PDF of the coefficients *y* conditioned to the event *m'* can be approximated by the PDF of *y* conditioned to the presence of the null sequence, $f_Y(y|0)$. The likelihood ration $l(y)$ becomes:

$$l(y) = f_Y(y|m) / f_Y(y|0). \tag{3}$$

Assuming that the information bits *b* and the coefficients in *m* are independent of each other, as well as the DWT coefficients used to carry the watermark. The PDF $f_Y(y|m)$ is obtained by integrating out the 2^{Nb} possible bit sequences.

$$\begin{aligned} f_Y(y|m) &= \prod_{k=1}^{N_b} f_Y(y_k|m_k) \\ &= \prod_{k=1}^{N_b} f_Y(y_k|m_k, -1)\, p(b_k = -1) + f_Y(y_k|m_k, +1)\, p(b_k = +1). \end{aligned} \tag{4}$$

By assuming that $p(b_k = -1) = p(b_k = +1) = 1/2$, equation (4) can be written as follows:

$$l(y)=\frac{\prod_{k=1}^{N_b}\frac{1}{2}\left[\prod_{i\in B_k}\frac{1}{1-\gamma m_{ki}}f_X\left(\frac{y_{ki}}{1-\gamma m_{ki}}\right)+\prod_{i\in B_k}\frac{1}{1+\gamma m_{ki}}f_X\left(\frac{y_{ki}}{1+\gamma m_{ki}}\right)\right]}{\prod_{k=1}^{N_b}\left[\prod_{i\in B_k}f_X\left(y_{ki}\right)\right]} \tag{5}$$

Further simplification can be made by taking the natural logarithm of the likelihood ratio, thus the decision rule can be expressed by

$$\begin{aligned} z(y)=\sum_{k=1}^{N_b}\Bigg\{&-\ln(2)+\ln\Bigg[\prod_{i\in B_k}\left(\frac{1}{1-\gamma m_{ki}}\right)f_X\left(\frac{y_{ki}}{1-\gamma m_{ki}}\right)-f_X\left(y_{ki}\right)\\ &+\prod_{i\in B_k}\left(\frac{1}{1+\gamma m_{ki}}\right)f_X\left(\frac{y_{ki}}{1+\gamma m_{ki}}\right)-f_X\left(y_{ki}\right)\Bigg]\Bigg\} \end{aligned} \tag{6}$$

For an optimum behavior of the ML detector, it is necessary to describe the PDF of the DWT coefficients of the original image. An initial investigation using various distributions such as Laplacian, Gaussian and Generalized Gaussian has found that the Generalized Gaussian PDF is the most suitable distribution that can reliably model the DWT coefficients of the fingerprint images. It has been found that the Generalized Gaussian can also be used to model the coefficients for each block B_k. The central Generalized Gaussian PDF is defined as:

$$f_X(x_i;\alpha,\beta)=\left(\beta\big/2\alpha\Gamma\left(1/\beta\right)\right)\exp\left(-\left(|x_i|/\alpha\right)^\beta\right) \tag{7}$$

where $\Gamma()$ is the Gamma function, i.e., $\Gamma(z)=\int e^{-t}t^{z-1}dt$, $z>0$. The parameter α is referred to as scale parameter and models the width of the PDF peak (standard deviation) and β is called the shape parameter and it is inversely proportional to the decreasing rate of the peak. Note that $\beta=1$ yields the Laplacian distribution and $\beta=2$ yields the Gaussian one. The parameter α and β are estimated as described in [12].

Inserting (7) in (6), the decision rule for the Generalized Gaussian model is expressed by:

$$\begin{aligned} z(y)=\sum_{k=1}^{N_b}\Bigg\{&-\ln(2)+\ln\Bigg[\prod_{i\in B_k}\left(\frac{1}{1-\gamma m_{ki}}\right)\exp\left[\left(\frac{|y_{ki}|}{\alpha_{B_k}}\right)^{\beta_{B_k}}\left[1-\left|\frac{1}{1-\gamma m_{ki}}\right|^{\beta_{B_k}}\right]\right]\\ &+\prod_{i\in B_k}\left(\frac{1}{1+\gamma m_{ki}}\right)\exp\left[\left(\frac{|y_{ki}|}{\alpha_{B_k}}\right)^{\beta_{B_k}}\left[1-\left|\frac{1}{1+\gamma m_{ki}}\right|^{\beta_{B_k}}\right]\right]\Bigg]\Bigg\} \end{aligned} \tag{8}$$

The decision rule reveals that an image is watermarked by the sequence m (H_0 is accepted) only if $z(y)$ exceeds a threshold λ.

4 Decision Threshold

The Neyman-Pearson criterion is used in this work to obtain the threshold λ in such a way that the missed detection probability is minimised, subject to a fixed false alarm probability P^*_{FA}. Fixing the value of P^*_{FA}, the threshold λ can be obtained using the relation:

$$P^*_{FA} = P(z(y) > \lambda | H_1) = \int_{\lambda}^{+\infty} f_z(z(y))\, dz \tag{9}$$

where $f_z(z(y))$ is the PDF of z conditioned to the event H_1. The problem now is to derive a good estimate of $f_z(z(y))$. One idea is to use Monte Carlo simulations to estimate the false alarm probability for different values of λ and then choose the threshold λ which leads to the desired false alarm. However, this approach is very computationally intensive, especially when Generalized Gaussian PDF is used to model the coefficients because the parameters β and α are calculated numerically. Another simpler solution may be used to derive the threshold λ, by relying on the central limit theorem and assuming that the PDF of $z(y)$ can be assumed Gaussian with mean $\mu_z = E[z(y)]$ and $\delta_z^2 = V[z(y)]$ [9]. Equation (9) can be written as:

$$P^*_{FA} = \frac{1}{2} erfc\left(\frac{\lambda - \mu_z}{\sqrt{2\delta_z^2}} \right) \tag{10}$$

where $erfc()$is the complementary error function, so:

$$\lambda = erfc^{-1}(2P^*_{FA})\sqrt{2\delta_z^2} + \mu_z . \tag{11}$$

The mean μ_z and the variance δ_z^2 are estimated numerically by evaluating $z(y)$ for n unreal sequences $\{ m_i : m_i \in [-1, 1]; 1 \le i \le n \}$, so that

$$\hat{\mu}_z = \frac{1}{n} \sum_{i=1}^{n} z_i \tag{12}$$

and

$$\hat{\delta}_z^2 = \frac{1}{n-1} \sum_{i=1}^{n} (z_i - \hat{\mu}_z)^2 \tag{13}$$

where z_i represents the log likelihood ratio corresponding to the sequence m_i and n is the number of the fake sequences used to evaluate z. the selection of n involves a trade-off between computational complexity and accuracy of results. The higher the n, the better the estimates of μ_z and δ_z^2 but the higher computational complexity is and the less used in real applications, and inversely.

5 Experimental Results

The experiments were carried out using real fingerprint images of size 448×478 with different quality chosen from 'Fingerprint Verification Competition' (Db3_a,FVC

2000)[13] . Each image is transformed by DWT using Daubechies wavelet at the 3rd level to obtain low resolution subband (LL_3), and high resolution horizontal (HL_3), vertical (LH_3) and diagonal (HH_3) subbands. For reasons of imperceptibility and robustness, the watermark is embedded in the HL_3, LH_3, HH_3 subbands. Each subband is partitioned into blocks of size 16×16 (256 coefficients/block). A blind detection is used so that the parameters α and β of each block used are directly estimated from the DWT coefficients of the watermarked image because it was assumed that the watermarked image is close to the original one (strength γ<<1). For all experiments, we choose 0.20 for γ and 10^{-7} for P_{FA}.

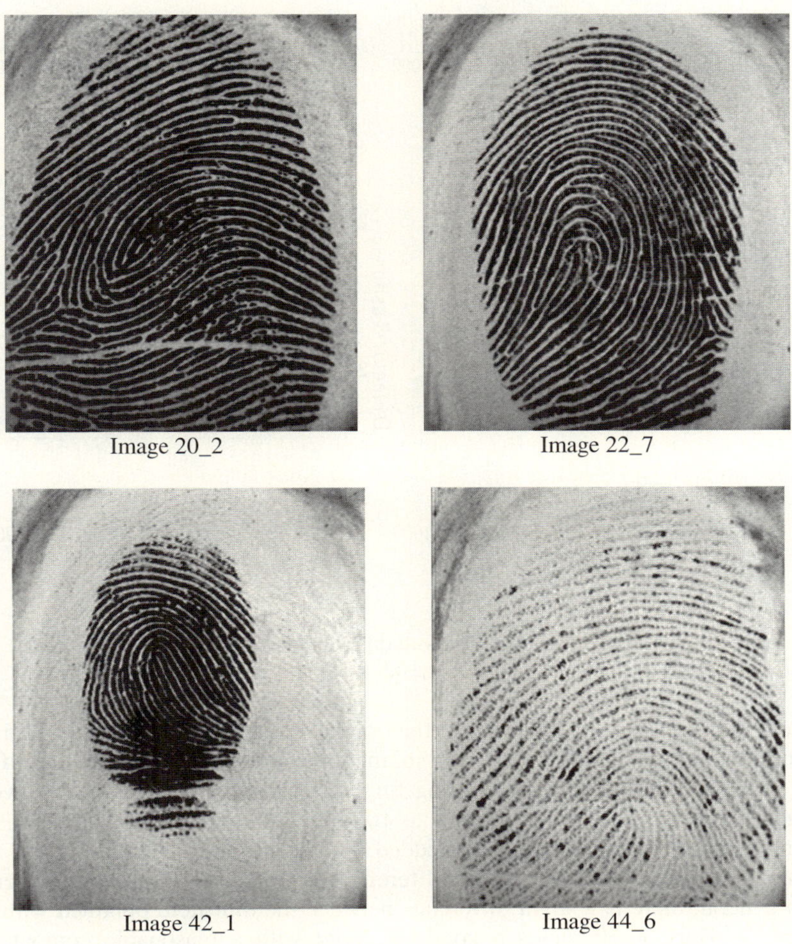

Fig. 1. Test images

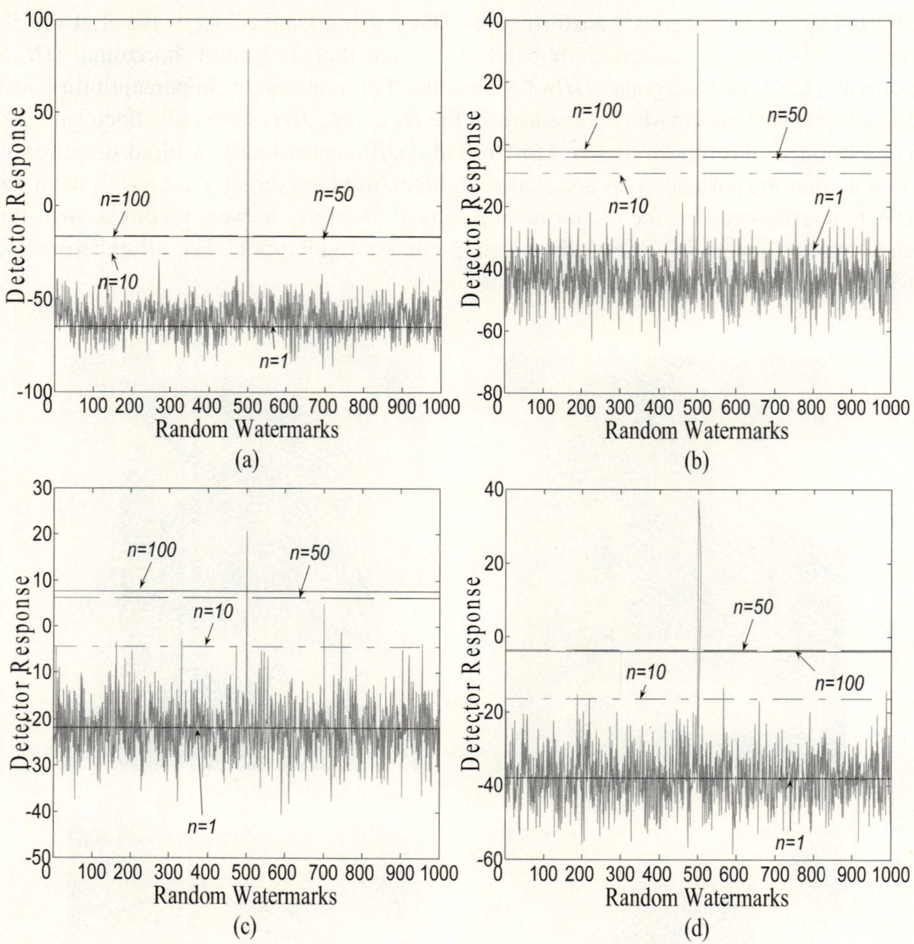

Fig. 2. Response of the watermark detector with different thresholds calculated with n=1, 10, 50, 100. (a) Image 20_2, (b) Image 22_7, (c) Image 42_1, (d) Image 44_6. γ=0.20 and P_{FA}=10^{-7}.

The first experiment is to determine the optimal value of *n*, necessary to derive the threshold λ with low complexity. To do so, the threshold λ is computed with different values of *n* (*n*=1, 10, 50, 100) and using fingerprint images of Fig. 1. We have also computed the responses of the detector to 1000 random watermarks where only one watermark among them is actually embedded. The results are plotted in Fig. 2.

The results obtained show that the different thresholds get closer when *n* increases and, in general, there is a slight difference between the threshold obtained with *n*=50 and *n*=100. Thus, n=50 yields a good threshold with a reasonable computational complexity. Further, the Fig. 2 shows that the correct response is much higher than those responses of the fake watermarks.

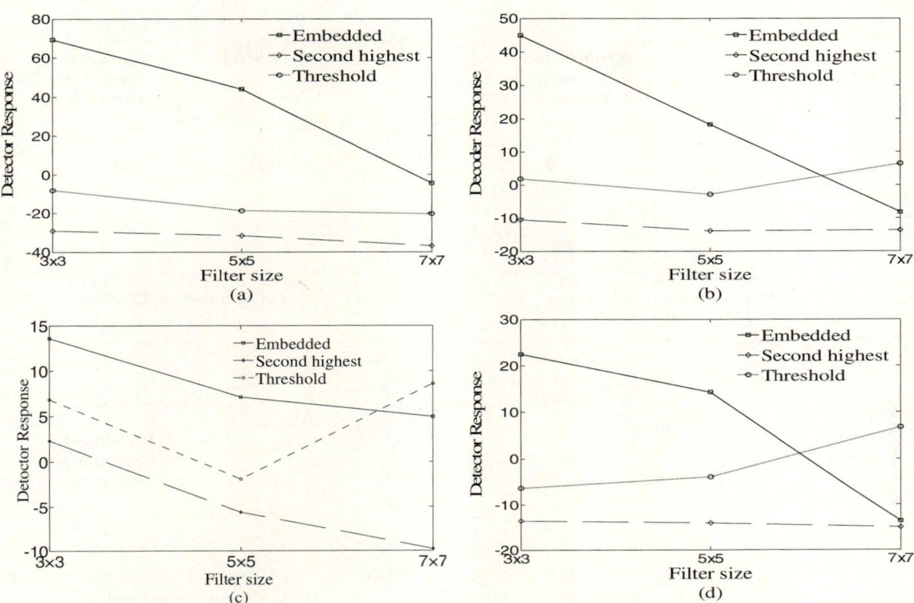

Fig. 3. Robustness against image filtering (mean filtering). Results refer to: (a) Image 20_2, (b) Image 22_7, (c) Image 42_1, (d) Image 44_6. with: γ=0.20, n=50 and P_{FA}=10^{-7}.

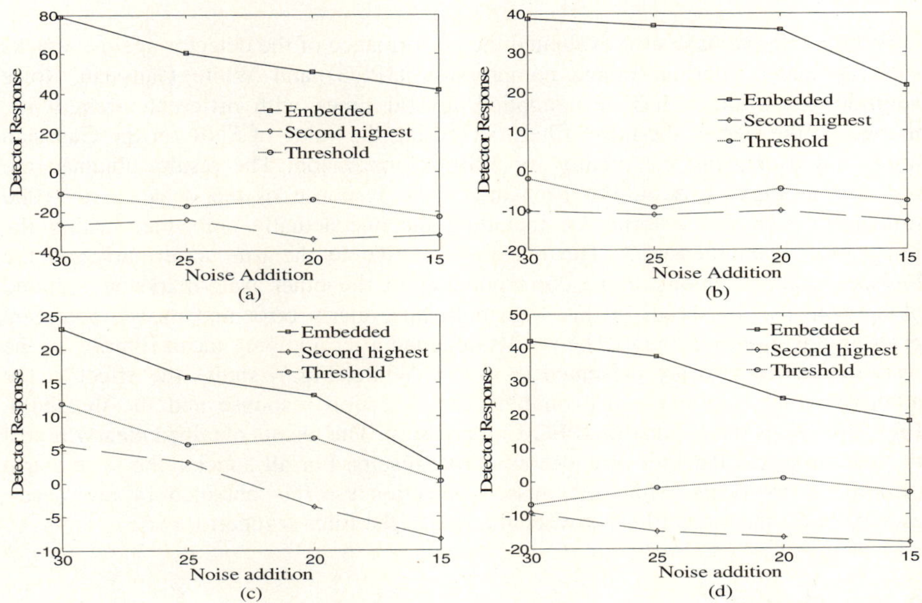

Fig. 4. Robustness against Gaussian noise addition. Results refer to: (a) Image 20_2, (b) Image 22_7, (c) Image 42_1, (d) Image 44_6. with: γ=0.20, n=50 and P_{FA}=10^{-7}.

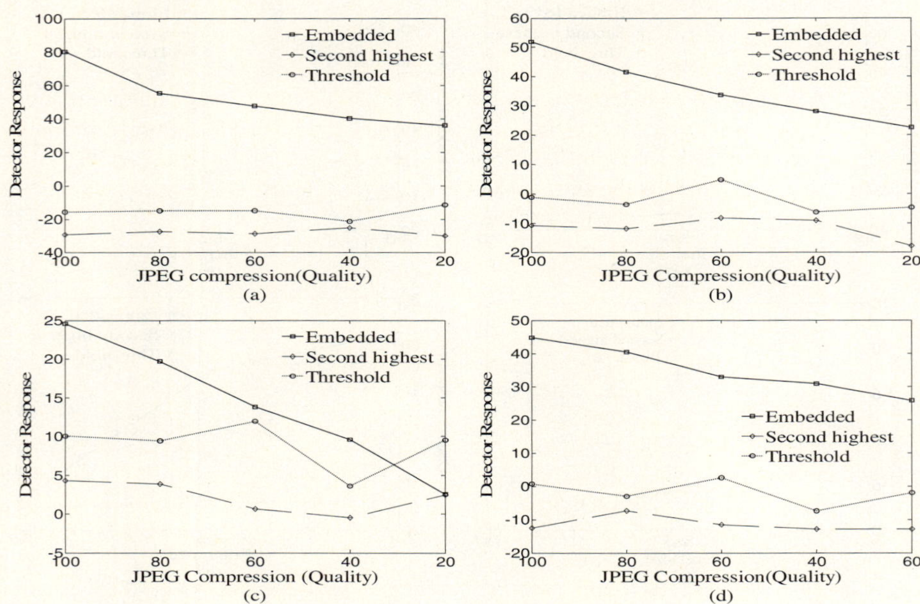

Fig. 5. Robustness against JPEG compression. Results refer to: (a) Image 20_2, (b) Image 22_7, (c) Image 42_1, (d) Image 44_6. with: γ=0.20, n=50 and $P_{FA}=10^{-7}$.

With n=50, we have also evaluated the performance of the detector against attacks such as mean filtering, image compression (JPEG) and White Gaussian Noise addition. Each attack has been applied several times with different strength i.e. increasing the size of the mean filter, decreasing the value of SNR for the Gaussian noise and decreasing the quality for JPEG compression. The results obtained are reported in Figs. 2, 3, 4. For each attack the response of the detector for 1000 randomly generated watermarks, including the one actually embedded within the image, has been measured. The response relative to the true watermark and the highest response among those corresponding to the other watermarks are plotted along with the threshold. In this way, both false alarm error and missed detection error are taken into account. The results obtained after applying mean filtering to the watermarked images are presented in Fig. 3. While, Fig. 4 shows the effect of the additive white Gaussian noise on both the detection response and the threshold. Fig. 5. provides the results for JPEG Compression. The results obtained clearly reveal that the proposed detector provides attractive results. For all attacks, the false alarm error does not occur while the missed detection error is obtained in few cases, especially for the mean filtering when the size of the filter is superior to 5.

6 Conclusion

In this paper, an optimum detector, based on the ML approach, for fingerprint image watermarking in the DWT domain has been proposed. The Generalized Gaussian

PDF has been used to model the statistical behavior of the DWT coefficients. The experiments reveals that the proposed detector provides very attractive results and the detecting error probability is very low, even in the presence of attacks. Also, the results confirm that the Generalized Gaussian is the most suitable distribution that can reliably model the DWT coefficients of fingerprint images. Further more, the quality of fingerprint images have an influence on the performance of the detector; we notice that the detector provides the best results for the images of good quality, where the ridges are very clear and represents the major part of the image.

References

1. Ratha, N.K., Connell, J.H., Bolle, R.M.: Enhancing Security and Privacy in Biometrics-based Authentication systems. Proc. IBM Systems Journal 40 (2001)
2. Schneier, B.: The Uses and Abuses of Biometrics. Comm. ACM 42, 136 (1999)
3. Pankanti, S., Yeung, M.M.: Verification Watermarks on Fingerprint Recognition and Retreival. In: Proc. SPIE EI, San Jose, CA, vol. 3657, pp. 66–78 (1999)
4. Ratha, N.K., Connell, J.H., Bolle, R.M.: Secure Data Hiding in Wavelet Compressed Fingerprint Images. In: Proc. ACM Multimedia 2000 Workshops, Los Angeles, CA, pp. 127–130. ACM Press, New York (2000)
5. Uludag, U., Gunsel, B., Ballan, M.: A Spatial Method for Watermarking of Fingerprint Images. In: Proc. First Intl. Workshop on Pattern Recognition in Information Systems, Setúbal, Portugal, pp. 26–33 (2001)
6. Jain, A.K., Uludag, U.: Hiding Biometric Data. In: Proc. IEEE, vol. 25. IEEE Computer Society Press, Los Alamitos (2003)
7. Zebbiche, K., Ghouti, L., Khelifi, F., Bouridane, A.: Protecting Fingerprint Data using Watermarking. In: Proc. First AHS Conf., Istanbul, Turkey, pp. 451–456 (2006)
8. Hernandez, J.R., Amado, M., Perez-Gonzales, F.: DCT-Domain Watermarking Techniques for Still Images: Detector Performance Analysis and New Structure. IEEE Trans. Image Processing 9, 55–68 (2000)
9. Barni, M., Bartolini, F., De Rosa, A., Piva, A.: Optimum Decoding and Detecting of Multiplicative Watermarks. IEEE Trans. Signal Processing 51, 1118–1123 (2003)
10. Barni, M., Bartolini, F., De Rosa, A., Piva, A.: A New Decoder for the optimum recovery of nonadditive Watermarks. IEEE Trans. Image Processing 10, 357–372 (2001)
11. NG, T.M., Garg, H.K.: Wavelet Domain Watermarking using Maximum-Likelihood Detection. In: Proc. SPIE Conf. Security, Steganographie, Watermarking Multimedia, San Jose, CA, vol. 5306 (2004)
12. Do, M.N., Vetterli, M.: Wavelet-based Texture Retrieval using Generalized Gaussian and Kullback-Leibler. IEEE Trans. Image Processing 11, 146–158 (2002)
13. Fingerprint Verification Competition: http://bias.csr.unibo.it/fvc2000/download.asp

Fake Finger Detection Based on Thin-Plate Spline Distortion Model

Yangyang Zhang, Jie Tian, Xinjian Chen, Xin Yang, and Peng Shi

Center for Biometrics and Security Research, Key Laboratory of Complex Systems and Intelligence Science, Institute of Automation, Chinese Academy of Sciences, Graduate School of the Chinese Academy of Sciences, P.O. Box 2728 Beijing 100080 China
tian@ieee.org, jie.tian@ia.ac.cn
http://www.fingerpass.net

Abstract. This paper introduces a novel method based on the elasticity analysis of the finger skin to discriminate fake fingers from real ones. We match the fingerprints before and after special distortion and gained their corresponding minutiae pairs as landmarks. The thin-plate spline (TPS) model is used to globally describe the finger distortion. For an input finger, we compute the bending energy vector by the TPS model and calculate the similarity of the bending energy vector to the bending energy fuzzy feature set. The similarity score is in the range [0, 1], indicating how much the current finger is similar to the real finger. The method realizes fake finger detection based on the normal steps of fingerprint processing without special hardware, so it is easily implemented and efficient. The experimental results on a database of real and fake fingers show that the performance of the method is available.

Keywords: fake finger, distortion, Thin-plate Spline model, bending energy vector, fuzzy feature set.

1 Introduction

Fingerprints have been increasingly utilized to realize individual identification in the civilian's daily life due to the uniqueness, permanence and universality. On the other side, there are still some potential dangerous in fingerprint recognition systems. One of them is caused by fake or artificial fingers, which is crucial for authentication based on fingerprint systems and decreases their security. Many fingerprint capture devices are probably deceived by well-duplicated fake fingers [10]. Therefore it is necessary to detect fake fingers in the fingerprint system, which can ensure that only live fingerprints are capable of generating templates for enrollment and identification. Some approaches have been proposed to resolve the problem [1], [2]. R. Derakhshani et al. [1] utilized detection of a perspiration pattern over the fingertip to identify the fingerprint vitality. Nevertheless, the method experience difficulties in cases of perspiration disorders (too wet or dry) and other abnormal skin conditions. A. Antonelli et al. [2] proposed an approach based on the analysis of finger skin elasticity. They captured a sequence of fingerprints at high frame rate (at least 20 fps) and tracked the location of each block to

S.-W. Lee and S.Z. Li (Eds.): ICB 2007, LNCS 4642, pp. 742–749, 2007.

calculate the DistortionCode. However, it needs special fingerprint capture device and the location tracking among so many frames is time-consuming.

Different from the previous methods, we utilize the Thin-Plate Spline model to globally approach the finger distortion. During the capturing process, the finger was pressed against the sensor surface and deformed according to the force. Under the same pressure, the structure and materials of the fingers determine the distortion of fingerprints. For live fingers, the special way they distort is related to the elasticity of human skin, and the position and shape of the finger bone. It is difficult to simulate the live fingers precisely. Therefore when pressed against the surface of the capture sensor, the fake and real fingers distort in different ways. The distortion is one of the difficult problems in fingerprint recognition, but here it is utilized to discriminate live fingers from fake ones.

We match the fingerprints before and after special distortion to gain their corresponding minutiae pairs as landmarks and use the thin-plate spline (TPS) model to globally describe the finger distortion. The bending energy vector of the TPS model is employed to determine the nature of the finger, and to the best of our knowledge this is the first time for using TPS model in fake finger detection. For an input finger, we firstly compute its bending energy vector of the TPS model, then calculate the similarity of the bending energy vector to the trained bending energy fuzzy feature set. The similarity score is in the range [0, 1], indicating how much the current finger is similar to the real one (1 means real finger).

The rest of this paper is organized as follows: section 2 describes the proposed approach, section 3 reports the experiments carried out to validate the new technique, and section 4 draws our conclusion.

2 Fake Finger Detection Based on TPS Distortion Model

Previous works [1], [2] show that generally fake fingers are more rigid than skin and the deformation is lower even if made of highly elastic materials. The elasticity is the basis for discriminating fake fingers from real ones. When a real finger moves on the scanner surface, it produces larger distortion than the fake fingers. We use the Thin-plate Spline (TPS) model to describe the finger distortion.

2.1 Fingerprints Capture and Landmarks Extraction

In order to describe the distortions produced by the finger, the user is required to firstly place a finger onto the scanner surface without any superficial tension, then to apply some pressure in four directions: 0 deg, 90deg, 180 deg and 270 deg respectively. A sequence of acquired fingerprints are captured for each finger including the natural fingerprint F0 and the distorted ones $\{F1, F2, F3, F4\}$.

Before the computation of the TPS distortion model, the acquired fingerprint images are enhanced by the Hong's method [3] and analyzed to extract relevant features related to skin distortion. When the fingerprint is distorted, its minutiae, as the most popular local features in the fingerprint, have different removal according to their locations. If the minutiae distribute almost symmetrically all over the fingerprint, their displacement can represent the global distortion. In Ref. [4], a robust method is proposed to match the distorted fingerprints based on the local triangle features set. During the matching

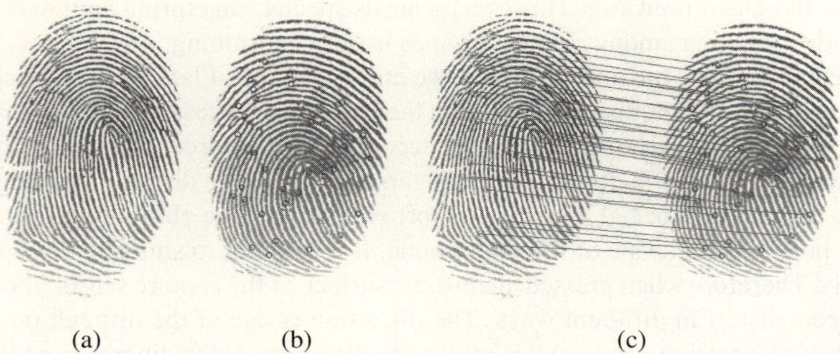

Fig. 1. (a) fingerprint F0 with extract minutiae; (b) fingerprint F3 with extracted minutiae; (c) the two fingerprints with corresponding minutiae paired

process, we can obtain a series of paired minutiae from two fingerprints before and after distortion. In the following, we utilize the paired minutiae as the landmark points to compute the parameters of TPS model. The process of the landmarks extraction is shown in Fig. 1.

2.2 Bending Energy Vector Calculation Based on TPS Model

The thin-plate spline (TPS) model calculate a 2D-2D map based on the arbitrary sets of corresponding points and is able to represent elastic deformations. A.M.Bazen et al. [5] and A. Ross et al. [6] applied thin-plate spline to model the elastic deformation of fingerprints. Since the live fingers have different distorted characteristics from fake ones, their TPS distorted features should have different characters under the same distortion condition caused by the same directional pressure. Given the displacements of a number of landmark points, the TPS model interpolates those points, while maintaining maximal smoothness. At each landmark point P_i, the displacement is represented by an additional z-coordinate. For each point (x, y) in original image, the TPS model describes the corresponding coordinates (x', y') in transformed image as $(f_x(x, y), f_y(x, y))$. The bending energy is given by the integral of the second-order partial derivatives over the entire surface and can be minimized by solving a set of linear equations. The TPS model for one of the transformed coordinates is given by the parameter vectors a and w:

$$f(x, y) = a_1 + a_2 x + a_3 y + \sum_{i=1}^{n} w_i \delta(|P_i - (x, y)|) \quad (1)$$

where the function $\delta(r)$ is adopted as the root function specially, $\delta(r) = -r^2 * log(r^2)$, a defines the affine part of the transformation, w gives an additional non-linear deformation, P_i is the ith landmark and n is the number of landmarks.

In fake finger detection, we take the paired minutiae as landmarks. However, the locations of landmarks maybe displaced a few pixels and false local matching maybe introduced because of the mistake in minutiae extraction algorithm. We use the approximating thin-plate splines model [11] to introduce some insensitivity to these errors. It allows a smoother transformation instead of entirely interpolating all the landmarks.

$$Q = (K + \lambda I) * W + P * \alpha \tag{2}$$

where I is $n * n$ identify matrix,λ refers to the weight of the optimization of landmark distance and smoothness. If we adopts large λ, only the affine transformation is left.

The TPS parameters W and α that minimize the bending energy satisfy the following linear equation:

$$\begin{bmatrix} q_{x,1} & q_{y,1} \\ \vdots & \vdots \\ q_{x,n} & q_{y,n} \end{bmatrix} = \begin{bmatrix} \lambda & \delta(r_{12}) + \lambda & \cdots & \delta(r_{1n}) + \lambda \\ \delta(r_{21}) + \lambda & \cdots & \cdots & \delta(r_{2n}) + \lambda \\ \cdots & \cdots & \cdots & \cdots \\ \delta(r_{n1}) + \lambda & \delta(r_{n2}) + \lambda & \cdots & \lambda \end{bmatrix} \begin{bmatrix} w_{x,1} & w_{y,1} \\ \vdots & \vdots \\ w_{x,n} & w_{y,n} \end{bmatrix} + \begin{bmatrix} 1 & p_{x,1} & p_{y,1} \\ \vdots & \vdots & \vdots \\ 1 & p_{x,n} & p_{y,n} \end{bmatrix} \begin{bmatrix} a_{x,1} & a_{y,1} \\ a_{x,2} & a_{y,2} \\ a_{x,3} & a_{y,3} \end{bmatrix} \tag{3}$$

where n is the number of landmarks, $r_{ij} = |P_i - P_j|$ represents the distance between the landmarks i and j, $P_i = (p_{x,i}, p_{y,i})$ is the ith landmark in the natural image, $Q_i = (q_{x,i}, q_{y,i})$ is the corresponding point in the distorted image.

When applied to fake finger detection, the TPS model must be attached with some modification. The affine part of typical TPS model defined by the matrix α allows the image to translate, rotate and scale. When the fingerprint distorts, its affine transformation can be defined by the vector $\Delta T = (\Delta x, \Delta y, \Delta\theta)$, where $\Delta\theta$ is the rotation angle and $(\Delta x, \Delta y)$ are the translations in x and y coordinates. We realize the global alignment of two fingerprints based on multiple reference minutiae [9]. Then we calculate the transformation matrix α as :

$$\alpha = \begin{bmatrix} \Delta x & sin(\Delta\theta) & cos(\Delta\theta) \\ \Delta y & cos(\Delta\theta) & -sin(\Delta\theta) \end{bmatrix} \tag{4}$$

The global bending energy E is calculated as the sum of the bending energy of X and Y transformed coordinates, which are respectively denoted by E_x and E_y. According to [8], the bending energy for one of the coordinates is estimated as following:

$$E_x = \int\int_{R^2} ((\frac{\partial^2 f_x}{\partial x^2})^2 + 2 * (\frac{\partial^2 f_x}{\partial x \partial y})^2 + (\frac{\partial^2 f_x}{\partial y^2})^2) dxdy \tag{5}$$

The value of bending energy E_x is proportional to $W_x^T K W_x$, where $W_x = (K + \lambda I)^{-1}(Q_x - P_x * \alpha_x)$. The bending energy is zero only when all the components of W are zero. In this case, there is just rigid transformation between two fingerprints.

We compute the bending energy of the finger in four directions: 0 deg, 90 deg, 180 deg and 270 deg respectively. The bending energy vector V is composed of these four bending energy defined as $E_0, E_{90}, E_{180}, E_{270}$. The obtained bending energy vector characterizes the deformation of a finger under a specific condition. Fig. 2 illustrates the main steps of the bending energy vector computation. A sequence of fingerprints

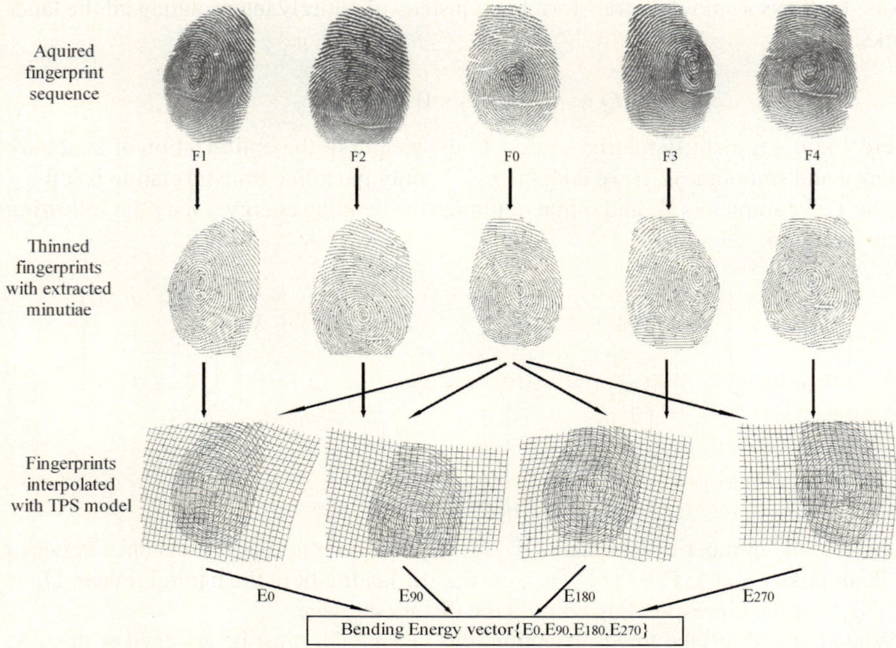

Fig. 2. The main steps of the bending energy vector computation

is captured and their minutiae are extracted from the thinned images. We respectively calculate the TPS models based on the paired landmarks between the natural fingerprint and the other four distorted fingerprints. The natural fingerprint F0 is distorted into the fingerprint skeletons in the third row by the corresponding TPS models. F0 is covered with griding before interpolating to represent the distortion of the TPS models clearly.

2.3 Fuzzy Similarity Measure

The fuzzy similarity based on bending energy vector method is applied to discriminate a real one from a fake finger. For an input finger, we compute the similarity between the current bending energy vector and the trained fuzzy feature set during the enrollment. The similarity score is in the range $[0, 1]$, indicating how much the current finger is similar to the real one(1 means real finger).

All elements in bending energy vector space of real finger construct real finger's fuzzy feature set $\tilde{V}$.We define z_r as he center of fuzzy feature set:

$$z_r = \frac{\Sigma_{v \in \tilde{V}} v}{Vol(\tilde{V})} \tag{6}$$

where $Vol(\tilde{V})$ denotes the size of $\tilde{V}$, z_r is essentially the mean of all elements of feature set. While averaging over all features in a feature set increases the robustness of fuzzy feature, at the same time, lots of useful information is submerged into the smoothing process because a set of feature vectors are mapped to a single feature vector.

Building or choosing a proper membership function is application dependent. The most commonly used prototype membership functions are cone, exponential, and Cauchy functions [7]. In the proposed algorithm, the modified Cauchy function is chosen due to its good expression and high-computational efficiency.

The membership function of bending energy vector e to real finger's fuzzy feature set $\tilde{V} : C_r(e) \rightarrow [0, 1]$, is defined as:

$$C_r(e) = \begin{cases} 1 & \text{if } h(e - z_r) = True \\ \dfrac{1}{1 + (\dfrac{\|e - z_r\|}{m})^a} & \text{otherwise} \end{cases} \quad (7)$$

where m and a , $m > 0$, $a \geq 0$, $\boldsymbol{z}_r$ is the center location of the fuzzy set. $h(e - z_r) = True$, if and only if the value of each entry in feature vector is less than the valve of corresponding entry in feature vector z_r. m represents the width $\|e - z_r\|$ of the function, and a determines the smoothness of the function. Generally, m and a describe the grade of fuzziness of the corresponding feature. It is obvious that the farther a feature vector moves away from the cluster center, the lower the degree of membership to the fuzzy feature.

Likewise, all elements in bending energy vector space of fake finger construct the fuzzy feature set $\tilde{U}$. We define the membership function of bending energy vector e to fake finger's fuzzy feature set $\tilde{U} : C_f(e) \rightarrow [0, 1]$.

Consequently, the similarity of the bending energy vector to the fuzzy feature sets is defined as $Sim(e) = (1 - p) * C_r(e) + p * (1 - C_f(e))$, where $p \in [0, 1]$ adjusts the significance of $C_r(e)$ and $C_f(e)$.

3 Experimental Results

A database of fingerprint sequences is collected to evaluate the fake fingerprint detection approach. 120 fake fingers are manufactured (made of silicone AL20) starting from fingers of the 20 cooperating volunteers and ten sequences are recorded for each finger. We also capture the same-scaled fingerprint sequences from the corresponding real fingers. All the fingerprints are acquired through CrossMatch V300 (Optical sensor). The database is divided into two disjoint sets: the training set (20 real/fake fingers) used to select the parameters of the approach and the test set (100 real/fake fingers) used to measure the performance. The matching where the number of landmarks exceeds a certain threshold $nThr$ (In our experiments $nThr$ = 15) is taken into account so that the fake-detection performance is evaluated more accurately. Fig. 3 shows the distribution of the number of landmarks N and the bending energy E in fake and real fingerprint matching.

Let FAR be the proportion of transactions with a fake finger that are incorrectly accepted and FRR be the proportion of transactions with a real finger that are incorrectly rejected. The Equal Error Rate (EER) of the proposed approach measured in the above experiments is 4.5%. Fig. 4 displays the performance diagram of our algorithm.

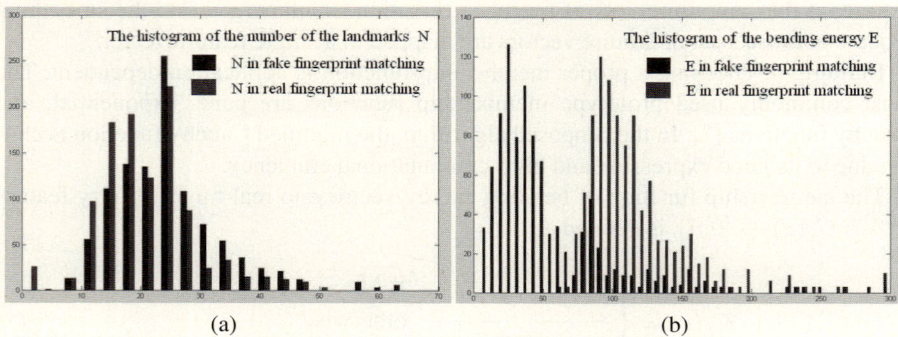

(a) (b)

Fig. 3. The distribution of the number of landmarks and the bending energy

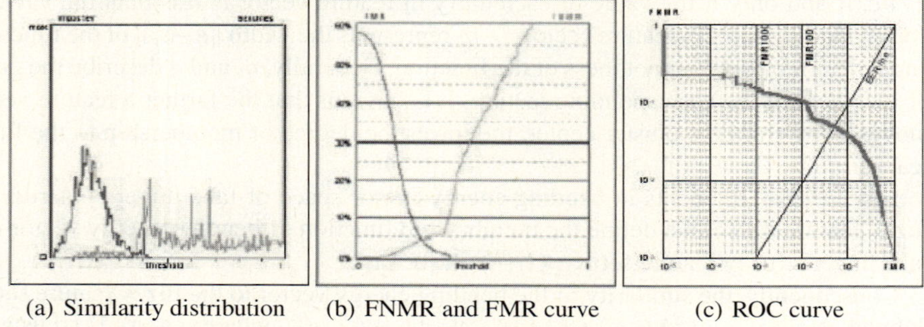

(a) Similarity distribution (b) FNMR and FMR curve (c) ROC curve

Fig. 4. The performance of our algorithm (red curve is for fake fingers, green curve is for real ones)

The experimental results prove that when real fingers move on a scanner surface they mostly produce a larger distortion than the fake fingers.The proposed method is easily implemented without needing any additional hardware. It is based on normal steps of fingerprint identification, including matching the fingerprints and gaining their corresponding minutiae pairs. The decision is made based on the similarity of the input finger's bending energy vector to the bending energy fuzzy feature set so it is efficient. The experimental results on the database of real and fake fingers show that the performance of the method is available.

4 Conclusion

The distortion is one of the difficult problems in fingerprint recognition, but in this paper it is used to discriminate live finger from fake ones. The proposed method uses the thin-plate spline (TPS) model to realize fake fingers detection. The bending energy vector of the TPS model is used to determine the nature of the finger. For an input finger, we firstly compute the bending energy vector of the TPS model, then calculate the similarity of the bending energy vector to the trained bending energy fuzzy feature set. The experimental results on the database of real and fake fingers confirm that the performance of the method is very promising. Nevertheless, the performance of the method relies on the accuracy of minutiae extraction and pairing.

Acknowledgments. This paper is supported by the Project of National Science Fund for Distinguished Young Scholars of China (No. 60225008), the Key Project of National Natural Science Foundation of China (No. 60332010 and 60575007), the Project for Young Scientists' Fund of National Natural Science Foundation of China (No.60303022), and the Project of Natural Science Foundation of Beijing (No.4052026).

References

1. Derakhshani, R., Schuckers, S.A.C., Hornak, L.A., O'Gorman, L.: Determination of vitality from a non-invasive biomedical measurement for use in fingerprint scanners. Pattern Recognition 36(2), 383–396 (2003)
2. Antonelli, A., Cappelli, R., Maio, D., Maltoni, D.: A new approach to fake finger detection based on skin distortion. In: Zhang, D., Jain, A.K. (eds.) Advances in Biometrics. LNCS, vol. 3832, pp. 221–228. Springer, Heidelberg (2005)
3. Hong, L., Wan, Y., Jain, A.K.: Fingerprint image enhancement: algorithms and performance evaluation. IEEE Trans. Pattern Analysis Machine Intelligence 20(8), 777–789 (1998)
4. Chen, X.J., Tian, J., Yang, X.: An algorithm for distorted fingerprint matching based on local triangle features set. IEEE Trans. on Information, Forensics and Security 1(2) (2006)
5. Bazen, A.M., Gerez, S.H.: Fingerprint matching by thin-plate spline modelling of elastic deformations. Pattern Recognition 36(8), 1859–1867 (2003)
6. Ross, A., Dass, S., Jain, A.K.: A deformable model for fingerprint matching. Pattern Recognition 38(1), 95–103 (2005)
7. Hoppner, F., Klawonn, F., Kruse, R., Runkler, T.: Fuzzy cluster analysis: methods for classification, Data Analysis and Image Recognition. John Wiley & Sons, Chichester (1999)
8. Bookstein, F.L.: Principal warps: Thin-plate splines and the decomposition of deformations. IEEE Transactions on Pattern Analysis and Machine Intelligence 2(6), 567–585 (1989)
9. Zhu, E., Yin, J.P., Zhang, G.M.: Fingerprint matching based on global alignment of multiple reference minutiae. Pattern Recognition 38(10), 1685–1694 (2005)
10. Matsumoto, T.H., Yamada, K., Hoshino, S.: Impact of Artificial 'Gummy' Fingers on. Fingerprint Systems. In: Proceedings of SPIE, vol. 4677 (2002)
11. Rohr, K., Fornefett, M., Stiehl, H.S.: Approximating Thin-Plate Splines for Elastic Registration: Integration of Landmark Errors and Orientation Attributes. In: Proceedings of the 16th International Conference on Information Processing in Medical Imaging, pp. 252–265 (1999)

Robust Extraction of Secret Bits from Minutiae

Ee-Chien Chang[1] and Sujoy Roy[2]

[1] School of Computing, National University of Singapore, Singapore
changec@comp.nus.edu.sg
[2] Institute for Infocomm Research, Singapore
sujoy@i2r.a-star.edu.sg

Abstract. Our goal is to extract *consistent* bits from the same fingerprint in a noisy environment. Such bits can then be used as a secret key in several cryptographic applications. In order to correct inevitable noise during scanning and processing, a known approach extracts and publishes an additional information, known as secure sketch from the minutiae. During subsequent scanning, the sketch aids in correcting the noise to give the consistent bits. However, for minutiae (represented as 2D point set), known constructions produce sketches that are large, and are difficult to adapt to slight variations of the 2D point representation. Furthermore, even with simplified model on the noise and distribution of the minutiae, it is not clear what is the entropy of the bits extracted. To overcome the problems, we suggest using a locality preserving hash in sketch construction. We give a method that produces a small sketch and thus suitable for applications involving mobile devices. Since the sketch size is small, with a reasonable assumption, we can estimate the entropy of the secret bits extracted. In addition, we can incorporate statistical properties of the noise, and distribution of the minutiae in fine-tuning the method. Our method also includes registration of fingerprints. Experiments conducted on 4000 fingerprint images from the NIST 4 database show promising results. Assuming that an intermediate representation is uniformly distributed, with FNMR = 0.09% we are able to extract about 8 secret bits (by a conservative estimate) or 10 bits (with certain assumption on the underlying codebook).

Keywords: Secure sketch, Fuzzy vault, Locality preserving hash, Cryptography.

1 Introduction

Fingerprints are probably one of the most widely used biometrics today. A typical fingerprint based authentication system, when given a template (obtained during enrollment) and a query (obtained during verification), decides whether the query is authentic by measuring its distance from the template. A less well studied application extracts a sequence of bits from the template, and such bits are then served as a secret key in other cryptographic operations. For example, one may use the secret bits to encrypt a file. During decryption of the file, the *exactly same* sequence needs to be extracted from the query. Note that when

S.-W. Lee and S.Z. Li (Eds.): ICB 2007, LNCS 4642, pp. 750–759, 2007.

used as a key in cryptographic applications, the representative sequence has a stronger requirement, that their match must be *exact*, i.e., two similar minutiae must map to the exactly same bit sequence. This requirement is much more restrictive than the requirement of similarity (not necessarily exact match) between the minutiae, as in typical authentication systems. In this paper, our goal is to extract consistent bits from minutiae.

In order to achieve consistency, a technique, known as fuzzy commitment[9], secure sketch[7], shielding function[10] and helper data[13], extracts an additional information from the template during enrollment. We follow notations by Dodis et al. [7] and call the additional information a sketch. The sketch has to be made public. In the example on encryption, the sketch is to be stored in clear in the header information of the encrypted file. During verification, the sketch is employed to remove the noise, in a similar role as the parity check bits of an error correcting code. Since the sketch is published in clear, it has to be secure in the sense that it does not reveal too much about the original template.

Relationship with traditional authentication system. Note that a system which is able to extract consistent bits, can be adopted (although not preferable) to serve the purpose of a typical biometric authentication system. This is done by simply using the bits as the template: two templates are declared to be a match iff their extracted bits are exactly the same. Hence, if the systems is able to extract m consistent bits, the false match rate (FMR) of the corresponding authentication system is 2^{-m}. Since biometric authentication system is relatively more extensively studied, the performance of bit extraction system is unlikely to out-perform the state-of-the art biometric authentication system in terms of false match rate (FMR) and false non-match rate (FNMR). In other words, if the state-of-the-art authentication system achieves FMR of 0.1% at a particular FNMR, it is unlikely that we can extract more than 10 bits(with the same FNMR). Although 10 bits is too small for cryptographic operations and thus seems pessimistic, we could employ multi-modals to increase the bits size. Some previous works claim to extract significantly more bits from a single fingerprint. However, these claims may be based on simplified noise models, or the claims may not consider information leaked by the sketch and information leaked during alignment. The relationship between the FMR with the bits size is also discussed by Buhan et al. [1] from another perspective.

Challenging issues in sketch construction. The design of a secure sketch heavily depends on the notion of similarity between templates, which is related to the associated underlying metric space. Although there are near optimal constructions for some metrics like Hamming distance for binary strings [9,7], and set-difference for sets [8,7,2], extending such constructions to the more "complicated" metric for minutiae is not straightforward. This is because the sketch has to handle both white noise, which corresponds to Hamming distance, and replacement noise, which corresponds to set-difference [6,3].

Clancy et al. [6] proposed a sketch construction for fingerprint that uses *chaff points.* Essentially, a large set of random points (known as the chaff points) is first generated, and the union of the chaff points and the minutiae is the sketch. The chaff points-based approach is adopted in a few other schemes [12,13,3]. However, it is very difficult to analyze the security achieved by this approach. Without rigorous analysis, it is not clear how many secret bits can be extracted. Indeed, an attack is proposed by Chang et al. [4] which demonstrates that the information revealed by the sketch is more than what was previously estimated. Although there are constructions with provable bounds on entropy loss[3] (based on formulation by Dodis et. al.[7]), it is not clear how effective are those constructions in practice. Furthermore, although the original minutiae are hidden, specific important information is revealed. For example, a point that does not appear in the sketch is definitely not in the original.

Besides the difficulty in analyzing the security of chaff points-based approach, there are also a few practical issues. Firstly, the sketch should be small so as to be fitted into mobile devices like smart card. Chaff points-based methods give large sketch since the size has a tradeoff with the security. Secondly, since the template is not available during verification, it is not clear how to align the query. Earlier works typically assumed that the fingerprints are already aligned with the exception of some recent works by Uludag et al. [13], which employ orientation field flow curves for alignment. Thirdly, previous works assume simplified models of noise and distribution of the minutiae. It is not clear how to fine-tune chaff generation for different noise models, and different statistical models of the minutiae.

Main idea in our construction. To handle the above mentioned issues, we propose applying a locality-preserving transformation[1] on the minutiae to a vector space of real coefficients. The function is locality preserving in the sense that two close-by data in the original metric space remains close to each other in the transformed space. Besides being locality-preserving, the function should decorrelate the original and give mutually independent real coefficients. We decorrelate the original by applying Principle Component Analysis so that the coefficients are pair-wise independent.

Note that we do not propose a new representation for fingerprint. Instead, we apply a transformation that preserves distance information of a well-accepted representation for fingerprints, and then extract bits from the transformed data.

Below are some advantages of the proposed method.

1. The transformation provides a way to map the minutiae to a metric space, whereby sketch can be easily constructed. It is fairly easy to adapt our transformation to different variants of minutiae representation. For example, if the orientation of each minutia is to be included, it is easy to modify the transformation to accustom this variation.
2. The transformation "diffuses" certain information on each individual minutia. In particular, some important specific information, for e.g. total number of minutiae, possible locations of the minutiae etc, are diffused and not leaked out.

[1] Also known as biometric embedding[7].

3. Our method is able to handle a wider class of noise models. As we shall see later, we use a maximum likelihood decoding to search for the the secret bits. As long as the noise model is able to facilitate maximum likelihood decoding, it can be incorporated.
4. Our method can also handle a more general model of minutiae distribution. This is achieved by applying PCA in the transformed domain.
5. As opposed to the chaff points-based method, no randomness is injected during the sketch construction. As a result, the size of our secure sketch is small.

Our method includes registration of fingerprints. This is achieved by including singular (core/delta) points[5] in the final sketch. These points carry global information and are independent of the minutiae, and thus unlikely to reveal any information of the minutiae, whereby the secret bits are extracted.

Our experimental data set consists of 2000 pairs of fingerprints from the NIST 4 database, using 100 pairs as training data and the rest as test data. Experimental studies show that the method can extract 10 consistent bits with FNMR of 0.09% and the total sketch size is around 320 bits. Hence, if this bit extraction system is adopted to serve in the traditional authentication system, its FNMR is 0.09% and FMR is 0.1%, which is close to typical authentication systems.

2 Proposed Method

2.1 Enrollment/Sketch Construction

Step 1. Extracting minutiae and singular points. Given a fingerprint, the set of minutiae $\mathbf{x}$ is extracted. Next, the singular (core and delta) points of the fingerprint are extracted using the complex filter based method proposed by Nilsson et al. [11].

Step 2. Locality Preserving Hash. Herein the set of minutiae $\mathbf{x}$ are mapped to a vector $\mathbf{v}$ in $\mathbb{R}^k$. This step consists of two transformations, M_1 and M_2, where M_1 maps the minutiae to a real vector, and M_2 de-correlates the vector and keeps only k coefficients. The final output is

$$\mathbf{h}_{\mathbf{x}} = M_2(M_1(\mathbf{x})).$$

The transformations M_2, M_1 and the parameter k are chosen during the design stage. First, a set $\mathcal{L}$ of 2D lines are selected, where$|\mathcal{L}| = q$ is some integer greater than k. Given the set $\mathbf{x}$, and a line $\ell \in \mathcal{L}$, we can obtain an integer which is the difference of number of points on the two sides of the line. Since there are q lines in $\mathcal{L}$, given $\mathbf{x}$, we obtain q integers. Let $\mathbf{v} = (v_1, v_2, \ldots, v_q)$ where v_i is the integer obtained corresponding to the i-th line in $\mathcal{L}$. Let M_1 denote this transformation, that is $\mathbf{v} = M_1(\mathbf{x})$.

Using knowledge of the statistical distribution of $\mathbf{v}$ (derived from a large collection of fingerprints), Principle Component Analysis (PCA) can be carried out to derive a linear transformation that de-correlate the coefficients in $\mathbf{v}$. By keeping only k decorrelated coefficients, we obtain the linear transformation M_2.

The q lines in $\mathcal{L}$ are randomly chosen during the design stage. One could choose the lines with certain properties, for example, equally spaced horizontal and vertical lines. One could also choose much more lines, i.e., using a larger q. Nevertheless, experiments suggest that the final performance is similar. The prior knowledge of the statistical distribution can be obtained from a database of samples. For example, the NIST fingerprint database [14] provides ample fingerprints to estimate the distribution of $M_1(\mathbf{x})$.

Step 3. Convert $\mathbf{h}_\mathbf{x}$ *to bits.* The sequence $\mathbf{h} = (h_1, h_2, \ldots, h_k)$ is converted to k bits $\mathbf{b} = (b_1, b_2, \ldots, b_k)$, where $b_i = 0$ iff $h_i < 0$, for each i.

Note that the PCA ensures that coefficients of $\mathbf{h}_\mathbf{x}$ are pairwise uncorrelated. Hence we assume that the k-bits $\mathbf{b}$ are uniformly distributed, and its entropy is k.

Step 4. Extract consistent bits and secure sketch. This step requires a codebook $\mathcal{C} = \{\mathbf{C}_i\}_{i=1}^{2^m}$ where each $\mathbf{C}_i$ is a k-bits string and m is a parameter to be decided during the design stage. The message associated to the codeword $\mathbf{C}_i$ is its index i. Given the k-bits sequence $\mathbf{b}_\mathbf{x}$, its nearest codeword $\mathbf{c}_\mathbf{r}$, with respect to Hamming distance, is determined. The message associated to $\mathbf{c}_r$ is output as the consistent bits. The sketch is the bit sequence

$$s_\mathbf{x} = \mathbf{b}_\mathbf{x} \oplus \mathbf{c}_r,$$

where $\oplus$ is the xor operations.

The codebook is determined during the design stage, and m an important parameter needs to be determined. In our implementation, in order to facilitate experimental studies for different values of k and m, we use a random codebook. That is, the codewords are randomly chosen during the design stage. To improve the performance, for a particular k and m, a good error correcting code can be used as the codebook. The use of xor operation here seems abrupt. This is a common technique in sketch construction for binary strings with Hamming distance as the underlying metric[7,9]

The message can be represented as a m-bits string. It is not necessary that the entropy of the message is m. We will discuss this further in Section 3. Alternatively, instead of taking the message as the secret, we can also use $\mathbf{c}_r$ as the secret bits. However, there is high redundancy in the k-bits $\mathbf{c}_r$.

Step 5. Publish the final sketch. The final sketch consists of the sketch $s_\mathbf{x}$, and the singular (core and delta) points information. The final sketch is then made public, for example, by storing it in the header of the encrypted file.

2.2 Verification

Now, given a query fingerprint and the final sketch (recall that the final sketch consists of the singular points, and the sketch $s_\mathbf{x}$, we want to extract the consistent bits.

Step 1. Alignment. Same as Step 1 in enrollment, the minutiae $\mathbf{y}$ and singular points of the query are extracted. Next, using the extracted singular points, and the singular points in the final sketch, alignment is carried out.

Step 2 & 3. Obtain $\mathbf{h_y}$ *and* $\mathbf{b_y}$. The same steps (Step 2 & 3) in the enrollment are carried out to obtain the k-bits $\mathbf{b_y}$.

Step 4. Maximum Likelihood Decoding. Together with the sketch $s_\mathbf{x}$, compute

$$\widetilde{\mathbf{b}} = \mathbf{b_y} \oplus s_\mathbf{x}.$$

Next, using maximum likelihood decoding, find the most likely codeword $\mathbf{c}_r$ that gives $\widetilde{\mathbf{b}}$ (the method is to be described below). The message corresponding to $\mathbf{c}_r$ is the consistent bits.

Given the 100 pairs of fingerprints (original $\mathbf{x}$ and noisy version $\mathbf{y}$) as training data, we compute the k-bits $\mathbf{b_x}$ and $\mathbf{b_y}$. Next, every pair is compared to note the corresponding bit flip for every bit. This gives an estimate of the probability p_j that the j-th bit flips under noise. During maximum likelihood decoding, for each codeword $\mathbf{C}_i = (c_1, c_2, \ldots, c_k)$, we estimate the probability P_i that $\widetilde{\mathbf{b}}_i = (\widetilde{b_1}, \widetilde{b_2}, \ldots, \widetilde{b_k})$ is a noisy version of the codeword.

$$P_i = \prod_{j=1}^{k} p_j^{\widetilde{b}_j \oplus c_j} (1 - p_j)^{(1 - \widetilde{b}_j \oplus c_j)}.$$

The codeword with largest P_i is chosen as the most likely codeword.

2.3 Remark

In sum, during the design stage, we determine a set of lines $\mathcal{L}$, and perform PCA to obtain two transformations M_1 and M_2. A codebook $\mathcal{C}$, and the probability of bit flip p_j is also determined during the design stage. There are two important parameters: k, the number of transformed bits, and $m = \log_2 |\mathcal{C}|$, where $|\mathcal{C}|$ is the number of codewords.

There is a subtle difference between enrollment and verification. During enrollment, the nearest word is determined with respect to the usual Hamming distance. However, during verification, we employ maximum likelihood decoding, which is essentially finding the nearest code with respect to a weighted Hamming distance.

3 Experiments and Analysis

Parameters. The performance of our method is evaluated based on the tradeoff that can be achieved by varying the two parameters. (1) k, the number of PCA coefficients retained, and (2) $|\mathcal{C}|$ the size of the codebook needed. For each set of parameters, we measure (1) the entropy of the sketch, denoted by $|s|$ and (2) FNMR of the system.

Recall that we assume that the k-bits $\mathbf{b}$ are uniformly distributed. If the entropy of the sketch is $|s|$, then the entropy of the consistent bits will be $k - |s|$. However, it is not easy to estimate the sketch entropy. In this paper, we use a conservative estimate (i.e. a upper bound). Thus $k - |s|$ could underestimate the number of consistent bits. From another perspective, the sketch is essentially the syndrome with respect to the error correcting code. If we further assume that the syndrome is independent from the message, then $\log_2 |\mathcal{C}|$ is the number of consistent bits.

Data Set and Experimental setup. Experiments were conducted on a database of 4000 fingerprints from the NIST fingerprint database[14], which consists of two scans of 2000 fingerprints. 100 fingerprint pairs were taken as training data for modeling the noise and distribution of minutiae. The remaining 1900 pairs were left as test data. Minutiae were extracted from the image using *mindtct*, a minutia extraction software provided with the NIST package. The extracted minutiae information consists of the 2D coordinates, the orientation and the quality of the minutiae. Only high quality minutiae were selected based on a threshold. The final set consisted of around 50 to 60 minutiae, and it would require at least 800 bits to represent the minutiae.

The singular points for alignment is extracted using complex filters filters[11]. Figure 1(a) depicts the singular points detected in one of the fingerprint scans.

The sketch size $|s|$ is estimated by first counting the number of 1's among the sketches $s_{\mathbf{x}}$ for all fingerprints in the test data. Now, we can estimate the probability that a bit in the sketch is 1, which in turn give the entropy of the k-bit $s_{\mathbf{x}}$.

Effect of PCA and the noise model. A total of $q = 600$ lines were chosen to perform locality preserving hash and then PCA is applied to generate 600 coefficients. The PCA attempts to decorrelate the coefficients and make them pairwise

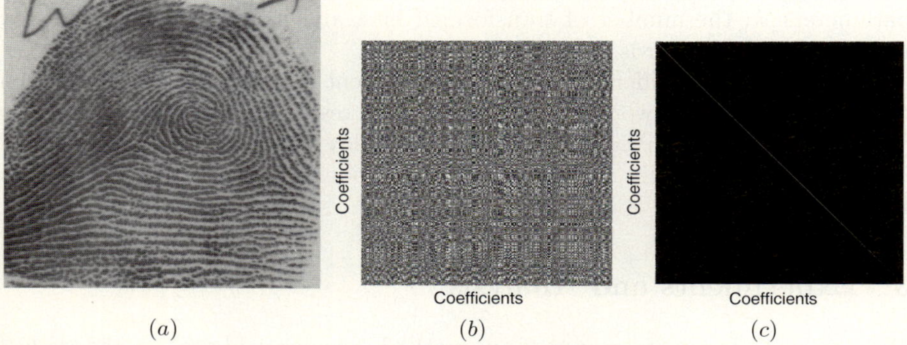

Fig. 1. (a) Singular point (core and delta) detection results for a fingerprint from the NIST database. (b) Covariance matrix of coefficient vectors (for 1900 fingerprint pairs of dimension 600) before applying PCA (c) Covariance matrix of coefficient vectors (for 1900 fingerprint pairs of dimension 600) after applying PCA.

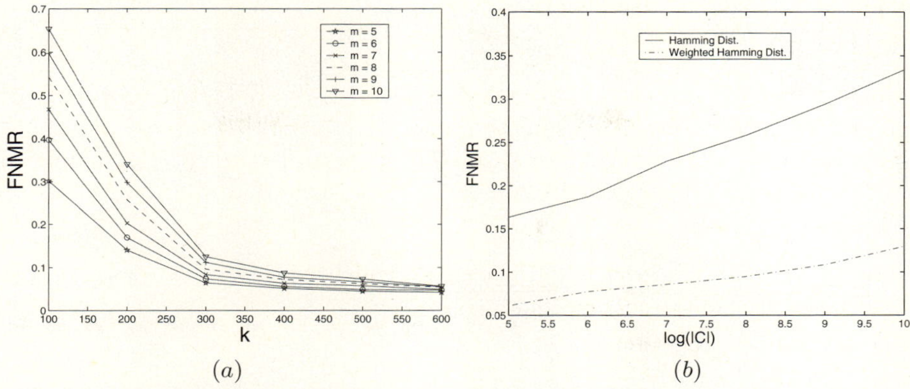

Fig. 2. (a) FNMR vs. k, for different values of $log_2(|\mathcal{C}|)$. (b) FNMR vs. k under hamming and weighted hamming distance. Illustrates the efficacy of using knowledge of noise is designing a distance function.

independent so that the bits in $\mathbf{b_x}$ would be uncorrelated. Figure 1(b)-(c) depicts an image of the covariance matrix of the coefficients for 1900×2 test fingerprints, before and after applying PCA. The high intensity along the diagonal of the covariance matrix image in Figure 1(c) is indicative of the statistical independence of the coefficients. The low intensity of the off-diagonal elements indicate low correlation.

Figure 2(b) illustrates the affect of weighted hamming distance and hamming distance on FNMR. Clearly, from the graph, using the noise model derived from the training data improves the FNMR.

Relationship among different parameters. Fig. 2 (a) shows the FNMR for different k and $|\mathcal{C}|$. As expected, FNMR reduces with larger k. This is expected because using more bits should preserve more distance information. FNMR also reduces with lesser codewords in $\mathcal{C}$. This is because with lesser codewords, the distances among them increase and thus more tolerance to noise. A line drawn parallel to the x-axis gives the number of coefficients k, that need to be retained for a given requirement on FNMR and $log_2|\mathcal{C}|$.

Figure 3(a) depicts the change in FNMR with $log_2(|\text{FMR}|)$ for different sizes of k. Note that for a 10 bit consistent key (i.e., codebook of size 2^{10}) for $k = 300$ bits, FNMR=0.09 (~ 0.1), which is very close to the FNMR obtained in typical biometric authentication systems. Figure 3 (b) depicts the change in sketch size $|s|$ for different k and $log_2|\mathcal{C}|$. An straight line draw parallel to the y-axis gives the sketch size for a given constraint on k and $|\mathcal{C}|$.

An observation is that to extract more bits, the size of the sketch $|s|$ has to be higher otherwise it leads to high FNMR. When k is around 300 bits we expect to be able to extract 10 bits with FNMR ~ 0.1, which is around the FNMR of typical authentication systems. For larger values of k, the FNMR does not improve significantly, hence 300 is a good tradeoff.

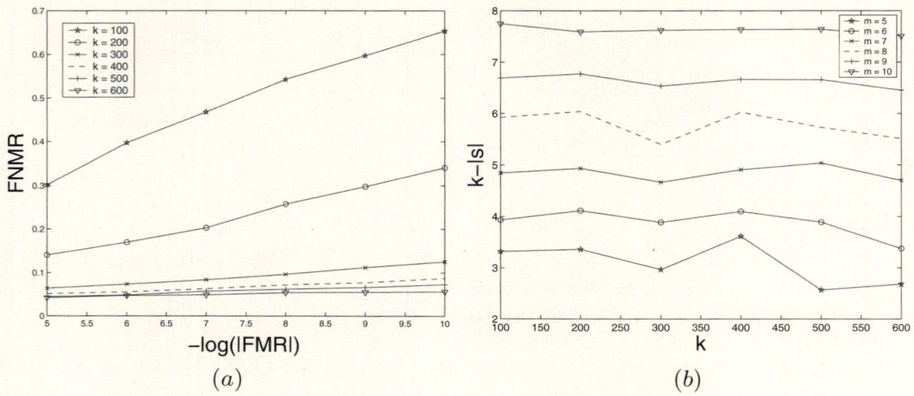

Fig. 3. (a) FNMR vs. $log_2(|\text{FMR}|)$ for different values of k. (b) $k - |s|$ vs. k. Since $|s|$ may be overestimated, this gives a lower bound on the number of consistent bits.

4 Conclusion

In this paper, a method for generating consistent bits from minutiae is proposed. Such bit sequences can be used as secret keys in cryptographic operations that require the exact sequence from different scans. Compared to known bit extraction methods, our proposed method allows for registration of the fingerprints using information (singular points) that is independent of the secret and thus does not leak any information about the minutiae. A locality preserving transformation followed by a PCA is performed on the minutiae to generate a binary sequence. Although some information is thrown away during the transformation, some of the obvious advantages of the method are that information is diffused and the binary sequence generated is robust. Unlike existing techniques, no randomness is injected during sketch construction and thus the sketch size is small. We show the use of a maximum-likelihood based distance measure for decoding that can incorporate different noise models. Experimental results verify the efficacy of our proposed method.

References

1. Buhan, I., Doumen, J., Hartel, P.H., Veldhuis, R.N.J.: Fuzzy extractors for continuous distributions. In: ASIACCS, pp. 353–355 (2007)
2. Chang, E.-C., Fedyukovych, V., Li, Q.: Secure sketch for multi-sets. Cryptology ePrint Archive, Report 2006/090 (2006)
3. Chang, E.-C., Li, Q.: Hiding secret points amongst chaff. In: Vaudenay, S. (ed.) EUROCRYPT 2006. LNCS, vol. 4004. Springer, Heidelberg (2006)
4. Chang, E.-C., Shen, R., Teo, W.: Finding the original point set hideen among chaff. In: Proc. ACM Sym on Information, Computer and Communications Security. ACM Press, New York (2006)

5. Chikkerur, S., Ratha, N.: Impact of singular point detection on fingerprint matching performance. In: IEEE AUTOID. IEEE Computer Society Press, Los Alamitos (2005)
6. Clancy, T.C., Kiyavash, N., Lin, D.J.: Secure smartcardbased fingerprint authentication. In: ACM SIGMM workshop on Biometrics methods and applications, pp. 45–52. ACM Press, New York (2003)
7. Dodis, Y., Reyzin, L., Smith, A.: Fuzzy extractors: How to generate strong keys from biometrics and other noisy data. In: Cachin, C., Camenisch, J.L. (eds.) EUROCRYPT 2004. LNCS, vol. 3027, pp. 523–540. Springer, Heidelberg (2004)
8. Juels, A., Sudan, M.: A fuzzy vault scheme. In: IEEE Intl. Symp. on Information Theory. IEEE Computer Society Press, Los Alamitos (2002)
9. Juels, A., Wattenberg, M.: A fuzzy commitment scheme. In: ACM Conf. on Computer and Communications Security, pp. 28–36. ACM Press, New York (1999)
10. Linnartz, J.-P.M.G., Tuyls, P.: New shielding functions to enhance privacy and prevent misuse of biometric templates. In: Kittler, J., Nixon, M.S. (eds.) AVBPA 2003. LNCS, vol. 2688, pp. 393–402. Springer, Heidelberg (2003)
11. Nilsson, K.: Localization of corresponding points in fingerprints by complex filtering. PhD thesis, Chalmers University of Technology, Sweden (2005)
12. Verbauwhede, I.M., Yang, S.: Secure fuzzy vault based fingerprint verification system. In: 38th Asilomar Conf. on Signals, Systems, and Computers, vol. 1, pp. 577–581 (2004)
13. Uludag, U., Jain, A.: Securing fingerprint template: fuzzy vault with helper data. In: Proc. IEEE Workshop on Privacy Research In Vision. IEEE Computer Society Press, Los Alamitos (2006)
14. Watson, C., Garris, M., Tabassi, E., Wilson, C., McCabe, R., Janet, S.: NIST fingerprint image software 2. NIST Special Database (2006)

Fuzzy Extractors for Minutiae-Based Fingerprint Authentication

Arathi Arakala*, Jason Jeffers, and K.J. Horadam

School of Mathematical and Geospatial Sciences
RMIT University
368-374 Swanston Street, Melbourne 3000
{arathi.arakala,jason.jeffers,Kathy.Horadam}@ems.rmit.edu.au

Abstract. We propose an authentication scheme using fingerprint biometrics, protected by a construct called a Fuzzy Extractor. We look at a new way of quantizing and digitally representing the minutiae measurements so that a construct called PinSketch can be applied to the minutiae. This is converted to a Fuzzy Extractor by tying some random information to the minutiae measurements. We run a matching algorithm at chosen quantization parameters and show that the authentication accuracy is within acceptable limits. We demonstrate that our authentication system succeeds in protecting the users' identity.

1 Introduction

Storage of an un-encrypted enrolled biometric template in a database for authentication is a privacy and security threat (demonstrated by [1] for the fingerprint biometric). Several primitives have been proposed to protect biometric templates by performing template comparison in the encrypted domain ([2], [3], [4], [5] and [6]). Prior work in building practical fingerprint authentication systems using the above ideas ([7] and [8]) use a frequency domain approach, either partially or completely to handle pre-alignment issues . Jeffers and Arakala [9] have studied the feasibility of using translation and rotation invariant structures to build a pre-alignment free Fuzzy Vault using minutiae information alone. In this paper, we extend that work to perform pre-alignment free matching and use Fuzzy Extractors to execute the matching in the encrypted domain.

2 Fuzzy Extractors

A Fuzzy Extractor is a cryptographic construct defined in [6], which enables two inputs to be compared in the encrypted domain and returns a successful match if the two inputs are within a limited distance from each other in a specific metric space. It is a combination of a primitive called a *Secure Sketch* and a *Strong*

* This paper is for the BBSPA competition. It forms part of the PhD thesis of the first author, taken under the supervision of the other two authors.

S.-W. Lee and S.Z. Li (Eds.): ICB 2007, LNCS 4642, pp. 760–769, 2007.

Randomness Extractor. During the enrolment of an error prone, non uniformly distributed input, the Secure Sketch generates some public information related to the input called a 'Sketch' which by itself cannot be used to recover the input. The Randomness Extractor is used to map the non uniform input to a uniformly distributed string. The seed for the Randomness Extractor along with the Sketch will be stored publicly. When a query must be matched to the input, the Fuzzy Extractor uses the public Sketch of the input along with the query to reconstruct the input exactly. The Fuzzy Extractor's reconstruction procedure will be designed such that if the query is within a specified distance from the input, the reconstruction will succeed. The reconstructed input will then be mapped to the same string using the same seed stored along with the Sketch. The public storage of the Sketch and the seed do not substantially compromise the security of the input as they cannot be used to recover the input without a query which is 'close' to the input. In this paper, we build our Fuzzy Extractor using a Secure Sketch construct called PinSketch defined in [6], which is based on the set difference metric in a large universe setting. We convert this to a Fuzzy Extractor by using a a simple pairwise independent hash function.

PinSketch performs error correction using binary $[n, k, \delta]$ BCH codes where n is the number of bits in the codeword, k is the number of bits in the message and δ is the minimum distance of the codeword. Each input X will be a word of length $n = 2^m - 1$. During enrollment, the Syndrome of X denoted by Synd(X) will be computed and will be stored as the public Sketch of X.When a query X' is to be compared with X, Synd(X) is retrieved and the following recovery procedure takes place:

- Compute Synd(X')
- Set $\sigma =$ Synd(X)− Synd(X')
- Find a vector v such that Synd(v)= σ and $|\text{Supp}(v)| \leq ((\delta - 1)/2)$[1]
- If X and X' differ in no greater than $((\delta - 1)/2)$ positions, then $v = X - X'$. We can get back X exactly by computing $X' + v$

3 Our Scheme

The novelty of our scheme is that we perform translation and rotation invariant minutiae-based matching in the encrypted domain. In our scheme, every fingerprint will be defined by the *Descriptor* of each minutia extracted from it. Each minutia's *Descriptor* is comprised of two parts: a vector describing the minutia's global position in a polar coordinate system centered on the core and 5 vectors representing the local positions of the five nearest neighboring minutiae in a polar coordinate system centered on the minutia in consideration. The components of each descriptor will be encrypted using an instance of a Fuzzy Extractor.

[1] A binary vector v can be represented by a list of its non zero positions, called its Support Set, denoted by Supp(v).

Quantization of the Global Reference Frame. Every minutia, M_i's, global position will be described by its radial distance from the core, R_i and the angle Θ_i made by M_i with respect to the 0° axis, which is aligned with the orientation of the core (see Fig. 1(a)). The polar coordinate frame is quantized with the radial width of each quantum as R_{tol} and the angular range of each quantum as Θ_{tol}. Let the maximum radial measure of the frame be R_{max}.The quanta will be numbered from 1 to GQ_{max} where $GQ_{max} = ((R_{max}/R_{tol}) \cdot (360°/\Theta_{tol}))$ is the total number of quanta in the global reference frame.

Quantization of the Local Reference Frame. Each Minutia M_i will be described by the five distances and five relative angles between a neighbor $n_i^j, 1 \leq j \leq 5$ and itself, in a polar coordinate system with M_i at the origin and M_i's ridge orientation aligned to the 0° axis (see Fig. 1(b)). This reference frame is quantized with each quantum having radial width d_{tol} and angular range θ_{tol}. If d_{max} is the maximum radial distance in this reference frame, the quanta will be numbered from 1 to LQ_{max} where $LQ_{max} = ((d_{max}/d_{tol}) \cdot (360°/\theta_{tol}))$ is the maximum number of quanta in this local reference frame.

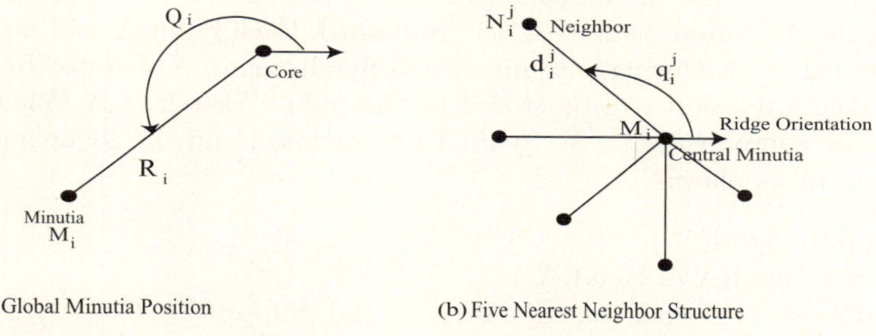

Fig. 1. Global Position and Local Structure of a Minutia

Compensating for Non-Linear Distortion in Minutiae Positions. Each minutia, by virtue of its position in a global or local reference frame, will lie in some quantum q. Non-linear distortions in minutia position may cause it to move to a different quantum when compared to its corresponding minutia in the enrolled fingerprint. We propose a novel scheme to match corresponding minutiae positions when such movement occurs. Every local or global position will be described by a set of quanta. This set, which includes q where a minutia lies and the 8 quanta that surround it is called a *Position Set.* The shaded regions in 2(a) give an example of the elements of the Position Set for a Minutia's global position. If non-linear distortion causes a minutia to move to any one of the eight surrounding quanta, the resulting Position Set will differ from the correct Position set by a maximum of 10 elements. An illustration of this is given in Fig. 2(b), (c) and (d). Hence two minutiae positions are considered to match if the set difference between their Position Sets is less than or equal to 10. For minutiae that lie in the first tier (core is one of the corners) of the quantized frame, a

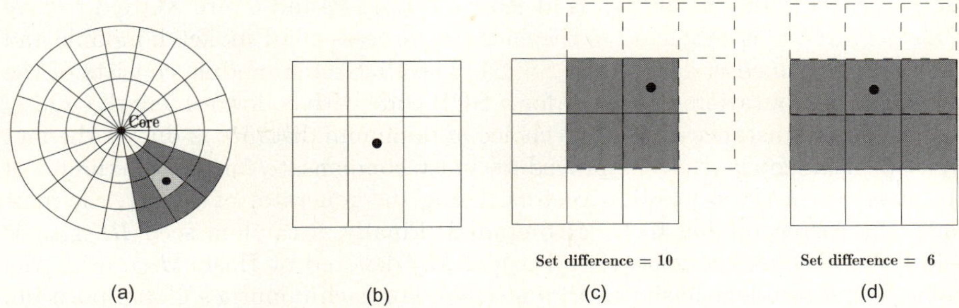

Fig. 2. Error tolerance in minutia position

similar compensation for movement results in a maximum set difference of 7. Thus, by setting the maximum allowable set difference to 10 we permit slightly more position variation in minutiae lying in the inner quanta.

Binary Representation and Matching Condition. The global Position Set of a Minutia M_i will be represented by a binary vector P_i, called its *Position Vector*, having length equal to GQ_{max} and with 1 in every position except those corresponding to the elements in its Position Set. Similarly, each of M_i's neighbors will be represented by the binary Position Vector of length LQ_{max} corresponding to each of their local Position Sets. A minutia in the enrolled fingerprint matches a minutia in the query fingerprint if:

1. The global Position Sets (Position Vectors) of the two minutiae have a set difference (Hamming distance) of not more than 10.
2. At least four out of the five neighbors in their corresponding Five Nearest Neighbor structures will have a set difference (Hamming distance) not more than 10 , when local Position Sets (Position Vectors) of corresponding neighbors are compared.

3.1 Encrypted Matching of Minutiae Points

If N minutiae were extracted from a fingerprint, the un-encrypted fingerprint template will consist of N *Descriptors*, one for each minutia. For a minutia M_i, its Descriptor comprises of a binary global Position Vector P_i and five binary local Position vectors $N_i^j, 1 \leq j \leq 5$. To perform matching in the encrypted domain, each global Position Vector is protected by using a Fuzzy Extractor realization called FE_{global} . Each set of five local Position Vectors is also protected by a Fuzzy Extractor realization called FE_{local}. The block diagrams of FE_{global} and FE_{local} are depicted in Fig. 3 and Fig. 4 respectively.

FE_{global} **Enrolment:** The enrolment stage consists of 3 modules - An XOR module, the PinSketch encoding module and a pairwise independent hash function module. In order to encrypt the global position of minutia M_i, P_i is given as input to FE_{global}. A codeword C is randomly chosen from a BCH Code

BCH_1 whose codeword length is at least GQ_{max}. P_i and C are XORed to give $PE_i = P_i \oplus C$. C is subjected to the encoding process of a PinSketch module and the result obtained is denoted by SS(C). The PinSketch module consists of the syndrome computation procedure for a BCH code with codeword length GQ_{max} and minimum distance of 21. The choice of minimum distance is due to the fact that the PinSketch recovery procedure must compensate for a a maximum of 10 bit errors between position vectors. Using the generator of BCH_1, the message M_C corresponding to C is computed. Finally, a random seed RS_{global} is selected and is used to generate a Hash of M_C denoted by Hash(M_C), using the pairwise independent hash function module. For each minutia's global position, PE_i, SS(C), Hash(M_C) and RS_{global} form part of the publicly stored template.

FE_{global} **Verification:** The Verification stage also consists of 3 modules - An XOR module, the Recovery module of PinSketch and a pairwise independent hash function module. When a minutia in the query fingerprint is compared with minutia M_i of the enrolled finger, the global Position Vector of the query minutia, P_i', is first compared. To perform the comparison, the public template information corresponding to P_i is retrieved and the following procedure takes place:

1. Compute $P_i' \oplus PE_i$. Let this be denoted as E_i.
2. E_i is passed through the recovery procedure of the PinSketch module. This consists of a BCH decoder which will decode to the nearest valid codeword of BCH_1. If P_i' was within a Hamming distance of 10 bits to P_i, the decoder would correctly decode to the codeword C. This is because $P_i' \oplus PE_i = P_i' \oplus P_i \oplus C$. Let $P_i' \oplus P_i = e_i$. When $|e_i| \leq 10$, the BCH decoder will successfully decode $E_i = C + e_i$ to C. Let the decoded word be denoted by C'.
3. Using the generator of BCH_1, $M_{C'}$, the message corresponding to C' is computed and passed through the pairwise independent hash function module using the same random seed RS_{global} to get Hash($M_{C'}$). If Hash(M_C)= Hash($M_{C'}$), the minutiae are said to match in their global position.

FE_{local} **Enrolment:** For each local Position vector of a neighbor $N_i^j, 1 \leq j \leq 5$ of minutia M_i, a random codeword CC_i^j is picked from a BCH code BCH_2 whose codeword length is at least LQ_{max} and minimum distance is 21. Each pair of N_i^j and CC_i^j are successively passed through the XOR module to get five words $NE_i^j, 1 \leq j \leq 5$. Each CC_i^j is passed through the encoding module of the PinSketch$_1$ to get five syndromes denoted by SS(CC_i^j),$1 \leq j \leq 5$. Using the generator of BCH_2, the five messages corresponding to the five random codewords are computed $mm_i^j, 1 \leq j \leq 5$.

The five messages are considered as a set L=$\{mm_i^j, 1 \leq j \leq 5\}$. L can now be considered as a binary string of length equal to $2^{|mm_i^j|}$, with ones occurring at positions corresponding to the elements in the set. L is passed through the enrolment procedure of PinSketch$_2$ which works over a BCH code BCH_3 of length $2^{|mm_i^j|}$ and minimum distance 5, to get SS(L). The minimum distance of 5 for

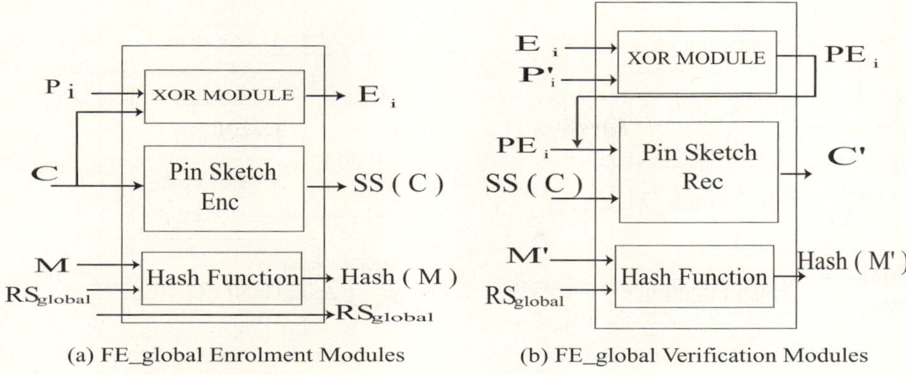

(a) FE_global Enrolment Modules (b) FE_global Verification Modules

Fig. 3. Block diagram for FE_{global}

BCH_3 is chosen because we seek to correct 2 set difference errors between the set L and the set that will be obtained from the minutia in the query fingerprint(and hence 2 bit errors between their binary characteristic vectors).

The five messages are ordered and concatenated to form a single word MM. A random seed RS_{local} is used to generate the Hash of MM using the pairwise independent hash function. Thus, the pattern of the local Five Nearest Neighbor Structure for minutia M_i is defined by $NE_i^j, 1 \leq j \leq 5$, SS(CC_i^j),$1 \leq j \leq 5$, SS(L),Hash(MM) and RS_{local} in the publicly stored template.

FE_{local} **Verification**: Our criteria for matching two local structures, requires four out of the five neighbor positions to match. This allows for one insertion and one deletion of minutiae between two structures that are compared. There are 5! ways to map the structure of the minutia in the enrolled fingerprint with that of the minutia in the query fingerprint. We call each such mapping as a *Permutation*. For each Permutation, there will be a one to one correspondence between the neighbors in the two structures that are being compared. In a certain Permutation, let $N_i^{j'}$ be the query structure's neighbor corresponding to N_i^j. The following procedure is performed:

1. Compute $N_i^{j'} \oplus NE_i^j, 1 \leq j \leq 5$. Let each be denoted as $F_i^j, 1 \leq j \leq 5$.
2. Each F_i^j is passed through the recovery module of PinSketch$_1$ to correct 10 bit position errors. On decoding, we will have five estimates of the codewords $CC_i^{j'}, 1 \leq j \leq 5$.
3. Using the generator of BCH_2 , we obtain the corresponding message words $mm_i^{j'}, 1 \leq j \leq 5$. They form the set L'.
4. L' is passed through the recovery procedure of PinSketch$_2$, which will correct 2 set difference errors between L and L'. The resulting set of 5 messages are ordered in the same way as during enrolment and concatenated to form MM'.
5. Finally the random seed RS_{local} is used to compute Hash(MM') using the pairwise independent hash function module.If Hash(MM') equals Hash(MM), the

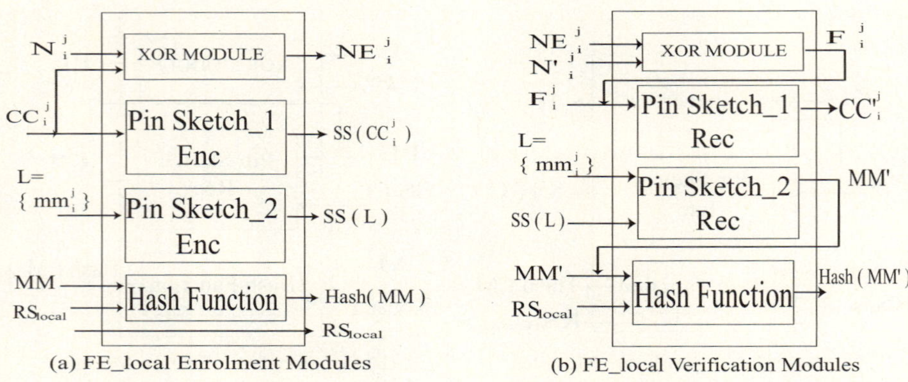

(a) FE_local Enrolment Modules (b) FE_local Verification Modules

Fig. 4. Block Diagram for FE_{local}

local structures are said to match. All possible Permutations are tried until a match is found. If no Permutation yields a match, then the local structures of the corresponding minutiae do not match.

When two fingerprints are compared, the global positions of corresponding minutiae are compared first. Only on obtaining a match in global position are the minutiae tested for match in the shape of the local structure. If sufficient number of minutiae match in both global position and local structure, the two fingerprints are considered as successful match.

4 Experiment Description

Our algorithm was run separately on two fingerprint databases. One was a privately collected database consisting of 74 distinct fingerprint impressions with 5 samples of each, weakly aligned[2]. Weak alignment means that a horizontal line through the core dividing the fingerprint in half, does not vary by more than a specified angle from the scanner's horizontal. For this database, this angle was 20°. The fingerprints were rolled, off-line, inked impressions scanned using a Mitsubishi Diamond View DV648U flatbed scanner set at 600 dpi. The core and minutiae (roughly 30 per fingerprint impression) were identified by eye and their Cartesian coordinates and orientation were recorded. The second database was the public FVC2000 Database 1a comprising of 100 fingerprints and 8 samples of each. We used Neurotechnologija's feature extraction SDK to determine the coordinates and orientation of the minutiae and core.

Quantization Parameters: The quantization parameters for each database had to be separately tuned. For the privately collected database, we chose R_{tol} and d_{tol} to be 40 pixels, Θ_{tol} and θ_{tol} were taken to be 20° and R_{max} and d_{max}

[2] Many fingerprint scanners enforce weak alignment by virtue of their fingerprint capture technique.

were set to 300 pixels. With these parameters, the maximum number of quanta in both the local and global frames was 126 i.e $GQ_{max} = LQ_{max} = 126$. For the public database, we chose R_{tol} and d_{tol} to be 20 pixels and kept Θ_{tol} and θ_{tol} at $20°$. This gave $GQ_{max} = LQ_{max} = 270$.

BCH Codes: For the privately collected database, the smallest BCH code length covering 126 quanta was 127. As we needed to correct 10 errors (Section 3), we chose both BCH_1 and BCH_2 to be BCH(127,64,21). BCH_3 was chosen to have a codeword length of 2^{64} and minimum distance of 5. For FVC2000 Database 1a, we chose BCH_1 and BCH_2 to be BCH(511,421,21) and BCH_3 to have a codeword length of 2^{421} and minimum distance of 5.

Hash function: We used a simple pairwise independent hash function described as follows: If P is the Message Space, K is the Key Space and T is the Tag Space, the Hash Function $Hash$ is defined as $Hash : K \times P \rightarrow T$. For our implementation, the message p, tag t and a key pair (k_1,k_2), each in GF(2^m), where m is a positive integer, are related by the function t = Hash(p) = $k_1 \times p + k_2$ [10]. The multiplication occurs over GF(2^m) and p corresponds to m_C or MM in the FE_{global} or FE_{local} respectively. The key pair (k_1,k_2) corresponds to RS_{global} or RS_{local} respectively. For the privately collected database, we worked over GF(2^{64}) and for FVC2000 Database 1a we used GF(2^{421}) as the fields from which p, k_1 and k_2 were drawn.

Software. The software has been written in C++ and run on the Windows platform on a Pentium 4, 3 GHz machine. We used the public domain software written by Harmon and Reyzin [11] for syndrome computation and syndrome decoding of BCH codes. Victor Shoup's NTL library [12] was used for performing Finite Field computations.

5 Results and Analysis

Applying the above parameters to the fingerprints in our database, we evaluated the *False Non Match Rate(FNMR)* and *False Match Rate(FMR)* at different match Thresholds. The graph is shown in Fig. 5. For the privately collected database, we observe that Equal Error occurs at a Threshold of 18 and the error is roughly 10%. However, for FVCDatabase 1a we found the error at Equal Error Point was closer to 15%. We observed that the low Genuine Acceptance Rate and higher error in the FVC2000 database compared to our privately collected database was due to the error introduced by the feature extractor in extracting minutiae and the core location. False non matches particularly occurred when the extractor found double cores in the fingerprint.

Security Analysis: In the privately collected Database, the quantization frame used for global and local minutia positions gave exactly 126 possibilities each for the global and local binary position vectors, which an intruder could easily list. There are 126^4 possibilities for a FNN structure shape, as the intruder needs to get four out of the five neighbor positions correctly. If operating at the equal error

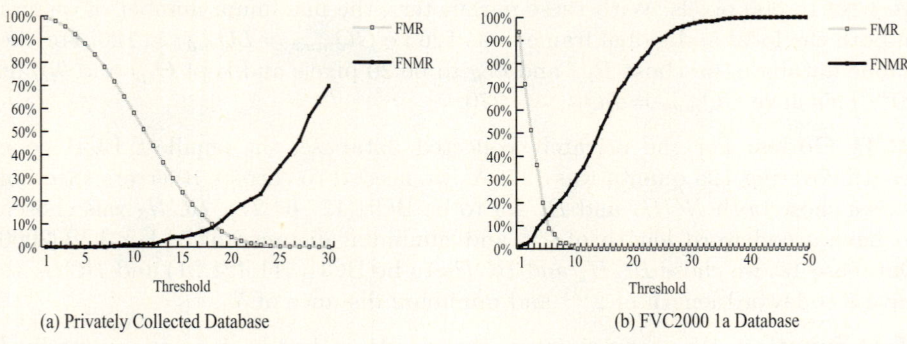

Fig. 5. FMR and FNMR curves

threshold, a minimum of 19 such structures need to be found to have a successful authentication. Thus the entropy of the fingerprint with such a representation scheme is $log_2(126^4 \times 19) = 32$ bits approx. For the FVC2000 database, the stricter quantization resulted in 270 possibilities for the local or global position vectors. Using a similar argument as before, the entropy of a fingerprint in this representation method would be $log_2(270^4 \times 6) = 34$ bits approx. Recovering an approximate reconstruction of the point pattern without the ridge orientations will be insufficient to reconstruct the fingerprint as described in [1] and trace a person's identity. Hence the identity of a user is protected under our scheme. However, an attacker who could hack into the feature extractor module could use this estimated point pattern to masquerade as the genuine enrolled user by overriding the feature extractor. A safeguard against such an attack would be to ensure that the feature extraction and matching algorithms be done at a secure site.

6 Conclusion and Future Work

We have demonstrated a working proof of concept of a secure minutia-based authentication system. The equal error rate is promising enough to encourage further research into faster matching, better quantization parameters and minutiae representation schemes. We will perform a full security analysis on this system and study methods (finer quantization and codes with larger error correcting capability) to improve its security. We will also test the system with alternate minutia structures to obtain better performances at equal error.

Acknowledgements. This research was supported by a grant from the Australian Department of Defence, which includes a scholarship for the first author. We are deeply grateful to Assoc. Prof. Serdar Boztas for useful discussions on pairwise independent hash functions. We also thank the anonymous reviewers for their comments which helped us to significantly improve our paper.

References

1. Ross, A., Shah, J., Jain, A.K.: Towards reconstructing fingerprints from minutiae points. In: Proc. SPIE, Biometric Technology for Human Identification II, vol. 5779, pp. 68–80 (March 2005)
2. Juels, A., Wattenberg, M.: A fuzzy commitment scheme. In: Tsudik, G. (ed.) Sixth ACM Conference on Computer and Communications Security, pp. 28–36. ACM Press, New York (1999)
3. Juels, A., Sudan, M.: A Fuzzy vault scheme. In: Proc. of IEEE ISIT, Lausanne, Switzerland, June 30-July 5, 2002, p. 408. IEEE Press, Los Alamitos (2002)
4. Linnartz, J.-P., Tuyls, P.: New shielding functions to enhance privacy and prevent misuse of biometric templates. In: Kittler, J., Nixon, M.S. (eds.) AVBPA 2003. LNCS, vol. 2688, pp. 393–402. Springer, Heidelberg (2003)
5. Tuyls, P., Goseling, J.: Capacity and Examples of Template-Protecting Biometric Authentication Systems. In: Maltoni, D., Jain, A.K. (eds.) BioAW 2004. LNCS, vol. 3087, pp. 158–170. Springer, Heidelberg (2004)
6. Dodis, Y., Ostrovsky, R., Reyzin, L., Smith, A.: Fuzzy Extractors: How to Generate Strong Keys from Biometrics and Other Noisy Data, Cryptology ePrint Archive, Report, 2003/235 (2003), Available `http://eprint.iacr.org`
7. Uludag, U., Jain, A.K.: Securing fingerprint template: fuzzy vault with helper data. In: Proc. IEEE Workshop on Privacy Research In Vision, NY, June 22, 2006, p. 163 (2006)
8. Tuyls, P., Akkermans, A.H.M., Kevenaar, T.A.M., Schrijen, G.-J., Bazen, A.M., Veldhuis, R.N.J.: Practical Biometric Authentication with Template Protection. In: Kanade, T., Jain, A., Ratha, N.K. (eds.) AVBPA 2005. LNCS, vol. 3546, pp. 436–446. Springer, Heidelberg (2005)
9. Jeffers, J., Arakala, A.: Minutiae-based Structures for a Fuzzy Vault. In: Proc. of 2006 Biometrics Symposium, MD, USA, September 19-21, 2006 (2006)
10. Shoup, V.: A Computational Introduction to Number Theory and Algebra, p. 125. Cambridge University Press, Cambridge (2005)
11. Harmon, K., Reyzin, L.: Implementation of algorithms from the paper Fuzzy Extractors: How to Generate Strong Keys from Biometrics and Other Noisy Data[Accessed October 3, 2006], [Online] Available: `http://www.cs.bu.edu/~reyzin/code/fuzzy.html`
12. Shoup, V.: NTL: A Library for doing Number Theory [Accessed October 9, 2006], [Online] Available: `http://shoup.net/ntl`

Coarse Iris Classification by Learned Visual Dictionary

Xianchao Qiu, Zhenan Sun, and Tieniu Tan

Center for Biometrics and Security Research
National Laboratory of Pattern Recognition, Institute of Automation
Chinese Academy of Sciences
P.O. Box 2728, Beijing, P.R. China, 100080
{xcqiu,znsun,tnt}@nlpr.ia.ac.cn

Abstract. In state-of-the-art iris recognition systems, the input iris image has to be compared with a large number of templates in database. When the scale of iris database increases, they are much less efficient and accurate. In this paper, we propose a novel iris classification method to attack this problem in iris recognition systems. Firstly, we learned a small finite dictionary of visual words(clusters in the feature space), which are called Iris-Textons, to represent visual primitives of iris images. Then the Iris-Texton histograms are used to represent the global features of iris textures. Finally, K-means algorithm is used for classifying iris images into five categories. Based on the proposed method, the correct classification rate is 95% in a five-category iris database. By combining this method with traditional iris recognition algorithm, our system shows better performance in terms of both speed and accuracy.

1 Introduction

The iris of human eye is the annular part between the black pupil and the white sclera, in which texture is extremely rich. Some examples are shown in Fig. 1. Iris texture is random and unique to each subject[1,2,3], so iris recognition has become one of the most important biometric solutions for personal identification nowadays.

There have been many schemes for iris representation and matching in the recent literature. Daugman[1] extracts iris textures using 2-D Gabor filter. The obtained phase information is encoded to a 2048-bit feature vector. The matching process is done using XOR operation. Wildes[3] suggests using 4-level Laplacian Pyramid to analyze iris textures and using normalized correlation for the matching process. Ma et al.[2] designs a bank of circular symmetric filters to capture the discriminating information along the angular direction of iris image.

All these methods use local features of iris image as the distinctive characteristic, so they can achieve very good recognition results. But all of them require the input iris image to be matched with a large number of irises stored in a database. This matching procedure is very time consuming, especially when the iris database grows large. In order to reduce the search time and computational

S.-W. Lee and S.Z. Li (Eds.): ICB 2007, LNCS 4642, pp. 770–779, 2007.

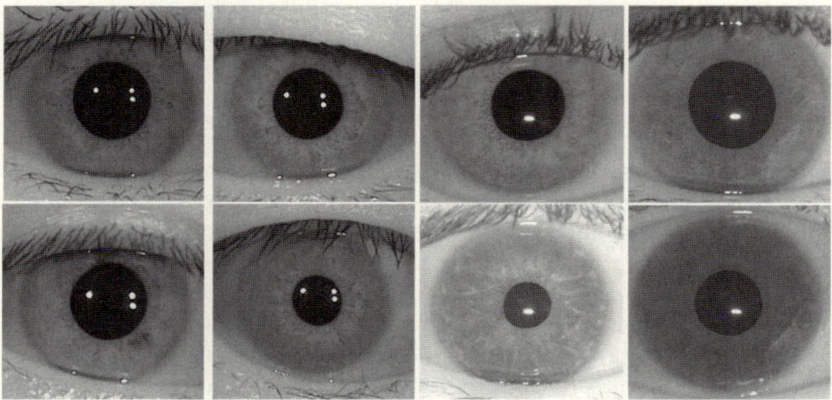

Fig. 1. Examples of iris images from CASIA and UBATH iris databases

complexity, it is desirable to classify irises in an accurate and consistent manner such that the input iris needs to be matched only with a subset of the irises in the database. Yet few attempts have been made to perform automatic iris classification.

In this paper, we propose a novel iris classification approach based on an visual-dictionary-learning algorithm. The main purpose of this paper is to find the global characteristics of iris images to classify irises into several categories, and reduce the number of iris templates that need to be searched when looking for a matching iris. Firstly, compact and yet discriminative visual features, we call them Iris-Textons here, are automatically learned from a set of training images. Then the Iris-Texton histogram was used to represent the global characteristics of iris images. Finally, a K-means classifier classify an input iris into one of five iris categories.

The remainder of this paper is organized as follows. Related work is presented in Section 2. The proposed method is discussed in Section 3. Experimental results are presented and discussed in Section 4 prior to conclusions in Section 5.

2 Related Work and Background

2.1 Iris Classification

Unlike iris classification, much work has been done on fingerprint and palmprint classification. For example, Karu et al.[4] uses the information such as number, type and location of singular points to classify fingerprint images. Wu et al.[5] use directional line detectors to extract the principal lines and then classify palmprints into six categories according to the number of the principal lines and the number of their intersections. Recently, many researchers pay more attention to iris classification. Yu et al.[6] use box-counting method to estimate the fractal dimensions of the iris, then classify iris images into four categories in accordance with the fractal dimensions. Fu et al.[7] use artificial color filter to detect the color information of iris images, and use it to improve iris recognition accuracy and shorten the searching time.

2.2 Texton Theory

Textons are defined as mini-templates that represent certain appearance primitives in images. The definition of texton is governed by a sound model of images in [8]. In fact, a small number of textons can be learned from training images as repeating appearance primitives. Then the texton histogram is used as a kind of global feature of an image. For a single texton, it characterizes the primitive texture pattern which shows the local feature of texture. For a texton histogram generated by a group of textons, it shows the statistical properties of texture, which is a kind of global feature. Therefore, the texton histogram method incorporates both local and global features in texture pattern. In practice, texton theory is widely used for texture recognition and object classification[9], and it shows high classification accuracy. So we extend Texton theory to represent the global feature of the texture-like iris patterns for coarse iris classification in this paper.

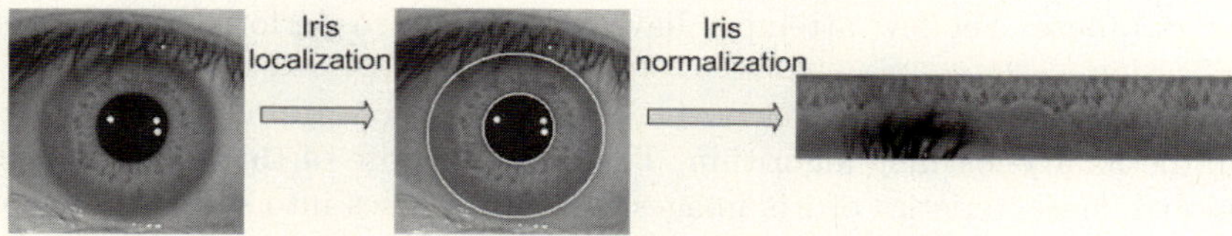

Fig. 2. Preprocessing of iris images

3 Coarse Iris Classification

In this paper, coarse iris classification system includes three basic modules: image preprocessing, feature extraction, and classification. Detailed descriptions of these modules are as follows.

3.1 Image Preprocessing

Image preprocessing plays a very important role in an iris recognition system. Fig. 2 illustrates the main preprocessing steps involving localization, normalization and enhancement. More details can be found in [2]. In our experiment, the size of normalized iris image is 80×512. After preprocessing, translation, scale and illumination variations between different iris images could be complemented.

3.2 Feature Extraction

In this paper, feature extraction process includes two steps. Firstly, we learn a small, finite dictionary of visual words in iris images, which are called Iris-Textons. Secondly, Iris-Texton histograms are used as feature vectors to represent the global characteristics of iris images.

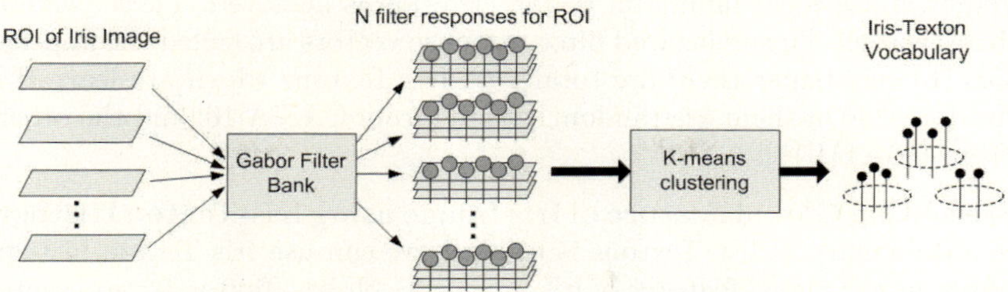

Fig. 3. Learning the vocabulary of Iris-Textons

Learning the Dictionary of Iris-Textons. A schematic diagram illustrating the steps of learning the dictionary of Iris-Textons is shown in Fig. 3. The first step taken to learn a dictionary is filtering. As we know, the Gabor Filters have received considerable attention because the characteristics of certain cells in the visual cortex of some mammals can be approximated by these filters. In addition these filters have been shown to possess optimal localization properties in both spatial and frequency domain and thus are very suited for texture classification problems. Therefore we can characterize a texture by its responses to a set of orientation and spatial-frequency selective Gabor filters that cover the whole frequency space. Typically, an input image (ROI) $I(x,y)$ is convolved with a 2D Gabor filter (here we only use even Gabor filters) to obtain a Gabor filtered image $r(x,y)$.

$$r(x,y) = \iint I(x_1,y_1)h(x-x_1,y-y_1)dx_1dy_1 \tag{1}$$

The computational models of 2D Gabor filters are:

$$h(x,y) = g(x,y) \cdot \cos[2\pi f(x\cos\theta + y\sin\theta)] \tag{2}$$

where $g(x,y)$ is an isotropic Gaussian function given by

$$g(x,y) = \frac{1}{2\pi\sigma^2} \cdot exp[-\frac{x^2+y^2}{2\sigma^2}]. \tag{3}$$

f and θ are the spatial frequency and orientation respectively. In our experiments, there are a total of 40 even Gabor filters (8 orientations and 5 scales). Each pixel is then transformed to a N= 40 dimensional vector.

The second step is to cluster the filter response vectors into a small set of prototypes, Iris-Textons. These vectors are clustered using a vector quantization algorithm, in particular K-means. K-means method try to find K centers such that after assigning each data vector to the nearest center, the sum of the squared distance from the centers is minimized. It is a greedy algorithm which iteratively performs the following two operations: (1)assign data vectors to the nearest of the K centers; (2)update each of the K centers to the mean of the data vectors assigned to it. These two steps are continued until the algorithm converges and a local minimum of the criterion is achieved. These centers are the Iris-Textons. The associated filter response vectors are called the appearance vectors. In this paper there are totally 64 Iris-Textons which are learned from 400 images, 200 of them are random selected from CASIA[10] and the other 200 are from UBATH[11].

Representing Global Feature of Iris Image using Iris-Texton Histogram. Once a dictionary of Iris-Textons is learned, we can use Iris-Texton histograms to represent the global features of iris images. Each Iris-Texton is represented by the mean of the vectors in this cluster and it is one bin in the texton histogram. For a pixel of iris image, we get a $N = 40$ dimensional vector by Gabor filtering and concatenation, and assigned it to the bin which is the nearest texton. The Iris-Texton histogram is a mapping of 40-dimensional vectors to 64 different Iris-Textons. We can see that the frequent variations of textons denote the richness of micro-textures in iris image. When proper filters are chosen, the Iris-Texton histogram is sufficient in characterizing the global features of iris images. The procedure of computing Iris-Texton Histograms is show in Fig. 4.

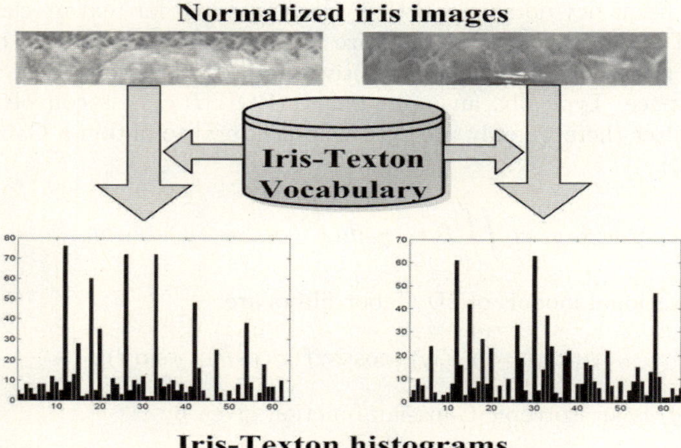

Fig. 4. The procedure of computing Iris-Texton Histograms

3.3 Classification Based on Iris-Texton Histograms

Now the iris textures are presented by Iris-Texton histograms. Our intuition is that iris images can be classified into several categories according to their global features. Here we run k-means algorithm again to achieve proper iris clusters. The k-means algorithm is popular because it is easy to implement and its time complexity is $O(n)$, where n is the number of patterns. In this paper, the Chi-square statistic is used to evaluate the dissimilarity of two texton histograms H1 and H2:

$$\chi^2(H1, H2) = \sum_{i=1}^{59} \frac{(H1_i - H2_i)^2}{H1_i + H2_i} \tag{4}$$

Because it is possible that $H1_i + H2_i = 0$, the summation only includes the non-zero bins.

Compared with parametric classification principles, non-parametric classification strategy is more flexible and avoid the assumption on the distribution of input data. Chi-square is a non-parametric statistic to test the goodness-of-fit of two distributions. The strength of Chi-square statistic suitable for our application is that it is a rough estimation of confidence. This feature makes Chi-square robust against the noises in iris data, such as deformation and occlusions.

If the number of categories is too small, it is impossible to reduce the searching time much, but if the number is too large, it is very difficult to keep high correct classification rate. As a tradeoff, we must choose a proper number in experiments. The choosing of this number will be discussed in next section.

4 Experimental Results and Discussions

4.1 Iris Databases

Extensive experiments were carried out to evaluate the effectiveness and accuracy of the proposed method on a large mixed iris database. It consists of two open iris image databases, CASIA[10] and University of Bath(UBATH)[11] databases. The CASIA iris database includes 8000 images from 400 different eyes of 200 subjects. There are 20 images for each eye. The UBATH iris database has the same size with CASIA, it also has 8000 images from 400 different eyes, 20 images for each eye. So the mixed database is large and includes 16000 images of 800 eyes.

4.2 Results and Discussions

In the first experiment, we randomly select one image from each eye in the mixed database to form the training set, and then the remain images to form the testing set. If the iris images from the same eye are classified into the same category, it means the result is correct. So a statistical test is carried out to measure the accuracy of the proposed algorithm. Correct Classification Rate(CCR), which is simply the percentage of correctly classified irises, is then examined.

Because we use K-means algorithm to find cluster centers, it is very important to choose a proper number of categories, K. If K is too small, it is impossible to reduce the searching time much, but if K is too large, it is very difficult to keep high Correct Classification Rate(CCR) and it may result in that some categories have many iris samples and others have very few. The relation between the number of categories and the CCR was show in Fig. 5. The distributions of irises in each category according to different K are listed in Table 1. As a tradeoff, we choose five as the K in our experiments. In the training process, the training set is clustered into five categories by the K-means algorithm. Then the testing set is used to estimate the performance of this classifier. We only need to calculate the distance between the testing sample and the centers of categories, and choose the shortest one as the testing sample's category label.

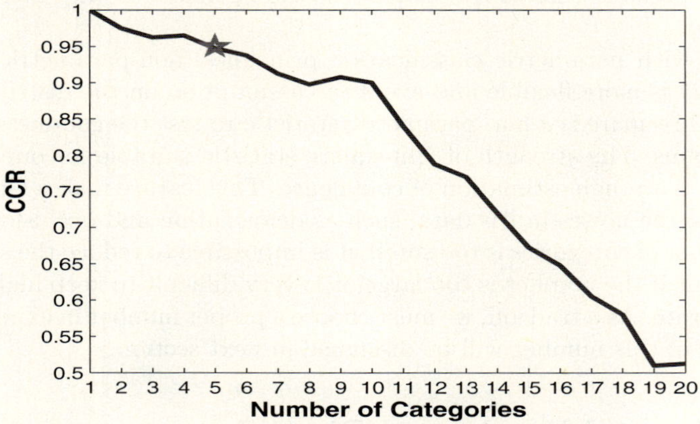

Fig. 5. Relationship between number of categories and CCR

The experimental results are shown in Table 2. The correct classification rate of our method is 95.0% on the large mixed database. And we have neither too much iris templates, nor too few iris templates in any category. It means that the proposed approach has good classification performance. Some examples of each iris category after processing are shown in Fig. 6.

Table 1. Distribution of each category according to different K

K	Distribution of each category (%)						
	Cat. 1	Cat. 2	Cat. 3	Cat. 4	Cat. 5	Cat. 6	Cat. 7
4	34.8	15.6	20.6	29.0	-	-	-
5	**14.3**	**12.2**	**30.5**	**25.6**	**17.4**	-	-
6	26.2	16.4	22.0	15.7	4.9	14.8	-
7	16.8	14.4	25.8	12.5	20.3	6.6	3.5

Table 2. Distribution of each category and Correct Classification Rate on our database.

Database	Number of Eyes	Distribution of each category (%)					CCR(%)
		Cat. 1	Cat. 2	Cat. 3	Cat. 4	Cat. 5	
CASIA & UBATH	800	14.3	12.2	30.5	25.6	17.4	**95.0**

The greatest benefit of using coarse iris classification is to reduce the time in searching. According to the CCR and the distribution of irises in five categories in the first experiment, we can evaluate the size of the database to decide when to use the coarse classification. Suppose N is the database size, T_1 is the time of local feature extraction, T_2 is the time used for coarse iris classification, T_3 is the matching time of two local features and the matching time of global feature can be ignored. In our method, $T_1 = 45ms$, $T_2 = 660ms$ and $T_3 = 1.1ms$ on a

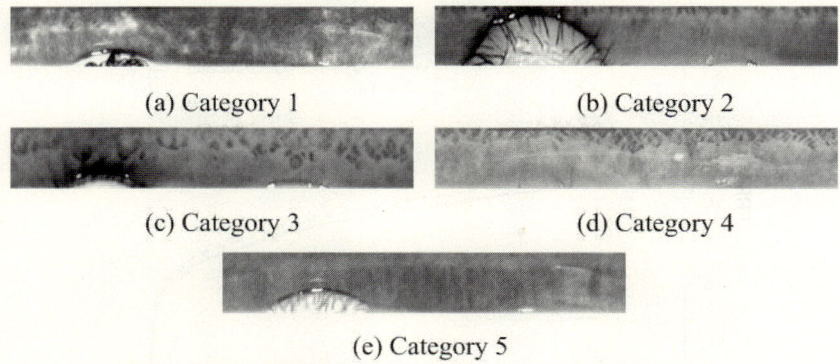

(a) Category 1 (b) Category 2 (c) Category 3 (d) Category 4 (e) Category 5

Fig. 6. Examples of each iris category after processing

PC of Pentium-4 2.8GHz CPU with Matlab. If the computational cost for iris classification is less than the reduced matching time, then coarse iris classification should be adopted.

The objective of iris identification is to find the corresponding templates in central database as soon as possible, so we test how long we need to search until we could reach the genuine template in each identification task. If we query a image without iris classification, the average searching time is:

$$T_{without} = T_1 + 0.5 * N * T_3 \tag{5}$$

By using iris classification, under condition of CCR equals 95.0% and all categories have the same number of templates, the average search time is:

$$T_{with} = T_1 + T_2 + (95.0\% * 0.2 + 5.0\% * 1) * 0.5 * N * T_3 \tag{6}$$

Let $T_{without} = T_{with}$, we can easily obtain that $N = 1579$. It shows that when the database size N is bigger than 1579, the coarse classification can reduce the computational time of the identification system. For an iris database contains 10,000 iris templates, the average searching time can be reduced almost 63% of the original searching time by using coarse iris classification. If the database grows even larger, this method can reduce the computational time dramatically.

The second benefit of using coarse iris classification is to improve the accuracy of an iris recognition algorithm. We complement local features based method with global features, the iris category labels, to strengthen the robustness of iris recognition system. The iris categories can work like a kind of "soft" biometric traits. Although the categories lacks the distinctiveness to identify an iris image uniquely and reliably, they provide some evidence about the iris identity that could be beneficial. In this study, all iris images is classified into five categories by Iris-Texton histograms, and Iris-Texton histograms represent the global features of iris images, so the category information is complement to local features which are used by state-of-the-art iris recognition methods. By the User Weighting fusion method[12], the accuracy and robustness of an iris recognition system can

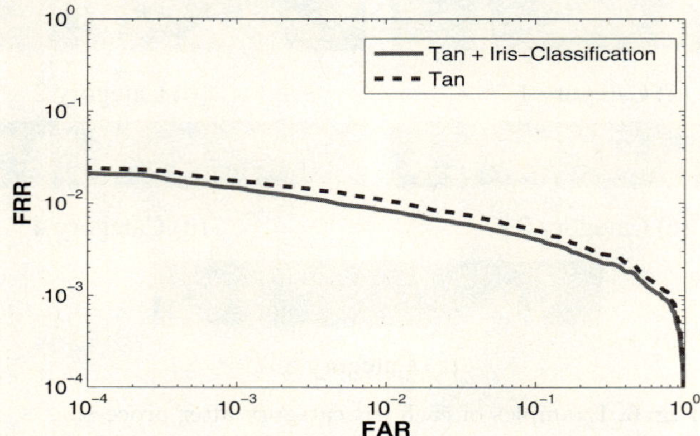

Fig. 7. Comparison of ROC curves of different iris recognition methods

be improved. For the purpose of comparison, the ROCs(receive operating curve) of Tan's[2] and the proposed methods are show in Fig. 7. After introducing coarse iris classification into our iris recognition systems, the equal error rate(EER) is reduced from 1.1% to 0.88%.

5 Conclusion

In this paper, we have presented a novel method for automatic iris coarse classification based on global texture analysis with Iris-Texton histograms. The main contributions of this paper include: (1)A visual dictionary containing typical textons is learned from iris images. Each Iris-Texton characterizes a kind of frequently appeared local patches in iris images. So the global texture feature of an iris image are well presented by the distribution of its Iris-Textons. (2)We show that iris images could be coarsely classified with histograms of Iris-Textons. The experimental results on a large mixed database proves that global features is complementary to local features which are commonly used by iris recognition algorithms. By combining two kinds of features, we get a faster, more accurate and more robust iris recognition system.

In the future, we will also try other approaches to improve the classification accuracy. In addition, we think the global features should play a defining role in the issues on iris coarse classification. So we will try to find out which kind of feature is powerful.

Acknowledgements

This work is funded by research grants from the National Basic Research Program (Grant No. 2004CB318110), Natural Science Foundation of China (Grant No. 60335010, 60121302, 60275003, 60332010, 69825105, 60605008), Hi-Tech

Research and Development Program of China (Grant No.2006AA01Z193) and the Chinese Academy of Sciences.

References

1. Daugman, J.: High confidence visual recognition of persons by a test of statistical independence. IEEE TRANS. PAMI 15(11), 1148–1161 (1993)
2. Ma, L., Tan, T., Wang, Y., Zhang, D.: Personal identification based on iris texture analysis. IEEE TRANS. PAMI 25(12), 1519–1533 (2003)
3. Wildes, R.P.: Iris recognition: An emerging biometric technology. Proceedings of the IEEE 85(9), 1348–1363 (1997)
4. Karu, K., Jain, A.K.: Fingerprint classification. Pattern Recognition 29(3), 389–404 (1996)
5. Wu, X., Zhang, D., Wang, K., Huang, B.: Palmprint classification using principal lines. Pattern Recognition 37, 1987–1998 (2004)
6. Yu, L., Zhang, D., Wang, K., Yang, W.: Coarse iris classification using box-counting to estimate fractal dimensions. Pattern Recognition 38, 1791–1798 (2005)
7. Fu, J., Caulfield, H.J., Yoo, S.-M., Atluri, V.: Use of artificial color filtering to improve iris recognition and searching. Pattern Recognition Letters 26, 2244–2251 (2005)
8. Zhu, S.-C., Guo, C.-E., Wang, Y., Xu, Z.: What are textons? International Journal of Computer Vision 62(1-2), 121–143 (2005)
9. Winn, J., Criminisi, A., Minka, T.: Object categorization by learned universal visual dictionary, vol. 2, pp. 1800–1807 (2005)
10. CASIA iris image database (2003), http://www.sinobiometrics.com
11. University of Bath iris image database, http://www.bath.ac.uk/elec-eng/pages/sipg/irisweb/
12. Jain, A.K., Ross, A.: Learning user-specific parameters in a multibiometric system, pp. 57–60 (2002)

Nonlinear Iris Deformation Correction Based on Gaussian Model

Zhuoshi Wei, Tieniu Tan, and Zhenan Sun

Center for Biometrics and Security Research
National Laboratory of Pattern Recognition, Institute of Automation
Chinese Academy of Sciences. P.O. Box 2728, Beijing, P.R. China, 100080
{zswei,tnt,znsun}@nlpr.ia.ac.cn

Abstract. Current iris recognition systems can achieve high level of success under restricted conditions, while they still face challenges of utilizing images with heavy deformation caused by illumination variations. Developing methods to alleviate the deformation becomes a necessity, since the requirement of uniform lighting is often not practical. This paper introduces a novel algorithm to counteract elastic iris deformation. In the proposed algorithm, for nonlinear iris stretch, the distance of any point in the iris region to the pupil boundary is assumed to be the corresponding distance under linear stretch plus an additive deviation. Gaussian function is employed to model the deviation. Experimental results on two databases with nonlinear deformation demonstrate the effectiveness of the algorithm. The proposed iris deformation correction algorithm achieves a lower Equal Error Rate (EER), compared to the other two linear and nonlinear normalization methods in the literature, making the system more robust in realistic environments.

1 Introduction

Since last decade, researchers have put great efforts in automatical personal identification based on biometrics. Iris pattern is considered as one of the most reliable biometric modalities due to the abundant distinctive information preserved in the iris texture. Current iris recognition systems can achieve good performance under restricted conditions. However, they still encounter challenges in realistic environments with significantly large illumination variations. Pupil dilation and contraction caused by illumination change make the iris texture undergoes nonlinear deformation. Iris normalization is important to iris recognition as it intends to reduce the effect of iris deformation. As the majority of iris recognition systems employ linear normalization, which is unsatisfactory in handling nonlinear iris distortion, it is necessary to develop nonlinear normalization methods to counteract the deformation.

Although iris recognition has been investigated over the past decade, only a few works focus on the deformation issue. Daugman [1] used a Rubber-sheet model based normalization which linearly project the annular iris region into a fixed rectangle: $I(x(r,\theta), y(r,\theta)) \rightarrow I(r,\theta)$. Yuan and Shi [2] employed a iris

S.-W. Lee and S.Z. Li (Eds.): ICB 2007, LNCS 4642, pp. 780–789, 2007.

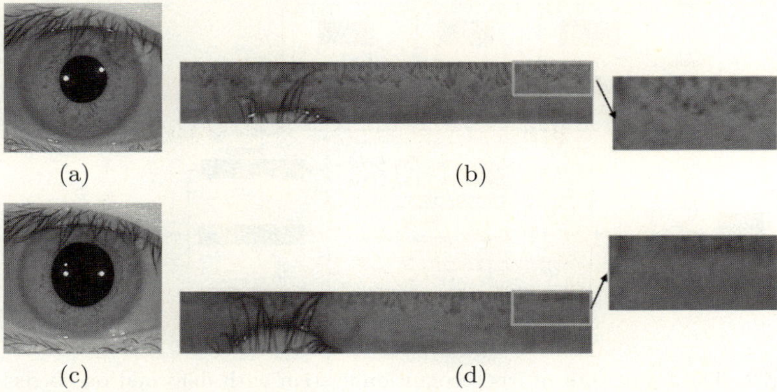

Fig. 1. Deformed image samples which can not align well under linear normalization

meshwork model proposed by Wyatt [3], and from which they deduced the relationship of iris collagen fibers between different pupil sizes. Li [4] used local calibration to alleviate iris distortion. Most of the existing systems employ Daugman's [1] linear iris normalization algorithm. However, some heavily deformed images still pose a challenge to linear normalization. Fig. 1 shows an example. Fig. 1(a) and Fig. 1(c) are two images captured from the same iris, but with very different pupil sizes. They can not align well under linear normalization, which is shown in Fig. 1(b) and Fig.1(d), especially in the zoomed region.

Human iris is an internal organ that is visible externally. The movement of iris (mainly dilation/contraction) controls the pupil size and thus dominates the amount of light that enter the eye through the pupil. According to [3], pupil diameter may range from a minimum of about 1.5mm to a maximum of over 7mm. Such distortion of iris texture may enlarge intra-class variations or increase the False Reject Rate (FRR). A major goal of this paper is to introduce a novel method to compensate elastic iris deformation. Motivated by Wyatt's [3] iris mesh model, we use a nonlinear deformation correction algorithm that utilizes Gaussian function to approximate the additive deviation of nonlinear iris stretch. The effectiveness of the algorithm is confirmed by experiments on two databases, both of which are collected under illumination changes. Our method achieves better recognition performance than the other two methods.

The rest of this paper is organized as follows. Section 2 describes the proposed nonlinear deformation correction algorithm. Section 3 gives the experimental results and discussion. Section 4 concludes the paper.

2 Nonlinear Iris Deformation Correction

A complete framework of iris recognition system with deformation correction is plotted in Fig. 2.

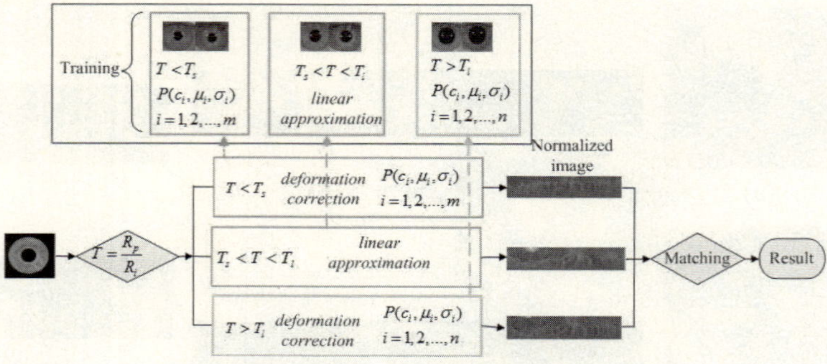

Fig. 2. The framework of iris recognition system with deformation correction

2.1 Iris Model

Iris collagen fibers are generally considered as radial components, which is also the assumption made by linear normalization methods. With the stretch of these radial fibers, the fibers near pupil boundary would undergo larger deformation than those fibers near iris boundary. One disadvantage of this assumption lies in the contradiction that iris structure requires very good mobility whereas iris collagen fibers are relatively inextensible tissues.

In this paper, we employ a meshwork "skeleton" of iris structure which was proposed by Rohen [5]. In the "skeleton" model, a series of fibrous arcs (left arcs and right arcs) which connect pupil boundary and iris boundary are interweaving together to form iris structure, as Fig. 3 shows. We do not consider iris meshwork model as exactly the human iris structure. But we believe that it is more reasonable in two aspects: first, this structure is much more complicated than the over-simplified radial one. It is highly flexible and fits for the pupil movements. Second, while the radial fibers go through acute change with pupil diameter varies, which makes people easy to feel fatigable, the meshwork model provides a possibility that the length of each arc undergoes less change.

As the meshwork model is also employed by Yuan and Shi [2], we give a brief comparison to these two employments. In Yuan's method, they made several assumptions: 1, the angles (θ in Fig. 4(a)) that correspond to iris fibrous arcs is 90°; 2, the fibrous arcs are part of circle so that the relationship between linear and nonlinear stretch can be acquired by solving two equations of circles. In the proposed method, we do not make such constraints because the angle θ would hardly remain constant and fibrous arcs would hardly remain as circles during the frequent change of pupil diameter. Instead we use a flexible assumption (Eq. 1) and acquire iris deformation model by statistical learning. Experimental results show that the proposed method is more reasonable in dealing with the deformation problem.

Fig. 4(a) illustrates the basic idea of the meshwork model. Suppose the solid line in Fig. 4(a) represents one fibrous arc in linear stretch model, and the dashed line represents the same arc in nonlinear stretch model. In Wyatt's treatment

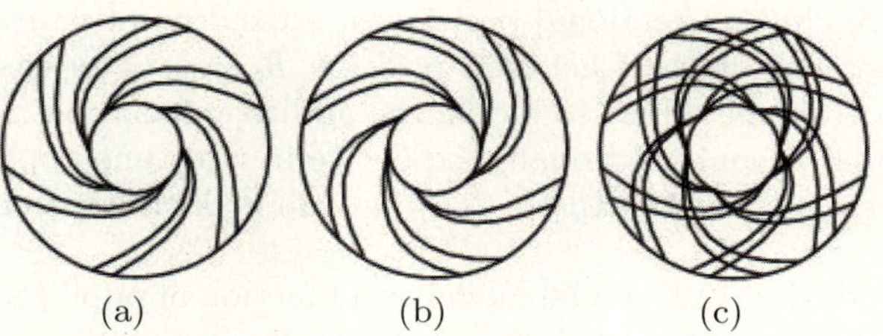

Fig. 3. Iris meshwork model described by Rohen [5]. (a) Left arcs. (b) Right arcs. (c) The meshwork model.

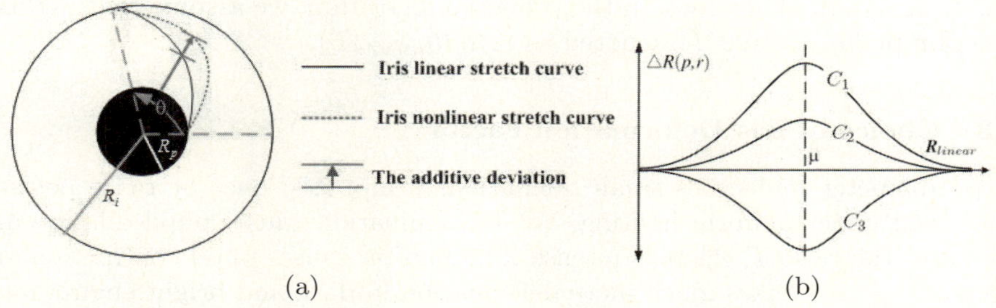

Fig. 4. (a) The relationship between linear and nonlinear iris stretch in Wyatt's work [3]. (b) The Gaussian model for additive deviation.

[3] to nonlinear stretch, a point in any position of iris region can be described as:

$$R_{nonlinear} = R_{linear} + \triangle R(p,r), \tag{1}$$

where R_{linear} is the position in linear stretch, and $\triangle R$ is the additive deviation related to R_{linear} (denotes as r) and pupil dilation (denotes as p). This deviation is described by a 6th-order polynomial in Wyatt's work [3], which is somewhat arbitrary as long as it is smooth enough to provide any flexibility to support elastic iris deformation.

2.2 Additive Deviation in Nonlinear Iris Stretch

As mentioned by Wyatt [3], the treatment described by Eq.1 is proved to be the easiest using fractional radial position instead of absolute radial position as a variable. Fractional position is defined as:

$$f = \frac{R - R_p}{R_i - R_p}, \tag{2}$$

here R is the distance of any point in iris region to the pupil center. R_p and R_i denote pupil radius and iris radius respectively, as Fig. 4(a) shows. In the remaining part of this paper, we use fractional position to refer to each variable in Eq.1.

In linear stretch, the fractional position of a fixed point is invariant as pupil size varies, therefore linear fractional position R_{linear} is an easily determined part. The key problem is how to model the additive deviation $\triangle R$. As the 6th-order polynomial is computationally expensive in real-time applications, we intend to find a simple way to express $\triangle R$ that can make the system both efficient and accurate.

Generally speaking, $\triangle R$ can be model as a function of pupil radius R_p and linear fractional position R_{linear}, since iris radius R_i is a relatively stable variable. However, due to the flexible distance from the camera during image acquisition, iris radius R_i often presents different values. Considering the influence of R_i, we use the ratio of pupil radius to iris radius $T = \frac{R_p}{R_i}$ to measure the degree of iris deformation. Therefore, in the proposed algorithm, we assume that $\triangle R$ is a function of R_{linear} and T, denoted as $\triangle R(R_{linear}, T)$.

2.3 Choice of Iris Deformation Factor

Pupil diameter undergoes small oscillations ("hippus") once or twice per second, even under uniform lighting. Weak illumination causes pupil dilation and increases the ratio T whereas intense illumination causes pupil contraction and decreases T. Iris takes much more deformation in dark and bright environment than in normal environment. According to our statistics, the ratio T of most irises stay in an interval $[T_s, T_l]$ under uniform lighting. In the proposed method, we use linear normalization to approximate iris stretch when T is in the threshold $[T_s, T_l]$. Otherwise, iris images are treated as nonlinear stretch.

As a measuring parameter, when $T > T_l$, pupil dilates and iris compresses. The larger T is, the heavier iris deforms. On the contrary, when $T < T_s$, pupil contracts and iris extends. The smaller T is, the heavier iris deforms. In the proposed algorithm, we set $(\frac{T_s+T_l}{2} - T)$ as a factor of the additive deviation $\triangle R$, indicating how heavily the deformation is while compared to the non-deformed images. However, the choice of this deformation factor is not unique. Here we assume the deviation is described as:

$$\triangle R = C \times F(R_{linear}), \tag{3}$$

here $C = (\frac{T_s+T_l}{2} - T)$, and $F(R_{linear})$ is a function of R_{linear}.

2.4 The Gaussian Model for Deviation

As how to model iris collagen fibers movement is still an open problem, we learn $F(R_{linear})$ via training. The training data set: $D_{k,m} = \{D_{i,j} | i = 1, 2, ..., k; j = 1, 2, ..., m\}$ contains 600 iris images with $k = 10$ subjects, and each subject has an image sequence which contains $m = 60$ images captured under gradually varying illumination. Some image samples are shown in Fig. 6(a). We apply the following procedure to obtain $F(R_{linear})$:

1. Given an image sequence: $D_i = \{D_{i,1}, D_{i,2}, ..., D_{i,m}\}$, we mark n prominent points on every iris image (shown in Fig. 6(a)) and obtain their nonlinear stretch positions $R_{nonlinear}$ by measuring the distance between each point and the pupil boundary.
2. Divide iris region into three annular regions equally, as illustrated in Fig. 6(b). According to their distance to pupil boundary, we use three sets $\{P_{in}\}$, $\{P_{mid}\}$ and $\{P_{out}\}$, respectively, to denote the location within each region.
3. Group all the points into the three sets $\{P_{in}\}$, $\{P_{mid}\}$ or $\{P_{out}\}$ using the Nearest Neighbor clustering method.

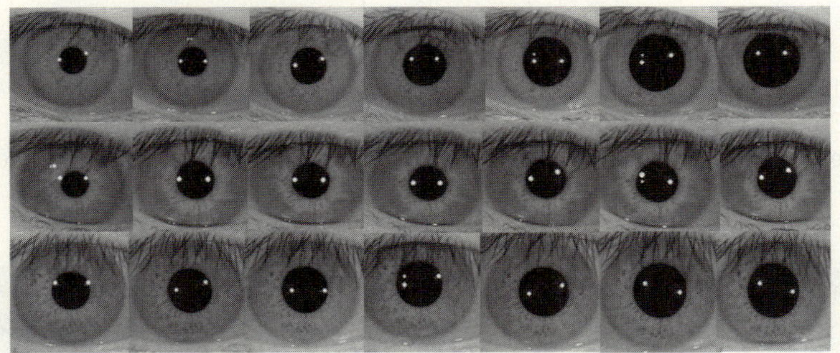

Fig. 5. Iris image samples with heavy elastic deformation

As nonlinear stretch positions $R_{nonlinear}$ is obtained by locating the points manually and linear stretch positions R_{linear} is approximated by iris stretch under uniform lighting, $\triangle R$ can be acquired by simply applying Eq. 1. Fig. 6(c) depicts the relationship between $\triangle R$ and pupil dilation $T = \frac{R_p}{R_i}$. It shows that when pupil size is appropriate (T is around 0.47), the deviation reaches the lowest. When pupil contracts, $\triangle R$ presents a positive deviation. Otherwise pupil dilates and $\triangle R$ presents a negative deviation.

Fig. 6(c) also shows that the degree of deformation is varying from regions. Texture in the middle region $\{P_{mid}\}$ suffers more deformation than texture near pupil/iris boundary (regions $\{P_{in}\}/\{P_{out}\}$). We rearrange the value of $\triangle R$ to estimate its relation to R_{linear}, shown in Fig. 6(d), which expresses iris deformation from another perspective.

The relationship between $\triangle R$ and R_{linear} can be approximated as Gaussian function (solid line in Fig. 6(d)), with the mean around the center of R_{linear}. $\triangle R$ apparently should be equal to 0 at pupil boundary or iris boundary, that is to say, the additive deviation should be subjected to: $\triangle R = 0$, when $R_{linear} = 0$ or 1. In this case σ should be chosen less than $\mu/3$, so that $N(\mu, \sigma^2)$ is out of the interval of $[\mu - 3\sigma, \mu + 3\sigma]$, which leads to $\triangle R \approx 0$ when $R_{linear} = 0$ or 1. In the proposed algorithm, μ and σ are learned from training while obeying these rules.

The index C_i $(i = 1, 2, 3, \cdots)$ in Fig. 6(d) is the deformation factor described in Eq. 3, indicating the degree of deformation. For each different C, there is a different curve to represent the deviation. If $C > 0$, pupil contracts, iris extends, and $\triangle R$ appears to be a positive deviation. On the contrary, $C < 0$, pupil dilates, iris compresses, and $\triangle R$ appears to be a negative deviation.

Finally $F(R_{linear})$ is expressed as Gaussian function, and a deformed image can be corrected by compensating the additive deviation $\triangle R$, which can be described as:

$$\begin{aligned} \triangle R &= C \times F(R_{linear}) = C \times N(\mu, \sigma^2) \\ &= C \times \frac{1}{\sqrt{2\pi}\sigma} \exp\{-\frac{(R_{linear} - \mu)^2}{2\sigma^2}\}. \end{aligned} \tag{4}$$

Once the additive deviation $\triangle R$ is chosen as Gaussian function, shown in Fig. 4(b), nonlinear iris stretch model is able to be measured. The fractional position of each point under nonlinear stretch is computed based on Eq. 1. According to Eq. 4, every deformed image has 3 parameters to be determined. We denote these parameters as $P(c_i, \mu_i, \sigma_i)$, which is mentioned in our framework (see Fig. 2).

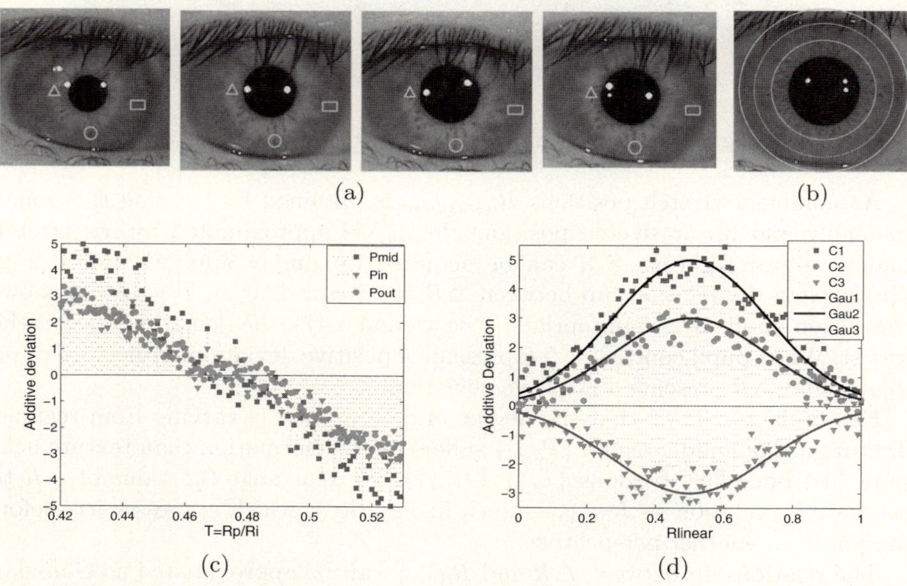

Fig. 6. Illustration of training. (a)Recording the location of iris prominent points. (b)The three annular regions. (c)The relationship between $\triangle R$ and $T = \frac{R_p}{R_i}$. (d)The relationship between $\triangle R$ and R_{linear}.

3 Experiments and Discussion

In this section the proposed nonlinear iris deformation correction algorithm is evaluated on two databases, both of which possess large pupil size variations.

We incorporated the proposed algorithm with Daugman's [1] iris localization and Ma's [6] feature extraction algorithm into one recognition system. To eliminate other influences, we only adopt clear images in the experiment. Daugman's Rubber-sheet model and Yuan's nonlinear normalization are also implemented on the same database for comparison.

3.1 Experiments on DB1

To evaluate the effectiveness of the proposed algorithms in different lighting condition, we collected a database (denote as DB1) under gradually changing illumination using a hand held device produced by OKI. It contains 30 classes and each class contains 60 images. Samples of 3 subjects' images are given in Fig.5, which shows that there is heavy deformation within each class. $T = \frac{R_p}{R_i}$ ranges from a minimum of 0.2353 to a maximum of 0.5902 in DB1. The within class deformation in DB1 is heavier than any other publicly available databases, therefore it is quite challenge. Ten arbitrary classes are selected for training, leaving

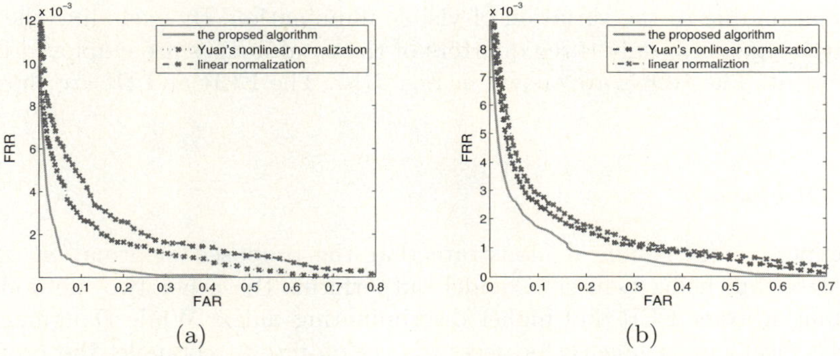

Fig. 7. (a) ROC curve in DB1. (b) ROC curve in CASIA-IrisV3-Lamp

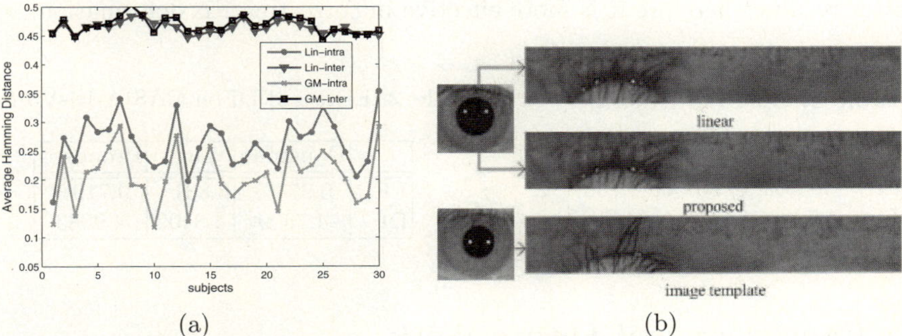

Fig. 8. (a) Hamming distance (HD) of Linear(Lin) method vs. Gaussian model(GM) correction. (b) A sample iris texture with GM correction that align better with the image template. (Lin vs. Tem: 0.459HD; GM vs. Tem: 0.375HD)

the rest 20 classes for testing. All possible intra-class and inter-class comparisons are made to evaluate the recognition performance. The ROCs (receiver of operating curves) of the three methods are shown in Fig.7(a). The EER (equal error rate) and discriminating index [1] ($DI = \frac{|\mu_1 - \mu_2|}{\sqrt{\frac{(\sigma_1^2 + \sigma_2^2)}{2}}}$) are shown in Table 1. The benefits of our approach are well illustrated in Fig. 8(a), which plots the average intra/inter-class Hamming distances of the 30 classes in DB1. This figure shows that our method can reduce the intra-class distance while maintaining the inter-class distance. Fig. 8(b) shows a corrected iris sample that align better with the image template in the case of a genuine match.

3.2 Experiments on CASIA-IrisV3-Lamp Database

To get a more convincing result, our second experiment is based on a larger database. We take 400 classes of iris images from CASIA-IrisV3-Lamp [7] database. Each class contains 20 images, 10 of which were captured with a lamp on and the other 10 with the lamp off. So images of this database also contain nonlinear deformation due to the variation of visible illumination. By excluding the poor quality image data, only three quarters of the total images are employed in the experiment. The ROCs are shown in Fig. 7(b). The EER and DI are shown in Table 2.

3.3 Discussion

The experimental results demonstrate that the proposed deformation correction algorithm using Gaussian model outperforms the other two methods, by obtaining a lower EER and higher discriminating index. While Daugman's [1] Rubber-sheet model linearly projects iris region into a rectangle, the proposed Gaussian deformation correction model makes use of iris structure and it can better alleviate the distortion. Compare to Yuan's [2] nonlinear normalization, the proposed method uses a more simple and flexible approach, but achieves better results, therefore it is more effective in correcting iris deformation.

Table 1. EER and DI on DB1

	Daugman	Yuan	Proposed
EER	1.058%	0.857%	0.733%
DI	4.7094	4.8213	4.9913

Table 2. EER and DI on CASIA-IrisV3-Lamp

	Daugman	Yuan	Proposed
EER	0.973%	0.831%	0.719%
DI	4.7509	4.8409	4.9083

4 Conclusion and Future Work

In this paper, we have proposed a novel method to correct nonlinear iris deformation. In this algorithm, iris images are corrected by compensating the additive deviation between nonlinear and linear iris stretch. The additive deviation is described by Gaussian function, which is chosen via training. Experimental results demonstrate that the proposed algorithm can resist considerable iris deformation and yield better results than the other two approaches. Therefore it makes iris recognition system more robust to the external stimulus, such as illumination variations.

How to deal with iris deformation problem has only been addressed by a few literatures, and we think this issue hold great importance in iris recognition. In the future, we will try to tackle the problem not only from iris model but also the appearance of iris images. Hopefully it can deepen our understanding of iris deformation and improves the recognition performance.

Acknowledgement

This work is funded by research grants from the National Basic Research Program (Grant No. 2004CB318110), the Natural Science Foundation of China (Grant No. 60335010, 60121302, 60275003, 60332010, 69825105, 60605008) and the Chinese Academy of Sciences.

References

1. Daugman, J.: High confidence visual recognition of persons by a test of statistical independence. IEEE Transactions on Pattern Analysis and Machine Intelligence 15(11), 1148–1161 (1993)
2. Yuan, X., Shi, P.: A non-linear normalization model for iris recognition. In: Advances in Biometric Person Authentication, pp. 135–141 (2005)
3. Wyatt, H.J.: A 'minimum-wear-and-tear' meshwork for the iris. Vision Research 40, 2167–2176 (2000)
4. Li, X.: Modeling intra-class variation for nonideal iris recognition. In: International Conference on Biometrics 2006, pp. 419–427 (2006)
5. Rohen: Der bau der regenbogenhaut beim menschen undeinigen saugern. Gegenbaur Morphology Journal 91, 140–181 (1951)
6. Ma, L., Tan, T., Wang, Y., Zhang, D.: Personal identification based on iris texture analysis. IEEE Transactions on Pattern Analysis and Machine Intelligence 25(12), 1519–1533 (2003)
7. CASIA-IrisV3: `http://www.cbsr.ia.ac.cn/IrisDatabase.htm`

Shape Analysis of Stroma for Iris Recognition*

S. Mahdi Hosseini[1], Babak N. Araabi[1], and Hamid Soltanian-Zadeh[1,2]

[1] Control and Intelligent Processing Center of Excellence, School of ECE, Univesity of Tehran, P.O. Box 14395-515, Tehran, Iran
[2] Image Analysis Lab., Radiology Dept., Henry Ford Health System, Detroit, MI 48202, USA
sm.hosseini@ece.ut.ac.ir, {araabi,hszadeh}@ut.ac.ir

Abstract. In this paper, a new shape analysis approach for iris recognition is proposed. First, the extracted iris images from eye portrait are enhanced by image deblurring filter which computes restoration using FFT-based Tikhonov filter with the identity matrix as the regularization operator. This procedure produces a smooth image in which shape of pigmented fibro vascular tissue known as Stroma is depicted easily. Then, an adaptive filter is defined to extract these shapes. In the next step, shape analysis techniques are applied in order to extract robust features from contour of the shapes such as support functions and radius vectors. These features are invariant under iris localization and mapping. Finally, a feature strip code is defined for every iris image. Introduced algorithm is applied to UBIRIS databank. Experimental results show efficiency of the proposed method by achieving an accuracy of 95.08% on first session of UBIRIS.

Keywords: Biometric Recognition, Stroma, Tikhonov Filter, Shape Analysis.

1 Introduction

Literature of iris recognition is dominated by wavelet methods. First method was proposed by Daugman [1, 2] which used multiscale quadrature wavelets to extract texture phase structure information of the iris. Ma et al. [3–4] adopted a well-known texture analysis method (multichannel Gabor filtering) to capture both global and local details in iris. Wildes et al. [5] with a Laplacian pyramid constructed in four different resolution levels and the normalized correlation for matching designed their system. Tisse et al. [6] combined the original image and Hilbert transform to demodulate the iris texture. 2D Haar wavelet was used by Lim et al. [7] and applied an LVQ neural network for classification. Kumar et al. [8] developed correlation filters to measure the consistency of iris images from the same eye. The correlation filter of each class was designed using the two-dimensional Fourier transforms of training images. Bae et al. [9] projected the iris signals onto a bank of basis vectors derived by independent component analysis and quantized the resulting projection coefficients as features. Gu et al. [10] used a multiorientation features via both spatial

* This paper is for BBSPA competition.

S.-W. Lee and S.Z. Li (Eds.): ICB 2007, LNCS 4642, pp. 790–799, 2007.

and frequency domains and a nonsymmetrical SVM to develop their system. They extracted features by variant fractal dimensions and steerable pyramids for orientation information.

Although there exists different feature extraction methods based on wavelet approaches for iris recognition, nevertheless, extra developments are needed to reach highly accurate results in huge size databanks. Besides, most of the approaches are sensitive to iris localization and distortion during iris extraction, where this matter causes in error during template matching. By the definition, other approaches should be considered to extract robust features. Studying the anatomy of iris would assist us to sense it more reliable and obtain more suitable features.

Iris contains two different layers. The thin innermost layer is called the iris pigment epithelium (IPE) and consists of a compact array of opaque cells. The outermost layer is referred to as the iris stroma, which contains more loosely arranged cells, including melanocytes that synthesize the pigment melanin [11]. Iris stroma is the unique characteristic which identifies a person where the following shapes can be considered to process them in the form they appear.

In this paper, we introduce a new method in order to extract the iris stroma shapes in binarized portrait from gray image which is adaptive to light luminance. Gaussian fitting through gray image histogram and detecting threshold boundaries is the essential key for the implemented adaptive filtering. Section 2 reviews the state of art of shape analysis methodology in order to apply it to iris recognition. Nevertheless, Section 3 implements the above method to analyze the unique iris stroma shapes. In Section 4 we set up a feature code for every person's iris, where after all, we apply and evaluate our algorithm to UBIRIS [12] as a databank for classification. Finally, Section 5 concludes the paper.

2 Shape Analysis and Invariant Features

Shape analysis techniques have been of interest in computer vision and intensively developed over the past decades. Shape is a difficult concept, invariant of geometrical transformations such as translation, rotation, size changes and reflection [13]. The normal description of a shape can be defined by functional approach which is explained in Section 2.1.

2.1 Functional Approach

The function description of a figure is appropriate for many applications because of its advantages over other methods such as [13]:

- *Effective data reduction:* frequently only a few coefficients of the approximation functions are needed for a rather precise form description, where it causes less computation time in processing the algorithm.
- *A convenient description and intuitive characterization of complex forms:* this leads to considering whole complexity of figure's shape as useful features.

As a functional approach, two distinct features are introduced here to apply them in extracting features from iris images which are *Radius-Vector Functio*n and *Support Function.*

Regarding *radius-vector function*, a reference point O in the interior of the figure X is selected which is called the center of gravity. Next, the appropriate reference line l crossing the reference point O is chosen parallel to the x- or y-axes. The radius-vector function $r_X(\varphi)$ is then the distance from the reference point O.

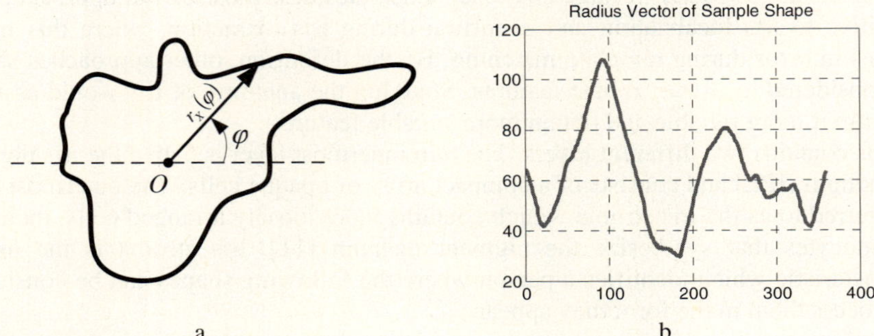

Fig. 1. a. Figure of a sample shape and definition of radius-vector function **b.** Radius-Vector Function of a sample shape

It is necessary, for polar description, that the figure remains star-shaped with respect to O. This means that there only exists one point of p for every angle. In fact, it is not obligatory to describe a figure in polar coordinates. Here, we used all points of figure as potential features and normalized the radius-vector function. For example, in Fig. 1.b, the number of the points is normalized to 360 points, though this value is completely arbitrary.

It is important to know how Radius-Vector Function depends on geometrical transformations such as *translation, size changes, rotation,* and *reflection*. Above function shows the following features [13]:

1. is invariant under translation: $r_{X+t}(\varphi) = r_X(\varphi)$ where $X + t$ is X translated by a vector t;
2. depends on the size of figure $X : r_{\lambda X}(\varphi) = \lambda r_X(\varphi)$ where λX is the figure X zoomed by a factor λ. Nevertheless, this matter can be solved by normalizing the radius function;
3. is not invariant under reflection;
4. depends on the orientation of the figure $X : r_X(\varphi) = r_Y(\varphi - \alpha)$ where Y is Figure X rotated by an angle α.

The last two seems disadvantages of the radius-vector function. In particular, the fourth argument declares dependency of the function to orientation.

Nevertheless, orientation is not a problem in iris recognition even by mapping the extracted iris from polar to Cartesian coordinates, see Fig. 2, because orientation in polar coordinates is the same as translation in Cartesian coordinates.

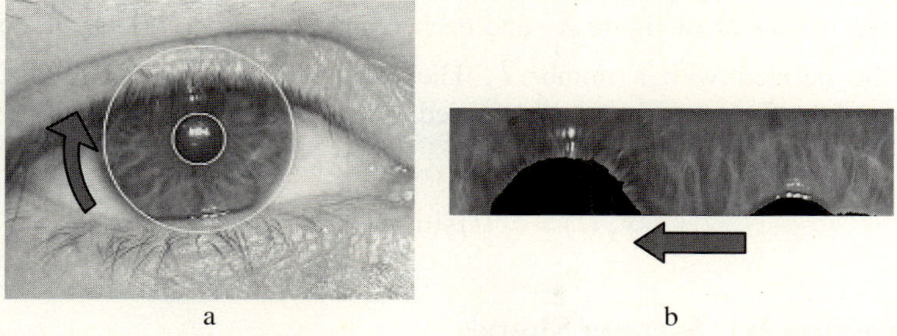

Fig. 2. a. Orientation in polar coordinate **b.** Translation in Cartesian coordinates corresponds to orientation in polar coordinates

Obviously, the third problem, which refers to reflection, will not happen if a distinct definition is introduced for extracting a shape like iris. Usually in iris recognition neither extracted iris nor mapped iris do not reflect the shape, see [15].

The second functional approach to figure description is Support Function. For a figure X, let g_φ be an oriented line through the origin O with direction φ, $0 \le \varphi \le 2\pi$. Let $g_\varphi^\perp$ be the line orthogonal to g_φ so that the figure X lies completely in the half-plane determined by $g_\varphi^\perp$ with $g_\varphi^\perp \cap X \neq \varnothing$, which is opposite to the direction of g_φ. The absolute value of the support function equals to the distance from O to $g_\varphi^\perp$ and the support function $S_X(\varphi)$ is negative if the figure lies behind $g_\varphi^\perp$ as seen from the origin. If O is an element of the figure X, then $S_X(\varphi) \ge 0$ for all φ [13], see Fig. 3.

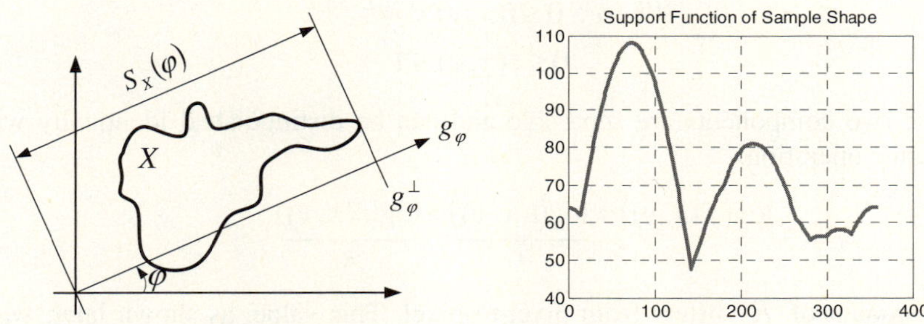

Fig. 3. a. Support Function Description **b.** Support Function of the sample shape

All of the four benefits in the above discussion are appropriate for the support function. This parameter can be calculated as follows:

$$s_X(\varphi) = \max_{0 \le l \le L}\left[x_X(l)\cos(\varphi) + y_X(l)\sin(\varphi)\right] \tag{1}$$

L is the perimeter of figure X and each point $(x_X(l), y_X(l))$ of the contour of X can be defined with a number l. The relation between polar and Cartesian coordinate of the figure thus can be identified by:

$$\begin{aligned} x_X(l) &= r_X(l)\cos(\varphi_l) \\ y_X(l) &= r_X(l)\sin(\varphi_l) \end{aligned} \tag{2}$$

3 Extracting Iris Stroma Shapes

As noted in Section 1, the iris stroma is the outermost layer of iris and has unique characteristic for each individual. It has to be segmented to extract the related features such as radius-vector and support function. Iris stroma is usually a thin layer where by implementing a filter, it should be extracted precisely. Most captured iris images are noisy due to light luminance of camera flash. UBIRIS [12] is databank with dominant noise. The authors of the databank presented a table to discuss the noise factors, see [16]. They introduced the first session of the databank as 11% noisy databank regarding Focus, Reflection-Area and Visible-Iris-Area, simultaneously with 17.06%, 5.4% and 10.71% noise factors. In this paper, we implement an adaptive filter in order to eliminate the above noises.

The portrait of an image consists of two components: a) the amount of source illumination incident on the scene being viewed; and b) the amount of illumination reflected by the objects in the scene [17]. These components are called the Illumination and Reflectance and are denoted by $i(x, y)$ and $r(x, y)$ respectively. Production of the two components called the gray value $f(x, y)$:

$$\begin{aligned} & f(x, y) = i(x, y) r(x, y) \\ & Where\colon\ 0 \le i(x, y) < \infty \\ & \qquad 0 \le r(x, y) \le 1 \end{aligned} \tag{3}$$

These two components are separable and can be distinguished identically with a logarithmic operation:

$$\log(f(x, y)) = \underbrace{\log(i(x, y))}_{I} + \underbrace{\log(r(x, y))}_{R} \tag{4}$$

The amount of R differs from pixel-to-pixel. This value, as shown later, will be adaptively eliminated and only illumination incident I will remain as appropriate value to generate a binary image.

The image smoothed after logarithmic operation in order to distribute focus noise factors along the image. Tikhonov Filter [18] is a suitable tool to denoise the related noise of the images where deblurs an image with identity matrix as the regularization operator known as mask. After deblurring, the high frequency noises of the image removed by a lowpass filter. The whole procedure of the implemented algorithm is shown in Fig. 4. As shown, the image generated by Tikhonov filter is nicely smooth and iris stroma is smoothly depicted.

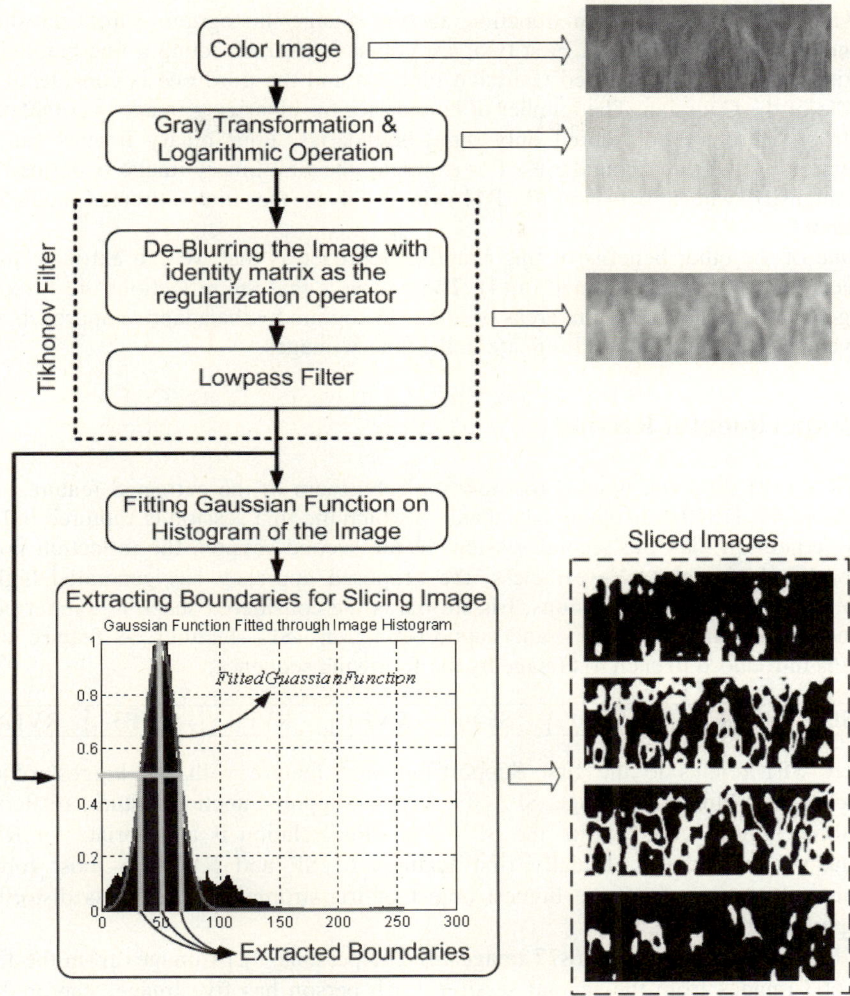

Fig. 4. The implemented algorithm block diagram for extracting iris stroma

After smoothing iris template, we need to extract iris stroma by considering the fact that the reflection noise is not yet removed from the image. A simple method is to binarize image with several distinct thresholds. However, the histogram of incident illumination I is not a fixed distribution. It changes from person to person. This fact causes problem during thresholding the images where in some sample of binarized templates, there exists just tiny shapes which are not suitable for shape analysis. To solve the problem, we proposed an adaptive approach in which the image histogram is fitted by a Gaussian function. This is because almost the entire iris gray levels are clustered around a distinct intensity value which relates to iris stroma. In other words, the variance of the intensity values of the iris image is small.

After fitting a Gaussian function to the image histogram, three threshold boundaries can be extracted. First two, are gotten from intersecting a line parallel to x-axis which bisects the fitted Gaussian function and the third one is considered by middle of the Gaussian. The number of boundaries for binarizing image is completely arbitrary. Here we considered only three boundaries. Four binary images can be generated by the three boundaries. For example, the first binary image is defined by the intensity values between [0, B1] where B1 is the first extracted boundary threshold.

One of the other benefits of this adaptive approach is that we can extricate from reflectance components defined in (4). The reason is that the reflections are fused in image and gather in maximum areas of image histogram by the adaptive approach, the above noises automatically illuminate in the binary images.

4 Experimental Results

UBIRIS [12] databank is used to show the robustness of the extracted features. As noted before, UBIRIS is a noisy databank in which the first session is captured in less noisy condition than the second session. In the second session, the reflection noise factor has high value. Nevertheless, the proposed approach has generated highly accurate results for both sessions. Iris stroma is the considered shape to extract both radius-vector-function—RVF—and support-function—SF—features. A feature strip code is introduced to each iris image by the following sequence:

SF1	SF2	SF3	SF4	RVF1	RVF2	RVF3	RVF4

Where SF1 relates to the first Support-Function feature with the biggest object detected from binary iris image. SF2-SF4 are the Support-Function features related to the three biggest objects after the SF1. The same relation is appropriate for RVF (radius-vector-function). Usually first features of SF and RVF are most robust because they come from the biggest object of iris stroma and have less distortion compared with the other ones.

UBIRIS [12] consists of 1877 images of 241 persons, 1214 images from the first and 663 images from the second session. Each person has five images captured in different time sequences. Table 1 shows the classification results for both sessions of UBIRIS in 3 different conditions with to two, three and four test data. The best accuracy is obtained from the first session (first condition) with 95.08% accuracy. We realized that the images with high noise levels, especially on reflection, failed in the experimental step. The other important fact is that degradation of the results from the first to the second sessions is not high showing the robustness of proposed algorithm to noisy images. False acceptance rate is one of the important facts to realize the behavior of accuracy of applied contribution by allowing system to verify the failed images in several attempts. For example, for the first session of UBIRIS after 2 attempts, the accuracy result increases to 98%. Fig. 5 shows the related argument.

Table 1. Classification results for UBIRIS databank considering three different situation

Conditions	1st Session of UBIRIS	2nd Session of UBIRIS	Degradation
1 Test Images & 4 Comparing Images	**95.08%**	**91.37%**	**3.71%**
2 Test Images & 3 Comparing Images	**93.00%**	**88.12%**	**4.88%**
3 Test Images & 2 Comparing Images	**86.09%**	**81.06%**	**5.03%**
4 Test Images & 1 Comparing Image	**78.39%**	**70.19%**	**8.22%**

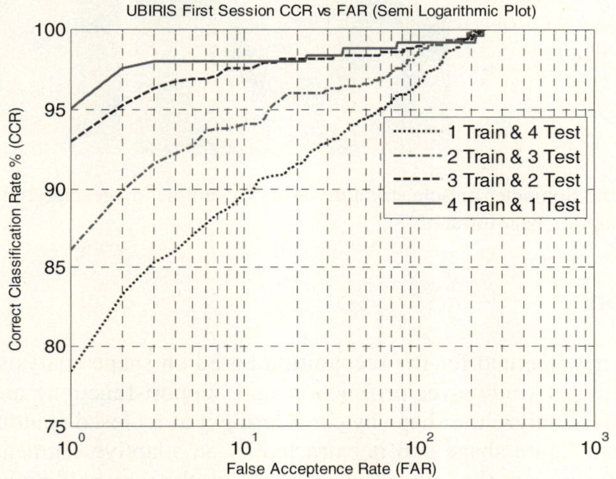

Fig. 5. CCR versus Classification attempt numbers for the first session of UBIRIS

CASIA [19] might be the most popular databank in iris recognition, where the images have been captured in near infrared. In CASIA, due to near infrared imaging, reflections do not influence the images, and they are less noisy as compared with those images captured in visible light. Applying our developed algorithm to CASIA, however, results in very poor performance. The best result of shape analysis on CASIA led on 38.88% accuracy for 1 FAR, see Fig. 6.

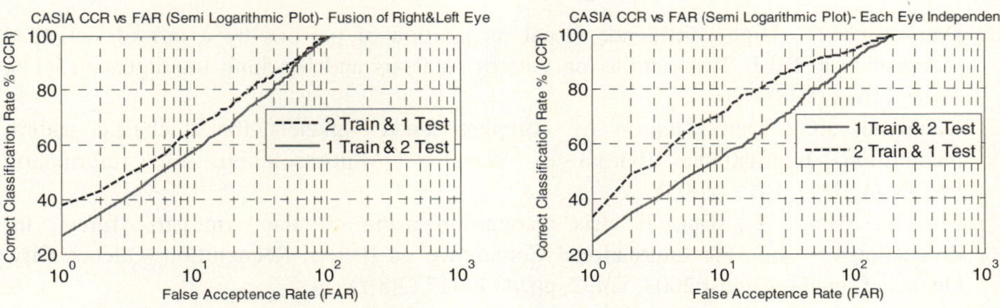

Fig. 6. a. CCR of CASIA with fusion of Left and Right eyes **b.** CCR of CASIA Each eye independent

The reason for lack of performance of our stroma shape analysis based method on CASIA lay in the fact that near infrared imaging suppress most of the information one may get from Stroma patterns. Fig. 7 compares two typical images from UBIRIS and CASIA. One can examine that the pattern generated by the radial muscles in stroma almost disappear on infrared imaging.

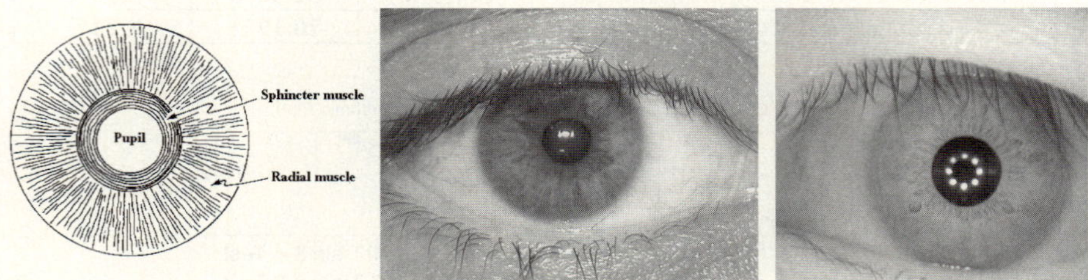

Fig. 7. a. Radial and Sphincter muscle structure of iris **b.** Sample image captured in visible light c. sample image capture near infrared

5 Conclusion

In this paper, a new method for iris recognition based on shape analysis is proposed. Two shape attributes (radius-vector-function and support-function) are introduced. These two features analyze the shape by considering it as a closed contour. Iris stroma is considered as a figure shape and is extracted by an adaptive segment filter which fits a Gaussian function to the image histogram. Next, the thresholding boundaries are found to create binary images for shape analysis. In the analysis step, the biggest objects are considered for the analysis. Results of accuracy on UBIRIS depicts an accuracy of 95.08% for two test images and three comparison images of 241 individuals (total of 1214 images). Currently, we consider the fusion of our proposed shape analysis based signatures with existing iris signatures for iris recognition in a hierarchical scheme.

References

1. Daugman, J.G.: High confidence visual recognition of persons by a test of statistical independence. IEEE Transactions on Pattern Analysis and Machine Intelligence 15(11), 1148–1161 (1993)
2. Daugman, J.G.: Demodulation by complex-valued wavelets for stochastic pattern recognition. International Journal of Wavelets, Multiresolution, and Information Processing 1(1), 1–17 (2003)
3. Ma, L., Wang, Y., Tan, T.: Iris recognition using circular symmetric filters. In: Proceedings of the 16th International Conference on Pattern Recognition, Quebec City, Quebec, Canada, August 2002, vol. 2, pp. 414–417 (2002)
4. Ma, L., Tan, T., Wang, Y., Zhang, D.: Personal identification based on iris texture analysis. IEEE Transactions on Pattern Analysis and Machine Intelligence 25(12), 1519–1533 (2003)

5. Wildes, R.P., Asmuth, J.C., Green, G.L., et al.: A machinevision system for iris recognition. Machine Vision and Applications 9(1), 1–8 (1996)
6. Tisse, C., Martin, L., Torres, L., Robert, M.: Person identification technique using human iris recognition. In: Proceedings of the 15th International Conference on Vision Interface (VI '02), Calgary, Canada, May 2002, pp. 294–299 (2002)
7. Lim, S., Lee, K., Byeon, O., Kim, T.: Efficient iris recognition through improvement of feature vector and classifier. ETRI Journal 23(2), 61–70 (2001)
8. Kumar, B.V.K.V., Xie, C., Thornton, J.: Iris verification using correlation filters. In: Kittler, J., Nixon, M.S. (eds.) AVBPA 2003. LNCS, vol. 2688, pp. 697–705. Springer, Heidelberg (2003)
9. Bae, K., Noh, S.-I., Kim, J.: Iris feature extraction using independent component analysis. In: Kittler, J., Nixon, M.S. (eds.) AVBPA 2003. LNCS, vol. 2688, pp. 838–844. Springer, Heidelberg (2003)
10. Gu, H.-Y., Zhuang, Y.-T., Pan, Y.-H.: An iris recognition method based on multi-orientation features and nonsymmetrical SVM. Journal of Zhejiang University: Science 6A(5), 428–432, A0505 (2005)
11. Imesch, P.D., Wallow, I.H.L., Albert, D.M.: The color of the human eye: A review of morphologic correlates and of some conditions that affect iridial pigmentation. Survey of Ophthal. 41, 117–123 (1997)
12. Proença, H., Alexandre, L.A.: UBIRIS: a noisy iris image database. In: Roli, F., Vitulano, S. (eds.) ICIAP 2005. LNCS, vol. 3617, pp. 3–540. Springer, Heidelberg (2005)
13. Kindratenko, V.: Development and Application of Image Analysis Techniques for identification and Classification of Microscopic Particles. Ph.D. Thesis, University of Antwerp, Belgium (1997), http://www.ncsa.uiuc.edu/ kindr/phd/index.pdf
14. Stoyan, D., Stoyan, H.: Fractals, Random Shapes and Point Fields (Methods of Geometrical Statistics). John Wiley & Sons, Chichester (1995)
15. Hosseini, S.M., Araabi, B.N., Poursaberi, A.: A Super Fast and Accurate method for Iris Segmentation Based on Effect of Retina Color on Pupil. In: 2nd IAPR/IEEE International Conference on Biometrics, Seoul, Korea, August 27-29 (2007) (submitted)
16. Proença, H., Alexandre, L.A.: Iris segmentation methodology for non-cooperative Recognition. IEE Proc.-Vis. Image Signal Process 153(2) (April 2006)
17. Gonzalez, R.C., Woods, R.E.: Digital Image Processing, 2nd edn. Prentice Hall Inc., Englewood Cliffs (2002)
18. Hansen, P.C., Nagy, J.G., O'Leary, D.P.: Deblurring Images - Matrices, Spectra and Filtering, SIAM, Philadelphia (2006)
19. Institute of Automation, Chinese Academy of Sciences, CASIA Iris Image Database, CASIA-IrisV1 and CASIA-IrisV3: http://www.cbsr.ia.ac.cn/IrisDatabase.htm

Biometric Key Binding: Fuzzy Vault Based on Iris Images

Youn Joo Lee[1], Kwanghyuk Bae[1], Sung Joo Lee[1], Kang Ryoung Park[2], and Jaihie Kim[1]

[1] Department of Electrical and Electronic Engineering, Yonsei University, Biometrics Engineering Research Center
{younjoo,paero,sungjoo,jhkim}@yonsei.ac.kr
[2] Division of Digital Media Technology, Sangmyung University, Biometrics Engineering Research Center
parkgr@smu.ac.kr

Abstract. Recently, crypto-biometric systems have been studied for solving the key management problem of cryptographic systems and protecting templates in biometric systems at the same time. The fuzzy vault system is a well-known crypto-biometric system. We propose a new method of applying iris data to the fuzzy vault. Our research has following two advantages and contributions. First, in order to solve the variation problem of the extracted iris features, we introduce a pattern clustering method. Second, in order to produce unordered sets for fuzzy vault, we use the iris feature extraction algorithm based on ICA (Independent Component Analysis). Experimental results showed that 128-bit cryptographic keys as well as the iris templates were secure with the fuzzy vault scheme.

Keywords: Fuzzy Vault Scheme, Pattern Clustering, Independent Component Analysis (ICA).

1 Introduction

In general, cryptographic systems suffer from the key management problem [1], which refers to dealing with the storage of cryptographic keys and the secure generation of these keys. To overcome these problems, current cryptographic systems have stored keys in storage devices such as smartcards, computers or servers, to be released only by password-based authentication [1]. Therefore, the security level of cryptographic keys has depended on how robust a user's password is to brute force attacks [2] and how robust a user's stored keys are to physical attacks. Passwords are generally short and simple so that users can memorize them easily. Hence, password-based authentication always involves the threat of passwords being cracked by brute force attacks. Also, passwords may be shared, lost or forgotten. These problems can be solved by using biometric-based authentication. Some reasons for this are because biometric features are generally difficult to be copied, shared and distributed, and they usually require users to present at the time and point of authentication [1]. However, if stored keys can be released from storage devices by using simple biometric

S.-W. Lee and S.Z. Li (Eds.): ICB 2007, LNCS 4642, pp. 800–808, 2007.

matching, there still remains the risk of the keys and biometric templates being compromised by physical attacks. For example, if an attacker strikes a storage device, stored keys and templates can be readily compromised. To overcome these problems, a crypto-biometric system is needed, which merges cryptographic keys with user's biometric data, using cryptography. In crypto-biometric systems, keys and templates are combined and then stored in storage devices. Therefore, attackers cannot obtain keys without knowing the specific user's biometric data, so the keys and biometric templates can remain secure. The fuzzy vault scheme, as proposed by Juels and Sudan [3], is well known as a form of cryptography that binds cryptographic keys and biometric templates.

In this paper, we focus on applying iris data to a fuzzy vault scheme. We propose a method of extracting iris features suitable to fuzzy vault and then implementing our system. To extract invariant iris features, we used an iris feature extraction algorithm based on Independent Component Analysis (ICA) [4-5] and a pattern clustering technique. Our fuzzy vault system was achieved by combining iris data with a 128-bit Advanced Encryption Standard (AES) key [2].

The remainder of this paper is organized as follows: section 2 describes works related to the fuzzy vault scheme. In section 3, we discuss how to extract iris features that can be applied to the fuzzy vault scheme as well as the procedures necessary to implement the fuzzy vault based on the iris data. Experimental results are presented in section 4, and conclusions are drawn in section 5.

2 Related Works

Juels and Sudan [3] first proposed a fuzzy vault scheme which encrypted and decrypted secret information securely, using a fuzzy unordered set. When encrypting the secret data, these researchers first generated a polynomial (p) by encoding secret data (for example, by using the secret data (which corresponds to secret key) as the coefficients of the polynomial). Next, they projected the components (which corresponds to biometric data) of the unordered set as x-axis coordinates on this polynomial (p) and produced genuine point pairs $(x_i, p(x_i))$, $i = 1,2,\ldots,n$, where n refers to the size of the unordered set (X) on the polynomial (p). Then, chaff points which did not exist on the polynomial (p) were generated in order to protect the genuine point set $\{(x_i, p(x_i)), i = 1,2,\ldots,n\}$. Finally, they created a vault which was a mixture of the genuine and the chaff point set. To access secret data from the vault, an unordered set (Y) was used, which had to be almost equal to set X. If the difference between set X and set Y was very small, the genuine point set was discriminated from the vault by set Y. Finally, the polynomial (p) was perfectly reconstructed and the secret data was generated securely. In general, cryptographic systems require correct cryptographic keys in order to decrypt secret data. On the other hand, fuzzy vault scheme allows the fuzziness of the unordered sets (which act as secret keys), which means that biometric data can be used as unordered sets because biometric data contain the intra-variations of the same person. However, the fuzzy vault scheme also requires pre-aligned biometric templates that are properly aligned with the input biometric data [1].

Most previous works [1][6-9] that were based on Juels and Sudan's fuzzy vault scheme used fingerprint data. This is because fingerprints are reliable biometric features, and it is also easy to extract the proper features for the fuzzy vault. Clancy *et al.* [6] proposed a fingerprint-based fuzzy vault system. They used the location set of minutiae as an unordered set [3] and assumed that there were no great variations between the template and the query minutiae set. Uludag *et al.* [1] introduced a modified fuzzy vault system that did not require Reed-Solomon decoding and allowed manual alignment between the template and query fingerprint data. However, they also proposed a new method to automatically align the template and query fingerprint data with helper data [7]. Shibata *et al.* [8] proposed a minutiae-based fingerprint fuzzy vault system that used the clustering technique to automatically align fingerprint data. Yang *et al.* [9] proposed automatic fingerprint verification based on the fuzzy vault scheme. Freire-Santos *et al.* [10] proposed the implementation of the fuzzy vault system based on hand-written signatures. These researchers did not assume the pre-alignment of biometric data. Last, Feng *et al.* [11] proposed a fuzzy vault system that used face data.

3 Proposed Method

In this section, we present our method of generating unordered sets (a locking set and an unlocking set) and the implementation of our fuzzy vault system. Fig. 1 shows a block diagram of the proposed fuzzy vault system. Details explanations about Fig.1 are shown in section 3.2 and 3.3.

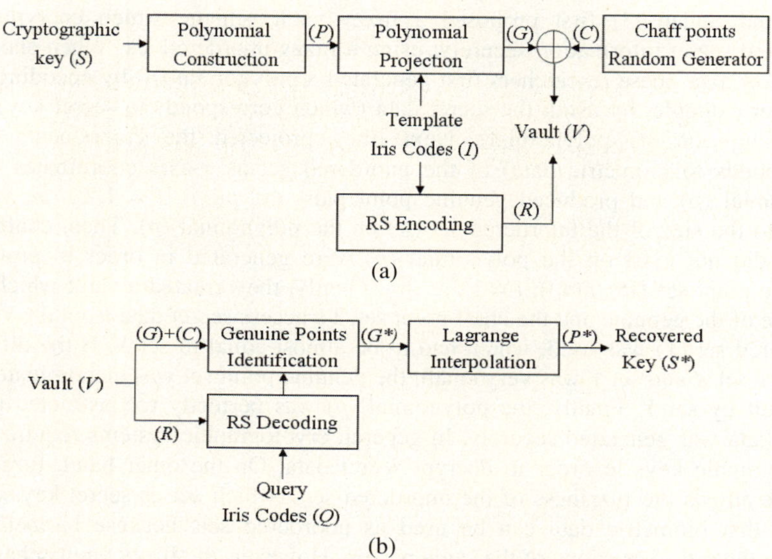

Fig. 1. Fuzzy vault system based on iris data: (a) locking the vault, (b) unlocking the vault

3.1 Feature Extraction

In order to generate an unordered set from iris data, we chose an algorithm [4-5] based on ICA. One reason is that ICA method is suitable for extracting multiple and local iris feature vectors from iris data. Another reason is that the performance of ICA method [4-5] is similar to the performance of Daugman's method [12]. Finally, instead of a global feature vector such as a 2048-bit iris code [12], we obtained multiple iris feature vectors from multiple iris image blocks using ICA method [4-5] because multiple input values are required for fuzzy vault system. The iris feature extraction process took place as follows: the first step was to localize the iris region in a captured eye image using a conventional circular edge detection method [4], as shown in Fig. 2(a). The second step was to transform the localized iris region into a polar coordinate to obtain the iris features invariant to translation and rotation. Then, we selected two iris regions which were not occluded by eyelids, eyelashes and specular reflections, as regions of interest for feature extraction, in the localized iris image at a polar coordinate, as shown in Fig. 2(b) [4].

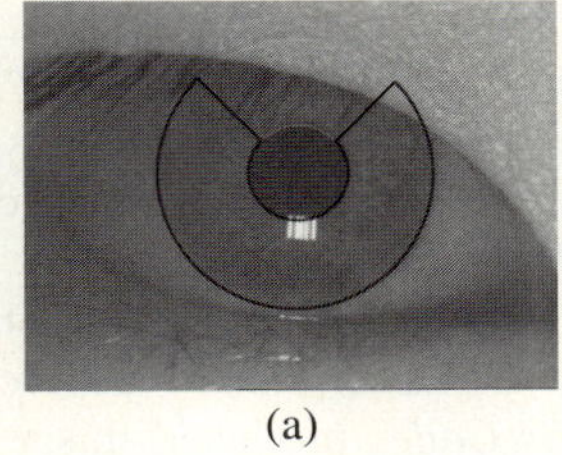

(a)

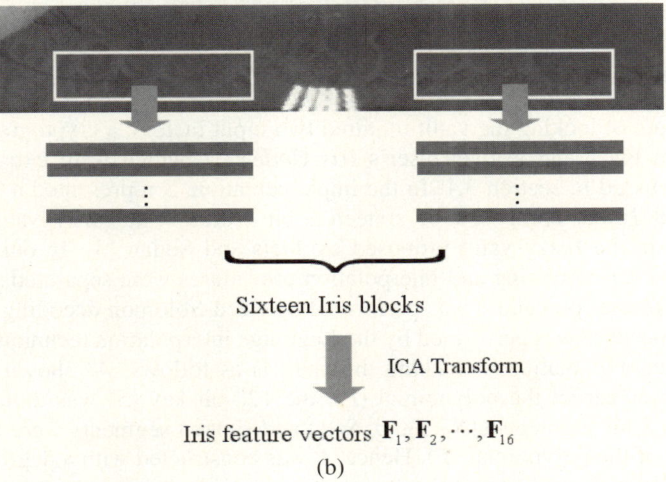

(b)

Fig. 2. Iris feature extraction: (a) localized iris image, (b) dividing two selected iris regions into sixteen iris image sub-regions (blocks) in the localized iris image of a polar coordinate and extracting an iris feature vector from each iris image block

The last step was to divide each region into eight iris image blocks and to extract sixteen iris feature vectors from sixteen iris image blocks by using the ICA algorithm [4-5], as shown in Fig. 2(b). Here, sixteen extracted iris feature vectors were quantized to be 27-bit binary codes with a sign of ICA coefficients [4-5].

We used sixteen feature vectors (sixteen 27-bit binary codes) because a polynomial of 15 degrees was used in our fuzzy vault system (see section 3.2). However, we could not use a set of sixteen feature vectors as an unordered set because iris data generally contains intra-class variations and the elements of an unordered set must be elements of a finite field, often called the *Galois Field* (GF) [13] in accordance with Reed-Solomon codes (RS codes) [14-15], used for error correcting in fuzzy vault [3]. Therefore, we used a pattern clustering technique to reduce the variations between the iris templates and the input iris data, and proposed a method of generating a set of *Iris Codes* which were proper for an unordered set.

The set of *Iris Codes* was generated as follows: to produce a locking set [3], we obtained five eye images from the same user for clustering. Next, we made a cluster using five extracted iris feature vectors for each iris block. For clustering, the K-means algorithm [16] was used because the number of classes was known. After clustering, each user had a cluster for each iris block. Namely, one user obtained sixteen clusters for sixteen iris blocks. Last, to generate the *Iris Codes*, we assigned a random integer of the finite field GF(2^8) to a prototypes of each cluster for each user. In our system, because we aimed at assigning 16 coefficients to 128 bits (for security level of fuzzy vault scheme to brute-force attacks, we do not use less than sixteen coefficients such as 8 or 4 coefficients), each coefficient had 8 bits, consequently. So, the *Galois Field* was defined as GF(2^8) based on the principle of Reed-Solomon coding. Each user's sixteen *Iris Codes* produced this way were represented by 8-bit words and were the elements of the locking set. Also, an unlocking set consisted of the *Iris Codes* to be found by matching the input iris feature vectors with the prototypes of each cluster map.

3.2 Locking the Vault

The procedure of locking the vault required two input factors: a cryptographic key (S) as shown in Fig.1 and a given user's *Iris Codes* (I), which were extracted by the method discussed in section 3.1. In the implementation, S represented a 128-bit AES key [2] and I was composed of sixteen 8-bit words. Our fuzzy vault system is different from the fuzzy vault proposed by Juels and Sudan [3]. In our fuzzy vault system, the error correcting and interpolation procedures were separated, as shown in Fig. 1. The former procedure was performed by Reed-Solomon decoding [14-15] and the latter procedure was performed by the Lagrange interpolation technique [17].

A Detailed explanation of locking the vault is as follows. As shown in Fig. 1, S was used to construct the polynomial (P): the 128-bit key (S) was divided into no-overlapping 8-bit segments ($\{S_1, S_2, \ldots, S_{16}\}$) and sixteen segments were then used as coefficients of the polynomial (P). Hence, P was constructed with a degree $d = 15$ ($d = (B/l)-1$, where B represented the length of a key and l represented a bit-length of elements in a finite field): $P(x) = S_1 + S_2x + \ldots + S_{16}x^{15}$. Then, three sets ($G$, C, R) were generated, as shown in Fig. 1(a).

The first set was a genuine set G, which was formed by evaluating the polynomial $P(x)$ in terms of the *Iris Codes* ($I = \{c_1, c_2, \ldots, c_{16}\}$): $G = \{(c_1, P(c_1)), (c_2, P(c_2)), \ldots, (c_{16}, P(c_{16}))\}$. The set G was used to reconstruct the polynomial during unlocking. So, the size of the set G had to be sixteen (degree of the polynomial + 1) or more. The second set was the chaff point set C which had a significant role in protecting the genuine set G. The set C was generated randomly in the range of the finite field, with the constraint that their values on the x-axis could not overlap with the *Iris Codes* (I) and they could not be located on the polynomial (P). The last set was the redundancy set (R), obtained by RS encoding. The set R was used to correct errors at the time of unlocking the vault [15]. The set R was composed of 8-bit redundant symbols, and the number of symbols was determined as twice the number of errors to be corrected [15]. Finally, the three sets (G, C, R) were combined to create a vault (V) which was stored in a device such as a smartcard or a server.

3.3 Unlocking the Vault

To generate the cryptographic key (S), a user unlocked the vault with his (or her) queried *Iris Codes* (Q). Unlocking also needed two inputs: the vault (V) created at locking and the queried *Iris Codes* (Q), as shown in Fig. 1. The vault (V) was obtained from a storage device and the *Iris Codes* (Q) was generated using the procedure discussed in section 3.1. However, the *Iris Codes* (Q) contained some errors because of the variations of the iris images taken under different conditions in spite of using the clustering method. Therefore, at the beginning of unlocking the vault, we corrected the errors of the *Iris Codes* (Q) using the RS decoding algorithm [14-15].

At this time, set R (the redundancy set obtained by RS encoding, as shown in Fig. 1(a)) was also used for decoding. Then, if outcome (Q^*) of RS decoding was equal to a user's *Iris Codes* (I), the genuine set G (which was formed by evaluating the polynomial $P(x)$ by the *Iris Codes* (I), as described in section 3.2) was perfectly identified from G+C (here, C represents the set of chaff points, as shown in Fig. 1(a)). Namely, the set G^* of Fig. 1(b) was equal to the set G. We then reconstructed the polynomial (P^*) with the set G^* by using Lagrange interpolation [17], a simple method that interpolates a polynomial with point pairs on the polynomial. When the point pairs were $(x_1, y_1), (x_2, y_2), \ldots, (x_{d+1}, y_{d+1})$, the corresponding polynomial was obtained as follows:

$$P(x) = \frac{f(x)}{(x-x_1)f'(x_1)} y_1 + \frac{f(x)}{(x-x_2)f'(x_2)} y_2 + \cdots + \frac{f(x)}{(x-x_{d+1})f'(x_{d+1})} y_{d+1} . \quad (1)$$

Here, $f(x) = (x- x_1)(x- x_2)\ldots(x- x_{d+1})$, $f'(x)$ represented a derivative of $f(x)$ and the degree of this polynomial was d (in our case, d was 15). In our paper, a set of point pairs was the genuine set G^* and a polynomial $P^*(x) = S^*_1 + S^*_2 x + \ldots + S^*_{16} x^{15}$ was reconstructed by Lagrange interpolation. Finally, all coefficients of the polynomial were concatenated as $S^*_1 S^*_2 \ldots S^*_{16}$ and the secret key S^* was recovered perfectly.

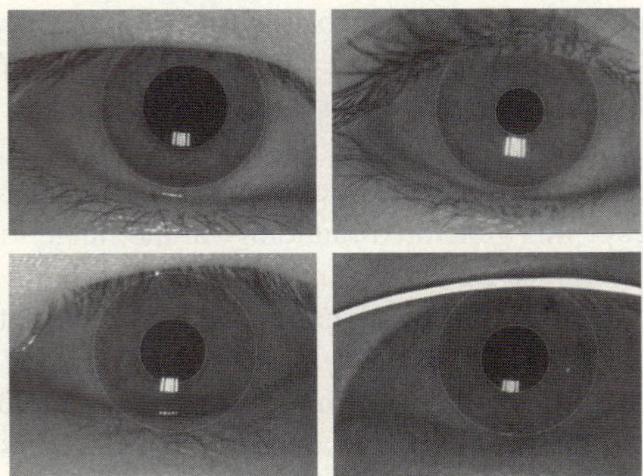

Fig. 3. Iris image examples from the BERC iris database (version 1)

4 Experimental Results

4.1 Iris Database

We used the BERC iris database (version 1) [18] to evaluate the proposed method. The BERC iris database (version 1) consists of 990 images: 10 images for each 99 individuals [4-5]. Fig. 3 shows some examples of the BERC iris database, captured at a resolution of 640×480 pixels and 8-bit gray information. These images were captured by our hand-made iris recognition camera, which contained a monochrome CCD sensor with a fixed focal lens, and an 850nm IR (Infra-Red) illuminator [4-5].

In our experiments, half of ten iris sample images per class were used for training and the remaining images were used for authentication. So, the number of authentic tests was 4,000 and the number of imposter tests was 16,000. We assumed that the difference between the iris templates and the input iris data was not great.

4.2 Experimental Results

In our experiments, the criteria of system performance were the False Rejection Rate (FRR) and the False Acceptance Rate (FAR). The FRR was defined as the error rate obtained when a legitimate user's cryptographic key was not generated when the user tried to obtain his or her key using his or her iris image and vault. The FAR was defined as the error rate obtained when a legitimate user's cryptographic key was generated when an illegitimate attacker attempted to steal a key using his or her iris image with a legitimate user's vault. The similarity between a queried iris feature vector and the prototype of each cluster was evaluated by Hamming distance.

In the conventional cryptographic system to which we tried to apply our fuzzy vault system, the FAR was more important than the FRR, because its main purpose is to make secret key for encryption system which can be used for banking service etc. So, a certain number of False Rejection cases can be accepted, such as when genuine users fail to input correct passwords. Therefore, in our experiments, we considered the minimum FRR value when the FAR was set to 0% as the optimal result.

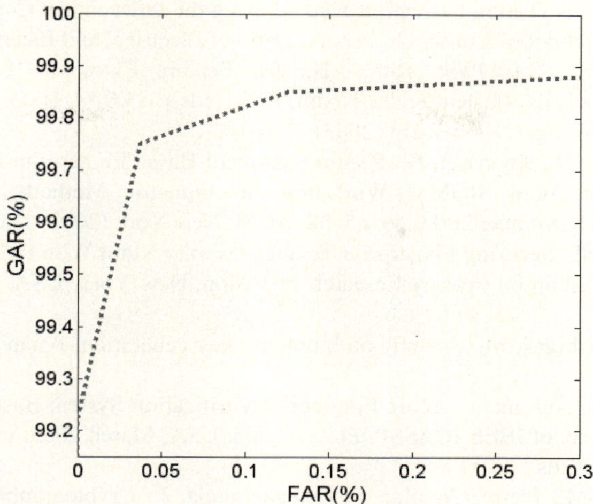

Fig. 4. ROC curves of the proposed fuzzy vault system

Fig. 4 shows the ROC curves. As shown in Fig. 4, when the FAR was set to 0%, the FRR was 0.775% (when the Genuine Acceptance Rate (GAR) was 99.225%), correcting eight errors among the sixteen queried *Iris Codes*.

5 Conclusions

The fuzzy vault system refers to a cryptographic method that encrypts and decrypts secret data with an unordered set. This cryptographic method can be used in combination with biometrics because it permits only a few variations of the unordered set by using error-correcting codes. In this paper, we proposed a new way of implementing the fuzzy vault system based on iris data.

In future work, we will evaluate our proposed method with regard to various input iris images (e.g., rotation, translation and blurring).

Acknowledgments. This work was supported by the Korea Science and Engineering Foundation (KOSEF) through the Biometrics Engineering Research Center (BERC) at Yonsei University.

References

1. Uludag, U., Pankanti, S., Jain, A.K.: Fuzzy Vault for Fingerprints. In: Proceedings of Audio- and Video-based Biometrics, December 4, 2006 DRAFT 31 Person Authentication, Rye Town, USA, July 2005, pp. 310–319 (2005)
2. Trappe, W., Washington, L.C.: Introduction to Cryptography with coding theory. Prentice-Hall, Upper Saddle River, NJ.
3. Juels, A., Sudan, M.: A fuzzy vault scheme. In: ACM Conference on Computer and Communications Security, CCS 2002. ACM, New York (2002)

4. Bae, K.H.: An Iris Feature Extraction Method using the Independent Component Analysis. The Graduate School of Yonsei University, Dept. of Electrical and Electronic Eng. (2002)
5. Bae, K.H., Noh, S.I., Park, Kim, J.H.: Iris Feature Extraction Using Independent Component Analysis. In: Kittler, J., Nixon, M.S. (eds.) AVBPA 2003. LNCS, vol. 2688, pp. 838–844. Springer, Heidelberg (2003)
6. Clancy, T., Lin, D., Kiyavash, N.: Secure Smartcard-Based Fingerprint Authentication. In: Proceedings of ACM SIGMM Workshop on Biometric Methods and Applications, Berkley, USA, November 2003, pp. 45–52. ACM, New York (2003)
7. Uludag, U., et al.: Securing Fingerprint Template: Fuzzy Vault With Helper Data. In: Proc. of CVPR Workshop on Privacy Research In Vision, New York, USA, June 2006, p. 163 (2006)
8. Shibata, Y., Nishigak, M.: A study on biometric key generation. Asian Biometrics Forum (2006)
9. Yang, S., et al.: Automatic Secure Fingerprint Verification System Based on Fuzzy Vault Scheme. In: Proc. of IEEE ICASSP, Philadelphia, USA, March 2005, vol. 5, pp. 609–612. IEEE, Los Alamitos (2005)
10. Freire-Santos, M., Fierrez-Aguilar, J., Ortega-Garcia, J.: Cryptographic Key Generation Using Handwritten Signature. In: Proceedings of Biometric Technologies for Human Identification III, Orlando, USA, April 2006, vol. 6202, pp. 225–231 (2006)
11. Feng, Y.C., Yuen, P.C.: Protecting Face Biometric Data on Smartcard with Reed-Solomon Code. In: Proceedings of CVPR Workshop on Privacy Research In Vision, New York, USA, June 2006, p. 29 (2006)
12. Daugman, J.: How iris recognition works. IEEE Trans. Circuits Syst. Video Techno. 14(1), 21–30 (2004)
13. Wicker, S.B.: Error Control Systems for Digital Communication and Storage. Prentice-Hall, Englewood Cliffs, NJ (1995)
14. Sylvester, J.: Reed-Solomon Codes (January 2001), Available from http://www.elektrobit.co.uk
15. Sklar, B.: Reed-Solomon Codes (accessed on 2007.2.10),.Available at, http://www.informit.com/content/images/art_sklar7_reed- solomon/elementLinks/art_sklar7_reed-solomon.pdf
16. Duda, R.O., Har, P.E., Stork, D.G.: Pattern Classification, 2nd edn. Wiley-Interscience, Chichester (2001)
17. Kreyszig, E.: Advanced Engineering Mathematics, 8th edn. Wiley, Chichester (1999)
18. (accessed on 2007.1. 2) http://berc.yonsei.ac.kr

Multi-scale Local Binary Pattern Histograms for Face Recognition

Chi-Ho Chan, Josef Kittler, and Kieron Messer

Centre for Vision, Speech and Signal Processing,
University of Surrey, United Kingdom
{c.chan,j.kittler,k.messer}@surrey.ac.uk

Abstract. A novel discriminative face representation derived by the Linear Discriminant Analysis (LDA) of multi-scale local binary pattern histograms is proposed for face recognition. The face image is first partitioned into several non-overlapping regions. In each region, multi-scale local binary uniform pattern histograms[1] are extracted and concatenated into a regional feature. The features are then projected on the LDA space to be used as a discriminative facial descriptor. The method is implemented and tested in face identification on the standard Feret database and in face verification on the XM2VTS database with very promising results.

1 Introduction

Nowadays, face identification and verification are an integral part of the infrastructure needed for diverse business and security sectors. However, the performance of most current systems is detrimentally affected by two factors: 1) large variability in facial appearance of an individual due to changes in pose, expression and age, as well as ambient light condition and camera parameters, and 2) high dimensionality of the problem with a small sample size training. For tackling the above problems, one of the important strategies is to represent a face image by projecting it into a "good" feature space which captures the intrinsic attributes of face and simplifies the face manifolds of the raw image space. The most popular representations proposed for this purpose include Eigenface, Fisherface, Wavelets (Gabor and Haar).

Recently, the local binary pattern (LBP) operator, introduced by Ojala et.al [10], has gained reputation as a powerful and attractive texture descriptor showing excellent results in terms of accuracy and computational complexity in many empirical studies. The LBP method has already been applied for instance to visual inspection, image retrieval, motion detection, remote sensing, biomedical image analysis, and outdoor scene analysis. Ahonen et al. [9] applied a LBP representation to face recognition and achieved very good results on the FERET database. In their method, the face image is first partitioned into small regions from which LBP histograms are extracted and concatenated into a single, spatially enhanced feature histogram representing the local texture and global shape of face images. The recognition is performed using a nearest-neighbor classifier.

[1] This paper is for BBSPA competition.

S.-W. Lee and S.Z. Li (Eds.): ICB 2007, LNCS 4642, pp. 809–818, 2007.

Later, Zhang et al. [2] identified two shortcomings of Ahonen's approach. First, the size of the feature space in Ahonen's method was limited by fixing the position and size of the local region. Second, the region weighting was manually optimized. Therefore, they proposed to use a boosting classifier [2][12] to select discriminative histograms from a pool which is obtained by extracting the LBP histograms by shifting and scaling a local window over pairs of intra-personal and inter-personal face images. Comparative studies with Ahonen's method on the FERET database FB protocol showed similar results in accuracy but as fewer regional histograms are used, the dimensionality of the representation space is lower. However, shifting and scaling the local window will result in an over-complete representation requiring a prohibitive amount of time for training. In addition, the accuracy is dependent on a predefined feature number or a predefined recognition rate, and thus is not optimal. Other interesting contributions include the work of Rodriguez and Marcel [14] who proposed a generative approach for face verification based on applying a LBP histogram as the face descriptor. Shan et al. [8] advocated the use of a linear discriminant analysis (LDA) classifier on LBP local histograms and showed that their results outperformed the Ahonen's method. However, the small size (4x8) of the local region for computing the histogram tends to degrade the accuracy in the presence of face localization errors. Also, our results show that the accuracy of directly applying LDA on the uniform LBP local histograms is better than for their method. The reason is the way the pattern labels are grouped as already mentioned by Ojala et.al [10] who pointed out that the histogram of uniform patterns provides better discrimination in comparison to the histogram of all individual patterns. The definition of uniform LBP will be introduced in the next section.

For multiresolution analysis, Zhang et al [11] proposed to apply LBP on Gabor wavelets, called MHLVP or LGBPHS, for face recognition and have very impressive results on the FERET database, but the computational complexity and the feature dimension are very high. In this paper, an alternative but a much simple discriminative descriptor containing the information from a multresolution analysis is proposed. The novel descriptor is formed by projecting the local information combined from multiple LBP operators into the LDA space. The recognition is performed by measuring the dissimilarity of the gallery and probe descriptors using normalized correlation. We evaluate the proposed algorithm on the Feret and XM2VTS databases and show that it exhibits superior performance in both face identification and face verification scenarios. The paper first introduces the basic LBP histogram and then describes the multi-scale LBP with LDA for face recognition. The experimental setup is then introduced and the results discussed.

2 Face Description with Multi-scale LBP

2.1 Basic Uniform Local Binary Patterns

The LBP operator, shown in Equation 1, a powerful texture measure with a low-computational complexity, extracts information which is invariant to local gray-scale variations of the image. During the LBP operation, the value of current pixel, g_c, is applied as a threshold to each of the neighbors, $g_p(p=0,\ldots.P-1)$ to obtain a binary number. A local binary pattern is obtained by first concatenating these binary numbers and then converting the sequence into the decimal number. Using circular neighborhoods and linearly interpolating the pixel values allows the choice of any radius, R, and number of pixels in the neighborhood, P, to form an operator.

$$LBP_{P,R}(x,y)=\sum_{p=0}^{P-1}s(g_p-g_c)2^P \quad (1)$$

where, $$s(x)=\begin{cases}1 & x\geq 0\\ 0 & x<0\end{cases}$$

A subset of these 2^P binary patterns, called uniform patterns, can be used to represent spot, flat area, edge and corner. The uniformity measure, U(x), presented in Equation 2 records the number of spatial transitions in the binary pattern, and the uniform pattern is a binary pattern which contains at most two bitwise transitions, i.e., U(x)≤2. The uniform pattern contains in total (P-1)P+2 binary patterns. It consists of two types of patterns, namely (P-1)P rotational patterns, such as edges and two non-rotational patterns, such as a bright spot or a flat area. Other patterns, where U(x)>2, are regarded as non-uniform patterns. The uniform LBP operator, $LBP^{u2}_{P,R}$, is defined as.

$$LBP^{u2}_{P,R}(x,y)=\begin{cases}I\left(LBP_{P,R}(x,y)\right) & \text{if } U(LBP_{P,R})\leq 2,\\ & \mathrm{I(z)}\in\left[0,(P-1)P+1\right]\\ (P-1)P+2 & \text{otherwise}\end{cases} \quad (2)$$

where, $U(LBP_{P,R})=\left|s(g_{P-1}-g_c)-s(g_0-g_c)\right|+\sum_{p=1}^{P}\left|s(g_p-g_c)-s(g_{P-1}-g_c)\right|$

Superscript u2 shown in Equation 2 indicates that the definition relates to uniform patterns with a U value of at most 2. If U(x) is smaller than 2, the current pixel will be labeled by an index function, I(z). Otherwise, it will be labeled as (P-1)P+2. The index function, I(z), containing (P-1)P+2 indices, is used to assign a particular index to each of the uniform patterns.

Some researchers used the LBP operator as one of the face normalization techniques [1] and then directly applied a LDA classifier to the LBP image. However, such an approach will fail in the presence of an image translation or even rotation. The histogram approach which first summarizes the LBP image statistically has been proposed to alleviate these problems. As keeping the information about the spatial relation of facial regions is very important for face recognition, the face image is first divided into several small non-overlapping regions of the same size. Uniform pattern histograms are computed over the regions and then concatenated into a single histogram representing the face image.

2.2 Multi-scale Local Binary Patterns

By varying the sampling radius, R and combining the LBP images, a multiresolution representation based on LBP, called multi-scale local binary patterns [10] can be obtained. This representation has been suggested for texture classification and the results reported for this application show that its accuracy is better than that of the single scale local binary pattern method. In general, this multiresolution representation can be realized in two ways. First, it can be accomplished by increasing the neighborhood size of the operator. Alternatively one can down-sample the original image with interpolation or low-pass filtering and then apply an LBP operator of fixed radius. However, the general problem associated with the multiresolution analysis is the high dimensionality of the representation combined with the small training sample size. It limits the total number of LBP operators to at most of 3. One of the approaches [13] is to employ a feature selection technique to minimize redundant information. We propose another method which achieves dimensionality reduction by feature extraction.

2.3 Our Approach

In our approach, we combine the multi-scale local binary pattern representation with Linear Discrminant Analysis, LDA. Uniform local binary pattern operators at R scales are first applied to a face image. This generates a grey level code for each pixel at every resolution. The resulting LBP images, shown in Fig. 1, are cropped to the same size and divided into non-overlapping sub-regions, M_0, M_1,..M_{J-1}. The regional pattern histogram for each scale is computed based on Equation 3.

$$H^{\mu 2}_{P,r,j}(i) = \sum_{(x',y')\in M_j} B\left(LBP^{\mu 2}_{P,r}(x',y') = i\right) \tag{3}$$

$$where, \quad i \in [0,(P-1)P+2), r \in [1,R], j \in [0,J), \;\; and \;\; B(x) = \begin{cases} 1 & when\ x = 0 \\ 0 & otherwise \end{cases}.$$

B(x) is a Boolean indicator. The set of histograms computed at different scales for region, M_j, provides regional information. By concatenating these histograms into a single histogram, we obtain the final multiresolution regional face descriptor presented in Equation 4.

$$F_j = \left[H^{\mu 2}_{P,1,j} \quad H^{\mu 2}_{P,2,j} \quad ..... \quad H^{\mu 2}_{P,R,j}\right] \tag{4}$$

This regional facial descriptor can be used to measure the face similarity by summing the similarities between all the regional histograms. However, by directly applying the similarity measurement to the multi-scale LBP histogram [10], the performance will be compromised. The reason is that this histogram is of high dimensionality and contains redundant information. By adopting the idea from [7], the dimension of the descriptor can be reduced by employing principal component analysis (PCA) before LDA. PCA is used to extract the statistically independent information as a basis for LDA to derive discriminative facial features. Thus a regional discriminative facial descriptor, D_j, is defined by projecting the histogram information, F_j, into LDA space W_j^{lda}, i.e.

$$D_j = \left(W_j^{lda}\right)^T F_j \tag{5}$$

After the projection, the similarity measurement presented below is obtained by summing the similarity, i.e. normalized correlation, of regional discriminative descriptors.

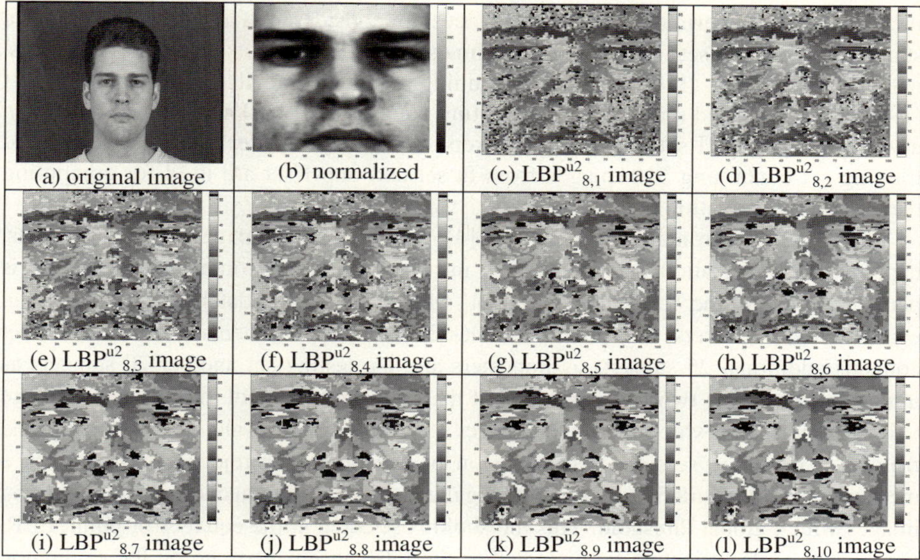

Fig. 1. a) original image, b) cropped and normalized face image, c-l) LBP^{u2} images at different radii. (Note: Gray: non-uniform pattern, White: dark spot, Black: bright spot, Other colors: rotational uniform patterns where 8 brightness levels of color denote the rotational angle).

$$Sim(I, I') = \sum_j \frac{D_j D_j'}{\|D_j\| \|D_j'\|} \tag{6}$$

This discriminative descriptor gives 4 different levels of locality: 1) the local binary patterns contributing to the histogram contain information at the pixel level, 2) the patterns at each scale are summed over a small region to provide information at a regional level, 3) the regional histograms at different scales are concatenated to produce multiresolution information, 4) the global description of face is established by concatenating the regional discriminative facial descriptors.

3 Experimental Setup

The goals of identification and verification systems are different. Whereas the goal of identification is to recognize an unknown face image, verification validates a person's identity by comparing the captured face image with her/his image template(s) stored in the system database. However, most researchers only evaluate their algorithm either in identification or verification scenario, which makes them very difficult to compare with others. In order to ensure a reproducibility of the experiments and comparability with other methods, we tested our approach on the well-known, FERET and XM2VTS, databases using common protocols.

In the FERET database [6], the open-source publicly available CSU face identification evaluation framework [3] was utilized to test the performance of our method. In this experiment, only frontal faces are considered. They are divided into a standard gallery (fa set) containing 1196 images of 1196 subjects, and four probe sets, namely the fb set (1195 images containing different facial expressions), fc set (194 images acquired under different lighting conditions), dup I set (722 images taken a week later), dup II set (234 images taken at least a year later). The CSU standard training set containing 510 images from fa set and dup I set are used for computing the LDA transformation matrix, W_j^{lda}.

The XM2VTS frontal face database [4] contains 2360 images of 295 subjects, captured for verification over 4 sessions in a controlled environment. The testing is performed using the Lausanne protocol which splits the database into training, evaluation and test sets. The training set has 200 subjects as clients, the evaluation set contains additional 25 subjects as imposters and the testing set another 70 subjects as imposters. There are two configurations of the Lausanne Protocol. In our work, we use Configuration I, in which the client images for training and evaluation were acquired from the first three sessions. The decision of acceptance or rejection is based on a measurement of similarity between the gallery and the average of client's training images with a global threshold. This threshold is selected at the equal error point, EER, at which the false rejection rate is equal to the false acceptance rate on the evaluation set. For both XM2VTS and Feret databases, face images are extracted with the provided groundtruth eye positions and scaled to a size of 142×120 (rows × columns). The cropped faces are photometrically normalized by histogram equalization.

In total, four parameters are available to optimize the performance of our method. The first one is the LBP parameter, the circularly symmetric neighborhood size, P. A large neighborhood increases the length of the histogram and slows down the computation of the similarity measure while small neighborhood may result in information loss. We have selected a neighborhood of P=8, containing 59 patterns for LBP^{u2}. The second parameter is the total number of multi-scale operators. A small number of operators cannot provide sufficient information for face recognition, while a large radius operator not only reduces the size of the corresponding LBP images, but also decreases the number of uniform patterns which tends to degrade the system accuracy. In our experiments, R is set to 10, which means that ten LBP operators are employed to represent the face image. After extracting the LBP images, they are then cropped to the same size. The third parameter is the number of the regions, k. A large number of small regions increases the computation time as well as degrading the system accuracy in the presence of face localization errors. A big region increases the loss of spatial information. In this work, an image is partitioned into k×k non-overlapped rectangle size regions where k is optimized empirically. The last parameter controls the PCA transformation matrix. In general, some of the higher-order eigenvectors are removed because they do not contribute to the accuracy of face recognition and the measure also saves the computation time. In our experiments, the number of eigenvectors kept is determined by the requirement to retain 98% of the energy of the signal [3].

4 Results and Discussions

4.1 Experiments in Face Identification: FERET Database

In this test, the recognition rate at rank1 and two statistical measures are used to compare the performance of the methods. The measures are the mean recognition rate with 95% confidence interval and the probability of the algorithm outperforming another. The probability is denoted by P(Alg 1 > Alg 2). These measures are computed by permuting the gallery and probe sets, see [3] for details. The results with PCA, BIC and EBGM in the CSU system as benchmarks [3] are reported in Table 1 for comparison.

The result of the $LBP^{u2}_{8,2}$ regional histograms method with chi-squared similarity measurement (LBPH_Chi) [9], $LBP^{u2}_{8,2}$ regional histograms projected on LDA space with normalized correlation (LBPH+LDA) and our proposed method (MLBPH+LDA) with different k×k regions are plotted in Fig. 2. Comparing the mean recognition rate with LBPH_Chi and LBPH+LDA, applying LDA to the representation generated by uniform pattern regional histograms clearly improves the performance, but employing the multi-scale LBP improves the recognition rate even further. As expected for the LBP histogram based methods, the mean recognition rate is reduced as the window size increases because of the loss of the spatial information, but for our method, the mean recognition rate is robust for a wide range of $16 \geq k > 3$

Table 1. Comparisons on the probe sets and the mean recognition rate of the permutation test with 95% confidence interval on the FERET database with CSU Standard training set

	k	Fb	Fc	Dup1	Dup2	Lower	Mean	Upper
MLBPH+LDA	11	0.986	0.711	0.722	0.474	0.844	0.885	0.925
LBPH+LDA	16	0.977	0.747	0.710	0.491	0.819	0.856	0.900
LBPH_Chi	16	0.964	0.588	0.648	0.487	0.744	0.791	0.838
PCA_MacCos		0.853	0.655	0.443	0.218	0.662	0.721	0.775
Bayesian_MP		0.818	0.351	0.508	0.299	0.669	0.720	0.769
EBGM_Optimal		0.898	0.418	0.463	0.244	0.621	0.664	0.712

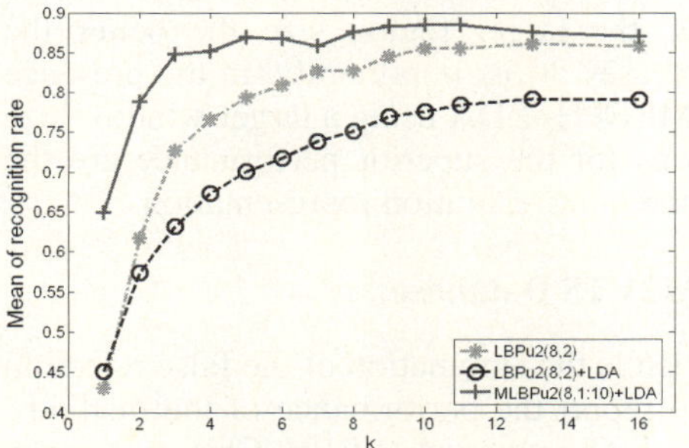

Fig. 2. The mean recognition rate with 95% confidence interval for three LBP methods against different k×k regions.

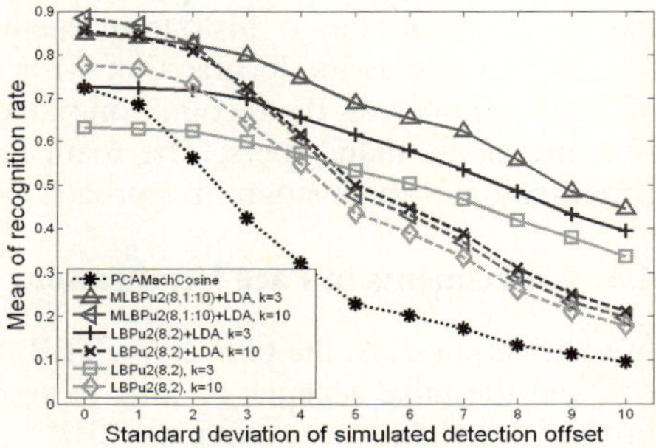

Fig. 3. The mean recognition rate with 95% confidence interval for LBP based methods and PCA MahCosine against varying the standard deviation of the simulated localization error.

regions. For example the mean recognition rate with k=3 is 84.8%, while k=11 is 88.5%. In other words, changing the number of regions, k, only affects the length of the feature vector and the computation time. In the presence of the face localization inaccuracies, the performance of the face recognition method involving spatial information as an input parameter degrades; however our proposed method using smaller k can be expected to maintain the recognition accuracy. These finding are discussed further in Section 4.2.

In Table 1, the parameter k of the LBP-based method is optimized from the point of view of accuracy and compared with other methods. LBP with LDA based methods clearly outperform the others in all statistical tests and all probe sets. Comparing MLBP and LBP both with LDA, the accuracy is not significantly different, but MLBPH+LDA is slightly better as P(*MLBPH+LDA>LBPH+LDA*)= 0.898.

4.2 Robustness to Face Localization Error

A generic face recognition system first localizes and segments a face image from the background before recognizing it. However, a perfect face localization method is very difficult to achieve, and therefore a face recognition method capable of working well in the presence of localization errors is highly desired. In order to evaluate the effect of face localization error on the recognition rate of our method achieved on the FERET database comparatively, PCA MachCosine, LBPH+LDA and LBPH+Chi face recognition methods are also implemented. The training images and gallery images, fa set, are registered using the groundtruth eye coordinates but the probe sets (fb, fc, Dup 1 and 2) are registered using simulated eye coordinates which are the groundtruth eye location displaced by a random vector perturbation (ΔX, ΔY). These vectors are uncorrelated and normally distributed with a zero mean and standard deviation, σ, from 0 to 10. For LBP based methods, a large region size parameter, k=3, and a small region size, k=10, are tested. The recognition rates of LBP based methods using the respective values of parameter k, with PCA MachCosine against the standard deviation of the simulated localization error are plotted in Fig. 3. Clearly, the recognition rates of local region based methods outperform that of PCA. Projecting LBP histograms on LDA spaces provides better recognition rate than the error achieved in the original histogram space, in spite of the localization error. Also, for the local region based histogram methods, the larger region size the better the recognition rate as the localization error increases. Most importantly, in the presence of localization error, the recognition rate of MLBPH+LDA using a larger window size is more robust than others. The main reasons for the superior performance are the combination of the histogram approach and the multiresolution representation.

4.3 Experiments in Face Verification: XM2VTS Database

In verification tests, the total error, TER, which is the summation of the false rejection rate and the false acceptance rate, is used to report the performance of the methods. In this experiment, we compare $LBP^{u2}_{8,2}$ with Chi-squared (LBPH_Chi), histogram intersection (LBPH_HI), and our proposed method (MLBPH+LDA) together with the Adaboost classifier for LBPH [2] (LBPH+Adaboost). Rodriguez [14] found that the total error rate of LBPH-Adaboost giving 7.88% on the test set, is similar to that of LBPH-Chi, namely 6.8%. Nevertheless, we found that the error rate of LBPH-Adaboost can be reduced to 5.263% if 300 regional histograms (features) are used.

Table 2. Total Error Rate, TER, according to Lausanne protocol for configuration 1

	k	Manual Registration		Automatic Registration	
		Eva Set (%)	Test Set (%)	Eva Set (%)	Test Set (%)
MLBPH+LDA	3	1.74	1.48	1.53	1.99
LBPH+LDA	6	8.39	6.74		
LBPH_Chi [9]	7	11.11	8.27		
LBPH_HI	7	10.28	7.94		
LBPH+AdaBoost [2]		7.37	5.26		
LBPH_MAP [14]			2.84		
LBP+LDA [1]			9.12		
LBP+HMM [1]			2.74		
ICPR2000-Best [5]		5.00	4.80	14.00	13.10
AVBPA03-Best [5]		2.21	1.47	4.98	3.86
ICB2006-Best [5]		1.63	0.96	2	2.07[2]

Table 2 reports the comparative results of the above mentioned methods, as well as of Rodriguez methods [14][1], and the performance of the best ICPR2000[5], the best AVBPA2003[5] and the best ICB2006[5] algorithms with the Lausanne protocol Configuration 1.

Compared to other LBP based methods, it is clear that our proposed method, MLBPH+LDA, performs better. However, the result of our method in manual registration is not better than that in ICB2006, in which the features were extracted by convoluting the gabor filters, 5 scales and 8 orientation, on the face image. Since the method in ICB2006 uses face images of better resolution than ours, we can expect that the face manifolds of the gabor feature space are simpler and the associated error rate is lower. Nevertheless, our method is more robust than others in the presence of face localization inaccuracies as shown in Table 2.

5 Conclusions

In a real face recognition system, a face image is detected, registered and then identified. However, the accuracy of automatic face localization is not perfect and therefore face recognition methods working successfully in the presence of localization error are highly desired. In this paper, a discriminative descriptor containing the information from a multiresolution analysis of face image is proposed. The descriptor is formed by projecting the local face image information acquired by multiple LBP operators, into the LDA space. The recognition is performed by measuring the dissimilarity of the gallery and probe descriptors. Our proposed method has been implemented and compared with existing LBP methods as well ass other well known benchmarks in the application of face identification and verification using the FERET and XM2VTS databases following their standard protocols. In face identification performed on the FERET database, the experimental results clearly show that the mean recognition rate of 88.5%, with a 95% confidence interval, delivered by our method outperforms other state-of-the-art contenders. In particular, our method achieved the overall best result of 98.6% recognition rate in the

[2] Note: There is a mistake in the TER of the best algorithm reported in ICB 2006, where TER, 1.57, is not equal to the summation of false acceptance rate, 0.57 and the false rejection rate, 1.57.

experiment involving the varying facial expression probe set (fb set) while delivering comparative results to other LBP based methods for other probe sets. Also under the simulated localization error test, our proposed method is clearly more robust than others because it benefits from the multiresolution information captured by the regional histograms. The proposed method has also been tested in the verification mode on the XM2VTS database. With manual registration it achieved the third best result, TER=1.48% on the test set, but with fully automatic registration outperformed all the other methods by a small margin, achieving, TER=1.99%. In conclusion, our method achieves a comparable result with the state-of-art benchmark methods, on manually annotated face but it is more robust in the presence of localization errors.

Acknowledgements

A partial support from the EU Network of Excellence Biosecure and from the ESPRC Grant GR/S98528/01 is gratefully acknowledged.

References

1. Heusch, G., Rodriguez, Y., Marcel, S.: Local Binary Patterns as an Image Preprocessing for Face Authentication. In: Proc FGR 2006, pp. 9–14 (2006)
2. Zhang, G., Huang, Z., Li, S.Z.: Boosting local binary pattern (LBP)-based face recognition. In: SinoBiometrics 2004, pp. 179–186 (2004)
3. Beveridge, J.R., Bolme, D., Teixeira, M., Draper, B.: The CSU Face Identification Evaluation System User's Guide: Version 5.0, Technical Report, C.S. Dept., CSU (2003)
4. Messer, K., Matas, J., Kittler, J., Jonsson, K.: XM2VTSDB: The extended M2VTS database. In: Akumuri, S., Kullman, C. (eds.) AVBPA'99, pp. 72–77 (1999)
5. Messor, K., Kittler, J., Short, J., Heusch, G., Cardinaux, F., Marcel, S., Rodriguez, Y., Shan, S., Su, Y., Gao, W., Chen, X.: Performance Characterisation of Face Recognition Algorithms and Their Sensitivity to Severe Illumination Changes. In: ICB2006, pp. 1–11 (2006)
6. Philips, P.J., Moon, H.J., Rizvi, S.A., Rauss, P.J.: The FERET Evaluation Methodology for Face Recognition Algorithms. PAMI 22(10), 1090–1104 (2000)
7. Belhumeur, P.N., Hespanha, J.P., Kriegman, D.J.: Eigenfaces vs. Fisherfaces: Recognition using Class Specific Linear Projection. In: Buxton, B.F., Cipolla, R. (eds.) ECCV 1996. LNCS, vol. 1065, pp. 45–56. Springer, Heidelberg (1996)
8. Shan, S., Zhang, W., Su, Y., Xhen, X., Gao, W.: Ensemble of Piecewise FDA based on Spatial Histogram of Local (Gabor) Binary Patterns for Face Recognition. In: ICPR (2006)
9. Ahonen, T., Hadid, A., Pietikäinen, M.: Face description with local binary patterns: Application to face recognition. PAMI 28(12), 2037–2041 (2006)
10. Ojala, T., Pietikäinen, M., Mäenpää, T.: Multiresolution Gray-Scale and Rotation Invariant Texture Classification with Local Binary Patterns. PAMI 24(7), 971–987 (2002)
11. Zhang, W., Shan, S., Zhang, H., Gao, W., Chen, X.: Multi-resolution histogram of local variation patterns (MHLVP) for Robust Face Recognition. In: Kanade, T., Jain, A., Ratha, N.K. (eds.) AVBPA 2005. LNCS, vol. 3546, pp. 937–944. Springer, Heidelberg (2005)
12. Huang, X., Li, S.Z., Wang, Y.: Jensen-Shannon Boosting Learning for Object recognition. In: Proceeding of CVPR (2005)
13. Raja, Y., Gong, S.: Sparse Multiscale Local Binary Patterns. In: Proc. 17th BMVC (2006)
14. Rodriguez, Y., Marcel, S.: Face authentication using adapted local binary pattern histogram. In: Leonardis, A., Bischof, H., Pinz, A. (eds.) ECCV 2006. LNCS, vol. 3954, pp. 321–332. Springer, Heidelberg (2006)

Histogram Equalization in SVM Multimodal Person Verification

Mireia Farrús, Pascual Ejarque, Andrey Temko, and Javier Hernando

TALP Research Center, Department of Signal Theory and Communications
Technical University of Catalonia, Barcelona, Catalonia
{mfarrus,pascual,temko,javier}@gps.tsc.upc.edu

Abstract. It has been shown that prosody helps to improve voice spectrum based speaker recognition systems. Therefore, prosodic features can also be used in multimodal person verification in order to achieve better results. In this paper, a multimodal recognition system based on facial and vocal tract spectral features is improved by adding prosodic information. Matcher weighting method and support vector machines have been used as fusion techniques, and histogram equalization has been applied before SVM fusion as a normalization technique. The results show that the performance of a SVM multimodal verification system can be improved by using histogram equalization, especially when the equalization is applied to those scores giving the highest EER values.

Keywords: speaker recognition, multimodality, fusion, support vector machines, histogram equalization, prosody, voice spectrum, face.

1 Introduction

Multimodal biometric systems, which involve the combination of two or more human traits, are used to achieve better results than the ones obtained in a monomodal recognition system [1]. In a multimodal recognition system, fusion is possible at three different levels: feature extraction level, matching score level and decision level. Fusion at the score level matches the monomodal scores of different recognition systems in order to obtain a single multimodal score, and it is the preferred method by most of the systems.

Matching score level fusion is a two-step process which consists of a previous score normalization and the fusion itself [2-5]. The normalization process transforms the non homogeneous monomodal scores into a comparable range of values. Z-score is a conventional affine normalization technique which transforms the scores into a distribution with zero mean and unitary variance [3, 5]. Histogram equalization (HE) is used as a non linear normalization technique which makes equal the statistics of the monomodal scores. HE can be seen as an extension to the whole statistics of the mean and variance equalization performed by the z-score normalization.

The fusion process is a combination of the previously normalized scores. In this paper, two fusion methods are used and compared: matcher weighting and support vector machines. In matcher weighting method, each monomodal score is weighted by a factor proportional to its recognition result. A support vector machine is a binary

S.-W. Lee and S.Z. Li (Eds.): ICB 2007, LNCS 4642, pp. 819–827, 2007.

classifier based on a learning fusion technique, where scores are seen as input patterns to be labeled as accepted or rejected.

The aim of this work is to improve the results obtained in our recent work based on the fusion of prosody, voice spectrum and face features where different step strategies were applied [6]. The improvement is achieved with previous histogram equalization as a normalization of the scores in a SVM based fusion.

In the next section, the monomodal information sources used in this work are described. Z-score and histogram equalization are presented in section 3. Matcher weighting fusion technique and support vector machines are reviewed in section 4 and, finally, experimental results are shown in section 5.

2 Monomodal Sources

2.1 Voice Information

In multimodal person recognition only short-term spectral features are normally used as voice information. However, it has been demonstrated that voice spectrum based systems can be improved by adding prosodic information [7].

Spectral parameters are those which only take into account the acoustical level of the signal, like spectral magnitudes, formant frequencies, etc., and they are more related to the physical traits of the speaker. Cepstral coefficients are the usual way to represent the short-time spectral envelope of a speech frame in current speaker recognition systems. However, Frequency Filtering (FF) parameters, presented in [8] and used in this work, become an alternative to the use of cepstrum in order to overcome some of its disadvantages.

Several linguistic levels like lexicon, prosody or phonetics are used by humans to recognize others with voice. These levels of information are more related to learned habits and style, and they are mainly manifested in the dialect, sociolect or idiolect of the speaker. Prosodic parameters, in particular, are manifested as sound duration, tone and intensity variation. Although these features don't provide very good results when they are used alone, they give complementary information and improve the results when they are fused with vocal tract spectrum based systems. The prosodic recognition system used in this task consists of a total of 9 prosodic scores already used in [9]:

- number of frames per word averaged over all words
- average length of word-internal voiced segments
- average length of word-internal unvoiced segments
- mean F0 logarithm
- maximum F0 logarithm
- minimum F0 logarithm
- F0 range (maximum F0 – minimum F0) logarithm
- F0 "pseudo slope": (last F0 – first F0) / (number of frames in word)
- average slope over all segments of a piecewise linear stylization of F0

2.2 Face Information

Facial recognition systems are based on the conceptualization that a face can be represented as a collection of sparsely distributed parts: eyes, nose, cheeks, mouth, etc. Non negative matrix factorization (NMF), introduced in [10], is an appearance-based face recognition technique based on the conventional component analysis techniques which does not use the information about how the various facial images are separated into different facial classes. The most straightforward way in order to exploit discriminant information in NMF is to try to discover discriminant projections for the facial image vectors after the projection. The face recognition scores used in this work have been calculated in this way with the NMF-faces method [11], in which the final basis images are closer to facial parts.

3 Histogram Equalization

Z-score (ZS) is one of the most conventional normalization methods, which transforms the scores into a distribution with zero mean and unitary variance Denoting as a the raw matching from the set A of all the original monomodal biometric scores, the z-score normalized biometric is computed as:

$$x_{ZS} = \frac{a - mean(A)}{std(A)} \tag{1}$$

where *mean(A)* is the statistical mean of A and *std(A)* the standard deviation.

Histogram equalization (HE) is a general non parametric method to match the cumulative distribution function (CDF) of some given data to a reference distribution. This technique can be seen as an extension of the statistical normalization made by the z-score to whole biometric statistics.

Histogram equalization is a widely used non linear method designed for the enhancement of images. HE employs a monotonic, non linear mapping which re-assigns the intensity values of pixels in the input image in order to control the shape of the output image intensity histogram to achieve a uniform distribution of intensities or to highlight certain intensity levels.

This method has been also developed for the speech recognition adaptation approaches and the correction of non linear effects typically introduced by speech systems such as microphones, amplifiers, clipping and boosting circuits and automatic gain control circuits [12, 13].

The objective of HE is to find a non linear transformation to reduce the mismatch of the statistics of two signals. In [14, 15] this concept was applied to the acoustic features to improve the robustness of a speaker verification system. On the other hand, in this paper HE is applied to the scores. N intervals with the same probability are assigned in the distributions of both signals. Each interval in the reference distribution, $x \in [q_i, q_{i+1}[$, is represented by $(x_i, F(x_i))$. x_i is the average of the scores and $F(x_i)$ is the maximum cumulative distribution value:

$$x_i = \frac{\sum_{j=1}^{k_i} x_{ij}}{k_i}, \qquad F(x_i) = \frac{K_i}{M} \tag{2}$$

where x_{ij} are the scores in the interval, k_i is the number of scores in the interval, K_i is the number of data in the interval $[q_0, q_{i+1}[$, and M is the total amount of data.

All the scores in each interval of the source distributions are assigned to the corresponding interval in the reference distribution. $F(x_i)$ sets the boundaries $[q'_i, q'_{i+1}[$ of the intervals in the distribution to be equalized. These boundaries limit the interval of values that fulfils the following condition: $F(q_i) \leq F(y) < F(q_{i+1})$, and all the values of the source signal lying in the interval $[q'_i, q'_{i+1}[$ will be transformed to their corresponding x_i value.

4 Fusion Techniques and Support Vector Machines

One of the most conventional fusion techniques is the matcher weighting (MW) method, where each monomodal score is weighted by a factor proportional to each biometric recognition rate, so that the weights for more accurate matchers are higher than those of less accurate matchers. When using the Equal Error Rates (EER) the weighting factor for every biometric is proportional to the inverse of its EER. Denoting w_m and e_m the weighting factor and the EER for the m-th biometric x_m and M the number of biometrics, the final fused score u is expressed as [1, 3]:

$$u = \sum_{m=1}^{M} w_m x_m \qquad \text{where} \qquad w_m = \frac{\frac{1}{e_m}}{\sum_{m=1}^{M} \frac{1}{e_m}} . \tag{3}$$

In contrast to the MW that is a linear and a data-driven fusion method, non linear and machine learning based methods may lead to a higher performance. Learning based fusion can be treated as a pattern classification problem in which the scores obtained with individual classifiers are seen as input patterns to be labeled as 'accepted' or 'rejected'.

Recent works on statistical machine learning have shown the advantages of discriminative classifiers like SVM [16] in a range of applications. Support vector machine (SVM) is a state-of-the-art binary classifier. Given a linearly separable two-class training data, SVM finds an optimal hyperplane that splits input data in two classes, maximizing the distance of the hyperplane to the nearest data points of each class.

However, data are normally not linearly separable. In this case, non linear decision functions are needed, and an extension to non linear boundaries is achieved by using specific functions called kernel functions [17]. Kernel functions map the data of the input space to a higher dimensional space (feature space) by a non linear transformation. The optimal hyperplane for a non linearly separable data is defined by:

$$f(x) = \sum_{i=1}^{N} \alpha_i t_i \mathrm{K}(x, x_i) + b \tag{4}$$

where t_i are labels, K is a chosen kernel function and $\sum_{i=1}^{N} \alpha_i t_i = 0$. The vectors x_i are the support vectors, which determine the optimal separating hyperplane and correspond to the points of each class that are the closest to the separating hyperplane.

5 Recognition Experiments

In the next section, the monomodal recognition systems used in the fusion experiments are described. Experimental results by using different normalization and fusion techniques are shown in section 5.2.

5.1 Experimental Setup

Recognition experiments have been performed with the Switchboard-I speech database [18] and the video and speech XM2VTS database of the University of Surrey [19]. Switchboard-I database, which is a collection of 2430 two-sided telephone conversations among 543 speakers from all areas of the United States, has been used for the speaker recognition experiments. Speaker scores have been obtained by using two different systems: a voice spectrum based recognition system and a prosody based recognition system.

The spectrum based speaker recognition system used is a 32-component GMM system with diagonal covariance matrices; 20 Frequency Filtering parameters were generated with a frame size of 30 ms and a shift of 10 ms, and 20 corresponding delta and acceleration coefficients were included.

In the prosody based recognition system a 9-feature vector was extracted for each conversation side. The mean and standard deviation over all words were computed for each individual feature. The system was tested using the k-Nearest Neighbor classifier (with k=3), comparing the distance of the test feature vector to the k closest vectors of the claimed speakers and the distance of the test vector to the k closest vectors of the cohort speakers, and using the symmetrized Kullback-Leibler divergence as a distance measure.

In both spectral and prosodic systems, each speaker model was trained with 8 conversation sides. Training was performed using splits 1-3 of the Switchboard-I database, and splits 4-6 were provided the cohort speakers and the UBM. Both systems were tested with one conversation-side according to NIST's 2001 Extended Data task.

Face recognition experiments were performed with the XM2VTS database, which is a multimodal database consisting of face images, video sequences and speech recordings of 295 subjects. Only the face images have been used in our experiments. In order to evaluate the verification algorithms on the database, the evaluation protocol described in [19] was followed. The well-known Fisher discriminant criterion was constructed as [20] in order to discover discriminant linear projections and to obtain the facial scores.

Fusion experiments have been done at the matching score level. Since both databases contain biometric characteristics belonging to different users, a chimerical database has been created to perform the experiments. A chimerical database is an artificial database created using two or more monomodal biometric characteristics from different individuals to form artificial (or chimerical) users. In this paper, the chimerical database consists of 30661 users created by combining 179 different voices of the Switchboard-I database with 270 different faces of the XM2VTS database. The scores were then split in two equal sets (development and test) for each recognition system, obtaining a total amount of 46500 scores for each set (16800 clients and 29700 impostors).

The kernel function used in the SVM was a Gaussian radial basis function. Scores are always equalized to the histogram corresponding to the best scores involved in the fusion; i.e. those scores that provided the lowest EER. A 1000-interval histogram was applied before each SVM fusion, and both SVM and HE-SVM techniques are compared to a baseline system which uses MW fusion and z-score normalization.

5.2 Verification Results

Monomodal systems. Table 1 shows the EER obtained for each prosodic feature in the prosody based recognition system. As it can be seen in the table, features based on fundamental frequency measurements achieve the lowest EER.

Table 1. EER for each prosodic feature

Features	EER (%)
Log (#frames/word)	30.3
Average length of word-internal voiced segments	31.5
Average length of word-internal unvoiced segments	31.5
Log(mean_F0)	19.2
Log(max_F0)	21.3
Log(min_F0)	21.5
Log(range_F0)	26.6
F0 'pseudo-slope'	38.3
Average slope over all segments of PWL stylization of F0	28.7

The EER obtained in each monomodal recognition system are shown in Table 2. Note that fusion is only used in the prosodic system, where there are 9 prosodic scores to be combined. In this case, fusion is carried out in one single step, and the results of the three types of fusion mentioned above are presented: (1) matching score fusion with z-score normalization, (2) support vector machines and (3) support vector machines with a previous histogram equalization.

Table 2. EER (%) for each monomodal recognition system

Source		EER (%)
Prosody	ZS-MW	15.66
	SVM	14.65
	HE-SVM	13.39
Voice spectrum		10.10
Face		2.06

Bimodal systems. Table 3 shows the fusion results for two bimodal systems: a prosody based system fused with the voice spectral recognition system, and a voice spectrum based system fused with the face recognition system, using the same fusion methods as above. As in the monomodal systems (Table 2), matcher weighting fusion is slightly worse than the support vector machines.

Table 3. EER (%) for each bimodal recognition system

Source	ZS-MW	SVM	HE-SVM
Prosody + voice spectrum	7.44	6.84	6.25
Voice spectrum + face	1.83	0.99	1.02

Trimodal system. In [6] several strategies were proposed by fusing the monomodal scores in one, two and three steps. In those experiments the best results were achieved in a two-step configuration, where the 9 prosodic scores were fused in the first step and the obtained scores were then fused in the second step with voice spectral and facial scores (Fig. 1).

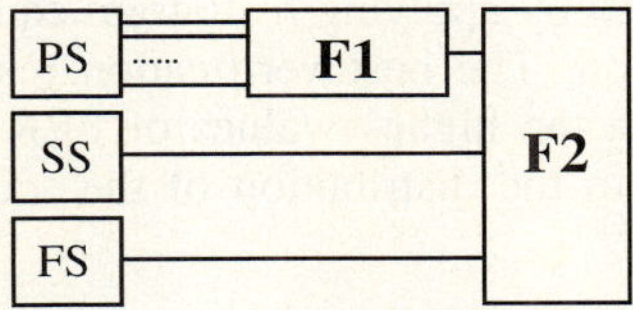

Fig. 1. Two-step fusion

The EER for the selected two-step fusion are presented in Table 4. Once again, matcher weighting fusion method is clearly outperformed by support vector machines.

Table 4. EER (%) for the trimodal system

Fusion technique	EER (%)
ZS-MW	1.493
SVM	0.647

In our trimodal system, equalization has been applied in all the possible combinations:

(1) HE before the first fusion (equalization of the prosodic scores)
(2) HE before the second fusion (equalization of the three modalities)
(3) HE before both fusions F1and F2

The results are shown in Table 5 and they are compared to the non equalized SVM fusion.

Table 5. EER (%) applying HE before SVM fusion

Fusion technique	F1	F2	EER (%)
SVM	-	-	0.647
	HE	-	0.630
	-	HE	0.649
	HE	HE	**0.613**

As it can be seen in the table, the best result is achieved when histogram equalization is used before F1 and F2. By equalizing only the prosodic scores, the performance of the system is also improved. On the other hand, equalization before the second fusion does not improve the performance of the system.

6 Conclusions

In this work, the use of prosody improves the performance of a bimodal system based on vocal tract spectrum and face features. The experiments show that support vector machines based fusion is clearly better than matcher weighting fusion method. In addition, results are improved by applying histogram equalization as a normalization technique before SVM fusion. The best verification results are achieved when the histogram of the scores with the highest values of EER (the prosodic scores in our experiments) are equalized to the distribution of the scores that provide the lowest EER.

References

1. Bolle, R.M., et al.: Guide to Biometrics, p. 364. Springer, New York (2004)
2. Fox, N.A., et al.: Person identification using automatic integration of speech, lip and face experts. In: ACM SIGMM 2003 Multimedia Biometrics Methods and Applications Workshop, Berkeley, CA. ACM, New York (2003)
3. Indovina, M., et al.: Multimodal Biometric Authentication Methods: A COTS Approach. In: MMUA. Workshop on Multimodal User Authentication, Santa Barbara, CA (2003)
4. Lucey, S., Chen, T.: Improved audio-visual speaker recognition via the use of a hybrid combination strategy. In: The 4th International Conference on Audio- and Video- Based Biometric Person Authentication, Guildford, UK (2003)
5. Wang, Y., Tan, T.: Combining fingerprint and voiceprint biometrics for identity verification: and experimental comparison. In: Zhang, D., Jain, A.K. (eds.) ICBA 2004. LNCS, vol. 3072. Springer, Heidelberg (2004)
6. Farrús, M., et al.: On the Fusion of Prosody, Voice Spectrum and Face Features for Multimodal Person Verification. In: ICSLP, Pittsburgh (2006)
7. Campbell, J.P., Reynolds, D.A., Dunn, R.B.: Fusing high- and low-level features for speaker recognition. In: Eurospeech (2003)
8. Nadeu, C., Hernando, J., Gorricho, M.: On the decorrelation of filter bank energies in speech recognition. In: Eurospeech (1995)
9. Peskin, B., et al.: Using prosodic and conversational features for high-performance speaker recognition: Report from JHU WS'02. In: ICASSP (2003)

10. Lee, D.D., Seung, H.S.: Algorithms for non-negative matrix factorization. In: Advances in Neural Information Processing Systems: Proceedings of the 2000 Conference. MIT Press, Cambridge (2001)
11. Zafeiriou, S., Tefas, A., Pitas, I.: Discriminant NMF-faces for frontal face verification. In: IEEE International Workshop on Machine Learning for Signal Processing, Mystic, Connecticut, IEEE, Los Alamitos (2005)
12. Hilger, F., Ney, H.: Quantile based histogram equalization for noise robust speech recognition. In: Eurospeech, Aalborg, Denmark (2001)
13. Balchandran, R., Mammone, R.: Non parametric estimation and correction of non linear distortion in speech systems. In: ICASSP (1998)
14. Pelecanos, J., Sridharan, S.: Feature warping for robust speaker verification. In: ODYSSEY-2001 (2001)
15. Skosan, M., Mashao, D.: Modified Segmental Histogram Equalization for robust speaker verification. Pattern Recognition Letters 27(5), 479–486 (2006)
16. Cristianini, N., Shawe-Taylor, J.: An introduction to support vector machines (and other kernel-based learning methods). Cambridge University Press, Cambridge (2000)
17. Burges, C.J.C.: A tutorial on support vector machines for pattern recognition. Data Mining and Knowledge discovery 2, 121–167 (1998)
18. Godfrey, J.J., Holliman, E.C., McDaniel, J.: Switchboard: Telephone speech corpus for research and development. In: ICASSP (1990)
19. Lüttin, J., Maître, G.: Evaluation Protocol for the Extended M2VTS Database (XM2VTSDB). In: IDIAP, Martigny, Switzerland (1998)
20. Belhumeur, P.N., Hespanha, J.P., Kriegman, D.J.: Eigenfaces vs. Fisherfaces: Recognition using class specific linear projection. IEEE Transactions on Pattern Analysis and Machine Intelligence 19(7), 711–720 (1997)

Learning Multi-scale Block Local Binary Patterns for Face Recognition

Shengcai Liao, Xiangxin Zhu, Zhen Lei, Lun Zhang, and Stan Z. Li

Center for Biometrics and Security Research &
National Laboratory of Pattern Recognition,
Institute of Automation, Chinese Academy of Sciences,
95 Zhongguancun Donglu, Beijing 100080, China
{scliao,xxzhu,zlei,lzhang,szli}@nlpr.ia.ac.cn
http://www.cbsr.ia.ac.cn

Abstract. In this paper, we propose a novel representation, called Multi-scale Block Local Binary Pattern (MB-LBP), and apply it to face recognition. The Local Binary Pattern (LBP) has been proved to be effective for image representation, but it is too local to be robust. In MB-LBP, the computation is done based on average values of block subregions, instead of individual pixels. In this way, MB-LBP code presents several advantages: (1) It is more robust than LBP; (2) it encodes not only microstructures but also macrostructures of image patterns, and hence provides a more complete image representation than the basic LBP operator; and (3) MB-LBP can be computed very efficiently using integral images. Furthermore, in order to reflect the uniform appearance of MB-LBP, we redefine the uniform patterns via statistical analysis. Finally, AdaBoost learning is applied to select most effective uniform MB-LBP features and construct face classifiers. Experiments on Face Recognition Grand Challenge (FRGC) ver2.0 database show that the proposed MB-LBP method significantly outperforms other LBP based face recognition algorithms.

Keywords: LBP, MB-LBP, Face Recognition, AdaBoost.

1 Introduction

Face recognition from images has been a hot research topic in computer vision for recent two decades. This is because face recognition has potential application values as well as theoretical challenges. Many appearance-based approaches have been proposed to deal with face recognition problems. Holistic subspace approach, such as PCA [14] and LDA [3] based methods, has significantly advanced face recognition techniques. Using PCA, a face subspace is constructed to represent "optimally" only the face; using LDA, a discriminant subspace is constructed to distinguish "optimally" faces of different persons. Another approach is to construct a local appearance-based feature space, using appropriate image filters, so the distributions of faces are less affected by various changes. Local features analysis (LFA) [10], Gabor wavelet-based features [16,6] are among these.

S.-W. Lee and S.Z. Li (Eds.): ICB 2007, LNCS 4642, pp. 828–837, 2007.

Recently, Local Binary Patterns (LBP) is introduced as a powerful local descriptor for microstructures of images [8]. The LBP operator labels the pixels of an image by thresholding the 3×3-neighborhood of each pixel with the center value and considering the result as a binary string or a decimal number. Recently, Ahonen et al proposed a novel approach for face recognition, which takes advantage of the Local Binary Pattern (LBP) histogram [1]. In their method, the face image is equally divided into small sub-windows from which the LBP features are extracted and concatenated to represent the local texture and global shape of face images. Weighted Chi square distance of these LBP histograms is used as a dissimilarity measure of different face images. Experimental results showed that their method outperformed other well-known approaches such as PCA, EBGM and BIC on FERET database. Zhang et al [17] propose to use AdaBoost learning to select best LBP sub-window histograms features and construct face classifiers.

However, the original LBP operator has the following drawback in its application to face recognition. It has its small spatial support area, hence the bit-wise comparison therein made between two single pixel values is much affected by noise. Moreover, features calculated in the local 3×3 neighborhood cannot capture larger scale structure (macrostructure) that may be dominant features of faces.

In this work, we propose a novel representation, called Multi-scale Block LBP (MB-LBP), to overcome the limitations of LBP, and apply it to face recognition. In MB-LBP, the computation is done based on average values of block subregions, instead of individual pixels. This way, MB-LBP code presents several advantages: (1) It is more robust than LBP; (2) it encodes not only microstructures but also macrostructures of image patterns, and hence provides a more complete image representation than the basic LBP operator; and (3) MB-LBP can be computed very efficiently using integral images. Considering this extension, we find that the property of the original uniform LBP patterns introduced by Ojala et al [9] can not hold to be true, so we provide a definition of statistically effective LBP code via statistical analysis. While a large number of MB-LBP features result at multiple scales and multiple locations, we apply AdaBoost learning to select most effective uniform MB-LBP features and thereby construct the final face classifier.

The rest of this paper is organized as follows: In Section 2, we introduce the MB-LBP representation. In Section 3, the new concept of uniform patterns are provided via statistical analysis. In Section 4, A dissimilarity measure is defined to discriminate intra/extrapersonal face images, and then we apply the AdaBoost learning for MB-LBP feature selection and classifier construction. The experiment results are given in Section 5 with the FRGC ver2.0 data sets [11]. Finally, we summarize this paper in Section 6.

2 Multi-scale Block Local Binary Patterns

The original LBP operator labels the pixels of an image by thresholding the 3×3-neighborhood of each pixel with the center value and considering the result as

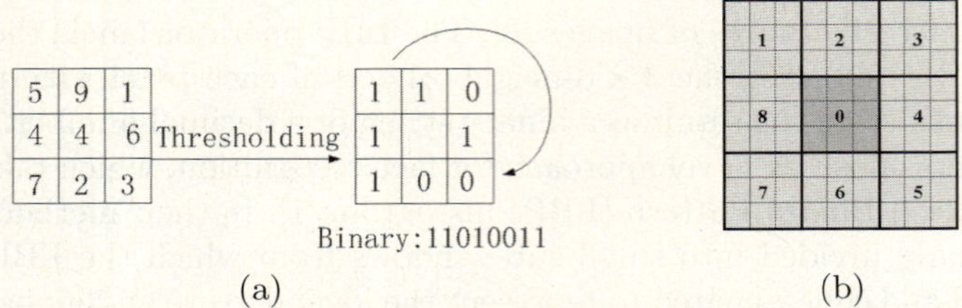

Fig. 1. (a) The basic LBP operator. (b) The 9×9 MB-LBP operator. In each sub-region, average sum of image intensity is computed. These average sums are then thresholded by that of the center block. MB-LBP is then obtained.

a binary string or a decimal number. Then the histogram of the labels can be used as a texture descriptor. An illustration of the basic LBP operator is shown in Fig. 1(a). Multi-scale LBP [9] is an extension to the basic LBP, with respect to neighborhoods of different sizes.

In MB-LBP, the comparison operator between single pixels in LBP is simply replaced with comparison between average gray-values of sub-regions (*cf.* Fig. 1(b)). Each sub-region is a square block containing neighboring pixels (or just one pixel particularly). The whole filter is composed of 9 blocks. We take the size s of the filter as a parameter, and $s \times s$ denoting the scale of the MB-LBP operator (particularly, 3×3 MB-LBP is in fact the original LBP). Note that the scalar values of averages over blocks can be computed very efficiently [13] from the summed-area table [4] or integral image [15]. For this reason, MB-LBP feature extraction can also be very fast: it only incurs a little more cost than the original 3×3 LBP operator.

Fig. 2 gives examples of MB-LBP filtered face images by 3×3, 9×9 and 15×15 blocks. From this example we can see what influence parameter s would make. For a small scale, local, micro patterns of a face structure is well represented, which may beneficial for discriminating local details of faces. On the

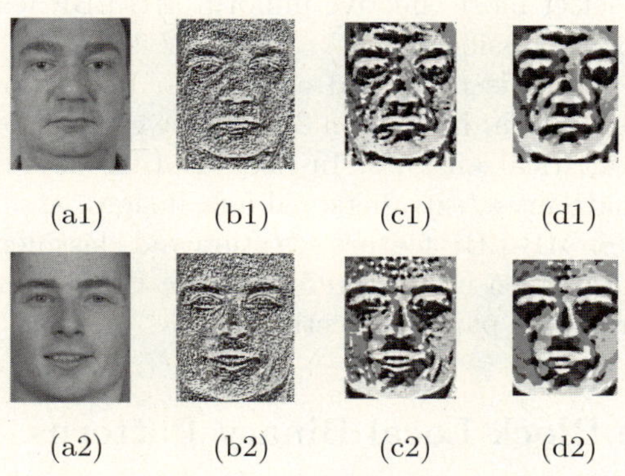

Fig. 2. MB-LBP filtered images of two different faces. (a) original images; (b) filtered by 3×3 MB-LBP (c) filtered by 9×9 MB-LBP; (d) filtered by 15×15 MB-LBP.

other hand, using average values over the regions, the large scale filters reduce noise, and makes the representation more robust; and large scale information provides complementary information to small scale details. But much discriminative information is also dropped. Normally, filters of various scales should be carefully selected and then fused to achieve better performance.

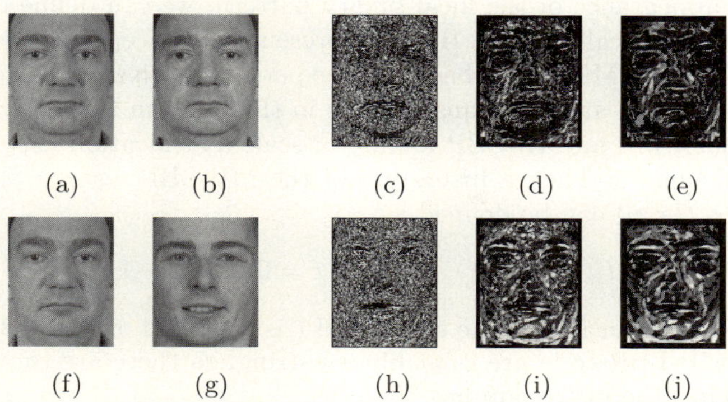

Fig. 3. Differential images. (a)(b) are the original intra-personal images, (c)(d)(e) are the corresponding differential images generated by 3×3, 9×9 and 15×15 MB-LBP operators. And (f)(g) are the original extra-personal images, (h)(i)(j) are the corresponding differential images generated by 3×3, 9×9 and 15×15 MB-LBP operators.

Fig. 3 demonstrates MB-LBP features for intra-personal and extra-personal difference images (brighter pixels indicate greater difference). Using differential images, We also have another way to demonstrate the discriminative power of MB-LBP. We see that when scale of the MB-LBP filter become larger, thought both intra-personal variance and extra-personal variance decrease, it is more clear that with larger scale MB-LBP, intra-personal differences are smaller than that of the extra-personal.

3 Statistically Effective MB-LBP (SEMB-LBP)

Using the "uniform" subset of LBP code improves the performance of LBP based methods. A Local Binary Pattern is called uniform if it contains at most two bitwise transitions from 0 to 1 or vice versa when the binary string is considered circular [9]. It is observed that there are a limited number of transitions or discontinuities in the circular presentation of the 3×3 texture patterns; according to Ojala, this uniform patterns are fundamental properties of local image texture, they provide a vast majority amount all patterns: 90% for (8,2) type LBP, 70% for (16,2) type [9].

However, the original definition of uniform LBP patterns based on the transition of pixel values can not be used for MB-LBP with blocks containing more than a single pixel. The reason is obvious: the same properties of circular continuities in 3×3 patterns can not hold to be true when parameter s becomes larger. Using average gray-values instead of single pixels, MB-LBP reflects the statistical properties of local sub-region relationship. The lager parameter s becomes, the harder for the circular presentation to be continuous.

So we need to redefine uniform patterns. Since the term uniform refers to the uniform appearance of the local binary pattern, we can define our uniform MB-LBP via statistical analysis. Here, we present the concept of Statistically Effective MB-LBP (SEMB-LBP), based on the percentage in distributions, instead of the number of 0-1 and 1-0 transitions as in the uniform LBP.

Denote $f_s(x, y)$ as an MB-LBP feature of scale s at location (x, y) computed from original images. Then a histogram of the MB-LBP feature $f_s(\cdot, \cdot)$ over a certain image $I(x, y)$ can be defined as:

$$H_s(l) = 1_{[f_s(x,y)=l]}, \qquad \ell = 0, \ldots, L-1 \tag{1}$$

where $1_{(S)}$ is the indicator of the set S, and ℓ is the label of the MB-LBP code. Because all MB-LBP code are 8-bit binary string, so there are total L $= 2^8 =$ 256 labels. Thus the histogram has 256 bins.

This histogram contains information about the distribution of the MB-LBP features over the whole image. The histograms, with the large still training set of the FRGC ver2.0, for the scales 3×3, 9×9, 15×15, and 21×21 are shown in Fig. 4. We sort the bins of a histogram according to its percentage in the histogram. A statistical analysis shows the following:

- For the 3×3 LBP operator, the top 58 bins correspond to the so-called uniform patterns;
- However, for MB-LBP filters with block containing more than one pixel, the top 58 bins are not the same as those for the 3×3 LBP filters.

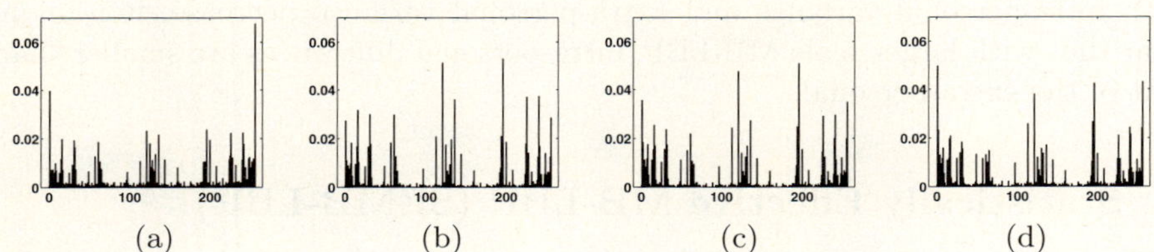

Fig. 4. Histograms of MB-LBP labels on the large still training set of the FRGC ver2.0. (a)3×3, (b)9×9, (c)15×15, and (d)21×21.

To reflect the uniform appearance of MB-LBP, we define the statistically effective MB-LBP (SEMB-LBP) set of scale s as follows:

$$SEMB\text{-}LBP_s = \{\ell | Rank[H_s(l)] < N\} \tag{2}$$

where Rank$[H_s(l)]$ is the index of $H_s(l)$ after descending sorting, and N is the number of uniform patterns. For the original uniform local binary patterns, N

= 58. However, in our definition, N can be assigned arbitrarily from 1 to 256. Large value of N will cause the feature dimensions very huge, while small one loses feature variety. Consequently, we adopt N = 63 for a trade-off. Labeling all remaining patterns with a single label, we use the following notation to represent SEMB-LBP:

$$u_s(x,y) = \{ \begin{array}{ll} Index_s[f_s(x,y)], & if \quad f_s(x,y) \in SEMB\text{-}LBP_s \\ N, & otherwise \end{array} \tag{3}$$

where $Index_s[f_s(x,y)]$ is the index of $f_s(x,y)$ in the set $SEMB\text{-}LBP_s$ (started from 0).

4 AdaBoost Learning

The above SEMB-LBP provides an over-complete representation. The only question remained is how to use them to construct a powerful classifier. Because those excessive measures contain much redundant information, a further processing is needed to remove the redundancy and build effective classifiers. In this paper we use Gentle AdaBoost algorithm [5] to select the most effective SEMB-LBP feature.

Boosting can be viewed as a stage-wise approximation to an additive logistic regression model using Bernoulli log-likelihood as a criterion [5]. Developed by Friedman et al, Gentle AdaBoost modifies the population version of the Real AdaBoost procedure [12], using Newton stepping rather than exact optimization at each step. Empirical evidence suggests that Gentle AdaBoost is a more conservative algorithm that has similar performance to both the Real AdaBoost and LogitBoost algorithms, and often outperforms them both, especially when stability is an issue.

Face recognition is a multi-class problem whereas the above AdaBoost learning is for two classes. To dispense the need for a training process for faces of a newly added person, we use a large training set describing intra-personal or extra-personal variations [7], and train a "universal" two-class classifier. An ideal intra-personal difference should be an image with all pixel values being zero, whereas an extra-personal difference image should generally have much larger pixel values. However, instead of deriving the intra-personal or extra-personal variations using difference images as in [7], the training examples to our learning algorithm is the set of differences between each pair of local histograms at the corresponding locations. The positive examples are derived from pairs of intra-personal differences and the negative from pairs of extra-personal differences.

In this work, a weak classifier is learned based on a dissimilarity between two corresponding histogram bins. Once the SEMB-LBP set are defined for each scale, histogram of these patterns are computed for calculating the dissimilarity: First, a sequence of m subwindows $R_0, R_1, \ldots, R_{m-1}$ of varying sizes and locations are obtained from an image; Second, a histogram is computed for each SEMB-LBP code i over a subwindow R_j as

$$H_{s,j}(i) = 1_{[u_s(x,y)=i]} \cdot 1_{[(x,y)\in R_j]}, \qquad i = 0, \ldots, N, j = 0, \ldots, m-1 \tag{4}$$

The corresponding bin difference is defined as

$$D(H^1_{s,j}(i), H^2_{s,j}(i)) = |H^1_{s,j}(i) - H^2_{s,j}(i)| \quad i = 0, \ldots, N \tag{5}$$

The best current weak classifier is the one for which the weighted intra-personal bin differences (over the training set) are minimized while that of the extra-personal are maximized.

With the two-class scheme, the face matching procedure will work in the following way: It takes a probe face image and a gallery face image as the input, and computes a difference-based feature vector from the two images, and then it calculates a similarity score for the feature vector using the learned AdaBoost classifier. Finally, A decision is made based on the score, to classify the feature vector into the positive class (coming from the same person) or the negative class (different persons).

5 Experiments

The proposed method is tested on the Face Recognition Grand Challenge (FRGC) ver2.0 database [11]. The Face Recognition Grand Challenge is a large face recognition evaluation data set, which contains over 50,000 images of 3D scans and high resolution still images. Fig. 5 shows a set of images in FRGC for one subject section. The FRGC ver2.0 contains a large still training set for training still face recognition algorithms. It consists of 12,776 images from 222 subjects. A large validation set is also provided for FRGC experiments, which contains 466 subjects from 4,007 subject sessions.

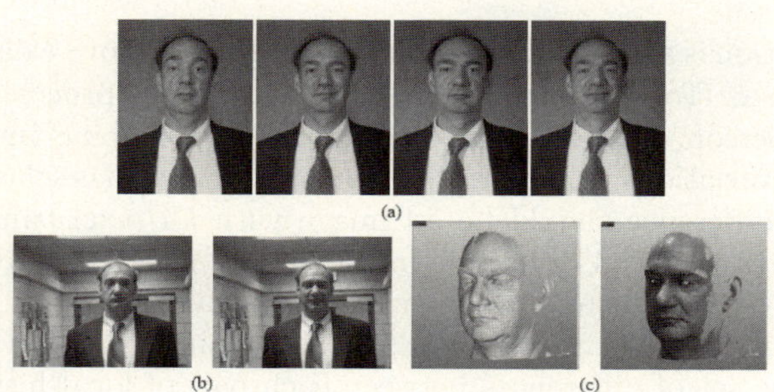

Fig. 5. FRGC images from one subject session. (a) Four controlled still images, (b) two uncontrolled stills, and (c) 3D shape channel and texture channel pasted on the corresponding shape channel.

The proposed method is evaluated on two 2D experiments of FRGC: Experiment 1 and Experiment 2. Experiment 1 is designed to measure face recognition performance on frontal facial images taken under controlled illumination. In this experiment, only one single controlled still image is contained in one biometric sample of the target or query sets. Experiment 2 measures the effect of multiple still images on performance. In Experiment 2, each biometric sample contains four controlled images of a person taken in a subject session. There are 16 matching scores between one target and one query sample. These scores are averaged to give the final result.

There are total 16028 still images both in target and query sets of experiment 1 and 2. In the testing phase, it will generate a large similarity matrix of 16028 by 16028. Furthermore, three masks are defined over this similarity matrix, thus three performance results will obtained, corresponding to Mask I, II, and III. In mask I all samples are within semesters, in mask II they are within a year, while in mask III the samples are between semesters, i.e., they are of increasing difficulty.

In our experiments, All images are cropped to 144 pixels high by 112 pixels wide, according to the provided eyes positions. A boosting classifier is trained on the large still training set. The final strong classifier contains 2346 weak classifiers, e.g. 2346 bins of various sub-region SEMB-LBP histograms, while achieving zero error rate on the training set. The corresponding MB-LBP filter size of the first 5 learned weak classifiers are s = 21, 33, 27, 3, 9. We find that a middle level of scale s has a better discriminative power.

To compare the performances of LBP based methods, we also evaluate Ahonen et al's LBP method [1] and Zhang et al's Boosting LBP algorithm [17]. We use $LBP^{u2}_{8,2}$ operator as Ahonen's, and test it directly on FRGC experiment 1 and 2 since their method needs no training. For Zhang's approach, we train an AdaBoost classifier on the large still training set in the same way of our MB-LBP. The final strong classifier of Zhang's contains 3072 weak classifiers, yet it can not achieve zero error rate on the training set.

The comparison results are given in Fig. 6, and Fig. 7 describes the verification performances on a receiver operator characteristic(ROC) curve (mask III). From the results we can see that MB-LBP outperforms the other two algorithms on all experiments. The comparison proves that MB-LBP is a more robust representation than the basic LBP. Meanwhile, because MB-LBP provides a more complete image representation that encodes both microstructure and macrostructure, it can achieve zero error rate on the large still training set, while generate well on the validation face images. Furthermore, we can also find that MB-LBP performs well on Mask III, which means that it is robust with time elapse.

	Experiment 1			Experiment 2		
	Mask I	Mask II	Mask III	Mask I	Mask II	Mask III
MB-LBP	**98.07**	**97.04**	**96.05**	**99.78**	**99.58**	**99.45**
Zhang's LBP	84.17	80.35	76.67	97.67	96.73	95.84
Ahonen's LBP	82.72	78.65	74.78	93.62	90.54	87.46

Fig. 6. Verification performance (FAR=0.1%) on FRGC Experiment 1 and 2

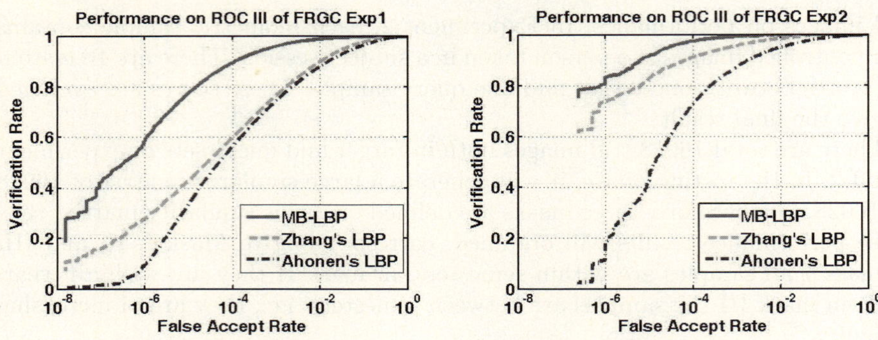

Fig. 7. ROC performance on FRGC Experiment 1 and 2

6 Summary and Conclusions

In this paper, we present a Multi-scale Block Local Binary Pattern (MB-LBP) based operator for robust image representation. The Local Binary Pattern (LBP) has been proved to be effective for image representation, but it is too local to be robust. The Multi-scale Block Local Binary Patterns (MB-LBP) use sub-region average gray-values for comparison instead of single pixels. Feature extraction for MB-LBP is very fast using integral images. Considering this extension, uniform patterns may not remain the same as those defined by Ojala et al [9]. To reflect the uniform appearance of the MB-LBP, we define our Statistically Effective MB-LBP (SEMB-LBP) via statistical analysis. Simply using absolute difference between the same bin of two histograms as dissimilarity measure, we finally apply AdaBoost learning to select the most effective weak classifiers and construct a powerful classifier. Experiments on FRGC ver2.0 show that MB-LBP significantly outperforms other LBP based method.

Since MB-LBP can be viewed as a certain way of combination using 8 ordinal rectangle features, our future work may be combining eight or more ordinal features [2] in a circular instead of rectangle features. While ordinal filters are sufficient and robust for comparison of image regions, we expect that this kind of combination will be more powerful for image representation.

Acknowledgements. This work was supported by the following funding resources: National Natural Science Foundation Project #60518002, National Science and Technology Supporting Platform Project #2006BAK08B06, National 863 Program Projects #2006AA01Z192 and #2006AA01Z193, Chinese Academy of Sciences 100-people project, and the AuthenMetric Collaboration Foundation.

References

1. Ahonen, T., Hadid, A., Pietikainen, M.: Face recognition with local binary patterns. In: Proceedings of the European Conference on Computer Vision, Prague, Czech, pp. 469–481 (2004)

2. Balas, B., Sinha, P.: Toward dissociated dipoles: Image representation via non-local comparisons. In: CBCL Paper #229/AI Memo #2003-018, MIT Computer Science and Artificial Intelligence Laboratory, Cambridge, MA, USA (August 2003)
3. Belhumeur, P.N., Hespanha, J.P., Kriegman, D.J.: Eigenfaces vs. Fisherfaces: Recognition using class specific linear projection. IEEE Transactions on Pattern Analysis and Machine Intelligence 19(7), 711–720 (1997)
4. Crow, F.: Summed-area tables for texture mapping. In: SIGGRAPH, vol. 18(3), pp. 207–212 (1984)
5. Friedman, J., Hastie, T., Tibshirani, R.: Additive logistic regression: a statistical view of boosting. Technical report, Department of Statistics, Sequoia Hall, Stanford Univerity (July 1998)
6. Liu, C., Wechsler, H.: Gabor feature based classification using the enhanced fisher linear discriminant model for face recognition. IEEE Transactions on Image Processing 11(4), 467–476 (2002)
7. Moghaddam, B., Nastar, C., Pentland, A.: A Bayesain similarity measure for direct image matching. Media Lab Tech Report No.393, MIT (August 1996)
8. Ojala, T., Pietikainen, M., Harwood, D.: A comparative study of texture measures with classification based on feature distributions. Pattern Recognition 29(1), 51–59 (1996)
9. Ojala, T., Pietikainen, M., Maenpaa, M.: Multiresolution gray-scale and rotation invariant texture classification with local binary patterns. IEEE Transactions on Pattern Analysis and Machine Intelligence 24(7), 971–987 (2002)
10. Penev, P., Atick, J.: Local feature analysis: A general statistical theory for object representation. Neural Systems 7(3), 477–500 (1996)
11. Phillips, P.J., Flynn, P.J., Scruggs, T., Bowyer, K.W., Chang, J., Hoffman, K., Marques, J., Min, J., Worek, W.: Overview of the face recognition grand challenge. In: Proceedings of IEEE Computer Society Conference on Computer Vision and Pattern Recognition. IEEE Computer Society Press, Los Alamitos (2005)
12. Schapire, R.E., Singer, Y.: Improved boosting algorithms using confidence-rated predictions. In: Proceedings of the Eleventh Annual Conference on Computational Learning Theory, pp. 80–91 (1998)
13. Simard, P.Y., Bottou, L., Haffner, P., Cun, Y.L.: Boxlets: a fast convolution algorithm for signal processing and neural networks. In: Kearns, M., Solla, S., Cohn, D. (eds.) Advances in Neural Information Processing Systems, vol. 11, pp. 571–577. MIT Press, Cambridge (1998)
14. Turk, M.A., Pentland, A.P.: Eigenfaces for recognition. Journal of Cognitive Neuroscience 3(1), 71–86 (1991)
15. Viola, P., Jones, M.: Robust real time object detection. In: IEEE ICCV Workshop on Statistical and Computational Theories of Vision, Vancouver, Canada, July 13, 2001 (2001)
16. Wiskott, L., Fellous, J., Kruger, N., Malsburg, C.v.d.: Face recognition by elastic bunch graph matching. IEEE Transactions on Pattern Analysis and Machine Intelligence 19(7), 775–779 (1997)
17. Zhang, G., Huang, X., Li, S.Z., Wang, Y., Wu, X.: Boosting local binary pattern (LBP)-based face recognition. In: Li, S.Z., Lai, J.-H., Tan, T., Feng, G.-C., Wang, Y. (eds.) SINOBIOMETRICS 2004. LNCS, vol. 3338, pp. 180–187. Springer, Heidelberg (2004)

Horizontal and Vertical 2DPCA Based Discriminant Analysis for Face Verification Using the FRGC Version 2 Database

Jian Yang[1,2] and Chengjun Liu[1]

[1] Department of Computer Science,
New Jersey Institute of Technology, Newark, NJ 07102
[2] Department of Computer Science,
Nanjing University of Science and Technology,
Nanjing 210094, P.R. China
{csjyang,chengjun.liu}@njit.edu

Abstract. This paper presents a horizontal and vertical 2D principal component analysis (2DPCA) based discriminant analysis (HVDA) method for face verification. The HVDA method, which derives features by applying 2DPCA horizontally and vertically on the image matrices (2D arrays), achieves high computational efficiency compared with the traditional PCA and/or LDA based methods that operate on high dimensional image vectors (1D arrays). The HVDA method further performs discriminant analysis to enhance the discriminating power of the horizontal and vertical 2DPCA features. Finally, the HVDA method takes advantage of the color information across two color spaces, namely, the *YIQ* and the YC_bC_r color spaces, to further improve its performance. Experiments using the Face Recognition Grand Challenge (FRGC) version 2 database, which contains 12,776 training images, 16,028 controlled target images, and 8,014 uncontrolled query images, show the effectiveness of the proposed method. In particular, the HVDA method achieves 78.24% face verification rate at 0.1% false accept rate on the most challenging FRGC experiment, i.e., the FRGC Experiment 4 (based on the ROC III curve).

Keywords: Principal Component Analysis (PCA), Biometric Experimentation Environment (BEE), Face Recognition Grand Challenge (FRGC), Fisher Linear Discriminant Analysis (FLD or LDA), feature extraction, face verification, biometrics, color space.

1 Introduction

Principal component analysis (PCA) is a classical technique widely used in pattern recognition. Sirovich and Kirby first applied PCA to represent pictures of human faces [1], and Turk and Pentland further proposed the well-known Eigenfaces method for face recognition [2]. Since then, PCA has become a popular method for face recognition. Due to its simplicity and robustness, PCA was chosen as the baseline algorithm for the Face Recognition Grand Challenge (FRGC) evaluation [10].

S.-W. Lee and S.Z. Li (Eds.): ICB 2007, LNCS 4642, pp. 838–847, 2007.

PCA-based techniques usually operate on vectors. That is, before applying PCA, the 2D image matrices should be mapped into pattern vectors by concatenating their columns or rows. The pattern vectors generally lead to a high-dimensional space. For example, an image with a spatial resolution of 128×128 defines a 16, 384-dimensional vector space. In such a high-dimensional vector space, computing the eigenvectors of the covariance matrix is very time-consuming. Although the singular value decomposition (SVD) technique is effective for reducing computation when the training sample size is much smaller than the dimensionality of the images [1, 2], it does not help much when the training sample size becomes large. For example, for the FRGC version 2 database, the number of training images is 12,776. If all these training images are used, PCA has to compute the eigenvectors of a $12{,}776 \times 12{,}776$ matrix. It should be mentioned that the Fisherfaces method [3] also encounters the same problem as PCA does, since the Fisherfaces method requires a PCA step before applying the Fisher linear discriminant analysis (FLD or LDA).

Compared with PCA, the two-dimensional PCA method (2DPCA) [4] is a more straightforward technique for dealing with 2D images (matrices), as 2DPCA works on matrices (2D arrays) rather than on vectors (1D arrays). Therefore, 2DPCA does not transform an image into a vector, but rather, it constructs an *image covariance matrix* directly from the original image matrices. In contrast to the covariance matrix of PCA, the size of the image covariance matrix of 2DPCA is much smaller. For example, if the image size is 128×128, the *image covariance matrix* of 2DPCA is still 128×128, regardless of the training sample size. As a result, 2DPCA has a remarkable computational advantage over PCA.

The original 2DPCA method, which focuses on the columns of images and achieves the optimal image energy compression in horizontal direction, however, overlooks the information that might be contained in the image rows. In this paper, we embed both kinds of image information (in rows and columns) into a discriminant analysis framework for face recognition. Specifically, we first perform the *image-column based* 2DPCA (*horizontal 2DPCA*) and the *image-row based* 2DPCA (*vertical 2DPCA*), and then apply LDA for further feature extraction. The proposed framework is called Horizontal and Vertical 2DPCA based Discriminant Analysis (HVDA).

FRGC is the most comprehensive face recognition efforts so far organized by the US government, which consists of a large amount of face data and a standard evaluation method, known as the Biometric Experimentation Environment (BEE) system [10, 6]. The FRGC version 2 database contains both controlled and uncontrolled high resolution images, and the BEE baseline algorithm reveals that the FRGC Experiment 4 is the most challenging experiment, because it evaluates face verification performance of controlled face images versus uncontrolled face images. As the training set for FRGC version 2 database consists of 12,776 high resolution images, face recognition methods have to deal with high-dimensional images and very large data sets [11]. The proposed HVDA method has the computational advantage over the conventional PCA and/or LDA based methods, such as the Eigenfaces and the Fisherfaces methods, for dealing with high resolution images and large training data sets due to the computational efficiency of 2DPCA.

Recent research in face recognition shows that color information plays an important role in improving face recognition performance [7]. Different color spaces as well as various color configurations within or across color spaces are investigated and assessed using the FERET and the FRGC Version 2 databases. The experimental results reveal that the color configuration YQC_r, where Y and Q color components are from the YIQ color space and C_r is from the YC_bC_r color space, is most effective for the face recognition task. This color configuration, together with an LDA method, achieves 65% face verification rate at 0.1% false accept rate on FRGC Experiment 4 using the FRGC Version 2 database. This paper, thus, applies the HVDA method in the YC_bC_r color space for improving face recognition performance.

2 Horizontal and Vertical 2DPCA

This section outlines the two versions of 2DPCA, namely the horizontal 2DPCA and the vertical 2DPCA.

2.1 Horizontal 2DPCA

Given image $\mathbf{A}$, an $m \times n$ random matrix, the goal of 2DPCA is to find a set of orthogonal projection axes $\mathbf{u}_1, \cdots, \mathbf{u}_q$ so that the projected vectors $\mathbf{Y}_k = \mathbf{A}\mathbf{u}_k$ ($k = 1, 2, \cdots, q$) achieve a maximum total scatter [4]. The *image covariance* (*scatter*) *matrix* of Horizontal 2DPCA is defined as follows [4]:

$$\mathbf{G}_t = \frac{1}{M}\sum_{j=1}^{M}(\mathbf{A}_j - \overline{\mathbf{A}})^{\mathrm{T}}(\mathbf{A}_j - \overline{\mathbf{A}}) \tag{1}$$

where M is the number of training images, $\mathbf{A}_j$ is an $m \times n$ matrix denoting the j-th training image, and $\overline{\mathbf{A}}$ is the mean image of all training images.

The optimal projection axes $\mathbf{u}_1, \cdots, \mathbf{u}_q$ are chosen as the orthonormal eigenvectors of $\mathbf{G}_t$ corresponding to q largest eigenvalues $\lambda_1, \lambda_2, \cdots, \lambda_q$ [4]. After the projection of images onto these axes, i.e.,

$$\mathbf{X}_k = (\mathbf{A} - \overline{\mathbf{A}})\mathbf{u}_k, \; k = 1, 2, \cdots, q, \tag{2}$$

we obtain a family of *principal component vectors*, $\mathbf{Y}_1, \cdots, \mathbf{Y}_q$, which form an $m \times q$ feature matrix $\mathbf{B} = [\mathbf{X}_1, \cdots, \mathbf{X}_q]$. Let $\mathbf{U} = [\mathbf{u}_1, \cdots, \mathbf{u}_q]$, and Equ. (2) becomes

$$\mathbf{B} = (\mathbf{A} - \overline{\mathbf{A}})\mathbf{U} \tag{3}$$

The feature matrix $\mathbf{B}$ contains the horizontal 2DPCA features of image $\mathbf{A}$.

2.2 Vertical 2DPCA

If the input of 2DPCA is the transpose of the $m \times n$ image $\mathbf{A}$, then the *image covariance matrix* defined in Eq. (1) becomes

$$\mathbf{H}_t = \frac{1}{M}\sum_{j=1}^{M}(\mathbf{A}_j - \overline{\mathbf{A}})(\mathbf{A}_j - \overline{\mathbf{A}})^{\mathrm{T}} \tag{4}$$

Now, $\mathbf{H}_t$ is an $m \times m$ non-negative definite matrix. Let $\mathbf{v}_1, \cdots, \mathbf{v}_p$ be the orthonormal eigenvectors of $\mathbf{H}_t$ corresponding to the p largest eigenvalues. After projecting $\mathbf{A}^T$ onto these eigenvectors, we have

$$\mathbf{Y}_k = (\mathbf{A} - \overline{\mathbf{A}})^T \mathbf{v}_k, \ k = 1, 2, \cdots, p \tag{5}$$

Let $\mathbf{V} = [\mathbf{v}_1, \cdots, \mathbf{v}_p]$ and $\mathbf{C}^T = [\mathbf{Y}_1, \cdots, \mathbf{Y}_p]$, then we have

$$\mathbf{C}^T = (\mathbf{A} - \overline{\mathbf{A}})^T \mathbf{V} \text{ and } \mathbf{C} = \mathbf{V}^T (\mathbf{A} - \overline{\mathbf{A}}) \tag{6}$$

$\mathbf{C} = \mathbf{V}^T (\mathbf{A} - \overline{\mathbf{A}})$ contains the vertical 2DPCA features of image **A**.

Horizontal 2DPCA operates on image rows while Vertical 2DPCA operates on image columns, as image columns become image rows after the transpose operation.

3 Horizontal and Vertical 2DPCA Based Linear Discriminant Framework

This section discusses the Horizontal and Vertical 2DPCA based Discriminant Analysis (HVDA) method, which applies the YQC_r color configuration defined by combining the component images across two color spaces: YIQ and YC_bC_r.

3.1 Fisher Linear Discriminant Analysis

The between-class scatter matrix $\mathbf{S}_b$ and the within-class scatter matrix $\mathbf{S}_w$ are defined as follows [13]

$$\mathbf{S}_b = \frac{1}{M} \sum_{i=1}^{c} l_i (\mathbf{m}_i - \mathbf{m}_0)(\mathbf{m}_i - \mathbf{m}_0)^{\mathrm{T}} \tag{7}$$

$$\mathbf{S}_w = \frac{1}{M} \sum_{i=1}^{c} \frac{l_i}{l_i - 1} \sum_{j=1}^{l_i} (\mathbf{x}_{ij} - \mathbf{m}_i)(\mathbf{x}_{ij} - \mathbf{m}_i)^{\mathrm{T}} \tag{8}$$

where $\mathbf{x}_{ij}$ denotes the j-th training sample in class i; M is the total number of training samples, l_i is the number of training samples in class i; c is the number of classes; $\mathbf{m}_i$ is the mean of the training samples in class i; $\mathbf{m}_0$ is the mean across all training samples.

If the within-class scatter matrix $\mathbf{S}_w$ is nonsingular, the Fisher discriminant vectors $\boldsymbol{\varphi}_1, \boldsymbol{\varphi}_2, \cdots, \boldsymbol{\varphi}_d$ can be selected as the generalized eigenvectors of $\mathbf{S}_b$ and $\mathbf{S}_w$ corresponding to the d ($d \le c-1$) largest generalized eigenvalues, i.e., $\mathbf{S}_b \boldsymbol{\varphi}_j = \lambda_j \mathbf{S}_w \boldsymbol{\varphi}_j$, where $\lambda_1 \ge \lambda_2 \ge \cdots \ge \lambda_d$. These generalized eigenvectors can be obtained using the classical two-phase LDA algorithm [13].

In small sample size cases, the within-class scatter matrix $\mathbf{S}_w$ is singular because the training sample size is smaller than the dimension of the image vector space. To address this issue of LDA, A PCA plus LDA strategy, represented by Fisherfaces [3], was developed. In Fisherfaces, $N-c$ principal components are chosen in the PCA phase and then LDA is implemented in the $N-c$ dimensional PCA space.

To improve the generalization performance of the Fisherfaces method, the Enhanced Fisher Model (EFM) is developed [5]. The EFM method applies a criterion to choose the number of principal components in the PCA to avoid overfitting of the PCA plus LDA framework. In particular, a proper balance should be preserved between the *data energy* and the *eigenvalue magnitude* of the within-class scatter matrix. While the spectral energy should be preserved, the trailing eigenvalues of the within-class scatter matrix should not be too small in order to prevent the amplification of noise. It should be pointed out that this criterion is still applicable even when the within-class scatter matrix $\mathbf{S}_w$ is nonsingular.

3.2 Horizontal and Vertical 2DPCA Based Discriminant Analysis (HVDA)

In our algorithm, the horizontal feature matrix **B** derived by Horizontal 2DPCA and the vertical feature matrix **C** from Vertical 2DPCA are processed, respectively, by the EFM method for further feature extraction. The extracted features then apply the cosine similarity measure to calculate the similarity score between any pair of query and target images. After similarity score normalization, two kinds of normalized scores, i.e., the normalized scores from the horizontal discriminant features and the normalized scores from the vertical discriminant features, are fused at the classification level. The proposed HVDA framework is illustrated in Fig. 1. Some details on cosine similarity measure, score normalization and fusion strategy are presented below.

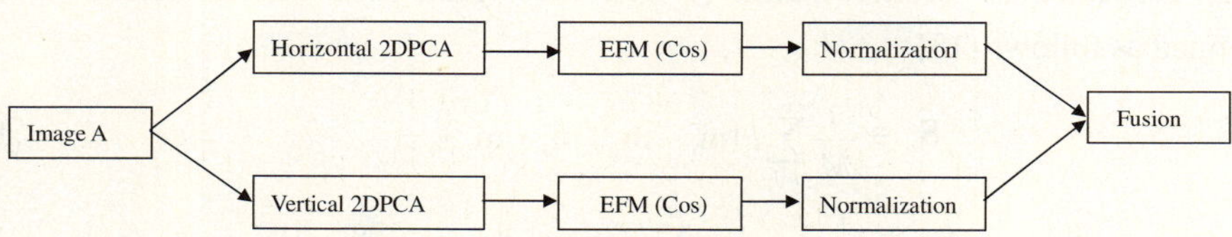

Fig. 1. Illustration of the proposed HVDA framework

The cosine similarity measure between two vectors $\mathbf{x}$ and $\mathbf{y}$ is defined as follows:

$$\delta_{\cos}(\mathbf{x},\mathbf{y}) = \frac{\mathbf{x}^T\mathbf{y}}{\|\mathbf{x}\|\cdot\|\mathbf{y}\|} \tag{9}$$

where $\|\cdot\|$ is the notation of Euclidian norm.

Suppose that there are M target images $\mathbf{x}_1, \mathbf{x}_2, \cdots \mathbf{x}_M$. For a given query image $\mathbf{y}$, we can obtain a similarity score vector $\mathbf{s} = [\mathbf{s}_1, \mathbf{s}_2, \cdots, \mathbf{s}_M]^T$ by calculating the Cosine similarity measure between each pair of $\mathbf{x}_i$ and $\mathbf{y}$. Based on the horizontal discriminant features, we can obtain the horizontal similarity score vector $\mathbf{s}^h$ and, based on vertical discriminant features, we can calculate the vertical similarity score vector $\mathbf{s}^v$. Each score vector is normalized by means of the z-score normalization technique [8]. The normalized scores are as follows:

$$\mathbf{s}_i^{new} = \frac{\mathbf{s}_i - \mu}{\sigma}, \tag{10}$$

where μ is the mean of $\mathbf{s}_1, \mathbf{s}_2, \cdots, \mathbf{s}_M$ and σ is their standard deviation. After score normalization, the horizontal similarity score vector $\mathbf{s}^h$ and the vertical similarity score vector $\mathbf{s}^v$ are fused using the sum rule, that is, the final similarity score vector is $\mathbf{s}^h + \mathbf{s}^v$.

3.3 HVDA in YQC_r Color Space

Recent research on color spaces for face recognition reveals that some color configurations, such as YQC_r, can significantly improve the FRGC baseline performance [7]. YQC_r is defined by combining the component images across two color spaces: YIQ and YC_bC_r.

YIQ is a color space formerly used in the National Television System Committee (NTSC) television standard [14]. The Y component represents the luminance information and I and Q represent the chrominance information. Remember that in the YUV color space, the U and V components can be viewed as x and y coordinates within the color space. I and Q can be viewed as a second pair of axes on the same graph, rotated 33° clockwise. Therefore, IQ and UV represent different coordinate systems on the same plane. The YIQ system is intended to take advantage of human color-response characteristics. YIQ is derived from the corresponding RGB space as follows:

$$\begin{bmatrix} Y \\ I \\ Q \end{bmatrix} = \begin{bmatrix} 0.2990 & 0.5870 & 0.1140 \\ 0.5957 & -0.2745 & -0.3213 \\ 0.2115 & -0.5226 & 0.3111 \end{bmatrix} \begin{bmatrix} R \\ G \\ B \end{bmatrix} \tag{11}$$

The YC_bC_r color space is developed as a part of the ITU-R Recommendation B.T. 601 for digital video standard and television transmissions [14]. It is a scaled and offset version of the YUV color space. Y is the luminance component and C_b and C_r are the blue and red chrominance components, respectively. YC_bC_r is derived from the corresponding RGB space as follows:

$$\begin{bmatrix} Y \\ C_b \\ C_r \end{bmatrix} = \begin{bmatrix} 16 \\ 128 \\ 128 \end{bmatrix} + \begin{bmatrix} 65.4810 & 128.5530 & 24.9660 \\ -37.7745 & -74.1592 & 111.9337 \\ 111.9581 & -93.7509 & -18.2072 \end{bmatrix} \begin{bmatrix} R \\ G \\ B \end{bmatrix} \tag{12}$$

Our HVDA method first works on the three color components Y, Q and C_r to derive the similarity scores, and then fuses the normalized similarity scores using the sum rule.

4 Experiments

We evaluate our HVDA method using the FRGC version 2 database and the associated Biometric Experimentation Environment (BEE) [10]. The FRGC version 2 database contains 12,776 training images, 16,028 controlled target images, and 8,014 uncontrolled query images for the Experiment 4. The controlled images have good image quality, while the uncontrolled images display poor image quality, such as large illumination variations, low resolution of the face region, and possible blurring. It is these uncontrolled factors that pose the grand challenge to the face recognition performance. The BEE system provides a computational-experimental environment to support a challenge problem in face recognition or biometrics, which allows the description and distribution of experiments in a common format. The BEE system uses the PCA method that has been optimized for large scale problems as a baseline algorithm, which applies the *whitened cosine distance* measure for its nearest neighbor classifier [10]. The BEE baseline algorithm shows that Experiment 4, which is designed for indoor controlled single still image versus uncontrolled single still image, is the most challenging FRGC experiment. We therefore choose FRGC Experiment 4 to evaluate our method. In our experiment, the face region of each image is first cropped from the original high-resolution still images and resized to 64x64. Fig. 2 shows some example images used in our experiments.

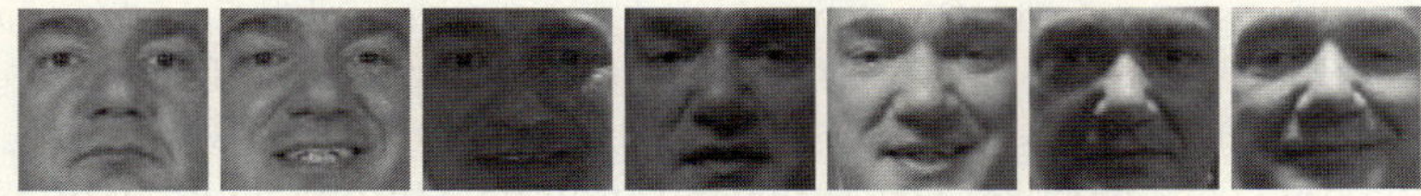

Fig. 2. Example cropped images in FRGC version 2

According to the FRGC protocol, the face recognition performance is reported using the Receiver Operating Characteristic (ROC) curves, which plot the Face Verification Rate (FVR) versus the False Accept Rate (FAR). The ROC curves are automatically generated by the BEE system when a similarity matrix is input to the system. In particular, the BEE system generates three ROC curves, ROC I, ROC II, and ROC III, corresponding to images collected within semesters, within a year and between semesters, respectively [12]. The similarity matrix stores the similarity score of every query image versus target image pair. So, the size of the similarity matrix is $T \times Q$, where T is the number of target images and Q is the number of query images.

The proposed HVDA method is trained using the standard training set of the FRGC Experiment 4. In the 2DPCA phase, we choose q=19 in horizontal 2DPCA transform and p=19 in vertical 2DPCA transform, respectively. In the EFM phase, we choose 1000 principal components in the PCA step and 220 discriminant features in the LDA step. The resulting similarity matrix is analyzed by the BEE system and the three ROC curves generated are shown in Fig. 3. The verification rates (%) when the False Accept Rate is 0.1% are listed in Table 1. Table 1 also includes the verification rates reported in recent papers for comparison [7, 9]. These results show that the

HVDA method achieves better face verification performance than those reported before. In addition, we can see that the fusion of Horizontal 2DPCA based Discriminant Analysis (HDA) and Vertical 2DPCA based Discriminant Analysis (VDA) can significantly improve the verification performance.

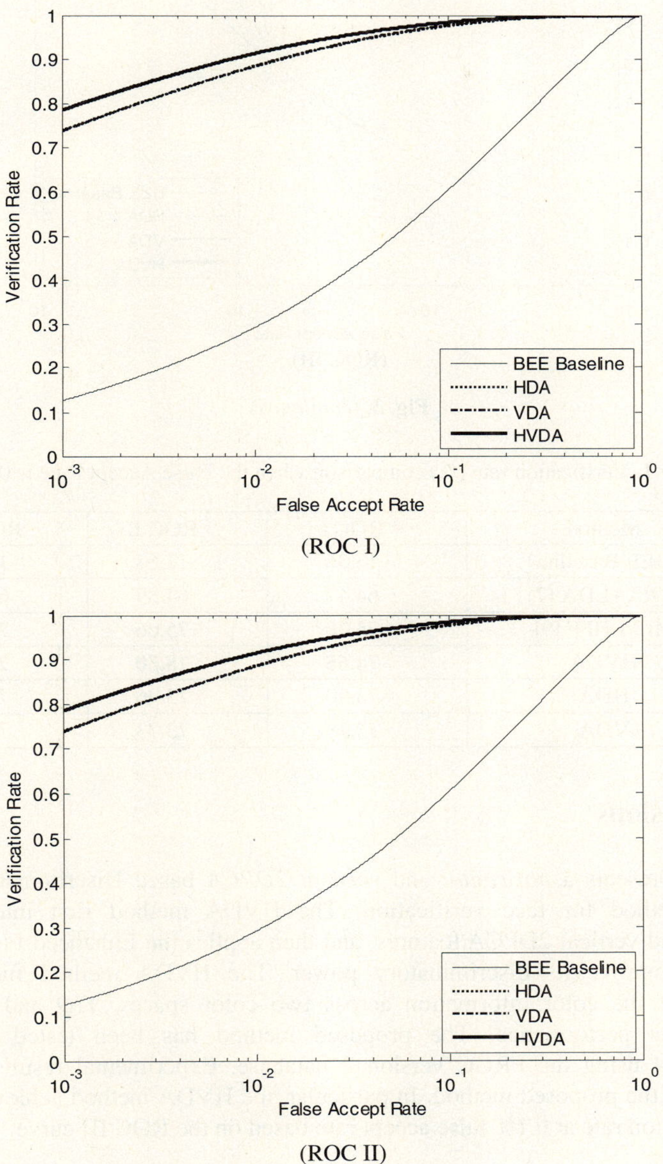

Fig. 3. ROC curves corresponding to the HDA, VDA, and HVDA methods and the BEE Baseline algorithm

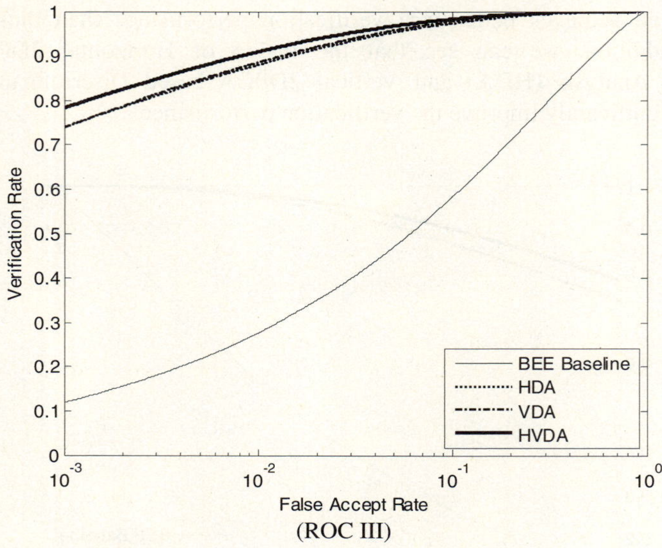

(ROC III)

Fig. 3. (*continued*)

Table 1. Verification rate (%) comparison when the False Accept Rate is 0.1%

Method	ROC I	ROC II	ROC III
BEE Baseline	13.36	12.67	11.86
YQC_r +LDA [7]	64.47	64.89	65.21
MFM-HFF [9]	75.70	75.06	74.33
HVDA	**78.65**	**78.50**	**78.24**
HDA	73.90	73.96	73.89
VDA	73.38	73.73	73.97

5 Conclusions

This paper presents a *horizontal* and *vertical 2DPCA* based Discriminant Analysis (HVDA) method for face verification. The HVDA method first integrates the horizontal and vertical 2DPCA features, and then applies the Enhanced Fisher Model (EFM) to improve its discriminatory power. The HVDA method further takes advantage of the color information across two color spaces, *YIQ* and YC_bC_r for enhancing its performance. The proposed method has been tested on FRGC Experiment 4 using the FRGC version 2 database. Experimental results show the feasibility of the proposed method. In particular, the HVDA method achieves 78.24% face verification rate at 0.1% false accept rate based on the ROC III curve.

Acknowledgments. This work was partially supported by the NJCST/NIJT grant, and by Award No. 2006-IJ-CX-K033 awarded by the National Institute of Justice, Office of Justice Programs, US Department of Justice. Dr. Yang was also supported by the National Science Foundation of China under Grants No. 60503026, No. 60472060, No. 60473039, and No. 60632050.

References

1. Sirovich, L., Kirby, M.: Low-dimensional procedure for characterization of human faces. J. Optical Soc. Of Am. 4, 519–524 (1987)
2. Turk, M., Pentland, A.: Eigenfaces for recognition. J. Cognitive Neuroscience 3(1), 71–86 (1991)
3. Belhumeur, P.N., Hespanha, J.P., Kriengman, D.J.: Eigenfaces vs. Fisherfaces: Recognition using class specific linear projection. IEEE Trans. Pattern Anal. Machine Intell. 19(7), 711–720 (1997)
4. Yang, J., Zhang, D., Frangi, A.F., Yang, J.-Y.: Two-Dimensional PCA: a New Approach to Face Representation and Recognition. IEEE Transaction on Pattern Analysis and Machine Intelligence 26(1), 131–137 (2004)
5. Liu, C., Wechsler, H.: Robust coding schemes for indexing and retrieval from large face databases. IEEE Trans. Image Processing 9(1), 132–137 (2000)
6. Liu, C.: Capitalize on Dimensionality Increasing Techniques for Improving Face Recognition Grand Challenge Performance. IEEE Trans. Pattern Analysis and Machine Intelligence 28(5), 725–737 (2006)
7. Shih, P., Liu, C.: Improving the Face Recognition Grand Challenge Baseline Performance Using Color Configurations Across Color Spaces. In: IEEE International Conference on Image Processing (ICIP 2006), Atlanta, GA, October 8-11 (2006)
8. Jain, A., Nandakumar, K., Ross, A.: Score normalization in multimodel biometric systems. Pattern Recognition 38, 2270–2285 (2005)
9. Hwang, W., Park, G., Lee, J.: Multiple face model of hybrid Fourier feature for large face image set. In: Proc. IEEE Conf. Computer Vision and Pattern Recognition. IEEE Computer Society Press, Los Alamitos (2006)
10. Phillips, P.J., Flynn, P.J., Scruggs, T., Bowyer, K.W., Chang, J., Hoffman, K., Marques, J., Min, J., Worek, W.: Overview of the Face Recognition Grand Challenge. In: Proc. IEEE Conf. Computer Vision and Pattern Recognition. IEEE Computer Society Press, Los Alamitos (2005)
11. Phillips, P.J., Flynn, P.J., Scruggs, T., Bowyer, W.W.: Preliminary Face Recognition Grand Challenge Results. In: Proceedings of the 7th International Conference on Automatic Face and Gesture Recognition (FGR'06) (2006)
12. Phillips, P.J.: FRGC Third Workshop Presentation. In: FRGC Workshop, (February 2005)
13. Fukunaga, K.: Introduction to Statistical Pattern Recognition, 2nd edn. Academic Press, London (1990)
14. Buchsbaum, W.H.: Color TV Servicing, 3rd edn. Prentice Hall, Englewood Cliffs, NJ (1975)

Video-Based Face Tracking and Recognition on Updating Twin GMMs

Li Jiangwei and Wang Yunhong

Intelligence Recognition and Image Processing Laboratory,
Beihang University, Beijing, P.R. China
{jwli,yhwang}@buaa.edu.cn

Abstract. Online learning is a very desirable capability for video-based algorithms. In this paper, we propose a novel framework to solve the problems of video-based face tracking and recognition by online updating twin GMMs. At first, considering differences between the tasks of face tracking and face recognition, the twin GMMs are initialized with different rules for tracking and recognition purposes, respectively. Then, given training sequences for learning, both of them are updated with some online incremental learning algorithm, so the tracking performance is improved and the class-specific GMMs are obtained. Lastly, Bayesian inference is incorporated into the recognition framework to accumulate the temporal information in video. Experiments have demonstrated that the algorithm can achieve better performance than some well-known methods.

Keywords: Face Tracking, Face Recognition, Online Updating, Bayesian Inference, GMM.

1 Introduction

Recently, more and more research interesting has been transferred from image-based face detection and recognition [1-2] to video-based face tracking and recognition [3-5]. Compared to image-based face technologies, multiple frames and temporal continuity contained in video facilitate face tracking and recognition. However, large variations of image resolution and pose, poor video quality and partial occlusion are the main problems video-based face technologies have encountered. To deal with these difficulties, many researchers have presented their solutions [3-5], which adopted various strategies to fully use temporal and spatial information in video.

The capability of online learning is very favorable for video-based algorithms. The models can be updated when new sample comes, so the memory is saved without preserving the sample, and the model turns to fit current and future patterns with the time elapsing. Among all video-based face technologies, only a few algorithms [3,4] introduced the updating mechanism into their framework.

In this paper, we propose a new framework for video-based face tracking and recognition based on online updating Gaussian Mixture Models (GMMs). At any instance, we use the new sample to update two GMMs, called as "twin GMMs". As

S.-W. Lee and S.Z. Li (Eds.): ICB 2007, LNCS 4642, pp. 848–857, 2007.

shown in Fig. 1, in the training stage, according to different requirements of face tracking and recognition, we design twin initial models, namely tracking model and recognition model. Then, use the tracking model to locate the face of the incoming frame. At each instance, the detected face is learned to update both twin models with different updating rules. By learning all frames in the sequence, the recognition model gradually evolves to the class-specific model, and the tracking model becomes more powerful by merging the learned samples into its framework. In the testing stage, given the testing video, the recognition score is calculated by accumulating the current likelihood and previous posteriors using Bayesian inference.

For most traditional methods, they train gallery models in batch modes and then use it to perform recognition. Contrastively, with online sequential updating, our learning mechanism saves memory loads and is more adaptive for real-time applications. Moreover, the recognition approach based on Bayesian inference effectively captures temporal information. Experimental results show that our algorithm can effectively track and recognize faces in video even with large variations.

Note the differences between our algorithm and some existing updating methods [3, 4]. In our paper, we emphasize the necessity of designing different models to deal with different tasks. Compared to [3, 4], we note the distinctions between face tracking and recognition, so twin models with various initialization and learning strategies for each task are proposed. It is fairly a delicate learning mechanism. Furthermore, with our learning mechanism, the evolved class-specific models for distinct individuals have different forms. These advantages make the algorithm flexible.

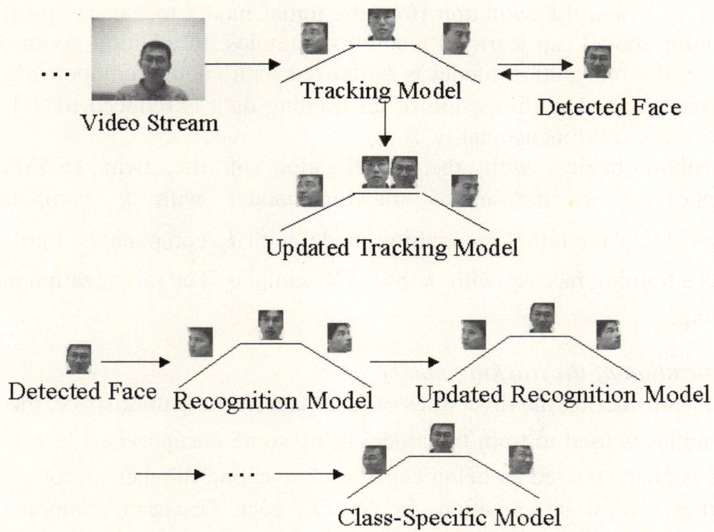

Fig. 1. Online updating twin models

2 The Framework of Updating

GMM is a special form of HMM and have been well studied for many years. The GMM assumes the probability that the observed data belongs to this model takes the following form:

$$G(\vec{x}) = p(\vec{x} \mid \lambda_l) = \sum_{m=1}^{l} \alpha_m N(\vec{x}, \mu_m, \theta_m) \tag{1}$$

where $N(\vec{x}, \mu_m, \theta_m)$ denotes the multi-dimensional normal distribution with the mean μ_m and the covariance matrix θ_m, and α_m is the weight of the corresponding component, satisfying:

$$\alpha_m \geq 0, m = 1, \cdots, l, \text{ and } \sum_{m=1}^{l} \alpha_m = 1 \tag{2}$$

In the following, we begin with the initialization of the twin GMMs. Then will show how to learn the incoming sample to update the twin models in the training stage.

2.1 Initialization

Motivated by the distinctions between face tracking and face recognition, it is necessary to initialize the face tracking model and the face recognition model in different ways. For face tracking, considering there exists numerous variations in face pattern, the initial tracking model must train on a large scale of data samples. For face recognition, to fasten the evolution from the initial model to a class-specific model, the recognition model can learn on much less samples. In addition, to ensure proper convergence, the recognition model is initialized with enough components to spread over the face space. The dimension of all training data is reduced to d by PCA to prevent "the curse of dimensionality".

The method begins with the initialization of the twin GMMs. Denote $G_T(\vec{x}) = p(\vec{x} \mid \lambda_{l_1})$ as the initial tracking model with l_1 components and $G_R(\vec{x}) = p(\vec{x} \mid \lambda_{l_2})$ the initial recognition model with l_2 components. Further assume there exists a training face set with p (p>5000) samples. The initialization proceeds as the following:

- ***Initialization of the tracking model***

For $G_T(\vec{x})$, considering the diversities of face patterns in feature space, the whole set with p samples is used to train the model using some unsupervised learning method [6], which is characterized as being capable of selecting number of components and not requiring careful initialization. In $G_T(\vec{x})$, each Gaussian component can be treated as a pose manifold. Since it is random for a face in video being a certain pose, we discard the learned weight coefficients for all components and fix them as $1/l_1$, namely all components in $G_T(\vec{x})$ are equally weighted. So the initial parameters of

$G_T(\vec{x})$ are $\{l_1, \frac{1}{l_1}, \mu_{(m,0)}, \theta_{(m,0)}\}$, where l_1 is the number of components, and $\frac{1}{l_1}$, $\mu_{(m,0)}$ and $\theta_{(m,0)}$ are initial weight, mean and covariance of each Gaussian components.

- ***Initialization of the recognition model:***

For $G_R(\vec{x})$, we randomly select l_2 points from the set as the mean vectors, and initialize the weight $\alpha_{(m,0)} = 1/l_2$. To weaken the influence of the training data on class-specific models, only $q(q << p)$ samples are selected from the set to compute the initial covariance matrix:

$$\theta_{(m,0)} = \frac{1}{10d} trace(\frac{1}{q}\sum_{i=1}^{q}(\vec{x}_i - m)(\vec{x}_i - m)^T)I \tag{3}$$

where $m = \frac{1}{q}\sum_{i=1}^{q}\vec{x}_i$ is the mean of the selected samples and I is the d-dimensional identity matrix. So the initial parameters of $G_R(\vec{x})$ are $\{l_2, \alpha_{(m,0)}, \mu_{(m,0)}, \theta_{(m,0)}\}$, where l_2 is the number of components, and $\alpha_{(m,0)}$, $\mu_{(m,0)}$ and $\theta_{(m,0)}$ are initial weight, mean and covariance of each Gaussian components.

Generally, as face variations of an individual are much less than variations of all individuals, the number of Gaussian components in the initial tracking model should be more than that in the initial recognition model, i.e., $l_1 > l_2$. This is beneficial for the fast evolution of $G_R(\vec{x})$ from initial recognition model to class-specific models as well.

2.2 Updating Process

In the training stage, with the initial tracking model $G_T(\vec{x})$, we can use the model to continuously track the face. Denote $\{I_0, \cdots, I_t, \cdots I_N\}_i$ the ith incoming video sequence. The updating process can be expressed as:

$$G_T(\vec{x}) \oplus \{I_0, \cdots I_t, \cdots, I_N\}_i \ -> G_T(\vec{x}), \ G_R(\vec{x}) \oplus \{I_0, \cdots I_t, \cdots, I_N\}_i \ -> G_i(\vec{x}) \tag{4}$$

where $\oplus$ is the operator of incremental updating, and $G_i(\vec{x})$ is the class-specific model for the ith sequence.

In video, the dynamics between frames can facilitate the tracking process. It is formulated as a Gaussian function:

$$\mathrm{K}(s_t, s_{t-1}) = \exp\{-(s_t - s_{t-1})C_{t-1}^{-1}(s_t - s_{t-1})\} \tag{5}$$

where s_t is the current state variable, including face position and pose information. From the current frame I_t, according to Eq.(5), draw y image patches around the previous position of the detected face as face candidates and normalize them into d-dimensional vectors $\{F_{(1,t)},\cdots,F_{(r,t)},\cdots,F_{(y,t)}\}$. The face is detected with maximum likelihood rule:

$$F_t^* = \arg\max_i G_T(F_{(i,t)}) \tag{6}$$

After we obtain the face, we use it to update both models. Note that the twin models should be updated in different ways:

- ***Updating of the tracking model:***

Give the model $G_T(\vec{x})$ with the parameter $\{l,\frac{1}{l},\mu_{(m,t-1)},\theta_{(m,t-1)}\}$ at time $t-1$, where m is the *mth* Gaussian component. For the new sample F_t^*, we first find its ownership:

$$o_{(m,t)}(F_t^*) = N(F_t^*,\mu_{(m,t-1)},\theta_{(m,t-1)}),\quad m^* = \arg\max_m o_{(m,t)}(F_t^*) \tag{7}$$

In Eq.(7), the probability of F_t^* in the m^*th component is largest. All weights keep invariant, and only update the parameters of the m^* component with the rate λ_T:

$$\varsigma = F_t^* - \mu_{(m^*,t-1)},\quad \mu_{(m^*,t)} = \mu_{(m^*,t-1)} + \lambda_T o_{(m^*,t)}(F_t^*)\varsigma$$

$$\text{and } \theta_{(m^*,t)} = \theta_{(m^*,t-1)} + \lambda_T o_{(m^*,t)}(F_t^*)(\varsigma\varsigma^T - \theta_{(m^*,t-1)}) \tag{8}$$

To facilitate face tracking in current video and simultaneously avoid over-fitting, we keep the weights of all components invariant and only update the mean and the covariance of the component with highest ownership score. These will prevent the model converging to a class-specific model so as to still keep good tracking performance when the following video comes.

- ***Updating of the recognition model:***

For $G_R(\vec{x})$, we use some existing technique for updating. There are several incremental learning methods for GMM [7,8], while only [8] can update the model one by one. So the method in [8] is used.

Assume the parameter is $\{l_{t-1},\alpha_{(m,t-1)},\mu_{(m,t-1)},\theta_{(m,t-1)}\}$ at time $t-1$. As the new data F_t^* comes, for each component, we first calculate its ownership confidence score:

$$o_{(m,t)}(F_t^*) = \alpha_{(m,t-1)} N(F_t^*,\mu_{(m,t-1)},\theta_{(m,t-1)}) / G_R(\vec{x}) \tag{9}$$

Then use the score to update the corresponding weight:

$$\alpha_{(m,t)} = \alpha_{(m,t-1)} + \lambda_R\left(\frac{o_{(m,t)}(F_t^*)}{1-l_{t-1}C} - \alpha_{(m,t-1)}\right) - \lambda_R \frac{C}{1-l_{t-1}C} \tag{10}$$

In Eq.(10), λ_R determines the updating rate, and $C = \lambda N/2$ is a constant, where $N = d + d(d+1)/2$ is the number of parameters specifying each mixture component.

Check all $\alpha_{(m,t)}$. If $\alpha_{(m,t)} < 0$, it means too few data belong to the component m, so cancel this component, set $l_t = l_{t-1} - 1$ and renormalize $\alpha_{(m,t)}$. The remaining parameters are updated as:

$$\varsigma = F_t^* - \mu_{(m,t-1)},\ \mu_{(m,t)} = \mu_{(m,t-1)} + \lambda_R \frac{o_{(m,t)}(F_t^*)}{\alpha_{(m,t-1)}} \varsigma,$$

$$\text{and } \theta_{(m,t)} = \theta_{(m,t-1)} + \lambda_R \frac{o_{(m,t)}(F_t^*)}{\alpha_{(m,t-1)}} (\varsigma\varsigma^T - \theta_{(m,t-1)}) \tag{11}$$

Then use the new parameter $\{l_t, \alpha_{(m,t)}, \mu_{(m,t)}, \theta_{(m,t)}\}$ for next updating.

2.3 Updating Results

Except for above updating rules, note the following additions: (1) For the face recognition model, to learn more intra-personal patterns and tolerate face location error, at any instance, the model is updated with more generated virtual samples by locating the face with errors and mirror operation. (2) Two models should be updated with different updating rate. Generally, the updating rate of the face recognition model is much faster than that of the face tracking model, i.e., $\lambda_T << \lambda_R$. Given limited samples, this will accelerate the evolution from the face recognition model to class-specific models.

With this framework, both the twin models are updated gradually. As in learning, the detection capability of the tracking model is enhanced. The parameters are adjusted to fit the current video data, and this will benefit the following tracking. The recognition model evolves to the class-specific model. With its own initial and updating rules, the recognition model can converge to proper face models. Fig.2 shows an example of evolution result given an image sequence. The left image is the initial recognition model and the right is the evolved class-specific model. The result looks encouraging for good fitness of video data. Compared to those existing methods [3,4], the component number in a class-specific model is not pre-fixed and totally determined by the learned video data. So our updating mechanism is flexible to model the real video image data distribution.

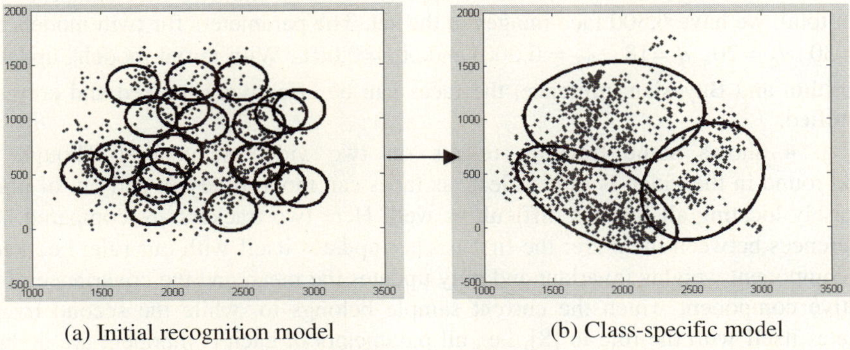

(a) Initial recognition model (b) Class-specific model

Fig. 2. An online updating example

3 Recognition Framework

Repeatedly applying the algorithm to J sequences $\{1,\cdots,i,\cdots,J\}$, we can obtain J class-specific GMMs $\{G_1(\vec{x}),\cdots,G_i(\vec{x}),\cdots,G_J(\vec{x})\}$. In the testing stage, we incorporate temporal continuity into the recognition framework. By assuming constant identity, using time recursion and Bayes rule, when the tracked face F_t^* comes, its identity i^* is determined with the evolution of posterior probability:

$$\begin{aligned} i^* &= \arg\max_i p(i \mid F_t^*, F_{0:t-1}^*) \\ &= \eta \arg\max_i p(F_t^* \mid i) \cdot p(i \mid F_{t-1}^*, F_{0:t-2}^*) \\ &= \eta \arg\max_i G_i(F_t^*) \cdot p(i \mid F_{t-1}^*, F_{0:t-2}^*) \end{aligned} \tag{11}$$

In the above framework, we do not use the priors of personal pose transitions to improve recognition performance as in [4]. We argue that these statistical priors are too reliant on the dynamics of head moving of the training video to be used as a reliable cue when recognize the testing video. Also, we can use the sample F_t^* to update both the tracking model and the i^* th class-specific model based on the confidence measure of the recognition result.

4 Experimental Results

In this section, we will evaluate both tracking and recognition performance with the described algorithm on our collected database. The database is composed of 56 video sequences of 25 people. Each person has at least two sequences, one for gallery and one for probe. The remaining 6 sequences are used to train both the twin initial models. Some examples of the database are shown in Fig. 3.

When train initial twin models, we manually crop the face and generate the mirror image from the remaining 6 sequences, then normalize them into 23×28 pixels. In addition, we enlarge the training set by appending some standard face databases into it. In total, we have 6,500 face images in the set. The parameters for twin models are: $l_1 = 30$, $l_2 = 20$, $d = 18$, $\lambda_T = 0.0001$ and $\lambda_R = 0.001$. With initial models, updating algorithm and Bayesian inference, the faces can be effectively tracked and correctly identified.

Fig. 4 shows some tracking results on two video sequences. Though the background in the video is rather clear, as faces can move freely in and out of plane, precisely locating all faces is difficult as well. Here two trackers are compared. The differences between them are: the first tracker updates itself with our rule, i.e., keeps the component weights invariant and only updates the mean and the covariance of the relative component which the current sample belongs to, while the second tracker updates itself with the rule in [8], i.e., all parameters of each component are updated with the learning of samples. As shown in Fig.4, both of two trackers can properly detect the faces of the first video. When tracks the second sequence, only the first tracker still keeps good performance. This is because with the learning rule of the first tracker, it can fit the current video data by adjusting the parameters of the relative component, and simultaneously, it avoids over-fitting by keeping all component weights invariant and only adjusting the relative component. Compared to the first tracker, after learning one sequence, the second tracker tunes its parameters to completely cater for the learned sequence, so fails to be robust to the next sequence. This experiment indicates the importance of designing different rules for the initialization and updating of the tracking model.

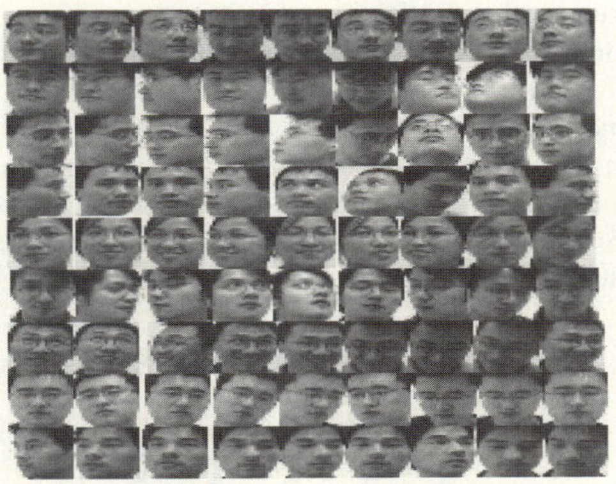

Fig. 3. Some examples in the database

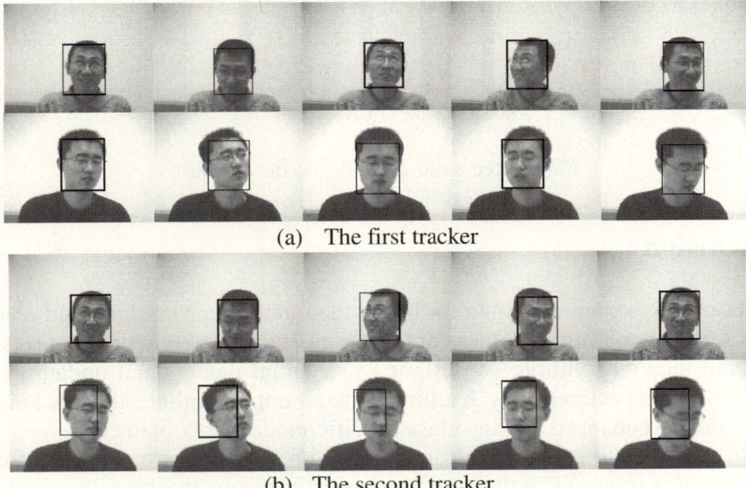

(a) The first tracker

(b) The second tracker

Fig. 4. Some tracking results on the database

The next experiment is to verify the recognition performance of our algorithm. The testing database contains 7852 frames from 25 sequences. The faces are detected using our proposed tracker. Five frame-based algorithms are compared: our algorithm BGMM (class-specific GMMs with Bayesian inference), GMM (class-specific GMMs without Bayesian inference), PCA, LDA and NN (Nearest neighbor). We take the optimal number of eigenvectors for PCA and LDA, namely 643 and 24, respectively. The experimental results are shown in Fig. 5, where the recognition rates for all methods are listed on the top. From the experimental results, we can note that:

(1) Compared to GMM, PCA, LDA and NN, our algorithm achieves best recognition rate of 94.0%. It indicates the success of our algorithm. The initial recognition model can converge to proper class-specific model after the training sequence is learned. Furthermore, the application of Bayesian inference is important as well. It can accumulate historical recognition information.

(2) The recognition rate of GMM is slightly lower than that of PCA and LDA. It is mainly due to more parameters need to be estimated in GMM. However, on one hand, GMM can fit any complex video data distribution so have great potential to improve performance. On the other hand, the use of class-specific model based on GMM is reasonable as its component number is completely determined by the training data distribution. So GMM is used instead of subspace [4] for updating.

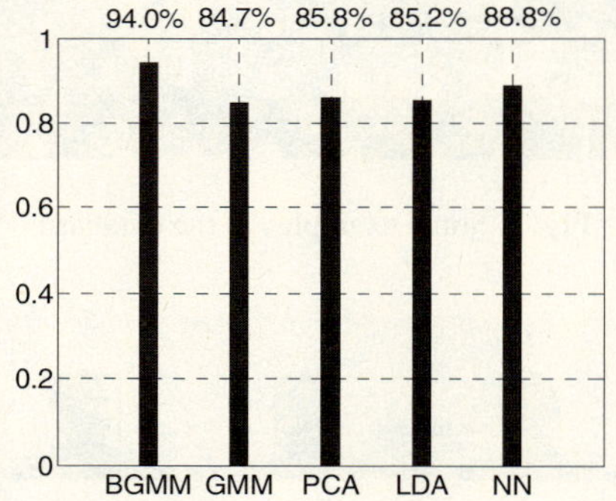

Fig. 5. Recognition results on the database

5 Conclusion

This paper has presented a method for both video-based face tracking and recognition based on GMM updating. We have noted the distinctions between the tasks of face tracking and face recognition, so designed two initial models and update them with different rules, respectively. By learning video samples online, the tracking model will be gradually enhanced and the class-specific models are obtained.

Note the samples in recognition can be used for updating as well. In the future, we will focus on this issue. With the current learning mechanism, the component number in GMM will decrease with time elapse. However, if necessary, some of them may have to be split to better fit the data. Another future issue is to develop the corresponding solution for this problem.

Acknowledgments. This work was supported by Program of New Century Excellent Talents in University, National Natural Science Foundation of China (No. 60575003, 60332010), Joint Project supported by National Science Foundation of China and Royal Society of UK (60710059), and Hi-Tech Research and Development Program of China (2006AA01Z133).

References

[1] Zhao, W., Chellappa, R., Rosenfeld, A., Phillips, P.J.: Face Recognition: A Literature Survey. Technical Reports of Computer Vision Laboratory of University of Maryland (2000)

[2] Li, S., Jain, A. (eds.): Handbook of Face Recognition. Springer, Heidelberg (2004)

[3] Liu, X., Chen, T.: Video-Based Face Recognition Using Adaptive Hidden Markov Models. In: Proceedings of Computer Vision and Pattern Recognition (2003)

[4] Lee, K.C., Kriegman, D.: Online Learning of Probabilistic Appearance Manifolds for Video-based Recognition and Tracking. In: Proceedings of Computer Vision and Pattern Recognition (2005)

[5] Aggarwal, G., Chowdhury, A., Chellappa, R.: A System Identification Approach for Video-based Face Recognition. In: Proceedings of International Conference on Pattern Recognition (2004)

[6] Figueiredo, M., Jain, A.K.: Unsupervised Learning of Finite Mixture Models. IEEE Transaction on Pattern Analysis and Machine Intelligence 24(3) (2002)

[7] Wu, J., Hua, X., Zhang, H., Zhang, B.: An Online-Optimized Incremental Learning Framework for Video Semantic Classification. ACM Multimedia (2004)

[8] Zivkovic, Z., Heijden, F.: Recursive Unsupervised learning of Finite Mixture Models. IEEE Transaction on Pattern Analysis and Machine Intelligence 26(5) (2004)

Fast Algorithm for Iris Detection

Jan Mazur

Institute of Telecommunications Teleinformatics and Acoustics,
Wroclaw University of Technology
Janiszewskiego 7/9, 50-372 Wroclaw, Poland
jan.mazur@pwr.wroc.pl

Abstract. The paper presents a fast algorithm for iris detection. The idea behind the algorithm comes from well-known Daugman's circular edge detector based on smoothed integro-differential operators. We use *binning* instead of convolution which is a bit more suitable for new generation of application processors (e.g. AP7000 from Atmel)and new CMOS imagers offering binning on demand. We also reformulated the inner function of the operator. These two steps allow for finding geometrical parameters of iris somewhat faster and with, we believe, comparable robustness offered by Daugman's solution. In the paper the idea, the implementation and some results of rough tests of the code running on AP7000 *application processor* are presented. Also, possible improvements are discussed.

Keywords: binning, iris segmentation, integro-differential operator.

1 Introduction

For many years biometrics based on iris pattern has been proving its reliability, stability and its relative robustness against spoofing. False acceptance ratio (FAR) and false rejection ratio (FRR) achieved with this method are still far lower than those achieved with other (even combined) methods of biometric identification/verification [1].

This causes that in many applications that need very high level of security iris based biometrics is considered to be very attractive and relatively cheap solution. Multi-media embedded platforms with mobile banking/trading seem to be the first non-PC solutions offering iris recognition on board. One of the first, if not the first device (PDA) on the market was Iris-SDi [8]. Also, last November OKI announced its new iris-based recognition technology and showed examples of general optical camera-equipped PDA and mobile phone that can utilize this technology [7]. For fast PCs running at 2GHz or more, efficiency of the algorithm processing an iris pattern is usually not an issue and even then manufacturers estimate the time of capturing the iris image within a range of a second and the same time range they reserve for iris identification [9].

Typical application processor used in most of mobile devices is running at a clock of only a couple of hundreds MHz and without hardware-implemented

S.-W. Lee and S.Z. Li (Eds.): ICB 2007, LNCS 4642, pp. 858–867, 2007.

floating-point arithmetics. This makes real difficulties with efficient and relatively cheap implementation of biometric algorithms. In case of iris recognition one of the most challenging task is to localize the iris precisely and within a reasonable time. Up to now a number of quite well-performing algorithms has been proposed [2][4][5], though they are designed with the assumption that the image frame is given and it resides in memory. This is quite obvious approach with CCD imagers, although modern CMOS imagers, especially those designed as a system on chip (SOC) devices, can offer additional processing power that can be utilized by a biometric algorithm. One of the function usually offered by CMOS imagers is *binning* that, combined with windowing property, can decrease resolution dynamically to allow for faster processing, if required.

Binning can roughly be considered as a kind of joined process of convolution using flat mask and decimation, what makes it much faster than typical decimation with non-flat mask as the latter requires multiplication-summation operations and binning requires summation operation only. This is the main reason we have used binning in reformulation of the well-known Daugman's circular edge detector based on compact (not to say elegant) in form integro-differential operator [2].

In this paper we present the idea of the proposed algorithm, we try then to explain why binning is justified and what are the pros and cons of such an approach. Also, we present some preliminary results and we point out to possible improvements as well as extensions of the proposed method.

2 Proposed Solution

2.1 Statement of the Problem

For locating an iris Daugman in [2] proposes an integro-differential operator in the following form

$$\max_{(r,x_0,y_0)} \left| G_\sigma(r) * \frac{\partial}{\partial r} \oint_{r,x_0,y_0} \frac{I(x,y)}{2\pi r} ds \right| \tag{1}$$

where (r, x_0, y_0) are searched parameters (radius r and center (x_0, y_0)), $G_\sigma(r)$ is a smoothing Gaussian function of scale σ and $I(x, y)$ is an input image. The operator works as a circular edge detector, blurred at a scale defined by σ, that searches for a maximum of the given integral derivative of the input image. The whole procedure is iterative in a space spanned by all three searched parameters r, x_0, y_0 and in successively finer scales of analysis. To speed up the computations and to make the above operator more robust Daugman proposes a slight nonlinear modification and reformulates the operator so that it eventually takes the following (discrete) form

$$\max_{(n\Delta r,x_0,y_0)} \left| \sum_k \left\{ \frac{(G_\sigma(a_0) - G_\sigma(a_1)) \sum_m I(b_x, b_y)}{\Delta r \sum_m I(c_x, c_y)} \right\} \right| \tag{2}$$

with $a_0 = (n-k)\Delta r$, $a_1 = (n-k-1)\Delta r$, $b_x = k\Delta r\cos(m\Delta\phi) + x_0$, $b_y = k\Delta r\sin(m\Delta\phi) + y_0$, $c_x = (k-2)\Delta r\cos(m\Delta\phi) + x_0$, and $c_y = (k-2)\Delta r\sin(m\Delta\phi) + y_0$,

In other words for each (r, x_0, y_0) we deal with two sums over m (in numerator and denominator) and one sum over k with one multiplication in it (in numerator). In the following section we show how to modify (simplify) expression 2 to obtain a faster and, we believe, simpler algorithm that should be more easily implementable in integer arithmetics or even (partially) in assembly code, if required.

2.2 Idea of the Proposed Solution

Basically our algorithm follows the scheme proposed by Daugman in that we construct a kind of circular edge detector, though we do not use convolution as such and coarse-to-fine strategy we implement as a series of binned images, like those shown in fig. 1. Each image in the series (except the input image $I^{(0)}$) is obtained from that of higher resolution by binning the source image with a specified binning factor so that $I^{(k)} = \mathcal{B}\{I^{(k-1)}, f\}$, where f is the binning factor. In the example given in fig.1 all three binning factors defining the transitions

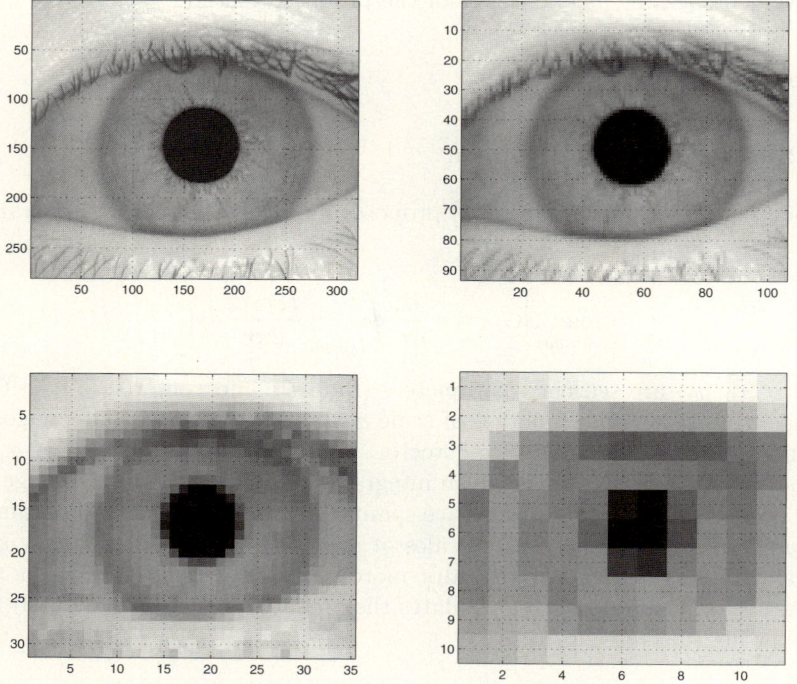

Fig. 1. An example series of binned images. The source image (upper left) comes from CASIA V1 database.

from one image to the other were set to 3, though in general their values can (or even should) be optimized for the best performance.

To implement circular edge detection we define a simple function

$$\sum_{(x,y)\in C} \langle \nabla I(x,y), \overrightarrow{r} \rangle \tag{3}$$

where $\langle .,. \rangle$ denotes inner product, $\nabla I(x,y)$ denotes the gradient of input image I at the point of analysis (x,y) and $\overrightarrow{r}$ is a vector rotating around the potential center (x_0, y_0) of the searched circle and defining the coordinates of the point of analysis as

$$x = x_m = x_0 + [r \cos \alpha_m] \tag{4}$$

$$y = y_m = y_0 + [r \sin \alpha_m] \tag{5}$$

where $\alpha_m = 2\pi m/M$ and M is the number of points taken into integration over the circle. Symbol $[\cdot]$ denotes integer value operator.

Gradient ∇I of the input image is defined by simple differences in two orthogonal directions and it is computed on demand as follows

$$\nabla I = (I_x, I_y) \tag{6}$$

$$I_x(x,y) = I(x+1,y) - I(x-1,y) \tag{7}$$

$$I_y(x,y) = I(x,y+1) - I(x,y-1) \tag{8}$$

The drawback of (3) is that it is up to the length $r = |\overrightarrow{r}|$ so that it prefers circles of larger radiuses. To avoid this problem we introduce vector $\overrightarrow{v} = \overrightarrow{r}/r$ so that $v = 1$ and the eventual version of (3) takes the form

$$\sum_{m=0}^{M-1} \langle \nabla I(x_m, y_m), \overrightarrow{v}_m \rangle \tag{9}$$

where $\overrightarrow{v}_m = (\cos \alpha_m, \sin \alpha_m)$.

The algorithm is as follows

1. Get an input image I.
2. Create a series of binned images so that $I_k = \mathcal{B}\{I_{k-1}, f\}$, $k = 1..K$
3. For I_K (i.e. the most binned image in the series) find a minimum and assume it is a center $(x_0^{(K)}, y_0^{(K)})$ of the pupil. This step may require smoothing with a small (3x3) Gaussian mask. Set $r^{(K)} = 2$; this is true for all CASIA images and in case the size of the most binned image is about 10 x 10 pixels. In other cases this value should be adjusted.
4. For each image $I^{(k)}$ $k = 0..K$ starting from K to 0 (i.e. from more to less binned images)

(a) construct a set of potential centers around the point defined by initial values obtained as the result of the previous stage

$$(x_0^{(k)}, y_0^{(k)}) \in C^{(k)} \tag{10}$$

where

$$C^{(k)} = \{(\hat{x}_0^{(k)} - [f_k/2])..(\hat{x}_0^{(k)} + [f_k/2])\} \times \{(\hat{y}_0^{(k)} - [f_k/2])..(\hat{y}_0^{(k)} + [f_k/2])\} \tag{11}$$

(b) construct a set of potential radiuses

$$r^{(k)} \in \{(\hat{r}^{(k)} - [f_k/2])..(\hat{r}^{(k)} + [f_k/2])\} \tag{12}$$

(c) find (we omit the upper k index for editorial purpose)

$$(\check{r}, \check{x}, \check{y}) = \arg\max_{(r,x,y)} \sum_{m=1}^{M} (I_x(x_m, y_m)\cos\alpha_m + I_y(x_m, y_m)\sin\alpha_m) \tag{13}$$

5. Recompute $(\check{r}^{(k)}, \check{x}^{(k)}, \check{y}^{(k)})$ to the finer grid using f_k

$$(\hat{r}^{(k-1)}, \hat{x}^{(k-1)}, \hat{y}^{(k-1)}) = f_k(\check{r}^{(k)}, \check{x}^{(k)}, \check{y}^{(k)}) \tag{14}$$

In much the same way we search for external radius of an iris and for the center if required.

In the following sections we present and discuss the results of some rough tests and we point out to possible enhancements of the proposed method.

3 Results

The algorithm presented in the previous section has been implemented in C and it runs on AP7000, a 133MHz application processor.

We have tested the algorithm using CASIA V1 and V3 database[1] [6]. The results of some preliminary tests are summarized in table 1. We assumed $M = 64$ (i.e. the number of points of integration) at all stages, but for $M = 32$ the quality seems to stay the same, so the real times can possibly be approximately half of those shown in the table. The results given concern inner and outer circle and their respective centers; they do not cover other processing sometimes performed like eyelid detection.

The most important parameter in the proposed algorithm to be set up is the area of potential centers of pupil. In the tests performed we assumed that the actual center of pupil is covered by the area of the darkest pixel in the frame of the lowest resolution (in our case: L_3). In higher resolution frame (one level up) this area is covered by a number of pixels that is up to the relevant binning factor. In our case this factor equals 3, hence nine pixels (a 3×3 matrix treated as a central

[1] Portions of the research in this paper use the CASIA-IrisV1 and CASIA-IrisV3 collected by the Chinese Academy of Sciences Institute of Automation (CASIA).

Table 1. Execution times obtained for three cases C_1, C_2 and C_3 (see text for explanation). *Tk* denotes the time required for computations on k-th level of binning.

	C_1	C_2	C_3
Binning	50ms	50ms	50ms
T1+T2+T3	10ms	20ms	30ms
T0	10ms	20ms	30ms

point and the neighborhood of ±1 pixel) in the frame L_2 matches the area of one pixel in L_3. This matrix is the set of potential centers of the pupil. At the same time we set the potential range of pupil's radius and for these three parameters the algorithm finds the best solution. Having found the new coordinates of the center of pupil and new radius, we iterate this scheme until we will find the searched parameters in the frame of highest resolution. Theoretically, it should be enough to take into account only those pixels in L_i that cover the area of exactly one pixel in L_{i+1}. Unfortunately, this is often not true because pixels in lower resolution are greatly affected by their respective neighbors and hence the area of potential centers in higher resolution frames should be generally larger than the area covered by one pixel in the lower resolution frame.

We considered the following three cases:

C1 - neighborhood of ±1 pixel for all stages,
C2 - neighborhood of ±2 pixel for stages L1 and L2
C3 - neighborhood of ±2 pixel for all stages

The times given in table 1 are very roughly estimated, especially for small values, as the program was running under linux and the least step of clock() function used to measure the execution time was 10ms.

In fig. 2a we show an example of image with found circles drawn. In fig. 2b we show the zoomed version of the image from the left with visible path of centers recomputed to the highest resolution (i.e. the original resolution of the image). In the given example centers of both inner and outer circle of iris were searched. It is, however possible to assume that pupil and iris are coaxial and finding of center of outer circle can be omitted. This, of course, reduces the total time of computations.

Two main issues have been addressed in the tests we have performed. One of the issues was the execution time. The other issue was the accuracy with which parameters are estimated. In the following figures we try to summarize the behavior of the proposed algorithm. In fig. 3 we show correct estimation of parameters in case of white noise added to the images. The proposed algorithm is relatively immune to additive noise. This feature can be important when working in low light conditions.

On the other hand, there is a number of clear images (i.e. with no noise added) for which the proposed algorithm found the parameters incorrectly. In the rough tests made on more than 400 images taken from CASIA V3-INT database about 20%-25% of images have been processed incorrectly. For these images the inner

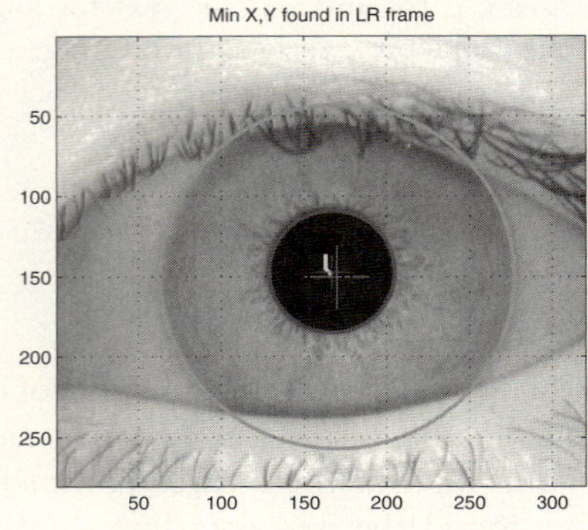

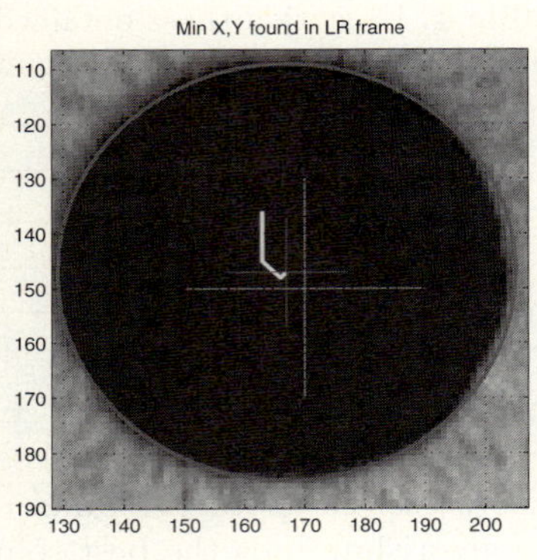

Fig. 2. An example of image with the inner and outer boundary drawn (a) and inner and outer centers drawn (b). The light curve shows the path of centers obtained in each of 4 stages of processing.

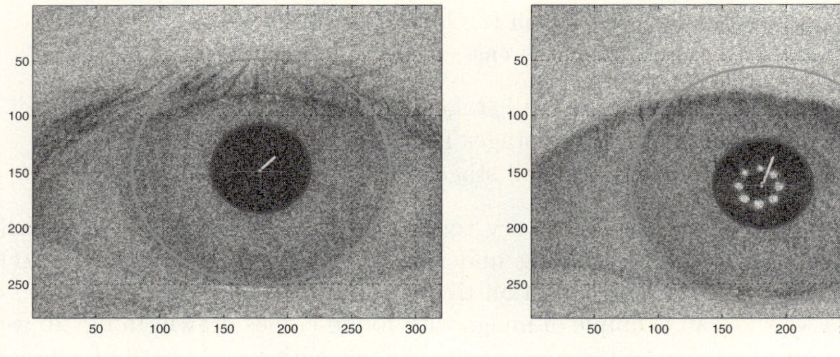

Fig. 3. An example of images from: a) CASIA V1 database b) CASIA V3-INT database with additive noise

or outer radius of the iris and/or centers of pupil have been found incorrectly. In fig. 4a the center of the pupil and pupil's radius have been found incorrectly. The initial guess of center coordinates is here affected by two factors: first, too bright pupil area due to existing reflections and second, relatively dark area of eyelashes. This moves the found center to the upper left part of the pupil and because of neighborhood values taken into account, this is too far from the real center of the pupil and the algorithm finds the best pupil's radius but only in the given range. The center of outer circle is only allowed to move a couple of pixels from the center of inner circle, so it also finds the radius incorrectly as the best solution in the given range. Note that in the proposed method initial estimation of pupil's center is critical. Due to reasonable constraints all parameters will be found incorrectly, if pupil's center can not be estimated with enough accuracy.

In fig. 4b only the inner radius of the iris has been found incorrectly. This is because in the mean sense (as we integrate) the set of lamps reflected from the pupil can be considered as relatively sharp edge; sharper than any other in the considered set of potential centers and radiuses. Note, that the real edge of the pupil can be even sharper but due to assumed constraints concerning the set of potential centers and the range of potential radiuses chosen in each frame of different resolutions, the one that was found is the best solution. To overcome this kind of errors we could set the minimal value of inner radius to be large enough or we could decrease the intensity of the reflection of lamps. In general, significant number of all the errors came from the fact that pupil reflecting the lamps could not be assumed to be the darkest area in the given image. Also, some nonlinear mappings of intensity could help to reduce the number of errors coming from reflections.

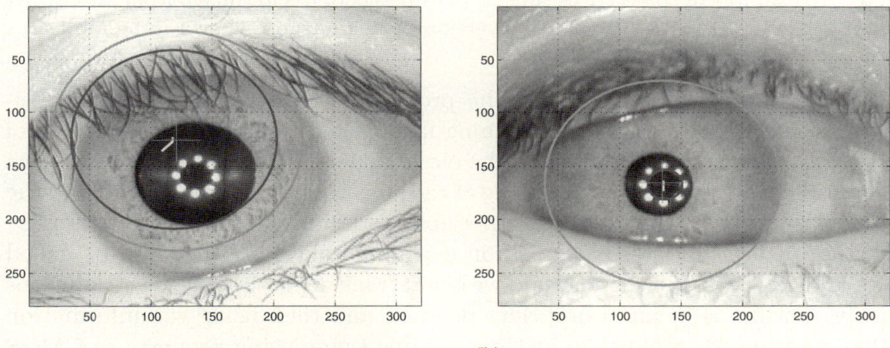

Fig. 4. An example of incorrect estimation of: a) the center of the pupil and - implicitly - the rest of parameters, b) inner radius of an iris,.

The tests concerning part of CASIA V3-LAMP database resulted in a slight smaller error rates of about 15%-20%. A reason for that is the reflections in images of CASIA V3-Lamp occupy relatively smaller area than reflections in CASIA-V3 int. An example of correct estimation of parameters from CASIA V3-Lamp and CASIA V3-Int has been shown in fig. 5a and fig. 5b, respectively.

4 Discussion

The results presented in table 1 shows that the most computationally intensive is binning. What can be done here to decrease the time of computations is to analyze the code and optimize it taking into account that in case of binning we basically run (almost) empty loops. The other possibility is to interface the imager and the processor with a small FPGA or even CPLD device utilizing its capability of running parallel computations. Also, application processors usually have some kind of hardware-implemented accelerator for fixed point or integer arithmetics that can be used to speed up the algorithm.

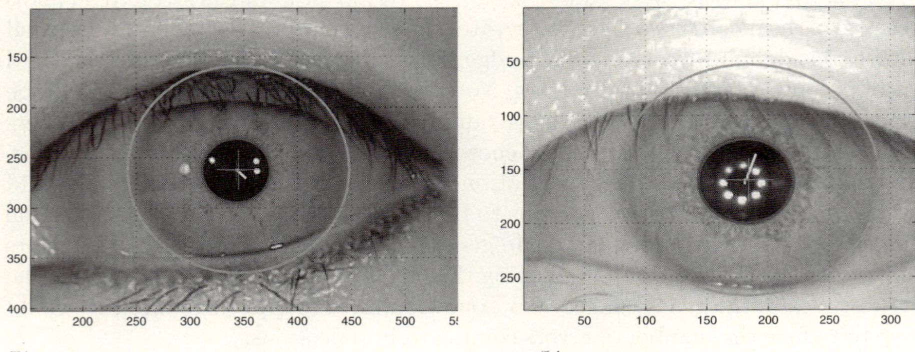

Fig. 5. An example of correctly estimated parameters of iris for image from: a) CASIA V3-LAMP, b) CASIA V3-INT (a noisy version of this image is shown in fig. 3b)

From algorithmic point of view, the proposed solution requires many optimizations, including the choice of binning factors and, implicitly, the number of stages, the number (M) of points on the circle taken for integration and the area of potential centers as well as the range of radiuses that are considered to find the best solution. Undersampling is also possible, especially in higher resolutions.

Further, a new method of aquisition can be employed, that could be called "track and get". With such a method we could track an iris in very low resolutions (quickly) until it is in an appropriate position and then using the information on that position we could take just part of one (windowing property of CMOS imagers), high resolution frame. This would reduce the number of binning stages and consequently the time required for making unneeded binned images. This would also reduce the time required for finding searched parameters. In effect, doing so, we would virtually move a part of the algorithm to the imager equipped with binning capabilities.

5 Conclusion

In the paper we have presented a fast algorithm for iris detection or, more precisely, for finding geometrical parameters of an iris. Basically the algorithm is a reformulation of Daugman's circular detector based on integro-differential operator [2]. The idea behind the proposed method comes from technology and it tries to utilize features of modern imagers usually equipped with so called *binning*, though it does not require an imager to have this function implemented. We also proposed a relatively simple measure of circularity that can be easily implemented in assembly code, if required.

The results obtained showed that initial guess of pupil's center (in the lowest resolution considered) is critical for the algorithm to work properly. The results also showed that a number of parameters should be adjusted and their values are up to the resolution of the imager, processor that is to be used and the required efficiency. Optimizing those parameters, possibly utilizing the parallelism offered by small FPGA or CPLD device, should make the proposed algorithm fast enough to be implemented in small, cost effective mobile devices. The eventual time required for finding geometrical parameters of an iris with the use of the (optimized) method proposed and the optimized code should be no more than 100ms for a typical 1.3-2.0 Mpix imager.

References

1. Jain, A., Bolle, R., Pankanti, S. (eds.): Biometrics: Personal Identification in a Networked Society. Kluwer, Norwell (1999)
2. Daugman, J.G.: High Confidence Visual Recognition of Persons by a Test of Statistical Independence. IEEE Trans. Pattern Analysis and Machine Intelligence 15(11), 1148–1161 (1993)
3. Daugman, J.G.: The importance of being random: statistical principles of iris recognition. Pattern Recognition 36(2), 279–291
4. Cho, D.H., Park, K.R., Rhee, D.W.: Real-Time Iris Localization for Iris Recognition in Cellular Phone, snpd-sawn. In: Sixth Int. Conf. on Software Engineering, Artificial Intelligence, Networking and Parallel/Distributed Computing and First ACIS Int. Workshop on Self-Assembling Wireless Networks (SNPD/SAWN'05), pp. 254–259 (2005)
5. Feng, X., Fang, C., Ding, X., Wu, Y.: Iris Localization with Dual Coarse-to-fine Strategy. In: icpr.18h Int. Conf. on Pattern Recognition (ICPR'06), pp. 553–556 (2006)
6. `http://www.cbsr.ia.ac.cn/IrisDatabase.htm`
7. `http://www.oki.com/en/press/2006/z06114e.html`
8. `http://www.iridiantech.com/products.php?page=4`
9. `http://www.oki.com/jp/FSC/iris/en/m_features.html`

Pyramid Based Interpolation for Face-Video Playback in Audio Visual Recognition

Dereje Teferi and Josef Bigun

School of Information Science, Computer, and Electrical Engineering (IDE)
Halmstad University, P.O. Box 823, SE-301 18
Halmstad, Sweden
{Dereje.Teferi,Josef.Bigun}@ide.hh.se

Abstract. Biometric systems, such as face tracking and recognition, are increasingly being used as a means of security in many areas. The usability of these systems depend not only on how accurate they are in terms of detection and recognition but also on how well they withstand attacks. In this paper we developed a text-driven face-video signal from the XM2VTS database. The synthesized video can be used as a means of playback attack for face detection and recognition systems. We use Hidden Markov Model to recognize the speech of a person and use the transcription file for reshuffling the image sequences as per the prompted text. The discontinuities in the new video are significantly minimized by using a pyramid based multi-resolution frame interpolation technique. The playback can also be used to test liveness detection systems that rely on lip-motion to speech synchronization and motion of the head while posing/speaking. Finally we suggest possible approaches to enable biometric systems to stand against this kind of attacks. Other uses of our results include web-based video communication for electronic commerce.

1 Introduction

Biometrics is the study of automated methods for uniquely identifying and recognizing humans based upon one or more intrinsic physiological or behavioral traits. The traits used for recognition include, face, fingerprints, hand geometry, gait, handwriting, iris, retina, voice etc. Biometric systems are in use in applications such as security, finance, banking etc [1], [2].

The need for increased security is becoming apparent at all levels as transaction fraud and security breaches became more and more a threat. It is increasingly reported, in research and development, that biometrics systems have high level of accuracy in identifying and recognizing people. However, its application is not as widespread as expected. One drawback is that biometric data of a person (such as face, speech, etc) are not secret and cannot be replaced anytime the user wants to or whenever they are compromised by a third party. The problem of spoofing is minimal if the authentication system works with the help of a human supervisor as in border control where the presented trait can be visually checked to see if it is genuine or fake. However, the risk is high

S.-W. Lee and S.Z. Li (Eds.): ICB 2007, LNCS 4642, pp. 868–877, 2007.

for remotely controlled biometric applications such as banking and e-commerce that use the internet [3]. The risk of spoofing on automated biometric systems can be reduced significantly by combining multiple traits into the system and incorporating liveness detection.

Biometric system attacks may occur in a number of points throughout the process of enrollment, identification or verification (Fig 1). The attacks could be set off at the sensor, network, algorithm, the template database etc. These vulnerable points of a biometric system are discussed in detail in [4]. This work presents a possible playback attack targeting points two of the verification process.

Since the purpose of this research is not to attack biometric systems but to prevent them from such, we conclude with solutions to differentiate playback videos from that of live ones.

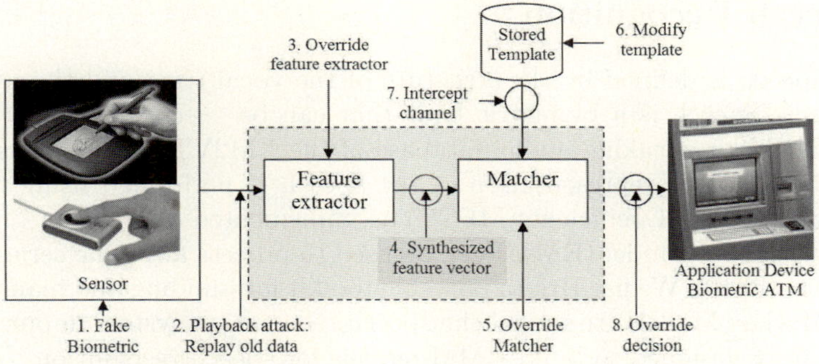

Fig. 1. Possible attack points of a biometric system

Technological advances in audio-video capture and processing have enabled the development of sophisticated biometric systems. As such it has also presented opportunities for more vicious system attacks. Impersonation can be done, for example, by audio-video playback and application of image processing techniques without the presence of the real client.

The actual presence of the client can be assured to a certain degree by liveness detection systems. Liveness detection is an anti-spoofing mechanism to protect biometric systems [5], [4]. It is performed by, for example, face part detection and optical flow of lines to determine liveness score [5], analysis of fourier spectra of the face image [6], lip-motion to speech synchronization[7], body temperature, on the spot random queries such as pronouncing of random sequences of digits, iris size scanning under varying illumination etc.

Text-prompted liveness detection and audio-video based recognition systems use random digits as their text prompts. This is because random numbers are easier to read for the client than random texts and numbers are easier to synthesize. Accordingly, the digit speaking image sequences of the XM2VTS database are used in this work for the experiment. XM2VTS is a 295 subject audio-video database that offers synchronized video and speech data for research in multimodal recognition systems [8]. In this paper we developed a text prompted face-video synthesis for testing the capability of liveness detection and audio-visual person verification systems against attacks.

We use HMM based speech recognizer to identify the locations, in order of 10^{-7} of a second, of each digit spoken by the subject. The pre-recorded image sequence is then reshuffled according to system prompt (or digits entered). However, the process of shuffling creates discontinuities between digits in the new image sequence. This discontinuity between the last frame of a digit and the first frame of the next digit is minimized by interpolating frames in between using a pyramid based multiresolution frame interpolation method. This method reported a better result, for the attacker, by reducing the *block effect* and *false match* as illustrated in Fig 6.

2 Speech Recognition

Human speech is defined by the structure of the vocal tract and the use of the vocal cords. Speech is a biometric trait that can be used to uniquely identify people. The digit speaking audio database of the XM2VTS database is used in this work. Vectorial representation of the speech is performed using the Mel-Frequency Cepstral Coefficients(MFCC) as implemented in [9].

Hidden Markov Model (HMM) can be used to process any time series such as that of speech [10]. We use Htk (a portable toolkit for building and manipulating Hidden Markov Models) to model the speech recognition system in our work 2. Htk is mainly designed to build HMM models for speech recognition.

The waveform files are converted into a sequence of discrete equally spaced acoustic parameter vectors using MFCC according to a defined configuration. The configuration in our HMM model has a sampling period of 10 ms, a window size of 25 ms while the number of cepectral coefficients is set to 12. A prototype HMM model with 39 feature vectors and 3 left-right states is defined and used for the training.

The final HMM model constructed from a series of trainings is used for the speech recognition as shown in 2. A speech signal is passed to the HMM model for recognition of the digits. The result - a transcription file - is used to reshuffle the image sequences according to the system prompt.

3 Motion Estimation for Frame Interpolation

Motion estimation is the process of finding optimal motion vectors that describe the movement of pixels or blocks of pixels from frame to frame in an image sequence. A number of motion estimation techniques are discussed in [11], [12], and [13]. We use motion estimation to calculate motion vectors for interpolating new frames to reduce the discontinuity in the image sequence. The discontinuity occurs due to the rearrangement of sequence of frames according to the prompted text.

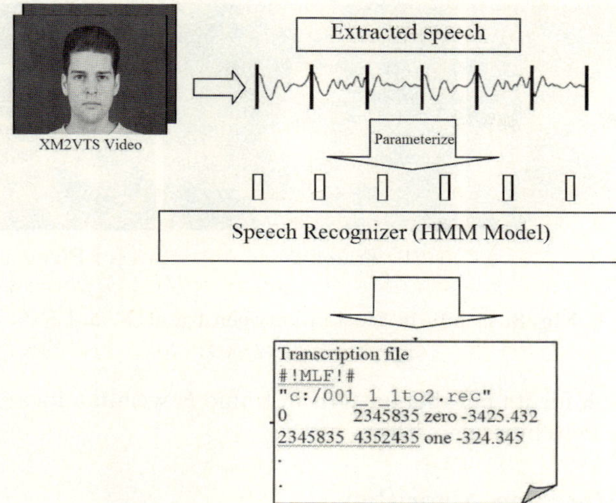

Fig. 2. Speech Recognition System

Motion estimation is a common technique used in video compression. A video usually have some redundant data between adjacent frames within a certain period of time $(t_1 - t_0)$. The redundancy is small for fast paced and complex motion of objects and background in the video and high otherwise. This redundancy is exploited to compress the video. That is a reference frame (sometimes known as the independent frame) is taken from a sequence every n frame apart. Then the middle frames are predicted from these frames as well as from previously predicted frames by the codec. The codec actually uses the motion vector and prediction error to reconstruct the *dependent* frames. Forward prediction, where the new frames are predicted from previous frames, or backward prediction, where the new frames are predicted from future frames, or both can be used for estimation of the new frames in the middle. Many codecs use this method for video compression.

Typical audio visual recognition systems use head-shoulder video as an input. Moreover, it is not too difficult to acquire video of a person uttering the 10 digits. Given such a sequence an attacker could proceed as discussed below.

Assuming the video is captured with a stationary camera, the background will be near-constant. Therefore, little information is lost or added between adjacent frames, such as teeth, mouth and eyes. That is, there is a high probability that most part of a frame exist in another frame although translated to a different location. First, the points in motion are extracted using absolute difference between the two frames (Fig 3).

$$AD = |\mathbf{F}(k,l) - \tilde{\mathbf{F}}(k,l)| \quad (1)$$

Now that we know the points in motion, the motion vector (MV) is calculated only for blocks around these points. For each block around a point in motion on

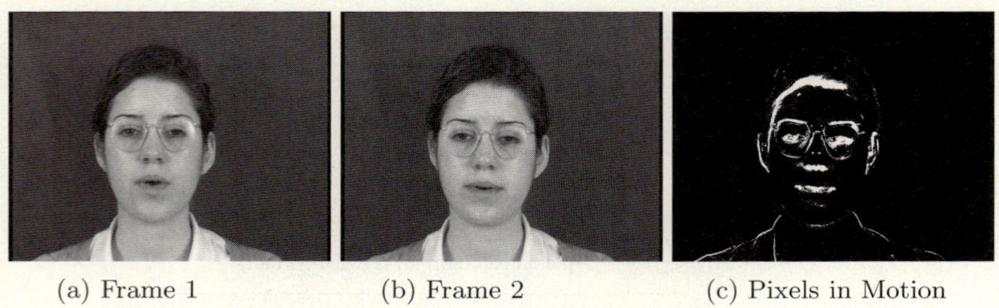

(a) Frame 1 (b) Frame 2 (c) Pixels in Motion

Fig. 3. Points in Motion between frame $\mathbf{F}$ and $\tilde{\mathbf{F}}$

frame $\mathbf{F}$, we look for its parallel pattern in frame $\tilde{\mathbf{F}}$ within a local neighborhood by using block matching algorithm.

3.1 Block Matching Algorithm

Block matching is a standard technique used by video compression techniques to encode motion in image sequences. A review of block matching algorithms is given in [13], [12], and [14]. The motion vector calculated from the block matching algorithm is used for frame interpolation. This method of using motion of objects between frames for interpolation is referred to as motion compensated frame interpolation (MCFI) [15].

Non-overlapping blocks are created over the points in motion of frame $\mathbf{F}$ (*the frame at time* t_0) and a search area is defined on frame $\tilde{\mathbf{F}}$ (*the frame at time* t_1). The search area is larger than the size of the block by *expected* displacement e of the object in motion (Fig 4). Then, Schwartz inequality is applied to find the most parallel pattern for the block in frame $\mathbf{F}$ from the search area in frame $\tilde{\mathbf{F}}$.

Let $\mathbf{f}$ and $\tilde{\mathbf{f}}$ be vectorial representations of patterns from frames $\mathbf{F}$ and $\tilde{\mathbf{F}}$ and $<,>$ be the scalar product defined over the vector space. Then, we have

$$|<\mathbf{f},\tilde{\mathbf{f}}>| \leq \|\mathbf{f}\|\|\tilde{\mathbf{f}}\|$$

$$cos(\theta) = \frac{|<\mathbf{f},\tilde{\mathbf{f}}>|}{\|\mathbf{f}\|\|\tilde{\mathbf{f}}\|} = \frac{|\mathbf{f}^T\tilde{\mathbf{f}}|}{\|\mathbf{f}\|\|\tilde{\mathbf{f}}\|} \leq 1 \tag{2}$$

where $\mathbf{f} = (f_1, f_2, ..., f_{k-1}, f_k, f_{k+1}, ...)$ and $\tilde{\mathbf{f}} = (\tilde{f}_1, \tilde{f}_2, ..., \tilde{f}_{k-1}, \tilde{f}_k, \tilde{f}_{k+1}, ...)$ are vector forms of the 2D pattern $\mathbf{f}$ and $\tilde{\mathbf{f}}$ from frames $\mathbf{F}$ and $\tilde{\mathbf{F}}$ respectively and $cos(\theta) \in [0,1]$ is the similarity measure between the patterns.

The most parallel pattern $\tilde{\mathbf{f}}$ in the frame $\tilde{\mathbf{F}}$ is found by maximizing $cos(\theta)$. This can be done by repetitive scalar products. That is the pattern $\mathbf{f}$ from frame $\mathbf{F}$ is glided over a neighborhood of *expected* parallel local neighborhood of $\tilde{\mathbf{f}}$ in the frame $\tilde{\mathbf{F}}$ and the most similar pattern is selected as a match.

The motion vector for the point at the center of pattern $\mathbf{f}$ is calculated as the displacement between pattern $\mathbf{f}$ and pattern $\tilde{\mathbf{f}}$ as illustrated in Fig. 4. That is:

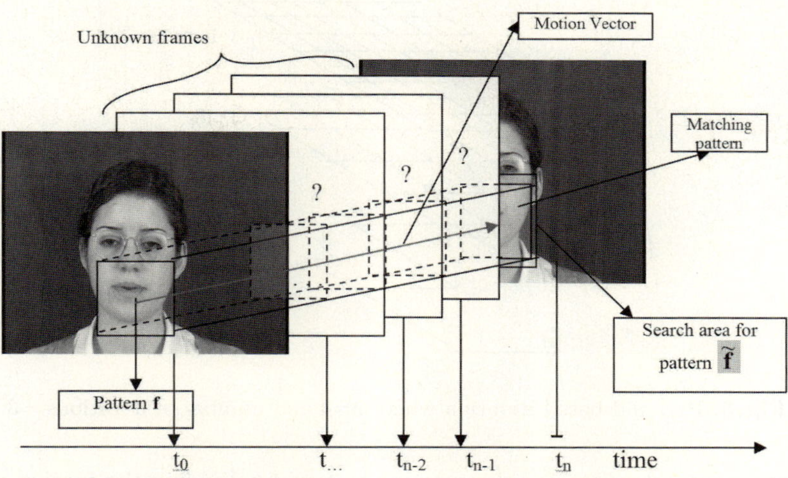

Fig. 4. Motion Vector and unknown frames in a sequence

$$MV(k,l) = x + iy \tag{3}$$

Where x and y are the horizontal and vertical displacements respectively of the block/pattern **f** , *(k,l)* is the index for the center of pattern **f** and $i = \sqrt{-1}$.

3.2 Pyramid Based Approach for Block Matching

Using large block size while calculating the motion vectors above gives rise to what is known as *block effect* in the interpolated frame. Whereas making the block size small may result in multiple similarities and a probable choice of a *false match* for the motion vector.

To solve this problem, a pyramid based frame interpolation method which makes use of both large as well as small size blocks hierarchically is employed to calculate the motion vector in the right direction. That is, initially large block size is used to get a crude directional information on which way the block is moving. Here it is unlikely to get a false match as the size of the block is very large. This motion vector is used to determine the appropriate search area in the next step of the the block matching process so that the probability of a false match is minimal. The search area is also reduced to a smaller local neighborhood because we have information on where to look for the pattern. Then, we reduce the size of the block by a factor of n and calculate the motion vector again (Fig 5). The motion vector calculated for each block is again used to determine where the search area should be in the next iteration. This process is repeated until a satisfactory result is achieved in the interpolated frame.

The final complex valued motion vector matrix is used to interpolate the new frames between $\mathbf{F}$ and $\tilde{\mathbf{F}}$. The number of frames to be interpolate d depends on the norm of the motion vector and is determined at run-time. For a length 2

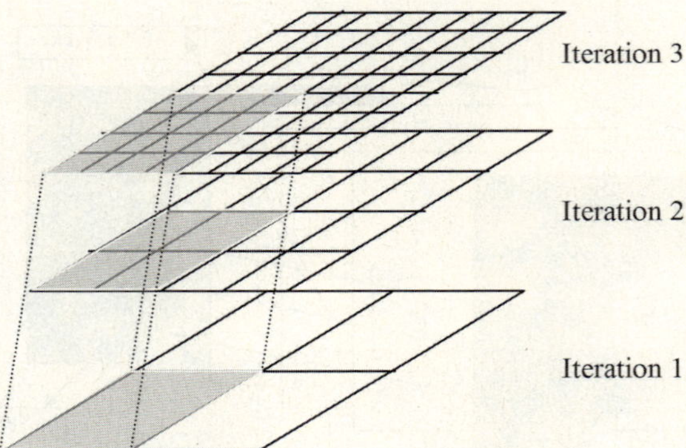

Fig. 5. Pyramid based iteration where n=4 and number of iterations =3

time units, the actual frame interpolation is done by dividing the motion vector at point (k,l) by 2 and moving the block in frame $\tilde{\mathbf{F}}$ centered at $(k{+}x,l{+}y)$ to the new frame at $(k{+}x/2,l{+}y/2)$. Then the block at the new location in frame $\tilde{\mathbf{F}}$ is moved back the same distance. That is, let $\mathbf{F}$ be the frame at t_0, $\tilde{\mathbf{F}}$ the frame at t_1 and $\mathbf{F}^{'}$ be the frame at $\frac{(t_1-t_0)}{2}$, then

$$\mathbf{F}^{'}(k+x/2,l+y/2) = \tilde{\mathbf{F}}(k+x,l+y) \quad (4)$$

$$\mathbf{F}^{'}(k,l) = \tilde{\mathbf{F}}(k+x/2,l+y/2) \quad (5)$$

where x and y are the real and imaginary parts of the motion vector at (k,l).

Consecutive interpolations are made in analogous manner. The motion vector is adjusted and a new frame is created as necessary between frames $\mathbf{F}$ and $\mathbf{F}^{'}$ as well as between $\mathbf{F}^{'}$ and $\tilde{\mathbf{F}}$. This process continues until all the necessary frames are created.

4 Video Synthesis

Audio data is extracted from the input audio-video signal and forwarded to the speech recognizer. The recognizer uses the HMM models for the recognition and returns a transcription file containing the start and end time of each digit spoken in the audio signal. A search for the prompted text is done against the transcription file and the time gap of each prompted digits within the video signal is captured. Then, the image sequences are arranged according to the order of the prompted text.

The discontinuity between the image sequences of each digit is minimized by interpolating frames using the pyramid based multiresolution frame interpolation technique summarized in section 3. The interpolated frames are attached to a silence sound and are inserted to their proper locations in the video signal to decrease the discontinuity of utterances. Finally, the video is played to represent the digit sequence prompted by the system.

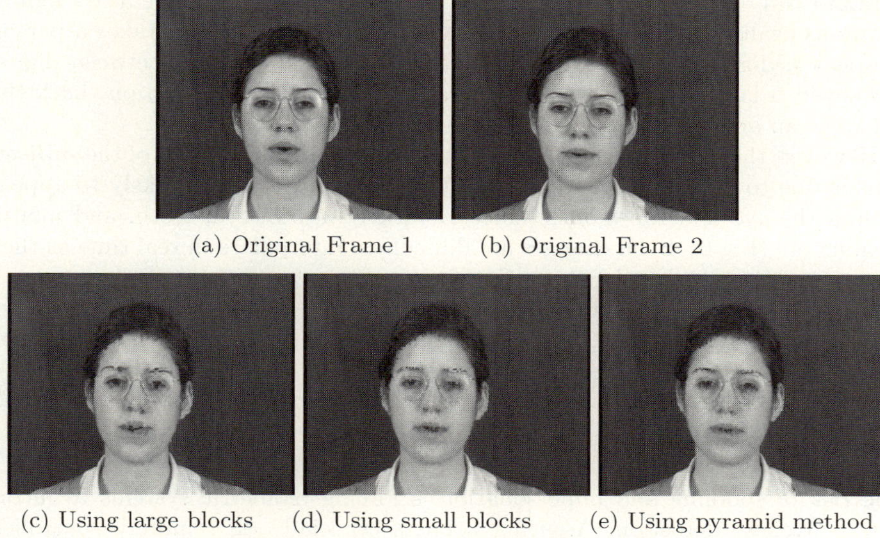

Fig. 6. Results of the various frame interpolation methods

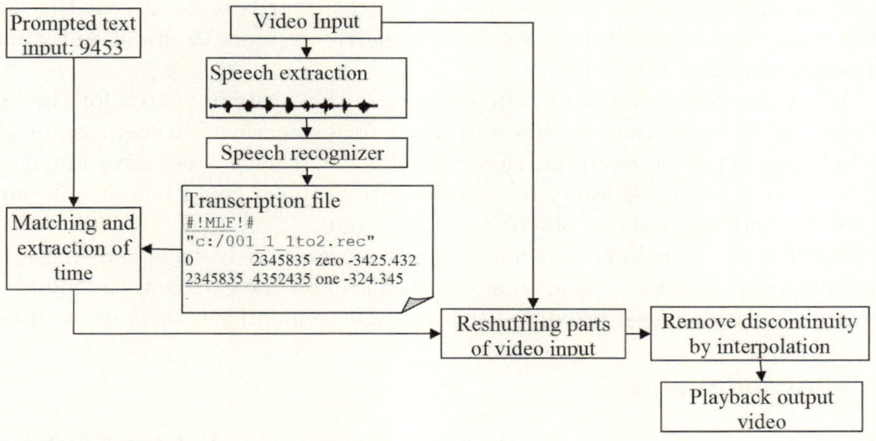

Fig. 7. Process flowchart

5 Experiment

The experiments are conducted on all the digit speaking face videos of the XM2VTS database. The accuracy of the text-prompted video signal is mainly dependent on the performance of the speech recognition system. The accuracy of our HMM based speech recognition system is 94%. The pyramid based frame interpolation algorithm gives optimal result when the final block size of the pyramid is 3. The discontinuity of the reshuffled video signal is reduced significantly as evaluated by the human eye, the authors. The time it takes a person to speak a digit is enough to interpolate the necessary frames between digits. Moreover, a laptop computer as a portable DVD can be used to playback the video for an audio visual recognition system.

However, there is still visible blur around the eye and the mouth of the subject. This is due to the fact that differences between the frames are likely to appear around the eye and the mouth, such as varied state of eye, teeth, and mouth opening etc (Fig 6). Such changes are difficult to interpolate in real time as they do not exist in both the left and right frames.

Biometric authentication and liveness detection systems that make use of motion information of face, lip and text prompted audio-video are easy targets of such playback attacks described here.

6 Conclusion

The risk of spoofing and impersonation is forcing biometric systems to incorporate liveness detection. Assuring liveness especially on remotely controlled systems is a challenging task. The proposed method shows a way to produce playback attacks against text-prompted systems using audio and video in real time. The result shows that assuring liveness remotely by methods that rely on apparent motion can be targets of such attacks. Our results suggest the need to increase the sophistication level of biometric systems to stand up against advanced playback attacks.

Most video-based face detection and recognition systems search for the best image from a sequence of images and use it for extracting features assuming it will yield a better recognition. However, this could have a negative impact as some of those blurry or faulty frames that are dropped could be our only hope to tell if a video-signal is a playback or a live one.

Therefore, we conclude that audio visual recognition systems can withstand such playback attacks by analyzing the area around the eyes and the mouth of the new frames between prompted text or digit to identify if they are *artificial*.

Acknowledgment

This work has been sponsored by the Swedish International Development Agency (SIDA).

References

1. Jain, A., Ross, A., Prebhakar, S.: An Introduction to Biometric Recognition. IEEE Transactions on Circuits and Systems for Video Technology, Special Issue on Image- and Video-Based Biometrics 14(1) (January 2004)
2. Ortega-Garcia, J., Bigun, J., Reynolds, D., Gonzalez-Rodriguez, J.: Authentication Gets Personal with Biometrics. IEEE Signal Processing Magazine 21(2), 50–62 (2004)

3. Faundez-Zanuy, M.: Biometric Security Technology. IEEE Aerospace and Electronic Systems Magazine 21(6), 15–26 (2006)
4. Ratha, N.K., Connell, J.H., Bolle, R.M.: Enhancing Security and Privacy in Biometrics-Based Authentication Systems. IBM Systems Journal 40(3), 614–634 (2001)
5. Kollreider, K., Fronthaller, H., Bigun, J.: Evaluating Liveness by Face Images and the Structure Tensor. In: AutoID 2005: Fourth Workshop on Automatic Identification Advanced Technologies, pp. 75–80. IEEE Computer Society Press, Los Alamitos (2005)
6. Li, J., Wang, Y., Tan, T., Jain, A.K.: Live Face Detection Based on the Analysis of Fourier Spectra. In: Jain, A.K., Ratha, N.K. (eds.) Biometric Technology for Human Identification. Proceedings of the SPIE, vol. 5404, pp. 296–303 (August 2004)
7. Faraj, M., Bigun, J.: Person Verification by Lip-Motion. In: Computer Vision and Pattern Recognition Workshop (CVPRW), pp. 37–45 (June 2006)
8. Messer, K., Matas, J., Kitler, J., Luettin, J., Maitre, G.: XM2VTSDB: The Extended M2VTS Database. In: 2nd International Conference on Audio and Video-based Biometric Person Authentication (AVBPA), pp. 72–77 (1999)
9. Veeravalli, A.G., Pan, W., Adhami, R., Cox, P.G.: A Tutorial on Using Hidden Markov Models for Phoneme Recognition. In: Thirty-Seventh Southeastern Symposium on System Theory, SSST 2005 (2005)
10. Young, S., Evermann, G., Gales, M., Hein, T., Kershaw, D., Moore, G., Odell, J., Ollason, D., Povey, D., Valtchev, V., Woodland, P.: The htk Book. for Version 3.3 (April 2005), `http://htk.eng.cam.ac.uk/docs/docs.shtml`
11. Bigun, J.: Vision with Direction: A Systematic Introduction to Image Processing and Computer Vision. Springer, Heidlberg (2006)
12. Jain, J., Jain, A.K.: Displacement Measurement and its Application in Interframe Image Coding. IEEE Transactions on Communication COM 29, 1799–1808 (December 1981)
13. Cheng, K.W., Chan, S.C.: Fast Block Matching Algorithms for Motion Estimation. In: ICASSP-96: IEEE International Conference on Acoustic Speech and Signal Processing, vol. 4(1), pp. 2311–2314. IEEE Computer Society Press, Los Alamitos (1996)
14. Aly, S., Youssef, A.: Real-Time Motion Based Frame Estimation in Video Lossy Transmission. In: Symposium on Applications and the Internet, pp. 139–146 (January 2001)
15. Zhai, J., Yu, K., Li, J., Li, S.: A Low Complexity Motion Compensated Frame Interpolation Method. In: IEEE International Symposium on Circuits and Systems. ISCAS 2005, vol. 5, pp. 4927–4930. IEEE Computer Society Press, Los Alamitos (2005)

Face Authentication with Salient Local Features and Static Bayesian Network

Guillaume Heusch[1,2] and Sébastien Marcel[1]

[1] IDIAP Research Institute, rue du Simplon 4, 1920 Martigny, Switzerland
[2] Ecole Polytechnique Fédérale de Lausanne (EPFL), 1015 Lausanne, Switzerland
{heusch,marcel}@idiap.ch

Abstract. In this paper, the problem of face authentication using salient facial features together with statistical generative models is adressed. Actually, classical generative models, and Gaussian Mixture Models in particular make strong assumptions on the way observations derived from face images are generated. Indeed, systems proposed so far consider that local observations are independent, which is obviously not the case in a face. Hence, we propose a new generative model based on Bayesian Networks using only salient facial features. We compare it to Gaussian Mixture Models using the same set of observations. Conducted experiments on the BANCA database show that our model is suitable for the face authentication task, since it outperforms not only Gaussian Mixture Models, but also classical appearance-based methods, such as Eigenfaces and Fisherfaces.

1 Introduction

Face recognition has been an active research area since three decades, and a huge variety of different systems are now capable to recognize people based on their face image, at least in so-called controlled conditions (good illumination, fixed pose). Existing algorithms are often divided into two categories, depending on the information they use to perform the classification: appearance-based methods (also called *holistic*) are typically using the whole face as input to the recognition system. On the other hand, feature-based methods are considering a set of local observations derived from a face image. Such observations may be geometric measurements (distance between the eyes, etc.), particular blocks of pixels, or local responses to a set of filters for instance.

Examples of appearance-based systems include the well-known Principal Component Analysis (PCA) [19], Linear Discriminant Analysis (LDA) [4] as well as Independent Component Analysis (ICA) [3] to name a few. These projection techniques are used to represent face images as a lower-dimensional vector, and the classification itself is actually performed by comparing these vectors according to a metric in the subspace domain (or using a more sophisticated classification technique, such as Multi-Layer Perceptron or Support Vector Machines). On the other hand, feature-based approaches are trying to derive a model of an individual's face based on local observations. Examples of such systems include

S.-W. Lee and S.Z. Li (Eds.): ICB 2007, LNCS 4642, pp. 878–887, 2007.

the Elastic Bunch Graph Matching (EBMG) [20], recent systems using Local Binary Patterns (LBP) [1] [17], and also statistical generative models: Gaussian Mixture Models (GMM) [6] [13], Hidden Markov Models (HMM) [15] [18] or its variant [5] [14].

Face recognition systems using local features were empirically shown to perform better as compared to holistic methods [5] [12] [13]. Moreover, they also have several other advantages: first, face images are not required to be precisely aligned. This is an important property, since it increases robustness against imprecisely located faces, which is a desirable behaviour in real-world scenarios. Second, local features are also less sensitive to little variations in pose and in illumination conditions.

In this paper we will focus on statistical generative models and propose a new model, based on static Bayesian Networks, especially dedicated to the data we have to deal with, that is the human face. Actually, we think that classical statistical models (GMM and HMM), although successful, are not really appropriate to properly describe the set of local observations extracted from a face image. Indeed, GMM as applied in [5] are modelling the distribution of overlapping blocks among the whole face image, thus considering each block to be independent with respect to the others. Furthermore, it was shown in [13] that better results are obtained by modelling each part of the face using a different GMM. However, the model likelihood is computed as the product of the GMM likelihood, hence again considering the different face parts independently.

Obviously, this is not the case due to the nature of the "face object". Consider the two eyes for instance: the block containing one eye is likely to be related somehow to the block containing the other eye. Going one step further, HMM-based approaches, as well as its variant (2D-HMM, coupled HMM) are able to add structure to the observations and therefore usually perform better. Examples of embbeded *dynamic* Bayesian Networks (which are nothing else but an extension of the HMM framework) applied to face recognition can be found in [14]. However, such systems cannot introduce *causal relationships* between observations themselves, they mainly act on their ordering. By using *static* Bayesian Networks, it is then possible to model causal relationships between a set of different observations represented by different variables. Hence, in this contribution we propose a first attempt, to our knowledge, to derive a statistical generative model based on this paradigm and especially dedicated to the particular nature of the human face. Conducted experiments on the BANCA [2] database show a performance improvement over a GMM-based system making the independence assumption between different facial features.

The remaining of this paper is organized as follows. Section 2 describes the general framework to perform face authentication with statistical models. Then, Bayesian Networks are briefly introduced before presenting the proposed generative model used to represent a face. The BANCA database, the experimental framework and obtained results are discussed in Sec. 4. Finally, the conclusion is drawn in Sec. 5, and some possible future research directions are outlined.

2 Face Authentication Using Generative Models

In the framework of face authentication, a client claims its identity and supports the claim by providing an image of its face to the system. There are then two different possibilities: either the client is claiming its real identity, in which case it is referred to as a *true client*, either the client is trying to fool the system, and is referred as an *impostor*. In this open-set scenario, subjects to be authenticated may or may not be present in the database. Therefore, the authentication system is required to give an opinion on whether the claimant is the true client or an impostor. Since modelling all possible impostors is obviously not feasible, a so-called *world-model* (or universal background model) [5] [10] is trained using data coming from different identities, and will be used to simulate impostors.

More formally, let us denote $\lambda_{\bar{C}}$ as the parameter set defining the world-model whereas λ_C represents the client-specific parameters. Given a client claim and its face representation X, an opinion on the claim is given by the following log-likelihood ratio:

$$\Lambda(X) = \log P(X|\lambda_C) - \log P(X|\lambda_{\overline{C}}) \quad (1)$$

where $P(X|\lambda_C)$ is the likelihood of the claim coming from the true client and $P(X|\lambda_{\overline{C}})$ is representing the likelihood of the claim coming from an arbitrary impostor. Based on a threshold τ, the claim is accepted if $\Lambda(X) \geq \tau$ and rejected otherwise.

In order to find the parameters $\lambda_{\overline{C}}$ of the world model, and since we are dealing with model containing unobserved (or hidden) variables, the well-known Expectation-Maximisation (EM) algorithm [9] in the Maximum Likelihood (ML) learning framework is used. However, when it comes to client parameter estimation, ML learning cannot be reliably used due to the small amount of available training data for each client, instead the Maximum A Posteriori (MAP) criterion is used [10] [5]. In this case, client-specific parameters are *adapted* from the world-model parameters (i.e. the prior) using client data in the following manner:

$$\lambda_C^{MAP} = \alpha \cdot \lambda_C^{ML} + (1 - \alpha) \cdot \lambda_{\overline{C}} \quad (2)$$

where λ_C^{ML} denotes the client parameters obtained from a Maximum Likelihood estimation. The adaptation parameter α is used to weight the relative importance of the obtained ML statistics with respect to the prior.

3 Proposed Model

3.1 Bayesian Networks

In this section, we will briefly describe the framework used to build the statistical generative model to represent a face. Bayesian networks (also known as belief networks) provide an intuitive way to represent the joint probability distribution over a set of variables: random variables are represented as nodes in a directed acyclic graph, and links express *causality relationships* between these variables.

More precisely, defining $Pa(X_i)$ as the parents of the variable X_i, the joint probability encoded by such a network over the set of variables $\mathbf{X} = (X_1, ..., X_n)$ is given by the following chain rule:

$$P(\mathbf{X}) = \prod_{i=1}^{n} P(X_i|Pa(X_i)) \tag{3}$$

Hence, a Bayesian Network is fully defined by the *structure* of the graph and by its *parameters*, which consists in the conditional probability distributions of each variable given its parents. Note however that a variable may have no parents, in which case its probability distribution is a prior distribution.

Inference. The task of inference in Bayesian Networks consists in computing probabilities of interest, once evidence has been entered into the network (i.e. when one or more variables has been observed). In other words, entering evidence consists in either fixing the state of a discrete variable to one of its possible value or to assign a value in the case of a continuous variable. We are then interested in finding the effect this evidence has on the distribution of the others unobserved variables.

There are many different algorithm allowing to perform inference, the most renowned is certainly the belief propagation due to Pearl [16], which is a generalisation of the forward-backward procedure for HMM. However, it becomes problematic when applied to multiply-connected networks. Another more generic method is the Junction Tree algorithm [8], which allows to compute such posterior probabilities in any kind of networks and is also the most efficient algorithm to perform exact inference.

Learning. Learning in Bayesian Networks refers either to structure learning, parameters learning or both [11]. In our case, we are considering networks of fixed structure. Hence, parameters are learned using the classical EM algorithm [9] with either the ML or the MAP criterion described previously (Sec. 2).

3.2 Face Representation

Figure 1 depicts the proposed model to represent a face using salient facial features. Shaded nodes are representing visible observations (eyebrows, eyes, nose and mouth) derived from the face image, whereas white nodes are representing the hidden *causes* that generated these observations. This model can be understood as follows: a face is described by a set of unknown dependencies between eyebrows and eyes (node BE), eyes and nose (node EN) and nose and mouth (node NM). These combinations then generate a certain type of facial features (such as a small nose, or broad lips for instance) which are represented by the nodes at the second level. And finally, these types of facial features then generate the corresponding observations.

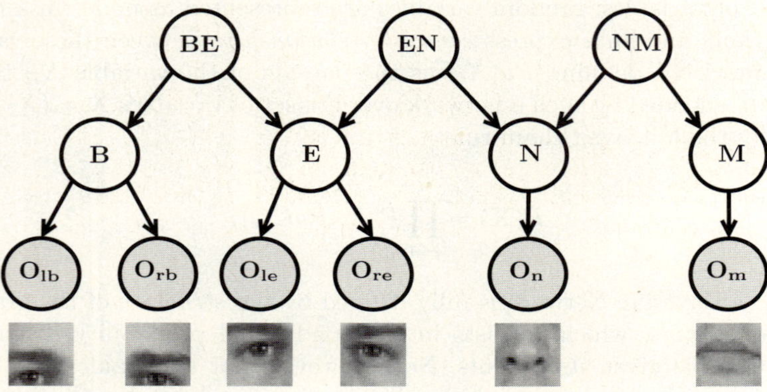

Fig. 1. Static Bayesian Network for Face Representation

In this network, hidden nodes are discrete-valued and observed nodes are multivariate gaussians. The likelihood of the face representation defined by $X = (O_{lb}, O_{rb}, O_{le}, O_{re}, O_n, O_m)$ is obtained by first inferring the distribution of the hidden variables once observations has been entered in the network, and then by summing out over the states of the hidden variables. Note that our model introduce relationships between observations: if the node O_{le} is observed, information about the node O_{re} can be inferred through the node E node for instance.

4 Experiments and Results

4.1 The BANCA Database

The BANCA database [2] was especially meant for multi-modal biometric authentication and contains 52 clients (English corpus), equally divided into two groups g1 and g2 used for development and evaluation respectively. Each corpus is extended with an additional set of 30 other subjects and is referred as the *world model*. Image acquisition was performed with two different cameras: a cheap analogue webcam, and a high-quality digital camera, under several realistic scenarios: controlled (high-quality camera, uniform background, controlled lighting), degraded (webcam, non-uniform background) and adverse (high-quality camera, arbitrary conditions). Figure 2 shows examples of the different acquisition scenarios.

In the BANCA protocol, seven distinct configurations for the training and testing policy have been defined. In our experiments, the configuration referred as Match Controlled (Mc) has been used. Basically, it consists in training the system with five images per client acquired during the first contolled session. Then, the testing phase is performed with images acquired during the remaining sessions under the controlled scenario.

(a) controlled (b) degraded (c) adverse

Fig. 2. Example of the different scenarios in the BANCA database

4.2 Experimental Framework

Each image was first converted to grayscale and processed by an Active Shape Model (ASM) in order to locate the facial features [7]. Then, histogram equalization was applied on the whole image so as to enhance its contrast. Blocks centered on a subset of facial features were extracted (Fig. 1), and in order to increase the amount of training data, shifted versions were also considered. Hence, in our experiments we use the original extracted block as well as 24 other neighbouring blocks, resulting from extractions with shifts of 2, 3 and 4 pixels in each directions. Each block is finally decomposed in terms of 2D Discrete Cosine Transform (DCT) in order to build the final observation vectors.

Face authentication is subject to two types of error, either the true client is rejected (false rejection) or an impostor is accepted (false acceptance). In order to measure the performance of authentication systems, we use the Half Total Error Rate (HTER), which combines the False Rejection Rate (FRR) and the False Acceptance Rate (FAR) and is defined as:

$$HTER = \frac{(FAR + FRR)}{2} \quad [\%] \tag{4}$$

Hyperparameters, such as the threshold τ, the dimension of the DCT feature vectors, the cardinality of the hidden nodes and the adaptation parameter α were selected using the validation set along a DET curve at the point corresponding to the Equal Error Rate (EER), where the false acceptance rate equals the false rejection rate. HTER performance is then obtained on the evaluation set with these selected hyperparameters.

4.3 Results

Here we present face authentication results obtained with the proposed model based on Bayesian Networks (BNFACE), and also with a baseline GMM system. Since the main assumption that drove us towards our approach was to state that blocks containing facial features should not be treated independently, we reproduced the experiment with the so-called *Partial Shape Collapse* GMM (PSC-GMM) first presented in [13]. However, and in order to yield a fair comparison, we use exactly the same set of features produced for our model, and hence did not take into account the nose bridge and both cheek regions used in [13]. In our experiments, DCT feature vectors of dimensions 64 were used, and the cardinality of the discrete variables was set to 3 at the first level and to 8 at the second level. Regarding the PSC-GMM model, we used 512 gaussians for each of the six GMM corresponding to the six extracted facial features, as suggested in [13].

In Tab. 1, we report the results obtained by our approach (BNFACE), by our implementation of the PSC-GMM and by the GMM approach as published in [5]. Note that in [5] only the results on g2 are available. The proposed BNFACE model outperforms the corresponding PSC-GMM approach on both sets of the BANCA database. Moreover, obtained results on the test set g2 are better than those obtained with a single GMM [5]. This comparison is interesting since this GMM-based system uses much more features extracted from the whole face image. Note also that our model contains the less client-specific parameters to be learned.

Table 1. HTER Performance on the Mc protocol of the BANCA database

FA system	HTER on g1 [%]	HTER on g2 [%]	number of parameters
BNFACE	9.01	5.41	5225
PSC-GMM	11.31	11.34	$6 \cdot 33280$
GMM [5]	not available	8.9	9216

Since results presented in [13] are reported in terms of EER on a graph, we also compare EER performance on both development and test sets in Tab. 2. Note however that the numeric results from [13] are estimated from the graph, and are thus subject to little imprecisions. Once again, we noticed that the proposed approach performs better than using the PSC-GMM with the same features, as can also be seen on DET curves (Fig. 3). However, results of the original PSC-GMM are better. It can be explained by the fact that it uses more features than our model to perform the face authentication task. Note also that our model provide better performance than classical appareance-based models such as Eigenfaces and Fisherfaces as provided in [13].

Table 2. EER Performance on the Mc protocol of the BANCA database

FA system	EER on g1 [%]	EER on g2 [%]
BNFACE	9.01	4.84
PSC-GMM	11.31	6.92
PSC-GMM [13]	3.9	4.1
Fisherfaces [13]	10.2	11.5
Eigenfaces [13]	13.8	14.0

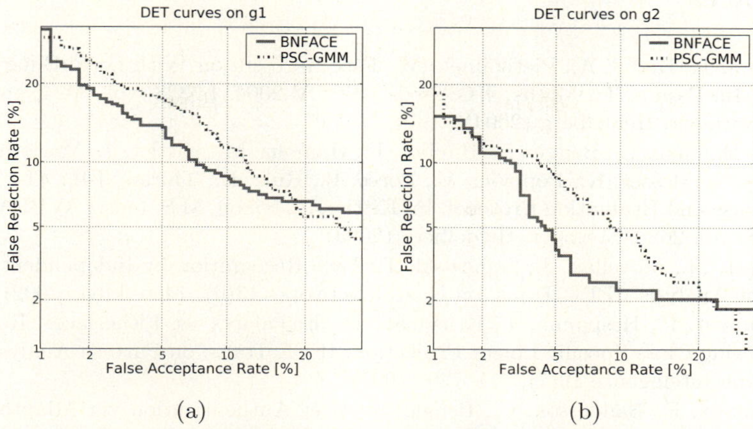

Fig. 3. DET curves obtained on the Mc protocol of the BANCA database for the BNFACE (solid line) and the PSC-GMM (dashed line) models

5 Conclusion and Future Directions

In this paper, we proposed a new statistical generative model to represent human faces, and applied it to the face authentication task. The main novelty of our approach consists in introducing dependencies between observations derived from salient facial features. As shown by the conducted experiments on a benchmark database, our main hypothesis seems to be verified, since our model performs better than systems relying on the independence assumption between facial features. Moreover, obtained results also compares favourably against classical holistic methods such as Eigenfaces and Fisherfaces.

However, this work is a preliminary attempt to use static Bayesian Networks in face recognition and many issues are still open. Indeed, future research directions are manifold. First, causal relationships between facial features are not known (at least to our knowledge) and finding the right structure for the network is not straightfoward. Second, it will be interesting to use other facial features possibly carrying more discriminative information, such as skin texture for instance, and incorporate it into a network.

Acknowledgments

This work has been funded by the GMFace project of the Swiss National Science Foundation (SNSF) and the Swiss National Center of Competence in Research (NCCR) on Interactive Multimodal Information Management (IM2). Softwares were implemented using the TorchVision library[1] and experiments were carried out using the PyVerif framework.[2]

[1] http://torch3vision.idiap.ch

[2] http://pyverif.idiap.ch

References

1. Ahonen, T., Hadid, A., Pietikäinen, M.: Face Recognition With Local Binary Patterns. In: Pajdla, T., Matas, J(G.) (eds.) ECCV 2004. LNCS, vol. 3024, pp. 469–481. Springer, Heidelberg (2004)
2. Bailly-Baillière, E., Bengio, S., Bimbot, F., Hamouz, M., Kittler, J., Mariéthoz, J., Matas, J., Messer, K., Popovici, V., Porée, F., Ruiz, B., Thiran, J-P.: The Banca Database and Evaluation Protocol. In: Kittler, J., Nixon, M.S. (eds.) AVBPA 2003. LNCS, vol. 2688. Springer, Heidelberg (2003)
3. Bartlett, M., Movellan, J., Sejnowski, T.: Face Recognition by Independent Component Analysis. IEEE Trans. on Neural Networks 13(6), 1450–1464 (2002)
4. Belhumeur, P., Hespanha, J., Kriegman, D.: Eigenfaces vs. Fisherfaces: Recognition Using Class Specific Linear Projection. IEEE Trans. on Pattern Analysis and Machine Intelligence 19(7), 711–720 (1997)
5. Cardinaux, F., Sanderson, C., Bengio, S.: User Authentication via Adapted Statistical Models of Face Images. IEEE Trans. on Signal Processing 54(1), 361–373 (2005)
6. Cardinaux, F., Sanderson, C., Marcel, S.: Comparison of MLP and GMM classifiers for face verification on XM2VTS. In: Kittler, J., Nixon, M.S. (eds.) AVBPA 2003. LNCS, vol. 2688. Springer, Heidelberg (2003)
7. Cootes, T.F., Taylor, C.J., Cooper, D., Graham, J.: Active Shape Models: Their Training and Applications. Computer Vision & Image Understanding 61(1), 38–59 (1995)
8. Cowell, G., Dawid, P., Lauritzen, L., Spiegelhalter, J.: Probabilistic Networks and Expert Systems. Springer, Heidelberg (1999)
9. Dempster, A., Laird, N., Rubin, D.: Maximum Likelihood From Incomplete Data via the EM Algorithm. The Journal of Royal Statistical Society 39, 1–37 (1977)
10. Gauvain, J.-L., Lee, C.-H.: Maximum A Posteriori Estimation for Multivariate Gaussian Mixture Observations of Markov Chains. IEEE Transactions on Speech and Audio Processing 2(2), 291–298 (1994)
11. Heckerman, D.: Tutorial on Learning With Bayesian Networks. In: Learning in Graphical Models, ch. A, pp. 301–354. MIT Press, Cambridge (1999)
12. Heisele, B., Ho, P., Wu, J., Poggio, T.: Face Recognition: Component-based versus Global Approaches. Computer Vision and Image Understanding 91(1), 6–21 (2003)
13. Lucey, S., Chen, T.: A GMM Parts Based Face Representation for Improved Verification through Relevance Adaptation. In: IEEE Intl. Conf. on Computer Vision and Pattern Recognition (CVPR), pp. 855–861. IEEE Computer Society Press, Los Alamitos (2004)
14. Nefian, A.: Embedded Bayesian Networks for Face Recognition. In: IEEE Intl. Conference on Multimedia and Expo. (ICME). IEEE Computer Society Press, Los Alamitos (2002)
15. Nefian, A., Hayes, M.: Hidden Markov Models for Face Recognition. In: IEEE Intl. Conf. on Acoustics, Speech, and Signal Processing (ICASSP), vol. 5, pp. 2721–2724. IEEE Computer Society Press, Los Alamitos (1998)
16. Pearl, J.: Probabilistic Reasoning in Intelligent Systems: Networks of Plausible Inference. Morgan Kaufmann, San Francisco (1988)
17. Rodriguez, Y., Marcel, S.: Face Authentication Using Adapted Local Binary Pattern Histograms. In: Leonardis, A., Bischof, H., Pinz, A. (eds.) ECCV 2006. LNCS, vol. 3954, pp. 321–332. Springer, Heidelberg (2006)

18. Samaria, F., Young, S.: HMM-based Architecture for Face Identification. Image and Vision Computing 12(8), 537–543 (1994)
19. Turk, M., Pentland, A.: Face Recognition Using Eigenfaces. In: IEEE Intl. Conf. on Computer Vision and Pattern Recognition (CVPR), pp. 586–591. IEEE Computer Society Press, Los Alamitos (1991)
20. Wiskott, L., Fellous, J.-M., Krüger, N., Von Der Malsburg, C.: Face Recognition By Elastic Bunch Graph Matching. In: 7th Intl. Conf. on Computer Analysis of Images and Patterns (CAIP), pp. 456–463 (1997)

Fake Finger Detection by Finger Color Change Analysis

Wei-Yun Yau[1], Hoang-Thanh Tran[2], Eam-Khwang Teoh[2], and Jian-Gang Wang[1]

[1] Institute for Infocomm Research, 21 Heng Mui Keng Terrace, Singapore
[2] Nanyang Technological University, EEE, Singapore
wyyau@i2r.a-star.edu.sg, tranhoangthanh@pmail.ntu.edu.sg, eekteoh@ntu.edu.sg, jgwang@i2r.a-star.edu.sg

Abstract. The reliability of a fingerprint recognition system would be seriously impacted if the fingerprint scanner can be spoofed by a fake finger. Therefore, fake finger detection is necessary. This work introduces a new approach to detect fake finger based on the property of color change exhibited by a real live finger when the finger touches a hard surface. The force exhibited when the finger presses the hard surface changes the blood perfusion which resulted in a whiter color appearance compared to a normal uncompressed region. A method to detect and quantify such color change is proposed and used to differentiate a real finger from the fakes. The proposed approach is privacy friendly, fast and does not require special action from the user or with prior training. The preliminary experimental results indicate that the proposed approach is promising in detecting the fake finger made using gelatin which is particularly hard to detect.

Keywords: Fake finger, Color change, blood perfusion.

1 Introduction

The identity of an individual is a very critical "asset" of that individual that facilitates the person when performing myriad daily activities such as financial transactions, access to places and buildings and to computerized accounts. However, the traditional means of identity authentication using tokens such as card and key or personal identification number and password is becoming vulnerable to identity thefts. Therefore, the ability to correctly authenticate an individual using biometrics is becoming important. Unfortunately, the biometric system is also not fool-proof. It is subjected to various threats including attack at the communication channels (such as replay attacks), the software modules (such as replacing the matching module), the database of the enrolled users and the sensor with fakes [1], [2].

Recently, several researchers have shown that it is possible to spoof the fingerprint recognition system with fake fingers [3],[4]. These include enhancing the latent prints on the finger scanner with pressure and/or background materials to creating fingerprint molds using materials such as silicon, gelatin and Play-Doh as well as the use of cadaver fingers [5]. In order to counter such spoof attacks, fingerprint recognition

S.-W. Lee and S.Z. Li (Eds.): ICB 2007, LNCS 4642, pp. 888–896, 2007.

system vendors have considered several approaches to detect the liveness of the finger. In general, these approaches can be classified into the following three categories [6]:

1. *Analysis of skin details in the acquired images*: minute details of the fingerprint images are used, ex: detecting sweat pores [5] and coarseness of the skin texture. A high resolution sensor is usually needed. Furthermore, sweat pores and skin texture varies with finger type, such as those dry and wet fingers and thus these approaches usually have large false error.
2. *Analysis of static properties of the finger*: additional hardware is used to capture information such as temperature, impedance or other electrical measurements, odor, and spectroscopy [12] where multiple wavelengths are exposed and the spectrum of the reflected light is analyzed to determine the liveness of the finger. Except for the spectroscopy technique, the other approaches can be easily defeated. However, the spectroscopy technique requires the use of expensive sensing mechanism.
3. *Analysis of dynamic properties of the finger*: analyzes the properties such as pulse oximetry, blood pulsation, perspiration, skin elasticity and distortion [6]. The former two approaches can only detect a dead or an entire fake finger but cannot differentiate false layer attached to the finger. In addition, it may reveal the medical condition of the user. To measure the perspiration, the user has to place the finger on the sensor for quite some time and may not be feasible for people with dry finger. A summary of the various liveness detection approaches is given in [7],[8].

Most of the approaches except the spectroscopy and the skin distortion techniques are not able to detect fake finger layer made using gelatin as gelatin contains moisture and has property such as electrical property quite similar to human skin. However, the spectroscopy technique requires expensive equipment while measuring the skin distortion requires the user to touch and twist the finger which is not user-friendly and will require user training. In this paper, the mold made using gelatin will be investigated as this is the most difficult attack to detect and that the attacker can easily destroy any proof by just eating the gelatin mold.

This paper proposed the use of the dynamic property of the skin color. As the finger is pressed on the hard surface of the fingerprint scanner, there occurs change in the color of the skin at the region in contact with the scanner. Such color change is dynamic and occurs only in a live finger. A method to detect and measure the color change is proposed and used to differentiate between a real and fake finger. Section 2 describes the property of the finger color change while Section 3 describes the approaches used to detect and measure the color change. This is followed by Section 4 describing the experimental results before Section 5 concludes the paper.

2 Finger Color Change

The main idea of our proposed approach to detect fake finger described in this paper is based on the change in the color of the finger portion in contact with any hard surface, such as when the finger is pressed on the finger scanner. As a real live finger is pressed on the hard surface of the scanner, the applied force will cause interaction among the fingernail, bone and tissue of the fingertip. This will alter the hemodynamic state of the finger, resulting in various patterns of blood volume or perfusion [9]. Such pattern is observable at the fingernail bed [9],[10] and at the surrounding skin region in contact with the scanner. The compression of the skin tissue at the contact region with the scanner will cause the color of the region to change to whiter and less reddish compared to the normal portion. This is because blood carries hemoglobin which is red in color. When the finger is pressed onto the hard surface, the amount of blood that can flow to the skin region in contact with the surface is limited due to the force exerted which constricts the capillaries at the fingertip. With less blood flow, the color of the skin region will change to less reddish, resulting in whiter appearance compared to the normal finger. Figure 1 shows the property of the color change before (Fig. 1a and 1c) and after the finger is pressed on a hard surface (Fig. 1b and 1d). For comparison, Figure 2 shows the color of the fake finger made using gelatin before and after the finger is pressed.

As shown in figures 1 and 2, the portion of the finger in contact with the hard surface will show change in color. We postulate this property to be true even for people

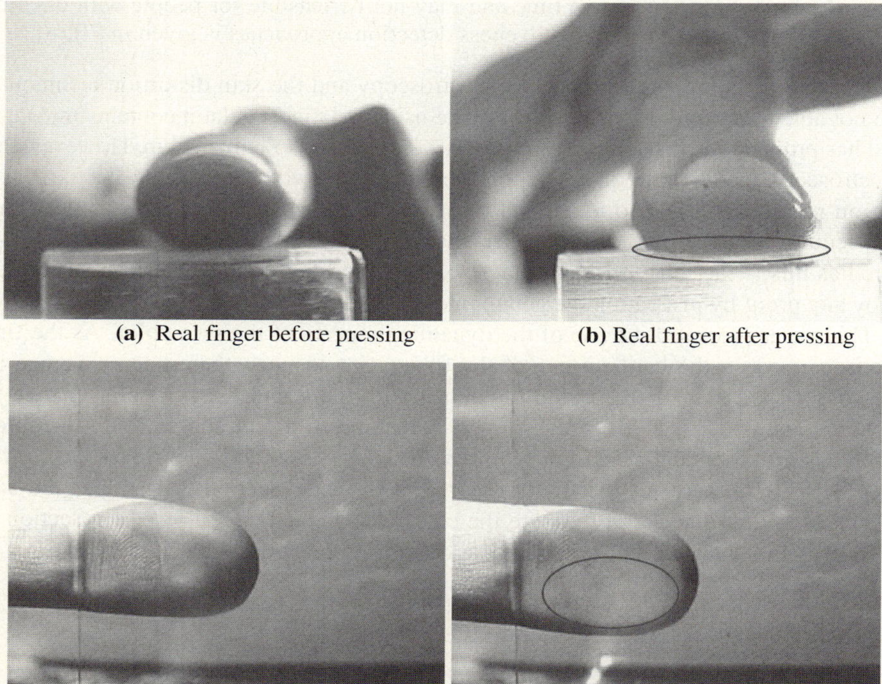

(a) Real finger before pressing (b) Real finger after pressing

(c) Real finger before pressing (d) Real finger after pressing

Fig. 1. Images of a real finger before and after pressing on a hard surface

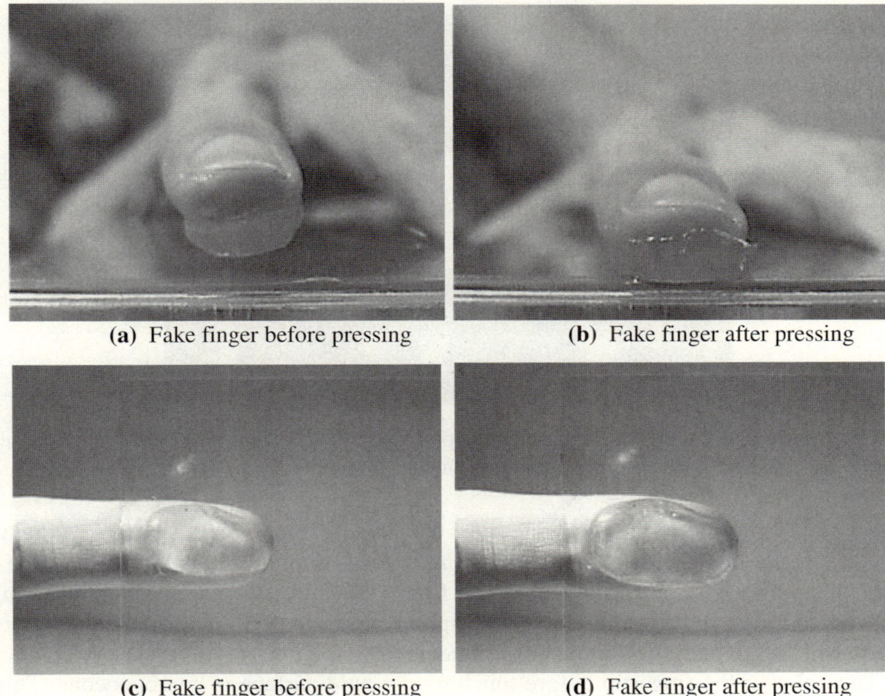

(a) Fake finger before pressing (b) Fake finger after pressing

(c) Fake finger before pressing (d) Fake finger after pressing

Fig. 2. Images of a fake finger before and after pressing on a hard surface

of different age, ethnicity or gender and is not sensitive to the type or condition of the skin, such as dry, wet or oily. However, a fake finger will not have such a property as mold will contact the surface first and the user will have to be careful when pressing the soft gelatin mold on the hard surface. As this property is dynamic and repeatable for all live fingers, it can be used to detect the liveness of the finger. The proposed method will only require the use of ordinary low cost digital camera, such as those commonly used in the mobile phones or PCs.

3 Fake Finger Detection Methodology

To quantify the change in the color of the finger, we first model the background region using a Gaussian model when the finger is not present. When a substantial change is detected, a finger is present. This image is saved as the initial image, I_I. Then, the images are continuously captured until the finger is pressed on the sensor and then lift off. The finger image with the entire finger pressed on the sensor, which gives the largest contact area, is taken as the desired image, I_D. Image I_I is then aligned to I_D based on the tip and the medial axis of the finger as shown in figure 3. The tip is defined as the point where the medial axis of the fingertip cuts the border of the fingertip.

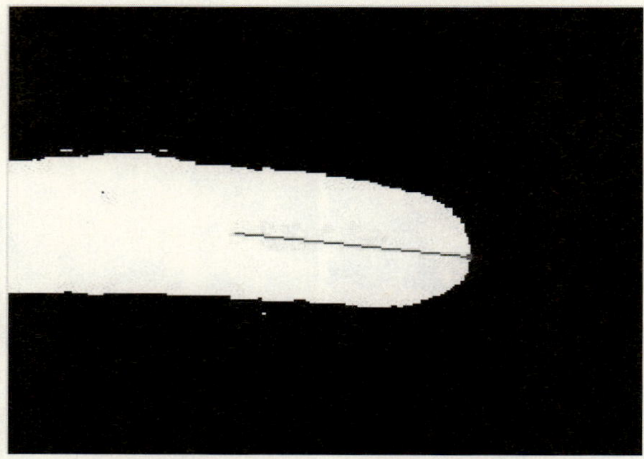

Fig. 3. Alignment of finger using the finger tip. The red line is the medial axis while the red square dot at the boundary between the finger and background is the tip point.

Subsequently, the foreground region of the finger is smoothed using an averaging filter. Then the region is divided into $n_1 \times n_2$ non-overlapping square blocks of size $s \times s$, beginning from the medial axis of the finger. Since we are interested in detecting the color change only, we convert the original image in RGB into CIELa*b* color space which provides good results experimentally.

The color of the fingertip before touching the hard surface is homogeneous. Thus we regard the chrominance component of all the $n_1 \times n_2$ blocks in the initial image I_I (before pressing) can be modeled using a single Gaussian distribution, μ_o, σ_o. This would be taken as the reference chrominance value for the normal un-pressed fingertip region, R_o. For each block in the pressed image I_D, clustering using hierarchical k-means [11] is performed on the chrominance component. Then the dominant clusters with homogeneous chrominance value of center μ_1 and standard deviation σ_1 different from μ_o, σ_o found from the $n_1 \times n_2$ blocks is taken as the reference value for the compress region R_1 of a pressed fingertip. This is then repeated for all the k images of I_I and I_D in the training sets to obtain the overall reference value for the normal $R_o(\mu_{ro}, \sigma_{ro})$ and pressed region $R_1(\mu_{r1}, \sigma_{r1})$ of the individual.

Given a pixel $x_{i,j}$, its similarity with respect to the normal R_o or pressed region R_1 can be quantified using the distance measure:

$$D^t_{i,j}(x_{i,j}|\mu_{rt}, \sigma_{rt}) = \sqrt{\frac{(x_{i,j} - \mu_{rt})^2}{\sigma^2_{rt}}} \quad ; t = 0,1 \tag{1}$$

The pixel $x_{i,j}$ is assigned to its proper region, R, based on the following thresholding operation:

$$R(x_{i,j}) = \begin{cases} 0 & D^o_{i,j} < \alpha_o \\ 1 & D^1_{i,j} < \alpha_1 \\ 2 & \text{otherwise} \end{cases} \tag{2}$$

where α_o, α_1 are the thresholds for the similarity measure to the region R_o and R_1 respectively.

For each block n in the $n_1 \times n_2$ blocks of I_I and I_D, the likelihood that n belongs to the category normal (R_0), pressed (R_1) or otherwise (R_2) can be obtained from the dominant homogeneous region assigned to the pixels in it as:

$$R(n_{i,j}) = \text{mod}(R(x_{i,j})|_{x_{i,j} \in n_{i,j}}) \tag{3}$$

When verifying the liveness of a finger, the category assigned to each of the $n_1 \times n_2$ blocks in images I_I and I_D is determined using equations (2) and (3). Then the finger is considered real if it satisfies the following criteria:

$$R(n_{i,j}|_{I_I}) \in R_o \ \forall n|_{I_I} \ \cap \ \text{mod}(R(n_{i,j}|_{I_D})) \notin R_2 \ \cap \ \sum R(n_{i,j}|_{I_D} - n_{i,j}|_{I_I}) > \alpha_R \tag{4}$$

where α_R is the threshold for real finger verification.

4 Experimental Results

In order to evaluate the proposed approach, a database of images was collected using the prototype setup shown in figure 4.

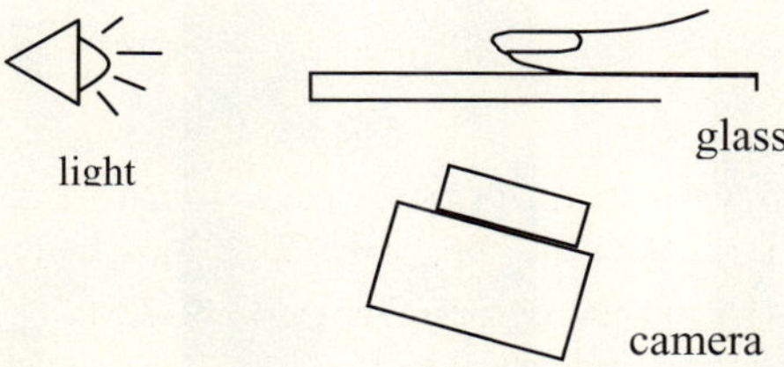

Fig. 4. Prototype system setup for data collection. The camera used is a PC camera with 0.5M pixel resolution while the light source is obtained from a series of LED.

The images were collected from 25 human subjects using white LED light source. Prior to any capture, the background image without the presence of finger was first captured. Then two images were acquired from each subject, one before the finger pressed the glass and the other after the finger pressed the glass. No guidance was given to the subjects on how they should press their finger except that they were told to press as if they were using a fingerprint recognition system. This was then repeated with the subject wearing a gelatin mold to simulate fake finger. A new gelatin mold was made for each subject since the gelatin mold quality deteriorates with time. Thus we have a total of 50 images (before and after pressing) for real fingers and another 50 images (before and after pressing) for fake fingers in the dataset. All these images were used in the performance evaluation of the proposed system.

Based on this dataset, we are able to correctly detect all real fingers and achieving 80% accuracy in detecting the fake finger as fake. Table 1 show the result obtained.

Table 1. Result for real and fake finger detection

	Correct detection rate	False detection rate
Real finger	100%	0%
Fake finger	80%	20%

Figure 5 shows some sample results obtained for the real and fake finger respectively. The errors in detecting the fake finger occur when the gelatin mold is made very thin and properly stuck to the real finger before touching the glass surface or due to error in the segmentation process. We found that in some cases, the fake finger has been detected even before pressing it. This is because the mold is not well made with bubbles which will be rejected as the homogeneity constraint of the finger is not valid anymore.

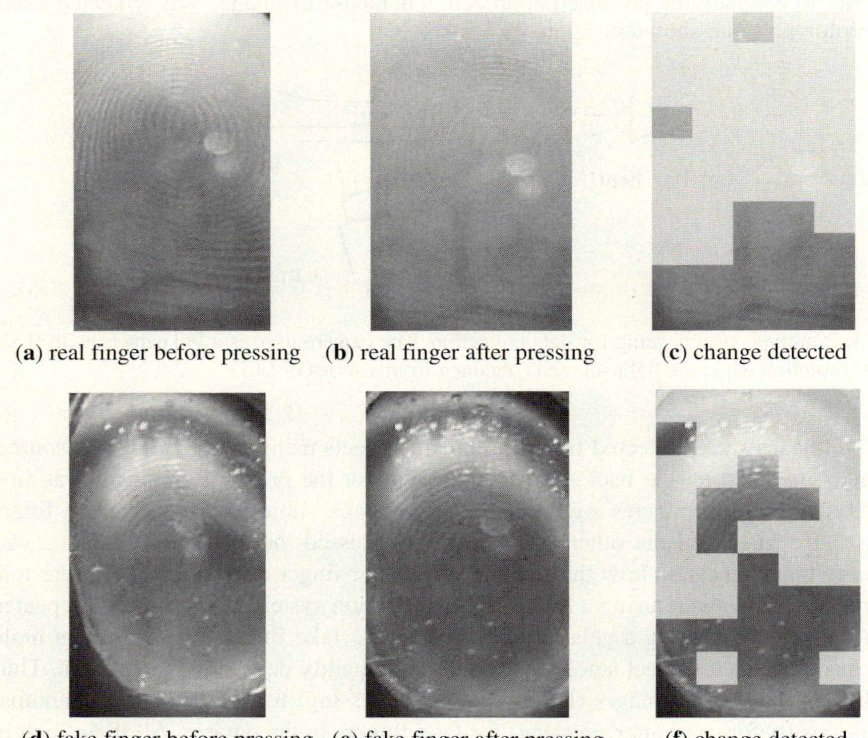

Fig. 5. Results of color change detection obtained on a real and the corresponding fake finger of the same subject. The colored part is the detected change.

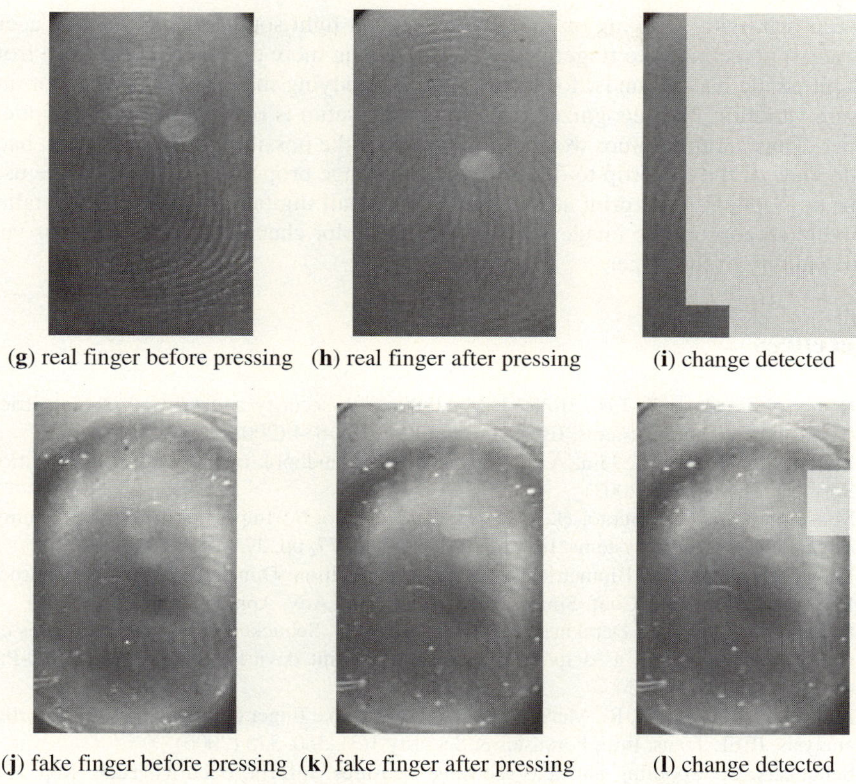

(**g**) real finger before pressing (**h**) real finger after pressing (**i**) change detected

(**j**) fake finger before pressing (**k**) fake finger after pressing (**l**) change detected

Fig. 5. (*continued*)

The advantages of the proposed method are that it is fast since the capture is done real time and does not have to wait for perspiration to set in as in [5]. It also does not require the use of expensive hardware as in [12] and has no implication on the privacy of the user as it does not reveal the medical condition of the person. In addition, it also does not require careful interaction of the user with the scanner as in [6] and thus can be readily deployed for mass users without prior user training.

5 Conclusion and Future Works

This paper presented a new approach to detect fake finger based on the property of color change exhibited by a real live finger when the finger touches a hard surface. Such condition arises naturally due to blood perfusion which is universal. The proposed approach is privacy friendly, fast and does not require special action from the user with prior training. The preliminary experimental results indicate that the proposed approach is promising in detecting the fake finger made using gelatin which is particularly hard to detect.

We are currently working on the use of different light source to improve the accuracy rate of detecting fake finger as well as collecting more data, including those from different ethnic backgrounds, for the purpose of studying the effect of skin color and pressure variation. We recognized that the current setup is only applicable for optical scanner. Thus another future work is to investigate the possibility of using front, back or side view of the fingertip to detect the color change property. These views are useful for non-optical fingerprint scanners where a small digital camera can be installed to capture an appropriate image for detecting the color change property and thus verify the validity of the finger.

References

1. Ratha, N.K., Connell, J.H., Bolle, R.M.: Enhancing security and privacy in biometrics-based authentication systems. IBM Syst. J. 40(3), 614–634 (2001)
2. Maltoni, D., Maio, M., Jain, A.K., Prabhakar, S.: Handbook of Fingerprint Recognition. Springer, Heidelberg (2003)
3. Matsumoto, T., Matsumoto, H., Yamada, K., Hoshino, S.: Impact of artificial "Gummy" fingers on fingerprint systems. In: Proc. SPIE, vol. 4677, pp. 275–289 (2002)
4. Putte, T., Keuning, J.: Biometrical fingerprint recognition: Don't get your fingers burned. In: Proc. 4th Working Conf. Smart Card Research and Adv. App., pp. 289–303 (2000)
5. Partthasaradhi, S.T.V., Derakhshani, R., Hornak, L.A., Schuckers, S.A.C.: Time-series detection of perspiration as a liveness test in fingerprint devices. IEEE Trans. SMC-Part C 35(3), 335–343 (2005)
6. Antonelli, A., Cappelli, R., Mario, D., Maltoni, D.: Fake finger detection by skin distortion analysis. IEEE Trans. Info. Forensics & Security 1(3), 360–373 (2006)
7. Schuckers, S.: Spoofing and anti-spoofing measures. Inform. Security Tech. Rep. 7(4), 56–62 (2002)
8. Valencia, V., Horn, C.: Biometric liveness testing. In: Woodward Jr., J.D., Orlans, N.M., Higgins, R.T. (eds.) Biometrics, McGraw Hill, New York (2002)
9. Mascaro, S.A., Asada, H.H.: The common patterns of blood perfusion in the fingernail bed subject to fingertip touch force and finger posture. Haptics-e 4(3), 1–6 (2006)
10. Mascaro, S.A., Asada, H.H.: Understanding of fingernail-bone interaction and fingertip hemodynamics for fingernail sensor design. In: Proc. 10th Int. Symp. Haptic Interfaces for Virtual Environment and Teleoperator Systems, pp. 106–113 (2002)
11. Duda, R.O., Hart, P.E., Stork, D.G.: Pattern Classification. Wiley, Chichester (2001)
12. Nixon, K., et al.: Novel spectroscopy-based technology for biometric and liveness verification. In: Proc. SPIE, vol. 5404, pp. 287–295 (2004)

Feeling Is Believing: A Secure Template Exchange Protocol

Ileana Buhan, Jeroen Doumen, Pieter Hartel, and Raymond Veldhuis

University of Twente, Enschede, The Netherlands
{ileana.buhan,jeroen.doumen,pieter.hartel,
r.n.j.veldhuis}@utwente.nl

Abstract. We use grip pattern based biometrics as a secure side channel to achieve pre-authentication in a protocol that sets up a secure channel between two hand held devices. The protocol efficiently calculates a shared secret key from biometric data. The protocol is used in an application where grip pattern based biometrics is used to control access to police hand guns.

Keywords: Ad-hoc authentication, fuzzy cryptography, biometrics.

1 Introduction

We are developing smart guns with grip pattern biometrics [11] for the police, to reduce the risk of officers being shot with their own weapon in case of a take away situation [7]. In this scenario a police handgun authenticates the owner by grip pattern biometrics integrated with the grip of the gun. Police officers often work in teams of two and each officer must be able to fire the other officer's weapon. Normally, teams are scheduled in advance so that appropriate templates can be loaded into the weapons at the police station. However, in emergency situation this is not possible; in this case police officers have to team up unprepared and exchange templates in the field. Biometric data is sensitive information thus during the exchange the templates must be protected. Officers may work with colleagues from other departments, even from neighboring countries, so a shared key, or a public key infrastructure where the certificate associated with these keys must be verifiable on-site is not realistic. Also, one cannot expect a police officer to perform some complicated interfacing operation with his gun in the field.

In this paper we present a solution that is both simple and effective. Each police officer owns a gun, that holds the owners stored biometric grip pattern template and is equipped with a grip pattern sensor and a short range radio. The users swap the devices, so that each device can measure the grip pattern of the other user. The devices are then returned to their owners. Each device now contains a genuine template of its owner and a measurement of the other user, called guest. The devices calculate a common key from the owner's template and the guest measurement. The act of the guest putting her hand on the user's device corresponds to sending a message on a secure side channel. Therefore, we have termed our protocol Feeling is Believing (FiB).

Securing the exchange of biometric templates is an instance of the *pairing problem*. As described by Saxena [9] the *pairing problem* is to enable two devices, which share no prior context, to agree upon a security association that they can use to protect their

S.-W. Lee and S.Z. Li (Eds.): ICB 2007, LNCS 4642, pp. 897–906, 2007.

subsequent communication. Secure pairing must be resistant to a man-in-the-middle adversary who tries to impersonate one or both of these devices in the process. To achieve secure pairing one cannot rely on any previously shared secret information. This problem can be solved in cryptography by the issue of certificates. As said before, due to the ad-hoc nature of the pairings we cannot rely on an existing communications channel to a certification authority that could validate certificates. Our approach is to use an additional physically authenticated side channel which is governed by humans.

Related Work. Balfanz *et al.*[9] propose physical contact between devices. This type of channel has the property that the user can control precisely which devices are communicating. The authors extend this approach to location limited channels where they propose short range wireless infrared communication where the secret information is communicated when devices are in the line of sight. McCune *et al.* [6] propose to use a visual channel and make photographs of the hash codes of the public keys. This represents a major breakthrough especially from the point of user friendliness. In the same line of work, Googrich *et al.* [4] propose a human assisted authentication audio channel as a secure side channel. They use a text to speech engine for vocalizing a sentence derived from the hash of a device's public key. The pre-authentication channel is used mostly to authenticate public-keys. The hash of the public key is either vocalized [4] or photographed [6]. Others [12,10], use a Diffie-Hellman like key agreement scheme where short sequences transmitted on the private channel authenticate the key sent on the main channel. Our protocol is a Diffie-Hellman like protocol in the sense that both parties equally contribute to the session key. FiB achieves mutual authentication and the partial keys are extracted from the biometric identification data of the individual.

Contribution. FiB can perform secure biometric template exchange in an ad-hoc situation, its main merit being user friendliness. We stress that the application domain for FiB is more general than the gun application. FiB can securely exchange template for any type of biometric system. FiB is formally verified to prove the security and origin authentication of templates. The workload of an intruder who is trying to guess the session key is evaluated in 9 different scenarios. To the best of our knowledge, this is the first time that a biometric is used as a location limited channel. Using biometrics and cryptography together brings up challenges. Biometric data is usually noisy. However the noise is not reproducible or uniformly random thus cryptography algorithms have difficulties in adjusting to this noise. We propose a new method for correcting errors in the keys generated from biometric data using a user specific error profile.

2 FiB Protocol Description

FiB solves the problem of secure template exchange and provide a solution for securing the ad-hoc transfer of private information between mobile, biometrically enabled devices in a scenario where no pre-distributed keys are available. The main threat is an intruder loading his template into one of the participating devices. Thus, we require the authorization of the device owner before his template is transferred. To preserve the privacy of the biometric template, it must be encrypted before being sent out.

Fuzzy Key Extraction. Before we turn to the protocol, we introduce the main tool. A fuzzy extractor as defined by Dodis *et al.* [1] is a public function that extracts robustly a binary sequence K from a noisy measurement F with the help of some public string H. Enrollment is performed by a function Gen, which on the input of the noise free biometric T and the chosen binary string K will compute a public string $H = \texttt{Gen}(T, K)$. During authentication, a second function Reg takes as input a noisy measurement F and the public string H and outputs a binary string $K' = \texttt{Reg}(F, H)$. In a perfect world, $K' = K$ but in reality they might be slightly different. However, we expect that keys are close in terms of their Hamming distance when T and F are similar enough. Both T and F are multidimensional feature vectors and while for most of the features the authentication will work correctly, for some feature the noise might be too large. We write $K' = K + e$, where we assume that the Hamming weight of the error e, denoted with $\texttt{wt}(e)$ satisfies $\texttt{wt}(e) \leq t, 0 \leq t \ll n$.

FiB Protocol preliminaries. Before we delve into the description of the protocol, which represents the core of our solution, we describe the context. Enrollment of users takes place before the protocol starts. During enrollment a low noise measurement T is taken, for each user. A key K of length n is generated and function Gen(T,K) outputs the helper data H. Then the user specific error profiles E is computed. The error profile is used by the protocol to lower the error rates of the biometric system, see subsection 4. This information is loaded into the device of the user. After the enrollment we have achieved that: (1) the identity of the user can be verified by his own device, and (2) a device is prepared to run the FiB protocol which allows secure template transfer so that *another device* can verify the identity of the user.

The Protocol. The principals that interact during the protocol are two devices D_a and D_b. Before the protocol starts each device knows the data of its owner, i.e. the template, the helper data constructed from the template, the key and the error profile. Hence initially D_a knows $\{T_a, H_a, K_a, E_a\}$ and D_b knows $\{T_b, H_b, K_b, E_b\}$. The message flow of the FiB protocol is shown in Figure 1. By $K'_a||K'_b$ we mean a combination of K'_a and K'_b, for example concatenation.

Actions of device D_a (Initiator). We assume that D_a starts the protocol. When an unknown grip pattern is detected, D_a broadcasts its helper data H_a on the wireless channel. H_a is constructed such that it does not reveal any significant information about T or K. Upon receiving message 4 from D_b, D_a uses the received H_b and F_b to extract $K_b^{'}$. The second part of the message is used to help D_a recover $K_a^{'}$. Since K_a and K'_a are close, D_a can use the error profile E_a to recover K'_a by flipping carefully chosen bits in K_a until it can successfully decrypt $\{F_a\}_{K'_a}$. Since D_a can recognize a measurement coming from its own user, D_a can check the decryption results. When D_a successfully finds $K_a^{'}$ it sends message 7 to D_b. D_a verifies in step 11 that T_b matches the measurement received on the secure side channel in step 1.

Actions of device D_b (Responder). Device D_b receives H_a and detects an unknown grip pattern, F_a. The rest of the operations are similar to those of D_a. Both participants have to perform the same amount of computation.

FiB is a solution that offers confidentiality during data transfer and authentication. However, FiB does not guarantee what happens to the templates *after* the protocol ends.

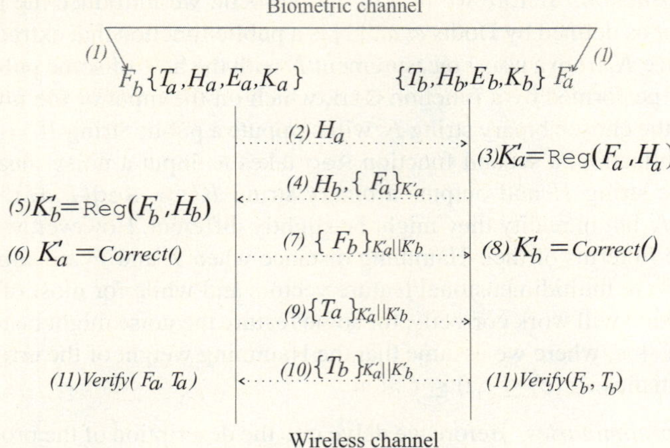

Fig. 1. FiB protocol

We emphasize that loading a template into ones device is similar to handing over a key to the device. At any time the owner of the template can access that device. In the scenario of the smartgun we assume that the sensitive information is stored in a tamper resistant storage environment where the templates cannot be "taken out".

3 Security Evaluation for FiB Protocol

There are two distinct, rigorous views of cryptography that have been developed over the years. One is a formal approach where cryptographic operations are seen as black box functions represented by symbolic expressions and their security properties are modelled formally. The other is based on a detailed computational model where cryptographic operations are seen as strings of bits and their security properties are defined in terms of probability and computational complexity of successful attacks. In the following we look at both aspects of security.

3.1 Formal Verification of the FiB Protocol with CoProVe

We have formally verified that FiB satisfies secrecy of the templates and mutual authentication. The adversary, named Eve, is a Dolev-Yao [3] intruder that has complete control of the communication channel. She can listen to, or modify messages on the main communication channel between the devices but cannot access the secure side channel. The tool used for this purpose is the constraint based security protocol verifier CoProVe by Corin and Etalle [2]. An earlier version of the protocol was verified and found buggy, the published version of the protocol above fixes the flaw found. A (security) protocol is normally verified using a model of the protocol, to avoid getting bogged down in irrelevant detail. The quality of the model then determines the accuracy of the verification results. The basic difference between a protocol and a model lies in the assumptions made when modelling the protocol. We believe that the following assumptions are realistic:

1. *No biometric errors.* We assume that the correction mechanism always works perfectly and thus the initiator knows the key used by the sender. Thus, we look only at complete protocol rounds. When the initiator cannot work out the key the protocol is aborted. In this case we assume that Eve cannot work out the key either.
2. *Modelling the secure side channel.* We assume that when the protocol starts device D_a knows F_a and device D_b knows F_b while Eve knows neither because she cannot eavesdrop on the secure side channel.
3. *Classifier based verification in step 11 removed.* Because systems without an equational theory such as CoProVe cannot compare two terms, the last check before accepting a template cannot be modelled. This check prevents an intruder modifying messages 9 and 10 in the protocol.

We have verified the model in figure 1 with the assumptions above. We argue that the above abstractions do not affect the secrecy and the authentication property. Verification with CoProVe explores a scenario in which one of the parties involved in the protocol plays the role of the initiator (i.e. the party staring the protocol) and the other plays the role of the responder. A third party, the intruder learns all message exchanged by the initiator and the responder. The intruder can devise new messages and send them to honest participants as well as replay or delete messages. Should the intruder learn a secret key and a message encrypted with that key, then the intruder also knows the message. This is the classical Dolev-Yao intruder [3].

We have explored two scenarios that we believe to be realistic and representative for real attacks. In the first scenario two honest participants Alice and Bob are plagued by a powerful intruder who is assumed to know T_b (because the intruder might have communicated with Bob in a previous session).

In the scenario the intruder tries to load her own template T_i into D_a so as to be able to fire weapon T_a. This impersonation attack is found to be impossible by CoProVe under the assumption that the intruder does not know F_a or T_a. This is a realistic assumption since these are not transmitted in clear and the key used to encrypt is computed from data sent over the secure side channel. Verification thus shows that the intruder cannot impersonate D_b even though the intruder has knowledge of T_b.

In the second scenario one participant, Alice, has to deal with the intruder, who does not have useful initial knowledge. This scenario represents the case that Alice's device was stolen and the intruder tries to load his template into Alice's device and use it. Verification shows that T_a remains secret when Alice is the initiator of the protocol. This means that an intruder cannot trick Alice into disclosing her template data if she does not provide the intruder a sample of her biometric data. When Alice is the responder and the intruder has full access to the device (i.e. the intruder can submit his own biometric data), T_a will not be disclosed. This is because before the device sends anything useful on the wireless link the device will check whether his owner is there after step 3.

As a result in both scenarios we have verified the security and authentication authentication of responder to the initiator and authentication of initiator to responder.

3.2 Intruder's Computational Effort of Guessing $K'_a||K'_b$.

To derive keys from fuzzy data we use a semi-known plain text attack in steps 6 and 8, to recover the session key. This approach can raise a couple of natural questions: "If both Alice (device D_a) and Bob (device D_b) have to guess the session key, how much more difficult is for Eve (the intruder) to do the same?", "What happens if Eve already knows the templates of Alice and or Bob?", "What kind of guarantees is this protocol offering?" To answer these questions we study the following scenarios:

AE(0) No previous contact between Alice and Eve.
AE(1) Eve records a measurement of Alice's biometric.From the helper data sent out in the clear Eve constructs K''_a.
AE(2) Eve had a protocol run with Alice and knows T_a and Eve can construct K_a.

We denote by $W(x \to y)$ the average number of trials that Eve, has to do to guess y when she knows x using the best guessing strategy. We analyze Eve's workload to guess K'_a in the three scenarios above.

In scenario $AE(2)$, Eve knows K_a and has to guess $K'_a = K_a + e$ where $\texttt{wt}(e) \leq t$. Since Eve has no information about the noise distribution, she has to correct up to t errors. As the key length is n, there are $\binom{n}{i}$ different error patterns if the actual number of errors is i, thus on average she will have to guess:

$$W(K_a \to K'_a) \approx \frac{1}{2}\sum_{i=0}^{t}\binom{n}{i} + \frac{1}{2}.$$

In scenario $AE(1)$, Eve knows K''_a and has to guess K'_a where $K''_a = K_a + e'$, thus $K''_a = K'_a + e' + e$. Since $\texttt{wt}(e' + e) \leq 2t$, Eve has workload:

$$W(K''_a \to K'_a) \approx \frac{1}{2}\sum_{i=0}^{2t}\binom{n}{i} + \frac{1}{2}.$$

In scenario $AE(0)$ Eve has no information on Alice thus she has to brute force all possibilities. Thus the number of trials is approximately:

$$W(0 \to K'_a) \approx \frac{2^n + 1}{2}.$$

Scenarios for Bob are analogous:

BE(0) No previous contact between Bob and Eve.
BE(1) Eve records a measurement of Bob.
BE(2) Eve had a previous round with Bob thus knows T_b and can construct K_b.

Eve's workload for guessing K'_b is equal to guessing K'_a in the analogous scenario. To achieve her goal of loading her template in one of the devices, Eve has to guess $K'_a||K'_b$ in all scenarios. Table 1 summarizes her workload. In each row we have the information that Eve knows about Bob and in the column the information that Eve knows about Alice. Due to the message flow in the protocol (see figure 1), Eve might have an advantage if she has information about Alice. Eve can intercept message (4), $\{F_a\}_{K'_a}$ and recover K'_a if the biometrics allows for taking a decision on whether two measurements come from the same individual. This explains the plus sign between the work of guessing K'_a and the work of guessing K'_b in the columns where Eve has some

Table 1. Guesswork required for Eve to compute the session key

	AE(0)	AE(1)	AE(2)
BE(0)	$W(0 \to K'_a) \cdot W(0 \to K'_b)$	$W(K''_a \to K'_a) + W(0 \to K'_b)$	$W(K_a \to K'_a) + W(0 \to K'_b)$
BE(1)	$W(0 \to K'_a) \cdot W(K''_b \to K'_b)$	$W(K''_a \to K'_a) + W(K''_b \to K'_b)$	$W(K_a \to K'_a) + W(K''_b \to K'_b)$
BE(2)	$W(0 \to K'_a) \cdot W(K_b \to K'_b)$	$W(K''_a \to K'_a) + W(K_b \to K'_b)$	$W(K_a \to K'_a) + W(K_b \to K'_b)$

knowledge about Alice. We can estimate an upper bound for the work load of Alice and Bob according to Pliam's [8] equation:

$$W_{Alice}(K_a \to K'_a) \leq \frac{1}{2}(\sum_{i=0}^{t} \binom{n}{i} + 1) - \frac{1}{2}\sum_{i=0}^{t} \binom{n}{t} \cdot \sum_{j=1}^{n} |E_j(\sigma, q) - \frac{1}{2^n}|.$$

Here $E_j(\sigma, q)$ represents the distribution of the noise, which is described below. The best case scenario for Eve, however unlikely, is [BE(2),AE(2)] when she had a previous round with both Alice and Bob. Even though she has both K_a and K_b her workload is at least twice as high compared to Alice or Bob. Moreover while for Eve all error patterns are equally likely, Alice and Bob have the error profile that makes recovery faster.

4 Experimental Validation with Real Life Data

The *Correct* function used during the FiB protocol uses a semi-known plain text attack to recover the key. We link the keys used in the protocol to the biometric data of a user using the template protection scheme proposed by Linnartz and Tuyls [5]. The purpose of using this function is to lower the error rate of the system by flipping bits on the result of function Reg in the order defined by the user specific user profile E.

Key search algorithm. In classical symmetric cryptography to decrypt a message encrypted with a key K one must posses K. In particular, with a key K' that differs only in one bit from K, decryption will fail. The FiB protocol uses this apparent disadvantage of symmetric key cryptography as an advantage: K' is used to form the session key. The noise of the measurements is used as random salt [13] for the session key. The key search algorithm makes it possible to recover K'. We start the key search by assuming there are no errors in $K^{'}$, and we use $K^{'}$ for decryption. If decryption fails we assume that we have a one bit error. We start flipping one bit of the key according to the position indicated by the error profile, until we have exhausted the error profile. Then we assume that two bits are wrong and we try all combinations of two bits from the error profile. Finally if we reach the limit on the number of trials we assume that the key is coming from an intruder. The recovery of K' is a semi-known plain text attack. When the correct value of $K^{'}$ is discovered the initiator will recognize the message encrypted with $K^{'}$. This is possible since the encrypted message is a biometric template. The initiator of the protocol possesses a fresh measurement of this template and hence is able to recognize a correct match. The verification is performed by a classifier based matching algorithm designed for this particular biometrics.

Error profile computation. Linnartz et *al.* [5] propose a multiple quantization level system with odd-even bands. The embedding of binary data is done by shifting the template distribution to the center of the closest even-odd q interval if the value of the key bit is a 1, or to the center of an odd-even q interval if the value of the key bit is a 0. The calculation $\texttt{Gen}(t_i, k_i) = h_i$ proceeds component wise as follows, where $i = 1, n$:

$$\texttt{Gen}(t_i, k_i) = h_i = \begin{cases} (2p + \frac{1}{2}) \cdot q - t_i, & k_i = 1 \\ (2p - \frac{1}{2}) \cdot q - t_i, & k_i = 0. \end{cases}$$

where $p \in \mathbb{Z}$ is chosen such that $h_i \leq 2q$. During authentication the key is recovered by computing:

$$\texttt{Reg}(f_i, h_i) = \begin{cases} 1, & 2pq \leq f_i + h_i < (2p+1)q \\ 0, & (2p-1)q \leq f_i + h_i < 2pq. \end{cases}$$

However, during $\texttt{Reg}$ whenever the difference between the measured f_i value and the template t_i is greater than $\frac{q}{2}$ we get an error in the key computation. Each key bit is extracted independently. Thus, the error profile is a vector of length n. The i-th value of the error profile represents the probability of the i-th key bit to be computed wrongly. We assume that the features are independent and normally distributed. The error profile is computed component-wise, using the function:

$$E_i(\sigma, q) = \sigma\, 2\sqrt{2} \sum_{i=0}^{\infty} \int_{\frac{(1+4i)}{2\sqrt{2}} \frac{q}{\sigma}}^{\frac{(3+4i)}{2\sqrt{2}} \frac{q}{\sigma}} e^{-x^2} dx \approx \sigma\, 2\sqrt{2} \int_{\frac{q}{\sigma\, 2\sqrt{2}}}^{\frac{3q}{\sigma\, 2\sqrt{2}}} e^{-x^2} dx,$$

During enrollment several different measurement have to be made for each user. The error profile is based on the fact that in practical situations the estimated standard deviation is different for different user. To compute the error profile we use the same data after dimensionality reduction that the classifier based matcher use.

Results. We implemented the key extraction described above. We wanted to see the influence of the correction mechanism on the overall error rates. The evaluation is performed on real life grip pattern biometric data collected from 41 police officers. A detailed description of this biometric can be found in Veldhuis *et al.* [11]. Each of the 41 officers contributed 25 different measurements. Approximately 75% of these samples(18), are used for training the algorithm and 25% (7) are used for testing. First, we reduce the dimensionality of the data to 40 independent features. For training and testing we use the same data that is used for verification by the classifier based recognition algorithm.Second, we embed the key bits using Linnartz and Tuyls scheme above. Figures 2 presents the results obtained from the collected data. We offer three conclusions from this evaluation. The first conclusion is, as expected, the larger the quantization step the lower the FRR but the higher the FAR. We tested 8 different values for q, ranging from 1 to 5 in increments of 0.5. We did not try larger values for q because the FAR becomes unacceptably large. The second conclusion is that the influence of the correction algorithm is significant. For example for $q = 3$, without correction the FRR=13.93% and the FAR=0%. When we correct 1 bit the FRR goes down to 5.92%,

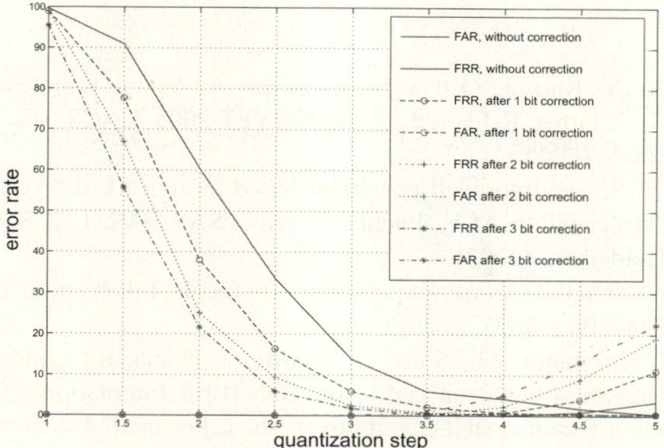

Fig. 2. Results on grip pattern data

while the FAR retains the same value 0%. After correcting 2 bits the FRR goes down to 2.43% while the FAR remains equal to 0%. Correcting 3 bits further reduces the FRR to 1.74% while the FAR increases only slightly to 0.07%. The third conclusion is that the correction mechanism is stable, meaning that the effect of correction is independent of the time when data in collected. Data was collected during two sessions and the performance of the correction algorithm is similar on both sets.

5 Conclusions

The contributions of this paper are threefold. Firstly, we propose FiB a protocol that can exchange biometric templates securely even though no prior security association exists between the participants. We are confident in the guarantees offered by FiB because we formally verify the protocol to prove security and origin authentication. Also, from the information theoretic point of view the workload of Eve is at least double of that of Alice or Bob in the unlikely scenario where Eve has interacted with Alice and Bob and where Eve possess the same key material. Moreover, in this case the biometric has to be favorable to Eve in that she has to be able to verify wheatear two noisy measurements are coming from the same user or not. Secondly, for the first time we propose to use biometrics as a secure side channel. The advantage of using biometrics compared to any other types of side channels is the extreme user friendliness. Thirdly, a new correction mechanism for correcting biometric errors based on user specific error profile is proposed. We present an evaluation of the performance in terms of FAR and FRR and we show that the correction algorithm significantly improves the overall results. Our experiments show that by correcting only 1 bit in the overall key the FRR is reduced by approximately 50% while the FAR is not increased significantly. We believe that our approach can be applied to other types of biometrics.

Acknowledgements

The authors would like to thank Ricardo Corin and Sandro Etalle for helping formally verify the protocol using CoProVe.

References

1. Boyen, X., Dodis, Y., Katz, J., Ostrovsky, R., Smith, A.: Secure remote authentication using biometric data. In: Cramer, R.J.F. (ed.) EUROCRYPT 2005. LNCS, vol. 3494, pp. 147–163. Springer, Heidelberg (2005)
2. Corin, R., Etalle, S.: An improved constraint-based system for the verification of security protocols. In: Hermenegildo, M.V., Puebla, G. (eds.) SAS 2002. LNCS, vol. 2477, pp. 326–341. Springer, Heidelberg (2002)
3. Dolev, D., Yao, A.: On the security of public key protocols. Information Theory, IEEE Transactions on 29, 198–208 (1983)
4. Goodrich, M.T., Sirivianos, M., Solis, J., Tsudik, G., Uzun, E.: Loud and clear: Human-verifiable authentication based on audio. In: 26th IEEE International Conference on Distributed Computing Systems (ICDCS 2006), Lisboa, Portugal, 4-7 July 2006, p. 10. IEEE Computer Society Press, Los Alamitos (2006)
5. Linnartz, J.P, Tuyls, P.: New shielding functions to enhance privacy and prevent misuse of biometric templates. In: Kittler, J., Nixon, M.S. (eds.) AVBPA 2003. LNCS, vol. 2688, pp. 393–402. Springer, Heidelberg (2003)
6. McCune, J., Perrig, A., Reiter, M.: Seeing-is-believing: using camera phones for human-verifiable authentication. In: Security and Privacy, 2005 IEEE Symposium on, pp. 110–124. IEEE Computer Society Press, Los Alamitos (2005)
7. NJIT: Personalized weapons technology project, progress report. Technical report, New Jersey Institute of Technology (April 2001)
8. Pliam, J.O.: Guesswork and variation distance as measures of cipher security. In: Heys, H.M., Adams, C.M. (eds.) SAC 1999. LNCS, vol. 1758. Springer, Heidelberg (2000)
9. Saxena, N., Ekberg, J., Kostiainen, K., Asokan, N.: Secure device pairing based on a visual channel (short paper). SP, 306–313 (2006)
10. Vaudenay, S.: Secure communications over insecure channels based on short authenticated strings. In: Shoup, V. (ed.) CRYPTO 2005. LNCS, vol. 3621, pp. 309–326. Springer, Heidelberg (2005)
11. Veldhuis, R.N.J., Bazen, A.M., Kauffman, J.A., Hartel, P.H.: Biometric verification based on grip-pattern recognition. In: Security, Steganography, and Watermarking of Multimedia Contents VI, Proceedings of SPIE, San Jose, California, USA, January 18-22, 2004, vol. 5306, pp. 634–641 (2004)
12. Wong, F.L., Stajano, F.: Multi-channel protocols for group key agreement in arbitrary topologies. In: 4th IEEE Conference on Pervasive Computing and Communications Workshops (PerCom 2006 Workshops), Pisa, Italy, 13-17 March 2006, pp. 246–250. IEEE Computer Society Press, Los Alamitos (2006)
13. Wu, T.D.: The secure remote password protocol. In: Proceedings of the Network and Distributed System Security Symposium, NDSS 1998, San Diego, California, USA. The Internet Society (1998)

SVM-Based Selection of Colour Space Experts for Face Authentication

Mohammad T. Sadeghi[1], Samaneh Khoshrou[1], and Josef Kittler[2]

[1] Signal Processing Research Lab., Department of Electronics
University of Yazd, Yazd, Iran
[2] Centre for Vision, Speech and Signal Processing
School of Electronics and Physical Sciences
University of Surrey, Guildford GU2 7XH, UK
{M.Sadeghi,J.Kittler}@surrey.ac.uk

Abstract. We consider the problem of fusing colour information to enhance the performance of a face authentication system. The discriminatory information potential of a vast range of colour spaces is investigated. The verification process is based on the normalised correlation in an LDA feature space. A sequential search approach which is in principle similar to the "plus L and take away R" algorithm is applied in order to find an optimum subset of the colour spaces. The colour based classifiers are combined using the SVM classifier. We show that by fusing colour information using the proposed method, the resulting decision making scheme considerably outperforms the intensity based verification system.

1 Introduction

The spectral property of the skin albedo is known to provide useful biometric information for face recognition. Measured in terms of colour, it has been exploited directly in terms of features derived from the colour histogram [7]. Such features are then used to augment the face feature space in which the matching of a probe image against a template is carried out. Alternatively, the spectral information can be used indirectly, by treating each R, G, B colour channel as a separate image. The face matching scores computed for the respective channels are then combined to reach the final decision about the probe image identity. This indirect approach has the advantage that an existing face recognition system can simply be applied to create the respective colour space experts, without any structural redesign. This indirect approach has been investigated extensively in [13] [6]. In these studies the colour face experts were designed in different colour spaces, such as R, G, B, the intensity image, normalised green and an opponent colour channel, or colour channels decorrelated by the Principal Component Analysis (PCA). The merits of the information conveyed by the various channels individually, as well as their combined effect, have been evaluated. It has been demonstrated that some of the colour spaces provide more powerful representation of the face skin properties than others, offering significant improvements in performance as compared to the raw intensity image. In

S.-W. Lee and S.Z. Li (Eds.): ICB 2007, LNCS 4642, pp. 907–916, 2007.

this paper we extend the work to other colour representations suggested in the literature. In total, 15 different colour spaces are considered, giving rise to 45 different colour channels. Assuming that face experts based on all these channels are available, it is pertinent to ask which channels provide complementary information and how the expert scores should be fused to achieve the best possible performance of the face recognition system. In [12] the fusion problem was solved by selecting the best expert or a group of experts dynamically with the help of a gating function learnt for each channel. In the present study we formulate the colour expert fusion problem as a feature selection problem. The colour spaces for fusion are selected using a sequential search approach similar to the Plus L and Take Away R algorithm.

An important contributing factor in the selection algorithm is the "fusion rule" used for combining the colour based classifiers. In [11] untrained methods such as averaging and voting schemes were used for this purpose. However, in different applications it has been demonstrated that trained approaches such as Support Vector Machines (SVMs) have the potential to outperform the simple fusion rules, especially when a large enough training data is available. The main aim of this paper is to study the performance of the proposed colour selection algorithm using the SVM classifiers. Surprisingly good results are obtained using the proposed method.

The paper is organised as follows. In the next section different colour spaces adopted in different machine vision applications are reviewed. The face verification process is briefly discussed in Section 3. The proposed method of colour space selection is described in Section 4. The experimental set up is detailed in Section 5. Section 6 presents the results of the experiments. Finally, in Section 7 the paper is drawn to conclusion.

2 Colour Spaces

For computer displays, it is most common to describe colour as a set of three primary colours: Red, Green and Blue. However, it has been demonstrated that in different applications using different colour spaces could be beneficial. In this section some of the most important colour spaces are reviewed. Considering the R, G, B system as the primary colour space, we can classify the other colour spaces into two main categories: Linear and Nonlinear transformation of the R, G,B values.

2.1 Linear Combination of R,G,B

CMY-based colour space is commonly used in colour printing systems. The name CMY refers to cyan, magenta and yellow. The RGB values can be converted to CMY values using:

$$C = 255 - R, \quad M = 255 - G, \; Y = 255 - B \tag{1}$$

There are several CIE-based colour spaces,but all are derived from the fundamental XYZ space [2]. A number of different colour spaces including YUV,

YIQ, YES and YC_bC_r are based on separating luminance from chrominance (lightness from colour). These spaces are useful in compression and other image processing applications. Their formal definition can be found in [2].

$I1I2I3$ or Ohta's features [8] were first introduced for segmentation as optimised colour features and are shown in equations:

$$I1 = \frac{R+G+B}{3.0}, \quad I2 = R - B, \quad I3 = 2G - R - B \tag{2}$$

LEF Colour Space defines a colour model that combines the additivity of the RGB model with the intuitiveness of the hue-saturation-luminance models by applying a linear transformation to the RGB cube.

2.2 Nonlinear Combination of R,G,B

The chromaticities for the normalised RGB are obtained by normalising the RGB values with the intensity value, I:

$$r = R/I, \quad g = G/I, \quad b = B/I \tag{3}$$

where $I = (R+G+B)/3$. Similar equations are used for normalising the XYZ values. The result is a 2D space known as the CIE chromaticity diagram. The opponent chromaticity space is also defined as

$$rg = r - g, \quad yb = r + g - 2b \tag{4}$$

Kawato and Ohya [5] have used the ab space which is derived from NCC rg-chromaticities as:

$$a = r + g/2, \quad b = \sqrt{3}/(2g) \tag{5}$$

In [16], two colour spaces namely $P1$ and $P2$ have been defined by circulating the r, g and b values in equation 4. Log-opponent (or Log-opponent chromaticity) space has been applied to image indexing in [1]. The space is presented by equations:

$$Ln_{rg} = \ln(R/G) = \ln R - \ln G$$
$$Lnyb = ln(\frac{R.G}{B^2}) = \ln R + \ln G - 2\ln B \tag{6}$$

TSL (Tint - Saturation - Lightness) colour space is also derived from NCC rg-chromaticities.

$l1l2l3$ colour space as presented in [4] has been adopted for colour-based object recognition. Many people find HS-spaces (HSV, HSB, HSI, HSL) intuitive for colour definition. For more information about the relevant equations used in this study, the reader is referred to [3].

3 Face Verification Process

The face verification process consists of three main stages: face image acquisition, feature extraction, and finally decision making. The first stage involves sensing and image preprocessing the result of which is a geometrically registered and photometrically normalised face image. Briefly, the output of a physical sensor (camera) is analysed by a face detector and once a face instance is detected, the position of the eyes is determined. This information allows the face part of the image to be extracted at a given aspect ratio and resampled to a pre-specified resolution. The extracted face image is finally photometrically normalised to compensate for illumination changes.

The raw colour camera channel outputs, R, G and B are converted according to the desired image representation spaces. In this study different colour spaces reviewed in the previous section were considered.

In the second stage of the face verification process the face image data is projected into a feature space. The final stage of the face verification process involves matching and decision making. Basically the features extracted for a face image to be verified, $\mathbf{x}$, are compared with a stored template, $\boldsymbol{\mu}_i$, that was acquired on enrolment. In [14], it was demonstrated that the Gradient Direction (GD) metric or Normalised Correlation (NC) function in the Linear Discriminant Analysis (LDA) feature space works effectively in the face verification systems. In this study we adopted the NC measure in the LDA space. The score, s, output by the matching process is then used for decision making. In our previous studies [11] [6], global or client specific thresholding method were used for decision making. In this work, the above mentioned thresholding methods are compared to decision making using the Support Vector Machines.

If the score computation is applied to different colour spaces separately, we end up with a number of scores, $s_k = s(\mathbf{x}_k), \ \ k = 1, 2, \ldots, N$ which then have to be fused to obtain the final decision. The adopted fusion method is studied in the next section.

4 Colour Space Selection

One of the most exciting research directions in the field of pattern recognition and computer vision is classifier fusion. Multiple expert fusion aims to make use of many different designs to improve the classification performance. The approach we adopted for selecting the best colour space(s) is similar in principal to the sequential feature selection methods in pattern recognition [10]. In this study, the Sequential Forward Selection (SFS), Sequential Backward Selection (SBS) and Plus'L' and Take away 'R' algorithms were examined for selecting an optimum subset of the colour spaces. Two untrained fusion rules, the sum rule and the voting scheme and a trained fusion method, the Support Vector Machines are used in order to combine the scores of the colour based classifiers. The selection procedure keeps adding or taking away features (colour spaces in our case) until the best evaluation performance is achieved. The selected colour spaces are then used in the test stage.

4.1 Support Vector Machines

A Support Vector Machine is a two-class classifier showing superior performance to other methods in terms of Structural Risk Minimisation [15]. For a given training sample $\{\mathbf{x}_i, y_i\}$, $i = 1, ..., N$, where $\mathbf{x}_i \in R^D$ is the object marked with a label $y_i \in \{-1, 1\}$, it is necessary to find the direction $\mathbf{w}$ along which the margin between objects of two classes is maximal. Once this direction is found the decision function is determined by threshold b:

$$y(\mathbf{x}) = sgn(\mathbf{w} \cdot \mathbf{x} + b) \tag{7}$$

The threshold is usually chosen to provide equal distance to the closest objects of the two classes from the discriminant hyperplane $\mathbf{w} \cdot \mathbf{x} + b = 0$, which is called the optimal hyperplane. When the classes are linearly non-separable some objects can be shifted by a value δ_i towards the right class. This converts the original problem into one which exhibits linear separation. The parameters of the optimal hyperplane and the optimal shifts can be found by solving the following quadratic programming problem:

$$\begin{aligned} & \textit{minimise } \mathbf{w} \cdot \mathbf{w} + C \sum_{i=1}^{N} \delta_i \\ & \textit{subject to:} \\ & y_i(\mathbf{w} \cdot \mathbf{x}_i + b) \geq 1 - \delta_i, \quad \delta_i \geq 0 \quad i = 1, ..., N \end{aligned} \tag{8}$$

where parameter C defines the penalty for shifting the objects that would otherwise be misclassified in the case of linearly non separable classes.

The QP problem is usually solved in a dual formulation

$$\begin{aligned} & \textit{minimise } \sum_{i=1}^{N} \alpha_i - \frac{1}{2} \sum_{i=1}^{N} \sum_{j=1}^{N} \alpha_i \alpha_j y_i y_j \mathbf{x}_i \cdot \mathbf{x}_j \\ & \textit{subject to:} \\ & \sum_{i=1}^{N} \alpha_i y_i = 0, \quad 0 \leq \alpha_i \leq C \quad i = 1, ..., N \end{aligned} \tag{9}$$

Those training objects $\mathbf{x}_i$ with $\alpha_i > 0$ are called Support Vectors, because only they determine direction $\mathbf{w}$:

$$\mathbf{w} = \sum_{i=1,\ \alpha_i > 0}^{N} \alpha_i y_i \mathbf{x}_i \tag{10}$$

The dual QP problem can be rapidly solved by the Sequential Minimal Optimisation method, proposed by Platt [9]. This method exploits the presence of linear constraints in (9). The QP problem is iteratively decomposed into a series of one variable optimisation problems which can be solved analytically.

For the face verification problem, the size of the training set for clients is usually less than the one for impostors. In such a case, the class of impostors is represented better. Therefore, it is necessary to shift the optimal hyperplane towards the better represented class. In this work, the size of the shift is determined in the evaluation step considering the Equal Error Rate criterion.

5 Experimental Design

The aim of the experiments is to show that by fusing the sensory data used by component experts, the performance of the multiple classifier system improves considerably. We use the XM2VTS database [1] and its associated experimental protocols for this purpose.

The XM2VTS database is a multi-modal database consisting of face images, video sequences and speech recordings taken of 295 subjects at one month intervals. Since the data acquisition was distributed over a long period of time, significant variability of appearance of clients, e.g. changes of hair style, facial hair, shape and presence or absence of glasses, is present in the recordings.

For the task of personal verification, a standard protocol for performance assessment has been defined. The so called Lausanne protocol splits randomly all subjects into a client and impostor groups. The client group contains 200 subjects, the impostor group is divided into 25 evaluation impostors and 70 test impostors. The XM2VTS database contains 4 sessions. Eight images from 4 sessions are used.

From these sets consisting of face images, training set, evaluation set and test set are built. There exist two configurations that differ by a selection of particular shots of people into the training, evaluation and test sets. The training set is used to construct client models. The evaluation set is selected to produce client and impostor access scores, which are used for designing the required classifier. The score classification is done either by the SVM classifier or by thresholding. The thresholds are set either globally (GT) or using the client specific thresholding (CST)technique [6]. According to the Lausanne protocol the threshold is set to satisfy the Equal Error Rate criterion, i.e. the operating point where the false rejection rate (FRR) is equal to the false acceptance rate (FAR). False acceptance is the case where an impostor, claiming the identity of a client, is accepted. False rejection is the case where a client, claiming his true identity, is rejected. The evaluation set is also used in fusion experiments (classifier combination) for training. The SVM-based sequential search algorithms pick the best colour spaces using this set of data.

Finally the test set is selected to simulate realistic authentication tests where impostor's identity is unknown to the system. The performance measures of a verification system are the False Acceptance rate and the False Rejection rate.

The original resolution of the image data is 720×576. The experiments were performed with a relatively low resolution face images, namely 64×49. The results reported in this article have been obtained by applying a geometric face registration based on manually annotated eyes positions. Histogram equalisation was used to normalise the registered face photometrically.

[1] http://www.ee.surrey.ac.uk/Research/VSSP/xm2vtsdb/

6 Experimental Results

Table 1 shows the performance of the face verification system using the individual colour spaces considering the first configuration of the Lausanne protocol. The decision boundary in the NC space was determined using the SVMs. The values in the table indicate the FAR and FRR in both evaluation and test stages. As we expect, the best performance is obtained neither in the original RGB spaces nor in the intensity space. Some other colour spaces such as U in the YUV space or opponent chromaticities individually can lead to better results. Table 2 shows some results of the same experiments considering the second XM2VTS protocol configuration.

As mentioned earlier, in similar experiments the global or client specific thresholding techniques were used for decision making. Figure 1 contains plots of the total error rate in different colour spaces in the evaluation and test stages. These results demonstrate that although in most of the cases, the SVMs work better than the GT technique, but the CST leads to better or comparable results.

Table 1. Identity verification results using different colour spaces. Classification boundary was determined using the SVMs.(configuration 1).

subspace	R	G	B	I	H	Sat	Val	r	g
FAR Eval	2.19	1.97	1.75	2.14	1.92	1.76	2.19	1.93	1.48
FRR Eval.	2.17	2	1.83	2.17	1.83	1.66	2.16	1.83	1.5
FAR Test	2.41	1.97	1.97	2.17	1.84	1.81	2.46	2.08	1.47
FRR Test	1.5	1.75	1.75	1.25	0.5	1.25	2	0.75	1
subspace	b	T(TSL)	S(TSL)	L(TSL)	V(YUV)	rg	U(YUV)	Cr	I2
FAR Eval.	1.69	1.52	1.31	2.11	2.31	1.49	1.91	1.82	2.31
FRR Eval	1.66	1.5	1.33	2.166	2.33	1.5	1.83	1.83	2.33
FAR Test	1.73	1.32	1.53	2.1491	2.26	1.60	1.75	2.21	2.3
FRR Test	1.25	1	1.75	1.5	0.75	1.25	0	1.5	0.75
subspace	I3	E(LEF)	F(LEF)	X(CIE)	Y(CIE)	Z(CIE)	Y(YES)	E(YES)	S(YES)
FAR Eval.	1.67	2.1	1.66	2.27	2.11	2	2.05	1.82	2
FRR Eval.	1.6	2.166	1.67	2.33	2.166	2	2	1.83	2
FAR Test	1.69	2.21	1.60	2.38	2.14	2.25	2.10	1.65	1.82
FRR Test	0.75	0.5	0.5	1.25	1.5	1.75	1.5	0.75	0.25
subspace	I(YIQ)	Q(YIQ)	a(ab)	b(ab)	Lnrg	Lnyb	l1	l2	l3
FAR Eval.	2.17	1.85	1.79	1.52	1.22	1.49	2.05	2.35	1.71
FRR Eval.	2.16	1.83	1.83	1.5	1.16	1.5	2	2.33	1.67
FAR Test	2.48	1.75	1.92	1.58	1.35	1.59	1.74	2.46	1.58
FRR Test	1.5	0.75	1.25	1.2500	1.75	1.25	1	1.25	1.50
subspace	LHSL)	Xn	Yn	Zn	C(CMY)	M(CMY)	Y(CMY)	bg	
FAR Eval.	2.33	1.80	1.65	1.52	2.47	2.02	1.74	1.66	
FRR Eval.	2.33	1.83	1.66	1.5	2.5	2	1.83	1.66	
FAR Test	2.42	1.90	1.69	1.57	2.79	2.02	1.97	1.73	
FRR Test	1	1	1.25	0.5	1.75	1.75	1.75	0.75	

Table 2. Identity verification results using some of the colour spaces (configuration 2)

subspace	R	G	B	I	H	S	V	r	g	b
FAR Eval.	1.26	1.25	1.25	1.24	1.25	1.23	1.25	1.36	0.74	1.34
FRR Eval.	1.25	1.25	1.25	1.25	1.25	1.25	1.25	1.25	0.75	1.25
FAR Test	1.65	1.67	1.87	1.80	1.14	1.71	1.61	2.02	0.76	1.67
FRR Test	1.5	1.5	1.5	1.5	0.5	1	1.5	1.5	0.5	0.75

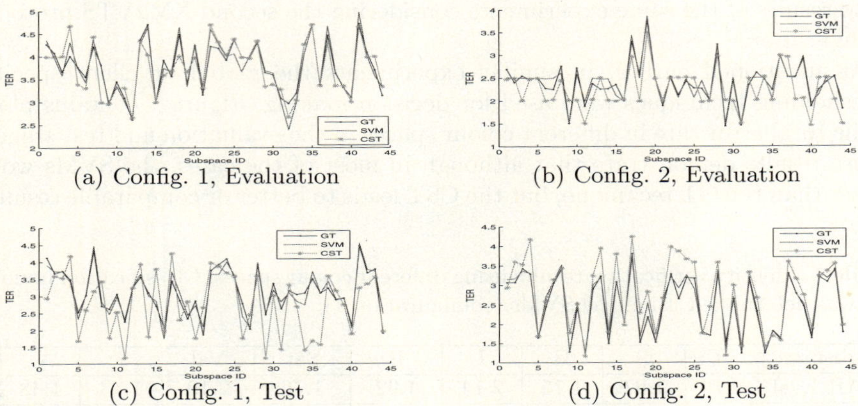

(a) Config. 1, Evaluation (b) Config. 2, Evaluation

(c) Config. 1, Test (d) Config. 2, Test

Fig. 1. Verification results in different colour spaces. The decision boundary has been determined using GT, SVMs or CST.

In the next step, the adopted search method, Plus 'L' and Take away 'R' algorithm was used for selecting a subset of colour spaces. Figure 2 shows the resulting error rates for different number of colour spaces in Configurations 1 and 2. In the search algorithm $L = 2$ and $R = 1$. Before fusing, the scores associated to each colour space were appropriately normalised. The normalised scores were then considered as a feature vector. The SVM classifier was finally used for decision making.

Table 3 contains the fusion results obtained using the adopted "Plus 2 and take away 1" algorithm for Configurations 1 and 2. These results were obtained by score fusion using the averaging rule or the SVMs. Note that using the search algorithm, colour spaces are selected from the evaluation data for the whole data set. However, the algorithm is flexible so that, for different conditions, different spaces can be adopted adaptively. In the case of the experimental protocols of the XM2VTS database using the SVM classifier Lnrg, a(ab), V(HSV) spaces have been selected for the first configuration while b(ab),U(YUV), bg(opp-chroma), Cr, X(CIE),I, V(HSV), H(HSV) and S(YES) have been adopted for the second one. These results first of all demonstrate that the proposed colour selection algorithm considerably improves the performance of the face verification system. Moreover, they also show that although not much gain in performance can be

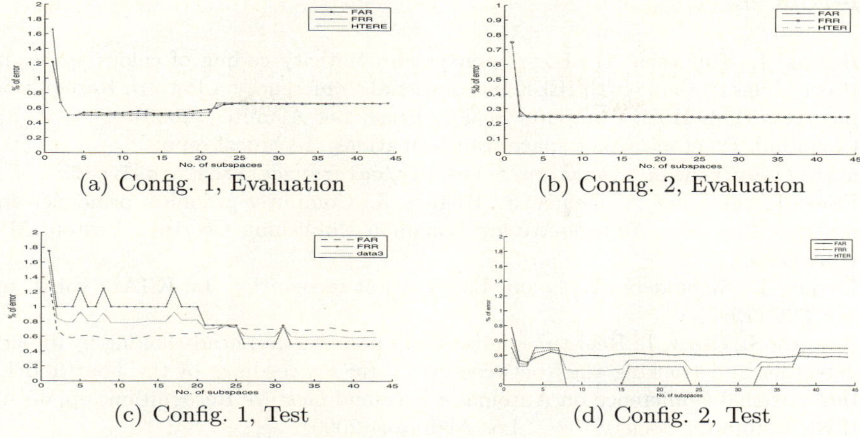

(a) Config. 1, Evaluation (b) Config. 2, Evaluation

(c) Config. 1, Test (d) Config. 2, Test

Fig. 2. SVM-based Plus 2 and Take away 1 results

Table 3. Verification results using the proposed colour selection and fusion methods

Configuration	Fusion rule	Evaluation			Test		
		FAR	FRR	TER	FAR	FRR	TER
1	Averaging	0.48	0.5	0.98	0.55	1	1.55
	SVMs	0.5	0.5	1	0.59	1	1.59
2	Averaging	0.19	0.25	0.44	0.27	0.25	0.52
	SVMs	0.24	0.25	0.49	0.38	0	0.38

obtained from SVMs in the colour spaces individually (figure 1) , combining the colour based classifiers using SVMs would overall be beneficial.

7 Conclusions

We addressed the problem of fusing colour information for face authentication. In a face verification system which is based on the normalised correlation measure in the LDA face space, an SVM-based sequential search approach similar to the "plus L, and take away R" algorithm was applied in order to find an optimum subset of the colour spaces. Using the proposed method, the performance of the verification system was considerably improved as compared to intensity only or the other colour spaces. Within the framework of the proposed method, we showed that fusing colour based classifiers using SVMs outperforms the simple averaging rule.

Acknowledgements. The financial support from Iran Telecommunication Research Centre is gratefully acknowledged. A partial support from the EU Network of Excellence Biosecure and from the EPSRC Grant GR/S98528/01 is also gratefully acknowledged.

References

1. Berens, J., Finlayson, G.: Log-opponent chromaticity coding of colour space. In: Proceedings of the Fourth IEEE International Conference on Pattern Recognition, pp. 1206–1211. IEEE Computer Society Press, Los Alamitos (2000)
2. Colantoni, P., et al.: Color space transformations. Technical report, http://www.raduga-ryazan.ru/files/doc/colorspacetransform95.pdf
3. Foley, J., van Dam, A., Feiner, S., Hughes, J.: Computer graphics: principles and practice, 2nd edn. Addison-Wesley Longman Publishing Co. Inc., Boston, MA, USA (1996)
4. Gevers, T., Smeulders, A.: Colour based object recognition. In: ICIAP, vol. 1, pp. 319–326 (1997)
5. Kawato, S., Ohya, J.: Real-time detection of nodding and head-shaking by directly detecting and tracking the "between-eyes". In: Proceedings of the Fourth IEEE International Conference on Automatic Face and Gesture Recognition, pp. 40–45. IEEE Computer Society Press, Los Alamitos (2000)
6. Kittler, J., Sadeghi, M.: Physics-based decorrelation of image data for decision level fusion in face verification. In: Roli, F., Kittler, J., Windeatt, T. (eds.) MCS 2004. LNCS, vol. 3077, pp. 354–363. Springer, Heidelberg (2004)
7. Marcel, S., Bengio, S.: Improving face verification using skin colour information. In: 16th International Conference on Pattern Recognition, vol. 2, pp. 20378–20382 (2002)
8. Ohta, Y., Kanade, T., Sakai, T.: Colour information for region segmentation. Computer Graphics and Image Processing 13(3), 222–241 (1980)
9. Platt, J.: Sequential minimal optimization: A fast algorithm for training support vector machines. Technical Report 98-14, Microsoft Research, Redmond, Washington (April 1998)
10. Pudil, P., Novovicova, J., Kittler, J.: Floating search methods in feature selection. Pattern Recognition Letters 15, 1119–1125 (1994)
11. Sadeghi, M., Khoshrou, S., Kittler, J.: Colour feature selection for face authentication. In: Proceedings of the International Conference on Macine Vision Applications, MVA'07, Japan, May 2007 (2007)
12. Sadeghi, M., Khoshrou, S., Kittler, J.: Confidence based gating of colour features for face authentication. In: Proceedings of the 7th International Workshop on Multiple Classifier System, MCS'07, Czech Republi, May 2007, pp. 121–130 (2007)
13. Sadeghi, M., Kittler, J.: A comparative study of data fusion strategies in face verification. In: The 12th European Signal Processing Conference, Vienna, Austria, 6-10 September 2004 (2004)
14. Sadeghi, M., Kittler, J.: Decision making in the LDA space: Generalised gradient direction metric. In: The 6th International Conference on Automatic Face and Gesture Recognition, Seoul, Korea, May 2004, pp. 248–253 (2004)
15. Vapnik, V.: The Nature of Statistical Learning Theory. Springer, New York (1995)
16. Vertan, C., Cuic, M., Boujemaa, N.: On the introduction of a chrominance spectrum and its applications. In: Proceedings of the First International Conference on Colour in Graphics and Image Processing, 1-4 October 2000, pp. 214–218 (2000)

An Efficient Iris Coding Based on Gauss-Laguerre Wavelets

H. Ahmadi[1,2], A. Pousaberi[1], A. Azizzadeh[3], and M. Kamarei[1]

[1] Dept. of Electrical and Computer Engineering,University of Tehran
[2] Dept. of Electrical and Computer Engineering, University of British Columbia
[3] Research Center, Ministry of Communication, Tehran, Iran
noubari@ece.ubc.ca, a.poursaberi@ece.ut.ac.ir, azad@itrc.ac.ir, kamarei@ut.ac.ir

Abstract. In this paper preliminary results of a new iris recognition algorithm using Gauss-Laguerre filter of circular harmonic wavelets are presented. Circular harmonic wavelets (CHWs) applied in this paper for iris pattern extraction, are polar-separable wavelets with harmonic angular shape. The main focus of this paper is on iris coding using Gauss-Laguerre CHWs which constitute a family of orthogonal functions satisfying wavelet admissibility condition required for multiresolution pyramid structure. It is shown that Gauss-Laguerre wavelets having rich frequency extraction capabilities are powerful tools for coding of iris patterns. By judicious tuning of Laguerre parameters, a 256-byte binary code is generated for each iris. A fast matching scheme based on Hamming distance is used to compute the similarity between pairs of iris codes. Preliminary experimental results on CASIA and our database indicate that the performance of the proposed method is highly accurate with zero false rate and is comparable with Daugman iris recognition algorithm well publisized in literature.

Keywords: Biometrics, Iris recognition, Gauss-Laguerre wavelets, Circular harmonic wavelets.

1 Introduction

Security and surveillance of information and personnel is becoming more and more important recently, in part due to the rapid development of information technology (IT) and its wide spread applications in all aspects of daily life. For surveillance of personnel, biometrics as a science of personal identification that utilize physical/biological or behavioral characteristics of an individual, are now widely used in numerous security applications. For a biometric system to be a valid candidate for use in human identification, it is required that it embodies any number of unique characteristics of an individual that remain consistent during the life of a person. Fingerprints, voiceprints, retinal blood vessel patterns, face, iris pattern, handwriting are examples of biometrics that can be used in place of non-biometric methods. Iris-based biometrics is considered to provide a high accuracy personal identification mainly due to rich texture of iris pattern as well as nonintrusive nature of biometric extraction [1].

S.-W. Lee and S.Z. Li (Eds.): ICB 2007, LNCS 4642, pp. 917–926, 2007.

Iris recognition is based on the visible features of the human iris (see Fig. 1) that include rings, furrows, freckles, and the iris corona. These unique features are protected by the body's own mechanisms and can not be modified without risk. As such iris features are considered to be the highly accurate and reliable biofeatures for personal identification [1] and has been a subject of wide attentions during the last decade. Standard iris recognition process consists of the following three major steps.

- Preprocessing step which includes image capturing, image filtering and enhancement (optional) followed by iris localization, normalization, de-noising and image enhancement.
- Iris feature extraction stage.
- Iris feature classification

Several algorithms have been proposed by numerous groups for iris-based biometrics of which the most publisized and accepted algorithm, belongs to John Daugman [2]. Daugman used multiscale quadrature wavelets to extract phase structure information of the iris texture and generate a 2048-bit iris code. For identification the difference between a pair of iris codes is evaluated using Hamming distance criteria. In Daugman scheme, it has been shown that a Hamming distance of less than 0.34 measured with any of iris templates in database was acceptable for identification. Since introduction of Daugman algorithm, numerous attempts have been made by other groups to arrive at compatible or alternative algorithms and several claims have been made on the adequacy of these algorithms for iris recognition. Daugman used the following three innovations for feature extraction and subsequent coding:

1. An Integro-differential scheme for iris segmentation.
2. A Cartesian to polar transformation followed by normalization.
3. A 256 binary code based on Gabor filters.

These three steps have also been utilized by other research groups in which alternative algorithms including modification of Gabor filters have been proposed. Among them, algorithms proposed by Wildes [3], Ma [4] are claimed to be comparable with Daugman scheme in accuracy of recognition. In this paper, we present an alternative iris coding scheme which utilizes Gaussian-Laguerre filters during iris coding where it is shown that results are commensurable with those of Daugman. The proposed algorithm using Gaussian-Laguerre wavelets first introduced in this paper was tested using CASIA data base as well as data generated by this research group. The rich information of Gaussian Laguerre filter in various frequency bands enables an extraction of the necessary iris patterns in an effective manner and generates a meaningful unique code for each individual. The proposed algorithm includes also an algorithm based on Radon transformation for iris localization which is computationally efficient and contributes significantly to increase the speed of iris localization. In the sequel, a brief reference is made to some of the related research works on iris-based biometrics followed with an overview of our proposed algorithm in Section 2. Description of circular harmonic wavelets (CHW) is included in Section 3. Image preprocessing for segmentation, feature extraction and pattern matching are

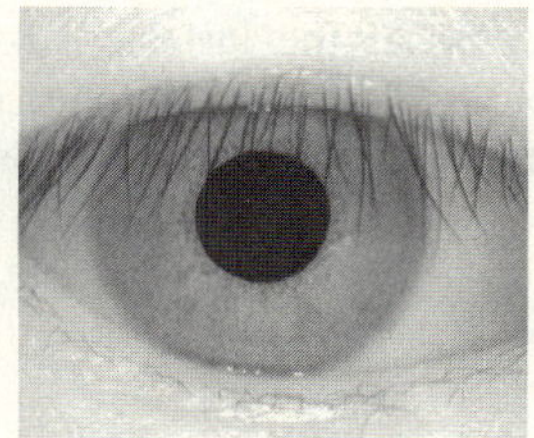
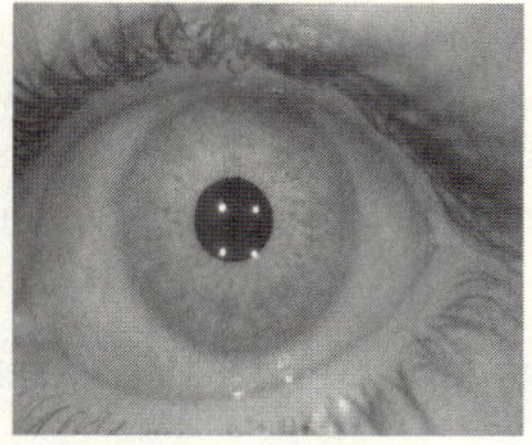

Fig. 1. Typical iris images, (left) CASIA data base, (right) Our captured iris image

given in Sections 4 and 5, respectively. Experimental results on Iris databases are reported in Section 6. Further works are described in Section 7. Finally Section 7 concludes this paper.

2 A Brief Overview of Literature and Proposed Scheme

Biometrics using iris features is relatively new with most of the works done during last decade. A pioneering work was done by John Daugman [2] in which multiscale quadrature wavelets were used to extract texture phase structure information of the iris to generate a 2,048-bit iris code. Euclidean distance was used to evaluate the difference between a pair of iris representations. It was shown that, a Hamming distance of lower than 0.34 with any of iris templates in database will suffice for identification. Ma et al.[4],[5] adopted a well-known texture analysis method (multichannel Gabor filtering) to capture both global and local details in an iris image. They studied Gabor filter families for feature extraction. Wildes et al. [3] considered Laplacian pyramid constructed in four different resolution levels and used their normalized correlation for matching Boles and Boashash [6] used a zero-crossing of 1D wavelet at various resolution levels to distinguish the texture of the iris. Tisse et al. [7] constructed the analytic image (a combination of the original image and its Hilbert transform) to demodulate the iris texture. Lim et al. [8] used 2D Haar wavelet and quantized the 4th level high frequency information to form an 87-binary code length as feature vector and applied a LVQ neural network for classification. Woo Nam et al. [9] exploited a scale-space filtering to extract unique features that uses the direction of concavity of image from an iris image. A modified Haralick's co-occurrence method with multilayer perceptron has also been introduced for extraction and classification of the iris images [10]. In a prior work carried-out by this group Daubechies2 wavelets were utilized for the analysis of local patterns of iris [11] [12].

A typical automatic iris recognition system (AIRS) requires an implementation of several steps as indicated in Fig. 2. At first step, an imaging system must be designed to capture a sequence of iris images with sufficient details from the subject. After image capturing, image preprocessing is to be applied on the images which includes several important steps stages consisting of identification of boundaries of iris, image enhancement, normalization and coordinate transformation. To implement an automatic iris recognition system (AIRS), we used a new algorithm for iris segmentation that is considered to perform faster than the currently reported methods. This was followed by a new iris feature extraction and coding algorithm using

Laguerre Gaussian wavelets. For matching process as the last step in identification process and for comparing iris code with database, Hamming distance between class of each iris code and input code was utilized. Descriptions of details of proposed algorithms are given in sections that follow.

3 Gaussian Laguerre Wavelets

The circular harmonic wavelets (CHWs) are polar-separable wavelets, with harmonic angular shape. They are steerable in any desired direction by simple multiplication with a complex steering factor and as such they are referred to self-steerable wavelets. The CHWs were first introduced in [14] which utilizes concepts from circular harmonic functions (CHFs) employed in optical correlations for rotation invariant pattern recognition. The same functions also appear in harmonic tomographic decomposition and have been considered for the analysis of local image symmetry. In addition; recently, CHFs have been employed for the definition of rotation-invariant pattern signatures [8]. A family of orthogonal CHWs forming a multiresolution pyramid referred to as circular harmonic pyramid (CHP) is utilized for coefficient generation and coding. In essence, each CHW pertaining to the pyramid represents the image by translated, dilated and rotated versions of a CHF. At the same time, for a fixed resolution, the CHP orthogonal system provides a local representation of the given image around a point in terms of CHFs. The self-steerability of each component of the CHP can be exploited for pattern analysis in presence of rotation (other than translation and dilation) and, in particular, for pattern recognition, irrespective of orientation [15].

CHFs are complex, polar separable filters characterized by harmonic angular shape, a useful property to build rotationally invariant descriptors. A scale parameter is also introduced to perform a multiresolution analysis. The Gauss-Laguerre filters (CHFs) which constitute a family of orthogonal functions satisfying wavelet

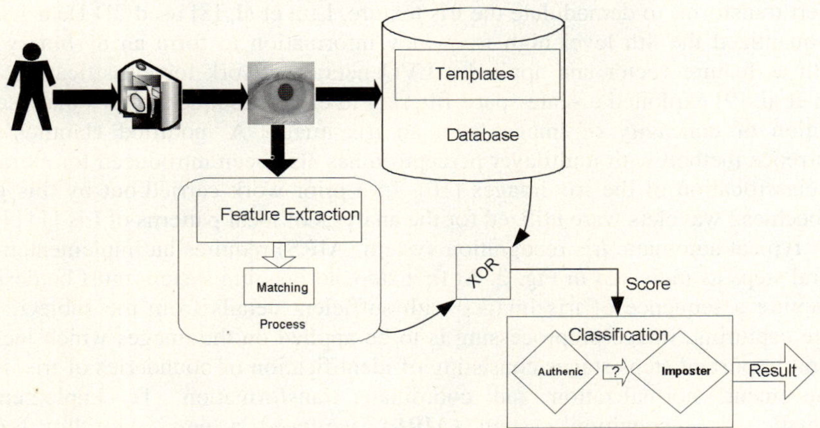

Fig. 2. Flow diagram of system for eye localization and iris segmentation

admissibility condition required for multiresolution wavelet pyramid analysis are used. Similar to Gabor wavelets, any image may be represented by translated, dilated and rotated replicas of Gauss-Laguerre function. For a fixed resolution, the Gauss-Laguerre CHFs provide a local representation of the image in the polar coordinates system centered at a given point, named pivot. This representation is called the Gauss-Laguerre transform [16]. A Circular harmonic function is a complex polar separable filter characterized by a harmonic angular shape, which is represented in polar coordinates as:

$$L_k^{(n)}(r,\theta) = h(r).e^{in\theta} \tag{1}$$

where $h(r)$ is:

$$h(r) = (-1)^k \, 2^{\frac{(|n|+1)}{2}} \, \pi^{\frac{|n|}{2}} \left[\frac{k!}{(|n|+k)!} \right]^{\frac{1}{2}} r^{|n|} L_k^n(2\pi r^2) e^{-\pi r^2} \tag{2}$$

Here r and θ are polar coordinates and $L_k^{(n)}(.)$ is the generalized Laguerre polynomial as follows:

$$L_k^n(r) = \sum_{h=0}^{k} (-1)^k \binom{n+k}{k-h} \frac{r^h}{h!} \tag{3}$$

For different radial order k and angular order n, these functions called Gauss-Laguerre (GL) functions and from an orthogonal basis set under the Gaussian function. As any CHF, GL functions are self-steering, i.e. they rotate by an angle ϕ when multiplied by factor $e^{jn\phi}$. In particular, the real and imaginary part of each GL function form a geometrically in phase-quadrature pair. Moreover, GL functions are isomorphous with their Fourier transform. It is shown [15] that each GL function defines an admissible dyadic wavelet. Thus, the redundant set of wavelets corresponding to different GL functions constitutes a self-steering pyramid, useful for local and multiscale image analysis. The real part of GL function is depicted in Fig. 3. For better visualization, the resolution of filter is enhanced. GL pyramid (real part CHW) is also shown in Fig. 4.

An important feature of GL functions as applied to iris recognition system is that GL function with various degrees of freedom can be tuned to significant visual features. For examples, for $n=1$, GLS are tuned to edges, for $n=2$ to ridges, for $n=3$ to equiangular forks, for $n=4$ to orthogonal crosses, irrespective of their actual orientation. Let $I(x,y)$ be the observed image. For every site of the plane, it is possible to perform the GL analysis by convolving it with each properly scaled GL function,

$$g_{jnk}(x,y) = \frac{1}{a2^j} L_k^n\left(\frac{r\cos\theta}{a2^j}, \frac{r\sin\theta}{a2^j}\right) \tag{4}$$

where $a2^j$ are the dyadic scale factors.

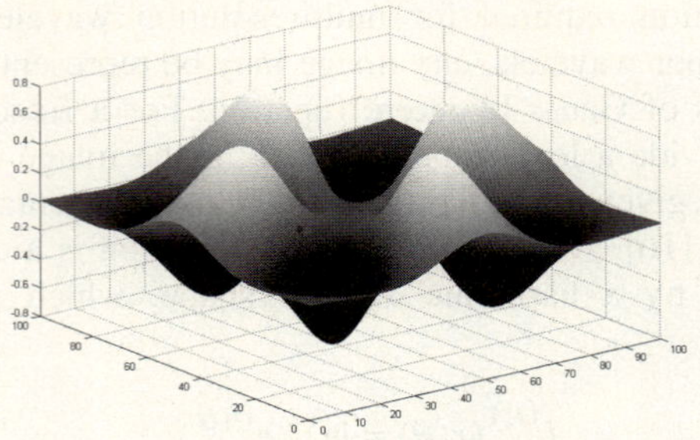

Fig. 3. Real part of GL function for $n = 4, k = 0, j = 2$

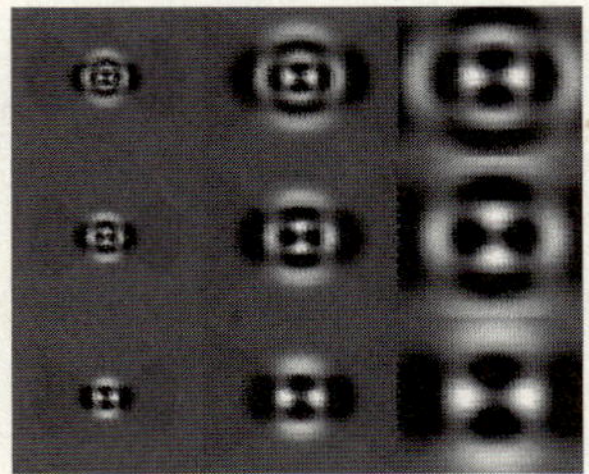

Fig. 4. GL pyramid. Real part of CHW for $n = 2, k = 0,1,2, j = 0,1,2$.

4 Image Preprocessing

Preprocessing in iris recognition consists of three steps: iris edge detection, normalization and enhancement. A captured image contains not only the iris but also contains segments of eyelid, eyelash, pupil and sclera that all are considered to be not desirable. Distance between camera and eye, environment light conditions (dilation of pupil) can influence the size of iris. Therefore, image preprocessing is a necessary step before any feature extraction step can be applied to overcome these problems. However, in the proposed algorithm due to its robustness against illumination and contrast effects, we have not considered enhancement or noise removal during iris preprocessing.

4.1 Iris Localization

Iris boundaries are considered to be composed of two non concentric circles. For iris recognition, it is necessary to determine inner and outer boundaries, radius and centers. Several approaches have been proposed using iris edge detection. Our method is based on iris localization using Radon transform and locally searching for iris image. The details of the approach are in [13]. The key contribution of the Radon transformation and consequent local search approach is its fast response in identifying the iris boundaries. For instance, time of detection on CASIA image database [17] was only .032 seconds in average evaluated on a platform of 2.2 Intel CPU, 512 M

RAM and MATLAB source code. In comparison, our approach exhibited a high order of success rate and time consuming between existed methods. The results of detection on two databases [13], show high order of reliability on iris segmentation.

4.2 Iris Normalization

Different image acquisition process and conditions can influence the results of identification. The dimensional incongruities between eye images are mostly due to the stretching of the iris caused by pupil expansion/ contraction from variation of the illuminations. Other factors that contribute to such deformations include variance of camera and eye distance, rotation of the camera or head. Hence a solution must be contrived to remove these deformations. The normalization process, projects iris region into a constant dimensional ribbon so that two images of the same iris under different conditions have characteristic features at the same spatial location. Daugman [2] suggested a normal Cartesian to Polar transform that remaps each pixel in iris area into a pair of polar coordinates (r,θ) where r and θ is on the interval $[0 \quad 1]$ and $[0 \quad 2\pi]$ respectively. In this paper, we have used Daugman's approach on the images of size of 512×128 and 12.5% of lower part of the normalized image was discarded.

5 Feature Extraction

As stated earlier, GL functions provide self steering pyramidal analysis structure that can be used to extract iris features and for iris coding efficiently. Using GL functions where by proper choice of their parameters, it is possible to generate a set of redundant wavelets that enable an accurate extraction of complex texture features of an iris. Redundancy of wavelet transform and a higher degree of freedom in selecting parameters of GL function as compared with those of Gabor wavelets, makes GL function highly suitable for iris feature extraction. Self steering pyramid structure of LG–based image analysis is distinctly different from Gabor wavelets where by choosing the parameters of GL functions, we are able to carryout both local and multiscale image analysis of a given image in a more effective manner .To take advantage of the degrees of freedom provided by LG function, it is necessary that the parameters of the filters be tuned to significant visual features and iris texture patterns so that it can extract desirable frequency information of iris patterns. In our experiment it was found that for $n = 2$, quality results were obtained where several simulations runs were carried out to verify the selection of parameters in which filters were convolved directly with the mapped iris image. Other parameters in this manner were also adjusted by trial and error and observing the simulation results. The output of filtered image is a complex value code that contains information of iris for coding. Based on the sign of each entry, we assign +1 to positive and 0 to others codes. Finally a 2048 binary bite is generated for each iris a sample of the code is depicted in Fig. 5. For matching process, Hamming distance is used. Rotation is considered here by shifting code versus templates in database. We take into account 12 bite shifts in both direction (left and right) and 2 bit shifts upwards and downwards. The minimum distance between input code and all codes in database for each class is assigned for decision making.

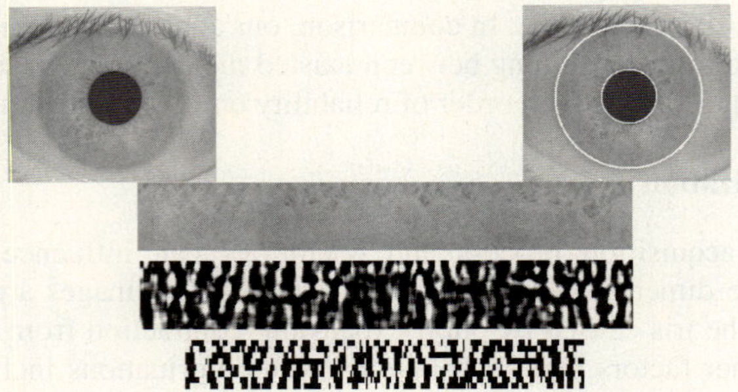

Fig. 5. Step by step of flowchart. (from left to right – up to down) input image, segmented iris, normalized iris, complex-valued iris code, binary code.

6 Experimental Results

To evaluate the performance of the proposed algorithm, our alghoritm was tested on two iris databases: a) CASIA Database [17] and a) set of iris image collected locally using using an iris camera system built at the research lab. Our preliminary database constructed locally has 280 images from 40 distinct subjects. Three images were taken at the first session followed by 4 images that were taken at second session. Our local iris imaging system was a modified webcam with Infrared lighting. For each iris class,

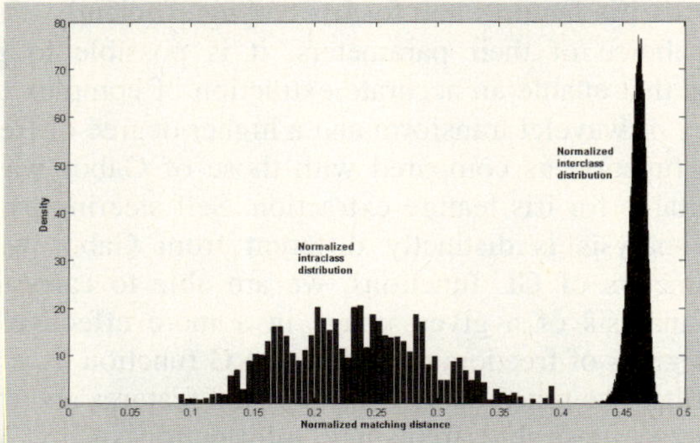

Fig. 6. The distribution of distance between authorized abd imposter users. A reasonable separation is exist between them.

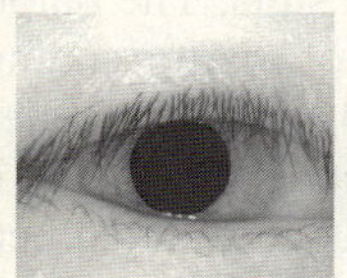 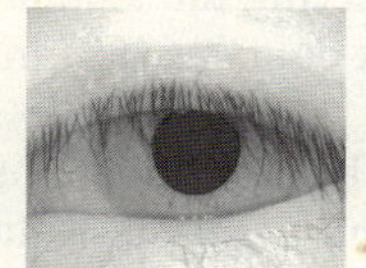 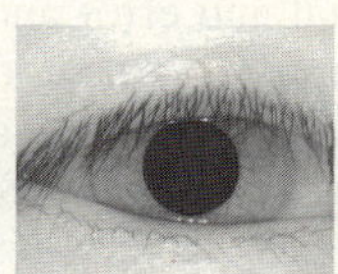 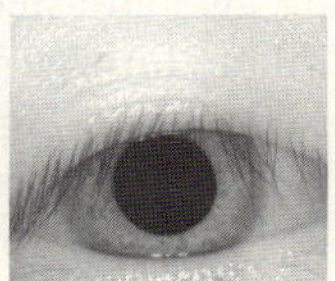

Fig. 7. Four iris images that failed in verification process. As can be seen, all are heavily occluded with eyelids and eyelashes.

we choose three samples taken at the first session for training and all samples captured at second sessions serve as test samples. This is also consistent with the widely accepted practice for testing biometrics algorithms [18]. We tested the proposed algorithms in two modes of. identification and verification. In identification tests, correct classification rate was 100% and complete separabality between interclass and intraclass distances is achived in both databases. In verification mode, a 1:1 search for each image was done. The algoritm was able to succesfully verify each input image except in case of 4 iris images in CASIA and 0 image in our local database. The discrepency and the error can easily be attributed to poor image quality and image capturing process. Fig. 6 shows the distribution of intra-class and inter-class matching distance of algorithm. The four images that failed for correct identification, are shown in Fig. 7 and as it can be seen, images are extremely occluded or has excessive pupil dilation. The system was implemented by MATLAB, 1.8GHz Intel processor, 256M RAM. The entire time of process including localization, preprocessing and normalization, feature extraction and matching is only (.2+.05+.15+.05=.45 Seconds).

7 Further Works

This paper outlines the results of our preliminary attempt for designing an effective iris recognition system for personal identification. As such we plan modifications in the system to improve the system both in hardware and in software algorithm. In our future, we will attempt to improve identification results for which image enhancement will be incorporated during preprocessing stage. Such preprocessing is anticipated to increase classification accuracy i.e. increase of separation distance between inter and intra classes. It is also planned to examine a new scheme in XOR classification in which a circular shifting to simulate eye rotation will be considered. Masking of the eyelids and eyelashes is also planned as part of future works.

8 Conclusion

In this paper, a new and an efficient algorithm for fast iris recognition is proposed for which Gaussian-Laguerre (LG) Wavelets have been utilized. Gauss-Laguerre filter is conceived to be more compatible for extraction of iris texture information as compared with commonly used Gabor filter. By adjusting Laguerre parameters and applying to normalized iris, a 256-byte in binary form is generated for each individual. An Exclusive OR classifier was used to perform and evaluate matching score. Despite of the absence of iris enhancement and denoising during image preprocessing, the results showed that the algorithm is sufficiently robust against contrast and illumination factors. Experimental results on a set of two databases indicated superior performance of the LG based algorithm in both identification and verification modes.

References

1. Jain, A., Bolle, R., Pankanti, S.: Biometrics: Personal Identification in a Networked Society. Kluwer Academic Publishers, Dordrecht (1999)
2. Daugman, J.: High Confidence Visual Recognition of Persons by a Test of Statistical Independence. IEEE Trans. PAMI 15, 1048–1061 (1993)

3. Wildes, R.P.: Iris Recognition: An Emerging Biometric Technology. In: Proc. IEEE, vol. 85, pp. 1348–1363 (1997)
4. Ma, L., Tan, T., Wang, Y., Zhang, D.: Efficient Iris Recognition by Characterizing Key Local Variations. IEEE Trans. Image Processing 13 (2004)
5. Ma, L., Wang, Y., Tan, T.: Personal Iris Recognition Based on Multichannel Gabor Filtering. In: ACCV2002, Melbourne Australia (2002)
6. Boles, W., Boashash, B.: A Human Identification Technique Using Images of the Iris and Wavelet Transform. IEEE Trans. Signal Processing 46, 1085–1088 (1998)
7. Tisse, C., Martin, L., Torres, L., Robert, M.: Person Identification Technique Using Human Iris Recognition. In: Proc. Vision Interface, pp. 294–299 (2002)
8. Lim, S., Lee, K., Byeon, O., Kim, T.: Efficient Iris Recognition through Improvement of Feature Vector and Classifier. ETRI Journal 23 (2001)
9. Nam, K.W., Yoon, K.L., Bark, J.S., Yang, W.S.: A Feature Extraction Method for Binary Iris Code Construction. In: Proc. 2nd Int. Conf. Information Technology for Application (2004)
10. Jaboski, P., Szewczyk, R., Kulesza, Z.: Automatic People Identification on the Basis of Iris Pattern Image Processing and Preliminary Analysis. In: Proc. Int. Conf. on Microelectronics, Yugoslavia, vol. 2, pp. 687–690 (2002)
11. Poursaberi, A., Araabi, B.N.: A Half-Eye Wavelet Based Method for Iris Recognition. In: Proc. 5th Int. Conf. Intelligent Systems Design and Applications (ISDA), Wroclaw Poland (2005)
12. Poursaberi, A., Araabi, B.N.: Iris Recognition for Partially Occluded Images: Methodology and Sensitivity Analysis. J. Applied Signal Processing (to be published in February 2006)
13. Torkamani, A., Azizzadeh, A.: Iris Detection as Human Identification. J. IET Image Processing Journal (to be published 2007)
14. Jacovitti, G., Neri, A.: Multiscale Image Features Analysis with Circular Harmonic Wavelets. In: Proc. SPIE 2569, Wavelets Appl. Signal Image Process, vol. 2569, pp. 363–372 (1995)
15. Jacovitti, G., Neri, A.: Multiresolution Circular Harmonic Decomposition. IEEE Trans. Signal Processing 48, 3242–3247 (2000)
16. Capdiferro, L., Casieri, V., Jacovitti, G.: Multiple Feature Based Multiscale Image Enhancement. In: Proc. IEEE DSP. IEEE Computer Society Press, Los Alamitos (2002)
17. www.sinobiometrics.com
18. Mansfield, T., Kelly, G., Chandler, D., Kane, J.: Biometric Product Testing Final Report. In: issue 1.0, Nat'l Physical Laboratory of UK (2001)

Hardening Fingerprint Fuzzy Vault Using Password*

Karthik Nandakumar, Abhishek Nagar, and Anil K. Jain

Department of Computer Science & Engineering, Michigan State University,
East Lansing, MI – 48824, USA
{nandakum,nagarabh,jain}@cse.msu.edu

Abstract. Security of stored templates is a critical issue in biometric systems because biometric templates are non-revocable. Fuzzy vault is a cryptographic framework that enables secure template storage by binding the template with a uniformly random key. Though the fuzzy vault framework has proven security properties, it does not provide privacy-enhancing features such as revocability and protection against cross-matching across different biometric systems. Furthermore, non-uniform nature of biometric data can decrease the vault security. To overcome these limitations, we propose a scheme for hardening a fingerprint minutiae-based fuzzy vault using password. Benefits of the proposed password-based hardening technique include template revocability, prevention of cross-matching, enhanced vault security and a reduction in the False Accept Rate of the system without significantly affecting the False Reject Rate. Since the hardening scheme utilizes password only as an additional authentication factor (independent of the key used in the vault), the security provided by the fuzzy vault framework is not affected even when the password is compromised.

Keywords: Biometric template security, fuzzy vault, hardening, password, fingerprint, minutiae, helper data.

1 Introduction

Biometric systems have attained popularity because they provide a convenient and reliable way to authenticate a user as opposed to traditional token-based (e.g., smart cards) and knowledge-based (e.g., passwords) authentication. However, it is now well-known that biometric systems are vulnerable to attacks. One of the most serious attacks is against the stored templates. A stolen biometric template cannot be easily revoked and it may be used in other applications that employ the same biometric trait. Table 1 presents a summary of the approaches that have been proposed for biometric template protection. We propose a hybrid approach where the biometric features are hardened using password before a secure sketch (fuzzy vault) is constructed.

1.1 Fuzzy Vault Framework

Fuzzy vault [1] is a cryptographic framework that binds the biometric template with a uniformly random key to build a secure sketch of the template. Only the secure sketch

* Research supported by ARO grant no. W911NF-06-1-0418.

S.-W. Lee and S.Z. Li (Eds.): ICB 2007, LNCS 4642, pp. 927–937, 2007.

Table 1. Summary of biometric template protection approaches

Template Protection Approaches	Methodology	Advantages	Limitations
Encryption	Template is encrypted using well-known cryptographic techniques	Matching algorithm and accuracy are unaffected	Template is exposed during every authentication attempt
Non-invertible transform (e.g., [2, 3])	*One-way function* is applied to the biometric features	Since transformation occurs in the same feature space, matcher need not be redesigned	Usually leads to increase in the FRR
Hardening / Salting (e.g., [4])	*User-specific external randomness* is added to the biometric features	Increases the entropy of biometric features resulting in low FAR	If the user-specific random information is compromised, there is no gain in entropy
Key generation (e.g., [5])	A key is derived directly from biometric features	Most efficient and scalable approach	Tolerance to intra-user variations is limited, resulting in high FRR
Secure sketch (e.g. [1, 6-9])	A sketch is derived from the template; sketch is secure because template can be reconstructed only if a *matching* biometric query is presented	More tolerant to intra-user variations in biometric data; can be used for securing external data such as cryptographic keys	Template is exposed during successful authentication. Non-uniform nature of biometric data reduces security
Proposed hardened fuzzy vault	A *hybrid* approach where the biometric features are hardened (using password) before a secure sketch (vault) is constructed	Hardening increases the entropy thereby improving the vault security; also enhances user privacy	Not user-friendly; user needs to provide both the password and the biometric during authentication

(vault) is stored and if the original template is "uniformly random", it is infeasible (or computationally hard) to retrieve either the template or the key without any knowledge of the user's biometric data.

The fuzzy vault scheme can secure biometric features that are represented as an unordered set. Let $\mathbf{M}^{\mathbf{T}} = \{x_1, x_2, ..., x_r\}$ denote a biometric template with r elements. The user selects a key K, encodes it in the form of a polynomial P of degree n and evaluates the polynomial P on all the elements in $\mathbf{M}^{\mathbf{T}}$. The points lying on P $\left(\{(x_i, P(x_i))\}_{i=1}^{r}\right)$ are hidden among a large number (s) of random chaff points that do not lie on P $\left(\{(x_j, y_j) \mid x_j \neq x_i, \forall i = 1, ..., r, y_j \neq P(x_j)\}_{j=1}^{s}\right)$. The union of genuine and chaff point sets constitutes the vault $\mathbf{V}$. In the absence of user's biometric data, it is computationally hard to identify the genuine points in $\mathbf{V}$, and hence the template is secure. During authentication, the user provides a biometric query denoted by $\mathbf{M}^{\mathbf{Q}}$ $= \{x'_1, x'_2, ..., x'_r\}$. If $\mathbf{M}^{\mathbf{Q}}$ overlaps substantially with $\mathbf{M}^{\mathbf{T}}$, the user can identify many points in $\mathbf{V}$ that lie on the polynomial. If the number of discrepancies between $\mathbf{M}^{\mathbf{T}}$ and $\mathbf{M}^{\mathbf{Q}}$ is less than $(r-n)/2$, Reed-Solomon decoding can be applied to reconstruct P and the authentication is successful. On the other hand, if $\mathbf{M}^{\mathrm{T}}$ and $\mathbf{M}^{\mathrm{Q}}$ do not have sufficient overlap, it is infeasible to reconstruct P and the authentication is unsuccessful. The vault is called *fuzzy* because it can be decoded even when $\mathbf{M}^{\mathrm{T}}$ and $\mathbf{M}^{\mathrm{Q}}$ are not exactly the same; this fuzziness property compensates for intra-user variations observed in biometric data. Security of the fuzzy vault framework has been studied in [1, 6] and bounds on the entropy loss of the vault have been established.

1.2 Limitations of Fuzzy Vault Framework

Though the fuzzy vault scheme has proven security properties [1, 6], it has the following limitations.

(i) The security of the vault can be compromised if the same biometric data is re-used for constructing different vaults (with different polynomials and random chaff points) [10, 11]. If a person has access to two vaults obtained from the same biometric data, he can easily identify the genuine points in the two vaults by correlating the abscissa (x) values in the two vaults. Due to this reason, the *vault is not revocable*, i.e., if a vault is compromised, a new vault cannot be created from the same biometric data by merely binding it with a different key. Further, this vulnerability *allows cross-matching of templates across different systems*. Thus, the fuzzy vault framework does not have privacy-enhancing properties.

(ii) It is possible for an attacker to exploit the *non-uniform* nature of biometric features and develop attacks based on statistical analysis of points in the vault.

(iii) Since the number of chaff points in the vault is much larger than the number of genuine points, it is possible for an adversary to substitute a few points in the vault using his own biometric features [10, 11]. This allows both the original user and the adversary to be successfully authenticated using the same identity. Thus, an *adversary can deliberately increase the false accept rate* of the system.

(iv) As a genuine user is being authenticated, his *original template is exposed temporarily*, which may be gleaned by an attacker.

While better fuzzy vault constructions that do not involve chaff points [6] can prevent vulnerabilities (ii) and (iii), they do not address limitations (i) and (iv). By using a password as an additional factor for authentication, the above limitations of a fuzzy vault system can be easily alleviated. In this paper, we propose a scheme for hardening a fingerprint-based fuzzy vault using password. One of the main advantages of password-based hardening is enhanced user privacy. Further, the proposed scheme has been designed such that *password is only an additional layer of authentication and the security provided by the basic fuzzy vault framework is not affected even if the password is compromised.* Hence, the proposed approach provides higher level of security as long as the password is secure. When the password is compromised, template security falls to the same level as in the fuzzy vault.

2 Hardening Fuzzy Vault Using Password

Our vault hardening scheme consists of three main steps (see Fig. 1). Firstly, a random transformation function derived from the user password is applied to the biometric template. The transformed template is then secured using the fuzzy vault framework. Finally, the vault is encrypted using a key derived from the password.

Random transformation of the template using password enhances user privacy because it enables the creation of revocable templates and prevents cross-matching of templates across different applications. The distribution of transformed template is statistically more similar to uniform distribution than the distribution of original template. This provides better resistance against attacks on the vault. Furthermore, the additional variability introduced by password-based transformation decreases the similarity between transformed templates of different users. This reduces the False Accept Rate of the system substantially. If we assume client-server architecture for the biometric system (as shown in Fig. 1) where feature extraction and transformation are applied at the client side and matching is performed at the server, the server never sees the original template. Only the transformed template would be revealed during successful vault decoding and the original template is never exposed at the server.

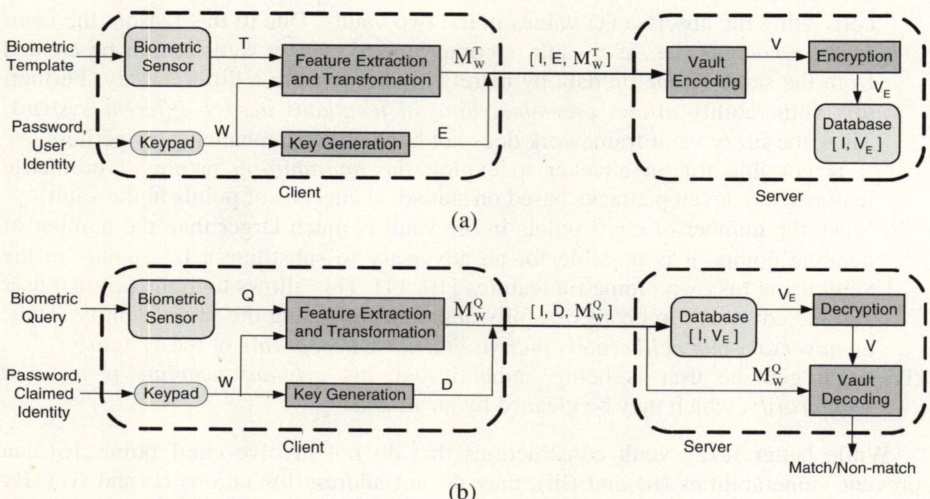

Fig. 1. Operation of the hardened fuzzy vault. (a) Enrollment and (b) authentication stages. In this figure, I represents the identity of the user, W is the user password, M^T (M^Q) represents the biometric template (query), M_W^T (M_W^Q) represents the template (query) after transformation using the password, E and D represent the encryption and decryption keys generated from the password and V and V_E represent the plaintext and encrypted vaults.

Two common methods for cracking a user password are dictionary attacks and social engineering techniques. In the proposed system, password is implicitly verified during authentication by matching the transformed biometric features. Even if an adversary attempts to guess the password, it is not possible to verify the guess without knowledge of the user's biometric data. This provides resistance against dictionary attacks to learn the password. However, it is still possible to glean the user password through social engineering techniques. Therefore, password based transformation alone is not sufficient to ensure the security of the biometric template. Due to this reason, we use the fuzzy vault framework to secure the transformed biometric template. Note that the *key used in constructing the fuzzy vault that secures the transformed template is still uniformly random and independent of the password.* Therefore, even if the password is compromised, the security of the vault is not affected and it is computationally hard for an attacker to obtain the original biometric template. Finally, the vault is encrypted using a key derived from the password. This prevents substitution attacks against the vault because an adversary cannot modify the vault without knowing the password or the key derived from it.

3 Fingerprint-Based Fuzzy Vault Implementation

A number of techniques have been proposed for constructing a fuzzy vault using fingerprint minutiae (e.g., [13, 14]). The proposed hardening scheme is based on the fingerprint-based fuzzy vault implementation described in [12] which has the highest genuine accept rate and a very low false accept rate among the known implementations of fingerprint-based fuzzy vault. In this implementation, the Reed-Solomon polynomial reconstruction step is replaced by a combination of Lagrange interpolation and Cyclic Redundancy Check (CRC) based error detection. Each minutia point is represented as an element in the Galois field GF(2^{16}) by applying the following procedure. Let (u, v, θ) be the attributes of a minutia point, where u and v indicate the row and column indices in the image, and θ represents the orientation of the minutia with respect to the horizontal axis. The minutia attributes are uniformly quantized and expressed as binary strings Q_u, Q_v and Q_θ of lengths B_u, B_v and B_θ bits, respectively. The values of B_u, B_v and B_θ are chosen to be 6, 5 and 5, respectively, so that a 16-bit number can be obtained by concatenating the bit strings Q_u, Q_v and Q_θ.

A fixed number (denoted by r) of minutiae are selected based on their quality. A randomly generated key K of size $16n$ bits is represented as a polynomial P of degree n. The polynomial P is evaluated at the selected minutiae and these points constitute the locking set. A large number (denoted by s, $s >> r$) of chaff points are randomly generated and the combined set of minutiae and chaff is randomly reordered to obtain the vault **V**. To facilitate the alignment of query minutiae to the template, we extract and store a set of high curvature points (known as *helper data*) from the template image. The helper data itself does not leak any information about the minutiae, yet contains sufficient information to align the template and query fingerprints [12].

During authentication, the helper data extracted from the query image is aligned to the template helper data using trimmed Iterative Closest Point (ICP) algorithm [15]. Aligned query minutiae are used to coarsely filter out the chaff points in the vault. A minutiae matcher [16] is then applied to find correspondences between the query minutiae and the remaining points in the vault. Vault points having a matching minutia in the query constitute the unlocking set. For interpolation of a polynomial of degree n, at least (n+1) projections are needed. Therefore, if the size of the unlocking set is less than (n+1), it leads to authentication failure. If the unlocking set has (n+1) or more elements, all possible subsets of size (n+1) are considered. Each of these subsets gives rise to a candidate polynomial and CRC-based error detection identifies the valid polynomial. If a valid polynomial is found, the authentication is successful.

4 Hardened Fuzzy Vault Implementation

The key component of a hardened fingerprint-based fuzzy vault scheme is the feature transformation module which transforms the minutiae features using a password. We employ simple operations of translation and permutation as the transformation functions because they do not affect the intra-user variability of the minutiae features thereby maintaining the false reject rate to a great extent.

4.1 Minutiae Transformation

We assume that the password is of length 64 bits (8 characters) which is divided into 4 units of 16 bits each. We classify the minutiae into 4 classes by grouping minutiae lying in each quadrant of the image into a different class and assign one password unit to each class. We generate a permutation sequence of 4 numbers by applying a one way function on the password. Using this sequence, we permute the 4 quadrants of the image such that the relative positions of minutiae within each quadrant are not changed. Each 16-bit password unit is assumed to be in the same format as a 16-bit minutia representation described in section 3. Hence, the password unit can be divided into three components T_u, T_v and T_θ of lengths B_u, B_v and B_θ bits, respectively. The values of T_u and T_v are considered as the amount of translation along the vertical and horizontal directions, respectively, and T_θ is treated as the change in minutia orientation. The new minutiae attributes are obtained by adding the translation values to the original values modulo the appropriate range, i.e., $Q'_u = (Q_u + T_u) \bmod (2\wedge B_u)$, $Q'_v = (Q_v + T_v) \bmod (2\wedge B_v)$ and $Q'_\theta = (Q_\theta + T_\theta) \bmod (2\wedge B_\theta)$. To prevent overlapping of minutiae from different quadrants, the minutia location is wrapped around in the respective quadrant if it has been translated beyond the boundary. The effect of minutiae transformation using password is depicted in Fig. 2.

4.2 Encoding Hardened Vault

The transformed minutiae are encoded in a vault using the procedure described in section 3. The vault and helper data are further encrypted using a key generated from the password. This layer of encryption prevents an impostor without knowledge of the password from modifying the vault.

4.3 Decoding Hardened Vault

During authentication, the encrypted vault and helper data are first decrypted using the password provided by the user. The template and query helper data sets are aligned and the password-based transformation scheme described in section 4.1 is applied to the aligned query minutiae. Good quality minutiae are then selected for decoding the vault.

Apart from the well-known factors like partial overlap, non-linear distortion and noise that lead to differences in the template and query minutiae sets of the same user, the password-based transformation scheme introduces additional discrepancies. If a minutia lies close to the quadrant boundary, the same minutiae may fall in different quadrants in the template and the query due to imperfect alignment. This reduces the number of minutiae correspondences and leads to a small decrease in the genuine accept rate. Another problem arising due to imperfect alignment is that the same minutia point may appear at opposite ends of the quadrants in the template and the query after the transformation. This is because the minutiae are translated within their respective quadrants modulo the quadrant size. To address this problem, we add a border of width 15 pixels around each quadrant and minutiae within 15 pixels of the quadrant boundary are duplicated on the border at the opposite end of the quadrant.

5 Experimental Results

The proposed password-based fuzzy vault hardening scheme has been tested on the FVC2002-DB2 and MSU-DBI fingerprint databases. FVC2002-DB2 [17] is a public domain database with 800 images (100 fingers × 8 impressions/finger) of size 560×296. Only the first two impressions of each finger were used in our experiments; the first impression was used as the template to encode the vault and the second impression was used as the query in vault decoding. The MSU-DBI database [18] consists of 640 images (160 fingers × 4 impressions/finger) of size 640×480. Two impressions of each finger collected six weeks apart were used in our experiments.

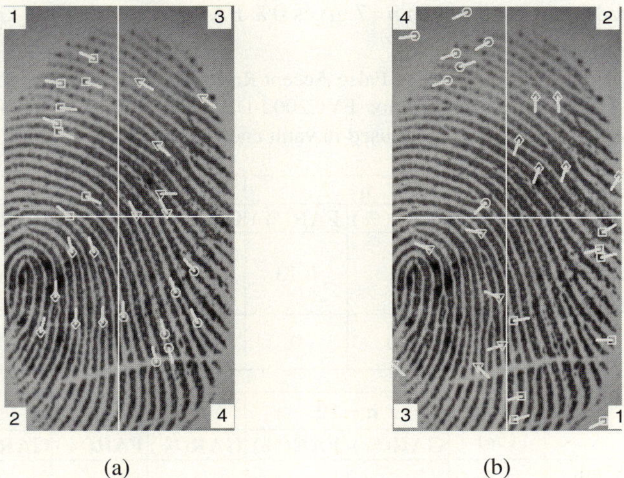

Fig. 2. Minutiae transformation using password. (a) and (b) show the original and transformed minutiae, respectively. The number at each corner indicates the permutation of quadrants.

The criteria used for evaluating the performance are failure to capture rate (FTCR), genuine accept rate (GAR) and false accept rate (FAR). When the number of minutiae in the template and/or query fingerprint is less than the required number of genuine points, we call it as failure to capture. The parameters used in vault implementation were chosen as follows. Since the number of minutiae varies for different users, using a fixed value of r (the number of genuine minutiae used to construct the vault) across all users leads to large FTCR. To overcome this problem, we fix the range of r (set to

18-24 and 24-30 for the FVC and MSU databases, respectively) and determine its value individually for each user. The number of chaff points (s) is chosen to be 10 times the number of genuine points in the vault. The choice of n requires a compromise between the vault security and the acceptable values of GAR and FAR.

Table 2 shows that the proposed system leads to a small decrease in the GAR for all values of n. This is due to misclassification of a few minutiae at the quadrant boundaries and the inability of the minutiae matcher to effectively account for non-linear deformation in the transformed minutiae space. Although the minutiae matcher [16] used here can tolerate deformation to some extent by employing an adaptive bounding box, it is designed to work in the original minutiae space where the deformation is consistent in a local region. Since minutiae transformation makes the deformation inconsistent in all the regions, the number of correspondences found by the matcher decreases. Fig. 3 shows a pair of images for which the vault without hardening could be decoded, but the hardened vault could not be decoded.

From Table 2, we also observe that the FAR of the system is zero for all values of n. This is due to the transformation of minutiae using password which makes the distribution of minutiae more random and reduces the similarity between minutiae sets of different users. This enables the system designer to select a wider range of values for n without compromising the FAR. For example, for the FVC database, the original fuzzy vault required n=10 to achieve 0% FAR (corresponding GAR is 86%). For the hardened fuzzy vault, even n=7 gives 0% FAR (corresponding GAR is 90%).

Table 2. Genuine Accept Rates (GAR), False Accept Rates (FAR) and Failure to Capture Rates (FTCR) of the hardened fuzzy vault for FVC2002-DB2 and MSU-DBI databases. Here, n represents the degree of the polynomial used in vault encoding.

		FTCR (%)	n = 7		n = 8		n = 10	
			GAR(%)	FAR(%)	GAR(%)	FAR(%)	GAR(%)	FAR(%)
FVC2002 – DB2	Vault without hardening	2	91	0.13	91	0.01	86	0
	Hardened vault	2	90	0	88	0	81	0
		FTCR (%)	n = 10		n = 11		n = 12	
			GAR(%)	FAR(%)	GAR(%)	FAR(%)	GAR(%)	FAR(%)
MSU-DBI	Vault without hardening	5.6	85	0.08	82.5	0.02	78.8	0
	Hardened vault	5	80.6	0	75.6	0	73.8	0

6 Security Analysis

The hardened fuzzy vault system has two independent layers of security, namely, password and biometric. An impostor can gain access to the system only if both these layers of security are compromised simultaneously. Now, we shall analyze the security of the system if one of the layers is compromised.

Compromised Password: Suppose an impostor gains access to the password of a genuine user. The impostor can at most generate the decryption key that allows him to decrypt the vault. However, to be successfully authenticated, he still would have to decode the vault by identifying the genuine minutia points from the vault, which is computationally hard. Suppose an attacker attempts a brute-force attack on the proposed system by trying to decode the vault using all combinations of (n+1) points in the vault. If n = 10, r = 30 and s = 300, the total number of possible combinations is C(330,11); among these combinations, C(30,11) combinations will successfully decode the vault. The expected number of combinations that need to be evaluated is 2×10^{12} which corresponds to ~ 40 bits of security. Security can be improved by adding a larger number of chaff points (e.g., when s = 600 in the above system, we can achieve ~ 50 bits of security) at the expense of increased storage requirements. Further improvement in the template security can be achieved by replacing the random permutation and translation functions (that are invertible) by a non-invertible transform [2]. Though non-invertible transforms usually result in a decrease in GAR, they can provide an additional 50-70 bits of security [2] if the goal is to prevent an attacker from learning the original biometric template of the genuine user.

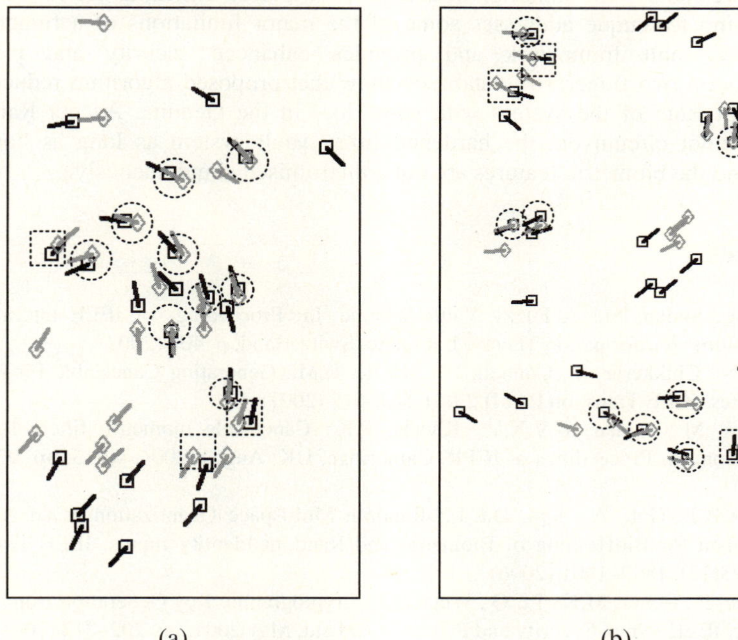

Fig. 3. An example of false reject in password-based vault hardening. (a) Template and aligned query minutiae prior to hardening and the corresponding minutiae matches found by the matcher, (b) Template and query minutiae after vault hardening and the corresponding minutiae matches found by the matcher. While the minutiae matches marked with circles were found in both (a) and (b), the matches marked with squares were detected *only* in (a) and *not* in (b). Since the number of minutia correspondences prior to hardening is 12, the vault can be successfully decoded because *n* was set to 10. After hardening, the number of minutia matches is only 9; hence, the vault cannot be decoded for *n* = 10.

Compromised Biometric: Suppose an impostor gains access to the biometric template of a genuine user through covert means (e.g., lifting a fingerprint impression of the genuine user without his knowledge), he will still have to guess the password to be authenticated. The guessing entropy of an 8-character password is between 18-30 bits [19]. Although this level of security may be insufficient in practical applications, it is still better than the fuzzy vault framework and most of the other approaches presented in Table 1 which offer no security when the biometric is compromised.

When an adversary does not have any knowledge of the user password and biometric data, then the security of the hardened fuzzy vault is the combination of the security provided by the password and biometric layers. If n = 10, r = 30, s = 300 and password is 8-character long, the security of the hardened vault is between 58-70 bits.

7 Summary

We have proposed an algorithm to harden a fingerprint-based fuzzy vault based on user password. Based on permutations and translations generated from the user password, we modify the minutiae in a fingerprint before encoding the fuzzy vault. Our hardening technique addresses some of the major limitations of a fingerprint-based fuzzy vault framework and provides enhanced security and privacy. Experiments on two fingerprint databases show that proposed algorithm reduces the False Accept Rate of the system with some loss in the Genuine Accept Rate. An impostor cannot circumvent the hardened fuzzy vault system as long as both the password and the biometric features are not compromised simultaneously.

References

1. Juels, A., Sudan, M.: A Fuzzy Vault Scheme. In: Proceedings of IEEE International Symposium on Information Theory, Lausanne, Switzerland, p. 408 (2002)
2. Ratha, N., Chikkerur, S., Connell, J.H., Bolle, R.M.: Generating Cancelable Fingerprint Templates. IEEE Trans. on PAMI 29(4), 561–572 (2007)
3. Savvides, M., Kumar, B.V.K.V., Khosla, P.K.: Cancelable biometric filters for face recognition. In: Proceedings of ICPR, Cambridge, UK, August 2004, vol. 3, pp. 922–925 (2004)
4. Teoh, A.B.J., Goh, A., Ngo, D.C.L.: Random Multispace Quantization as an Analytic Mechanism for BioHashing of Biometric and Random Identity Inputs. IEEE Trans. on PAMI 28(12), 1892–1901 (2006)
5. Monrose, F., Reiter, M.K., Li, Q., Wetzel, S.: Cryptographic Key Generation from Voice. In: Proc. IEEE Symp. Security and Privacy, Oakland, May 2001, pp. 202–213 (2001)
6. Dodis, Y., Reyzin, L., Smith, A.: Fuzzy Extractors: How to Generate Strong Keys from Biometrics and Other Noisy Data. In: Proceedings of International Conference on Theory and Applications of Cryptographic Techniques, May 2004, pp. 523–540 (2004)
7. Hao, F., Anderson, R., Daugman, J.: Combining Crypto with Biometrics Effectively. IEEE Trans. on Computers 55(9), 1081–1088 (2006)
8. Sutcu, Y., Li, Q., Memon, N.: Protecting Biometric Templates with Sketch: Theory and Practice. IEEE Trans. on Information Forensics and Security 2007 (to appear)

9. Draper, S.C., Khisti, A., Martinian, E., Vetro, A., Yedidia, J.S.: Using Distributed Source Coding to Secure Fingerprint Biometrics. In: Proc. of IEEE International Conference on Acoustics, Speech and Signal Processing, Hawaii, vol. 2, pp. 129–132 (April 2007)
10. Boult, T.E., Scheirer, W.J., Woodworth, R.: Fingerprint Revocable Biotokens: Accuracy and Security Analysis. In: Proc. of CVPR, Minneapolis (June 2007)
11. Scheirer, W.J., Boult, T.E.: Cracking Fuzzy Vaults and Biometric Encryption, Univ. of Colorado at Colorado Springs, Tech. Rep. (February 2007)
12. Nandakumar, K., Jain, A.K., Pankanti, S.: Fingerprint-based Fuzzy Vault: Implementation and Performance, Michigan State Univ. Tech. Rep. TR-06-31 (2006)
13. Yang, S., Verbauwhede, I.: Automatic Secure Fingerprint Verification System Based on Fuzzy Vault Scheme. In: Proceedings of IEEE International Conference on Acoustics, Speech, and Signal Processing, Philadelphia, USA, March 2005, vol. 5, pp. 609–612 (2005)
14. Uludag, U., Pankanti, S., Jain, A.K.: Fuzzy Vault for Fingerprints. In: Proceedings of Fifth International Conference on AVBPA, Rye Town, USA, July 2005, pp. 310–319 (2005)
15. Chetverikov, D., Svirko, D., Stepanov, D., Krsek, P.: The Trimmed Iterative Closest Point Algorithm. In: Proc. of ICPR, Quebec City, Canada, August 2002, pp. 545–548 (2002)
16. Jain, A.K., Hong, L., Bolle, R.: On-line Fingerprint Verification. IEEE Trans. on PAMI 19(4), 302–314 (1997)
17. Maio, D., Maltoni, D., Wayman, J.L., Jain, A.K.: FVC2002: Second Fingerprint Verification Competition. In: Proc. of ICPR, Quebec City, August 2002, pp. 811–814 (2002)
18. Jain, A.K., Prabhakar, S., Ross, A.: Fingerprint Matching: Data Acquisition and Performance Evaluation. Michigan State Univ. Tech. Rep. TR99-14 (1999)
19. Burr, W.E., Dodson, D.F., Polk, W.T.: Information Security: Electronic Authentication Guideline. NIST Special Report 800-63 (April 2006)

GPU Accelerated 3D Face Registration / Recognition

Andrea Francesco Abate, Michele Nappi, Stefano Ricciardi, and Gabriele Sabatino

Dipartimento di Matematica e Informatica, Università degli Studi di Salerno, 20186, Fisciano (SA), Italy
{abate,mnappi,sricciardi,gsabatino}@unisa.it

Abstract. This paper proposes a novel approach to both registration and recognition of face in three dimensions. The presented method is based on normal map metric to perform either the alignment of captured face to a reference template or the comparison between any two faces in a gallery. As the metric involved is highly suited to be computed via vector processor, we propose an implementation of the whole framework on last generation graphics boards, to exploit the potential of GPUs applied to large scale biometric identification applications. This work shows how the use of affordable consumer grade hardware could allow ultra rapid comparison between face descriptors through their highly specialized architecture. The approach also addresses facial expression changes by means of a subject specific weighting masks. We include preliminary results of experiments conducted on a proprietary gallery and on a subset of FRGC database.

1 Introduction

Three dimensional face representation is object of growing interest from the biometrics research community, as witnessed by the large number of approaches to recognition proposed in the last years, whose main focus has been accuracy and robustness, often considering the computing time required a minor issue. This fact is easily understandable considering the serious challenges related to face recognition which sometimes push researchers to exploit metrics involving time intensive computing. According to literature, 3D based methods can exploit a plurality of metrics [1], some of which, like Eigenface [2], Hausdorff distance [3] and Principal Component Analysis (PCA) [4], have been originally proposed for 2D recognition and then extended to range images. Other approaches instead, have been developed specifically to operate on 3D shapes [5], like those exploiting Extended Gaussian Image [6], the Iterative Closest Point (ICP) method [7], canonical image [8] or normal map [9]. One line of work is represented by multi-modal approaches, which typically combine 2D (intensity or colour) and 3D (range images or geometry) facial data and in some case different metrics, to improve recognition accuracy and/or robustness over conventional techniques [10-12]. However, as the diffusion of this biometric increases, the need for one-to-many comparison on large galleries becomes more frequent and crucial to many applications. Unfortunately, a matching time in the range of seconds (or even minutes) is not rare in 3D face recognition, so, as claimed by Bowyer et al. in their 2006 survey “one attractive line of research involves methods to speed up the 3D

S.-W. Lee and S.Z. Li (Eds.): ICB 2007, LNCS 4642, pp. 938–947, 2007.

matching" [1]. To this regard the launch of multi-core CPUs on the market could be appealing to biometric systems developers, but the reality is that not many of the most established face recognition algorithm can take advantage of multithreading processing and, even in case this is possible, the overall theoretical speedup is by a factor 2 or 4 (for PC and workstation class machines), while database size could possibly grow by even orders of magnitude.

It is worth to note that one of the most stable technological trend in the last years for PCs and workstations has been the leap in both computing power and flexibility of specialized processors on which graphics board are based on: the Graphical Processing Units (GPUs). Indeed, GPUs arguably represent today most powerful and affordable computational hardware, and they are advancing at an incredible rate compared to CPUs, with performances growing approximately from 1.7 to 2.3 times/year versus a maximum of 1.4 times/year for CPUs. As an example, the recent G80 GPU core from Nvidia Corp. (one of the market leaders together with ATI Corp.) features approximately 681 millions of transistors resulting in a highly parallel architecture based on 128 programmable processors, 768 MB of VRAM with 86 GB/sec of transfer rate over a 384 bit wide bus.

The advantages in using these specialized processors for general purpose applications, a task referred as General Purpose computation on GPU or GP-GPU, have been marginal until high level languages for GPU programming have emerged. Nevertheless, as GPUs are inherently vector processors and not real general-purpose processing units, not every algorithm or data structure is suited to fully exploit this potential. In this paper, we present a method to register and recognize a face in 3D by means of the same normal map metric. As this metric represents geometry in terms of coloured pixels, it is particularly suited to take full advantage of vector processors, so we propose a GPU implementation aimed to maximize the comparison speed for large scale identification applications. This paper is organized as follows. In section 2. the proposed methodology is presented in detail. In section 3. experimental results are shown and briefly discussed. The paper concludes in section 4.

2 Description of Proposed Methodology

In the following subsections 2.1 to 2.4. we describe in depth the proposed face recognition approach and its implementation via GPU. A preliminary face registration is required for the method to perform optimally but, as it is based on the same metric exploited for face matching, we first describe the normal map based comparison, then we expose the alignment algorithm, and the adaptation necessary to efficiently compute the metric through GPU.

2.1 Representing Face Through Normal Map and Comparing Faces Through Difference Map

Whether a subject has to be enrolled for the first time or a new query (a subject which has to be recognized) is submitted to the recognition pipeline, a preliminary face capture is performed and the resulting range image is converted in a polygonal mesh M. We intend to represent face geometry storing normals of mesh M in a bidimensional matrix N with dimension $l \times m$. To correlate the 3D space of normals to the 2D domain of matrix N we project each vertex in M onto a 2D surface using a spherical projection (opportunely adapted to mesh size). Then we sample the mesh by means of mapping coordinates and quantize the length of the three scalar components of each normal as an RGB coded color, storing it in a bitmap N by means of the same coordinates as array indexes. More precisely, we assign to each pixel (i, j) in N, with $0 \leq i < l$ and $0 \leq j < m$, the three scalar components of the normal to the point of the mesh surface with mapping coordinates $(l/i, m/j)$. The resulting sampling resolution is $1/l$ for the s range and $1/m$ for the t range. The normal components are stored in pixel (i, j) as RGB colour components.

We refer to the resulting matrix N as the normal map of mesh M. A normal map with a standard colour depth of 24 bit allows 8 bit quantization for each normal component, this precision proved to be adequate for the recognition process. To compare the normal map N_A from input subject to another normal map N_B previously stored in the reference database, we compute the angle included between each pairs of normals represented by colours of pixels with corresponding mapping coordinates, and store it in a new *Difference Map D* with components r, g and b opportunely normalized from spatial domain to colour domain, so $0 \leq r_{N_A}, g_{N_A}, b_{N_A} \leq 1$ and $0 \leq r_{N_B}, g_{N_B}, b_{N_B} \leq 1$. The value θ, with $0 \leq \theta < \pi$, is the angular difference between the pixels with coordinates (x_{N_A}, y_{N_A}) in N_A and (x_{N_B}, y_{N_B}) in N_B and it is stored in D as a grey-scale image (see Fig. 1). To reduce the effects of residual face misalignment during acquisition and sampling phases, we calculate the angle θ using a $k \times k$ (usually 3×3 or 5×5) matrix of neighbour pixels.

Summing every grey level in D results in histogram $H(x)$ that represent the angular distance distribution between mesh M_A and M_B. On the X axis we represent the resulting angles between each pair of comparisons (sorted from 0° degree to 180° degree), while on the Y axis we represent the total number of differences found. This means that two similar faces will have an histogram $H(x)$ with very high values on little angles, while two distinct faces will have differences more distributed. We define a similarity score through a weighted sum between H and a Gaussian function G, as in (3) where σ and k change recognition sensitivity .

$$similarity\_score = \sum_{x=0}^{k} \left(H(x) \cdot \frac{1}{\sigma\sqrt{2\pi}} e^{-\frac{x^2}{2\sigma^2}} \right) \tag{1}$$

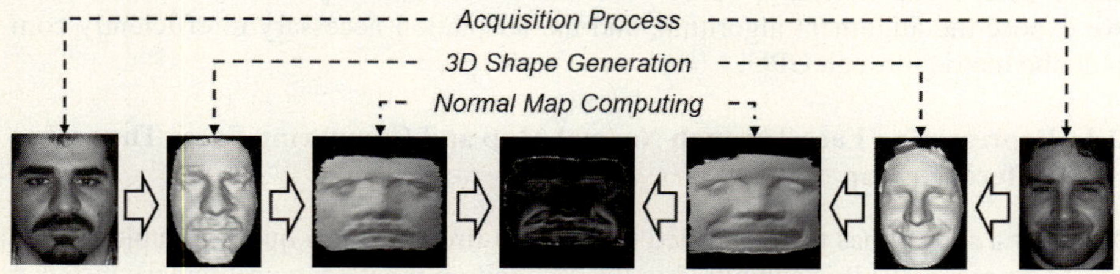

Fig. 1. Face capture, Normal Map generation and resulting Difference Map for two subjects

2.2 Face Registration

A precise registration of captured face is required by normal map based comparison to achieve the best recognition performance. So, the obvious choice could be to use the most established 3D shape alignment method, the Iterative Closest Point (ICP), to this aim. Unfortunately ICP is a time expensive algorithm. The original method proposed by Chen and Medioni [13] and Besl and McKay [14] features a O(N2) time complexity, which has been lowered to O(Nlog(n)) by other authors [15] and further reduced by means of heuristic functions or by shape voxelization and distance pre-computing in its most recent versions [16]. Nevertheless the best performance in face recognition applications are in the range of many seconds to minutes, depending on source and target shape resolution. As the whole normal-map based approach is aimed to maximize the overall recognition speed reducing the comparison time, we considered ICP not suited to fit well into this approach.

So we introduce pyramidal-normal-map based face alignment. A pyramidal-normal-map is simply a set of normal maps relative to the same 3D surface ordered by progressively increasing size (in our experiments each map differs from the following one by a factor of 2). Our purpose is to exploits this set of local curvature descriptors to perform a fast and precise alignment between two 3D shapes, measuring the angular distance (on each axis) between an unregistered face and a reference template and reducing it to a point in which it does not significantly affect recognition precision. The template is a generic neutral face mesh whose centroid corresponds to the origin of the reference system. To achieve a complete registration the captured face has to match position and rotation of reference template.

Scale matching, indeed, is not needed as the spherical projection applied to generate the normal map is invariant to object size. The first step in the alignment procedure is therefore to compute face's centroid which allows to match reference template position offsetting all vertices by the distance from centroid to the axis origin. Similarly, rotational alignment can be obtained through a rigid transformation of all vertices once the angular distance between the two surface has been measured. As we intend to measure this distance iteratively and with progressively greater precision, we decide to rotate the reference template instead of captured face. The reason is simple: because the template used for any alignment is always the same, we can precompute for every discrete step of rotation the relative normal map once and offline, drastically reducing the time required for alignment. Before the procedure begins, a set-up is required to compute a pyramidal normal map for the captured face (a set of four normal maps with size ranging from 16x16 to 128x128 has proved to be adequate in our tests). At this time the variables controlling the iteration are initialised, like the initial size m of normal maps, the angular range reduction factor k, and R, the maximum angular range for the algorithm to operate, i.e. the maximum misalignment allowed between the two surfaces. We found that for biometric applications a good compromise between robustness and speed is reached setting this value to 180°, with k=4, but even R=360° can be used if required.

With the first iteration, the smallest normal map in the pyramid is compared to each of k^3 pre-computed normal maps of the same size relative to the coarsest rotation steps of template. The resulting difference maps are evaluated to find the one with the highest similarity score, which represent the better approximation to alignment (on each axis) for that level of pyramid. Then the template is rotated according to this first estimate. The next iteration starts from this approximation comparing the next normal map in the pyramid (with size m=m*2) to every template normal map of corresponding size found within a range which has now its centre on the previous approximation and whose width has been reduced by a factor k. This scheme is repeated for i iterations until the range's width fall below a threshold value T. At this point the sum of all i approximations found for each axis is used to rotate the captured face, thus resulting in its alignment to the reference template (see Fig. 2).

Using the above mentioned values for initialisation, four iterations (i=4) with angular steps of 45°, 11,25°, 2.8° and 0.7° are enough to achieve an alignment adequate for recognition purpose. As the number of angular steps is constant for each level of iteration, the total number of template normal maps generated offline for i iterations is ik^3, and the same applies to the total number of comparisons. It has to be noted that the time needed for a single comparison (difference map computing), is independent by mesh resolution but it depends on normal map size instead, whereas the time needed to precompute each template's normal map depends on its polygonal resolution.

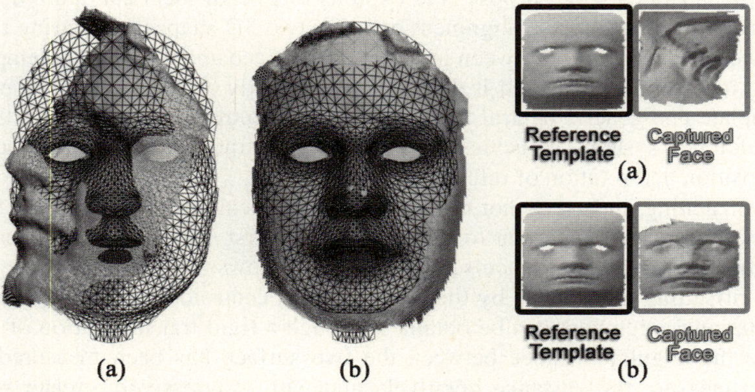

Fig. 2. Face captured (shaded) and reference template (wireframe) before (left) and after (center) alignment. Right: normal maps before (up) and after (bottom) alignment

The template does not need to have the same resolution and topology of captured face, it is sufficient it has a number of polygons at least greater than the number of pixels in the largest normal map in the pyramid and a roughly regular distribution of vertices. Finally, another advantage of proposed algorithm is that no preliminary rough alignment is needed by the method to converge if the initial face misalignment (for each axis) is within R.

2.3 Storing Facial Expressions in Alpha Channel

To improve robustness to facial expressions we introduce the expression weighting mask, a subject specific pre-calculated mask aimed to assign different relevance to different face regions. This mask, which shares the same size of normal map and difference map, contains for each pixel an 8 bit weight encoding the local face surface rigidity based on the analysis of a set facial expressions of the same subject (see Fig. 3). In fact, for each subject enrolled, eight expressions (a neutral plus seven variations) are acquired and compared to the neutral face resulting in seven difference maps. More precisely, given a generic face with its normal map N_0 (neutral face) and the set of normal maps N_1, N_2, …, N_n (the expression variations), we first calculate the set of difference map D_1, D_2, …, D_n resulting from {`$N_0$ - $N_1$', `N_0 - N_2', …, `N_0 – N_n'}.The average of set {D_1, D_2, …, D_n} is the expression weighting mask which is multiplied by the difference map in each comparison between two faces. We can augment each 24 bit normal map with the Expression Weighting Mask normalized to 8 bit. The resulting 32 bit per pixel bitmap can be conveniently managed via various image formats like the Portable Network Graphics format (PNG) which is typically used to store for each pixel 24 bit of colour and 8 bit of alpha channel (transparency) in RGBA format. When comparing any two faces, the difference map is computed on the first 24 bit of colour info (normals) and multiplied to the alpha channel (mask).

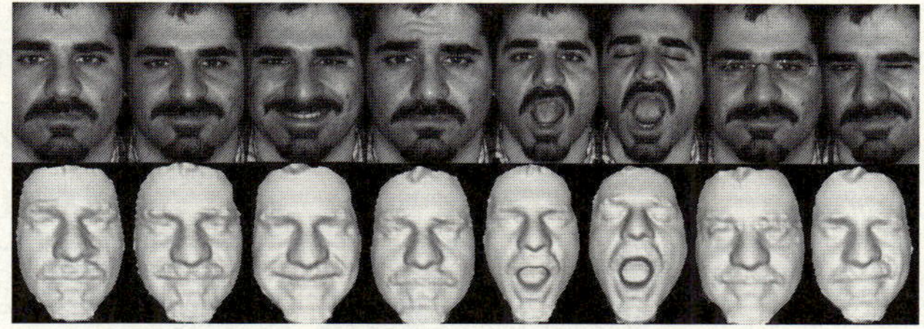

Fig. 3. Facial expressions exploited in Expression Weighting Mask

2.4 Implementing the Proposed Method Via GP-GPU

As briefly explained in the introduction to this paper, GPUs can vastly outperform CPUs for some computational topics, but two key requirements have to be satisfied: (1) the algorithm and the data types on which it operates should conform as much as possible to the computational architecture of GPU and to its specialized memory, the VRAM; (2) the data exchange with main memory and CPU should be carefully planned and minimized where possible. Because the descriptor used in our approach to face recognition is a RGBA coded bitmap the second part of first requirement is fully satisfied, but the first part is not so trivial. Indeed if the comparison stage of two normal maps requires pixel to pixel computation of a dot product, a task easily performed on multiple pixels in parallel via pixel shaders, the computation of histogram and similarity score for their algorithmic nature is not so suited to be efficiently implemented on GPU. This is mainly due to the lack of methods to access and to write in VRAM as we could easily do in RAM via CPU.

For this reason we decided to split the face comparison step from the rank assignment step, by means of a two-staged strategy which relies on GPU to perform a huge number of comparisons in the fastest possible time, and on CPU to work on the results produced from GPU to provide rank statistics, thanks to its general purpose architecture. We addressed the second requirement by an optimised arrangement of descriptors which minimize the number of data transfers from and to the main memory (RAM) and, at the same time, allows vector units on GPU to work efficiently (see

Fig. 4). Indeed we arranged every 1024 normal maps (RGBA, 24+8 bit) in a 32x32 cluster, resulting in a single 32 bit 4096x4096 sized bitmap (assuming each descriptor is sized 128x128 pixels). This kind of bitmap reaches the maximum size a GPU can manage at the moment, allowing to reduce by a factor 1,000 the number of exchanges with VRAM . The overhead due to descriptor arrangement is negligible as this task is performed during enrolment when normal map and expression weighting mask are computed and stored in the gallery. Up to 15,000 templates could be stored within 1GB of VRAM. On a query, the system load the maximum allowed amount of clusters from main memory to available free VRAM, then the GPU code is executed in parallel on any available pixel shader unit (so computing time reduction is linear in the number of shader units) and the result is write in a specifically allocated Frame-Buffer-Object (FBO) as a 32x32 cluster of difference maps. In the next step the FBO is flushed to RAM and the CPU start to compute the similarity score of each difference map storing each score and its index. This scheme repeats until all template clusters have been sent to and processed by GPU and all returning difference map clusters have been processed by CPU. Finally the sorted score vector is outputted. We implemented this algorithm through the Open GL 2.0 library and GLSL programming language.

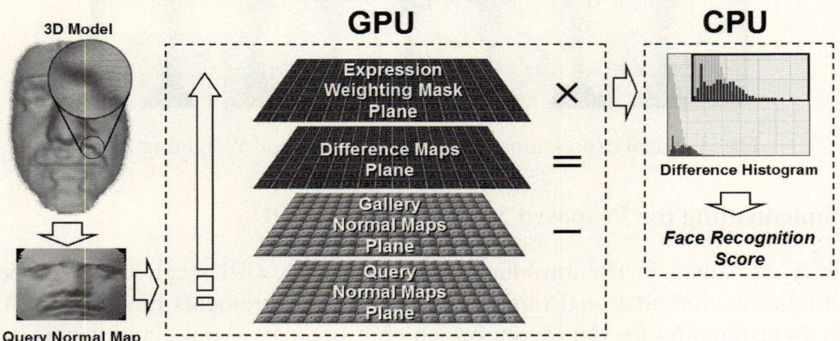

Fig. 4. Schematic representation of GPU accelerated normal map matching

3 Experiments

To test the proposed method four experiments using two different 3D face datasets have been conducted. We built the first dataset acquiring 235 different individuals (138 males and 97 females, age ranging from 19 to 40) in an indoor environment by means of a structured light scanner, the Mega Capturor II from Inspeck Corp.. For each subject eight expressions has been captured (including the neutral one) and each resulting 3D surface has an average of 60-80.000 polygons, with a minimum detail of about 1.5 millimetres. For the second dataset we used 1024 face shapes from release 2/experiment 3s of FRGC database, disregarding texture data. This dataset has undergone a pre-processing stage including mesh subsampling to one fourth or original resolution, mesh cropping to eliminate unwanted details (hair, neck, ears, etc.) and mesh filtering to reduce capture noise and artifacts. For all experiments we set σ =4.5 and k=50 for the Gaussian function and the normal map size is 128×128 pixels.

The first experiment, whose results are shown in Fig. 5-a., measures the overall recognition accuracy of proposed method through the Receiver Operating Characteristic (ROC) curve. The histogram compares the baseline algorithm (blue column, implemented exploiting the FRGC framework and applied on the preprocessed dataset described above) respectively to: proposed method on FRGC dataset using embedded alignment info (violet column), proposed method on FRGC dataset with pyramidal-normal-map based alignment (green column) and proposed method and alignment on our gallery allowing the use of expression weighting mask (orange). The result shown in the third column (green) is slightly better than the one measured on the second column (violet) as the alignment performed by proposed algorithm has proved to be more reliable than the landmarks embedded in FRGC. The best score is achieved in the fourth column (orange) as in this case we exploit both proposed alignment method and the weighting mask to better address expression variations.

The second experiment is meant to measure alignment accuracy, using the first dataset with 235 neutral faces for gallery and 705 (235*3) opened mouth, closed eyes and smile variations as probes. Moreover, the probes have been rotated of known angles on the three axis to stress the algorithm. The results are shown on Fig. 5-b. where after four iterations, 95.1% of probes have been re-aligned with a tolerance of less than two degree and for 73.1% of them the alignment error is below one degree.

The purpose of the third group of experiments is to measure the effect of posing variations and probe misalignment on recognition performance without the alignment step. Also in this case we used the neutral faces for gallery and opened mouth, closed eyes and smile variations, additionally rotated of known angles, as probes. The results in Fig. 5-c. show that for a misalignment within one degree the recognition rate is 98.1%, which drops to 94.6% if misalignment reaches two degrees. As the average computational cost of a single comparison (128x128 sized normal maps) is about 3 milliseconds for an Amd Opteron 2,6 GHz based PC, the total time needed to alignment is slightly more than 0.3 seconds, allowing an almost real time response. The overall memory requirement to completely store the template's precomputed normal maps is just 4 Mbytes. Finally, the fourth experiment shows in Fig. 6. how many templates can be theoretically compared to the query within 1 second if they could fit entirely in VRAM, proving how time wise the GPU based version of proposed method easily outperform any CPU based solution, whatever the processor chosen. To this aim we replicated the 1024 templates from FRGC subset to fill in all available VRAM. The system was able to compare about 85,000 templates per second (matching one-to-15,360 in 0,18 sec. on GeForce 7950 GTX/1024 with 32 pixel shaders) versus about 330 of CPU based version (AMD). In the same figure we compare the performance of different CPUs and GPUs including recently released GPU cores based on specs reported from the two main manufacturers (NVidia 8800 GTS and 8800 GTX featuring 96 and 128 programmable unified shaders respectively). Comparing these results to ICP based registration and recognition methods (typically requiring from a few seconds to tens of seconds for a single one-to-one match) clearly shows that the proposed approach is worth using it, at least timewise, regardless to the dataset dimension, as in a real biometric application the pre-processing phase (mesh

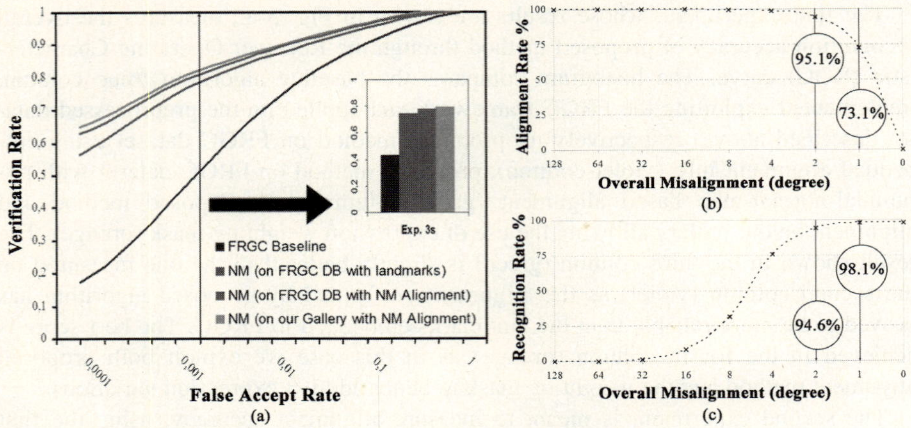

Fig. 5. ROC curve (a), alignment accuracy (b) and its relevance to recognition (c)

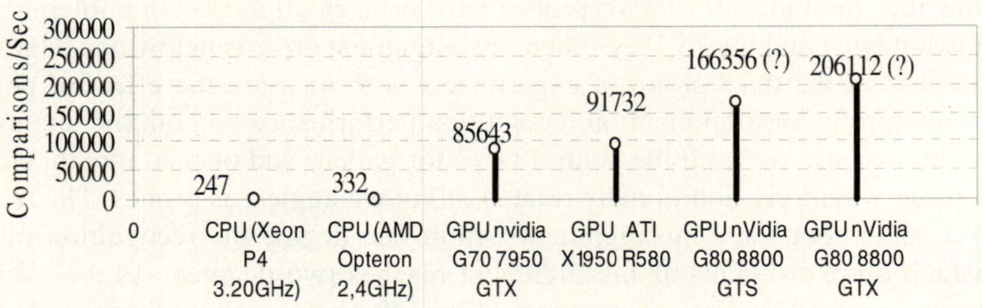

Fig. 6. Number of comparisons/sec for various computational hardware. In the graph CPU means only CPU is exploited, while GPU means that CPU (AMD Opteron 2,4 GHz) + GPU work together according to proposed scheme. (?) is just an estimate based on specs.

subsampling, filtering, cropping performed within 1 second in the tested framework) has to be performed only once at enrolment time.

4 Conclusions and Future Works

We presented a 3D face registration and recognition method optimized for large scale identification applications. The proposed approach showed good accuracy and robustness and proved to be highly suited to take advantage of GPU architecture, allowing to register a face and to compare it to many thousands of templates in less than a second.

As the recent release of Nvidia “Cuda” GPU based programming environments promises further advances in term of general purpose capability, we are currently working to fully implement the method on GPU, including those stages (as normal map and histogram computing) which are still CPU based in this proposal.

References

[1] Bowyer, K.W., Chang, K., Flynn, P.A.: A survey of approaches and challenges in 3D and multi-modal 3D + 2D face recognition. In: Computer Vision and Image Understanding, vol. 101, pp. 1–15. Elsevier, Amsterdam (2006)

[2] Zhang, J., Yan, Y., And Lades, M.: Face Recognition: Eigenface, Elastic Matching, and Neural Nets. Proc. of the IEEE 85(9), 1423–1435 (1997)

[3] Achermann, B., Bunke, H.: Classifying range images of human faces with Hausdorff distance. In: 15-th International Conference on Pattern Recognition, September 2000, pp. 809–813 (2000)

[4] Hesher, C., Srivastava, A., Erlebacher, G.: A novel technique for face recognition using range images. In: Seventh Int'l Symposium on Signal Processing and Its Applications (2003)

[5] Lu, X., Colbry, D., Jain, A.K.: Three-dimensional model based face recognition. In: 7th IEEE Workshop on Applications of Computer Vision, pp. 156–163 (2005)

[6] Tanaka, H.T., Ikeda, M., Chiaki, H.: Curvature-based face surface recognition using spherical correlation principal directions for curved object recognition. In: Third International Conference on Automated Face and Gesture Recognition, pp. 372–377 (1998)

[7] Medioni, G., Waupotitsch, R.: Face recognition and modeling in 3D. In: IEEE International Workshop on Analysis and Modeling of Faces and Gestures (AMFG 2003), October 2003, pp. 232–233 (2003)

[8] Bronstein, A.M., Bronstein, M.M., Kimmel, R.: Expression-invariant 3D face recognition. In: Kittler, J., Nixon, M.S. (eds.) AVBPA 2003. LNCS, vol. 2688, pp. 62–70. Springer, Heidelberg (2003)

[9] Abate, A.F., Nappi, M., Ricciardi, S., Sabatino, G.: Fast face recognition based on normal map. In: Proceedings of ICIP 2005, IEEE International Conference on Image Processing, Genova, Italy, July 2005. IEEE Computer Society Press, Los Alamitos (2005)

[10] Tsalakanidou, F., Tzovaras, D., Strintzis, M.G.: Use of depth and color eigenfaces for face recognition. Pattern Recognition Letters 24(9-10), 1427–1435 (2003)

[11] Papatheodorou, T., Rueckert, D.: Evaluation of Automatic 4D Face Recognition Using Surface and Texture Registration. In: Proceedings of the Sixth IEEE International Conference on Automatic Face and Gesture Recognition, Seoul, Korea, May 2004, pp. 321–326. IEEE Computer Society Press, Los Alamitos (2004)

[12] Gokberk, B., Salah, A.A., Akarun, L.: Rank-based decision fusion for 3D shape-based face recognition. In: Kanade, T., Jain, A., Ratha, N.K. (eds.) AVBPA 2005. LNCS, vol. 3546, pp. 1019–1028. Springer, Heidelberg (2005)

[13] Chen, Y., Medioni, G.: Object modeling by registration of multiple range images. Image and Vision Computing 10, 145–155 (1992)

[14] Besl, P., McKay, N.: A method for registration of 3-D shapes. IEEE Transaction on Pattern Analysis and Machine Intelligence 14, 239–256 (1992)

[15] Jost, T., Hügli, H.: Multi-resolution ICP with heuristic closest point search for fast and robust 3D registration of range images. In: Fourth International Conference on 3-D Digital Imaging and Modeling, October 06 - 10, 2003, pp. 427–433 (2003)

[16] Yan, P., Bowyer, K.: A Fast Algorithm for ICP-Based 3D Shape Biometrics. In: Proceedings of the ACM Workshop on Multimodal User Authentication, December 2006, pp. 25–32. ACM, New York (2006)

Frontal Face Synthesis Based on Multiple Pose-Variant Images for Face Recognition

Congcong Li, Guangda Su, Yan Shang, and Yingchun Li

Electronic Engineering Department, Tsinghua University, Beijing, 100084, China
lcc@mails.tsinghua.edu.cn

Abstract. Pose variance remains a challenging problem for face recognition. In this paper, a stereoscopic synthesis method for generating a frontal face image is proposed to improve the performance of automatic face recognition system. Through this method, a frontal face image is generated based on two pose-variant face images. Before the synthesis, face pose estimation, feature point extraction and alignment are executed on the two non-frontal images. Benefited from the high accuracy of pose estimation and alignment, the composed frontal face retains the most important features of the two corresponding non-frontal face images. Experiment results show that using the synthetic frontal image achieves a better recognition rate than using the non-frontal ones.

Keywords: Face recognition, pose estimation, face alignment, stereoscopy, texture synthesis.

1 Introduction

In recent years, techniques on face recognition have been developed a lot. Many algorithms have achieved satisfying recognition performance in controlled conditions under which faces are in frontal pose with harmonious illumination and neutral expression. However, there are still many open problems when face recognition technology is put into real world applications. The face recognition vender test (FRVT) 2002 reports [1] that recognition under illumination, expression and pose variations still remains challenging. Results show that recognition rate decreases sharply when face rotates to a large angle.

Aiming to improve face recognition performance under pose variance, face synthesis has been considered a lot. There have been considerable discussions of synthesizing face image in novel views which can be roughly divided into two categories: those based on 3D head model and those based on 2D image statistics [2].

One common way to synthesize novel views of a face is to recover its 3D structure. Many current algorithms utilize a morphable 3D model to generate face images of novel views from a single image. These methods face a problem in common: when only one face image is available, the texture within occluded region becomes undefined. Vetter et al. [3, 4] use the linear object class approach to deal with this

S.-W. Lee and S.Z. Li (Eds.): ICB 2007, LNCS 4642, pp. 948–957, 2007.

problem. It is assumed that a new face's texture can be represented as a linear combination of the texture from a group of example faces in the same view, and the combination coefficients can be used to synthesize the face image in another view. However, another difficulty appears. Since the generated texture is a linear combination of the textures in training database, some individual characteristic information would be lost, such as little scar, beauty spot, and so on.

Methods based on 2D images can also produce promising results for face synthesis. Stereopsis and projective geometry are often utilized. The utilization of these techniques highly depends on whether most face region is visible in all source images. While building statistical models for face images, AAM (Active Appearance Models) [5] and ASM (Active Shape Models) [6] are widely used. Both methods can help extract corresponding feature points for different facial images.

In this work, we present a whole scheme from pose-variant image capture to novel frontal image synthesis and recognition. This scheme generates a frontal facial image based on multiple pose-variant facial images. Pose estimation algorithm and ASM algorithm for face alignment are both improved to ensure the synthetic accuracy. The synthesis stage is divided into shape reconstruction and texture synthesis. Shape reconstruction is carried out mainly based on stereoscopy and partly assisted by a trained model. The proposed scheme solves the following problems:

1. It transforms the 2-D rotated facial images to a 2-D frontal view which is proven more suitable for face recognition by our experimental results.
2. Since the synthesis is based on more than one image, the texture contained in the two input images can cover most of the face so that details are retained;
3. It overcomes the computationally extensive problem of synthesis, and thus is suitable for real-time face identification applications;

The rest of the paper is organized as follows: Section 2 provides an overview of the proposed method; Section 3 introduces briefly the pose estimation method and Section 4 introduces the face alignment method, both of which affect the final accuracy of face reconstruction. Section 5 demonstrates the synthetic process, including shape reconstruction and texture synthesis. Experiment results are given in Section 6, and this paper is concluded in section 7.

2 Overview of the Proposed Scheme

Aiming to generate a frontal-pose face image for recognition, an integrated scheme is designed, including image collection, image preprocessing, pose estimation, face alignment, facial shape reconstruction and texture synthesis, as shown in Fig. 1.

The Multi-Channel Image Input & Process Module by Tsinghua University captures face image and performs face detection parallelly in four channels. Face synthesis will be carried on based on the input images with the help of pose estimation and face alignment.

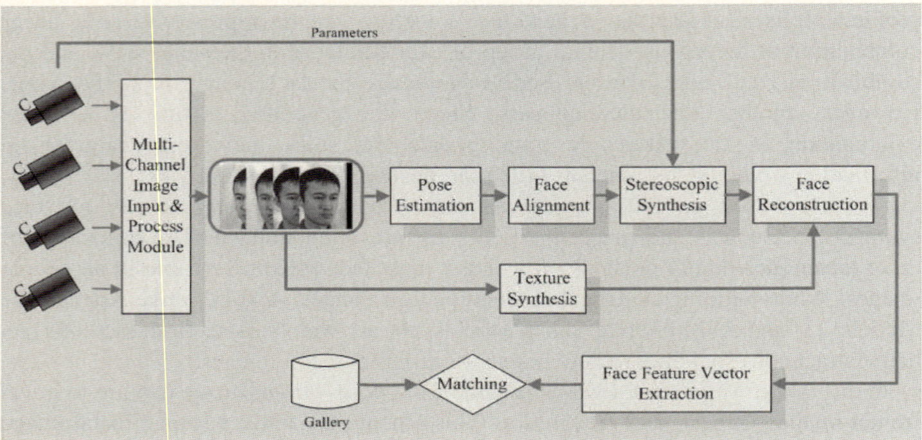

Fig. 1. Overview of the proposed scheme

3 Pose Estimation

In order to reconstruct a frontal face, the first step is to estimate poses of the input face images. The face images are preprocessed through feature-positioning and normalization. They are rectified and normalized geometrically according to the automatically located key-point positions. In the geometric normalization step, not only the eyes but also the chin middle point are located automatically. Then each face image is scaled and rotated so that the eyes are positioned in a horizontal line and the distance between the chin point and the center of the eyes equals a predefined length. After that, the face image is cropped to a given size. The examples of training images in TH face database [7] are shown in Fig.2. We collect 780 images of 60 people with left-right poses ranging from -45 degree to 45 degree at intervals of 15 degree and with up-down poses ranging from -20 degree to 20 degree at intervals of 10 degree.

It is essential to extract features from images utilizing the composite PCA (principle component analysis) and projecting face images to their eigenspace. Given a set of samples $X_i \in \mathbb{R}^N$ represented face images by column vectors. The transformation

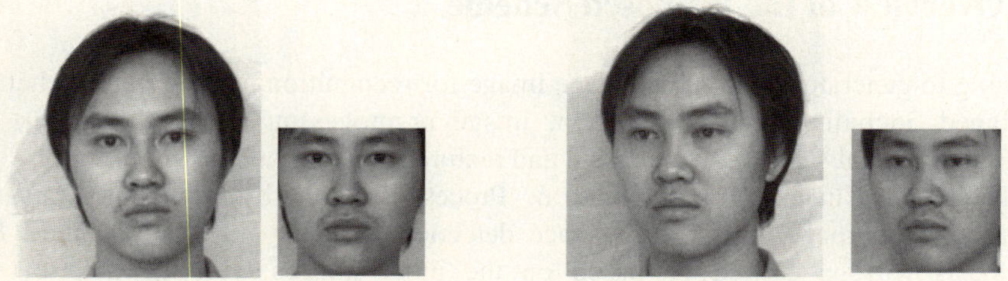

Fig. 2. The training face images in TH database and their corresponding normalized images

matrix can be formed by using eigenvectors which normalized to unit matrix T . The projection of X_i into the N-dimensional subspace can be expressed as

$$\alpha = \{\alpha_1, \cdots, \alpha_N\} = X_i^T \cdot T \tag{1}$$

The shape feature is shown in Fig. 3. The feature points represent geometric characteristic. AB and $A'B'$ are the distance between two eyes when pose angle is 0 and β degree respectively. Set radius as 1.

$$A'E' = A'B' = \sin(\theta + \beta) + \sin(\theta - \beta) = 2\sin\theta\cos\beta \tag{2}$$

Since distance $AB = 2\sin\theta$, then pose angle

$$\beta = \arccos(\frac{A'E'}{AB}) \tag{3}$$

Set weights of two weight parameters α and β after two groups of features are gained. The new eigenvector ξ is

$$\xi = p \cdot \alpha + q \cdot \beta \text{ , where } p + q = 1 \tag{4}$$

SVM (support vector machine) is used to find the optimal linear hyperplane by which the expected classification error for unseen test samples is minimized [8]. According to the structural risk minimization principle, a function that classifies the training data accurately will generalize best regardless of the dimensionality of the input space.

Each training sample x_i is associated with coefficient a_i .Those samples whose coefficient a_i is nonzero are Support Vectors (SV) of the optimal hyperplane. $f(x)$ is an optimal SVM classified function. $y_i \in (+1, -1)$.

$$f(x) = \sum_{\text{vector}} y_i a_i K(x_i, x) + b \tag{5}$$

Where K is a kernel function. Here we use linear kernel, $\phi(x_i) = x_i$, then $K(x_i, x_j) = x_i \cdot x_j = x_i^T x_j$.

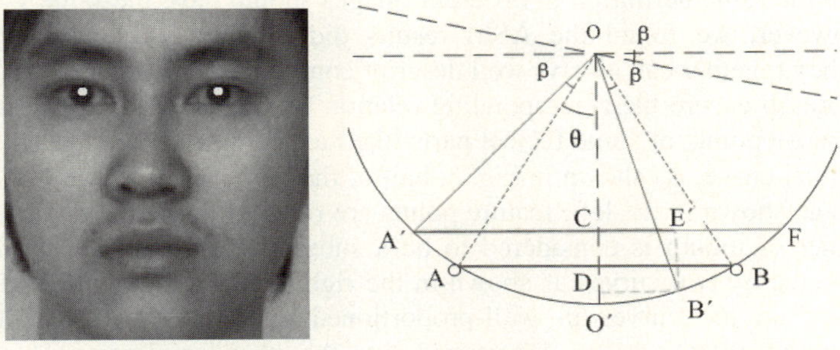

Fig. 3. Shape feature points and the configuration of pose variance

The PCA projection values of samples to eigenspace are used as SVM input parameters and the optimal hyperplane that correctly separates data points is found. Combining the PCA and SVM classifier, we can draw better classification results, thus more accurate pose angle estimation.

4 Face Alignment

An improved ASM (active shape models) method is chosen to extract the face feature points in this paper. It is hard for the conventional ASM to get accurate result on each feature point; what's more, the performance depends heavily on the initial positions of the landmarks. According to the facial structure, the edge information and facial part information are introduced to the matching process of ASM, which improved the performance of ASM [9, 10].

The face images are first normalized and totally 105 feature points extracted by the improved ASM algorithm are selected to represent the face shape feature, as shown in Fig. 4.

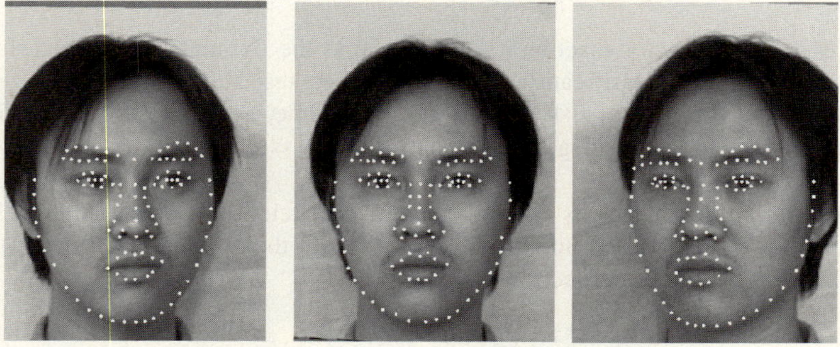

Fig. 4. Feature points extracted by the improved ASM algorithm

Although the improved ASM algorithm provides fine alignment, the accuracy of points can still be ameliorated. For images with different left-right poses, feature points with the same definition in different images should have the same y-coordinate value. However, we found the ASM results did not always meet this principle, although they together can always well descript contours of facial parts.

Therefore, to ensure the corresponding relation between feature points in different images, feature points of some facical parts like face contour are connected and fitted by polynomial curve. As shown in Fig. 5, half of the contour is fitted at two stages. At the first stage shown in the left, feature points are roughly fitted and the point parallel to the corner of mouth is considered to be a subsection point. Then the contour is fitted separated by two curves as shown in the right. Then the contour feature points are adjusted on the curves in well-proportioned distribution. Besides fitting the contour, similar operations are also carried onto the other facial parts. The alignment of the face feature points provides an important basis for shape reconstruction of frontal face, which will be mentioned in the next section.

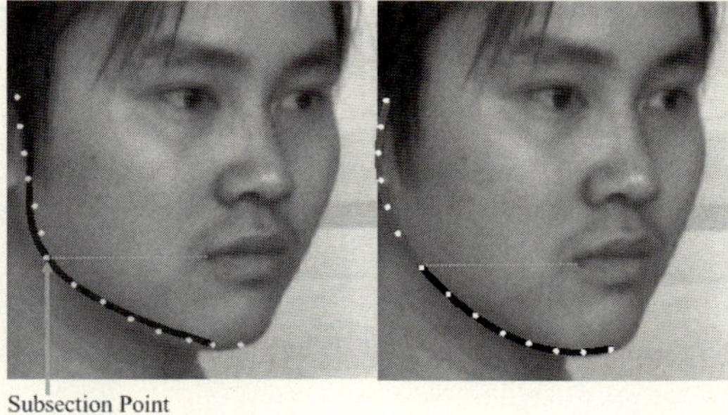

Fig. 5. A two-stage fitting to the contour with polynomial curves

5 Face Synthesis

A face image can be separated into shape information and texture information. If we have these two kinds of information, we can reconstruct a facial image.

5.1 Shape Reconstruction

The shape of the novel frontal facial image is reconstructed based on the aligned feature points extracted from the source images. Two-view stereoscopy is introduced into the shape reconstruction, as shown in the Fig. 6 below.

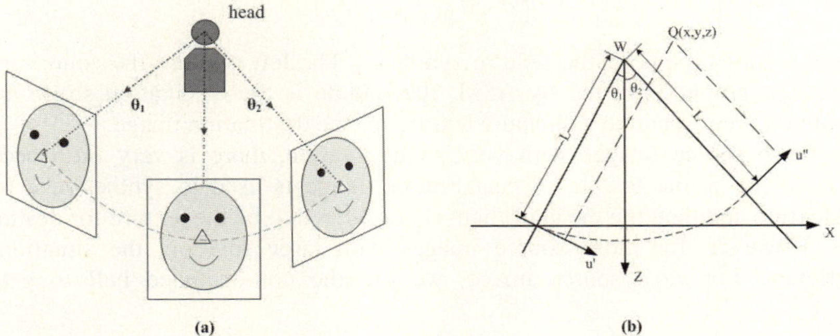

Fig. 6. Demonstration of the stereoscopy of shape reconstruction

For those feature points that are occluded in the source image with large rotation, we utilize a mean 3D model generated by 30 training subjects to reproduce their positions. We assume the shape of a human face is symmetric in horizontal direction. So we can generate positions of feature points in the occluded part from the viewable part in the same image with the help of this model. Although the model-based generated feature point positions are only approximations to their actual positions, the accuracy of these positions can be improved by a series of detailed iterative measures.

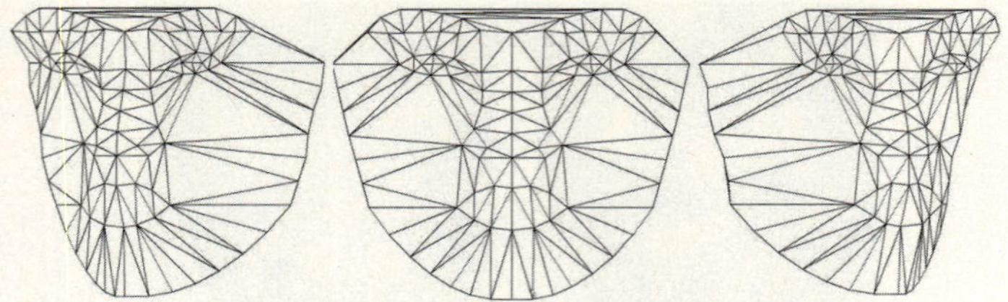

Fig. 7. A mean 3D model in our experiment

5.2 Texture Synthesis

For each source image and the reconstructed image, after feature points are positioned, triangularization is introduced to depart the face into multiple triangles. The triangularization follows the same principle and is realized by applying Delaunay triangularization [11] to a standard frontal shape. The standard frontal image can be a mean shape from a series of training images. Then the triangle based affine transform is used to span the source face images to fit the destination shape. Equation (6) describes this affine transform process. Here (x', y') is the corresponding coordinate in the destination image of a point (x, y) in the source image. Since the coordinates of vertexes of the corresponding triangles in the source and destination images are known, the affine transform in Equation (6) can be solved.

$$\begin{bmatrix} x' \\ y' \end{bmatrix} = \begin{bmatrix} a & b \\ c & d \end{bmatrix} \begin{bmatrix} x \\ y \end{bmatrix} + \begin{bmatrix} O_x \\ O_y \end{bmatrix} \tag{6}$$

Fig.8 is an example of the texture synthesis. The left two are the source images with feature points extracted by ASM; the middle is the destination shape and its triangulation; the right one is the pure texture for the destination image.

For those source images with very small rotation, there is very little occluded region. So the whole texture of each source image is used to synthesize a frontal facial texture and then the mean of them is considered to be the texture for destination image. However, for those source images with large rotation, the situation will be different. For each source image, we use the non-occluded half to generate

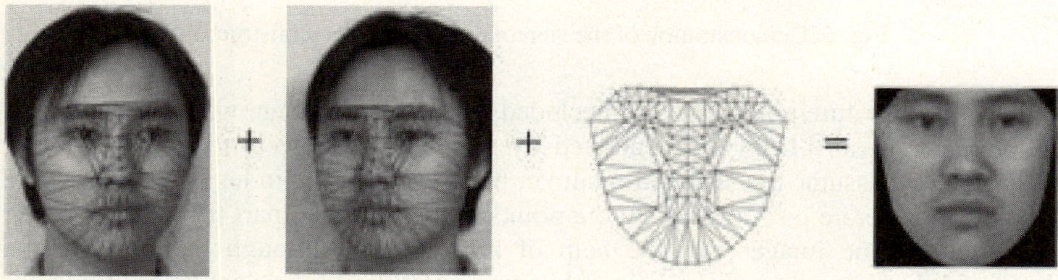

Fig. 8. Process of texture synthesis

respectively texture of half the destination image, and a smooth filter is applied to the boundary in the middle.

6 Experiment Results

In this section we describe our experiment results on TH face database [7]. The proposed synthesis method is used to generate frontal facial images based on different sets of facial images with different poses. Then the performance of face recognition based on the synthetic images is tested and compared with that based on the original face-rotated images, as shown in Table 1 on the next page.

Experiments are based on an identification task. The task is completed by common Gabor-PCA algorithm, which is trained by using another 600 frontal images from TH face database. The recognition rate means the fraction of probes that have ranked first in the identification task. The gallery consists of images of 2000 people with one frontal image per person from TH face database. Probe sets include image sets of different facial poses and the synthetic face image sets. Each probe set contains 200 face images and would be used to test recognition performance respectively.

In our experiments, the mean time cost of the proposed method is tested. The one-time completion of the whole scheme is 0.98 second averagely. This indicates that this method can be used for real-time identification applications.

Fig. 9 and Fig. 10 show some examples of the facial synthetic results. Fig. 9 gives two examples of face synthesis based on images with left-right rotation angles (yawing angles). Fig. 10 gives three examples of face synthesis based on images with up-down rotation angles (pitching angles). For each person, the first two columns are original images with rotation; the third column is the synthetic frontal facial image generated from the two images in the same row by our method; the fourth row is the real frontal facial image for the same person which is presented here for comparison.

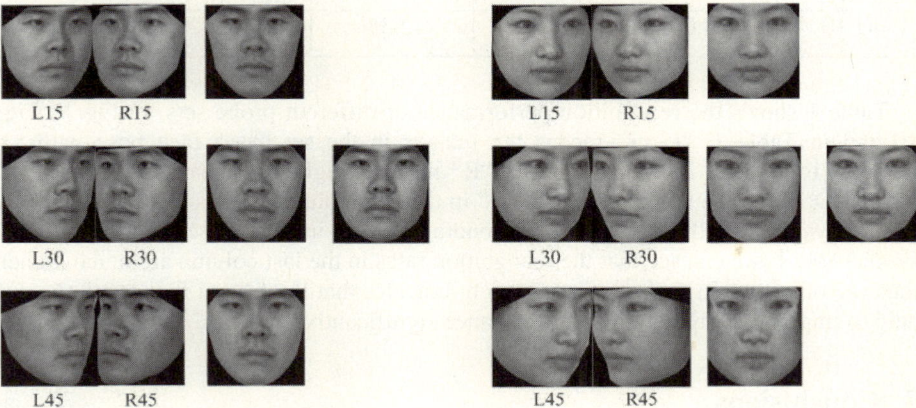

Fig. 9. Examples of face synthesis based on images with different yawing angles (left-right rotation angles)

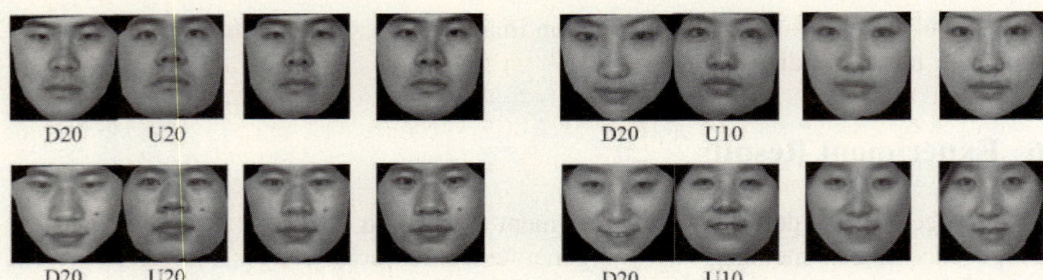

Fig. 10. Examples of face synthesis based on images with different pitching angles (up-down rotation angles)

Table 1. Recognition performance of the original image sets and the synthetic image sets

Original Image Set	Recognitio n Rate	Original Image Set	Recognitio n Rate	Synthetic Image Set	Recognitio n Rate
L 15	71.4%	R 15	70.1%	L 15+R 15	**88.5%**
L 30	58.2%	R 30	57.8%	L 30+R 30	**76.5%**
L 45	25.0%	R 45	25.2%	L 45+R 45	**52.6%**
L 15	71.4%	R 30	57.8%	L 15+R 20	**85.6%**
L 15	71.4%	R 45	25.2%	L 15+R 45	**79.0%**
L 30	58.2%	R45	25.2%	L 30+R 45	**62.7%**
U 10	62.5%	D 10	62.8%	U 10+D 10	**79.9%**
U 20	45.0%	D 20	42.3%	U 20+D 20	**66.7%**
U 10	64.0%	D 20	42.3%	U 10+D 20	**70.9%**

Table 1 shows the recognition performance of different probe sets. In Fig. 9, Fig. 10 and in Table 1, "L xx" means the images in the set has a face pose with xx degree's rotation to its left. Similarly, "R" means "Right", U means "Up" and "D" means "Down". The name "L xx + R yy" in the fifth column means that images in the set are synthesized through the corresponding images in "L xx" set and "R yy" set. From Table.1, we can see that the recognition rates in the last column are much higher than the other two in the same row, which indicates that the frontal face synthesis did help to improve the recognition performance significantly.

7 Conclusions

In this paper, we proposed a scheme for pose-variant face recognition. In order to overcome the difficulty brought by the non-frontal face images, a stereoscopic synthesis method is presented to generate a frontal face image based on two pose-variant face images, which are captured at the same time. To ensure the accuracy of shape reconstruction, we introduced an eigenspace analysis and SVM classification combined method for facial pose estimation and an improved ASM method for facial feature point extraction and alignment. With more than one input images, the whole face texture is nearly totally covered so that the synthesized frontal face can retain the individual texture characteristics. Although a small quantity of unavoidable estimation and alignment errors may affect the final reconstruction accuracy, experiment results show that most of the information important for recognition has been retained and helps to improve the recognition performance. Without expensive time cost, this method is suitable for real-time identification applications.

References

1. Phillips, P.J., Grother, P., Ross, J., Blackburn, D., Tabassi, E., Bone, M.: Face Recognition Vendor Test 2002: Evaluation Report. (March 2003)
2. Du, Y., Lin, X.: Multi-view face image synthesis using factorization models. In: International Workshop on Human-Computer Interaction (2004)
3. Vetter, T., Poggio, T.: Linear object classes and image synthesis from a single example image. IEEE Transactions on Pattern Analysis and Machine Intelligence 19(7), 733–742 (1997)
4. Cootes, T., Edwards, G., Taylor, C.: Active appearance models. IEEE Trans. Pattern Analysis and Machine Intelligence 23(6), 681–685 (2001)
5. Cootes, T., Taylor, C., Cooper, D., et al.: Active shape models ~ their training and application. Computer Vision and Image Understanding 61(1), 38–59 (1995)
6. Vetter, T.: Synthesis of novel views from a single face image. International Journal of Computer Vision 28(2), 103–116 (1998)
7. Li, C., Su, G., Meng, K., Zhou, J.: Technology Evaluations on TH-FACE Recognition System. In: Zhang, D., Jain, A.K. (eds.) Advances in Biometrics. LNCS, vol. 3832, pp. 589–597. Springer, Heidelberg (2005)
8. Vapnik, V.: Statistical Learning Theory. John Wiley & Sons, New York (1998)
9. Gu, H., Su, G., Du, C.: Feature Points Extraction from Faces. In: Image and Vision Computing (IVCNZ'03), pp. 154–158 (2003)
10. Du, C., Su, G., Lin, X., Gu, H.: An Improved Multi-resolution Active Shape Model for Face Alignment. Jounal of Optoelectronics. Laser 15(12), 706–710 (2004) (in Chinese)
11. Hassanpour, R., Atalay, V.: Delaunay Triangulation based 3D Human Face Modeling from Uncalibrated Images. In: Int. C. Computer Vision and Pattern Recognition, p. 75. IEEE Comput. Soc. Press, Los Alamitos (2004)

Optimal Decision Fusion for a Face Verification System

Qian Tao and Raymond Veldhuis

Signals and Systems Group, Faculty of EEMCS
University of Twente, The Netherlands

Abstract. Fusion is a popular practice to increase the reliability of the biometric verification. In this paper, optimal fusion at decision level by AND rule and OR rule is investigated. Both a theoretical analysis and the experimental results are given. Comparisons are presented between fusion at decision level and fusion at matching score level. For our face verification system, decision fusion proves to be a simple, practical, and effective approach, which significantly improves the performance of the original classifier.

1 Introduction

Fusion is a popular practice to increase the reliability of the biometric verification by combining the outputs of multiple classifiers. Often, fusion is done based on these matching scores, because this combines a good performance with a simple implementation. In decision fusion, each classifier outputs an accept or reject decision and the fusion is done based on these decisions. The diagram of decision fusion can be drawn as in Fig. 1.

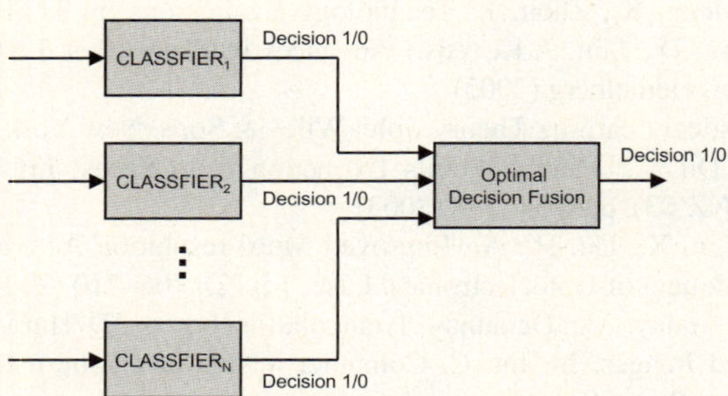

Fig. 1. Diagram of optimal decision fusion

In literature fusion at matching score level is more frequently discussed [2] [3] [6] [5]. In this paper, however, we will show that fusion at decision level by AND rule and OR rule can be applied in a optimal way such that it always gives an improvement in terms of error rates over the classifiers that are fused. Here optimal is taken in Neyman-Pearson sense [9]: at a given false-reject rate α, the decision-fused classifier has a false-reject rate β that is minimal and never larger than the false-reject rates of the classifiers that are fused at the same α.

S.-W. Lee and S.Z. Li (Eds.): ICB 2007, LNCS 4642, pp. 958–967, 2007.

In this paper we apply the optimal decision fusion to a likelihood-ratio-based face verification system. At decision level the classifier outputs binary values: 0 for reject and 1 for accept. At matching score level, the classifier outputs the log likelihood ratio. Optimal decision fusions by AND rule and OR rule are compared to matching score fusion by sum rule.

This paper is organized as follows. In Section 2 theoretical analysis on optimal decision fusion is given. In Section 3 the application on face verification is described, and the results of optimal decision fusion on this system are shown. Section 4 gives the conclusions.

2 Optimal Decision Fusion

2.1 Optimal Decision Fusion Theory

Suppose we have two (or more) classifiers which output binary decisions. Assume that the decisions are statistically independent. (Note that this independency may arise from independent classifiers, or independent samples.)

Each decision D_i is characterized by two error probabilities: the first is the probability of a false accept, the false-accept rate (FAR), α_i, and the second is the probability of a false reject, the false-reject rate (FRR), β_i. To analyze the AND rule it is more convenient to work with the detection probability or detection rate $p_{d,i} = 1-\beta_i$. It is assumed that $p_{d,i}$ is a known function of α_i, $p_{d,i}(\alpha_i)$, known as the ROC (Receiver Operating Characteristic). In practice, the ROC has to be derived empirically. After application of the AND rule to decisions $D_i, i = 1, ..., N$, we have, under the important assumption that all decisions are statistically independent, that

$$\alpha = \prod_{i=1}^{N} \alpha_i \tag{1}$$

$$p_d(\alpha) = \prod_{i=1}^{N} p_{d,i}(\alpha_i) \tag{2}$$

with α the false-accept rate and p_d the detection rate of the fused decision, respectively. Optimal AND rule fusion can be formally defined by finding

$$\hat{p}_d(\alpha) = \max_{\alpha=\prod_{i=1}^{N}\alpha_i} \prod_{i=1}^{N} p_{d,i}(\alpha_i) \tag{3}$$

(3) means that the resulting detection rate p_d at a certain α is the maximal value of the product of the detection rates at some combination of α_i 's under the condition that $\alpha = \prod_{i=1}^{N} \alpha_i$. In other words, the α_i 's of component classifiers are tuned so that the fused classifier can give maximal detection rate at a fixed $\alpha = \prod_{i=1}^{N} \alpha_i$. Likewise, if we define the reject rate for the impostors $p_{r,i} = 1 - \alpha_i$, the optimal decision fusion by OR rule can be similarly formulated

$$\hat{p}_r(\beta) = \max_{\beta=\prod_{i=1}^{N}\beta_i} \prod_{i=1}^{N} p_{r,i}(\beta_i) \tag{4}$$

where $\hat{p}_d(\alpha)$ and $\hat{p}_r(\beta)$ are the optimized ROCs by AND rule and OR rule, respectively.

For AND rule, it is easily proved that the optimized detection rate $\hat{p}_d(\alpha)$ is never smaller than any of the $p_{d,i}$'s at the same FAR α

$$\hat{p}_d(\alpha) \geq p_{d,i}(\alpha) \qquad i = 1, ..., N \tag{5}$$

Because, by definition

$$\begin{aligned} \hat{p}_d(\alpha) &= \max_{\alpha=\prod_{i=1}^{N}\alpha_i} \prod_{i=1}^{N} p_{d,i}(\alpha_i) \\ &\geq \prod_{j=1}^{N} p_{d,j}(\alpha_j) \Big|_{\prod_{i=1}^{N}\alpha_i=\alpha} \end{aligned} \tag{6}$$

As it holds for any classifier that, $p_{d,i}(1) = 1$, (5) readily follows by setting $\alpha_j = \alpha$ and $\alpha_i = 1, i \neq j$. For OR rule, it can be similarly proved that the optimized reject rate $\hat{p}_r(\beta)$ is never smaller than any of the $p_{r,i}$'s at the same FRR β.

By solving the optimization problem in (3) and (4), the operation points for every component classifiers are obtained, hence the fused classifier which yields the optimal performance in the Neyman-Pearson sense. Because in real situations, the ROCs, i.e. $\hat{p}_d(\alpha)$ or $\hat{p}_r(\beta)$, are characterized by a set of discrete operation points rather than analytically, the optimization in (3) and (4) must be solved in a numerical way. In [11] the problem is reformulated in a logarithmic domain as an unconstrained Lagrange optimization problem.

2.2 Optimal Decision Fusion on Identical Classifiers

In this section we will discuss, in particular, the optimal decision fusion on identical classifiers. This is a very useful setting in real applications, as will be shown in Section 3. Fusion on identical classifiers, in practice, means that given one classifier and multiple independent input samples, we make optimal fusion on the multiple output decisions.

In this paper, for simplicity, we analyze optimal fusion on two decisions. Fusion on three or more decisions can be done in a similar manner. Because the classifiers are identical, we have that $p_{d,1} = p_{d,2}$ and the optimization problem can be formulated to

$$p_{\text{fusion}}(x;\alpha) = p_d(x) \cdot p_d(\frac{\alpha}{x}) \tag{7}$$

$$\hat{p}_{\text{fusion}}(\alpha) = \max_{\alpha \leq x \leq 1} \{p_{\text{fusion}}(x;\alpha)\} \tag{8}$$

where x is a changing variable in the search process, and $\hat{p}_{\text{fusion}}(\alpha)$ is the detection rate at α under optimal AND fusion.

The optimum can be found by looking for the stationary point where the derivative of (7) w.r.t x is zero. As this derivative can be written

$$p'_{\text{fusion}}(x;\alpha) = p'_d(x)p_d(\frac{\alpha}{x}) - \frac{\alpha}{x^2}p_d(x)p'_d(\frac{\alpha}{x}) \tag{9}$$

Obviously when $x = \sqrt{\alpha}$, i.e. $\alpha_1 = \alpha_2 = \sqrt{\alpha}$, the derivative reaches zero. However, for some ROCs and for some α, this stationary point corresponds to a minimum, then the optimum is found at the border, either $\alpha_1 = 1$ or $\alpha_2 = 1$, which means only one of the two ROCs is taken.

In practice, therefore, under the optimal situation, either the two component classifiers work on identical operation points, or one of them does not effect at all. Although the former situation happens more often in practice, the later one does occur in certain cases.

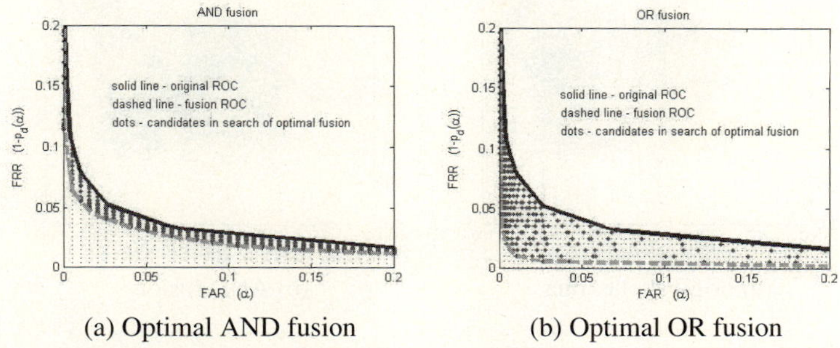

(a) Optimal AND fusion (b) Optimal OR fusion

Fig. 2. Optimal decision fusion on ROC, example 1

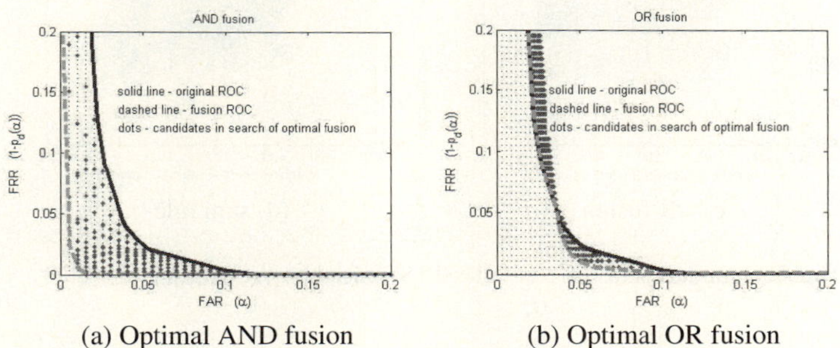

(a) Optimal AND fusion (b) Optimal OR fusion

Fig. 3. Optimal decision fusion on ROC, example 2

Examples are shown to illustrate the optimal decision fusion. Fig. 2 and Fig. 3 show two examples of optimal decision fusion. In both figures, the solid line represents the original ROC, the dots represent the candidates in search of optimal point by (7) with different x, and the dashed line represents the resulting optimal ROC. Improvements of performance can be clearly seen in both cases. Furthermore, it can be observed that OR rule is more suitable for the ROC in Fig. 2, and AND rule is more suitable for the ROC in Fig. 3. In Fig. 3 (b) we can see that for a certain range of α, the two component classifiers are not working on the same operation point, , but one of the two is taken.

To better explain the improvement brought by fusion, Fig. 4 visualizes different decision boundaries of the original classifier, AND fusion, OR fusion, and the sum rule. The crosses represent the scattering of two independent matching scores (in this case the logarithm likelihood ratio) for the user, and the circles represent the scattering of two independent matching scores for the impostors. In Fig. 4 (b) (c) (d), fusion facilitates decision boundaries spanning across a two dimensional space, where the two "clouds" are better separated compared to the case of a one dimensional space in Fig. 4 (a) (in which only one dimension is valid). Even better separation can be expected in higher dimensional spaces.

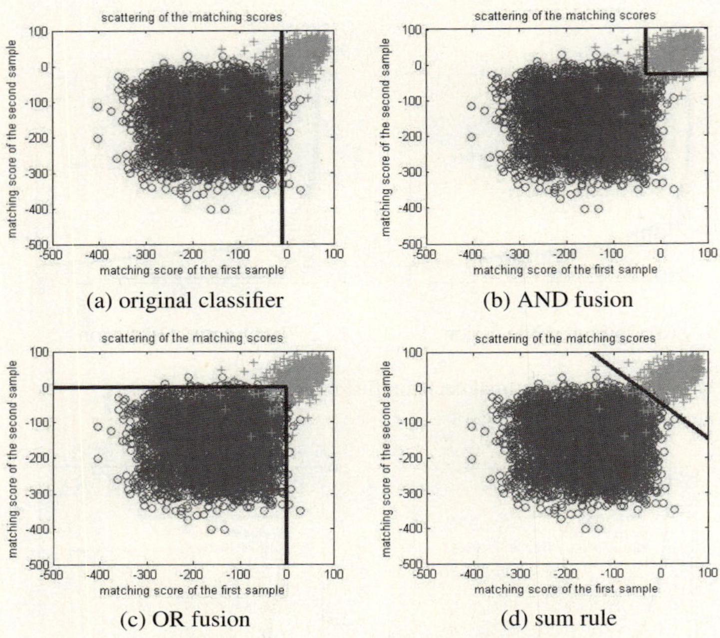

(a) original classifier (b) AND fusion

(c) OR fusion (d) sum rule

Fig. 4. Boundaries of different classifiers based on the original classifier

3 Application of Optimal Decision Fusion on a Face Verification System

3.1 The Face Verification System on a Mobile Device

In Section 2 the optimal decision fusion theory has been presented. In this section we describe a real application of a biometric verification system, on which the optimal decision fusion will be applied.

In a larger context, our biometric verification system acts as a link between a user and a private PN (personal network), via an intermediate MPD (mobile personal device) [7]. To achieve high security for the PN, it is specially demanded, among other requirements, that the authentication should be done not only at logon time, but also ongoing, in order to prevent the scenario that a MPD is taken away by the impostors after logged in by the user.

We use the face as the biometrics, and a camera on the MPD as the biometric sensor. In our standard system, features are extracted from each frame of face image, and a decision of YES or NO is made. In our original face recognition system, face detection is done by Viola-Jones method [10], face registration is done by aligning prominent facial landmarks detected also by Viola-Jones method. Illumination normalization is done by apply local binary patterns (LBP) [4] [1] as an preprocessing method. A likelihood ratio classifier is used which is based on the relative distribution between the user and the background data [8]. As the user-specific distribution has to be learned from extensive user training data which is beyond most public face databases, we collected our dataset under laboratory conditions. More than 500 frames of face images are collected per subject. (The database is still under construction, but the data used in this paper is available on request.)

In our new system with decision fusion, multiple frames with certain intervals are taken as the input, and the decision is made based on optimal fusion. It can be argued that the independency assumption is rendered less true when the intervals are chosen too small, but we will show that even in case of partial dependency, the decision fusion brings improvements to the performance of the system.

3.2 Experiments Setup

In the experiments, the face images are collected with a frequency of 5 frames per second, and stored as a function of time. For each subject, the data are independently collected in different sessions under different illuminations. Examples of the cross session data are shown by Fig. 5.

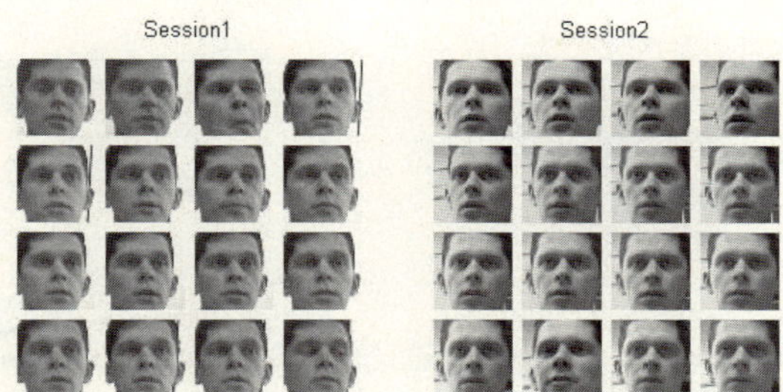

Fig. 5. The face data of a user collected in different sessions

We use the data of two independent sessions for training and testing. Firstly, the classifier is trained on the first session. Secondly, the classifier is tested on the second session, and a ROC is obtained. The ROC represents the component classifier in the decision fusion. Then optimal decision fusion is then made on the ROC according to (3) or (4). Finally, the optimal decision fusion scheme is tested on multiple inputs from the second session, with each component classifier working on its optimal operation points.

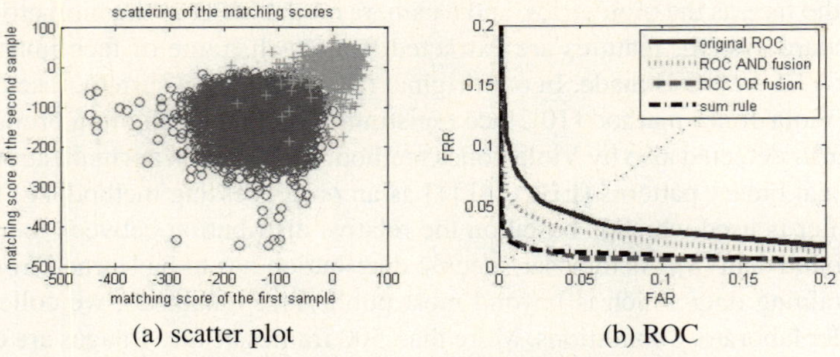

(a) scatter plot (b) ROC

Fig. 6. Experiment results with randomly chosen samples

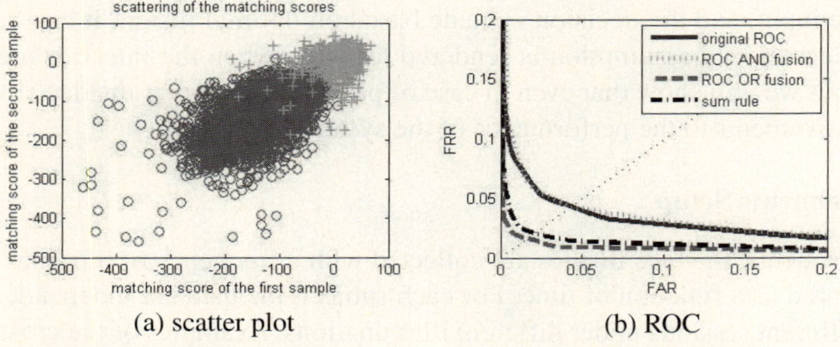

(a) scatter plot (b) ROC

Fig. 7. Experiment results with samples chosen at a time interval of 0.5 second

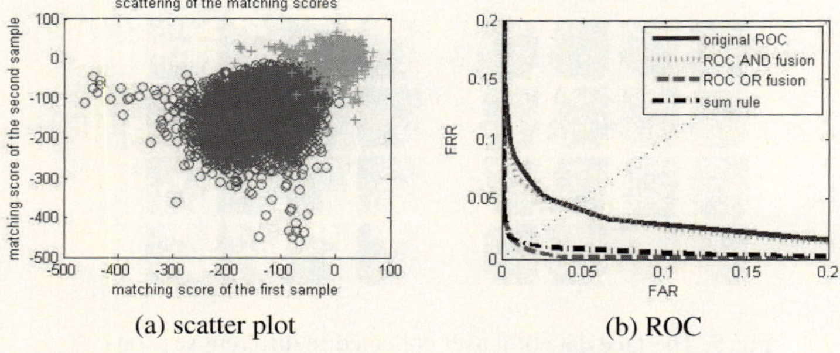

(a) scatter plot (b) ROC

Fig. 8. Experiment results with samples chosen at a time interval of 15 second

3.3 Results on Optimal Decision Fusion

In the following experiments, optimal decision fusion is done on two samples. The samples are taken in three ways. (1) The two samples are randomly taken; (2) The two samples are taken on a short interval of 0.5 second; (3) The two samples are taken on a longer interval of 15 second. For comparison, we also do sum rule matching score fusion, which is the theoretically optimal scheme for logarithm likelihood ratio matching scores. Fig. 6, Fig. 7, and Fig. 8 shows the results of these three sampling ways, respectively.

Improvements in performance can be clearly seen from Fig. 6, Fig. 7, and Fig. 8, with the EER (equal error rate) reduced to less than half of the original value. In Fig. 7 and Fig. 8 there exists certain correlation between the two samples, but despite this partial independency, OR rule still works very well and yields a performance comparable to or even better than the sum rule matching score fusion. The scatter plot indicates that in certain cases, a corner-shaped OR rule boundary is favored over a straight-line sum rule boundary.

3.4 Outliers and OR-Rule Optimal Decision Fusion

Outliers, in face verification, means the face images which belong to the user, but deviate from the user distribution because of extraordinary expressions or poses. Outliers occur in biometric verification, and cause rejections of the user. In our ongoing face verification system on a MPD, this harms the convenience aspect of the system [7]. Fig. 9 illustrates the outlier faces rejected by the original classifier.

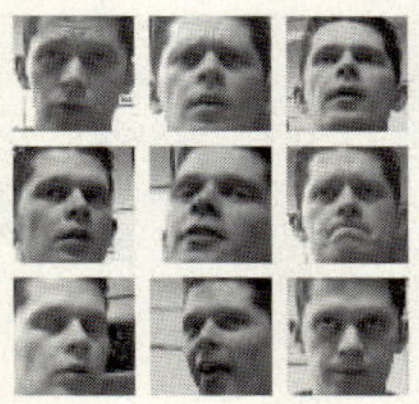

Fig. 9. Outliers in user data which are rejected by the classifier

The optimal decision fusion by OR rule, fortunately, can effectively reduce the FRR cause by the outliers at almost no expenses of FAR. Suppose the outlier distribution of the genuine user sample x is denoted by $\Psi_{Go}(x)$, with a prior probability of a small quantity p_o, and suppose the distribution of the genuine user sample in normal cases is $\Psi_G(x)$, with a prior probability of $1 - p_o$. Taking into acount the outlier distribution, the probability $\Psi(x)$ of a genuine user sample x can be expressed by

$$\Psi(x) = (1 - p_o) \cdot \Psi_G(x) + p_o \cdot \Psi_{Go}(x) \tag{10}$$

For two samples x_1 and x_2, assuming independency, their joint probability is

$$\begin{aligned} \Psi(x_1, x_2) &= (1 - p_o)^2 \cdot \Psi_G(x_1)\Psi_G(x_2) + p_o^2 \cdot \Psi_{Go}(x_1)\Psi_{Go}(x_2) \\ &+ p_o n(1 - p_o) \cdot \Psi_{Go}(x_1)\Psi_G(x_2) + p_o(1 - p_o) \cdot \Psi_G(x_1)\Psi_{Go}(x_2) \end{aligned} \tag{11}$$

The four terms in (11) describe the probability of the four different joint occurrences of the two samples, corresponding to Fig. 10. Note the second term, which describes the simultaneous occurrences of two outliers, is extremely small due to p_o^2. In this case, OR rule boundary denoted by the solid line works better than the sum rule boundary denoted by the dotted line, with fewer false rejections. Real examples in our experiments also confirms the advantage of OR rule, as shown in Fig. 11. In this experiment, the cross session data are more extensive, therefore the outlier effects are more prominent.

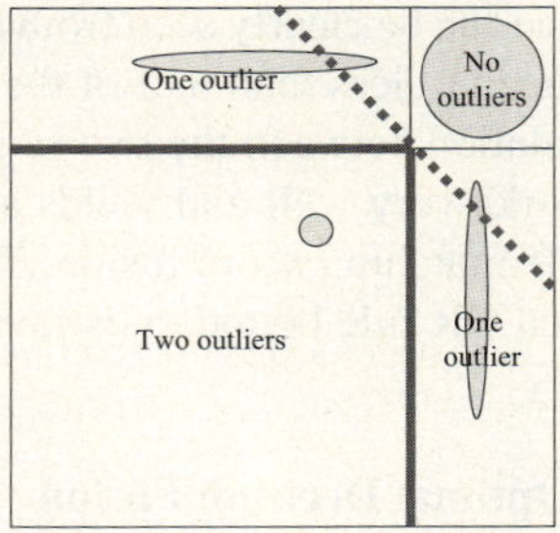

Fig. 10. The distribution of the two samples in fusion, taking into account the outlier distribution. The solid lines are the OR rule boundary, and the dotted line is the sum rule boundary.

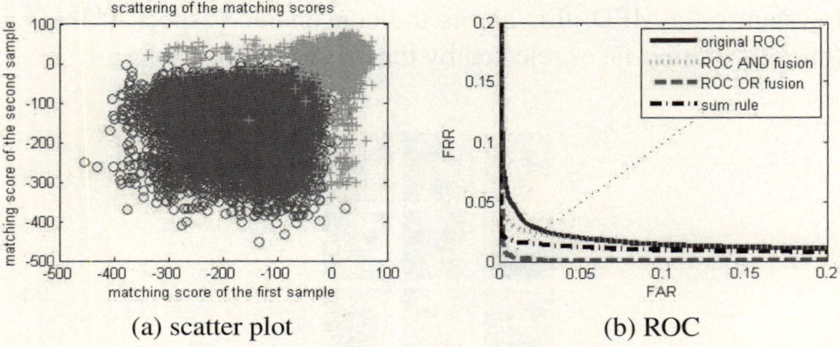

(a) scatter plot (b) ROC

Fig. 11. Experiment results with samples with outliers

It can be seen that in realistic situations, in presence of outliers, the OR rule works best. Comparing the OR rule performance with the sum rule performance in Fig. 11 (b), it can be seen that the FRR is effectively reduced at the same FAR.

4 Conclusions

In this paper, optimal fusion at decision level by AND rule and OR rule is proposed and investigated. Both the theoretical analysis and the experimental results are given, showing optimal decision fusion can always give an improvement to the performance of the original classifier. For our face verification system, decision fusion proves to be a simple, practical, and effective approach, which significantly improves the performance of the system. The improvements brought by optimal decision fusion on FAR with respect to a fixed FRR (or FRR with respect to FAR) is very desirable for biometric systems.

References

1. Heusch, G., Rodriguez, Y., Marcel, S.: Local binary patterns as image preprocessing for face authentication. In: IEEE International Conference on Automatic Face and Gesture Recognition. IEEE Computer Society Press, Los Alamitos (2006)
2. Kittler, J., Hatef, M., Duin, R., Matas, J.: On combining classifiers. IEEE Transactions on Pattern Analysis and Machine Intelligence 20(3), 226–239 (1998)

3. Kittler, J., Li, Y., Matas, J., Sanchez, M.: Combining evidence in multimodal personal identity recognition systems. In: Bigün, J., Borgefors, G., Chollet, G. (eds.) AVBPA 1997. LNCS, vol. 1206. Springer, Heidelberg (1997)
4. Ojala, T., Pietikainen, M., Maenpaa, T.: Multiresolution gray-scale and rotation invariant texture classification with local binary patterns. IEEE Transactions on Pattern Analysis and Machine Intelligence 24(7), 971–987 (2004)
5. Ross, A., Jain, A.: Information fusion in biometrics. 24(13) (2003)
6. Ross, A., Nandakumar, K., Jain, A.: Handbook of Multibiometrics. Springer, Heidelberg (2006)
7. Tao, Q., Veldhuis, R.: Biometric authentication for mobile personal device. In: First International Workshop on Personalized Networks, San Jose, USA (2006)
8. Tao, Q., Veldhuis, R.: Verifying a user in a personal face space. In: 9th Int. Conf. Control, Automation, Robotics, and Vision, Singapore (2006)
9. van Trees, H.L.: Detectioin, Estimation, and Modulation Theory. John Wiley and Sons, New York (1969)
10. Viola, P., Jones, M.: Robust real-time face detection. International Journal of Computer Vision 57(2), 137–154 (2004)
11. Zhang, W., Chang, Y., Chen, T.: Optimal thresholding for key generation based on biometrics. In: International Conference on Image Processing (2004)

Robust 3D Head Tracking and Its Applications

Wooju Ryu and Daijin Kim

Intelligent Multimedia Laboratory, Dept. of Computer Science and Engineering,
Pohang University of Science and Technology (POSTECH), Pohang, Korea
{wjryu,dkim}@postech.ac.kr

Abstract. The head tracking is a challenging work and a useful application in the field of computer vision. This paper proposes a fast 3D head tracking method that is working robustly under a variety of difficult conditions. First, we obtain the pose robustness by using the 3D cylindrical head model (CHM) and dynamic template. Second, we also obtain the robustness about the fast head movement by using the dynamic template. Third, we obtain the illumination robustness by modeling the illumination basis vectors and by adding them to the previous input image to adapt the current input image. Experimental results show that the proposed head tracking method outperforms the other tracking method using the fixed and dynamic template in terms of the small pose error and the higher successful tracking rate and it tracks the head successfully even if the head moves fast under the rapidly changing poses and illuminations in a speed of 10-15 frames/sec. The proposed head tracking method has a versatile applications such as a head gesture TV remote controller for the handicapped people and a drawing tool by the head movement for the entertainment.

1 Introduction

For the 3D head tracking, many researchers have used simple geometric head models such as a cylinder [1], [2], an ellipsoid [3], or a head-like 3D shape [4] to recover the global head motion. They assume that the shape of the head model does not change during tracking, which means that it does not have the shape parameters. The global head motion can be represented by a rigid motion, which can be parameterized by 6 parameters; three for 3D rotation and three for 3D translation. Therefore, the number of the model parameters is only 6. Among three different geometric 3D head models, we take the cylindrical head model due to the robustness to the pose variation and the general applicability and the simplicity. It is more appropriate to approximate the 3D shape of the generic faces than the ellipsoid model. Also, it requires a small number of parameters and its fitting performance is less sensitive to their initialization than the head-like 3D shape model.

To be more robust about the extreme pose and fast head movement, dynamic template technique has been proposed [2]. Although the dynamic template technique can treat the extreme head movement, it has a problem that can fail the head tracking due to the accumulated fitting error. To remedy this problem, [2]

S.-W. Lee and S.Z. Li (Eds.): ICB 2007, LNCS 4642, pp. 968–977, 2007.

proposed the re-registration technique that stored the reference frames and used them when the fitting error became large. The dynamic template may cover the gradually changing illumination because the template is updated every frames. However, it can not cover all kinds of illumination changes, specifically for the rapidly changing illumination. [1] removed the illumination effects by adding the illumination basis vectors to the template. This approach can cover the rapidly changing illumination.

We derive a novel full-motion recovery under perspective projection that combines the dynamic template and re-registration technique [2] and the removal of illumination effect by adding the illumination basis vectors [1]. Also, we update the reference frames according to the illumination condition of input image. This approach provides a new head tracking method which is robust to the extreme head poses, the fast head movement, the rapidly changing illumination.

2 Full Motion Recovery Under the Rapidly Changing Illuminations

2.1 Full Motion Recovery

The cylinder head model assumes that the head is shaped as a cylinder and the face is approximated by the cylinder surface. The 3D cylinder surface represented as $\mathbf{x} = [x \;\; y \;\; z]^{\mathrm{T}}$ and the 2D image pixel coordinate is represented as $\mathbf{u} = [u \;\; v]^{\mathrm{T}}$. If we take the perspective projection function, the 2D image pixel coordinate $\mathbf{u}$ is given by

$$\mathbf{u} = P(\mathbf{x}) = \frac{f_L}{z}[x \;\; y]^{\mathrm{T}}, \tag{1}$$

where f_L is the focal length.

When the cylinder surface point $\mathbf{x}$ is transformed by the rigid motion vector $\mathbf{p}$, the rigid transformation function $M(\mathbf{x}; \mathbf{p})$ of $\mathbf{x}$ can be represented by

$$M(\mathbf{x}; \mathbf{p}) = R\mathbf{x} + T, \tag{2}$$

where $R \in \mathbb{R}^{3\times 3}$ and $T \in \mathbb{R}^{3\times 1}$ are the 3D rotation matrix and the 3D translation vector, respectively. We take the twist representation [8], whose detailed derivation is given in [9]. According to the twist representation, the 3D rigid motion model $M(\mathbf{x}; \mathbf{p})$ is given by

$$M(\mathbf{x}; \mathbf{p}) = \begin{bmatrix} 1 & -w_z & w_y \\ w_z & 1 & -w_x \\ -w_y & w_x & 1 \end{bmatrix} \begin{bmatrix} x \\ y \\ z \end{bmatrix} + \begin{bmatrix} t_x \\ t_y \\ t_z \end{bmatrix} \tag{3}$$

where $\mathbf{p} = [\, w_x \;\; w_y \;\; w_z \;\; t_x \;\; t_y \;\; t_z \,]^{\mathrm{T}}$ is the 3D full head motion parameter vector. The warping function $W(\mathbf{x}; \mathbf{p})$ in Eq. (??) is completely defined by using $P(\mathbf{x})$ and $M(\mathbf{x}; \mathbf{p})$ as

$$W(\mathbf{x}; \mathbf{p}) = P(M(\mathbf{x}; \mathbf{p})) \tag{4}$$

$$= \begin{bmatrix} x - yw_z + zw_y + t_x \\ xw_z + y - zw_x + t_y \end{bmatrix} \frac{f_L}{-xw_y + yw_x + z + t_z} \tag{5}$$

When we consider the illumination basis vectors, the objective function for the robust 3D head tracking is given by

$$\mathit{minimize} \sum_{\mathbf{x}} [I(W(\mathbf{x};\mathbf{p}),t) - \sum_{i=1}^{b_N}(q_i+\Delta q_i)\mathbf{b}_i(\mathbf{x}) - I(W(\mathbf{x};\mathbf{p}+\Delta\mathbf{p}),t+1)]^2, \quad (6)$$

where $\mathbf{p}$ and q_i are the 3D rigid motion parameter and the $i-th$ illumination coefficient, respectively, and $\Delta\mathbf{p}$ and Δq_i are the updated parameters computed by solving optimization problem.

2.2 Linear Approximation

To solve the Eq. (6), we need to approximate the nonlinear equation to the linear equation about the $\Delta\mathbf{p}$ and $\Delta\mathbf{q}$ as

$$\begin{aligned} & I(W(\mathbf{x};\mathbf{p}),t) - \sum_{i=1}^{b_N}(q_i+\Delta q_i)\mathbf{b}_i(\mathbf{x}) - I(W(\mathbf{x};\mathbf{p}+\Delta\mathbf{p}),t+1) \\ \approx\ & I(W(\mathbf{x};\mathbf{p}),t) - I(W(\mathbf{x};\mathbf{p}),t+1) \\ & - \sum_{i=1}^{b_N} q_i\mathbf{b}_i(\mathbf{x}) - \sum_{i=1}^{b_N}\Delta q_i\mathbf{b}_i(\mathbf{x}) - \nabla\mathbf{I}\frac{\partial\mathbf{W}}{\partial\mathbf{p}}\Delta\mathbf{p}. \end{aligned} \quad (7)$$

Let us define the error image, the steepest descent image, and the Hessian matrix H as

$$E(\mathbf{x}) = I(W(\mathbf{x};\mathbf{p}),t) - I(W(\mathbf{x};\mathbf{p}),t+1) - \sum_{i=1}^{b_N} q_i\mathbf{b}_i(\mathbf{x}) \quad (8)$$

$$SD(\mathbf{x}) = [\nabla\mathbf{I}\frac{\partial\mathbf{W}}{\partial p_1},\ldots,\nabla\mathbf{I}\frac{\partial\mathbf{W}}{\partial p_6},\mathbf{b}_1(\mathbf{x}),\ldots,\mathbf{b}_{b_N}(\mathbf{x})] \quad (9)$$

$$H = \sum_{\mathbf{x}} SD(\mathbf{x})^{\mathrm{T}} SD(\mathbf{x}). \quad (10)$$

Then, the model parameters $[\,\Delta\mathbf{p}\ \ \Delta\mathbf{q}\,]^{\mathrm{T}}$ can be obtained as

$$\begin{bmatrix}\Delta\mathbf{p}\\ \Delta\mathbf{q}\end{bmatrix} = H^{-1}\sum_{\mathbf{x}} SD(\mathbf{x})^{\mathrm{T}} E(\mathbf{x}). \quad (11)$$

2.3 Parameter Update

At every frame, we iteratively update the parameters $\Delta\mathbf{p}$ and $\Delta\mathbf{q}$ simultaneously. Before the iterative process, we need to set the previous input image patch as the current template and set the initial parameters $\mathbf{p}=\mathbf{p}_0$ and $\mathbf{q}=0$, where $\mathbf{p}_0$ is the previous motion parameters. At every iteration, we compute the new error image and the steepest descent image. When computing the new error image, the parameter $\mathbf{p}$ in the first term $I(W(\mathbf{x};\mathbf{p}),t)$ should be kept as $\mathbf{p}_0$ because it is used as the template image. Table 1 summarizes the overall process of the iterative parameter update of $\mathbf{p}$ and $\mathbf{q}$, where ϵ_1 and ϵ_2 are the threshold values.

Table 1. Overall process of the parameter update

(1) Set the previous input image patch as template image.
(2) Initialize the parameters as $\mathbf{p} = \mathbf{p}_0$ and $\mathbf{q} = 0$.
(3) Compute $E(\mathbf{x})$ and $SD(\mathbf{x})$.
(4) Compute the Hessian matrix H.
(5) Compute the incremental parameter $\Delta\mathbf{p}$ and $\Delta\mathbf{q}$.
(6) Update the parameter by $\mathbf{p} \leftarrow \mathbf{p} + \Delta\mathbf{p}$ and $\mathbf{q} \leftarrow \mathbf{q} + \Delta\mathbf{q}$.
(7) If $\Delta\mathbf{p} < \lvert\epsilon_1\rvert$ and $\Delta\mathbf{q} < \lvert\epsilon_2\rvert$ then stop. Otherwise goto (3).

3 Robust 3D Head Tracking

The dynamic template and re-registration method firstly suggested in [2] for robust head tracking. In this chapter we will review the dynamic template and explain how to generate illumination basis vectors and the modified re-registration algorithm under the rapidly changing illumination.

3.1 Dynamic Template

We briefly review the dynamic template method for the robust head tracking [2]. Since the fixed template can not cover the all kinds of head motions, we consider the dynamic template to obtain the long-term robustness of head motion. The cylindrical model can not represent the head shape exactly, the template from the initial frame can not cover the current input image when the head pose is extremely changed. The dynamic template method assumes that the previous input image patch is the current template image.

3.2 Illumination Basis Vectors

Although the dynamic template approach can cover the gradually changing illumination, it can not cover the rapidly changing illumination effectively. To tackle the rapidly changing illumination, we propose to use the linear model. To build illumination model, we generate the head images whose illuminations are changed in five different directions(left, right, up, down, and front side), collect illumination images, and apply the principle component analysis (PCA) to the collected images after subtracting the mean image.

3.3 Re-registration

We describe what frames are referenced and how to execute the re-registration process with the illumination vectors are considered. While tracking the head motion, the fitting error can be accumulated. Therefore, when the fitting error is over a certain threshold value, we need to re-register to prevent the accumulation error. In the early step of tracking, before accumulation error is over the threshold value, we record the input image I and its motion parameter $\mathbf{p}$

as the reference frames (reference DB). The reference frames are classified with the head pose w_x, w_y, w_z and each class in the reference DB is represented by one reference frame. When the re-registration is executed, the reference frame which corresponds to the current head pose is selected from the reference DB. If the illumination is changed, we can not use the old reference DB because the current input image has different illumination condition with the reference frame. Therefore we update the reference DB when the norm of the illumination parameter $\mathbf{q}$ is larger than a threshold value, after the re-registration is performed.

4 Experimental Results

We developed the illumination-robust 3D head tracking system using the real-time algorithm explained above. We used the desktop PC(Pentium IV 3.2GHz) and Logitech Web Camera. The average tracking speed is about the 10 frames per second when the illumination basis vectors are used and is about 15 frames per second when they are not used. To initialize automatically, we used the face and eye detector based on MCT+Adaboost [10] and AAM face tracker to find face boundary and face feature points.

4.1 Extreme Pose and Fast Head Movement

In this experiments, we compared the 3D head tracking using the fixed and dynamic template.

First, we captured the test sequence with extreme head motion about the tilting and yawing. Fig. 1-(a) shows the result of the 3D head tracking, where each row corresponds to the 3D head tracking using the fixed template and the 3D head tracking using the dynamic template, respectively. As you see, the 3D head tracking using the fixed template starts to fail from the $48-th$ frame and loses the head tracking completely at the $73-th$ frame. After the $73-th$ frame, the tracking can not be performed any more. However, we can get a stable head tracking throughout the entire frames using the dynamic template. Fig. 1-(b) compared the measured 3D head poses (tilting, yawing, rolling) when the poses changed much, where the left and right column correspond to the fixed template and the dynamic template, respectively, and the ground truth poses are denoted as the dotted line.

Second, we evaluated our head tracking system when the head move very fast. The test sequence has 90 frames with one tilting and two yawings. Fig. 2-(a) shows the result of 3D head tracking using the test image sequence. While the tracking using the fixed template is failed at frame 31, the tracking using the dynamic template is succeeded throughout the whole test sequence. Fig. 2-(b) compared the measured 3D head poses when the head moves fast.

As you see in the above experiments, the fixed template produces the large measurement error in the 3D head poses, but the dynamic template produces the very accurate 3D head pose measurements.

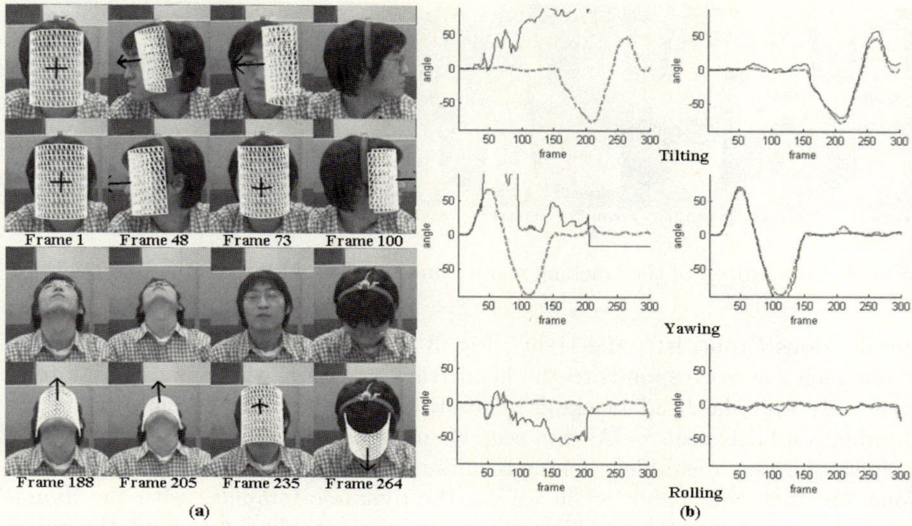

Fig. 1. Comparison of the head tracking results and the measured 3D head poses in the case of changing poses

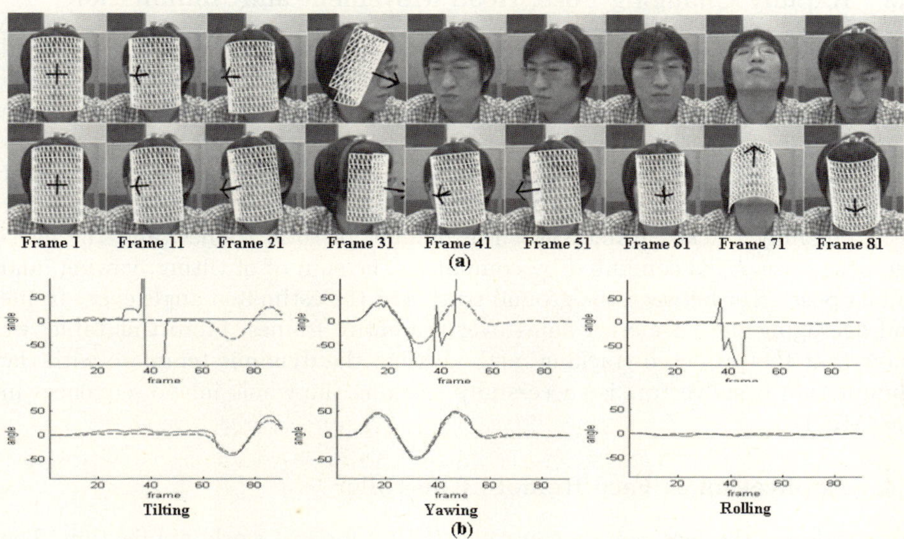

Fig. 2. Comparison of head tracking results and the measured 3D head poses in the case of the fast head movement

4.2 Rapidly Changing Illumination

We tested how the proposed head tracking system is executed when the illumination condition is changed rapidly. The test sequence has three rapidly changing

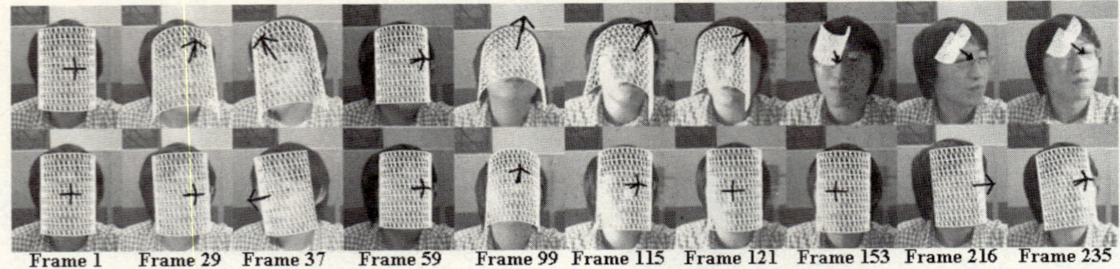

Fig. 3. Comparison of the tracking results under the rapidly changing illumination

illuminations (front, left, and right). Fig. 3 compares the head tracking results, where each row corresponds to the head tracking result with the dynamic template only and the head tracking result with the dynamic template using the illumination basis vectors. As you see, when we use the dynamic template only, it shows the very unstable tracking results under the rapidly changing illuminations. On the other hand, when we use the dynamic template with the illumination basis vectors, the tracking results are very stable throughout the entire frames even though the illumination condition changes rapidly.

4.3 Rapidly Changing Pose, Head Movement and Illumination

To test the proposed head tracking methods more faithful, we built the head moving database[1] of the 15 different peoples which includes five different illuminations (left, right, up, down, and front). The ground truth of the head rotation is measured by the 3D object tracker (Fastrak system). Table 4.3 summarizes the head tracking experiments on the IMH DB, where the number in each test sequence denotes the number of frames, r_{track} denotes the ratio of the number of successfully tracked frames over the number of total frames, and the average pose error E_p is computed by computing the sum of of tilting, yawing, and rolling pose error between the ground truth and the estimated angle every frame and averaging the pose error sums over the entire frames. From this table, we know that the proposed tracking method using the dynamic template with the illumination basis vectors is successfully tracking the whole image sequences in the IMH DB.

4.4 Application 1: Face Remote Controller

We developed the face remote controller (FRC) for real world application. The FRC is the remote controller which is controlled by the head gesture instead of the hand. The head gestures are used for moving the current cursor to the left, right, up, and down side, where the cursor is designated to move discretely between buttons. And, the eye blinking is used for generating the button click event. We apply the FRC to a TV remote controller system using the CCD camera that can zoom in/out and is located on the top of the TV. The TV

[1] We call this database the IMH DB [11].

Table 2. The tracking results on the IMH DB

	Fixed template	Dynamic template	Dynamic template with the illumination basis vectors
Seq. 1 (679)	$r_{track} = 0.05$	$r_{track} = 0.89$	$r_{track} = 1$ $E_p = 3.89$
Seq. 2 (543)	$r_{track} = 0.1$	$r_{track} = 0.54$	$r_{track} = 1$ $E_p = 3.34$
Seq. 3 (634)	$r_{track} = 0.06$	$r_{track} = 0.26$	$r_{track} = 1$ $E_p = 3.75$
Seq. 4 (572)	$r_{track} = 0.07$	$r_{track} = 0.44$	$r_{track} = 1$ $E_p = 4.81$
Seq. 5 (564)	$r_{track} = 0.06$	$r_{track} = 0.9$	$r_{track} = 1$ $E_p = 5.75$
Seq. 6 (663)	$r_{track} = 0.08$	$r_{track} = 0.39$	$r_{track} = 1$ $E_p = 4.41$
Seq. 7 (655)	$r_{track} = 0.07$	$r_{track} = 0.48$	$r_{track} = 1$ $E_p = 3.89$
Seq. 8 (667)	$r_{track} = 0.05$	$r_{track} = 0.88$	$r_{track} = 1$ $E_p = 4.29$
Seq. 9 (588)	$r_{track} = 0.09$	$r_{track} = 0.38$	$r_{track} = 1$ $E_p = 4.49$
Seq. 10 (673)	$r_{track} = 0.23$	$r_{track} = 0.48$	$r_{track} = 1$ $E_p = 2.92$
Seq. 11 (672)	$r_{track} = 0.07$	$r_{track} = 0.42$	$r_{track} = 1$ $E_p = 5.30$
Seq. 12 (504)	$r_{track} = 0.04$	$r_{track} = 0.59$	$r_{track} = 1$ $E_p = 8.21$
Seq. 13 (860)	$r_{track} = 0.37$	$r_{track} = 0.53$	$r_{track} = 1$ $E_p = 5.38$
Seq. 14 (694)	$r_{track} = 0.13$	$r_{track} = 0.72$	$r_{track} = 1$ $E_p = 2.19$
Seq. 15 (503)	$r_{track} = 0.25$	$r_{track} = 0.58$	$r_{track} = 1$ $E_p = 3.79$

watcher sits in the chair which is approximately 5 meters far from the TV. Fig. 4 shows how to perform the cursor movement and button click with the head gesture and the eye blinking, and how the FRC is applied to the TV remote controller system.

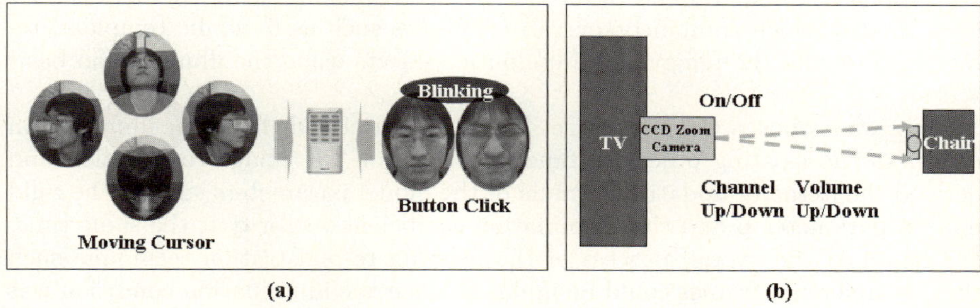

Fig. 4. Cursor movement and click using the head gesture and the eye blinking

4.5 Application 2: Drawing Tool by Head Movement

We also applied the head movement to develop a drawing tool. Basically, we use the head movement instead of the mouse or tablet pen to move the mouse cursor, where the center point on the front cylinder surface is used as the position of the mouse cursor. We define three state as "Wait", "Move", and "Draw" to organize the drawing tool by the head movement (DTHM). When the state is "Wait", the DTHM system does nothing and just wait for the eye blinking. Once

Fig. 5. Drawing tool by head movement

the eye blinking has been occurred in the state of "Wait", the DTHM system changes the state from "Wait" to "Move". In the state of "Move", we can move the mouse cursor where you want to start drawing. If there are no movements in the state of "Move" for some time, the state is changed from "Move" to "Draw", and then we can draw a shape by moving the head. If you want to stop drawing and move mouse cursor, stop head moving and wait for some time until the state is changed from "Draw" to "Move". Fig. 5 shows how to execute the DTHM system. Initially, the system is in the state of "WAIT" and changes to the "Move" state by blinking the eye. Then, the system is changed to the "Draw" state by doing nothing for some time and we draw the "R" character by moving the cursor appropriately. We change the state from the "Draw" to "Move" to move the cursor to the next drawing position.

5 Conclusion

We proposed a new framework for the 3D head tracking using the 3D cylinder head model, which combined several techniques such as dynamic template, re-registration, and the removal of illumination effects using the illumination basis vectors.

Also, we proposed the new object function that added the linear illumination model to the existing objective function based on LK image registration and derived the iterative updating formula of the model parameters such as the rigid motion parameter $\mathbf{p}$ and the illumination coefficient vector $\mathbf{q}$ at the same time. We modified the overall process of the existing re-registration technique such that the reference frames could be updated when the illumination condition was changed rapidly.

We performed many intensive experiments of 3D head tracking using the IMH DB. We evaluated the head tracking performance in term of the pose error and the successful tracking rate. The experiment results showed that the proposed head tracking method was the most accurate and stable among other tracking methods using the fixed and dynamic template.

We also developed the face TV remote controller for the handicapped people and the drawing tool by head movement for the entertainment to prove the versatile applicability of the proposed 3D head tracking method.

Acknowledgement

This work was financially supported by the Ministry of Education and Human Resources Development(MOE), the Ministry of Commerce, Industry and Energy(MOCIE) and the Ministry of Labor(MOLAB) through the fostering project of the Lab of Excellency. Also, it was partially supported by the Intelligent Robotics Development Program, one of the 21st Century Frontier R&D Programs funded by the Ministry of Commerce, Industry and Energy of Korea.

References

1. Cascia, M., Sclaroff, S., Athitsos, V.: Fast, reliable head tracking under varying illumination: An approach based on robust registration of texture-mapped 3d models. IEEE Trans. Pattern Analysis and Machine Intelligence(PAMI) 22, 322–336 (2000)
2. Xiao, J., Moriyama, T., Kanade, T., Cohn, J.: Robust full-motion recovery of head by dynamic templates and re-registration techniques. International Journal of Imaging Systems and Technology 13, 85–94 (2003)
3. Basu, S., Essa, I., Pentland, A.: Motion regularization for model-based head tracking. In: Proceedings of the International Conference on Pattern Recognition(ICPR), vol. 3, p. 611 (1996)
4. Malciu, M., Preteux, F.: A robust model-based approach for 3d head tracking in video sequences. In: Proceedings of the Fourth IEEE International Conference on Automatic Face and Gesture Recognition, p. 169. IEEE Computer Society Press, Los Alamitos (2000)
5. Lucas, B., Kanade, T.: An iterative image registration technique with an application to stereo vision. In: Proceedings of the 7th International Joint Conference on Artificial Intelligence (IJCAI), pp. 674–679 (1981)
6. Baker, S., Matthews, I.: Lucas-Kanade 20 Years On: A Unifying Framework: Part 1, tech. report CMU-RI-TR-02-16, Technical Report. Robotics Institute, Carnegie Mellon University (2002)
7. Baker, S., Gross, R., Matthews, I.: Lucas-Kanade 20 Years On: A Unifying Framework: Part 3, tech. report CMU-RI-TR-03-35, Technical Report. Robotics Institute, Carnegie Mellon University (2003)
8. Bregler, C., Malik, J.: Tracking people with twists and exponential maps. In: IEEE Conference on Computer Vision and Pattern Recognition(CVPR), pp. 8–15. IEEE Computer Society Press, Los Alamitos (1998)
9. Murray, R., Li, Z., Sastry, S.: A Mathematical Introduction to Robotic Manipulation. CRC Press, Boca Raton, USA (1994)
10. Froba, B., Ernst, A.: Face detection with the modified census transform. In: Proceedings of the IEEE Conference on Automatic Face and Gesture Recognition, pp. 91–96. IEEE Computer Society Press, Los Alamitos (2004)
11. Ryu, W., Sung, J., Kim, D.: Asian Head Movement Video Under Rapidly Changing Pose, Head Movement and Illumination AHM01, Technical Report. Intelligent Multimedia Lab, Dep. of CSE, POSTECH (2006)

Multiple Faces Tracking Using Motion Prediction and IPCA in Particle Filters

Sukwon Choi and Daijin Kim

Intelligent Multimedia Laboratory, Dept. of Computer Science & Engineering, Pohang University of Science and Technology (POSTECH), Pohang, Korea
{capriso,dkim}@postech.ac.kr

Abstract. We propose an efficient real-time face tracking system that can track fast moving face and cope with the illumination changes. To achieve these goals, we use the active appearance model(AAM) to represent the face image due to its simplicity and flexibility and take the particle filter framework to track the face image due to its robustness. We modify the particle filter framework as follows. To track fast moving face, we predict the motions using motion history and motion estimation, hence we can reduce the required number of particles. For observation model, we use active appearance model(AAM) to obtain an accurate face region, and update the model using incremental principle component analysis(IPCA). Occlusion handling scheme incorporates motion history to handle the moving face with occlusion. We have expanded our application to multiple faces tracking system. Experimental results present the robustness and effectiveness of the proposed system.

1 Introduction

Many research groups in the computer vision society have been interested in the topics related to the human face such as face detection, face recognition, face tracking, etc. Among them, face tracking is an important work that can be applied to several applications such as human-computer interaction, facial expression recognition, and robotics, etc.

There are several works that is related to the face tracking. Bayesian filters such as Kalman filter [1] and particle filter [2], [3], [4] are the most popular techniques for face tracking. The Kalman filter assumes that the state transition model obeys the Gaussian function. On the other hand, the particle filter assumes arbitrary model. The particle filter shows better performance on face tracking because the dynamics of the moving face obeys the non-linear/non-Gaussian function. Particle filter consists of observation model and state transition model. The observation model has to measure the likelihood of each particle. For this purpose, we need an appearance model. There are several researches about face modeling algorithm. Turk *et al.* [5] use PCA for eigenface analysis. Jepson *et al.* [6] introduce an online learning algorithm, namely online appearance model (OAM), which assumes that each pixel can be explained with mixture components, and Zhou *et al.* [7] modify it. However, these approaches cannot cope

S.-W. Lee and S.Z. Li (Eds.): ICB 2007, LNCS 4642, pp. 978–987, 2007.

with the facial variations such as illumination or expression. Cootes *et al.* [8] introduce AAM to represent the face using eigenface approach. The drawback of AAM is that all variations cannot be trained during training phase. Hamlaoui *et al.* [9] expand Zhou's work and use AAM as their appearance model, but there is no scheme to update the observation model.

The state transition model describes the dynamics of the moving objects between two frames. There are two ways to approximate the motion model: using a trained motion model by learning from video examples and using a fixed constant-velocity model. However, these approaches do not work well when the objects are moving very fast. The image registration technique introduced by Lucas and Kanade [10] is another approach that can be used for object tracking. However, their method is a gradient-based approach, which often traps into the local minimum. Zhou *et al.* [7] use adaptive velocity model to track the object effectively. However, if the particles are insufficient or the variance is relatively small, fast moving face cannot be tracked.

We propose to use IPCA [11], [12], [13] and motion prediction model to track the fast moving faces under the illumination change. This tracking system is expanded to multiple faces tracking for real-time system.

This paper is organized as follows: We review the particle filter in Section 2. In Section 3 and Section 4, we explain the observation model and the state transition model. We present how to handle the occlusion while the face is moving in Section 5. Section 6 shows how we expanded our system for multiple faces tracking. Next, the experimental results are presented in Section 7 and the conclusions are drawn in Section 8.

2 Particle Filter

The particle filter tries to estimate the states $\{\boldsymbol{\theta}_1, \ldots, \boldsymbol{\theta}_t\}$ recursively using sampling technique. To estimate the states, the particle filter approximates the posterior distribution $p(\boldsymbol{\theta}_t|Y_{1:t})$ with a set of samples $\{\boldsymbol{\theta}_t^{(1)}, \ldots, \boldsymbol{\theta}_t^{(P)}\}$ and a noisy observation $\{Y_1, \ldots, Y_t\}$. The particle filter consists of two components, observation model and state transition model. They can be defined as:

$$\begin{array}{rl} State\ Transition\ Model: & \boldsymbol{\theta}_t = F_t(\boldsymbol{\theta}_{t-1}, U_t), \\ Observation\ Model\ \ : & Y_t = H_t(\boldsymbol{\theta}_t, V_t). \end{array} \tag{1}$$

The transition function F_t approximates the dynamics of the object being tracked using the previous state $\boldsymbol{\theta}_{t-1}$ and the system noise U_t. The measurement function H_t models a relationship among the noisy observation Y_t, the hidden state $\boldsymbol{\theta}_t$, and the observation noise V_t. We can characterize transition probability $p(\boldsymbol{\theta}_t|\boldsymbol{\theta}_{t-1})$ with the state transition model, and likelihood $p(Y_t|\boldsymbol{\theta}_t)$ with the observation model. We use maximum a posteriori (MAP) estimate to get the state estimate $\hat{\boldsymbol{\theta}}_t$.

3 Observation Model

The observation model in the particle filter finds the relationship between the observed data and the state. We use AAM to represent the face image due to its simplicity and flexibility. We design the observation likelihood using the warped image and the reconstructed image of AAM. To make the observation model cope with the illumination change, we use IPCA to update the AAM basis vectors.

3.1 AAM-based Observation Model

We use the AAM for our observation model. Let us define the reconstructed image at time t as $\hat{I}_t$, and the warped image at time t as $\tilde{I}_t$. The AAM tries to minimize the AAM error, which is the distance between the reconstructed image and the warped image. Thus, we approximate the AAM error using Mahalanobis distance between $\hat{I}_{t-1}$ and $\tilde{I}_t$. To prevent the observation likelihood of a good particle from being spoiled by a few outliers, we use the robust statistics [14] to decrease the weight of outliers. The observation likelihood looks as :

$$p(I_t|\boldsymbol{\theta}_t) \propto exp\left(-\sum_{l=1}^{N} \rho \left(\frac{\tilde{I}_t(l) - \hat{I}_{t-1}(l)}{\sigma_R(l)} \right) \right), \tag{2}$$

$$where \quad \rho(x) = \begin{cases} \frac{1}{2}x^2, & \text{if } |x| < \xi \\ \xi|x| - \frac{1}{2}\xi^2, & \text{if } |x| \geq \xi \end{cases}, \tag{3}$$

where N is the number of pixels in the template image, l is the pixel index, the σ_R is the standard deviation of reconstruction image, and ξ is a threshold that determines whether the pixel is an outlier or not.

We select the best particle, which has the largest observation likelihood, as the MAP estimate.

3.2 Update Observation Model

After estimating the state, we perform AAM fitting to get the accurate face region and then we can get the 2D global pose parameter $\hat{\boldsymbol{\theta}}_t$. Then, we need to update the observation model to cope with the illumination change. Before we update the observation model, we need to check the goodness of fitting to determine whether we need to update the observation model or not. The AAM error is not appropriate for measuring the goodness of fitting, because the ill-fitted result and the illumination changes both increases the AAM error. For this purpose, we use the number of outliers using OAM. A pixel is declared as an outlier if the normalized pixel value, which is normalized by the mean and the variance of the OAM component, is larger than certain threshold ξ. We get the number of outliers for each component and take the average number of outliers, $N_{outlier}$. If $N_{outlier}$ is smaller than certain threshold N_0, then we can update the AAM basis vectors using IPCA with new input image $\tilde{I}_t$.

4 State Transition Model

The state transition model describes the dynamics of moving object. In our system, we use motion history and motion estimation to predict the location of the face with low computation.

4.1 Motion Prediction Model Using Motion History

We implemented the tracking system of Zhou *et al.* [7] and evaluated the tracking performance and operating speed. Fig. 1-(a) shows the tracking performance when 20 particles are used to track the fast moving face, where the vertical axis denotes the pixel displacement between two consecutive frames and the circles denote the cases of failed tracking. We can see that the their tracking algorithm often fails when the pixel displacement between two consecutive frames is greater than 20. Fig. 1-(b) shows the average operating speed when the number of particles is changed. The number of particles should be less than 30 to guarantee the 15 frame per second. To realize the real-time face tracking, we propose the adaptive state transition model using the motion prediction model using the motion history.

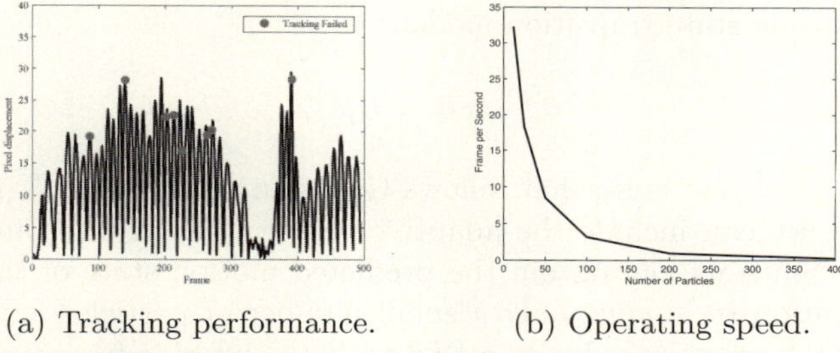

(a) Tracking performance. (b) Operating speed.

Fig. 1. Tracking experimentation results of Zhou *et al.*[7] algorithm

We assume that the dynamics of moving face obeys the constant acceleration model. Then, the velocity $\mathbf{v}_{t-1}$ and the acceleration $\mathbf{a}_{t-1}$ at the time $t-1$ is obtained as:

$$\mathbf{v}_{t-1} = \hat{\boldsymbol{\theta}}_{t-1} - \hat{\boldsymbol{\theta}}_{t-2}, \tag{4}$$

$$\mathbf{a}_{t-1} = \mathbf{v}_{t-1} - \mathbf{v}_{t-2}, \tag{5}$$

where $\boldsymbol{\theta}_{t-1}$ is the motion state that is the global 2D pose parameter of the AAM fitted image at the time $t-1$. The motion velocity at the current time is predicted by the motion velocity and the acceleration at the previous time. Then, the velocity of moving face at the time t and the effective velocity $\bar{\mathbf{v}}$ between the two consecutive frames can be obtained as:

$$\tilde{\mathbf{v}}_t = \mathbf{v}_{t-1} + \mathbf{a}_{t-1}, \tag{6}$$

$$\bar{\mathbf{v}}_t = \frac{\mathbf{v}_{t-1} + \tilde{\mathbf{v}}_t}{2}. \tag{7}$$

In real situation, the actual motion of moving face does not obey the constant velocity model. So, the effective velocity obtained from the motion history model may be overestimated or underestimated. To overcome this problem, we suggest to use the motion prediction model that performs the motion estimation technique [15] around the estimated motion state $\bar{\boldsymbol{\theta}}_t = \hat{\boldsymbol{\theta}}_{t-1} + \bar{\mathbf{v}}_t$.

In the motion estimation technique, each macroblock in the current frame is compared to a macroblock in the reference frame to find the best matching macroblock. To achieve this goal, block matching criterion such as the mean absolute error(MAE) or the mean squared error(MSE) are usually used. The computational load of finding the best matching macroblock is proportional to the size of macroblock.

To reduce the computation, we use the face detector based on Adaboost [16]. We can obtain the predicted motion state of the face $\boldsymbol{\theta}'_t$ by applying motion estimation technique around $\bar{\boldsymbol{\theta}}_t$. If the face detector fails, we use $\bar{\boldsymbol{\theta}}_t$ as the predicted motion state of the face as:

$$\tilde{\boldsymbol{\theta}}_t = \begin{cases} \bar{\boldsymbol{\theta}}_t, & \textit{if the face is detected,} \\ \boldsymbol{\theta}'_t, & \textit{if the face is not detected.} \end{cases} \tag{8}$$

The particles are distributed around the predicted motion state of the face $\tilde{\boldsymbol{\theta}}_t$ as in the following state transition model.

$$\boldsymbol{\theta}_t^{(p)} = \tilde{\boldsymbol{\theta}}_t + U_t^{(p)}, \tag{9}$$

where U_t is the system noise that follows Gaussian distribution $N(0, \sigma_t^2)$.

Optionally, we can include the adaptive velocity model into our state transition model. Since we can obtain the predicted motion state of the face using motion estimation technique, only a small number of particles is required. So, we can apply the adaptive velocity model without suffering from the heavy computational load. The particles are generated as:

$$\boldsymbol{\theta}_t^{(p)} = \tilde{\boldsymbol{\theta}}_t + V_{LS}\{I_t; \tilde{\boldsymbol{\theta}}_t\} + U_t^{(p)}, \tag{10}$$

where $V_{LS}\{I_t; \tilde{\boldsymbol{\theta}}_t\}$ is a function that computes the adaptive velocity at the starting point $\tilde{\boldsymbol{\theta}}_t$ in the input image I_t.

4.2 Noise Variance and Number of Particles

We adaptively changes the noise variance and the number of particles. They are proportional to the Mahalanobis distance, D_t, between $\hat{I}_t$ and $\tilde{I}_t$ at $\hat{\boldsymbol{\theta}}_t$.

$$\sigma_t = \sigma_0 \times \frac{D_t}{D_0}, \quad P_t = P_0 \times \frac{D_t}{D_0}. \tag{11}$$

We restrict the range of standard deviation as $[\sigma_{min}, \sigma_{max}]$ and the number of particles as $[P_{min}, P_{max}]$ to ensure certain degree of frame rate and performance.

5 Occlusion Handling

Our system detects occlusion using the number of outliers. If the face is occluded, the number of outliers $N_{outlier}$ is larger than certain threshold, N_0, because the occlusion makes large number of outliers. When the occlusion is declared, we will get a bad tracking result if we use adaptive velocity model or face detector. Hence, we stop these methods and use only motion history with maximizing the number of particles and the variance. We can generate a new set of particles based on the Eq. (12).

$$\boldsymbol{\theta}_t^{(p)} = \bar{\boldsymbol{\theta}}_t + U_t^{(p)}. \tag{12}$$

6 Multiple Faces Tracking

We presented single face tracking algorithm so far. We have expanded our single face tracking algorithm to multiple faces tracking.

To check a new incoming face, we periodically invoke face detector. We use face detector based on Adaboost [16] learning. If we find a new face, then we detect eyes in the face region. With geometric information of eyes' position, we initialize the parameters of AAM, and perform AAM fitting. The result of the AAM fitting is used to initialize a new tracker. The overall procedure of multiple faces tracking algorithm is not quite different from the single tracking case. We use motion prediction model, and perform AAM fitting on the MAP estimate, then update the observation model if possible, for each tracker.

7 Experimental Results

We implemented the proposed system in Windows C++ environment. Our system processes at least 15 frames per second for single face tracking in Pentium 4 CPU with 3.0 GHz and 2 GB RAM with Logitech Web Camera. All the experiments in this section uses the parameters in the following manner. We captured the test sequences of size 320×240 with 15 fps. The size of AAM template image is 45×47, and we used 5 shape/appearance basis vectors each. We set ξ as 1.7 to declare outlier, and N_0/N as 0.18 to declare occlusion. We performed 3 experiments to prove the robustness of the proposed face tracking system. In the first experiment, we showed that the proposed system is robust and effective in terms of the moving speed of faces, the required number of samples, and the tracking performance. The second experiment showed the performance of the tracking system under the occlusions. In the last experiment, we showed that our system can also handle the multiple faces tracking problem.

7.1 Tracking Fast Moving Face

We captured the test sequences with high/medium/low speed of moving face. We compared the face tracking system that uses the motion prediction model and the adaptive velocity model.

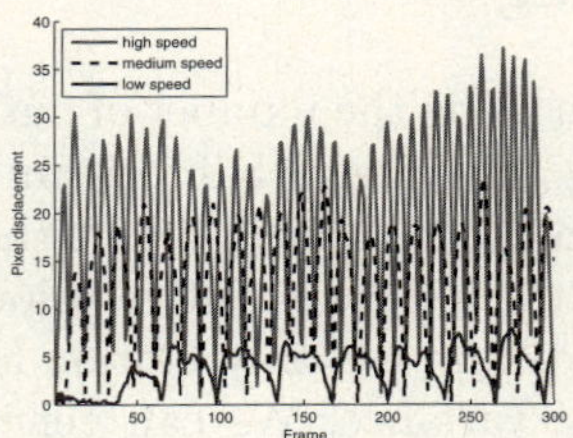

Fig. 2. The pixel displacement of the face in test sequences with high/medium/low speed of moving face

We obtained the pixel displacement of the face for each sequence as in Fig. 2. Tracking is performed using 20 particles. The horizontal axis denotes the frame number, and the vertical axis denotes the pixel displacement of the face. To measure the tracking accuracy, we compute the error between the estimated location and the ground truth of the face as $e_g = \sqrt{(q_x - g_x)^2 + (q_y - g_y)^2}$, where q_x, q_y are the horizontal/vertical translations of the estimated location of the face, and g_x, q_y are the translations of the ground truth. Fig. 3 compares the graph of e_g from each velocity models. As you can see, e_g of the motion prediction model shows lower value when the face moves fast. Fig. 4 shows the result of

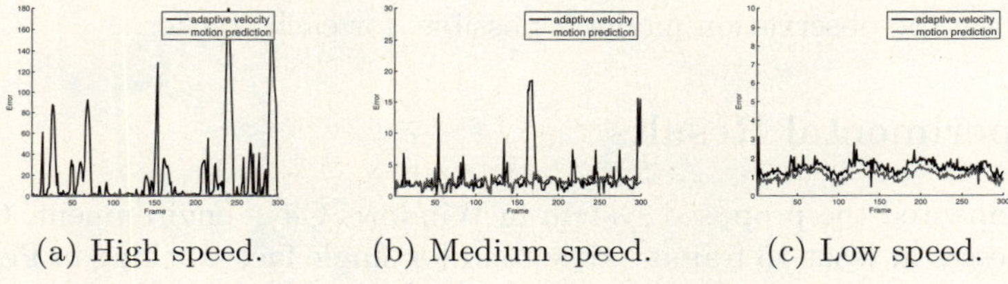

(a) High speed. (b) Medium speed. (c) Low speed.

Fig. 3. Tracking accuracy under the various speed of moving face

the face tracking using the test sequence with high speed of moving face. The motion prediction model successfully tracks the face, while the adaptive velocity model fails to track the face.

To compare the required number of particles, we performed another tracking experiment using the range of the number of particles as [10, 60] and use 20 particles at initialization. Fig. 5 shows the required number of particles and the AAM error of the tracking systems with the two velocity models.

As shown in Fig. 5, we need fewer particles with the motion prediction model due to its better tracking performance, so we can save computations.

7.2 Occlusion Handling

We present the performance of our occlusion handling method. As shown in Fig. 6, the moving face is heavily occluded. On the upper right corner of each

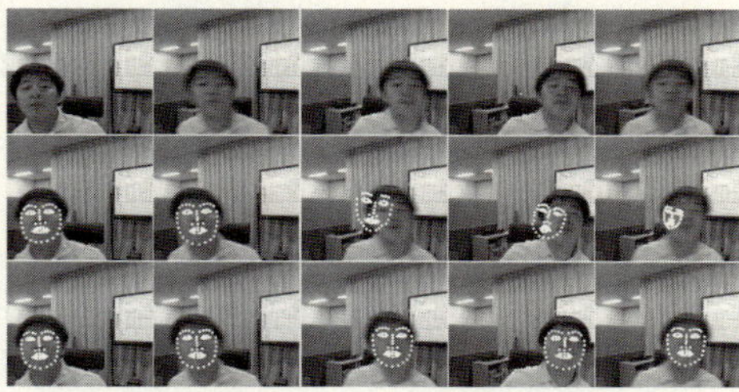

Fig. 4. 1st row : original test sequence, 2nd row : tracking result of the adaptive velocity model, 3rd row : tracking result of the motion prediction model, 1-5 column : frame 155, 158, 161, 164, 167

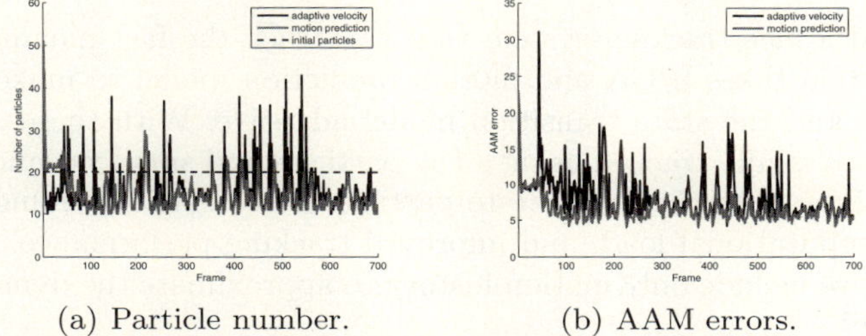

(a) Particle number. (b) AAM errors.

Fig. 5. The required number of particles and the AAM error

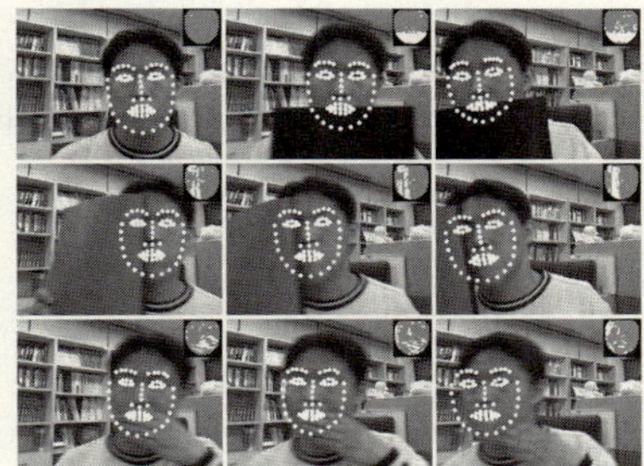

Fig. 6. Occlusion handling, 1st row : frame 43, 56, 65, 2nd row : frame 277, 281, 285, 3rd row : frame 461, 463, 465

Fig. 7. Tracking results, 1st row : frame 190, 200, 210, 2nd row : frame 230, 330, 350

image, we can see small template image that displays outliers with white pixels. Our occlusion detection scheme detected outliers and occlusion successfully.

7.3 Multiple Faces Tracking

In this section, we present our multiple faces tracking system. Fig. 7 shows that our system is expanded to a multiple faces tracking system. We can see that scale, rotation, and translation of three faces are changing, but our system shows good tracking performance.

8 Conclusion

We presented a face tracking system that can track the fast moving face. The proposed system takes IPCA and motion prediction model to make the observation model and the state transition model adaptive. With these approaches, the face is successfully tracked using a few particles and small variance. We have found that these approaches generate particles more efficiently, and saved unnecessary computational load, and improved tracking performance. In the case of occlusion, we include only motion history to approximate the dynamics of the occluded face.

Our system has implemented and tested in real-time environment. The experimental results of the proposed face tracking system show the robustness and effectiveness in terms of the moving speed of faces, the required number of samples, the tracking performance, and occlusion handling. Also, we have applied our system and found that the system can handle the multiple faces properly.

Acknowledgement

This work was partially supported by the Korea Science and Engineering Foundation (KOSEF) through the Biometrics Engineering Research Center (BERC) at Yonsei University. Also, it was partially supported by the Intelligent Robotics Development Program, one of the 21st Century Frontier R&D Programs funded by the Ministry of Commerce, Industry and Energy of Korea.

References

1. Azarbayejani, A., Pentland, A.: Recursive estimation of motion, structure and focal length. IEEE Transactions on Pattern Analysis and Machine Intelligence 17, 562–575 (1995)
2. Doucet, A., Godsill, S.J., Andrieu, C.: On sequential Monte Carlo sampling methods for Bayesian filtering. Statistics and Computing 10(3), 197–209 (2000)
3. Arulampalam, S., Maskell, S., Gordon, N., Clapp, T.: A tutorial on particle filters for online nonlinear/non-Gaussian Bayesian tracking. IEEE Transactions on Signal Processing 50(2), 174–189 (2002)

4. Okuma, K., Taleghani, A., de Freitas, N., Little, J., Lowe, D.: A boosted particle filter: Multitarget detection and tracking. In: Proceddings of European Conference on Computer Vision, pp. 28–39 (2004)
5. Turk, M., Pentland, A.: Eigenfaces for recognition. Journal of Cognitive Neuroscience 3(1), 72–86 (1991)
6. Jepson, A.D., Fleet, D.J., El-Maraghi, T.: Robust online appearance model for visual tracking. IEEE Transactions on Pattern Analysis and Machine Intelligence 25(10), 1296–1311 (2003)
7. Zhou, S., Chellappa, R., Moghaddam, B.: Visual tracking and recognition using appearance-adaptive models in particle filters. IEEE Transactions on Image Processing 13(11), 1491–1506 (2004)
8. Cootes, T.F., Edwards, G.J., Taylor, C.J.: Active appearance models. In: Proceedings of 5th European Conference on Computer Vision, pp. 484–498 (1998)
9. Hamlaoui, S., Davoine, F.: Facial action tracking using particle filters and active appearance models. In: Joint sOc-EUSAI conference, pp. 165–169 (2005)
10. Lucas, B.D., Kanade, T.: An iterative image registration technique with an application to stereo vision. In: Proceedings of the 7th International Joint Conference on Artificial Intelligence, pp. 674–679 (1981)
11. Hall, P., Marshall, D., Martin, R.: Incremental eigenanalysis for classification. In: Proceedings of British Machine Vision Conference, pp. 286–295 (1998)
12. Artac, M., Jogan, M., Leonardis, A.: Incremental PCA for on-line visual learning and recognition. In: International Conference on Pattern Recognition, pp. 781–784 (2002)
13. Ross, D.A., Lim, J., Yang, M.-H.: Adaptive probabilistic visual tracking with incremental subspace update. In: Proceedings of 8th European Conference on Computer Vision, vol. 2, pp. 470–482 (2004)
14. Huber, P.J.: Robust statistics. John Wiley, Chichester (1982)
15. Bhaskaran, V., Konstantinides, K.: Image and video compression standards. Kluwer Academic Publishers, Dordrecht (1997)
16. Froba, B., Ernst, A.: Face detection with the modified census transform. In: Sixth IEEE International Conference on Automatic Face and Gesture Recognition. IEEE Computer Society Press, Los Alamitos (2004)

An Improved Iris Recognition System Using Feature Extraction Based on Wavelet Maxima Moment Invariants

Makram Nabti and Ahmed Bouridane

Institute for Electronics, Communications and Information Technology (ECIT), School of Electronics, Electrical Engineering and Computer Science, Queen's University Belfast, Northern Ireland, UK, BT7 1NN.
{mnabti01,a.bouridane}@qub.ac.uk

Abstract. Human recognition technology based on biometrics has received increasing attention over the past decade. Iris recognition is considered to be the most reliable biometric authentication system and is becoming the most promising technique for high security. In this paper, we propose a multiscale approach for iris localization by using wavelet modulus maxima for edge detection, a fast and a compact method for iris feature extraction based on wavelet maxima components and moment invariants. The features are represented as feature vector, thus allowing us to also propose a fast matching scheme based on exclusive OR operation. Experimental results have shown that the performance of the proposed method is very encouraging and comparable to the well known methods used for iris texture analysis.

Keywords: biometrics, iris recognition, multiscale edge detection, wavelet maxima, moment invariants.

1 Introduction

Consistent automatic recognition of individuals has long been an important goal, and it has taken on new importance in recent years. The use of biometric signatures, instead of tokens such as identification cards or computer passwords, continues to gain increasing attention as a means of identification and verification of individuals for controlling access to secured areas, materials, or systems because an individual's biometric data is unique and cannot be transferred. Biometrics is automated methods of identifying a person or verifying the identity of a person based on a physiological or behavioral characteristic. Examples of physiological characteristics include hand, finger images, facial characteristics, and iris recognition. Signature verification and speaker verification are examples of behavioral characteristics [2,3]. Biometrics have the potential for high reliability because it is based on the measurement of an intrinsic physical property of an individual

The iris is an overt body that is available for remote (i.e., noninvasive) assessment. The variability of features of any one iris is well enough constrained to make possible a fully automated recognition and verification system based upon machine vision, and even identical twins have distinct iris features[2].

S.-W. Lee and S.Z. Li (Eds.): ICB 2007, LNCS 4642, pp. 988–996, 2007.

The iris is an annular area between the pupil and the white sclera in the eye; it has a rich texture based on interlacing features, called the texture of the iris. This texture is well known to provide a signature that is unique to each subject. Compared with other biometric signatures mentioned above, the iris is generally considered more stable and reliable for identification [3].

The authentication system based on iris recognition is reputed to be the most accurate among all biometrics methods because of its acceptance, reliability and accuracy. Ophthalmologists originally proposed that the iris of the eye might be used as a kind of optical fingerprint for personal identification [1]. Their proposal was based on clinical results that every iris is unique and it remains unchanged in clinical photographs. The human iris begins to form during the third month of gestation. The structure is complete by the eighth month of gestation, but pigmentation continues into the first year after birth. It has been discovered that every iris is unique and no two people even two identical twins have uncorrelated iris patterns [3], and is stable throughout the human life. It is suggested in recent years that the human irises might be as distinct as fingerprint for different individuals, leading to the idea that iris patterns may contain unique identification features.

A number of groups have explored iris recognition algorithms and some systems have already been implemented and put into commercial practice by companies such as Iridian Technologies, whose system is based on the use of Daugman's algorithm.

1.1 Related Work

Most works on personal identification and verification using iris patterns have been done in the 1990s; Daugman [1] developed the feature extraction process based on information from a set of 2-D Gabor filter. He generated a 256byte code by quantizing the local phase angle according to the outputs of the real and imaginary parts of the filtered image, the Wildes system made use of Laplacian pyramid constructed with four different resolution levels to generate iris code [4]. It also exploited a normalized correlation based on goodness-of-match values and Fisher's linear discriminant for pattern matching. Boles [5] implemented the system operating the set of 1-D signals composed of normalized iris signatures at a few intermediate resolution levels and obtaining the iris representation of these signals via the zerocrossing of the dyadic wavelet transform. Tan [6] generates a bank of 1D intensity signals from the iris image and filters these 1D signals with a special class of wavelet. The positions of local sharp variations are recorded as the features.

1.2 Outline

In this paper, we first present a multiscale approach for edge detection based on wavelet maxima which can provide significant edges where noise disappears with an increase of the scales (to a certain level), with less texture points producing local maxima thus enabling us to find the real geometrical edges of the image thereby yielding an efficient detection of the significant circles for inner and outer iris boundaries and eyelids. A new approach has been proposed for feature extraction to making a feature vector compact and efficient by using wavelet maxima components and moment invariants technique to present our feature vector which is invariant to translation, rotation, and scale changes. A fast matching scheme based on the exclusive OR operation has been carried out.

The remainder of this paper is organized as follows. Section 2 describes iris localization step using our proposed multiscale edge detection approach. Mapping and normalization step are presented in Section 3. Feature extraction and matching are given in Section 4 and Section 5, respectively. Experimental results and discussions are reported in Section 6. Section 7 concludes this paper.

2 Iris Localization

Image acquisition captures the iris as part of a larger image that also contains data derived from the immediately surrounding eye region. Therefore, prior to performing iris pattern matching, it is important to localize that portion of the acquired image that corresponds to the iris. Figure 1 depicts the portion of the image derived from inside the limbus (the border between the sclera and the iris) and outside the pupil (iris is from CASIA iris database).

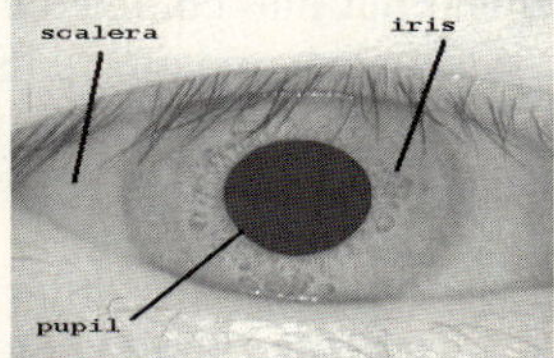

Fig. 1. Eye image

If the eyelids are occluding part of the iris, then only that portion of the image below the upper eyelid and above the lower eyelid should be included. The eyelid boundary also can be irregular due to the presence of eyelashes. From these suggestions, it can be said that, in iris segmentation problems, a wide range of edge contrasts must be taken in consideration, and iris segmentation must be robust and effective.

2.1 Multiscale Edge Detection

In our proposed method [10], a multistage edge detection is used to extract the points of sharp variations (edges) with modulus maxima and where the local maxima are detected to produce only single pixel edges. The resolution of an image is directly related to the appropriate scale for edge detection. A high resolutions and a small scale will result in noisy and discontinuous edges; low resolution and a large scale will result in undetected edges. The scale controls the significance of edges to be shown. Edges of higher significance are more likely to be preserved by the wavelet transform across the scales. Edges of lower significance are more likely to disappear when the scale increases.

Mallat, and Hwang [7, 8] proved that the maxima of the wavelet transform modulus can detect the location of the irregular structures. The wavelet transform characterizes the local regularity of signals by decomposing signals into elementary building blocks that are well localized both in space and frequency. This not only explains the underlying mechanism of classical edge detectors, but also indicates a way of constructing optimal edge detectors under specific working conditions.

2.2 Proposed Method

Assume f(x, y) is a given image of size M×N. At each scale j with j>0 and $S_0 f$ = f(x,y), the wavelet transform decomposes $S_{j-1} f$ into three wavelet bands : a lowpass band $S_j f$, a horizontal highpass band $W_j^H f$ and a vertical highpass band $W_j^V f$. The three wavelet bands ($S_j f$, $W_j^H f$, $W_j^V f$) at scale j are of size M×N, which is the same as the original image, and all filters used at scale j (j>0) are upsampled by a factor of 2^j compared with those at scale zero.

In addition, the smoothing function used in the construction of a wavelet reduces the effect of noise. Thus, the smoothing step and edge detection step are combined together to achieve the optimal result.

At each level of wavelet decomposition the modulus $M_j f$ of the gradients can be computed by:

$$M_j f = \sqrt{\left|W_j^H f\right|^2 + \left|W_j^V f\right|^2} \tag{1}$$

and the associated phase $A_j f$ is obtained by:

$$A_j f = \tan^{-1}\left(\frac{W_j^V}{W_j^H}\right) \tag{2}$$

A Hough transform is then used to localize iris and pupil circles. The eyelids are isolated using the horizontal multiscale edges (figure2-b) with a linear Hough transform while the eyelashes are isolated using a thresholding technique (figure 3).

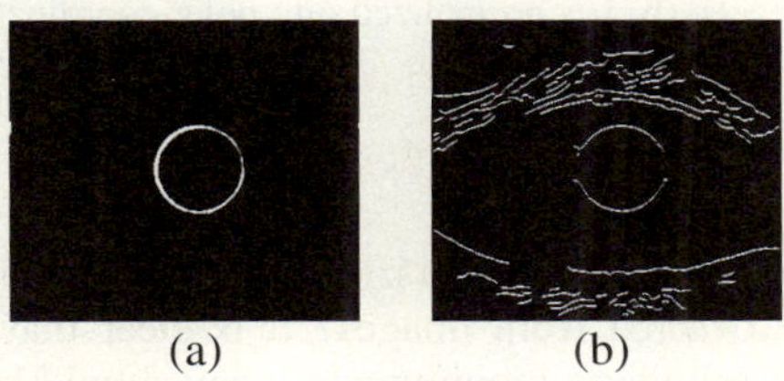

Fig. 2. Edge detection, (a) pupil edge detection, (b) Edges for eyelids detection

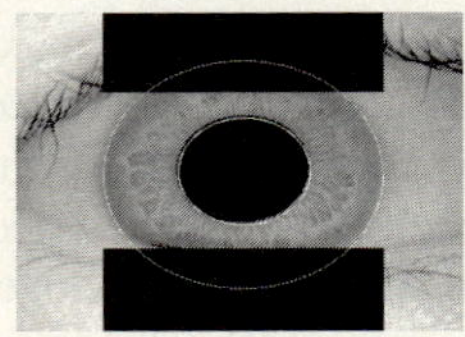

Fig. 3. Iris localization, Black regions denote detected eyelid and eyelash regions

3 Iris Normalization

After determining the limits of the iris in the previous phase, the iris should be isolated and stored in a separate image. The dimensional variations between eye images are mainly due to the stretching of the iris caused by pupil dilation from varying levels of illumination, images capture distances, head incline, and other factors. Regarding this reasons it is necessary to normalize iris region, for this purpose all the points within the boundary of the iris are remapped (figure 4) from Cartesian coordinates to polar coordinates (r,θ) as:

$$I(x(r, \theta), y(r, \theta)) \longrightarrow I(r, \theta) \tag{3}$$

where r is on the interval [0,1] and θ is angle [0,2π].

In this model a number of data points are selected along each radial line and this is defined as the radial resolution. The number of radial lines going around the iris region is defined as the angular resolution as in (figure 4-a).

In the new coordinate system, the iris can be represented in a fixed parameter interval (figure 4-b).

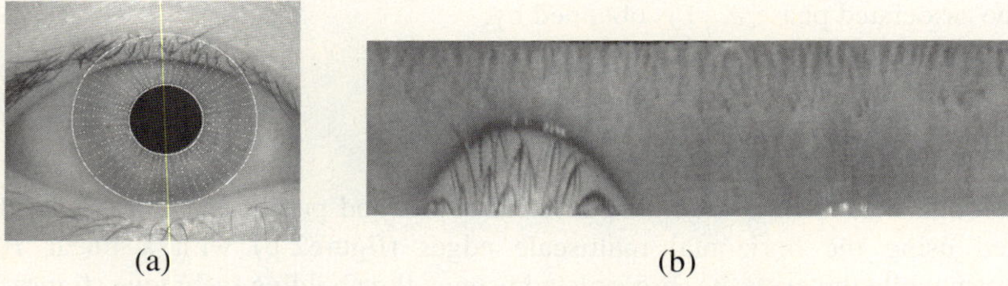

(a) (b)

Fig. 4. Normalized iris, (a) Normalized iris portion with radial resolution of 15 pixels, and angular resolution of 60 pixels, (b) Iris normalized into polar coordinates

4 Feature Extraction

Feature extraction is the crucial step in an iris recognition system, therefore what kind of features should be extracted from images? It is clear that the extracted features should meet at least the following requirements: they should be significant, compact, and fast to compute. For these reasons and to achieve a compact and efficient feature vector, wavelet maxima components and moment invariants techniques are used.

4.1 Wavelet Maxima Components for Feature Extraction

Wavelet decomposition provides a very elegant approximation of images and a natural setting for the multi-level analysis. Since wavelet transform maxima provide useful information about textures and edges analysis [7], we propose to use this technique for fast feature extraction by using the wavelet components.

Wavelet maxima have been shown to work well in detecting edges which are likely the key features in a query; moreover this method provides useful information about texture features by using horizontal and vertical details.

4.2 Proposed Method

As described in [7] to obtain the wavelet decomposition a pair of discrete filters H, G has been used as follows:

Table 1. Response of filters H, G

H	0	0	0.125	0.375	0.375	0,125	0
G	0	0	0	-2	2	0	0

At each scale s, the algorithm decomposes the normalized iris image I(x,y) into I(x, y, s) , W_v (x y, s) and W_h (x,y,s) as shown in figures (5,6) .

- I(x, y, s) : the image smoothed at scale s.

- W_h (x, y, s) and W_v (x, y, s) can be viewed as the two components of the gradient vector of the analyzed image I(x,y) in the horizontal and vertical direction, respectively.

At each scale s (s=0 to s=S-1 where S is the number of scales or decomposition) image I(x, y) is smoothed by a lowpass filter:

$$I(x, y, s+1) = I(x, y, s) * (H_s , H_s) \tag{4}$$

The horizontal and vertical details are obtained respectively by:

$$W_h (x, y, s) = \frac{1}{\lambda_s} . I(x, y, s) * (G_s , D) \tag{5}$$

$$W_v (x\ y, s) = \frac{1}{\lambda_s} . I(x, y, s) * (D, G_s) \tag{6}$$

- We denote by D the Dirac filter whose impulse response is equal to 1 at 0 and 0 otherwise.

- We denote by A * (H, L) the separable convolution of the rows and columns, respectively, of image A with the 1-D filters H and L.

- G_s, H_s are the discrete filters obtained by appending 2^s-1 zeros between consecutive coefficients of H and G.

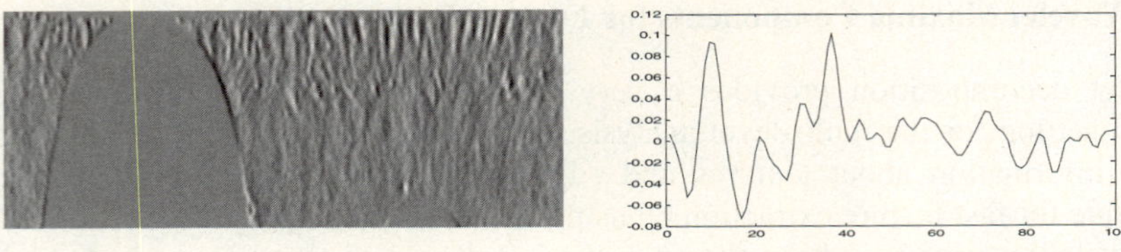

Fig. 5. Wavelet maxima vertical components at scale 2 with intensities along specified column

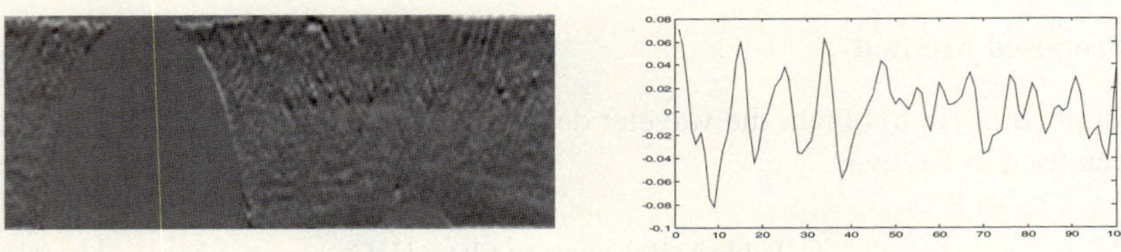

Fig. 6. Wavelet maxima horizontal components at scale 2 with intensities along specified column

- λ_s, as explained in [7] due to discretization, the wavelet modulus maxima of a step edge do not have the same amplitude at all scales as they should in a continuous model. The constants λ_s compensate for this discrete effect.

4.3 Moment Invariants for Feature Vector Representation

The theory of moments provides an interesting series expansion for representing objects. This is also suitable to mapping the wavelet maxima to vectors so that their similarity distance can be measured in a simple way [9].

Certain functions of moments are invariant to geometric transformations such as translation, scaling, and rotation. Such features are useful in the identification of objects with unique signatures regardless of their location, size, and orientation [9].

A set of seven 2-D moment invariants that are insensitive to rotation, translation and scaling [9] have been computed for each horizontal and vertical wavelet maxima component from scale 1 to scale 5 . Therefore, ten wavelet maxima components (i.e., H1,V1,H2,V2,H3,V3,H4,V4,H5,V5) are obtained thus making a feature vector size of 70 (7x10) for every iris image.

5 Matching

It is important to present the obtained vector in a binary code because it is easier to determine the difference between two binary code-words than between two number vectors.In fact, Boolean vectors are always easier to compare and to manipulate.

We have applied Hamming Distance matching algorithm for the recognition of two samples. It is basically an Exclusive OR (XOR) function between two bit patterns. Hamming Distance is a measure, which delineates the differences, of iris codes. Every bit of the presented iris code is compared to every bit of referenced iris code so that if the two bits are the same e.g. two 1's or two 0's, the system assigns a value '0' to that comparison and if the two bits are different, the system assigns a value '1' to that comparison. The equation for iris matching is as follows:

$$HD = \frac{1}{N} \sum P_i \oplus R_i \tag{7}$$

where N is dimension of feature vector, P_i is the ith component of the presented feature vector while R_i is the ith component *of* referenced feature vector. The Match Ratio between two iris templates is computed by:

$$Ratio = \left(\frac{T_z}{T_b} \right) * 100 \tag{8}$$

where T_z is total number of zeros calculated by the Hamming distance vector and T_b is the total number of bits in iris template.

6 Results and Analysis

The proposed algorithm have been assessed using the CASIA iris image database, which consists of 80 persons, 108 set eye images and 756 eye images. From the results shown in Table 2, we can find that Daugman's method and the proposed method have the best performance, followed by Li Ma and Tan method.

Table 2. Accuracy and speed Comparison

Methods	Daugman	Tan	Proposed
Correct recognition rate (%)	99.90	99.23	99.50
Speed (ms)	310	110	85

Daugman analyzed the iris texture by computing and quantizing the similarity between the quadrature wavelets and each local region, which requires that the size of the local region must be small enough to achieve high accuracy. In [6] special class of wavelet to represent local texture information of the iris has been adopted. Our proposed method achieves higher accuracy based on a texture analysis method using wavelet maxima modulus for edge detection to localize the iris region and wavelet maxima components for feature extraction.

The result of this feature extraction is a set of moments (7 elements) at different wavelet maxima decomposition levels for each iris image those features called in the proposed method as wavelet maxima moments. These features significantly represent iris images; they are compact and can be easily used to compute similar distances. Finally, wavelet maxima moments are invariant to all affine transforms namely translation, scaling and rotation.

From the point of view complexity, as shown in Table 2, our proposed method clearly outperforms the other two. In particular, it can be said that, although Daugman's method achieves a very slightly better recognition rate (+0.4%) our proposed method is about 3.65 times faster. Compared against Tan's method, our proposed solution achieves a better recognition rate (+0.5%) and is about 1.3 times faster. It is worth noting that the speed results were obtained on a PC running Windows OS with a 1.8 MHz clock speed. Implementations were carried out under MATLAB tools.

7 Conclusion

In this paper, we propose some optimized and robust methods for improving the accuracy of human identification system based on the iris patterns from the practical viewpoint. To achieve this some efficient methods based on a multiscale edge detection approach using wavelet maxima modulus and wavelet maxima moments have been presented. Our extracted features are invariant to all affine transforms namely translation, scaling and rotation. Through various experiments, we show that the proposed methods can be used for personal identification systems in an efficient way.

References

1. Daugman, J.: High Confidence Visual Recognition of Persons by a Test of Statistical Independence. IEEE Trans. Pattern Analysis and Machine Intelligence 15(11), 1148–1161 (1993)
2. Jain, A., Maltoni, D., Maio, D., Wayman, J.: Biometric systems, Technology, Design and Performance Evaluation. Springer, London (2005)
3. Muron, A., pospisil, j.: The human iris structure and its usages. Physica 39, 87–95 (2000)
4. Wildes, R.: Iris Recognition: An Emerging Biometric Technology. Proc. IEEE 85, 1348–1363 (1997)
5. Boashash, B., Boles, W.: A Human Identification Technique Using Images of the Iris and Wavelet Transform. IEEE Trans. Signal Processing 46(4), 1185–1188 (1998)
6. Ma, L., Tan, T., et al.: Efficient Iris Recognition by Characterizing Key Local Variations. IEEE Trans. on Image Processing 13, 739–750 (2004)
7. Mallat, S., Hwang, W.: Singularity Detection and Processing with Wavelets. IEEE Trans. Information Theory 38(2), 617–643 (1992)
8. Mallat, S.: A Wavelet Tour of Signal Processing, 2nd edn. Academic Press, London (1998)
9. Jain, A.K.: Fundamentals of digital image processing. Prentice-Hall, Inc., Englewood Cliffs (1989)
10. Nabti, M., Ghouti, L., Bouridane, A.: An efficient iris segmentation technique based on a multiscale approach, Special issue on advances in biometrics. The Mediterranean Journal of Computers and Networks 2(4), 151–159 (2006)

Color-Based Iris Verification

Emine Krichen, Mohamed Chenafa, Sonia Garcia-Salicetti, and Bernadette Dorizzi

Institut National des Télécommunications, 9 Rue Charles Fourier 91160 Evry France
{emine.krichen,sonia.salicetti,bernadette.dorizzi}@int-evry.fr

Abstract. In this paper we propose a novel iris recognition method for iris images acquired under normal light illumination. We exploit the color information as we compare the distributions of common colors between a reference image and a test image using a modified Hausdorff distance. Tests have been made on the UBIRIS public database and on the IRIS_INT database acquired by our team. Comparisons with two iris reference systems in controlled scenario show a significant improvement when using color information instead of texture information. On uncontrolled scenarios, we propose a quality measure on colors in order to select good images from bad ones in the comparison process.

Keywords: Iris recognition; Hausdorff distance; quality measure, Gaussian Mixture Models.

1 Introduction

Iris acquisition is a challenging task. Indeed, a small and in most of the cases dark object has to be acquired from a relative long distance (from 35cm to 3m). Iris is also a moving target, hidden in another moving object (the eye) almost covered by eyelids, bounded nearly in the middle by a dark hole (the pupil) which can dilate and contract depending on the illumination intensity during the acquisition process. These dilations and contractions of the pupil induce changes in iris texture which unfortunately are nonlinear.

Nevertheless, the most challenging problem is that iris is located behind the cornea, a very high reflective mirror, which makes impossible to acquire irises in normal light without some constraints and extra tools. Figure 1 (left) shows an iris acquired under normal illumination conditions and without any particular constraint. Reflections do not permit any accurate processing in this case. One solution would be the use of a strong source of illumination on the eye (typically a flash). Figure 1 (middle image) shows the kind of images obtained using this technique with normal light illumination. Reflections are then mostly deleted, except the ones resulting from the use of the flash itself. Despite the relative good quality of this image, in general, these alternatives are not sufficient for a performant texture analysis.

In practice, near infrared illumination is considered to be the most appropriate for iris acquisition. Indeed, it allows tackling the problem of cornea reflection. Moreover, near infrared waves penetrate the cornea and allow getting very good quality iris images with all the richness of the iris texture, even with dark irises. Figure 1 (right

S.-W. Lee and S.Z. Li (Eds.): ICB 2007, LNCS 4642, pp. 997–1005, 2007.

image) shows an iris image acquired under near infrared illumination. As can be seen the image quality is substantially higher than the one of the two irises previously presented. All commercial iris solutions are running today on images acquired under this kind of illumination [1].

However, there are applicative situations where we have at disposal a color camera with more or less high resolution. This is the case on PDA and smartphones. Our aim, in this article is to study whether it is possible to use these cameras and more especially the color information of the iris to produce a system sufficiently accurate to perform iris identity verification.

Very few works report results on this type of images. In [2], we proposed a small modification of the standard iris techniques by using wavelet packets instead of the classic Gabor wavelet. We ran preliminary experiments on a private database using a 3 million pixels camera, indoor and with a flash (figure 1 (middle) is an image from such database). We also studied the contribution of color information to the wavelet method. We showed that the mean of the inter-class distribution using color information is higher than the one obtained with grey level images. In other publications [3] presenting experiments on normal light images, researchers just transform color irises into grey level ones and apply on this type of images the algorithms they developed previously for near infrared images.

Our paper is organised as follows: section 2 describes all the modules composing our proposed algorithm, including iris segmentation, normalization and recognition. In section 3 we introduce the databases on which we have run our experiments namely IRIS_INT and UBIRIS. UBIRIS [4] is an iris database acquired under normal light illumination. It is a public database, which contains about 250 persons, some of them with 2 sessions. In the second session, irises are acquired under uncontrolled mode (outdoor, uncontrolled illumination, ...). Experimental results will be given in section 4. Also, as benchmarking tools for our system, we consider two reference iris systems, Masek [6] (used by NIST) and OSIRIS, a new reference system developed by our team in the framework of BioSecure. We demonstrate that the use of color information can highly outperform methods only based on texture information. We also propose a global quality measure on color images in order to select test images during the matching process. Finally, conclusions are given and future works is discussed.

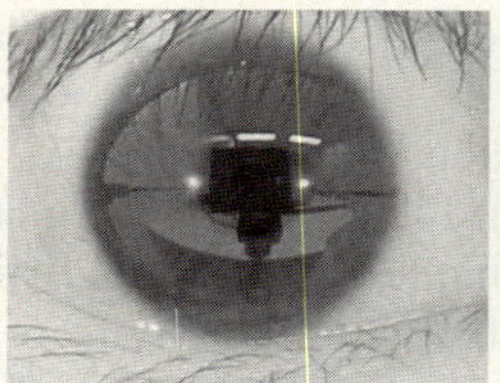
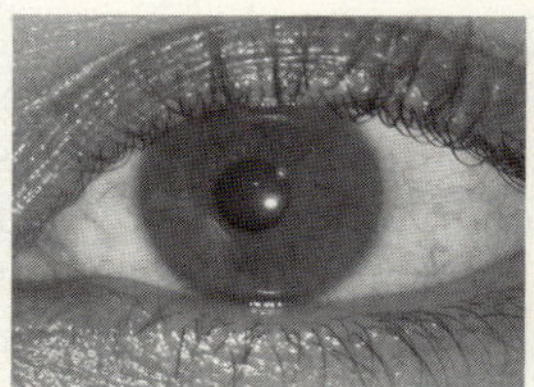
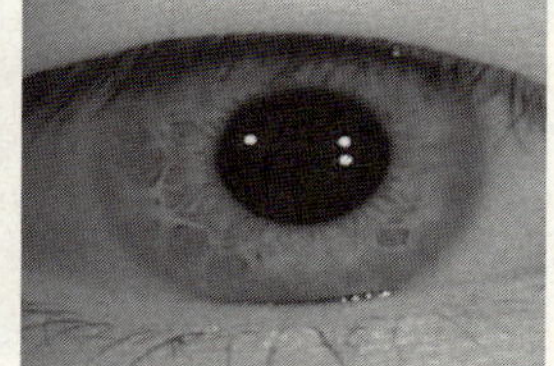

Fig. 1. Iris acquisition under normal light conditions without any restrictions (left image), normal light iris acquisition under a controlled scenario with a flash (middle image from IRIS_INT database) and near infrared iris acquisition (right image from CASIAv2 database)

2 Iris Recognition on Color Images

The iris rim is segmented from original iris images using the Hough Transform method proposed and explained in [5] and developed in open source by Masek [6]. Once iris and pupil circles have been detected, we normalize the iris rim using the rubber sheet model proposed by J. Daugman in [7]. The segmentation and normalization processes are shown in Figure 2.

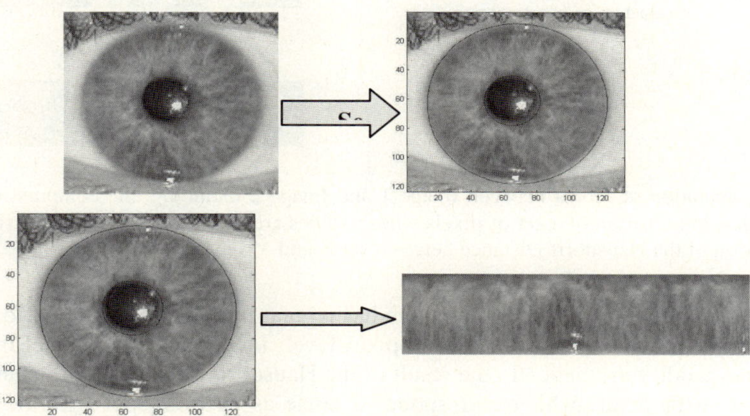

Fig. 2. Iris segmentation (Top images): the iris and pupil contours are considered as circles and are detected using the Hough Transform. Iris normalization (Bottom images): the iris is normalized using the rubber sheet model.

Our iris recognition method is composed of several steps: first we need to compress the colors present in the reference image into a fixed number of colors. We have used the minimum variance quantization in order to reduce the number of colors [9]. From each original image, we produce a compressed image with its corresponding color map (figure 3). Both information will be used in the next stages.

We need to compress the number of colors of the images because of the fact that at least 10.000 colors are present in the iris image even in dark and poorly textured irises. This makes any color-based method very heavy to develop.

Once the reference iris image is compressed, we process the test image using the color map obtained for the reference image. We assign each color in the map to the nearest color present in the test iris image using the 3 dimensional color cube (RGB space). Then, for each color in the map, we compare the distributions of the corresponding pixel positions in the reference and test images. This comparison is made using a modified Hausdorff Distance [8].

The Hausdorff Distance is an asymmetric distance which measures the maximum distance of each point of a set to the nearest point in the other set. Formula 1 shows the original expression of the Hausdorff Distance between set *X* and set *Y* where *x* is an element of *X*, *y* of *Y* and *d* denotes the Euclidian distance.

$$d_H(X,Y) = \max\left\{\sup_{x \in X} \inf_{y \in Y} d(x,y), \sup_{y \in Y} \inf_{x \in X} d(x,y)\right\}. \quad (1)$$

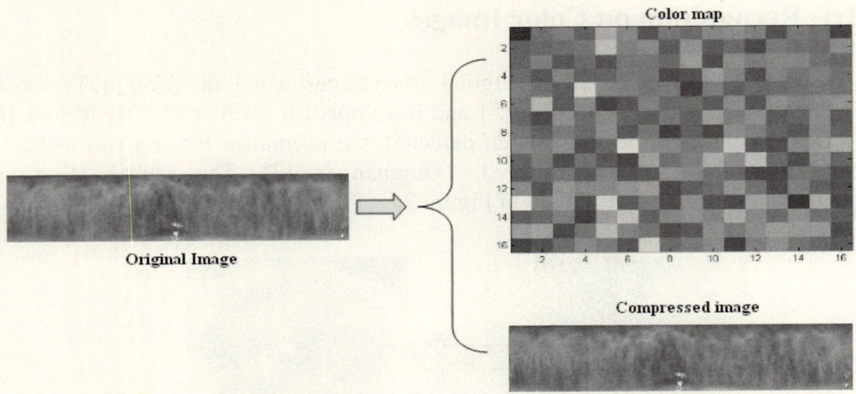

Fig. 3. Calculation of scores between Image 1 and Image 2 including: the compression of the two images; the creation of a set of pixels whose values are equal to each color and finally the computation of the Hausdorff Distance between set X and Y

This formula of the Hausdorff distance has a great limitation if we want to apply it to our problem because it works at the pixel level; indeed, only one pixel that is an outlier can modify dramatically the result of the Hausdorff Distance. For instance, this will occur with pixels which correspond to noise as eyelids, spot light reflections, eyelashes … for these reasons, we have used a modified form of the Hausdorff Distance in which we took the minimum between the Hausdorff distance calculated between X and Y on one hand and Y and X on another hand, and we computed the average between the Euclidian distances of elements of one set to the elements of the other set. This modified Hausdorff Distance is expressed in Formula 2:

$$d_{H\,\mathrm{mod}}(X,Y) = \min\left[\frac{1}{Nx}\sum_{X}\inf_x d(x,y), \frac{1}{Ny}\sum_{Y}\inf_y d(y,x)\right] \qquad (2)$$

Finally, the score between two images is computed by averaging the modified Hausdorff distances obtained for each color, on all possible colors c of the map (see Formula 3). Xc and Yc are the pixel positions corresponding to color c respectively in the reference image Iref and the test image Itest.

$$S(Iref, Itest) = mean_c(d_{H\,\mathrm{mod}}(X_c, Y_c)) \qquad (3)$$

In order to accelerate our algorithm, only distributions with comparable pixels size are used for comparison. The whole recognition process is described in Figure 4.

Based on the dominant color of the iris, we made a coarse pre-classification between irises. We notice that two main classes of colors are present in the iris images (blue and brown images). The Hue distribution (form the HSV color space instead of RGB color space [10]) can be used to automatically classify the irises into 2 classes. The Hue value indicates the nature of the color and is expressed in terms of angle (degrees). For brown irises, the Hue distribution falls into the range of 0° (90% of the

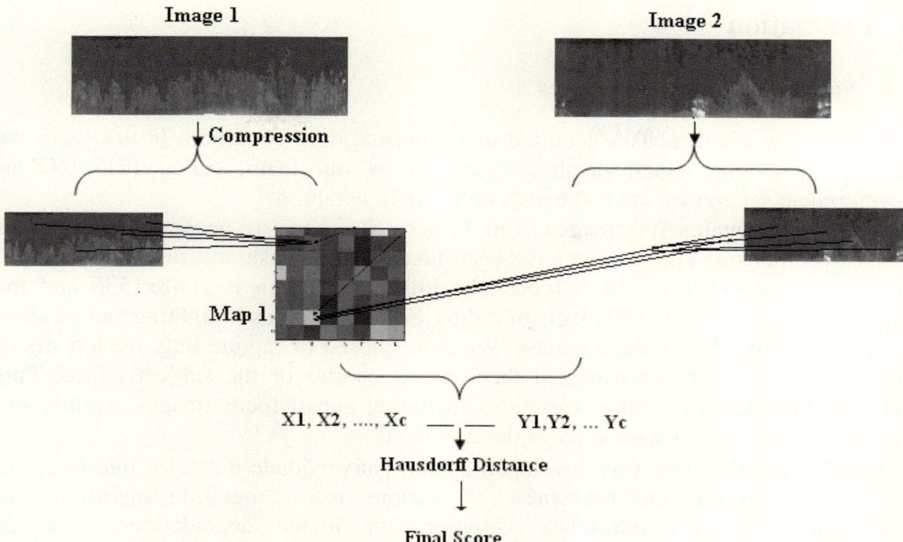

Fig. 4. Scores computation between Image 1 and Image 2 including: the compression of the two images; the creation of a set of pixels whose values correspond to a given color and finally the computation of the modified Hausdorff Distance between set X (reference) and Y (test)

irises in the databases at hand) while the Hue values for blue irises varies around 200°. Figure 5 shows one Hue distribution of each class.

In order to classify the two kinds of irises (brown and blue irises) we have used a simple Gaussian Mixture Model [12] with 3 Gaussians for each class. Some images may contain eyelids occlusion; as eyelids fall in range of 300 to 360°, these images can affect the Hue distribution by introducing a new peak (see Figure 5 right). As the discrimination between the 2 classes is mainly due to other values range of the distribution, eyelids don't affect the classification capacity of the GMM.

In order to pre-classify an iris test image, we select the class (brown or blue) corresponding to the GMM giving the highest probability. After this pre-classification, only comparisons between reference and test irises belonging to the same class are performed (the reference image is stored with its associated class label). In case no comparison is performed, a maximum score is given to the corresponding test image.

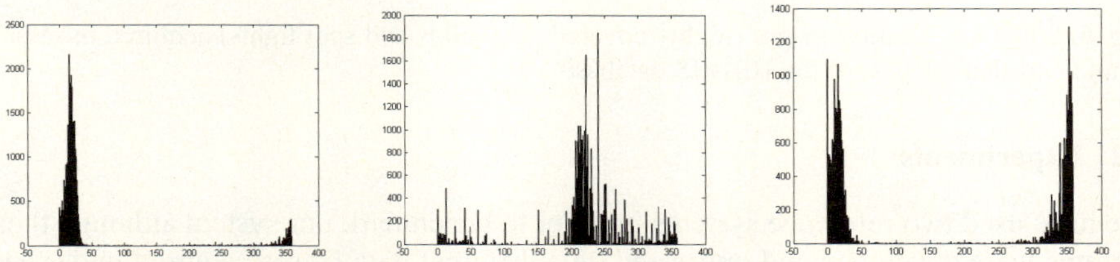

Fig. 5. Brown iris Hue histogram (left image), blue iris Hue histogram (middle image) and brown iris with strong Eyelids presence (right image)

3 Evaluation

3.1 Normal Light Iris Databases

There are few iris databases acquired under normal light condition. In this work we have used a quite small database acquired by our team, called IRIS_INT as development set and we made the tests on UBIRIS database.

IRIS_INT contains 700 images from 70 persons. There are between 7 and 23 iris images per person. The images have been taken with a flash at a distance of 20-30 cms; the camera has a 23mm focus, the image resolution is 2048x1536 and the captured irises have 120-150 pixels of radius. Some variations in lighting and position have been introduced in the database. We have chosen to capture only the left iris of each person. In fact, we acquired the top left quarter of the subject's face. This database includes some other variations including out of focus images, eyelids and eyelashes occlusions, lenses and eyeglasses effects.

UBIRIS iris database was developed by the Universidade da Beira Interior, with the aim of testing the robustness of various iris recognition algorithms to degradations. Several intra-class variations or image degradations, such as illumination, contrast, reflections, defocus, and occlusions are present in this database. The database contains 1,877 gray-level images from 241 persons, captured in two different sessions. Some images are shown in Figure 6.

In the first session, noise factors are minimized as the irises are acquired indoor, in a controlled illumination environment (dark room). Images are available at two different resolutions, a high resolution (800*600) and a low resolution (200*150). In our experiments we used the smallest resolution available in order to simulate PDA or smartphone limitation in terms of resolution. Indeed, if we consider the half top of a face acquired with a PDA or smartphone camera of 2 megapixels, an iris in average will be represented by an image of size 400*300 which doubles the resolution that we consider.

We have used 1727 images from the 1,877 which are available. The deleted images correspond to very degraded images (closed eye, blurring, occlusion).

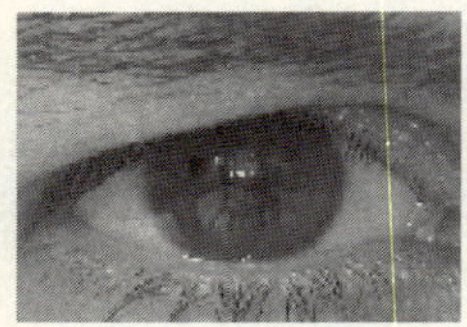 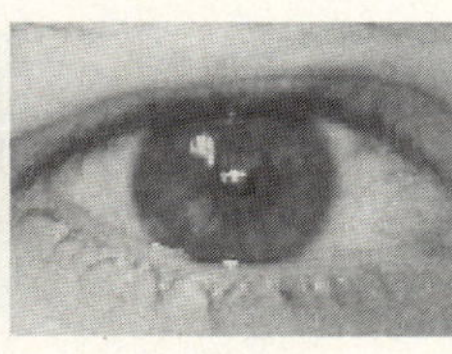  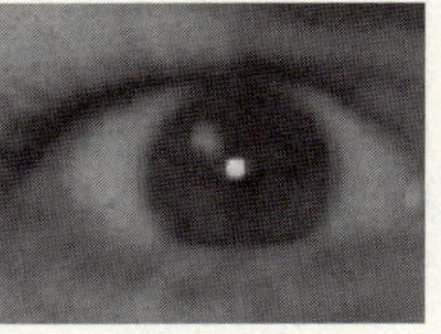

Fig. 6. Some low quality images (highly covered by eyelids and spot lights) acquired in session 2 (uncontrolled images) of the UBIRIS database

3.2 Experiments

We have used two reference systems in order to benchmark our system although those systems were developed and optimized on a different data (irises acquired under near infrared illumination). These two systems; Masek [6] from *the University of Western*

Australia, and OSIRIS developed under the BioSecure European Network of Excellence [11] correspond to implementations of Daugman's work [7] although none of them can pretend to be equivalent to Daugman's system in terms of optimization and recognition performance.

In the present work, all developments are made on IRIS_INT database while tests are made on UBIRIS database. We developed two different protocols (or scenarios) on UBIRIS. In the first protocol, called "controlled scenario", we only consider images from the first session, that is images acquired indoor, in a dark room under controlled illumination conditions. In the second protocol, "called uncontrolled scenario", images of the first session are used as references while those of the second session are used as test images. In both cases, only one image is considered as reference.

Development experiments. We made all possible comparisons between images of IRIS_INT database. It has allowed us to optimize some parameters in the system such as the number of colors in the compressed images. We considered from 30 to 300 colors in the color map, and the best results were obtained for color maps of 60 colors. Indeed, if too many colors are considered, the similarity between reference and test images of the same person is lost. On the other hand if too few colors are considered the essential information to discriminate a client and an impostor will be also lost. Also in this case too many pixel positions will be associated to each color in the color map, which increasing considerably the computational load when computing the modified Hausdorff distances.

Controlled scenario. For the controlled scenario on the UBIRIS database we obtain 1.2% of EER, and 2.1% of FRR with 0.1% of FAR. These results are very encouraging as both OSIRIS and MASEK perform poorly on the same data (of course on grey-level images), from 5 to 10 times worst than our color-based approach (see Table1). Such a difference between systems can only be explained by the fact that color carries some information which is definitively lost when we just use grey-level images and texture information only. Indeed, the quality of texture information is bad and not sufficient for such analysis. Also, the bad performance of both Masek and OSIRIS confirm that texture-based methods suffer greatly from the low resolution of the images (small size of irises, a radius lower than 50 pixels).

Uncontrolled scenario. Uncontrolled illumination changes affect both color and texture of the image. Tests show a huge performance degradation compared to the controlled scenario, up to 22% of FRR at 0.1% of FAR for our color-based approach that still outperforms significantly OSIRIS and Masek. Table 1 summarizes the performance obtained in each scenario and with the three different systems.

Table 1. Benchmarking performances on UBIRIS database under different scenarios with Color-based system, OSIRIS and Masek systems

	Controlled scenario		Uncontrolled scenario	
	EER	FRR	EER	FRR
Color	1.2	2.1	8	22
OSIRIS	5	10	14.5	40
Masek	7.1	20	25	80

To cope with bad quality images of this uncontrolled scenario, like images which are covered by a high number of spot lights as shown in Figure 6, we introduce a quality measure on iris images at the acquisition step. This way images would be rejected right after acquisition and thus not processed by the system; system performance would this way be increased. In fact, in the UBIRIS database brown irises suffer much more from illumination changes than blue irises: for brown irises the 'red' colors (range 0°-50°) turn to purple in most cases (less than 360°). Therefore, to detect bad quality images we only use the GMM trained on brown irises (acquired in the controlled scenario) for the two classes separation by applying a threshold on the probability given by the GMM.

Figure 7 shows the distribution of the resulting GMM probabilities on brown irises, when considering all the brown iris images from both the first session (red points) and the second session (blue points). The principle to select test images by the proposed quality measure is the following: only irises that have a probability comparable to those obtained on iris images of the first session (controlled scenario) are kept. Irises from the first session have a minimum probability of 0.42; so we fixed the selection threshold at 0.4. This means that irises with a probability lower than 0.4 are rejected and not considered in the test process. Using this selection process, 80% of brown irises from the second session (uncontrolled scenario) are rejected. The EER falls from 8% to 1.5%, and FRR reaches 3.8% at FAR of 0.1% (versus 22% without considering the selection process).

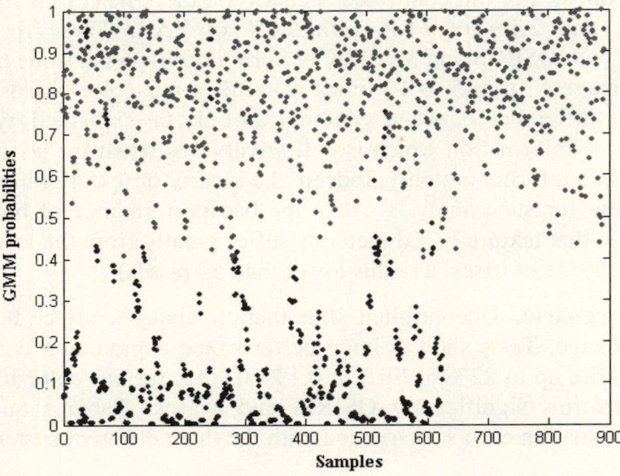

Fig. 7. GMM probabilities on brown irises from session1 (Red) and Session2 (Blue)

4 Conclusions

In this paper we presented a novel iris verification method entirely based on the color information, using the minimum variance principle for iris color reduction and a modified Hausdorff distance for matching. We also proposed a pre-selection method based on the use of Gaussian Mixture Models that characterize two classes of colors (blue and brown or more generally clear and dark) for iris images encoded in the Hue axis of the HSV color space. These models are also used to detect images corrupted by a variety of strong illumination effects. Our tests show that in the controlled acquisition mode our system outperforms significantly two iris reference systems based on texture information. Nevertheless, in uncontrolled conditions, tests show a huge decrease in performance for our method although it remains better than those obtained with texture-based systems (22% vs. 40% and 80%). In order to cope with image degradation, typical in the uncontrolled scenario, we proposed a quality measure based on the GMMs above mentioned to reject bad quality images. This selection process drastically improves the results of our approach reducing the error rates roughly by a factor 6, while rejecting 80% of the images acquired in uncontrolled conditions.

Future work will be focused on fusion strategies of texture-based systems and our color-based approach on images acquired under normal illumination conditions.

References

1. http://www.iridiantech.com/index2.php
2. Emine Krichen, M., Mellakh, A., Garcia-Salicetti, S., Dorizzi, B.: Iris Identification Using Wavelet Packets. In: 17th International Conference on Pattern Recognition (ICPR 2004), Cambridge, UK, 23-26 August 2004, vol. 4, pp. 335–338 (2004)
3. Sun, Z., Wang, Y., Tan, T., Cui, J.: Improving iris recognition accuracy via cascaded classifiers. IEEE Transactions on Systems, Man, and Cybernetics, Part C 35(3), 435–441 (2005)
4. http://iris.di.ubi.pt
5. Wildes, R.: Automated iris recognition: An emerging biometric technology. Proceedings of the IEEE 85 (9), 1348–1363 (1997) Awarded IEEE Donald G. Fink Prize Paper Award
6. http://www.csse.uwa.edu.au/ pk/studentprojects/libor/
7. Daugman, J.: How iris recognition works. IEEE Transactions on Circuits and Systems fo Video Technology 14(1) (January 2004)
8. Dubuisson, M.-P., Jain, A.K.: A modified Hausdorff distance for object matching. Pattern Recognition (1994). In: Conference A: Computer Vision & Image Processing, Proceedings of the 12th IAPR International Conference, 9-13 October 1994, vol. 1, pp. 566–568 (1994)
9. Mathworks, Inc., Matlab Image Processing Toolbox, Ver. 2.2 Natick, MA (1999)
10. Smith, A.R.: Color Gamut Transform Pair. Computer Graphics 12(3), 12–19 (1978)
11. http://www.biosecure.info

Real-Time Face Detection and Recognition on LEGO Mindstorms NXT Robot*

Tae-Hoon Lee

Center for Cognitive Robotics, Korea Institute of Science and Technology,
39-1 Hawolgok-dong, Seongbuk-gu, Seoul 136-791, Republic of Korea

Abstract. This paper addresses a real-time implementation of face recognition system with LEGO Mindstorms NXT robot and wireless camera. This system is organized to capture an image sequence, find the features of face in the images, and recognize and verify a person. Moreover, this system can collect the facial images of various poses due to movable robot, which enables this system to increase performance. The current implementation uses the LDA(Linear Discriminant Analysis) learning algorithm considering the number of training data. We have made several tests on video data, and measured the performance and the speed of the proposed system in real environment. Finally, the result has confirmed that the proposed system is better than conventional PC-based systems.

Keywords: LEGO Mindstorms NXT robot, real-time face recognition.

1 Introduction

During the past few years, we have witnessed the explosion in interest and progress in automatic face recognition technology. Face recognition technologies have been developed and come into our life. For instance, applications such as intelligent building, PC security system based on face analysis start to appear in recent years.

For applying face recognition technologies to real applications, many kinds of systems have been developed before 21 century. In the early 1990s, Gilbert et al. introduced a real-time face recognition system using custom VLSI hardware for fast correlation in an IBM compatible PC[2]. Five years later, Yang et al. introduced a parallel implementation of face detection algorithm using a TMS320C40 chip[3]. On the other hand, IBM introduced a commercial chip, ZISC which can compute the classification in RBF(Radial Basis Function) based neural network[4].

However, these efforts did not make successful results because they could not cope with real problems caused by illumination change, pose variation, human aging, lens distortion, and so forth. So recent face researches are focused on solving these problems. For illumination invariant face recognition, S. Zhou and

---

* This research was performed when the author was a summer student intern at the Center for Cognitive Robotics, Korea Institute of Science and Technology.

S.-W. Lee and S.Z. Li (Eds.): ICB 2007, LNCS 4642, pp. 1006–1015, 2007.

R. Chellappa proposed rank constraint recognition[5] and A. Georghiades et al. proposed 'Illumination cone'. For pose variation, R. Gross proposed 'Eigen light-fields'[7] and 3D face recognition based on morphable model was proposed by V. Blanz and T. Vetter[8].

These approaches deal with illumination changes using multiple training data from database, which have already collected in well-structured studio. However, it can be difficult to collect these facial data in real environment. The limited number of registered facial images is also one of the reason why the recognition rate decreases. Since face recognition system has generally a fixed position, it requires well-posed and frontal faces. Recently for overcoming this limitation, many researches have been reported[1].

In order to solve training data problem, we adopt movable camera using wireless camera and collect more training data instead of improving learning algorithms. We can collect multiple facial data in different poses and conditions using active robot, which is controlled by predefined rules. Then LDA can categorize these data into each manifold.

The remaining parts of this paper are organized as follows: In Section 2, we introduce the hardware structure regarding the movable camera. Our face recognition processes by the LDA learning are presented in Section 3. In Section 4, the applicability of the proposed method is illustrated via some experiments. Finally, in Section 5, concluding remarks are given.

2 Hardware Design

Most of face recognition system is running using non-movable camera. Therefore it has a defect that can not deal with various face pose. In order to cope

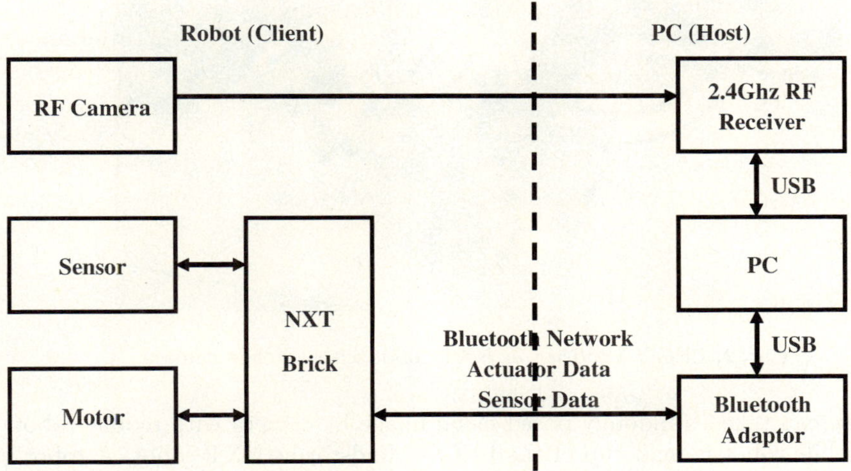

Fig. 1. The block diagram of the proposed system

with diverse facial images, the face recognition system has to train many faces collected from well-designed studio or recognize a well-posed frontal face. Considering these restricted conditions, we construct a prototype system based on LEGO Mindstorms NXT robot with wireless camera. The LEGO Mindstorms NXT is well known as a tiny embedded system for students[9]. This system can collect arbitrarily posed facial images and train them.

In this section, we introduce our system's hardware architecture. This system is composed of server and client system as shown in Fig. 1. The former is exactly same as the conventional PC, which plays a role on face recognition process and the latter consists of a camera and a LEGO Mindstorms NXT robot. Two systems can communicate with each other via Bluetooth.

The LEGO Mindstorms NXT brick has a 32-bit Atmel ARM7 processor with Atmel AVR coprocessor. Each processor has 256KB Flash memory and 512 byte memory respectively. Additionally it has Bluetooth module for wireless communication, which a server can control its motor module. The LEGO Mindstorms NXT robot has too small memory to recognize a person(See Table 1. So we attached a wireless camera and make communication between the server and the camera using radio frequency(RF) devices. Host system analyzes the video frames and sends the control signal to LEGO Mindstorms NXT robot for collecting data while moving around. The LEGO Mindstorms NXT robot is decorated with LEGO blocks and camera, which is shown in Fig. 2.

Fig. 2. LEGO Mindstorms NXT robot with wireless camera

So we can take a randomly posed facial image by camera with mobile robot. Our mobile robot is made up of the LEGO Mindstorms NXT robot. A robot's controller is NXT Brick that is small embedded system that play a role in the brain of LEGO Mindstorms NXT robot. Specification of this hardware is shown as Table 1[15].

Table 1. Specification of LEGO Mindstorms NXT

Processor	32-bit ARM7 250MHz
RAM	64 Kilo Byte
Storage	256 KB Flash Memory
Controller	Atmel AVR microcontroller 4MHz
RAM	512 Byte
Display	100x64 pixel LCD matrix
Input	four 6-wire cable digital platform
Output	three 6-wire cable digital platform

As mentioned, face recognition process requires high performance computing power. However, NXT brick has low computing power. Since we can not process image information on the NXT Brick, we implemented host PC-based face recognition system and construct wireless communication between robot and PC. On this system, the wireless camera captures video frames and send them to host PC. Robot works as actuator of camera by the signal from host PC. In other words, we take pictures using the wireless camera and transfer image data through radio frequency using transmitter. On the PC, our program receives an image from USB RF Receiver, processing image data and controlling robot using Bluetooth and RF communications.

3 Face Analysis

3.1 Face Detection and Feature Extraction

As the first step of the entire process, face detection affects greatly the overall system performance. In fact, a successful face detection is prerequisite to the success of following face recognition and verification tasks. Our system extracts faces using OpenCV face detector[14]. OpenCV face detector uses Haar cascade classifier. This algorithm was proposed by P. Viola and M. Jones[13]. Basically this approach is based on Adaboost, which is known as one of the best performance and quality methods. We have trained much enough faces with various poses that is also collected by movable robots. After face detection, we adjust the size of facial image into default rectangle, and extract the face region with ellipse mask because face image contains background area. And then we apply the histogram equalization processing. It is known that the histogram equalization is effective under quite a different illumination condition. Even if it could not normalize locally illuminated shape, it works in general illumination changes by windows and lights in indoor environment.

3.2 Face Classification

The classification of feature vectors in face images needs a essential compression of large images into a small vector. We used PCA(Principal Component Analysis)[11] and LDA as feature extractors. Firstly, PCA is mathematically considered as an orthogonal linear transformation, which is a kind of a mapping function into other space. In pattern recognition fields, PCA is used for dimensionality reduction. In this paper, facial images (40×40) are represented as a 1×1600 vector. Since we collected many images per person, a face is considered as a vector of high dimension. Let the training set of N face images be $\Gamma_1, \Gamma_2, \Gamma_3, \cdots, \Gamma_N$. The average face of the training set is

$$\Psi = \frac{1}{N} \sum_{i=1}^{N} \Gamma_i. \tag{1}$$

Each face differs from the average by the vector

$$\Phi_i = \Gamma_i - \Psi. \tag{2}$$

For a Φ^T with zero empirical mean by Equation 2, the PCA transformation is given by

$$Y = W^T \Phi = \Sigma V^T. \tag{3}$$

where W^T is a transformation matrix and $W \Sigma V^T$ is the sigular value decomposition of Φ.

We can consider Y as a vector of a face in new space and recognize a person using this vector. Generally, PCA shows a good transformation and largely distributed vectors. However, it has a demerit if there are many data in same class. In this paper, we should find another method because we consider several posed faces in same persons.

LDA is a class specific method that it tries to shape the scatter in order to make it more reliable for classification. This method selects a transformation matrix, W of Equation 3 in such a way that the ratio of the between-class scatter and the within-class scatter is maximized. Let the between-class scatter matrix be defined as

$$\mathbf{S_B} = \sum_{i=1}^{c} \mathbf{N_i} (\mu_i - \mu)(\mu_i - \mu)^T \tag{4}$$

and the within-class scatter matrix be defined as

$$\mathbf{S_W} = \sum_{i=1}^{c} \sum_{x_k \in X_i} (x_k - \mu_i)(x_k - \mu_i)^T \tag{5}$$

where μ_i is the mean image of class X_i, and N_i is the number of samples in class X_i. If $\mathbf{S_W}$ is nonsingular, the optimal projection W_{opt} is chosen as the matrix with orthonormal columns which maximizes the ratio of the determinant of the between-class scatter matrix of the projected samples to the determinant of the within-class scatter matrix of the projected samples, i.e.,

$$W_{opt} = argmax_W \frac{|W^T S_B W|}{|W^T S_W W|} = [W_1 W_2 \cdots W_m] \tag{6}$$

where $W_i|i = 1, 2, \cdots, m$ is the set of generalized eigenvectors of $\mathbf{S_B}$ and $\mathbf{S_W}$ corresponding to the m largest generalized eigenvalues $\lambda_i|i = 1, 2, \cdots, m$, i.e.,

$$\mathbf{S_b} w_i = \lambda \mathbf{S_W} w_i, \qquad i = 1, 2, \cdots, m \tag{7}$$

Note that there are at most $c - 1$ nonzero generalized eigenvalues, and so an upper bound on m is $c - 1$, where c is the number of classes. LDA has error rates lower than PCA and required less computation time[11]. When the number of training samples per class is small, it is known that PCA has better result than LDA[12]. In this paper, we use more than 20 images per one class.

4 Experimental Results and Analysis

We performed several experiments to verify our approaches. Firstly, we collected 281 facial images. Secondly, we did preprocessing including histogram equalization and masking. Finally we recognized an input person by matching it with all trained faces. We can identify a person by selecting the index, which has the minimum error. In this experiment, we perform this process repeatedly. One of 7 trained persons was randomly inserted and the system recognized the detected facial image repeatedly.

4.1 Collecting Facial Images

For collecting facial images, wireless camera is used in order to enable to transfer video stream through radio frequency. This device is made up of wireless camera and RF receiver. The detailed information is explained in Table 2[16].

Table 2. Specification of wireless camera

Image Sensor	1/4" Color CCD
Horizontal Resolution	300 TV lines
Sync	Internal
PAL	625 lines interlaced
NTSC	525 lines interlaced
Light Sensitivity	10 Lux
Signal to Noise Ratio	42dB or more
Gamma	0.45
Frequency	2.410GHz, 2.430GHz, 2.450GHz and 2.470GHz

In this paper, the robot moves around and collects facial images on the desk. It has tried to track a face and move a little step until it loses a face region. If it loses a face region, it returns a previous status and position to try it again. Server system carries the whole algorithm out and controls the robot by analyzed signal. Server system extracts facial images using OpenCV face detector and normalizes the size of faces into $40 \times 40(pixels)$ in every captured images.

4.2 Performance in Face Recognition

We have performed experiments with captured images in real-time with our prototype system. We used a data set of 7 persons(more than 20 images per a person) for training and tried to recognize persons with newly captured images in indoor environment.

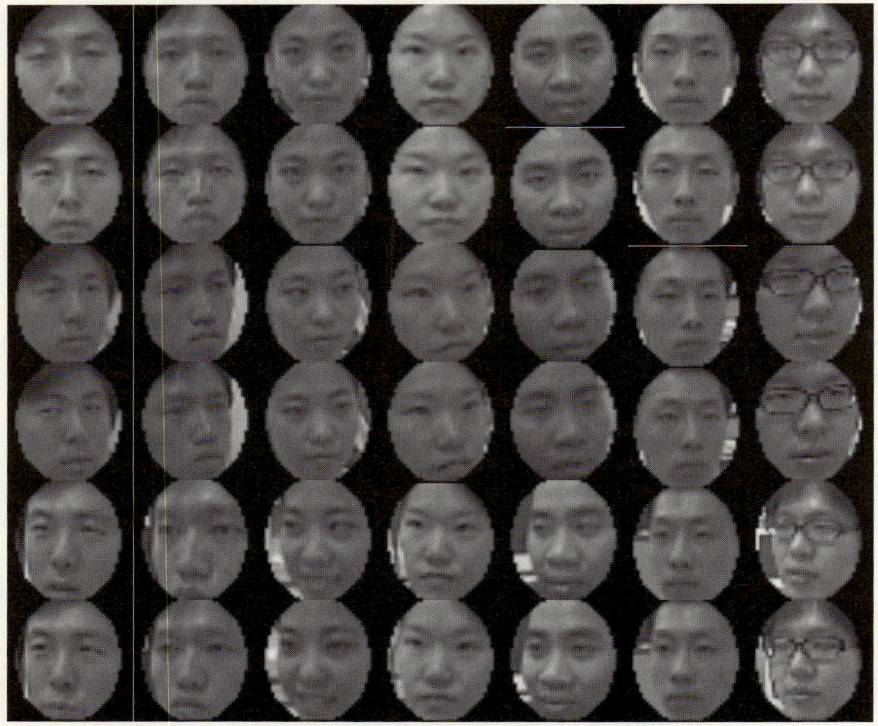

Fig. 3. Examples of collected facial images

This system can detect a face and recognize a person at 12-16 frame rates. This speed was measured from user-input to final stage with the result being dependent on the number of objects in an image. The system captures a frame from wireless camera through Bluetooth, preprocesses it, detects a face, extracts feature vectors and identifies a person. These whole stages have to be operated in real-time. In this system, movable robot always tries to train a manifold of each person. In a general way, even though training stage take much time, it is done in background process and user can not be aware of this process. We also measured the processing time of each stages using internal timer and the results were shown in Table 3. Even though the training stage takes too much time to perform in real-time, we can turn the process into background running and we would make it as if it were

Table 3. Speeds of each process

Process	Time
Face detection	111 ms
Preprocessing(masking and histogram Equalization)	67 ms
PCA training	250 ms
LDA training	221 ms
Classification	38 ms

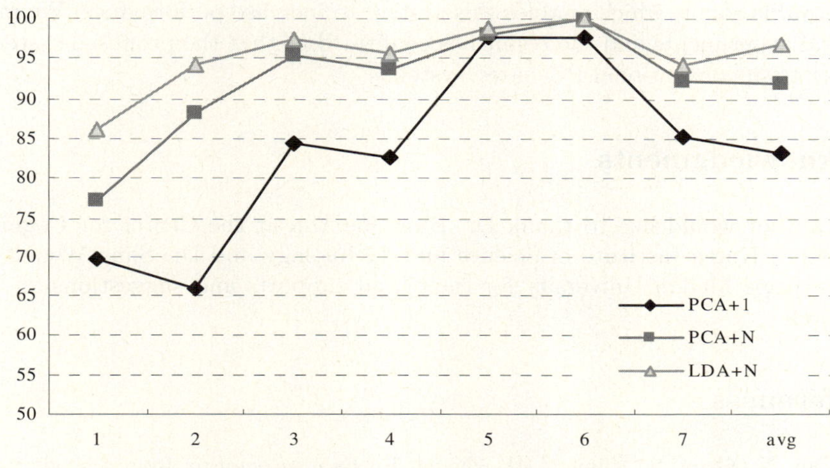

Fig. 4. Experimental results

done in real-time. We can also carry it out in real-time if the number of persons in training is small enough without other efforts.

The recognition performance of the system is highly dependent on accuracy of face extraction. In the next test, we measured the classification accuracy assuming correct face extraction, which means that we throw away the data wrongly extracted by OpenCV face detector.

This experiment was done by comparing three approaches in order to verify the effect of multiple training data. One is that we use the PCA method with only one image per person for training(PCA+1). Another is that we use the PCA method with n images per person(PCA+N). The other is that we use the LDA method with more than n images per person for training(LDA+N).[1] All of them use just an image for testing. The result in Fig. 4 shows that the LDA method with collected training images makes the result the best.

5 Conclusions

Until now, most of face recognition system have a fixed camera. Therefore they can not deal with various face pose. In order to cope with diverse facial images,

[1] In this paper, N=20 was used.

the face recognition system has to train many faces collected from well-designed studio or recognize a well-posed frontal face. In this paper, we construct a prototype system to throw these restricted conditions away.

In order to collect facial images enough in real environments, we organized several components such as a conventional PC, movable robot using LEGO Mindstorms NXT robot, and RF wireless communication. This system can actively capture an image sequence, find the features of face in the images, and recognize a person. In addition, it can collect the facial images of various poses due to movable robot, which enables this system to increase performance. We made several experiments and the result has confirmed us that the proposed system is better than conventional PC-based systems.

Acknowledgments

The author would like to thank Dr. Bum-Jae You at the Center for Cognitive Robotics, Korea Institute of Science and Technology and Dr. Sang-Woong Lee at Carnegie Mellon University for their kind supports and suggestions for this research.

References

1. Tan, X., Chen, S., Zhou, Z.-H., Zhang, F.: Face recognition from a single image per person: A survey. Pattern Recognition 39(9), 1725–1745 (2006)
2. Gilbert, J.M., Yang, W.: A Real-Time Face Recognition System Using Custom VLSI Hardware. In: Proc. of Computer Architectures for Machine Perceptron Workshop, New Orleans, USA, pp. 58–66 (1993)
3. Yang, F., Paindavoine, M., Abdi, H.: Parallel Implementation on DSPs of a Face Detection Algorithm. In: Proc. of International Conference on the Software Process, Chicago, USA (1998)
4. IBM ZISC036 Data Sheet: http://www.ibm.com
5. Zhou, S., Chellappa, R.: Rank constrained recognition under unknown illuminations. In: IEEE International Workshop on Analysis and Modeling of Faces and Gestures (2003)
6. Georghiades, A., Belhumeur, P., Kriegman, D.: From Few to Many: Illumination Cone Models for Face Recognition under Variable lighting and Pose. IEEE Transactions. on Pattern Analysis and Machine Intelligence 23(6), 643–660 (2001)
7. Gross, R., Matthews, I., Baker, S.: Appearance-Based Face Recognition and Light-Fields. IEEE Transactions on Pattern Analysis and Machine Intelligence 26(4), 449–465 (2004)
8. Blanz, V., Vetter, T.: Face Recognition Based on Fitting a 3D Morphable Model. IEEE Transactions on Pattern Analysis and Machine Intelligence 25(9), 1063–1074 (2003)
9. Sharad, S.: Introducing Embedded Design Concepts to Freshmen and Sophomore Engineering Students with LEGO MINDSTORMS NXT. In: IEEE International Conference on Microelectronic System Education, pp. 119–120. IEEE Computer Society Press, Los Alamitos (2007)

10. LEGO Mindstorms NXT Hardware Developers Kit: http://mindstorms.lego.com/overview/nxtreme.aspx
11. Turk, M., Pentland, A.: Eigen faces for recognition. Journal of Cognitive Neuroscience 3, 71–86 (1991)
12. Martinez, A.M., Kak, A.C.: PCA versus LDA. IEEE Transaction on Pattern Analysis and Machine Intelligence 23(2), 228–233 (2001)
13. Viola, P., Jones, M.: Robust Real-time Face Detection. International Journal of Computer Vision 57(2) (2004)
14. http://sourceforge.net/projects/opencvlibrary/
15. http://mindstorms.lego.com/
16. http://www.miracleon.com/products/cm32c.php

Speaker and Digit Recognition by Audio-Visual Lip Biometrics

Maycel Isaac Faraj and Josef Bigun

Halmstad University, School of Information Science,
Computer and Electrical Engineering (IDE)
Halmstad University, Box 823, SE-301 18 Halmstad
{maycel.faraj,josef.bigun}@ide.hh.se

Abstract. This paper proposes a new robust bi-modal audio visual digit and speaker recognition system by lip-motion and speech biometrics. To increase the robustness of digit and speaker recognition, we have proposed a method using speaker lip motion information extracted from video sequences with low resolution (128 ×128 pixels). In this paper we investigate a biometric system for digit recognition and speaker identification based using line-motion estimation with speech information and Support Vector Machines. The acoustic and visual features are fused at the feature level showing favourable results with digit recognition being 83% to 100% and speaker recognition 100% on the XM2VTS database.

1 Introduction

In recent years, some techniques have been suggested that combine visual features to improve the recognition rate in acoustically noisy environments that have background noise or cross talk among speakers [1][2][3][4][5]. The present work is a continuation of [6]. The dynamic visual features are suggested based on the shape and intensity of the lip region [7][8][9][10][11] because changes in the mouth shape including the lips and tongue carry significant phoneme-discrimination information. So far the visual representation has been based on shape models to represent changed mouth shapes that rely exclusively on the accurate detection of the lip contours, often a challenging task under varying illumination conditions and rotations of the face. Another disadvantage is the fluctuating computation time due to the iterative convergence process of the contour extraction. The motion in dynamic lip images can be modelled by moving-line patterns generating planes in space-time that encode the normal velocity of lines also known as *normal image velocity*, further details can be read in [6][12].

Here we use direct feature fusion to obtain the audio-visual observation vectors by concatenating the audio and visual features. The observation sequences are then modelled with a Support Vector Machine (SVM) classifier for digit and speaker recognition respectively. The studies [13][14] [15] reported good performance with Support Vector Machine (SVMs) classifiers in recognition, whereas traditional methods for speaker recognition are GMMs [16] and artificial neural networks [17]. By investigating SVM instead of the more common GMM [6],

S.-W. Lee and S.Z. Li (Eds.): ICB 2007, LNCS 4642, pp. 1016–1024, 2007.

we wanted to study the performance influence of the classification method on speaker recognition and digit recognition.

In previous work [6], we introduced a novel feature extraction method for lip motion used in a speaker verification system as a framework for the well known Gaussian Mixture Models. Here, we extended previous work [6] by studying a novel quantization technique for lip features. Furthermore, a digit recognition is presented together with a biometric speaker identification using SVM classifier. An extension of this work as journal article is under review $IEEET.onComputers$. The remainder of the paper is organized as follows. In Section 2 we describe briefly the lip-motion technique for the mouth region along with our quantization (feature-reduction) method, followed by acoustic feature extraction in Section 3. Section 4 describes SVM classifier used for digit and speaker recognition along with the database and the experimental setup in Section 5. Finally experimental results are shown with a discussion of the experiments and the remaining issues, Section 6 and 7.

2 Visual Features by Normal Image Velocity

Bigun et al. proposed a different motion estimation technique based on an eigenvalue analysis of the multidimensional structure tensor [18], allowing the minimization process of fitting a line or a plane to be carried without the Fourier Transform. Applied to optical-flow estimation, known as the 3D structure-tensor method, the eigenvector belonging to the largest eigenvalue of the tensor is directed in the direction of the contour motion, if motion is present. However, this method can be excessive for applications that need only line-motion features. We assume that the local neighbourhood in the lip image contains parallel lines or edges as this is supported by real data [19]. Lines in a spatio-temporal image translated with a certain velocity in the normal direction will generate planes with a normal that can be estimated in a total-least-square-error (TLS) sense as the local directions of the lines in 2D manifolds using complex arithmetic and convolution [18]. The velocity component of translation parallel to the line cannot be calculated; this is referred to as the *aperture problem.* We denote the normal unit vector as $\mathbf{k} = (k_x, k_y, k_t)^T$ and the projection of $\mathbf{k}$ to the x–y coordinate axes represents the direction vector of the line's motion. The normal, $\mathbf{k}$, of the plane will then relate to the velocity vector $v\mathbf{a}$ as follows

$$\mathbf{v} = v\mathbf{a} = -\frac{k_t}{k_x^2+k_y^2}(k_x, k_y)^T =$$

$$-\frac{1}{(\frac{k_x}{k_t})^2 + (\frac{k_y}{k_t})^2}\left(\frac{k_x}{k_t}, \frac{k_y}{k_t}\right)^T, \qquad (1)$$

where $\mathbf{v}$ is the *normal image flow.* The normal velocity estimation problem becomes a problem of solving the tilts $(\tan\gamma_1 = \frac{k_x}{k_t})$ and $(\tan\gamma_2 = \frac{k_y}{k_t})$ of the motion plane in the xt and yt manifolds, which is obtained from the eigenvalue analysis of the 2D structure tensor, [18]. Using complex numbers and smoothing, the angles

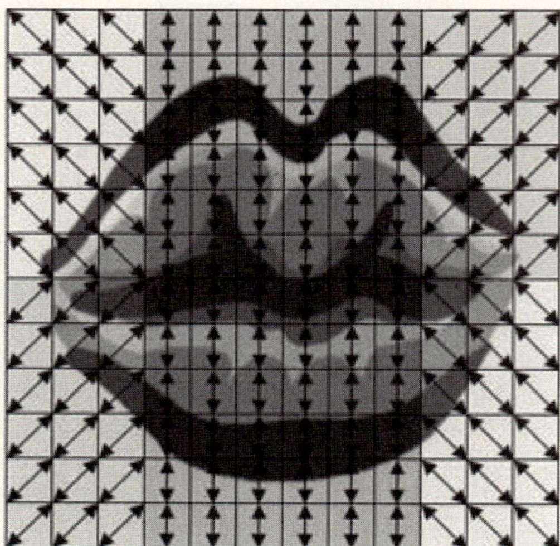

Fig. 1. Illustration of velocity estimation quantification and reduction

of the eigenvectors are given effectively as complex values such that its magnitude is the difference of the eigenvalues of the local structure tensor in the xt manifold, whereas its argument is twice the angle of the most significant eigenvector approximating $2\gamma_1$. The function f represents the continuous local image, whose sampled version can be obtained from the observed image sequence. Thus, the arguments of $\tilde{u}_1$ and $\tilde{u}_2$ deliver the TLS estimations of γ_1 and γ_2 in the local 2D manifolds xt and yt respectively, but in the double angle representation [20], leading to the estimated velocity components as follows.

$$\frac{k_x}{k_t} = \tan\gamma_1 = \tan(\frac{1}{2}\arg(\tilde{u}_1)) \Rightarrow \tilde{v}_x = \frac{\tan\gamma_1}{\tan^2\gamma_1 + \tan^2\gamma_2} \tag{2}$$

$$\frac{k_y}{k_t} = \tan\gamma_2 = \tan(\frac{1}{2}\arg(\tilde{u}_2)) \Rightarrow \tilde{v}_y = \frac{\tan\gamma_2}{\tan^2\gamma_1 + \tan^2\gamma_2} \tag{3}$$

The tilde over v_x and v_y denote that these quantities are estimations of v_x and v_y. With the calculated 2D-velocity feature vectors, $(v_x, v_y)^T$, in each mouth-region frame (128×128 pixels) we have dense 2D-velocity vectors. To extract statistical features from the 2D normal velocity and to reduce the amount of data without degrading identity-specific information excessively, we reduce the 2D velocity feature vectors $(v_x, v_y)^T$ at each pixel to 1D scalars where the expected directions of motion are 0°, 45°, −45° – marked with 3 different greyscale shades in 6 regions in Fig. 1. The motion vectors within each region become real scalars that take the signs + or − depending on which direction they move relative to their expected spatial directions (differently shaded boxes).

$$f(p,q) = \|(v_x(p,q), v_y(p,q))\| * sgn(\angle(v_x(p,q), v_y(p,q))),\ p,q = 0\ldots127. \tag{4}$$

The next step is to quantize the estimated velocities from arbitrary real scalars to a more limited set of values. We found that direction and speed quantization significance reduces the impact of noise on the motion information around the lip area. The quantized speeds are obtained from the data by applying a mean approximation as follows.

$$g(l,k) = \sum_{p,q=0}^{N-1} f(Nl+p, Nk+q),\ \ p,q = 0\ldots(N-1),\ l,k = 0\ldots(M-1) \quad (5)$$

where N and M represent the window size of the boxes (**Fig. 1**) and the number of boxes, respectively. The statistics of lip-motion are represented by 144-dimensional $(M \times M)$ feature vectors. The original dimension before reduction is $128 \times 128 \times 2 = 32768$.

3 Acoustic Features

The Mel-Frequency Cepstral Coefficient (MFCC) is a commonly used instance of the filter-bank–based features [21] that can represent the speech spectrum. Here, the input signal is pre-emphasized and divided into 25-ms frame every 10 ms. A Hamming window is applied to each frame that is computed by (MFCC) vectors from the FFT-based, mel-warped, log-amplitude filter bank followed by a cosine transform and cepstral filtering. The speech features in this study were the MFCC vectors generated by the Hidden Markov Model Toolkit (HTK) [22] processing the data stream from the XM2VTS database. This MFCC vector contains 12 cepstral coefficients extracted from the Mel-frequency spectrum of the frame with normalized log energy, 13 delta coefficients (velocity), and 13 delta-delta coefficients (acceleration).

4 Classification by Support Vector Machine

The SVM formulation is based on the Structural Risk Minimization principle, which minimizes an upper bound on the generalization error, as opposed to the Empirical Risk Minimization [23][24]. An SVM is a discrimination-based binary method using a statistical algorithm. The background idea in training an SVM system is finding a hyperplane $\mathbf{w} \cdot \mathbf{x} + b = 0$, as a decision boundary between two classes. For linearly separable training dataset labelled pairs $\mathbf{x}_i, y_i, i = 1, \ldots, l$, where $\mathbf{x}_i \in \Re^n$ and $\mathbf{y} \in \{1,\text{-}1\}^l$, the following equation is verified for each observation data (feature vector).

$$d_i(w^T \mathbf{x}_i + b) \geq 1 - \xi_i \ for\ i = 1, 2, ..., l\ \xi_i > 0, \quad (6)$$

where d_i is the label for sample data $\mathbf{x}_i$ which can be +1 or -1; $\mathbf{w}_i$ and b are the weights and bias that describe the hyperplane; ξ represents the number of data samples left inside the decision area, controlling the training errors. In our experiment we use the inner-product kernel function as RBF kernel

$$K(\mathbf{x}, \mathbf{y}) = \exp(-\gamma \left\| \mathbf{x} - \mathbf{y} \right\|^2), \gamma > 0, \tag{7}$$

When conducting digit-classification experiments, we will need to choose between multiple classes. The best method of extending the two-class classifiers to multi-class problems appears to be application dependent. For our experiments we use the *one against one* approach. It simply constructs for each pair of classes an SVM classifier which separates those classes. All tests in this paper were performed using the SVM toolkit [25].

5 XM2VTS Database

All experiments in this paper are conducted on the XM2VTS database, currently the largest publicly available audio-visual database [26]. The XM2VTS database contains images and speech of 295 subjects (male and female), captured over 4 sessions. In each session, the subject is asked to pronounce three sentences when recording the video sequence; we use only "0 1 2 3 4 5 6 7 8 9". It is worth noting that the XM2VTS data is difficult to use as is for digit recognition experiments because the speech or lip motions are not annotated. Before defining a protocol we thus needed to annotate both speech and visual data, which we did nearly 100% automatically by speech segmentation. For each speaker of the XM2VTS database, the utterance " 0 1 2 3 4 5 6 7 8 9" was divided into single-digit sub sequences 0 to 9. We used Hidden Markov models to automatically segment the digit sequences furthermore we manually verified and corrected the segmentation results so as to eliminate the impact of database segmentation errors when interpreting our recognition results. We propose two protocol setups for the XM2VTS database; protocol 1 is the well known Lausanne protocol [26], used for speaker identification and protocol 2 which is used for digit recognition. Protocol 2 is also suggested by other studies [14].

Protocol 1 – the training contains 225 subjects with 200 subjects as clients using and 25 subjects as impostors using sessions 1, 2 and 3. The training group is also used in evaluation. For the testing session 4 of the training group are used and with yet another 70 subjects as impostors. *Protocol 2* – the speakers were involved both in training SVMs and testing SVMs, we used 4 different pronunciations for training and testing. The training and test samples were completely disjoint.

6 Experimental Results

We want to quantify the performance of our visual features in speaker recognition and digit recognition as a stand-alone and audio-complementary modality. First the text-prompted speaker-recognition test using protocol 1 are presented and then the digit-recognition system test results using protocol 2 are presented. In our experiments we use direct fusion at feature level, which are detailed in [19].

Table 1. Speaker identification rate by SVM using word "7" for 295 speakers

Kernel	Audio recognition rate	Visual recognition rate	Audio-Visual recognition rate
RBF	92%	80%	100%

6.1 Speaker-Identification System by SVM

A smaller dataset of 100 speakers was tested for all digits and the most significant word for the speaker recognition rate was digit "7" which gave the highest recognition rate. The experiment follows protocol 1 using all 295 speakers:

- Partition the database for training, evaluation, and testing according to protocol 1.
- Train the SVM for an utterance so that the classification score, L (the mean of the classification equation 6 for an utterance), is positive for the user and negative for impostors.
- L is compared to a threshold T.
  - Find the threshold T such that False Acceptance is equal to False Rejection using the evaluation set.
  - Using the threshold T, the decision L is made according to the rule: if $L > T$ accept the speaker else reject her/him.

However, protocol 1 is desired for verification (1:1 matching). To perform identification (1:many matching) we proceed as follows:

- Identify the speaker from a group of speakers
  - We construct classifiers to separate each speaker from all other speakers in the training set.
  - The speaker identity is determined by the classifier that yields the largest likelihood score.

Table 1 shows the results of using SVM classifiers with RBF kernel function using only one word (digit) to recognize the speaker identity. The recognition performance obtained when using coefficients both from dynamic image and speech are considerably higher than when using a single modality based on speech parameters. These results show that our features can perform well in identification problems.

6.2 Digit Recognition System by SVM

In Table 2, we illustrate all systems based on only acoustic, only visual and merged audio visual feature information. We obtain the best recognition rate for digits "1, 6, and 7" 100%. One cause why the results in Table 2 vary is that there is not enough information (especially visual information) for certain utterances. This is not surprising because the XM2VTS database was collected for identity recognition and not digit recognition. During the segmentation we could verify that when

Table 2. Digit-recognition rate of all digits using protocol 2 in one against one SVM

Word	Audio features	Visual features	Audio-Visual features
0	89%	70%	92%
1	90%	77%	100%
2	86%	60%	89%
3	90%	75%	96%
4	89%	55%	85%
5	90%	50%	83%
6	100%	90%	100%
7	93%	100%	100%
8	91%	54%	83%
9	90%	49%	85%

uttering the words from 0 to 9 in a sequence without silence between words, the words "4, 5, 8, 9" are pronounced in shorter time-lapses and the amount of visual data is notably less in comparison to other digits. Additionally amount of speech for each speaker differ when uttering the same word or digit depending on the manner and speed of the speaker. Digit recognition give $\approx 68\%$ and audio-visual features give $\approx 90\%$ for overall recognition.

7 Conclusion and Discussion

In this paper we described a system utilizing lip movement information in dynamic image sequences of numerous speakers for robust digit and speaker recognition by no use of iterative algorithm or assuming successful lip-contour tracking. In environments such as airports, outside traffic, train station etc. the automatic digit recognition or speaker recognition system based on only acoustic information would with high probability be unsuccessful. Our experimental results support the importance of adding lip motion representation in speaker or digit recognition systems that can be installed for instance in mobile devices as a complement to acoustic information.

We presented a novel lip-motion quantization and recognition results of lip-motion features as standalone and as a complement to audio for speaker and digit recognition tasks using extensive tests. Improvements of recognition rate based on audio utilizing our motion features for digit as well as identity are provided. Our main goal is to present an effective feature level extraction for lip movement sequences which in turn can be used for identification and digit recognition as shown here and also for speaker verification [19] using an different state-of-art approach GMM.

From a visual information classification performance perspective, the digit utterance in the XM2VTS database contained less relevant information for the digits "4, 5, 8, 9". The poor recognition performance of these digits indicate that XM2VTS database does not contain sufficient amounts of visual information on lip movements. Not surprisingly, if the visual feature-extraction is made on sufficient amount of visual speech data, the available modelling for recognition tasks appears to be sufficient for successful recognition.

References

1. Potamianos, G., Neti, C., Gravier, G., Garg, A., Senior, A.: Recent advances in the automatic recognition of audiovisual speech. Proceedings of the IEEE 91(9), 1306–1326 (2003)
2. Brunelli, K.R., Falavigna, D.: Person identification using multiple cues. IEEE Transactions on Pattern Analysis and Machine Intelligence 17(10), 955–966 (1995)
3. Chibelushi, C., Deravi, F., Mason, J.: A review of speech-based bimodal recognition. IEEE Transactions on Multimedia 4(1), 23–37 (2002)
4. Duc, B., Fischer, S., Bigun, J.: Face authentication with sparse grid gabor information. In: IEEE International Conference Acoustics, Speech, and Signal Processing, vol. 4(21), pp. 3053–3056 (1997)
5. Tang, X., Li, X.: Video based face recognition using multiple classifiers. In: Sixth IEEE International Conference on Automatic Face and Gesture Recognition FGR2004, pp. 345–349. IEEE Computer Society, Los Alamitos (2004)
6. Faraj, M.I., Bigun, J.: Person verification by lip-motion. In: 2006 Conference on Computer Vision and Pattern Recognition Workshop (CVPRW), pp. 37–45 (2006)
7. Luettin, J., Maitre, G.: Evaluation protocol for the extended m2vts database xm2vtsdb (1998). In: IDIAP Communication 98-054, Technical report R R-21, number = IDIAP - (1998)
8. Dieckmann, U., Plankensteiner, P., Wagner, T.: Acoustic-labial speaker verification. In: Bigün, J., Borgefors, G., Chollet, G. (eds.) AVBPA 1997. LNCS, vol. 1206, pp. 301–310. Springer, Heidelberg (1997)
9. Jourlin, P., Luettin, J., Genoud, D., Wassner, H.: Acoustic-labial speaker verification. In: Bigün, J., Borgefors, G., Chollet, G. (eds.) AVBPA 1997. LNCS, vol. 1206, pp. 319–326. Springer, Heidelberg (1997)
10. Chen, T.: Audiovisual speech processing. IEEE Signal Processing Magazine 18(1), 9–21 (2001)
11. Liang, L., Zhao, X.L.Y., Pi, X., Nefian, A.: Speaker independent audio-visual continuous speech recognition. In: IEEE International Conference on Multimedia and Expo., 2002. ICME 02. Proceedings, vol. 2, pp. 26–29 (2002)
12. Kollreider, K., Fronthaler, H., Bigun, J.: Evaluating liveness by face images and the structure tensor. In: AutoID 2005: Fourth Workshop on Automatic Identification Advanced Technologies, pp. 75–80. IEEE Computer Society Press, Los Alamitos (2005)
13. Wan, V., Campbell, W.: Support vector machines for speaker verification and identification. In: Proceedings of the 2000 IEEE Signal Processing Society Workshop, Neural Networks for Signal Processing X, vol. 2, pp. 775–784 (2000)
14. Gavat, I., Costache, G., Iancu, C.: Robust speech recognizer using multiclass svm. In: 7th Seminar on Neural Network Applications in Electrical Engineering. NEUREL 2004, pp. 63–66 (2004)
15. Clarkson, P., Moreno, P.: On the use of support vector machines for phonetic classification. In: IEEE International Conference on Acoustics, Speech, and Signal Processing, ICASSP, vol. 2, pp. 585–588. IEEE Computer Society Press, Los Alamitos (1999)

16. Reynolds, D., Quatieri, T., Dunn, R.B.: Speaker verification using adapted gaussian mixture models. Digital Signal Processing 10(1-3), 19–41 (2000)
17. Farrell, K., Mammone, R., Assaleh, K.: Speaker recognition using neural networks and conventional classifiers, vol. 2(1), pp. 194–205. IEEE-Computer Society Press, Los Alamitos (1994)
18. Bigun, J., Granlund, G., Wiklund, J.: Multidimensional orientation estimation with applications to texture analysis of optical flow. IEEE-Trans. Pattern Analysis and Machine Intelligence 13(8), 775–790 (1991)
19. Faraj, M.I., Bigun, J.: Audio-visual person authentication using lip-motion from orientation maps. (Article accepted for publication in Pattern Recognition Letters: February 2, 2007) (2007)
20. Granlund, G.H.: In search of a general picture processing operator. Computer Graphics and Image Processing 8(2), 155–173 (1978)
21. Davis, S., Mermelstein, P.: Comparison of parametric representations for monosyllabic word recognition in continuously spoken sentences. IEEE transactions on Acoustics, Speech, and Signal Processing 28(4), 357–366 (1980)
22. Young, S., Kershaw, D., Odell, J., Ollason, D., Valtchev, V., Woodland, P.: The htk book (for htk version 3.0) (2000), `http://htk.eng.cam.ac.uk/docs/docs.shtml`
23. Vapnik, V.N.: The Nature of Statistical Learning Theory. Springer, Heidelberg (1995)
24. Burges, C.J.: A tutorial on support vector machines for pattern recognition. Data Mining and Knowledge Discovery 2(2), 121–167 (1998)
25. Chang, C.C., Lin, C.J.: Libsvm-a library for support vector machines. software (2001), available at `http://www.csie.ntu.edu.tw/cjlin/libsvm`
26. Messer, K., Matas, J., Kittler, J., Luettin, J.: Xm2vtsdb: The extended m2vts database. In: Second International Conference of Audio and Video-based Biometric Person Authentication, ICSLP'96, pp. 72–77 (1999)

Modelling Combined Handwriting and Speech Modalities

Andreas Humm, Jean Hennebert, and Rolf Ingold

Université de Fribourg, Boulevard de Pérolles 90, 1700 Fribourg, Switzerland
{andreas.humm, jean.hennebert, rolf.ingold}@unifr.ch

Abstract. We are reporting on consolidated results obtained with a new user authentication system based on combined acquisition of online handwriting and speech signals. In our approach, signals are recorded by asking the user to say what she or he is simultaneously writing. This methodology has the clear advantage of acquiring two sources of biometric information at no extra cost in terms of time or inconvenience. We are proposing here two scenarios of use: spoken signature where the user signs and speaks at the same time and spoken handwriting where the user writes and says what is written. These two scenarios are implemented and fully evaluated using a verification system based on Gaussian Mixture Models (GMMs). The evaluation is performed on MyIdea, a realistic multimodal biometric database. Results show that the use of both speech and handwriting modalities outperforms significantly these modalities used alone, for both scenarios. Comparisons between the spoken signature and spoken handwriting scenarios are also drawn.

1 Introduction

Multimodal biometrics has raised a growing interest in the industrial and scientific communities. The potential increase of accuracy combined with better robustness against forgeries makes indeed multimodal biometrics a promising field. In our work, we are interested in building multimodal authentication systems using speech and handwriting as modalities. Speech and handwriting are indeed two major modalities used by humans in their daily transactions and interactions. Also, these modalities can be acquired simultaneously with no inconvenience, just asking the user to say what she/he is signing or writing. Finally, speech and handwriting taken alone do not compare well in terms of performance against more classical biometric systems such as iris or fingerprint. Merging both biometrics will potentially lead to a competitive system.

1.1 Motivations

Many automated biometric systems based on speech alone have been studied and developed in the past, as reviewed previously [1]. Numerous biometric systems based on signature have also been studied and developed in the past [2][3]. Likewise biometric systems based on online handwriting were not so numerous, however, we can refer to [4] or [5] as examples of state-of-the-art systems.

S.-W. Lee and S.Z. Li (Eds.): ICB 2007, LNCS 4642, pp. 1025–1034, 2007.

Our proposal here is to record speech and handwriting signals where the user reads aloud what she or he is writing. Such acquisitions are referred here and in our related works as CHASM for **c**ombined **h**andwriting **a**nd **s**peech **m**odalities[1]. In this work, we have been defining two scenarios. In the first one, called **spoken signatures**, a bimodal signature with voice is acquired. In this case, the user is simply asked to say the content of the signature, corresponding in most of the case to his or her name. This scenario is similar, in essence, to text-dependent password based systems where the signature and speech content remains the same from access to access. Thanks to the low quantity of data requested to build the biometric templates, this scenario would fit in commercial applications running, for example, in banks. In the second scenario, called **spoken handwriting**, the user is asked to write and read synchronously the content of several lines of a given random piece of text. This scenario is less applicable in the case of commercial applications because of the larger quantity of data requested to build models. However, it could be used for forensic applications. Comparisons that we will draw between these scenarios will, of course, have to be weighted due to the difference of quantity of data.

Our motivation to perform a synchronized acquisition is multiple. Firstly, it avoids doubling the acquisition time. Secondly, the synchronized acquisition will probably give better robustness against intentional imposture. Indeed, imitating simultaneously the voice and the writing of somebody has a much higher cognitive load than for each modality taken separately. Finally, the synchronization patterns (i.e. where do users synchronize) or the intrinsic deformation of the inputs (mainly the slowdown of the speech signal) may be dependent on the user, therefore bringing an extra piece of useful biometrics information.

1.2 Related Work

Several related works have already shown that using speech and signature modalities together permits significant improvements in authentication performances in comparison to systems based on speech or signature alone. In [6], a tablet PC system based on online signature and voice modalities is proposed to ensure the security of electronic medical records. In [7], an online signature verification system and a speaker verification system are also combined. Both sub-systems use Hidden Markov Models (HMMs) to produce independent scores that are then fused together. In [8], tests are reported for a system where the signature verification part is built using HMMs and the speaker verification part uses either dynamic time warping or GMMs. The fusion of both systems is performed at the score level and results are again better than for the individual systems. In [9], the SecurePhone project is presented where multimodal biometrics is used to secure access and authenticate transactions on a mobile device. The biometric modalities include face, signature and speech signals.

The main difference between these works and our CHASM approach lies in the acquisition procedure. In our case, the speech and signature data streams

[1] We note here that such signals could also be used to recognize the content of what is said or written. However, we focus here on the task of user authentication.

are recorded simultaneously, asking the user to actually say the content of the signature or text. Our procedure has the advantage of shortening the enrollment and access time for authentication and will potentially allow for more robust fusion strategies upstream in the processing chain. This paper is actually reporting on consolidated evaluation results of our CHASM approach. It presents novel conclusions regarding comparison of performance of spoken signature and spoken handwriting. Individual analysis and performance evaluation of spoken signatures and spoken handwriting have been presented in our related works [10][11][12].

The remainder of this paper is organized as follows. In section 2, we give an overview of MyIDea, the database used for this work and of the evaluation protocols. In section 3 we present our modelling system based on a fusion of GMMs. Section 4 presents the experimental results. Finally, conclusions and future work are presented.

2 CHASM Database

2.1 MyIDea Database

CHASM data have been acquired in the framework of the MyIDea biometric data collection [13][14]. MyIDea is a multimodal database that contains many other modalities such as fingerprint, talking face, etc. The "set 1" of MyIDea is already available for research institutions. It includes about 70 users that have been recorded over three sessions spaced in time. This set is here considered as a development set. A second set of data is planned to be recorded in a near future and will be used as evaluation set in our future work[2].

CHASM data have been acquired with a WACOM Intuos2 graphical tablet and a standard computer headset microphone (Creative HS-300). For the tablet stream, (x, y)-coordinates, pressure, azimuth and elevation angles of the pen are sampled at 100 Hz. The speech waveform is recorded at 16 kHz and coded linearly on 16 bits. The data samples are also provided with timestamps to allow a precise synchronization of both streams. The timestamps are especially important for the handwriting streams as the graphical tablet does not send data samples when the pen is out of range.

In [15], we provide more comments on spoken signature and spoken handwriting data and on the way users synchronize their acoustic events with signature strokes. In [16], we report on a usability survey conducted on the subjects of MyIDea. The main conclusions of the survey are the following. First, all recorded users were able to perform the signature or handwriting acquisition. Speaking and signing or writing at the same time did not prevent any acquisition from happening. Second, the survey shows that such acquisitions are acceptable from a usability point of view.

---

[2] The data set used to perform the experiments reported in this article has been given the reference MYIDEA-CHASM-SET1 by the distributors of MyIDea.

2.2 Recording and Evaluation Protocols

Spoken signatures. In MyIDea, six *genuine* spoken signatures are acquired for each subject per session. This leads to a total of 18 true acquisitions after the three sessions. After acquiring the genuine signatures, the subject is also asked to imitate six times the signature of another subject. Spoken signature imitations are performed in a gender dependent way by letting the subject having an access to the static image and to the textual content of the signature to be forged. The access to the voice recording is not given for imitation as this would lead to a too difficult task considering the high cognitive load and would be practically infeasible in the limited time frame of the acquisition. This procedure leads to a total of 18 *skilled forgeries* after the three sessions, i.e. six impostor signatures on three different subjects. Two assessment protocols have been defined on MyIDea with the objective of being as realistic as possible (see [16] for details). The first one is called **without time variability** where signatures for training and testing are taken from the same session. The second protocol is called **with time variability** where the signatures for training are taken from the first session while for testing they are taken from a different session. To compare with the skilled forgeries described above, we also test with *random forgeries* taking the accesses from the remaining users. These protocols are strictly followed here.

Spoken handwriting. For each of the three sessions, the subject is asked to read and write a random text fragment of about 50 to 100 words. The subject is allowed to train for a few lines on a separated sheet in order to be accustomed to with the procedure of talking and writing at the same time. After acquiring the genuine handwriting, the subject is also asked to imitate the handwriting of another subject (same gender) and to synchronously utter the content of the text (skilled forgeries). In order to do this, the imitator has access to the *static* handwriting data of the subject to imitate. The access to the voice recording is also not given for imitation. This procedure leads to a total of three impostor attempts on different subjects after the three sessions. An assessment protocol for spoken handwriting is also available with MyIDea [16] and is followed for the realization of the tests in this paper. In short, this protocol trains the models on data from session one and test it on data from sessions two and three. As for spoken signatures, we also test against skilled forgeries and random forgeries. It actually corresponds to a **text-prompted scenario** where the system prompts the subject to write and say a random piece of text each time an access is performed. This kind of scenario allows the system to be more secure against spoofing attacks where the forger plays back a pre-recorded version of the genuine data. This scenario also has the advantage of being very convenient for the subject who does not need to remember any password phrase.

3 System Description

As illustrated on Fig. 1, our system models independently the speech and handwriting signals to obtain a score that is finally fused.

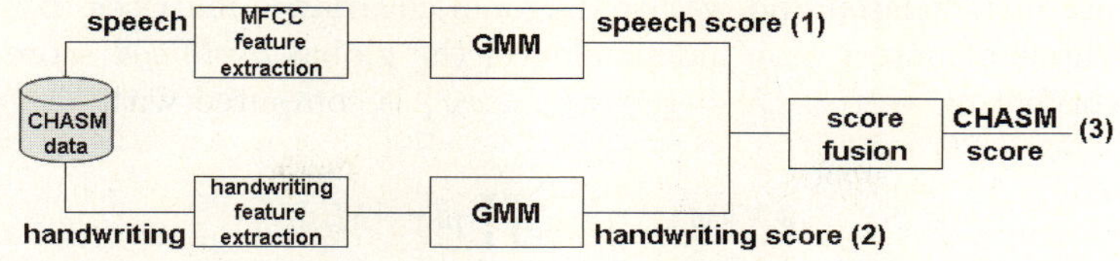

Fig. 1. CHASM handwriting system

3.1 Feature Extraction

For each point of the handwriting, we extract 25 dynamic features based on the x and y coordinates, the pressure and angles of the pen in a similar way as in [17] and [10]. This feature extraction was actually proposed to model signatures. However it can be used without modification in the case of handwriting as nothing specific to signature was included in the computation of the features. The features are mean and standard deviation normalized on a per user basis.

For the speech signal, we compute 12 Mel Frequency Cepstral Coefficients (MFCC) and the energy every 10 ms on a window of 25.6 ms. We realized that the speech signal contains a lot of silence which is due to the fact that writing is usually more slow than speaking. It is known, in the speech domain, that silence parts impair the estimation of models. We therefore implemented a procedure to remove all the silence parts of the speech signal. This silence removal component is using a classical energy-based speech detection module based on a bi-Gaussian model. MFCC coefficients are mean and standard deviation normalized using normalization values computed on the speech part of the data.

3.2 GMMs System

GMMs are used to model the likelihoods of the features extracted from the handwriting and from the speech signal. One could argue that GMMs are actually not the most appropriate models in this case as they are intrinsically not capturing the time-dependent specificities of speech and handwriting. However, a GMM is well appropriated to handle the text-independent constraint of the spoken handwriting scenario. We also wanted to have similar types of models for both scenarios to draw fair comparisons. Furthermore, GMMs are well-known flexible modelling tools able to approximate any probability density function.

With GMMs, the probability density function $p(x_n|M_{client})$ or *likelihood* of a D-dimensional feature vector x_n given the model of the client M_{client}, is estimated as a weighted sum of multivariate Gaussian densities

$$p(x_n|M_{client}) \cong \sum_{i=1}^{I} w_i \mathcal{N}(x_n, \mu_i, \Sigma_i) \quad (1)$$

in which I is the number of mixtures, w_i is the weight for mixture i and the Gaussian densities $\mathcal{N}$ are parameterized by a mean $D \times 1$ vector μ_i, and a $D \times D$ covariance matrix, Σ_i. In our case, we make the hypothesis that the features are uncorrelated and we use diagonal covariance matrices. By making the hypothesis of observation independence, the global *likelihood* score for the sequence of feature vectors, $X = \{x_1, x_2, ..., x_N\}$ is computed with

$$S_c = p(X|M_{client}) = \prod_{n=1}^{N} p(x_n|M_{client}) \quad (2)$$

The likelihood score S_w of the hypothesis that X is **not** from the given client is here estimated using a world GMM model M_{world} or *universal background model* trained by pooling the data of many other users. The decision whether to reject or to accept the claimed user is performed comparing the ratio of client and world score against a global threshold value T. The ratio is here computed in the log-domain with $R_c = \log(S_c) - \log(S_w)$. The training of the client and world models is usually performed with the Expectation-Maximization (EM) algorithm that iteratively refines the component weights, means and variances to monotonically increase the likelihood of the training feature vectors. Another way to train the client model is to adapt the world model using a Maximum A Posteriori criterion (MAP) [18].

In our experiments we used the EM algorithm to build the word model by applying a simple binary splitting procedure to increase the number of Gaussian components through the training procedure. The world model is trained by pooling the available genuine accesses in the database[3]. In the results reported here, we used MAP adaptation to build the client models. As suggested in many papers, we perform only the adaptation of the mean vector μ_i, leaving untouched the covariance matrix Σ_i and the mixture coefficient w_i.

3.3 Score Fusion

We obtain the spoken handwriting (*sh*) score by applying a weighted summation of the handwriting (*hw*) and speech (*sp*) log-likelihood ratios with $R_{c,sh} = W_{sp}R_{c,sp} + W_{hw}R_{c,hw}$. This is a reasonable procedure if we assume that the local observations of both sub-systems are independent. This is however clearly not the case as the users are intentionally trying to synchronize their speech with the handwriting signal. Time-dependent score fusion procedures or feature fusion followed by joint modelling would be more appropriate than the approach taken here. More advanced score recombination could also be applied such as, for example, using classifier-based score fusion. We report here our results with or without using a *z-norm* score normalization preceding the summation. The z-norm is here applied globally on both speech and signature scores for all test accesses, in a user-independent way. As the mean and standard deviation of the z-norm are estimated a posteriori on the same data set, z-norm results are of course unrealistic but give an optimistic estimation of what could be the fusion performances with such a normalisation.

[3] The skilled forgeries attempts are excluded for training the world model as it would lead to optimistic results. Ideally, a fully independent set of users would be preferable, but this is not possible considering the small number of users (≈ 70) available.

4 Experimental Results

We report our results in terms of Equal Error Rates (EER) which are obtained for a value of the threshold T where the impostor False Acceptation and client False Rejection error rates are equal.

4.1 Spoken Signature

Table 1 summarizes the results with our best MAP system (128 Gaussians for the client and world models) in terms of ERR for the different protocols. The following conclusions can be drawn. The speech modelisation performs equally well as the signature in the case of single session experiments (without time variability). However, when multi-session accesses are considered, signature performs better than speech. Signature and speech modalities suffer from time-variability but in different degrees. It is probable that users show a larger intra-variability for the speech than for the signature modality. This could be here even more amplified as users are probably not used to slow down the speech to the pace of handwriting. Another explanation could be in the acquisition conditions that are more difficult to control in the case of the speech signal: different position of the microphone, environmental noise, etc. Another conclusion from Table 1 is that skilled forgeries decrease systematically and significantly the performance in comparison to random forgeries. For the protocol *with time variability*, a drop of about 200% relative performance is observed for the signature modality and about 50% for the speech modality. We have to note here that the skilled forgers do not try to imitate the voice of the user but actually say the genuine verbal content which is very probably the source of the loss of performance. Also from Table 1, we can conclude that the sum fusion, although very straightforward, brings systematically a clear improvement in the results, in comparison to the modalities taken alone. Interestingly, the z-norm fusion is better than the sum fusion for the protocol without time variability and is worse in the case of the protocol *with time variability.* An interpretation of this is proposed in [11].

4.2 Spoken Handwriting

Table 2 summarizes the results with our best MAP system (256 Gaussians for the client and world models), comparing random versus skilled forgeries. The

Table 1. Summary of spoken signature results in terms of terms of Equal Error Rates. Protocol with and without time variability, skilled and unskilled forgeries.

time variability	without		with	
forgeries	random	skilled	random	skilled
signature	0.4 %	3.9 %	2.7 %	7.3 %
speech	0.8 %	2.7 %	12.4 %	17.1 %
sum fusion (.5/.5)	**0.2 %**	**0.9 %**	**1.7 %**	**5.0 %**
z-norm fusion (.5/.5)	**0.1 %**	**0.7 %**	**2.3 %**	**8.6 %**

Table 2. Spoken handwriting results in terms of terms of Equal Error Rates, with time variability. Comparison of random versus skilled forgeries.

forgeries	random	skilled
handwriting	4.0 %	13.7 %
speech	1.8 %	6.9 %
sum fusion (.5/.5)	**0.7 %**	**6.9 %**
z-norm fusion (.5/.5)	**0.3 %**	**4.0 %**

following conclusions can be drawn. For the handwriting, skilled forgeries decrease the performances in a significant manner. This result is actually understandable as the forger is intentionally imitating the handwriting of the genuine user. For the speech signal, skilled forgeries also decreases the performance. As the forger do not try to imitate the voice of the genuine user, this result can be surprising. However, it can be explained as the forger is actually saying the exact same verbal content as the one used by the user at training time. When building a speaker model, the characteristics of the speaker are of course captured, but also, to some extent, the content of the speech signal itself. Results using the z-norm fusion are also reported in Table 2, showing an advantage against the sum fusion.

As a conclusion of these experiments with spoken handwriting, we can reasonably say that the speech modelisation performs on average better than the handwriting. Intuitively, one could argue that this is understandable as the handwriting is a gesture that is more or less fully learned (behavioral biometric) while speech contains information that are dependent on learned and physiological features (behavioral and physiological biometric).

4.3 Comparison of Spoken Signatures and Spoken Handwriting

We are able here to do a comparison of results obtained with spoken signatures and spoken handwriting data as our experiments are performed using the same database, with the same users and the same acquisition conditions. Results of spoken handwriting in Table 2 can be compared with results of spoken signatures in Table 1, for the protocol *with time variability.* The signature modality of spoken signatures provides better results than the handwriting modality of spoken handwriting. This can be explained in the following way. Handwriting is a taught gesture that is crafted to be understood by every person. In school, every child learns in more or less the same way to write the different characters. In contrast, a signature is built to be an individual characteristic of a person that should not be imitable and that is used for authentication purposes. A comparison of the speech modality of Table 1 and 2 shows that spoken handwriting provides better results than spoken signatures. An explanation for this lies in the quantity of speech data available. While the average length of the speech is about two seconds for signature, spoken handwriting provides about two minutes of speech. The speech model is therefore more precise for spoken handwriting than for spoken signature. Now, if we compare the z-norm fusion of Table 1 and 2, we can observe that spoken handwriting performs better than spoken signatures. However, we should pay attention that this conclusion is also dependent on the quantity of data. If we would have less handwriting data, the conclusion may also be reversed.

5 Conclusions and Future Work

We presented consolidated results obtained with a new user authentication system based on combined acquisition of online handwriting and speech signals. It has been shown that the modelling of the signals can be performed advantageously using GMMs trained with a MAP adaptation procedure. A simple fusion of GMM scores lead to significant improvements in comparison to systems where the modalities would be used alone. From a usability point of view, this gain of performance is obtained at no extra cost in terms of acquisition time, as both modalities are recorded simultaneously. The proposed bi-modal speech and handwriting approach seems then to be a viable alternative to systems using single modalities. In our future work, we plan to investigate the use of more robust modelling techniques against time variability and forgeries. We have identified potential directions such as HMMs, time-dependent score fusion, joint modelling, etc. Also, as soon as an extended set of spoken signature data will be available, experiments will be conducted according to a development/evaluation set framework. We will also investigate if the biometrics performances are impaired due to the signal deformations induced by the simultaneous recordings.

Acknowledgments. We warmly thank Asmaa El Hannani for her precious help with GMMs based systems. This work was partly supported by the Swiss NSF program "Interactive Multimodal Information Management (IM2)", as part of NCCR and by the EU BioSecure IST-2002-507634 NoE project.

References

1. Reynolds, D.: An overview of automatic speaker recognition technology. In: Proc. IEEE ICASSP, vol. 4, pp. 4072–4075 (2002)
2. Plamondon, R., Lorette, G.: Automatic signature verification and writer identification - the state of the art. Pattern Recognition 22(2), 107–131 (1989)
3. Leclerc, F., Plamondon, R.: Automatic signature verification: the state of the art–1989-1993. Int'l J. Pattern Rec. and Art. Intelligence 8(3), 643–660 (1994)
4. Liwicki, M., Schlapbach, A., Bunke, H., Bengio, S., Mariéthoz, J., Richiardi, J.: Writer identification for smart meeting room systems. In: Proceedings of the 7th International Workshop on Document Analysis Systems, pp. 186–195 (2006)
5. Nakamura, Y., Kidode, M.: Online writer verification using kanji handwriting. In: Gunsel, B., Jain, A.K., Tekalp, A.M., Sankur, B. (eds.) MRCS 2006. LNCS, vol. 4105, pp. 207–214. Springer, Heidelberg (2006)
6. Krawczyk, S., Jain, A.K.: Securing electronic medical records using biometric authentication. In: Kanade, T., Jain, A., Ratha, N.K. (eds.) AVBPA 2005. LNCS, vol. 3546, pp. 1110–1119. Springer, Heidelberg (2005)

7. Fuentes, M., et al.: Identity verification by fusion of biometric data: On-line signature and speech. In: Proc. COST 275 Workshop on The Advent of Biometrics on the Internet, Rome, Italy, November 2002, pp. 83–86 (2002)
8. Ly-Van, B., et al.: Signature with text-dependent and text-independent speech for robust identity verification. In: Proc. Workshop MMUA, pp. 13–18 (2003)
9. Koreman, J., et al.: Multi-modal biometric authentication on the securephone pda. In: Proc. Workshop MMUA, Toulouse (2006)
10. Humm, A., Hennebert, J., Ingold, R.: Gaussian mixture models for chasm signature verification. In: 3rd Joint Workshop on Multimodal Interaction and Related Machine Learning Algorithms, Washington (2006)
11. Hennebert, J., Humm, A., Ingold, R.: Modelling spoken signatures with gaussian mixture model adaptation. In: 32nd ICASSP, Honolulu (2007)
12. Humm, A., Ingold, R., Hennebert, J.: Spoken handwriting verification using statistical models. In: Accepted for publication ICDAR (2007)
13. Dumas, B., et al.: Myidea - multimodal biometrics database, description of acquisition protocols. In: proc. of Third COST 275 Workshop (COST 275), Hatfield (UK) (October 27 - 28 2005), pp. 59–62 (2005)
14. Hennebert, J., et al.: Myidea database (2005), `http://diuf.unifr.ch/go/myidea`
15. Humm, A., Hennebert, J., Ingold, R.: Scenario and survey of combined handwriting and speech modalities for user authentication. In: 6th Int'l. Conf. on Recent Advances in Soft Computing (RASC 2006), Canterburry, Kent, UK, pp. 496–501 (2006)
16. Humm, A., Hennebert, J., Ingold, R.: Combined handwriting and speech modalities for user authentication. Technical Report 06-05, University of Fribourg, Department of Informatics (2006)
17. Van Ly, B., Garcia-Salicetti, S., Dorizzi, B.: Fusion of hmm's likelihood and viterbi path for on-line signature verification. In: Biometrics Authentication Workshop, Prague (May 15th 2004)
18. Reynolds, D., Quatieri, T., Dunn, R.: Speaker verification using adapted gaussian mixture models. Digital Signal Processing 10, 19–41 (2000)

A Palmprint Cryptosystem

Xiangqian Wu[1], David Zhang[2], and Kuanquan Wang[1]

[1] School of Computer Science and Technology,
Harbin Institute of Technology (HIT), Harbin 150001, China
{xqwu, wangkq}@hit.edu.cn
http://biometrics.hit.edu.cn

[2] Biometric Research Centre, Department of Computing,
Hong Kong Polytechnic University, Kowloon, Hong Kong
csdzhang@comp.polyu.edu.hk

Abstract. Traditional cryptosystems are based on passwords, which can be cracked (simple ones) or forgotten (complex ones). This paper proposes a novel cryptosystem based on palmprints. This system directly uses the palmprint as a key to encrypt/decrypt information. The information of a palmprint is so complex that it is very difficult, if not impossible, to crack the system while it need not remember anything to use the system. In the encrypting phase, a 1024 bits binary string is extracted from the palmprints using differential operations. Then the string is translated to a 128 bits encrypting key using a Hash function, and at the same time, an error-correct-code (ECC) is generated. Some general encryption algorithms use the 128 bits encrypting key to encrypt the secret information. In decrypting phase, the 1024 bits binary string extracted from the input palmprint is first corrected using the ECC. Then the corrected string is translated to a decrypting key using the same Hash function. Finally, the corresponding general decryption algorithms use decrypting key to decrypt the information. The experimental results show that the accuracy and security of this system can meet the requirement of most applications.

1 Introduction

Information security is becoming increasingly important in nowadays. Cryptology is one of the most effective ways to enhance the information security. In the traditional cryptosystems, information is encrypted using passwords. The simple passwords are easy to be memorized while they are also easy to be cracked. And the complex passwords are difficult to be cracked while they are also difficult to be remembered. In order to overcome this problem, some biometric feature-based encrypting/decrypting algorithms have been developed [1, 2, 3, 4, 5, 6, 7].

The palmprint is a relatively new biometric feature [8, 9, 10, 11, 12, 13] and has several advantages compared with other currently available features [14]: palmprints contain more information than fingerprint, so they are more distinctive; palmprint capture devices are much cheaper than iris devices; palmprints also contain additional distinctive features such as principal lines and wrinkles,

S.-W. Lee and S.Z. Li (Eds.): ICB 2007, LNCS 4642, pp. 1035–1042, 2007.

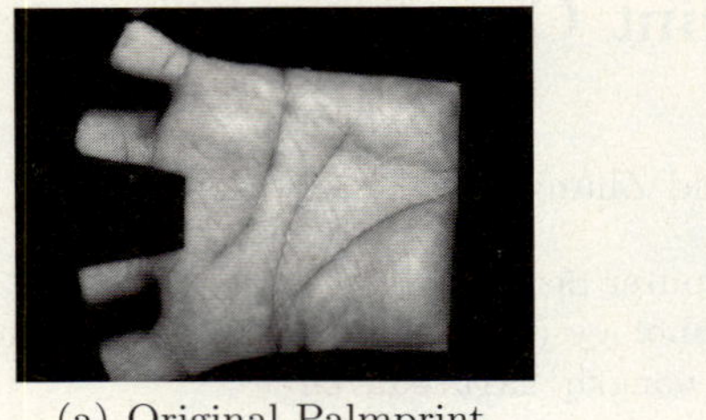
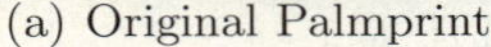
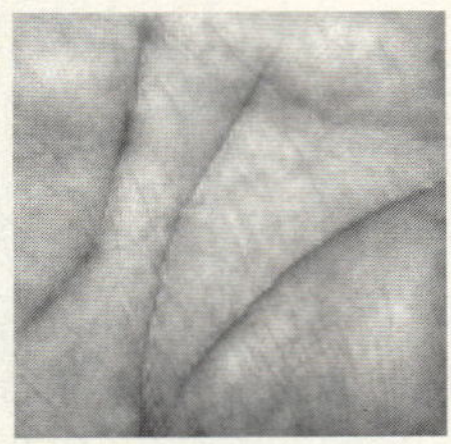

(a) Original Palmprint (b) Cropped Image

Fig. 1. An example of the palmprint and the normalized image

which can be extracted from low-resolution images; a highly accurate biometrics system can be built by combining all features of palms, such as palm geometry, ridge and valley features, and principal lines and wrinkles, etc. Therefore, it is suitable to use palmprints to implement a cryptosystem. Up to now, we failed to find any literature to discuss palmprint encryption. In this paper, we will use error-correcting theory to design a palmprint cryptosystem.

When palmprints are captured, the position and direction of a palm may vary so that even palmprints from the same palm may have a little rotation and translation. Furthermore, palms differ in size. Hence palmprint images should be orientated and normalized before feature extraction and matching. In this paper, we use the preprocessing technique described in [13] to align and normalize the palmprints. After preprocessing, the central part of the image, which is 128×128, is cropped to represent the whole palmprint. Fig. 1 shows a palmprint and the normalized image.

The rest of this paper is organized as follows. Section 2 describes the feature extraction and matching. Section 3 presents the palmprint cryptosystem. Section 4 contains some experimental results and analysis. And Section 5 provides some conclusions.

2 Feature Extraction and Matching

2.1 DiffCode Extraction

Let I denote a palmprint image and G_σ denote a 2D Gaussian filter with the variance σ. The palmprint is first filtered by G_σ as below:

$$I_f = I * G_\sigma \tag{1}$$

where $*$ is the convolution operator.

Then the difference of I_f in the horizontal direction is computed as following:

$$D = I_f * b \tag{2}$$

$$b = [-1, 1] \tag{3}$$

where $*$ is the convolution operator.

Finally, the palmprint is encoded according to the sign of each pixel of D:

$$C(i,j) = \begin{cases} 1, & \text{if } D(i,j) > 0; \\ 0, & \text{otherwise.} \end{cases} \tag{4}$$

C is called DiffCode of the palmprint I. The size of the preprocessed palmprint is 128×128. Extra experiments shows that the image with 32×32 is enough for the DiffCode extraction and matching. Therefore, before compute the DiffCode, we resize the image from 128×128 to 32×32. Hence the size of the DiffCode is 32×32. Fig. 2 shows some examples of DiffCode. From this figure, the DiffCode preserves the structure information of the lines on a palm.

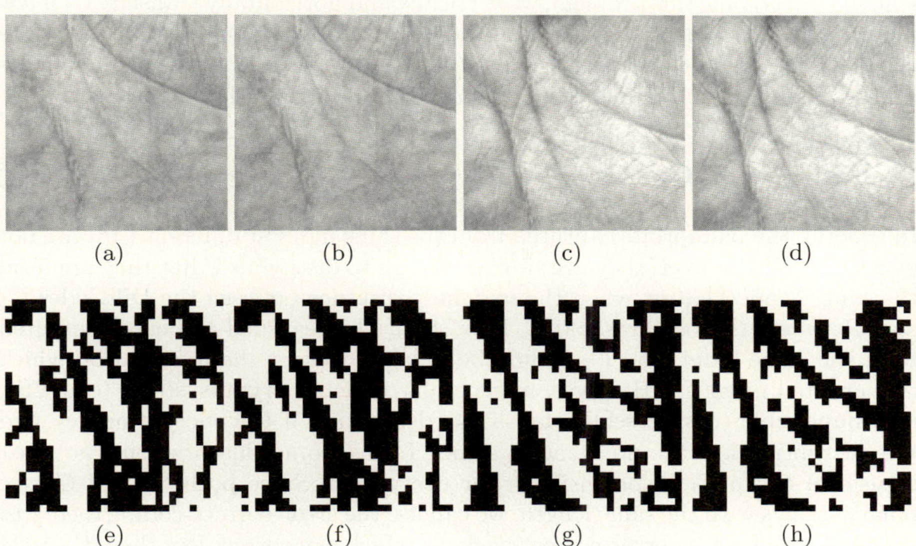

Fig. 2. Some examples of DiffCodes. (a) and (b) are two palmprint samples from a palm; (c) and (d) are two palmprint samples from another palm; (e)-(h) are the DiffCodes of (a)-(d), respectively.

2.2 Similarity Measurement of DiffCode

Because all DiffCodes have the same length, we can use Hamming distance to define their similarity. Let C_1, C_2 be two DiffCodes, their Hamming distance ($H(C_1, C_2)$) is defined as the number of the places where the corresponding values of C_1 and C_2 are different. That is,

$$H(C_1, C_2) = \sum_{i=1}^{32} \sum_{j=1}^{32} C_1(i,j) \otimes C_2(i,j) \tag{5}$$

where $\otimes$ is the logical **XOR** operation.

The matching distance of two DiffCodes C_1 and C_2 is defined as the normalized Hamming distance:

$$D(C_1, C_2) = \frac{H(C_1, C_2)}{32 \times 32} \tag{6}$$

Actually, $D(C_1, C_2)$ is the percentage of the places where C_1 and C_2 have different values. Obviously, $D(C_1, C_2)$ is between 0 and 1 and the smaller the matching distance, the greater the similarity between C_1 and C_2. The matching score of a perfect match is 0. Because of imperfect preprocessing, there may still be a little translation between the palmprints captured from the same palm at different times. To overcome this problem, we vertically and horizontally translate C_1 a few points to get the translated C_1^T , and then, at each translated position, compute the matching distance between C_1^T and C_2. Finally, the final matching distance is taken to be the minimum matching distance of all the translated positions.

3 Palmprint Cryptosystem

In general, the palmprints captured from the same hand at different time are not exactly same. However, they are similar enough to distinguish that they are from the same hand. That is, when the matching distance between the DiffCodes C_1 and C_2 is less than a threshold T, they should be regarded as being computed from the same hand, and C_2 should be able to decrypt the information which is encrypted using C_1. However, in general symmetric cryptosystems (eg.AES), it is impossible to successfully finish the decryption if the encrypting key and the decrypting key are not exactly same. To overcome this problem, we must transform C_2 to C_1 before using it for decryption. Since both C_1 and C_2 are binary strings with the same length, we can use the error-correct-coding theory to encode C_1 and get its error-correcting code, which can correct less than $T \times 1024$ errors, and then use this error-correcting code to correct C_2. If the matching distance between C_1 and C_2 is less than T, which means that C_1 and C_2 are from the same hand, C_2 can be exactly transformed to C_1 using the error-correcting code. And then the corrected C_2 can be used for decryption.

The principle of the palmprint cryptosystem is shown in Fig. 3. In the encrypting phase, the $32 \times 32 = 1024$ bits DiffCode is extracted from the palmprints. Then the DiffCode is encoded to a fix length palmprint key (HC) using a Hash function (eg. MD5), and at the same time, an error-correct-code (ECC) of the DiffCode is generated using an existed algorithm (eg. BCH). Some general encryption algorithms (eg. AES) use this palmprint key to encrypt the secret information S. In decrypting phase, the 1024 bits DiffCode extracted from the input palmprint is first corrected using the ECC. Then the corrected string is encoded to a palmprint key (HC) using the same Hash function. Finally, the corresponding general decryption algorithms use this key to decrypt theinformation (S).

To overcome the translation problem, we can get the 144×144 central part of the palmprint in the preprocessing of decryption phase, and then resize it to 36×36 to compute DiffCode. That is, in decryption phase, we get a DiffCode

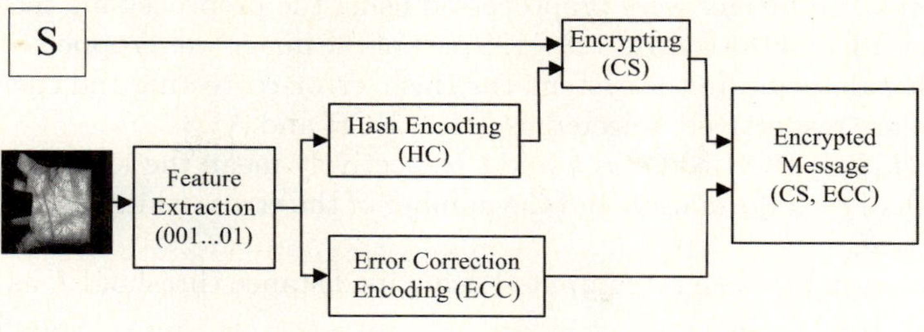

(a) Encrypting Phase

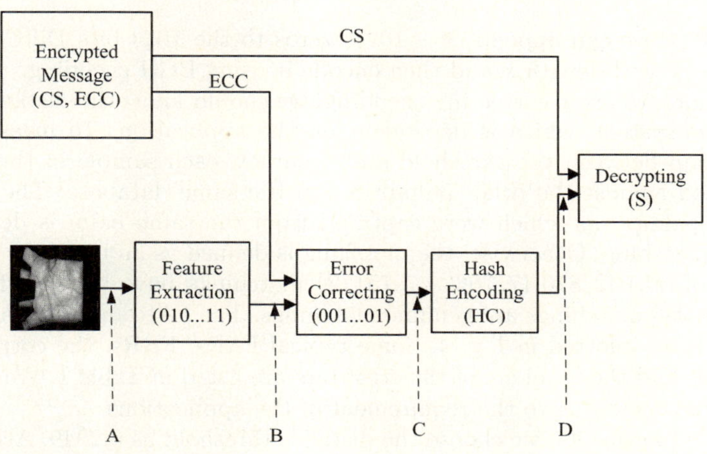

(b) Decrypting Phase

Fig. 3. Palmprint cryptosystem

with 36×36 size. From this larger DiffCode, we can get 25 DiffCodes with 32×32, which are used one by one for decryption until success. This process is equivalent to the translation the DiffCode vertically and horizontally from -2 to $+2$ points.

4 Experimental Results and Analysis

We employed the PolyU Palmprint Database [15] to test our system. This database contains 7,752 grayscale images captured from 386 different palms by a CCD-based device. These palmprints were taken from people of different ages and both sexes and were captured twice, at an interval of around two months, each time taking about 10 images from each palm. Therefore, This database contains about 20 images of each palm. The size of the images in the database is 384×284. In our experiments, all images were preprocessed using the preprocessing technique described in [13] and the central 128×128 part of the image was cropped to represent the whole palmprint. In the system, the Hash, error-correcting and encrypting algorithms are respectively selected as MD5, BCH and AES.

For a (n, k, t) BCH code, n, k and t respectively mean the length of the code, the length of the information and the number of the errors which can be corrected by this code.

For our system, t can be computed using its distance threshold T as following:

$$t = 1024 \times T. \tag{7}$$

And k should satisfy the following conditions:

$$k \geqslant 1024 \tag{8}$$

If $k > 1024$, we can append $(k - 1024)$ zeros to the 1024 bits DiffCode to get the message with length k and then encode it using BCH encoding.

Therefore, to error-correcting encoding, we should know the distance threshold of the system, which is dependent on the application. To investigate the relationship between the threshold and accuracy, each sample in the database is matched against the other palmprints in the same database. The matching between palmprints which were captured from the same palm is defined as a genuine matching. Otherwise, the matching is defined as an impostor matching. A total of $30,042,876$ $(7,752 \times 7,751/2)$ matchings have been performed, in which $74,086$ matchings are genuine matchings. The FAR and FRR at different thresholds are plotted in Fig. 4. Some typical FARs, FRRs, the corresponding thresholds and the numbers of the error bits are listed in Table 1. We can select a threshold according to the requirement of the applications.

In our experiments, we choose the distance threshold as 0.2949. According to Table 1, the corresponding FAR, FRR and the number of errors which should be corrected are 0.0012% , 3.0169%, and 302. According to the theory of BCH error-correcting-code, $(4095, 1412, 302)$ BCH code can be used in our system. Now we analyze the attacks to this system.

If the attack happens at Point A (See Fig. 3), that is, the attacker uses some palmprints to attack the system. In this case, the possibility to successfully decrypt the message is about $0.0012\% \approx 10^{-5}$, which means that to decrypt the message, a cracker has to find about 10^5 different palmprints to try, which is very difficult to get so many palmprints in a short time.

If the attack happens at Point B (See Fig. 3), that is, the cracker attacks the system by directly generating the DiffCode for the error-correcting. The possibility to successfully decrypt the message in this way is p:

$$p = \frac{C_{1024}^{302} + C_{1024}^{301} + \cdots + C_{1024}^{1} + C_{1024}^{0}}{2^{1024}} \approx 2^{-134} \tag{9}$$

If the attack happens at Point C (See Fig. 3), that is, the cracker generates the corrected DiffCode to attack the system, the possibility to success is 2^{-1024}.

If the attack happens at Point D (See Fig. 3), that is, the cracker generates the hashed code to attack the system, the possibility to success is 2^{-128}.

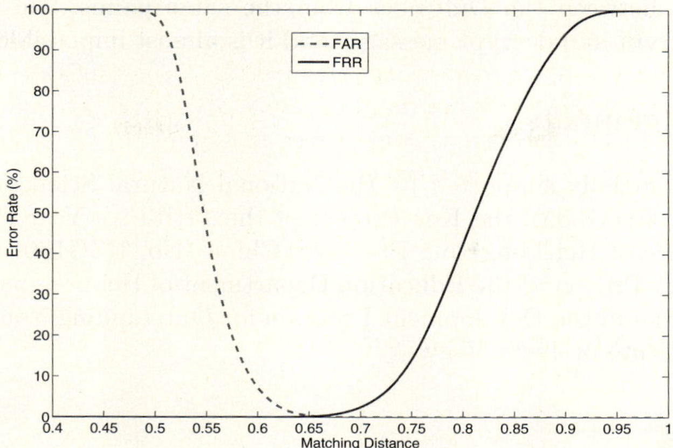

Fig. 4. The FAR and FRR at Different Threshold

Table 1. Typical FAR, FRR, corespoding thresholds and number of error bits

Threshold	Number of Error Bits	FAR (%)	FRR (%)
0.3799	389	2.6862	0.0240
0.3750	384	2.0133	0.0283
0.3701	379	1.4784	0.0382
0.3652	374	1.0976	0.0523
0.3604	369	0.7799	0.0764
0.3555	364	0.5458	0.1018
0.3496	358	0.3786	0.1386
0.3447	353	0.2558	0.2150
0.3398	348	0.1663	0.2899
0.3350	343	0.1092	0.3791
0.3301	338	0.0663	0.4964
0.3252	333	0.0399	0.6973
0.3203	328	0.0238	0.9038
0.3154	323	0.0135	1.2277
0.3096	317	0.0075	1.5445
0.3047	312	0.0042	1.9533
0.2998	307	0.0022	2.4370
0.2949	302	0.0012	3.0169
0.2900	297	0.0006	3.6788
0.2852	292	0.0003	4.4751

5 Conclusions

This paper proposed a almprint cryptosystem. This system extracted binary DiffCode feature from palmprint and used the error-correcting theory to remove the difference between the DiffCodes from the same palms. The system can effectively encrypt and decrypt messages and it is almost impossible to crack it.

Acknowledgements

This work is partially supported by the National Natural Science Foundation of China (No. 60441005), the Key-Project of the 11th-Five-Year Plan of Educational Science of Hei Longjiang Province, China (No. HZG160), the Science and Technology Project of the Education Department of Hei Longjiang Province (No. 11523026) and the Development Program for Outstanding Young Teachers in Harbin Institute of Technology.

References

1. Uludag, U., Pankant, S., Prabhakar, S., Jain, A.K.: Biometric cryptosystems: issues and challenges. Proceedings of the IEEE 92, 948–960 (2004)
2. Freire-Santos, M., Fierrez-Aguilar, J., Ortega-Garcia, J.: Cryptographic key generation using handwritten signature. In: Proc. of SPIE, Biometric Technologies for Human Identificatin III (2006)
3. Uludag, U., Pankant, S., Jain, A.K.: Fuzzy vault for fingerprints. In: Kanade, T., Jain, A., Ratha, N.K. (eds.) AVBPA 2005. LNCS, vol. 3546, pp. 310–319. Springer, Heidelberg (2005)
4. Monrose, F., Reiter, M.K., Li, Q., Wetzel, S.: Using voice to generate cryptographic keys. In: A Speaker Odyssey, The Speaker Recognition Workshop, pp. 202–213 (2001)
5. Juels, A., Sudan, M.: A fuzzy vault scheme. In: Proc. IEEE International Symposium on Information Theory, IEEE Computer Society Press, Los Alamitos (2002)
6. Soutar, C., Roberge, D., Stojanov, S.A., Gilroy, R., Kumar, B.V.K.V.: Biometric encryption. ICSA Guide to Cryptography (1999)
7. Monrose, F., Reiter, M.K., Li, Q., Lopresti, D.P., Shih, C.: Towards speech-generated cryptographic keys on resource constrained devices. In: Proc. 11th USENIX Security Symposium, pp. 283–296 (2002)
8. Zhang, D.: Palmprint Authentication. Kluwer Academic Publishers, Dordrecht (2004)
9. Wu, X., Zhang, D., Wang, K.: Palmprint Recognition. Scientific Publishers, China (2006)
10. Wu, X., Wang, K., Zhang, D.: Fisherpalms based palmprint recognition. Pattern Recognition Letters 24, 2829–2838 (2003)
11. Duta, N., Jain, A., Mardia, K.: Matching of palmprint. Pattern Recognition Letters 23, 477–485 (2001)
12. Han, C., Chen, H., Lin, C., Fan, K.: Personal authentication using palm-print features. Pattern Recognition 36, 371–381 (2003)
13. Zhang, D., Kong, W., You, J., Wong, M.: Online palmprint identification. IEEE Transactions on Pattern Analysis and Machine Intelligence 25, 1041–1050 (2003)
14. Jain, A., Ross, A., Prabhakar, S.: An introduction to biometric recognition. IEEE Transactions on Circuits and Systems for Video Technology 14, 4–20 (2004)
15. PolyU Palmprint Palmprint Database (http://www.comp.polyu.edu.hk/~biometrics/)

On Some Performance Indices for Biometric Identification System

Jay Bhatnagar and Ajay Kumar

Biometrics Research Laboratory
Department of Electrical Engineering
Indian Institute of Technology Delhi, New Delhi, India
jbhatnagar@ee.iitd.ac.in, ajaykr@ieee.org

Abstract. This paper investigates a new approach to formulate performance indices of biometric system using information theoretic models. The performance indices proposed here (unlike conventionally used FAR, GAR, DET etc.) are scalable in estimating performance of large scale biometric system. This work proposes a framework for identification capacity of a biometric system, along with insights on number of cohort users, capacity enhancements from user specific statistics etc. While incorporating feature level information in a rate-distortion framework, we derive condition for optimal feature representation. Furthermore, employing entropy measures to distance (hamming) distribution of the encoded templates, this paper proposes an upper bound for false random correspondence probability. Our analysis concludes that capacity can be the performance index of a biometric system while individuality expressed in false random correspondence can be the performance index of the biometric trait and representation. This paper also derives these indices and quantifies them from system parameters.

Keywords: Identification capacity, Joint source-channel coding, Individuality, FRC (false random correspondence probability).

1 Introduction

There has been significant interest in large scale applications of biometrics for secure personal authentication. Proposing scalable performance indices for large scale identification systems using biometrics is a challenging problem in biometrics research. The challenge lies in devising indices and evolving their interdependence to convey security, accuracy, privacy and such other measurable characteristics of biometric systems. Authors in [1] discuss system specific indices such as FAR, FRR, GAR, ROC etc. as measures for the imperfect accuracy in relation to signal capacity and representation limitations. However, error rates are performance indices that are dependent on choice of: threshold, user at that threshold. Further, error rates are computed by integrating region from known distributions (genuine and imposter). It will be computationally efficient (for reasons of scalability) to develop average performance measure of biometric identification system. If such a measure can be computed incorporating constrained statistical information instead of complete distributions, then it leads to efficient tools in proposing performance models [2].

S.-W. Lee and S.Z. Li (Eds.): ICB 2007, LNCS 4642, pp. 1043–1056, 2007.

Information conveyed in biometric is considered to be inherent part of individuality of a person, and a natural code generated from user specific characteristics – physiological or behavioral. A population of user biometric templates which is uniquely indexed (uniqueness) and maximally separable (distinctiveness) is desirable for reliable identification, however this may not guarantee security [1]. It is well known that in practical applications, user biometric data does not provide error free (perfect) identification. Loss of uniqueness and distinctiveness can be attributed to: (1) statistical variations in biometric data of a user (in-class) and, (2) statistical variations in the biometric data after inter-user comparisons. Authors of [3] allude the need to model information content (statistical measure) of biometric template in relation to the number of users that can be reliably identified. In the same work [3], the above reference to information content is stated as template capacity or inherent signal capacity (and individuality) of a biometric. Authors in [4] use Kullback-Leibler` divergence or the relative entropy $D(p \parallel u)$ between (p) population distribution and (u) user distribution per feature to model uniqueness and individuality for face biometric. The approach of [4] demonstrates one of the few important distance measures from information theory perspective. Capacity and error rates have been widely known in information theory literature [2]. For the framework proposed here, Capacity represents: how many users on average can be reliably recognized by the identification system, for a given data base and noise model. Restated, capacity ties the decision accuracy in terms of number of users to database quality and system noise. Similarly, individuality sets a limit to identification capacity in absence of noise (in-class).

The key contributions of this paper can be summarized as follows:

(i) Formulate and quantify capacity of a biometric identification system (section 3)
(ii) Estimate the average number of cohort users from the capacity derived in (i)
(iii) Derive false random correspondence probability with optimality for feature representation (section 4)

Biometric signals of our interest could be at feature level or score level (class genuine and imposter). Several reasons motivate the choice of matching score and feature template, respectively, in the proposed analysis of capacity and individuality. Due to higher dimensionality, it is computationally difficult to extract accurate cross-user information (inter-class statistics) at feature level; though the same can be tractable using matching scores. Also, with number of users tending to infinity (in the asymptote), the i.i.d. (independent identically distributed) assumption for feature vectors is weakened due to correlation present in multiple biometric acquisitions. Traditionally, signal received at the channel output is used for making decision in communication system [2]. Analogously, for biometric system it is matching score which represents the signal space used for decision making and not the query template itself. Therefore, in the framework for capacity of biometric system it is proposed to employ statistics from matching scores. Uniqueness and distinctiveness are statistical properties of biometric feature template and the feature representation, which together define individuality in this work. Hence, discussion on individuality (section 4) entails feature level information.[1]

[1] Information: refers Shannon measure for statistical information, expressed in terms of entropy [2].

2 Motivation: Review of Noisy Source-Channel Model

In the basic information model given by Shannon [5], i.i.d (independent identically distributed) symbols S from source with self information or entropy given by $H(S)$ are transmitted on a memoryless additive white Gaussian noise channel given by N. Information theorems define maximum and minimum bounds on information rates for achievable reliability and fidelity, respectively [2]. Reliability (capacity) gives an average measure of erroneous decisions due to noisy observations made over an unreliable channel. Reliability measures the accuracy in identifying source constrained by the channel noise. Fidelity, gives an average measure of error in representation of the biometric source. The information theorems on source coding and information capacity cover these concepts [2]. A generalized form of information theorems is the joint source-channel coding theorem [6], which marks need for a combined source-channel model. This result states that a loss in signal-to-noise ratio (alternately, loss of discernability) at the source coder has an equivalent measure in loss of channel reliability (increase in bit error rate of the channel), also known as the source-channel separation principle. The separation principle provides us with a framework to decompose class genuine (also, class imposter) separately as source statistics and noise statistics, which otherwise may be perceived only as source distribution. We now formulate capacity of biometric identification system. **Biometric system capacity:** is the maximum information (max. number of users) per use of the noisy identification channel (in-class, inter-class variations) that can be guaranteed near zero error rate for identification. **Capacity** (pattern recognition context)**:** The term capacity is measured as the maximum average mutual information on observation space of all measurable patterns X containing k, which maximizes the occurrence of a pattern of class k given the distribution of k. Average mutual information gives an average measure of statistics for optimal decision rule (maximum likelihood) [2].

$$C =: \max \overline{I}(S;X), \forall p(S). \quad (1)$$

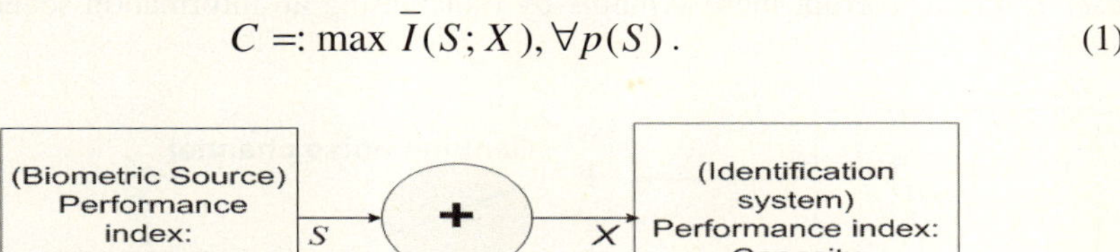

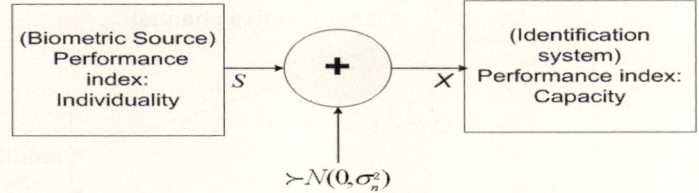

Fig. 1. Schematic of Biometric systems as identification channel

The linear channel model shown in above figure assumes Gaussian noise $N \succ (0, \sigma_N^2)$ and desired signal modeled with statistics $S \succ (0, \overline{S_G})$. The resulting expression for capacity can be shown [2] as given by:

$$\overline{C} = \frac{1}{2}\log_2\left(1 + \frac{\overline{S_G}}{\sigma_N^2}\right). \quad (2)$$

The main reasons that influence choice of Gaussian are [4]: (a) Closed form expression is analytically tractable, (b) Tends to be a good reflection of real world distributions, and (c) Has the highest entropy for given variance and is useful in estimating bounds. In this paper *variance* has been used interchangeably for *statistics*. In context of the proposed approach signal statistics will cover all desired information or signals of interest for identification. Similarly, noise statistics will capture the mechanisms that restrict reliable identification.

3 A New Framework for Capacity

In this section we combine tools discussed so far to develop a model for estimating capacity of the biometric system. From a signal theory perspective [7], *M* registered users are required to be represented by an *M*-ary signal probability space. However, measures on the signal space of matching scores can be uniquely defined for a single user. A challenging problem in formulating capacity with score level information for *M*-users is that different users registered in the biometric system have different sample spaces (or class distributions) and a unique probability space cannot apparently be defined. The following model removes this shortcoming and facilitates use of score level signals to formulate a new framework for biometric system capacity.

Figure 2 depicts a model for estimating identification capacity. Let $\{\hat{g}_m\}$ & $\{\hat{i}_m\}$ denote the median scores taken from genuine and imposter distributions for user $m \in M$; for which the respective distributions peak. Let *A* be the *desired user* transmitting information sequence $\{\hat{g}_m\}$ and let *B* be the *interfering user* trying to corrupt these symbols by transmitting an information sequence $\{\hat{i}_m\}$.

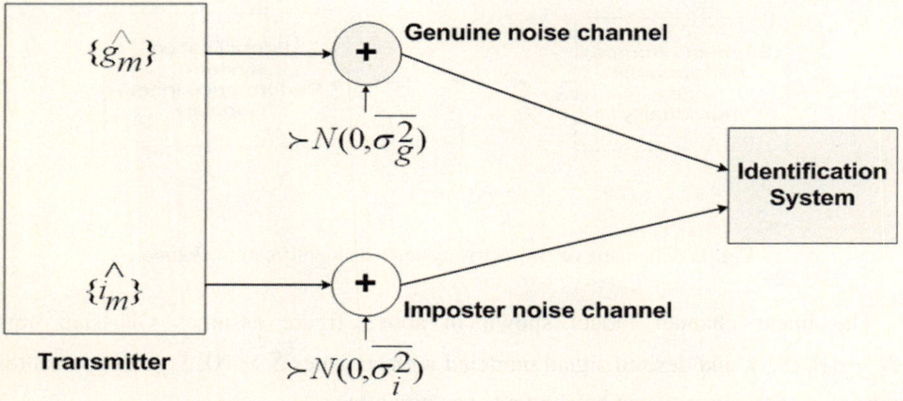

Fig. 2. A two channel biometric identification system

Thus for each transmitted genuine signal from $\{\hat{g}_m\}$ in the indexing order *m*, *B* transmits an interference symbol by transmitting the same indexed imposter signal from $\{\hat{i}_m\}$. Further, information symbols $\{\hat{g}_m\}$ and $\{\hat{i}_m\}$ are subject to random spreading given by additive white Gaussian channels. The spreading for *A* is from a genuine Gaussian channel $\succ N(0,\sigma^2_{g(m)})$ and that for *B* is from imposter Gaussian channel $\succ N(0,\sigma^2_{i(m)})$ .Variances given by $\overline{\sigma^2_g}, \overline{\sigma^2_i}$ respectively are averages for genuine and imposters from all enrolled users *M*. (Figure 2) and denote the average trend to model the biometric system[2] noise. This almost completes formulating the model for *M*-ary hypotheses on a single probability space [8]. The resulting model looks Neyman-Pearson type used in jamming/intrusion systems, with target *A* and interferer *B*. Figure 3 is simplified form of Figure 2 incorporating a the worst case additive noise $\succ N(0,\overline{\sigma^2_i})$ for both sets of information sequences. Figure 4 illustrates a useful statistical distance measure between $\{\hat{g}_m\} = s_1$ and $\{\hat{i}_m\} = s_2$ given by d_m. Discernability (decidability index) improves with increase in d_m. As observed in Figure 3, the transmitter is a 2-ary or binary hypothesis transmitter for *M* signal pairs that are randomly spaced, since d_m is a random variable. The resulting average signal energy for randomly chosen signal pair can be given: $(s_1^2 + s_2^2)/2 \cong 2.5d_m^2$, on the assumption that $s_1 \cong d_m$. The average for *M*-ary set of signal pairs can be given as $2.5\overline{d_m^2}$.

This completes formulating the model for biometric identification channel. Therefore, the signal to noise ratio as required in (2) can be expressed as:

$$\frac{\overline{S_G}}{\sigma_N^2} = \frac{2.5\overline{d^2}}{\max(\overline{\sigma_g^2}, \overline{\sigma_i^2})} \quad . \tag{3}$$

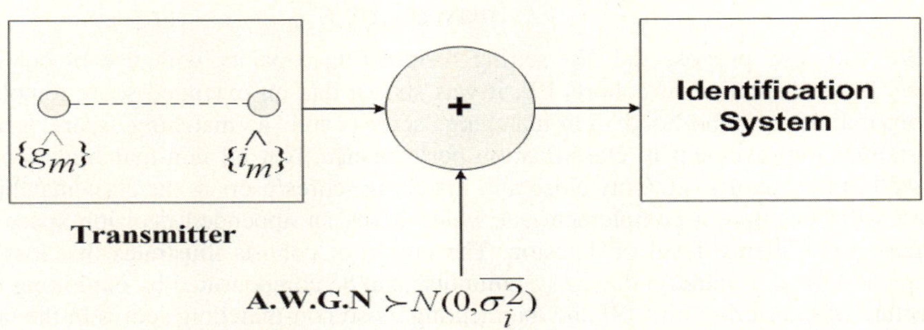

Fig. 3. A Generalized model for biometric identification system with random coding

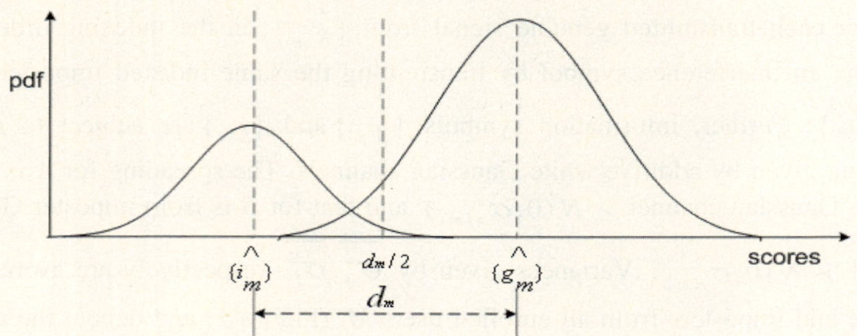

Fig. 4. Statistical distance measures and distributions for user *m*

The achievable rate *R* of identification channel can be given using (2):

$$C_1 = \frac{1}{2}\log_2[1+\frac{2.5\overline{d^2}}{\max(\overline{\sigma_g^2},\overline{\sigma_i^2})}]. \tag{4}$$

For model variations to incorporate new information/statistics (independent to & additional of existing signal statistics) and its effect on capacity, variance of new statistics can be added in the numerator of the log argument in (4), similarly any additions to noisy statistics can be accounted in the denominator. One such example is that of capacity improvement from incorporating quality indices at score level. If we apply the fact that the median (peak) genuine scores are different for different users, then the variability of the peaking of matching score from different users, offers a user-specific measure to improve classification performance [9]. Performance improvement using this signal statistics can be given by extracting the variance of the peaks of genuine scores from all *M* users, denoted as $\hat{\sigma}_g^2$. Then under revised frame work new system capacity can be given by:

$$C_2 = \frac{1}{2}\log_2[1+\frac{\hat{\sigma}_g^2 + 2.5\overline{d^2}}{\max(\overline{\sigma_g^2},\overline{\sigma_i^2})}]. \tag{5}$$

We will now propose the last setting formulating capacity with use of cohorts *score*. In the inception of cohorts [9], it was shown that an extended score template incorporating neighborhood non-matching scores and a matching score gives substantial improvement in classification performance. Not all non-matching scores do well in the cohorts set. Only close non-matching scores/users to the class matching score will constitute a complement set which gives an appended decision space or increased confidence level of decision. The notion of cohorts illustrates that loss of uniqueness (and, accuracy) due to system noise can be compensated by exploiting the structure of interfering bins [9] and augmenting close non-matching scores in the new decision space. It is proposed to employ one possible selection of cohorts using 3σ bound. 3σ rule is a loose probability bound in Markov sense [8], in that it includes all scores lying within 33 % probability about the mean/median genuine score. Markov inequality is a weak approximation as it gives the loosest bound in estimating the spread of a random variable about its median. The rule of 3σ will select $\pm\sigma,\pm 2\sigma,\pm 3\sigma$ points about the peak matching (genuine) score for each user to estimate cohorts. Also towards the tails of the class genuine distribution, a non-matching score may not give accurate information on the class/ class neighbors. Denote the average of such M-variances as $\overline{\sigma_c}^2$.

$$C_3 = \frac{1}{2}\log_2[1 + \frac{\overline{\sigma_c^2} + \hat{\sigma}_g^2 + 2.5\overline{d^2}}{\max(\overline{\sigma_g^2}, \overline{\sigma_i^2})}]. \tag{6}$$

From the definition of identification capacity the number of users (χ) that can be identified reliably.

$$\chi = CM. \tag{7}$$

If, $C \in [0,1]$, then $1-\overline{C} = C \in [0,1]$. This gives the complement set $\overline{C}$, of the maximum average unreliability of the identification channel. In terms of average number of close/unreliable users, it can be formulated that;

$$N = \overline{C}M, N \le M. \tag{8}$$

For a fixed number of users M, greater the value of C, smaller is the useful cohort set given by (8). This is particularly the case with highly individual biometrics. For highly individual biometrics, C is expected to be closer to 1 than 0.5 (also, validated by results for capacity in section 5). However, the actual number of (useful) close cohorts for users varies with user. A variation of (4) as given below can provide per user capacity. The user specific cohort requirement can be obtained as follows:

$$C_m = \frac{1}{2}\log_2[1 + \frac{2.5d_m^2}{\max(\sigma_{g(m)}^2, \sigma_{i(m)}^2)}]. \tag{9}$$

Similarly, extrema of identification capacity for biometric system can be proposed to give peak capacity and minimum capacity based on the following expressions obtained from system parameters.

$$(\frac{\overline{S_G}}{\sigma_N^2})_{\max} = (\frac{2.5d_m^2}{\max(\sigma_{g(m)}^2, \sigma_{i(m)}^2)})_{\max}, \quad (\frac{\overline{S_G}}{\sigma_N^2})_{\min} = (\frac{2.5d_m^2}{\max(\sigma_{g(m)}^2, \sigma_{i(m)}^2)})_{\min} \tag{10}$$

4 Individuality and False Random Correspondence Probability

In biometrics literature, the individuality is related to and expressed in terms of probability of false random correspondence [10]. The prototype proposed in [10] for random correspondence of fingerprint defines a tolerance area which actually is tolerable distortion measure, as we introduce later in this section. Random correspondence was introduced in [10] as the limiting error rate arising from intra class variability given noisy versions of a user template. Infact, intra class variability contains some measure of random correspondence along with system noise. For a really noisy biometric system, attributing intra class variability to random correspondence may be quite inaccurate. **Individuality:** As minimum information computed on population statistics comprising of templates from all users (one per user), subject to hamming distortion given by δ. **FRC (false random correspondence):** Probability that two different user templates are δ similar, for which the rate distortion and distortion rate exist and are equivalent.

In documenting iris as a highly individual biometric, Daugman [11] used variability measures at feature level characterized for Gabor features. However, after [11] not much work on random correspondence in the literature employed entropy or entropy rate (rate distortion theory). A plausible explanation for the above could be that the Daugman's approach in [11] used an exhaustive database on which probability measures and variability were shown to fit a binomial distribution for normalized hamming distances (scores) owing to encoding scheme from the Gabor features. Thus [11] illustrated an empirical model for uniqueness of iris which was an accurate asymptote for population statistics. We point here that encoding refers to feature representation method and its binarization. Author in [11] showed that encoding iris based on Iris code of Gabor features gives code with binomial distribution (independent realizations of many Bernoulli) with peak at 0.5 which signifies maximum source entropy code for the binomial family. By encoding variations based on hamming distance, source coding used in [11] applies a hamming distortion metric to locally source code partitions of the template along a trajectory in the iris. This condition also provides a maximally spaced code book as entropy of hamming distance (which is binomial distributed) peaks at 0.5 for best uniqueness, a clairvoyant choice in favor of the Gabor representation. It is therefore good to infer that uniqueness/individuality is dependent on the choice for representation of feature statistics. Applying rate-distortion concepts [12] it is proposed that approach employed in [11] and the approach in [10] are two related manifestations of a more general approach. Furthermore, it is analytically difficult to accurately evolve parametric models for larger number of features and/or larger population that can be generalized for all biometrics [12]. In this section the rate-distortion frame work will be revived to propose that: 1) individuality is a property of the source that can be measured in representation statistics (source coding features) given some minimum distortion, 2) individuality is related to false random correspondence probability for a distortion constraint δ. The purpose is to seek the minimum information rate for an average distortion constraint or the average information rate for minimum distortion (both are equivalent approaches in giving optimal source representation [12]).For a choice of representation method (PCA, LDA, Gabor etc.) and given a distortion constraint, smaller the rate-distortion more efficient is the representation technique. In that sense, rate-distortion is a direct measure of individuality. We propose to use a minimum limiting distortion to generate a source code book and study the distance distribution on this code book to formulate false random correspondence. This approach is rationally similar to that discussed in [2]. The following corollary is useful in providing the analytical basis to false random correspondence based on distance measures.

Corollary 1. Given a source code book $\hat{F}$ that lies in the rate-distortion region for avg. minimum distortion $\overline{D}$, If the distribution of hamming metric defined on source code book $\hat{F}$ denoted by $\{d_i\}, \forall i \in I \geq KM$ follows a binomial distribution with probability = 0.5, then minimum of achievable rate condition is implied.

Proof: We use result proved as bound for rate-distortion in **appendix A**

$$I(f_k;\hat{f}_k) \geq h(f_k) - h(f_k - \hat{f}_k). \tag{11}$$

$$I(f_k;\hat{f}_k) \geq \frac{1}{2}\log_e(2\pi e)\sigma_k^2 - h(f_k - \hat{f}_k). \tag{12}$$

We use the following inequality for any source coding model [14]

$$h(f_k) \geq h(\hat{f}_k) \approx h(d_k) \geq h(f_k - \hat{f}_k) . \tag{13}$$

$h(d_k)$, denotes the entropy of hamming distance distribution, hamming distance computed between code vectors for feature $k \in K$ .The variability/uncertainty in d_k denotes average hamming distortion, for equivalent to variance of f_k. $h(d_k) \geq h(f_k - \hat{f}_k)$ is important to tighten the inequality further in (12).

Also, for *k* independent observations (appendix B).

$$\sum_{\forall k \in K} I(f_k;\hat{f}_k) \geq \sum_{\forall k \in K} \frac{1}{2}\log_e(2\pi e)\sigma_k^2 - h(d_k) = R(\overline{D}) \tag{14}$$

Given $d_k \in (0,1,....,N)$ is a discrete random variable, $\{d_k\}$ gives independent realizations of *K* random variables for *K* different features.

We define, $d_i = \sum_{\forall k \in K} d_k ; i \in I$. This gives realizations from independent *K* partitions and hence independent random variables. (14) shows addition of hamming metrics from *K* partitions (features) of *M*-templates to give the hamming distance distribution for $\hat{F}$. We characterize the independence of hamming metrics { d_i } by binomial distribution parameterized by $\succ (p, I)$ [8]. Minimization of (14) is possible if entropy $h(d_i) = \sum_{k \in K} h^{(m)}(d_k)$ is maximum, entropy for binomial $\succ (p, I)$ maximizes for p = 0.5, proving the corollary. (Indexing by *m* denotes a template-*m* which can have a maximum *I* as hamming metric in distance computations across the *M* template population). Therefore, a minimum rate achievability using (14) can also be viewed as the condition for accurately transferring uniqueness from source statistics onto the space of representation statistics, given the distortion constraint. Conversely, a source representation for which the above condition is achieved with equality gives optimal rate-distortion. As a simple illustration, we cite the Iris code and its optimality in capturing uniqueness of iris biometric using a Gabor representation [11].

The corollary with propositions presented in this section help in formulating the false random correspondence probability of a biometric. If, we approximate $H(F) \cong H(\hat{F}) = h(d)$ Since, $h(d) \geq H(\overline{D})$, Define, $d_i \leq \delta; \delta > 0$; where δ denotes tolerable hamming distortion which is binary hamming metric for tolerable distortion given by $\overline{D}$.The tolerable hamming threshold given by δ corresponds to conditional entropy given by $h(d / d \leq \delta)$. An exponent of conditional entropy to base 2 gives the average total number of sequences that lie within a hamming distance of δ. This gives an analytical expression for the average false random correspondence probability as:

$$P\,(\text{false correspondence}) = \frac{2^{h(d/d \leq \delta)}}{2^{h(d)}}. \tag{15}$$

Clearly, from (15), increase in δ reflects greater distortion, thereby increasing the numerator with conditional entropy in the exponent. This results in a higher false correspondence. The basic form of entropy function will depend on the *choice* of feature representation. Thus, uniqueness is dependent on the choice of feature representation. An interesting observation from this section is in noting that (15) is the zero noise reliability of the biometric system. Thus, (15) defines a minimum (best) error rate of noiseless biometric system, for a target population.

5 Experiments

In order to estimate the capacity formulated in section 3, we perform experiments on real biometric samples. Hand images of 100 users (10 images of each user) employed in [13] were used to simultaneously extract palmprint and hand geometry features. The feature extraction for each of the modalities is same as detailed in [13]. Class genuine and imposter score distributions, using Euclidean distance, were generated to extract the following parameters: $\overline{\sigma_i^2}$, $\overline{d^2}$, $\overline{\sigma_g^2}$, $\hat{\sigma}_g^2$ and $\overline{\sigma_c^2}$. Table-1 as given below shows system parameters.

Some significant insights can be acquired from Table 2 which shows capacity and number of cohort users based on formulae (6), (7), (8) and (9). Capacity increase from incorporating user specific statistics and cohorts is about twice the capacity prior to the additional statistics, this explains improved identification performance of the biometric system as a result of incorporating additional information gains. Clearly,

Table 1. System parameters from the experiments

Biometric Modality	$\overline{\sigma_g^2}$	$\overline{\sigma_i^2}$	$\overline{d^2}$	$\hat{\sigma}_g^2$	$\overline{\sigma_c^2}$
Palmprint	1.5e+4	6.3e+4	2.2e+4	1.4e+4	3.5e+4
Hand geometry	2.988	7.652	1.295	0.893	2.55

Table 2. System capacity and required number of cohorts

Biometric Modality	C_1	C_2	C_3	N_1	N_2
Palmprint	0.45	0.53	0.7	55	47
Hand geometry	0.25	0.31	0.45	75	69

palmprint gives a superior identification performance, based on measurements for the database. The difference in identification capacity between palmprint and hand geometry remains approximately the same for every additional statistic. N_1 is smaller than N_2, and indicates the number of cohorts users for two distinct cases when (1) raw capacity, (2) capacity with user specific statistics.

6 Conclusions

This paper formulates a new frame work for performance indices of biometric identification system. Section 3 proposed system level performance index namely the identification capacity. It was also illustrated in section 3, that boosting capacity is possible using extra information/ variability from statistics such as user quality, and cohorts. Capacity is useful to compare noisy performance at systems level and hence can be considered as a local performance index. Exp0erimental results in section 5 gave real values to capacity for the input statistics and inference on number of cohort users. Section 4 formulates a generalized approach for false random correspondence (and, individuality) using rate-distortion and hamming distortion measure. Individuality is a global performance index, in that it gives the upper limit to performance of the biometric trait for a noiseless biometric system. It is also important to point here that information theoretic approach relies mainly on statistical averages; hence performance indices such as capacity & false random correspondence indicate average trends.

Several open problems spring from this analysis, the most natural is in asking how capacity can be related to a minimum test sample size and training sample size to guarantee a stable ROC, since both capacity & reliability are system performance indices like ROC. Study of individuality is apparently closer to the theory of evolution than information theory. Our future work will consider extending the current analysis to other biometric traits such as fingerprint, iris, face, and gait and study the resulting performance measures from experimental work. A more challenging problem will be to evolve performance indices for multi biometric system that employ various types of fusion principles.

Acknowledgement

This work is partially supported by the research grant from Ministry of Information and Communication Technology, Government of India, grant no. 12(54)/2006-ESD.

References

1. Jain, A.K., Pankanti, S., Prabhakar, S., Hong, L., Ross, A., Wayman, J.L.: Biometrics: A Grand Challenge. In: Proc. ICPR, UK, vol. II, pp. 935–942 (2004)
2. Gallager, R G.: Information Theory and Reliable Communication. John Wiley, Chichester (1968)
3. Jain, A.K., Ross, A., Pankanti, S.: Biometrics: A Tool for Information Security. IEEE Trans. Information Forensics and Security 1(2), 125–143 (2006)
4. Adler, A., Youmaran, R., Loyka, S.: Towards a Measure of Biometric Information (February 2006), http://www.sce.carleton.ca/faculty/adler//publications
5. Slepian, D.: Key Papers in the Development of Information Theory. IEEE Press, New York (1974)
6. Vembu, S., Verdú, S., Steinberg, Y.: The Source-Channel Separation Theorem Revisited. IEEE Trans. Information Theory 41(1), 44–54 (1995)
7. Simon, M., Hinedi, S., Lindsey, W.: Digital communication Techniques: Signal Design and Detection. Prentice-Hall, NJ (1995)
8. Feller, W.: An Introduction to Probability Theory and Applications. John Wiley & Sons, Chichester (1971)
9. Aggarwal, G., Ratha, N., Bolle, R.M.: Biometric Verification: Looking Beyond Raw Similarity Scores. In: Workshop on Biometrics (CVPR), New York, pp. 31–36 (2006)
10. Pankanti, S., Prabhakar, S., Jain, A.K.: On the Individuality of Fingerprints. IEEE Trans. PAMI 24(8), 1010–1025 (2002)
11. Daugman, J.: Probing the uniqueness and randomness of Iris Codes: Results from 200 billion iris pair comparisons. Proc. of the IEEE 94(11), 1927–1935 (2006)
12. Cover, T M., Thomas, J A.: Elements of Information Theory. John Wiley & Sons, Chichester (1991)
13. Kumar, A., Zhang, D.: Feature selection and combination in biometrics. In: Kanade, T., Jain, A., Ratha, N.K. (eds.) AVBPA 2005. LNCS, vol. 3546, pp. 813–822. Springer, Heidelberg (2005)

Appendix A

Definitions:

$R(\overline{D})$: Rate distortion function is the infinum of achievable rates *R,* such that $R(\overline{D})$ is in the rate-distortion region of the source (*K*-feature statistics for all *M* users) for the corresponding distortion constraint $\overline{D}$.

We rephrase the need of Gaussian assumption to source coding (based on estimation theory) - For Gaussian distribution under mean sq. error, the conditional mean of { $\hat{f}$ } is optimal estimator of source { f }; $f \in F, \hat{f} \in \hat{F}$. Furthermore, mean square distortion $\overline{D}$ as the distortion measure in Gaussian frame work is adopted for following reasons:1) generally useful for image information, 2) gives the minimum rate for representation error(tightened by the fact that rate at min. distortion is equivalent to distortion at min. rate), which is required in formulating individuality. Though the population statistics for *F* need not actually be Gaussian, we employ Normal approximation to *M*-user statistics to deduce the achievable worse case lower bound for rate-distortion $R(\overline{D})$.

Problem: To formulate rate distortion $R(\overline{D})$ in source coding Feature statistics of *K*-different features per template, for *M* user population, approx. by Gaussian (for large number of users); and for avg. distortion measure given by $\overline{D} \geq E\left|F - \hat{F}_k\right|^2 ; k \in K$

Hence, to show that:

$$R(\overline{D}) = \min \sum_{k=1}^{K} \frac{1}{2} \log_e \frac{\sigma_k^2}{D_k} ; \sum_{\forall k \in K} D_k = \overline{D}$$

Solution:

Let the *K*- different features per template be i.i.d (For non-i.i.d we subtract a template self-covariance from σ_k^2 , in the numerator of the result to prove). Idea is to source code each $k \in K$ features and then concatenate the *K* code blocks to generate the template code. We prove the stated result for $k = 1$, which can be easily generalized under uncorrelated ness to $k = K$.

$$I(f_k; \hat{f}_k) = h(f_k) - h(f_k / \hat{f}_k)$$

$$= \frac{1}{2} \log_e (2\pi e) \sigma_k^2 - h(f_k - \hat{f}_k / \hat{f}_k)$$

$$\geq \frac{1}{2} \log_e (2\pi e) \sigma_k^2 - h(f_k - \hat{f}_k) ; \text{(Conditioning reduces entropy)}$$

$$= \frac{1}{2}\log_e(2\pi e)\sigma_k^2 - h(N(0, E(f_k - \hat{f}_k)^2);$$

$$\geq \frac{1}{2}\log_e(2\pi e)\sigma_k^2 - \frac{1}{2}\log_e(2\pi e)D_k$$

$$R(D_k) = \frac{1}{2}\log_e[\frac{\sigma_k^2}{D_k}] = \inf I(f_k; \hat{f}_k)$$

For K independent variables (feature sets) can be generalized as below:

$$R(\overline{D}) = \sum_{\forall k} R(D_k) = \sum_{\forall k} \frac{1}{2}\log_e[\frac{\sigma_k^2}{D_k}] = \inf I(F; \hat{F})$$

Automatic Online Signature Verification Using HMMs with User-Dependent Structure

J.M. Pascual-Gaspar and V. Cardeñoso-Payo

ECA-SIMM, Dpto. Informática, Universidad de Valladolid,
Campus Miguel Delibes s/n, 47011 Valladolid, Spain
{jmpascual,valen}@infor.uva.es

Abstract. A novel strategy for Automatic online Signature Verification based on hidden Markov models (HMM) with user-dependent structure is presented in this work. Under this approach, the number of states and Gaussians giving the optimal prediction results are independently selected for each user. With this simple strategy just three genuine signatures could be used for training, with an EER under 2.5% obtained for the basic set of raw signature parameters provided by the acquisition device. This results increment by a factor of six the accuracy obtained with the typical approach in which claim-independent structure is used for the HMMs.

1 Introduction

Signature verification is of particular importance within the framework of biometrics, because of its long standing tradition in many identity verification scenarios[1]. In on-line Automatic Signature Verification (ASV) systems, the signer uses special hardware to produce her signature, so that a time sequence of parameters (position, inclination, pressure, ...) is generated by the device and can be processed by a system in order to characterize spatial and temporal features of the signature. These features are to be useful to build a model or template which could be later used to verify the claimed identity of the same signer with a minimum controlled risk that a forged signature could be taken as genuine. This particular instance of a pattern recognition problem is heavily influenced by intra and inter-user variability affecting the signing process, so that proper selection of a good model for every signature is a key step of any signature verification system.

Hidden Markov Models (HMM) is a widely used probabilistic framework when modelling patterns of temporal sequences. It has been successfully applied to speech recognition tasks [2], on-line handwriting [3] and on-line signature verification [4,5]. A HMM can be roughly described as a graph of interconnected emitting states which topology is defined by means of a transition matrix, made of probability values for every particular state-to-state transition, and where the probability of emission of a given output value is usually modelled by a superposition of Gaussian distributions.

S.-W. Lee and S.Z. Li (Eds.): ICB 2007, LNCS 4642, pp. 1057–1066, 2007.

The number of states in the model and the number of Gaussian distributions associated to each state constitute the *structural parameters* of the model. Fixing these structural parameters is a highly specialized problem-dependent task carried out by domain experts, since it is hard to find general efficient algorithms to infer these parameters from the data being modelled.

Given the structure of the model, the classical Baum-Welch algorithm (see [2]) can be successfully applied to estimate the values of the transition probabilities and of the weights and statistical moments of the Gaussians which provide the maximum expected likelihood for the observed time sequence. These values represent what we call the *statistical parameters* of the model.

Table 1 provides a view of the current state of the art in ASV using different modelling alternatives and sometimes combining local and global signature parameters. This gives a reference point of the expected accuracy of present and future systems.

Table 1. Some ASV systems, its error rates and employed techniques

Author	Date	Employed technique	% Error
Nelson et al. [6]	1994	Distance based	EER: 6
Yang et al. [5]	1995	HMM	FR: 1.75, FA: 4.44
Kashi et al. [7]	1997	HMM	EER: 2.5
Nalwa [8]	1997	Own algorithm	EER: between 2 and 5
DiLeece et al. [9]	2000	Multiexpert system	FR: 3.2, FA: 0.55
Jain et al. [10]	2002	String matching	FR: 3.3, FA: 2.7
Igarza et al. [11]	2003	HMM	EER: 9.25
Ortega et al. [12]	2003	HMM	EER: 0.98
Hansheng et al. [13]	2004	Linear regression (ER_2)	EER: 0.2
Fierrez-Aguilar et al. [14]	2005	Local and Global fusion	EER: 0.24

In this work we evaluate the influence of a claim-dependent selection of the structural parameters of the HMM on the accuracy of the automatic ASV. In section 2, a brief discussion of user dependent and user independent structure selection is made. The signature database used in this work is described in section 3 and the set of experiments is presented in section 4. Results and discussion section 5 will show that user dependent selection of the optimal model structure provides average EER below 2.5%, even for skilled forgeries. If we take into account that these experiments were carried out using just 5 raw signature parameters and 3 training signatures per user, we find the final accuracy values really promising and competitive with state of the art ASV systems.

2 User-Dependent Structure of HMMs

HMMs have been successfully applied to high-accuracy ASV systems for the last decade [15,11,5]. Although these systems differ in several important aspects (e.g. signature pre-processing techniques, signature database characteristics, likelihood and score normalization techniques, ...), they always share a common architectural strategy, since they are based on a global set of structural parameters which, in most cases, are experimentally evaluated using all possible signatures of the database. The structure of the model which provides the best overall performance over all signers is selected. This is what we refer as *ASV approach based on HMM with user-independent structure* (HMM-UIS).

As an alternative to the HMM-UIS approach, the selection of the best structural parameters of the model could be carried out independently for each user, exploiting specific characteristics of the signature. This is what we call *ASV based on HMM with user-dependent structure* (HMM-UDS). Under this approach, the model would be adapted to the user or, at least, to a given class of users sharing a set of statistically similar features. Although some heuristics have been evaluated to guide this selection, in the present paper we will concentrate in an exhaustive search procedure of the optimal model structure. Although this approach is not directly usable in practical systems, we can use the results as an upper bound for the best accuracy which could be obtained when switching to a UDS.

To further support our view of the importance of a user-dependent selection of the structural parameters of the model, we include Figure 1 to illustrate the correlation between form and structural parameters of the HMM in a given fictitious stroke of a signature. The five subfigures illustrate five different ways of covering a sample signature trace with states, each with the same fixed number of Gaussians. The same number of degrees of freedom ($N_S \times N_G = 16$ has been used in all cases, starting with the coarse-grained solution of figure 1-b), in which there is no dynamic modelling provided by state change, to the one in figure 1-f), where 16 states are used to model the stroke dynamics. For a given number of degrees of freedom, it should be expected that the model with lower number of Gaussians would perform better when using raw features without time derivatives, since it will better resemble time evolution of the stroke.

At the same time, the number of states will be highly influenced by the amount of statistically different samples available to initialize the model. As a consequence, the compromise between N_S and N_G is to be highly influenced both by the geometric and temporal characteristics of the signature and by the observable variability of features along it over the set of training samples. This is what motivated the experimental study we will present in the following sections.

3 Data Acquisition and Pre-processing

All the experiments have been carried out using the MCYT signature database [16], which contains on-line signatures acquired with a WACOM Intuos A6 USB digital tablet. A total of 333[1] different users contributed to the database, each of them producing 25 genuine signatures across five time-spaced sessions in which

[1] While the delivered and filtered version of MCYT database contains just 330 signatures, the raw complete original version was used in this study.

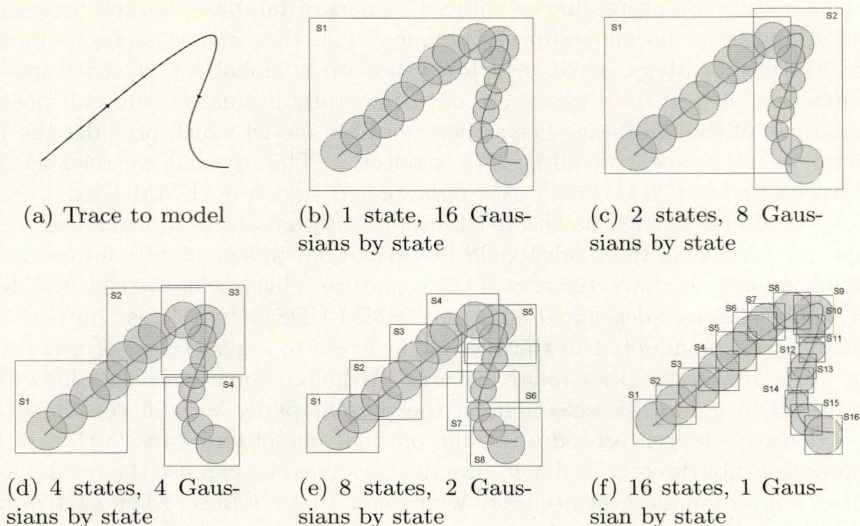

(a) Trace to model (b) 1 state, 16 Gaussians by state (c) 2 states, 8 Gaussians by state

(d) 4 states, 4 Gaussians by state (e) 8 states, 2 Gaussians by state (f) 16 states, 1 Gaussian by state

Fig. 1. Samples of how to model a signature's stroke

each user also produced 25 'over-the-shoulder' skilled forgeries of 5 different users. With this procedure, a total of $333 \times (25 + 25) = 16650$ signatures were produced, 8325 genuine and 8325 skilled forgeries. The input tablet provided a series of 100 vector samples per second, each vector including the raw parameters we used in this experiment: pen coordinates X and Y, pressure level P and pen orientation in terms of azimuth and elevation (see [16] for further details).

Table 2. MCYT global statistics summary

Gen (For)	Mean	σ (%)	Max.	Min.
Length (cm)	23.98 (24.25)	18% (38%)	47.51 (71.28)	6.12 (3.44)
Duration (s)	5.79 (7.15)	41% (74%)	20.20 (53.06)	0.57 (0.50)
Speed (cm/s)	5.71 (4.59)	28% (56%)	19.46 (23.96)	1.29 (0.51)

The basic statistics of relevant global signature parameters for this database are shown in Table 2, both for genuine instances and forgeries. The signature length results to be the most stable feature and the easiest to reproduce, while duration and speed show higher deviation both intra and, specially, inter-user. A geometric normalization is performed to remove the absolute position offsets, since a grid of cells was used during the acquisition process to capture several signatures per sheet.

4 Experimental Setup

A single experiment can be defined as a function $E(N_U, N_S, N_G, I_K) \rightarrow EER$ depending on the user identity N_U, the number of states N_S, the number of

Gaussians per state N_G, and the kind of forgery considered in the evaluation phase I_K ($K = S, R$, S:skilled, R:random). In each experiment the same three multi-session signatures were used for training (the first ones from each of the 3 central sessions).

Two collections of experiments have been carried out in order to compare HMM-UIS and HMM-UDS strategies. In both of them a Bakis Left-To-Right-noskip topology was chosen for the HMMs and EER was used as the objective function for the optimization in HMM-UDS strategy.

In the first collection of experiments, the HMM-UIS strategy was evaluated using 49 $M_{UIS} = (N_S, N_G)_{7x7}$ different structure configurations, both N_S and N_G ranging from 1 to 64 in steps of power of 2. The average EER obtained with each model was calculated and also the number of users for whom a model structure could be trained was annotated. This is a relevant parameter, since not for every user is always possible to initialize a model with any number of states and Gaussians. In these experiments, we evaluated EER using only random forgeries.

In the second collection of experiments, we evaluated the influence of the selection of optimal values for N_S and N_G independently for each user (HMM-UDS). Here, the models were trained using the same experimental conditions used in the first collection, to allow comparison between both approaches. A set of 555 possible structures were evaluated for each user $M_{UDS} = (N_S, N_G)_{111x5}$, the number of states ranging from 1 to 111 and the number of Gaussians from 1 to 5. From these models, the optimal model (M_{opt}) was selected as the one that brought the lowest EER or the lower number of states for equal EER values. The average EER over all the M_{opt} models was taken as the global average accuracy. Evaluation was carried out using both random and skilled forgeries in this case.

5 Results and Discussion

Table 3 shows error rates using the 49 models of the M_{UIS} test matrix. The number in parenthesis in each cell represents the number of users N_{VU} for whom a valid model structure was trainable. As expected, N_{VU} decreases as the number of degrees of freedom N_{FD} increases, since for some users there are not enough initialization data. Six of these configurations (N_{FD} = 1024, 2048 and 4096) were not trainable for any user and are shown as empty cells in the table.

Since any ASV system should balance accuracy and good generalization capabilities, the model structure with lowest EER and for which all subjects in the database can be trained is chosen: the configuration composed of 32 states and one Gaussian by state. This HMM-UIS configuration produced an EER of 16.29% using just three training samples. Of course, better EER exist in the table, but they come at the cost of smaller generalization capabilities, since the number of valid trainable users is really small.

Table 4 shows error rates obtained using the HMM-UDS approach, which are clearly lower than the ones in the HMM-UIS approach. The adaptation of the number of states individually for each user drastically improved the accuracy of

Table 3. Errors as %EER with HMM-UIS approach tested using random forgeries

$N_S \setminus N_G$	**1**	**2**	**4**	**8**	**16**	**32**	**64**
1	$36.43_{(333)}$	$35.19_{(333)}$	$33.08_{(333)}$	$31.88_{(333)}$	$30.19_{(333)}$	$28.64_{(333)}$	$28.29_{(324)}$
2	$35.55_{(333)}$	$33.93_{(333)}$	$31.77_{(332)}$	$30.11_{(324)}$	$28.21_{(306)}$	$27.61_{(287)}$	$29.92_{(260)}$
4	$34.80_{(333)}$	$32.40_{(327)}$	$29.84_{(319)}$	$27.88_{(310)}$	$26.76_{(277)}$	$29.53_{(210)}$	$37.47_{(90)}$
8	$31.11_{(333)}$	$29.71_{(330)}$	$26.80_{(312)}$	$25.83_{(287)}$	$27.28_{(241)}$	$35.91_{(104)}$	$42.59_{(7)}$
16	$24.20_{(333)}$	$23.74_{(321)}$	$22.38_{(306)}$	$22.90_{(254)}$	$30.47_{(99)}$	$55.88_{(9)}$	
32	$\mathbf{16.29}_{(333)}$	$16.27_{(309)}$	$15.85_{(259)}$	$16.36_{(107)}$	$21.04_{(8)}$		
64	$11.82_{(324)}$	$11.48_{(262)}$	$8.94_{(107)}$	$8.56_{(7)}$			

Table 4. Results with HMM-UDS models

N_G	**% EER ($I_K = R$)**	**% EER ($I_K = S$)**
1	3.83	3.29
2	3.46	3.29
3	4.08	3.42
4	4.63	3.71
5	4.96	3.59
$N_{G\text{opt.}}$	**2.33**	**2.06**

the system, although the impact of the number of Gaussians by state was not so relevant as the influence of the optimization of the number of states.

Average EER using both random and skilled forgeries is shown in this table and, again, just 3 signatures were always used for training. The first five rows at the table represent the error when N_G was fixed and the optimum number of states was selected. As expected, the best results arise for models with low N_G values (1 and 2). The last row shows the average error obtained when both the number of states and the number of Gaussians by state are selected to optimize EER. With this 'two-dimension' optimization the error rate is reduced by 33% and 37% for random and skilled forgeries respectively.

Figure 2 shows the histograms of N_S and N_G for the experiments with random (a,b)and skilled forgeries (c,d). From figures fig. 2-a and fig.2-c it can be seen that the upper limit of 111 states per model can be increased in future works expecting better results from it because many models reached their best performance with the highest values of N_S. With respect the number of Gaussians distributions it seems that for random forgeries (fig. 2-b) a low number of Gaussians per state performs better, however in the case of skilled forgeries (fig. 2-d) a higher number of Gaussians discriminate better this kind of impostor.

To illustrate the relationship between signature complexity and number of states, signatures with different visual complexities are plotted in figure 3 besides their optimal number of states (one Gaussian per state was used in these signatures).

After all these experiments, we came to the conclusion that a reliable ASV-HMM system must be accurate for the majority of users, reporting a low mean error rate, and also that is very important for the real application acceptance

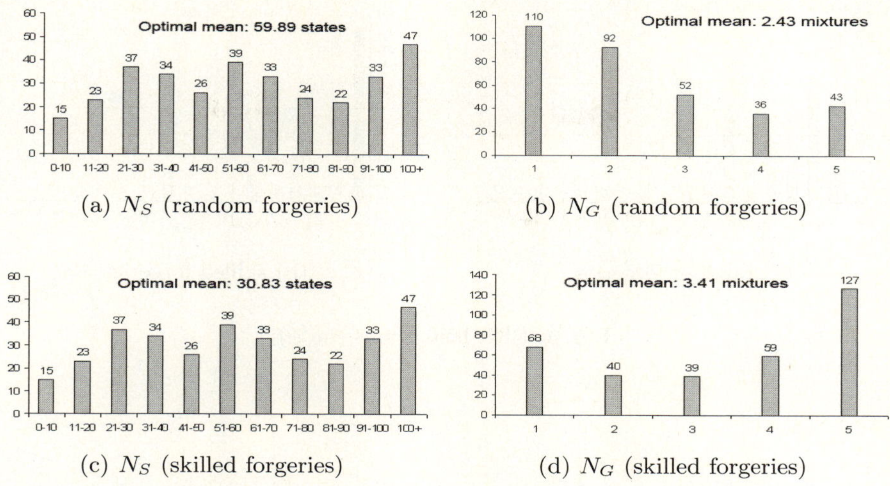

(a) N_S (random forgeries) (b) N_G (random forgeries)

(c) N_S (skilled forgeries) (d) N_G (skilled forgeries)

Fig. 2. N_S and N_G histograms for random forgeries (a,b) and skilled forgeries (c,d) tests

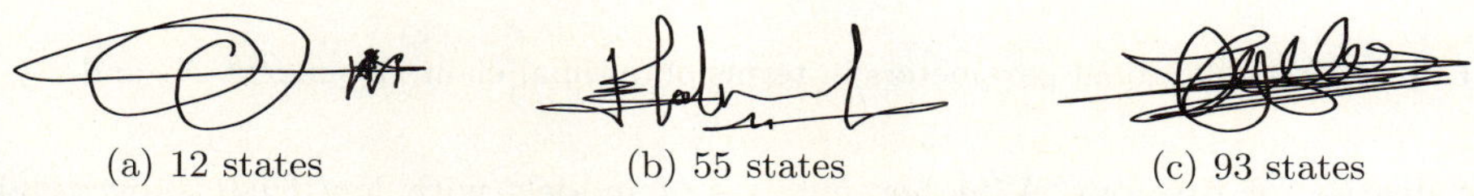

(a) 12 states (b) 55 states (c) 93 states

Fig. 3. Samples of signatures modelled using the HMM user-dependent structure approach

that the system works properly for very different types of signatures, not being desirable the existence of users getting high errors rates because their signatures are simplistic or inconsistent.

The histogram in figure 4-a) illustrates the distribution of the number of users sharing a same EER interval when random forgeries were used. We emphasize the following three results: a) a high number of users yield no verification errors (28% of the models give 0% EER); b) 86% of the models have an EER lower than 5%; c) only three models report EER over 15%, 15.81% being the worst EER result of our system.

Table 4 shows that no significant differences are found with respect to the random case when skilled forgeries were used. In fact, only a slight improvement can be depicted, which could be attributed to the fact that forged signatures were produced without information on the signature dynamics, which is difficult to infer for complex signatures. In spite of these similar average EER results, the appearance of the EER histogram in figure 4-b) is completely different to the one in random forgeries. Many of the genuine signatures of the users resulted to be difficult to forge when a different optimal number of states and Gaussians is chosen for each user, since the dynamics are hidden in these optimal number

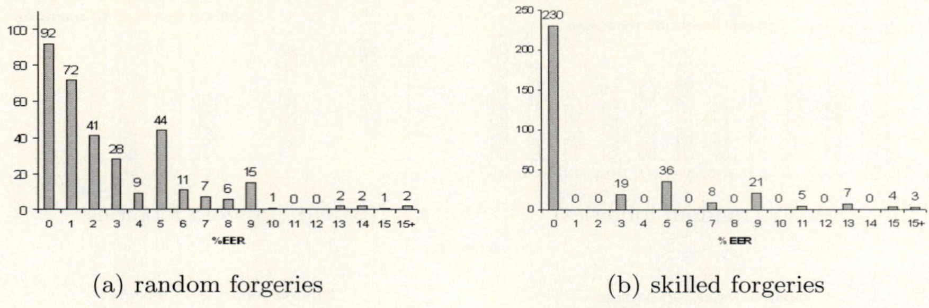

(a) random forgeries (b) skilled forgeries

Fig. 4. EER histograms (in %)

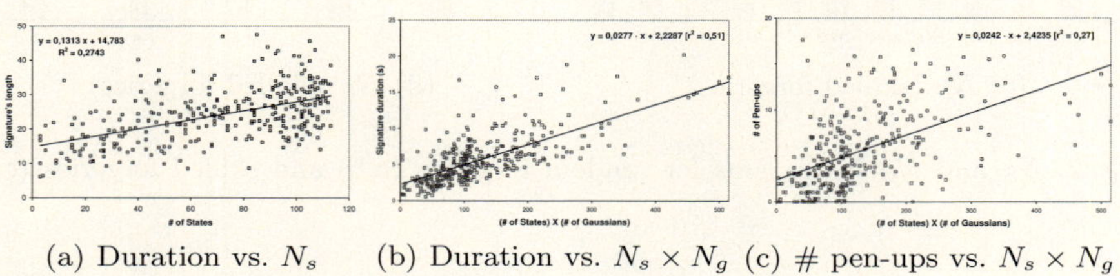

(a) Duration vs. N_s (b) Duration vs. $N_s \times N_g$ (c) # pen-ups vs. $N_s \times N_g$

Fig. 5. Relevant global parameters in terms of optimal claim-dependent N_s and N_g

of degrees of freedom. A higher number of models with low EER show (230 producing 0% EER), although there also exists a group of users which produced simplistic or non-consistent signatures easier to forge, leading to a final average EER similar to the one found in random forgeries. This might have been clearly improved with a higher control over the acquisition process.

Recent studies on the combination of local and global features for ASV have provided reference rankings on the relevance of several global features [15]. The total length of a signature and the number of strokes (or the basically equivalent number of pen-ups) are shown to be the most relevant of these global parameters.

In order to test the correlation between the optimum number of degrees of freedom (N_S, N_G) of the user dependent models and the value of these global parameters for a given user, we have carried out a linear correlation analysis shown in figure 5.

In these figures, we prove that there is a reasonably good linear correspondence ($r^2 = 0.51$) between the length of a signature and the number $N_S \times N_G$, which could provide a basic guideline on a more efficient model selection strategy. As for the number of pen-ups, there is not such a clear correspondence. This could be related to the fact that independent strokes could be better modelled after separate HMM models and then the results merged, compared to a single HMM based model as the one we are using here. Even less information can be extracted about the correspondence between signature length and optimum number of states. In any case, we conclude that further research is worthy on the correspondence between global signature parameters and optimum structural parameters of the models.

6 Conclusions

In this work, we provided experimental evidences of the fact that data driven user dependent structure optimization of the HMM models could bring lower EER in ASV systems. The influence of two relevant structural parameters, the number of states N_S in the model and the number of Gaussians by state N_G, was evaluated and N_S was the parameter which provided better observable improvement. HMM-UDS strategies lead to more accurate and reliable ASV systems using a smaller number of training signatures, which always represents an advantage for practical use cases. User adaptation shows to cope well with intra-user variability while providing good inter-user discrimination.

An EER of 2.33% for random forgeries and 2.06% for skilled forgeries has been obtained. This represents a factor of 6 gain over the HMM-UIS strategy for the random forgery scenario within the same experimental conditions. Since optimization was carried out using an exhaustive search, it might not be useful in practical systems. Nevertheless, the results provide an lower bound for the best obtainable EER which encourages for further experimentation on data driven model selection strategies. Also, a better parameterization including time-dependent features will of course provide an overall increase of accuracy, according to the results found in other works [15].

Acknowledgements

This work has been partially supported by the Spanish Ministry of Education, under contract TIC2003-08382-C05-03 and by the Consejería de Educación de la Junta de Castilla y León, under research project VA053A05.

References

1. Plamondon, R., Srihari, S.N.: On-line and off-line handwriting recognition: A comprehensive survey. Transactions on pattern analysis and machine intelligence 22(1), 63–84 (2000)
2. Rabiner, L.R.: A tutorial on hidden markov models and selected application in speech recognition. Proceedings of IEEE 77(2), 257–286 (1989)
3. Hu, J., Brown, M.K., Turin, W.: Hmm based on-line handwriting recognition. IEEE Trans. Pattern Anal. Mach. Intell. 18(10), 1039–1045 (1996)
4. Fierrez-Aguilar, J.: Adapted Fusion Schemes for Multimodal Biometric Authentication. PhD thesis, Esc. Técnica Superior de Ing. de Telecomunicación (2006)
5. Yang, L., Widjaja, B.K., Prasad, R.: Application of hidden markov models for signature verification. Pattern Recognition 28(2), 161–170 (1995)
6. Nelson, W., Turin, W., Hastie, T.: Statistical methods for on-line signature verification. IJPRAI 8(3), 749–770 (1994)

7. Kashi, R.S., Hu, J., Nelson, W.L., Turin, W.: On-line handwritten signature verification using hidden markov model features. Document Analysis and Recognition 2 (1997)
8. Nalwa, V.S.: Automatic on-line signature verification. Proceedings of the IEEE 85(2), 215–239 (1997)
9. Lecce, V.D., Dimauro, G., Guerriero, A., Impedovo, S., Pirlo, G., Salzo, A.: A multi-expert system for dynamic signature verification. In: Kittler, J., Roli, F. (eds.) MCS 2000. LNCS, vol. 1857, pp. 320–329. Springer, Heidelberg (2000)
10. Jain, A., Griess, F., Connell, S.: On-line signature verification. Pattern Recognition 35(12), 2963–2972 (2002)
11. Igarza, J.J., Goirizelaia, I., Espinosa, K., Hernáez, I., Méndez, R., Sánchez, J.: Online handwritten signature verification using hidden markov models. In: Sanfeliu, A., Ruiz-Shulcloper, J. (eds.) CIARP 2003. LNCS, vol. 2905, pp. 391–399. Springer, Heidelberg (2003)
12. Ortega-Garcia, J., Fierrez-Aguilar, J., Martin-Reillo, J., Gonzalez-Rodriguez, J.: Complete signal modeling and score normalization for function-based dynamic signature verification. In: Kittler, J., Nixon, M.S. (eds.) AVBPA 2003. LNCS, vol. 2688, pp. 658–667. Springer, Heidelberg (2003)
13. Lei, H., Palla, S., Govindaraju, V.: Er2: An intuitive similarity measure for online signature verification. In: IWFHR '04: Proceedings of the Ninth International Workshop on Frontiers in Handwriting Recognition (IWFHR'04), Washington, DC, USA, pp. 191–195. IEEE Computer Society Press, Los Alamitos (2004)
14. Fierrez-Aguilar, J., Nanni, L., Lopez-Peñalba, J., Ortega-Garcia, J., Maltoni, D.: An on-line signature verification system based on fusion of local and global information. In: Kanade, T., Jain, A., Ratha, N.K. (eds.) AVBPA 2005. LNCS, vol. 3546, pp. 523–532. Springer, Heidelberg (2005)
15. Fierrez-Aguilar, J., Krawczyk, S., Ortega-Garcia, J., Jain, A.K.: Fusion of local and regional approaches for on-line signature verification. In: Li, S.Z., Sun, Z., Tan, T., Pankanti, S., Chollet, G., Zhang, D. (eds.) IWBRS 2005. LNCS, vol. 3781, pp. 188–196. Springer, Heidelberg (2005)
16. Ortega, J., Fierrez, J., Simon, D., Gonzalez, J., Hernaez, I., Igarza, J.J., Vivaracho, C., Escudero, D., Moro, Q.: Mcyt baseline corpus: a bimodal biometric database. IEEE Proc. Visual Image Signal Processing 150(6), 395–401 (2003)

A Complete Fisher Discriminant Analysis for Based Image Matrix and Its Application to Face Biometrics

R.M. Mutelo, W.L. Woo, and S.S. Dlay

School of Electrical, Electronic and Computer Engineering
University of Newcastle
Newcastle upon Tyne, NE1 7RU
United Kingdom
{risco.mutelo,w.l.woo,s.s.dlay}@ncl.ac.uk

Abstract. This paper presents a Complete Orthogonal Image discriminant (COID) method and its application to biometric face recognition. The novelty of the COID method comes from 1) the derivation of two kinds of image discriminant features, image regular and image irregular, in the feature extraction stage and 2) the development of the Complete OID (COID) features-based on the fusion of the two kinds of image discriminant features used in classification. Firstly, the COID method first derives a feature image of the face image with reduced dimensionality of the image matrix by means of two dimensional principal component analysis and then performs discriminant analysis in a double discriminant subspaces in order to derive the image regular and irregular features making it more suitable for small sample size problem. Finally combines the image regular and irregular features which are complementary for achieving better discriminant features. The feasibility of the COID method has been successfully tested using the ORL images where it was 73.8% more superior to 2DFLD method on face recognition.

Keywords: Biometrics, Face Recognition, Fisher Discriminant Analysis (FDA), two dimensional Image, Feature extraction, image representation.

1 Introduction

Over the last few years, biometrics has attracted a high interest in the security technology marketplace. Biometric technologies use physiological or behavioural characteristics to identify and authenticate users attempting to gain access to computers, networks, and physical locations. The fastest growing areas of advanced security involve biometric face recognition technologies. Biometric face recognition technology offers great promise in its ability to identify a single face, from multiple lookout points, from a sea of hundreds of thousands of other faces. However building an automated face recognition system is very challenging. In real world applications, particularly in image recognition, there is a lot of small sample size (SSS) problems in observation space (input space). In such problems, the number of training samples is less than the dimension of feature vectors. A good face recognition methodology should consider representation as well as classification issues. Straightforward image

S.-W. Lee and S.Z. Li (Eds.): ICB 2007, LNCS 4642, pp. 1067–1076, 2007.

projection techniques such two-dimensional principal component analysis (2DPCA) [1], two dimensional reduction PCA (2D RPCA) [2], two dimensional FLD [3, 4] are among the most popular methods for representation and recognition.

This paper introduces a novel Complete Orthogonal Image discriminant (COID) method for biometric face representation and recognition. The novelty of the COID method comes from 1) the derivation of two kinds of image discriminant features, image regular and image irregular, in the feature extraction stage and 2) the development of the Complete OID (COID) features based on the fusion of the two kinds of image discriminant features used in classification. In particular, the COID method first derives a feature image of the face image with reduced dimensionality of the image matrix by means of two dimensional principal component analysis and then performs discriminant analysis in a double discriminant subspaces in order to derive the image regular and irregular features making it more suitable for small sample size problem. The 2DPCA transformed face images preserves the spatial structure that defines the 2D face image and exhibit strong characteristics features with reduced noise and redundancies. Whereas, 2DFLD would further reduce redundancy and represent orthogonal discriminant features explicitly.

2 Outline of 2DPCA and 2DFLD

Given a set of M training samples $\mathbf{X}_1, \mathbf{X}_{2,} \cdots, \mathbf{X}_M$ in the input space $\Re^{m \times n}$. The aim is to project image $\mathbf{X}_i$, an $m \times n$ face matrix, onto $\mathbf{B}_i$ by the following linear transformation

$$\mathbf{Y}_i = \mathbf{X}_i \mathbf{B} \tag{1}$$

Thus, we obtain an an $m \times d$ dimensional projected matrix $\mathbf{Y}_i$, which is the feature matrix of the image sample $\mathbf{X}_i$. In the 2DPCA method, the total scatter $\mathbf{S}_t$ of the projected samples is introduced to measure the discriminatory power of the projection vector $\mathbf{B}$. The total scatter of the projected samples can be characterized by the trace of the scatter matrix of the projected feature vectors. Whereas in 2DFLD the between class scatter $\mathbf{S}_b$ and the within-class scatter $\mathbf{S}_w$ matrices of the projected samples are introduced. From this point of view, we adopt the following criterion:

$$J(\beta_i) = \beta^T \mathbf{S}_t \beta \tag{2}$$

$$J(\varphi_i) = \frac{\varphi_i^T \mathbf{S}_b \varphi_i}{\varphi_i^T \mathbf{S}_w \varphi_i}, \varphi_i \neq 0 \tag{3}$$

where β_i and φ_i are the unitary vector that maximizes the 2DPCA criterion (2) and the 2DFLD criterion (3) which are called the optimal projection axis, β_{opt} and φ_{opt}. In general, it is not enough to have only one optimal projection axis. We usually need to select a set of projection axes, $\mathbf{B} = \lfloor \beta_1, \beta_{2,} \cdots, \beta_d \rfloor$ and $\mathbf{B} = \lfloor \varphi_1, \varphi_{2,} \cdots, \varphi_d \rfloor$, subject to the orthonormal constraints. The scatter matrices can be defined as follows:

$$\mathbf{S}_t = \frac{1}{M}\sum_{i=1}^{M}(\mathbf{X}_i - \mathbf{X}_0)^T(\mathbf{X}_i - \mathbf{X}_0) \tag{4}$$

$$\mathbf{S}_b = \frac{1}{M}\sum_{j=1}^{C}L_i(\overline{\mathbf{X}}_i - \mathbf{X}_0)^T(\overline{\mathbf{X}}_i - \mathbf{X}_0) \tag{5}$$

$$\mathbf{S}_w = \frac{1}{M}\sum_{i=1}^{C}\sum_{j=1}^{L_i}(\mathbf{X}_{ij} - \overline{\mathbf{X}}_i)^T(\mathbf{X}_{ij} - \overline{\mathbf{X}}_i) \tag{6}$$

where $\mathbf{X}_{ij}$ denotes the j th training sample in class i, L_i is the number of training samples in class i, $\overline{\mathbf{X}}_i$ is the mean of the training samples in class i, C is the number of image classes, $\mathbf{X}_0$ is the global mean across all training samples.

3 Complete Orthogonal Image Discriminant Approach

In this section, we examine the problem in the whole *input space* rather than in the space transformed by 2DPCA first.

3.1 Fundamentals

Suppose we have a set of *M* training samples $\mathbf{X}_1, \mathbf{X}_{2,} \cdots, \mathbf{X}_M$ in the input space of size $m \times n$, by definition the $rank(\mathbf{X}_i) = \min(m,n)$. From the denominator in (3), we have

$$\begin{aligned} rank(\mathbf{S}_w) &= rank\left(\frac{1}{M}\sum_{i=1}^{C}\sum_{j=1}^{L_i}(\mathbf{X}_{ij} - \overline{\mathbf{X}}_i)^T(\mathbf{X}_{ij} - \overline{\mathbf{X}}_i)\right) \\ &\le (M - C)\cdot \min(m,n) \end{aligned} \tag{7}$$

So that $\mathbf{S}_w$ is non-singular when

$$M \ge c + \frac{n}{\min(m,n)} \tag{8}$$

If the within-class covariance operator $\mathbf{S}_w$ is invertible, $\varphi_i^T \mathbf{S}_w \varphi_i > 0$ always holds for every nonzero vector φ_i. Therefore, the Fisher criterion can be directly employed to extract a set of optimal discriminant vectors. However, in some case it is almost impossible to make $\mathbf{S}_w$ invertible because of the limited amount of training samples in real-world applications. This means that there always exist vectors satisfying $\varphi_i^T \mathbf{S}_w \varphi_i = 0$. In [5], it is shown that these vectors are from the null space of $\mathbf{S}_w$ for the vectorized fisher discriminant approach. These vectors turn out to be very effective if they satisfy $\varphi_i^T \mathbf{S}_b \varphi_i > 0$ at the same time [5]. The positive image between-class scatter matrix makes the data become well separable when the within-class scatter matrix is zero. In such a case, the Fisher criterion degenerates into the following between-class covariance criterion:

$$J_b(\varphi_i) = \varphi_i^T \mathbf{S}_b \varphi_i, (\|\varphi_i\| = 1) \tag{9}$$

As a special case of the Fisher criterion, it is reasonable to use the image between class scatter to measure the discriminatory ability of a projection axis when the image within-class covariance is zero.

3.2 Optimal Orthogonal Image Discriminant Vectors

The input space $\Re^{m\times n}$ is relatively large and mostly empty (containing noise and redundancies), it is computationally intensive to calculate the optimal discriminant vectors directly. Our strategy is to reduce the feasible solution space (search space) where two kinds of discriminant vectors might hide. Suppose $\beta_1, \beta_{2,} \cdots, \beta_d$ are eigenvectors corresponding to the largest positive eigenvalues of $\mathbf{S}_t$. We can define the subspace $\psi_t = span\{\beta_1, \beta_2, \cdots, \beta_d\}$ and its orthogonal complementary space is denoted by $\psi_{\frac{\perp}{t}} = span\{\beta_{d+1}, \beta_{d+2}, \cdots, \beta_n\}$. The eigenvectors $\{\beta_{d+1}, \beta_{d+2}, \cdots, \beta_n\}$ are relatively close to zero. In 2DPCA these eigenvectors are considered to contain very little or no discriminant information. Since $n = rank(\mathbf{S}_t)$, non of the eigenvalues of $\mathbf{S}_t$ are negative. Therefore, we refer to $\psi_{\frac{\perp}{t}}$ in this paper as the positive null space of $\mathbf{S}_t$. Since $\Re^{mxn} = \psi_t \oplus \psi_{\frac{\perp}{t}}$, it follows that for an arbitrary vector $\varphi_i \in \Re^{m\times n}$, φ_i can be uniquely represented in the form $\varphi_i = \phi_i + \varsigma_i$ with $\boldsymbol{\varphi}_i \in \psi_t$ and $\varsigma_i \in \psi_{\frac{\perp}{t}}$. We can define the mapping . $\Re^{m\times n} \to \psi_t$ using

$$\varphi_i = \phi_i + \varsigma_i \to \phi_i \tag{10}$$

where ϕ_i is the orthogonal projection of φ_i onto ψ_t. The eigenvectors ς_i have eigenvalues relatively close to zero, thus discarded in 2DPCA. It follows that $J(\varphi_i) = J(\phi_i)$. Since the new search space is much smaller (less dimensionality), it is easer to derive discriminant vectors from it. The aim at this point is to calculate Fisher optimal discriminant vectors in the reduced search space ψ_t. According to linear algebra theory [6], ψ_t is isomorphic to $m\times d$ dimensional matrix space $\Re^{m\times d}$. The corresponding isomorphic mapping is

$$\varphi_i = \mathbf{B}\eta_i \text{ , where } \mathbf{B} = (\beta_1, \beta_2, \cdots, \beta_d), \eta_i \in \Re^{m\times d} \tag{11}$$

Under the isomorphic mapping $\varphi_i = \mathbf{B}\eta_i$, the criterion function (3) and (9) in the subspace is, converted into

$$J(\varphi_i) = \frac{\eta_i^T (\mathbf{B}^T \mathbf{S}_b \mathbf{B}) \eta_i}{\eta_i^T (\mathbf{B}^T \mathbf{S}_w \mathbf{B}) \eta_i} \text{ and } J_b(\varphi_i) = \eta_i^T (\mathbf{B}^T \mathbf{S}_b \mathbf{B}) \eta_i \tag{12}$$

$$J(\eta_i)=\frac{\eta_i^T\hat{\mathbf{S}}_b\eta_i}{\eta_i^T\hat{\mathbf{S}}_w\eta_i}, \eta_i \neq 0 \text{ and } J_b(\eta_i)=\eta_i^T\hat{\mathbf{S}}_b\eta_i, \|\eta_i\|=1 \tag{13}$$

where $\hat{\mathbf{S}}_b=\mathbf{B}^T\mathbf{S}_b\mathbf{B}$ and $\hat{\mathbf{S}}_w=\mathbf{B}^T\mathbf{S}_w\mathbf{B}$. This means that $J(\eta_i)$ is a generalized Rayleigh quotient and $J_b(\eta_i)$ Rayleigh quotient in the isomorphic space $\Re^{m\times d}$. Now, the problem of calculating the optimal discriminant vectors in subspace ψ_t is transformed into the extremum problem of the (generalized) Rayleigh quotient in the isomorphic space $\Re^{m\times d}$. Therefore we can obtain the discriminant feature matrix $\mathbf{\Pi}_j$ by the following transformation:

$$\mathbf{\Pi}_j=\mathbf{X}_j\mathbf{T} \tag{14}$$

where $$\begin{aligned}\mathbf{T} &=(\varphi_1,\varphi_2,\cdots,\varphi_q)=(\mathbf{B}\eta_1,\mathbf{B}\eta_2,\cdots,\mathbf{B}\eta_q)\\ &=\mathbf{B}(\eta_1,\eta_2,\cdots,\eta_q)\end{aligned}$$

The transformation in (14) can be divided into two transformations:

$$\mathbf{Y}_j=\mathbf{X}_j\mathbf{B}, \text{ where } \mathbf{B}=(\beta_1,\beta_2,\cdots,\beta_d) \tag{15}$$

$$\mathbf{\Pi}_j=\mathbf{Y}_j\mathbf{\Lambda}, \text{ where } \mathbf{\Lambda}=(\eta_1,\eta_2,\cdots,\eta_q) \tag{16}$$

The transformation (15) is exactly 2DPCA [1]. Looking back at (13) and considering the two matrices $\hat{\mathbf{S}}_b$ and $\hat{\mathbf{S}}_w$ are the between class and within-class scatter matrices in $\Re^{m\times d}$. Therefore, 2DPCA is firstly used to reduce dimension of the input space. Low dimensionality is important for learning, performing 2DFLD on the transformed images results in better generalization to unseen images.

3.3 Two Kinds of Image Discriminant Features

Our strategy is to split the space $\Re^{m\times d}$ into two subspaces: the positive null space and the range space of $\hat{\mathbf{S}}_w$ and then use the Fisher criterion to derive the image regular discriminant features from the range space and use the between-class scatter criterion to derive the image irregular discriminant matrices from the null space. Suppose $\alpha_1,\alpha_2,\cdots,\alpha_d$ are the orthonormal eigenvectors of $\hat{\mathbf{S}}_w$ and the first q ones correspond to largest positive eigenvalues. We define the subspace, $\mathbf{\Theta}_w=span\{\alpha_1,\alpha_2,\cdots,\alpha_q\}$, the ranger space and it's orthogonal complementary space is $\mathbf{\Theta}_{\frac{\perp}{w}}=span\{\alpha_{q+1},\alpha_{d+2},\cdots,\alpha_d\}$. Since for the nonzero vector η_i in $\mathbf{\Theta}_{\frac{\perp}{w}}$, the image within class scatter and between class scatter becomes $\eta_i^T\hat{\mathbf{S}}_w\eta_i=0$ and $\eta_i^T\hat{\mathbf{S}}_b\eta_i>0$. Therefore the Fisher criterion $J_b(\eta_i)=\eta_i^T\hat{\mathbf{S}}_b\eta_i$ is used to derive the discriminant feature matrix. On the other hand, for every nonzero vector η_i in $\mathbf{\Theta}_w$ satisfies $\eta_i^T\hat{\mathbf{S}}_w\eta_i>0$, it is feasible to derive the optimal regular discriminant vectors from $\mathbf{\Theta}_w$ using the standard Fisher criterion $J(\eta_i)$. To calculate the optimal image regular discriminant vectors in $\mathbf{\Theta}_w$. The dimension of $\mathbf{\Theta}_w$ is $m \times q$, space $\mathbf{\Theta}_w$ is isomorphic to the matrix space $\Re^{m \times q}$ and the corresponding isomorphic mapping is

$$\eta = \mathbf{B}_1 \xi \text{ , where } \mathbf{B}_1 = (\alpha_1, \alpha_2, \cdots, \alpha_q) \tag{17}$$

Under this mapping, the Fisher criterion $J(\eta_i)$ is converted into

$$\bar{J}(\xi_i) = \frac{\xi_i^T \tilde{\mathbf{S}}_b \xi_i}{\xi_i^T \tilde{\mathbf{S}}_w \xi_i}, \xi_i \neq 0 \tag{18}$$

where $\tilde{\mathbf{S}}_b = \mathbf{B}_1^T \hat{\mathbf{S}}_b \mathbf{B}_1$ and $\tilde{\mathbf{S}}_w = \mathbf{B}_1^T \hat{\mathbf{S}}_w \mathbf{B}_1$. Thus the generalized eigenvector of the generalized eigenequation is $\tilde{\mathbf{S}}_b \xi_i = \lambda_i \tilde{\mathbf{S}}_w \xi_i$. Let $\vartheta_1, \vartheta_2, \cdots, \vartheta_f$ be the f largest eigenvectors of $\tilde{\mathbf{S}}_w^{-1} \tilde{\mathbf{S}}_b$, we can obtain the image regular discrminant vectors $\bar{\eta}_i = \mathbf{B}_1 \vartheta_i, i = 1, \cdots, f$ using (17). Similarly, the optimal image irregular discriminant vectors within $\mathbf{\Theta}_{\frac{1}{w}}$ is isomorphic to the matrix space $\Re^{m \times (d-q)}$ and the corresponding isomorphic mapping is

$$\eta = \mathbf{B}_2 \xi \text{ , where } \mathbf{B}_2 = (\alpha_{q+1}, \alpha_{q+2}, \cdots, \alpha_d) \tag{19}$$

Under this mapping, the Fisher criterion $\hat{J}_b(\eta_i)$ is converted into

$$\hat{J}_b(\xi_i) = \xi_i \breve{\mathbf{S}}_b \xi_i, \|\xi_i\| = 1 \tag{20}$$

where $\breve{\mathbf{S}}_b = \mathbf{B}_2^T \hat{\mathbf{S}}_b \mathbf{B}_2$. Letting $\upsilon_1, \upsilon_2, \cdots, \upsilon_f$ be the eigenvectors of $\breve{\mathbf{S}}_b$ corresponding to f largest eigenvalues. We have $\hat{\eta}_i = \mathbf{B}_2 \upsilon_i$ the optimal irregular discriminant vectors with respect to $\hat{J}_b(\eta)$. The linear discriminant transformation in (16) can be performed in $\Re^{m \times d}$. After the projection of the image sample $\mathbf{Y}_j$ onto the regular discriminant vectors $\bar{\eta} = (\bar{\eta}_1, \bar{\eta}_2, \cdots, \bar{\eta}_f)$, we can obtain the image regular discriminant feature matrix:

$$\mathbf{\Pi}^1 = \mathbf{Y}_j (\bar{\eta}_1, \bar{\eta}_2, \cdots, \bar{\eta}_f) = \mathbf{X}_j \mathbf{B}_1 \vartheta \tag{21}$$

where $\mathbf{B}_1 = (\alpha_1, \alpha_2, \cdots, \alpha_q)$, $\vartheta = (\vartheta_1, \vartheta_2, \cdots, \vartheta_f)$. After the projection of the sample $\mathbf{Y}_j$ onto the irregular discriminant vectors $\hat{\eta}_1, \hat{\eta}_2, \cdots, \hat{\eta}_f$, we can obtain the image irregular discriminant feature matrix:

$$\mathbf{\Pi}^2 = \mathbf{Y}_j (\hat{\eta}_1, \hat{\eta}_2, \cdots, \hat{\eta}_f) = \mathbf{X}_j \mathbf{B}_2 \boldsymbol{\upsilon} \tag{22}$$

where $\mathbf{B}_2 = (\alpha_{q+1}, \alpha_{q+2}, \cdots, \alpha_d)$, $\upsilon = (\upsilon_1, \upsilon_2, \cdots, \upsilon_f)$.

3.4 Fusion of Two Kinds of Discriminant Features

We propose a simple fusion strategy based on a summed normalized distance. The distance between two arbitrary feature matrices,

$$D(\mathbf{\Pi}^i, \mathbf{\Pi}^j) = \sum_{z=1}^{f} \sqrt{\left(\sum_{k=1}^{q} \left(\mathbf{T}_{zk}^i - \mathbf{T}_{zk}^j \right)^2 \right)} \tag{23}$$

where $\mathbf{\Pi}^i = [\mathbf{T}_1^i, \mathbf{T}_2^i, ... \mathbf{T}_f^i]$ and $\mathbf{\Pi}^j = [\mathbf{T}_1^j, \mathbf{T}_2^j, ... \mathbf{T}_f^j]$. For a given image sample we denote a feature matrix $\mathbf{\Pi} = \left[\mathbf{\Pi}^1, \mathbf{\Pi}^2\right]$, where $\mathbf{\Pi}^1$, $\mathbf{\Pi}^2$ are the regular and irregular discriminant feature matrices of the same pattern. The summed normalized-distance between sample $\mathbf{\Pi}$ and the training sample $\mathbf{\Pi}_r = \left[\mathbf{\Pi}_r^1, \mathbf{\Pi}_r^2\right]$ is defined by

$$\overline{D}(\mathbf{\Pi}, \mathbf{\Pi}_r) = \theta_r \frac{D(\mathbf{\Pi}^1, \mathbf{\Pi}_r^1)}{\sum_{g=1}^{M} D(\mathbf{\Pi}^1, \mathbf{\Pi}_g^1)} + \theta_i \frac{D(\mathbf{\Pi}^2, \mathbf{\Pi}_r^2)}{\sum_{g=1}^{M} D(\mathbf{\Pi}^2, \mathbf{\Pi}_g^2)} \tag{24}$$

where θ_r and θ_i are the fusion coefficient. These coefficients determine the weight of regular discriminant information and irregular information in the decision level.

4 Results and Discussions

Our analysis was performed on the Olivetti Research Laboratory (ORL) face database which contains 40 persons, each person has 10 different images. For some subjects, the images were taken at different times, which contain quite a high degree of variability in lighting, facial expression (open/closed eyes, smiling/nonsmiling etc), pose (upright, frontal position etc), scale, and facial details (glasses/no glasses). Examples of sample images from the ORL face database are shown in Fig. 1.

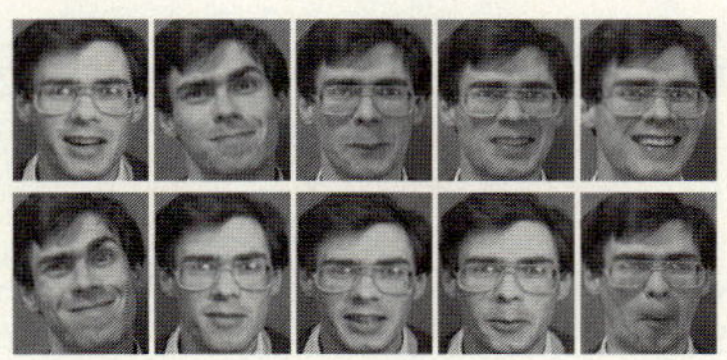

Fig. 1. Example ORL images with spatial resolution. 112 × 92Note that the images vary in pose, size, and facial expression.

4.1 ORL Face Database

Firstly, an analysis was performed using one image samples per class for training. Thus, the total number of training samples is 40 and testing samples is 360. That is, the total number of training samples and number of image classes are both 40. According to (8) the image within scatter matrix $\hat{\mathbf{S}}_w$ is singular. It is almost impossible to make $\tilde{\mathbf{S}}_w$ invertible because of the limited amount of training samples used here as it is the usual case in real-world applications. That is, there always exist vectors satisfying $\xi_i \tilde{\mathbf{S}}_w \xi_i = 0$. The 2DLDA method is inapplicable since $\tilde{\mathbf{S}}_w$ is

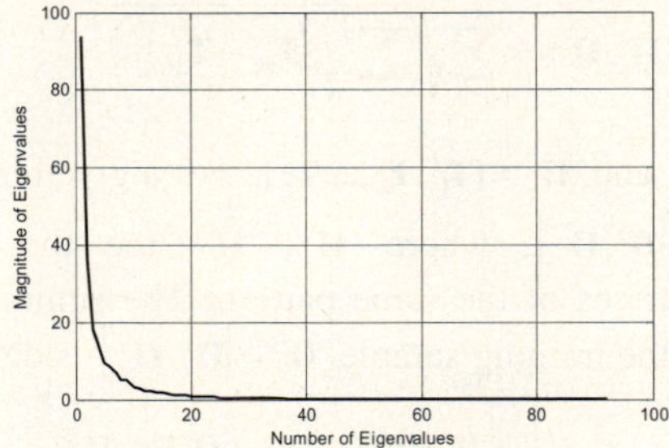

Fig. 2. Mmagnitudes of the eigenvalues in descending order from $\mathbf{S}_t$ for 2DPCA

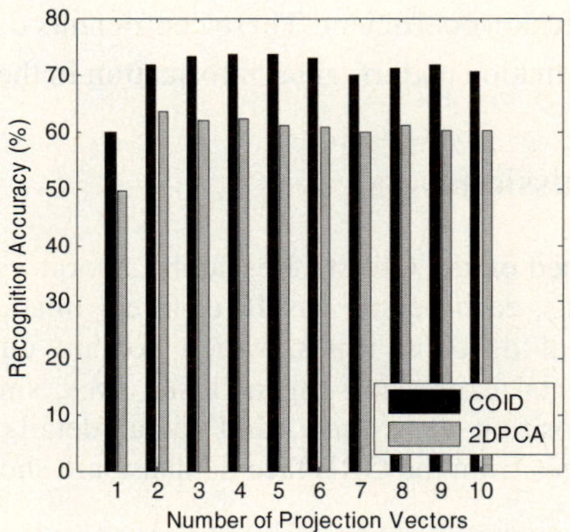

Fig. 3. Face Recognition performance for the COID method and 2DPCA. The 2DFLD method is inapplicable when a limited number of training samples is given.

singular thus suffers from the SSS problem. Therefore 2DPCA and COID methods were used for feature extraction. The size of image scatter matrix $\mathbf{S}_t$ was 92 × 92 and the $rank(\mathbf{S}_t)$ = 92, the largest d principal components are used as projection axes. According to section 3.2, most of the discriminant information is reserved. From Fig. 2, it is reasonable to use the 10 eigenvectors corresponding to the largest eigenvalues. The 2DPCA transformed feature matrix $\mathbf{Y}_j$ is of size 112 × 10, thus, it follows that $\tilde{\mathbf{S}}_b$ and $\tilde{\mathbf{S}}_w$ are 10 × 10. However, the $rank(\hat{\mathbf{S}}_w)=0$, therefore the positive null space $\mathbf{\Theta}_{\frac{\perp}{w}}$ is used to extract the optimal discriminant vector where $\mathbf{B}_1=0$ and $\mathbf{B}_2=(\boldsymbol{\alpha}_1,\boldsymbol{\alpha}_2,\cdots,\boldsymbol{\alpha}_{10})$ since q = 0. The results in Fig. 3 lead to the following findings: 1) the classification performance with the COID outputs is better than that achieved by the 2DPCA method. The best performance of 73.6% was achieved by COID and 2DPCA obtained an accuracy of 63.6%. The difference is that COID evaluates a smaller discriminant scatter matrix $\tilde{\mathbf{S}}_b$ of size 10 × 10 more accurately, in

Table 1. CPU Times (seconds) for feature extraction at top recognition accuracy for training

	2DPCA	2DLDA	Image Irregular	Image Regular	COID
Accuracy (%)	86.9	88.0	77.5	84.38	89.9
Dimensions	112×4	112×2	112×2	112×2	112×2
Feature Extraction time (seconds) *Pentium IV, 3.00GHz, RAM 496Mb*	0.438	0.562	1.143	1.260	2.150

contrast to the scatter matrix of 2DPCA of size 92 × 92. 2) The recognition accuracy increases as the number of eigenvectors $\mathbf{B}_2 = (\boldsymbol{\alpha}_1, \boldsymbol{\alpha}_2, \cdots, \boldsymbol{\alpha}_{10})$ used are increased. In particular, the face recognition perform of COID becomes stable when 4 and 5 eigenvectors are used where a top recognition accuracy of 73.6%. After which the recognition accuracy decreases as noise and redundancies are introduced by the smaller eigenvectors making the system unstable. Similar trend is also observed for 2DPCA.

We then analysed the performance of 2DPCA [1], 2DFLD [3] and COID when two image samples per class are used for training and all the remaining image samples per class for testing. Again 10 eigenvectors were used to transform the 2DPCA space. Then spaces $\mathbf{\Theta}_w = span\{\alpha_1, \alpha_2, \cdots, \alpha_4\}$ and $\mathbf{\Theta}_{\underset{w}{\perp}} = span\{\alpha_5, \alpha_6, \cdots, \alpha_{10}\}$ were defined as in section 3.2. The fusion coefficients θ_r =2 and θ_i = 0.8 were used combine the two kinds of discriminant information. The results in table 1 lead to the findings: 1) the COID method performs better than 2DPCA, 2DLDA methods with an accuracy of 89.9% correct recognition when 112×2 features are used. In addition, the dimensions of the feature matrix for COID method are comparable to 2DPCA and 2DLDA. 2) Although the image regular features show superior performance to the irregular feature, they are complementary to each other as shown by the COID results. As the discriminatory power depends on both the within class and between class covariance matrices, regular feature contain more discriminatory information. However, COID (compared to 2DPCA and 2DLDA) takes more time for feature extraction as it requires a two phase process which derives the discriminant information from double discriminant subspace making it a more powerful discriminant approach.

5 Conclusions

A novel Complete Orthogonal Image discriminant (COID) is developed. The COID method performs discriminant analysis in double discriminant subspaces: regular and irregular. The novelty of the OID method comes from 1) the derivation of the two kinds of image discriminant features, image regular and image irregular, in the feature extraction stage and 2) the development of the Complete OID (COID) features-based on the fusion of the two kinds of image discriminant features used in classification. In particular, the COID method first derives a feature image of the face image with reduced dimensionality of the image matrix by means of two dimensional principal component analysis. This low dimensionality is important for the discriminant learning leading to better generalization to unseen images, as the number of examples required for attaining a given level of performance grows exponentially with the dimensionality of the underlying representation space. The reason behind integrating the 2DPCA and the 2DFLD representations are twofold. Firstly, the 2DPCA transformed face images preserves the spatial structure that defines the 2D face image and exhibit strong characteristics features with reduced noise and redundancies. Lastly, 2DFLD would further reduce redundancy and represent orthogonal discriminant features explicitly. Since the image regular and irregular features are complementary for achieving better discriminant features there combined together in order to enhance the performance. In addition, the results show that COID is more suitable for Small Sample Size (SSS) problem due to its double discriminant subspace.

References

[1] Yang, J., Zhang, D., Frangi, A.F., Yang, J.-y.: dimensional PCA: a new approach to appearance-based face representation and recognition. Pattern Analysis and Machine Intelligence, IEEE Transactions 26, 131–137 (2004)

[2] Mutelo, R.M., Khor, L.C., Woo, W.L., Dlay, S.S.: Two-dimensional reduction PCA: a novel approach for feature extraction, representation, and recognition, presented at Visualization and Data Analysis 2006 (2006)

[3] Li, M., Yuan, B.: 2D-LDA: A statistical linear discriminant analysis for image matrix. Pattern Recognition Letters 26, 527–532 (2005)

[4] Yang, J., Zhang, D., Yong, X., Yang, J.-y.: Two-dimensional discriminant transform for face recognition. Pattern Recognition 38, 1125–1129 (2005)

[5] Chen, L.-F., Liao, H.-Y.M., Ko, M.-T., Lin, J.-C., Yu, G.-J.: A new LDA-based face recognition system which can solve the small sample size problem. Pattern Recognition 33, 1713–1726 (2000)

[6] Kreyszig, E.: Introductory Functional Analysis with Applications. John Wiley & Sons, Chichester (1978)

SVM Speaker Verification Using Session Variability Modelling and GMM Supervectors

M. McLaren, R. Vogt, and S. Sridharan

Speech and Audio Research Laboratory
Queensland University of Technology, Brisbane, Australia
{m.mclaren,r.vogt,s.sridharan}@qut.edu.au

Abstract. This paper demonstrates that modelling session variability during GMM training can improve the performance of a GMM supervector SVM speaker verification system. Recently, a method of modelling session variability in GMM-UBM systems has led to significant improvements when the training and testing conditions are subject to session effects. In this work, session variability modelling is applied during the extraction of GMM supervectors prior to SVM speaker model training and classification. Experiments performed on the NIST 2005 corpus show major improvements over the baseline GMM supervector SVM system.

1 Introduction

Commonly, text-independent speaker verification systems employ Gaussian mixture models (GMMs) trained using maximum a-posteriori (MAP) adaptation from a universal background model (UBM) to provide state-of-the-art performance [1,2,3]. The GMM-UBM approach involves generative modelling whereby the distribution that produced some observed data is determined.

A major challenge in the design of speaker verification systems is the task of increasing robustness under adverse conditions. During the GMM training process, adverse effects due to session variability contribute to errors in the distribution estimation.

Recently, a method was proposed to directly model session variability in telephony speech during model training and testing [4,5]. The main assumption is that session effects can be represented as a set of offsets from the true speaker model means. A further assumption is that the offsets are constrained to a low-dimensional space. Session variability modelling attempts to directly model the session effects in the model space, removing the need for discrete session categories and data labelling required for regular handset, channel normalisation and feature mapping [6,7]. Direct modelling of session effects has led to a significant increase in robustness to channel and session variations in GMM-based speaker verification systems. Results show a reduction of 46% in EER and 42% in minimum detection cost over baseline GMM-UBM performance on the Mixer corpus of conversational telephony data [5].

Session variability modelling aims to relate the session effects across the mixture components of a model. For this technique, the speaker dependent information of a model's mixture components can be conveniently represented as a

S.-W. Lee and S.Z. Li (Eds.): ICB 2007, LNCS 4642, pp. 1077–1084, 2007.

GMM mean supervector formed through the concatenation of the GMM component means.

In contrast to the traditional GMM-UBM classifier, the support vector machine (SVM) is a two-class, discriminative classifier whereby the maximum margin between classes is determined. SVMs utilise a kernel to linearly separate two classes in a high-dimensional space. A SVM speaker verification system recently presented by Campbell et al. has utilised GMM mean supervectors as features to provide performance comparable to state-of-the-art GMM-UBM classifiers [8].

The fundamental differences between GMM and SVM classification bring into question whether techniques used to improve GMM systems based on *distribution estimation* can also enhance SVM classification based on *margin maximisation*. This paper aims to demonstrate that robust modelling techniques developed for generative modelling can improve the performance of discriminative classifiers. The approach taken involves modelling session variability in the GMM mean supervector space prior to SVM speaker model training and classification.

A description of the common GMM-UBM system and recent research into session variability modelling is presented in Section 2. A brief summary of support vector machines is presented in Section 3 along with details regarding the extraction of session variability modelled supervectors for SVM training. Presented in Section 4 is the experimental configuration with the results of the system evaluated using the NIST 2005 database in Section 5.

2 Modelling Session Variability in the GMM Mean Supervector Space

2.1 The GMM-UBM Classifier

In the context of speaker verification, GMMs are trained using features extracted from a speech sample to represent the speech production of a speaker. In such a system, MAP adaptation is employed to adapt only the means of the UBM to model a speaker [1]. The classifier computes a likelihood ratio using the trained speaker model and the UBM, giving a measure of confidence as to whether a particular utterance was produced by the given speaker. GMM-UBM classifiers provide state-of-the-art performance when coupled with a combination of robust feature modification and score normalisation techniques [3,9].

The GMM likelihood function is,

$$g(x) = \sum_{c=1}^{C} \omega_c \mathcal{N}(\boldsymbol{x}; \boldsymbol{\mu}_c, \boldsymbol{\Sigma}_c), \tag{1}$$

where $\boldsymbol{\omega}_c$ are the component mixture weights, $\boldsymbol{\mu}_c$ the means, and $\boldsymbol{\Sigma}_c$ the covariances of the Gaussians. A mean supervector can be obtained by concatenating each of the mean vectors, $\boldsymbol{\mu} = \left[\boldsymbol{\mu}_1^T \cdots \boldsymbol{\mu}_C^T\right]$. As only the means are adapted during speaker model training, the speaker model can be compactly represented by the common UBM and a speaker dependent GMM mean supervector offset.

2.2 Session Variability Modelling

Attempts to directly model session variability in GMM-UBM based speaker verification systems have provided significant performance improvements when using telephony speech [5]. The purpose of session variability modelling is to introduce a constrained offset of the speaker's mean vectors to represent the effects introduced by the session conditions. In other words, the Gaussian mixture model that best represents the acoustic observations of a particular recording is the combination of a session-independent speaker model and an additional session-dependent offset from the true model means. This can be represented in terms of the GMM component means supervectors as

$$\boldsymbol{\mu}_h(s) = \boldsymbol{m} + \boldsymbol{y}(s) + \boldsymbol{U}\boldsymbol{z}_h(s). \tag{2}$$

Here, the speaker s is represented by the offset $\boldsymbol{y}(s)$ from the speaker independent (or UBM) mean supervector $\boldsymbol{m}$. To represent the conditions of the particular recording (designated with the subscript h), an additional offset of $\boldsymbol{U}\boldsymbol{z}_h(s)$ is introduced where $\boldsymbol{z}_h(s)$ is a low-dimensional representation of the conditions in the recording and $\boldsymbol{U}$ is the low-rank transformation matrix from the constrained session variability subspace to the GMM mean supervector space.

Speaker models are trained through the simultaneous optimisation of the model parameters $\boldsymbol{y}(s)$ and $\boldsymbol{z}_h(s), h = 1, ..., H$ over a set of training observations. The speaker model parameters are optimised according to the *maximum a posteriori* (MAP) criterion often used in speaker verification systems [10,2]. The speaker offset $\boldsymbol{y}(s)$ has a prior as described by Reynolds [1] while the prior for each of the session factors $\boldsymbol{z}_h(s)$ is assumed to belong to a standard normal distribution, $\mathcal{N}(\boldsymbol{0}, \boldsymbol{I})$.

An efficient procedure for the optimisation of the model parameters is described in [5]. The session variability vectors are not actually retained to model the speaker but their estimation is necessary to accurately estimate the true speaker means. A similar optimisation process is used during testing.

3 Support Vector Machines

A support vector machine (SVM) performs classification by mapping observations to a high-dimensional, discriminative space while maintaining good generalisation characteristics [11]. SVM training involves the positioning of a hyperplane in the high-dimensional space such that the maximum margin exists between classes; a procedure unlike distribution estimation for GMMs. The term *support vectors* refers to the training vectors which are located on or between the class boundaries and, as a result, contribute to the positioning of the separating hyperplane. A kernel function $K(\boldsymbol{X}_a, \boldsymbol{X}_b) = \phi(\boldsymbol{X}_a) \cdot \phi(\boldsymbol{X}_b)$ is used to compare observations in the high-dimensional space to avoid explicitly evaluating the mapping function $\phi(\boldsymbol{X})$.

3.1 A GMM Supervector SVM Speaker Verification System

In the context of speaker verification, it is necessary to be able to compare two utterances of varying lengths when using SVMs. A method of achieving this is to train a GMM through mean adaptation to represent each utterance, from which mean supervectors can be extracted. SVMs using GMM supervectors as feature vectors have demonstrated promising capabilities when only feature mapping and feature normalisation are applied [8].

The process of producing a GMM mean supervector to represent an utterance can be viewed as a kernel. Essentially, features from a variable length sequence of feature vectors are being transformed from the input space to the SVM *feature space*. In the given context, the SVM feature space has a dimension determined by the length of the GMM mean supervector.

The SVM system implemented in this work uses the mean offsets from a gender dependent UBM as input supervectors for SVM classification. That is, the supervector representing utterance $\boldsymbol{X}_a$ is the difference between the supervector $\boldsymbol{\mu}_a$ extracted from the mean adapted GMM trained from $\boldsymbol{X}_a$ and the supervector $\boldsymbol{m}$ taken from the gender dependent UBM. The motivation for removing the UBM mean bias is to reduce the rounding errors accumulated when equating dot products of floating point representations in high dimensions.

The input supervectors are also scaled to have unit variance in each dimension based on statistics from the background dataset. The aim of this process is to allow each dimension of the supervector an equal opportunity to contribute to the SVM.

The SVM kernel using background data scaling can then be formulated as,

$$K(\boldsymbol{X}_a, \boldsymbol{X}_b) = (\boldsymbol{\mu}_a - \boldsymbol{m})^T \boldsymbol{B}^{-1} (\boldsymbol{\mu}_b - \boldsymbol{m}), \tag{3}$$

where $\boldsymbol{B}$ is the diagonal covariance matrix of the background data. This background dataset is a collection of non-target speakers used to provide negative examples in the SVM training process.

3.2 Incorporating Session Variability into GMM Supervectors

The session variability modelling technique described in Section 2.2 is employed during GMM training to estimate and remove the contribution of the session conditions from the adapted model means. The trained model means can then be represented in GMM supervector form by $\boldsymbol{y}(s)$ in (2). This session-independent speaker model provides a method of incorporating session variability modelling into SVM classification. This differs from Campbell's nuisance attribute projection (NAP) in which subspaces in the SVM kernel contributing to variability are removed through projection [12].

The following experiments attempt to model session variability into the GMM supervectors during GMM training in order to demonstrate the possible advantages that such techniques for generative modelling may impart on discriminative classification.

4 Experiments

Evaluation of the proposed method was conducted using the NIST 2005 speaker recognition corpus consisting of conversational telephone speech from the Mixer Corpus. Focus was given to 1-sided training and testing using the common evaluation condition, restricted to English dialogue as detailed in the NIST evaluation plan [13]. The performance measures used for system evaluation were the equal error rate (EER) and minimum decision cost function (DCF)

Further experiments involving score-normalisation were conducted on the systems to aid in the comparison of the GMM and SVM domains [6]. A set of 55 male and 87 female T-Norm models were trained to estimate the score normalisation parameters.

4.1 GMM-UBM System

As a point of reference, a baseline GMM-UBM system was implemented. The system uses MAP adaptation with an adaptation factor of 8 and feature-warped MFCC features with appended delta coefficients [7]. Throughout the trials, 512 GMM mixture components were used. Gender dependent UBMs were trained using a diverse selection of 1818 utterances from both Mixer and Switchboard 2 corpora.

The GMM-UBM system employing the session variability modelling technique presented in [5] used gender dependent transform matrices $\boldsymbol{U}$ with a session subspace dimension of $R_s = 50$ trained from the same data as was used to train the UBMs.

4.2 GMM Supervector SVM System

The training of SVM speaker models required the production of several sets of utterance supervectors. A GMM mean supervector was produced to represent each *(1)* utterance in the background data set, *(2)* training utterance and *(3)* testing utterance. The background dataset consisted of all utterances used to train the UBMs.

The difference between the standard SVM and the session variability modelling SVM system is the method used to train the GMMs to represent each utterance prior to extraction of the supervectors. The baseline SVM system used standard MAP adapted GMMs to represent each utterance while the session SVM system employed session variability modelling training. In the latter system, session variability modelling was applied to the GMM of each utterance including those in the background data set.

For both systems, the supervectors were used to train one-sided SVM speaker models using LIBSVM [14]. A single supervector was used to represent the target training utterance while non-target training utterances were represented by the gender dependent background data set.

The SVM employed a linear-based kernel using background data scaling as detailed in (3).

5 Results

A comparison of performance between different system configurations is shown in Figure 1 with resulting EER and minimum DCF points detailed in Table 1. Results of systems including score normalisation are also detailed in this table.

These results show that a distinct performance gain can be achieved in discriminative classifiers when robust modelling techniques are applied during generative model training. This is evident by the observed performance variation between the two discriminative classifiers. The minimum DCF of the SVM system was reduced from .0258 to .0185 when session variability modelling was applied; a 28% relative improvement. In terms of EER, the session SVM system has a gain of 13% over the reference SVM configuration.

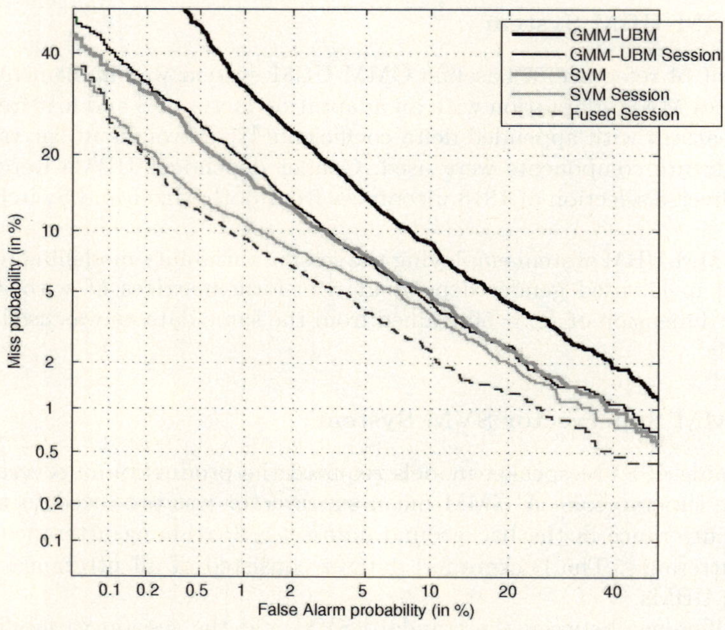

Fig. 1. DET plot for the 1-side condition comparing GMM-UBM and GMM mean supervector SVM systems, with and without session variability modelling

A comparison between the reference GMM-UBM and SVM systems shows the SVM configuration having a gain of 38% in minimum DCF and 30% in EER over the GMM-UBM. Similarly, an improvement of 35% and 10% in minimum DCF and EER respectively is found between the two session configurations.

A significant improvement is shown through the GMM supervector SVM classification over the baseline GMM-UBM configuration which reflects the findings in [12]. Noteworthy is the performance of the reference SVM system being similar to that of the session GMM-UBM system throughout the mid to high false alarm range.

Table 1. Minimum DCF and EER results for 1-side condition for GMM-UBM and GMM mean supervector SVM systems, including T-Norm results

System	Standard		T-Norm	
	EER	Min. DCF	EER	Min. DCF
Reference GMM-UBM	9.15%	.0418	9.95%	.0392
Session GMM-UBM	6.23%	.0286	5.58%	.0239
Reference SVM	6.38%	.0258	6.15%	.0240
Session SVM	5.58%	.0185	5.26%	.0189
Session Fused	4.41%	.0168	4.74%	.0160

Table 1 shows that a significant advantage was found through the application of T-Norm to the session GMM-UBM configuration, supporting previous results indicating that the session GMM-UBM system responds particularly well to score normalisation [5]. Conversely, the session SVM system showed little change through the normalisation technique while the reference GMM-UBM and SVM configurations both showed similar, moderate improvements when applying score-normalisation. The modest improvements due to T-Norm for the session SVM system suggests that this system may produce scores that are less prone to output score variations across different test utterances.

The scores from both the session GMM-UBM and the session SVM system were linearly fused to minimise the mean-squared-error. The DET plot demonstrates that performance is further boosted through this process. The fused system gave a relative improvement of 9% in minimum DCF and 21% in EER over the session SVM configuration. This result indicates that complementary information is found between the two systems despite session variability modelling being incorporated in both. Applying T-Norm to this fused system provided mixed results.

Future work will investigate further score normalisation methods for the GMM mean supervector SVM system using session variability modelling. A comparison between Campbell's method of nuisance attribute projection (modelling session variability in the SVM kernel) with GMM supervectors [12] and the work presented in this paper would also be of interest.

6 Conclusions

This paper has demonstrated that employing robust modelling techniques during GMM training improves the performance of a GMM mean supervector SVM speaker verification system. This is of interest due to the fundamental differences between the two classification systems; GMM's based on distribution estimation versus margin maximisation in SVM classification.

Applying session variability modelling during the training of the GMM mean supervectors for SVM classification showed significant performance gains when evaluated using the NIST 2005 SRE corpus and was superior to the session GMM-UBM configuration. Fusion of the session GMM-UBM and session SVM systems displayed performance above either configuration on its own.

Acknowledgments. This research was supported by the Australian Research Council (ARC) Discovery Grant Project ID: DP0557387.

References

1. Reynolds, D.A., Quatieri, T.F., Dunn, R.B.: Speaker Verification Using Adapted Gaussian Mixture Models. Digital Signal Processing 10(1), 19–41 (2000)
2. Gauvain, J.L., Lee, C.H.: Maximum a posteriori estimation for multivariate Gaussian mixture observations of Markov chains. IEEE Transactions on Speech and Audio Processing 2(2), 291–298 (1994)
3. Przybocki, M., Martin, A.: NIST Speaker Recognition Evaluation Chronicles. In: Odyssey Workshop (2004)
4. Kenny, P., Dumouchel, P.: Experiments in speaker verification using factor analysis likelihood ratios. In: Odyssey: The Speaker and Language Recognition Workshop, pp. 219–226 (2004)
5. Vogt, R., Sridharan, S.: Experiments in Session Variability Modelling for Speaker Verification. IEEE International Conference on Acoustics, Speech and Signal Processing 1, 897–900 (2006)
6. Auckenthaler, R., Carey, M., Lloyd-Thomas, H.: Score normalization for text-independent speaker verification systems. Digital Signal Processing 10(1), 42–54 (2000)
7. Pelecanos, J., Sridharan, S.: Feature warping for robust speaker verification. Proc. Speaker Odyssey 2001 (2001)
8. Campbell, W.M., Sturim, D.E., Reynolds, D.A.: Support vector machines using GMM supervectors for speaker verification. Signal Processing Letters 13(5), 308–311 (2006)
9. Vogt, R.: Automatic Speaker Recognition Under Adverse Conditions. PhD thesis, Queensland University of Technology, Brisbane, Queensland (2006)
10. Reynolds, D.A.: Comparison of background normalization methods for text-independent speaker verification. Proc. Eurospeech 97 (1997)
11. Cortes, C., Vapnik, V.: Support-vector networks. Machine Learning 20(3), 273–297 (1995)
12. Campbell, W.M., Sturim, D.E., Reynolds, D.A., Solomonoff, A.: SVM Based Speaker Verification using a GMM Supervector Kernel and NAP Variability Compensation. IEEE International Conference on Acoustics, Speech and Signal Processing 1, 97–100 (2006)
13. The NIST 2006 Speaker Recognition Evaluation Plan (2006), Available at `http://www.nist.gov/speech/tests/spk/2004/SRE-04_evalplan-v1a.pdf`
14. Chang, C.C., Lin, C.J.: LIBSVM: a library for support vector machines. (2001), Software available at `http://www.csie.ntu.edu.tw/~cjlin/libsvm`

3D Model-Based Face Recognition in Video

Unsang Park and Anil K. Jain

Department of Computer Science and Engineering
Michigan State University
3115 Engineering Building
East Lasing, MI 48824, USA
{parkunsa,jain}@cse.msu.edu

Abstract. Face recognition in video has gained wide attention due to its role in designing surveillance systems. One of the main advantages of video over still frames is that evidence accumulation over multiple frames can provide better face recognition performance. However, surveillance videos are generally of low resolution containing faces mostly in non-frontal poses. Consequently, face recognition in video poses serious challenges to state-of-the-art face recognition systems. Use of 3D face models has been suggested as a way to compensate for low resolution, poor contrast and non-frontal pose. We propose to overcome the pose problem by automatically (i) reconstructing a 3D face model from multiple non-frontal frames in a video, (ii) generating a frontal view from the derived 3D model, and (iii) using a commercial 2D face recognition engine to recognize the synthesized frontal view. A factorization-based structure from motion algorithm is used for 3D face reconstruction. The proposed scheme has been tested on CMU's Face In Action (FIA) video database with 221 subjects. Experimental results show a 40% improvement in matching performance as a result of using the 3D models.

Keywords: Face recognition, video surveillance, 3D face modeling, view synthesis, structure from motion, factorization, active appearance model.

1 Introduction

Automatic face recognition has now been studied for over three decades. While substantial performance improvements have been made in controlled scenarios (frontal pose and favorable lighting conditions), the recognition performance is still brittle with pose and lighting variations [12, 13]. Until recently, face recognition was mostly limited to one or more still shot images, but the current face recognition studies are attempting to combine still shots, video and 3D face models to achieve better performance. In particular, face recognition in video has gained substantial attention due to its applications in deploying surveillance systems. However, face images captured in surveillance systems are mostly off-frontal and have low resolution. Consequently, they do not match very well with the gallery that typically contains frontal face images.

S.-W. Lee and S.Z. Li (Eds.): ICB 2007, LNCS 4642, pp. 1085–1094, 2007.

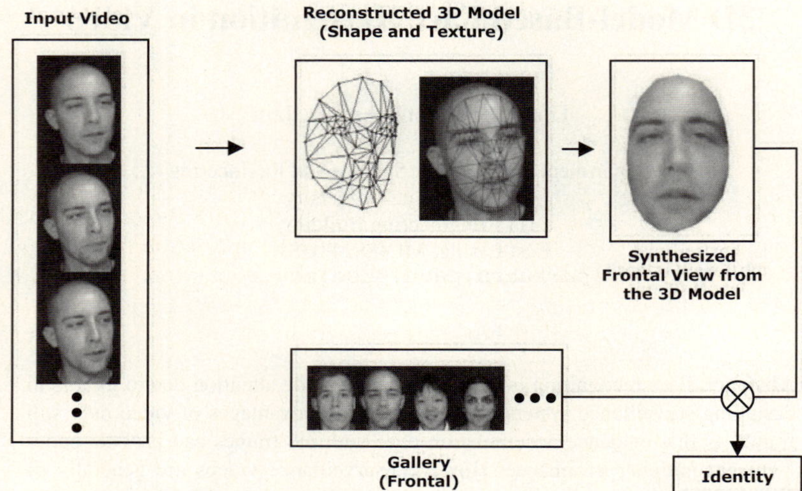

Fig. 1. Face recognition system with 3D model reconstruction and frontal view synthesis

There have been two main approaches to overcome the problem of pose and lighting variations: (i) view-based and (ii) view synthesis. View-based methods enroll multiple face images under various pose and lightings and match the probe image with the gallery image with most similar pose and lighting conditions [1, 2]. View-synthesis methods generate synthetic views from the input probe images with similar pose and lighting conditions as in gallery data to improve the matching performance. The desired view can be synthesized by learning the mapping function between pairs of training images [3] or by using 3D face models [4, 11]. The parameters of the 3D face model in the view synthesis process can also be used for face recognition [4]. Some of the other approaches for face recognition in video utilize appearance manifolds [14] or probabilistic models [15], but they require complicated training process and have been tested only on a small database.

The view-synthesis method is more appealing than the view-based method in two respects. First, it is not practical to collect face images at all possible pose and lighting conditions for the gallery data. Second, the state-of-the-art face recognition systems [5] perform the best in matching two near-frontal face images.

We propose a face recognition system that identifies the subject in a video which contains mostly non-frontal faces. We assume that only the frontal pose is enrolled in gallery data. This scenario is commonly observed in practical surveillance systems. The overall system is depicted in Fig. 1. One of the main contributions of the proposed work is to utilize 3D reconstruction techniques [6, 7, 8] for the purpose of handling the pose variation in the face recognition task. Unlike the morphable model based approach [4], comprehensive evaluations of 3D reconstruction from 2D images for the face recognition task have not been reported. Most of the effort in 3D face model reconstruction from 2D video has focused on accurate facial surface reconstruction, but the application of the resulting model for recognition has not been extensively explored. The contributions of our work are: (i) quantitative evaluation of the performance of factorization algorithm in structure from motion, (ii) view-synthesis using structure from motion and its use in face recognition, and (iii) evaluation on a public domain video database (CMU's Face In Action database [10]) using a commercial state-of-the-art face recognition engine (FaceVACS from Cognitec [5]).

2 3D Face Reconstruction

Obtaining a 3D face model from a sequence of 2D images is an active research problem. Morphable model (MM) [4], stereography [19], and Structure from Motion (SfM) [17, 6] are well known methods in 3D face model construction from 2D images or video. MM method has been shown to provide accurate reconstruction performance, but the processing time is overwhelming for use in real-time systems. Stereography also provides good performance and has been used in commercial applications [19], but it requires a pair of calibrated cameras, which limits its use in many surveillance applications. SfM gives reasonable performance, ability to process in real-time, and does not require a calibration process, making it suitable for surveillance applications. Since we are focusing on face recognition in surveillance video, we propose to use the SfM technique to reconstruct the 3D face models.

2.1 Tracking Facial Feature Points

We use 72 facial feature points that outline the eyes, eyebrows, nose, mouth and facial boundary. While the actual number of feature points is not critical, there needs to be sufficient number of points to capture the facial characteristics. Number of points used in face modeling using AAM vary in the range 60~100. The predefined facial feature points are automatically detected and tracked by the Active Appearance Model (AAM) [18], which is available as a SDK in public domain [9]. We train the AAM model on a training database with about ± 45° yaw, pitch and roll variations. As a result, the facial feature points from a face image within ±45° variations can be reliably located in the test images. The feature points detected in one frame are used as the initial locations for searching in the next frame, resulting in more stable point correspondences. An example of feature point detection is shown in Fig. 2.

2.2 3D Shape Reconstruction

The Factorization method [6] is a well known solution for the Structure from Motion problem. There are different factorization methods depending on the rigidity of the object [7, 8], to recover the detailed 3D shape. We regard the face as a rigid object and treat the small expression changes as noise in feature point detection, resulting in recovering only the most dominant shape from video data.

We use orthographic projection model that works reasonably well for face reconstruction when the distance between camera and object is a few meters. Under orthographic projection model, the relationship between 2D feature points and 3D shape is given by

$$W = M \cdot S, \tag{1}$$

$$W = \begin{bmatrix} u_{11} & u_{12} & \cdots & u_{1p} \\ u_{21} & u_{22} & \cdots & u_{2p} \\ & & \vdots & \\ u_{f1} & u_{f2} & \cdots & u_{fp} \\ v_{11} & v_{12} & \cdots & v_{1p} \\ v_{21} & v_{22} & \cdots & v_{2p} \\ & & \vdots & \\ v_{f1} & v_{f2} & \cdots & v_{fp} \end{bmatrix}, \; M = \begin{bmatrix} i_{1x} & i_{1y} & i_{1z} \\ i_{2x} & i_{2y} & i_{2z} \\ & \vdots & \\ i_{fx} & i_{fy} & i_{fz} \\ j_{1x} & j_{1y} & j_{1z} \\ j_{2x} & j_{2y} & j_{2z} \\ & \vdots & \\ j_{fx} & j_{fy} & j_{fz} \end{bmatrix}, \; S = \begin{bmatrix} S_{x1} & S_{x2} & \cdots & S_{xp} \\ S_{y1} & S_{y2} & \cdots & S_{yp} \\ S_{z1} & S_{z2} & \cdots & S_{zp} \end{bmatrix}, \tag{2}$$

where, u_{fp} and v_{fp} in W represent the row and column pixel coordinates of pth point in the fth frame, each pair of $\boldsymbol{i}_f^T = [i_{fx}\ i_{fy}\ i_{fz}]$ and $\boldsymbol{j}_f^T = [j_{fx}\ j_{fy}\ j_{fz}]$ in M represents the rotation matrix with respect to the fth frame, and S represents the 3D shape. The translation term is omitted in Eq. (1) because all 2D coordinates are centered at the origin. The rank of W in Eq. (2) is 3 in the ideal noise-free case.

The solution of Eq. (1) is obtained by a two-step process: (i) Find an initial estimate of M and S by singular value decomposition, and (ii) apply metric constraints on the initial estimates. By a singular value decomposition of W, we obtain

$$W = U{\cdot}D{\cdot}V^T \approx U'D'V'^T, \tag{3}$$

where U and V are unitary matrices of size 2F×2F and P×P, respectively and D is a matrix of size 2F×P for F frames and P tracked points. Given U, D and V, U' is the first three columns of U, D' is the first three columns and first three rows of D and V'^T is the first three rows of V^T, to impose the rank 3 constraint on W. Then, M' and S' that are the initial estimates of M and S are obtained as

$$M' = U'{\cdot}D'^{1/2},$$
$$S' = D'^{1/2}{\cdot}V'^T. \tag{4}$$

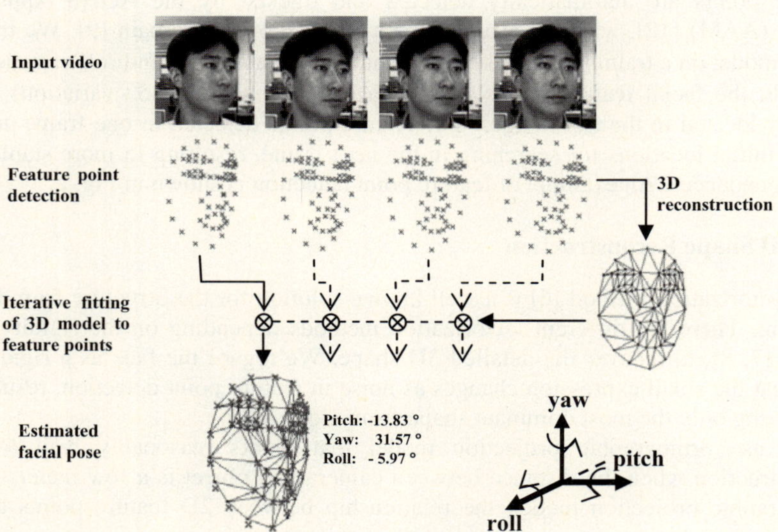

Fig. 2. Pose estimation scheme

To impose the metric constrains on M', a 3×3 correction matrix A is defined as

$$([\boldsymbol{i}_f\ \boldsymbol{j}_f]^{\mathrm{T}} \cdot A) \cdot (A^T \cdot [\boldsymbol{i}_f\ \boldsymbol{j}_f]) = E, \tag{5}$$

where $\boldsymbol{i}_f$ is the fth $\boldsymbol{i}$ vector in the upper half rows of M, $\boldsymbol{j}_f$ is the fth $\boldsymbol{j}$ vector in the lower half rows of M and E is a 2×2 identity matrix. The constraints in Eq. (5) need to be imposed across all frames. There are one $\boldsymbol{i}_f$ and $\boldsymbol{j}_f$ vectors in each frame, which generate three constraints. Since $A \cdot A^T$ is a 3x3 symmetric matrix, there are 6 unknown variables. Therefore, at least two frames are required to solve Eq. (5). In practice, to obtain a robust solution, we need more than two frames and the solution is obtained by the least squared error method. The final solution is obtained as

$$M = M' \cdot A,$$
$$S = A^{-1} \cdot S', \tag{6}$$

where M contains the rotation information between each frame and the 3D object and S contains the 3D shape information. We will provide the lower bound evaluation of the performance of Factorization method on synthetic and real data in Section 3.

2.3 3D Facial Pose Estimation

We estimate the facial pose in a video frame to select the best texture model for the 3D face construction. The video frame with facial pose close to frontal is a good candidate for texture mapping because it covers most of the face area. If a single profile image is used for texture mapping, the quality of the 3D model will be poor in the occluded region. When a frame in a near-frontal pose is not found, two frames are used for texture mapping. There are many facial pose estimation methods in 2D and 3D domains [20]. Because the head motion occurs in 3D domain, 3D information is necessary for accurate pose estimation. We estimate the facial pose in [yaw, pitch, roll] (YPR) values as shown in Fig. 2. Even though all the rotational relationships between the 3D shape and the 2D feature points in each frame are already obtained by the matrix M in factorization process, it reveals only the first two rows of the rotation matrix for each frame, which generates inaccurate solutions in obtaining YPR values especially in noisy data. Therefore, we use the gradient descent method to iteratively fit the reconstructed 3D shape to the 2D facial feature points.

2.4 Texture Mapping

We define the 3D face model as a set of triangles and generate a VRML object. Given the 72 points obtained from the reconstruction process, 124 triangles are generated. While the triangles can be obtained automatically by Delaunay triangulation process [16], we use a predefined set of triangles for efficiency sake because the number and configuration of the feature points are fixed. The corresponding set of triangles can be obtained from the video frames with a similar process. Then, the VRML object is generated by mapping the triangulated texture to the 3D shape. The best frame to be used in texture mapping is selected based on the pose estimation as described earlier. When all the available frames deviate

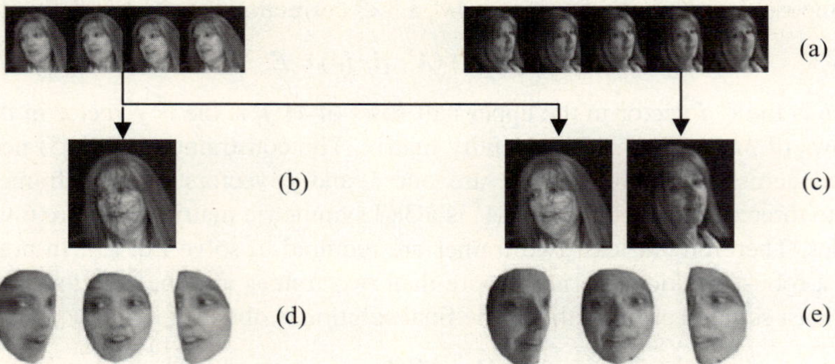

Fig. 3. Texture mapping. (a) a video sequence used for 3D reconstruction; (b) single frame with triangular meshes; (c) two frames with triangular meshes; (d) reconstructed 3D face model with one texture in (b); (e) reconstructed 3D face model with two texture mappings in (c). The two frontal poses in (d) and (e) are correctly identified in matching experiment.

significantly from the frontal pose, two frames are used for texture mapping as described in Fig. 3. Even though both the synthetic frontal views in Figs. 3 (d) and (e) are correctly recognized, the one in (e) looks more realistic. When more than one texture is used for texture mapping, a sharp boundary is often observed across the boundary where two different textures are combined because of the difference in illumination. However, the synthetic frontal views are correctly recognized in most cases regardless of this artifact.

3 Experimental Results

We performed a number of experiments to i) evaluate the lower performance bound of the Factorization algorithm in terms of the rotation angle and number of frames in synthetic and real data, ii) reconstruct 3D face models on a large public domain video database, and iii) perform face recognition using the reconstructed 3D face models.

3.1 3D Face Reconstruction with Synthetic Data

We first evaluate the performance of the Factorization algorithm using synthetic data. A set of 72 facial feature points are obtained from a ground truth 3D face model. A sequence of 2D coordinates of the facial feature points are directly obtained from the ground truth. We take the angular values for the rotation in steps of 0.1° in the range (0.1°, 1°) and in steps of 1° in the range (1°, 10°). The number of frames range from 2 to 5. The RMS error between the ground truth and the reconstructed shape is shown in Fig. 4 (a). While the number of frames required for the reconstruction in the noiseless case is two (Sec. 2.2), in practice more frames are needed to keep the error small. As long as the number of frames is more than two, the errors are negligible.

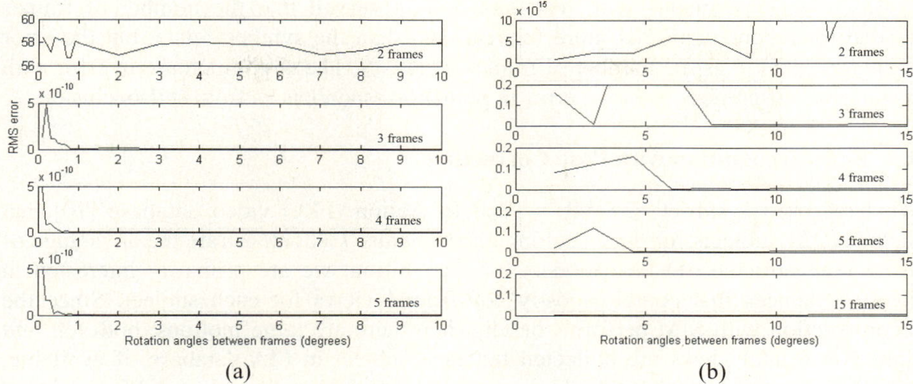

Fig. 4. (a) RMS error between reconstructed shape and ground truth. (b) RMS error between reconstructed and ideal rotation matrix, M_s.

3.2 3D Face Reconstruction with Real Data

For real data, noise is present in both the facial feature point detection and the correspondences between detected points across frames. This noise is not random and its affect is more pronounced at points of self-occlusion and on the facial boundary. Since AAM does use feature points on the facial boundary, the point correspondences are not very accurate in the presence of self-occlusion. Reconstruction experiments are performed on real data with face rotation from -45° to +45° across 61 frames. We estimate the rotation between successive frames as 1.5° (61 frames varying from -45° to +45°) and obtain the reconstruction error with rotation in steps of 1.5° in the range (1.5°, 15°). The number of frames used is from 2 to 61. A direct comparison between the ground truth and the reconstructed shape is not possible in case of real data because the ground truth is not known. Therefore, we measure the orthogonality of M to estimate the reconstruction accuracy. Let M be a 2F×3 matrix as shown in Eq. (3) and $M(a{:}b,c{:}d)$ represent the sub matrix of M from rows a to b and columns c to d. Then, $M_s = M \times M'$ is a 2Fx2F matrix where all elements in $M_s(1{:}F,\ 1{:}F)$ and $M_s(F+1{:}2F,\ F+1{:}2F)$ are equal to 1 and all elements in $M_s(1{:}F,\ F+1{:}2F)$ and $M_s(F+1{:}2F,\ 1{:}F)$ are equal to 0 if M is truly an orthogonal matrix. We measure the RMS difference between the ideal M_s and the calculated M_s as the reconstruction error. The reconstruction error for real data is shown in Fig. 4 (b).

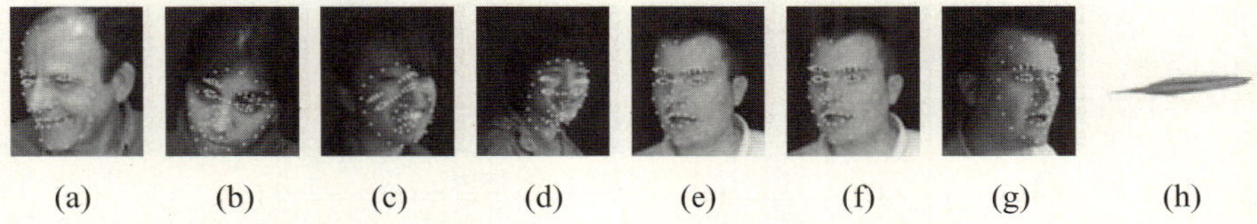

(a) (b) (c) (d) (e) (f) (g) (h)

Fig. 5. Examples where 3D face reconstruction was not successful. (a), (b), (c) and (d) Failure of feature point detection using AAM; (e), (f) and (g) Deficiency of motion cue, resulting in (h) a failure of SfM to reconstruct the 3D face model.

Based on experiments with real data, it is observed that the number of frames needed for reconstruction is more for real data than the synthetic data, but the error decreases quickly as the number of frames increases. The slight increase in error with larger pose differences is due to error in point correspondences from self-occlusion.

3.3 Face Recognition with Pose Correction

We have used a subset of CMU's Face In Action (FIA) video database [10] that includes 221 subjects for our matching experiments. To demonstrate the advantage of using reconstructed 3D face models for recognition, we are primarily interested in video sequences that contain mostly non-frontal views for each subject. Since the reconstruction with SfM performs better when there are large motions, both left and right non-frontal views are collected for each subject in FIA database, if available, resulting, on average, about 10 frames per subject. When there is a sufficient inter-frame motion and the feature point detection performs well, it is possible to obtain the 3D face model from only 3 different frames, which in consistent with the results shown in Fig. 4. The number of frames that is required for the reconstruction can be determined based on the orthogonality of M.

We successfully reconstructed 3D face models for 197 subjects out of the 221 subjects in the database. The reconstruction process failed for 24 subjects either due to poor facial feature point detection in the AAM process or the deficiency of motion cue, which caused a degenerate solution in the factorization algorithm. Example images where AAM or SfM failed are shown in Fig. 5. The failure occurs due to large pose or shape variations that were not represented in the samples used to train the AAM model. All the reconstructed 3D face models are corrected in their pose to make all yaw, pitch, and roll values equal to zero. The frontal face image can be obtained by projecting the 3D model in the 2D plane. Once the frontal view is synthesized, FaceVACS® face recognition engine from Cognitec [5] is used to generate the matching score. This engine is one of the best commercial 2D face recognition systems. The face recognition results for frontal face video, non-frontal face video

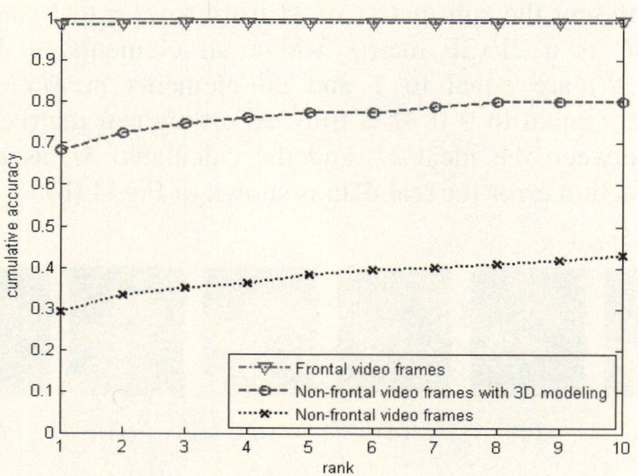

Fig. 6. Face recognition performance with 3D face modeling

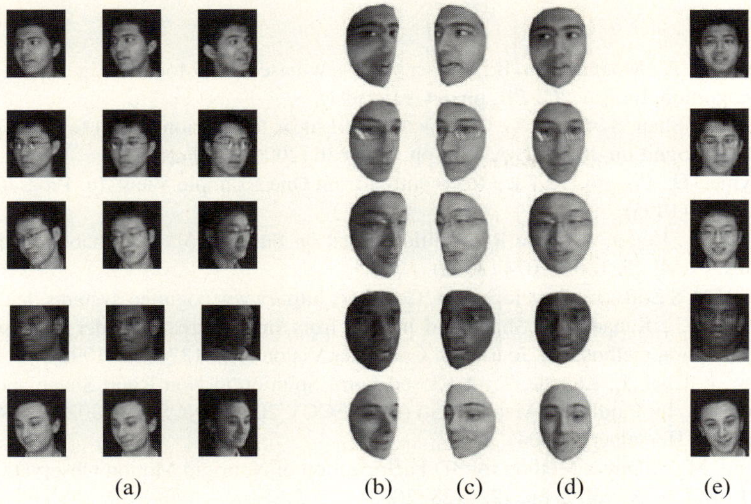

Fig. 7. 3D model-based face recognition results on six subjects (Subject IDs in the FIA database are 47, 56, 85, 133, and 208). (a) Input frames; (b), (c) and (d) reconstructed 3D face models at right, left, and frontal views, respectively; (e) frontal images enrolled in the gallery database. All the frames in (a) are not correctly identified, while the synthetic frontal views in (d) obtained from the reconstructed 3D models are correctly identified for the first four subjects, but not for the last subject (#208). The reconstructed 3D model of the last subject appears very different from the gallery image, resulting in the recognition failure.

and non-frontal face video with 3D face modeling are shown in Fig. 6 based on 197 subjects for which the 3D face reconstruction was successful. The CMC curves show that the FaceVACS engine does extremely well for frontal pose video but its performance drops drastically for non-frontal pose video. By using the proposed 3D face modeling, the rank-1 performance in non-frontal scenario improves by about 40%. Example 3D face models and the synthesized frontal views from six different subjects are shown in Fig. 7.

4 Conclusions

We have shown that the proposed 3D model based face recognition from video provides a significantly better performance, especially when many non-frontal views are observed. The proposed system synthesizes the frontal face image from the 3D reconstructed models and matches it against the frontal face enrolled in the gallery. We have automatically generated 3D face models for 197 subjects in the Face In Action database (session 1, indoor, camera 5) using the SfM factorization method. The experimental results show substantial improvement in the rank-1 matching performance (from 30% to 70%) for video with non-frontal pose. The entire face recognition process (feature point tracking, 3D model construction, matching) takes ~10 s per subject on a Pentium IV PC for 320x240 frames. We are working to improve the matching speed and the texture blending technique to remove the sharp boundary that is often observed when mapping multiple textures.

References

[1] Pentland, A., Moghaddam, B., Starner, T.: View-based and Modular Eigenspace for Face Recognition. In: Proc. CVPR, pp. 84–91 (1994)

[2] Chai, X., Shan, S., Chen, X., Gao, W.: Local Linear Regression (LLR) for Pose Invariant Face Recognition. In: Proc. AFGR, pp. 631–636 (2006)

[3] Beymer, D., Poggio, T.: Face Recognition from One Example View. In: Proc. ICCV, pp. 500–507 (1995)

[4] Blanz, V., Vetter, T.: Face Recognition based on Fitting a 3D Morphable Model. IEEE Trans. PAMI 25, 1063–1074 (2003)

[5] FaceVACS Software Developer Kit, Cognitec, http://www.cognitec-systems.de

[6] Tomasi, C., Kanade, T.: Shape and motion from image streams under orthography: A factorization method. Int. Journal of Computer Vision 9(2), 137–154 (1992)

[7] Xiao, J., Chai, J., Kanade, T.: A Closed-Form Solution to Non-Rigid Shape and Motion Recovery. In: Pajdla, T., Matas, J(G.) (eds.) ECCV 2004. LNCS, vol. 3024, pp. 668–675. Springer, Heidelberg (2004)

[8] Brand, M.: A Direct Method for 3D Factorization of Nonrigid Motion Observation in 2D. In: Proc. CVPR, vol. 2, pp. 122–128 (2005)

[9] Stegmann, M.B.: The AAM-API: An Open Source Active Appearance Model Implementation. In: Ellis, R.E., Peters, T.M. (eds.) MICCAI 2003. LNCS, vol. 2879, pp. 951–952. Springer, Heidelberg (2003)

[10] Goh, R., Liu, L., Liu, X., Chen, T.: The CMU Face In Action (FIA) Database. In: Zhao, W., Gong, S., Tang, X. (eds.) AMFG 2005. LNCS, vol. 3723, pp. 255–263. Springer, Heidelberg (2005)

[11] Zhao, W., Chellappa, R.: SFS Based View Synthesis for Robust Face Recognition. In: Proc. FGR, pp. 285–292 (2000)

[12] Phillips, P.J., Grother, P., Micheals, R.J., Blackburn, D.M., Tabassi, E., Bone, J.M.: FRVT: 2002: Evaluation Report, Tech. Report NISTIR 6965, NIST (2003)

[13] Phillips, P.J., Flynn, P.J., Scruggs, T., Bowyer, K.W., Worek, W.: Preliminary Face Recognition Grand Challenge Results. In: Proc. AFGR, pp. 15–24 (2006)

[14] Lee, K., Ho, J., Yang, M., Kriegman, D.: Video-based face recognition using probabilistic appearance manifolds. CVPR I, 313–320 (2003)

[15] Zhou, S., Krueger, V., Chellappa, R.: Probabilistic recognition of human faces from video. Computer Vision and Image Understanding 91, 214–245 (2003)

[16] Barber, C.B., Dobkin, D.P., Huhdanpaa, H.: The Quickhull Algorithm for Convex Hulls. ACM Trans. Mathematical Software 22(4), 469–483 (1996)

[17] Ullman, S.: The Interpretation of Visual Motion. MIT Press, Cambridge, MA (1979)

[18] Matthews, I., Baker, S.: Active Appearance Models Revisited. International Journal of Computer Vision 60(2), 135–164 (2004)

[19] Maurer, T., Guigonis, D., Maslov, I., Pesenti, B., Tsaregorodtsev, A., West, D., Medioni, G.: Performance of Geometrix ActiveIDTM 3D Face Recognition Engine on the FRGC Data. In: Proc. CVPR, pp. 154–160 (2005)

[20] Tu, J., Huang, T., Tao, H.: Accurate Head Pose Tracking in Low Resolution Video. In: Proc. FGR, pp. 573–578 (2006)

Robust Point-Based Feature Fingerprint Segmentation Algorithm

Chaohong Wu, Sergey Tulyakov, and Venu Govindaraju

Center for Unified Biometrics and Sensors (CUBS)
SUNY at Buffalo, USA

Abstract. A critical step in automatic fingerprint recognition is the accurate segmentation of fingerprint images. The objective of fingerprint segmentation is to decide which part of the images belongs to the foreground containing features for recognition and identification, and which part to the background with the noisy area around the boundary of the image. Unsupervised algorithms extract blockwise features. Supervised method usually first extracts point features like coherence, average gray level, variance and Gabor response, then a Fisher linear classifier is chosen for classification. This method provides accurate results, but its computational complexity is higher than most of unsupervised methods. This paper proposes using Harris corner point features to discriminate foreground and background. Shifting a window in any direction around the corner should give a large change in intensity. We observed that the strength of Harris point in the foreground area is much higher than that of Harris point in background area. The underlying mechanism for this segmentation method is that boundary ridge endings are inherently stronger Harris corner points. Some Harris points in noisy blobs might have higher strength, but it can be filtered as outliers using corresponding Gabor response. The experimental results proved the efficiency and accuracy of new method are markedly higher than those of previously described methods.

1 Introduction

The accurate segmentation of fingerprint images is key component to achieve high performance in automatic fingerprint recognition systems. If more background areas are included into segmented fingerprint of interest, more false features are possibly introduced into detected feature set; If some parts of foreground are excluded, useful feature points may be missed. There are two types of fingerprint segmentation algorithms: unsupervised and supervised. Unsupervised algorithms extract blockwise features such as local histogram of ridge orientation [1,2], gray-level variance, magnitude of the gradient in each image block [3], Gabor feature [4,5]. Practically, the presence of noise, low contrast area, and inconsistent contact of a fingertip with the sensor may result in loss of minutiae or more spurious minutiae. Supervised method usually first extracts several features like coherence, average gray level, variance and Gabor response [5,6,7], then a simple linear classifier is chosen for classification. This method provides accurate results, but its computational complexity is higher than most unsupervised methods.

Segmentation in low quality images faces several challenging technical problems. First problem is the presence of noise caused by dust and grease on the surface of live-scan fingerprint scanners. Second problem is ghost images of fingerprints remaining

S.-W. Lee and S.Z. Li (Eds.): ICB 2007, LNCS 4642, pp. 1095–1103, 2007.

from the previous image acquisition [7]. Third problem is low contrast fingerprint ridges generated through inconsistent contact press or dry/wet finger surface. Fourth problem is indistinct boundary if the features in the fixed size of window are used. Final problem is segmentation features being sensitive to the quality of image.

This paper proposes using Harris corner point features [8,9] to discriminate foreground and background. The Harris corner detector was developed originally as features for motion tracking, it can reduce significantly amount of computation compared to tracking every pixel. It is translation and rotation invariant but not scale invariant. We found that the strength of a Harris point in the foreground area is much higher than that of a Harris point in the background area. Some Harris points in noisy blobs might have higher strength, but it can be filtered as outliers using corresponding Gabor response. The experimental results proved the efficiency and accuracy of new method are much better than those of previously described methods. Furthermore, this segmentation algorithm can detect accurate boundary of fingerprint ridge regions, which is very useful in removing spurious boundary minutiae, and most current segmentation methods can not provide consistent boundary minutiae filtering.

2 Features for Fingerprint Segmentation

Feature selection is the first step for designing fingerprint segmentation algorithm. There are two general types of features used for fingerprint segmentation, i.e., block features and pointwise features. In [5,10] selected point features include local mean, local variance or standard deviation, and Gabor response of the fingerprint image. Local mean is calculated as $Mean = \sum_w I$, local variance is calculated as $Var = \sum_w (I - Mean)^2$, w is window size centered the processed pixel. The Gabor response is the smoothed sum of Gabor energies for eight Gabor filter responses. Usually the Gabor response is higher in the foreground region than that in the background region. The coherence feature indicates how strong the local window gradients centered the processed point in the same dominant orientation. Usually the coherence will be much higher in the foreground than in the background, but it may be influenced significantly by boundary signal and noisy signal. Therefore, single coherence feature is not sufficient for robust segmentation. Systematic combination of those features is necessary.

$$Coh = \frac{|\sum_w (G_{s,x}, G_{s,y})|}{|\sum_w (G_{s,x}, G_{s,y})|} = \frac{\sqrt{(G_{xx} - G_{yy})^2 + 4G_{xy}^2}}{G_{xx} + G_{yy}} \tag{1}$$

Because pointwise-based segmentation method is time consuming, blockwise features are usually used in the commercial automatic fingerprint recognition systems. Block mean, block standard deviation, block gradient histogram [1,2], block average magnitude of the gradient [11] are most common block features for fingerprint segmentation. In [12] gray-level pixel intensity-derived feature called block clusters degree(CluD) is introduced. *CluD* measures how well the ridge pixels are clustering.

$$E(x, y) = \log \left\{ \int_r \int_\theta |F(r, \theta)|^2 \right\} \tag{2}$$

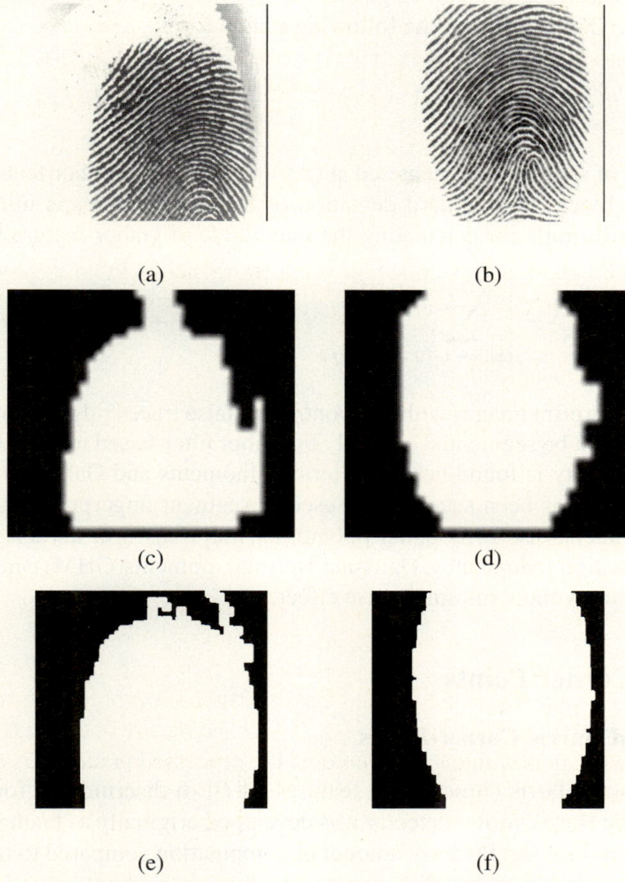

Fig. 1. (a) and (b) are two original images, (c) and (d) are FFT energy maps for images (a) and (b), (e) and (f) are Gabor energy maps for images (a) and (b), respectively

Texture features, such as Fourier spectrum energy [6], Gabor features [4,13] and Gaussian-Hermite Moments [14], have been applied to fingerprint segmentation. Ridges and valleys in a fingerprint image are generally observed to possess a sinusoidal-shaped plane wave with a well-defined frequency and orientation [15], and non-ridge regions does not hold this surface wave model. In the areas of background and noisy regions, it is assumed that there is very little structure and hence very little energy content in the Fourier spectrum. Each value of energy image E(x,y) indicates the energy content of the corresponding block. The fingerprint region may be differentiated from the background by thresholding the energy image. The logarithm values of the energy is used to convert the large dynamic range to a linear scale(Equation 2). The region mask is obtained by thresholding $E(x, y)$. However, uncleaned trace finger ridges and straight stripes are unfortunately included into regions of interest (Figure 1(c)).

Gabor filter-based segmentation algorithm is now most often used method [4,13]. An even symmetric Gabor filter has the following spatial form:

$$g(x, y, \theta, f, \sigma_x, \sigma_y) = exp\{-\frac{1}{2}[\frac{x_\theta^2}{\sigma_x^2} + \frac{y_\theta^2}{\sigma_y^2}]\}cos(2\pi f x_\theta) \quad (3)$$

For each block of size $W \times W$ centered at (x,y), 8 directional Gabor features are computed for each block, the standard deviation of 8 Gabor features is utilized for segmentation. The formula for calculating the magnitude of Gabor feature is defined as,

$$G(X, Y, \theta, f, \sigma_x, \sigma_y) = \left| \sum_{x_0=-w/2}^{(w/2)-1} \sum_{y_0=-w/2}^{(w/2)-1} I(X + x_0, Y + y_0) g(x_0, y_0, \theta, f, \sigma_x, \sigma_y) \right| \quad (4)$$

However, fingerprint images with low contrast or false traces ridges or noisy complex background can not be segmented correctly by Gabor filter-based method (Figure 1(e)).

In [14], similarity is found between Hermite moments and Gabor filter. Gaussian-Hermite Moments has been successfully used to segment fingerprint images in [14]. Orthogonal moments use orthogonal polynomials as transform kernels and produce minimal information redundancy, Gaussian Hermite moments(GHM) can represent local texture feature without minimal noise effect.

3 Harris Corner Points

3.1 Review of Harris-Corner-Points

We propose using Harris corner point features [8,9] to discriminate foreground and background. The Harris corner detector was developed originally as features for motion tracking, it can reduce significantly amount of computation compared to tracking every pixel. Shifting a window in any direction around the corner should give a large change in intensity. Corner points provide repeatable points for matching, so some efficient methods have been designed [8,9]. Gradient is ill defined at a corner, so edge detectors perform poorly at corners. However, in the region around a corner, gradient has two or more different values. The corner point can be easily recognized by looking a small window. Shifting a window around a corner point in any direction should give a large change in gray-level intensity,

Given a point I(x,y), and a shift(Δx, Δy), the auto-correlation function E is defined as:

$$E(x, y) = \sum_{w(x,y)} [I(x_i, y_i) - I(x_i + \Delta x, y_i + \Delta y)]^2 \quad (5)$$

where w(x,y)is window function centered on image point(x,y). For a small shifts [Δx,Δy], the shifted image is approximated by a *Taylor expansion* truncated to the first order terms,

$$I(x_i + \Delta x, y_i + \Delta y) \approx I(x_i, y_i) + [I_x(x_i, y_i) I_y(x_i, y_i)] \begin{bmatrix} \Delta x \\ \Delta y \end{bmatrix} \quad (6)$$

where $I_x(x_i, y_i)$ and $I_y(x_i, y_i)$ denote the partial derivatives in x and y, respectively. Substituting approximation Equation 6 into Equation 5 yields,

$$\begin{aligned} E(x,y) &= \textstyle\sum_{w(x,y)}[I(x_i,y_i) - I(x_i+\Delta x, y_i+\Delta y)]^2 \\ &= \textstyle\sum_{w(x,y)} \left(I(x_i,y_i) - I(x_i,y_i) - [I_x(x_i,y_i)I_y(x_i,y_i)] \begin{bmatrix} \Delta x \\ \Delta y \end{bmatrix} \right)^2 \\ &= \textstyle\sum_{w(x,y)} \left(-[I_x(x_i,y_i)I_y(x_i,y_i)] \begin{bmatrix} \Delta x \\ \Delta y \end{bmatrix} \right)^2 \\ &= \textstyle\sum_{w(x,y)} \left([I_x(x_i,y_i)I_y(x_i,y_i)] \begin{bmatrix} \Delta x \\ \Delta y \end{bmatrix} \right)^2 \\ &= [\Delta x, \Delta y] \begin{bmatrix} \sum_w (I_x(x_i,y_i))^2 & \sum_w I_x(x_i,y_i)I_y(x_i,y_i) \\ \sum_w I_x(x_i,y_i)I_y(x_i,y_i) & \sum_w (I_y(x_i,y_i))^2 \end{bmatrix} \begin{bmatrix} \Delta x \\ \Delta y \end{bmatrix} \\ &= [\Delta x, \Delta y] M(x,y) \begin{bmatrix} \Delta x \\ \Delta y \end{bmatrix} \end{aligned} \tag{7}$$

That is,

$$E(\Delta x, \Delta y) = [\Delta x, \Delta y] M(x,y) \begin{bmatrix} \Delta a \\ \Delta y \end{bmatrix} \tag{8}$$

where M(x,y) is a 2×2 matrix computed from image derivatives, called auto-correlation matrix which captures the intensity structure of the local neighborhood.

$$M = \sum_{x,y} w(x,y) \begin{bmatrix} (I_x(x_i,y_i))^2 & I_x(x_i,y_i)I_y(x_i,y_i) \\ I_x(x_i,y_i)I_y(x_i,y_i) & (I_y(x_i,y_i))^2 \end{bmatrix} \tag{9}$$

3.2 Strength of Harris-Corner Points of a Fingerprint Image

In order to detect interest points, the original measure of corner response in [8] is :

$$R = \frac{det(M)}{Trace(M)} = \frac{\lambda_1 \lambda_2}{\lambda_1 + \lambda_2} \tag{10}$$

The auto-correlation matrix (M) captures the structure of the local neighborhood. Based on eigenvalues(λ_1, λ_2) of M, interest points are located where there are two strong eigen values and the corner strength is a local maximum in a 3×3 neighborhood. To avoid the explicit eigenvalue decomposition of M, $Trace(M)$ is calculated as $I_x^2 + I_y^2$, $Det(m)$ is calculated as $I_x^2 I_y^2 - (I_x I_y)^2$, and

$$R = Det(m) - k \times Trace(M)^2 \tag{11}$$

To segment the fingerprint area (foreground) from the background, the following "corner strength" measure is used, because there is one undecided parameter k in equation(11).

$$R = \frac{I_x^2 I_y^2 - I_{xy}^2}{I_x^2 + I_y^2} \tag{12}$$

3.3 Harris-Corner-Points Based Fingerprint Image Segmentation

We found that the strength of a Harris point in the fingerprint area is much higher than that of a Harris point in background area, because boundary ridge endings inherently possess higher corner strength. Most high quality fingerprint images can be easily segmented by choosing appropriate threshold value. In Figure 2, a corner strength of 300 is selected to distinguish corner points in the foreground from those in the background. Convex hull algorithm is used to connect harris corner points located in the foreground boundary.

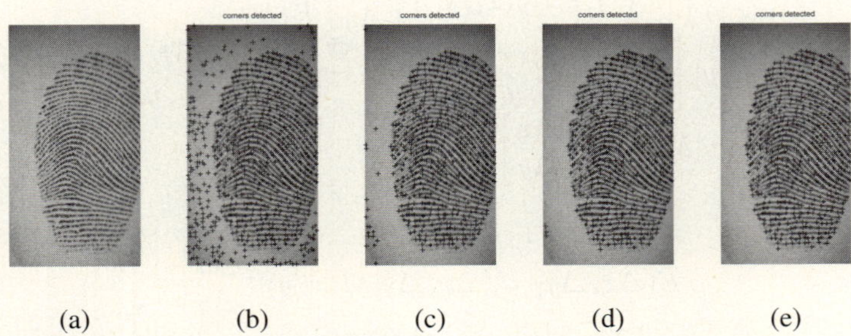

(a) (b) (c) (d) (e)

Fig. 2. A fingerprint with harris corner strength of (b)10, (c)60, (d)200, and (e)300. This fingerprint can be successfully segmented using corner response threshold of 300.

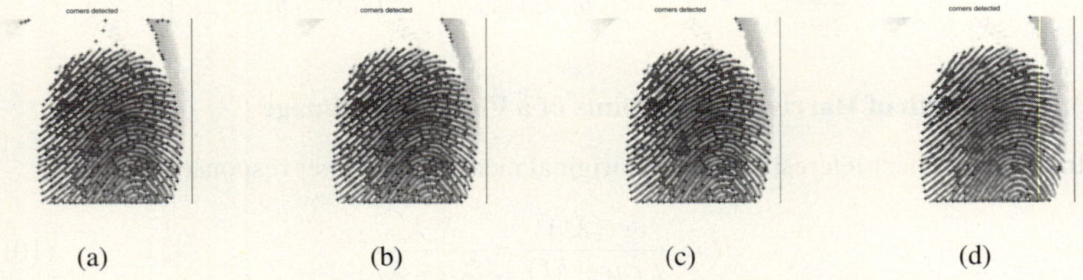

(a) (b) (c) (d)

Fig. 3. A fingerprint with harris corner strength of (a)100, (b)500, (c)1000, (d) 1500 and (e)3000. Some noisy corner points can not be filtered completely even using corner response threshold of 3000.

It appears relatively easy for us to segment fingerprint images for following image enhancement, feature detection and matching. However, two technical problems need to be solved. First, different "corner strength" thresholds are necessary to achieve good segmentation results for different qualities images based on image characteristical analysis. Second, Some Harris points in noisy blobs might have higher strength, it can not be segmented by choosing simply one threshold. When single threshold is applied to all the fingerprint images in one whole database, not all the corner points in the background in a fingerprint image are removed, some corner points in noisy regions can not be thresholded even using high threshold value (Figure 3). In order to deal with such situations, we implemented a heuristic selection algorithm using corresponding Gabor response (Figure 4).

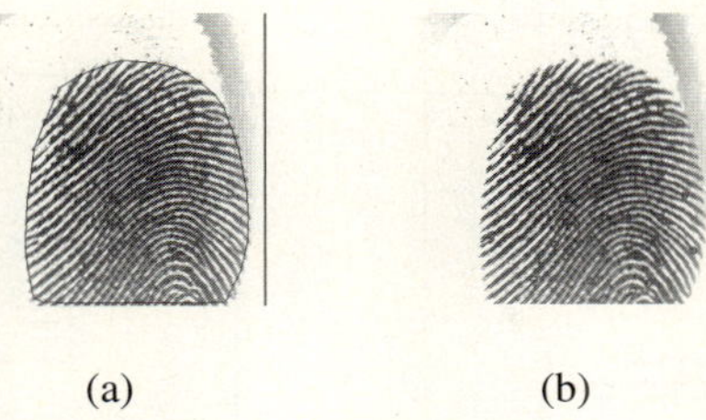

(a) (b)

Fig. 4. Segmentation result and final feature detection result for the image shown in the Figure 1(a). (a) Segmented fingerprint marked with boundary line, (b) final detected minutiae.

4 Experimental Results

The proposed methodology is tested on FVC2002 DB1 and DB4, each database consists of 800 fingerprint images (100 distinct fingers, 8 impressions each). Image size is 374×388 and the resolution is 500dpi. To evaluate the methodology of adapting a gaussian kernel to the local ridge curvature of a fingerprint image, we modified Gabor-based fingerprint enhancement algorithm [15,16] with two kernel sizes: the smaller one in high-curvature regions and the larger one in pseudo-parallel ridge regions, minutiae are detected using chaincode-based contour tracing [17], the fingerprint matcher developed by Jea et al. [18] is used for performance evaluation.

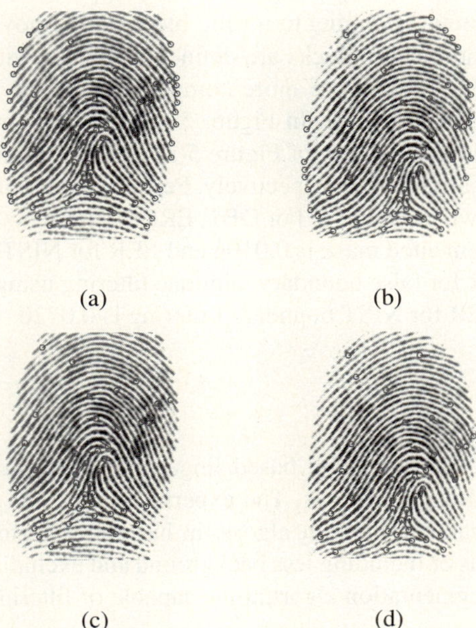

(a) (b)

(c) (d)

Fig. 5. Boundary spurious minutiae filtering. (a) and (b) incomplete filtering using NIST method, (c) and (d) proposed boundary filtering.

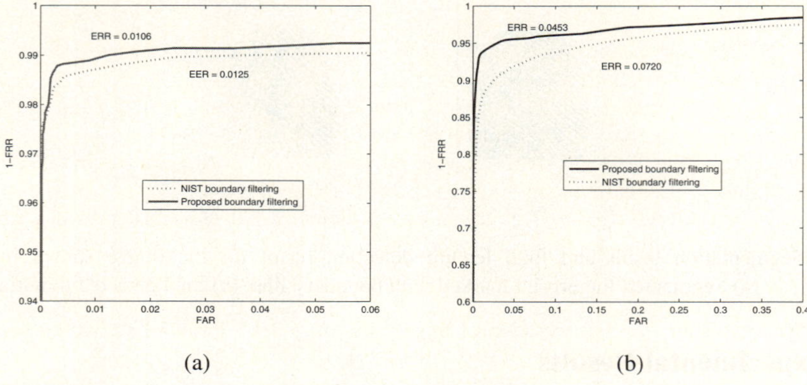

Fig. 6. ROC curves for (a) FVC2002 DB1 and (b) FVC2002 DB4

Our methodology has been tested on low quality images from FVC2002. To validate the efficiency of proposed segmentation method, current widely-used Gabor filter-based segmentation algorithm [4,13] and NIST segmentation [19] are utilized for comparison.

The proposed segmentation method have a remarkable advantage over current methods in terms of boundary spurious minutiae filtering. Figure 5 (a) and (b) show unsuccessful boundary minutiae filtering using NIST method [19], which is implemented by removing spurious minutiae pointing to invalid block and removing spurious minutiae near invalid blocks, and invalid blocks are defined as blocks with no detectable ridge flow. However, boundary blocks are more complicated, so the method in [19] fails to remove most boundary minutiae. In Figure 5 (c) and (d) show the filtering results of proposed method. In comparison of Figure 5(a) against (c) and (b) and (d), 30 and 17 boundary minutiae are filtered, respectively. Performance evaluations for FVC2002 DB1 and DB4 are shown in Figure 6. For DB1, ERR for false boundary minutiae filtering using proposed segmented mask is 0.0106 and EER for NIST boundary Filtering is 0.0125. For DB4, ERR for false boundary minutiae filtering using proposed segmented mask is 0.0453 and EER for NIST boundary Filtering is 0.0720.

5 Conclusions

In this paper, a robust interest point based fingerprint segmentation is proposed for fingerprints of varied image qualities. The experimental results compared with those of previous methods validate that our algorithm has better performance even for low quality images, in terms of including less background and excluding less foreground. In addition, this robust segmentation algorithm is capable of filtering efficiently spurious boundary minutiae.

References

1. Mehtre, B.M., Chatterjee, B.: Segmentation of fingerprint images – a composite method. Pattern Recognition 22(4), 381–385 (1989)
2. Mehtre, B.M., Murthy, N.N., Kapoor, S., Chatterjee, B.: Segmentation of fingerprint images using the directional image. Pattern Recognition 20(4), 429–435 (1987)
3. Ratha, N.K., Chen, S., Jain, A.K.: Adaptive flow orientation-based feature extraction in fingerprint images. Pattern Recognition 28(11), 1657–1672 (1995)
4. Alonso-Fernandez, F., Fierrez-Aguilar, J., Ortega-Garcia, J.: An enhanced gabor filter-based segmentation algorithm for fingerprint recognition systems. In: Pan, Y., Chen, D.-x., Guo, M., Cao, J., Dongarra, J.J. (eds.) ISPA 2005. LNCS, vol. 3758, pp. 239–244. Springer, Heidelberg (2005)
5. Bazen, A., Gerez, S.: Segmentation of fingerprint images. In: Proc. Workshop on Circuits Systems and Signal Processing (ProRISC 2001), pp. 276–280 (2001)
6. Pais Barreto Marques, A.C., Gay Thome, A.C.: A neural network fingerprint segmentation method. In: Fifth International Conference on Hybrid Intelligent Systems(HIS 05), p. 6 (2005)
7. Zhu, E., Yin, J., Hu, C., Zhang, G.: A systematic method for fingerprint ridge orientation estimation and image segmentation. Pattern Recognition 39(8), 1452–1472 (2006)
8. Harris, C., Stephens, M.: A combined corner and edge detector. In: Proc. in Alvey Vision Conference, pp. 147–151 (1988)
9. Mikolajczyk, K., Schmid, C.: Scale affine invariant interest point detectors. International Journal of Computer Vision 60(1), 63–86 (2004)
10. Klein, S., Bazen, A.M., Veldhuis, R.: fingerprint image segmentation based on hidden markov models. In: 13th Annual workshop in Circuits, Systems and Signal Processing, in Proc. ProRISC 2002 (2002)
11. Maio, D., Maltoni, D.: Direct gray-scale minutiae detection in fingerprints. IEEE Transactions on Pattern Analysis and Machine Intelligence 19(1), 27–40 (1997)
12. Chen, X., Tian, J., Cheng, J., Yang, X.: Segmentation of fingerprint images using linear classifier. EURASIP Journal on Applied Signal Processing 2004(4), 480–494 (2004)
13. Shen, L., Kot, A., Koo, W.: Quality measures of fingerprint images. In: Proc. Int. Conf. on Audio- and Video-Based Biometric Person Authentication, pp. 266–271 (2001)
14. Wang, L., Suo, H., Dai, M.: Fingerprint image segmentation based on gaussian-hermite moments. In: Li, X., Wang, S., Dong, Z.Y. (eds.) ADMA 2005. LNCS (LNAI), vol. 3584, pp. 446–454. Springer, Heidelberg (2005)
15. Hong, L., Wan, Y., Jain, A.K.: "Fingerprint image enhancement: Algorithms and performance evaluation". IEEE Transactions on Pattern Analysis and Machine Intelligence 20(8), 777–789 (1998)
16. Wu, C., Govindaraju, V.: Singularity preserving fingerprint image adaptive filtering. In: International Conference on Image Processing, pp. 313–316 (2006)
17. Wu, C., Shi, Z., Govindaraju, V.: Fingerprint image enhancement method using directional median filter. In: Biometric Technology for Human Identification. SPIE, vol. 5404, pp. 66–75 (2004)
18. Jea, T.Y., Chavan, V.S., Govindaraju, V., Schneider, J.K.: Security and matching of partial fingerprint recognition systems. In: SPIE Defense and Security Symposium. SPIE, vol. 5404 (2004)
19. Watson, C.I., Garris, M.D., Tabassi, E., Wilson, C.L., MsCabe, R.M., Janet, S.: User's Guide to NIST Fingerprint Image Software2(NFIS2). NIST (2004)
20. Otsu, N.: A threshold selection method from gray level histograms. IEEE Transactions on Systems, Man and Cybernetics 9, 62–66 (1979)

Automatic Fingerprints Image Generation Using Evolutionary Algorithm

Ung-Keun Cho, Jin-Hyuk Hong, and Sung-Bae Cho

Dept. of Computer Science, Yonsei University
Biometrics Engineering Research Center
134 Sinchon-dong, Seodaemun-ku
Seoul 120-749, Korea
{bearoot,hjinh}@sclab.yonsei.ac.kr, sbcho@cs.yonsei.ac.kr

Abstract. Constructing a fingerprint database is important to evaluate the performance of an automatic fingerprint recognition system. Because of the difficulty in collecting fingerprint samples, there are only few benchmark databases available. Moreover, various types of fingerprints should be required to get a fair assessment on how robust the system is against various environments. This paper presents a novel method that generates various fingerprint images automatically from only a few training samples by using the genetic algorithm. Fingerprint images generated by the proposed method include similar characteristics of those collected from the corresponding real environment. Experiments with real fingerprints verify the usefulness of the proposed method.

Keywords: fingerprint identification performance evaluation, genetic algorithm, image filtering, image generation.

1 Introduction

Due to the persistence and individuality of fingerprints, the fingerprint recognition has become a popular personal identification technique [1]. Recently, people consider it important to evaluate the robustness of those systems for practical application [2]. Performance evaluation, mostly dependent on benchmark databases, is a difficult process, because of the lack of public fingerprint databases involving large samples. Except for some popular fingerprint databases such as NIST database [3] and FVC databases [2], researchers usually rely on a small-scale database collected by themselves to evaluate their system. The construction of fingerprint databases requires an enormous effort so as to be incomplete, costly and unrealistic [4]. Moreover, the database should include samples collected from various environments in order to estimate the robustness of the system under realistic applications [5].

In order to measure the performance of fingerprint recognition systems from various points of view, researchers proposed several performance evaluation protocols and databases. Jain, *et al.* developed a twin-test by measuring the similarity of identical twins' fingerprints [6], while Pankanti, *et al.* theoretically estimated the individuality of fingerprints [1]. Hong, *et al.* reviewed performance evaluation for

S.-W. Lee and S.Z. Li (Eds.): ICB 2007, LNCS 4642, pp. 1104–1113, 2007.

biometrics systems including fingerprint verification systems [7]. Khanna and Weicheng presented benchmarking results using NIST special database 4 [3], and Maio, *et al.* initiated several competitions of fingerprint verification such as FVC [2]. Simon-Zorita, *et al.* collected MCYT Fingerprint Database in consideration of position variability control and image quality [5].

There were some works on the generation of synthetic images for constructing databases with little cost and effort. FaceGen [9] is a modeler for generating and manipulating human faces. It manages shape, texture, expression, phones, and accessories (hair, glasses), and it can also reconstruct 3D face from single images and were used to test face recognition techniques [10]. Cappelli, *et al.* developed a software (SFinGE) [4] that heuristically generated fingerprint images according to some parameters, where the synthetic databases were used as one of benchmark databases in FVC [2].

In this paper, we propose a novel method that generates fingerprint images from only a few initial samples, in which the images get similar characteristics to ones manually collected from the corresponding real environment. When a target environment is given, the proposed method constructs a set of filters that modifies an original image so as to become similar to that collected in the environment. A proper set of filters is found by the genetic algorithm [8,11], where the fitness evaluation is conducted using various statistics of fingerprints to measure the similarity.

2 Proposed Method

2.1 Overview

The proposed method works similar to that of a simple genetic algorithm as shown in Fig. 1, and fitness evaluation optimizes a filter set that generates fingerprint images corresponding to a given environment. In the initialization step are set the parameters for the genetic algorithm including the population size, the maximum number of generations, the length of chromosomes, selection strategy, selection rate, crossover rate and mutation rate. The length of chromosomes means the size of a filter composed, where each gene in the chromosome represents the corresponding filter in the pool of filters. A target environment should be also determined in initialization so that the proposed method can generate images having the similar characteristics of fingerprints collected by that environment. Only a few samples are required to calculate several statistics for the target environment to evaluate a chromosome.

After initializing population, the proposed method iteratively conducts fitness evaluation, selection, crossover and mutation until a terminal condition is satisfied, in which the last 3 steps work the same as the genetic algorithm. Especially, the fitness of a chromosome is estimated according to the similarity between a few real images from the target environment and images generated after filtering. The value of each gene means a filter to apply for images of the training database. If we collect some samples from an environment which we target, the proposed method automatically analyzes the environment and finds out a set of proper filters without any expert knowledge.

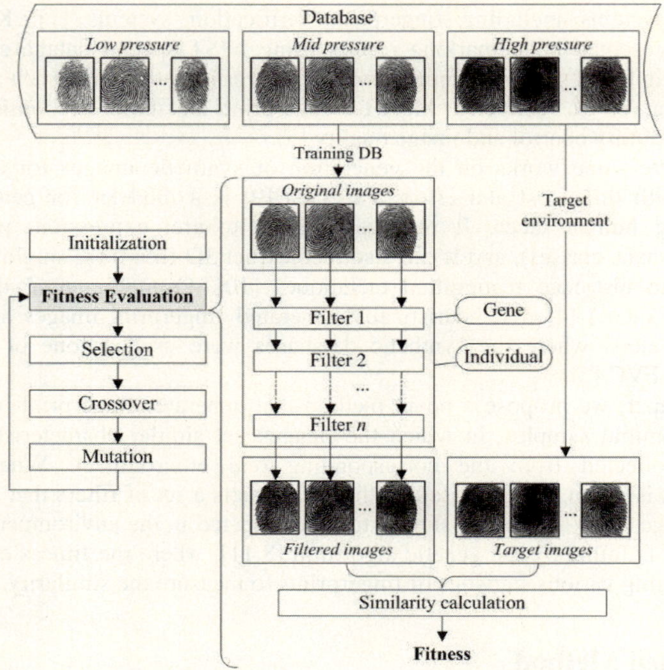

Fig. 1. Overview of the proposed method

2.2 Image Filter Pool

Popular image filters are used to produce similar effects from real environments. Even though each filter has a simple effect as shown in Table 1, they might produce various results when appropriately compounding with each other. The order and type of filters used in the filter set are determined by the genetic algorithm, because it is practically impossible to test all the cases of composition.

Table 1 shows the description of image filters used in this paper. They are widely used to reduce noises, smooth images, or stress the focus of images [12]. Typically, there are several categories of image filters such as histogram-based filters, mask filters and morphological filters. Various parameters like mask types make the effect of filtering more diverse. Total 70 filters construct the pool of filters.

Table 1. Image filters used in this paper

Group	Filter	Index
Histogram	Brightness (3 values), Contrast (3 values), Stretch, Equalize, Logarithm	1~9
Mask	Blur (6 masks), Sharper (4 masks), Median (10 masks)	10~29
Morphology(10 masks)	Erosion, Dilation, Opening, Closing	30~69
	None	0

2.3 Fitness Evaluation

The fitness of a filter set is estimated by measuring the similarity between fingerprints collected from the target environment and images generated by the composite filter. Several representative features of fingerprints, such as the mean and variance of images, directional contrasts [13], average ridge thickness and interval [14], singularities [13] and minutiae [1], are used to design the fitness evaluation function. As mentioned before, fingerprints are easily affected by an input environment, where the statistics of fingerprints obtained might manifest the environment. Table 2 shows the features of fingerprint images and the reason to use these features for evaluating the fitness.

Table 2. Features of fingerprint images for fitness evaluation

Feature	Description	Purpose
Mean	The mean of gray values	Measurement of whole gray level
Variance	The variance of gray values	Uniformity of gray values
Directional contrast	The mean of block directional difference	Distinctness between ridges and valleys
Thickness	The mean of ridge thickness	Measurement of ridge thickness
Interval	The mean of valley thickness	Measurement of valley thickness
Singularity	The region of discontinuous directional field	Major features of fingerprints
Minutiae	Ending and bifurcation point of ridges	Major features of fingerprint recognition

There are 4 directional contrasts obtained by estimating the block directional difference in 8 cardinal directions without regard for the opposite direction.

Singularity is detected by the Poincare index [13], which is a popular method to compute core and delta points based on the orientation field. According to the result by the algorithm and human experts, 3 types of singularities are defined as follows:

– Missing singularity: A set of real singularities which the algorithm cannot detect.
– Spurious singularity: A set of points which the algorithm detects but are not real.
– Paired singularity: A set of real singularities which the algorithm detects well.

Minutiae points are extracted through the process of Gabor filtering, binarization and thinning the ridges [1]. Minutiae including ending and bifurcation and nothing can be detected by the algorithm and identified by human experts, respectively, so as to define 8 types of combinations as follows: ending-ending, ending-bifurcation, ending-nothing, bifurcation-ending, bifurcation-bifurcation, bifurcation-nothing, nothing-ending, nothing-bifurcation.

With these various statistics for fingerprints, the fitness evaluation function, in which weights are heuristically determined, is defined as follows. The statistics of the target environment is calculated from the environment database. All the values are normalized from 0 to 1.

$$\begin{aligned} fitness(i) = {} & w_1 \times (mean_i - mean_{\text{target}}) \\ & + w_2 \times (variance_i - variance_{\text{target}}) \\ & + w_3 \times \sum_{j=1}^{4} (contrast_i^j - contrast_{\text{target}}^j) \\ & + w_4 \times (thickness_i - thickness_{\text{target}}) \\ & + w_5 \times (interval_i - interval_{\text{target}}) \\ & + w_6 \times \sum_{c \in singularityType} (singularity_i(c) - singularity_{\text{target}}(c)) \\ & + w_7 \times \sum_{c \in minutiaeType} (minutiae_i(c) - minutiae_{\text{target}}(c)) \end{aligned} \tag{1}$$

3 Experimental Results

3.1 Experimental Environment

The usability of the proposed method is verified by comparing the fingerprints collected from real environments with those generated. A fingerprint database, used in this work, is constructed by Computer Vision Laboratory in Inha University, in which three fingerprints images were captured from each finger according to the input pressure (high (H), middle (M) and low (L)) [15]. Forty two fingerprint images of fourteen fingers are used for the training data, while forty five fingerprint images of fifteen fingers are for the test data. In the experiment, we aim to generate the fingerprints of high and low pressures from those of middle pressure. With the training data, two filter sets (M→H, M→L) are evolved by the proposed method for each environment. Real fingerprints of high and low pressures in the training data are used to calculate the statistics of target environments as shown in Fig. 1. After evolution, the test data is used to estimate the performance of the proposed method by measuring the similarity between the real fingerprints of high and low pressures and those generated by the filters from fingerprints of middle pressure.

Fig. 2 shows the distribution of features for the training data. The input pressure affects the value of fingerprint features, which might also influence the performance of fingerprint recognition. The ridges of highly pressed fingerprints are easily connected so as to produce spurious bifurcation points, while fingerprints of low pressure are apt to generate spurious ending points. It is natural that the thickness and interval of ridges are divided to the input pressure. On the other side, singularity is less affected by the input pressure since it is calculated by the global feature like orientation. The fingerprints, collected in the environment of middle input pressure, show good performance in extracting minutiae points rather than the others. Especially, 'real ending-extracted bifur' and 'real bifur-extracted ending' of minutiae strongly show the trend of effects of the input pressure.

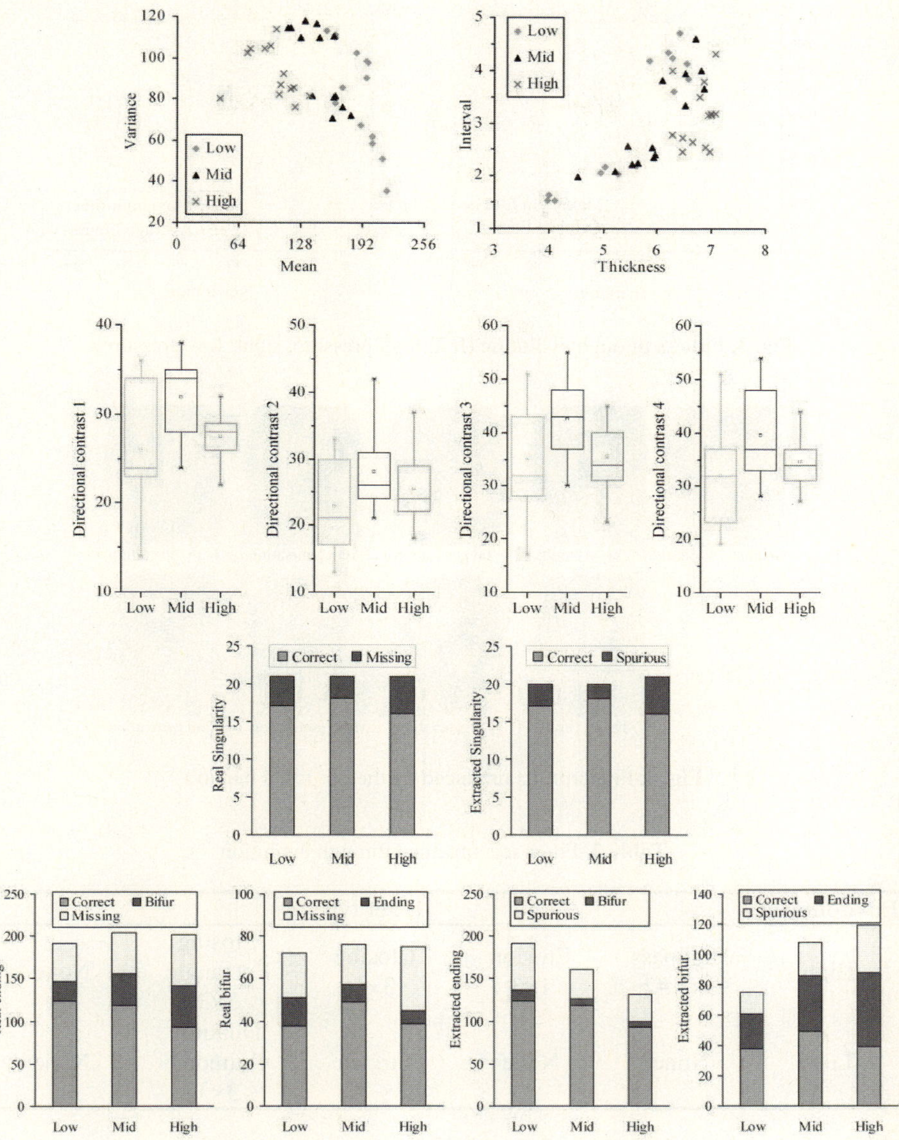

Fig. 2. Minutiae analysis of the training data

3.2 Analysis of the Process of Evolution

Parameters of the genetic algorithm in the experiment are set as follows: 100 generations, 50 populations, 5 gene lengths, 0.7 selection rate, 0.7 crossover rate and 0.05 mutation rate. At most five filters are used to compose a filter set because the size of chromosomes is set as five. Roulette-wheel selection is used as a basic

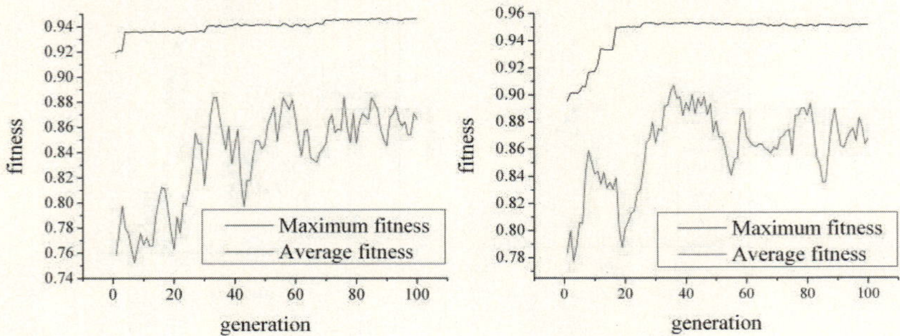

Fig. 3. Fitness through evolution (left: high pressure, right: low pressure)

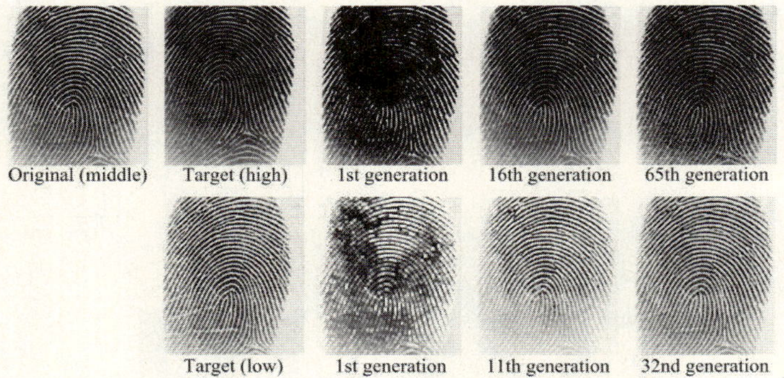

Fig. 4. Fingerprints produced by the proposed method

Table 3. Filter sets obtained through evolution

Environment	Filter type				
High	Highpass 3×3 #2	Erosion 1×3	Closing 3×1	Closing Rectangle 3×3	None
Low	None	None	Stretch	Dilation Diamond 3×3	None

selection mechanism. Weights used in the fitness function are set as (1, 1, 1, 2, 2, 1, 3), since the ridge information is highly affected by the input pressure.

Better filter sets are obtained by the proposed method through evolution as shown in Fig. 3. The maximum and average fitness increase as the generation grows for both target environments. Fig. 4 shows the resulting fingerprints that show similar figures to those collected from the target environments, while table 3 presents the best filter sets obtained in the last generation.

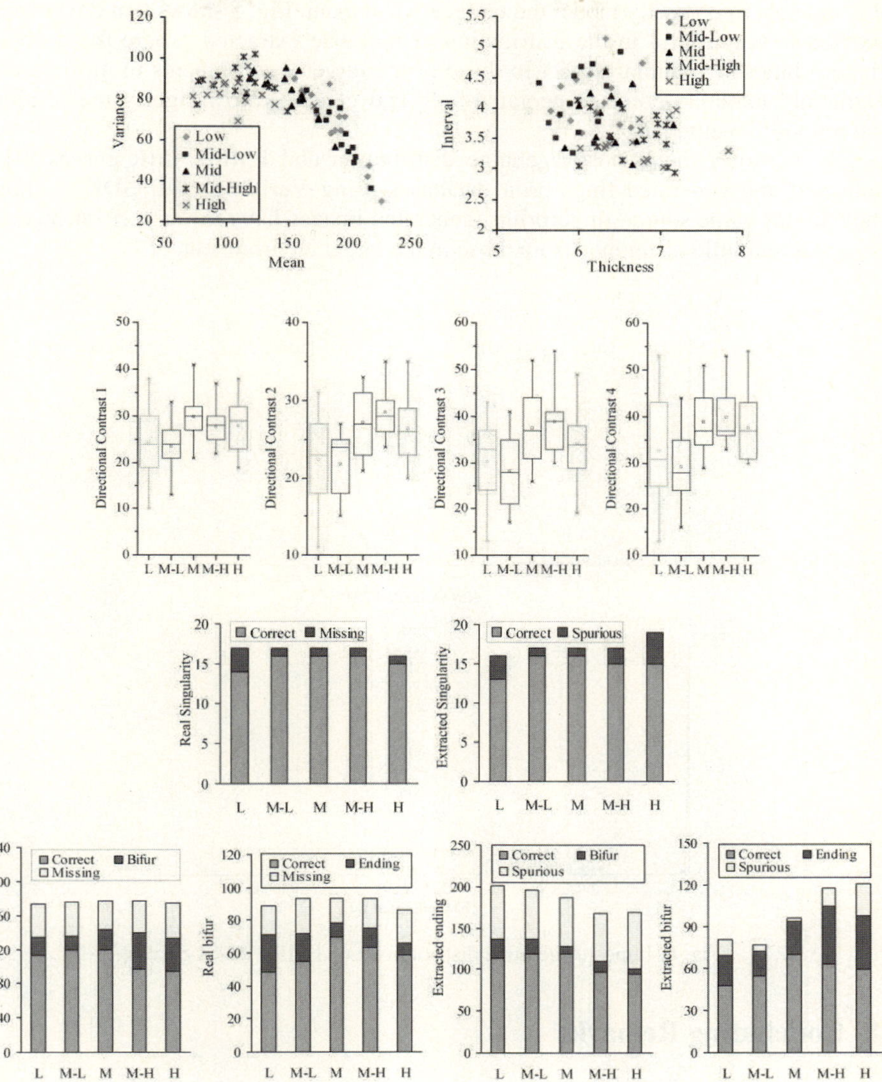

Fig. 5. Minutiae analysis of the test data

3.3 Analysis of Generated Fingerprints

We have analyzed the resulting fingerprints by comparing with fingerprints collected from the target environment. As shown in Fig. 5, the statistics of the fingerprints of middle pressure has been changed to be close to those calculated from the target environments, especially for mean, directional contrasts, ridge thickness and interval. Since singularity is hardly dependent on the orientation of original images, however, it is not able to correctly model the target environment. Fig. 5 shows that the proposed method is very useful in the distribution of minutiae extracted, where the generated fingerprints show similar aspect to those of the target environments in most cases of extracting minutiae points. Generated-high and generated-low signify the results of the proposed method.

Fig. 6 shows the impostor/genuine distribution and FMR/FNMR curves [4] on collected and generated fingerprint databases using VeriFinger 4.2 SDK. Although they are the same source fingerprints, generated images have lower performance than originals and little difference from those in the target environment.

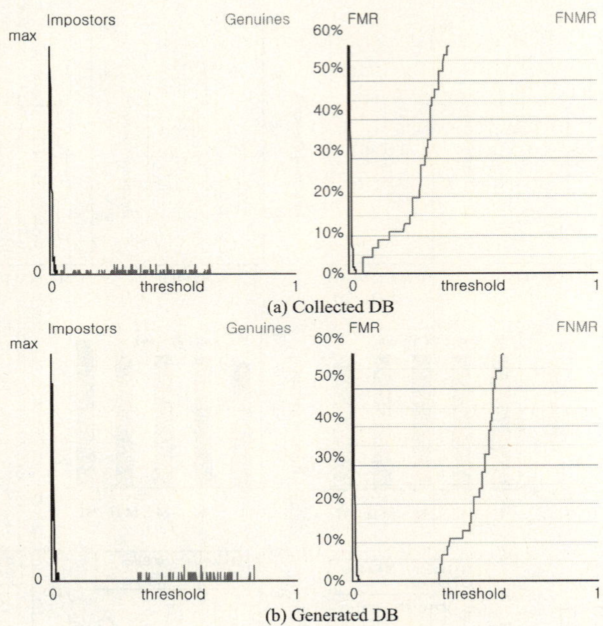

Fig. 6. Impostor/genuine distribution and FMR/FNMR curves

4 Concluding Remarks

In this paper, we have proposed a novel method that automatically generates fingerprint images by using the genetic algorithm. Various simple image filters are used to construct a composite filter where the genetic algorithm searches their proper types and order. We have conducted experiments on the real database collected according to the input pressure, where the fingerprints generated by the proposed method showed the similar characteristics to those collected from real environments in terms of various statistics of fingerprint images. The generated images might be used to evaluate the performance of fingerprint recognition systems. Moreover, the proposed method has the applicability to the fingerprint image enhancement by modifying the fitness evaluation module.

As the future work, in order to generate realistic fingerprints more precisely, we will develop a fingerprint model that characterizes them with various measures. Heuristic filters that deform fingerprints might be used to include various effects into them.

Acknowledgments. This work was supported by the Korea Science and Engineering Foundation (KOSEF) through the Biometrics Engineering Research Center (BERC) at Yonsei University.

References

[1] Pankanti, S., Prabhakar, S., Jain, A.: On the individuality of fingerprints. IEEE Trans. Pattern Analysis and Machine Intelligence 24(8), 1010–1025 (2002)

[2] Cappelli, R., Maio, D., Maltoni, D., Wayman, J.L., Jain, A.K.: Performance evaluation of fingerprint verification systems. IEEE Trans. Pattern Analysis and Machine Intelligence 28(1), 3–18 (2006)

[3] Khanna, R., Weicheng, S.: Automated fingerprint identification system (AFIS) benchmarking using the National Institute of Standards and Technology (NIST) Special Database 4. In: Proc. 28th Int. Carnahan Conf. on Security Technology, pp. 188–194 (1994)

[4] Maltoni, D.: Generation of Synthetic Fingerprint Image Databases. In: Ratha, N., Bolle, R. (eds.) Automatic Fingerprint Recognition Systems, Springer, Heidelberg (2004)

[5] Simon-Zorita, D., Ortega-Garcia, J., Fierrez-Aguilar, J., Gonzalez-Rodriguez, J.: Image quality and position variability assessment in minutiae-based fingerprint verification. IEEE Proc. Vision, Image Signal Process 150(6), 402–408 (2003)

[6] Jain, A., Prabhakar, S., Pankanti, S.: On the similarity of identical twin fingerprints. Pattern Recognition 35(11), 2653–2663 (2002)

[7] Hong, J.-H., Yun, E.-K., Cho, S.-B.: A review of performance evaluation for biometrics systems. Int. J. Image and Graphics 5(2), 501–536 (2005)

[8] Goldberg, D.: Genetic Algorithm in Search, Optimization and Machine Learning. Addison Wesley, Reading (1989)

[9] Blanz, V., Vetter, T.: A Morphable Model for the Synthesis of 3D Faces. In: Proceedings of Computer Graphics SIGGRAPH, pp. 187–194 (1999)

[10] Orlans, N., Piszcz, A., Chavez, R.: Parametrically controlled synthetic imagery experiment for face recognition testing. In: Proc. of the 2003 ACM SIGMM workshop on Biometrics methods and applications, pp. 58–64 (2003)

[11] Cho, U.-K., Hong, J.-H., Cho, S.-B.: Evolutionary singularity filter bank optimization for fingerprint image enhancement. In: Rothlauf, F., Branke, J., Cagnoni, S., Costa, E., Cotta, C., Drechsler, R., Lutton, E., Machado, P., Moore, J.H., Romero, J., Smith, G.D., Squillero, G., Takagi, H. (eds.) EvoWorkshops 2006. LNCS, vol. 3907, pp. 380–390. Springer, Heidelberg (2006)

[12] Gonzalez, R., Woods, R.: Digital Image Processing. Addison-Wesley, Reading, MA (1992)

[13] Karu, K., Jain, A.: Fingerprint Classification. Pattern Recognition 29(3), 389–404 (1996)

[14] Lim, E., Jiang, X., Yau, W.: Fingerprint quality and validity analysis. IEEE Int. Conf. on Image Processing 1, 22–25 (2002)

[15] Kang, H., Lee, B., Kim, H., Shin, D., Kim, J.: A study on performance evaluation of fingerprint sensors. In: Proc. 4th Int. Conf. Audio-and Video-based Biometric Person Authentication, pp. 574–583 (2003)

Audio Visual Person Authentication by Multiple Nearest Neighbor Classifiers

Amitava Das

Microsoft Research – India
196/36 2nd Main, Sadashivnagar, Bangalore 560 080, India
amitavd@microsoft.com

Abstract. We propose a low-complexity audio-visual person authentication framework based on multiple features and multiple nearest-neighbor classifiers, which instead of a single template uses a set of codebooks or collection of templates. Several novel highly-discriminatory speech and face image features are introduced along with a novel "text-conditioned" speaker recognition approach. Powered by discriminative scoring and a novel fusion method, the proposed MCCN method delivers not only excellent performance (0% EER) but also a significant separation between the scores of client and imposters as observed on trials run on a unique multilingual 120-user audio-visual biometric database created for this research.

Keywords: Speaker recognition, face recognition, audio-visual biometric authentication, fusion, multiple classifiers, feature extraction, VQ, Multimodal.

1 Introduction

Multimodal biometric authentication is attracting lots of interest these days as it offers significantly higher performance and more security than unimodal methods using a single biometric. Multimodal methods also make the system more robust to sensor failures and adverse background conditions such as poor illuminations or high background noise. However, proper fusion of multiple biometrics remains a challenging and crucial task. Amongst the various multimodal biometric methods reported so far, Audio-Visual person authentication [3-8][17] offers some more unique advantages. First of all, it uses two biometrics (speech and face image), which people share quite comfortably in everyday life. No additional private information is given away. These biometrics are not associated with any stigma (unlike fingerprints which are taken for criminals as well). These are contact-free and the sensors for these are everywhere thanks to the worldwide spread of camera-fitted mobile phones. Another unique advantage of this combination is that the combined use of an intrinsic biometric (face) along with a performance biometric (voice) offers a heightened protection from imposters, while providing flexibility in terms of changing of 'password'.

The challenges faced by audio-visual authentication are: a) poor performance by face recognition, especially for expression, pose and illumination variation, b) poor performance in speaker recognition in noise, c) increased complexity of the system,

S.-W. Lee and S.Z. Li (Eds.): ICB 2007, LNCS 4642, pp. 1114–1123, 2007.

and d) lack of proper fusion method to exploit best of the two biometrics. Some other requirements for any biometric systems are: a) training material should be low and enrollment should be fast, b) enrollment of a new user should not require any massive re-estimation, c) ease of using the system during enrollment and actual usage, d) complexity to be minimal so that it can be scaled up to handle a large number of users or run it in an embedded device, e) high accuracy , or in other words a significant separation between client and imposter score distributions f) robustness to multiple sessions of testing g) ability to change "password", and h) robustness to various imposter attacks.

Majority of the recent audio-visual biometric authentication methods [3-8] use separate speech and face based classifiers and then apply various late fusion methods [12] such as sum, product, voting, mixture-of-experts, etc, to fuse the scores of the two modes. A few recent methods (e.g. [8]) proposed a feature level fusion as well. For the speech mode, various text-independent speaker recognition methods, using GMM [11] or VQ [10], are predominantly used. These methods offer lower complexity than HMM [13] or DTW[14] based text-dependent speaker recognition methods. Performance of the Text-dependent methods are better accuracy but they require lots of training data. For the face-mode, majority of the methods [1] are essentially variations of PCA-based [2] approach. Since PCA-based methods suffer severely from pose and illumination variations, various pose normalization methods [1] were proposed using 2D or 3D models followed by a PCA based dimension reduction and a nearest neighbor matching of the reduced-feature template. Several methods (e.g. [9]) use multiple frames of a video and analyze different trajectories or face dynamics in the feature space for face recognition. Note that all these methods mentioned here require quite high complexity and some methods, especially the HMM-based ones, need a massive amount of training data as well. PCA based methods also face the problem of re-estimation -- every time a new user is enrolled.

In this paper, we propose a low-complexity multimodal biometric authentication framework based on multiple features and multiple nearest neighbor classifiers (MNNC). The proposed MNNC framework uses multiple features and for each feature uses a set of codebooks or collection of templates (opposed to a single template). We used it here for audio-visual person authentication, but MNNC can be used for any detection/verification task involving multiple classifiers. We also introduce several new speech and face features and a novel "text-conditioned" speaker recognition approach. Coupled with a discriminative scoring and a novel fusion method the proposed MNNC method delivers excellent performance (0% EER) as well as a non-overlapping distribution of the client and imposter scores, as demonstrated on trials run on a unique 120 people multilingual MSRI Bimodal Biometric database. The proposed method meets all the requirements mentioned above, while operating at very low complexity. A real-time AV-LOG person authentication system prototype is created based on this research, which is being used by employees of our organization on a trial basis.

This paper is organized as follows: Section 2 details the basic architecture, describes the computation of the scoring & fusion method. Section 3 presents the various feature extraction methods. Section 4 presents details of the MSRI database, experimental set up, followed by the results. Finally the summary and conclusions are presented in section 5.

2 Person Authentication by Multiple Nearest Neighbor Classifiers

In the proposed architecture, multiple features $\mathbf{F_1}, \mathbf{F_2}, \mathbf{F_3}, \ldots, \mathbf{F_L}$, are extracted from the various biometrics used. For each feature $\mathbf{F_i}$ we have a dedicated nearest neighbor classifier, which compares $\mathbf{F_i}$ with a set of codebooks, one for each of the N users enrolled, and computes a score $\mathbf{R_i}$ and multiply it with a suitable weight. A suitable fusion method combines various scores $\mathbf{R_i}$ to form a final score $\mathbf{R_{final}}$, which is then compared with a threshold to decide to accept or reject the identity claim.

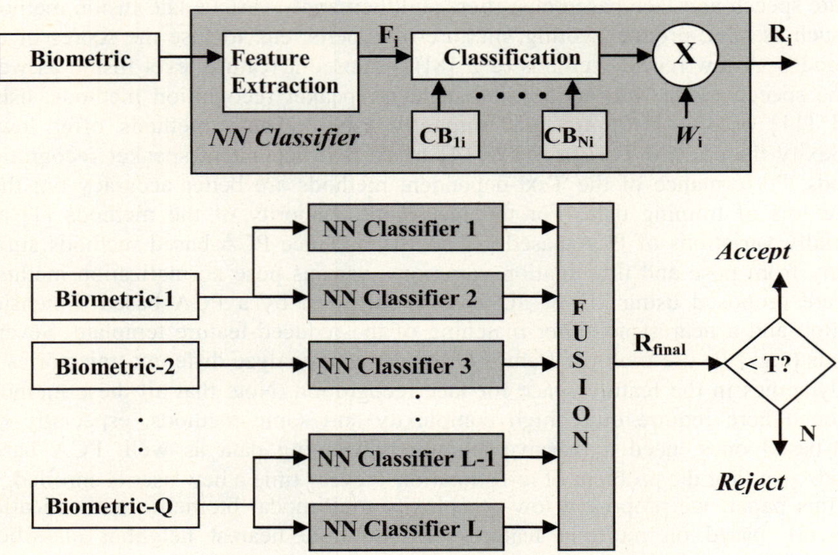

Fig. 1. Architecture of the proposed MNNC framework

2.1 Score Computation for Person Authentication

During enrollment, for each user P_j and for each feature vector $\mathbf{F_i}$, a codebook $\mathbf{CB_{ij}}$, is designed from the feature vector ensemble $[\mathbf{F_{i1}}\ \mathbf{F_{i2}}\ \mathbf{F_{i3}} \ldots \mathbf{F_{iT}}]$ of size T obtained from the training data. Any standard clustering method such as K-means can be used to design the codebooks.

During authentication, a set of Q biometric samples are presented (Figure 1), along with an identity claim, 'k'. We need to verify whether the feature set $[\mathbf{F_1}\ \mathbf{F_2}\ \mathbf{F_3} \ldots \mathbf{F_L}]$, extracted from the biometric samples, belongs to person P_k or not. We present next the scoring method for person verification (the basic idea can be extended to the person-identification problem as well).

Let us consider just a single Nearest Neighbor classifier, which has N codebooks $\boldsymbol{CB_k}$ k=1,2,..,N, for the N users enrolled to the system. Each $\boldsymbol{CB_k}$ has M codevectors, $\boldsymbol{CB_k} = [\boldsymbol{C_{km}}]$, m=1,2,..,M.

Given a feature vector **F** (one of the L feature vectors $\mathbf{F}_i$, i=1,2..L, we drop the index "i" here for convenience) and a claim "k", we find a similarity-dissimilarity ratio R as follows :

Step1: Given the identity claim, k, compute two distances, D_{true} & D_{imp}, as follows:

*D_{true} = minimum distance of **F** from the codebook $\mathbf{CB}_k$ of claimed person Pk, $D_{true} = \min \{D_{km}\}$, where $D_{km} = ||\mathbf{F} - \mathbf{C}_{km}||^2$, m=1,2,...,M, $\mathbf{C}_{km}$ being the codevector of codebook $\mathbf{CB}_k$.*

*D_{imp} = minimum distance of **F** from the set of codebooks of all other persons except person P_k or $D_{imp} = \min \{D_{im}\}$, where $D_{im} = ||\mathbf{F} - \mathbf{C}_{nm}||^2$, m=1,2,,M; n=1,2,..N & n not equal to k.*

Note that, when a sequence of feature vectors [F_{ij}, j=1,2,3...J] are given (as in case of the MFCC sequence of all the J frames of a speech utterance), D_{imp} and D_{true} are computed by first computing the D_{imp} and D_{true} distance for each feature vector F_{ij} and then accumulate them, e.g. $D_{true}(J) = D_{true}(F_{i1}) + D_{true}(F_{i2}) + ... + D_{true}(F_{iJ})$.

Step2: Compute the score as $R = D_{true} / D_{imp}$

In conventional person verification using a single feature, this score R will be compared against a threshold T and the identity claim will be rejected/accepted if R is greater/less than T. In our system, we compute this ratio R_i for each of the L features $\mathbf{F}_i$ i=1,2,..,L and then fuse them. If all the users being tested are pre-enrolled, it can be shown that for a client, R_i should be less than 1 and for an imposter, it should be greater than 1. Note that, R_i is essentially a likelihood ratio measure.

2.2 Fusion Methods Used in the Proposed MNNC Framework

Knowing the unique property of the scores $\mathbf{R}_i$, it makes sense to use the product rule, i.e. $R_{final} = R_1 x R_2 x..x\ R_L$. This should perform well, separating the true and imposter distributions. However, often one or two feature scores will misbehave making the product score to be inaccurate. Therefore, we propose a "trend-modified-product' (TMP) rule described below:

1. *Given the scores, find whether the majority is greater than 1 (indicated by a flag J=0) or the majority is less than 1 (indicated by a flag J=1).*
2. *If J equals 1, then final-score is a product of those scores which are less than a threshold (THmin), else if (J=0) then the final-score is a product of scores Ri which are greater than a threshold (THmax).*

With the features we proposed here (section 3), we observed that usually only one or two feature scores fail at the most, and most of the times the majority trend (J=0) is observed. This helps TMP to work well. To illustrate this, we show the results of a sample speaker verification trial (Table 1). TMP does work better (lower EER; better client-imposter score separation) than product rule in this example.

Table 1. Results of MNNC based speaker verification using product rule & TMP

Only Speech	MFCC: CBsize=4; Dim=9; CMD: CBsize=10; Dim=9							
	EER	FAR	FRR	Mc	Mi	D(Mc,Mi)	Dovlp	Dsep
Product Fusion	5.5	61.6	61.7	1.31	30.24	29.24	24	-
TMP Fusion	0.75	1	20.5	0.75	45.4	44.4	6	-

2.3 MNNC Based Audio-Visual Person Authentication System -- AVLOG

We designed a real-time person authentication system called AVLOG for log-in and other access-control applications. The biometrics used here are speech utterances of a user-selected password and multiple profiles of the user's face. During testing and enrollment, a person is asked to look at 3 to 5 (this number is a system parameter) spots on the screen and a single web-cam captures the multiple profiles. Then the person is asked to speak his password. During enrollment, 4 samples of the password are taken. During testing the user needs to say the password only once. A password is a set of 4 words, such as address, names, etc – something which is easy to remember and preferably spoken in the native language of the person. As a result, the passwords are unique (very unlikely to be the same) and phonetically and linguistically quite different from each other. We call this approach "text-conditioning" speaker recognition, which differs from the conventional 'text-dependent' or 'text-independent' approaches. Details of feature extraction methods are presented next.

3 Feature Extraction Details

We want to keep the training and test data to the minimum, so the challenge is how to extract multiple meaningful features from limited data. For face, we use multiple poses, and for each pose we use a highly discriminatory "transformed pose feature" (TFP) [16] which captures the essence of a person's face quite well. For speech we use the conventional MFCC (Mel-Frequency-Cepstral-Coefficient) as well as introduce a novel speech feature called Compressed MFCC Dynamics (CMD).

3.1 Speech Feature 1: Text-Conditioned MFCC

Text conditioning (use of unique password per user) leads to a high discrimination and the extracted MFCC sequences become more separable. Figure 2 shows the effect of the proposed text-conditioning approach. It shows the MFCCs of the two passwords of two users plotted in a 2-D MFCC (MFCC component 1 & 2) space. Conventional case (any password) on the left shows overlapping, while the text-conditioned case on the right shows distinct separation of data from two speakers.

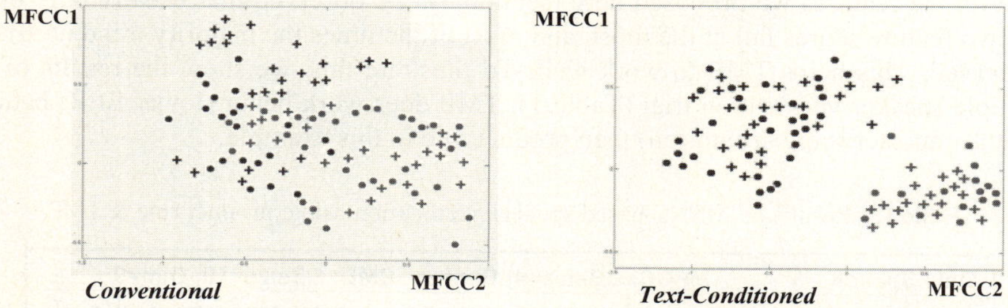

Fig. 2. Scatter plots of 2 MFCC components; Blue dot/cross → two utterances of speaker-1, Red dot/cross → two utterances of speaker-2. Note that text-conditioned data are separable.

Table 2. Speaker identification accuracies of TIVQ & TCVQ for various codebook size(N) and code-vector dimension (K) for experiments run on the MSRI database

	TIVQ			TCVQ		
	K=8	K=8	K=13	K=8	K=8	K=13
N=4	51.4	60.1	65.9	97.8	98.3	97.4
N=8	76.2	81.7	84	100	100	100
N=64	93.1	94.9	95.6	100	100	100

Text-conditioning allows a simple VQ-based classifier perform significantly better than the conventional text-independent VQ (TIVQ) speaker recognition systems [10] at significantly less complexity. We call our speaker-recognition method 'text-conditioned VQ' or TCVQ. Table 2 compares the identification accuracies of TCVQ against TIVQ for various codebook sizes and dimensions for trials run on our MSRI database. The discriminatory power of text-conditioned MFCC feature allows TCVQ to outperform TIVQ, while using lesser number of codebook parameters -- amounting to lower complexity and memory usage [17].

Text-conditioned MFCC offers two other advantages as evident in Figure 3: a) there is a significantly wider separation of the client from imposters and b) the system can quit earlier (without processing the entire utterance) while giving 100% accuracy.

3.2 Speech Feature 2: Compressed MFCC Dynamics (CMD) Signature

When a person says something, his or her characteristics are best captured in the dynamics of the utterance. Traditionally researchers used a combination of 13-dimension MFCC, 13 delta-MFCC & 13-delta-delta-MFCC or a total of 39 dimension vector to capture such dynamics. This gives a little benefit but makes the feature space very large -- increasing confusability and complexity.

We introduce a novel speech feature called "Compressed-MFCC-Dynamics" or CMD, which captures the above-mentioned speech dynamics efficiently. The CMD is computed as follows. The set of MFCCs are collected from the entire utterance to form a 2-D array called MFCCgram (Figure 4). On this 2-D array, we apply DCT and then keep a small set (M) of DCT coefficients. This fixed M-dimension (typically M=15 works well) vector forms the CMD. Figure 4 shows the MFCCgram and the CMD parameters for 3 users and their 2 passwords. Figure 4 clearly shows how well the CMD feature captures speaker characteristics. Note the similarities within a

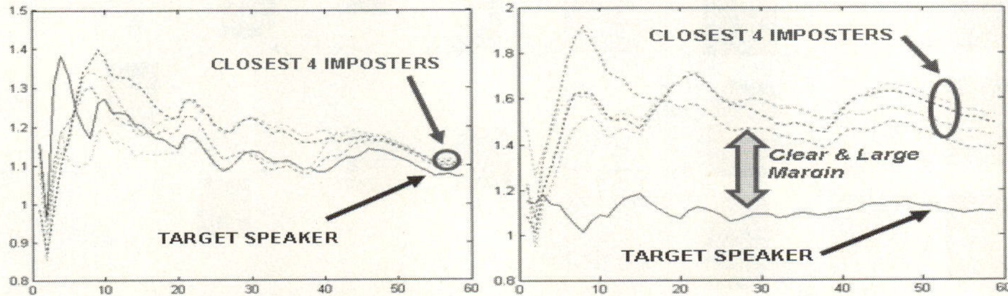

Fig. 3. Plot of accumulated distance of target speaker(client) and 4 closest imposters over time (expressed as speech frame numbers) – plotted for conventional (left) MFCC and text-conditioned (right) MFCC

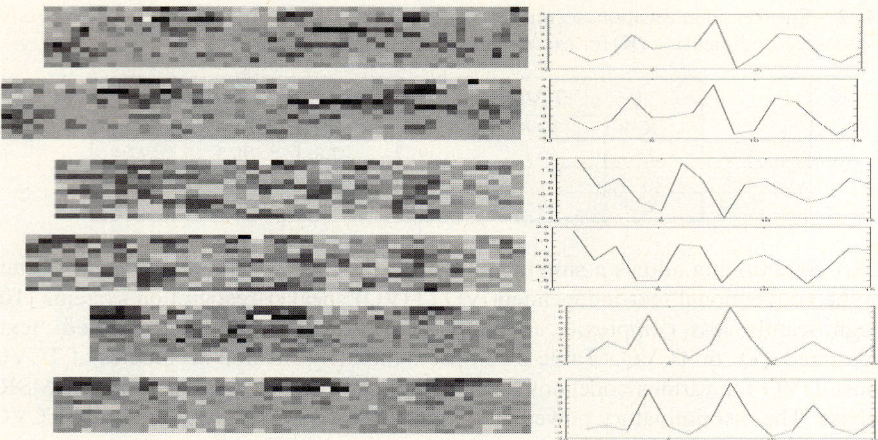

Fig. 4. MFCCgram and the corresponding CMD signatures of two utterances of the passwords of 3 speakers of the MSRI database. CMD dimension=15.

speaker and the differences across speakers. Note that MFCCgram is variable in X dimension, but CMD has a fixed dimension ¯ easy for designing classifiers˙

3.3 Face Image Feature: Transformed Face Profile (TFP)

The face features are extracted in a manner similar to the CMD. From each face profile, after face detection [15] DCT is applied on the cut gray image. A set of selected DCT coefficients is stored [16] as the Transformed Face Profile (TFP) signature. Figure 5 shows the discriminatory power of TFP across users and their ability to form natural clusters in a 3D TFP space (formed by two selected maxima and one minimum). Also note how well TFP tolerates expression variations.

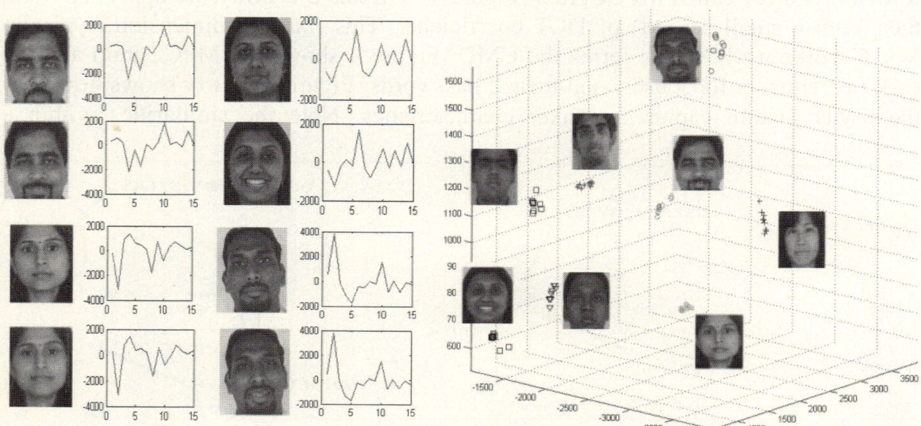

Fig. 5. Left: Central profile faces and the corresponding TFP signatures for 4 users Right: Clustering of 3 TFP points (2 maxima, 1 minima) for 10 central-profile samples of 8 users

4 Database, Experiments and Results

Due to our text-conditioning requirements (unique password for each user) we could not use any conventional audio-visual databases. We therefore created a unique multilingual audio-visual biometric MSRI database which captured 3 face profiles (left, center and right) and unique multi-lingual passwords from 120 people. For each user, there are 10 training and 10 test samples of the password and 10-20 face images for each profile. The face images are captured with digital camera in normal office lighting condition and there are decent expression variations.

For the proposed MNNC method, we report results for only the person verification task. The system can easily be configured for both closed-set and open-set person identification tasks. The various system parameters are: MFCC-codebook-size, MFCC dimension, number of CMD's, CMD dimension, no of TFP's and TFP dimension. The results presented in Table 3 are for the individual biometrics as well as the combined audio-visual system.

Only a minimal number of system parameters are used, leading to a storage of only 486 numbers per user and approximately 4000 multiply-add operations for each user-trial. In comparison, a 128x39 Text-independent VQ speaker recognition sub-system alone would have needed 5000 numbers per user to be stored and about $5x10^5$ multiply-adds per user-trial.

Table 3. Performance of the proposed MNNC method. Shown here are the EER, FAR, FRR as well as the means of the client and imposter distributions (Mc, Mi), the distance between them D(Mc, Mi) and the amount of overlap, D_{ovlp}, (or non-overlap, D_{sep}) between the tails of the distributions of client and imposter scores.

Only Speech	MFCC: CBsize=4; Dim=9; CMD: CBsize=10; Dim=9							
	EER	FAR	FRR	Mc	Mi	D(Mc,Mi)	D_{ovlp}	D_{sep}
MFCC	0.83	0.8	2.5	0.9	1.28	0.28	0.2	-
CMD	13.5	87	0.25	1.67	13.1	12.1	32.5	-
Product Fusion	5.5	61.6	61.7	1.31	30.24	29.24	24	-
TMP Fusion	0.75	1	20.5	0.75	45.4	44.4	6	-
Only Face	CBsize=8; Dim=15							
	EER	FRR	FAR	Mc	Mi	D(Mc,Mi)	D_{ovlp}	D_{sep}
Left TFP	4.6	13	24	0.59	36	35	2.11	-
Center TFP	7.8	16	41	0.64	43.2	42.2	3.34	-
Right TFP	3.3	21.7	8.3	0.43	48.1	47.1	1.5	-
TMP Fusion	0.09	0.09	0.09	0.22	1.8E+07	1.8E+07	1.3	-
Speech+Face	Speech: MFCC-CB-size=4;Dim=9; CMD number=10;Dim=9 Face: TFP number=8, TFP Dim=15							
	EER	FRR	FAR	Mc	Mi	D(Mc,Mi)	D_{ovlp}	D_{sep}
Product Fusion	0	0	0	0.33	6E+08	6E+08	-	10
TMP Fusion	0	0	0	0.11	7.5E+08	7.5E+08	-	44

From the results in Table 3. the following observations can be made:

a) Combination of multiple features and multiple biometrics gives better results than unimodal methods using a single biometric

b) Proposed trend-modified-fusion (TMP) does provide better client-to-imposter separation than the conventional product fusion

c) The MCCN framework proposed here performs quite well, significantly separating the score distributions of the client and imposters (no overlap; 0% EER)

The proposed MNNC method requires very low complexity. To provide some insight into this, let us compare the storage and computation requirements of MNNC with two hypothetical AV biometric systems using PCA [2] for face and text-independent VQ for speech [10] and PCA for face and a high performance text-dependent DTW based system (as in[14]) for speech. As mentioned earlier, these sub-systems are the most popular ones used in audio-visual authentication systems proposed recently. The MIPS-complexity is expressed here in terms of the number of multiply-add operations per user-trial (for 120 users) and the memory-complexity is expressed in terms of number of real constants required to be stored per user. For the MIPS part, PCA complexity dominates, for the memory, the DTW method dominates. As see in Table 4, the proposed MCCN method requires significantly less complexity and storage per user than any of these conventional methods.

Table 4. Complexity and memory usage comparison of MCCN with conventional methods

METHOD	MIPS	Memory	Comments
VQ+PCA	10^8	O(6000)	4 sec test utterance; CBsize=128; dim=39; PCA - 60 size eigenvalue per profile; 40x40 size image
DTW+PCA	10^8	O(30000)	5-template DTW, 4 second test utterance; Method as in [14]; PCA as above
MCCN	O(4000)	O(500)	4 second test utterance; other parameters as in Table 3

5 Summary and Conclusions

We proposed a low-complexity high-performance audio-visual person authentication method based on multiple features and a multiple nearest neighbor classifier framework. Few novel speech and face features were proposed, which are highly compact and discriminatory. Use of a judicious fusion method combined with the discrimination power of the features led the proposed method to achieve high performance (0% EER) and a wide separation (no-overlap) of the score-distributions of the client and imposters. We created a unique multilingual 120-user bimodal audio-visual MSRI biometric database to test our proposed approach. A real-time AVLOG access control system has been built using the basic principles proposed here and the system is being tested by various employees of our organization. The performance of the real-time prototype is similar to the data presented here. We also have versions which are robust to background noise. Our current and future focus includes: a) mobile and small-foot-print embedded implementation, b) expanding our database to more number of users and c) investigating few more promising features.

Acknowledgment

The databases used in this research has been prepared by interns working at MSRI.

References

1. Zhao, W.Y., et al.: Face recognition: A Literature Survey. ACM Comp. Surveys, 399–458 (2003)
2. Turk, M., Pentland, A.: Eigenfaces for Recognition. Journal of cognitive neuroscience 3, 71–86 (1991)
3. Chibelushi, C., et al.: A Review of Speech Based Bimodal Recognition. IEEE trans. Multimedia, 23–37 (2002)
4. Kanak, A., et al.: Joint Audio Video Processing for Biometric Speaker Identification. In: Proc. ICASSP-03 (2003)
5. Marcel, S., et al.: Bi-Modal Face & Speech Authentication: A Bio Login Demonstration System. In: Proc. MMUA-06 (May 2006)
6. Hazen, T., et al.: Multi-modal Face and Speaker Identification on Handheld Device. In: Proc. MMUA (May 2003)
7. Yacoub, S., et al.: Fusion of Face and Speech Data for Person identity Verification. IEEE trans. neural Network (September 1999)
8. Wu, Z., Cai, L., Meng, H.: Multi-level Fusion of Audio and visual Features for Speaker identification. In: Proc. ICB 2006, pp. 493–499 (2006)
9. Biuk, Z., Loncaric, S.: Face Recognition from Multi-pose Image Sequence. In: Proc. 2nd Int'l. Symp. on Image and Signal Processing and Analysis, pp. 319–324 (2001)
10. Soong, F.K., Rosenberg, A.E., Juang, B.-H., Rabiner, L.R.: A vector quantization approach to speaker recognition. AT&T Journal 66, 14–26 (1987)
11. Reynolds, D., et al.: Speaker Verification using adapted GMM. Digital Signal Processing 10(1-3) (2000)
12. Kittler, J., et al.: Combining Evidence in Multimodal personal identity recognition systems. In: Proc. Int. Conf. on Audio & Video Based Person Authentication (1997)
13. Das, A., Ram, V.: Text-dependent speaker-recognition – A survey and State of the Art. Tutorial presented at ICASSP-2006, Toulouse (May 2006)
14. Ram, V., Das, A., Kumar, P.: Text-dependent speaker-recognition using one-pass dynamic programming. In: Proc. ICASSP, Toulouse, France (May 2006)
15. Viola, P., Jones, M.: Robust Real-time Object Detection. In: Proc. ICCV-2001 (2001)
16. Das, A., et al.: Face Recognition from Images with high Pose Variations by Transform Vector Quantization. In: Kalra, P., Peleg, S. (eds.) ICVGIP 2006. LNCS, vol. 4338, pp. 674–685. Springer, Heidelberg (2006)
17. Das, A., et al.: Audio Visual Biometric Recognition by Vector Quantization. In: Proc. IEEE/ACL SLT workshop (December 2006)
18. Das, A.: Audio-Visual Biometric Recognition. In: ICASSP07 (accepted tutorial) (2007)

Improving Classification with Class-Independent Quality Measures: *Q-stack* in Face Verification

Krzysztof Kryszczuk and Andrzej Drygajlo

Swiss Federal Institute of Technology Lausanne (EPFL), Signal Processing Institute
`http://scgwww.epfl.ch/`

Abstract. Existing approaches to classification with signal quality measures make a clear distinction between the single- and multiple classifier scenarios. This paper presents an uniform approach to dichotomization based on the concept of stacking, *Q-stack*, which makes use of class-independent signal quality measures and baseline classifier scores in order to improve classification in uni- and multimodal systems alike. In this paper we demonstrate the application of *Q-stack* on the task of biometric identity verification using face images and associated quality measures. We show that the use of the proposed technique allows for reducing the error rates below those of baseline classifiers in single- and multi-classifier scenarios. We discuss how *Q-stack* can serve as a generalized framework in any single, multiple, and multimodal classifier ensemble.

Keywords: statistical pattern classification, quality measures, confidence measures, classifier ensembles, stacking.

1 Introduction

Biometric identity verification systems frequently face the challenges of non-controlled data acquisition conditions. In such conditions biometric signals may suffer from quality degradation due to extraneous, identity-independent factors. It has been demonstrated in numerous reports that a degradation of biometric signal quality is a frequent cause of significant deterioration of classification performance [1,2,3], also in multimodal systems, which systematically outperform their unimodal counterparts [4,1,5].

Seeking to improve the robustness of classifiers to degraded data quality, researchers started to incorporate quality measures into the classification process, at the same time making a clear distinction between using quality information in single classifier [2,6,7,3], as opposed to multi-classifier and multimodal biometric systems [1,5,8,9]. The application of quality measures in a multimodal system received far more attention, with a dominant intuitive notion that a classifier that has a higher quality data at its disposal ought to be more credible than a classifier that operates on noisy signals [1]. In [5] Toh et al. mention that introduction of quality measures provide additional degrees of freedom which helps maximize class separation but neither they explicitly state the actual reason for this improved separation nor do they suggest if and how should this effect

S.-W. Lee and S.Z. Li (Eds.): ICB 2007, LNCS 4642, pp. 1124–1133, 2007.

apply to single classifier systems. However, the impact of signal quality measures on classification performance of a single classifier has also been noticed. In [3] Gales and Young propose to use parallel model architecture to account for varying speech quality in speaker verification. In [2,6] adaptive threshold selection helps reduce errors. In turn, while quality-dependent model or threshold selection/adaptation is shown to work for single classifiers, the method is not generalized to multiple classifier systems.

We argue that in fact the very same mechanisms governs the use of quality measures in single- and multi-classifier systems alike, and propose a quantitative rather than intuitive perspective on the role of quality measures in classification. In [10] we have proposed *Q-stack*, a novel theoretical framework of improving classification with class-independent quality measures. $Q - stack$ is based on the concept of classifier stacking [11]. In the scheme of $Q - stack$ a classifier ensemble is used in which the first classifier layer is made of the baseline unimodal classifiers, and the second, stacked classifier operates on features composed of the normalized similarity scores and the relevant quality measures. The concept of concatenating scores and quality measures into one feature vector was previously used in [9], but only in the context of multimodal fusion using a likelihood ratio-based classifier. In [10] we have demonstrated using synthetic datasets that $Q - stack$ allows for improved class separation using class-independent quality measures for both uni- and multi-modal classification, provided that a statistical dependence exists between the features of the stacked classifier. The nature of the stacked classifier is chosen depending on the actual structure of the classified data. The importance of the dependence between classification scores and quality measures was also stressed in [7], but its implications are not extended beyond error prediction for a single classifier.

In this paper we present $Q-stack$ as a general framework of classification with quality measures that is applicable to uni-, multiple-classifier and multimodal biometric verification. We demonstrate the principles and performance of $Q - stack$ on a real biometric dataset, the face part of the BioSec database [12], using two different face image matchers, a quality measure that is correlated with the classification scores of one of the matchers, and three different stacked classifiers. We give evidential support to following hypotheses:

1. A score-dependent quality measure provides an additional dimension in which a stacked classifier can separate the classes better than the baseline classifier that uses only the similarity scores.
2. Proposed method allows to improve biometric verification in single- and multi-classifier scenarios alike.
3. In a multi-classifier system, the quality measure needs to be dependent on at least one classifier in order to observe the benefits of $Q - stack$.

The paper is structured as follows. Section 2 describes the principles of the proposed method of $Q - stack$. In Section 3 we treat on the application of $Q-stack$ to uni- and multi-classifier face matching, and we give the experimental results with their discussion. Section 4 concludes the paper.

2 $Q - Stack$ - Using Quality Measures to Improve Classification

Consider two class data-generating processes A and B, which generate features subjected to k arbitrary base classifiers $C_{1,2,...,k}$, each returning a scalar similarity score $x_{1,2,...,k}$. Concatenate these scores to $\mathbf{x} = [x_1, x_2, ..., x_k]$, where vector $\mathbf{x}$ is an instance of a multivariate random variable X. The distribution of X is affected by a noise-generating process N that interacts according to some function γ with the class-generating processes A and B, causing signal degradation. The nature of γ needs not be given explicitly [10]. Instead, the interaction between A, B and N manifests itself in the impact of noise instances n on the corresponding observed score instances $\mathbf{x}$. Consequently, a causal dependence between N and X can be observed. In practice it may not be feasible to measure n directly. Instead, a set of j scalar quality measures $\mathbf{qm} = qm_1, qm_2, ..., qm_j$ can be collected, where $\mathbf{qm}$ denotes an instance of a random variable QM. By definition, QM is dependent on N, and therefore it also inherits a dependence on X. At the same time, quality measures do not carry class-selective information, $p(\mathbf{qm}|A) = p(\mathbf{qm}|B)$.

Let us now concatenate the training scores $\mathbf{x}$ and the relevant quality measures $\mathbf{qm}$ into *evidence vectors* $\mathbf{e} = [\mathbf{x}, \mathbf{qm}]$, and analyze the separation between classes A and B in the $(k + j)$-dimensional *evidence space* defined by all components of the evidence vectors. Under the assumption of equal priors, $P(A) = P(B)$, class separation can be expressed in terms of divergence between class-conditional joint distributions of $p(\mathbf{e}|A)$ and $p(\mathbf{e}|B)$. In [13] Koval et al. have shown that divergence between joint class-conditional distributions is greater for dependent, than for independent classification features. Consequently, since $p(QM|A) = p(QM|B)$ the existence of statistical dependencies between X and QM grants that

$$\int_{-\infty}^{\infty} |p(\mathbf{x}|B) - p(\mathbf{x}|A)| \, d\mathbf{x} < \int_{-\infty}^{\infty} |p(\mathbf{e}|B) - p(\mathbf{e}|A)| \, d\mathbf{e}. \tag{1}$$

A detailed proof of (1) is beyond the frames of this paper. An intuitive understanding of this result is shown in Figure 1. Here, the evidence consists of one class-selective score and one quality measure, $\mathbf{e} = [x, qm]$. In both subplots the marginal class-conditional distributions of evidence remain unchanged. The variables of X and QM are independent in the left, and dependent in the right subplot. Note that in the independent case the class separation is defined entirely by $p(\mathbf{x}|A)$ and $p(\mathbf{x}|B)$. In the presence of a dependence between X and QM classes A and B are clearly better separated. For more details the reader is referred to [10].

As a consequence of (1), classification in the evidence space is guaranteed to be more accurate than using base scores $\mathbf{x}$ alone, as long as there is a dependence between X and QM. For classification in the evidence space the scores of the base classifiers $\mathbf{x}$ become part of the feature vector for a new stacked classifier [11], hence the coined name $Q - stack$. The stacked classifier can be chosen arbitrarily, depending on the actual joint distributions of evidence $\mathbf{e}$.

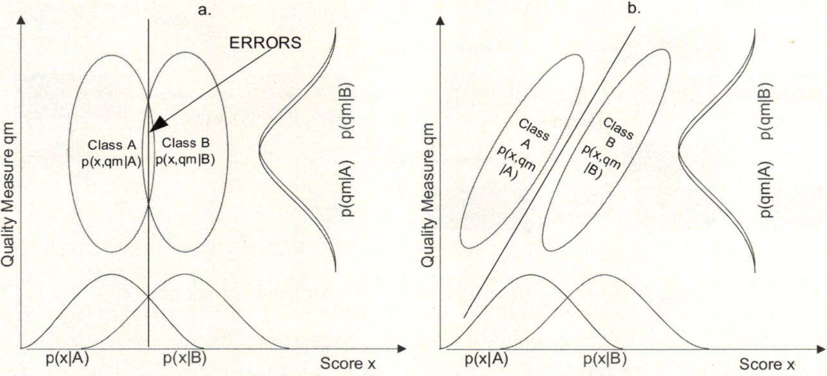

Fig. 1. Graphical representation of the impact of dependence between scores x and quality measures qm on class separation in the evidence space $e = [x, qm]$: a. independent x and qm, b. dependent x and qm.

Figure 2 shows a block diagram of $Q - stack$ applied in a single-classifier scenario. Features extracted from a single signal are classified by a single base classifier. At the same time, quality measures (one or more) are collected. Classification scores and quality measures are combined into evidence vectors and classified by a stacked classifier operating in the evidence space. In Figure 3 the very same structure is applied to multimodal classification. Two signals are classified in parallel, resulting in score vector $\mathbf{x}$, which is further combined together with the respective quality measures into an evidence vector $\mathbf{e} = [\mathbf{x}, \mathbf{qm}]$. The evidence vector $\mathbf{e}$ becomes a feature vector for the stacked classifier. Note that if no quality measures are present, the architecture shown in Figure 3 simply performs a multimodal score-level fusion.

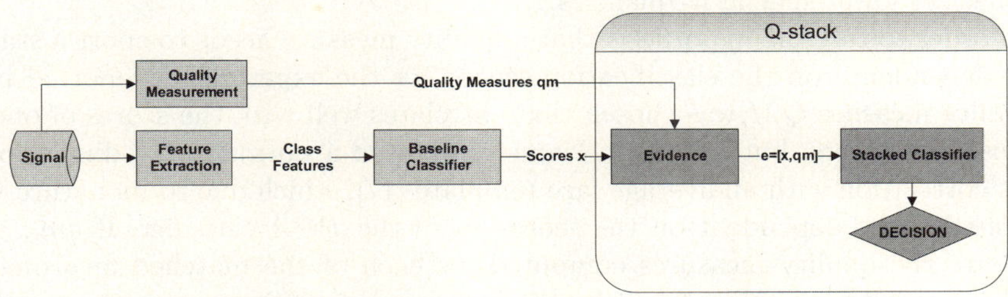

Fig. 2. Q-stack in single base classifier scenario

3 Q-Stack for Face Verification

The experiments presented here give an embodiment of the proposed method of $Q - stack$. We show that the improvements in the system performance do indeed hinge on the statistical dependencies of the signal quality measures on

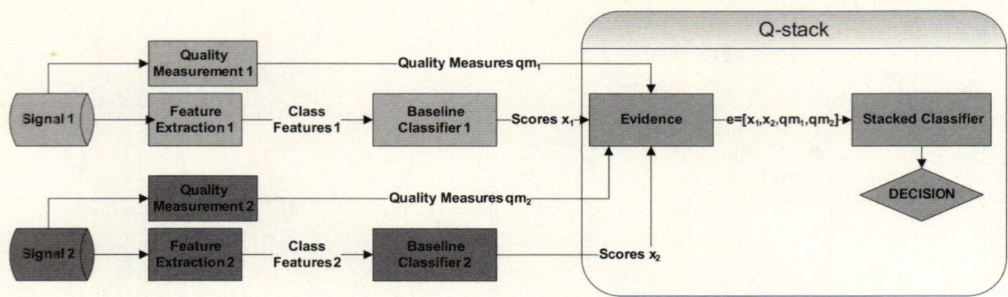

Fig. 3. Q-stack in multimodal/multiclassifier scenario

the corresponding classifier scores, using an example of face matching. In our experiments we used face images of 200 subjects (training set: 50 subjects, testing set: 150 subjects) from the BioSec database, baseline corpus. For the details regarding the BioSec database the reader is referred to [12]. The experiments presented in this paper involve one-to-one sample matching. All face images have been registered manually in order to avoid the impact of face localization algorithms on the matching performance. All images have been photometrically normalized [14].

In our experiments we used the following two face matchers: 1. *DCT* - local *DCTmod*2 features and a Bayes classifier based on the feature distributions approximated by Gaussian Mixture Models (GMM)[15] (scores produced by the *DCT* matcher denoted as x_1), 2. *PCA* - Mahalanobis distance between global *PCA* feature vectors [16]. The *PCA* projection space was found using all images from the training dataset. The scores produced by the *PCA* matcher are denoted as x_2. The two face matchers were chosen since they both operate on very different features. The local *DCTmod*2 features encode mostly high spacial frequencies, while the projection of the face images on the *PCA* subspace emphasizes lower spacial frequencies.

In order to test the hypothesis that a quality measure needs to sport a statistical dependence on the classification scores, for the experiments reported here a quality measure *QM* was chosen that correlates well with the scores of one of the used matchers, but not both. Namely, we used a normalized 2-dimensional cross correlation with an average face template [17], which due to its nature was expected to be dependent on the scores x_2 of the *PCA* classifier. If qm_α and qm_β are the quality measures computed for each of the matched face images then the resulting combined quality measure used as evidence was computed as $qm = \sqrt{qm_\alpha qm_\beta}$, following [1].

In order to maintain a consistent notation with Section 2 and with [10] denote here the class of genuine client match scores as *Class A*, and the class of the imposter match scores as *Class B*. The class-conditional distributions of classifier scores x_1 (*DTC* matcher), x_2 (*PCA* matcher), and quality measures *QM* are shown in Figure 4. The distributions of the quality measures in Figure 4 *c* show that indeed the used quality measures are class-independent and cannot help separate classes on their own.

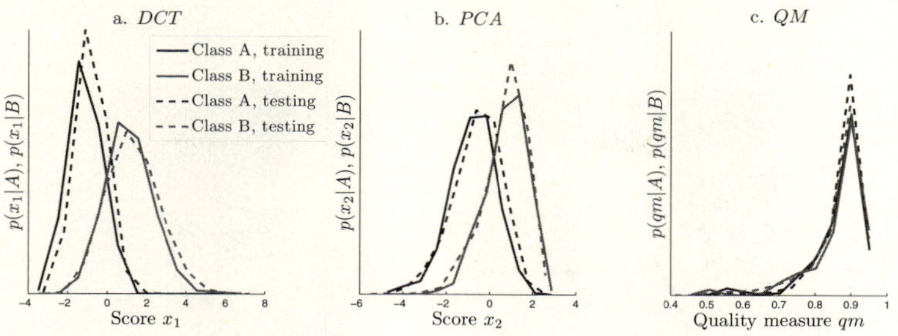

Fig. 4. Class-conditional distributions of scores x_1, x_2 and quality measures qm

Table 1. Correlation coefficients between evidence components x_1, x_2, qm

	Training				*Testing*		
	x_1	x_2	qm		x_1	x_2	qm
x_1	1.00	0.57	0.02	x_1	1.00	0.36	-0.11
x_2	0.57	1.00	0.46	x_2	0.36	1.00	0.50
qm	0.02	0.46	1.00	qm	-0.11	0.50	1.00

As we have discussed before, a quality measure needs to be dependent on the scores in order to improve the class separation. Since correlation between random variables entails dependence, we computed the pair-wise Pearson's correlation coefficients between x_1, x_2 and qm for both the training and testing data sets - see Table 1. A strong correlation is evident between the scores x_1 and x_2, which is a consequence of the fact that both classifiers operate on the same input signals. However, the quality measure QM is strongly correlated only with the scores x_2 originating from the PCA classifier.

The experiments were conducted as follows. First, the baseline classifiers DCT and PCA were trained using the dedicated training data set of the BioSec database, disjoint from the testing set, originating from a separate set of users, and quality measures qm were collected. The proposed method of $Q-stack$ was applied to evidence vectors composed of $\mathbf{e} = [x_1, qm]$, $\mathbf{e} = [x_2, qm]$, $\mathbf{e} = [x_1, x_2]$ and $\mathbf{e} = [x_1, x_2, qm]$. The combinations of $\mathbf{e} = [x_1, qm]$ and $\mathbf{e} = [x_2, qm]$ are examples of $Q-stack$ applied to a single classifier. The evidence vector $e = [x_1, x_2]$ is $Q-stack$ with only score-level evidence from two classifiers, which is equivalent to multi-classifier fusion [4]. Finally, the evidence vector $\mathbf{e} = [x_1, x_2, qm]$ represents $Q-stack$ applied to multi-classifier fusion with quality measures. Scores x_1, x_2 and quality measures qm were normalized to zero mean and unit variance using normalization parameters estimated on the training dataset. Three different stacked classifiers that separated $e|A$ from $e|B$ were used: Support Vector Machines classifier with a Radial Base Function kernel (SVM), a Bayes classifier using Gaussian approximations of the class-conditional distributions ($Bayes$), and a Linear Discriminant-based classifier (LDA).

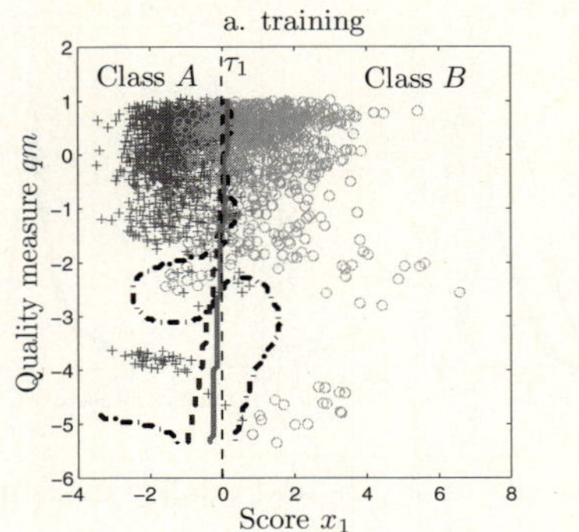

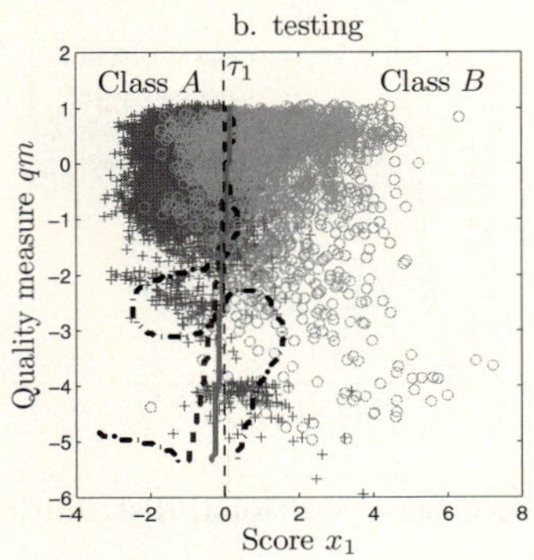

Fig. 5. Class separation in the evidence space $\mathbf{e} = [x_1, qm]$ for the DCT classifier. Bold lines show the $Q-stack$ decision boundaries for following stacked classifiers: SVM (dash-dot), Bayes (dashed) and LDA (solid). Thin dashed line marked τ_1 shows the corresponding decision boundary of the baseline DCT classifier.

Figure 5 shows the application of $Q-stack$ to the DCT classifier with evidence vector $\mathbf{e} = [x_1, qm]$ and Figure 6 shows the application of $Q-stack$ to the PCA classifier, evidence vector $\mathbf{e} = [x_1, qm]$ for both the training (a) and testing (b) datasets. The solid lines in both figures show the class decision boundaries for the corresponding stacked classifiers, optimized on the testing dataset. The thin dashed lines marked τ_1 and τ_2 represent baseline classification boundaries for x_1 and x_2, respectively. In Figures 5 and 6 the areas confined by the bold ($Q-stack$) and the thin lines show the loci of observations that can be classified more accurately by $Q-stack$ than by the baseline classifiers (τ_1 and τ_2). The gains in accuracy due to the classification in the space of evidence $\mathbf{e}$ rather than in the score space x_1 or x_2 are summarized in Table 2. Classification results are reported in terms of total classification accuracy AC, Half-Total Error Rate $HTER$ [4] and error rates for individual classes ER_A and ER_B, obtained on the testing dataset.

A weak correlation between the quality measure and the scores x_1 of the DCT classifier (Table 1) result in marginal improvements in classification accuracy. Indeed, as it is shown in Figure 5, the $Q-stack$ decision boundary does not deviate much from the baseline classification boundary given by $x_1 = \tau_1$. The exception here is the stacked SVM classifier, whose shape of the decision boundary suggests overfitting. Strong correlation between the the quality measure QM and the scores x_2 of the PCA classifier is reflected in a $Q-stack$ decision boundaries that deviate consistently and significantly from that of the baseline classifier given by $x_2 = \tau_2$ (Figure 6). Large areas confined by the $Q-stack$ and τ_2 decision bounds suggest a significant improvement of classification accuracy in the $\mathbf{e} = [x_2, qm]$ space compared with the baseline classifier. This improvement is indeed consistent for all stacked classifiers.

In the case of classification in the $\mathbf{e} = [x_1, x_2]$ space, $Q-stack$ is equivalent to any trained classifier fusion method: here using SVM, Bayesian and LDA classifiers. The results shown in Table 2 show an improvement in classification

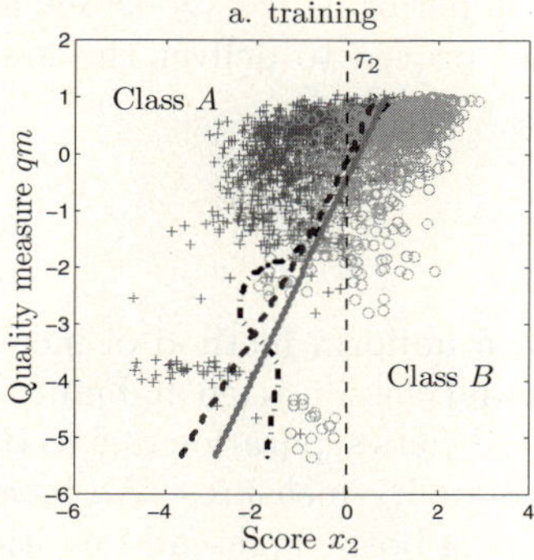

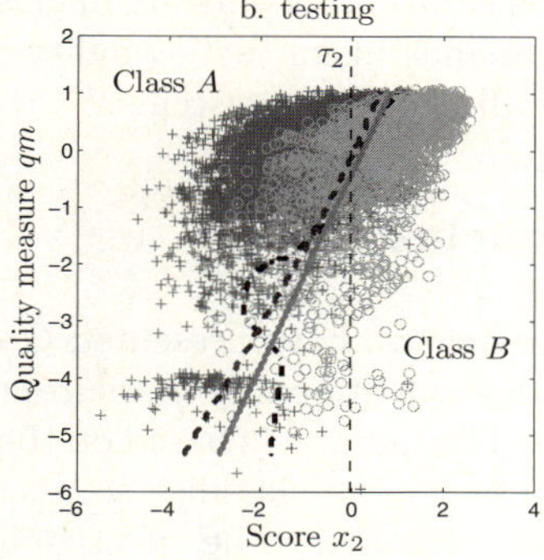

Fig. 6. Class separation in the evidence space $\mathbf{e} = [x_2, qm]$ for the PCA classifier. Bold lines show the $Q - stack$ decision boundaries for following stacked classifiers: SVM (dash-dot), Bayes (dashed) and LDA (solid). Thin dashed line marked τ_2 shows the corresponding decision boundary of the baseline PCA classifier.

Table 2. Comparison of classification performance achieved by the baseline classifiers and using the proposed $Q - stack$ method. Experimental results reported for the SVM, $Bayes$ and LDA stacked classifiers operating in the evidence space.

	$Accuracy[\%]$	$HTER[\%]$	$ER_A[\%]$	$ER_B[\%]$
Baseline				
DCT: $\mathbf{e} = [x_1]$	83.97	14.92	13.21	16.64
PCA: $\mathbf{e} = [x_2]$	70.62	26.68	15.25	13.36
SVM				
$DCT + QM$: $\mathbf{e} = [x_1, qm]$	84.97	14.95	14.83	15.07
$PCA + QM$: $\mathbf{e} = [x_2, qm]$	79.23	20.68	20.54	20.82
$DCT + PCA$: $\mathbf{e} = [x_1, x_2]$	87.41	12.73	12.96	12.51
$DCT + PCA + QM$: $\mathbf{e} = [x_1, x_2, qm]$	87.78	12.12	11.96	12.28
LDA				
$DCT + QM$: $\mathbf{e} = [x_1, qm]$	83.85	14.83	12.79	16.88
$PCA + QM$: $\mathbf{e} = [x_2, qm]$	77.32	21.53	19.75	23.31
$DCT + PCA$: $\mathbf{e} = [x_1, x_2]$	85.91	13.06	11.46	14.66
$DCT + PCA + QM$: $\mathbf{e} = [x_1, x_2, qm]$	88.68	11.57	11.96	11.19
Bayes				
$DCT + QM$: $\mathbf{e} = [x_1, qm]$	84.85	14.65	13.88	15.43
$PCA + QM$: $\mathbf{e} = [x_2, qm]$	76.41	21.56	18.42	24.7
$DCT + PCA$: $\mathbf{e} = [x_1, x_2]$	86.23	13.04	11.92	14.17
$DCT + PCA + QM$: $\mathbf{e} = [x_1, x_2, qm]$	87.03	12.3	11.25	13.34

accuracy over both baseline systems, which is an expected result. The classification results for $\mathbf{e} = [x_1, x_2]$ serve as multi-classifier baseline for the comparison with the results obtained by applying $Q - stack$ to fusion with $\mathbf{e} = [x_1, x_2, qm]$. Despite the fact that QM correlates well only with x_2 but not with x_1, adding the quality measure to the evidence vector ($\mathbf{e} = [x_1, x_2, qm]$) resulted in further consistent improvements in classification performance. $Q - stack$ applied to multi-classifier fusion with quality measures proved to deliver the lowest error rates of all compared systems.

4 Conclusions

In this paper we have presented $Q - stack$, a uniform method of incorporating class-independent quality measures in unimodal classification and multi-classifier systems. The method is based on the improved class separation due to the dependence between the classifier scores and the quality measures. We have demonstrated the method to be effective in improving both single- and multi-classifier face verification. We have also shown that the benefits that can be expected of the application of $Q - stack$ hinge on the statistical dependencies between the quality measures and the baseline classifier similarity scores, and on a proper selection of the stacked classifier according to the class-conditional evidence distributions. The method generalizes well to other modalities - we have obtained promising results also for fingerprint and speech modalities. Multiple quality measures can be incorporated by simply adding them into the evidence vector. The results suggest that particular attention must be paid to the development of classifier-quality measure ensembles, rather than classifier-independent quality measures alone.

Acknowledgments

This work was partially funded by the Swiss National Science Foundation ($SNSF$) and National Centre of Competence in Research ($NCCR$)$IM2.MPR$. We wish to thank Prof. Javier Garcia-Ortega (UAM) for making the face part of the BioSec database available for our experiments.

References

1. Fierrez-Aguilar, J.: Adapted Fusion Schemes for Multimodal Biometric Authentication. PhD thesis, Universidad Politecnica de Madrid (2006)
2. Kryszczuk, K., Drygajlo, A.: Gradient-based image segmentation for face recognition robust to directional illumination. In: Visual communications and image processing 2005, Beijing, China, July 12-15, 2005 (2005)
3. Gales, M.J.F., Young, S.J.: Robust continuous speech recognition using parallel model compensation. IEEE Transactions on Acoustics, Speech and Signal Processing 4(5) (1996)
4. Bengio, S., Marcel, C., Marcel, S., Mariethoz, J.: Confidence measures for multimodal identity verification. Information Fusion 3(4), 267–276 (2002)
5. Toh, K.A., Yau, W.Y., Lim, E., Chen, L., Ng, C.H.: Fusion of auxiliary information for multi-modal biometrics authentication. In: Proceedings of International Conference on Biometrics, Hong Kong. LNCS, pp. 678–685. Springer, Heidelberg (2004)

6. Wein, L., Baveja, M.: Using fingerprint image quality to improve the identification performance of the U.S. VISIT program. In: Proceedings of the National Academy of Sciences (2005)
7. Grother, P., Tabassi, E.: Performance of biometric quality measures. IEEE Transactions on Pattern Analysis and Machine Intelligence 29(4), 531–543 (2007)
8. Poh, N., Heusch, G., Kittler, J.: On combination of face authentication experts by a mixture of quality dependent fusion classifiers. In: Proceedings of th 7th International Workshop on Multiple Classifier Systems, Prague, Czech Republic (2007)
9. Nandakumar, K., Chen, Y., Dass, S.C., Jain, A.K.: Quality-based score level fusion in multibiometric systems. In: Proceedings of International Conference on Pattern Recognition, Hong Kong, China, vol. 4, pp. 473–476 (2006)
10. Kryszczuk, K., Drygajlo, A.: Q-stack: uni- and multimodal classifier stacking with quality measures. In: Proceedings of the International Workshop on Multiple Classifier Systems, Prague, Czech Republic (2007)
11. Wolpert, D.: Stacked generalization. Neural Networks 5, 241–259 (1992)
12. Fierrez, J., Ortega-Garcia, J., Torre-Toledano, D., Gonzalez-Rodriguez, J.: Biosec baseline corpus: A multimodal biometric database. Pattern Recognition 40(4), 1389–1392 (2007)
13. Koval, O., Voloshynovskiy, S., Pun, T.: Error exponent analysis of person identification based on fusion of dependent/independent modalities. In: Proceedings of SPIE Photonics West, Electronic Imaging 2006, Multimedia Content Analysis, Management, and Retrieval 2006 (EI122) (2006)
14. Gross, R., Brajovic, V.: An image preprocessing algorithm for illumination invariant face recognition. In: Kittler, J., Nixon, M.S. (eds.) AVBPA 2003. LNCS, vol. 2688, Springer, Heidelberg (2003)
15. Sanderson, C.: Automatic Person Verification Using Speech and Face Information. PhD thesis, Griffith University, Queensland, Australia (2003)
16. Turk, M.A., Pentland, A.P.: Eigenfaces for recognition. Journal of Cognitive Neuroscience 3(1), 71–86 (1991)
17. Kryszczuk, K., Drygajlo, A.: On combining evidence for reliability estimation in face verification. In: Proc. of the EUSIPCO 2006, Florence (September 2006)

Biometric Hashing Based on Genetic Selection and Its Application to On-Line Signatures

Manuel R. Freire, Julian Fierrez, Javier Galbally, and Javier Ortega-Garcia

Biometric Recognition Group - ATVS,
Escuela Politecnica Superior, Universidad Autonoma de Madrid
C/ Francisco Tomas y Valiente 11, E-28049 Madrid, Spain
{m.freire,julian.fierrez,javier.galbally,javier.ortega}@uam.es

Abstract. We present a general biometric hash generation scheme based on vector quantization of multiple feature subsets selected with genetic optimization. The quantization of subsets overcomes the dimensionality problem of other hash generation algorithms, while the feature selection step using an integer-coding genetic algorithm enables to exploit all the discriminative information found in large feature sets. We provide experimental results of the proposed hashing for verification of on-line signatures. Development and evaluation experiments are reported on the MCYT signature database, comprising 16, 500 signatures from 330 subjects.

Keywords: Biometric Hashing, Biometric Cryptosytems, Feature Selection, Genetic Algorithms.

1 Introduction

The application of biometrics to cryptography is receiving increasing attention from the research community. Cryptographic constructions known as *biometric cryptosystems* using biometric data have been recently proposed, exploiting the advantages of authentication based on something that you are (e.g., your fingerprint or signature), instead of something that you know (e.g., a password) [1,2].

A review of the state of the art in biometric cryptosystems is reported in [2]. It establishes a commonly accepted classification of biometric cryptosystems, namely: (*i*) *key release*, where a secret key and a biometric template are stored in the system, the key being released after a valid biometric match, and (*ii*) *key generation*, where a template and a key are combined into a unique token, such that it allows reconstructing the key only if a valid biometric trait is presented. This last scheme has the particularity that it is also a form of cancelable biometrics [3] (i.e., the key can be changed), and it is secure against system intruders since the stored token does not reveal information from neither the key nor the biometric.

Within key generation biometric cryptosytems, the biometric template can be extracted using a *biometric hashing* scheme, where a binary string is obtained from the biometric sample (see Fig. 1). In this arquitecture, biometric cryptosystems have stronger security constraints than biometric hashing schemes, where the extraction of a stable binary representation of the biometric is generally priorized.

S.-W. Lee and S.Z. Li (Eds.): ICB 2007, LNCS 4642, pp. 1134–1143, 2007.

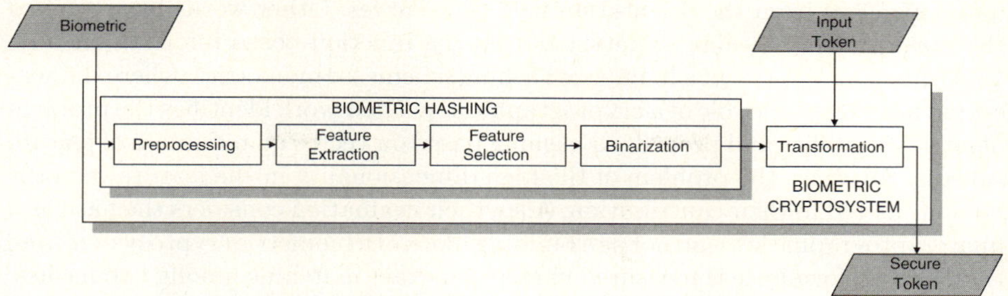

Fig. 1. A generic biometric cryptosystem, where the biometric is binarized using a biometric hashing scheme

We present a biometric hashing scheme based on genetic selection, extending the idea of feature subset concatenation presented in [4]. In that previous work, there was no clear indication of which of all the possible feature subsets should be used for the biometric hash. Moreover, there is a need for a dimensionality reduction criterion when dealing with high-dimensional vectors. We provide a solution to this problem using feature subset selection based on a genetic algorithm (GA) [5], leading to a practical implementation of biometric hashing.

The proposed hash generation scheme can be applied to any biometric trait represented as a fixed-sized feature vector. In this work, we present a case study for the application of this scheme to the verification of on-line signatures, where dynamic information of the signing process is available. Within biometric hashing, handwritten signature has an interesting application in authentication and identity management, due to its widespread social and legal acceptance [6,7].

This paper is structured as follows. In Sect. 2 we outline related work on hashing and biometric cryptosystems. The proposed hashing scheme is presented in Sect. 3.1, and the feature selection algorithm using GA is detailed in Sect. 3.2. A case study in biometric hash generation from on-line signatures is reported in Sect. 4. Finally, some conclusions and future work are discussed in Sect. 5.

2 Related Work

Several biometric cryptosystems for key generation have been proposed in the literature. The *fuzzy vault* scheme [8] establishes a framework for biometric cryptosystems. In this construction, a secret (typically, a random session key) is encoded using an unordered set of points A, resulting in an indivisible vault V. The original secret can only be reconstructed if another set B is presented and overlaps substantially with A. The fuzzyness of this construction fits well with the intra-variability of biometrics. Uludag et al. [9] proposed a biometric cryptosystem for fingerprints based on the fuzzy vault, where the encoding and the decoding sets were vectors of minutiae data. Their scheme was further developed in [10], where the fuzzy vault for fingerprints is enhanced with helper data extracted from the orientation field flow curves. Other works have applied the fuzzy vault to on-line signature data using function-based information [11].

Hoque et al. [4] present a biometric hashing scheme for biometrics, where the generated hash plays the role of a cryptographic key. Their work identifies the problem of intra-variability and proposes a hashing based on vector quantization of feature subsets. However, the problem of the high dimensionality in the feature vector is not considered in their contribution. Also, their evaluation considers the hash as a final cryptographic key and not as a building block of a biometric cryptosystem, and therefore performance is measured in terms of exact matching among two hashes. Another approach was presented in [12], where Vielhauer et al. propose a biometric hashing scheme for statistical features of on-line signatures. Their work is based on user-dependent helper data, namely an Interval Matrix. Vielhauer and Steinmetz further applied this scheme to biometric hash generation using handwriting [13].

Another approach to crypto-biometrics using handwritten signature is Bio-Hashing, where pseudo-random tokens and biometrics are combined to achieve higher security and performance [14,15]. This scheme has also been applied to face biometrics in [16].

Information-theoretical approaches to crypto-biometrics have also been presented. One example is the work of Dodis et al. [17], where a theoretical framework is presented for cryptography with fuzzy data (here, biometrics). They propose two primitives: a *secure sketch*, which produces public information about a biometric signal that does not reveal details of the input, and a *fuzzy extractor*, wich extracts nearly uniform randomness from a biometric input in an error-tolerant way helped by some public string. Also, they propose an extension of the fuzzy vault which is easier to evaluate theoretically than the original formulation of Juels and Sudan [8].

3 Biometric Hash Generation

We present a biometric hash generation scheme based on the concatenation of binary strings extracted from a set of feature vector subsets. We extend the previous work by Hoque et al. [4], where vector quantization is applied to feature subsets, which are further concatenated to form the biometric hash. We provide a solution for high-dimensional vectors by means of feature selection based on an integer-coding genetic algorithm.

3.1 Feature Subset Concatenation

Given a feature vector $\mathbf{x} = [x_1, \ldots, x_N]$ with $x_i \in \mathcal{R}$, a biometric hash $\mathbf{h} = [h_1, \ldots, h_L]$ with $h_i \in \{0, 1\}$ of dimension L is extracted. Let $\mathbf{x}^j$ with $j = 1, \ldots, D$ be formed by a subset of features of $\mathbf{x}$ of dimension M $(M < N)$, with possibly overlapping features for different j. Let C^j be a codebook obtained by vector quantization of feature subset $\mathbf{x}^j$ using a development set of features $\mathbf{x}^j_{k=1,\ldots,K}$. We define $\mathbf{h}$ for an input feature vector $\mathbf{x}_T$ as:

$$\mathbf{h}(\mathbf{x}_T) = \underset{j=1,\ldots,D}{\text{concat}} \left(f(\mathbf{x}^j_T, C^j) \right) \tag{1}$$

where f is a function that assigns the nearest-neighbour codewords, and concat$(\cdot)$ denotes the concatenation of binary strings.

The codebooks C^j are computed with vector quantization as follows. Let $\mathbf{x}^j_{k=1,\ldots,K}$ be feature vector subsets forming a development set. The k-means algorithm is used to compute the centroids of the underlying clusters, for a given number of clusters Q. Then, centroids are ranked based on their distance to the mean of all centroids. Finally, binary codewords of size $q = \log_2 Q$ are defined as the position of each centroid in the ranking using Gray coding [18].

3.2 Feature Selection Using Genetic Algorithms

GA are non-deterministic methods inspired in natural evolution, which apply the rules of selection, crossover and mutation to a population of possible solutions in order to optimize a given fitness function [5]. In the present work, a GA with integer coding is implemented in order to obtain the best subsets of M features. Integer coding has been used instead of binary coding, since the last one does not fit well when the number of features is fixed.

Algorithm 1. Feature subset selection using GA

```
Input: n, S, θ
Output: A
  F ← S
  A ← ∅
  for i ← 1 to n do
    B ← GA(F) {Call GA, returns a sorted list of candidate subsets}
    for all b ∈ B do
      if b ∩ a ≤ θ, ∀a ∈ A then
        A ← A ∪ b
      end if
    end for
    N ← ∅
    for all a ∈ A do
      N ← N ∪ a
    end for
    N ← unique(N) {Remove repeated items}
    F' ← ∅
    for j ← 1 to |F|/2 do
      F' ← F' ∪ N_j
    end for
    F ← F − F'
  end for
```

The proposed iterative algorithm for feature subset selection using GA is presented in Algorithm 1. Note that the proposed algorithm can be easily modified to use a different feature selection technique such as SFFS [19].

In words, Algorithm 1 receives the number of iterations n, the initial feature set S, and the threshold θ, which represents the maximum number of overlapped features permitted among different subsets. For the feature set F, initially equal to S, the feature selection algorithm is called (here, the GA). From the output (a sorted list of subsets of size M), subsets are selected iteratively if no previously selected subset overlaps with the one at hand in more than a certain threshold θ. This way, the threshold settles the degree of correlation allowed among the different subsets.

In the proposed scheme, the fitness function of the GA has been defined as $f = \text{EER}^{-1}$, where the EER is computed for skilled forgeries from a development set different to the training set used for vector quantization (see Sect. 4.1).

After the subsets selection, the half of the features with the best performance are removed from F, and the algorithm is iterated. This strategy was followed in order to avoid the possible loss of not so discriminative sets of features, that nevertheless provide complementary information to the previously selected features.

4 Case Study: Biometric Hash Generation from Feature-Based Information of On-Line Signatures

4.1 Signature Database and Experimental Protocol

The MCYT on-line signature corpus is used for the experiments [20]. This database contains 330 users with 25 genuine signatures and 25 skilled forgeries per user, captured in four acquisition sites. Forgers were asked to imitate after observing the static image of the signature to imitate, they tried to copy them at least 10 times, and then they wrote the forgeries naturally without breaks or slowdowns.

For the experiments presented here, we have followed a 2-fold cross-validation strategy. The database has been divided into two sets: a *development* set, formed by the even users, and an *evaluation* set, with the odd users. The development set has been further partitioned into: *training* set (for vector quantization), with the even users of the development set, and *testing* set (for GA optimization), with the rest.

Evaluation experiments were conducted as follows. A binary hash was generated for each genuine signature in the database, and compared to the hashes of the remaining genuine signatures of the user at hand, all her skilled forgeries, and the first genuine signature of the remaining users (random forgeries).

Genuine and impostor matching scores were calculated using the similarity function $s_H(\mathbf{h}_1, \mathbf{h}_2) = q_{\max} - d_H(\mathbf{h}_1, \mathbf{h}_2)$, where d_H represents Hamming distance and $\mathbf{h}_1$ and $\mathbf{h}_2$ are binary vectors of size $q_{\max}$ [21]. The EER between genuine and either skilled of random forgeries using this similarity measure is used as the performance criterion of the hashing scheme. Examples of the matching of genuine and skilled hashes are included in Fig. 2.

4.2 Feature Extraction from On-Line Signatures

For the experiments we use an on-line signature representation based on global features [7]. In particular, a 100-dimensional global feature vector is extracted from each on-line signature [22], including features based on timing information, number of strokes, geometry, etc.

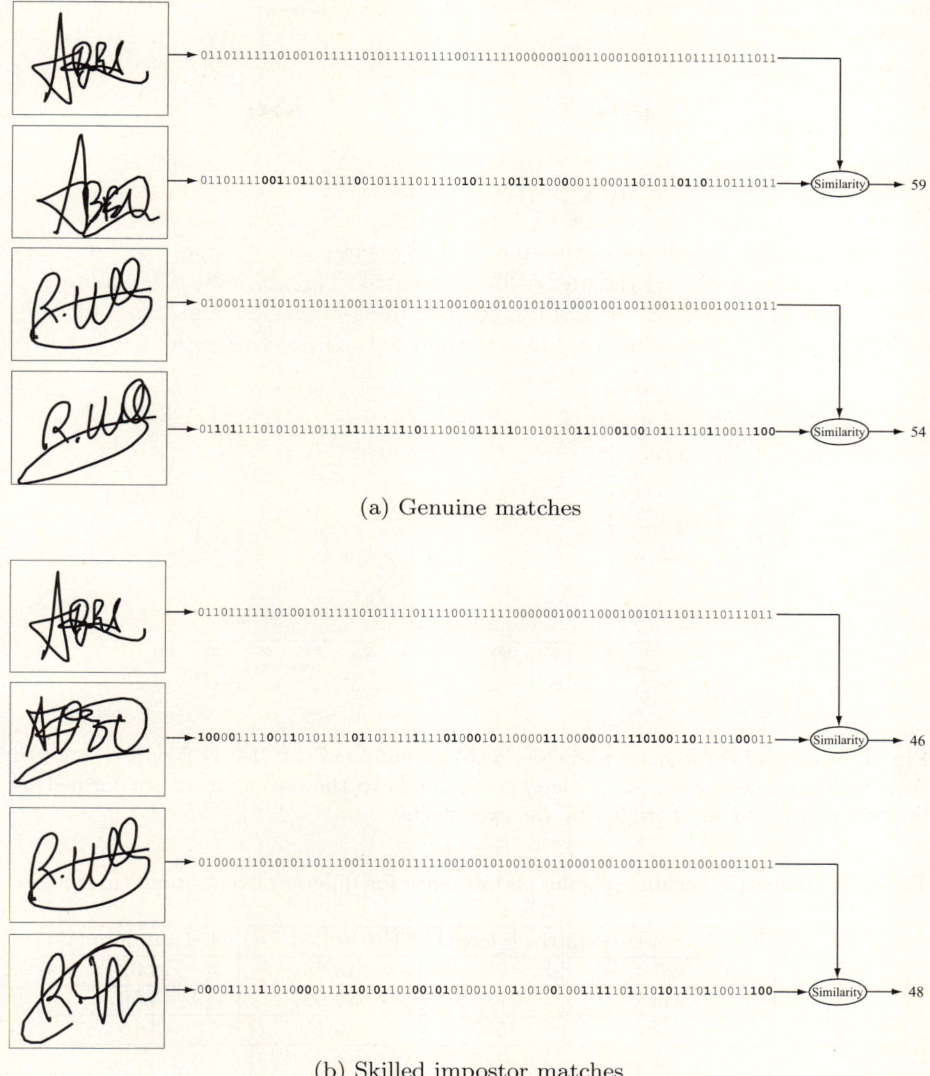

(a) Genuine matches

(b) Skilled impostor matches

Fig. 2. Examples of the matching between a genuine template and a genuine test hash (a), and between a genuine template and a skilled forgery (b). The binary strings correspond to the real hashes obtained with overlap $\theta = 0$. Different bits are represented in **bold**.

Each feature x_i is normalized into the range $[0, 1]$ using *tanh*-estimators [23]. The normalization is given by:

$$x'_i = \frac{1}{2}\left\{\tanh\left(0.1\left(\frac{x_i - \mu_i}{\sigma_i}\right)\right) + 1\right\} \quad (2)$$

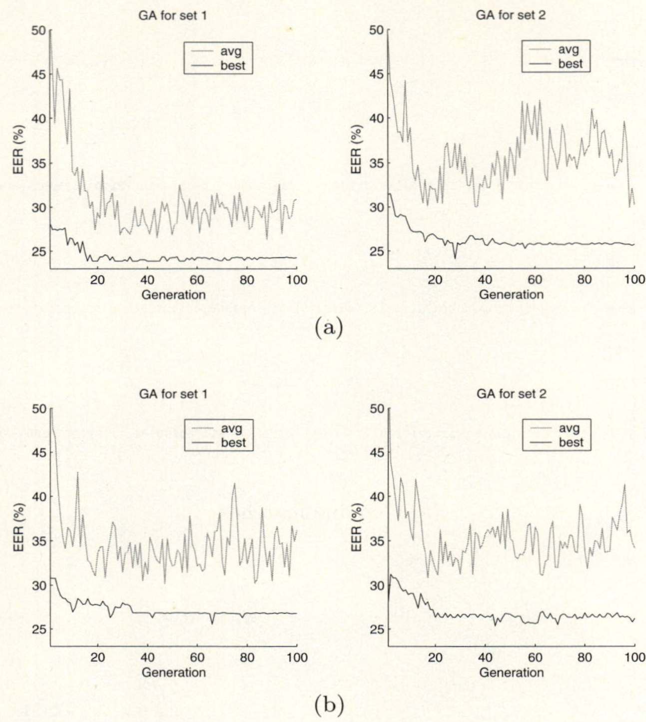

Fig. 3. Results of the first (a) and second (b) execution of the GA. Following the 2-fold cross-validation approach, set 1 (left) corresponds to the development set formed by the odd users, and set 2 (right) by the even users.

Table 1. Biometric hashing scheme performance for different overlapping threshold θ

Overlap (θ)	Number of subsets	Hash length	EER skilled (%)	EER random (%)
0	25	75	18.83	8.02
1	171	513	12.99	3.50
2	530	1590	12.15	3.16

where μ_i and σ_i are the mean and the standard deviation of the feature x_i for the genuine signatures in the database.

4.3 Implementation of the Genetic Algorithm

In the proposed integer-coding genetic selection, a string of the genetic population is represented by a vector of length M, where M is the dimension of the subsets to be found. Each element of the string is an integer in the range $[1, 100]$ and corresponds to a feature in the original set.

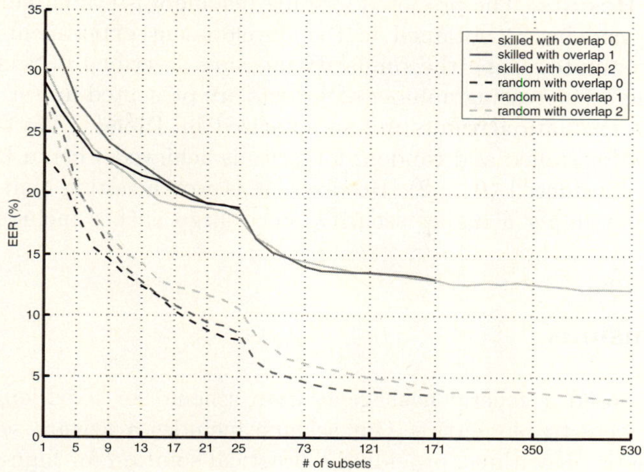

Fig. 4. EER (in %) for increasing number of subsets of the biometric hash for overlapping threshold $\theta = 0$, 1 and 2, respectively

The configuration set of the genetic algorithm is the following:

– Population size: 100, randomly generated in the first generation.
– String size: 4, representing the number M of features in the subset.
– Stop condition: after completing 100 generations.
– Selection: binary tournament.
– Crossover: one-point, with 85% probability.
– Mutation: mutated elements are randomly assigned a value in the range $[1, 100]$ that is not present in the string, with 5% probability.

The output of our genetic algorithm is the whole set of the strings produced along the evolution of the GA, sorted by descending order of fitness.

4.4 Experimental Results

Development Experiments. Algorithm 1 was executed for parameters $n = 2$, $S = [1, 100]$ and $\theta = 0$, 1, and 2, respectively. The number of clusters in the k-means algorithm was fixed to 8. As a result, codewords extracted from each subset have a bit size of $\log_2 8 = 3$.

In Fig. 3(a) we present the evolution of the first iteration of the feature subset selection algorithm, corresponding to an execution of the genetic algorithm. We observe that the best string (feature subset) converges to an EER value of about 24% for skilled forgeries. Results of the second execution are presented in Fig. 3(b). Interestingly, the best EER is only slightly worse when considering the 50 features discarded from the first iteration.

Evaluation Results. The proposed hashing scheme was evaluated for the subsets and the codebooks obtained in the development experiments. Matching scores were computed using the similarity measure described in Sect. 4.1.

EERs using an increasing number of subsets are presented in Fig. 4 for $\theta = 0$, 1 and 2. The evaluation results are summarized in Table 1. We observe that the best EER for skilled and random forgeries is achieved when a high number of subsets is considered ($\theta = 2$). However, it is worth noting that a big hash length does not imply a higher security, since large hashes include redundant information.

5 Conclusions

We have proposed a general hash generation scheme for fixed-length feature-based approaches to biometrics. Our scheme includes a feature selection step based on genetic algorithms, providing a practical solution for high-dimensional feature vectors. The proposed scheme can be used as a building block of biometric cryptosystems.

Experiments have been conducted on signature data from the MCYT database using 2-fold cross-validation. We have studied the effect of using subsets with a variable number of overlapping features. We observed that the best EER is achieved with the configuration that involves more feature subsets (overlapping threshold of 2).

A future direction of this research will be the comparison of the GA with other feature selection strategies. Also, the effect of other parameters as the quantization size or the subset length will be considered. The redundancy of the resulting hashes is also yet to be studied, as well as the application of the proposed hashing to other biometrics.

Acknowledgements

This work has been supported by Spanish Ministry of Education and Science (project TEC2006-13141-C03-03) and BioSecure NoE (IST-2002-507634). M. R. F. is supported by a FPI Fellowship from Comunidad de Madrid. J. F. is supported by a Marie Curie Fellowship from European Commission. J. G. is supported by a FPU Fellowship from the Spanish Ministry of Education and Science.

References

1. Jain, A.K., Ross, A., Pankanti, S.: Biometrics: A tool for information security. IEEE Trans. on Information Forensics and Security 1(2), 125–143 (2006)
2. Uludag, U., Pankanti, S., Prabhakar, S., Jain, A.K.: Biometric cryptosystems: Issues and challenges. Proceedings of the IEEE 92(6), 948–960 (2004)
3. Bolle, R.M., Connell, J.H., Ratha, N.K.: Biometric perils and patches. Pattern Recognition 35(12), 2727–2738 (2002)

4. Hoque, S., Fairhurst, M., Howells, G., Deravi, F.: Feasibility of generating biometric encryption keys. Electronics Letters 41(6), 309–311 (2005)
5. Goldberg, D.E.: Genetic Algorithms in Search, Optimization and Machine Learning. Addison-Wesley Longman Publishing Co. Inc., Boston, MA, USA (1989)
6. Plamondon, R., Srihari, S.N.: On-line and off-line handwriting recognition: A comprehensive survey. IEEE Trans. PAMI 22(1), 63–84 (2000)
7. Fierrez, J., Ortega-Garcia, J.: On-line signature verification. In: Jain, A.K., Ross, A., Flynn, P. (eds.) Handbook of Biometrics (to appear)
8. Juels, A., Sudan, M.: A fuzzy vault scheme. Design Code. Cryptogr. 38(2), 237–257 (2006)
9. Uludag, U., Pankanti, S., Jain, A.K.: Fuzzy vault for fingerprints. In: Kanade, T., Jain, A., Ratha, N.K. (eds.) AVBPA 2005. LNCS, vol. 3546, pp. 310–319. Springer, Heidelberg (2005)
10. Uludag, U., Jain, A.K.: Securing fingerprint template: Fuzzy vault with helper data. In: Proc. CVPRW, p. 163. IEEE Computer Society, Los Alamitos (2006)
11. Freire-Santos, M., Fierrez-Aguilar, J., Ortega-Garcia, J.: Cryptographic key generation using handwritten signature. In: Proc. SPIE., vol. 6202, pp. 225–231 (2006)
12. Vielhauer, C., Steinmetz, R., Mayerhoefer, A.: Biometric hash based on statistical features of online signatures. In: Proc. ICPR., vol. 1, pp. 123–126 (2002)
13. Vielhauer, C., Steinmetz, R.: Handwriting: Feature correlation analysis for biometric hashes. EURASIP JASP 2004(4), 542–558 (2004)
14. Teoh, A.B., Goh, A., Ngo, D.C.: Random multispace quantization as an analytic mechanism for biohashing of biometric and random identity inputs. IEEE Trans. PAMI 28(12), 1892–1901 (2006)
15. Lumini, A., Nanni, L.: An improved biohashing for human authentication. Pattern Recognition 40(3), 1057–1065 (2007)
16. Ngo, D.C.L., Teoh, A.B.J., Goh, A.: Biometric hash: high-confidence face recognition. IEEE Trans. Circ. Syst. Vid. 16(6), 771–775 (2006)
17. Dodis, Y., Reyzin, L., Smith, A.: Fuzzy extractors: How to generate strong keys from biometrics and other noisy data. In: Cachin, C., Camenisch, J.L. (eds.) EUROCRYPT 2004. LNCS, vol. 3027, pp. 523–540. Springer, Heidelberg (2004)
18. Lin, S., Costello, D.J.: Error Control Coding, 2nd edn. Prentice-Hall, Inc. Upper Saddle River, NJ, USA (2004)
19. Pudil, P., Novovicova, J., Kittler, J.: Floating search methods in feature selection. Pattern Recogn. Lett. 15(11), 1119–1125 (1994)
20. Ortega-Garcia, J., et al.: MCYT baseline corpus: A bimodal biometric database. IEE Proc. Vision, Image and Signal Processing 150(6), 395–401 (2003)
21. Theodoridis, S., Koutroumbas, K.: Pattern Recognition. Academic Press, San Diego (2006)
22. Fierrez-Aguilar, J., et al.: An on-line signature verification system based on fusion of local and global information. In: Roli, F., Vitulano, S. (eds.) ICIAP 2005. LNCS, vol. 3617, pp. 523–532. Springer, Heidelberg (2005)
23. Jain, A.K., Nandakumar, K., Ross, A.: Score normalization in multimodal biometric systems. Pattern Recognition 38(12), 2270–2285 (2005)

Biometrics Based on Multispectral Skin Texture

Robert K. Rowe

Lumidigm, Inc, 801 University Blvd., SE, Suite 302, Albuquerque, NM 87106
Rob.Rowe@Lumidigm.com

Abstract. Multispectral imaging (MSI) of the skin provides information about both the surface and subsurface characteristics of the skin tissue. These multispectral characteristics may be described as textures and used to determine the identity of an individual. In this investigation, a multi-day, multi-person study was conducted to compare the performance of a matcher based on multispectral texture analysis with a conventional minutiae-based fingerprint matcher. Both matchers used MSI data from exactly the same area of the sensor. Performance of the two methods was compared for a range of simulated sensor areas. The performance of the textural matcher was nearly equivalent to that of the minutiae matcher for the larger sensor areas within the limited scope of this study. For small sensor areas, the performance of the texture matcher was significantly better than the minutia matcher operating over the identical small region.

Keywords: multispectral skin texture, skin biometrics, multispectral imaging, local consistency.

1 Introduction

Fingerprint-based biometric sensors are used across a broad range of applications, from law enforcement and civil identification to commercial access control and even in some consumer devices such as laptops and cell phones. In the latter cases, there is a need to reduce the size of the sensor in order to reduce the area of the device that the sensor occupies and also, generally, to reduce the cost of the sensor. However, the performance of a contact fingerprint sensor degrades as the size decreases [1]. Because of this, some manufacturers [2, 3, 4] produce long and narrow fingerprint sensors that simulate a larger-area sensor by combining a series of narrow images collected while the user "swipes" their finger across the sensor surface. Such a sensor configuration places a burden on the user and limits the applications in which this type of solution is considered.

One way to reduce the sensing area while maintaining a simple, single-touch user interface is to measure a property of the skin that is *locally consistent* while still being distinct from person to person. In this way, a small-area sensor would be able to perform a biometric match using a skin location never previously enrolled as long as the optical properties of the enrolled and tested skin sites were "similar enough".

In this paper, we examine the feasibility of using multispectral imaging (MSI) for small-area sensors. The matching is done using textural descriptors of the multispectral

S.-W. Lee and S.Z. Li (Eds.): ICB 2007, LNCS 4642, pp. 1144–1153, 2007.

data combined with a classification methodology that seeks to find characteristics of the data that are locally consistent. We test the performance of this matcher against that of a commercial minutiae matcher operating on fingerprint images developed from the same multispectral data used for the texture matcher.

2 Relationship to Other Work

A number of papers have been published in the area of using texture matching of fingerprints. For example, Jain [5] proposed a local texture analysis using Gabor filters applied to tessellated regions around the core point. Lee and Wang [6] and Hamamoto [7] also used Gabor filters localized at the core. Coetzee and Botha [8] and Willis and Myers [9] proposed a Fourier analysis fingerprint texture as the basis for biometric determinations. Tico et al. [10] applied wavelet analysis to fingerprint images to distinguish between them. Apart from differences in basis functions and other methodological matters, the key difference between these prior efforts and the one reported in this paper is that, to this investigator's knowledge, all prior investigations are based on conventional fingerprint images. As such, the observed textural pattern is extracted from a single image, which limits the information content and can be adversely affected by artifacts due to effects such as dry skin, poor contact between the skin and sensor, and other operationally important matters. In contrast, the present investigation is based on multiple images taken with a robust imaging methodology which contains information about both the surface and subsurface characteristics of the skin while minimizing sampling artifacts. In fact, the one data plane in the MSI stack most similar to conventional optical fingerprinting techniques was explicitly removed from the texture analysis in order to avoid the presence of spurious effects, as described later in this paper.

The topic of how to perform biometric matching using small-area fingerprint sensors is an active area of investigation. One common approach is to build up a large enrollment image by piecing together a series of small fingerprint images taken over multiple placements of the finger in a process known as *mosaicing* [1, 11]. Alternatively, some authors have combined the minutiae information together instead of the image themselves [12, 13, 14, 15]. In contrast to either of these approaches, the work described in this paper is associated with finding those characteristics of the multispectral skin texture that are locally consistent in order that an enrollment measurement may be made at one skin site and successfully verified at a different but nearby skin site.

One manufacturer of a facial recognition system [16] says they use "surface texture analysis" to augment and improve the performance of their commercial system. The major difference between such a surface-based method and the methods and systems described in this paper is that the MSI sensor has been developed to obtain a significant portion of information from features below the surface of the skin. Moreover, the plurality of wavelengths, illumination angles, and optical polarization conditions used in this investigation yields additional information beyond that available through simple surface reflectance measurements.

3 Multispectral Skin Sensing

3.1 Hardware and Raw MSI Data

In order to capture information-rich data about the surface and subsurface features of the skin of the finger, the MSI sensor collects multiple images of the finger under a variety of optical conditions. The raw images are captured using different wavelengths of illumination light, different polarization conditions, and different illumination orientations. In this manner, each of the raw images contains somewhat different and complementary information about the finger. The different wavelengths penetrate the skin to different depths and are absorbed and scattered differently by various chemical components and structures in the skin. The different polarization conditions change the degree of contribution of surface and subsurface features to the raw image. Finally, different illumination orientations change the location and degree to which surface features are accentuated.

Fig. 1 shows a simplified schematic of the major optical components of an MSI fingerprint sensor. Illumination for each of the multiple raw images is generated by one of the light emitting diodes (LEDs). The figure illustrates the case of polarized, direct illumination being used to collect a raw image. The light from the LED passes through a linear polarizer before illuminating the finger as it rests on the sensor platen. Light interacts with the finger and a portion of the light is directed toward the imager through the imaging polarizer. The imaging polarizer is oriented with its optical axis to be orthogonal to the axis of the illumination polarizer, such that light with the same polarization as the illumination light is substantially attenuated by the polarizer. This severely reduces the influence of light reflected from the surface of the skin and emphasizes light that has undergone multiple optical scattering events after penetrating the skin.

The second direct-illumination LED shown in Fig. 1 does not have a polarizer placed in the illumination path. When this LED is illuminated, the illumination light is randomly polarized. In this case the surface-reflected light and the deeply penetrating light are both able to pass through the imaging polarizer in equal proportions. As such, the image produced from this non-polarized LED contains a much stronger influence from surface features of the finger.

Importantly, all of these direct-illumination sources (both polarized and non-polarized) as well as the imaging system are arranged to avoid any critical-angle phenomena at the platen-air interfaces. In this way, each illuminator is certain to illuminate the finger and the imager is certain to image the finger regardless of whether the skin is dry, dirty or even in contact with the sensor. This aspect of the MSI imager is distinctly different from most other conventional fingerprint imaging technologies and is a key aspect of the robustness of the MSI methodology.

In addition to the direct illumination illustrated in Fig. 1, the MSI sensor also integrates a form of total internal reflectance (TIR) imaging. In this illumination mode, one or more LEDs illuminate the side of the platen. A portion of the illumination light propagates through the platen by making multiple TIR reflections at the platen-air interfaces. At points where the TIR is broken by contact with the skin, light enters the skin and is diffusely reflected. A portion of this diffusely reflected light is directed toward the imaging system and passes through the imaging polarizer

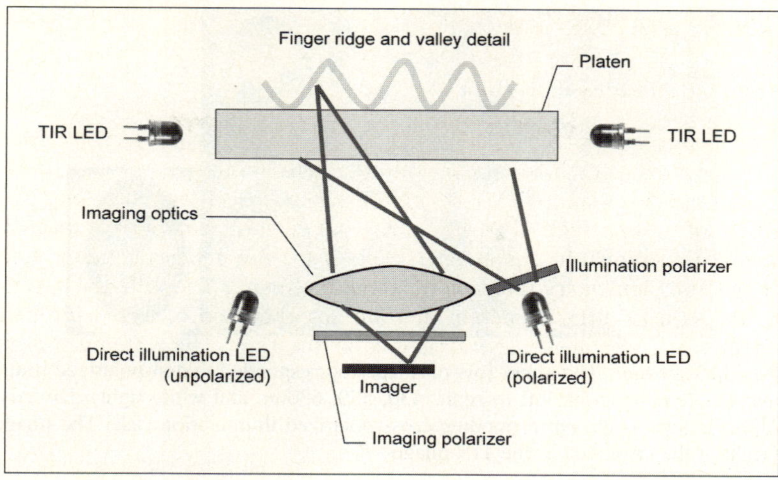

Fig. 1. Optical configuration of an MSI sensor. The red lines illustrate the direct illumination of a finger by a polarized LED.

(since this light is randomly polarized), forming an image for this illumination state. Unlike all of the direct illumination states, the quality of the resulting raw TIR image is critically dependent on having skin of sufficient moisture content and cleanliness making good optical contact with the platen, just as is the case with conventional TIR sensors.

In practice, MSI sensors typically contain multiple direct-illumination LEDs of different wavelengths. For example, the Lumidigm J110 MSI sensor used to collect the data used in this investigation has four direct-illumination wavelength bands (430, 530, and 630 nm as well as a white light) in both polarized and unpolarized configurations. When a finger is placed on the sensor platen, eight direct-illumination images are captured along with a single TIR image. The raw images are captured on a 640 x 480 image array with a pixel resolution of 525 ppi. All nine images are captured in approximately 500 mSec.

An example of the nine images captured during a single finger placement is illustrated in Fig 2. The upper row shows the raw images for unpolarized illumination wavelengths of 430, 530, and 630 nm, as well as white light. The lower row shows the corresponding images for the cross-polarized case as well as the TIR image. The grayscale for each of the raw images has been expanded to emphasize the features.

3.2 Composite Fingerprint Generation and Matching

It can be seen from Fig. 2 that there are a number of features present in the raw data including the textural characteristics of the subsurface skin, which appears as mottling that is particularly pronounced under blue (430 nm) and green (530 nm) illumination wavelengths. As well, the relative intensities of the raw images under each of the illumination conditions is very indicative of the spectral characteristics (i.e. color) of the finger or other sample (note that the relative intensities have been obscured in Fig. 2 to better show the comparative details of the raw images).

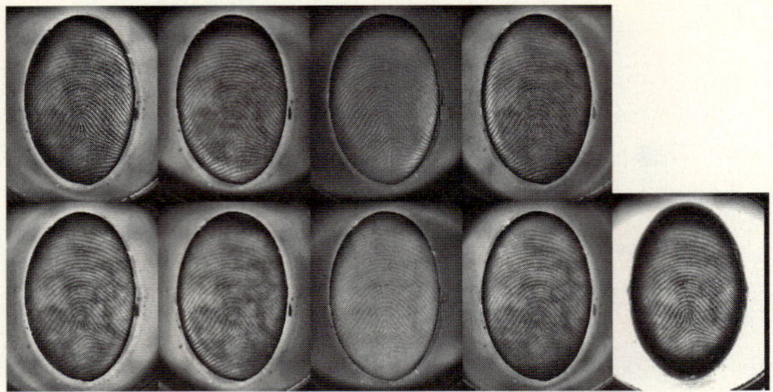

Fig. 2. Raw MSI images. The upper row of images corresponded to non-polarized illumination of various wavelengths (from left to right: 430, 530, 630nm and white light). Directly below each of these images is the corresponding cross-polarized illumination case. The image at the extreme right of the lower row is the TIR image.

The set of raw images shown in Fig. 2 can be combined together to produce a single representation of the fingerprint pattern. This fingerprint generation relies on a wavelet-based method of image fusion to extract, combine and enhance those features that are characteristic of a fingerprint. The wavelet decomposition method that is used is based on the dual-tree complex wavelet transform (DTCWT) [17]. Image fusion occurs by selecting and compiling the coefficients with the maximum absolute magnitude in the image at each position and decomposition level [18]. An inverse wavelet transform is then performed on the resulting collection of coefficients, yielding a single, composite image. An example of the result of applying the compositing algorithm to two placements of the same finger is given in Fig. 3.

The composite fingerprint images can then be used with conventional fingerprint matching software. For this investigation, a commercial minutiae-based feature extraction and matching routine (NEC, NECSAM FE4, ver. 1.0.2.0, PPC2003) was applied to the composite fingerprints as a control to compare to texture matching results.

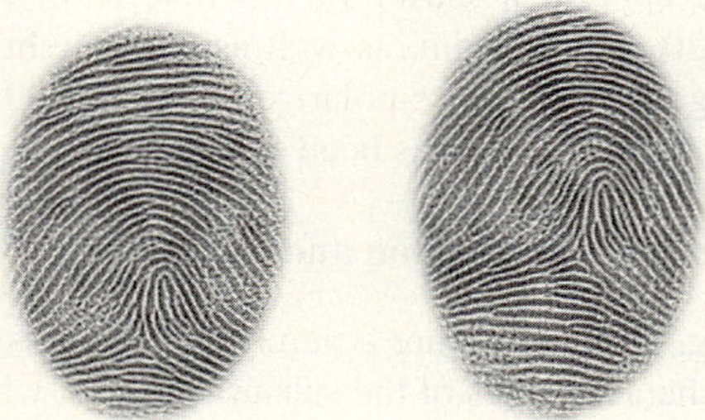

Fig. 3. Composite fingerprint images extracted from 2 different sets of multispectral data like those shown in Fig. 2

3.3 Multispectral Texture Analysis

The DTCWT process that was used to generate composite fingerprint images was also used to provide the spectral-textural features of the multispectral data. The coefficients from the third level of the DTCWT decomposition of the multispectral image stack were used as features for the texture analysis in this investigation. Since the strength and quality of the raw TIR image plane is highly variable (dependent on skin moisture, good contact, etc.), this plane was omitted from the multispectral texture analysis but not from the corresponding composite fingerprint.

Anderson et al. [19] have defined a set of image features based on a DTCWT decomposition that they refer to as inter-level products. These features represent the conjugate products of the DTCWT coefficients in two adjacent decomposition levels. They have also defined an inter-coefficient product (elsewhere in their publications it is referred to as "same-level product") that represents the conjugate product of adjacent coefficients in the same decomposition level. These conjugate products have been shown to represent the fundamental features of the image while being insensitive to translation and some amount of rotation.

In a similar way, we define an inter-image product, P, as the conjugate product of coefficients at some direction, d, decomposition level, k, generated by any 2 of the raw multispectral images, i and j, in a multispectral image stack at location x,y:

$$P_{i,j}(x,y,d,k) = C_i(x,y,k)\ C_j^*(x,y,k), \tag{1}$$

where $C_i(x,y,k)$ is the complex coefficient for image i at decomposition level k and location x,y while $C^*_j(x,y,k)$ is the conjugate of the corresponding complex value for image j.

For purposes of this investigation, we compiled all real and imaginary components of all the conjugate products generated from each unique image pair as a feature vector. For 8 raw image planes, this results in a 384 element vector (28 conjugate products/direction, 6 directions, 2 scalar values (real and imaginary) per product for $i{\neq}j$, plus 8 conjugate products/direction, 6 directions, 1 scalar value (real only) for $i{=}j$). In addition, the isotropic magnitudes of the coefficients were added to the feature vector, where the isotropic magnitude is simply the sum of the absolute magnitudes over the 6 directional coefficients. Finally, the mean DC values of each of the raw images over the region of analysis were added to the feature vector. Concatenating all of these values resulted in a 400-element feature vector at each element location.

4 Experimental Data and Analysis

Multispectral data were collected on 21 volunteers over a period of approximately 2 weeks. The participants were office workers whose ages ranged from the mid-20s to the mid-60s. They were of mixed gender and race. Each participant made two visits separated by at least one day. During a visit, each of the 4 fingers on the right hand was measured 3 times, yielding 12 multispectral data sets collected per person per visit. This resulted in a total dataset comprised of 504 multispectral image stacks taken over 84 unique fingers.

For purposes of this investigation, the data collected during a participant's first visit was treated as enrollment data and data from the second visit was used for testing. A summary of the spans of time between enrollment and verification for the 21 study participants is: 1 day (16 people), 3 days (2 people), 4 days (1 person), 5 days (1 person) and 11 days (1 person).

Since the dataset used for this analysis was of a relatively modest size, the biometric task that was tested was chosen to be personalization, which requires far less data than verification (or any other "open" formulation) to obtain stable results. In this testing scenario, there are N enrolled people and each test sample is assumed to be one of the enrollees. No attempt is made to determine or discriminate against non-enrolled test samples. The estimate for identity is simply the enrollment sample that is the closest match to the test sample.

Multiple, random trials were conducted to determine the performance of both the multispectral texture matcher as well as the fingerprint matcher used as a control for each tested condition. Each trial was based on enrollment by 6 randomly selected fingers from 6 randomly selected people. These same data were also used to build a classification model as described below. The data from the same fingers taken during the second visit for each of the 6 enrolled fingers were used for performance testing. In order to augment the calibration model, the data from one randomly selected finger from each of the other 15 people in the dataset who were not enrolled for a particular trial were included as part of the calibration dataset.

Multispectral texture analysis was performed on an element-by-element basis over a particular analysis region. Each analysis region comprised a contiguous area of the imager with pixel dimensions of 64 x 48. The number of analysis regions used for each of the 4 cases that were studied varied from 5 x 5 (320 x 240 pixels, 0.61" x 0.46") to 1 x 1 (64 x 48 pixels, 0.12" x 0.09"). In each of the cases studied, the comparison was made to a fingerprint that was generated from the multispectral data and masked to cover exactly the same area as used for the multispectral match. The four cases are illustrated and further described in Fig. 4. For all cases, the analysis regions were centered on the active image area.

The calibration data for a given analysis region was used as an input into a Fisher linear discriminant analysis (FLDA) algorithm to develop a classification model. Prior to processing the calibration data, the data were normalized such that the standard deviation of each of the elements of the feature vector was 1.0 over the calibration set. The same normalization factor was also applied to the test data.

The test samples were then matched to the enrollment samples by projecting the difference in feature vectors onto the FLDA factors and accumulating an RMS summary of the resulting projection. The differences were accumulated for all elements within an analysis region and for all analysis regions used in a particular case. The estimate of the identity of the test sample was then selected as the enrollment that had the smallest accumulated match value associated with it.

The comparison to fingerprint minutiae matching was done by masking the MSI-derived fingerprint to the same area as used for the corresponding MSI texture analysis. The minutiae matching was then performed between the test image and the 6*3 = 18 enrolled images. The ID of the enrolled image with the largest match value was recorded for that particular test image.

Fig. 4. Illustration of sensor sizes used in this study using the same images as in Fig 3. The largest sensor size is at the top and is 320 x 240 (0.61" x 0.46") followed by 192 x 144 (0.37" x 0.27"), 192 x 48 (0.37" x 0.09") and 64 x 48 (0.12" x 0.09") on the bottom.

5 Results

The performance of each test configuration was estimated by aggregating the results of 20 random trials conducted for each of the test conditions. The summary of these results is given in Fig. 5.

A comparison of the results of this study indicates that the performance of the multispectral texture matcher is approximately the same as the fingerprint matcher for

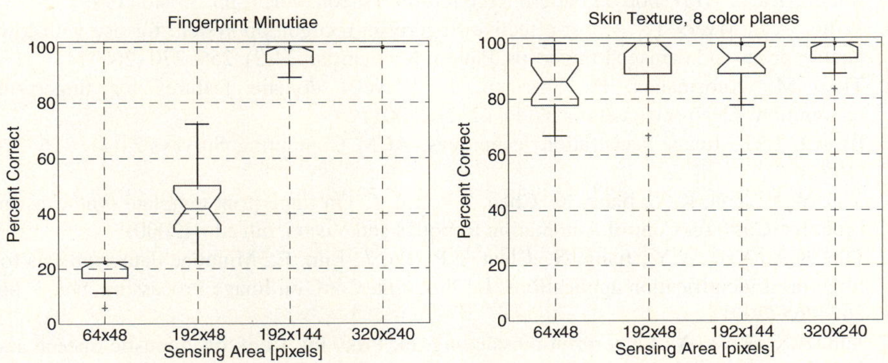

Fig. 5. Results for fingerprint matching (left) and multispectral skin texture matching (right) for 4 different sensor sizes. The boxes indicate the inner two quartiles of the 20 random trials and the red line is the median of the 20 trials. The notch indicates the uncertainty of the median at a 5% significance level.

the two largest sensor areas that were tested. Further work with larger datasets will be required to quantify the performance differences between a minutiae matcher and a multispectral texture matcher over the same, relatively large area of the finger.

However, the results from this modestly sized study do indicate that as the sensor size decreases, the performance of the texture-based matcher is maintained better than that of the minutiae-based matcher, which degrades sharply for the smallest sensor areas tested. This difference in performance is possibly due to the property of local consistency of the multispectral texture: skin proximal to the point of enrollment has approximately the same properties as the enrollment site itself. Therefore, placement-to-placement variation (which becomes more severe as the sensor size decreases) affects the texture matcher far less than the minutiae matcher.

References

1. Maltoni, D., Maio, D., Jain, A.K., Prabhakar, S.: Handbook of Fingerprint Recognition. Springer, Heidelberg (2003)
2. http://www.authentec.com
3. http://www.upek.com
4. http://www.atmel.com/products/biometrics/
5. Jain, A.K., Prabhakar, S., Hong, L., Pankanti, S.: Filterbank-based fingerprint matching. IEEE Transactions on Image Processing 9, 846–859 (2000)
6. Lee, C.J., Wang, S.D.: Fingerprint feature extraction using Gabor filters. Electronic Letters 35(4), 288–290 (1999)
7. Hamamoto, Y.: A Gabor filter-based method for fingerprint identification. In: Jain, L.C., Halici, U., Hayashi, I., Lee, S.B. (eds.) Intelligent Biometric Techniques in Fingerprint and Face Recognition, CRC Press, Boca Raton, FL (1999)
8. Coetzee, L., Botha, E.C.: Fingerprint recognition with a neural-net classifier. In: Proc. South African Workshop on Pattern Recognition, 1st edn. vol. 1, pp. 33–40 (1990)
9. Willis, A.J., Myers, L.: A cost-effective fingerprint recognition system for use with low-quality prints and damaged fingertips. Pattern Recognition 34(2), 255–270 (2001)
10. Tico, M., Kuosmanen, P., Saarinen, J.: Wavelet domain features for fingerprint recognition. Electronics Letters 37(1), 21–22 (2001)
11. Brown, L.G.: Image registration techniques. ACM Computing Surveys 24(4), 326–376 (1992)
12. Yau, W.Y., Toh, K.A., Jiang, X., Chen, T.P., Lu, J.: On fingerprint template synthesis. In: Proc. Int. Conf. on Control Automation Robotics and Vision, 6th edn. (2000)
13. Toh, K.A., Yau, W.Y., Jiang, X., Chen, T.P., Lu, J., Lim, E.: Minutiae data synthesis for fingerprint identification applications. In: Proc. Int. Conf. on Image Processing, vol. 3, pp. 262–265 (2001)
14. Jain, A.K., Ross, A.: Fingerprint mosaicking. In: Proc. Int. Conf. on Acoustic Speech and Signal Processing, vol. 4, pp. 4064–4067 (2002)
15. Ramoser, H., Wachmann, B., Bischof, H.: Efficent alignment of fingerprint images. In: Proc. Int. Conf. on Pattern Recognition (16th), vol. 3, pp. 748–751 (2002)
16. http://www.visionics.com/trends/skin.html

17. Kingsbury, N.: Complex wavelets for shift invariant analysis and filtering of signals. Journal of Appl. and Comput. Harmonic Analysis 10, 234–253 (2001)
18. Hill, P., Canagarajah, N., Bull, D.: Image fusion using complex wavelets. In: Proc. 13th British Machine Vision Conference, Cardiff, UK (2002)
19. Anderson, R., Kingsbury, N., Fauqueur, J.: Robust rotation-invariant object recognition using edge-profile clusters. submitted to European Conference on Computer Vision (May 2006)

Application of New Qualitative Voicing Time-Frequency Features for Speaker Recognition

Nidhal Ben Aloui[1,2], Hervé Glotin[1], and Patrick Hebrard[2]

[1] Université du Sud Toulon-Var Laboratoire LSIS
B.P. 20 132 - 83 957 La Garde, France
{benaloui,glotin}@univ-tln.fr
[2] DCNS - Division SIS,
Le Mourillon B.P. 403 - 83 055 Toulon, France
{nidhal.ben-aloui,patrick.hebrard}@dcn.fr

Abstract. This paper presents original and efficient Qualitative Time-Frequency (QTF) speech features for speaker recognition based on a med-term speech dynamics qualitative representation. For each frame of around 150ms, we estimate and binarize a suband voicing activity estimation of 6 frequency subands. We then derive the Allen temporal relations graph between these 6 time intervals. This set of temporal relations, estimated at each frame, feeds a neural network which is trained for speaker recognition. Experiments are conducted on fifty speakers (males and females) of a reference radio database ESTER (40 hours) with continuous speech. Our best model generates around 3% of frame class error, without using information of frame continuity, which is similar to state of the art. Moreover, our QTF generates a simple and light representation using only 15 integers for coding speaker identity.

1 Introduction

Classical models of speech recognition assume that a short term analysis of the acoustic signal is essential for accurately decoding the speech signal. Most of these systems are based on maximum likelyhood trained Gaussian mixture speaker models, with diagonal covariance matrices. They can use for example principal component analysis from the output of 24 mel frequency channels, or more usually around 256 components calculated from the cepstral coefficients and deltas [1], voice recognition feature for speaker recognition such as since such features compensate charactarics of speakers [2].

This paper presents an alternative view, where the time scale requires an accurate description, longer than the phonetic segment, wedded to the dynamics of TF voicing level intervals. We assume that voicing reflects a singular property of the modulation spectrum that may provide a qualitative framework to generate a speaker identity model.

S.-W. Lee and S.Z. Li (Eds.): ICB 2007, LNCS 4642, pp. 1154–1163, 2007.

A variety of studies have shown that intelligibility depends on the integrity of the low-frequency modulation spectrum [3]. Within reverberant environments the greatest impact of acoustic reflection is between 2 and 6Hz. An effect of reverberation is to jumble the spectral content of the acoustic signal across both time and frequency, particulary that portion of the spectrum below 1500Hz. Although, reverberation is known to interfere with intelligibility; the basis for its deleterious impact is not well understood. On the other hand, it has been established that phonological perception is a SB process [4]. Moreover, this can be linked to speech production dynamics [5]. This has inspired various algorithms for robust speech recognition [6, 7], also linked to the TF voicing level [6, 8]. This time-frequency dynamics seems therefore to be important in speech perception, and because a natural representation for timely events has been proposed by Allen J.F., we proposed a quantic time-frequency dynamics for robust speech features extraction paradigm [9], that an approach is presented here for a specific task of speaker recognition.

2 Features Extraction

2.1 Voicing Extraction

We use the voicing measure [6, 10], correlated with SNR and equivalent to the *harmonicity index* (HNR) [11, 12] to estimate the average voicing per utterance. It is extracted form the autocorrelogram of a demodulated signal. In the case of Gaussian noise, the correlogram of a noisy frame is less modulated than a clean one [11]. The peaks in the autocorrelogram of the demodulated frame isolate the various harmonics in a signal. This can be used to separate a mixture of harmonic noises and a dominant harmonic signal. It is interesting that such separation can be efficiently accomplished, using a time windows of duration in the same range as the average phoneme duration.

Before the autocorrelation we compute the demodulated signal after half wave rectification, followed by pass-band filtering in the pitch domain ([90,350]Hz). For each frame of 128ms, we calculate the ratio $R = R1/R0$, where $R1$ is the local maximum in time delay segment corresponding to the fundamental frequency, and $R0$ is the cell energy. This measure is strongly correlated with SNR in the 5-20dB range [11]. Figure 1 demonstrates explicitly the voicing levels for each SBs and each frame. These values will be thresholded to get qualitative dynamic features that will be used to estimate the speaker identity. The subband (SB) definitions are following Fletcher studies, followed by other ones like in ALLEN J.B. papers [4, 5, 6].[1] Here are the definitions of SB range (Hz):[216 778 ; 707 1631 ;1262 2709; 2121 3800 ; 3400 5400 ; 5000 8000].

---

[1] Note that ALLEN J.B and ALLEN J.F. are two different authors, the first worked on speech analysis, the second on generic time representation. Our model is based on both approaches.

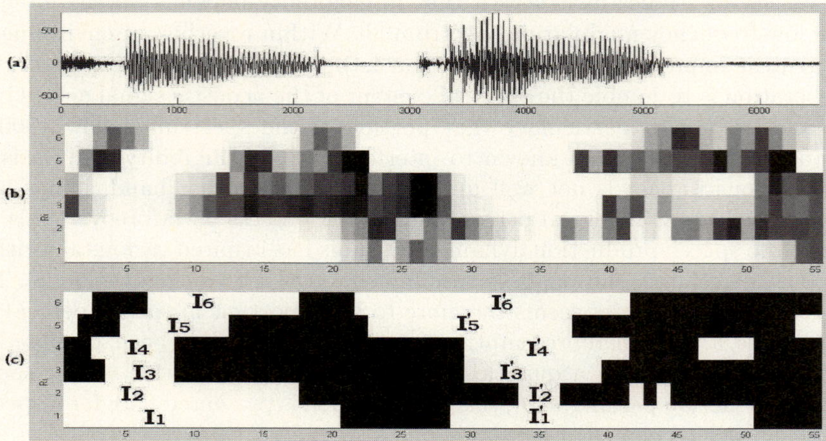

Fig. 1. From Voicing to the Allen's Interval : (a) voicing signal (b) the voicing level by SB (c) the binarized voicing levels by SB using ${}^{s}T_{b}$ threshold

2.2 Allen Interval Graphs

A temporal intervals algebra has been defined in [13, 14], where 13 atomic relations are depicted between two time intervals. From ours observations to the voicing levels by SB (cf fig. 1-(b)), we propose to apply the J.F. Allen's time representation for each SBs and each voicing activity regions (that can be 200 ms long). We present Allen's time relationships in the figure 2. X is the sliding interval which gives, progressively with Y, the 13 Allen intervals relations. We can define the algebric distance d between the two nearest interval to 1 and we increment it as we moved away from the interval relation. This will give us the numeric values for each relation that we use in this paper. The "b"symbol is coded into "1", "m"into "2", ... for the 13 relations of the figure 2. Moreover, the "no-relation" is also coded into "0", this can occured between two SBs if one or both have no frame with enough voicing level.

In order to obtain and to characterize exactly these six SB intervals we binarize the voicing matrix ${}^{s}M_{R}$ (s mean that for each speaker we build his own voicing matrix). First of all, we must find the best threshold for each sub-waveband to use it after. Indeed, after some experiences we have noticed that it is better to set one threshold for each SB. Thus we are looking for the best threshold which gives a fixed percent (30% , 50% and 70%) of 1 in each waveband by binarising the voicing matrix ${}^{s}M_{R}$. We first look for the threshold ${}^{s}T_{b_i}$ values in: $\Upsilon = \left[mean({}^{s}M_{R_{b_i}}) - \tau \ , \ mean({}^{s}M_{R_{b_i}}) + \tau \right]$, by steps of 0.01 with $\tau = 0.4$, such that:

$$\frac{Card({}^{s}R_{b_i}(t) \ > \ {}^{s}T_{b_i})}{Card({}^{s}w)} = P \pm \varepsilon, \tag{1}$$

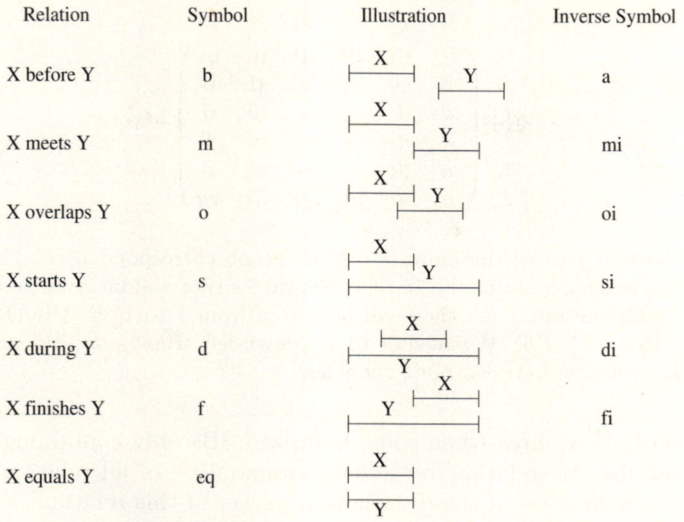

Relation	Symbol	Illustration	Inverse Symbol
X before Y	b	X Y	a
X meets Y	m	X Y	mi
X overlaps Y	o	X Y	oi
X starts Y	s	X Y	si
X during Y	d	X Y	di
X finishes Y	f	X Y	fi
X equals Y	eq	X Y	

Fig. 2. The interval construction structure with the 13 symbols. (no="no-relation").

where t is the time of speaker s, T is threshold used, b_i represents a SB with $i \in \{1..6\}$, and P defines the percent of 1 in the binarized interval. ε is a percent of tolerance ($\pm 1\%$), and ${}^s w$ is the total number of frames for speaker s.

If not any threshold value satisfies the previous conditions, then we set ${}^s T_{b_i} = mean({}^s M_{R_{b_i}})$.

After this iterative threshold research, we have generated per speaker voicing frame a threshold vector ${}^s T = [{}^s T_1 \;\; {}^s T_2 \;\; {}^s T_3 \;\; {}^s T_4 \;\; {}^s T_5 \;\; {}^s T_6]$, where T_i represents the threshold by SB. By applying ${}^s T$ to ${}^s M_R$ we obtain the binarized matrix, which a short sample is represented on Fig. 1-c. We then extract the Allen's graph per speaker for all frame having at least 4 binarized voicing interval simultaneously equal to 1.

The Allen graph corresponding to the figure 1-c is represented by atomic relation matrix in figure 3 (we characterize in bold the relations which are non redundant and useful). For each speaker, we obtain full graphs which will be used to discriminate one from the other by using a Multi-Layer Perceptron (MLP). In the next paragraph, we introduce a brief explanation of this method.

All Allen graphs are symmetric to the first diagonal (see 3). Each of the seven relations has an inverse relation in the same graph. This is due to the logic between two intervals: if the interval A is BEFORE B, in the same time we can assure that B IS AFTER A. Thus the useful information is contained in the 15 first relations which are ordered from left to the right, beginning from subband I'1 to subband I'5. For our example, one input vector at time t of our Multi Layer Perceptron Classifier is QTF(t)=[di di di oi oi d d d d s oi d oi f d]. We see on figure 4 the histogram of all QTF vectors for "Yves Decaens".

$$\begin{array}{c|cccccc} & I'_1 & I'_2 & I'_3 & I'_4 & I'_5 & I'_6 \\ \hline I'_1 & eq & \mathbf{di} & \mathbf{di} & \mathbf{di} & \mathbf{oi} & \mathbf{oi} \\ I'_2 & d & eq & \mathbf{d} & \mathbf{d} & \mathbf{d} & \mathbf{d} \\ I'_3 & d & di & eq & \mathbf{s} & \mathbf{oi} & \mathbf{d} \\ I'_4 & d & di & si & eq & \mathbf{oi} & \mathbf{f} \\ I'_5 & o & di & o & o & eq & \mathbf{d} \\ I'_6 & o & di & di & fi & di & eq \end{array}$$

Fig. 3. The second part of the figure 1-c Allen graph correspondences. The top-right triangle of this matrix contains the 15 relations values that will be given to an MLP for Id. speaker modelisation. Then they will be sorted from 1 to 15 as $1 = (I'1, I'2), 2 = (I'1, I'3), ..., 15 = (I'5, I'6)$. We needn't to use down-left triangle of this matrix due to the symmetric relation between both triangles.

The "no-relation" occures when some binarized SBs only containing zeros. We see that that the "no-relation"represents around 10% of all relations. See also Tab. 1 for an estimation of the discrimative power of this relation.

In figure 5 we present the log ratio of the QTF normalized distributions of two speakers (Yves Deceans and Patricia Martin), whos both have spoken about 50 minutes. It shows well the strong differences for certain relations and certain SB couples. We demonstrate in this paper that this information is discrimitive for a speaker identification task training a simple MLP.

For this purpose, we train with these 15 integers a MLP using the Torch toolbox [15]. It's a machine learning library written in simple C++ and distributed under BSD License. Torch is currently developed by IDIAP team. Torch has been designed to be essentially time efficient, modular, as it is a research oriented library. Our MLP is based on the Last Mean Square criterion (other Machine Learning algorithm could have been used, like Support Vector Machines SVM).

3 Database

Our experiments are conducted on a corpus issued from the Phase 1 of ESTER 2006 evaluation campaign (Evaluation Campaign for the Rich Transcription of French Broadcast News) [16]. ESTER implements three tasks, named transcription (T), segmentation (S) and information extraction (E). We have focused our work on SVL Speaker tracking and SRL Speaker diarization. This acoustic corpus Phase 1 is issued from two different sources, named France Inter (Inter) and Radio France International (RFI). It contains about 40 hours of manually transcribed radio broadcast news. This corpus is divided into three separated parts for training, developing and testing activities respectively. The training part (train) contains 30 hours and 40 minutes and the development part (dev) 4 hours and 40 minutes. The test part (test) contains 4 hours and 40 minutes. The unseen source in the test data is meant to evaluate the impact of the knowledge of the document source on performances.

4 Experimental Results and Interpretation

We give class error rate results left column in table 1, and their falsification in right columns in the same Table. We see that the best parametrisation is given for 70% of 'active'intervall in each SB, yielding to a class error rate of 2.5%. Comparison with ESTER Phase 1 results [17] are promising: we get the same order of speaker identification for this task on continous broadcast news.

Table 1. In the "Real Data" column are presented the class error results for the 50 speakers id. with different P values (MLP methods $P = 0.3, 0.5$ or 0.7). The best score is around 2.5%. In the "Falsified Data" column we find for comparison a model falsification with only two relations: no-relation versus all other relations (see text).

			Real data				Falsified data			
	Parameters		The_class_error				The_class_error			
MLP method	data Set Nb	nhu Nb	iter Nb	Train %	Dev %	Test %	iter Nb	Train %	Dev %	Test %
	-	300	1206	8.57	12.37	12.21	132	85.21	85.01	84.95
0.3	27338	600	1678	9.97	16.18	16.27	123	85.15	84.44	85.29
	-	**600**	**1472**	**8.20**	**13.62**	**13.30**	110	85.14	84.21	84.50
	-	1000	1242	26.16	32.93	33.68	**138**	**84.99**	**85.74**	**86.12**
	-	300	1431	8.58	13.32	13.11	**95**	**85.22**	**84.60**	**84.96**
0.5	27306	**600**	**1940**	**6.62**	**9.05**	**9.11**	140	85.23	85.33	84.80
	-	600	675	34.95	43.22	42.58	128	85.24	84.86	84.57
	-	1000	1560	10.20	15.17	15.11	130	85.07	85.24	85.70
	18166	600	874	1.56	2.68	3.01	159	86.03	86.74	86.03
0.7	-	300	819	1.49	2.7	2.92	141	85.75	86.56	85.90
	-	**600**	**873**	**1.44**	**2.55**	**2.46**	**149**	**86.11**	**86.41**	**86.25**
	-	1000	923	1.46	2.57	2.48	150	86.11	86.92	86.01

We run a falsification experimentation to verify if each relation encodes useful information, or if only the difference between "no-relation" and all other relations is relevant. Thus, in each set (train, dev and test), we have just used a 1 bit intput parameter for our MLP, replacing all atomic relations different to the "no-relation" by 1, and keeping all the no-relation (originaly coded by 0). The table 1 on the right gives this falsification results: we observe that the worst score is approximately 85%, telling that most of the coding information is given by the nature of the relations. But we also mesure that this is better than the random system (around 93% cf. formula[2]). This demonstrates that the no-relation contains by itself some speaker identity information.

[2] Let P_k be the frequency of the class C_k, the error rate of a random classifier is:

$$ER_{rand} = 1 - \sum_{k=1}^{c} (P_k)^2 = 1 - \sum_{k=1}^{c} \left(\frac{card(C_k)}{\sum_{k=1}^{c} card(C)} \right)^2$$

where c is the number of classes and $card(C_k)$ is the number of images in the class C_k.

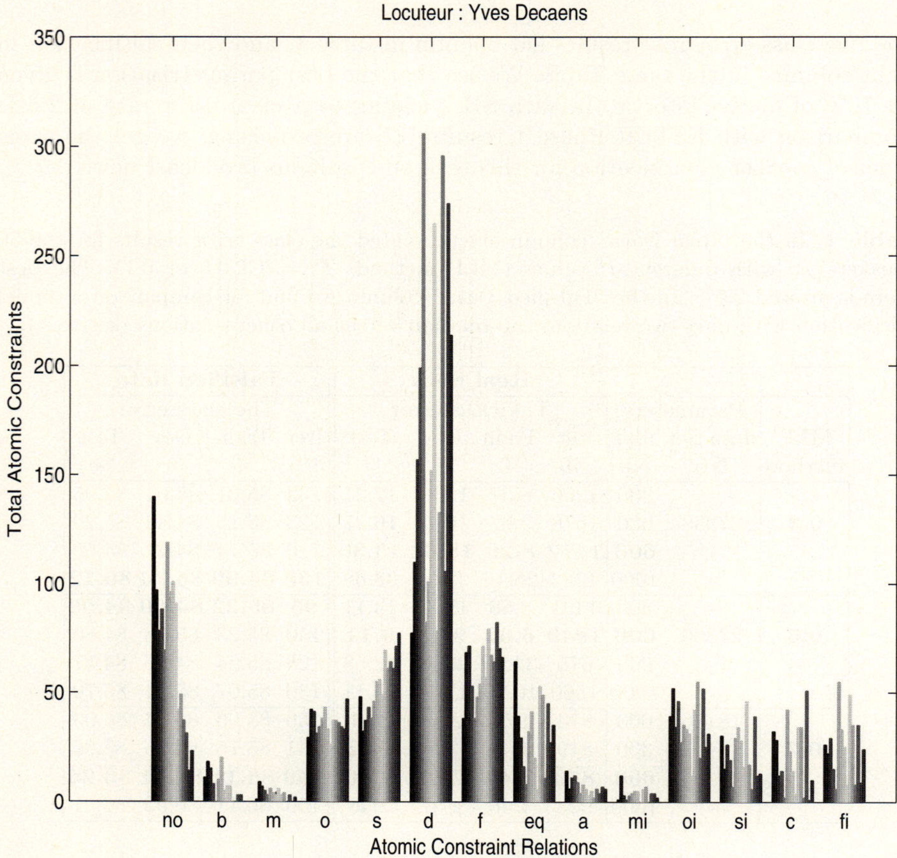

Fig. 4. Histogram of the QTF MLP inputs for the men speaker "Yves DECAENS". Each atomic relation is in abscissa from left to right (no:no-relation, b:before, m:meets, o:overlaps, s:starts, d:during, f:finishes, eq:equals, and respective symmetric ones: a, mi, oi, si, di, fi and eq). Each of the 15 MLP inputs (from left blue for the SB couple (I1,I2), to right red dark for the SB couple (I5,I6)). We note that the QTF distributions are varying more across relations than across each SB couples. The first input in dark blue on the left of each histogram (i.e for the couple (I1,I2)) has a majority of "no relation" and "during". The 15th input (node for couple (I5,I6)), in the right of each histogram, has a majority of "during" relation, ie the voicing interval in subband 5 is most of the time included in the voicing interval of SB 6. The "meeting" relations are not present for this speaker. The "equal" relation seems to be an informative kind of relation, showing great contrast across each SB couple.

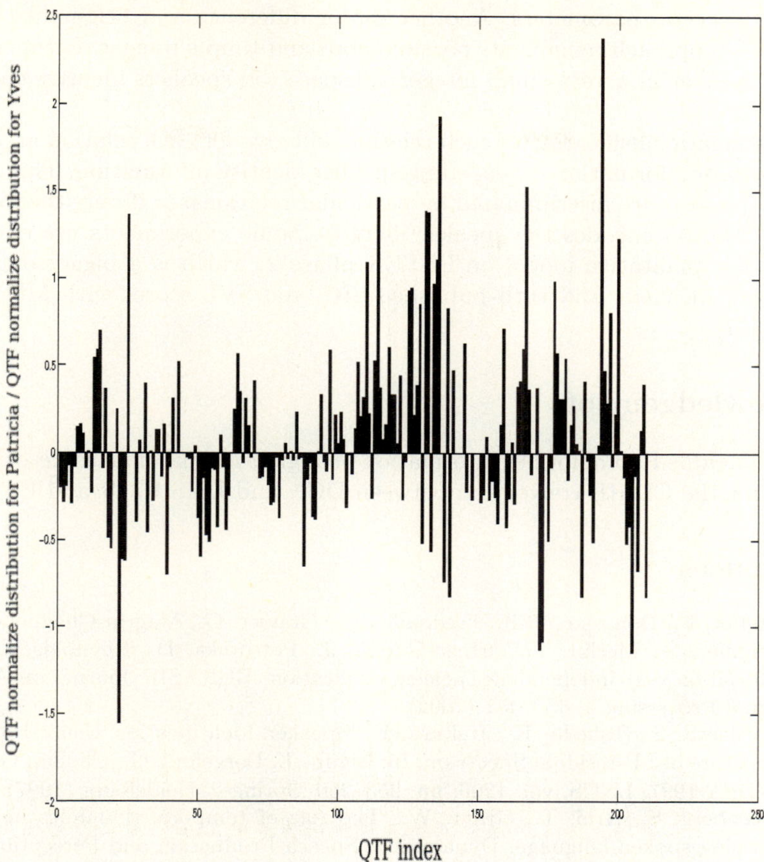

Fig. 5. This figure shows the logarithm (10) ratio between the QTF normalized distributions. The atomic relations and SB couples orders are the same than in previous figure. As we can see there are often large differences between at least half of the relations or SB couples. The MLP have learned with success each of these singularities distributions and then discriminats well speaker identity. Note that this figure represents only a part of the QTF processed information: it may exists another intra-frame discriminative information between the 15 parameters calculated on each frame, that is erased in this global histogram summing all training frames.

5 Discussion and Conclusion

A better optimisation could be obtained by combining different parameters for each subband. Moreover this preliminary iterative threshold research should be replaced by more global optimisation scheme. The total number of MLP weights is around 39000 (=600*(15+50)), which is smaller than usual parameters size. Nevertheless our approach generates the same order of errors than other experiments conducted on ESTER Phase 1 using classical MG HMM model on classical spectral parameters. Another major difference and originality of our qualitative approach remains its parcimonious and simple integer representation of each speaker in a very small integer subspace (50 speakers identity coded in $[0:13]^{15}$).

A systematic falsification of each relation will give for each relation an idea of its amount of information for encoding speaker identity information. This should show if speakers are discriminated by particular relations, or if only the joint set of each relation encodes the speaker identity. Some experiments are currently testing our qualitative model on ESTER phase 2, which is a bigger database, with more speakers, and with published SRL and SVL scores with MG HMM models [17].

Acknowledgements

We thank Odile Papini for her information on logical atomic time representation. ADER for the CIFRE convention between DCN and LSIS UMR and USTV.

References

[1] Bimbot, F., Bonastre, J.-F., Fredouille, C., Gravier, G., Magrin-Chagnolleau, I., Meignier, S., Merlin, T., Ortega-Garcia, J., Petrovska, D., Reynolds, D.A.: A tutorial on text-independent speaker verification. EURASIP Journal on Applied Signal Processing 4, 430–451 (2004)

[2] Hayakawa, S., Takeda, K., Itakura, F.: Speaker Identification Using Harmonic Structure of LP-residual Spectrum. In: Bigün, J., Borgefors, G., Chollet, G. (eds.) AVBPA 1997. LNCS, vol. 1206, pp. 253–260. Springer, Heidelberg (1997)

[3] Greenberg, S., Arai, T., Grant, W.: The role of temporal dynamics in understanding spoken language. Dynamics of Speech Production and Perception Nato Advanced Studies Series, Life and Behavioural Sciences 374, 171–190 (2006)

[4] Fletcher, H.: The nature of speech and its interpretation. J. Franklin Inst. 193(6), 729–747 (1922)

[5] Allen, J.B.: How do humans process and recognise speech. IEEE Trans. on Speech and Signal Processing 2(4), 567–576 (1994)

[6] Glotin, H.: Elaboration and comparatives studies of robust adaptive multistream speech recognition using voicing and localisation cues. Inst. Nat. Polytech Grenoble & EPF Lausanne IDIAP (2001)

[7] Morris, A., Hagen, A., Glotin, H., Bourlard, H.: Multi-stream adaptive evidence combination for noise robust ASR. int. journ. Speech Communication, special issue on noise robust ASR 17(34), 1–22 (2001)

[8] Glotin, H., Vergyri, D., Neti, C., Potamianos, G., Luettin, G.: Weighting schemes for audio-visual fusion in speech recognition. In: IEEE int. conf. Acoustics Speech & Signal Process (ICASSP) Salt Lake City-USA (September 2001)

[9] Glotin, H.: When Allen J.B. meets Allen J.F.: Quantal Time-Frequency Dynamics for Robust Speech Features. Research Report LSIS 2006.001 Lab Systems and Information Sciences UMR CNRS (2006)

[10] Glotin, H.: Dominant speaker detection based on harmonicity for adaptive weighting in audio-visual cocktail party ASR. In: Adaptation methods in speech recognition ISCA Workshop September, Nice (2001)

[11] Berthommier, F., Glotin, H.: A new SNR-feature mapping for robust multistream speech recognition. In: Proc. Int. Congress on Phonetic Sciences (ICPhS) Berkeley University Of California, Ed., San Francisco 1 of XIV August, pp. 711–715 (1999)
[12] Yumoto, E., Gould, W.J., Bear, T.: Harmonic to noise ratio as an index of the degree of hoarseness. The Acoustic Society of America 1971, 1544–1550 (1982)
[13] Allen, J.F.: An Interval-Based Representation of Temporal Knowledge. In: Proceedings of 7th IJCAI August, pp. 221–226 (1981)
[14] Allen, J.F.: Maintaining Knowledge About Temporal Intervals. Communications of the ACM 26(11), 832–843 (1983)
[15] Collobert, R., Bengio, S., Marihoz, J.: Torch: a modular machine learning software library. Laboratoire IDIAP IDIAP-RR 02-46 (2002)
[16] Gravier, G., Bonastre, J.F., Galliano, S., Geoffrois, E., Mc Tait, K., Choukri, K.: The ESTER evaluation campaign of Rich Transcription of French Broadcast News. In: Language Evaluation and Resources Conference (April 2004)
[17] Galliano, S., Geoffrois, E., Mostefa, D., Choukri, K., Bonastre, J.-F., Gravier, G.: The Ester Phase 2: Evaluation Campaign for the Rich Transcription of French Broadcast News. In: European Conf. on Speech Communication and Technology pp. 1149–1152 (2005)

Palmprint Recognition Based on Directional Features and Graph Matching

Yufei Han, Tieniu Tan, and Zhenan Sun

Center for Biometrics and Security Research
National Labrotory of Pattern Recognition,Institue of Automation
Chinese Acdamey of Sciences
P.O. Box 2728, Beijing, P.R. China, 100080
{yfhan,tnt,znsun}@nlpr.ia.ac.cn

Abstract. Palmprint recognition, as a reliable personal identity check method, has been receiving increasing attention during recent years. According to previous work, local texture analysis supplies the most promising framework for palmprint image representation. In this paper, we propose a novel palmprint recognition method by combining statistical texture descriptions of local image regions and their spatial relations. In our method, for each image block, a spatial enhanced histogram of gradient directions is used to represent discriminative texture features. Furthermore, we measure similarity between two palmprint images using a simple graph matching scheme, making use of structural information. Experimental results on two large palmprint databases demonstrate the effectiveness of the proposed approach.

1 Introduction

Biometrics identifies different people by their physiological and behavioral difference, such as face, iris, retinal, gait, etc [1]. As an alternative personal identity authentication method, it has attracted increasing attention during recent years. In the field of biometrics, palmprint is a novel but promising member. Most discriminating patterns of palmprint could be captured by low resolution capture devices, such as a low-cost CCD camera [3]. Large region of palm supplies stable line patterns which are difficult to be faked.

A key issue in palmprint analysis is finding a proper descriptor to represent its line patterns [5]. In previous work, local texture based approach is proved to be the most efficient [1,2,3,4,5,6]. Since line patterns of palmprint are always spread over different image areas, both description of local patterns and their spatial relation are important for describing palmprint in an accurate way. Therefore, component based image representation supplies a reasonable framework, following which we could design efficient palmprint recognition methods by adopting local image features.

In this paper, we introduce a novel approach for palmprint recognition which considers both texture information of local image regions and the spatial relationships between these regions. In our method, a straightforward extraction of image gradients vector is adopted across the whole palmprint image plane. Derived vector field is then divided into blocks. Statistical texture features of each block are encoded by a local

S.-W. Lee and S.Z. Li (Eds.): ICB 2007, LNCS 4642, pp. 1164–1173, 2007.

direction histogram (LDH) proposed in this paper, which describes distribution properties of the directional vectors. All localized blocks form a global graph. The similarity of two palmprint images is measured by a simple graph matching method, previously utilized in [9].

The remainder of this paper is organized as follows. Details about LDH scheme and the graph matching method are described in section 2 and 3 respectively. In section 4, experimental results are reported. Section 5 concludes the paper.

2 Local Direction Histogram Based Palmprint Description

Image gradient has been used as an efficient indicator of local image texture [8]. As reported in [7], it has a close relation with reflectance and surface normal of objects imaged, which decide inherent structures of corresponding image patches. Benefit from it, histogram of gradient directions has been widely used as a powerful image descriptor [10][11]. It captures characteristic patterns of local image region. In our work, we utilize histograms of oriented gradients to represent texture information of palmprint images.

We calculate gradient vectors by the first order Gaussian derivative operator ∇G, in order to avoid noise sensitivity caused by directly differentiation on original intensities. It should be noted that size of ∇G operator is chosen according to needs of applications. A proper choice makes good trade-off between noise tolerance and locality of description. For a local image region *W*, the gradient magnitude *M* and direction angle θ are expressed respectively as follows:

$$M = \sqrt{(\nabla G_x * W)^2 + (\nabla G_y * W)^2}$$
$$\theta = \tan^{-1}\left(\frac{\nabla G_y * W}{\nabla G_x * W}\right) \tag{1}$$

The whole procedure of palmprint feature extraction is illustrated in Fig.1. Before feature extraction and matching, input palmprint images are firstly normalized to regulate translation, rotation and scale variation among different palms, following the method employed in [3]. In our work, assuming the size of normalized palmprint image and ∇G operator is *N* by *N* and *m* by *m* respectively. After calculation of gradient vector on each sample region, the size of derived vector valued image is $(N-m+1)$ by $(N-m+1)$. To focus on local texture representation, we divide the whole vector field into $r*r$ square blocks, each of them has the side length of $(N-m+1)/r$.

For each block, we again divide it into 4 sub-regions with the same size. A 6-bin direction histogram is constructed covering the 360 degree range of gradient directions in each sub-region. Same as in [10], samples are added to the histogram, weighted by corresponding gradient magnitudes. This histogram contains information about distribution of the direction angles, which represents details of image structure in a statistical way. Besides, spatial information is also important for more efficient representation. So we combine histograms of these four neighboring regions to yield a 24-bin spatially enhanced histogram and normalize it to unit length, namely, local direction histogram, as shown in Fig. 2. Through this way, local statistical descriptions and their spatial arrangement are concatenated into a more discriminative texture feature of the block region. A more involve method to construct histograms is based on adding gradient vectors into bins with equal weights, rather than weighted by their magnitudes. The gradient magnitude is sensitive to changes in illumination settings, such as direction changes of light sources. In contrast, the direction angle is more stable under those variations. Through this scheme, we can improve robustness of texture representation. Both two types of histogram based features are evaluated in the experiment.

Finally, we take each block as a node of a graph map, associated with a local direction histogram, illustrated also in Fig.1. As a result, a palmprint image is represented by such a map in two different respects. Bins of local direction histograms represent statistical characteristics of texture patterns on the region level. Topology relations among nodes describe spatial layouts of blocks and thus produce a more global description of the whole image.

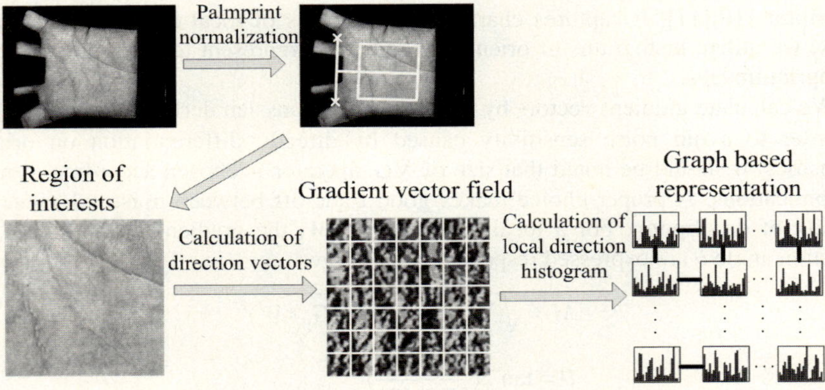

Fig. 1. Diagram of palmprint feature extraction

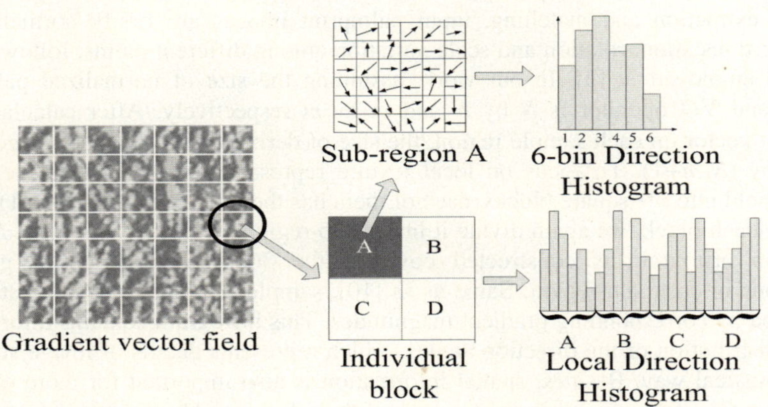

Fig. 2. Generation of local direction histogram

3 Graph Matching Approach

Each node of the graph representation has two attributes, local direction histogram feature associated with it, and its spatial relation with other nodes. It is a natural idea to measure similarity of two palmprint images by comparing nodes of corresponding graphs. In our work, we adopt a simple graph matching algorithms proposed by Sun et al [9]. Each node of one palmprint image is supposed to be the most similar with the corresponding one of another palmprint image, if these two are captured from the same palm. Similarly in [9], before any discussion, we define conditions that matching nodes should satisfy.

Assuming the graph representations of two palmprint images are $\{A_i\}$ and $\{B_j\}$ $(i, j = 1, 2 \ldots S)$ respectively, two matching nodes should have the same spatial position in each graph. Furthermore, texture patterns of matching node pair A_i and B_i should be most similar under a certain metric among all pairs composed by A_i and individual B_j $(i, j = 1, 2 \ldots S)$. Therefore, we count the number of matching pairs to evaluate resemblance between two images. The higher it is, the more likely the two images come from the same palm. Through this kind of procedure, we make full use of both texture and structure properties of each node to achieve accurate classification.

In our paper, we utilize the Chi-square distance between local direction histograms $\{LDHA_i\}$ and $\{LDHB_j\}$ $(i, j = 1, 2 \ldots S)$ to measure texture similarity of two nodes:

$$\chi^2(LDHA_i, LDHB_j) = \sum_{k=1}^{24} \frac{(LDHA_i^k - LDHB_j^k)^2}{LDHA_i^k + LDHB_j^k} \tag{2}$$

Based on this metric, Chi-square distance between histogram features of two matching nodes should be lower than a prefixed threshold [9]. Following pseudo codes illustrate how to compute the number of matching pairs N step by step:

```
Begin
  N = 0
  for each node Ai do
   {  for each node Bj do
      {  Compute χ²(LDHA_i, LDHB_j);  (j = 1,2...S)
         if χ²(LDHA_i, LDHB_j) < χ²(LDHA_i, LDHB_i)  (j ≠ i)
         break;
      }
  if χ²(LDHA_i, LDHB_i) is the minimal among all χ²(LDHA_i, LDHB_j)
        {  if χ²(LDHA_i, LDHB_i) < Threshold
                N = N+1;
        }
   }
End
```

To obtain normalized matching score ranging between 0 and 1, we can divide N by S, the total number of nodes in each graph map. In the following experiment, we directly employ N as the matching score for convenient.

4 Verification Experiments

In this section, we test the performance of the proposed approach on the PolyU Palmprint Database [12] and the CASIA Palmprint Database [13]. In the first dataset, images which belong to the same palm contain deformation of skin surface, such as contraction and stretching (see Fig. 7). Images in the second one are mostly captured with less such variations between intra-class samples.

4.1 Verification Experiment on the PolyU Palmprint Database

The PolyU database [12] contains 7,752 palmprint images from 386 palms. Each palm has two sessions of images. Average time interval between two sessions is two months. Light conditions and focus of the imaging device are changed between two occasions of image capturing [3], which is challengeable to robustness of recognition algorithms. After preprocessing, regions of interests, with the size of 128×128 are obtained. The ∇G operator has the size of 9 by 9. After gradient calculation, the whole vector valued image is divided into 6*6 = 36 blocks. All images are used to estimate intra-class distribution. We select five images randomly from each session to form inter-class samples. If a session contains less than five images, we make up totally ten samples from the class which the session belong to, including all images contained in the session. Therefore, 74,068 intra-class matching and 7,430,500 inter-class matching are involved in the experiment. In this experiment, we evaluate two LDH based methods. The first constructs histograms with samples weighted by their corresponding gradient magnitudes, while the second treats each sample with the same weight. The other three state-of-the-art algorithms, namely, fusion code [4], competitive code [5], ordinal code [6], are implemented for further comparing. Experimental results are denoted in Table 1 and Fig. 3.

Table 1. Comparisons of performances on the PolyU database

Algorithm	EER [14]	d' [14]
Fusion code [4]	0.21%	5.40
Competitive code [5]	0.04%	5.84
Ordinal code [6]	0.05%	6.90
Weighted LDH	0.10%	7.13
Non-weighted LDH	0.08%	6.12

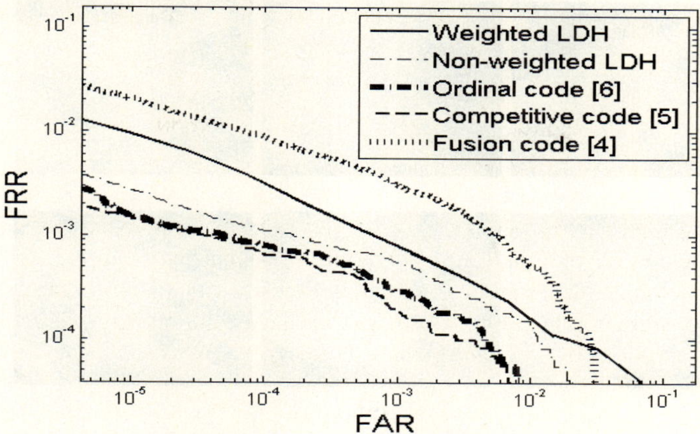

Fig. 3. ROC curves on the PolyU database

We named the first method " Weighted LDH " and the second " Non-weighted LDH " . As shown in Fig. 3, in terms of ROC curves, both of LDH based methods achieve comparable performances, compared with ordinal code [6] and competitive code [5]. Notably, they are more accurate than Fusion code [4]. Of the two proposed approaches, non-weighted LDH performs obviously better, which is more robust to intra-class appearance variations.

4.2 Verification Experiments on the CASIA Palmprint Database

The CASIA Palmprint database [13] contains 4,512 24-bit color palmprint images, coming from 564 palms. Each palm has 8 images. During image capturing, palms of subjects are required to be laid on a uniform-colored background (see in Fig. 4(a)). Then palmprint images are captured by a common CMOS camera above palms. There are no pegs to restrict postures and positions of palms. Original size of each image is 640×480. After preprocessing, we crop a square region with size of 176×176, as region of interests (ROI), show in Fig. 4(b). We again adopt 9×9 ∇G operator and divide the whole vector valued image into 6*6 = 36 blocks. All possible intra-class samples are used to simulate genuine distribution. One image is selected randomly from each class to estimate imposter distribution. Thus, totally 15,792 intra-class comparisons and 158,766 inter-class comparisons are implemented.

Tab 2 and Fig. 5 illustrate performances of two proposed LDH methods and the other three state-of-the-art algorithms. As we see, non-weighted LDH method achieves the highest accuracy, followed by weighted LDH, ordinal code [6], competitive code [5] and fusion code [4]. Compared with results in section 4.1, both two LDH based approaches perform better. That's because that deformation of skin surface (see Fig.7) existing in intra-class samples of the PolyU database [12] changes reflectance and geometrical structures of skin surface, which then declines similarities of local distributions of image gradient directions.

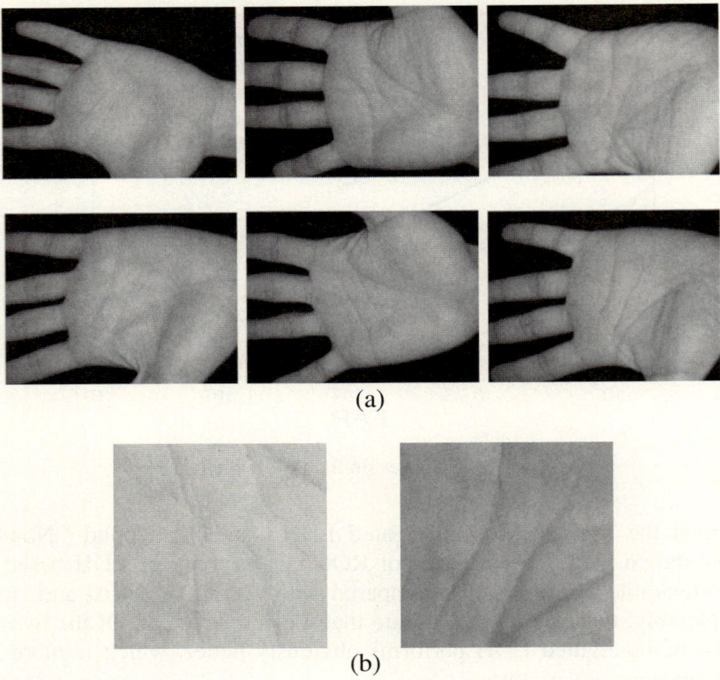

(a)

(b)

Fig. 4. (a) Palm images in the CASIA database (b) Cropped ROI

Table 2. Comparisons of performances on the CASIA database

Algorithm	EER [14]	*d'* [14]
Fusion code [4]	0.57%	3.73
Competitive code [5]	0.19%	3.82
Ordinal code [6]	0.08%	5.65
Weighted LDH	0.05%	9.30
Non-weighted LDH	0.04%	10.51

Furthermore, Fig. 6 describes the intra-class and inter-class matching score distributions using non-weighted LDH on the PolyU [12] and the CASIA [13] databases. As shown in the figure, for most intra-class samples, the number of matching block pairs is higher than ten, about 1/3 of the total blocks. Therefore, our approach only needs a fraction of the whole image area to deliver a valid classification. It can be used to handle palmprint images containing regions of occlusion or impaired palm skin. Compared with it, state-of-the-art algorithms [4][5][6] achieve successful recognition requiring most of the image region should be matched.

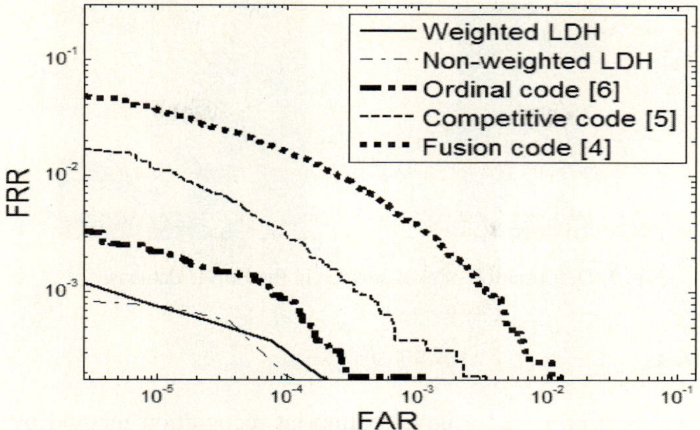

Fig. 5. ROC curves on the CASIA database

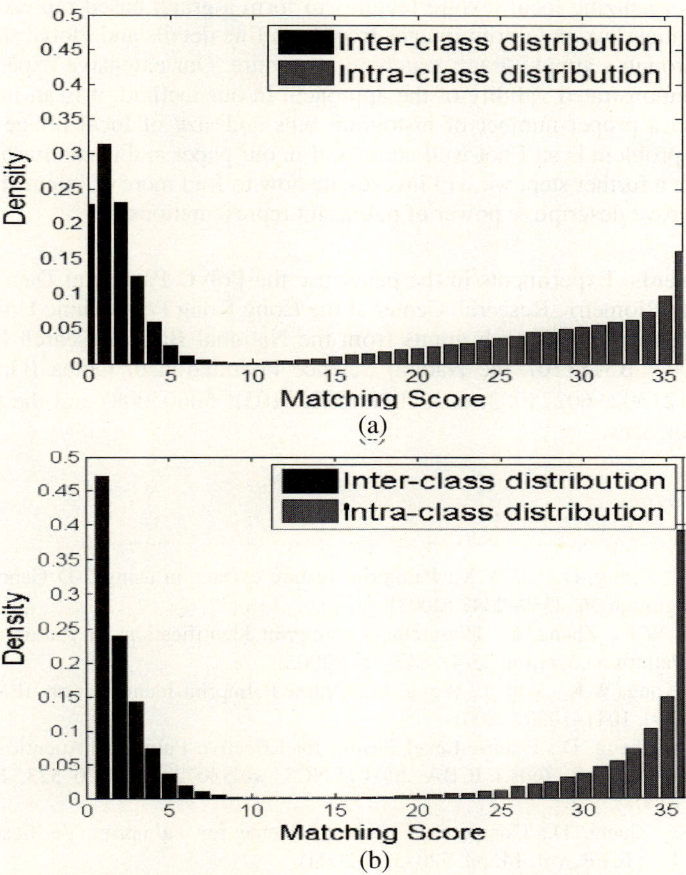

Fig. 6. Distribution of matching scores on the PolyU (a) and the CASIA (b) databases

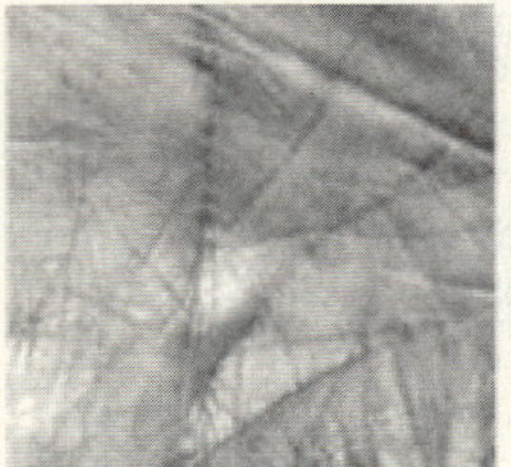
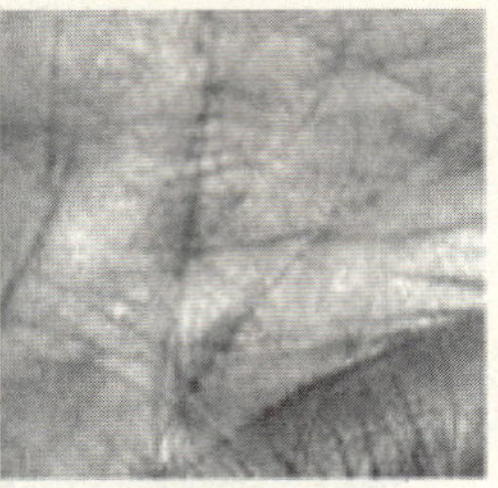

Fig. 7. Deformation of skin surface in the PolyU database

5 Conclusions

In this paper, we have proposed a novel palmprint recognition method by utilizing LDH based local texture descriptor and graph matching. It involves three main parts, namely, gradient vector calculation, local direction histogram generation and graph matching. By organizing local texture features to form a graph based representation, we can differentiate two palmprint images from both fine details and global structural information through a simple graph matching procedure. Our extensive experimental results have demonstrated validity of the approach. In our method, it is an important issue to choose a proper number of histogram bins and size of local image blocks. However, this problem is still not well addressed in our paper and needs further work in the future. In a further step, we will investigate how to find more efficient structural features to improve descriptive power of palmprint representations.

Acknowledgments. Experiments in the paper use the PolyU Palmprint Database 2nd collected by the Biometric Research Center at the Hong Kong Polytechnic University. This work is funded by research grants from the National Basic Research Program (Grant No. 2004CB318110), the Natural Science Foundation of China (Grant No. 60335010, 60121302, 60275003, 60332010, 69825105, 60605008) and the Chinese Academy of Sciences.

References

1. Kong, W.K., Zhang, D., Li, W.X.: Palmprint feature extraction using 2-D Gabor filters. Pattern recognition 36, 2339–2347 (2003)
2. You, J., Li, W.X., Zhang, D.: Hierarchical palmprint identification via multiple feature extraction. Pattern recognition 35(4), 847–859 (2002)
3. Zhang, D., Kong, W.K., You, J., Wong, M.: Online Palmprint Identification. IEEE Trans on PAMI 25(9), 1041–1050 (2003)
4. Kong, W.K., Zhang, D.: Feature-Level Fusion for Effective Palmprint Auentication. In: Zhang, D., Jain, A.K. (eds.) ICBA 2004. LNCS, vol. 3072, pp. 520–523. Springer, Heidelberg (2004)
5. Kong, W.K., Zhang, D.: Competitive Coding Scheme for Palmprint Verification. In: Proc.of the 17th ICPR, vol. 14, pp. 520–523 (2004)

6. Sun, Z.N., Tan, T.N., Wang, Y.H., Li, S.Z.: Ordinal Palmprint Representation for Personal Identification. In: Proc. of CVPR 2005, vol. 1, pp. 279–284 (2005)
7. Chen, H.F., Belhumeur, P.N., Jacobs, D.W.: In Search of Illumination Invariants. In: Proc. of CVPR 2000, vol. I, pp. 254–261 (2000)
8. Sun, Z.N., Tan, T.N., Wang, Y.H.: Robust Direction Estimation of Graident Vector Field for Iris Recognition. In: Proc. of ICPR 2004, vol. 2, pp. 783–786 (2004)
9. Sun, Z.N., Tan, T.N., Qiu, X.C.: Graph Matching Iris Image Blocks with Local Binary Pattern. In: Zhang, D., Jain, A.K. (eds.) Advances in Biometrics. LNCS, vol. 3832, pp. 366–372. Springer, Heidelberg (2005)
10. Lowe, D.G.: Distinctive Image Features from Scale-Invariant Keypoints. International Journal of Computer Vision(IJCV) 60, 90–110 (2004)
11. Dalal, N., Triggs, B.: Histograms of Oriented Gradients for Human Detection. In: Proc.of CVPR 2005, vol. 1, pp. 863–886 (2005)
12. PolyU Palmprint Database, http://www.comp.polyu.edu.hk/ biometrics/
13. CASIA Palmprint Database, http://www.cbsr.ia.ac.cn
14. Daugman, J., Williams, G.: A Proposed Standard for Biometric Decidability. In: Proc. CardTech/SecureTech Conference, Atlanta, GA, pp. 223–234 (1996)

Tongue-Print: A Novel Biometrics Pattern

David Zhang[1,*], Zhi Liu[2], Jing-qi Yan[2], and Peng-fei Shi[2]

[1] Biometrics Research Centre, Department of Computing, Hong Kong Polytechnic University, Kowloon, Hong Kong
[2] Institute of Image Processing and Pattern Recognition, Shanghai Jiao Tong University, Shanghai China
csdzhang@comp.polyu.edu.hk,{liu_zhi,jingqiy}@sjtu.edu.cn

Abstract. The tongue is a unique organ in that it can be stuck out of mouth for inspection, and yet it is otherwise well protected in the mouth and is difficult to forge. The tongue also presents both geometric shape information and physiological texture information which are potentially useful in identity verification applications. Furthermore, the act of physically reaching or thrusting out is a convincing proof for the liveness. Despite these obvious advantages for biometrics, little work has hitherto been done on this topic. In this paper, we introduce this novel biometric and present a verification framework based on the tongue-prints. The preliminary experimental results demonstrate the feasibility of the tongue biometrics.

Keywords: Biometrics, tongue-print, verification.

1 Introduction

The reliable automatic recognition of identities has long been an attractive goal, with biometrics [1][2], such as fingerprints, palmprints and iris images already being widely used in a number of identity recognition systems. The list of physiological and behavioral characteristics that have so far been developed and implemented in such systems is long and includes the face, iris, fingerprint, palmprint, hand shape, voice, signature and gait. However, how to counter the forge has been the common challenge for the traditional biometrics. Many of the traditional biometrics, however, are unreliable in that features may be forged, for example by using a fake iris. Actually, the tightened security required the noninvasive biometrics that are anti-counterfeiting and can provide liveness verification. Accordingly, it is very necessary to find some new biometrics to fill the requirements.

The tongue may offer a solution to this difficulty, having as it does many properties that make it suitable for use in identity recognition. To begin with, the tongue is unique to each person in its shape (see Fig. 1) and in its surface textures (see Fig. 2). Second, the tongue is the only internal organ that can quite normally and easily be exposed for inspection. This is useful because it is the exposed portion of the tongue that carries a great deal of shape and textural information that can be acquired in images that we call "tongue-print". Third, according to our long time observation, the shape of the individual tongue is constant, notwithstanding its instinctive squirm and

S.-W. Lee and S.Z. Li (Eds.): ICB 2007, LNCS 4642, pp. 1174–1183, 2007.

its physiological textures are invariant even as the coating of the tongue changes. Fourth, as the human tongue is contained in the mouth, it is isolated and protected from the external environment, unlike the fingers, for example. Finally, the process of tongue inspection is also a reliable proof of life.

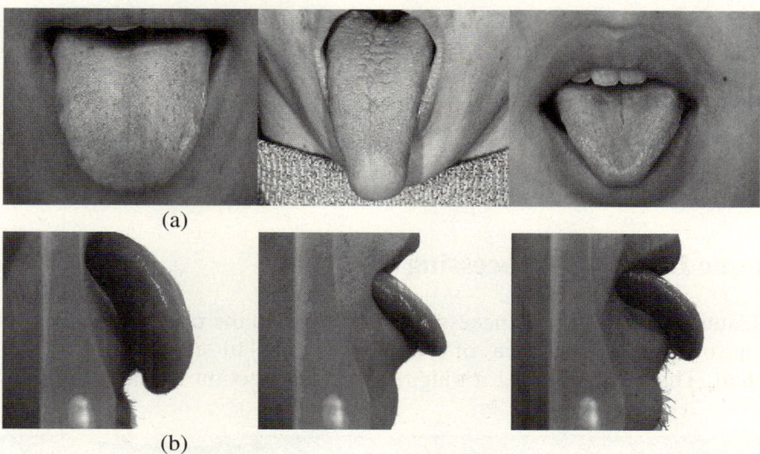

Fig. 1. Some samples with different shape from frontal and profile view. (a) Different shapes from the frontal view and (b) different shapes from the profile view.

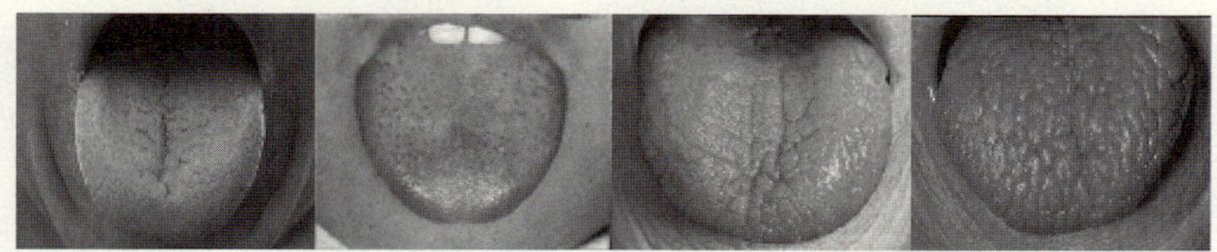

Fig. 2. Some samples with different textures

This promising combination of characteristics was the inspiration for the development of the on-line verification system based on the tongue-prints that is described here. This system extracts both the shape and textural features of the tongue and uses them for recognition. The shape vector represents the shape features of the tongue, specifically its length, bend, thickness, and width, and the curvature of its tip. The texture codes represent the textural features of the central part of the tongue. Fig. 3 gives a block diagram illustrating the framework. The modules are described in the following sections.

The remainder of this paper is organized as follows: Section 2 describes the preprocessing of tongue-print images. Section 3 introduces our feature extraction and recognition framework, describing how we extract shape features and analyze the texture of the tongue. Section 4 presents the experimental results. Section 5 offers our conclusion.

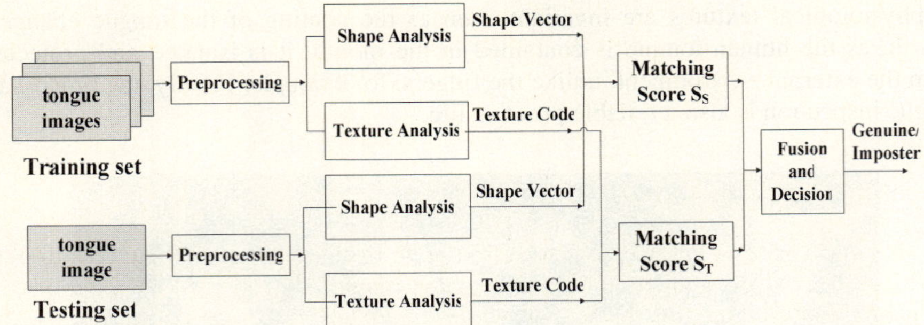

Fig. 3. The block diagram of our tongue-print verification procedure

2 Tongue Image Preprocessing

Before feature extraction, it is necessary to preprocess the captured tongue images to obtain an outline of the area of the tongue and to eliminate the non-tongue background. This is done using a tongue contour detection method described in our

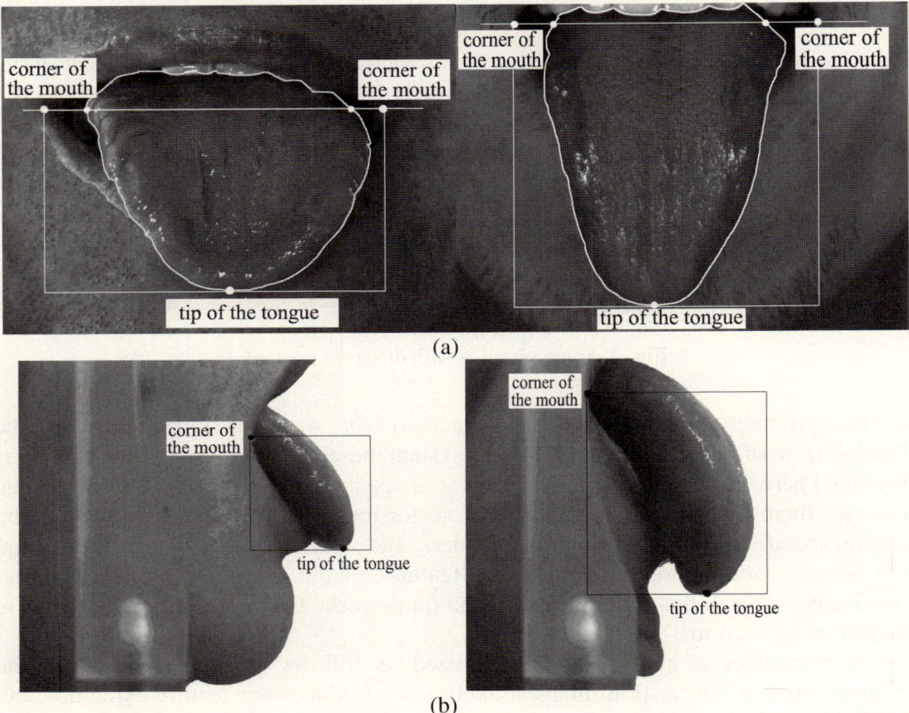

Fig. 4. The region we determined using corners of the mouth and tip of the tongue. (a) is the frontal view; and (b) is the profile view.

previous work [7][8] The corners of the mouth and the tip of the tongue (see Fig. 4) can then be used to determine the region of interest (ROI) in the captured tongue image. These ROI provide the main visual features of the tongue that are used in the subsequent procedures.

3 Tongue-Print Recognition

In this section we introduce a feature extraction and recognition framework that makes use of both the shape and texture of the tongue. The shape vector represents the geometrical features of the tongue while the texture codes represent the textural features of the central part of the tongue.

3.1 Shape Feature Extraction

The shape of the tongue (to be represented as a shape vector) is measured using a set of control points. The control points are P1, P2, …,P11, P_{tip} and P_m (shown in Fig. 5). These control points demarcate important areas of the ROI (here, the part below the segment $L_{P1,P2}$). The following describes how five measures, length, bend, thickness, width of the tongue, and the curvature of its tip, are formed as our measurement vectors:

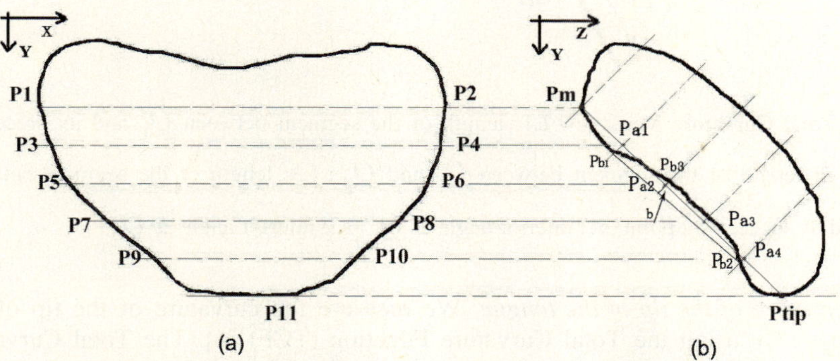

Fig. 5. The tongue feature model for the frontal and profile view images. (a) is the frontal view; and (b) is the profile view.

1) *Width:* We define four segments ($L_{P3,P4}$, $L_{P5,P6}$, $L_{P7,P8}$, $L_{P9,P10}$) that are parallel to the segment $L_{P1,P2}$ in the regions of interest mentioned above. And these segments follow the rule formularized by Eq. (1):

$$d(L_{P1,P2}, L_{P3,P4}) = d(L_{P3,P4}, L_{P5,P6}) = d(L_{P5,P6}, L_{P7,P8}) = d(L_{P7,P8}, L_{P9,P10}) \tag{1}$$

where $d(\bullet)$ represents the distance between two parallel segments. We then use the length of these five segments to construct the width vector $\overline{W}$.

2) *Length:* The length of the tongue in the profile view is defined by the distance between P_{tip} and P_m (P_{tip} denotes the tip of the tongue, and P_m denotes the corner of the mouth, as shown in Fig. 5 (b)) as follows:

$$Length = \left\| P_{tip} - P_m \right\|. \tag{2}$$

3) *Thickness:* Take a line between P_{tip} and P_m (shown in Fig. 5 (b)) and extend the lines ($L_{P3,P4}$, $L_{P5,P6}$, $L_{P7,P8}$, $L_{P9,P10}$) so that they intersect with the segment $L_{P_m P_{tip}}$. The points of intersection are labeled as: P_{a1} , P_{a2} , P_{a3} , P_{a4} . Crossing these points, we can get a set of orthogonal lines of the segment $L_{P_m P_{tip}}$. The lengths of these lines within the contour of the profile view are used for the thickness vector $\overline{T}$. In addition, the orthogonal lines that cross P_{a1} P_{a4} and P_{a2} respectively intersect the contour of the tongue at P_{b1} , P_{b2} and P_{b3} .

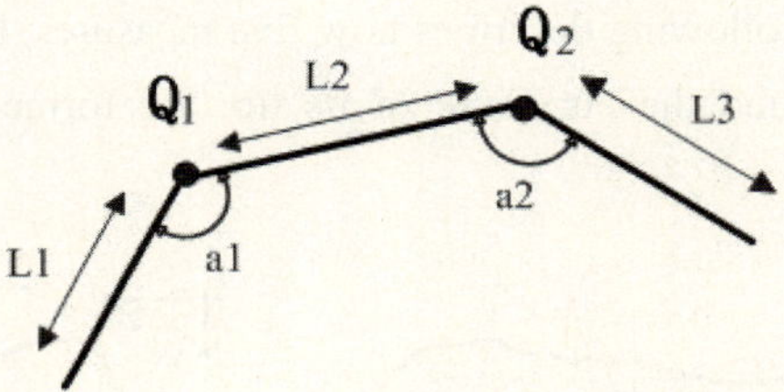

Fig. 6. Total Curvature Measures. L1: length of the segment between Q_1 and its preceding point; L2: length of the segment between Q_1 and Q_2 ; L3: length of the segment between Q_2 and its succeeding point; a1: interior angle at Q_1 ; a2: interior angle at Q_2 .

4) *Curvature of the tip of the tongue:* We measure the curvature of the tip of the tongue by using the Total Curvature Function (TCF) [6]. The Total Curvature Function is an approximate estimation method and it is defined for one segment between the two points Q_1 and Q_2 , as illustrated in Fig. 6. In this figure, the curvature at Q_1 can be formulated as:

$$C1 = a1/(L1 + L2) \tag{3}$$

and the curvature at Q_2 is formulated as:

$$C2 = a2/(L2 + L3). \tag{4}$$

Thus, the total curvature value of the segment L2 between Q_1 and Q_2 is formulated as:

$$TC = L2 * (C1 - C2)\,. \quad (5)$$

We then use these TC to build the vector $\overline{Cur}$ by using the curvature values at the control points $P3, P4, \dots P9, P10$ (shown in Fig. 5(a)).

5) *Bend:* The distance between the middle point P_{b3} and the segment $L_{P_{b1}P_{b2}}$ is formulated as in Eq. (6)

$$b = D(P_{b3}, L_{P_{b1}P_{b2}}) \quad (6)$$

where $D(\bullet)$ computes the distance between the P_{b3} and $L_{P_{b1}P_{b2}}$. Then, we can use b to describe the degree of bend of the tongue. The measurement of b is illustrated in Fig. 5(b).

As the components of these vectors are of different sizes and they have a large dynamic range, it is necessary to normalize them into a single, common range. The five measurement vectors are then combined to form the shape vector that represents the tongue shape.

3.2 Texture Feature Extraction

The textural features of the tongue are primarily found on the central part of its surface. To extract this information, we set up a sub-image of the segmented tongue image as a region of interest (ROI). This region is selected under the coordinates system $P_{corner}OP_{tip}$ with 256*256 pixels, corresponding to the rectangular area enclosed by the white line in Fig. 7 (a). To extract the texture features, we apply a powerful texture analysis tool, a two dimensional Gabor filter. Gabor filters have been widely used to extract local image features [9][10]. A 2-D Gabor filter in the spatial domain has the following general form [9]:

$$G(x,y,\theta,u,\sigma) = \frac{1}{2\pi\sigma^2}\exp\{\frac{x^2+y^2}{2\sigma^2}\}\exp\{2\pi i(ux\cos\theta + uy\sin\theta)\} \quad (7)$$

where $i = \sqrt{-1}$; u is the frequency of the sinusoidal wave; θ controls the orientation of the function; and σ is the standard deviation of the Gaussian envelope. Gabor filters are robust against variations in image brightness and contrast and can be said to model the receptive fields of a simple cell in the primary visual cortex. In order to make the Gabor filter more robust against brightness, it is set to zero DC (direct current) with the application of the following formula [9]:

$$G'(x,y,\theta,\mu,\sigma) = G(x,y,\theta,\mu,\sigma) - \frac{\sum_{i=-n}^{n}\sum_{j=-n}^{n} G(i,j,\theta,\mu,\sigma)}{(2n+1)^2} \quad (8)$$

where $(2n+1)^2$ is the size of the filter.

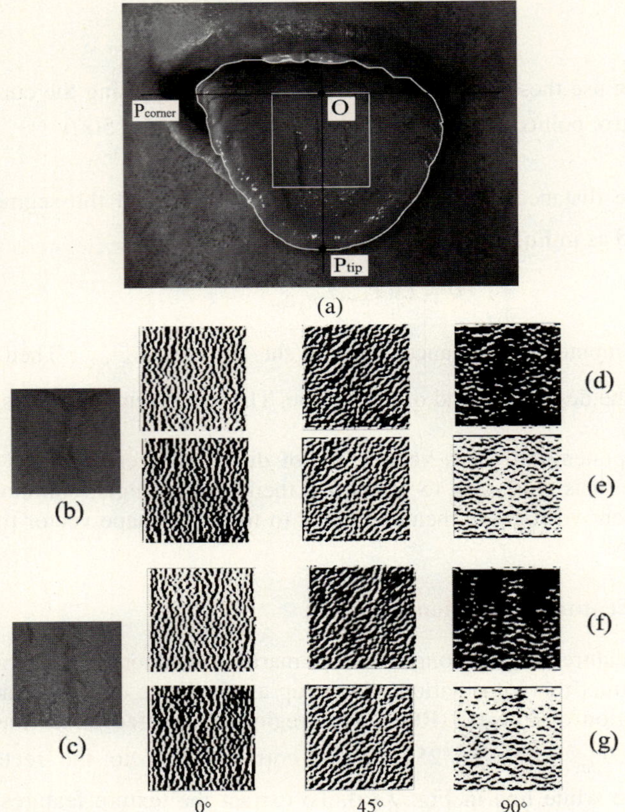

Fig. 7. (a) shows the ROI; (b) and (c) are original samples of the textures in the ROI. (d) and (f) are respectively the real parts of features from (b) and(c). (e) and (g) are the imaginary parts of (b) and (c).

An input tongue sub-image $I(x, y), x, y \in \Omega$ (Ω is the set of image points) is convolved with G'. Then, the sample point in the filtered image is coded to two bits, (b_r, b_i) using the following rules:

$$\begin{aligned} b_r &= 1 \quad \text{if } \mathrm{Re}[I \otimes G'] \geq 0 \\ b_r &= 0 \quad \text{if } \mathrm{Re}[I \otimes G'] < 0 \\ b_i &= 1 \quad \text{if } \mathrm{Im}[I \otimes G'] \geq 0 \\ b_i &= 0 \quad \text{if } \mathrm{Im}[I \otimes G'] < 0 \end{aligned} \tag{9}$$

Using this coding method means that only the phase information in the sub-images is stored in the texture feature vector. This texture feature extraction method was introduced by Daugman for use in iris recognition [11]. Fig. 7 (d)(e)(f)(g) show the features generated in this procedure

3.3 Recognition

In this step, the Mahalanobis distance is used for the tongue shape matching and the Hamming distance is used for the tongue texture code matching. Using these two kinds of distances gives us two matching scores. Because the shape feature vector and texture codes are non-homogeneous and are suitable for different matchers, in this tongue-print based verification method we exploit the matching score level fusion [3]. In our experience, the tongue shape information is more important than texture information. Thus, we apply the following strategy to get the decision results.

$$S = w_1 S_S + w_2 S_T \tag{10}$$

where S is the final matching score and the S_S , S_T are respectively the matching scores in the shape matching module and texture matching module and w_1 , w_2 are their corresponding weight values (in our study, $w_1 = 0.6$ and $w_2 = 0.4$).

4 Experiments and Results

4.1 Database

Our database contains 134 subjects. The subjects were recorded in five separate sessions uniformly distributed over a period of five months. Within each session ten image pairs for each subject, a front view and a profile view, were taken using our self-designed tongue-print capture device. In total, each subject provided 50 image pairs. We collected the tongue images from both men and women and across a wide range of ages. The distribution of the subjects is listed in Table 1. We called this tongue image database TB06.

Table 1. Composition of the tongue image database

	Sex		Age		
	male	female	20-29	30-39	40-49
Number of samples	89	45	81	32	21
Percentage (%)	66.4	33.6	60.4	23.9	15.7

4.2 Experimental Results

A matching is counted as a correct matching if two tongue images were collected from the same tongue; otherwise it is an incorrect matching. In our study, the Minimum Distance Classifier [12] is applied for its simplicity. The verification result is obtained using the matching score level fusion [3]. The performance of the verification system when using TB06 is represented by Receiver Operating Characteristic (ROC) curves, which are a plot of the genuine acceptance rate against the false acceptance rate for all possible operating points. From Fig. 8, we can see that combining shape and texture features for the tongue verification produces a better

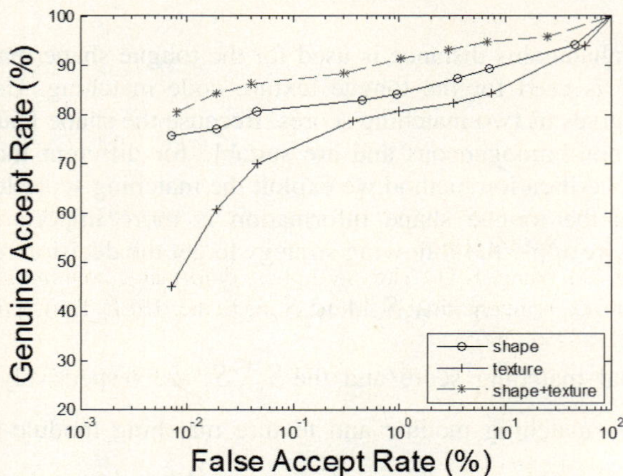

Fig. 8. ROC curve used to illustrate the verification test results

performance than using them singly. When the FAR is equal to 2.9%, we get the Genuine Accept Rate of 93.3%. These results demonstrate that the tongue biometric is feasible.

5 Conclusions

As the only internal organ that can be protruded from the body, the human tongue is well protected and is immune to forgery. The explicit features of the tongue cannot be reverse engineered, meaning that tongue verification protects the privacy of users better than other biometrics. This paper presents a novel tongue-print based verification approach. Using a uniform tongue image database containing sample images collected from 134 people, experiments produced a 93.3% recognition rate. These promising results suggest that tongue-prints of the human tongue qualify as a feasible new member of the biometrics family.

Acknowledgment

This work was supported in part by the UGC/CRC fund from the HKSAR Government, the central fund from the Hong Kong Polytechnic University and the NSFC fund under the contract No. 60332010.

References

1. Zhang, D.: Automated Biometrics—Technologies and Systems. Kluwer Academic, Boston (2000)
2. Jain, A., Bolle, R., Pankanti, S.: Biometrics: Personal Identification in Networked Society. Kluwer Academic, Boston (1998)

3. Ross, A., Jain, A., Qian, J.-Z.: Information Fusion in Biometrics. Pattern Recognition Letters 24(13), 2115–2125 (2003)
4. Hughe, G.E.: On the mean accuracy of statistical pattern recognizers. IEEE Transactions on Information Theory 14(l), 55–63 (1968)
5. Deng, J.-W., Tsui, H.T: A novel two-layer PCA/MDA scheme for hand posture recognition. In: Proceedings of 16th International Conference on Pattern Recognition, vol. 1, pp. 283–286 (2002)
6. Pikaz, A., Dinstein, I.: Matching of partially occluded planar curves. Pattern Recognition 28(2), 199–209 (1995)
7. Pang, B., Zhang, D., Wang, K.Q.: The bi-elliptical deformable contour and its application to automated tongue segmentation in Chinese medicine. IEEE Transactions on Medical Imaging 24(8), 946–956 (2005)
8. zhi, L., Yan, J.-q., Zhou, T., Tang, Q.-l.: Tongue Shape Detection Based on B-Spline. In: ICMLC2006, vol. 6, pp. 3829–3832 (2006)
9. Kong, W.K., Zhang, D., Li, W.: Palmprint feature extraction using 2-D Gabor filters. Pattern Recognition 36(10), 2339–2347 (2003)
10. Jain, A., Healey, G.: A multiscale representation including opponent color features for texture recognition. IEEE Transactions on Image Processing 7(1), 124–128 (1998)
11. Daugman, J.: High confidence visual recognition of persons by a test of statistical independence. IEEE Transactions on Pattern Analysis and Machine Intelligence 15(11), 1148–1161 (1993)
12. Jain, A.K., Duin, R.P.W., Mao, J.: Statistical Pattern Recognition: A Review. IEEE Transactions on Pattern Analysis and Machine Intelligence 22(1), 4–37 (2000)

Embedded Palmprint Recognition System on Mobile Devices

Yufei Han, Tieniu Tan, Zhenan Sun, and Ying Hao

Center for Biometrics and Security Research
National Labrotory of Pattern Recognition,Institue of Automation
Chinese Acdamey of Sciences
P.O. Box 2728, Beijing, P.R. China, 100080
{yfhan,tnt,znsun,yhao}@nlpr.ia.ac.cn

Abstract. There are increasing requirements for mobile personal identification, e.g. to protect identity theft in wireless applications. Based on built-in cameras of mobile devices, palmprint images may be captured and analyzed for individual authentication. However, current available palmprint recognition methods are not suitable for real-time implementations due to the limited computational resources of handheld devices, such as PDA or mobile phones. To solve this problem, in this paper, we propose a sum-difference ordinal filter to extract discriminative features of palmprint using only +/- operations on image intensities. It takes less than 200 ms for our algorithm to verify the identity of a palmprint image on a HP iPAQ PDA, about 1/10 of state-of-the-art methods' complexity, while this approach also achieves high accuracy on the PolyU palmprint database. Thanks to the efficient palmprint feature encoding scheme, we develop a real-time embedded palmprint recognition system, working on the HP PDA.

1 Introduction

There are about 1.5 billion mobile devices currently in use. With fast development of wireless network and embedded hardware, people enjoy the convenience of mobile commerce, mobile banking, mobile office, mobile entertainment, etc. However, at the same time, the risk of identity theft is increasing. The mostly used identity authentication method is password, but it can be cracked or forgotten. So biometrics is emerging to enhance the security of digital life. Fingerprint, face and voice recognition have been put into use on embedded mobile devices such as PDA and mobile phones. But they still have many disadvantages. For fingerprint recognition, only a small portion of mobile devices have a fingerprint sensor, and some people do not have clear fingerprints [1]. Face and voice recognition are sometimes not accurate and robust enough for personal recognition [1]. In contrast, palmprint could supply an alternative way for mobile authentication when these methods fail. According to work [2,3], large areas of human palms supply enough and robust representative features for identity authentication. Furthermore, palmprint recognition is testified to achieve high accuracy in real world use based on low-resolution (<100 dpi) images. As a result, using built-in cameras of PDA or mobile phones, it is possible to capture palmprint images adequate for further recognition.

S.-W. Lee and S.Z. Li (Eds.): ICB 2007, LNCS 4642, pp. 1184–1193, 2007.

Various palmprint recognition approaches have been proposed in the literatures [1-12]. Almost all available algorithms involve thousands of large-size convolutions or filtering, i.e. millions of multiplication operations of floating points. Although these algorithms can work well on PC, most embedded mobile devices can not afford such complex computations because of the limited computational resources on handheld apparatus. To the best of our knowledge, there is no work reported on palmprint recognition for embedded systems. We think the main bottleneck is the limited computational resources of mobile devices. To attack this problem, we propose a novel fast palmprint feature encoding algorithm, only involving +/- integer operations of pixel intensities, to make palmprint recognition applicable for mobile devices. The basic idea of our method is based on qualitative comparison of the average intensities of two elongated and orthogonal palmprint image regions, namely ordinal features [2]. Simple and fast as it is, our algorithm obtains high accuracy on PolyU palmprint database [13]. Based on the proposed approach, we develop a real-time palmprint recognition system, working on a HP rx3715 PDA.

The rest of the paper is organized as follows. We represent the total framework of the proposed system in Section 2. In Section 3, our fast palmprint encoding scheme is described. In Section 4, experiments are designed to test performance of the system. Section 5 concludes the paper.

2 System Overview

The architecture of the proposed system is denoted in the following diagram (see Fig. 1). We adopt a HP iPAQ rx3715 PDA as a computing platform of the system. This device contains a low-power 400MHZ StrongARM processor which lacks floating point unit. Besides, it equips with a built-in digital camera with the resolution of 100 dpi, which is used to capture palmprint images. The whole system is implemented using Microsoft Embedded Visual C++ 3.0 under Windows CE operating system. Two most important components of the system are image capture and feature encoding module. The former aims to obtain normalized palmprint images, decreasing the effect of image translation, rotation and scale variations. The latter derives a compact description of each palmprint image for further feature matching in a high speed.

After a user starts the system, the built-in camera is activated automatically. A continually updated preview frame (see Fig. 2 (a)) on screen can be used to adjust the distance and position between the user ' s palm and the camera. During image capturing, the root region of the middle finger, forefinger and ring finger is required to be aligned with the top border of the frame. The left and right borders of the frame are required to be aligned with the corresponding borders of the central region of a palm. Then images of the central region are obtained with little rotation, translation and scale variation. In the captured image, a fixed size sub-image is cropped from it at a fixed position, which is used for feature extraction, namely region of interest (ROI), as shown in Fig. 2(b). A mobile user could control his right or left hand to capture the palmprint image of left or right hand.

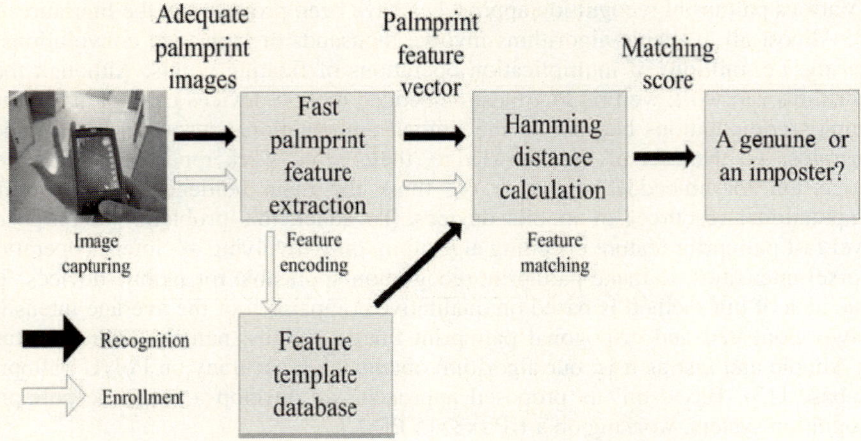

Fig. 1. System framework

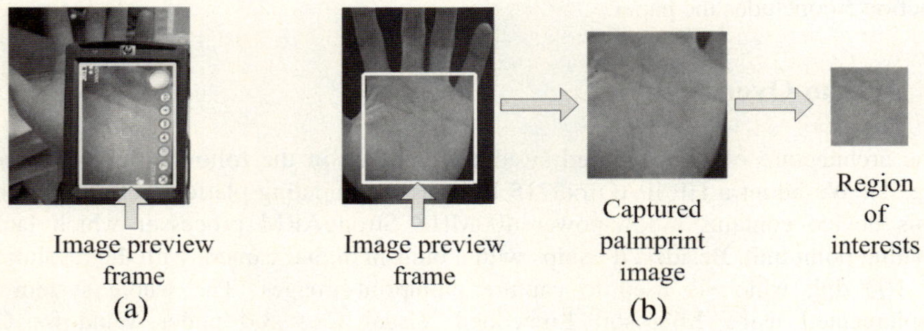

Fig. 2. An example of ROI generation. (a) Image preview frame;(b) Generation of ROI.

During enrollment, one user could choose either of his palms to be registered in the system. For each registered palm, the system captures three palmprint images. In our application, the size of each captured image is 160×120, and a 80×80 subimage is extracted as ROI. After feature extraction, three feature templates are compared with each other using hamming distance. Only if all obtained hamming distances are lower than a given threshold, the feature templates can be stored into a 256 MB SD card of PDA, which is used as the feature template database. Otherwise, the system will prompt that the enrollment procedure fails. During recognition, each input palmprint feature is compared with all feature templates stored in the system by fast hamming distance matching. If the minimal hamming distance is higher than a threshold, the user is classified as an imposter; otherwise, he is accepted as a registered user.

3 Sum-Difference Ordinal Filter

In our previous work, we proposed the orthogonal line ordinal feature (OLOF) [2] to represent negative line features of palmprints efficiently. The orthogonal line ordinal filter is designed as follows [2]:

$$F(x,y,\theta) = G(x,y,\theta) - G(x,y,\theta + \pi/2) \tag{1}$$

where

$$G(x,y,\theta) = \exp[-(\frac{x\cos\theta + y\sin\theta}{\delta_x})^2 - (\frac{-x\sin\theta + y\cos\theta}{\delta_y})^2] \tag{2}$$

which is a 2D Gaussian filter, and θ is the orientation of the Gaussian filter. To make its shape like a line, we controlled the parameters $\delta_x / \delta_y > 3$. After convolution between a local region and the ordinal filter, the filtering result is then encoded into 1 or 0 according to whether it is positive or negative. Thousands of ordinal codes are concatenated into a feature template. The OLOF describes orientation information of negative line segments in palmprints. Our fast palmprint feature encoding scheme uses simplified OLOF because the coefficients of the Gaussian function are floating point numbers and result in relative high computational cost on the PDA. So a novel ordinal filter is designed, namely, sum-difference ordinal filter (SDOF), which contains only integer coefficients instead. According to equation (1) and (2), the effective region for filtering of the OLOF [2] could be detected by projecting $F(x,y,\theta)$ to the image plane as follows:

$$g(x,y) = \{I(x,y) : |F(x,y,\theta)| \geq k, k > 0\}, \tag{3}$$

k is a fixed threshold, which is set empirically as following Eq.5.

According to Eq.3, we can obtain four discrete symmetric regions. One example is illustrated in Figure 3 (a). The square region in the example has a size of 35×35. Two regions are along the horizontal axis, while the other two along the vertical axis. Pairs along the same axis can be seen as the head and the tail of a line segment. In the SDOF, coefficients in horizontal parts are +1, while these in vertical parts are -1, represented as follows:

$$SDOF(x,y,\theta) = \begin{cases} 1 & F(x,y,\theta) \geq k \\ -1 & F(x,y,\theta) \leq -k \\ 0 & otherwise \end{cases} \tag{4}$$

where $k > 0$ and θ is the orientation of the filter. According to our experiments, we choose k as follows:

$$k = 0.005 \times E \tag{5}$$

where E is the maximum intensity of $G(x,y,\theta)$. For each ROI obtained, three sum-difference ordinal filters are performed on it as follows:

$$R(\theta) = SDOF(x, y, \theta) * I(x, y) \tag{6}$$

where $\theta = 0, \pi/6, \pi/3$. $I(x, y)$ denotes the local patch of ROI and * denotes the operator of convolution. Three bit binary codes are generated according to signs of $R(\theta)$. After the whole palmprint image filtered, numbers of these binary codes constitute a feature template, namely sum-difference ordinal code, as shown in Fig 3(b). In contrast to the orthogonal line ordinal filter [2], the feature extraction time can be reduced obviously, because there are only addition and subtraction involved in the convolution. Similarity between two feature templates is then measured by hamming distance. Simple as it is, like the orthogonal line ordinal code [2], sum-difference ordinal code also represents ordinal measures between two geometrical orthogonal line-like image regions, which is testified to be a robust and discriminating feature to describe negative line patterns in palmprint images, such as principle lines and wrinkles [2].

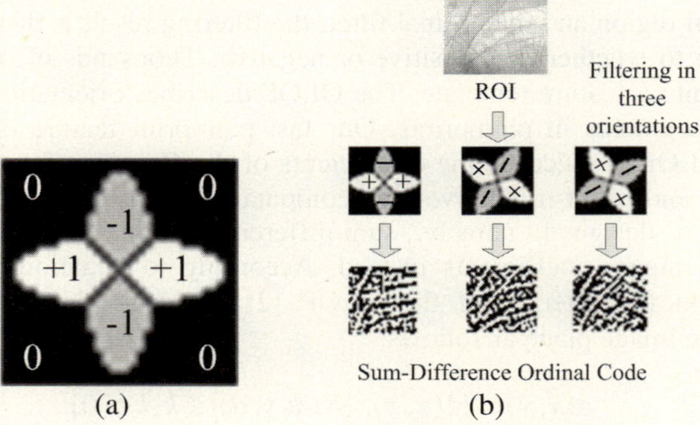

Fig. 3. An example of ordinal palmprint features extraction (a) Four symmetric regions; (b) Generation of sum-difference ordinal code

4 Experimental Results

This section consists of two parts. In section 4.1, we collect a palmprint image dataset using the proposed system, following the way shown in Fig. 2. Based on those images, we test performance of the system in the section, including accuracy of recognition and usability of the system. We also implement three state-of-the-art algorithms, fusion code [10], competitive code [11] and ordinal code [2] on PDA for further comparisons with the proposed sum-difference ordinal code. Besides, in section 4.2, we design a verification experiment on PolyU Palmprint Database [13] to test validity of the proposed approach in a further step.

4.1 Performance Evaluation of the System

We collect 400 gray-scale images from 40 subjects, with five images for each palm, Six examples are shown in Fig. 4(a). Fig. 4(b) shows an example of cropped ROI. The first three images of each palm are captured by the system as the enrolling images, while the other two are added further. Notably, unlike biometric systems used for entrance control, an identity authentication system of a PDA or mobile phone is usually utilized to confirm whether the current user is the owner of the mobile device. So there are only the owner's biometric features stored in the system. Therefore, we evaluate recognition accuracy of the system in terms of verification rate [14] of sum-difference ordinal code and total success rate [12], both obtained through one-to-one image matching. There are totally 800 intra-class comparisons and 3,160 inter-class comparisons. Due to large number of matching operations, all comparisons are performed on PC. We compare the average feature extraction time of the proposed algorithm with that of the other three methods [2][10][11] on the PDA. Table.1 lists performances of all four algorithms. Fig. 5 shows corresponding ROC curves. Fig.6 shows total success rate of our system varying with different threshold values. From experimental results illustrated in Tab.1 and Fig. 5, we can see that computational cost of sum-difference ordinal code is only a fraction of the others. In addition, it is the most accurate for identity verification.

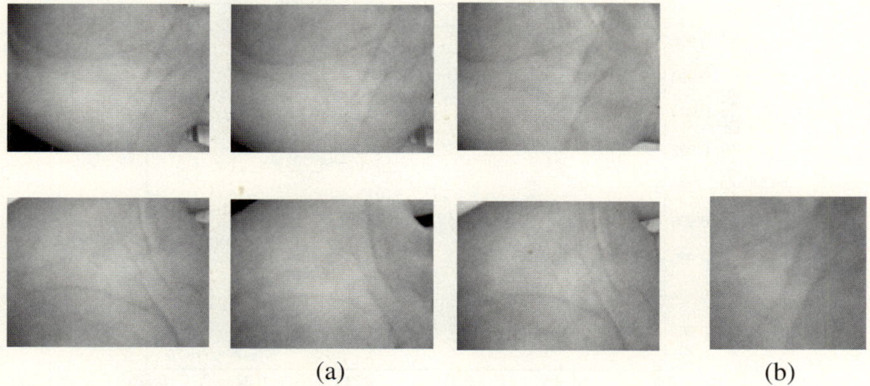

(a) (b)

Fig. 4. Examples of palmprint images captured by the proposed system (a) Palmprint images collected by the system; (b) Region of interests

Table 1. Performance comparison on images collected by the system

Algorithm	EER[14]	d'[14]	Feature extraction time on PDA
Fusion code[10]	3.8%	3.86	2296 ms
Competitive code[11]	1.1%	4.70	1627 ms
Ordinal code[2]	1.02%	4.70	803 ms
Sum-difference ordinal code	0.92%	4.76	180 ms

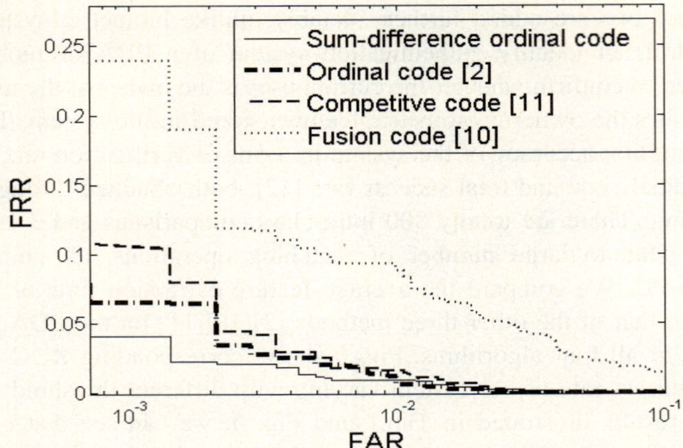

Fig. 5. ROC curves on images collected by the system

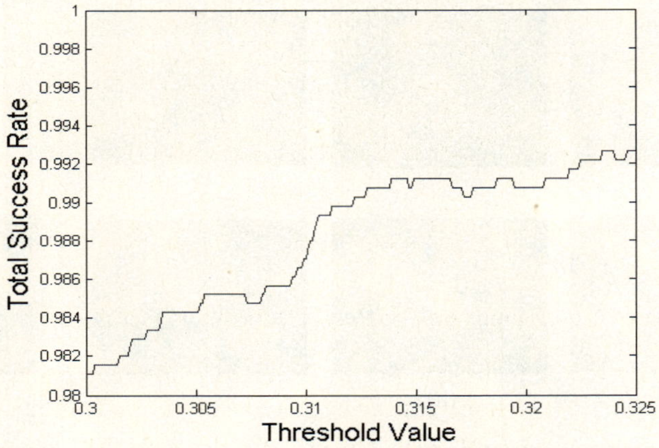

Fig. 6. Total success rate of our system

Total success rate (TSR) [12] is employed to evaluate recognition accuracy in a further step. It is calculated considering both correct accepted and correct rejected items:

$$TSR = 1 - \frac{FAR \times Amount\ of\ imposter + FRR \times Amount\ of\ genuine}{Total\ amount\ of\ matching} \tag{7}$$

As shown in Fig. 6, with proper choice of threshold value, our system achieves a total success rate of around 99%, using the efficient feature extraction method. Due to limit to accuracy of the alignment method used in the system, described in section 2, position and scale variations still exit in captured images, which may deteriorate performance of the system. Nevertheless, based on the fast feature encoding scheme, our system can deliver a real-time recognition in relatively high accuracy on the PDA.

Except for average feature time, we also record the enrollment duration of each subject during collecting images by the system, as shown in Fig. 7. It includes time for a complete successful enrolling procedure and depends mostly on interaction between users and the recognition system. Fast enrollment is very important for point-of-sale use. The minimum and mean enrollment duration values are 65.2 seconds and 76 seconds respectively. As we see in Fig. 7, most of subjects finish enrollment successfully in less than 78 seconds. Only one costs more than 100 seconds, due to his unfamiliarity with usage of PDA.

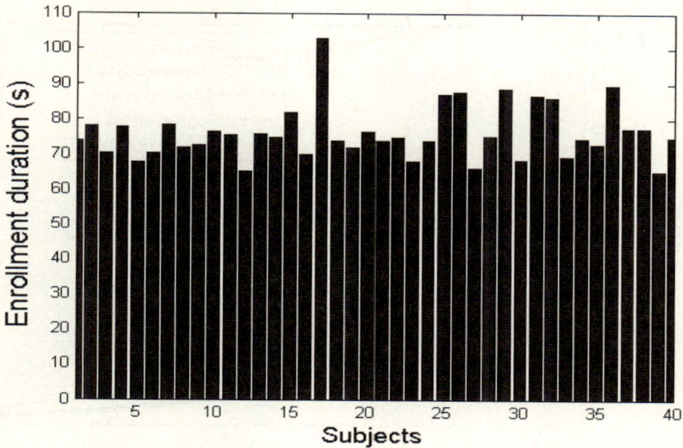

Fig. 7. Enrollment duration of 40 subjects

4.2 Verification Experiment on the PolyU Palmprint Database

There are totally 7,752 palmprint images from 386 different palms in the PolyU Palmprint database 2nd version [13]. Each palm has two sessions. The average time interval between each two session is about two months. We normalize original images into 128×128 ROI images [3]. Totally 74,068 intra-class comparisons and 7,430,500 inter-class comparisons are involved. All matching procedures are performed on a common PC. Fig. 8 and Table 2 show experimental results. For each of four algorithms, we measure its average feature extraction time on the PDA, as listed in Table 2. Compared with state-of-the-art palmprint recognition algorithms [2][10][11], sum-difference ordinal code achieves significantly high accuracy. Furthermore, it costs only about 1 second for feature extraction on one ROI image, much faster than the other three opponents. ROI images in the section are larger than those in section 4.1. As a result, they contains more discriminative features. Furthermore, there is less alignment error in images of the PolyU database [12] after preprocessing [3]. Thus, all four algorithms perform better. Results demonstrate that sum-difference ordinal code is not only suitable for fast palmprint recognition on PDA, but also on PC with image capture devices introduced in [3].

Table 2. Performance comparison on PolyU palmpirnt image database

Algorithm	EER[14]	d'[14]	Feature extraction time on PDA
Fusion code[10]	0.21%	5.40	13455 ms
Competitive code[11]	0.06%	5.64	8325 ms
Ordinal code[2]	0.07%	6.63	4421 ms
Sum-difference ordinal code	0.07%	6.58	1127 ms

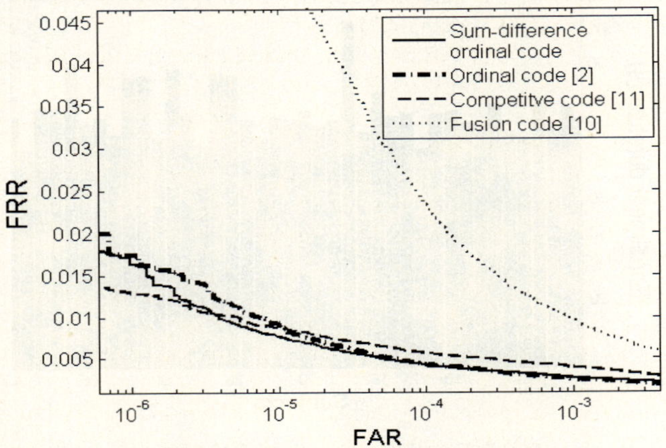

Fig. 8. ROC curves on PolyU database

5 Conclusions and Future Work

In this paper, we have proposed and developed a real-time palmprint recognition system for mobile devices, such as PDA. As far as we know, this is the first attempt to apply palmprint based identity check on such mobile devices. The core of the system is a fast palmprint feature encoding scheme using a sum-difference ordinal filter. The coefficients of the filter only involve 1s or 0s, so palmprint feature extraction could be implemented with only +/- operations of integers. The average feature extraction time is only 180ms on the HP PDA, almost ten times faster than the other three state-of-the-art methods in the experiments. Although our method is simple, the filter is able to extract the discriminative palmprint feature --- ordinal measures [2] between a negative line pattern and its geometric orthogonal region. So it is not surprised that our method has a good performance in the verification test. Benefit from the efficient approach and human-computer interface, the proposed system achieves accurate recognition and convenient use at the same time. We can further use such a technology to protect identity of mobile applications or enhance the security of wireless communication. However, how to design a suitable image alignment method to improve accuracy of the system is not well addressed in this paper. It is an important issue in our future work.

Acknowledgments. Experiments in the paper use the PolyU Palmprint Database ver.2 collected by the Biometric Research Center at the Hong Kong Polytechnic University. This work is funded by research grants from the National Basic Research Program (Grant No.2004CB318110), the Natural Science Foundation of China (Grant No. 60335010, 60121302, 60275003, 60332010, 69825105□60605008) and the Chinese Academy of Sciences.

References

1. Li, W., Zhang, D., Xu, Z.: Palmprint Identification by Fourier Transform. International Journal of PRAI 16(4), 417–432 (2002)
2. Sun, Z.N., Tan, T.N., Wang, Y.H., Li, S.Z.: Ordinal Palmprint Representation for Personal Identification. In: Proc. of CVPR 2005, vol. 1, pp. 279–284 (2005)
3. Zhang, D., Kong, W.K., You, J., Wong, M.: Online Palmprint Identification. IEEE Trans on PAMI 25(9), 1041–1050 (2003)
4. Zhang, D., Shu, W.: Two Novel Characteristics in Palmprint Verification: Datum Point Invariance and Line Feature Matching. Pattern Recognition 32(4), 691–702 (1999)
5. Duta, N., Jain, A.K., Mardia, K.V.: Matching of Palmprint. Pattern Recognition Letters 23(4), 477–485 (2001)
6. Lu, G., Zhang, D., Wang, K.: Palmprint Recognition Using Eigenpalms Features. Pattern Recognition Letters 24(9-10), 1463–1467 (2003)
7. Han, C.C., Cheng, H.L., Fan, K.C., Lin, C.L.: Personal Authentication Using Palmprint Features. Pattern Recognition 36(2), 371–381 (2003)
8. You, J., Kong, W.K., Zhang, D., Cheung, K.: On Hierarchical Palmprint Coding with Multi- features for Personal Identification in Large Databases. IEEE Trans on Circuit Systems for Video Technology 14(2), 234–243 (2004)
9. Zhang, L., Zhang, D.: Characterization of Palmprints by Wavelet Signatures via Directional Context Modeling. IEEE Trans on SMC-B 34(3), 1335–1347 (2004)
10. Kong, W.K., Zhang, D.: Feature-Level Fusion for Effective Palmprint Authentication. In: Zhang, D., Jain, A.K. (eds.) ICBA 2004. LNCS, vol. 3072, pp. 520–523. Springer, Heidelberg (2004)
11. Kong, W.K., Zhang, D.: Competitive Coding Scheme for Palmprint Verification. In: Proc. of the 17th ICPR, vol. 1, pp. 520–523 (2004)
12. Connie, T., Jin, A.T.B., Ong, M.G.K., Ling, D.N.C.: Automated palmprint recognition system. Image and Vision Computing 23, 501–515 (2005)
13. PolyU Palmprint Database, http://www.comp.polyu.edu.hk/ biometrics/
14. Daugman, J., Williams, G.: A Proposed Standard for Biometric Decidability. In: Proc. CardTech/SecureTech Conference, Atlanta, GA, pp. 223–234 (1996)

Template Co-update in Multimodal Biometric Systems

Fabio Roli[1], Luca Didaci[2], and Gian Luca Marcialis[1]

[1] University of Cagliari – Department of Electrical and Electronic Engineering
Piazza d'Armi – 09123 Cagliari (Italy)
[2] University of Cagliari – Department of Pedagogical and Philosophical Sciences
Via Is Mirrionis, 1 - 09123 Cagliari (Italy)
{roli,luca.didaci,marcialis}@diee.unica.it

Abstract. Performances of biometric recognition systems can degrade quickly when the input biometric traits exhibit substantial variations compared to the templates collected during the enrolment stage of users. This issue can be addressed using template update methods. In this paper, a novel template update method based on the concept of biometric co-training is presented. In multimodal biometric systems, this method allows co-updating the template galleries of different biometrics, realizing a co-training process of biometric experts which allows updating templates more quickly and effectively. Reported results provide a first experimental evidence of the effectiveness of the proposed template update method.

1 Introduction

As pointed out clearly by Uludag et al. [1], in real operational scenarios, input biometric data can exhibit substantial variations compared to the templates collected during the enrolment stage of users. In other words, we can have a large intra-class variability, due to changes of the environment conditions (e.g., illumination changes), aging of the biometric traits, variations of the interaction between the sensor and the individual (e.g., variations of the person pose), etc. This large intra-class variability can make the templates acquired during the enrolment session poorly representative of the biometric data to be recognized, so resulting in poor recognition performances. For example, Tan et al. pointed out, by experiments with the ORL face data base [2], that the performance of an eigenface-based face recogniser drops quickly when the enrolled templates become poorly representative. The authors reported similar results for the AR face data base [3]. Template update methods have been proposed to address this issue. In fingerprint recognition, Uludag et al. proposed two methods which can be used to update templates when new fingerprint impressions, labeled with the user's identity, become available [1]. One of the methods is based on a clustering strategy to choose a template set that best represents the intra-class variations, whilst the other selects templates that exhibit maximum similarity with the rest of the impressions. Both the methods work off-line (i.e., template updating is performed after a new batch of labelled data has been acquired) and are supervised (i.e., a supervisor has to label the new biometric data to be used for template updating). Some "semi-supervised" template updating methods have been also

S.-W. Lee and S.Z. Li (Eds.): ICB 2007, LNCS 4642, pp. 1194–1202, 2007.

proposed. With the term semi-supervised, we indicate those methods that update templates using both the initial set of labelled templates and a set of unlabelled data acquired during the on-line operation of the biometric system. Jiang and Ser [4], Ryu et al. [5], proposed some on-line and semi-supervised methods which update templates by a fusion process with impressions acquired on-line which are recognized as genuine with high reliability. Liu et al. proposed an on-line semi-supervised algorithm to update incrementally the eigenspace of a PCA-based face recognition system by exploiting unlabelled data acquired during the system's operation [6]. Roli and Marcialis developed an off-line semi-supervised method, using the learning method named "self-training", to update incrementally the templates and the eigenspace of a PCA-based face recognition system [3].

To our knowledge, so far template update methods have focused on unimodal biometric systems, and no method tailored to multimodal systems has been proposed. In addition, the performance of unimodal, semi-supervised, template update methods depends on two contrasting factors: the importance of updating templates using "difficult", but informative, new biometric data, and the difficulty to recognize correctly new input data that exhibit substantial variations compared to the current templates. It is easy to see that a template update method which exploits only high quality and easy to recognize input data may not be able to account for the variations of an user's biometric.

In this paper, a novel template update method tailored to multimodal biometric systems is proposed. This method exploits the concept of biometric co-training that the authors introduced in [7], and it is based on the semi-supervised learning method proposed by Blum and Mitchell [8]. In multimodal biometric systems, this method allows co-updating the template galleries of different biometrics, realizing a co-training process of biometric experts which allows updating templates also using "difficult", but informative, input data. Results reported in Section 4 provide a first experimental evidence of the effectiveness of the proposed template update method.

2 Template Co-update and Biometric Co-training

The template co-update method we developed was inspired by the semi-supervised learning method named co-training [8], and, therefore, it can regarded as a biometric co-training algorithm where two multimodal biometric experts co-train each other in order to update their template galleries. The key idea behind biometric co-training is a generalization to the problem of template update of the basic idea behind multi-modal biometrics [7]. In fact, the "complementary" performances of biometric recognizers using distinct biometric traits, for example, face and fingerprints, are one of the fundamental motivations for multi-modal biometrics [9]. Intuitively, each recognizer is expected to assign correct labels to certain input data which are difficult for the other. So far this idea was the basis for the design of multi-modal systems, but such idea has never been exploited in a learning context to implement a template update method. On the other hand, the complementary performances of two biometric recognizers can be indeed exploited in a semi-supervised learning context, by allowing the recognizers to co-train each other. A co-training approach to semi-supervised learning was proposed by Blum and Mitchell in 1998 [8]. Here we illustrate the basic idea behind the original co-training approach of Blum and Mitchell with a multi-modal biometric recognition example, which also allows us to explain how this semi-supervised learning method could be used to implement a template update method. Let us suppose that we have a multimodal biometric system made up of a face and a fingerprints recognition system, and a small set D_l of biometric data, labelled with the users' identities, acquired during the enrolment session. According to the Blum and Mitchell co-training algorithm, these two recognisers should be trained with the set D_l, and it is assumed that they will exhibit a low, but better than random, accuracy. In our biometric example, the set D_l should be used to create the initial template galleries, and, eventually, to initialize other parameters of the recognition system (e.g., computing the eigenspace in the case of a PCA-based face recogniser). During the on-line operation of the biometric system, a batch D_u (usually, much larger than D_l) of unlabelled data can be acquired (this data set is obtained simply by disregarding the labels assigned by the recognition system). The co-training algorithm assumes that each recognizer is applied to such unlabeled set D_u. For each recogniser, the unlabelled examples that are classified with the highest confidence are added to the training set D_l, so that the two recognisers contribute to increase the data set. Both the recognisers are re-trained with this augmented data set (e.g., by updating the face and fingerprint template galleries), and the process is repeated a specified number of times. Intuitively, co-training is expected to work because each recogniser may assign correct labels to certain examples, whilst it may be difficult for the other recogniser to do so. Therefore, each recogniser can increase the training set with examples which are very informative for the other recogniser. In few words, the two recognisers are expected to co-train each other. When the co-training process finishes, the two resulting recognisers can be combined by the product of their outputs.

It is worth noting that a fundamental assumption of the Blum and Mitchell co-training algorithm is that patterns are represented with two "redundantly sufficient" feature sets. This assumption means that the two feature sets should be conditionally independent, so that the examples which are classified with high confidence by one of the two recognisers are *i.i.d.* samples for the other, and both the feature sets should be sufficient to design an optimal recognition algorithm if we have enough labelled data. In multi-modal biometrics, using, for example, face and fingerprint data, this assumption is likely to be satisfied, at least at the extent which justifies the use of co-training for practical purposes.

Figure 1 illustrates the use of biometric co-training to co-update face and fingerprints galleries. A given bi-modal, face and fingerprint, input data could be difficult to classify correctly for the face recogniser using the available templates (e.g., due to an illumination change), while the fingerprint recogniser could be able to do easily because the user provided a good fingerprint impression. In Figure 1, this is the case of the first couple of face-fingerprint images on the right of the initial templates. In this case, the fingerprint recogniser could train the face recogniser, that is, the face template gallery could be updated using this difficult (and, therefore, "informative") face image which was acquired jointly with an easy fingerprint image. This update of the face template gallery would not be possible without co-training (because we are supposing that the input face image cannot be recognised correctly with the current templates in the gallery), or this would take much more time (i.e., one

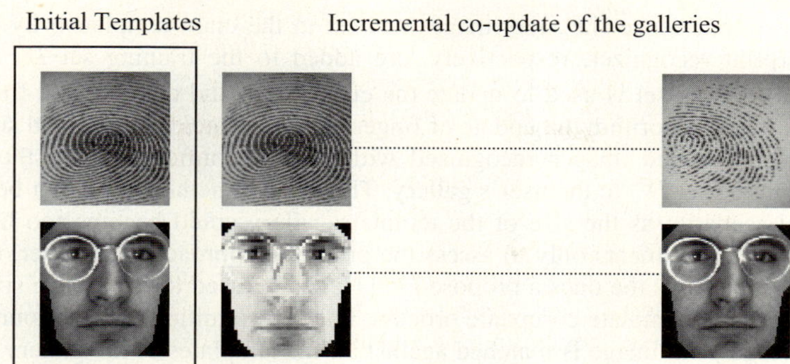

Fig. 1. An illustrative example of the use of biometric co-training to co-update face and fingerprints galleries. The first couple of images on the left are the initial face and fingerprint templates. Two examples of co-update of the galleries are shown on the right of the templates. These examples highlight how a difficult (and, therefore, "informative") biometric template can be added to a gallery, supposed that this input data comes in with a sample of the other biometrics which can be easily recognized using the initial template.

should wait for an incremental update of the gallery which makes possible to recognise correctly this difficult face input). The fingerprint recogniser can train the face recogniser in a similar way (see the case of the second couple, on the right of the initial templates, of input face-fingerprint images in Figure 1), so realizing a co-training process which allow updating templates more quickly and effectively.

3 Co-updating of Face and Fingerprint Recognition Systems

In order to investigate the practical use of a template co-update method based on the above biometric co-training concept, we first implemented a simple multi-modal identification system made up of a PCA-based face recognizer and a fingerprint recognizer using the "String" matching algorithm ("String" is a matching algorithm based on minutiae points). We used the standard versions of these two recognition algorithms [10, 11]. Then we implemented the template co-update algorithm in Figure 2 to update automatically the template galleries of these two recognizers. It is worth noting that our co-update algorithm also updates the eigenspace of the PCA-based face recognizer, as we experimented that this improves the overall performance of the multimodal system w.r.t. updating only the template galleries. The main steps of the co-updating algorithm we implemented are summarized in Figure 2. After the enrolment session, the set D_l, containing the face and fingerprint images acquired, labeled with the user's identity, is used to train the PCA-based face recognizer (i.e., the PCA transform is computed and the initial templates are created) and to create the initial fingerprint templates. Then, during the on-line operation, an unlabelled batch of data D_u is collected over a given period of time, simply by disregarding the labels assigned by the recognition system. This set D_u is used for the template co-update process as follows (Figure 2). According to the standard co-training approach, for each iteration of the algorithm, two sets D^1 and D^2 of unlabelled images recognized with highest confidence (i.e., the images nearest to the class templates) by the face and fingerprint recognizer, respectively, are added to the training set D_l, and this augmented training set is used to update the eigenspace, and the face and fingerprint templates. In our algorithm the update of fingerprint templates is performed simply by adding the unlabelled images recognized with highest confidence (i.e., the images contained in the set D^2) to the user's gallery. This simple method could not be used in a practical scenario, as the size of the template gallery could become too large (we used it in our experiments only to assess the proposed approach). However, template selection methods, as the ones a proposed in [1], can be used to reduce the size of the gallery during the template co-update process. In the recognition phase of our system, the input fingerprint image is matched against all the templates of the gallery, and the final matching score is computed as average of the individual scores. For each identity, the face template is simply the "mean" face, so template updating is very simple. However, more sophisticated methods, based on clustering, could be used for updating the face templates [1].

Finally, one should note that we are assuming that the template co-updating process is performed either when the system is not operating (e.g., during the night) or using a separate processing unit which allows carrying out co-updating in parallel with the recognition stage.

4 Experimental Results

The goal of our experiments was to evaluate the capability of the proposed co-updating algorithm to exploit a batch of unlabelled images, collected during a given session of the system operation, in order to update the face and fingerprint templates galleries, and the eigenspace of the PCA-based face recognizer. To this end, we carried out experiments with the AR and the FVC-2002 DB2 data sets on an identification task [12, 13]. The AR data set contains frontal view faces with different facial expressions, illumination conditions, and occlusions (sun glasses and scarf). Each person participated in two acquisition sessions, separated by two weeks time. Each session is made up of seven images per person. We selected 100 subjects (50 males and 50 females), and manually cropped face images and, after histogram stretching and equalization, resized them at 40x40 pixels. The FVC-2002 DB2 data set is made up of 800 fingerprints images, acquired with an optical sensor, belonging to 100 subjects. For each individual, eight fingerprint impressions have been acquired. We coupled the two data bases in two different ways in order to create two "chimerical" multi-modal data sets for our experiments. One of the chimerical data sets was created by selecting, for each user, one face image and one fingerprint impression as training set D_l, that is, as initial templates (in particular, the face templates were selected from the first acquisition session of the AR data base), and using the remaining seven fingerprint impressions and seven face images of the second AR session as unlabelled data set D_u. The other chimerical data set was created simply reversing the use of the AR images, that is, selecting the training data from the second session images and the unlabelled data from the first session images. In addition, for each data set, we performed two trials using either the face or the

In the enrolment session, collect a set D_l of labelled face and fingerprint images. A couple of face and fingerprint images is acquired for each user.
Compute the PCA transform and create the face templates using the set D_l
Create the fingerprint templates using the set D_l

During the on-line system operation, collect an unlabelled set D_u.

Co-update algorithm
Loop for N iterations:
Assign (pseudo)identity labels to a subset D^1 of images in D_u recognized with high confidence by the face recogniser
Assign (pseudo)identity labels to a subset D^2 of images in D_u recognized with high confidence by the fingerprint recogniser
Increase the training set $D_l \leftarrow D^1 \cup D^2$
Update PCA transform using the augmented labelled set D_l
Update face templates using the augmented labelled set D_l
Update fingerprint templates using the augmented labelled set D_l

Fig. 2. Co-updating algorithm of a PCA-based face recogniser and a fingerprint matcher using the "String" algorithm. The main steps of the algorithm are shown.

fingerprint recogniser as first algorithm, in the loop of the co-updating algorithm (Figure 2), which assigns (pseudo)labels to unlabelled data. In fact, even if, theoretically speaking, this order should not affect co-updating performances, we verified that it can do in this biometric application. In summary, the results which are going to report are the average of the results obtained with four trials (two data sets and two trials for each data set).

Figure 3 shows the percentage accuracy on the unlabelled data set D_u averaged on four trials. For this experiment, we point out that the initial galleries (before the template co-update process) contained only one face and fingerprint template per person. Performances are shown as function of the number of unlabelled data used during the iterations of the co-updating algorithm. Around one-hundred pseudo-labeled data were added to the training set during every iteration. Looking the two curves labelled "Co-updating-Fingerprint" and "Co-updating-Face" in Figure 3 one notes immediately the large difference of performance between the fingerprint and face recognizer at the beginning of the co-updating process, when no unlabeled data has been still used (90% vs. 48% of accuracy). This large difference is due to the use of a single template per person and the characteristics of the two data sets. For the AR face data set, the large differences between first and second session images make a single template per person poorly representative. Differently, for the FVC-2002 DB2 fingerprint data set, a single template per person is quite representative of the remaining seven fingerprint impressions, as the results of the past FVC-2002 competion pointed out [13]. It is worth noting that such a performance unbalance between a face and a fingerprint recogniser is a realistic scenario. In fact, large differences of performances have been reported in many works [9], and they could be indeed exhibited when a multi-modal system is created by adding a new face recognition module to a previously installed, and well trained, fingerprint recognition system. In this case, the face recognition module could initially exhibit performances much lower than the ones of the fingerprint module whose templates have been (re)updated by supervised (re)enrolment sessions over the time. It should be also noted that co-training can offer a solution to this kind of practical cases. In fact, the face recognizer, newly installed, could be co-trained by the fingerprint recognizer. Other scenarios, where performances are more balanced, are obviously possible, and we are investigating by experiments such cases.

Figure 3 shows clearly that the fingerprint and the face recogniser co-train each other, that is, their accuracies increase substantially with the number of unlabelled data exploited by co-training. As it could be expected, the face recogniser, whose initial templates were poorly representative, gets the greatest benefits from the co-updating process. It is also interesting to note that the combination of the two recognisers by product of their matching scores further increases the performance. From an application viewpoint, this results points out that the co-training process can allow to improve the recognition results previously achieved on a batch of input data. For example, in a person identification scenario such a system re-training could allow improving the identification results stored in the data base the day before. We assessed by experiments that co-training can also improve recognition accuracy on novel input data, acquired after the co-training process with the unlabeled set D_u. The benefits of co-training were also assessed in terms of the so called rank-order curves. For the sake of brevity, we do no report these results.

To investigate the practical operation of the proposed template co-updating algorithm, we analysed how the galleries of users' templates were updated and increased. We report this analysis only for the face galleries, as it is easier to understand the operation by the visual analysis and comparison of face galleries than analysing fingerprint galleries. We also compared the galleries created by our template co-update method with the ones created by the self-update method of face templates we proposed in [3]. Such method selects the unlabelled data to be used for template updating in a way similar to the one proposed for fingerprint template updating in [4,5]. Face templates are updated using the unlabelled images recognized with highest confidence (i.e., the images nearest to the current class templates). This comparison should help the reader to understand better the advantages of co-updating.

Figure 4 depicts an examples of the update of users' galleries by co-updating and self-updating. For each gallery, the first image on the left is the initial training image used as face template. The remaining images are the unlabelled images which were pseudo labelled and added to the galleries during the iterations of co-updating and self-updating. In Figure 4, if one compare the gallery depicted in the first row, created by co-updating, with the second row gallery, created by self-updating, it is easy note that our co-updating algorithm allows updating the gallery with "difficult" (and, therefore, "informative") face images quicker than self-updating. For example, the second image of the first row is a difficult image w.r.t. the initial template (illumination changed substantially); and, in fact, self-updating added this image only at the fourth iteration.

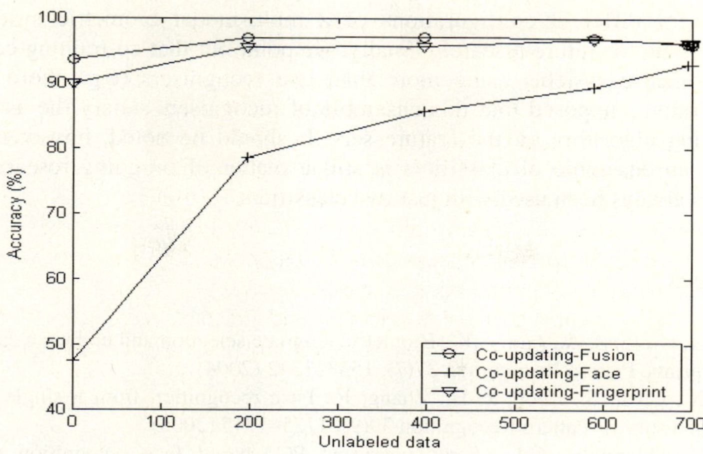

Fig. 3. Average accuracy on the unlabelled data set as function of the number of unlabelled data used in the co-updating algorithm of Figure 2. The curves "Co-updating-Fingerprint" and "Co-updating-Face" refer to the co-trained fingerprint and face recognition algorithms, respectively. The curve "Co-updating-Fusion" refers to the combination of the two algorithms by the product of their matching scores.

Example of the incremental update of a template gallery Co-updating vs. Self-updating

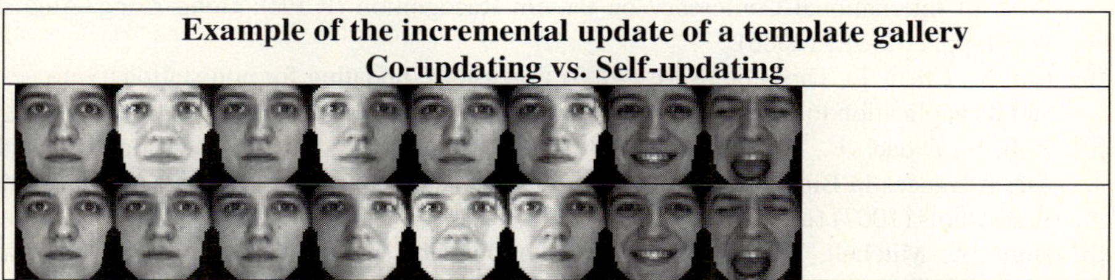

Fig. 4. Example of the incremental update of a face gallery. A comparison between the galleries created by co-updating and self-updating is shown. For all the galleries, the first image on the left is the initial training image used as face template. First row: gallery created by co-updating; second row: gallery created by self-updating for the same user.

5 Conclusions

In this paper, we presented a novel template update method. Our method exploits the concept of biometric co-training that can be regarded as an application of the semi-supervised learning method proposed by Blum and Mitchell. In multimodal biometric systems, this method allows co-updating the template galleries exploiting also"difficult", but informative, input data. Results reported in Section 4 provide a first experimental evidence of the effectiveness of the proposed template update method.

It is worth noting that, in a multi-modal biometric system, various system configurations are possible, depending on the application, the number of sensors, biometric traits, recognition algorithms, etc.. We believe that Investigating the use of co-training for different configurations of a multi-modal biometric system is an interesting issue for future research. Finally, we point out that co-training can be also used in biometric systems using more than two recognisers (e.g., more than two biometric traits), supposed that this ensemble of recognisers satisfy the assumptions of co-training algorithm on the feature sets. It should be noted, however, that co-training of an ensemble of classifiers is still a matter of on-going research, as co-training has always been used with just two classifiers.

References

[1] Uludag, U., Ross, A., Jain, A.K.: Biometric template selection and update: a case study in fingerprints. Pattern Recognition 37(7), 1533–1542 (2004)

[2] Tan, X., Chen, S., Zhou, Z.-H., Zhang, F.: Face recognition from a single image per person: a survey. Pattern Recognition 39(9), 1725–1745 (2006)

[3] Roli, F., Marcialis, G.L.: Semi-supervised PCA-based face recognition using self-training. In: Yeung, D.-Y., Kwok, J.T., Fred, A., Roli, F., de Ridder, D. (eds.) Structural, Syntactic, and Statistical Pattern Recognition. LNCS, vol. 4109, pp. 560–568. Springer, Heidelberg (2006)

[4] Jiang, X., Ser, W.: Online Fingerprint Template Improvement. IEEE Trans. PAMI 24(8), 1121–1126 (2002)

[5] Ryu, C., Hakil, K., Jain, A.K.: Template adaptation based fingerprint verification. In: Proc. of International Conference on Pattern Recognition (ICPR), Hong Kong, August, vol. 4, pp. 582–585 (2006)

[6] Liu, X., Chen, T., Thornton, S.M. (2003) Eigenspace updating for non-stationary process and its application to face recognition. Pattern Recognition, 1945–1959 (2003)

[7] Roli, F., Didaci, L., Marcialis, G.L.: Adaptive biometric systems that can improve with use, Advances in Biometrics. In: Ratha, N., Govindaraju, V. (eds.) Sensors, Systems and Algorithms (2007) (in press)

[8] Blum, A., Mitchell, T.: Combining labeled and unlabeled data with co-training. In: Proc. of the Workshop on Computational Learning Theory, pp. 92–100 (1998)

[9] Ross, A., Nandakumar, K., Jain, A.K.: Handbook of Multibiometrics. Springer, Heidelberg (2006)

[10] Turk, M., Pentland, A.: Eigenfaces for Face Recognition. Journal of Cognitive Neuroscience 3(1), 71–86 (1991)

[11] Jain, A.K., Hong, L., Bolle, R.: On-line Fingerprint Verification. IEEE Transactions on Pattern Analysis and Machine Intelligence 19(4), 302–314 (1997)

[12] Martinez, A., Benavente, R.: The AR Face Database. CVC Technical Report #24 (June 1998)

[13] Maio, D., Maltoni, D., Cappelli, R., Wayman, J.L., Jain, A.K.: FVC2002: Second Fingerprint Verification Competition. In: Proceedings 16th International Conference on Pattern Recognition (ICPR2002), Québec City, vol. 3, pp. 811–814 (2002)

Continual Retraining of Keystroke Dynamics Based Authenticator

Pilsung Kang, Seong-seob Hwang, and Sungzoon Cho*

Seoul National University, San 56-1, Shillim-dong, Kwanak-gu, 151-744, Seoul, Korea
{xfeel80,hss9414,zoon}@snu.ac.kr

Abstract. Keystroke dynamics based authentication (KDA) verifies a user based on the typing pattern. During enroll, a few typing patterns are provided, which are then used to train a classifier. The typing style of a user is not expected to change. However, sometimes it does change, resulting in a high false reject. In order to achieve a better authentication performance, we propose to continually retrain classifiers with recent login typing patterns by updating the training data set. There are two ways to update it. The *moving window* uses a fixed number of most recent patterns while the *growing window* uses all the new patterns as well as the original enroll patterns. We applied the proposed method to the real data set involving 21 users. The experimental results show that both the moving window and the growing window approach outperform the fixed window approach, which does not retrain a classifier.

1 Introduction

Password based user authentication has been widely used in security systems where a keyboard or a keypad is the main input device. When a user exposes his password or a third-party acquires the password, however, the authentication system becomes vulnerable to improper access trials. In order to cope with the vulnerability of password based user authentication, keystroke dynamics based authentication (KDA) has been proposed[1][2]. KDA considers keystroke dynamics together with password characters when authenticating an access attempt, i.e., it utilize a user's behavior as well as knowledge.

KDA involves three main processes as shown in Fig. 1. The enrollment process involves a user enrolling a certain number of keystroke typing patterns. The classifier building process involves constructing a classifier with the typing patterns collected in the enrollment process. The authentication process evaluates an access attempt with the classifier and takes an appropriate action: grant or deny access.

Recently, a number of methods for building high performance classifiers have been reported[3][4][5]. According to Peacock et al.[6], however, high performance classifiers reported in the literature were built with a large number of typing patterns. Most classifiers that they reviewed used more than 100 typing patterns

* Corresponding author.

S.-W. Lee and S.Z. Li (Eds.): ICB 2007, LNCS 4642, pp. 1203–1211, 2007.

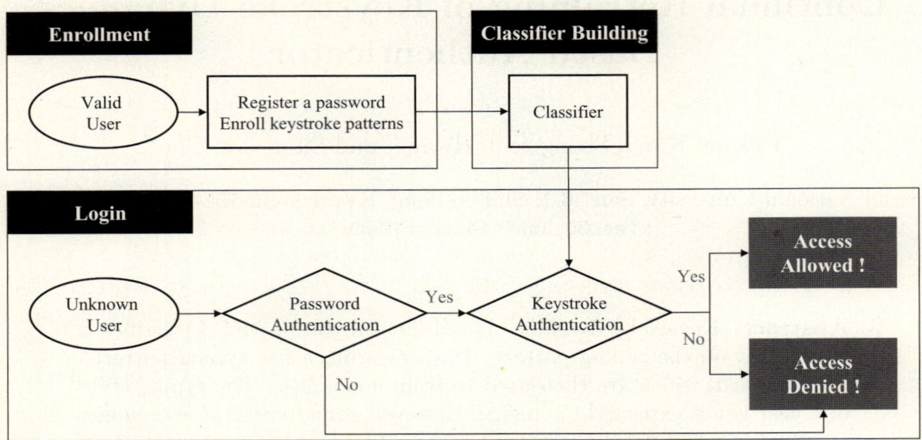

Fig. 1. Keystroke dynamics based authentication process

from each user to build the classifiers. Some even used more than 1,000 typing patterns. In practice, however, the number of patterns collected in the enrollment process should be no more than 10. Otherwise, a user may not choose to use the system at all. With such a small number of typing patterns, it is essential that the typing style of a user will not change in the future. It is often the case, however, that the typing style of a user changes. In this case, the performance of the classifier may degenerate. Fig. 2 shows the distances between the login patterns and the mean vector of the enroll patterns of three users involved in our experiment. The x-axis represents the index of login typing patterns. The larger the index is, the more recent the pattern is. The y-axis represents the Euclidian distance of the login pattern to the mean vector. The mean vector was calculated using 10 enroll patterns. User 9's typing style did not change over time since it shows little fluctuation (Fig. 2(a)). User 1 (Fig. 2(b)) is a typical user whose typing style changed gradually over time. The distance of the login patterns to the mean vector increased steadily. User 16 (Fig. 2(c)), on the other hand, surely changed his typing style, but no trend can be extracted since the

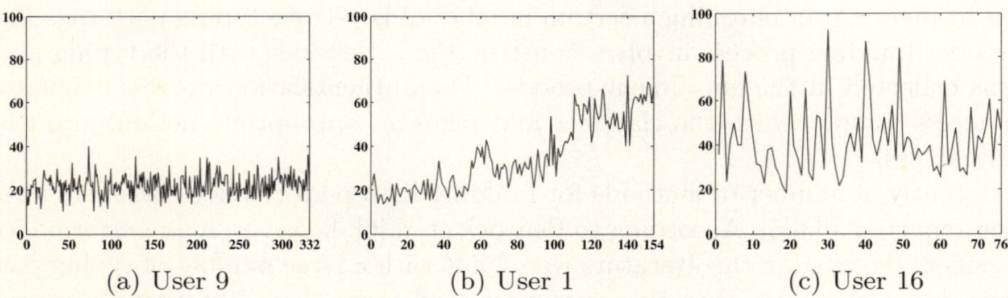

Fig. 2. Distance between login pattern and mean enroll pattern

distance neither increased nor decreased. The fluctuation is larger than the other users and many spikes are presented.

A remedy for changing typing style is to keep retraining the classifier. In this paper, we propose to update the training pattern set dynamically in order to accommodate the change of a user's typing behavior. In particular, we add "successful" login patterns to the training set and retrain the classifier. We propose two different ways of updating the training pattern set. The first is *"Moving window"*, where the number of training patterns is fixed. A recent pattern is added to the training set, while the least recent training pattern is removed. The second is *"Growing window"*, where a recent pattern keeps being added without any training pattern removed. Thus, the number of training patterns keeps increasing.

The rest of this paper is structured as follows. In section 2, we explain moving window and growing window followed by the experimental settings including authentication algorithm and data description in section 3. In section 4, we compare the performance of the classifiers based on two proposed methods and the *"Fixed window"*.[1] In section 5, with a conclusion, we discuss future work.

2 Updating Training Set

When KDA is employed in real systems, only a few number of typing patterns can be collected in the enrollment process. A small number of training patterns have a limitation that they can only represent a user's typing behavior at a particular time. If a user's typing style changes over time, newly available login patterns need to become a part of the training data set to retrain the classifier. We propose two ways of updating the training pattern set as follows.

2.1 Moving Window

In *moving window* method, the number of training patterns is fixed. When a new pattern is added to the training set, the oldest training pattern is removed. Let $TD_i = \{x_{m+1}, x_{m+2}, ..., x_{m+n}\}$ denote the training set at time period i, where n is the size of the training set. x_{m+1} is the oldest training pattern while x_{m+n} is the newest training pattern. With a new typing pattern x' available, TD_{i+1} is updated as follows:

$$\begin{aligned} &if \quad x' \quad is \quad granted \quad access \\ &\qquad TD_{i+1} = TD_i - \{x_{m+1}\} \cup \{x'\} \\ &else \\ &\qquad TD_{i+1} = TD_i \end{aligned} \tag{1}$$

If x' is granted access, it is added to TD_{i+1} while the oldest training pattern is removed. Otherwise, it is not added to TD_{i+1} so that the training data set

[1] *"Fixed window"* refers to the invariant training set consisting of the typing patterns collected in the enrollment process.

remains the same as TD_i. When a user's typing style changes, moving window can accommodate the change immediately. If the change between successive typing patterns is large but has no direction, however, moving window becomes unstable.

2.2 Growing Window

In *growing window* method, the number of training patterns is not fixed but increases. Ever when a new pattern is added to the training set, the oldest training pattern stays so that the growing window stores all the typing patterns that have been granted access as well as the original enroll patterns. The number of training patterns increases by one every time a new typing pattern is added. Let $TD_i = \{x_1, x_2, ..., x_n\}$ denote the training set at time i, where n is the size of the current training set. x_1 is the oldest training pattern, while x_n is the newest training pattern. With a new typing pattern x' available, TD_{i+1} is updated as follows:

$$\begin{aligned} &if \quad x' \quad is \quad granted \quad access \\ &\qquad TD_{i+1} = TD_i \cup \{x'\} \\ &else \\ &\qquad TD_{i+1} = TD_i \end{aligned} \tag{2}$$

If x' is granted access, it is added to TD_{i+1} while the oldest training pattern is not removed. So the number of training patterns becomes $n+1$. If x' is not granted access, on the other hand, it is not added to TD_{i+1} so that the training data set remains the same as TD_i. Since growing window method stores all possible training patterns, it reflects the change less than moving window when a user changes his typing style. If the change of typing patterns is not progressive and the scope of change is large, it can be more stable than moving window.

3 Experimental Settings

The data set used in our experiment originally appeared in Cho et al[4]. The data set consists of 21 users, each of whom has different number of training patterns from 76 to 388 as shown in Table 1. We used two types of features: duration (time between a key press and release) and interval (time between a key release and another key press). If a user uses a password with n characters, the length of the features becomes $2n-1$: n durations and $n-1$ intervals. Each user has 75 typing patterns of the valid user and 75 typing patterns of impostors. It is not easy to collect impostors' patterns in practice, thus, the subjects changed their roles such that a user tried to log in with other users' passwords. Initially, the earliest 10 patterns in the training set were used to build a classifier for all methods.

We employed K-Means algorithm based on Euclidian distance as the authentication classifier. The authentication algorithm is demonstrated in Fig. 3. First, K-means algorithm is performed using the training patterns so that the cluster membership of each training pattern is determined. Second, when the test

Table 1. Data description

User ID	Password	No. of features	No. of patterns	User ID	Password	No. of features	No. of patterns
1	90200jdg	15	164	12	dusru427	15	365
2	ahrfus88	15	260	13	i love 3	15	330
3	anehwksu	15	319	14	loveis.	13	207
4	autumnman	17	111	15	love wjd	15	101
5	beaupowe	15	76	16	manseiii	15	86
6	c.s.93/ksy	19	200	17	rhkdwo	11	205
7	dhfpql.	13	232	18	rla sua	15	101
8	dirdhfmw	15	309	19	tjddmswjd	17	337
9	dlfjs wp	15	342	20	tmdwnsl1	15	108
10	ditjdgml	15	151	21	yuhwa1kk	15	388
11	drizzle	13	299				

Step 1: Perform K-Means clustering with the training patterns

$[C_1, ..., C_K]$ = K-Means(X,K)

(C_K: the members belonging to K-th cluster)

(X: training patterns, K: the number of clusters)

Step 2: Find the closest cluster prototype of the test pattern y_j

$k = \arg_{i \in 1,\ldots,K} \min dist(y_j, P_i)$

(P_i: the prototype of the cluster C_i)

Step 3: Authentication

If $\mathrm{dist}(y_j, P_i) < M \times \frac{1}{|N_k|} \sum_{x_i \in C_k} dist(x_i, P_k)$

(N_k: the number of patterns in k-th cluster, M: Threshold coefficient)

grant access(y_j is considered as a valid user's typing pattern)

else

deny access(y_j is considered as an impostor's typing pattern)

Fig. 3. KDA authentication process

pattern is given, the nearest prototype to the test pattern is determined. Third, the average distance between training patterns belonging to their nearest prototype is calculated to estimate the threshold. If the distance between the test pattern and the nearest prototype is smaller than the threshold, the test pattern is granted access. Otherwise, it is denied access. In our experiment, we set the number of clusters (K) to 3.

There are two types of errors: false rejection rate (FRR) and false acceptance rate (FAR). FRR is the ratio of the valid user's attempts classified as impostors'. A high FRR indicates that the valid user's attempt is often rejected. A user may feel irritated if FRR is high. FAR is the ratio of impostors' attempts classified as the valid user's. The system is not secure when FAR is high. Since the purpose of KDA is to minimize both FRR and FAR, and one can be reduced at the cost of the other, we adopted equal error rate (EER, the value where FRR and FAR are equal[7]) for the performance measure.

4 Experimental Results

The EERs of all users using fixed window, moving window, and growing window are shown in Table 2. The average EER of fixed window is 4.8%. Both moving window and growing window, however, achieved average EER of 3.8%, which is 1.0% lower than that of fixed window. Since the variation of the users was fairly large, we investigated the effect of moving window and growing window on each user separately. First, we constructed a *win-draw-lose* table in order to estimate the relative dominance of moving window and growing window over fixed window (see Table 4). The EERs of moving window and growing window were compared for each user. If the difference was larger than 0.01, "win" or "lose" resulted. Otherwise, "draw" resulted. Five users lowered their EER with moving window while only one user resulted in a higher EER. Similarly, six users lowered their EER with growing window while none of the users resulted in a higher EER. Thus, we can conclude that both moving window and growing window improved EER over fixed window.

We also plotted the EER over time (Fig. 4) for three methods as the training data set is updated. The x-axis represents the index of typing patterns. A newer

Table 2. The average EER of fixed window, moving window, and growing window

User ID	Fixed window	Moving window	Growing window	User ID	Fixed window	Moving window	Growing window
1	0.173	0.107	0.126	12	0.000	0.000	0.000
2	0.027	0.026	0.027	13	0.040	0.033	0.016
3	0.000	0.000	0.000	14	0.093	0.090	0.081
4	0.000	0.001	0.000	15	0.227	0.117	0.149
5	0.080	0.057	0.075	16	0.133	0.149	0.129
6	0.053	0.041	0.044	17	0.000	0.002	0.001
7	0.013	0.013	0.013	18	0.040	0.035	0.031
8	0.000	0.005	0.003	19	0.000	0.000	0.000
9	0.013	0.013	0.013	20	0.013	0.013	0.013
10	0.000	0.000	0.000	21	0.000	0.000	0.000
11	0.107	0.096	0.082	**Average**	**0.048**	**0.038**	**0.038**

Table 3. Win-draw-lose table of moving window and growing window over fixed window

		Fixed Window		
		Win	Draw	Lose
Moving Window	Total Number	5	15	1
	User ID	1,5,6,11,15	-	16
Growing Window	Total Number	6	15	0
	User ID	1,6,11,13,14,15	-	-

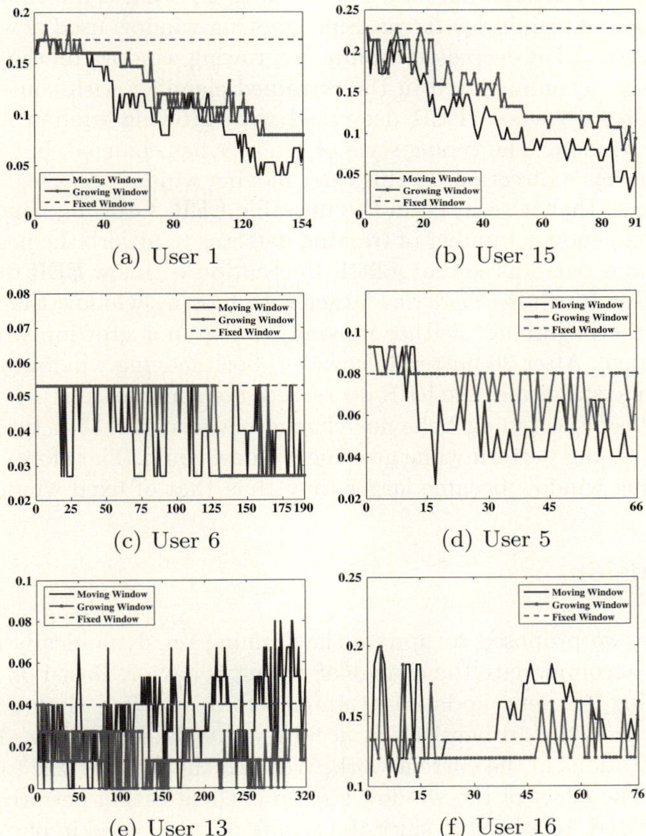

Fig. 4. EER for a sequence of login attempts of some users

pattern has a larger index. The y-axis represents the EER. The users plotted in Fig. 4(a,b,c) had better authentication performance with both moving window and growing window than fixed window. User 1 and User 15 are typical users whose typing style has changed over time. The EERs continuously decreased as the training patterns were updated. Lower EER was achieved by adjusting training patterns so as to accommodate the user's typing behavior change. Since moving window is more sensitive to typing change than growing window, its EER decreased more rapidly. User 6 has a different change pattern. The training patterns changed irregularly. Moving window accommodated the change as soon as a new pattern was added so that the fluctuation of the EER was rather large. Growing window, on the other hand, did not show much fluctuation of the EER since it used a large number of training patterns. Fig. 4(d) shows User 5 whose EER decreased with moving window but did not with growing window. Note that the training patterns numbered from 10 to 25 seem significantly different from the initial 10 training patterns. Since moving window used newly available patterns only, the EER decreased rapidly. In growing window, on the other hand, the change was accommodated in the retrained classifier with some delay. Fig. 4(e) shows User 13 whose EER decreased with growing window but did not with moving window. The typing style of the user has changed, but it is neither consistent nor has a direction. In this case, moving window *"chased"* after every single change so that it resulted in the unstable EER. Growing window, on the other hand, had enough number of training patterns to absorb the negative effect of a few spurious patterns so that a little fluctuation with low EER resulted. Fig. 4(f) shows User 16 whose EER was larger with moving window than with fixed window. At the beginning, neither moving window nor growing window could catch the change. After 20 patterns, however, both moving window and growing window became stable and the EER decreased. For some reason, moving window could not reflect the typing behavior change between the 35th typing pattern and the 65th typing pattern while growing window could. Therefore, the average EER of moving window became larger than than that of fixed window.

5 Conclusion

In this paper, we proposed to update the training set dynamically so that the classifier can accommodate the change of typing behavior. Based on the experiments involving 21 users, updating training sets by moving window or growing window improved the authentication accuracy over fixed window. There are a couple of limitations in the current work. We fixed the window size to 10 in moving window. The effect of the window size on authentication performance needs to be investigated. In addition, since the typing patterns used in our experiment were collected in a rather short period, data collection with longer period such as 6 months or 1 year should be investigated.

Acknowledgement

This work was supported by grant No. R01-2005-000-103900-0 from the Basic Research Program of the Korea Science and Engineering Foundation, the Brain

Korea 21 program in 2006 and 2007, and partially supported by Engineering Research Institute of SNU.

References

1. Gaines, R., Lisowski, W., Press, S., Shapiro, N.: Authentication by keystroke timing: some preliminary results. Rand Report R-256-NSF. Rand Corporation (1980)
2. Umphress, D., Williams, G.: Identity Verification through Keyboard Characteristics. International Journal of Man-Machine Studies 23, 263–273 (1985)
3. Obaidat, M., Sadoun, S.: Verification of computer users using keystroke dynamics. IEEE Transactions on Systems, Man and Cybernetics, Part B: Cybernetics 27(2), 262–269 (1997)
4. Cho, S., Han, C., Han, D., Kim, H.: Web-based keystroke dynamics identity verification using neural network. J. Organizational computing and electronics commerce 10(4), 295–307 (2000)
5. Brown, M., Rogers, S.J.: User Identification via keystroke characteristics of typed names using neural networks. Int. J. Man-Machine Studies 39, 999–1014 (1993)
6. Peacock, A., Ke, X., Wilkerson, M.: Typing Patterns: A Key to User Identification. IEEE Security & Privacy Magazine 5(2), 40–47 (2004)
7. Hwang, S., Lee, H., Cho, S.: mproving Authentication Accuracy of Unfamiliar Passwords with Pauses and Cues for Keystroke Dynamics-Based Authentication. In: Chen, H., Wang, F.-Y., Yang, C.C., Zeng, D., Chau, M., Chang, K. (eds.) WISI 2006. LNCS, vol. 3917, pp. 73–78. Springer, Heidelberg (2006)

Author Index

Printing: Mercedes-Druck, Berlin
Binding: Stein + Lehmann, Berlin

Lecture Notes in Computer Science

For information about Vols. 1–4563

please contact your bookseller or Springer

Vol. 4708: L. Kučera, A. Kučera (Eds.), Mathematical Foundations of Computer Science 2007. XVIII, 764 pages. 2007.

Vol. 4707: O. Gervasi, M.L. Gavrilova (Eds.), Computational Science and Its Applications – ICCSA 2007, Part III. XXIV, 1205 pages. 2007.

Vol. 4706: O. Gervasi, M.L. Gavrilova (Eds.), Computational Science and Its Applications – ICCSA 2007, Part II. XXIII, 1129 pages. 2007.

Vol. 4705: O. Gervasi, M.L. Gavrilova (Eds.), Computational Science and Its Applications – ICCSA 2007, Part I. XLIV, 1169 pages. 2007.

Vol. 4697: L. Choi, Y. Paek, S. Cho (Eds.), Advances in Computer Systems Architecture. XIII, 400 pages. 2007.

Vol. 4685: D.J. Veit, J. Altmann (Eds.), Grid Economics and Business Models. XII, 201 pages. 2007.

Vol. 4682: D.-S. Huang, L. Heutte, M. Loog (Eds.), Advanced Intelligent Computing Theories and Applications. XXVII, 1373 pages. 2007. (Sublibrary LNAI).

Vol. 4681: D.-S. Huang, L. Heutte, M. Loog (Eds.), Advanced Intelligent Computing Theories and Applications. XXVI, 1379 pages. 2007.

Vol. 4679: A.L. Yuille, S.-C. Zhu, D. Cremers, Y. Wang (Eds.), Energy Minimization Methods in Computer Vision and Pattern Recognition. XII, 494 pages. 2007.

Vol. 4673: W.G. Kropatsch, M. Kampel, A. Hanbury (Eds.), Computer Analysis of Images and Patterns. XX, 1006 pages. 2007.

Vol. 4671: V. Malyshkin (Ed.), Parallel Computing Technologies. XIV, 635 pages. 2007.

Vol. 4660: S. Džeroski, J. Todorovski (Eds.), Computational Discovery of Scientific Knowledge. X, 327 pages. 2007. (Sublibrary LNAI).

Vol. 4651: F. Azevedo, P. Barahona, F. Fages, F. Rossi (Eds.), Recent Advances in Constraints. VIII, 185 pages. 2007. (Sublibrary LNAI).

Vol. 4649: V. Diekert, M.V. Volkov, A. Voronkov (Eds.), Computer Science – Theory and Applications. XIII, 420 pages. 2007.

Vol. 4647: R. Martin, M. Sabin, J. Winkler (Eds.), Mathematics of Surfaces XII. IX, 509 pages. 2007.

Vol. 4645: R. Giancarlo, S. Hannenhalli (Eds.), Algorithms in Bioinformatics. XIII, 432 pages. 2007. (Sublibrary LNBI).

Vol. 4643: M.-F. Sagot, M.E.M.T. Walter (Eds.), Advances in Bioinformatics and Computational Biology. XII, 177 pages. 2007. (Sublibrary LNBI).

Vol. 4642: S.-W. Lee, S.Z. Li (Eds.), Advances in Biometrics. XX, 1216 pages. 2007.

Vol. 4639: E. Csuhaj-Varj'u, Z. Ésik (Eds.), Fundamentals of Computation Theory. XIV, 508 pages. 2007.

Vol. 4637: C. Kruegel, R. Lippmann, A. Clark (Eds.), Recent Advances in Intrusion Detection. XII, 338 pages. 2007.

Vol. 4635: B. Kokinov, D.C. Richardson, T.R. Roth-Berghofer, L. Vieu (Eds.), Modeling and Using Context. XIV, 574 pages. 2007. (Sublibrary LNAI).

Vol. 4634: H.R. Nielson, G. Filé (Eds.), Static Analysis. XI, 469 pages. 2007.

Vol. 4633: M. Kamel, A. Campilho (Eds.), Image Analysis and Recognition. XII, 1312 pages. 2007.

Vol. 4632: R. Alhajj, H. Gao, X. Li, J. Li, O.R. Zaïane (Eds.), Advanced Data Mining and Applications. XV, 634 pages. 2007. (Sublibrary LNAI).

Vol. 4628: L.N. de Castro, F.J. Von Zuben, H. Knidel (Eds.), Artificial Immune Systems. XII, 438 pages. 2007.

Vol. 4627: M. Charikar, K. Jansen, O. Reingold, J.D.P. Rolim (Eds.), Approximation, Randomization, and Combinatorial Optimization. XII, 626 pages. 2007.

Vol. 4626: R.O. Weber, M.M. Richter (Eds.), Case-Based Reasoning Research and Development. XIII, 534 pages. 2007. (Sublibrary LNAI).

Vol. 4624: T. Mossakowski, U. Montanari, M. Haveraaen (Eds.), Algebra and Coalgebra in Computer Science. XI, 463 pages. 2007.

Vol. 4622: A. Menezes (Ed.), Advances in Cryptology - CRYPTO 2007. XIV, 631 pages. 2007.

Vol. 4619: F. Dehne, J.-R. Sack, N. Zeh (Eds.), Algorithms and Data Structures. XVI, 662 pages. 2007.

Vol. 4618: S.G. Akl, C.S. Calude, M.J. Dinneen, G. Rozenberg, H.T. Wareham (Eds.), Unconventional Computation. X, 243 pages. 2007.

Vol. 4617: V. Torra, Y. Narukawa, Y. Yoshida (Eds.), Modeling Decisions for Artificial Intelligence. XII, 502 pages. 2007. (Sublibrary LNAI).

Vol. 4616: A. Dress, Y. Xu, B. Zhu (Eds.), Combinatorial Optimization and Applications. XI, 390 pages. 2007.

Vol. 4615: R. de Lemos, C. Gacek, A. Romanovsky (Eds.), Architecting Dependable Systems IV. XIV, 435 pages. 2007.

Vol. 4613: F.P. Preparata, Q. Fang (Eds.), Frontiers in Algorithmics. XI, 348 pages. 2007.

Vol. 4612: I. Miguel, W. Ruml (Eds.), Abstraction, Reformulation, and Approximation. XI, 418 pages. 2007. (Sublibrary LNAI).

Vol. 4611: J. Indulska, J. Ma, L.T. Yang, T. Ungerer, J. Cao (Eds.), Ubiquitous Intelligence and Computing. XXIII, 1257 pages. 2007.

Vol. 4610: B. Xiao, L.T. Yang, J. Ma, C. Muller-Schloer, Y. Hua (Eds.), Autonomic and Trusted Computing. XVIII, 571 pages. 2007.

Vol. 4609: E. Ernst (Ed.), ECOOP 2007 – Object-Oriented Programming. XIII, 625 pages. 2007.

Vol. 4608: H.W. Schmidt, I. Crnkovic, G.T. Heineman, J.A. Stafford (Eds.), Component-Based Software Engineering. XII, 283 pages. 2007.

Vol. 4607: L. Baresi, P. Fraternali, G.-J. Houben (Eds.), Web Engineering. XVI, 576 pages. 2007.

Vol. 4606: A. Pras, M. van Sinderen (Eds.), Dependable and Adaptable Networks and Services. XIV, 149 pages. 2007.

Vol. 4605: D. Papadias, D. Zhang, G. Kollios (Eds.), Advances in Spatial and Temporal Databases. X, 479 pages. 2007.

Vol. 4604: U. Priss, S. Polovina, R. Hill (Eds.), Conceptual Structures: Knowledge Architectures for Smart Applications. XII, 514 pages. 2007. (Sublibrary LNAI).

Vol. 4603: F. Pfenning (Ed.), Automated Deduction – CADE-21. XII, 522 pages. 2007. (Sublibrary LNAI).

Vol. 4602: S. Barker, G.-J. Ahn (Eds.), Data and Applications Security XXI. X, 291 pages. 2007.

Vol. 4600: H. Comon-Lundh, C. Kirchner, H. Kirchner (Eds.), Rewriting, Computation and Proof. XVI, 273 pages. 2007.

Vol. 4599: S. Vassiliadis, M. Berekovic, T.D. Hämäläinen (Eds.), Embedded Computer Systems: Architectures, Modeling, and Simulation. XVIII, 466 pages. 2007.

Vol. 4598: G. Lin (Ed.), Computing and Combinatorics. XII, 570 pages. 2007.

Vol. 4597: P. Perner (Ed.), Advances in Data Mining. XI, 353 pages. 2007. (Sublibrary LNAI).

Vol. 4596: L. Arge, C. Cachin, T. Jurdziński, A. Tarlecki (Eds.), Automata, Languages and Programming. XVII, 953 pages. 2007.

Vol. 4595: D. Bošnački, S. Edelkamp (Eds.), Model Checking Software. X, 285 pages. 2007.

Vol. 4594: R. Bellazzi, A. Abu-Hanna, J. Hunter (Eds.), Artificial Intelligence in Medicine. XVI, 509 pages. 2007. (Sublibrary LNAI).

Vol. 4592: Z. Kedad, N. Lammari, E. Métais, F. Meziane, Y. Rezgui (Eds.), Natural Language Processing and Information Systems. XIV, 442 pages. 2007.

Vol. 4591: J. Davies, J. Gibbons (Eds.), Integrated Formal Methods. IX, 660 pages. 2007.

Vol. 4590: W. Damm, H. Hermanns (Eds.), Computer Aided Verification. XV, 562 pages. 2007.

Vol. 4589: J. Münch, P. Abrahamsson (Eds.), Product-Focused Software Process Improvement. XII, 414 pages. 2007.

Vol. 4588: T. Harju, J. Karhumäki, A. Lepistö (Eds.), Developments in Language Theory. XI, 423 pages. 2007.

Vol. 4587: R. Cooper, J. Kennedy (Eds.), Data Management. XIII, 259 pages. 2007.

Vol. 4586: J. Pieprzyk, H. Ghodosi, E. Dawson (Eds.), Information Security and Privacy. XIV, 476 pages. 2007.

Vol. 4585: M. Kryszkiewicz, J.F. Peters, H. Rybinski, A. Skowron (Eds.), Rough Sets and Intelligent Systems Paradigms. XIX, 836 pages. 2007. (Sublibrary LNAI).

Vol. 4584: N. Karssemeijer, B. Lelieveldt (Eds.), Information Processing in Medical Imaging. XX, 777 pages. 2007.

Vol. 4583: S.R. Della Rocca (Ed.), Typed Lambda Calculi and Applications. X, 397 pages. 2007.

Vol. 4582: J. Lopez, P. Samarati, J.L. Ferrer (Eds.), Public Key Infrastructure. XI, 375 pages. 2007.

Vol. 4581: A. Petrenko, M. Veanes, J. Tretmans, W. Grieskamp (Eds.), Testing of Software and Communicating Systems. XII, 379 pages. 2007.

Vol. 4580: B. Ma, K. Zhang (Eds.), Combinatorial Pattern Matching. XII, 366 pages. 2007.

Vol. 4579: B. M. Hämmerli, R. Sommer (Eds.), Detection of Intrusions and Malware, and Vulnerability Assessment. X, 251 pages. 2007.

Vol. 4578: F. Masulli, S. Mitra, G. Pasi (Eds.), Applications of Fuzzy Sets Theory. XVIII, 693 pages. 2007. (Sublibrary LNAI).

Vol. 4577: N. Sebe, Y. Liu, Y.-t. Zhuang, T.S. Huang (Eds.), Multimedia Content Analysis and Mining. XIII, 513 pages. 2007.

Vol. 4576: D. Leivant, R. de Queiroz (Eds.), Logic, Language, Information and Computation. X, 363 pages. 2007.

Vol. 4575: T. Takagi, T. Okamoto, E. Okamoto, T. Okamoto (Eds.), Pairing-Based Cryptography – Pairing 2007. XI, 408 pages. 2007.

Vol. 4574: J. Derrick, J. Vain (Eds.), Formal Techniques for Networked and Distributed Systems – FORTE 2007. XI, 375 pages. 2007.

Vol. 4573: M. Kauers, M. Kerber, R. Miner, W. Windsteiger (Eds.), Towards Mechanized Mathematical Assistants. XIII, 407 pages. 2007. (Sublibrary LNAI).

Vol. 4572: F. Stajano, C. Meadows, S. Capkun, T. Moore (Eds.), Security and Privacy in Ad-hoc and Sensor Networks. X, 247 pages. 2007.

Vol. 4571: P. Perner (Ed.), Machine Learning and Data Mining in Pattern Recognition. XIV, 913 pages. 2007. (Sublibrary LNAI).

Vol. 4570: H.G. Okuno, M. Ali (Eds.), New Trends in Applied Artificial Intelligence. XXI, 1194 pages. 2007. (Sublibrary LNAI).

Vol. 4569: A. Butz, B. Fisher, A. Krüger, P. Olivier, S. Owada (Eds.), Smart Graphics. IX, 237 pages. 2007.

Vol. 4568: T. Ishida, S. R. Fussell, P. T. J. M. Vossen (Eds.), Intercultural Collaboration. XIII, 395 pages. 2007.

Vol. 4566: M.J. Dainoff (Ed.), Ergonomics and Health Aspects of Work with Computers. XVIII, 390 pages. 2007.

Vol. 4565: D.D. Schmorrow, L.M. Reeves (Eds.), Foundations of Augmented Cognition. XIX, 450 pages. 2007. (Sublibrary LNAI).

Vol. 4564: D. Schuler (Ed.), Online Communities and Social Computing. XVII, 520 pages. 2007.